T0215868

Lecture Notes in Computer Science   11124

Commenced Publication in 1973
Founding and Former Series Editors:
Gerhard Goos, Juris Hartmanis, and Jan van Leeuwen

More information about this series at http://www.springer.com/series/7410

Jan Camenisch · Panos Papadimitratos (Eds.)

Cryptology and Network Security

17th International Conference, CANS 2018
Naples, Italy, September 30 – October 3, 2018
Proceedings

Editors
Jan Camenisch (iD)
IBM Research - Zurich
Rüschlikon
Switzerland

Panos Papadimitratos (iD)
KTH Royal Institute of Technology
Stockholm
Sweden

ISSN 0302-9743   ISSN 1611-3349   (electronic)
Lecture Notes in Computer Science
ISBN 978-3-030-00433-0   ISBN 978-3-030-00434-7   (eBook)
https://doi.org/10.1007/978-3-030-00434-7

Library of Congress Control Number: 2018953695

LNCS Sublibrary: SL4 – Security and Cryptology

This Springer imprint is published by the registered company Springer Nature Switzerland AG
The registered company address is: Gewerbestrasse 11, 6330 Cham, Switzerland

Preface

A warm welcome to the 17th International Conference on Cryptology and Network Security (CANS)! Held in Naples, Italy, during September 30 – October 3, 2018, CANS 2018, the latest in a long series of conferences focusing on all aspects of cryptology and the security of data, networks, and computers, attracted cutting-edge results from world-renowned scientists in the area.

This year, the technical program featured 26 enticing papers, covering a range of topics from privacy, network protection, and malware, to cryptanalysis, cryptographic protocols, signature schemes, symmetric key cryptographic primitives, secret sharing, and cryptographic protocols. The program was presented in a single track, along with 4 invited talks. The exciting technical program is enriched by 4 keynote talks delivered by Prof. Pierangela Samarati (University of Milano), Prof. Abhi Shelat (Northeastern University), Prof. Ivan Visconti (Università degli Studi di Salerno), and Dr. Paolo Campegiani (Bit4id). Many thanks go to all keynote speakers!

Our call for papers attracted 79 qualified submissions from authors affiliated with a diverse set of organizations. The 49 members of the Technical Program Committee along with a selected group of external experts carefully reviewed all papers and selected 26 papers for presentation at the conference and inclusion in these proceedings. The review process was double-blind and it was carried out in a single stage. All papers received at least 3 reviews and approximately half of them received an additional fourth review.

CANS 2018 was a team effort. First of all, we would like to express our sincere gratitude to the Program Committee members and the external reviewers — their efforts were instrumental in constructing the strong technical program. Special thanks go to those that very effectively undertook the role of shepherds and helped to improve the few papers that were accepted conditionally. Needless to say, we wholeheartedly thank all the authors that submitted their research to the conference. Last but not least, our profound thanks go to the local organizing team, in particular, to Dr. Vincenzo Iovino and Dr. Giovanni Schmid for their prompt support in all matters, and to the Steering Committee, notably Prof. Yvo Desmedt, for their guidance.

Again, welcome to CANS 2018. We hope you enjoyed the program and that you had a splendid time in the beautiful city of Naples!

July 2018

Jan Camenisch
Panos Papadimitratos

Organization

Program Co-chairs

Jan Camenisch   IBM Research - Zurich, Switzerland
Panos Papadimitratos   KTH Royal Institute of Technology, Sweden

General Chair

Vincenzo Iovino   University of Luxembourg, Luxembourg

Organising Chair

Giovanni Schmid   CNR-Icar and Parthenope University, Italy

Publicity Chair

Giovanni Livraga   University of Milan, Italy

Local and Organizing Committee

Elena Pagnin   Chalmers University, Sweden
Giuseppe Persiano   University of Salerno, Italy

Steering Committee

Yvo Desmedt (Chair)   University of Texas at Dallas, USA
Juan A. Garay   Yahoo! Labs, USA
Amir Herzberg   Bar-Ilan University, Israel
Yi Mu   University of Wollongong, Australia
David Pointcheval   CNRS and ENS Paris, France
Huaxiong Wang   Nanyang Technological University, Singapore

Program Committee

Giuseppe Ateniese   Stevens Institute of Technology, USA
Tuomas Aura   Aalto University, Finland
Reza Azarderakhsh   Florida Atlantic University, USA
Lejla Batina   Radboud University, The Netherlands
Elisa Bertino   Purdue University, USA
Erik-Oliver Blass   Airbus Group Innovations, France
Sonja Buchegger   KTH Royal Institute of Technology, Sweden
Jan Camenisch   IBM Research - Zurich, Switzerland

Jing Deng	UNCG, USA
Rafael Dowsley	Aarhus University, Denmark
Manu Drijvers	IBM Research - Zurich, Switzerland
Rachid El Bansarkhani	TU Darmstadt, Germany
Ali El Kaafarani	University of Oxford, UK
Pooya Farshim	ENS, France
Elena Ferrari	University of Insubria, Italy
Chaya Ganesh	Aarhus University, Denmark
Peter Gaži	IST Austria, Austria
Esha Ghosh	Microsoft, USA
Dieter Gollmann	Hamburg University of Technology, Germany
Jan Hajny	VUT Brno, Czech Republic
Gerhard Hancke	City University of Hong Kong, SAR China
Amir Herzberg	Bar-Ilan University, Israel
Julia Hesse	TU Darmstadt, Germany
Vincenzo Iovino	University of Luxembourg, Luxembourg
Frank Kargl	Ulm University, Germany
Stefan Katzenbeisser	TU Darmstadt, Germany
Florian Kerschbaum	University of Waterloo, Canada
Stephan Krenn	AIT Austrian Institute of Technology, Austria
Ralf Kuesters	University of Stuttgart, Germany
Loukas Lazos	University of Arizona, USA
Zhe Lie	Nanjing University of Aeronautics and Astronautics, China
Panos Louridas	Athens University of Economics and Business and Greek Research and Technology Network, Greece
Songwu Lu	University of California, Los Angeles, USA
Evangelos Markatos	ICS-FORTH, Greece
Ivan Martinovic	University of Oxford, UK
Panos Papadimitratos	KTH Royal Institute of Technology, Sweden
Stefano Paraboschi	Universita di Bergamo, Italy
Alfredo Rial	University of Luxembourg, Luxembourg
Pierangela Samarati	University of Milan, Italy
Alessandra Scafuro	North Carolina State University, USA
Nolen Scaife	University of Florida, USA
Thomas Schneider	TU Darmstadt, Germany
Dominique Schroeder	Friedrich-Alexander-Universiät Erlangen-Nürnberg, Germany
Antonio Skarmeta Gomez	Universidad de Murcia, Spain
Claudio Soriente	NEC Laboratories Europe, Germany
Willy Susilo	University of Wollongong, Australia
George Theodorakopoulos	Cardiff University, UK
Ari Trachtenberg	Boston University, USA
Frederik Vercauteren	KU Leuven, Belgium

Additional Reviewers

Agrikola, Thomas
Al-Momani, Ala'A
Alkadri, Nabil
Bacis, Enrico
Bakos Lang, Elena
Bernal Bernabe, Jorge
Bernieri, Giuseppe
Beullens, Ward
Bonte, Charlotte
Büscher, Niklas
Cohn-Gordon, Katriel
D'Anvers, Jan-Pieter
Daemen, Joan
De Cristofaro, Emiliano
Demmler, Daniel
Engelmann, Felix
Etemad, Mohammad
Francati, Danilo
Galbraith, Steven
Geihs, Matthias
Genc, Ziya A.
Gunasinghe, Hasini
Hough, Patrick
Järvinen, Kimmo
Kaplan, Anna
Karmakar, Angshuman
Khovratovich, Dmitry
Kiss, Ágnes

Kleber, Stephan
Kopp, Henning
Liedtke, Julian
Makri, Eleftheria
Marin, Leandro
Markatou, Evangelia Anna
Massolino, Pedro Maat
Matousek, Matthias
Misoczki, Rafael
Mueller, Johannes
Neven, Gregory
Nguyen, Khoa
Nuñez, David
Rao, Fang-Yu
Rausch, Daniel
Renes, Joost
Rosenthal, Joachim
Sagirlar, Gokhan
Samardjiska, Simona
Shani, Barak
Shiehian, Sina
Simon, Mike
Slamanig, Daniel
Tkachenko, Oleksandr
Viet Xuan Phuong, Tran
Weinert, Christian
Zamyatin, Alexei

Contents

Signatures

Cryptanalysis

Cryptographic Primitives

Cryptographic Protocols

Privacy

Faster Privacy-Preserving Location Proximity Schemes

Kimmo Järvinen[1]($\boxtimes$), Ágnes Kiss[2]($\boxtimes$), Thomas Schneider[2]($\boxtimes$),
Oleksandr Tkachenko[2]($\boxtimes$), and Zheng Yang[3]($\boxtimes$)

[1] University of Helsinki, Helsinki, Finland
kimmo.u.jarvinen@helsinki.fi
[2] TU Darmstadt, Darmstadt, Germany
{kiss,schneider,tkachenko}@encrypto.cs.tu-darmstadt.de
[3] Singapore University of Technology and Design, Singapore, Singapore
zheng_yang@sutd.edu.sg

Abstract. In the last decade, location information became easily obtainable using off-the-shelf mobile devices. This gave a momentum to developing Location Based Services (LBSs) such as location proximity detection, which can be used to find friends or taxis nearby. LBSs can, however, be easily misused to track users, which draws attention to the need of protecting privacy of these users.

In this work, we address this issue by designing, implementing, and evaluating multiple algorithms for Privacy-Preserving Location Proximity (PPLP) that are based on different secure computation protocols. Our PPLP protocols are well-suited for different scenarios: for saving bandwidth, energy/computational power, or for faster runtimes. Furthermore, our algorithms have runtimes of a few milliseconds to hundreds of milliseconds and bandwidth of hundreds of bytes to one megabyte. In addition, the computationally most expensive parts of the PPLP computation can be precomputed in our protocols, such that the input-dependent online phase runs in just a few milliseconds.

Keywords: Location privacy · Proximity · Secure computation
Homomorphic encryption

1 Introduction

Nowadays, many mobile devices (e.g., smartphones or tablets) can easily measure and report precise locations in real time, so that several Location-Based Services (LBSs) over mobile networks have emerged in recent years. A basic LBS is location proximity detection that enables a user to test whether or not another user is nearby. This promising function has boosted the development of social applications to help users to find their nearby friends [22], Uber cars [17], or medical personnel in an event of emergency [33]. Although some users have nothing against sharing their location, many privacy-aware users want to protect it

© Springer Nature Switzerland AG 2018
J. Camenisch and P. Papadimitratos (Eds.): CANS 2018, LNCS 11124, pp. 3–22, 2018.
https://doi.org/10.1007/978-3-030-00434-7_1

from third parties. The reason for that are the possible privacy threats caused by location proximity detection [31] that may lead to serious consequences, including unintended tracking, stalking, harassment, and even kidnapping. Potential adversaries range from curious social media contacts to abusive family members and even professional criminals (e.g., burglars checking if a victim is at home), and sometimes the level of their technological skills may be high. Hence, it is desirable to provide location proximity detection services which preserve the privacy of the users' exact location. Furthermore, modern law (e.g., the EU General Data Protection Regulation (GDPR)[1]) obligates companies to better protect users' privacy. This affects companies such as smartphone manufacturers that frequently offer built-in LBSs and LBS providers that provide additional privacy-preserving LBSs based on the result of the Privacy-Preserving Location Proximity (PPLP) protocol, e.g., for advertising ongoing movies in nearby cinemas to friends in the vicinity.

1.1 Our Contributions

Our contributions are as follows:

Efficient PPLP Schemes. We design and evaluate practically efficient Euclidean distance-based Privacy-Preserving Location Proximity (PPLP) schemes (i) using a mix of Secure Two-Party Computation (STPC) protocols, (ii) using DGK encryption [7] and Bloom filters [4], and (iii) using exponential ElGamal encryption [13] over elliptic curves (ECs) and Bloom filters. This allows us to provide custom solutions for different PPLP applications with different requirements with respect to communication, computation, and runtime.

Optimizations. We present an optimization of the Boolean circuit for computing Euclidean and Manhattan distance for 32-bit values that reduces the number of AND gates by up to 22%.

Pre-computation. We consider two scenarios where (i) a precomputation scenario where two parties run a PPLP protocol on an ongoing basis, which allows pre-computations (e.g., overnight while charging) and substantially reduces computation and communication in the online phase, and (ii) an ad-hoc scenario where two strangers run a PPLP protocol only once (e.g., for mobile health care), and pre-computations are not possible.

Extensive Performance Evaluation. We give an extensive communication comparison of our PPLP protocols and the PPLP protocols presented in recent related work. Furthermore, we implement our most efficient protocols (two STPC-based and one EC-ElGamal-based algorithm) and give a runtime comparison of them and the most efficient recently introduced PPLP protocol of Hallgren et al. [15,16]. Additionally, we run our protocols in a real-world mobile Internet setting.

---

[1] https://www.eugdpr.org/.

1.2 Related Work

So far several solutions for privacy-preserving location proximity (PPLP) schemes have been proposed, e.g., [6,16,25,29–31,35–37]. In early literature [6], privacy-preserving location proximity computation is realized by an imprecise location-based range query that allows a user to approximately learn if any of its communication partners is within a fixed distance from her current location. To realize such queries, a user's cloaked location (i.e., the precise location of the user is put into a larger region) is sent to the service provider which handles the service request and sends back a probabilistic result to the user. However, this scheme may leak some location information since the service provider knows each individual is within a particular region.

Since then there is a large number of works (e.g., [12,31,31,35]) on using a (semi-)trusted third party for assisting the clients in location proximity detection. [30] introduces a PPLP solution called FriendLocator in the client-server setting. Here, each user first maps her location into a shared grid cell (granule), and the converted location is encrypted and sent to the location server who will blindly compute the proximity results for the user. Similar approaches relying on geographic grid are adopted in [12,31].

In the recent work [35], Zheng et al. proposed a novel scheme which is based on spatial-temporal location tags that are extracted from environmental signals. A user can learn a group of users that are within her vicinity region with the help of a semi-trusted server. However, collaborating with a third party (whose reputation is uncertain) for proximity detection may incur the risk of compromising location privacy or many other security issues. For better privacy protection, it would therefore be of great interest to develop PPLP schemes without requiring the existence of a (semi-)trusted third party.

Zhong et al. [36] present three PPLP protocols (called Louis, Lester and Pierre) [2]. Lester and Pierre do not rely on any third party. The common construction idea behind those protocols is to compute the location distance using additively homomorphic public key encryption (AHPKE) between two principals with a distance obfuscation technique. However, in all their schemes the users learn the mutual distance that might be sensitive information in many situations.

Narayanan et al. [25] show three PPLP protocols that reduce the proximity detection problem to private equality testing (in the first two protocols) or private set intersection (in the third protocol). Their protocols are run based on the location which is defined as a set of adjacent triangles of a hexagon (that divides a grid). The proximity detection is achieved by testing whether two users share at least one triangle. However, as discussed in [29], the protocols of [25] may introduce different errors in practice.

Šeděnka et al. [29] present three hybrid PPLP protocols that combine AHPKE schemes with secure two-party computation (STPC). Two users would first use the AHPKE scheme (e.g., Paillier [27]) to privately compute the distance of their locations (with different distance equations in each protocol), and then run a STPC protocol (e.g., the private inequality test protocol from [10], or garbled circuits [20]) to test whether the resulting location distance is within a pre-defined threshold. However, these PPLP protocols incur a high communication and computation overhead. Furthermore their protocols have multiple rounds of communication and using OT-based multiplication, which we use in our PPLP protocol $\mathsf{ABY_{AY}}$ (cf. Sect. 3.2), is substantially more efficient than AHPKE as shown in [8].

Hallgren et al. [16] develop a PPLP protocol built on only AHPKE to test whether two users' locations are within a given distance threshold (without a trusted third party). Their construction makes use of a similar distance obfuscation method as in [36]. The main difference is that Hallgren et al.'s scheme hides the exact distance between two users.

In recent work, Zhu et al. [37] propose two efficient PPLP schemes for different geometric situations (i.e., polygon or circle). However, their schemes are subject to linear equation solving attacks. Namely, a malicious sender who honestly follows the protocol execution can learn the location coordinates (x, y) of a receiver by solving the relevant linear equation (involving x and y) implied by the proximity answers returned by the receiver (in one query). The major problem of these schemes is that two equations share the same randomness which can be eliminated by a division. We show the attacks against Zhu et al.'s protocols in the full version [19, Appendix A].

2   Preliminaries

General Notations. We let κ be the security parameter and ρ be the statistical security parameter. Let $[n] = \{1, \ldots, n\}$ denote the set of integers between 1 and n. We write $a \xleftarrow{\$} S$ to denote the operation which samples a uniform random a element from set S. Let $\|$ denote the concatenation operation of two strings, $|a|$ denote the bit-length of a string a, and $\#S$ denotes the number of elements in set S.

Euclidean Distance. For computing the distance in our Privacy-Preserving Location Proximity (PPLP) protocols, we use Euclidean distance, which is computed as follows for two dimensions: $d \leftarrow \sqrt{(x_0 - x_1)^2 + (y_0 - y_1)^2}$. However, since the computation of square root is costly in secure computation, we calculate the squared Euclidean distance as $d^2 \leftarrow (x_0 - x_1)^2 + (y_0 - y_1)^2$ and compare it with the squared threshold $d^2 \overset{?}{<} T^2$ to determine if two users of the PPLP protocol are close to each other.

In the following, we review the cryptographic tools used in our paper.

2.1   Secure Two-Party Computation

We implement our PPLP protocols using the ABY framework for mixed-protocol Secure Two-Party Computation (STPC) [8]. We make use of two sharing types implemented in ABY: Yao and Arithmetic sharing.

Yao Sharing. Yao sharing denotes Yao's Garbled Circuits (GCs) protocol [32]. Using GCs, two mistrusting parties P_0 and P_1 can securely compute a public function f on their respective inputs x_0 and x_1. For this, P_0 garbles the plaintext Boolean circuit C (a Boolean circuit which represents f) into garbled circuit $\widetilde{C}$. P_0 sends $\widetilde{C}$ and its garbled inputs to P_1. P_1 obtains its garbled inputs using Oblivious Transfer (OT) [1,24], and P_1 evaluates $\widetilde{C}$. Depending on which party gets the output, either P_0 sends the decryption keys for the output to P_1, or P_1 sends the obtained garbled outputs to P_0, or both parties do this if they both get the output. We denote shares of input bit x as $((k^0, k^1), k^x)$, where P_0 holds both keys $\langle x \rangle_0^Y = (k^0, k^1)$ and P_1 holds the key that corresponds to its input bit x, i.e., $\langle x \rangle_1^Y = k^x$. In Yao sharing, evaluation of XOR gates is performed locally without communication [21], whereas evaluation of AND gates requires sending $2k$ bits [34].

Arithmetic Sharing. Arithmetic sharing denotes a generalization of the GMW protocol [14] for unsigned integer numbers in the ring $\mathbb{Z}_{2^\ell}$. In Arithmetic sharing, an integer x is shared between P_0 and P_1 as $x = \langle x \rangle_0^A + \langle x \rangle_1^A \mod 2^\ell$, where P_0 holds $\langle x \rangle_0^A$ and P_1 holds $\langle x \rangle_1^A$. The function to be evaluated is represented as arithmetic circuit, which operates on unsigned integer values and consists of addition, subtraction, and multiplication gates modulo 2^ℓ only. Addition and subtraction gates can be evaluated locally without interaction between the parties, whereas evaluation of multiplication gates requires interaction and OT-based precomputations [8].

Notation. A share of value x held by Party P_i in sharing $t \in \{A, Y\}$, where A denotes Arithmetic sharing and Y denotes Yao sharing, is written as $\langle x \rangle_i^t$. In protocol descriptions, the party index is omitted because both parties perform the same operations. Operation $\odot$ on shares $\langle x \rangle^t$ and $\langle y \rangle^t$ in sharing t is denoted as $\langle z \rangle^t = \langle x \rangle^t \odot \langle y \rangle^t$. We write a conversion of Yao sharing $\langle x \rangle^Y$ to Arithmetic sharing as $\langle x \rangle^A = Y2A(\langle x \rangle^Y)$ and a conversion of Arithmetic sharing to Yao sharing as $\langle x \rangle^Y = A2Y(\langle x \rangle^A)$.

2.2 Additively Homomorphic Public-Key Encryption Scheme

An additively homomorphic public-key encryption (AHPKE) scheme is a probabilistic encryption scheme which consists of the following three algorithms:

- **Key Generation** (KGen). Given the security parameter κ, the algorithm returns the public and private key pair (pk, sk).
- **Encryption** (Enc). This algorithm takes a message $m \in \mathcal{M}$ from a plaintext space $\mathcal{M}$ and a public key pk as inputs, and outputs a ciphertext $c \in \mathcal{C}$ where $\mathcal{C}$ is the ciphertext space.
- **Decryption** (Dec). This algorithm takes the secret key sk and a ciphertext as inputs, and outputs the plaintext m.

For two ciphertext $C_1 = \mathsf{Enc}(pk, m_1)$ and $C_2 = \mathsf{Enc}(pk, m_2)$, we have the following additively homomorphic properties:

$$\mathsf{Dec}(sk, C_1 \cdot C_2) = m_1 + m_2 \text{ and } \mathsf{Dec}(sk, C_1 \cdot C_2^{-1}) = m_1 - m_2.$$

Using the above homomorphic additions, it is also possible to efficiently compute multiplications and divisions by a plaintext value $v \in \mathcal{M}$ using the square-and-multiply algorithm:

$$\mathsf{Dec}(sk, C_1^v) = v \cdot m_1 \text{ and } \mathsf{Dec}(sk, C_1^{v^{-1}}) = m_1/v.$$

We require that the AHPKE schemes used in our implementations satisfy standard semantic security. In Table 1, we briefly review two concrete instantiations of AHPKE, i.e., the construction by Damgård et al. (DGK) [7] and Lifted ElGamal [9] instantiated with Elliptic Curve Cryptography (ECC). Let $EC : y^2 = x^3 + ax + b$ denote an elliptic curve over a prime field $\mathsf{GF}(p)$ with curve parameters $a, b \in \mathsf{GF}(p)$. When the modulus n is clear from the context, then the modular operation mod n may be omitted.

Table 1. Additively homomorphic public-key encryption (AHPKE) schemes used in this paper.

	DGK [7]	Lifted ElGamal [9]
$\mathsf{KGen}(\kappa)$	1. Choose two random large primes p, q s.t. $|p| = |q| = \kappa/2$ 2. $n := p \cdot q$ 3. Choose ℓ-bits prime u, s.t. $u|(p-1)$ and $u|(q-1)$ 4. Choose ϕ-bits primes (v_p, v_q), s.t. $v_p|(p-1)$ and $v_q|(q-1)$ 5. Choose (g, h) of orders (uv_pv_q, v_pv_q) 6. $pk = (n, g, h, u)$, $sk = (p, q, v_p, v_q)$	1. Choose ϕ-bits prime p 2. Choose points $P, Q \in EC$ 3. $y \xleftarrow{\$} \mathbb{Z}_p^*$, $Y = yP$ 4. $pk = (p, P, Q, Y)$, $sk = y$
$\mathsf{Enc}(pk, m)$	1. $r \xleftarrow{\$} \mathcal{R}_\mathsf{D} = \{0,1\}^{2.5\phi}$ 2. $C = g^m \cdot h^r \bmod n$	1. For $m \in \mathbb{Z}_p$, $r \xleftarrow{\$} \mathbb{Z}_p^*$ 2. $C = (R, V) = (rP, rY + mQ)$
$\mathsf{Dec}(sk, C)$	1. $C^{v_p} \bmod p = g^{v_p m} \bmod p$ 2. Calculate m by Pohlig-Hellman Alg. [28]	1. $mQ = V - yR$ Full decryption is not required

Bloom filter (BF) [4] is a probabilistic data structure that provides space-efficient storage of a set and that can efficiently test whether an element is a member of the set. The probabilistic property of BF may lead to false positive matches, but no false negatives. It is well-known that the more elements are added to the BF, the larger the probability of false positives gets. To reduce the false positive rate, we follow the approach of [26], i.e., a BF with $1.44\epsilon N$ bits for a set with size N has a false positive rate (FPR) of $2^{-\epsilon}$.

We review the algorithms of a Bloom filter as follows:

- **Filter initiation** (BF.init). On input a set size N, this algorithm initiates the Bloom filter of bit length $1.44\epsilon N$.
- **Element insertion** (BF.insert). This algorithm takes an element m as input, and inserts m into BF.
- **Element check** (BF.check). This algorithm returns 1 if an element m is in BF, and 0 otherwise.
- **Element change** (BF.Pos). This algorithm computes positions to be changed for element m in BF.

Random oracles were first introduced by Bellare and Rogaway [3] as a tool to prove security of a cryptographic scheme. In this work, we assume that the hash function is modeled as a random oracle. Basically, a random oracle is stateful, i.e., for a random oracle query $H(m)$ for some input $m \in \{0,1\}^*$, it proceeds as follows:

- With respect to the first query on m, the oracle just returns a truly random value r_m from the corresponding domain, and records the tuple (m, r_m) into its query list HList.
- If $m \in$ HList, then the oracle just returns its associated random value r_m recorded in HList.

3 Efficient PPLP Schemes from ABY

We show in this section how the ABY framework for Secure Two-Party Computation (STPC) [8] can be used for Privacy-Preserving Location Proximity (PPLP). For describing ABY-based protocols, we use the following notation described in Table 2. We design two protocols for PPLP: (i) based on Yao sharing only and (ii) based on a mix of Arithmetic and Yao sharing, which we describe in the following.

Table 2. Notation used for describing our ABY-based protocols.

Term	Description
P_0, P_1	Parties that perform secure computation
$t \in \{A, Y\}$	Sharing types: Arithmetic or Yao
$\langle x \rangle_i^t$	Share x in sharing t held by party P_i
$\langle z \rangle^t = \langle x \rangle^t \odot \langle y \rangle^t$	Operation $\odot$ on shares $\langle x \rangle^t$ and $\langle y \rangle^t$
$\langle x \rangle^Y = A2Y(\langle x \rangle^A)$	Sharing conversion from Arithmetic to Yao sharing

3.1   ABY$_Y$: A PPLP Scheme from Yao Sharing

The advantage of the Yao-based PPLP protocol is that it has a small and constant number of rounds, which makes it well-suited for high-latency networks. Since we operate on unsigned integers in ABY, we must make sure that no underflows occur for which we see two possible options for computing the Euclidean distance: (i) compute the extended equation of Euclidean distance, i.e., $x_0^2 + x_1^2 - 2x_0x_1 + y_0^2 + y_1^2 - 2y_0y_1$, or subtract the smaller coordinate from the larger coordinate, i.e., $(x_{max} - x_{min})^2 + (y_{max} - y_{min})^2$. PPLP calculation using the extended equation results in 6 multiplications (which are very expensive operations as they require a number of AND gates which is quadratic in the bitlength of the operands), whereas determining maxima requires only a linear overhead in the bitlength and only two expensive multiplications. This is why we choose and further improve approach (ii) as follows. The intuitive approach for the Yao-based Euclidean distance computation requires two MUX gates for each dimension for selecting x_{max} and x_{min} (resp. y_{max} and y_{min}). The functionality of multiplexer $c \leftarrow \text{MUX}(a, b, s)$ on inputs a and b, and selection bit s is defined as $c \leftarrow s == 0 ? a : b$. We slightly improve this circuit by observing that instead of individually selecting the maximum and the minimum, we can also swap the order of the two x values if $x_1 > x_0$ (and the same for the y values). Hence, we replace the two MUX gates by one Conditional Swap gate, which using the construction of [21] has the same costs as only *one* MUX gate (ℓ AND gates, where ℓ is the bitlength of the operands). The functionality of Conditional Swap $(a', b') \leftarrow \text{CondSwap}(a, b, s)$ on inputs a and b, and selection bit s is defined as $a' \leftarrow a \oplus [(a \oplus b) \wedge s]$, $b' \leftarrow b \oplus [(a \oplus b) \wedge s]$. Although this technique brings only slight performance improvement for Euclidean distance (0.4% fewer AND gates for 32-bit coordinates), it gains more significance when used in other privacy-preserving distance metrics, e.g., Manhattan distance (22% fewer AND gates for 32-bit coordinates).

In our Yao-based PPLP scheme (denoted as ABY$_Y$) given in Fig. 1, the following gates are used: $2(\text{GT}(\ell) + \text{CondSwap}(\ell) + \text{SUB}(\ell) + \text{MUL}(\sigma)) + ADD(\sigma)$, where $\text{GT}(\ell)$ is an ℓ-bit greater-than circuit (ℓ AND gates [20]), CondSwap(ℓ) is an ℓ-bit Conditional Swap gate (ℓ AND gates [21]), SUB(ℓ) is an ℓ-bit subtraction circuit (ℓ AND gates [20]), MUL(σ) is a σ-bit multiplication circuit ($2\sigma^2 - \sigma$ AND gates [20]), and ADD(σ) is a σ-bit addition circuit (σ AND gates [5]). The values ℓ and σ are the bitlengths of the computed values. In our setting, $\ell = 32$ bits (the bitlength of a coordinate) and $\sigma = 64$ bits (the bitlength of the resulting squared value).

The aforementioned gates result in the following communication requirements between parties: $6\ell + 4\sigma^2 - \sigma = 16512$ AND gates $= 528384$ bytes of communication with 256 bit communication per AND gate using the half-gates technique of [34]. This scheme requires 2 messages in the online phase.

3.2   ABY$_{AY}$: A PPLP Scheme from Arithmetic and Yao Sharing

We design a protocol for PPLP using a mix of Arithmetic and Yao sharing, which we denote as ABY$_{AY}$. The use of Arithmetic sharing is advantageous for

$$\langle isNear\rangle^Y \leftarrow \mathsf{ABY_Y}(\langle x_0\rangle^Y, \langle x_1\rangle^Y, \langle y_0\rangle^Y, \langle y_1\rangle^Y, \langle T\rangle^Y)$$

1 : $\langle gtX\rangle^Y \leftarrow \mathrm{GT}(\langle x_1\rangle^Y, \langle x_0\rangle^Y)$

2 : $swappedX \leftarrow \mathrm{CondSwap}(\langle x_0\rangle^Y, \langle x_1\rangle^Y, \langle gtX\rangle^Y)$

3 : $\langle x_{max}\rangle^Y \leftarrow swappedX[0]$

4 : $\langle x_{min}\rangle^Y \leftarrow swappedX[1]$

5 : $\langle gtY\rangle^Y \leftarrow \mathrm{GT}(\langle y_1\rangle^Y, \langle y_0\rangle^Y)$

6 : $swappedY \leftarrow \mathrm{CondSwap}(\langle y_0\rangle^Y, \langle y_1\rangle^Y, \langle gtY\rangle^Y)$

7 : $\langle y_{max}\rangle^Y \leftarrow swappedY[0]$

8 : $\langle y_{min}\rangle^Y \leftarrow swappedY[1]$

9 : $\langle d\rangle^Y \leftarrow (\langle x_{max}\rangle^Y - \langle x_{min}\rangle^Y)^2 + (\langle y_{max}\rangle^Y - \langle y_{min}\rangle^Y)^2$

10 : **return** $\langle d\rangle^Y < \langle T\rangle^Y$

Fig. 1. Our PPLP protocol $\mathsf{ABY_Y}$ using only Yao sharing in ABY [8].

this scheme—it (i) decreases the communication and computation overhead for the PPLP, and (ii) can decrease protocol runtimes in low-latency networks. However, $\mathsf{ABY_Y}$ can still be significantly faster in high-latency networks, such as LTE in areas with very poor signal reception, which is, however, uncommon in crowded areas where people usually meet. Our protocol requires the following gates: $6 \cdot \mathrm{MUL_A}(\sigma) + \mathrm{A2Y}(\sigma) + \mathrm{GT}(\sigma)$, where $\mathrm{MUL_A}(\sigma)$ is a σ-bit multiplication in Arithmetic sharing, $\mathrm{A2Y}(\sigma)$ is a σ-bit Arithmetic to Yao sharing conversion, $\mathrm{GT}(\sigma)$ is a σ-bit greater-than gate (σ AND gates [20]), and σ is the bitlength of the squared distance. Our protocol for mixed-protocol SMPC-based PPLP is shown in Fig. 2.

In total, 6 multiplication gates in Arithmetic sharing, 1 Arithmetic to Yao conversion gate, and σ AND gates in Yao sharing are required in this scheme. This results in $12\sigma^2 + 19\kappa\sigma$ bits of communication. In our setting with the bitlength of the squared value $\sigma = 64$, this yields 45056 bytes of communication, which is a factor $11\times$ improvement over $\mathsf{ABY_Y}$. However, this scheme requires 4 messages in the online phase ($2\times$ more than for $\mathsf{ABY_Y}$).

4   Efficient PPLP Schemes from Homomorphic Encryption

In this section, we show how to build efficient privacy preserving location proximity (PPLP) schemes which are suitable for mobile devices. In our construction, we will extensively use a one-way hash function $H : \{0,1\}^* \rightarrow \mathbb{Z}_p$ which will be modeled as a random oracle in the security analysis, where p is a large prime chosen in each scheme.

$$\langle \mathit{isNear} \rangle^Y \leftarrow \mathsf{ABY}_{\mathsf{AY}}(\langle x_0 \rangle^A, \langle x_1 \rangle^A, \langle y_0 \rangle^A, \langle y_1 \rangle^A, \langle T \rangle^Y)$$

1 : $\quad \langle x \rangle^A \leftarrow (\langle x_0 \rangle^A)^2 + (\langle x_1 \rangle^A)^2 - \langle x_0 \rangle^A \langle x_1 \rangle^A - \langle x_0 \rangle^A \langle x_1 \rangle^A$

2 : $\quad \langle y \rangle^A \leftarrow (\langle y_0 \rangle^A)^2 + (\langle y_1 \rangle^A)^2 - \langle y_0 \rangle^A \langle y_1 \rangle^A - \langle y_0 \rangle^A \langle y_1 \rangle^A$

3 : $\quad \langle d \rangle^Y \leftarrow \mathsf{A2B}(\langle x \rangle^A + \langle y \rangle^A)$

4 : $\quad$ **return** $\langle d \rangle^Y < \langle T \rangle^Y$

Fig. 2. Our PPLP protocol $\mathsf{ABY}_{\mathsf{AY}}$ using Arithmetic and Yao sharing in ABY [8].

OVERVIEW. We first give an overview of our constructions. Consider the general scenario that a party A at location with coordinates (x_A, y_A) wants to know whether the other party B at location (x_B, y_B) is close to her without learning any information about B's location. Intuitively, if the distance d between their locations are smaller than a threshold τ, then we can say that they are near. If set $T = \{d_1, \ldots, d_m\}$ denotes all possible Euclidean distances between two adjacent parties, then the location proximity problem is to determine whether d is in this public set or not. Since Euclidean distances are calculated as the sum of two squares $m = |T| \approx \lambda \cdot \frac{\tau^2}{\sqrt{2 \ln \tau}}$, where $\lambda = 0.7642$ is the Landau-Ramanujan constant, since we insert only unique elements in T that are smaller than or equal to τ^2 [11, Sect. 2.3].

However, the distance d should be also hidden from both parties to preserve privacy. Hence, we cannot let party A directly input the distance $x = d$ to test the location proximity. To protect the distance from A, we make use of additively homomorphic PKE scheme (either DGK or ElGamal shown in Table 1) to enable both parties to jointly compute a distance d based on party A's public key but B blinds d with two fresh random values (i.e., (r, s)). Namely, A will decrypt the ciphertext computed by B to get the blinded distance $\tilde{d} = s \cdot (r + d) \bmod p$ where p is a prime. Our distance obfuscation method is inspired by the Lester protocol [36], but is tailored to the additively homomorphic PKE schemes we use. To allow A to get the location proximity result, we further randomize the set T to another set $\mathcal{X} = \{x_1, \ldots, x_m\}$, s.t. $x_i = H(s \cdot (r + d_i) \bmod p)$. It is not hard to see that if $H(\tilde{d}) \in \mathcal{X}$, then $d \in T$. We use a Bloom filter to store the set $\mathcal{X}$ to reduce the storage and communication costs.

SECURITY MODEL. We consider the honest-but-curious (semi-honest) setting where both parties honestly follow the protocol specification without deviating from it in any way, e.g., providing malicious inputs. However, any party might passively try to infer information about the other party's input from the protocol messages. This model is formulated by ideally implementing the protocol with a Trusted Third Party (TTP) $\mathcal{T}$ which receives the inputs of both parties and outputs the result of the defined function. Security requires that, in the real implementation of the protocol (without a TTP), none of the parties learns more information than what is returned by $\mathcal{T}$ in the ideal implementation. Namely, for any semi-honest adversary that successfully attacks a real protocol, there must exist a simulator $\mathcal{S}$ that successfully attacks the same protocol in the ideal world. Let Dist be a function which takes as input the coordinates (x_A, y_A, x_B, y_B) of the two parties and outputs the distance d between them. In the following, we define an ideal functionality of PPLP.

An ideal functionality $\mathcal{F}_{\mathsf{PPLP}}$ of our upcoming PPLP protocol with private inputs x_A, y_A and x_B, y_B and a public distance set T with threshold $\tau \in \mathbb{N}$, is defined as:

$$\mathcal{F}_{\mathsf{PPLP}} : (x_A, y_A, T_i, x_B, y_B, \mathsf{T}) \rightarrow (\perp, (\mathsf{Dist}(x_A, y_A, x_B, y_B) \in \mathsf{T}?1 : 0)).$$

We say that a PPLP protocol Π securely realizes functionality $\mathcal{F}_{\mathsf{PPLP}}$ if: for all Probabilistic Polynomial Time (PPT) adversaries $\mathcal{A}$, there exists a PPT simulator $\mathcal{S}$, such that

$$\mathsf{REAL}(\Pi, \mathcal{T}, \mathcal{A}) \approx \mathsf{IDEAL}(\mathcal{F}_{\mathsf{PPLP}}, \mathcal{T}, \mathcal{S}),$$

where $\approx$ denotes computational indistinguishability.

4.1 Σ_{DGK}: A PPLP Scheme from DGK

We fist introduce our PPLP protocol Σ_{DGK} from DGK (KGen^{D}, Enc^{D}, Dec^{D} as shown in Table 1), which provides a fast pre-computation phase. This PPLP scheme running between two parties A and B is shown in Fig. 3. A learns the location proximity result, i.e., whether or not the distance between A and B is smaller than a pre-defined threshold T.

Remark 1. In our PPLP scheme, we consider some possible optimizations on generating the blinded distance. We separate the ciphertexts C_1, C_2, and C_3 into two steps. We observe that the exponentiations (e.g., $R_1 = h^{\widetilde{r}_1}$) related to the random values $(\widetilde{r}_1, \widetilde{r}_2, \widetilde{r}_3)$ of these ciphertexts can be precomputed. Note that each computation of $R_i = h^{\widetilde{r}_i}$ needs a full exponentiation with 2.5ϕ bits exponent (e.g., $\phi = 256$). In contrast, the size of the location coordinate and the blinded distance, i.e., the encrypted message, is much smaller, e.g., $\rho = 16$ bits. Hence, an exponentiation related to a message (e.g., g^{-2x_A}) can be done more efficiently online. For the online phase, we only need to compute the exponentiations related to the messages, so that only three exponentiations with 'small' exponents (depending on the message space) are required at party A. We can do similar pre-computations at party B. Furthermore, in order to compute the ciphertext C_d at party B, we can use simultaneous multi-exponentiation (with variable bases) [23, Algorithm 14.88] to speed up the computation. Then, the computation of C_d roughly needs 1.3 times that of a regular modular exponentiation.

Theorem 1. *If DGK is semantically secure and the hash function H is modeled as random oracle, then the proposed PPLP scheme Σ_{DGK} in Fig. 3 is a secure computation of $\mathcal{F}_{\mathsf{PPLP}}$ in the honest-but-curious model.*

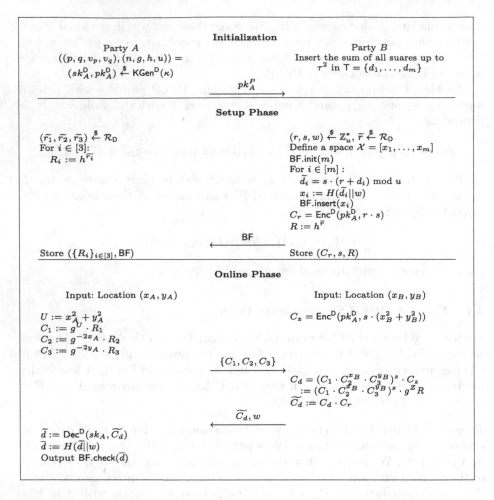

Fig. 3. Our PPLP protocol Σ_{DGK} using DGK encryption.

Proof. We present the security analysis with respect to two aspects: (i) no corrupted party B can learn the input set of an honest party A; (ii) no corrupted party A can learn the resulting distance. The security against corrupted party B is guaranteed by the security of DGK, since all inputs of A are encrypted. Hence, the simulator $\mathcal{S}$ can just replace the real ciphertexts with random ones. Any adversary distinguishing this change can be used to break DGK.

As for a corrupted party A, we claim that A cannot obtain any useful information from a blinded distance $\widetilde{d_i} = s \cdot (r + d_i)$ and the Bloom filter BF. We first show that the inputs (i.e., blinded distances) of the random oracles are unique in a query, so that each $\widetilde{d_i}$ is unique as well. Consider two possible blinded distances $\widetilde{d_1} = s \cdot (r + d_1)$ and $\widetilde{d_2} = s \cdot (r + d_2)$ in a location proximity query. Since each d_i is unique, so is $\widetilde{d_i}$. Hence, each x_i is generated by the random oracle with unique input in a query, so that it is independent of all others. In particular, there is no false negative. With respect to different queries, although A may obtain two distances $\tilde{d}_1 = s_1 \cdot (r_1 + d_1)$ and $\tilde{d}_2 = s_2 \cdot (r_2 + d_2)$ such that $\tilde{d}_1 = \tilde{d}_2$, these two distances are associated with different random numbers $w_1 \neq w_2$. Hence, the blinded distance $\tilde{d}$ and the random value w together would ensure the input of the random oracle to be unique through all queries with overwhelming probability. As a result, in the ideal world S could use randomly chosen strings to build a set $\mathcal{X}$ in a location proximity query instead of the results from the random oracle. Due to the properties of the Bloom filter, A cannot infer the position of a $\overline{d}_i$ (after decryption) in $\mathcal{X}$ from BF, where $\overline{d}_i = H(\tilde{d}_i \| t)$ is inserted in BF.

Furthermore, since a distance d is blinded by freshly chosen random values r and s, party A can neither infer r nor s from $\tilde{d}$ with an overwhelming probability. Thus, A cannot decrypt the distance nor test 'candidate' $\tilde{d}'$ (of her own choice) based on BF without knowing either r or s.

To summarize, the PPLP scheme is secure under the given assumptions.

4.2 Σ_{EIG}: A PPLP Protocol from ElGamal

In this section, we propose a PPLP protocol Σ_{EIG} from ElGamal ($\mathsf{KGen}^{\mathsf{E}}$, $\mathsf{Enc}^{\mathsf{E}}$, $\mathsf{Dec}^{\mathsf{E}}$ as shown in Table 1). The construction of Σ_{EIG} is similar to Σ_{DGK}. However, we observe that the full decryption in the online phase is not necessary for party A who only needs to know the location proximity result. Thus, we replace DGK with the ECC-based lifted ElGamal scheme which results in better online communication complexity. Moreover, when increasing the security parameter, the performance of ECC operations is better than that of arithmetic modulo an RSA modulus in DGK, so Σ_{EIG} is better suited for long-term security. The Σ_{EIG} PPLP protocol is shown in Fig. 4.

Theorem 2. *If ElGamal is semantically secure and the hash function H is modeled as random oracle, then the proposed PPLP scheme Σ_{EIG} in Fig. 4 is a secure computation of $\mathcal{F}_{\mathsf{PPLP}}$ in the honest-but-curious model.*

The proof of this theorem is analogous to that of Theorem 1 and thus omitted.

5   Comparison and Experimental Results

In this section, we compare our proposed protocols with the state-of-the-art PPLP protocol of Hallgren et al. [15,16]. We instantiate all primitives in our PPLP protocols to achieve a security level of $\kappa = 128$ bits. The secret-shared coordinates in our benchmarks are of bitlength $\ell = 32$ bit and the secret-shared squared results are of bitlength $\sigma = 64$ bit. However, we restrict the cleartext domain of the coordinates to $\{0, \ldots, 2^{31.5} - 1\}$ s.t. the squared Euclidean distance fits into a 64-bit unsigned integer. This is sufficient for any coordinates on earth with sub-meter accuracy.

We benchmark our prototype C++ implementations of our PPLP protocols on two commodity servers equipped with Intel Core i7 3.5 GHz CPUs and 32 GB

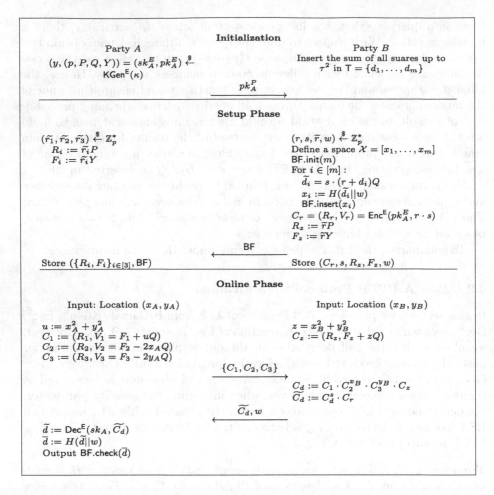

Fig. 4. Our PPLP protocol Σ_{EIG} using ElGamal encryption.

RAM. During our benchmarks, however, the maximum RAM requirements were in the order of a few dozen megabytes. The two machines are connected via Gigabit Ethernet. Each benchmarking result is averaged over 100 executions.

As shown in Table 3, our protocol Σ_{EIG} has the lowest online communication and also more efficient arithmetic than Σ_{DGK} due to the usage of ECC instead of modular arithmetic over a 3072-bit RSA modulus. Therefore, we implemented Σ_{EIG}, but not Σ_{DGK} because we expect its runtimes to be worse. When utilizing Bloom filters, we use a false positive rate of $2^{-\rho}$, where ρ is the statistical security parameter ($\rho = 40$) as before.

The underlying framework for our Σ_{EIG} implementation is the mcl library[2] that includes an optimized lifted ElGamal implementation. We use lifted

---

[2] https://github.com/herumi/mcl.

ElGamal encryption over the elliptic curve `secp256k1` with key size of 256 bits and 128-bit security. The mcl library supports point compression, and therefore each elliptic curve point can be represented by $256 + 1$ bits. An ElGamal ciphertext consists of two elliptic curve points, i.e., 514 bits in total.

5.1 Communication

We compare the communication of our protocols in Table 3. As can be seen from the table, the online communication and the setup communication of the ABY-based protocols is constant, whereas for the public-key based protocols the setup communication grows superlinearly with $\frac{\tau^2}{\sqrt{2\ln\tau}}$. The online round complexity of $\mathsf{ABY_Y}$, Σ_{DGK}, and Σ_{EIG} is minimal, but larger for $\mathsf{ABY_{AY}}$ due to the multiplication in Additive sharing and the conversion from Additive sharing to Yao sharing, which need additional rounds of interaction.

Table 3. Communication in Bytes and round complexities of our PPLP protocols for security level $\kappa = 128$ bit.

Protocol	$\mathsf{ABY_Y}$ (Sect. 3.1)	$\mathsf{ABY_{AY}}$ (Sect. 3.2)	Σ_{DGK} (Sect. 4.1)	Σ_{EIG} (Sect. 4.2)
Setup communication [Bytes]	209555	117155	$\approx 5.5 \frac{\tau^2}{\sqrt{2\ln\tau}}$	$\approx 5.5 \frac{\tau^2}{\sqrt{2\ln\tau}}$
Online communication [Bytes]	3656	3001	1056	288
# Sequential messages online	2	4	2	2

5.2 Benchmarks in a Local Network

In the following, we benchmark our protocols in a local Gigabit network with an average latency of 0.2 ms. We depict the runtimes and total communication of our PPLP protocols in Fig. 5. We exclude the runtimes for the base-OTs (0.48 s in the LAN setting) for $\mathsf{ABY_Y}$ and $\mathsf{ABY_{AY}}$, because they need to be run only for the first execution of the protocol and hence are a one-time expense. In the same manner, we exclude the one-time cost of generating the key pair and sending the public key in Σ_{DGK} and Σ_{EIG} (6 ms in the LAN setting).

Figure 5 confirms that the complexity of $\mathsf{ABY_Y}$ and $\mathsf{ABY_{AY}}$ is independent of τ, whereas the complexity of Σ_{EIG} grows superlinearly in τ. The online runtime also grows due to the growing size of the Bloom filter $\left(\approx 5.5 \frac{\tau^2}{\sqrt{2\ln\tau}}\right)$ and therefore the number of (non-cryptographic) hash functions that need to be computed. $\mathsf{ABY_{AY}}$ has the fastest online and setup runtime, and therefore, in total performance, it is substantially better than all other protocols.

As for the communication, Σ_{EIG} is more efficient than all other protocols for $\tau < 256$ (the communication of Σ_{DGK} is similar) and afterwards $\mathsf{ABY_{AY}}$ is again the most efficient. Thus, Σ_{EIG} and $\mathsf{ABY_{AY}}$ are beneficial for saving communication fees in mobile data networks which charge per KB. However, $\mathsf{ABY_{AY}}$ has more communication rounds (cf. Table 3), so it is unclear if it is also more efficient in high-latency networks which we will investigate next.

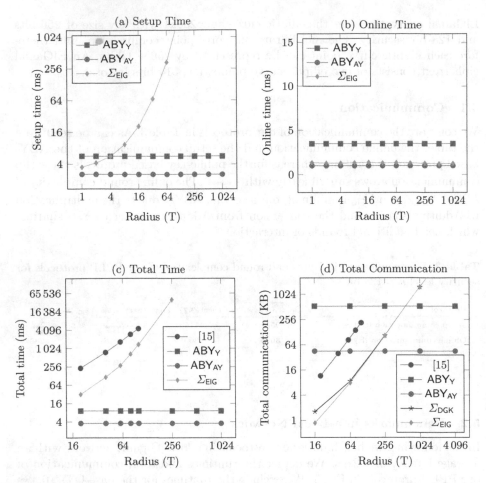

Fig. 5. Setup (a), online (b), and total (c) runtimes in milliseconds in a local Gigabit network with 0.2 ms average latency, and total communication (d) in Kilobytes of our PPLP schemes with security level $\kappa = 128$ bit in comparison with the ElGamal-based PPLP scheme of Hallgren et al. [15,16] with security level $\kappa = 112$ bit.

5.3 Benchmarks in a Simulated Mobile Network

To show the practicality of our PPLP protocols, we simulate a mobile Internet connection, where we restrict the network bandwidth to 16 Mbps and the network latency to 45 ms, which are typical average parameters for mobile Internet nowadays[3]. Although the mobile Internet is still much slower than the cable Internet, most of the developed countries already support LTE[4] that provides transfer channels with bandwidth of dozens of Mbps and a typical transfer latency of just a few dozen milliseconds. Moreover, free Wi-Fi is becoming ubiquitous especially

---

[3] https://opensignal.com.

[4] https://gsacom.com.

in big cities[5], which provides almost unlimited, fast, and low-latency access to PPLP. Thus, the prerequisites for using our algorithms greatly differ depending on the location of the deployment. Again, in the mobile Internet setting, we exclude the time needed for the base-OTs (0.75 s) and for generating the public key pair and sending the public key (0.05 s) as these are one-time expenses.

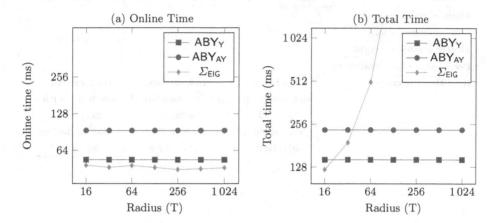

Fig. 6. Online (a) and total (b) runtimes in milliseconds of our PPLP protocols in the mobile Internet setting with 45 ms average network latency and 16 Mbps bandwidth.

We depict the online and total runtimes in the mobile Internet setting in Fig. 6. The online time for Σ_{EIG} is lowest due to the smallest communication and the minimal round complexity, followed by $\mathsf{ABY_Y}$ which also has minimal round complexity, but up to factor 12× more communication (cf. Table 3). The online time for $\mathsf{ABY_{AY}}$ is by factor 2× larger due to the larger round complexity. For the total runtimes, we see that Σ_{EIG} is the most efficient protocol for small thresholds of $\tau \leq 25$ from when on the constant runtime of $\mathsf{ABY_Y}$ with 143 ms is most efficient. The total runtime of $\mathsf{ABY_{AY}}$ is not competitive and almost twice as high as that of $\mathsf{ABY_Y}$ due to the higher round complexity[6].

5.4 Summary

We briefly summarize the properties of and use-cases for our PPLP protocols in Table 4. Since all our PPLP protocols have different strengths, we give possible use-cases in the following: $\mathsf{ABY_Y}$ is advantageous in high-latency networks withhigh bandwidth; $\mathsf{ABY_{AY}}$ is better-suited for low-latency networks

---

[5] https://wifispc.com.

[6] In the near future, today's 4G mobile networks will be replaced by 5G, which will significantly reduce the average network latency (average expected latency in 5G networks is around 1 ms [18]). Therefore, in low-latency 5G networks $\mathsf{ABY_{AY}}$ will potentially be most efficient (see Sect. 5.2).

with medium bandwidth and it is especially beneficial for computationally weak devices; Σ_{EIG} runs fast in any network types for small values of τ.

Table 4. Summary and use-cases of our most efficient PPLP protocols.

Protocol	ABY_{Y} (Sect. 3.1)	ABY_{AY} (Sect. 3.2)	Σ_{EIG} (Sect. 4.2)
Minimal online rounds	✓	✗	✓
Low communication	✗	✓	✓
Mostly symmetric crypto	✓	✓	✗
Performance independent of τ	✓	✓	✗
Resulting use cases	High latency, high bandwidth network; weak device; arbitrary τ	Low latency, medium bandwidth network; weak device; arbitrary τ	High latency, low bandwidth network; powerful device; small τ

6   Conclusion

In this work, we designed, implemented, and evaluated multiple practically efficient protocols for PPLP using STPC and AHPKE. Moreover, we introduced optimizations for our protocols: using Bloom filter [4] for our AHPKE-based protocols and using Conditional Swap [21] for our Boolean circuit-based protocols. We made extensive use of the pre-computation for computationally heavy parts of our protocols in the cases where the same parties perform PPLP several times, which substantially improves performance. Finally, we evaluated our most efficient protocols in a real-world mobile Internet setting and showed practical total runtimes of below 200 ms and online runtimes of below 50 ms. We leave implementation of our protocols on mobile devices as future work.

Acknowledgements. We thank Per Hallgren for providing the raw data of his benchmarks for comparison. This work has been co-funded by the DFG as part of project E4 within the CRC 1119 CROSSING, and by the German Federal Ministry of Education and Research (BMBF) and the Hessen State Ministry for Higher Education, Research and the Arts (HMWK) within CRISP. This work has been also co-funded by the INSURE project (303578) of Academy of Finland and by National Natural Science Foundation of China (Grant No. 61872051).

References

1. Asharov, G., Lindell, Y., Schneider, T., Zohner, M.: More efficient oblivious transfer and extensions for faster secure computation. In: CCS, pp. 535–548. ACM (2013)
2. Atallah, M.J., Du, W.: Secure multi-party computational geometry. In: Dehne, F., Sack, J.-R., Tamassia, R. (eds.) WADS 2001. LNCS, vol. 2125, pp. 165–179. Springer, Heidelberg (2001). https://doi.org/10.1007/3-540-44634-6_16
3. Bellare, M., Rogaway, P.: Random oracles are practical: a paradigm for designing efficient protocols. In: CCS (1993)
4. Bloom, B.H.: Space/time trade-offs in hash coding with allowable errors. Commun. ACM **13**(7), 422–426 (1970)
5. Boyar, J., Peralta, R., Pochuev, D.: On the multiplicative complexity of boolean functions over the basis $(\wedge, \oplus, 1)$. TCS **235**(1), 43–57 (2000)
6. Cheng, R., Zhang, Y., Bertino, E., Prabhakar, S.: Preserving user location privacy in mobile data management infrastructures. In: Danezis, G., Golle, P. (eds.) PETS 2006. LNCS, vol. 4258, pp. 393–412. Springer, Heidelberg (2006). https://doi.org/10.1007/11957454_23
7. Damgard, I., Geisler, M., Kroigard, M.: A correction to 'efficient and secure comparison for on-line auctions'. IJACT **1**(4), 323–324 (2009)
8. Demmler, D., Schneider, T., Zohner, M.: ABY - a framework for efficient mixed-protocol secure two-party computation. In: NDSS (2015)
9. ElGamal, T.: A public key cryptosystem and a signature scheme based on discrete logarithms. In: CRYPTO (1984)
10. Erkin, Z., Franz, M., Guajardo, J., Katzenbeisser, S., Lagendijk, I., Toft, T.: Privacy-preserving face recognition. In: Goldberg, I., Atallah, M.J. (eds.) PETS 2009. LNCS, vol. 5672, pp. 235–253. Springer, Heidelberg (2009). https://doi.org/10.1007/978-3-642-03168-7_14
11. Finch, S.R.: Mathematical Constants, vol. 93. Cambridge University Press, Cambridge (2003)
12. Freni, D., Ruiz Vicente, C., Mascetti, S., Bettini, C., Jensen, C.S.: Preserving location and absence privacy in geo-social networks. In: CIKM (2010)
13. El Gamal, T.: A public key cryptosystem and a signature scheme based on discrete logarithms. IEEE Trans. Inf. Theory **31**(4), 469–472 (1985)
14. Goldreich, O., Micali, S., Wigderson, A.: How to play any mental game. In: STOC (1987)
15. Hallgren, P.A.: Robust location privacy. Ph.D. thesis, Chalmers University of Technology (2017). http://www.cse.chalmers.se/research/group/security/pages/publications/perh-phd/phd-thesis.pdf
16. Hallgren, P.A., Ochoa, M., Sabelfeld, A.: InnerCircle: a parallelizable decentralized privacy-preserving location proximity protocol. In: PST (2015)
17. Hallgren, P.A., Orlandi, C., Sabelfeld, A.: PrivatePool: privacy-preserving ridesharing. In: CSF (2017)
18. Johansson, N.A., Wang, Y.-P.E., Eriksson, E., Hessler, M.: Radio access for ultra-reliable and low-latency 5G communications. In: ICC Workshop (2015)
19. Järvinen, K., Kiss, A., Schneider, T., Tkachenko, O., Yang, Z.: Faster privacy-preserving location proximity schemes. Cryptology ePrint Archive, Report 2018/694 (2018). http://ia.cr/2018/694
20. Kolesnikov, V., Sadeghi, A.-R., Schneider, T.: Improved garbled circuit building blocks and applications to auctions and computing minima. In: Garay, J.A., Miyaji, A., Otsuka, A. (eds.) CANS 2009. LNCS, vol. 5888, pp. 1–20. Springer, Heidelberg (2009). https://doi.org/10.1007/978-3-642-10433-6_1

21. Kolesnikov, V., Schneider, T.: Improved garbled circuit: free XOR gates and applications. In: Aceto, L., Damgård, I., Goldberg, L.A., Halldórsson, M.M., Ingólfsdóttir, A., Walukiewicz, I. (eds.) ICALP 2008. LNCS, vol. 5126, pp. 486–498. Springer, Heidelberg (2008). https://doi.org/10.1007/978-3-540-70583-3_40
22. Li, M., Ruan, N., Qian, Q., Zhu, H., Liang, X., Yu, L.: SPFM: scalable and privacy-preserving friend matching in mobile cloud. IEEE IoT J. 4(2), 583–591 (2017)
23. Menezes, A.J., Van Oorschot, P.C., Vanstone, S.A.: Handbook of Applied Cryptography. CRC Press, Boca Raton (1996)
24. Naor, M., Pinkas, B.: Efficient oblivious transfer protocols. In: SODA, pp. 448–457. ACM/SIAM (2001)
25. Narayanan, A., Thiagarajan, N., Lakhani, M., Hamburg, M., Boneh, D.: Location privacy via private proximity testing. In: NDSS (2011)
26. Pagh, A., Pagh, R., Rao, S.S.: An optimal bloom filter replacement. In: SODA (2005)
27. Paillier, P.: Public-key cryptosystems based on composite degree residuosity classes. In: Stern, J. (ed.) EUROCRYPT 1999. LNCS, vol. 1592, pp. 223–238. Springer, Heidelberg (1999). https://doi.org/10.1007/3-540-48910-X_16
28. Pohlig, S.C., Hellman, M.E.: An improved algorithm for computing logarithms over GF(p) and its cryptographic significance (corresp.). IEEE Trans. Inf. Theory 24(1), 106–110 (1978)
29. Šeděnka, J., Gasti, P.: Privacy-preserving distance computation and proximity testing on earth, done right. In: ASIACCS (2014)
30. Šikšnys, L., Thomsen, J.R., Šaltenis, S., Yiu, M.L., Andersen, O.: A location privacy aware friend locator. In: Mamoulis, N., Seidl, T., Pedersen, T.B., Torp, K., Assent, I. (eds.) SSTD 2009. LNCS, vol. 5644, pp. 405–410. Springer, Heidelberg (2009). https://doi.org/10.1007/978-3-642-02982-0_29
31. Siksnys, L., Thomsen, J.R., Saltenis, S., Yiu, M.L.: Private and flexible proximity detection in mobile social networks. In: MDM (2010)
32. Yao, A.C.: Protocols for secure computations. In: SFCS (1982)
33. Yu, W., Liu, Z., Chen, C., Yang, B., Guan, X.: Privacy-preserving design for emergency response scheduling system in medical social networks. Peer-to-Peer Netw. Appl. 10(2), 340–356 (2017)
34. Zahur, S., Rosulek, M., Evans, D.: Two halves make a whole. In: Oswald, E., Fischlin, M. (eds.) EUROCRYPT 2015. LNCS, vol. 9057, pp. 220–250. Springer, Heidelberg (2015). https://doi.org/10.1007/978-3-662-46803-6_8
35. Zheng, Y., Li, M., Lou, W., Hou, Y.T.: Location based handshake and private proximity test with location tags. IEEE Dependable Secure Comput. 14(4), 406–419 (2017)
36. Zhong, G., Goldberg, I., Hengartner, U.: Louis, lester and pierre: three protocols for location privacy. In: Borisov, N., Golle, P. (eds.) PET 2007. LNCS, vol. 4776, pp. 62–76. Springer, Heidelberg (2007). https://doi.org/10.1007/978-3-540-75551-7_5
37. Zhu, H., Wang, F., Lu, R., Liu, F., Fu, G., Li, H.: Efficient and privacy-preserving proximity detection schemes for social applications. IEEE Internet Things J. 5(4), 2947–2957 (2018). https://ieeexplore.ieee.org/document/8085131/

Computing Betweenness Centrality: An Efficient Privacy-Preserving Approach

Varsha Bhat Kukkala and S. R. S. Iyengar$^{(\boxtimes)}$

Indian Institute of Technology Ropar, Rupnagar, India
{varsha.bhat,sudarshan}@iitrpr.ac.in

Abstract. Betweenness centrality is a classic network measure used to determine prominent nodes in a network $G(V, E)$, where the edges capture a type of flow through the network (like information, material or money). Betweenness being a global centrality measure requires the entire network information to compute the centrality of even a single vertex. We consider the setting where the global network structure is not present centrally with a single individual. Rather, the data is distributed among many individuals, each having only a partial view of the network. Furthermore, confidentiality constraints prevent the individual parties from disclosing their share of the data, thus inhibiting the aggregation of the entire network for analysis. The current paper proposes a secure multiparty protocol to compute the betweenness centrality measure, in a privacy preserving manner, for the considered setting. Employing various optimizations, including oblivious data structures and oblivious RAM, we present a secure variant of the Brandes algorithm for computing betweenness centrality in unweighted networks. The protocol is designed in the semi-honest adversarial model under the two-party setting. We evaluate the performance of the designed protocol by implementing them in the Obliv-C framework for secure computation. We are the first to provide a benchmark for the implementations using the state of the art ORAM schemes and help identify the best schemes for input data of different sizes. Employing the Circuit ORAM and the Square-Root ORAM schemes, we report the complexity of the proposed protocol as $\mathcal{O}(|V||E|\log^3|E|)$ and $\mathcal{O}(|V||E|^{1.5}\log^{1.5}|E|)$ primitive operations respectively. The asymptotic complexity of Circuit ORAM is found to be the least, with an overhead of only $\mathcal{O}(\log^3|E|)$ compared to the traditional non-oblivious Brandes algorithm with complexity $\mathcal{O}(|V||E|)$.

Keywords: Privacy · Social network analysis
Secure multiparty computation · Betweenness centrality

1 Introduction

1.1 Motivation

Identifying the key players in a complex system modeled as a network $G(V, E)$ is often achieved by characterizing the network using centrality measures [11]. In

© Springer Nature Switzerland AG 2018
J. Camenisch and P. Papadimitratos (Eds.): CANS 2018, LNCS 11124, pp. 23–42, 2018.
https://doi.org/10.1007/978-3-030-00434-7_2

this regard, the notion of *betweenness centrality* was first introduced by Freeman in 1977 [10] as a measure to find central nodes in a communication network. Intuitively, this centrality measure quantifies the amount of information that flows through a node in a given network. A high centrality value is indicative of a large amount of flow through the corresponding node. The exact computation of the betweenness score is specified below.

Definition 1 *(Betweenness Centrality). In a directed unweighted graph $G(V, E)$, let σ_{st} represent the number of shortest paths from node s to node t and $\sigma_{st}(u)$ represent the number of shortest paths from s to t containing the node u. The betweenness centrality $C_B(u)$ of a node $u \in V$ is then defined as:*

$$C_B(u) = \sum_{\forall s,t: s \neq u \neq t} \frac{\sigma_{st}(u)}{\sigma_{st}} \tag{1}$$

Although the measure was initially defined for communication networks, today we find its applicability on a range of networks including collaboration networks [24], citation networks [22] and terrorist networks [19]. Given the wide applicability, many efficient algorithms have been designed for computing betweenness centrality over large scale complex networks [6,20]. Computing the betweenness centrality of a particular node requires complete knowledge of the network topology, since the shortest paths between every pair of nodes is to be accounted (see Definition 1). However, in many cases, the global structure of the network is unavailable with a single party (individual/organization). That is, we consider the scenario where the network data[1] is private to a set of parties, with each of them having only a partial view of the structure. This results in the global network being distributedly held by the set of parties. Further, privacy concerns prevent the parties from aggregating the network data, rendering it infeasible to compute betweenness centrality of nodes in the underlying network. The most appropriate scenario where such a setting is prevalent is that of a supply chain network (SCN). An SCN captures the supplier-consumer relationship between organizations. Nodes in the network are organizations, and an edge from node A to node B signifies the movement of material from organization A to organization B. Each organization is aware of only a subset of edges in the network (its incoming and outgoing edges) and hence the entire SCN is distributedly held. These contractual ties and the resulting structural position of an organization is kept private, to prevent competing organizations from taking advantage of the information [12]. On the contrary, knowledge of the entire SCN allows the organizations to better manage risk of cascading failures [16]. The betweenness centrality of an organization in an SCN is known to be correlated to the risk associated with it [12]. Thus, there is a need for organizations to be able to compute their betweenness centrality with respect to the underlying SCN, while not having to disclose their private data. Such a privacy-utility trade-off can be observed in other scenarios as well, including criminal networks [15], trust

---

[1] Network data here refers to the presence or absence of edges between nodes in the network.

networks [18], and transportation networks [1]. A major challenge in computing betweenness centrality of nodes in the above mentioned networks is the private and distributed nature of the data.

1.2 Problem Definition and Proposed Solution

The current paper considers the problem scenario where a set of n parties $P_1, P_2, \ldots, P_n$ collectively hold a graph $G(V, E)$. Each party P_i is representative of a set of nodes V_i and has a subgraph $G_i(V, E_i)$ as his private data such that $\bigcup_{i=1}^{n} E_i = E$. This shows that the set of nodes V in the graph is known to all the individuals, while the set of edges E is distributed across all the parties. These parties are interested in computing the betweenness centrality of nodes in V, such that no party's private data is compromised and each party P_i learns nothing apart from the centrality value of nodes in V_i. This is a typical instance of secure multiparty computation (MPC). It deals with the design of protocols that the set of parties can follow in order to securely compute a function f of their private data. In the current scenario, the function f that the parties are interested in is that of computing betweenness centrality scores of all the nodes in the network. The input to f would be the subgraphs that each party holds as his private data.

The solution to the addressed problem reduces to designing an efficient secure multiparty computation protocol to evaluate the betweenness centrality of nodes in the network. There are several generic constructions that allow the secure computation of any arbitrary function [5,7,13,27]. These constructions assume the circuit representation of the function and describe the secure evaluation of such a circuit. However, it is important to note that a direct translation of a RAM program to compute betweenness centrality into its equivalent circuit would incur a large blow-up in the complexity. This can be attributed to the extensive need for performing input dependent memory accesses. Thus, the direct use of generic circuit based solutions to evaluate a given function f securely is not often a practical approach. As an alternative, we design protocols in the RAM model of secure computation that combines *oblivious random memory access* (ORAM) schemes with circuit based MPC to facilitate better random memory accesses. Further, to make the most of the designed protocol, we propose a better graph representation which when combined with the underlying ORAM scheme leads to better efficiency. Thus, we tailor an efficient protocol to securely evaluate the betweenness centrality of nodes in a network.

1.3 Our Contribution

The current work extensively builds on the existing works in secure computation. However, the specific contributions of the current work include the following:

- Identifying a need for securely evaluating the betweenness centrality value, we study the performance of the classical algorithm by Brandes in the secure setting. This leads us to identifying the non-oblivious aspects of the algorithm.

- We are the first to provide a secure variant of the Brandes algorithm which is the most efficient algorithm for computing betweenness centrality. The complexity of the proposed algorithm is better than those reported previously in the literature. Additionally, the protocol accounts for the standard definition of the betweenness centrality, unlike other works in the literature. A detailed comparison of the current work with the previous works in the literature is provided in Sect. 7.
- We evaluate the performance of the designed protocol by implementing the same over Obliv-C [29], a well accepted framework for secure computation. We benchmark the performance of the Linear Scan ORAM, Square-Root ORAM and the Circuit ORAM schemes under varying input sizes. This further allows us to determine which of the ORAM schemes is best suited for an input of a given size.
- In order to design an efficient protocol for securely computing the betweenness centrality, rather than a direct translation of the Brandes algorithm using generic MPC protocols, we suggest several modifications. In this regard, we introduce a new data-oblivious representation to handle the input graph known as the *Edgelist* representation. This proves to be a more efficient alternative as compared to the standard adjacency matrix representation.

2 Preliminaries

2.1 Multiparty Computation

Consider a scenario where two or more individuals, each with some private input, are interested in computing a function of their collective inputs. Secure multiparty computation deals with the design of protocols (i.e. algorithms) that allows these individuals to collaboratively evaluate the function in such a way that they learn nothing apart from the final result. In order to deem such a protocol as *secure*, we prove that it preserves *privacy* and *correctness*. Privacy property guarantees that the protocol does not compromise any additional information other than what an individual can gather from his own input and the revealed output. Correctness, on the other hand, guarantees that the revealed output is in fact equal to the function evaluated on their collective inputs.

There are several generic protocols designed under different settings, that allow individuals to securely evaluate any computable function. These constructions usually describe how a function represented as either an arithmetic circuit [2,5] or as a Boolean circuit [13] can be collaboratively evaluated to reveal only the output. One such approach used in the implementation of the proposed protocol is that of Yao's garbled circuit protocol [28]. We duly note that our protocol is not designed specific to Yao's garbled circuit and can be evaluated using any of the generic MPC protocols. Hence, any protocol that facilitates the secure evaluation of the primitive operations assumed in the designed solution (i.e. arithmetic and logical operators) can be used to evaluate the designed protocol.

2.2 Garbled Circuits

Yao's garbled circuit protocol is basically a Boolean circuit based two party protocol for securely evaluating a function. The two parties agree upon a function f that they wish to collaboratively evaluate. One of the parties is referred to as the *generator* while the other as the *evaluator*. The generator is responsible for creating a garbled circuit equivalent of the function f, denoted as GC_f. The generator associates each input wire i of GC_f with two keys, k_i^0 for input bit 0 and k_i^1 for input bit 1. The generator now passes the circuit GC_f to the evaluator, along with one key $k_i^{b_i}$ corresponding to the appropriate input bit b_i for each of her input wire i. All that the evaluator now needs to evaluate GC_f is to obtain the garbled keys $k_j^{b_j}$ associated with each of her input wires j corresponding to the input bit b_j. This is obtained using an *oblivious transfer* (OT) gadget. The OT gadget is a two party protocol involving a sender having two private inputs m_0, m_1, and a receiver having a bit b as her private input. The protocol allows the receiver to learn only one of the private inputs of the sender, namely m_b, without the sender learning which of her inputs was transfered to the receiver. In this way, the generator behaves as the sender to obliviously transfer the keys corresponding to the input bits of the evaluator. Using GC_f and one garbled key per input wire, the evaluator computes the garbled output of the function f, which is decoded to obtain the true result.

2.3 RAM Secure Computation

When generic MPC protocols designed in the circuit model are used to securely evaluate RAM programs that perform intensive input dependent memory accesses, the inefficiency of circuit based solutions becomes apparent. In order to perform an oblivious memory access (i.e. keep the location of memory accessed secret), the circuit based solution would access the entire memory while retrieving only the value in the desired location. This immediately escalates the complexity of an $\mathcal{O}(1)$ access operation to $\mathcal{O}(n)$, where n is indicative of the size of the entire memory. In order to perform random memory accesses efficiently, RAM based secure computation incorporates the notion of an ORAM scheme into circuit based solutions. An ORAM scheme consists of an *initialization* protocol and an *access* protocol. Given an array of elements, the initialization protocol describes the process of storing the elements in an oblivious structure. Once initialized, the access protocol can be invoked to obliviously access a memory location. The protocol translates a given logical address into a sequence of physical memory locations that are accessed to retrieve the necessary array element. The security of an ORAM scheme guarantees that the memory access pattern during the initialization and access protocols does not leak any private data.

RAM based secure computation continues to be set in the circuit model, with the only difference that memory accesses are now performed by circuits that are designed to emulate the ORAM protocols. For example, in order to perform an oblivious access in a two party setting, the parties distributedly hold the state of the underlying ORAM. Using the secret logical array index to be accessed and the distributed ORAM state as private input, the two parties execute circuits to reveal the corresponding sequence of physical memory locations in the open. The security of the underlying ORAM scheme guarantees that this does not leak any private information. The parties then pass the elements retrieved from these physical locations as inputs to circuits that are further executed securely [14]. The Circuit ORAM [26] scheme has the best known asymptotic complexity for use in conjunction with MPC protocols. However, due the the large constants associated with Circuit ORAM complexity, the Square-Root ORAM [31] scheme is known to function the best for practical data sizes.

2.4 Security Model

An important aspect to be considered while designing MPC protocols is the underlying adversarial model. It describes the extent of corruption that is assumed from the parties. The protocols designed in the current work are for a two party setting, under the *semi-honest* adversarial model. That is, we assume that the protocol is run by two non-colluding parties who do not deviate from the given protocol. Thus, in the case that there are more than two parties who collectively hold the network data, we require that each of them provide shares of their private data to two representative parties. Upon receiving shares from all the parties, the two representative parties collectively hold the network distributedly and perform the computation on behalf of rest of the parties. This model is in contrast to the multiparty setting. Although the considered model is not as strong as the *malicious* adversarial model, where the parties are allowed to collude as well as deviate from the given protocol, previous works have shown that it suffices to work with semi-honest adversaries [12,15]. Further, we believe our solution is a first step towards efficiently performing social network analysis in a privacy preserving manner and leave the malicious adversarial model for future work.

2.5 Notation

We follow a few conventions in order to increase the readability of the designed protocol. First, it is important to note that the variables in the protocol can be categorized as *public* or *private*. Public variables are those whose values are known in the open, while private/secret variables represent garbled values which are distributedly held via shares by the two parties. Private variables are specified within angular brackets, such as $\langle x \rangle$. Similarly, we could also have an array of private data elements denoted as $\langle Array \rangle$. The ith index element of such an array would be referred to as $\langle Array \rangle_i$, where i is publicly known. The length of such an array would also be publicly known. Note that $\langle -1 \rangle$ is also a valid notation, shorthand for initializing a private variable whose value is -1. The left arrow $(\leftarrow)$ signifies the assignment of the right hand side expression to the private variable on the left. The protocol also uses oblivious conditional statements denoted by $\langle \textbf{if} \rangle$ and $\langle \textbf{else} \rangle$ constructs. In such a case, the truth assignment of the conditional is dependent on private variables. Hence, the body of an $\langle \textbf{if} \rangle$-$\langle \textbf{else} \rangle$ construct is always executed, independent of whether the conditional was evaluated as true or false. However, the instructions executed are effective only when the conditional was evaluated as true, else it results in a dummy execution [29].

There are also arrays that are maintained in an oblivious structure using an ORAM scheme. These are different from the private arrays described earlier. Here, the elements of the array are not indexed directly, rather are accessed using the ORAM protocols. Specifically, we use OramRead() and the OramWrite() functions to read and write to the elements of such arrays. The OramRead() function takes as input the name of the ORAM array and the private variable indicative of the logical address of the array element to be read. The contents of the specified address are returned as a private variable by the function. Similarly, the OramWrite() function takes three input parameters - the ORAM name, a private variable storing the logical address to which data is to be written and another private variable storing the new content to be written. The function replaces the contents of the specified address with the new contents and has no return value as such. Throughout the protocol, we assume that the private arrays as well as the ORAM arrays store data items that are integers. However, while computing betweenness centrality values, it is required for us to handle fractional values as well. These fractional values are dealt with by storing an integer representations of the same. The details of the representation are discussed further. We use a tilde over any array $\tilde{X}$ (private and ORAM) to denote that it in fact stores integer equivalent of fractional values.

2.6   Number Representation

An important aspect to be dealt with while designing secure protocols for computing betweenness centrality is to handle secure computation on real values. Despite the IEEE 754 floating-point representation being the standard used for representing reals, secure computation over this representation is a problem that continues to be addressed [25]. In the current work, we use the fixed point representation of real values as they are easy to implement and are efficient for use in secure computation due to the small sized circuits. Each real value r is mapped onto the integer $\phi(r) = \lceil r \times S \rceil$, where S denotes the scaling factor and determines the accuracy of the results. The scaling factor is taken sufficiently large to ensure no overflows occur. Using this representation, the operations of addition, subtraction, multiplications and division can be easily performed. Let r_1 and r_2 be two real values to be operated on. Then, it is easy to observe that the following holds:

$$\text{Addition: } \phi(r_1 + r_2) = \phi(r_1) + \phi(r_2)$$
$$\text{Subtraction: } \phi(r_1 - r_2) = \phi(r_1) - \phi(r_2)$$
$$\text{Multiplication: } \phi(r_1 \times r_2) = \left\lceil \frac{\phi(r_1) \cdot \phi(r_2)}{S} \right\rceil$$
$$\text{Division: } \phi(r_1/r_2) = \left\lceil \frac{\phi(r_1)}{\phi(r_2)} \cdot S \right\rceil$$

Thus, throughout the protocol, all the real values are dealt with using their integer representation. After the computation, the real valued results are retrieved by re-mapping the integer values to their corresponding real values.

3 Brandes Algorithm: The Traditional Approach to Computing Betweenness Centrality

Despite being established as a key measure of centrality since the 1980s, computing the betweenness centrality of nodes over a large network $G(V, E)$ was impractical. This was due to the high computational complexity of $\mathcal{O}(|V|^3)$ operations associated with the Floyd Warshall algorithm for computing all-pair shortest paths. Motivated to determine a more efficient algorithm for betweenness of nodes, Ulrik Brandes proposed an algorithm that takes $\mathcal{O}(|V||E|)$ time, having a space complexity of $\mathcal{O}(|V| + |E|)$ [6]. This algorithm, popularly known as *Brandes* algorithm, is more efficient when run on real world networks that are known to be very sparse, i.e. the number of edges ($|E|$) is of the order of number of nodes ($|V|$) [21]. In this section, we briefly describe the idea proposed by Brandes.

In the definition of betweenness (Definition 1), computing the centrality of a node $u \in V$ traditionally involves considering every pair of nodes $s, t \in V$ and counting the fraction of shortest paths between s and t that pass through u. This fraction is as defined below:

Definition 2 *(Pair Dependency). Given a pair of nodes $s, t \in V$, the pair dependency on an intermediary node u is denoted by $\delta_{st}(u)$. It is defined as the ratio of number of shortest paths between s and t that passes through u denoted as $\sigma_{st}(u)$ to the total number of shortest paths between s and t represented by σ_{st}.*

$$\delta_{st}(u) = \frac{\sigma_{st}(u)}{\sigma_{st}}$$

From the above definition it is clear that betweenness centrality of a node u is the sum over all of its pair dependencies $\left[C_B(u) = \sum_{s \neq t \neq u \in V} \delta_{st}(u) \right]$. Brandes, however, observed that it is possible to compute the betweenness of a node u without having to account for the pair dependency of each $s - t$ pair explicitly. Alternatively, he expressed betweenness centrality in terms of *dependency*, which he further showed can be efficiently computed in a recursive manner.

Definition 3 *(Dependency). Given a source vertex $s \in V$ and an intermediary vertex $u \in V$, the dependency of s on u is defined as the sum over the pair dependencies of the form $s - t$, for all $t \in V$. This is denoted by:*

$$\delta_{s\bullet}(u) = \sum_{t \in V} \delta_{st}(u)$$

Betweenness of a node can therefore be defined in terms of its dependency as:

$$C_B(u) = \sum_{s \neq u \in V} \delta_{s\bullet}(u) \tag{2}$$

Definition 4 *(Predecessor). Let $dist(u, v)$ denote the length of the shortest path from node u to node v. For a given source vertex $s \in V$, node $u \in V$ is said to be the predecessor of node v if $(u, v) \in E$ and $dist(s, v) = dist(s, u) + 1$. The set of all predecessors of v with respect to s is denoted by $P_s(v)$.*

Brandes established that the dependency of s on node u can be computed recursively using the dependency of s on all those nodes $v \in V$ for which u lies as immediate predecessors of v on the shortest paths from s to v. The recursive definition of dependency can be given as:

$$\delta_{s\bullet}(u) = \sum_{v:u \in P_s(v)} \frac{\sigma_{su}}{\sigma_{sv}}.(1 + \delta_{s\bullet}(v)) \tag{3}$$

With the help of the above recursion, we can compute the dependency of a node s on each vertex in two stages. First we perform a BFS traversal rooted at s to determine the number of shortest paths from s to each node $v \in V$. We then compute the dependency of nodes in the reverse order of their visit in the BFS traversal which allows for the recursive accumulation of the dependencies. Such a BFS traversal from each node as the root followed by computing the dependency in the reverse order of the traversal allows us to compute the betweenness of every node in the graph. The pseudocode for Brandes algorithm is given in Fig. 1.

Complexity

As seen in the pseudocode of Fig. 1, the initialization performed in steps 3–9 costs $\mathcal{O}(|V|)$ operations since we set a few variables with respect to each node. The steps 10–19 entails performing a BFS traversal starting from a given source node s and updating the list of predecessor of each node which costs $\mathcal{O}(|V|+|E|)$ operations. In steps 20–23, the stack S allows to process nodes in the reverse order of their visit during the BFS traversal. Further, we account each edge at most once while processing the predecessor of each node. Thus, computing the dependency of s on all nodes in steps 20–23 costs $\mathcal{O}(|V|+|E|)$ operations. Finally, accounting for the computed dependency in the betweenness centrality of the nodes in steps 24,25 costs $\mathcal{O}(|V|)$ operations. Therefore, the time complexity of an iteration of steps 2–25 is $\mathcal{O}(|E|)$. Since these steps are repeated $|V|$ number of times, the overall complexity of Brandes algorithm reduces to $\mathcal{O}(|V||E|)$.

4   Secure Betweenness Algorithm

We observe that the control flow of the algorithm and the sequence of memory accesses made during the run of Brandes algorithm (see Fig. 1) are particularly dependent on the input graph. Therefore, the control flow and the memory access patterns could in itself leak sensitive information. In order to hide the memory access pattern, each time we wish to access a dedicated memory location, we would have to scan through the entire memory. Thus, constructing a garbled circuit equivalent of Brandes algorithm will result in a large blow-up in

---

Input: Graph $G(V, E)$
Output: Betweenness centrality $C_B[v]$ for all $v \in V$
 1: Initialize betweenness value $C_B[v] \leftarrow 0$, for all $v \in V$
 2: **for** each node $s \in V$ as the source node **do**
 3:     Initialize the dependency $\delta[u] \leftarrow 0$ for all $u \in V$
 4:     Initialize an empty queue Q
 5:     Initialize an empty stack S
 6:     Initialize empty lists $pred[u]$, $\forall u \in V$ to store the list of predecessors of each node u.
 7:     Set the distance from s to u, $dist[u] \leftarrow -1$, $\forall u \in V \backslash s$
 8:     Set the count of shortest paths from s to u, $\sigma[u] \leftarrow 0$, $\forall u \in V \backslash s$
 9:     Begin the BFS from s by setting $dist[s] \leftarrow 0$, $\sigma[s] \leftarrow 1$ and enqueue s in Q
10:     **while** Q is not empty **do**
11:         Dequeue an element u from Q
12:         **for** each neighbor v of u **do**
13:             **if** v is unvisited **then**   ▷ i.e. $dist[v] == -1$
14:                 Set $dist[v] \leftarrow dist[u] + 1$
15:                 Push v onto stack S
16:                 Mark v as visited and enqueue in Q.
17:             **if** v is visited **then**   ▷ i.e $dist[v] == dist[u] + 1$
18:                 Update the predecessor list of v, $pred[v] \leftarrow pred[v] \bigcup \{u\}$
19:                 Increase the count of shortest paths to v, $\sigma[v] \leftarrow \sigma[v] + \sigma[u]$
20:     **while** S is not empty **do**
21:         Pop an element v from S
22:         **for** each predecessor u of v **do**
23:             Update dependency of u, $\delta[u] \leftarrow \delta[u] + (1 + \delta[v]) \frac{\sigma[u]}{\sigma[v]}$ ▷ Refer Eqn 3
24:     **for** each node $u \neq s$ **do**
25:         Update betweenness centrality of u with partial dependency, $C_B[u] \rightarrow C_B[u] + \delta[u]$

Fig. 1. Pseudocode for Brandes algorithm

the circuit complexity. We propose modifications to Brandes algorithm, which when run using primitives such as oblivious RAM, renders the control flow and memory access pattern independent of the input graph. Prior to describing the modifications, we enumerate over all the features of the Brandes algorithm that make it unsuitable for the *data-oblivious* setting. We suggest the reader refer to the pseudocode in Fig. 1, to better follow the issues raised. For each of the drawbacks, we describe modifications which can be efficiently evaluated using any of the generic MPC constructions such as Yao's garbled circuits.

1. *Adjacency list data structure:* Brandes algorithm assumes that the input graph is stored using an adjacency list graph representation. Although the representation is space efficient, the varying length of the list of neighbours of each node leaks the out-degree of nodes in the graph. As a solution, we employ a novel two tuple graph representation, termed the *edgelist* representation, which is oblivious to the graph structure. Edgelist uses space $O(|V|+|E|)$ and hence is asymptotically as efficient as the adjacency list representation. This representation leaks only the number of vertices and the number of edges in the graph.
2. *Input dependent for and while loop (Set 1):* For every source vertex $s \in V$, the number of *while* loop iterations executed (in Step 10) leaks the number of nodes reachable from s in the underlying graph. The control flow of the algorithm in the *for* loop in Step 12 also leaks the number of out-going links

of each vertex in the graph. As an alternative, the *while* and *for* loops in Steps 10 and 12 respectively can be coalesced into a single loop. Intuitively, loop coalescing combines the *for* and *while* loops into a functionally equivalent single *for* loop which is executed a publicly known number of times and is asymptotically as efficient as its previous counterpart.

3. *Input dependent for and while loop (Set 2):* The number of iterations of the *while* loop executed in Step 20 leaks the number of reachable nodes for each $s \in V$, as was in the case of the *while* loop in Step 10. The control flow of the *for* loop in Step 22 is data-dependent since the number of iterations executed of the loop, for each $v \in V$, is equal to the number of elements in the predecessor list $P[v]$ of v, which is dependent on the input graph. As a solution, we modify the Brandes algorithm by inserting edges in the stack S rather than vertices. This avoids the need for maintaining a predecessor list for each vertex. A detailed account of the modification in the classical algorithm is provided in Sect. 4.2.

4. *Conditional if-else statements:* In general, the control flow of an *if-else* statement would leak whether the condition evaluated in the *if* clause is true or false. The conditional *if-else* clauses in Steps 13 and 17 are dependent on secret variables, making the algorithm's control flow depend on the input data. To avoid this leakage, we employ the *oblivious-if* primitive ($\langle if \rangle$) introduced in Sect. 2.5. Intuitively, the $\langle if \rangle$ clause will execute both the *if* and *else* blocks of statements but ensures that the "effect" of only one block takes place depending on the condition of the clause.

5. *Memory accesses over data structures - array, linked list, stack and queue:* Memory accesses made to the arrays *dist*, σ and δ throughout the algorithm leaks the graph structure, i.e. the set of edges. We employ the ORAM primitive from Sect. 2.3 to hide array accesses over secret indices. To hide the memory access patterns of the queue Q, we implement it as an ORAM array of length $|V|$. The stack S of length $|V| + |E|$, on the other hand, is stored as an array of secret variables. We avoid the cost of storing S in the ORAM since the elements of the stack are accessed sequentially, independent of the input.

4.1   Edgelist Graph Representation

The adjacency matrix representation is the preferred graph representation for securely evaluating graph algorithms. This can be attributed to the fact that the representation leaks only the number of nodes in the graph, assuming that each entry of the matrix is protected. However, it is not space efficient when considering real world networks that tend to be very sparse. The *edgelist* graph representation serves as a space efficient representation for real world networks and is well suited for the running graph algorithms in the secure setting. The space complexity of the edgelist representation is $\mathcal{O}(|E| + |V|)$. Therefore, it fares better on real world networks, where $|E| = \mathcal{O}(|V|)$, than the adjacency matrix representation having $\mathcal{O}(|V|^2)$ complexity.

The network $G(V, E)$ (with number of nodes $|V|$ and edges $|E|$) is represented using a pair $(\mathcal{E}, Idx)$. The array $\mathcal{E}$ is of length $(|E| + 1)$ containing adjacency lists of all nodes concatenated and a null element ($\perp$) appended at the end. The array Idx is of length $(|V| + 1)$ and has an entry corresponding to each node $v \in V$ in the first $|V|$ entries, as defined below:

$$Idx[v] = \begin{cases} i & \text{if out-degree}(v) \neq 0 \text{ and the first neighbor of } v \text{ in } \mathcal{E} \text{ is } \mathcal{E}[i] \\ Idx[v + 1] & \text{if out-degree}(v) = 0 \text{ and } v \text{ is not the last node} \\ |E| + 1 & \text{if out-degree}(v) = 0 \text{ and } v \text{ is the last node} \end{cases}$$

The last entry, $Idx[|V| + 1]$ holds the value $|E| + 1$, as a pointer to the null element of the array $\mathcal{E}$. The edgelist graph representation is oblivious to the graph structure and reveals only the number of nodes and the number of edges in the network. The space complexity of the edgelist graph representation is $(|V| + |E| + 2)$, making it efficient for storing sparse graphs. It also overcomes the issues posed by the use of adjacency list representation, as described in Brandes algorithm.

4.2 The Proposed Algorithm

In order to ensure that the graph data structure does not leak sensitive information as well as is space efficient, the input for the proposed algorithm is assumed to be in the edgelist format. The components of the edgelist, i.e. the list of edges $\mathcal{E}$ and the list of pointers in Idx, are individually present as ORAM arrays of length $|E| + 1$ and $|V| + 1$ respectively. Similarly, we initialize an ORAM array each of length $|V|$ to store the node dependencies in $\tilde{\delta}$, distance from source node to a given node in $dist$ and count of shortest paths to a node in σ. Additionally, Q is an ORAM array of length $|V|$, that is used as a queue to store the sequence of nodes visited during the BFS traversal. Instead of maintaining a list of predecessors for each node, the length of which could vary depending on the input graph, we rely on a stack that holds the sequence of edges visited during BFS traversal. For this purpose, we use a private array $\langle S \rangle$ of length $|V| + |E| - 1$.

The exact computation of the centrality value is as described by the protocol in Fig. 2. The centrality value of each node is computed in stages. We first compute the dependence for each node with respect to a given source node which is then accumulated to obtain the betweenness centrality score of the respective nodes. Steps 4 to 40 in the protocol describe the method for doing the same. Steps 5–9 are required to trash the contents of the respective ORAMs that stored values with respect to the previous source node. This is done as an alternative to initializing new ORAM arrays each time. The *for* loop in steps 13–30 is responsible for performing a BFS traversal rooted at source node s, by exploring the edges stored in $\mathcal{E}$. The loop is executed a fixed public number of times, thus hiding the number of nodes reachable from the source node. Within the loop, the secret variable, $\langle u \rangle$ stores that node in the graph whose neighbours are currently being explored in the BFS traversal. In each iteration of the loop, we are either processing an edge of $\langle u \rangle$ (with neighbor $\langle v \rangle$) or we are updating the

Input: Graph $(\mathcal{E}, Idx)$ stored in the ORAM, with $\mathcal{E}, Idx$ as individual ORAM arrays

Output: The Betweenness values $\forall v \in V$ denoted by $\widetilde{C_B}[v]$

1: Initialize $\widetilde{(C_B)}_v \leftarrow 0$, for all $v \in V$
2: Initialize $\widetilde{\delta}$, $dist$, σ, Q each as an ORAM array of length $|V|$
3: Initialize an array $\langle S \rangle$ of length $|V| + |E| - 1$
4: **for** each node $s \in V$ as the source node **do**
5:     OramWrite($\widetilde{\delta}, u, \langle 0 \rangle$), $\forall u \in V$ ▷ Initialize dependency of all nodes
6:     OramWrite($dist, u, \langle -1 \rangle$), $\forall u \in V$ ▷ set the distance from s to u
7:     OramWrite($dist, s, \langle 0 \rangle$)   ▷ Reset the distance from s to s
8:     OramWrite($\sigma, u, \langle 0 \rangle$), $\forall u \in V$ ▷ Set the count of shortest paths from s to u
9:     OramWrite($\sigma, s, \langle 1 \rangle$)   ▷ Set the count of shortest paths from s to s
10:    $\langle ptr \rangle \leftarrow$ OramRead(Idx, s)   ▷ Pointer to keep track of elements read from $\mathcal{E}$
11:    OramWrite($Q, \langle 1 \rangle, s$)   ▷ Enqueue root node s in Q
12:    $\langle rear \rangle \leftarrow 1$, $\langle front \rangle \leftarrow 1$ ▷ Q pointers
13:    **for** $i = 1$ to $(|V| + |E| - 1)$ **do**
14:        $\langle e \rangle \leftarrow \langle \bot \rangle$ ▷ Initialize a null edge
15:        $\langle$**if**$\rangle$ $\langle rear \rangle \geq \langle front \rangle$ **then**   ▷ True if Q is not empty
16:            $\langle u \rangle \leftarrow$ OramRead($Q, \langle front \rangle$)
17:            $\langle$**if**$\rangle$ OramRead($Idx, \langle u+1 \rangle$) == $\langle ptr \rangle$ **then** ▷ True if all neighbors of u is seen
18:                $\langle front \rangle \leftarrow \langle front \rangle + 1$ ▷ u is removed from Q
19:                $\langle ptr \rangle \leftarrow$ OramRead(Idx,OramRead($Q, \langle front \rangle$))
20:            $\langle$**else**$\rangle$
21:                $\langle v \rangle \leftarrow$ OramRead($\mathcal{E}, \langle ptr \rangle$)   ▷ Current neighbor v of u updated
22:                $\langle ptr \rangle \leftarrow \langle ptr \rangle + 1$
23:                $\langle$**if**$\rangle$ (OramRead($dist, \langle v \rangle$)) == -1 **then**   ▷ True if v is not seen
24:                    $\langle rear \rangle \leftarrow \langle rear \rangle + 1$
25:                    OramWrite($Q, \langle rear \rangle, \langle v \rangle$)   ▷ Enqueue v in Q
26:                    OramWrite($dist, \langle v \rangle, $(OramRead($dist, \langle u \rangle$)) + 1)   ▷ Update $dist(s, v)$
27:                $\langle$**if**$\rangle$ (OramRead($dist, \langle v \rangle$)) == (OramRead($dist, \langle u \rangle$))+1 **then**
28:                    OramWrite($\sigma, \langle v \rangle, \langle$ OramRead($\sigma, \langle v \rangle$)+OramRead($\sigma, \langle u \rangle$) $\rangle$)
29:                    $\langle e \rangle \leftarrow (\langle u \rangle, \langle v \rangle)$
30:        $\langle S \rangle_i \leftarrow \langle e \rangle$ ▷ Push edge e (valid or null) into the stack
31:    **for** $i = (|V| + |E| - 1)$ to 1 **do**
32:        $\langle e \rangle \leftarrow \langle S \rangle_i$ ▷ Process edge e in reverse order to compute dependence
33:        $\langle$**if**$\rangle$ $\langle e \rangle \neq \langle \bot \rangle$ **then**   ▷ True if e is a valid edge
34:            $(\langle u \rangle, \langle v \rangle) \leftarrow \langle e \rangle$
35:            $\langle temp_1 \rangle \leftarrow \langle$OramRead($\sigma, \langle u \rangle$))/(OramRead($\sigma\langle v \rangle$))$\rangle$
36:            $\langle temp_2 \rangle \leftarrow \langle$OramRead($\widetilde{\delta}, \langle v \rangle + 1$)) $\times \langle temp_1 \rangle$
37:            $\langle temp_3 \rangle \leftarrow \langle$OramRead($\widetilde{\delta}, \langle u \rangle + 1$)) + $\langle temp_2 \rangle$
38:            OramWrite($\widetilde{\delta}, \langle u \rangle, \langle temp_3 \rangle$)
39:    **for** each node $u \in V \backslash s$ **do**
40:        $\widetilde{(C_B)}_u \leftarrow \widetilde{(C_B)}_u +$ OramRead($\widetilde{\delta}, \langle u \rangle$)

Fig. 2. Protocol for securely computing betweenness centrality

next node to be explored through updating the pointer variable $\langle ptr \rangle$. As there are $|E|$ number of edges and $\langle u \rangle$ can be updated a maximum of $|V| - 1$ times (excluding source node s), the loop is therefore executed for a total of $|V| + |E| - 1$ number of times. When processing an edge (steps 20–29), only those edges of $\langle u \rangle$ where $\langle u \rangle$ is the predecessor of its neighbor $\langle v \rangle$, are included as valid edges in $\langle S \rangle$. Else, we store a null($\bot$) edge. We use the array $\langle S \rangle$ as a stack to process valid edges in the reverse order in which they were added (steps 31–38). Since a valid edge $(\langle u \rangle, \langle v \rangle)$ implicitly accounts for the predecessor relationship, we compute the dependence of $\langle u \rangle$ using the dependence of $\langle v \rangle$. The correctness of this is described in detail in Sect. 5. Once the dependence of nodes is obtained, steps 39, 40 account for the dependence in the centrality score of each node.

Please note that the variables $\langle temp_i \rangle$ in the protocol are not necessary and is just used to increase the readability of the protocol.

5 Analytical Evaluation

5.1 Complexity

Traditionally, computing the betweenness centrality of nodes in a graph involved running a modified version of Floyd-Warshall algorithm. For computing the centrality value of a single node, this approach has a complexity of $\mathcal{O}(|V|^3)$ operations and requires $\mathcal{O}(|V|^2)$ space assuming the adjacency matrix representation. Since the approach is already data-oblivious, a naive implementation of the same using generic MPC protocols would incur a cost of $\mathcal{O}(|V|^4)$ operations to compute the centrality value of all the nodes. Similarly, a naive secure implementation of Brandes algorithm would have the asymptotic complexity of $\mathcal{O}(|V|^3|E|)$ operations using the adjacency matrix representation (i.e. $\mathcal{O}(|V||E|)$ operations while scanning $\mathcal{O}(|V|^2)$ memory each time). Thus, the algorithmic complexity also plays an important role in determining the cost of implementing the secure variant using generic constructions.

The algorithmic complexity of the designed protocol is governed by the two nested *for*-loops. The outer most *for*-loop is executed $|V|$ times while there are two inner *for*-loops which run $|V| + |E| - 1$ times each. This results in the complexity of $\mathcal{O}(|V||E|)$ operations on a memory of $\mathcal{O}(|E|)$ space in the ORAM. Thus, the overall asymptotic complexity of evaluating the protocol using the Square-Root ORAM and the Circuit ORAM schemes are $\mathcal{O}(|V||E|^{1.5} \log^{1.5} |E|)$ and $\mathcal{O}(|V||E| \log^3 |E|)$ respectively. Thus, we obtain better asymptotic complexity than any of the generic constrictions.

5.2 Security

In order to establish the security of the designed protocol, we must prove that it preserves privacy and it also correctly computes the betweenness centrality measure. The protocol majorly relies on the underlying ORAM scheme and is evaluated using Yao's garbled circuits. Thus, the privacy guarantees of the designed protocol are directly implied by the security properties of the ORAM scheme [26,31] and Yao's garbled circuit [23]. We guarantee security only in the semi-honest adversarial model, where we assume that the two parties do not deviate from the protocol nor do they collude. Although this is comparatively a weaker adversarial model than the malicious setting, it serves as a better solution than the current method of using a trusted third party who learns the entire network information. We believe that this is the much needed first step towards performing social network analysis without leaking any information apart from the desired output. We leave it as future work to modify the algorithms to support stronger adversarial models.

The correctness of the designed protocol is to be explicitly proved since its control flow is different from that of Brandes algorithm. Consider all the edges inserted into the stack $\langle S \rangle$ during an iteration of the *for*-loop in Step 4, corresponding to a particular root node $s \in V$. We define $level_s(k)$ to be the set of all edges $\langle e \rangle = (\langle u \rangle, \langle v \rangle)$ in $\langle S \rangle$ such that $dist(s, v) = k$, i.e., the set of all edges that are at level k in the BFS tree rooted at s. We further define for each $s \in V$, $d_{max}(s) = Max_{v \in V}\{dist(s, v)\}$, i.e., the maximum depth of the BFS tree rooted at s. We show that the designed protocol computes the dependencies with respect to a given source node s appropriately. In order to do so, we consider the dependencies computed in an iteration of the *for*-loop in Step 4. We hypothesize that the dependency $\delta_{s\bullet}(v)$ on vertex v, such that $dist(s, v) = k$, is correctly computed when all the edges in $level_s(k + 1)$ are popped from the stack $\langle S \rangle$. For every node $v \in V$ such that $dist(s, v) = d_{max}(s)$, the edge set $level_s(d_{max}(s) + 1) = \phi$ and the dependency $\delta_{s\bullet}(v)$ initialized to zero remains unchanged throughout the considered iteration. Thus the hypothesis is true for $k = d_{max}(s)$ as all nodes at depth $d_{max}(s)$ have their dependency correctly computed. This forms the base case of the argument through induction. Let us assume that our hypothesis is true for all nodes v which are at a distance k from source node s. Now, consider any node u such that $dist(s, u) = k - 1$. First we observe that the *if*-condition obliviously evaluated in Step-27 guarantees that every edge $\langle e \rangle = (\langle u \rangle, \langle v \rangle)$, where u is a predecessor of v is pushed onto the stack $\langle S \rangle$. The second observation is that since the edges are pushed onto the stack $\langle S \rangle$ in the order of the BFS traversal, we are guaranteed that all edges of $level_s(k)$ are popped before any edge in $level_s(k - 1)$ is popped. Thus, when the edge $\langle e \rangle = (\langle u \rangle, \langle v \rangle)$ is popped, the induction hypothesis guarantees that the dependency $\delta_{s\bullet}(v)$ is already correctly computed. This allows us to account the fraction of $v's$ dependency in computing $u's$ dependency (Steps 33–38) in accordance with recurrence in Eq. 3. Thus, when all the edges in $level_s(k - 1)$ are popped, every node v for which u is a predecessor is encountered and we are able to correctly compute the dependency $\delta_{s\bullet}(u)$ of node u. The designed protocol only alters the sequence in which the dependency of nodes is computed.

6 Experimental Evaluation

6.1 Setup

We evaluate the designed protocol for computing betweenness centrality under the semi-honest two party setting using Yao's garbled circuits. In order to implement and benchmark the same, we use *Obliv-C* [29], a C-language based framework for compiling and executing secure computation protocols through Yao's garbled circuits. There are several benefits to using the Obliv-C framework. First, it's performance under the 2PC setting is comparable to the best known frameworks so far, with the capability of executing approximately 5 million gates per second. Secondly, the framework incorporates several of the most recent optimizations for secure computation such as the use of free XOR [17], fixed-key blockciphers [4], half gates [30], efficient OT extensions [3], etc. Lastly, since the framework is C based, it inherently supports all the built-in data types of C-language. Given that our protocol is designed in the RAM model of secure computation, we require the secure implementations of different ORAM schemes. We use the implementations of the Circuit ORAM and the Square Root ORAM made available on Obliv-C itself. Additionally, we use the ACK library [9] in conjunction with Obliv-C in order to perform secure arithmetic operations on large integers. All the experiments were run on a 64-bit machine with Intel Xeon E7-8870 v3 CPU clocking at 2.10 GHz and 16 GB RAM under Ubuntu 16.04 operating system. All the codes were compiled using the gcc version 5.4.0 with the $-O3$ flag enabled. It is important to note that our benchmark is single threaded.

6.2   Datasets

Our protocol is designed to take advantage of the fact that real world networks are known to be sparse. Thus, we present the simulation results by considering sparse graphs of different sizes as input to the protocol. Each input graph is generated by fixing on the number of nodes (n) and number of edges (m), followed by choosing a graph uniformly at random from the set of all possible graphs on n nodes and m edges. This is commonly referred to as the $G_{n,m}$ model or the Erdos-Renyi model of graph generation. More specifically, while generating the random input graph, we assume the number of nodes to be a power of 2 $(|V| = 2^k)$ and the number of edges to be constant times the number of nodes $(|E| = 10 \times |V|)$ to ensure the sparsity. The factor of 10 is considered based on the datasets of real world social networks and communication networks as available on SNAP [21]. The average ratio of the number of edges to the number of nodes in these datasets was observed to be approximately 10. We begin with a graph having 32 nodes since it is the smallest possible graph that respects the above stated relation. All the results reported where the time taken is beyond 10^5 seconds are estimations made based on the computational and communicational complexity of the protocol.

6.3   Results

The asymptotic cost associated with each ORAM scheme is different. Thus, the choice of the ORAM scheme affects the running time of the designed algorithm in practice. Here, we analyze the effect of running the designed algorithm under different ORAM schemes for varying input sizes. Figure 3 clearly shows that the choice of the ORAM must be made with respect to the input size. The linear scan ORAM would be the best choice for running the algorithm on sparse graphs having lesser than 2^8 number of nodes. For those input graphs where the number of nodes are between 2^8 and 2^{15}, the Square-Root ORAM is the ideal choice. The Circuit ORAM performs the best for input graphs with nodes greater than 2^{15}. Similar results are obtained for graphs of different sparsity. Due to space constraints, we restrain to providing results for a specific sparsity and a detailed report will be provided in the full version of the paper.

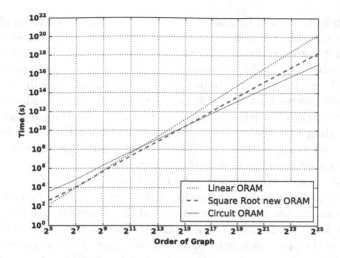

Fig. 3. ORAM analysis: For each ORAM scheme considered, we plot the overall running time of the designed algorithm for different input sizes. The order of the graph denotes the number of nodes in the graph. The plot is for graphs where $|E| = 10|V|$.

7   Related Work

The problem of investigating criminal networks in a privacy preserving manner has motivated the design of secure MPC protocols for closeness and betweenness centrality [15]. The problem has been studied in a setting where the underlying graph is distributedly held by a set of mutually distrusting parties. The proposed algorithm for computing betweenness is secure in the semi-honest adversarial model and uses the Floyd-Warshall algorithm for computing all pair shortest paths. They first obtain a pseudonymised version of the adjacency matrix, denoted by M, that is entry-wise encrypted using a thresholded homomorphic encryption scheme. They run the Floyd-Warshall algorithm on M while employing a secure comparison protocol at each step, in order to compute the *Min* function. The Floyd-Warshall algorithm takes $\mathcal{O}(|V|^3)$ steps, while each comparison operation is of $\mathcal{O}(\log|V|)$ complexity [8]. Thus, the overall complexity of the algorithm can be given by $\mathcal{O}(|V|^3 \log(|V|))$ operations for computing the centrality value of a node. This shows that the algorithm proposed in the current work has better asymptotic complexity. Further, the use of asymmetric key encryption in the former protocol renders it inefficient in comparison to the current protocol. It is important to note that the authors in this paper also assume a non-standard definition of betweenness. Hence, their algorithm cannot be directly employed to compute the standard measure betweenness centrality, unlike the protocol designed in the current paper. Betweenness centrality has also been studied in the context of supply chains. Fridgen and Garizy [12] identify betweenness centrality as a measure to find nodes that play a key role in supply chain risk management. Hence, the authors propose a privacy preserving algorithm for computing betweenness centrality of nodes in a supply chain network distributedly held by a set of organizations. The major focus of the work is to provide an artifact that helps securely compute the betweenness score, with no attention devoted to the complexity. They propose that the artifact be built using off-the-shelf generic MPC constructions, which as discussed previously are inefficient. The authors also fail to provide any proof of security for the designed algorithm. We believe that their solution is not private in accordance with the MPC definition, since the communication pattern between the parties leaks more information than just the betweenness centrality score. For example, in some instances, a party may be able to conclude regarding the presence or absence of edge between a neighboring node and a target node.

Thus, the current work proposes the best known protocol for securely computing betweenness centrality score so far. Additionally, we are the first to benchmark and evaluate the designed protocol with implementations. We prove the security and data-obliviousness of the designed protocol that guarantees that the control flow of the protocol is independent of the input. This in turn ensures that the protocol does not compromise the private data of the involved individuals.

8   Conclusion

In the current work, we consider the scenario where the network data is distributedly held by a set of individuals who are unwilling to disclose their share of the data. However, each of them is interested in computing the betweenness centrality of the nodes in the network. As a solution, we propose a privacy preserving approach for computing the centrality measure using the technique of secure multiparty computation. The protocol is designed for the two-party setting and proved secure under the semi-honest adversarial model. In order to achieve better efficiency, we propose an alternative graph representation called the edgelist representation to be used in conjunction with the state of the art ORAM schemes. Thus, the proposed algorithm performs better than the previous works reported in the literature that use the traditional representation of an adjacency matrix. This allows us to report an asymptotic complexity as low as $\mathcal{O}(|V||E|\log^3|E|)$ for the secure variant of the Brandes algorithm. We also provide the implementation of the designed algorithm along with the benchmarks for the performance of the various state of the art ORAM schemes as we vary the size of the input graph. The proposed protocol is known to be applicable for supply chain networks, interbank networks, criminal networks, etc. The current work is a step towards addressing the generalized problem of efficiently performing social network analysis in a privacy preserving manner. As future work, we wish to provide a complete suit of secure protocols for performing social network analysis.

References

1. Aly, A., Cuvelier, E., Mawet, S., Pereira, O., Van Vyve, M.: Securely solving simple combinatorial graph problems. In: Sadeghi, A.-R. (ed.) FC 2013. LNCS, vol. 7859, pp. 239–257. Springer, Heidelberg (2013). https://doi.org/10.1007/978-3-642-39884-1_21
2. Asharov, G., Lindell, Y.: A full proof of the BGW protocol for perfectly secure multiparty computation. J. Cryptol. **30**(1), 58–151 (2017)
3. Asharov, G., Lindell, Y., Schneider, T., Zohner, M.: More efficient oblivious transfer and extensions for faster secure computation. In: SIGSAC Conference on Computer & Communications Security, pp. 535–548. ACM (2013)
4. Bellare, M., Hoang, V.T., Keelveedhi, S., Rogaway, P.: Efficient garbling from a fixed-key blockcipher. In: Security and Privacy (SP), pp. 478–492. IEEE (2013)
5. Ben-Or, M., Goldwasser, S., Wigderson, A.: Completeness theorems for non-cryptographic fault-tolerant distributed computation. In: ACM symposium on Theory of Computing, pp. 1–10. ACM (1988)
6. Brandes, U.: A faster algorithm for betweenness centrality. J. Math. Sociol. **25**(2), 163–177 (2001)
7. Chaum, D., Crépeau, C., Damgard, I.: Multiparty unconditionally secure protocols. In: ACM Symposium on Theory of Computing, pp. 11–19. ACM (1988)
8. Damgård, I., Fitzi, M., Kiltz, E., Nielsen, J.B., Toft, T.: Unconditionally secure constant-rounds multi-party computation for equality, comparison, bits and exponentiation. In: Halevi, S., Rabin, T. (eds.) TCC 2006. LNCS, vol. 3876, pp. 285–304. Springer, Heidelberg (2006). https://doi.org/10.1007/11681878_15
9. Doerner, J.: The Absentminded Crypto Kit. https://bitbucket.org/jackdoerner/absentminded-crypto-kit.git
10. Freeman, L.C.: A set of measures of centrality based on betweenness. Sociometry **40**, 35–41 (1977)
11. Freeman, L.C.: Centrality in social networks conceptual clarification. Soc. Netw. **1**(3), 215–239 (1978)
12. Fridgen, G., Garizy, T.Z.: Supply chain network risk analysis-a privacy preserving approach. In: European Conference on Information Systems (ECIS) (2015)
13. Goldreich, O., Micali, S., Wigderson, A.: How to play any mental game. In: ACM Symposium on Theory of Computing, pp. 218–229. ACM (1987)
14. Gordon, S.D., Katz, J., Kolesnikov, V., Krell, F., Malkin, T., Raykova, M., Vahlis, Y.: Secure two-party computation in sublinear (amortized) time. In: ACM Conference on Computer and Communications Security, pp. 513–524. ACM (2012)
15. Kerschbaum, F., Schaad, A.: Privacy-preserving social network analysis for criminal investigations. In: Workshop on Privacy in the Electronic Society, pp. 9–14. ACM (2008)
16. Kim, Y., Choi, T.Y., Yan, T., Dooley, K.: Structural investigation of supply networks: a social network analysis approach. J. Oper. Manag. **29**(3), 194–211 (2011)
17. Kolesnikov, V., Schneider, T.: Improved garbled circuit: free XOR gates and applications. In: Aceto, L., Damgård, I., Goldberg, L.A., Halldórsson, M.M., Ingólfsdóttir, A., Walukiewicz, I. (eds.) ICALP 2008. LNCS, vol. 5126, pp. 486–498. Springer, Heidelberg (2008). https://doi.org/10.1007/978-3-540-70583-3_40
18. Krackhardt, D., Hanson, J.R.: 16 informal networks: the company behind the chart. In: Creative Management, p. 202 (2001)
19. Krebs, V.E.: Mapping networks of terrorist cells. Connections **24**(3), 43–52 (2002)

20. Lee, M.-J., Lee, J., Park, J.Y., Choi, R.H., Chung, C.W.: Qube: a quick algorithm for updating betweenness centrality. In: International Conference on World Wide Web, pp. 351–360. ACM (2012)
21. Leskovec, J., Krevl, A.: SNAP datasets: Stanford large network dataset collection, June 2014. http://snap.stanford.edu/data
22. Leydesdorff, L.: Betweenness centrality as an Indicator of the Interdisciplinarity of Scientific Journals. J. Am. Soc. Inf. Sci. Technol. **58**(9), 1303–1319 (2007)
23. Lindell, Y., Pinkas, B.: A proof of security of yao's protocol for two-party computation. J. Cryptol. **22**(2), 161–188 (2009)
24. Newman, M.E.J.: Scientific collaboration networks. II. Shortest paths, weighted networks, and centrality. Phys. Rev. E **64**(1), 016132 (2001)
25. Pullonen, P., Siim, S.: Combining secret sharing and garbled circuits for efficient private IEEE 754 floating-point computations. In: Brenner, M., Christin, N., Johnson, B., Rohloff, K. (eds.) FC 2015. LNCS, vol. 8976, pp. 172–183. Springer, Heidelberg (2015). https://doi.org/10.1007/978-3-662-48051-9_13
26. Wang, X., Chan, H., Shi, E.: Circuit ORAM: on tightness of the Goldreich-Ostrovsky lower bound. In: SIGSAC Conference on Computer and Communications Security, pp. 850–861. ACM (2015)
27. Yao, A.C.: Protocols for secure computations. In: Foundations of Computer Science, pp. 160–164. IEEE (1982)
28. Yao, A.C.-C.: How to generate and exchange secrets. In: Foundations of Computer Science, pp. 162–167. IEEE (1986)
29. Zahur, S., Evans, D.: Obliv-C: a language for extensible data-oblivious computation. IACR Cryptology ePrint Archive 2015:1153 (2015)
30. Zahur, S., Rosulek, M., Evans, D.: Two halves make a whole. In: Oswald, E., Fischlin, M. (eds.) EUROCRYPT 2015. LNCS, vol. 9057, pp. 220–250. Springer, Heidelberg (2015). https://doi.org/10.1007/978-3-662-46803-6_8
31. Zahur, S., Wang, X., Raykova, M., Gascón, A., Doerner, J., Evans, D., Katz, J.: Revisiting square-root ORAM: efficient random access in multi-party computation. In: Security and Privacy (SP), pp. 218–234. IEEE (2016)

HIKE: Walking the Privacy Trail

Elena Pagnin, Carlo Brunetta$^{(\boxtimes)}$, and Pablo Picazo-Sanchez

Chalmers University of Technology, Gothenburg, Sweden
{pagnin,brunetta,pablop}@chalmers.se

Abstract. We consider the problem of privacy-preserving processing of outsourced data in the context of user-customised services. Clients store their data on a server. In order to provide user-dependent services, service providers may ask the server to compute functions on the users' data. We propose a new solution to this problem that guarantees data privacy (*i.e.*, an honest-but-curious server cannot access plaintexts), as well as that service providers can correctly decrypt only –functions on– the data the user gave them access to (*i.e.*, service providers learn nothing more than the result of user-selected computations).

Our solution has as base point a new secure labelled homomorphic encryption scheme (**LEEG**). **LEEG** supports additional algorithms (**FEET**) that enhance the scheme's functionalities with extra privacy-oriented features. Equipped with **LEEG** and **FEET**, we define **HIKE**: a lightweight protocol for private and secure *storage, computation* and *disclosure* of users' data. Finally, we implement **HIKE** and benchmark its performances demonstrating its succinctness and efficiency.

Keywords: Homomorphic encryption
Privacy-preserving computation · Security protocol · GDPR

1 Introduction

We are living in the digital era, where people like to store their personal data in the cloud and get access to it any-time and anywhere. On the other hand, database maintainers and service providers develop an increasing interest for processing and extracting statistics from users's data. The usual setting is depicted in Fig. 1: users (or clients) agree to share their personal data with some service providers which, in exchange, returns customised services and improved user-dependent performances. Typical application scenarios are: e-Health environments (*e.g.*, keeping a blood pressure database that doctors can access to retrieve data) or smart trackers (*e.g.*, activity bands that keep track of users' performance and achieved goals).

In recent years, the cryptographic community has proposed new techniques for computing on outsourced data including Fully Homomorphic Encryption [12],

This work was partially supported by the Swedish Research Council (*Vetenskapsrådet*) through the grants PolUser (2015-04154) and PRECIS (621-2014-4845).

J. Camenisch and P. Papadimitratos (Eds.): CANS 2018, LNCS 11124, pp. 43–66, 2018.
https://doi.org/10.1007/978-3-030-00434-7_3

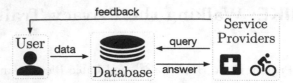

Fig. 1. The setting we consider: users send data to a database and enjoy some service. *Example 1* (e-Health): doctors can query for the average blood pressure in the last hour and alert the user in case of need. *Example 2* (sport): the service provider can query for the distance run until 'now' and feedback when the daily goal is achieved.

Verifiable Computation [10] or Multi-Key Homomorphic Signatures [8]. Beyond the obvious benefits, user-customised services may have undesirable drawbacks. In particular, service providers can collect data from thousands of clients, identify trends, profile users, and potentially sell their knowledge to third parties without the clients' consent or awareness.

In this paper, we define a model for user-customised services that addresses new privacy challenges inspired to the guidelines provided in the European *General Data Protection Regulation (GDPR)* [6]. This regulation sets clear boundaries on how data should be *collected, handled* and *processed* by protecting clients from possible miss-usages of their data by malicious service providers.

In particular, we give one of the *first attempts*[1] to *rigorously* formalise in *cryptographic* terms three of the main guidelines in the GDPR [6], namely: *(i)* the client's data is never stored in plaintext on public databases (art. 32); *(ii)* the client decides who can read her data (art. 15); *(iii)* the client has the *right to be forgotten, i.e.,* to request deletion of her data (art. 17).

Our Contributions. Our main contribution is the proposal and efficient instantiation of HIKE, a new cryptographic protocol that solves the problem of providing client-customised services. In details, our contributions are as follows:

(a) We present LEEG, a new labelled encryption scheme based on the elliptic-curve ElGamal scheme which supports homomorphic computation of multivariate linear polynomials.
(b) We define a set of additional algorithms that increase the versatility of LEEG, including an algorithm to cryptographically *destroy* encrypted data and a new procedure through which a chosen third party gets *decryption rights* for specific computations on encrypted data. We call this set of algorithms FEET as they extend the LEEG scheme.
(c) We then use LEEG and FEET in our HIKE protocol. HIKE is a novel lightweight protocol designed for application scenarios that involve users, servers, and service-providers. What makes this scenario different is that users' data need to be both privately and securely stored while allowing

---

[1] The only academic works we found related to the GDPR are [5,20], where the focus is on *technical* and *implementation* requirements. We could not find any work attempting to formalise and analyse the GDPR requirements in cryptographic terms.

service providers to perform simple statistics on specific portions of users' data.

(d) We prove that HIKE is secure with respect to our security model that includes notions that address three articles of the GDPR law, namely *(i)* user's data is *never* stored as *plaintext* in the server; *(ii)* the user has the power to decide *who* can *read* its data; *(iii)* the user can always ask the server to cryptographically destroy its data.

(e) We implement the HIKE protocol and empirically test its succinctness and efficiency. We provide a complete benchmark for all the algorithms involved. Our implementation is freely available at https://github.com/Pica4x6/HIKE.

Overview of our Technique. Our starting point is the ElGamal encryption scheme on elliptic curves [14,16]. We progressively change this scheme by introducing three *ideas*: (i) replacing the sampling of randomness in a ciphertext by using labels and Pseudo Random Function (PRF); (ii) modifying the labels to include the public key of the scheme, and; (iii) exploiting the structure of the new ciphertexts to define algorithms for special user-privacy oriented features.

In more detail, but still quite abstractly, the three ideas work as follows. A label is a *unique identifier* for a specific message and it contains the sender's *public key*, a *random curve point* and a *tag* that identifies the message. Idea (i) is to change *how* the randomness is generated during the encryption procedure. We replace the random sampling of ElGamal encryption with the evaluation of a secure pseudo-random function PRF_k on the label. For this change to work correctly, we also need to add the PRF key k to the user's secret key. The major implications of this change are: (1) we can get rid of the random component of classical ElGamal ciphertexts (thus achieving better succinctness), and (2) the new scheme has secret-key encryption.

Idea (ii) exploits the special structure of the labels and views the *"random curve point"* as the public key of the *designated-receiver* (*e.g.,* the service provider). By doing so, we can algebraically manipulate ciphertexts in meaningful ways and also allow data decryption for both the encryptor and the *designated-receiver* (the latter upon receiving a special data-dependent *token*).

The last idea (iii) is to combine (i) and (ii) and design a protocol which addresses: data-secrecy (similar notion to semantic security); token-secrecy (data owner have full control on *who* can decrypt their data), and; forgettability (data owners can ask for their data to be destroyed).

Related Work. Rivest *et al.* [23] introduced the concept of *Homomorphic Encryption (HE)* schemes as a set of algorithms that can be used to encrypt data, perform some computations on the ciphertexts, and directly decrypt the result of the computation.

For over 30 years, all secure proposals of HE schemes were only partially homomorphic, *i.e.,* they supported either additions or multiplications of ciphertexts [7,19]. The breakthrough result was due to Gentry [12] and started an avalanche of *Fully Homomorphic Encryption (FHE)* schemes [3,4,24,25]. However, most FHE schemes have major drawbacks due to key sizes and (or) efficiency. Albeit HE supports less expressive computations than FHE, as long as we are interested in simple statistics (*e.g.*, average, additions, least square fit of functions) on encrypted data, HE has better performances than FHE.

Barbosa *et al.* [2] introduced the notion of *Labelled Homomorphic Encryption (LabHE)* which combines HE with labels. This is an elegant approach to address the problem of privacy-preserving processing of outsourced data. In this paper, we follow their definitional framework but we avoid the presence of a *fully trusted party* that executes the initial setup and holds a master secret key. Albeit being less expressive than Barbosa *et al.*'s scheme, our protocol achieves full succinctness without relaying on any trusted party.

A concurrent and independent work by Fischer *et al.* [9] proposes a linearly homomorphic construction also based on ElGamal encryption scheme. The aim of [9] is to provide both information flow security and authentication while our scheme has a privacy-oriented cryptographic approach—since we do not consider authentication, and it achieves full ciphertext succinctness.

2   Preliminaries

Notation. For any finite set S, we denote by $x \xleftarrow{\$} S$ the uniformly random sampling of elements from S, and by $|S|$ as the size of the set. We denote by $[n]$ the set $\{1, \dots, n\}$, by $[0..q]$ the set $\{0, \dots, q\}$, and by $\{0,1\}^*$ the space of binary-strings of arbitrary length. For any linear function f on n variables we describe f as $f(x_1, \dots, x_n) = a_0 + \sum_{i \in [n]} a_i x_i$, for opportune values $a_i \in [0..q-1]$. We denote by λ the security parameter of cryptographic schemes and functions, and by ε a negligible function in λ, *i.e.*, $\varepsilon(\lambda) = O(\lambda^{-c})$ for every constant $c > 0$. We refer to computational feasibility (resp. infeasibility) of a problem if all known algorithm to solve the problem run in polynomial (resp. exponential) time.

Elliptic Curves. For prime p, let $\mathcal{E}$ be an elliptic curve over $\mathbb{F}_p$ and P be a generator point for the group $\mathbb{G}$ derived by $\mathcal{E}$. Let q be the order of $\mathbb{G}$, *i.e.*, $\mathbb{G} = <P> = \{\mathcal{O}, P, 2 \cdot P, \dots, (q-1) \cdot P\}$, where $\mathcal{O}$ is the point at infinity (identity element of $\mathbb{G}$). For security reasons, we require q to be a prime number or a non-smooth (*i.e.*, q is divisible by a large prime).

Problem 1 (Elliptic Curve Discrete Logarithm Problem [16]). Let p be a prime number and $\mathcal{E}$ be an elliptic curve over $\mathbb{F}_p$. Let $\mathbb{G}$ be the subgroup generated by a point $P \in \mathcal{E}$ such that $\mathbb{G} = <P>$ and $|\mathbb{G}| = q$ is prime or a non-smooth number. Given $Q \in \mathbb{G}$, the *Discrete Logarithm (DLog)* requires to find the value $m \in [0, \dots, q-1]$ such that $m \cdot P = Q$.

Pollard's Rho [21] is a well-known algorithm for solving the DLog problem. Its running time, however, is exponential in the group size, *i.e.*, $O(\sqrt{|\mathbb{G}|}) = O(2^{\frac{q}{2}})$.

Assumption 1. *Given $\mathbb{G}$, P and Q as in Problem 1, it is computationally infeasible to find a solution to the DLog.*

Problem 2 (Interval Discrete Logarithm Problem [22]). Let $\mathcal{E}$, $\mathbb{F}_p$, $\mathbb{G}$, P and Q be as in Problem 1. The *Interval Discrete Logarithm Problem (IDLP)* requires to find the value $m \in [0, \dots, q-1]$ such that $m \cdot P = Q$ knowing that $m \in [a, \dots, b]$ for $a, b \in [0, \dots, q-1]$.

Pollard's kangaroo algorithm [22] finds an existing solution to the IDLP problem in a given interval $[a, \dots, b]$ in time $O(2^{\frac{\Delta}{2}})$ where $\Delta = \lceil \log_2(b-a) \rceil$ is the number of bits in the binary representation of the interval length [17].

Assumption 2. *Solving the IDLP is computationally feasible for $\|[a..b]\| < 2^{22}$, while it is infeasible for larger intervals $\|[a..b]\| > 2^{160}$.*

Pseudo Random Functions (PRF) [15]. A PRF is a collection of keyed functions from a (possibly infinite) set A to a finite set B. Formally, let $\mathcal{F}$ be the set of all functions from A to B and $\mathcal{K}$ be a (finite) set of keys, a PRF family is a set of functions $\{\mathsf{PRF}_k : A \to B \mid k \in \mathcal{K}\}$ satisfying the following properties:

1. For any $a \in A$ and $k \in \mathcal{K}$, the function $\mathsf{PRF}_k(a)$ is efficiently computable.
2. No *Probabilistic Polynomial-Time (PPT)* algorithm can distinguish the function PRF_k (for $k \xleftarrow{\$} \mathcal{K}$) from a function $f \xleftarrow{\$} \mathcal{F}$.

In this paper, we regard HMAC-SHA256 as secure pseudo random function family for functions $\mathsf{PRF}_k : \{0,1\}^* \to \mathbb{Z}_q$ with $k \in \mathcal{K}$.

2.1   Labelled Homomorphic Encryption

The notion of labelled homomorphic encryption was introduced by Barbosa *et al.* to improve the efficiency of HE schemes [2]. The main idea is to combine homomorphic encryption [12] with labelled programs [11] to be able to compute on selected outsourced ciphertexts. A labelled program $\mathcal{P}$ is a tuple $(f, (\ell_1, \dots, \ell_n))$, such that $f : X^n \to X$ is a function of n variables and ℓ_i is a label for the i-th input of f. Labelled programs can be used to identify users' input to computations by imposing $\ell = (\mathsf{id}, \tau)$ for some user identifier id and tag τ [8]. We denote by $\mathcal{I}_\ell = (f, \ell)$ the *identity labelled program* on the label ℓ, *i.e.*, $f_\ell(x) = x$.

Formally, a labelled homomorphic encryption scheme $\mathsf{LabHE} = (\mathsf{KeyGen}, \mathsf{Enc}, \mathsf{Eval}, \mathsf{Dec})$ is defined by the following algorithms:

$\mathsf{KeyGen}(1^\lambda)$: on input the security parameter, it outputs a secret key sk and a (public) evaluation key ek that includes a description of a message space $\mathcal{M}$, a label space $\mathcal{L}$, and a class of admissible functions $\mathcal{F}$.

$\mathsf{Enc}(\mathsf{sk}, \ell, m)$: on input sk, a label ℓ, and a message m, it outputs a ciphertext ct.

$\mathsf{Eval}(\mathsf{ek}, f, \mathsf{ct}_1, \dots, \mathsf{ct}_n)$: on input ek, a function $f : \mathcal{M}^n \to \mathcal{M}$ in a set of admissible functions $\mathcal{F}$, and n ciphertexts. It returns a ciphertext ct.

$\mathsf{Dec}(\mathsf{sk}, \mathcal{P}, \mathsf{ct})$: on input sk, a labelled program $\mathcal{P} = (f, \ell_1, \dots, \ell_n)$ and a ciphertext ct, it outputs a message m.

Moreover, LabHE satisfies the properties of correctness, succinctness, (semantic) security and context hiding defined in as follows.

Definition 1 (Correctness [2]). *A LabHE scheme is said to be correct for a family of functions $\mathcal{F}$ if, for all keys $(\mathsf{ek}, \mathsf{sk}) \leftarrow \mathsf{KeyGen}(1^\lambda)$, all $f \subset \mathcal{F}$, any selection of labels $\ell_1, \ldots, \ell_n \in \mathcal{L}$, and messages $m_1, \ldots, m_n \in \mathcal{M}$, with corresponding ciphertexts $\mathsf{ct}_i \leftarrow \mathsf{Enc}(\mathsf{sk}, \ell_i, m_i)$, $i \in [n]$, and $\mathcal{P} = (f, (\ell_1, \ldots, \ell_n))$, it holds that:*

$$\Pr\left[\mathsf{Dec}\left(\mathsf{sk}, \mathcal{P}, \mathsf{Eval}(\mathsf{ek}, f, \mathsf{ct}_1, \ldots, \mathsf{ct}_n)\right) = f(m_1, \ldots, m_n)\right] \geq 1 - \varepsilon.$$

Definition 2 (Succinctness [2]). *A LabHE scheme is said to be succinct if there exists a fixed polynomial $\mathsf{poly}(\cdot)$ such that every honestly generated ciphertext (output by Enc or Eval) has bit-size size $\mathsf{poly}(\lambda)$.*

The security notion for LabHE schemes is inspired to the standard semantic security experiment proposed by Goldwasser and Micali [13].

Definition 3 (Context Hiding [2]). *A LabHE scheme is context-hiding if there exists a PPT algorithm $\mathcal{S}$ such that, for any $(\mathsf{ek}, \mathsf{sk}) \leftarrow \mathsf{KeyGen}(1^\lambda)$, $f \in \mathcal{F}$, any tuple of labels $\ell_1, \ldots, \ell_n \in \mathcal{L}$ and messages $m_1, \ldots m_n \in \mathcal{M}$ with corresponding ciphertexts $\mathsf{ct}_1 \leftarrow \mathsf{Enc}(\mathsf{sk}, \ell_i, m_i)$, if $m = f(m_1, \ldots, m_n)$ and $\mathcal{P} = (f, \ell_1, \ldots, \ell_n)$ then:*

$$\tfrac{1}{2} \cdot \sum_{\mathsf{ct}} \left|\mathsf{Prob}[\mathsf{Eval}(\mathsf{ek}, f, \mathsf{ct}_1, \ldots, \mathsf{ct}_n) = \mathsf{ct}] - \mathsf{Prob}[\mathcal{S}(1^\lambda, \mathsf{sk}, \mathcal{P}, m) = \mathsf{ct}]\right| < \varepsilon(\lambda).$$

Definition 4 (Semantic security for LabHE [2]). *A LabHE scheme is semantically secure if for any PPT algorithm $\mathcal{A}$ taking part to $\mathsf{Exp}^{\mathsf{sem.sec}}_{\mathsf{LabHE}, \mathcal{A}}$ in Fig. 2, it holds that:* $\mathsf{Adv}^{\mathsf{sem.sec}}_{\mathsf{LabHE}, \mathcal{A}}(\lambda) = \Pr\left[\mathsf{Exp}^{\mathsf{sem.sec}}_{\mathsf{LabHE}, \mathcal{A}}(\lambda) = 1\right] - \tfrac{1}{2} < \varepsilon.$

$\mathsf{Exp}^{\mathsf{sem.sec}}_{\mathsf{LabHE}, \mathcal{A}}(\lambda)$:

$b \xleftarrow{\$} \{0, 1\}, L_{\mathsf{lab}} = \emptyset$
$(\mathsf{ek}, \mathsf{sk}) \leftarrow \mathsf{KeyGen}(1^\lambda)$
$(\ell^*, m_0, m_1) \leftarrow \mathcal{A}^{O\mathsf{Enc}_{\mathsf{sk}}}(\mathsf{ek})$
if $\ell^* \in L_{\mathsf{lab}}$
    $\mathsf{ct} = \mathbf{error}$
else
    $\mathsf{ct} \leftarrow \mathsf{Enc}(\mathsf{sk}, \ell^*, m_b)$
    $L_{\mathsf{lab}} \leftarrow L_{\mathsf{lab}} \cup \ell^*$

$b' \leftarrow \mathcal{A}^{O\mathsf{Enc}_{\mathsf{sk}}}(\mathsf{ct})$

Output 1 if $b = b'$, and 0 otherwise.

$O\mathsf{Enc}_{\mathsf{sk}}(\ell, m)$:
if $\ell \in L_{\mathsf{lab}}$
    return $\mathbf{error}$
else $L_{\mathsf{lab}} \leftarrow L_{\mathsf{lab}} \cup \ell$
    return $\mathsf{ct} \leftarrow \mathsf{Enc}(\mathsf{sk}, \ell, m)$.

Fig. 2. The semantic-security experiment for LabHE schemes, and the $O\mathsf{Enc}$ oracle.

3   Labelled Elliptic-curve ElGamal (**LEEG**)

In its standard construction, the ElGamal encryption scheme [7] is defined on finite multiplicative groups and is only multiplicative-homomorphic. It is possible to obtain an additive-homomorphic version of ElGamal by using groups defined over an elliptic curve [14,16] and specific message encoding maps, discussed later in Sect. 7. Essentially, in the elliptic curve setting, exponentiations are replaced by multiplications and multiplications by additions. Security reduces to the hardness of computing the discrete logarithm on elliptic curves. For further details on ElGamal for elliptic curve groups see [14].

In this section, we define the first labelled and symmetric-key version of the additive-homomorphic ElGamal scheme that we refer to as LEEG (Labelled Elliptic-curve ElGamal). To ease the adoption of LEEG in our GDPR-oriented protocol HIKE in Sect. 5.1, we make a small adaptation to Barbosa *et al.*'s framework for LabHE. We introduce a SetUp algorithm that outputs some global public parameters pp, and make the KeyGen algorithm run on pp. This change is only syntactic if KeyGen is run once and brings with straightforward modifications to the definitions.

Definition 5 (LEEG). *The* LEEG *scheme is defined by the following five PPT algorithms:*

SetUp(1^λ): *on input the security parameter, the setup algorithm outputs* pp *that include: a λ-bit-size prime p, an elliptic curve $\mathcal{E}$ over $\mathbb{F}_p$ with a (prime) order-q group $\mathbb{G} \subseteq \mathcal{E}$, a generator P of the group $\mathbb{G}$, a set of admissible functions $\mathcal{F}$ (namely linear functions), a set of messages $\mathcal{M} \in [m]$, a set of message identifiers $\mathcal{T} = \{0,1\}^t$, a set of labels $\mathcal{L} = \mathbb{G} \times \mathbb{G} \times \mathcal{T}$, and a keyed-pseudorandom function family* PRF *from $\{0,1\}^*$ to $[0..q-1]$. The* pp *are input to all subsequent algorithms even if not stated explicitly.*

KeyGen(pp): *on input the public parameters the key generation algorithm selects a random element* sk $\stackrel{\$}{\leftarrow} [q-1]$ *and a random PRF key* k $\stackrel{\$}{\leftarrow} \mathcal{K}$. *It outputs the secret key* sk $= (sk, k)$.[2]

Enc(sk, ℓ, m): *on input a secret key* sk $= (sk, k)$, *a label $\ell = (sk \cdot P, Q, \tau)$ with $Q \in \mathbb{G}$ and message $m \in \mathcal{M}$ the encryption algorithm returns the ciphertext:*

$$\mathsf{ct} = m \cdot P + \mathsf{PRF}_k(\ell) \cdot sk \cdot Q \in \mathbb{G} \tag{1}$$

In case the input label has as first entry a value different from $sk \cdot P$ the algorithm returns error.

Eval($f, \mathsf{ct}_1, \ldots, \mathsf{ct}_n$): *on input a linear function $f(x_1, \ldots, x_n) = a_0 + \sum_{i \in [n]} a_i x_i$ and n ciphertexts ct_i, the evaluation algorithm returns the ciphertext:*

$$\mathsf{ct} = a_0 \cdot P + \sum_{i \in [n]} a_i \cdot \mathsf{ct}_i \in \mathbb{G} \tag{2}$$

Dec(sk, $\mathcal{P}, \mathsf{ct}$): *on input a secret key* sk $= (sk, k)$, *a labelled program $\mathcal{P} = (f, \ell_1, \ldots, \ell_n)$ for a linear function f with labels of the form $\ell_i = (sk \cdot P, Q_i, \tau_i)$,*

---

[2] In the original definition of Labelled Homomorphic Encryption [2], the KeyGen algorithm additionally outputs a public evaluation key. Since in our case this key is empty, we decided to skip it and have more succinct algorithm descriptions.

and a ciphertext ct, *the decryption algorithm computes:*

$$T = \text{ct} - sk \cdot \left(\sum_{i \in [n]} a_i \cdot \text{PRF}_k(\ell_i) \cdot Q_i \right) \in \mathbb{G} \qquad (3)$$

and returns $m = \log_P(T)$.

We note that LEEG is a fully dynamic scheme, indeed ciphertexts output by Eval can be used as input to new computations (as long as the new computation includes the initial labelled program).

Succinctness of LEEG. The succinctness of the LEEG scheme is immediate given that ciphertexts (output by Enc or Eval) are always one single group element in $\mathbb{G} \subseteq \mathcal{E}$. Further details regarding the actual bit-size for our implementation can be found in Sect. 7.

Correctness of LEEG. The correctness of LEEG is a straightforward computation.

Context-Hiding of LEEG. The context-hiding property of LEEG is straightforward since given sk, $\mathcal{P}$ and $m = f(\text{ct}_1, \ldots, \text{ct}_n)$ the simulator is able to reconstruct exactly the same ciphertext output by $\text{Eval}(f, \text{ct}_1, \ldots, \text{ct}_n)$ as $\mathcal{S}(\text{sk}, \mathcal{P}, m) := f(m_1, \ldots, m_n) \cdot P + sk \sum_{i \in [n]} a_i \text{PRF}_k(\ell_i) \cdot Q_i$.

Security of LEEG. The proof is rather simple and we provide here just an intuition, deferring the formal proof to Appendix A. First the challenger replaces PRF with a truly random function, that is, the values r are now taken uniformly at random from $[q - 1]$. At this point the security of the scheme becomes information theoretic.[3] We then prove the semantic security in the same way as for standard OTP-based schemes, *i.e.*, we show that the challenge ciphertext has the same probability of being an encryption of m_0 as of m_1.

4   FEET: Feature Extensions to the Labelled-Homomorphic El-Gamal EncrypTion Scheme

In this section we define FEET a set of additional algorithms that increase the versatility and use cases of LEEG. The new algorithms build on the following observation. Given a label $\ell = (Q_1, Q_2, \cdot)$ we can interpret its first component Q_1 as the public key of the user who is performing the encryption (that we call this data-owner), and Q_2 as the public key of another user (that we call intended receiver). By doing so, we can give a sensible meaning to the procedures and manipulate ciphertexts in such a way that decryption works correctly only for

---

[3] Indeed, even provided an oracle access to an efficient solver of the discrete logarithm problem, the only information the adversary would retrieve from the challenge cipher-text is a random message $m' = m_b + r \cdot sk$. This is possible because, differently from El Gamal ciphertexts, LEEG ciphertexts have a single component that combines message and randomness.

data encryptor statde in the first component of the label, and the *designated-receiver* identified by the second component of the label. Assuming the existence of a *Public Key Infrastructure (PKI)*, FEET exploits the algebraic structure of LEEG ciphertexts to perform two actions:

- Cryptographically *'delete'* data owner's ciphertexts from a database by making them un-decryptable, *i.e.,* even the original data-owner would retrieve a random message by decrypting a *destroyed* ciphertext.
- Allow the data-owner to generate a special piece of information (called *token*) that enables the intended receiver to decrypt the output of a specific labelled program run on the encryptor's data.

Definition 6 (FEET: set of additional algorithms for LEEG). *Let* LEEG = (SetUp, KeyGen, Enc, Dec, Eval) *be the labelled homomorphic encryption scheme of Definition 5, where the* KeyGen *algorithm is run multiple times and associates identities (identifiers* id*) to the keys it generates. We define:*

Destroy(ct): *on input a ciphertext* ct*, the destroy-cihpertext algorithm picks a random* $r \overset{\$}{\leftarrow} [0..q-1]$ *and outputs the destroyed ciphertext* ct$'$ = ct $+ r \cdot P$.
PublicKey(sk): *on input the secret key* sk = (sk, k) *output the corresponding public key* pk = $sk \cdot P$.
TokenGen(sk, $\mathcal{P}$): *on input a secret key* sk = (sk, k) *and a labelled program* $\mathcal{P}$ = $(f, \ell_1, ..., \ell_n)$ *the token generation algorithm checks if the labels are of the form* $\ell_i = (sk \cdot P, Q, \tau_i)$—*for a point* $Q \in \mathbb{G}$ *and some* $\tau_i \in \mathcal{T}$, $i \in [n]$. *If the condition is not satisfied, the algorithm returns* error; *otherwise, it parses* $f(x_1, ..., x_n) = a_0 + \sum_{i \in [n]} a_i x_i$ *and outputs:*

$$\text{tok} = sk \cdot \left(\sum_{i \in [n]} a_i \cdot \text{PRF}_k(\ell_i) \right) \cdot P \tag{4}$$

TokenDec(sk, ct, tok): *on input a secret key* sk = (sk, k), *a ciphertext* ct *and a token* tok*, the decryption-with-token algorithm outputs* $m' = \log_P (\text{ct} - sk \cdot \text{tok})$.

Information Theoretic Security of Destroy. We prove this property by showing that for any given message m and ciphertext ct$'$, ct$'$ is a possible 'destruction' of ct = Enc(sk, ℓ, m) for any label. More formally, for any $m \in \mathcal{M}$, $\ell = (sk \cdot P, \text{pk}, \tau)$ and ct$'$ $\in \mathbb{G}$ it holds that:

$$\text{Prob}[\text{Destroy}(\text{Enc}(sk, \ell, m)) = \text{ct}'] = \frac{|\{r : \text{ct}' = (m + r') \cdot P + sk \cdot r \cdot \text{pk}\}|}{|\mathbb{G}|} = \frac{1}{|\mathbb{G}|}$$

where the probability is taken over all possible random choices in the Destroy algorithm ($r' \in [0..q-1]$), and $r = \text{PRF}_k(\ell)$. In particular, for any pair of label-message couples $(\ell_0, m_0), (\ell_1, m_1)$ it holds that:

$$\text{Prob}[\text{Destroy}(\text{Enc}(sk_{id_0}, \ell_0, m_0)) = \text{ct}'] = \text{Prob}[\text{Destroy}(\text{Enc}(sk_{id_1}, \ell_1, m_1)) = \text{ct}'].$$

Therefore given a ct$'$ output by Destroy this could be generated by the ciphertext of *any* message $m \in \mathcal{M}$.

Correctness of TokenDec. In order to prove the correctness of the decryption-with-token algorithm we need to show that

$$\mathsf{TokenDec}(\mathsf{sk}_2, \mathsf{Eval}(f, \mathsf{ct}_1, \dots, \mathsf{ct}_n), \mathsf{TokenGen}(\mathsf{sk}_1, \mathcal{P})) = f(m_1, \dots, m_n)$$

where $\mathsf{ct}_i = \mathsf{Enc}(\mathsf{sk}_1, \ell_i, m_i)$, $\ell_i = (\mathsf{pk}_1, \mathsf{pk}_2, \tau_i)$ for some $\tau_i \in \mathcal{T}$, and $\mathcal{P} = (f, \ell_1, \dots, \ell_n)$. This is a straightforward computation and follows from Eq. (2), Eq. (4) and the fact that $\mathsf{pk}_i = sk_i \cdot P$.

Remark 1 (Composability of TokenGen*).* It is possible to combine two (or more) decryption tokens $\mathsf{tok}_1, \mathsf{tok}_2$ generated for distinct labelled programs $\mathcal{P}_1, \mathcal{P}_2$, to obtain a joint decryption token tok that enables the intended decryptor with public key $\mathsf{pk}_2 = Q$ (common to all the labels involved) to correctly decrypt in one-shot the ciphertext for any labelled program $\mathcal{P}$ such that $f = b_1 f_1 + b_2 f_2$, for any $b_1, b_2 \in [0..q-1]$. Intuitively, this property follows by the linearity of the sum. A detailed explanation can be found in Appendix B.

5   The HIKE Protocol

In this section, we introduce HIKE: a protocol that employs our LEEG scheme and its extra features FEET to achieve advanced properties relevant to real world applications.

In what follows, we present a use case for HIKE and defer the formal description to the Sect. 5.1. We consider a scenario with three types of actors: data-owners (called clients and denoted as C), a cloud server (denoted as S) that controls the database Δ where the clients' records are stored, and service providers (denoted as P). The work-flow of the interactions between these actors is depicted in Fig. 3. As a use case, consider clients with smart-watches used for tracking their sport performances. With HIKE clients can safely upload their data on the cloud, cancel previously uploaded records, retrieve their data (or functions of thereof) at any time. Moreover, clients can allow their personal trainer app to access specific aggregations of data to provide personalised performance feedback.

5.1   A Formal Description

Definition 7 (The HIKE protocol). *Let* LEEG $=$ (SetUp, KeyGen, Enc, Dec, Eval) *be the labelled homomorphic encryption scheme in Definition 5 enhanced with the algorithms* FEET $=$ (TokenGen, TokenDec, Destroy) *described in Definition 6. We assume a PKI that, at every run of the* KeyGen *algorithm, associates identities (identifiers* id*) to the freshly generated keys. The* HIKE *protocols is defined by the following procedures:*

Initialise(1^λ)*: on input the security parameter the initialisation procedure runs* SetUp(1^λ) $\rightarrow$ pp *and returns the public parameters. Implicitly, it also generates a database Δ and a public key infrastructure.*

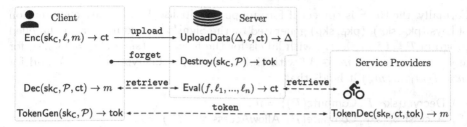

Fig. 3. Clients upload their encrypted data to the server (via an `upload` request). At any point in time, clients have the right to *destroy* their records in the database (via a `forget` request). In order to obtain aggregate information on the stored data, clients and service providers can ask the server to compute certain functions on the outsourced data and return the (encrypted) result (via a `retrieve` request). Finally, clients are always able to decrypt their own retrieved data, while service providers cannot decrypt directly. In order to decrypt the result of a computation $\mathcal{P} = (f, \ell_1, ..., \ell_n)$ on the client's data, the service provider needs to ask the client to generate a computation-specific decryption token (via a `token` request) that enables the designated service provider to decrypt.

SignUp(id): *on input a user identifier* id *the sign-up procedure returns* $\mathsf{sk}_{\mathsf{id}} \leftarrow$ KeyGen(pp) *and updates the public ledger (PKI) with* (id, $\mathsf{pk}_{\mathsf{id}}$) *where* $\mathsf{pk}_{\mathsf{id}} =$ PublicKey($\mathsf{sk}_{\mathsf{id}}$). *For correctness, this procedure outputs* $\bot$ *if user* id *was already present in the system.*

Encrypt(sk, ℓ, m): *on input a secret key* sk, *a label* ℓ *and a message* m *the encryption procedure returns the ciphertext* ct $=$ Enc(sk, ℓ, m).

UploadData($\Delta, \ell, \mathsf{ct}$): *on input a database* Δ, *a label* ℓ *and a ciphertext* ct *the upload data procedure performs* $\Delta = \Delta \cup \{(\ell, \mathsf{ct})\}$.

Forget(Δ, ℓ): *on input a database* Δ *and a label* ℓ *the forget-ciphertext procedure retrieves the record* (ℓ, ct) *from* Δ *and replaces it with* (ℓ, ct') *where* $\mathsf{ct}' \leftarrow$ Destroy(ct), *i.e.,it outputs* $\Delta = \Delta \setminus \{(\ell, \mathsf{ct})\} \cup \{(\ell, \mathsf{ct}')\}$.

Compute($\Delta, \mathcal{P}$): *on input a database* Δ *and a labelled program* $\mathcal{P} = (f, \ell_1, ..., \ell_n)$ *the retrieve-data (or aggregate data) procedure collects the ciphertexts* ct_i *corresponding to labels* ℓ_i *present in* Δ *and returns* ct $=$ Eval(pp, $f, \mathsf{ct}_1, ..., \mathsf{ct}_n$).

Decrypt(sk, $\mathcal{P}, \mathsf{ct}$): *on input a secret key* sk, *a labelled program* $\mathcal{P}$, *and a ciphertext* ct *the decryption procedure outputs* $m =$ Dec(sk, $\mathcal{P}, \mathsf{ct}$).

AllowAccess(sk, $\mathcal{P}$): *on input a user's secret key* sk *and a labeled program, the allow-access procedure returns* tok $=$ TokenGen(sk, $\mathcal{P}$).

AccessDec(sk, ct, tok) *on input a user's secret key* sk, *a ciphertext* ct *and a decryption token* tok, *the allowed-decryption procedure returns the output of* TokenDec(sk, ct, tok) $= m$.

5.2 Evaluation Correctness of HIKE

The evaluation correctness of our HIKE protocol essentially reduces to the correctness of the underlying LEEG scheme (Definition 5) and FEET (Definition 6).

Formally, the HIKE is correct if for any pp ← Initialise(1^λ), for any combination of keys ($\mathsf{pk_C, sk_C}$), ($\mathsf{pk_P, sk_P}$) generated by the SignUp procedure, for any labelled program $\mathcal{P} = (f, \ell_1, \ldots, \ell_n)$ with labels for the form $\ell = (sk_C \cdot P, Q = \mathsf{pk_P}, \cdot)$, for any set of messages $m_i \in \mathcal{M}$ with ciphertexts $\mathsf{ct}_i = \mathsf{Encrypt}(\mathsf{sk}, \ell_i, m_i)$, and for $m = f(m_1, \ldots, m_n)$ it holds that:

(1) $\mathsf{Decrypt}(\mathsf{sk_C}, \mathcal{P}, \mathsf{Compute}(\mathcal{P})) = m$.
(2) $\mathsf{AccessDec}\,(\mathsf{sk_P}, \mathsf{Compute}(\mathcal{P}), \mathsf{AllowAccess}(\mathsf{sk_C}, \mathcal{P})) = m$.

Condition *(1)* is equivalent to the evaluation correctness of the LEEG scheme given that the Compute procedure returns the output of LEEG's Eval algorithm and the Decrypt procedure runs LEEG's Dec algorithm.

Condition *(2)* is equivalent to the correctness of LEEG's additional algorithms given that AllowAccess returns the output of TokenGen, Compute returns the output of LEEG's Eval algorithm and AccessDec runs the TokenDec algorithm.

5.3   Interactions Between the Procedures of HIKE

We consider three categories of users taking part to the HIKE protocol:

Clients C: (or data owners), these users can run the procedures: SignUp, Encrypt, Decrypt and AllowAccess.
Server S: (or database maintainer), this user can run the procedures: UploadData, Compute and Forget.
Service providers P: (or third-party applications), these users can run the procedures: SignUp and AccessDec.

To simulate a real-world scenario, we allow users registered in the system to interact with each other. We model interaction via **requests** sent from one user to another and that there exists an authentication system to ensure this. Moreover, we assume that the target user reacts to the received request as follows:

upload: upload data requests can be performed by clients only and are directed to the server. Upon receiving an upload(ℓ, ct) request by a client C, the server checks if the submitted record is a new one , *i.e.,* if $(\ell, \cdot) \notin \Delta$. In this is the case, S runs UploadData($\Delta, \ell, \mathsf{ct}$) and returns **done** to C, otherwise S returns **error**.
forget: forget-ciphertext requests can be performed by clients only and are directed to the server. Upon receiving an forget(ℓ) request by a client C, the server checks that the label is a legit one for C, *i.e.,* that $\ell = (\mathsf{pk_C}, \cdot, \cdot)$ and that $(\ell, \cdot) \in \Delta$. If both conditions holds, S runs Forget(Δ, ℓ) and returns **done** to C, otherwise it returns **error**.
retrieve: retrieve-data requests can be performed by clients or by service providers and are directed to the server. Upon receiving a retrieve($\mathcal{P}$) request the server checks if the labelled program $\mathcal{P} = (f, \ell_1, \ldots, \ell_n)$ is well-defined, *i.e.,* if for every $i \in [n]$, $(\ell_i, \cdot) \in \Delta$ and $\ell_i = (\mathsf{pk}_h, \mathsf{pk}_k, \cdot)$ for some users registered in the systems. If the conditions hold, S runs Compute($\Delta, \mathcal{P}$) = ct and returns ct to whom performed the query, otherwise it returns **error**.

token: access-token requests can be performed by service providers only and are directed to clients only. Upon receiving a token($\mathcal{P}$) request, the client has the freedom to decide whether to reply consistently, running AllowAccess(sk, $\mathcal{P}$) = tok and returning tok to P, or to ignore the query returning error.

6   Security Model and Proofs for HIKE

Our security model builds on the setting introduced in Sect. 5.3 and covers three main goals:

(1) data-secrecy, *i.e.,* confidentiality of the clients' data;
(2) token-secrecy, *i.e.,* clients have full control on *who* can decrypt their data (only targeted service providers can decrypt, and no one else); and
(3) forgettability, *i.e.,* clients can ask for their data to be destroyed.

Interestingly, these security notions cover three of the requirements presented in the GDPR: the confidentiality of personal data (security of processing, art. 32), the clients' right of access (and share) data (art. 15), and; the right to ask for erasure of her personal data (*right to be forgotten*, art. 17) [6].

Adversarial Model. We denote malicious users with the user's category and the symbol *, *e.g.,* P*, and make the following assumptions:

– Clients C_i are *honest*, *i.e.,* they behave according to the interactions described in Sect. 5.3.
– The server S is *honest but curious*, *i.e.,* it behaves according to the interactions in Sect. 5.3 but tries to infer information about the clients' data (passive adversary).[4]
– Service Providers P_j can be *malicious* and deviate from the protocol in arbitrary ways.

We note that since anyone can generate and register keys in the protocol (using the PKI infrastructure), a malicious server corresponds to a malicious service provider that has access to an honest server (as the latter would reply to any retrieve request).

6.1   Data Secrecy

Our notion of data-secrecy is inspired to the definition of semantic-security for labelled homomorphic encryption by Barbosa *et al.* [2] but adapted to our protocol's setting. Intuitively, we require that the adversary $\mathcal{A}$, who controls a (malicious) server provider P* and holds a copy of the (encrypted) database Δ, should not be able to determine the plaintext associated to a database record (ℓ, ct). We formalise the notion through the data-secrecy experiment in Fig. 4.

---

[4] This assumption removes the theoretical need for the definition of forgettability in our security model. We include it for completeness.

Notably, $\mathcal{A}$ is given access to three oracles: $OSignUp$ to simulate users registering to the system, $OEncrypt$ to populate the database with adversarial chosen data (*i.e.*, $\mathcal{A}$ chooses the messages encrypted by a client). With abuse of notation we will write $\mathsf{pk}_{\mathsf{id}} \in L_{\mathsf{keys}}$ meaning that L_{keys} has an element of the form $(\mathsf{id}, \mathsf{sk}_{\mathsf{id}}, \mathsf{pk}_{\mathsf{id}})$.

$\mathsf{Exp}_{\mathsf{HIKE},\mathcal{A}}^{\mathsf{data-secrecy}}(\lambda):$

$b \xleftarrow{\$} \{0,1\}, L_{\mathsf{lab}} = L_{\mathsf{keys}} = \emptyset$
$\mathsf{pp} \leftarrow \mathsf{Initialise}(1^\lambda)$
$(\mathsf{id}^*, \mathsf{sk}_{\mathsf{id}^*}, \mathsf{pk}_{\mathsf{id}^*}) \leftarrow \mathcal{A}(\mathsf{pp})$
$L_{\mathsf{keys}} \leftarrow L_{\mathsf{keys}} \cup (\mathsf{id}^*, *, \mathsf{pk}_{\mathsf{id}^*})$

$(\ell^*, m_0, m_1) \leftarrow \mathcal{A}_{OEncrypt(\cdot,\cdot)}^{OSignUp(\cdot)}(\mathsf{pp})$
parse $\ell^* = (\mathsf{pk}_{\mathsf{id}}, \mathsf{pk}_{\mathsf{id}'}, \tau)$

if $\ell^* \in L_{\mathsf{lab}}$ or $\mathsf{pk}_{\mathsf{id}} = \mathsf{pk}_{\mathsf{id}^*}$ or $\mathsf{pk}_{\mathsf{id}}, \mathsf{pk}_{\mathsf{id}'} \notin L_{\mathsf{keys}}$
   $\mathsf{ct} = \mathbf{error}$
else
   $\mathsf{ct} \leftarrow \mathsf{Encrypt}(\mathsf{sk}_{\mathsf{id}}, \ell^*, m_b)$
   $L_{\mathsf{lab}} \leftarrow L_{\mathsf{lab}} \cup \{\ell_0^*, \ell_1^*\}$

$b^* \leftarrow \mathcal{A}_{OEncrypt(\cdot,\cdot)}^{OSignUp(\cdot)}(\mathsf{ct})$

if $b^* = b$ return 1, else return 0.

$OSignUp(\mathsf{id}):$
if $(\mathsf{id}, \cdot, \cdot) \in L_{\mathsf{keys}}$
   return $\mathbf{error}$
else
   $(\mathsf{id}, \mathsf{sk}_{\mathsf{id}}, \mathsf{pk}_{\mathsf{id}}) \leftarrow \mathsf{SignUp}(\mathsf{id})$
   $L_{\mathsf{keys}} \leftarrow L_{\mathsf{keys}} \cup (\mathsf{id}, \mathsf{sk}_{\mathsf{id}}, \mathsf{pk}_{\mathsf{id}})$
   return $\mathsf{pk}_{\mathsf{id}}$.

$OEncrypt(\ell, m):$
   parse $\ell = (\mathsf{pk}_{\mathsf{id}}, \mathsf{pk}_{\mathsf{id}'}, \tau)$
   if $\ell \in L_{\mathsf{lab}}$ or $\mathsf{pk}_{\mathsf{id}} = \mathsf{pk}_{\mathsf{id}^*}$
      or $(\cdot, \cdot, \mathsf{pk}_{\mathsf{id}}) \notin L_{\mathsf{keys}}$
   return $\mathbf{error}$
   else
      $L_{\mathsf{lab}} \leftarrow L_{\mathsf{lab}} \cup \ell$
      $\mathsf{ct} \leftarrow \mathsf{Encrypt}(\mathsf{sk}_{\mathsf{id}}, \ell, m)$
   return ct.

Fig. 4. The data-secrecy experiment and the oracles $OSignUp$ and $OEncrypt$.

Theorem 1. *The* HIKE *protocol achieves data-secrecy, i.e., for any PPT adversary* $\mathcal{A}$ *taking part to the experiment in Fig. 4, it holds that:*

$$\mathsf{Adv}_{\mathsf{HIKE},\mathcal{A}}^{\mathsf{data.sec}}(\lambda) = \Pr\left[\mathsf{Exp}_{\mathsf{HIKE},\mathcal{A}}^{\mathsf{data.sec}}(\lambda) = 1\right] - \frac{1}{2} \leq Q_{\mathsf{id}} \cdot \mathsf{Adv}_{\mathsf{LEEG},\mathcal{A}}^{\mathsf{sem.sec}}(\lambda),$$

where Q_{id} *is a bound on the total number calls to the sign-up oracle.*

Proof. We exhibit a reduction $\mathcal{B}$ that uses $\mathcal{A}$ to win the semantic-security experiment for the LEEG scheme. At the beginning the reduction samples $\mathsf{id}^* \in \mathsf{ID}$ as its guess for the identity that $\mathcal{A}$ will target during the game. (Note that $|\mathsf{ID}| = Q_{\mathsf{id}}$ is polynomial in this game). This step corresponds to $\mathcal{B}$ betting that $\mathcal{A}$ will choose the client id^* in its challenge labels.

When the semantic-security experiment starts, the reduction $\mathcal{B}$ (that is playing as an adversary) gets $\mathsf{ek} = (\mathsf{pk}^* = sk \cdot P, \mathsf{pp})$ from its challenger $\mathcal{C}$. Then $\mathcal{B}$ starts the data-secrecy experiment (as a challenger) by sending pp to $\mathcal{A}$. The adversary chooses an identity id^* and a pair of keys for it. $\mathcal{A}$ also sends $(\mathsf{id}^*, \mathsf{pk}_{\mathsf{id}^*})$ to $\mathcal{B}$. The reduction registers the (malicious) user id^* in the system $(L_{\mathsf{keys}} \leftarrow L_{\mathsf{keys}} \cup (\mathsf{id}^*, \cdot, \mathsf{pk}_{\mathsf{id}^*}))$ and replies to $\mathcal{A}$'s queries as follows.

Sign-up Queries: $\mathcal{B}$ forwards the queries to the $O\mathsf{SignUp}$.

Encryption Queries: $\mathcal{B}$ forwards the queries to the $O\mathsf{Encrypt}$ oracle unless $\ell = (\mathsf{pk}^\star, \mathsf{pk}, \tau)$, in which case $\mathcal{B}$ updates the list of queried labels $L_{\mathsf{lab}} \leftarrow L_{\mathsf{lab}} \cup \ell$, forwards (ℓ, m) as an encryption query to $\mathcal{C}$ and relays its reply to $\mathcal{A}$.

Let $(\ell^\star, m_0, m_1)$ be $\mathcal{A}$'s input to the challenge phase. If $\ell^\star \neq (\mathsf{pk}^\star, \cdot, \cdot)$ the reduction aborts (as $\mathcal{A}$ chose to challenge a different client than the one $\mathcal{C}$ has created). This event happens with probability $(1 - \frac{1}{Q_{\mathsf{id}}})$. Otherwise $\ell^\star = (\mathsf{pk}^\star, Q, \tau)$, $\mathcal{B}$ updates the list of queried labels $L_{\mathsf{lab}} \leftarrow L_{\mathsf{lab}} \cup \ell^\star$ and sends $(\ell^\star, m_0, m_1)$ to its challenger. Let ct denote $\mathcal{C}$'s reply, $\mathcal{B}$ sends ct to $\mathcal{A}$.

In the subsequent query phase $\mathcal{B}$ behaves as described above. At the end of the experiment, $\mathcal{B}$ outputs the same bit $b^\star$ returned by $\mathcal{A}$ for the data-secrecy experiment. Note that since $\mathcal{A}$ is given exactly the same challenge as in the semantic-security experiment, if $\mathcal{A}$ has a non-negligible advantage in breaking the data-secrecy of HIKE then $\mathcal{B}$ has the same non-negligible advantage in breaking the semantic security of LEEG, unless $\mathcal{B}$ aborts its simulation. Therefore we can conclude that: $\mathsf{Adv}^{\mathsf{sem.sec}}_{\mathsf{LEEG}, \mathcal{B}}(\lambda) \geq \left(\frac{1}{Q_{\mathsf{id}}} \right) \mathsf{Adv}^{\mathsf{data.sec}}_{\mathsf{HIKE}, \mathcal{A}}(\lambda).$ $\qquad\square$

6.2 Token Secrecy

Our notion of token-secrecy captures the idea that only the service provider P holding a valid decryption-token for a ciphertext that was created with P as intended recipient (*i.e.*, with associated label of the form $\ell = (\cdot, \mathsf{pk}_\mathsf{P}, \cdot)$) can decrypt the message correctly. In other words, the adversary $\mathcal{A}$ (as a malicious P*) should not be able to decrypt the result of any computation $\mathcal{P}^*$ for which it did not received decryption-tokens. We recall that by the token-composability property (Remark 1 in Sect. 4), given two decryption-tokens $\mathsf{tok}_\mathcal{P}$, $\mathsf{tok}_{\mathcal{P}'}$ for two labelled programs $\mathcal{P}$ and $\mathcal{P}'$, it is possible to generate decryption tokens for any linear combination of the programs $\mathcal{P}$ and $\mathcal{P}'$.

In the token-secrecy experiment, we make use of the same $O\mathsf{SignUp}$ oracle as in the experiment in Fig. 4; an $O\mathsf{Encrypt}'$ oracle which is the same as the $O\mathsf{Encrypt}$ in the experiment in Fig. 4 except that every time it would output a ciphertext ct it will also add the record to the database, *i.e.*, $\Delta \leftarrow \Delta \cup (\ell, \mathsf{ct})$ where ℓ is the label chosen by $\mathcal{A}$; and an additional $O\mathsf{Disclose}$ oracle, that enables $\mathcal{A}$ to get decryption-tokens of chosen (computations on) records. We allow the adversary to get decryption-tokens for any computation $\mathcal{P}$ as long as this does not contain the challenge labels.

Theorem 2. *The* HIKE *protocol achieves token-security, i.e., for any PPT adversary $\mathcal{A}$ taking part to the experiment in Fig. 5, it holds that:*

$$\mathsf{Adv}^{\mathsf{token.sec}}_{\mathsf{HIKE}, \mathcal{A}}(\lambda) = \Pr\left[\mathsf{Exp}^{\mathsf{token.sec}}_{\mathsf{HIKE}, \mathcal{A}}(\lambda) = 1 \right] - \frac{1}{2} \leq Q_{\mathsf{id}} \cdot \mathsf{Adv}^{\mathsf{sem.sec}}_{\mathsf{LEEG}, \mathcal{A}}(\lambda).$$

Due to the space limit, we moved proof of Theorem 2 to Appendix A.

$$\text{Exp}_{\text{HIKE},\mathcal{A}}^{\text{token.sec}}(\lambda):$$

$b \xleftarrow{\$} \{0,1\}, L_{\text{tok}} = L_{\text{lab}} = L_{\text{keys}} = \emptyset, \Delta = \emptyset$

$\text{pp} \leftarrow \text{Initialise}(1^\lambda)$

$(\text{id}^*, \text{sk}_{\text{id}^*}, \text{pk}_{\text{id}^*}) \leftarrow \mathcal{A}(\text{pp})$

$L_{\text{keys}} \leftarrow L_{\text{keys}} \cup (\text{id}^*, *, \text{pk}_{\text{id}^*})$

$O = \{OSignUp(\cdot), OEncrypt'(\cdot, \cdot), ODisclose(\cdot)\}$

$(\ell^*, m_0, m_1) \leftarrow \mathcal{A}^O(\text{pp})$

let $\ell^* = (\text{pk}_{\text{id}}, \text{pk}_{\text{id}'}, \tau)$

if $\ell^* \notin L_{\text{lab}}$ or $\ell^* \in L_{\text{tok}}$ or $\text{pk}_{\text{id}} = \text{pk}_{\text{id}^*}$

  or $\text{pk}_{\text{id}}, \text{pk}_{\text{id}'} \notin L_{\text{keys}}$

  $\text{ct} = \text{error}$

else

  $\text{ct} \leftarrow \text{Encrypt}(\text{sk}_{\text{id}}, \ell^*, m_b)$

  $L_{\text{tok}} \leftarrow L_{\text{tok}} \cup \ell^*, L_{\text{lab}} \leftarrow L_{\text{lab}} \cup \ell^*$

$b^* \leftarrow \mathcal{A}^O(\text{ct})$

if $b^* = b$ return 1, else return 0.

$OEncrypt'(\ell, m):$

parse $\ell = (\text{pk}_{\text{id}}, \text{pk}_{\text{id}'}, \tau)$

if $\ell \in L_{\text{lab}}$ or $\text{pk}_{\text{id}} = \text{pk}_{\text{id}^*}$

   or $(\cdot, \cdot, \text{pk}_{\text{id}}) \notin L_{\text{keys}}$

  return error.

$L_{\text{lab}} \leftarrow L_{\text{lab}} \cup \ell$

$\text{ct} \leftarrow \text{Encrypt}(\text{sk}_{\text{id}}, \ell, m)$

$\Delta \leftarrow \Delta \cup (\ell, \text{ct})$

return ct.

$ODisclose(\mathcal{P}):$

parse $\mathcal{P} = (f, \ell_1, \dots, \ell_n)$

with $\ell_i = (\text{pk}_{\text{id}}, \text{pk}_{\text{id}'}, \tau_i)$

if $\text{pk}_{\text{id}}, \text{pk}_{\text{id}'} \notin L_{\text{keys}}$ or $\text{pk}_{\text{id}} = \text{pk}_{\text{id}^*}$

   or $\ell_i \in L_{\text{tok}}$ for all $i \in [n]$

  return error.

$L_{\text{tok}} \leftarrow L_{\text{tok}} \cup \{\ell_1, \dots, \ell_n\}$

$\text{tok} = \text{AllowAccess}(\text{sk}_{\text{id}}, \mathcal{P})$

return tok.

Fig. 5. The token-secrecy experiment and the oracles $OEncrypt'$ and $ODisclose$

6.3 Forgettability

Our notion of forgettability (forget.sec) captures the idea that after a forget request, the target ciphertext does no longer decrypt to the original message. More precisely, there is no way to derive what the original message was from a destroyed ciphertext.

Our forget.sec experiment, in Fig. 6, uses the same oracles as the experiment in Fig. 5. Concretely, Experiment 6 is like the token-secrecy experiments (Fig. 5) until the challenge phase. In this phase the forget.sec adversary challenges $\mathcal{C}$ with one single new label ℓ. The challenger then randomly selects a message m, and encrypts it, generates the corresponding decryption token tok for $\mathcal{A}$, and runs the Forget procedure on the challenge ciphertext. Finally $\mathcal{C}$ returns to $\mathcal{A}$ the values (ct', tok). The

$$\text{Exp}_{\text{HIKE},\mathcal{A}}^{\text{forget.sec}}(\lambda):$$

$b \xleftarrow{\$} \{0,1\}, L_{\text{tok}} = L_{\text{lab}} = L_{\text{keys}} = \emptyset, \Delta = \emptyset$

$\text{pp} \leftarrow \text{Initialise}(1^\lambda)$

$(\text{id}^*, \text{sk}_{\text{id}^*}, \text{pk}_{\text{id}^*}) \leftarrow \mathcal{A}(\text{pp})$

$L_{\text{keys}} \leftarrow L_{\text{keys}} \cup (\text{id}^*, *, \text{pk}_{\text{id}^*})$

$O = \{OSignUp(\cdot), OEncrypt'(\cdot, \cdot), ODisclose(\cdot)\}$

$\ell^* \leftarrow \mathcal{A}^O(\text{pp})$

parse $\ell^* = (\text{pk}_{\text{id}}, \text{pk}_{\text{id}'}, \tau)$

if $\ell^* \notin L_{\text{lab}}$ or $\text{pk}_{\text{id}} = \text{pk}_{\text{id}^*}$ or $\text{pk}_{\text{id}}, \text{pk}_{\text{id}'} \notin L_{\text{keys}}$

  $\text{ct} = \text{error}$

else

  $m \xleftarrow{\$} \mathcal{M}$

  $\text{ct} \leftarrow \text{Encrypt}(\text{sk}_{\text{id}}, \ell^*, m)$

  $\text{ct}' \leftarrow \text{Destroy}(\text{ct})$

  $\Delta \leftarrow \Delta \cup (\ell^*, \text{ct}')$

  $\text{tok} \leftarrow \text{AllowAccess}(\text{sk}_{\text{id}}, \mathcal{I}_{\ell^*})$

  $L_{\text{tok}} \leftarrow L_{\text{tok}} \cup \{\ell^*\}; \ L_{\text{lab}} \leftarrow L_{\text{lab}} \cup \{\ell^*\}$

$m^* \leftarrow \mathcal{A}^O(\text{ct}', \text{tok})$

if $m^* = m$ return 1, else return 0.

Fig. 6. The forgettability experiment

adversary's goal is now to correctly guess the challenger's challenge message m.

Let m^* denote the output of $\mathcal{A}$ at the end of the experiment in Fig. 6, we say that $\mathcal{A}$ wins if $m^* = m$.

It is important to notice that the forget.sec experiment does not model an adversary that is able to obtain the original ciphertext ct, *e.g.*, via a database backup or some previous random `retrieve` request. The main reason for this restriction is the necessity to deploy an access control system on the database Δ which is of independent interest. On the other hand, to avoid an old-ciphertext to be reused, we can only suggest that the client C never distributes the decryption token of queries that involve the label corresponding to *forgotten* ciphertexts.

In a nutshell, our forgettability security statement below says that after a `forget` request the user's record encrypts a random message. In particular, we are able to show that HIKE's Forget procedure achieves information theoretic security in 'hiding' the original message m even under the presence of a malicious server.[5]

Theorem 3. *The* HIKE *protocol achieves perfect forgettability, i.e., for any PPT adversary $\mathcal{A}$ taking part to the experiment in Fig. 6, it holds that:*

$$\Pr\left[\mathsf{Exp}_{\mathsf{HIKE},\mathcal{A}}^{\mathsf{forget.sec}}(\lambda) = 1\right] = \frac{1}{|\mathcal{M}|}$$

Proof. The result follows trivially from the information theoretic security of the Destroy algorithm demonstrated in Sect. 4.   □

7   Implementation Details and Results

In this section, we discuss our *encoding map* from the message space to elliptic curve points. Afterwards, we describe the test-settings of our HIKE implementation with respect to different elliptic curve choices.

Encoding Messages on the Elliptic Curve. A typical design problem that arises when using *Elliptic Curve Cryptography (ECC)* is to define an injective map ϕ from a message space $\mathcal{M}$ to the subgroup $\mathbb{G}$ generated by a point P on an elliptic curve $\mathcal{E}$. This problem was firstly considered and *"solved"* by Koblitz in [16] by exploiting specific elliptic curves constructed over $\mathbb{F}_{2^n}$ for some appropriate n that depends on the message space dimension.

The main issue with Koblitz's map is that if we equip the message space $\mathcal{M}$ with an operation $\diamond$ and obtain the group $(\mathcal{M}, \diamond)$, then it is generally false that ϕ_K is a homomorphism between $(\mathcal{M}, \diamond)$ and $(\mathbb{G}, +)$, *i.e.*, there exists two messages $m_1, m_2 \in \mathcal{M}$ such that $\phi_K(m_1 \diamond m_2) \neq \phi_K(m_1) + \phi_K(m_2)$. A more natural homomorphism map is given by $\phi : \mathbb{Z}_q \to \mathbb{G}$ as $\phi(m) := m \cdot P$. The mapping is trivially a homomorphism when considering the message space as the natural group $(\mathbb{Z}_q, +)$. Unfortunately computing the inverse map ϕ^{-1} is exactly the DLog problem.

In our HIKE protocol we use this natural map to encode messages, and therefore the decryption procedure corresponds to solving an instance of the

---

[5] More precisely, if the server is honest-but-curious except with `forget` requests.

DLog problem. The apparent contradiction is addressed by the following observation. The security of HIKE relies on the hardness of solving the DLog problem (Assumption 1), but the efficiency of the decryption procedure is guaranteed by the feasibility of solving the IDLP in a particular interval (Assumption 2). In our implementation of HIKE, we consider the natural embedding ϕ and define a context-dependent message-space interval $\mathcal{M} = [a \dots b]$, for some $a, b \in \mathbb{N}$. This trick works whenever the decryption knows an approximation of the expected value. This is the case in most of the application scenarios we consider (*e.g.*, range of blood pressure values and range of kilometres run per day). Additionally, the technique does not work when the message space is too big (*e.g.*, floats of 64 bits) or not known.

To demonstrate our claim, we carried out one experiment to test that the decryption algorithm solves the IDLP in a reasonable time (see Fig. 7b) whereas a malicious adversary would still face the full DLog problem which is infeasible (see Fig. 7a). We implemented an extremely naive brute-force attack that checks, sequentially and incrementally, all the points of the selected interval. For this algorithm the *worst-case* in the interval $[a, \dots, b]$ is the point $b \cdot P$. In Fig. 7a, we empirically measure the running time of the our naive brute-force algorithm to solve the DLog problem with respect to the security parameter. As expected, the problem is exponentially hard. Then, in Fig. 7b, we focus on a specific message space, *i.e.*, numbers from 0 to 2^{22} as justified by Assumption 2, and plot the required time needed to decrypt a specific message.

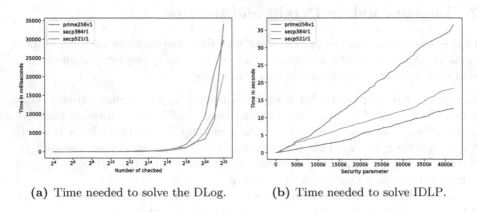

(a) Time needed to solve the DLog.   (b) Time needed to solve IDLP.

Fig. 7. Comparison between solving the DLog vs solving IDLP

HIKE Implementation. We have developed our HIKE scheme on Python by creating a new cryptographic scheme in the Charm Crypto framework [1]. The source code of HIKE is freely available at https://github.com/Pica4x6/HIKE. For the experiments, we used a MacBook Air with 2.2 GHz Intel Core i7 and 8 GB of RAM. We executed the experiments 100 times independently using the timeit library and report the average of the execution times in Table 1.

Table 1. Benchmark of HIKE scheme using the natural encoding map ϕ.

	KeyGen	Enc	Dec	Eval	PublicKey	TokenGen	TokenDec	Destroy
prime256v1	0.9 ms	280.0 ms	13442.4 ms	20.2 ms	5.3 ms	1293.2 ms	14.5 ms	6.4 ms
secp384r1	1.0 ms	399.7 ms	15149.3 ms	19.0 ms	70.1 ms	1521.0.0 ms	86.7 ms	73.9 ms
secp521r1	1.3 ms	426.6 ms	17102.7 ms	189.2 ms	66.4 ms	1837.5 ms	101.2 ms	68.0 ms

In addition, we evaluated the performances of HIKE using the three elliptic curves prime256v1, secp384r1 and secp521r1 that are recommended by the *National Institute of Standard and Technology (NIST)* [18]. Note that our implementation is agnostic to the definition of elliptic curve, thus it can be easily adapted to work with any type of elliptic curves defined in [1].

We remark that for every experiment, we randomly select a message in the HIKE message space dimension in which IDLP is feasible by our Assumption 2 and our empirical test in Fig. 7.

8   Conclusions and Directions for Future Work

In this paper, we proposed a new labelled homomorphic encryption scheme for multi-variate linear polynomial functions called LEEG. LEEG can be seen as a variant of ElGamal encryption on elliptic curve groups. We showed that LEEG supports additional features that are not commonly investigated for encryption scheme. We call this set of extra algorithms FEET, as it extends LEEG and improves its versatility. We then combined LEEG and FEET to make HIKE, a lightweight protocol designed for privately and securely store users' data while keeping it accessible to data owners and authorised service-providers. Application scenarios for HIKE include sport-tracking activity and simple e-Health alter systems. We deployed HIKE on Python and benchmarked its performance. Finally, we included in our security model some GDPR-inspired notions and proved that HIKE provides: *(i)* encrypted storage of the client's data; *(ii)* data owner's right to disclose information (including computation on data) to designated service-providers; and *(iii)* the right to be forgotten, *i.e.*, the possibility for data owners to request that selected records be made un-recoverable.

We identify some direction for further development of our HIKE protocol. First, since HIKE is based on a semantic-secure homomorphic encryption scheme, it cannot tolerate a malicious server. It would be interesting to design protocols with no trust on the server, thus providing both data confidentiality and integrity. Second, there are other extra features (not just FEET) that are worth developing. For example: generation of disclosure-tokens to allow any (chosen) third-party to decrypt a chosen computation on the user's data; introducing a trusted authority (*e.g.*, a legal entity) with the power of decrypting malicious users' data only if it collaborates with the designated service providers; enabling secure *"editable decryption"* to support the *rectification right* (art. 16 in GDPR). Third, it would be worth investigating multi-key properties in LEEG.

Such extension would for instance enable service-providers to perform statistic on data generated by different.

To the best of our knowledge, HIKE is the first cryptographic protocol proven to meet specific real-world privacy requirements, and we hope that it constitutes a springing-board for future works. We believe that a GDPR-oriented design of cryptographic protocols and primitives would facilitate developers implementation choices when designing new digital-services, as well as ensure cryptographically-proven security in the data-flow, leading to *privacy-by-design* solutions.

Acknowledgement. We thank the anonymous reviewers for their insightful comments and Erik-Oliver Blass for kindly shepherding us during this publication.

Appendix

A   Detailed Proofs

Semantic Security of LEEG. We want to prove that our LEEG scheme is semantically secure according to Barbosa *et al.*'s definition [2] (Definition 4).

Proof. Let $Q_{prf}(\lambda)$ be a bound on the total number of encryption queries performed by $\mathcal{A}$ during the security experiment. Let Game 0 be the semantic security experiment in Definition 4 where, for consistency with our definition of LEEG, the challenger runs $\mathsf{SetUp}(1^\lambda) \to \mathsf{pp}$ to obtain the public parameters of the scheme, then it runs $\mathsf{KeyGen}(\mathsf{pp}) \to \mathsf{sk} = (sk, \mathsf{k})$ and computes $\mathsf{pk} = sk \cdot P$. In addition, $\mathcal{C}$ ignores any query with label $\ell = (Q', Q, \tau)$ where $Q' \neq \mathsf{pk}$.

Let Game 1 be the same as Game 0 except that the challenger replaces every $\mathsf{PRF}_{\mathsf{k}}(\cdot)$ instance with the evaluation of a truly random function rand : $\mathbb{G} \times \mathbb{G} \times \mathcal{T} \to [0..q-1]$. It is quite easy to see that the difference between Game 1 and Game 0 is solely in the generation of the values r. Therefore the probability of $\mathcal{A}$ winning is the same in the two games, a part from a $Q_{prf}(\lambda)$ factor that comes from distinguishing the PRF instance from a truly random function. Thus

$$|\mathsf{Prob}[\mathsf{G}_0(\mathcal{A})] - \mathsf{Prob}[\mathsf{G}_1(\mathcal{A})]| \leq Q_{prf}(\lambda) \cdot \mathsf{Adv}_{\mathcal{A}}^{\mathsf{PRF}}(\lambda).$$

At this point, we observe that for any given ciphertext ct and label-message pair (ℓ, m) there is exactly one value $r \in [0..q-1]$ for which ct is an encryption of m for label ℓ. In particular, for every triple (ct, ℓ, m) it holds that

$$\mathsf{Prob}[\mathsf{Enc}(\mathsf{sk}, \ell, m) = \mathsf{ct}] = \frac{|r \in [0..q-1] : M + r \cdot sk \cdot Q = \mathsf{ct}|}{|[0..q-1]|} = \frac{1}{q},$$

where the probability is taken over all the possible values $r \xleftarrow{\$} [0..q-1]$. Since the above probability holds also for the challenge ciphertext ct^* we have that

$\mathsf{Prob}[\mathsf{Enc}(\mathsf{sk}, \ell_0, m_0) = \mathsf{ct}^*] = \mathsf{Prob}[\mathsf{Enc}(\mathsf{sk}, \ell_1, m_1) = \mathsf{ct}^*]$ (semantic security) and implies $\mathsf{Prob}[\mathsf{G}_1(\mathcal{A})] = \frac{1}{2}$. Therefore:

$$\mathsf{Prob}[\mathsf{G}_0(\mathcal{A})] \leq |\mathsf{Prob}[\mathsf{G}_0(\mathcal{A})] - \mathsf{Prob}[\mathsf{G}_1(\mathcal{A})]| + \mathsf{Prob}[\mathsf{G}_1(\mathcal{A})]$$

$$\leq Q_{\mathsf{prf}}(\lambda) \cdot \mathsf{Adv}_{\mathcal{A}}^{\mathsf{PRF}}(\lambda) + \frac{1}{2}$$

which proves the semantic security of LEEG, given that $Q_{\mathsf{prf}}(\lambda)$ is polynomial and $\mathsf{Adv}_{\mathcal{A}}^{\mathsf{PRF}}$ is negligible (by our security assumption on the PRF family).   □

Proof of Theorem 2. We want to prove our HIKE protocol achieves token secrecy, *i.e.*, that $\mathsf{Adv}_{\mathsf{HIKE},\mathcal{A}}^{\mathsf{token.sec}}(\lambda) \leq Q_{\mathsf{id}} \cdot \mathsf{Adv}_{\mathsf{LEEG},\mathcal{A}}^{\mathsf{sem.sec}}(\lambda)$.

Proof. We exhibit a reduction $\mathcal{B}$ that uses $\mathcal{A}$ to win the semantic-security experiment for the LEEG scheme. The reduction works exactly as the one in the proof of Theorem 1 a part for a couple of exceptions. First, this reduction holds an additional (private) list L_{rand}, that is empty at the beginning of the simulation. Second, $\mathcal{B}$ behaves differently (only) in the following cases:

Encryption Queries: $\mathcal{B}$ forwards the queries to the $O\mathsf{Encrypt}'$ oracle, unless $\ell = (\mathsf{pk}^\star, \mathsf{pk}, \tau)$. In case $\ell = (\mathsf{pk}^\star, \mathsf{pk}, \tau)$, the reduction does not have the secret key for encryption and token generation. In order to simulate the encryption and be consistent with future token-generation queries, $\mathcal{B}$ checks if $(\ell, r) \in L_{\mathsf{rand}}$ for some value $r \in [0..q-1]$. If so, $\mathcal{B}$ uses the existing values r to compute the ciphertext $\mathsf{ct} = (m \cdot P + r \cdot \mathsf{pk})$. Otherwise, $\mathcal{B}$ picks a random value $r \xleftarrow{\$} [0..q-1]$, updates $L_{\mathsf{rand}} \leftarrow L_{\mathsf{rand}} \cup (\ell, r)$, and computes $\mathsf{ct} = (m \cdot P + r \cdot \mathsf{pk})$. In any case, $\mathcal{B}$ updates the list of queried labels $L_{\mathsf{lab}} \leftarrow L_{\mathsf{lab}} \cup \ell$, and returns ct to $\mathcal{A}$. Note that ct has the same distribution as the output of $\mathsf{Enc}(\mathsf{sk}^\star, \ell, m)$, indeed for any r chosen by the reduction there exists a value $r' \in [0..q-1]$ such that $r = r' \cdot sk^\star$ mod q and thus $\mathsf{ct} = m \cdot P + r \cdot \mathsf{pk} = m \cdot P + r' \cdot \mathsf{sk}^\star \cdot \mathsf{pk}$. The latter series of equalities shows that $\mathcal{B}$'s simulation is still perfect.

Disclose Queries: $\mathcal{B}$ forwards to the $O\mathsf{Disclose}$ oracle all the queries $\mathcal{P} = (f, \ell_1 \dots, \ell_n)$ with $f(x_1, \dots, x_n) = a_0 + \sum_{i \in [n]} a_i x_i$, $\ell_i = (\mathsf{pk}, \mathsf{pk}', \tau_i)$ and $\mathsf{pk} \neq \mathsf{pk}^\star$. Otherwise, $\mathcal{P}$ contains labels of the form $\ell_i = (\mathsf{pk}^\star, \mathsf{pk}', \tau_i)$. The reduction performs the same checks as the $O\mathsf{Disclose}$ oracle, if any check fails $\mathcal{B}$ returns error. In case all conditions are met, $\mathcal{B}$ proceeds by checking if $(\ell_i, \cdot) \in L_{\mathsf{rand}}$ for all $i \in [n]$, in which case the reduction uses the randomness stored in L_{rand} to compute the token $\mathsf{tok} = (\sum_{i \in [n]} a_i r_i) \cdot \mathsf{pk}^\star$. Otherwise, for all those labels ℓ_j not present in L_{rand}, $\mathcal{B}$ samples a random element $r \xleftarrow{\$} [0..q-1]$ and updates the private list $L_{\mathsf{rand}} \leftarrow L_{\mathsf{rand}} \cup (\ell_j, r)$. At this point $(\ell_i, r_i) \in L_{\mathsf{rand}}$ for all the labels in the queried $\mathcal{P}$ and $\mathcal{B}$ can compute $\mathsf{tok} = (\sum_{i \in [n]} a_i r_i) \cdot \mathsf{pk}^\star$. In either case, $\mathcal{B}$ updates the list of queried token-labels, *i.e.*, $L_{\mathsf{tok}} \leftarrow L_{\mathsf{tok}} \cup (\ell_1, \dots, \ell_n)$, and returns tok to $\mathcal{A}$.

Let (ℓ^*, m_0, m_1) be $\mathcal{A}$'s input to the challenge phase. If $\ell^* \neq (\mathsf{pk}^\star, \cdot, \cdot)$ the reduction aborts ($\mathcal{A}$ chose to challenge a different client than the one $\mathcal{B}$ bet on). This event happens with probability $(1 - \frac{1}{Q_{\mathsf{id}}})$.

Otherwise $\ell^* = (\mathsf{pk}^*, Q, \tau)$, $\mathcal{B}$ updates the list of queried labels $L_{\mathsf{lab}} \leftarrow L_{\mathsf{lab}} \cup \ell^*$ and sends (ℓ^*, m_0, m_1) to its challenger $\mathcal{C}$ for the semantic security game. Let ct denote $\mathcal{C}$'s reply, $\mathcal{B}$ forwards ct to $\mathcal{A}$.

In the subsequent query phase $\mathcal{B}$ behaves as described above.

At the end of the experiment, $\mathcal{B}$ outputs the same bit b^* returned by $\mathcal{A}$ for the token.sec experiment. Note that since $\mathcal{A}$ is given exactly the same challenge as in the sem.sec experiment, if $\mathcal{A}$ has a non-negligible advantage in winning the token.sec experiment, then $\mathcal{B}$ has the same non-negligible advantage in breaking the semantic-security of LEEG, unless $\mathcal{B}$ aborts its simulation. Therefore we conclude that:

$$\mathsf{Adv}_{\mathsf{LEEG},\mathcal{B}}^{\mathsf{sem.sec}}(\lambda) \geq \left(\frac{1}{Q_{\mathsf{id}}}\right) \cdot \mathsf{Adv}_{\mathsf{HIKE},\mathcal{A}}^{\mathsf{token.sec}}(\lambda).$$ $\qquad\square$

B   Token Composability in FEET

In this appendix we show token composability for two labelled programs. The general case follows immediately.

Consider two labelled programs $\mathcal{P}_1 = (f_1, \ell_1, \dots, \ell_n)$ and $\mathcal{P}_2 = (f_2, \ell'_1, \dots, \ell'_{n'})$. For consistency, token composability requires that all the labels involved in $\mathcal{P}_1$ and $\mathcal{P}_2$ are of the form $\ell = (sk \cdot P, Q, \tau)$ for some opportune value of τ. Without loss of generality, we can set $f_1 = a_0 + \sum_{i \in [n]} a_i x_i$ and $f_2 = a'_0 + \sum_{j \in [n']} a'_j x_{\sigma(j)}$ for opportune coefficients $a_i, a'_j \in \mathcal{M}$, and an index-mapping function $\sigma : \mathbb{N} \to \mathbb{N}$ used to model the fact that the functions may be defined on a different set of variables. Let $I \subseteq \mathbb{N}$ be the set of indexes of common variables, formally:

$$I = \{i \in [n] \text{ such that } \sigma(j) = i \text{ for some } j \in [n']\}. \tag{5}$$

The composed labelled program $\mathcal{P} = b_1 \mathcal{P}_1 + b_2 \mathcal{P}_2$ is defined as $\mathcal{P} = (f, \tilde{\ell}_1, \dots, \tilde{\ell}_{\tilde{n}})$ with $f = b_1 f_1 + b_2 f_2$, $f(x_1, \dots, x_{\tilde{n}}) = (b_1 a_0 + b_2 a'_0) + \sum_{i \in I}(b_1 a_i + b_2 a'_i)x_i + \sum_{i \in [n] \setminus I} b_1 a_i x_i + \sum_{j \in [n'] \setminus \sigma(I)} b_2 a'_j x_j$ for any $b_1, b_2 \in \mathcal{M}$. We show that the combined token $\mathsf{tok} = b_1 \mathsf{tok}_1 + b_2 \mathsf{tok}_2$ is a valid decryption token for the composed labelled program $\mathcal{P}$, actually $\mathsf{tok} = \mathsf{TokenGen}(sk, \mathcal{P})$. In details:

$$\begin{aligned}
\mathsf{tok} &= b_1 \mathsf{tok}_1 + b_2 \mathsf{tok}_2 \\
&= sk \left(\sum_{i \in [n]} b_1 a_i r_i + \sum_{j \in [n']} b_2 a'_j r'_{\sigma(j)} \right) \cdot P \\
&= sk \left(\sum_{i \in I}(b_1 a_i + b_2 a'_i)r_i + \sum_{i \in [n] \setminus I} b_1 a_i r_i + \sum_{j \in [n'] \setminus \sigma(I)} b_2 a'_j r'_j \right) \cdot P \\
&= \mathsf{TokenGen}(sk, \mathcal{P})
\end{aligned}$$

The set I in the second last equality is the one defined in (5), that is $\ell_i = \ell'_{i=\sigma(j)}$ for all $i \in I$ and therefore $r_i = r'_i = \mathsf{PRF}_k(\ell_i)$. By the correctness of the TokenGen-TokenDec algorithms, we derive that tok is a valid decryption token for sk_2, $\mathsf{ct} = \mathsf{Eval}(f, \mathsf{ct}_1, \dots, \mathsf{ct}_{\tilde{n}})$. It is straightforward to generalise this reasoning to multiple labelled programs $\mathcal{P}_1, \dots \mathcal{P}_t$ as long as all the labels coincide on the first two entries.

References

1. Akinyele, J.A., et al.: Charm: a framework for rapidly prototyping cryptosystems. J. Cryptogr. Eng. **3**(2), 111–128 (2013)
2. Barbosa, M., Catalano, D., Fiore, D.: Labeled homomorphic encryption. In: Foley, S.N., Gollmann, D., Snekkenes, E. (eds.) ESORICS 2017. LNCS, vol. 10492, pp. 146–166. Springer, Cham (2017). https://doi.org/10.1007/978-3-319-66402-6_10
3. Brakerski, Z., Vaikuntanathan, V.: Efficient fully homomorphic encryption from (standard) LWE. SIAM J. Comput. **43**(2), 831–871 (2014)
4. Canetti, R., Raghuraman, S., Richelson, S., Vaikuntanathan, V.: Chosen-ciphertext secure fully homomorphic encryption. In: Fehr, S. (ed.) PKC 2017. LNCS, vol. 10175, pp. 213–240. Springer, Heidelberg (2017). https://doi.org/10.1007/978-3-662-54388-7_8
5. Connolly, A.: Freedom of encryption. S&P **16**(1), 102–103 (2018)
6. Council of the European Union, European Parliament. Regulation (EU) 2016/679 (General Data Protection Regulation) (2016). https://publications.europa.eu/en/publication-detail/-/publication/3e485e15-11bd-11e6-ba9a-01aa75ed71a1/language-en. Accessed May 2018
7. El Gamal, T.: A public key cryptosystem and a signature scheme based on discrete logarithms. In: CRYPTO, pp. 10–18 (1985)
8. Fiore, D., Mitrokotsa, A., Nizzardo, L., Pagnin, E.: Multi-key homomorphic authenticators. In: Cheon, J.H., Takagi, T. (eds.) ASIACRYPT 2016. LNCS, vol. 10032, pp. 499–530. Springer, Heidelberg (2016). https://doi.org/10.1007/978-3-662-53890-6_17
9. Fischer, A., Fuhry, B., Kerschbaum, F., Bodden, E.: Computation on encrypted data using data flow authentication. CoRR, abs/1710.00390 (2017)
10. Gennaro, R., Gentry, C., Parno, B.: Non-interactive verifiable computing: outsourcing computation to untrusted workers. In: Rabin, T. (ed.) CRYPTO 2010. LNCS, vol. 6223, pp. 465–482. Springer, Heidelberg (2010). https://doi.org/10.1007/978-3-642-14623-7_25
11. Gennaro, R., Wichs, D.: Fully homomorphic message authenticators. In: Sako, K., Sarkar, P. (eds.) ASIACRYPT 2013. LNCS, vol. 8270, pp. 301–320. Springer, Heidelberg (2013). https://doi.org/10.1007/978-3-642-42045-0_16
12. Gentry, C.: Fully homomorphic encryption using ideal lattices, pp. 169–178 (2009)
13. Goldwasser, S., Micali, S.: Probabilistic encryption & how to play mental poker keeping secret all partial information. In: STOC, pp. 365–377. ACM (1982)
14. Hoffstein, J., Pipher, J., Silverman, J.H., Silverman, J.H.: An Introduction to Mathematical Cryptography, vol. 1. Springer, New York (2008). https://doi.org/10.1007/978-0-387-77993-5
15. Katz, J., Lindell, Y.: Introduction to Modern Cryptography. CRC Press, Boca Raton (2014)
16. Koblitz, N.: Elliptic curve cryptosystems. Math. Comput. **48**(177), 203–209 (1987)
17. Montenegro, R., Tetali, P.: How long does it take to catch a wild kangaroo? In: STOC, pp. 553–560. ACM (2009)
18. NIST STS. Cryptographic Key Length Recommendation (2017). https://www.keylength.com/en/4/. Accessed May 2018
19. Paillier, P.: Public-key cryptosystems based on composite degree residuosity classes. In: Stern, J. (ed.) EUROCRYPT 1999. LNCS, vol. 1592, pp. 223–238. Springer, Heidelberg (1999). https://doi.org/10.1007/3-540-48910-X_16

20. Panjwani, M., Jäntti, M.: Data protection & security challenges in digital & it services: a case study. In: ICCA, pp. 379–383. IEEE (2017)
21. Pollard, J.M.: Monte Carlo methods for index computation (mod p). Math. Comput. **32**(143), 918–924 (1978)
22. Pollard, J.M.: Kangaroos, monopoly and discrete logarithms. J. Cryptol. **13**(4), 437–447 (2000)
23. Rivest, R.L., Adleman, L., Dertouzos, M.L.: On data banks and privacy homomorphisms. In: Foundations of Secure Computation. Academia Press, Orlando (1978)
24. Smart, N.P., Vercauteren, F.: Fully homomorphic encryption with relatively small key and ciphertext sizes. In: Nguyen, P.Q., Pointcheval, D. (eds.) PKC 2010. LNCS, vol. 6056, pp. 420–443. Springer, Heidelberg (2010). https://doi.org/10.1007/978-3-642-13013-7_25
25. van Dijk, M., Gentry, C., Halevi, S., Vaikuntanathan, V.: Fully homomorphic encryption over the integers. In: Gilbert, H. (ed.) EUROCRYPT 2010. LNCS, vol. 6110, pp. 24–43. Springer, Heidelberg (2010). https://doi.org/10.1007/978-3-642-13190-5_2

Internet Misbehavior and Protection

DNS-DNS: DNS-Based De-NAT Scheme

Liran Orevi[1]($\boxtimes$), Amir Herzberg[2,3], and Haim Zlatokrilov[4]

[1] Efi Arazi School of Computer Science,
Herzliya Interdisciplinary Center (IDC), Herzliya, Israel
liranorevi@gmail.com
[2] University of Connecticut, Mansfield, USA
[3] Bar Ilan University, Ramat Gan, Israel
[4] INCD, Tel Aviv, Israel

Abstract. Network Address Translation (NAT) routers aggregate the flows of multiple devices behind a single IP address. By doing so, NAT routers masquerade the original IP address, which is often viewed as a privacy feature, making it harder to identify the communication of individuals devices behind the NAT. *De-NAT* is the reverse process: re-identifying communication flowing into and out of the NAT. De-NAT can be used for traffic management, security, and lawful surveillance.

We show how DNS requests provide an effective De-NAT mechanism by observing queries to open resolver, in addition to 'classical' provider-based De-NAT. This new method allows de-NATing in cases where known schemes fail, e.g., in Windows 8 and 10, and by remote DNS resolvers. We analyze use cases where the suggested DNS based De-NAT is effective, suggest a De-NAT algorithm and evaluate its performance on real (anonymized) traffic. Another contribution is identifying the phenomena of *drum beats*, which are periodic DNS requests by popular applications and processes; these can allow long-term de-NATing, and also provide fingerprinting identifying specific devices and users. We conclude with recommendations for mitigating de-NATing.

1 Introduction

Mainly due to the shortage of IPv4 addresses, Network Address Translation (NAT) capabilities are a standard feature of edge routers, and used in most residential SOHO (Small Offices/Home Offices) networks and in many enterprise networks. Most residential NAT routers map multiple internal network addresses to one external network address. Specifically, the NAT maps (IP, port) pairs of the device in the local network, to a port, which is used together with external IP of the network. This mapping is maintained as long as this internal (IP, port) pair is in use; for TCP, this is typically as long as the TCP session is active. The exact method of mapping varies between NAT routers.

A typical configuration of a network using NAT is illustrated in Fig. 1. Devices connected to home network having internal address space (e.g. 192.168.x.x or

---

An updated version of this article, is available at https://tinyurl.com/linktoonline.

© Springer Nature Switzerland AG 2018
J. Camenisch and P. Papadimitratos (Eds.): CANS 2018, LNCS 11124, pp. 69–88, 2018.
https://doi.org/10.1007/978-3-030-00434-7_4

10.x.x.x) communicate with the Internet via a home router with NAT capabilities. The NAT-router receives an external IP from the service provider (e.g., 109.64.96.107 in Fig. 1). NAT devices often provide additional functions, e.g. a DNS proxy resolver, and almost always configure the devices' internal addresses (192.168.x.x) in the network using DHCP. Typically, service providers provide the configuration, including the addresses of a primary and secondary DNS resolvers. The DNS resolvers may be operated by the ISP or by a remote entity, typically a global open DNS server such as Google DNS or DynDNS.

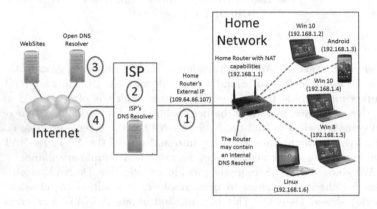

Fig. 1. Typical configuration of a home network using NAT.

NAT removes the internal IP address of the packets it sends to the ISP. For example, in Fig. 1, all communication uses the external IP address of the NAT-router (109.64.86.107).

As noted in RFC [SE01], This can be viewed as a privacy mechanism, making it hard to identity the specific device or user sending a particular packet, among all the devices and users using the NAT; such linkage is referred to as *de-NATing*.

This paper investigates a new scheme for de-NATing, i.e., clustering (all or specific types of) communication between a specific device or user within the home network and destinations outside the home network, i.e., in the Internet or hosted by the ISP, all flowing via the home router which provides NAT service. The De-NATing scheme we present can be performed at the ISP (number 2 in Fig. 1), at a remote DNS provider, e.g. open resolver (number 3 in Fig. 1), on the route to the ISP (number 1 in Fig. 1) or on the route from the ISP to the remote resolver (number 4 in Fig. 1).

There are multiple motivations for De-NATing. De-NATing can facilitate traffic management, when policies per NATed device should be applied, e.g. service providers might want to limit traffic generated by a single device, or control operations such as browsing by specific devices, typically for parental control or for security reasons. De-NATing can be applied for security applications, e.g., when a NATed device is discovered to run malware communicating with command and control servers, or to detect suspicious activity of a device. De-NAT can be also applied for lawful (or illegitimate) interception and surveillance. De-NATing has commercial applications, such as profiling the traffic coming from individual NATed devices. For instance, DNS providers or others might use such information to offer targeted advertisements, derived from the users' browsing history. De-NATing may help for network management, e.g., to know number of devices using same IP address. On the other hand, users who rely on NAT for some level of anonymity for their communication, believing they are indistinguishable from all other users of the same NAT, should know the potential limitations of this supposed-protection.

Several De-NATing methods have been published. The first step in most schemes is to identify the operating system of the sending device. This is often done using the IP TTL field; in devices using the Windows operating system, the initial TTL value of packets is typically 127, while in Android and Linux it is typically 63, and in iOS it is 255. This simple step may suffice to de-NAT a device if that device is the only one with that initial-TTL value in the SOHO network; and it is useful first step in de-NAT when there are devices using different operating systems in the network. We therefore focus on de-NAT traffic of devices, which all use the same operating-system.

Published De-NATing methods are based on two well-known side-channels:

IP-ID. A 16-bit field in IPv4 header, used to perform de-fragmentation. In the Windows 7 operation system and older versions, the IP-ID field is implemented as a simple counter and incremented for each packet coming out of a network interface.

TCP Timestamp. In various versions of the Linux based operating systems, the TCP Timestamp field is monotonically increasing with the elapsed time between packets.

We present a new De-NAT method which focuses on DNS requests. Specifically, we use the fact that the TCP/IP stack in some operating systems, including Windows 8, 10 (also observed in some Android devices), consistently increments the IP-ID field, when sending packets to the same destination IP. Since DNS requests sent to the DNS resolver are to the same destination IP, the value of the IP-ID field is monotonically increasing between DNS requests. Thus, tracking the values of the IP-ID allows to identify requests coming from a single device, i.e., to De-NAT the DNS requests. Furthermore, by correlating DNS requests to subsequent packets from/to the IP address resolved in the DNS query, an ISP can de-NAT most of the communication flowing out of and into the network behind the NAT.

This DNS-based De-NAT method is unique, in that it only requires the DNS requests, and not necessarily all traffic exiting the network. This means that de-NATing can be done not only by the ISP, but even by a remote open DNS resolver, if used, or by an eavesdropper on the communication from the network to the remote open resolver. Clearly, in such case, the DeNAT is only on the DNS requests and not on all connections, but it is important for many use cases. The use of open resolvers is quite common, therefore, this is a significant consideration for those concerned for their online privacy, and thinking they are hidden in the crowd behind NAT.

The following table summarizes the De-NAT schemes over operating systems and their side channels.

Table 1. De-NAT techniques

De-NAT scheme	Operating system	By whom?
IP-ID incremented for all packets [Bel02]	Win NT/XP/7	ISP only
TCP Time stamp [Bur07]	iOS, Android, Linux	ISP only
DNS-based De-DAT (This paper)	Win 8/10, Android	ISP or Open resolver

There are several challenges and concerns with this method. First, routers implementing NAT may treat DNS requests in different manners. For example, routers may cache DNS responses and therefore a DNS request may not occur before every DNS TTL elapses. Second, some routers may change the IP-ID of the DNS requests. Third, when there are multiple devices behind the NAT, collisions of IP-IDs values may occur. Finally it might not be trivial to relate the subsequent TCP/UDP connection, to the preceding DNS request. We address those challenges, and show that in spite of them, De-NAT can often be performed with high accuracy.

In Sect. 5.1, we show that the DNS requests of some applications have predictable and periodic patterns. These patterns, which we call *drum-beats*, can be used to fingerprint a device. Such fingerprinting can be used as a complementary technique to improve De-NATing, esp. over long periods of time. Some de-NATing signals persist even after a device restarts or migrates to another network. This is in contrast to all known methods of de-NATing, which require that the device stay connected to the same network and monitored continuously, without disruptions such as device restarts.

1.1   Related Works

The IP Identification field (IP-ID) is defined in [Pos81] and used for uniquely identifying the group of fragments of a single IP datagram. The specifications of the Domain Name System (DNS) are defined in [Moc87]. The RFC defines the DNS TTL field, which is the time to live measured in seconds. One should note that the DNS TTL field, which we refer to in this paper, is not related to the TTL field in IP headers, as defined in [Pos81].

The challenge of aggregating connections from a host behind NAT was addressed in several works. In [Bel02], Bellovin described a method for counting the number of hosts behind NAT by using the fact that the IP-ID field is implemented as a simple counter. With some modifications, this scheme can be used for de-NATing, i.e., aggregating connections generated from a single device. The simple counter implementation holds in older versions of the Windows operating system, such as Win-NT, Win-XP, Win-Vista and Win-7. However the implementation is different in many other operating systems, including newer versions of Windows, Linux, iOS, Android and more. The sequential IP-ID side-channel was used in other ways, e.g., covert-channels [Dan08] and off-path attacks on TCP/IP, DNS and privacy [GHS14, GH12].

Bursztein presented a different De-NAT scheme in [Bur07]. The scheme is based on the analysis of the TCP timestamp option to count the hosts behind a NAT. Bursztein shows this works for the Linux and BSD operating systems; we found that this scheme works also for the iOS and Android OSs. An adjustment to the method for separating TCP flows from each device in described in [WWM13].

De-NAT mechanism for general traffic, that covers multiple operating systems, requires the classification of connections to the originating OS, e.g. using the TTL IP header as described above; for other OS fingerprinting schemes, see [Bev04].

De-NATing is related to *user tracking*, where a passive adversary tracks users who use dynamic IP addresses, based on characteristic behavioral patterns; in particular, the schemes of [HBF13, KHLK16] focus on DNS requests. Those works focus on the use case where each user uses a different IP address each, as in mobile networks; this does not hold for users in the same network behind NAT. In [GFZ14] Machine Learning is used to address the De-NAT challenge. We believe that the user-behavior based schemes presented in these works can be used together with our schemes, to further improve the tracking and de-NAT capabilities, e.g. to allow re-identification of a device which was restarted (breaking the IP-ID tracing), or allowing identification of browsing by same user from different locations (e.g., home and office) or when the network's address changes (e.g., daily).

Several works discuss other privacy aspects of DNS, e.g., Shulman et el. [Shu14] describe pitfalls of DNS encryption.

1.2   Contributions

Our main contributions:

1. DNS-DNS, a new De-NATing scheme, based on tracking the IP-ID in DNS requests. It is the first De-NAT scheme which works for Windows 8 and 10 systems and on other observed operating systems that use incrementing IP-ID, such as Android 5.0.1.
2. DNS-DNS enables De-NATing of DNS requests by an open resolver, or an eavesdropper on the path to a remote (possibly open) resolver. Previous de-NAT schemes required involvement of the ISP, i.e., DNS-DNS can be deployed by many more attackers - for the common case of users of open resolvers.
3. DNS-DNS also leaks fingerprinting information, in particular, allows to differentiate between Windows 7 and Windows 8/10.

4. We show a simple method of time correlation between TCP connections to DNS requests. Using this method an eavesdropper can aggregate the traffic coming from a single device behind NAT.
5. We identify the phenomena of DNS periodic requests, which we call *Drum Beat* signals. We show how drum-beats can be used to improve the precision and recall of DNS-DNS. Some Drum-Beat signals persist following device restarts, thus enabling long-term de-NATing across restarts. Drum-beats may be applicable for additional remote privacy attacks, esp. on users of open-resolvers, such as fingerprinting.

2   The Behaviour of IP-ID in DNS Requests

The IP-ID field, defined in [Pos81], was introduced to facilitate de-fragmentation of an IP packet from its fragments. In some operating systems, e.g., iOS 10, the IP-ID is a random number, and in some others, e.g., several versions of Linux, it is set to zero for short packets. However, in many other operating systems, the IP-ID is incremented sequentially, either globally or for each destination. In particular, this is the case in Windows 8 and 10 systems, as we confirmed experimentally. Specifically, the IP-ID field is incremented by one, within the range of 1 to 33K, for packets sent to the same destination IP.

DNS requests are typically sent to a fixed IP address of the resolver (or, in some implementations, of primary and secondary resolvers). Thus, in those operating systems, the IP-ID field of DNS requests is incremental. Experiments showing this behavior in Windows 8, Windows 10 and Android 5.0.1 are shown in Fig. 2.

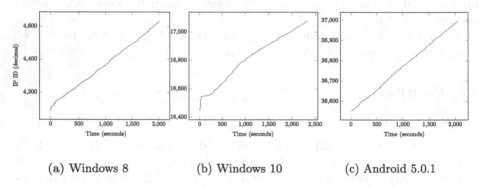

(a) Windows 8   (b) Windows 10   (c) Android 5.0.1

Fig. 2. IP ID of DNS queries over time on Windows 8, Windows 10 and Android 5.0.1

Note that since IP-ID is increased for every request, when many DNS requests are sent at the same time, e.g. when opening a web site, the graph shows fast growth in IP-ID in short period of time.

We experimentally validated that IP-IDs are increased by one for (almost) every request. Note that there are rare exceptions - a tiny fraction of larger or negative gaps in the IP-IDs numbers. The few larger positive gaps may be due to losses or reordering in communication or inside the capturing or sending device. The even fewer negative gaps may be due to out-of-order packets. The histogram in Fig. 3 shows the gaps between every two sequential DNS packets over an experiment with four devices, addressing the top 1000 Alexa web sites.

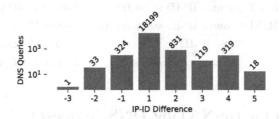

Fig. 3. Histogram of succeeding IP-ID differences

3   NAT-Routers and DNS Requests

The DNS-DNS scheme uses the fact that DNS requests use sequential IP-ID. In the previous section we showed that in many operating systems the IP-IDs are sequential. However, NAT-routers can handle DNS requests in different ways, some of which may have impact the de-NATing scheme. In particular, some NAT-routers may implement a DNS resolver proxy, or remove/change the IP-ID field; and some may be manually-configured to use an open resolver instead of or in addition to using the ISP's resolver. One should note that using open resolvers is a common practice. As an example, the DNS open resolver OpenDNS, serves 65 million daily users[1].

Table 2 shows the results of testing of several home routers (implementing NAT), for their handling of DNS requests. When using the ISP's resolver (statically-configured with ISP's DHCP setting the primary and secondary DNS resolvers), some routers replace or modify the IP-ID value in the request. In those cases, the De-NAT scheme described here would not work.

However, most routers we tested left the packets intact, and in particular did not change the IP-ID field; for those the DNS-based De-NAT scheme can be applied. Furthermore, in *all* devices we tested, the IP-ID was left intact - when the NAT was manually configured, e.g., by a user deciding to use an open resolver. This includes the two NAT devices which modify the IP-ID (using default configuration). Of course, users often do not change default values; but we believe that manual configuration of DNS resolver - in particular, to use an open resolver - is quite common.

Namely, in all these cases, i.e., when the NAT does not change the IP-ID field, the DNS-based de-NAT scheme can be applied by the open resolver, or any eavesdropper along the route to the resolver. Success depends then only on the operating system of the client device; see Table 1.

---

[1] Statistics at the front page of https://www.opendns.com/.

Table 2. Handling of IP-ID by different NAT-routers, for DNS requests sent to ISP's resolver or to an open resolver.

NAT-router	Statically configured ISP resolver	Manually configured open resolver
TP-Link TL-MR3220	Source IP-ID stays Intact	Source IP-ID stays Intact
TP-Link TL-WR740N 2	Source IP-ID stays Intact	Source IP-ID stays Intact
TP-Link TL-WR1042ND	Source IP-ID stays Intact	Source IP-ID stays Intact
Edimax N300	Sets IP-ID to zero	Source IP-ID stays Intact
NetGear WGR314	Creates new requests	Source IP-ID stays Intact

4   Algorithm for De-NATing DNS Requests

Assume an attacker is given the set of DNS requests coming out of a NAT-connected network; When can the attacker cluster the requests that originated from the same device (that is, De-NATing DNS requests)? We show that an attacker would normally succeed, when the devices in the network use per-destination-incrementing IP-ID. As shown in Fig. 2, this holds, at least, in devices using Windows 8/10 and Android 5.0.1 operating systems.

De-NATing DNS requests to a particular device can be implemented by clustering requests. DNS request shall be associated to a prior DNS request of a preceding, or close, IP-ID value. As Fig. 3 shows, the gaps between ID-IPs are expected to be up to 5, and vast majority of DNS requests IP-IDs are consecutive. For example, consider Fig. 4a representing the IP-ID values over time for three Windows 8/10 computers where the IP-IDs of DNS requests of each device are represented by a different color. This simple example shows that an algorithm for clustering DNS requests by the consecutive IP-IDs of each device will result in successful De-NATing.

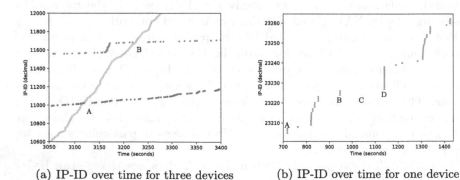

(a) IP-ID over time for three devices   (b) IP-ID over time for one device

Fig. 4. IP-ID over time for different devices

However, there are several algorithmic challenges. The first is how to handle out-of-order packets and gaps in IP-ID values. This challenge can be solved by allowing a larger set of 'possible increments' to the previous IP-ID in a sequence.

The second challenge, is how to handle 'collisions' of the sequences of IP-ID values, generated by multiple devices. An example is demonstrated by the areas A and B in Fig. 4a. That is, when two or more devices have similar or identical values of IP-IDs at the same time. How can one cluster a particular IP-ID of a DNS request to a specific device when there are multiple possibilities? Usually devices have different rates of sending queries at different times, and after the 'collision', we will be able to distinguish between queries from different devices and cluster them based on different IPID values. Then, the challenge would be to merge clusters before and after a 'collision'. For that matter, several methods can be implemented. We chose a method that accounts for the rate of the DNS requests coming from the same device. The rational is that the rate of DNS requests is usually quite stable at a given point of time. Hence, before and after the collision, the rate of IP-ID increase will remain stable. This method fits the case presented in Fig. 4a, however in some cases it might not be conclusive. This can be further enhanced by using other features such as the 'Drum-Beats' discussed in Sect. 5.

We next present a simple algorithm for De-NATing DNS request. The algorithm has two phases: *clustering* and *merging*. The *clustering phase* combines DNS queries based on gathering sequential and close IP-IDs of DNS requests into clusters. The merging phase uses rate interpolations to aggregate multiple clusters of the same device.

One should note that the algorithm deals with short term aggregation of packets. The algorithm does not handle well long-term scenarios, e.g., when IP-IDs are reinitiated due to computer restart, gaps in tracking due to technical issues or transition to other networks, e.g. from mobile to WiFi and vice verse. Directions to addressing these scenarios are discussed in Sect. 5.

4.1 Clustering

The *clustering phase* aggregates DNS queries into clusters, by accounting for close IP-IDs within a time frame. The assumption is that if for too long no sequential DNS queries were captured after the last query, a DNS query even if having a close IP-ID might belong to a different device. The time distance is a parameter of the algorithm.

Algorithm 1 presents the pseudo code of the *clustering* algorithm. The input to the *clustering* algorithm is the list *queries*, which is a list of *(time,IP-ID)* tuples, each tuple is called a *query*, and is extracted from each DNS query. We will now explain some of the variables used: *cluster* is a list of queries, that represents queries that originated from the same device. *clusters* is a set of *cluster*. new queries will usually be appended into one of the *cluster* in *clusters*. *x_cluster* is a list of *query*, used to save *query* related to collisions. *finishedClusters* is a set of *cluster* which will no longer be appended with new queries.

The algorithm tests each new query, to check whether it matches one of the previously identified *clusters*, This is done in lines 4 to 10, where the new query's *time* and IP-ID are examined against each *cluster*. For the *cluster*, the time of its last query and the highest IP-ID among its last n queries are used, where n is a constant. We've empirically selected a n to be 100, except when the *cluster* is *x_cluster*, then we selected n to be 1. The parameters that define the matching result are called *win_gap* and *win_time* for the IP-ID and time differences. Those were empirically defined to be 30 and 120 s respectively.

Lines 11 to 21 handle various cases based on the number of *clusters* the query was matched to. If no candidate cluster exists, a new cluster is created. If there is a single candidate cluster, the query would be added to it. In the case there are multiple candidate clusters (line 18), an IP-ID *'collision'* of multiple devices was discovered: in Fig. 5a the intersection areas A and B, are due to the proximity of IP-ID and time values, set by the window defined by the parameters *win_gap* and *win_time*, for both segments.

For queries within 'collision' areas, the algorithm cannot assign a cluster due to ambiguity. This case is handled in lines 18–21:

– Queries that may belong to two or more clusters in their proximity window are saved in *x_cluster*. The queries on *x_cluster* won't be associated with any device, and are painted black on areas A and B.
– Any clusters that were in the proximity window will not receive further queries (line 19).
– Following the intersection area of the collision, new queries will be saved in *x_cluster* until they are far enough from the intersection area. This is tested using l_{ipid}, l_t which contain the IP-ID and time of the last collision. When the IP-ID of a new query is far enough from l_{ipid}, l_t, the special cluster *x_cluster* will stop receiving queries (line 17) until the next collision. Note that in a system with a large number of devices, several 'collisions' may happen concurrently. Such systems will need to store data on more than one collision at the a time. We explain the algorithm assuming collisions do not happen concurrently, to simplify explanation.
– After the intersection area, new clusters will be created: on Fig. 5a, clusters F and E after area A, and clusters I and H after area B.

Merging of the clusters created after intersections, with the clusters before the intersections, is implemented in the **Merging** function ahead.

4.2   Merging

The *clustering phase* results in a set of clusters of DNS queries, each belong to a single device. However, there would usually be multiple clusters created for the same device as a result of collisions, as discussed above.

Another reason for having several clusters for a device is an inactivity period defined in the *clustering phase* by *win_time*. An example is the time difference illustrated in Fig. 4b. The queries from area A to area B are closer to each other

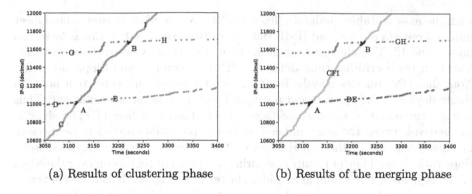

(a) Results of clustering phase   (b) Results of the merging phase

Fig. 5. Intermediate clusters and results of merging

Algorithm 1. Clustering

1: **procedure** CLUSTERING(*queries*)
2:     *clusters, finishedClusters, x_cluster* ← {}, l_t, l_{ipid} ← 0
3:     **for all** *query* ∈ *queries* **do**
4:         *close* ← {}
5:         **for all** *cluster* ∈ *clusters* ∪ *x_cluster* **do**
6:             t_c ←time of *cluster* last query
7:             i_c ←highest IP-ID between *cluster* last queries
8:             t_q ←time of *query*, i_q ←IP-ID of *query*
9:             **if** $(t_q - t_c < win\_time) \wedge (|i_q - i_c| < win\_gap)$ **then**
10:                 add *cluster* to *close* set
11:         **if** *close* is empty **then**
12:             *clusters* ← *clusters* ∪ {*query*}
13:         **if** *close* contains one cluster **then**
14:             add *query* to cluster
15:             **if** cluster is the *x_cluster* cluster **then**
16:                 **if** *query* IP-ID and time are far enough from l_t and l_{ipid} **then**
17:                     change *x_cluster* to stop accepting queries, until the next collision
18:         **if** *close* contains more than one cluster **then**
19:             move clusters in *close* from *clusters* to *finishedClusters*
20:             add *query* to *x_cluster*
21:             save collision IP-ID and time to l_t and l_{ipid}
        return *finishedClusters* ← *finishedClusters* ∪ *clusters*

---

than *win_time*. We used the value of 120 s, illustrated by the distance from B to C. However the time difference from area B to D is greater than *win_time*, meaning that the *clustering* algorithm will create a new cluster for the queries at area D rather than attaching them to the former queries of the same device. Therefore, we next apply the *merging phase*, to aggregate multiple clusters of the same device, separated by collisions, or due to periods of inactivity of the device resulting in a gap in the queries. The pseudo code of the *merging phase* algorithm is presented in Algorithm 2. The input to the *merging phase* is the *clusters* set which is the output of the *clustering* algorithm. For each *cluster*, the 'Merging' finds every possible candidate *cluster$_b$* for merging, and merges it with the most suitable candidate (lines 4 to 21). A candidate cluster should meet minimal criteria of time and IP-ID differences from the *cluster*, this is tested on lines 8 and 12. The clusters that meet these criteria are graded (lines 13 to 19) based on three criteria: time difference, IP-ID difference and Slope similarity. Note that DNS queries may be bursty, hence the slope isn't consistent across a single devices' DNS queries and a simple linear regression is insufficient. Thus a score composed of those three factors is calculated in line 17. The slope is calculated between the start and end regions of potential clusters to be merged, in lines 5 and 13. In the experiments we conducted on various traffic sources, slope ratio showed better results comparing to full linear regression over the edges of the segments. For example consider cluster C in Fig. 5a. It can be clustered, after the *x_cluster* marked by A, with clusters E and F. First, clusters should meet the minimal IP-ID and time requirements: line 8 disqualifies clusters D or G since they start before the end of cluster C, from being merged with the cluster. $60 \cdot win\_gap$ for i_{delta}, were used. The remaining clusters, e.g. E, F, I, G and H, are scored for possible merging. The clusters with the higher scores in terms of IP-ID and time are clusters F and E, out of them, cluster F will get a better slope score, and its total score, depending on the weights given for the time difference score s_i, IP-ID difference score s_t and slope score s_c (line 17) will be the highest (line 19). Thus, cluster C will be merged with cluster F, and this new merged cluster will be later merged with the cluster I for similar considerations. The result of the merging can be seen in Fig. 5b, where merged clusters are marked by combination of letters. That is, the three merged clusters, clusters C, F and I merged into the CFI merged-cluster, Clusters D and E are merged into the DE merged-cluster, and clusters G and H are merged into the GH merged-cluster. The result is very similar to the ground truth at Fig. 4a. The result of the *merging phase* are merged-clusters, each represents the De-NATed DNS queries of a single device.

4.3   Algorithm Results on Synthetic and Real Traffic

The algorithm was tested under synthetic scenarios and real traffic provided by SURFnet, the National Research and Education Network in the Netherlands. The results show overall consistency and are demonstrated in Fig. 6a on the real traffic provided by SURFnet, using 20 Windows 8/10 computers. In this figure, each color represents a single device as captured before NAT. Queries that were Successfully matched to their devices are colored in a non-black color, unique for each device, and queries that weren't successfully matched or queries that were discarded for being in intersections are colored in black. After the *clustering phase*, 155 clusters were identified due to collisions of IP-IDs coming from several devices and due to long periods where no DNS queries were observed. The *merging phase* aggregated the clusters into the final result of 37 merged-clusters. We will now explain how we quantify the algorithm's success.

Algorithm 2. Merging

1: **procedure** MERGING(*clusters*)
2:     **while** size of *clusters* decreases **do**
3:         **for all** *cluster* in clusters **do**
4:             $max_{score} \leftarrow 0$, $max_{cluster} \leftarrow \{\}$
5:             $s_1 \leftarrow$ slope of the queries at the end of *cluster*
6:             **for all** *cluster$_b$* in clusters (that aren't *cluster*) **do**
7:                 $t_s =$ time of first query in *cluster$_b$*, $t_e =$ time of last query in *cluster*
8:                 **if** $(t_s > t_e)$ **then**
9:                     $i_s =$ IP-ID of first query in *cluster$_b$*
10:                     $i_e =$ IP-ID of last query in *cluster*
11:                     $i_{diff} \leftarrow i_s - i_e$, $t_{diff} \leftarrow t_s - t_e$
12:                     **if** $(t_{diff} < t_{delta}$ & $i_{diff} < i_{delta})$ **then**
13:                         $s_b \leftarrow$ slope of the queries at the start of *cluster$_b$*
14:                         **if** $((s_b <= 0) \vee (s_1 <= 0))$ **then** $s_c = 0$
15:                         **else** $s_c \leftarrow$ minimum between s_b/s_1 and s_1/s_b
16:                         $s_t \leftarrow 1 \div (|t_{diff}| + \epsilon)$, $s_i \leftarrow |1 \div (i_{diff} + \epsilon)|$
17:                         $score \leftarrow$ weighted sum of s_c, s_t, s_i ▷ ϵ prevents zeros
18:                         **if** $score > max_{score}$ **then**
19:                             $max_{score} \leftarrow score$, $max_{cluster} \leftarrow cluster_b$
20:             add all queries in $max_{cluster}$ to the end of *cluster*, while keeping order
21:             $clusters \leftarrow clusters - max_{cluster}$
22:     **return** *clusters*   ▷ clusters returned shell be called merged-clusters

---

To quantify algorithm's success we used the following scheme:

- Each merged-cluster produced by the **Merging** is mapped to one of the ground truth devices. A merged-cluster is mapped to a device that has the most queries within that merged-cluster. If more than a single merged-cluster is assigned to a device, the one with the most queries from the device is chosen.
- The completed mapping has each device mapped to a single merged-cluster, and vice versa. We define two benchmarks, 'Total Coverage' measuring the ratio of successfully matched queries divided by the amount of queries, and 'Total Precision' measuring the ratio of successfully matched queries divided by the amount of queries in the merged-clusters they were part of:

$$\textbf{Total Coverage} = \frac{\sum_{d \in D} \sum_{q \in d} 1 \text{ if } q \in c(d)}{\sum_{d \in D} \sum_{q \in d} 1} \qquad (1)$$

$$\textbf{Total Precision} = \frac{\sum_{d \in D} \sum_{q \in d} 1 \text{ if } q \in c(d)}{\sum_{c \in C} \sum_{q \in c} 1} \qquad (2)$$

D is the set of devices, where each device d is a represented by a set of queries. C is the set of merged-clusters that were mapped to devices, where each merged-cluster c is a set of queries representing the device. Function $c(d)$ returns the merged-cluster mapped to the device d.

The Results: The Total Coverage ratio was 0.977, and the Total Accuracy was 0.996 (several merged-clusters weren't assigned to any device, so this number is higher). Meaning that the accuracy and coverage of DNS De-NATing are very high. Please note that the mostly black segment at IP-ID 25100 contains misidentifications, represented by the black points, is visually impressive but contains just a small percentage of the queries (392 queries from 55062 queries). So this segment has a low effect on the accuracy and coverage. Furthermore, a small improvement to the algorithm that solves the problem in this segment is explained in the following section.

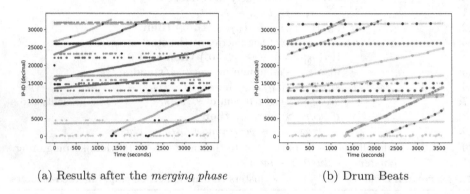

(a) Results after the *merging phase*   (b) Drum Beats

Fig. 6. Results and Drum Beats over 20 Win8/10 computers from SURFnet traffic

Detection of Misidentification of Several Devices as One: An extreme case of mismatch occurred with the merging of devices F and H in Fig. 6a, as the mostly black segment at IP-ID 25100. This segment was identified as the same merged-cluster by the *clustering* function. The reason was that both devices had very similar IP-ID values over a long period of time, and a similar frequency of DNS queries. The scenario of two devices that sending queries at very close IP-ID at the start of the De-NATing process isn't very rare. Assuming uniform distribution (given that IP-ID wraps around zero), Monte Carlo simulations showed that the chances of at least two devices having IP-ID differences of 15 or less, is close to 16% for 20 computers, and grows to about 50% for 39 computers.

Consider the following two extreme scenarios:

- One device changes at some high rate of R requests (packets) per second, and the other device has very slow rate - let's approximate it simply has fixed IP-ID X. In this case a collision will occur exactly once every P/R seconds where P is number of ports used ($<2^{16}$). With N such 'fixed' devices, we'll have a collision once every P/NR. this is identified by the *clustering* algorithm which divides the segments of the devices involved in the collision, and the *merging* algorithm which solves this case, by actually relying on the different rates of the segments to successfully merge between the segments of the same device.

- When devices collide, and their rates thereafter are similar. This is the case of devices H and F, where the two devices are accidentally being identified as one. Because the devices start from the same IP-ID (and time), and continue in roughly same rate, both *clustering* and *merging* algorithms fail to separate them. To address this case, an improvement to the algorithm is now presented.

The first step in solving this case is its identification: a simple way is to count the amount of negative IP-ID differences. We expect to see large amount of negative IP-ID differences, as usually one of the merged devices has a somewhat higher IP-ID, and when the second device sends a query after the first device, we'll see a shift from an higher IP-ID into a lower one, that will be identified as a negative difference, when we analyze the two devices as a single device. In the case of devices H and F, over 20% of the differences were negative. Comparing to the histogram on Fig. 3, this is unusually high, and indicates that presence of more than one device on the same merged-cluster. A simple solution is to run such detection for *Merging* function results and then rerun the algorithm once for each such merged-cluster as a single input, using a much finer IP-ID separation constant, in this case using IP-ID separation constant of 3 (instead of the original 30), managed to separate the devices, with results of coverage of 0.918 and accuracy of 1. In spite of this improvement, a larger quantity of devices increases the chances that the IPIDs of two devices will be so close after a collision that even a finer IP-ID separation will not succeed, and so a larger quantity of devices, reduces the chances of the algorithm's success.

5 Long Term De-NATing

The DNS De-NAT algorithm presented in the previous section should work well as long as the eavesdropper can track continuously the IP-IDs generated by devices behind NAT. However is it limited in scenarios such as device restart, where in many cases the IP-ID starts from another point, in scenarios when there are significant time gaps between DNS requests, or even in the case where there are gaps in interception due to technical limitations. To address these limitation for long term De-NATing additional layer of aggregation of merged-clusters is required. Such aggregation can be implemented by:

- Accounting for typical time differences of bursts of DNS requests in clusters using Machine Learning or other techniques.
- Accounting for past domains and aggregating merged-clusters to devices with highest probability based on domain frequency and/or domain classification.
- Use the DNS TTL field. The TTL denotes the number of seconds before the expiration of the record. Thus, if a domain is frequently used, every TTL seconds there will be a DNS request for that domain. This would be a strong hint for aggregation of merged-clusters, and may also be useful for linking between the requests of a device before and after rebooting (when the IP-ID is reset).
- Use the 'Drum beat' technique described hereafter.

5.1 DNS Drum Beats

We observed, in captures and in synthetic traffic generated by standard PCs, that DNS queries to some domains are send in very deterministic fixed time intervals, most likely due to implementation considerations. Such queries are typically originated from updates checking services (e.g. 'downloads.dell.com') or from sites that are opened on the browser and contain refresh constants or other scripts that are sending data at fixed intervals (e.g. 'data.cnn.com').

Also, in some cases DNS drum beats survive even computer restarts (e.g. 'downloads.dell.com') and are thus very helpful in long term De-NATing.

For some examples of Drum-Beats, we checked the frequencies of DNS queries over several computers. The fixed time gaps between DNS queries to some domains are shown on Table 3 and were consistent for hundreds of observations.

Table 3. Some DNS queries frequencies (Drum-Beats) to common domains

Domain	Query frequency (sec)
teredo.ipv6.microsoft.com	900
v10.vortex-win.data.microsoft.com	900
b.config.skype.com	3600
tpc.googlesyndication.com	315
s7.addthis.com	301
ping.chartbeat.net	Alternating 75 and 182
d2tpbry8f62bv9.cloudfront.net	Alternating 60 and 300
data.cnn.com	120
downloads.dell.com	600

In the SURFnet example discussed in Sect. 4.2, several domains had fixed intervals of 31 s with extremely small standard deviation of 0.0036 s (after removing outliers by taking the center 80% of the time differences). This repeated throughout the entire capture. Other domains had a mean of 120 s with standard deviation of less than 0.5 s. Figure 6b demonstrates this phenomena where most queries are painted in gray, but each DNS query sent to the same domain, with standard deviation divided by mean lower than 0.1, is marked with a different color per domain (outliers were not filtered out for this figure). It easy to see that time differences between these DNS queries are consistent. Clearly, this phenomena can be used to fingerprint devices and assist in merging cluster for long term.

6 Full Data De-NAT - Correlating TCP Connections to DNS Requests

In the case where the eavesdropping in done at the ISP or by interception on the route from the router to the Internet (see Fig. 1), in addition to the DNS

De-NATing, full data De-NAT can be performed. In the previous chapter we showed that one can aggregate DNS requests generated by a single Win 8/10 device behind NAT. To perform De-NAT of full devices traffic, the next challenge is to correlate between DNS requests and TCP connections. In this chapter we show that a short term correlation can be performed even by a greedy algorithm in high accuracy.

6.1 Basic Correlation Between DNS Queries and TCP Connections

Typically, a DNS query is issued by the TCP/IP stack to resolve the address for the TCP connection. From many experiments we conducted, in a typical Win 8/10 devices above 95% of TCP connections are preceded by DNS resolving queries. The remaining connections most likely use hard coded IP addresses.

We examined the correlation between DNS queries and TCP connections on computers addressing top 1000 Alexa websites. The time gaps between a DNS query to the beginning of the TCP stream to the requested destination are shown in Fig. 7a. Technically it shows the time difference after filtering out destinations with no preceding DNS query. As can be seen in Fig. 7a, less than 50% of the flows have about 0.13 second or less of time difference between the TCP syn and its relevant DNS query. Less than 16% of the flows have a difference of over a second and less that 6% have more that 8 s difference.

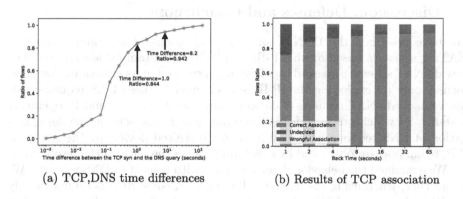

(a) TCP,DNS time differences   (b) Results of TCP association

Fig. 7. TCP and DNS time differences and DNS, TCP association algorithm

6.2 Associating TCP Streams to DNS Queries

Assuming the originating device aggregates of DNS queries are known by using the *clustering* algorithm presented in the previous section, the challenge is to associate the TCP streams with the DNS requests for full data De-NATing.

Based on the results of Fig. 7a, we present a naive algorithm to associate a TCP syn to its originating device. The algorithm associates a TCP syn to the **closest** DNS query that preceded it (the full implementation takes into account trivial details such as dealing with the DNS responses, which are used to match the IP destination of the TCP syn to that of the domain queried in the DNS query). If this time difference between a TCP syn and the closest DNS query for that domain is larger than some constant, we no longer assume they are related. In such case the TCP syn in not associated with any device, and is defined 'Undecided'.

The challenge is in setting the best constant, we refer to as 'Back time', for deciding the correlation time frames. If the time is too short, the algorithm may result in too many unassociated connections. On the other hand, if the time is too long and there are several computers there can be miss matching of correlating the DNS requests to the TCP streams in case of simultaneous requests to the same domains.

Results: We used the naive algorithm described above over four Win 8/10 devices addressing top 1000 Alexa web sites, The results are shown on Fig. 7b.

The ratio of the streams that were associated correctly, wrongfully associated, and undecided are shown over different values of 'Back Time'. We see that increasing the 'Back time' trades 'Undecided' with a mixture of both correct and failed associations. On an operative system, the specific value of 'Back Time' will be decided depending on the importance of avoiding wrongful association against the importance of improving the amount of the correct associations.

7   Discussion, Defenses and Conclusions

We have described the De-NAT problem and discussed new and known de-NATing schemes, based on the IP-ID and TCP Timestamp side channels. The new de-NAT scheme presented uses DNS requests, and in its current deployment, focuses only on exploiting the IP-ID side channel in these DNS requests; this allows us to de-NAT requests of devices using the Windows 8 and 10 operating systems, for which previous de-NAT schemes failed. The scheme enables aggregation of DNS requests generated by a single NATed device, by the resolvers' ISP, by an open-resolver, and by eavesdroppers on the path to the resolver.

We examined the behavior of home routers with respect to DNS requests. We found that, when using the default ISP's resolver, some routers do not modify the IP-ID in requests, facilitating the described de-NAT scheme. Please note that our aim is to show that this DeNat scheme works on some important scenarios, and it may not work on all types of routers and operation modes. When using a remote open resolver, *none* of the NAT-routers we tested modified the DNS requests. Namely, the remote open resolver, or an eavesdropper on the route, can use a DNS-based de-NAT scheme. An algorithm for DNS De-NAT was described and examined. The algorithm, tested on synthetic and real traffic, showed high level of De-NATing accuracy.

To address long term De-NATing that survive devices' restart or interception gaps, additional level of long term aggregation of DNS requests is required. Several methods were suggested along with a new method based on the periodic DNS requests to certain domains we refer to as 'Drum beats'.

For the case of eavesdropping at the service provider we showed a method to associate TCP flows to DNS requests. This allows for full traffic De-NAT.

We conclude that most current NAT-router devices, connecting SOHO networks, seem vulnerable to de-NATing, allowing the ISP or even a remote open-resolver or eavesdropper, to cluster most of the DNS requests of each specific device in the network. As we explained in the introduction, this has legitimate, desirable applications - but may be considered as a problem by users concerned about their privacy.

It is quite simple for NAT-routers to foil known de-NATing schemes, including our DNS-based de-NATing scheme. Focusing on our scheme, the best solution may be for the NAT-router to zero the IP-ID field; we do not expect that to cause any problem, since DNS requests are relatively short packets, and should not require fragmentation. Alternatively, the IP-ID field can be replaced by a pseudo-random permutation of it; this will be equally effective against possible random collisions with old fragments (from the same network). Notice, however, that some of the improvements to the scheme mentioned in Sect. 4, may yet be effective. A more robust defense against DNS-based de-NATing may be to run a DNS proxy in the NAT-router - this requires a bit more resources at the router, but provides robust defense and will have positive impact on performance.

Of course, in many cases, the person concerned about her privacy may not be able to pick or change the NAT-routers; e.g., consider public WiFi networks such as in cafe or hotel. This makes it more challenging to protect privacy against de-NATing. A possible solution may be to use a VPN, or even Tor or another anonymizing service. However, such solutions have significant overhead and may have undesirable impacts such as drawing attention to the user.

Acknowledgements. Many thanks to Amit Klein for his helpful comments. Many thanks to Roland van Rijswijk-Deij for his support during this project. This work was supported by the Israeli ministry of Science, grant number 3-11857. Part of the data that led to this research was provided by SURFnet, the National Research and Education Network in the Netherlands, https://www.surfnet.nl/en/.

References

[Bel02] Bellovin, S.M.: A technique for counting NATted hosts. In: Internet Measurement Workshop, pp. 267–272. ACM (2002)

[Bev04] Beverly, R.: A robust classifier for passive TCP/IP fingerprinting. In: Barakat, C., Pratt, I. (eds.) PAM 2004. LNCS, vol. 3015, pp. 158–167. Springer, Heidelberg (2004). https://doi.org/10.1007/978-3-540-24668-8_16

[Bur07] Bursztein, E.: Time has something to tell us about network address translation. In: Erlingsson,Ú., Sabelfeld, A. (eds.) Proceedings of the 12th Nordic Workshop on Secure IT Systems (NordSec 2007), Reykjavik, Iceland, October 2007

[Dan08] Danezis, G.: Covert communications despite traffic data retention. In: Christianson, B., Malcolm, J.A., Matyas, V., Roe, M. (eds.) Security Protocols 2008. LNCS, vol. 6615, pp. 198–214. Springer, Heidelberg (2011). https://doi.org/10.1007/978-3-642-22137-8_27

[GFZ14] Gokcen, Y., Foroushani, V.A., Zincir-Heywood, A.N.: Can we identify NAT behavior by analyzing traffic flows? In: 35th IEEE Security and Privacy Workshops, SPW 2014, San Jose, CA, USA, 17–18 May 2014, pp. 132–139 (2014)

[GH12] Gilad, Y., Herzberg, A.: Spying in the dark: TCP and tor traffic analysis. In: Fischer-Hübner, S., Wright, M. (eds.) PETS 2012. LNCS, vol. 7384, pp. 100–119. Springer, Heidelberg (2012). https://doi.org/10.1007/978-3-642-31680-7_6

[GHS14] Gilad, Y., Herzberg, A., Shulman, H.: Off-path hacking: the illusion of challenge-response authentication. IEEE Secur. Priv. **12**(5), 68–77 (2014)

[HBF13] Herrmann, D., Banse, C., Federrath, H.: Behavior-based tracking: exploiting characteristic patterns in DNS traffic. Comput. Secur. **39**, 17–33 (2013)

[KHLK16] Kirchler, M., Herrmann, D., Lindemann, J., Kloft, M.: Tracked without a trace: linking sessions of users by unsupervised learning of patterns in their DNS traffic. In: Proceedings of the 2016 ACM Workshop on Artificial Intelligence and Security, AISec@CCS 2016, Vienna, Austria, 28 October 2016, pp. 23–34 (2016)

[Moc87] Mockapetris, P.: Domain names - concepts and facilities, RFC 1034, November 1987

[Pos81] Postel, J.: Internet datagram protocol RFC791. USC/Information Sciences Institute, RFC 791, September 1981

[SE01] Srisuresh, P., Egevang, K.: Traditional IP network address translator (traditional NAT), RFC 3022, January 2001

[Shu14] Shulman, H.: Pretty bad privacy: pitfalls of DNS encryption. In: Ahn, G.-J., Datta, A. (eds.) WPES, pp. 191–200. ACM (2014)

[WWM13] Wicherski, G., Weingarten, F., Meyer, U.: IP agnostic real-time traffic filtering and host identification using TCP timestamps. In: LCN, pp. 647–654. IEEE Computer Society (2013)

CLEF: Limiting the Damage Caused by Large Flows in the Internet Core

Hao Wu[1,2]([✉])[iD], Hsu-Chun Hsiao[3][iD], Daniele E. Asoni[4][iD], Simon Scherrer[4][iD], Adrian Perrig[4][iD], and Yih-Chun Hu[1][iD]

[1] University of Illinois at Urbana Champaign, Champaign, USA
haowu.uiuc@gmail.com
[2] Rubrik, Inc., Palo Alto, USA
[3] National Taiwan University, Taipei, Taiwan
[4] ETH Zurich, Zürich, Switzerland

Abstract. The detection of network flows that send excessive amounts of traffic is of increasing importance to enforce QoS and to counter DDoS attacks. Large-flow detection has been previously explored, but the proposed approaches can be used on high-capacity core routers only at the cost of significantly reduced accuracy, due to their otherwise too high memory and processing overhead. We propose CLEF, a new large-flow detection scheme with low memory requirements, which maintains high accuracy under the strict conditions of high-capacity core routers. We compare our scheme with previous proposals through extensive theoretical analysis, and with an evaluation based on worst-case-scenario attack traffic. We show that CLEF outperforms previously proposed systems in settings with limited memory.

Keywords: Large-flow detection · Damage metric
Memory and computation efficiency

1 Introduction

Detecting misbehaving large network flows[1] that use more than their allocated resources is not only an important mechanism for Quality of Service (QoS) [29] schemes such as IntServ [5], but also for DDoS defense mechanisms that allocate bandwidth to network flows [4,19,23]. With the recent resurgence of volumetric DDoS attacks [3], the topics of DDoS defense mechanisms and QoS are gaining importance; thus, the need for efficient in-network accounting is increasing.

Unfortunately, per-flow resource accounting is too expensive to perform in the core of the network [12], since large-scale Internet core routers have an aggregate capacity of several Terabits per second (Tbps). Instead, to detect misbehaving flows, core routers need to employ highly efficient schemes which do not require

---

[1] As in prior literature [12,34], the term *large flow* denotes a flow that sends more than its allocated bandwidth.

© Springer Nature Switzerland AG 2018
J. Camenisch and P. Papadimitratos (Eds.): CANS 2018, LNCS 11124, pp. 89–108, 2018.
https://doi.org/10.1007/978-3-030-00434-7_5

them to keep per-flow state. Several approaches for large-flow detection have been proposed in this context; they can be categorized into probabilistic (i.e., relying on random sampling or random binning) and deterministic algorithms. Examples of probabilistic algorithms are Sampled Netflow [8] and Multistage Filters [11,12], while EARDet [34] and Space Saving [25] are examples of deterministic approaches.

However, previously proposed algorithms are able to satisfy the requirements of core router environments only by significantly sacrificing their accuracy. In particular, with the constraints on the amount of high-speed memory on core routers, these algorithms either can only detect flows which exceed their assigned bandwidth by very large amounts, or else they suffer from high false-positive rates. This means that these systems cannot prevent the performance degradation of regular, well-behaved flows, because of large flows that manage to stay "under the radar" of the detection algorithms, or because the detection algorithms themselves erroneously flag and punish the well-behaved flows.

As a numeric example, consider that for EARDet to accurately detect misbehaving flows exceeding a threshold of 1 Mbps on a 100 Gbps link, it would require 10^5 counters for that link. Maintaining these counters, together with the necessary associated metadata, requires between 1.6 MB and 4 MB of state[2], which exceeds typical high-speed memory provisioning for core routers, and would come at a high cost (for comparison, note that only the most high-end commodity CPUs approach the 1–4 MB range with their per-core L1/L2 memory, and the price tag for such processors surpasses USD 4000 [15]).

In this paper we propose a novel randomized algorithm for large flow detection called *Recursive Large-Flow Detection* (RLFD). RLFD works by considering a set of potential large flows, dividing this set into multiple subsets, and then recursively narrowing down the focus to the most promising subset. This algorithm is highly memory efficient, and is designed to have no false positives. To achieve these properties, RLFD sacrifices some detection speed, in particular for the case of multiple concurrent large flows. We improve on these limitations by combining RLFD with the deterministic EARDet, proposing a hybrid scheme called CLEF, short for *in-Core Limiting of Egregious Flows*. We show how this scheme inherits the strengths of both algorithms: the ability to quickly detect very large flows of EARDet (which it can do in a memory efficient way), and the ability to detect low-rate large flows with minimal memory footprint of RLFD.

To have a significant comparison with related work, we define a *damage* metric which estimates the impact of failed, delayed, and incorrect detection on well-behaved flows. We use this metric to compare RLFD and CLEF with previous proposals, which we do both on a theoretical level and by evaluating the amount of damage caused by (worst-case) attacks. Our evaluation shows that CLEF performs better than previous work under realistic memory constraints,

---

[2] The IP metadata consists of source and destination addresses, protocol number, and ports. Thus, it requires about 16 bytes and 40 bytes per counter for IPv4 and IPv6, respectively.

both in terms of our damage metric and in terms of false negatives and false positives.

To summarize, this paper's main contributions are the following: a novel, randomized algorithm, RLFD, that provides eventual detection of persistently large flows with very little memory cost; a hybrid detection scheme, CLEF, which offers excellent large-flow detection properties with low resource requirements; the analysis of worst-case attacks against the proposed large-flow detectors, using a damage metric that allows a realistic comparison with the related work.

2   Problem Definition

This paper aims to design an efficient large-flow detection algorithm that minimizes the *damage* caused by misbehaving flows. This section introduces the challenges of large-flow detection and defines a damage metric to compare different large-flow detectors. We then define an adversary model in which the adversary adapts its behavior to the detection algorithm in use.

2.1   Large-Flow Detection

A flow is a collection of related traffic; for example, Internet flows are commonly characterized by a 5-tuple (source/destination IP/port, transport protocol). A *large flow* is one that exceeds a flow specification during a period of length t. A flow specification can be defined using a leaky bucket descriptor $\mathsf{TH}(t) = \gamma t + \beta$, where $\gamma > 0$ and $\beta > 0$ are the maximum legitimate rate and burstiness allowance, respectively. Flow specifications can be enforced in two ways: *arbitrary-window*, in which the flow specification is enforced over every possible starting time, or *landmark-window*, in which the flow specification is enforced over a limited set of starting times.

Detecting every large flow exactly when it exceeds the flow specification, and doing so with no false positives requires per-flow state (this can be shown by the pigeonhole principle [32]), which is expensive on core routers. In this paper, we develop and evaluate schemes that trade timely detection for space efficiency.

As in prior work in flow monitoring, we assume each flow has a unique and unforgeable flow ID, e.g., using source authentication techniques such as accountable IPs [1], ICING [27], IPA [20], OPT [17], or with Passport [21]. Such techniques can be deployed in the current Internet or in a future Internet architecture, e.g., Nebula [2], SCION [36], or XIA [14].

Large-Flow Detection by Core Routers. In this work, we aim to design a large-flow detection algorithm that is viable to run on Internet core routers. The algorithm needs to limit damage caused by large flows even when handling worst-case background traffic. Such an algorithm must satisfy these three requirements:

- **Line rate:** An in-core large-flow detection algorithm must operate at the line rate of core routers, which can process several hundreds of gigabits of traffic per second.

- **Low memory:** Large-flow detection algorithms will typically access one or more memory locations for each traversing packet; such memory must be high-speed (such as on-chip L1 cache). Additionally, such memory is expensive and usually limited in size, and existing large-flow detectors are inadequate to operate in high-bandwidth, low-memory environments. An in-core large-flow detection algorithm should thus be highly space-efficient. Though perfect detection requires counters equal to the maximum number of simultaneous large flows (by the pigeonhole principle [32]), our goal is to perform effective detection with much fewer counters.
- **Low damage:** With the performance constraints of the previous two points, the large-flow detection algorithm should also minimize the damage to honest flows, which can be caused either by the excessive bandwidth usage by large flows, or by the erroneous classification of legitimate flows as large flows (false positives). Section 2.2 introduces our damage metric, which takes both these aspects into account.

2.2 Damage Metric

We consider misbehaving large flows to be a problem mainly in that they have an adverse impact on honest flows. To measure the performance of large flow detection algorithms we therefore adopt a simple and effective *damage* metric which captures the packet loss suffered by honest flows. This metric considers both (1) the direct impact of excessive bandwidth usage by large flows, and (2) the potential adverse effect of the detection algorithm itself, which may be prone to false positives resulting in the blacklisting of honest flows. Specifically, we define our damage metric as $D = D_{over} + D_{fp}$, where D_{over} (*overuse damage*) is the total amount of traffic by which all large flows exceed the flow specification, and D_{fp} (*false positive damage*) is the amount of legitimate traffic incorrectly blocked by the detection algorithm. The definition of the overuse damage assumes a link at full capacity, so when this is not the case the damage metric represents an over-approximation of the actual traffic lost suffered by honest flows. We note that the metrics commonly used by previous work, i.e., false positives, false negatives, and detection delay, are all reflected by our metric.

2.3 Attacker Model

In our attacker model, we consider an adversary that aims to maximize damage. Our attacker responds to the detection algorithm and tries to exploit its transient behavior to avoid detection or to cause false detection of legitimate flows.

Like Estan and Varghese's work [12], we assume that attackers know about the large-flow detection algorithm running in the router and its settings, but have no knowledge of secret seeds used to generate random variables, such as the detection intervals for landmark-window-based algorithms [9,10,12,13,16,24–26], and random numbers used for packet/flow sampling [12]. This assumption prevents the attacker from performing optimal attacks against randomized algorithms.

We assume the attacker can interleave packets, but is unable to spoof legitimate packets (as discussed in Sect. 2.1) or create pre-router losses in legitimate flows. Figure 1 shows the network model, where the attacker arbitrarily interleaves attack traffic (A) between idle intervals of legitimate traffic (L), and the router processes the interleaved traffic to generate output traffic (O) and perform large-flow detection. Our model does not limit input traffic, allowing for arbitrary volumes of attack traffic.

In our model, whenever a packet traverses a router, the large-flow detector receives the flow ID (for example, the source and destination IP and port and transport protocol), the packet size, and the timestamp at which the packet arrived.

Fig. 1. Adversary model.

3   Background and Challenges

In this section we briefly review some existing large flow detection algorithms, and discuss the motivations and challenges of combining multiple algorithms into a hybrid scheme.

3.1   Existing Detection Algorithms

We review the three most relevant large-flow detection algorithms, summarized in Table 1. We divide large flows into *low-rate large flows* and *high-rate large flows*, depending on the amount by which they exceed the flow specification.

EARDet. EARDet [34] guarantees exact and instant detection of all flows exceeding a high-rate threshold $\gamma_h = \frac{\rho}{m}$, where ρ is the link capacity and m is the number of counters. However, EARDet may fail to identify a large flow whose rate stays below γ_h.

Multistage Filters. Multistage filters [11,12] consist of multiple parallel stages, each of which is an array of counters. Specifically, *arbitrary-window-based Multistage Filter* (AMF), as classified by Wu et al. [34], uses leaky buckets as counters. AMF guarantees the absence of false negatives (no-FN) and immediate detection for any flow specification; however, AMF has false positives (FPs), which increase as the link becomes congested.

Flow Memory. Flow Memory (FM) [12] refers to per-flow monitoring of select flows. FM is often used in conjunction with another system that specifies which flows to monitor; when a new flow is to be monitored but the flow memory is full, FM evicts an old flow. We follow Estan and Varghese [12]'s random eviction. If the flow memory is large enough to avoid eviction, it provides exact detection. In practice, however, Flow Memory is unable to handle a large number of flows, resulting in frequent flow eviction and potentially high FN. FM's real-world performance depends on the amount by which a large flow exceeds the flow specification: high-rate flows are more quickly detected, which improves the chance of detection before eviction.

Table 1. Comparison of three existing detection algorithms. None of them achieve all desired properties.

Algorithm		EARDet	AMF	FM
No-FP		Yes	No*	Yes
No-FN	Low-rate	No**	Yes	No*
	High-rate	Yes	Yes	Yes***
Instant detection		Yes	Yes	Yes

*In our technical report [33] we show that Flow Memory has high FN and AMF has high FP for low-rate large flows when memory is limited.
**EARDet cannot provide no-FN when memory is limited.
***Flow Memory has nearly zero FN when large-flow rate is high.

3.2   Advantages of Hybrid Schemes

As Table 1 shows, none of the detectors we examined can efficiently achieve no-FN and no-FP across various types of large flows. However, different detectors exhibit different strengths, so combining them could result in improved performance.

One approach is to run detectors sequentially; in this composition, the first detector monitors all traffic and sends any large flows it detects to a second detector. However, this approach allows an attacker controlling multiple flows to rotate overuse among many flows, overusing a flow only for as long as it takes the first detector to react, then sending at the normal rate so that remaining detectors remove it from their watch list and re-starting with the attack.

Alternatively, we can run detectors in parallel: the hybrid detects a flow whenever it is identified by either detector. (Another configuration is that a flow is only detected if both detectors identify it, but such a configuration would have a high FN rate compared to the detectors used in this paper.) The hybrid inherits the FPs of both schemes, but features the minimum detection delay of the two schemes and has a FN only when both schemes have a FN. The remainder of this paper considers the parallel approach that identifies a flow whenever it is detected by either detector.

The EARDet and Flow Memory schemes have no FPs and are able to quickly detect high-rate flows; because high-rate flows cause damage much more quickly, rapid detection of high-rate flows is important to achieving low damage. Combining EARDet or Flow Memory with a scheme capable of detecting low-rate flows as a hybrid detection scheme can retain rapid detection of high-rate flows while eventually catching (and thus limiting the damage of) low-rate flows. In this paper, we aim to construct such a scheme. Specifically, our scheme will selectively monitor one small set at a time, ensuring that a consistently-overusing flow is eventually detected.

4 RLFD and CLEF Hybrid Schemes

In this section, we present our new large-flow detectors. First, we describe the *Recursive Large-Flow Detection* (RLFD) algorithm, a novel approach which is designed to use very little memory but provide eventual detection for large flows. We then present the data structures, runtime analysis, and advantages and disadvantages of RLFD. Next, we develop a hybrid detector, CLEF, that addresses the disadvantages of RLFD by combining it with the previously proposed EARDet [34]. CLEF uses EARDet to rapidly detect high-rate flows and RLFD to detect low-rate flows, thus limiting the damage caused by large flows, even with a very limited amount of memory.

4.1 RLFD Algorithm

RLFD is a randomized algorithm designed to perform memory-efficient detection of low-rate large flows; it is designed to scale to a large number of flows, as encountered by an Internet core router. RLFD is designed to limit the damage inflicted by low-rate large flows while using very limited memory. The intuition behind RLFD is to monitor subsets of flows, recursively subdividing the subset deemed most likely to contain a large flow. By dividing subsets in this way, RLFD exponentially reduces memory requirements (it can monitor m^d flows with $O(m + d)$ memory).

The main challenges addressed by RLFD include efficiently mapping flows into recursively divided groups, choosing the correct subdivision to reduce detection delay and FNs, and configuring RLFD to guarantee the absence of FPs.

Recursive Subdivision. To operate with limited memory, RLFD recursively subdivides monitored flows into m groups, and subdivides only the one group most likely to contain a large flow.

We can depict an RLFD as a *virtual counter tree*[3] (Fig. 2(a)) of depth d. Every non-leaf node in this tree has m children, each of which corresponds to a *virtual counter*. The tree is a full m-ary tree of depth d, though at any moment, only one node (m counters) is kept in memory; the rest of the tree exists only virtually.

---

[3] The terms "counter tree" and "virtual counter" are also used by Chen et al. [7], but our technique differs in both approach and goal. Chen et al. efficiently manage a sufficient number of counters for per-flow accounting, while RLFD manages an insufficient number of counters to detect consistent overuse.

Each flow f is randomly assigned to a path $PATH(f)$ of counters on the virtual tree, as illustrated by the highlighted counters in Fig. 2(b). This mapping is determined by hashing a flow ID with a keyed hash function, where the key is randomly generated by each router. Our technical report [33] explains how RLFD efficiently implements this random mapping.

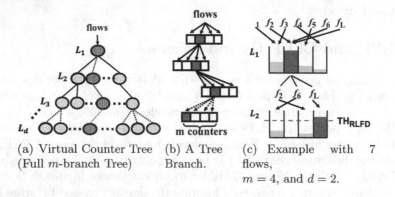

(a) Virtual Counter Tree (Full m-branch Tree) (b) A Tree Branch. (c) Example with 7 flows, $m = 4$, and $d = 2$.

Fig. 2. RLFD structure and example.

Since there are d levels, each leaf node at level L_d will contain an average of n/m^{d-1} flows, where n is the total number of flows on the link. A flow f is identified as a large flow if it is the only flow associated with its counter at level L_d and the counter value exceeds a threshold TH_{RLFD}. To reflect the flow specification $\mathsf{TH}(t) = \gamma t + \beta$ from Sect. 2.1, we set $TH_{RLFD} = \gamma T_\ell + \beta$, where T_ℓ is the duration of the period during which detection is performed at the bottom level L_d. Any flow sending more traffic than TH_{RLFD} during any duration of time T_ℓ must violate the large-flow threshold $\mathsf{TH}(t)$, so RLFD has no FPs. We provide more details about how we balance detection rate and the no-FP guarantee in our technical report [33].

RLFD considers only one node in the virtual counter tree at a time, so it requires only m counters. To enable exploration of the entire tree, RLFD divides the process into d periods; in period k, it loads one tree node from level L_k. Though these periods need not be of equal length, in this paper we consider periods of equal length T_ℓ, which results in a RLFD detection cycle $T_c = d \cdot T_\ell$.

RLFD always chooses the root node to monitor at level L_1; after monitoring at level L_k, RLFD identifies the largest counter C_{max} among the m counters at level L_k, and uses the node corresponding to that counter for level L_{k+1}. Our technical report [33] shows that choosing the largest counter detects large flows with high probability.

Figure 2(c) shows an example with $m = 4$ counters, $n = 7$ flows, and $d = 2$ levels. f_L is a low-rate large flow. In level L_1, the largest counter is the one associated with large flow f_L and legitimate flows f_2 and f_6. At level L_2, the flow set $\{f_L, f_2, f_6\}$ is selected and sub-divided. After the second round, f_L is detected because it violates the counter value threshold TH_{RLFD}.

Algorithm Description. As shown in Fig. 3(a), the algorithm starts at the top level L_1 so each counter represents a child of the root node. At the beginning of each period, all counters are reset to zero. At the end of each period, the algorithm finds the counter holding the maximum value and moves to the corresponding node, so each counter in the next period is a child of that node. Once the algorithm has processed level d, it repeats from the first level.

Figure 3(b) describes how RLFD processes each incoming packet. When RLFD receives a packet x from flow f, x is dropped if f is in the *blacklist* (a table that stores previously-found large flows). If f is not in the blacklist, RLFD hashes f to the corresponding counters in the virtual counter tree (one counter per level of the tree). If one such counter is currently loaded in memory, its value is increased by the size of the packet x. At the bottom level L_d, a large flow is identified when there is only one flow in the counter and the counter value exceeds the threshold TH_{RLFD}. To increase the probability that a large flow is in a counter by itself, we choose $d \geq \lceil \log_m n \rceil$ and use Cuckoo hashing [28] at the bottom level to reduce collisions. Once a large flow is identified, it is blacklisted: in our evaluation we calculate the damage D with the assumption that large flows are blocked immediately after having been added to the blacklist.

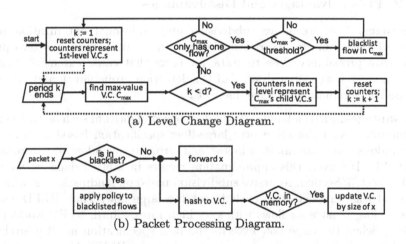

(a) Level Change Diagram.

(b) Packet Processing Diagram.

Fig. 3. RLFD decision diagrams. "V.C." stands for virtual counter.

4.2 RLFD Details and Optimization

We describe some of the details of RLFD and propose additional optimizations to the basic RLFD described in Sect. 4.1.

Hash Function Update. We update the keyed hash function by choosing a new key at the beginning of every initial level to guarantee that the assignment of flows to counters between different top-to-bottom detection cycles is independent and pseudo-random. For simplicity, in this paper we analyze RLFD assuming the random oracle model. Picking a new key is computationally inexpensive and needs to be performed only once per cycle.

Blacklist. When RLFD identifies a large flow, the flow's ID should be added to the blacklist as quickly as possible. Thus, we implement the blacklist with a small amount of L1 cache backed by permanent storage, e.g., main memory. Because the blacklist write only happens at the bottom-level period and the number of large flows detected in one iteration of the algorithm is at most one, we first write these large flows in the L1 cache and move them from L1 cache to permanent storage at a slower rate. By managing the blacklist in this way, we provide high bandwidth for blacklist writing, defending against attacks that overflow the blacklist.

Using Multiple RLFDs. If a link handles too much traffic to use a single RLFD, we can use multiple RLFDs in parallel. Each flow is hashed to a specific RLFD so that the load on each detector meets performance requirements. The memory requirements scale linearly in the number of RLFDs required to process the traffic.

4.3   RLFD's Advantages and Disadvantages

Advantages. With recursive subdivision and additional optimization techniques, RLFD is able to (1) identify low-rate large flows with non-zero probability, with probability close to 100% for flows that cause extensive damage (our technical report [33] analyzes RLFD's detection probability); and (2) guarantee no-FP, eliminating damage due to FP.

Disadvantages. First, a landmark-window-based algorithm such as RLFD cannot guarantee exact detection over large-flow specification based on arbitrary time windows [34] (landmark window and arbitrary window are introduced in Sect. 2.1). However, this approximation results in limited damage, as mentioned in Sect. 3. Second, recursive subdivision based on landmark time windows requires at least one detection cycle to catch a large flow. Thus, RLFD cannot guarantee low damage for flows with very high rates. Third, RLFD works most effectively when the large flow exceeds the flow specification in all d levels, so bursty flows with a burst duration shorter than the RLFD detection cycle T_c are likely to escape detection (where *burst duration* refers to the amount of time during which the bursty flow sends in excess of the flow specification).

4.4   CLEF Hybrid Scheme

We propose a hybrid scheme, CLEF, which is a parallel composition with one EARDet and two RLFDs (Twin-RLFD). This hybrid can detect both high-rate and low-rate large flows without producing FPs, requiring only a limited amount of memory. We use EARDet instead of Flow Memory in this hybrid scheme because EARDet's detection is deterministic, thus has shorter detection delay.

Parallel Composition of EARDet and RLFD. As described in Sect. 3.2, we combine EARDet and RLFD in parallel so that RLFD can help EARDet detect low-rate flat flows, and EARDet can help RLFD quickly catch high-rate flat and bursty flows.

Twin-RLFD Parallel Composition. RLFD is most effective at catching flows that violate flow specification across an entire detection cycle T_c. An attacker can reduce the probability of being caught by RLFD by choosing a burst duration shorter than T_c and an inter-burst duration greater than T_c/d (thus reducing the probability that the attacker will advance to the next round during its inter-burst period). We therefore introduce a second RLFD (RLFD$^{(2)}$) with a longer detection cycle $T_c^{(2)}$, so that a flow must have burst duration shorter than $T_c^{(1)}$ and burst period longer than $T_c^{(2)}/d$ to avoid detection by the Twin-RLFD (where RLFD$^{(1)}$ and $T_c^{(1)}$, are the first RLFD and its detection cycle respectively). For a given average rate, flows that evade Twin-RLFD have a higher burst rate than flows that evade a single RLFD. By properly setting $T_c^{(1)}$ and $T_c^{(2)}$, Twin-RLFD can synergize with EARDet, ensuring that a flow undetectable by Twin-RLFD must use a burst higher than EARDet's rate threshold γ_h.

Timing Randomization. An attacker can strategically send traffic with burst durations shorter than $T_c^{(1)}$, but choose low duty cycles to avoid detection by both RLFD$^{(1)}$ and EARDet. Such an attacker can only be detected by RLFD$^{(2)}$, but RLFD$^{(2)}$ has a longer detection delay, allowing the attacker to maximize damage before being blacklisted. To prevent attackers from deterministically maximizing damage, we randomize the length of the detection cycles $T_c^{(1)}$ and $T_c^{(2)}$.

5   Evaluation

We experimentally evaluate CLEF, RLFD, EARDet, and AMF-FM with respect to worst-case damage [33, Sect. 5.1]. We consider various large-flow patterns and memory limits and assume background traffic that is challenging for CLEF and RLFD. The experiment results confirm that CLEF outperforms other schemes, especially when memory is extremely limited.

5.1   Experiment Settings

Link Settings. Since the required memory space of a large-flow detector is sublinear to link capacity, we set the link capacity to $\rho = 1$ Gbps, which is high enough to incorporate the realistic background traffic dataset while ensuring the simulation can finish in reasonable time. We choose a very low threshold rate $\gamma = 12.5$ KB/s, so that the number of full-use legitimate flows $n_\gamma = \rho/\gamma$ is 10000, ensuring that the link is as challenging as a backbone link (as analyzed in our technical report [33]). The flow specification is set to $\mathsf{TH}(t) = \gamma t + \beta$, where β is set to 3028 bytes (which is as small as two maximum-sized packets, making bursty flows easier to catch).

The results on this 1 Gbps link allow us to extrapolate detector performance to high-capacity core routers, e.g., in a 100 Gbps link with $\gamma = 1.25\,\text{MB/s}$. Because CLEF's performance with a given number of counters is mainly related to the ratio between link capacity and threshold rate n_γ (as discussed in our technical report [33]), CLEF's worst-case performance will scale linearly in link capacity when the number of counters and the ratio between link capacity and threshold rate is held constant. AMF-FM, on the other hand, performs worse as the number of flows increases (according to our technical report [33]). Thus, with increasing link capacity, AMF-FM may face an increased number of actual flows, resulting in worse performance. In other words, AMF-FM's worst-case damage may be superlinear in link capacity. As a result, if CLEF outperforms AMF-FM in small links, CLEF will outperform AMF-FM by at least as large a ratio in larger links.

Background Traffic. We consider the worst background traffic for RLFD and CLEF: we determine the worst-case traffic in our technical report [33, Theorem 1]. Aside from attack traffic, the rest of the link capacity is completely filled with full-use legitimate flows running at the threshold rate $\gamma = 12.5\,\text{KB/s}$. The total number of attack flows and full-use legitimate flows is $n_\gamma = 10000$. Once a flow has been blacklisted by the large-flow detectors, we fill the idle bandwidth with a new full-use legitimate flow, to keep the link always running with the worst-case background traffic.

Attack Traffic. We evaluate each detector against large flows with various average rates R_{atk} and duty cycle θ. Their bursty period is set to be $T_b = 0.967\,\text{s}$. To evaluate RLFD and CLEF against their worst-case bursty flows ($\theta T_b < 2T_c$), large flows are allotted a relatively small bursty period $T_b = 4T_\ell = 0.967\text{s}$, where $T_\ell = \beta/\gamma = 0.242\,\text{s}$ is the period of each detection level in the single RLFD. In CLEF, RLFD$^{(1)}$ uses the same detection level period $T_\ell^{(1)} = T_\ell = 0.242\,\text{s}$ as well. Since RLFD usually has $d \geq 3$ levels and $T_c \geq 3T_\ell$, it is easy for attack flows to meet $\theta T_b < 2T_c$.

In each experiment, we have 10 artificial large flows whose rates are in the range of $12.5\,\text{KB/s}$ to $12.5\,\text{MB/s}$ (namely, 1 to 1000 times that of threshold rate γ). The fewer large flows in the link, the longer delay required for RLFD and CLEF to catch large flows; however, the easier it is for AMF-FM to detect large flows, because there are fewer FPs from AMF and more frequent flow eviction in FM. Thus, we use 10 attack flows to challenge CLEF and the results are generalizable.

Detector Settings. We evaluate detectors with different numbers of counters ($20 \leq m \leq 400$) to understand their performance under different memory limits. Although a few thousands of counters are available in a typical CPU, not all can be used by one detector scheme. CLEF works reasonably well with such a small number of counters and can perform better when more counters are available.

- **EARDet.** We set the low-bandwidth threshold to be the flow specification $\gamma t + \beta$, and compute the corresponding high-rate threshold, $\gamma_h = \frac{\rho}{m+1}$, for m counters as in [34].

- **RLFD**. A RLFD has d levels and m counters. We set the period of a detection level as $T_\ell = \beta/\gamma = 0.242\,\mathrm{s}^4$. $d = \lfloor 1.2 \times \log_m(n) \rfloor + 1$ to have fewer flows than the counters at the bottom level. The counter threshold of the bottom level is $TH_{RLFD} = \gamma T_\ell + \beta = 2\beta = 6056\,\mathrm{Bytes}$.
- **CLEF**. We allocate $m/2$ counters to EARDet, and $m/4$ counters to each RLFD. $\text{RLFD}^{(1)}$ and EARDet are configured like the single RLFD and the single EARDet above. For the $\text{RLFD}^{(2)}$, we properly set its detection level period $T_\ell^{(2)}$ to guarantee detection of most of bursty flows with low damage. The details of the single RLFD and CLEF are in our technical report [33].
- **AMF-FM**. We allocate half of the m counters to AMF and the rest to FM. AMF has four stages (a typical setting in [12]), each of which contains $m/8$ counters. All m counters are leaky buckets with a drain rate of γ and a bucket size β.

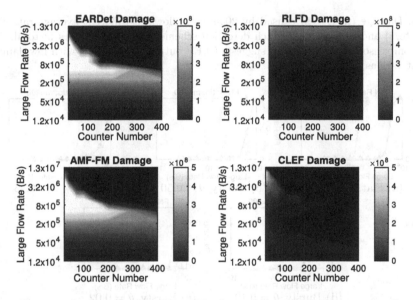

Fig. 4. Damage (in Bytes) caused by 200-s large flows at different average flow rate R_{atk} (in Byte/s) and duty cycle $\theta = 1.0$ (flat large flows) under detection of different schemes with different number of counters m. The larger the dark area, the lower the damage guaranteed by a scheme. Areas with white color are damage equals or exceeds 5×10^8. Figures of bursty flows are shown in our technical report [33]. CLEF outperforms other schemes in detecting flat flows, and has competitive performance to AMF-FM and EARDet over bursty flows.

5.2   Experiment Results

For each experiment setting (i.e., attack flow configurations and detector settings), we did 50 repeated runs and present the averaged results.

---

[4] If $T_\ell \ll \beta/\gamma$, it is hard for a large flow to reach the burst threshold β in such a short time; if $T_\ell \gg \beta/\gamma$, the detection delay is too long, resulting in excessive damage.

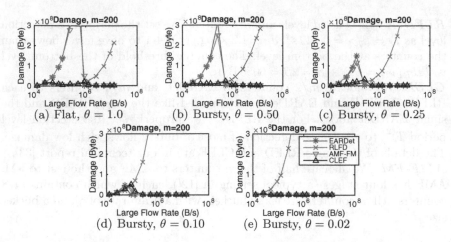

Fig. 5. Damage (in Bytes) caused by 200-s large flows at different average rate R_{atk} (in Byte/s) and duty cycle θ. Each detection scheme uses 200 counters in total. The clear comparison among schemes suggests CLEF outperforms others with low damage against various large flows.

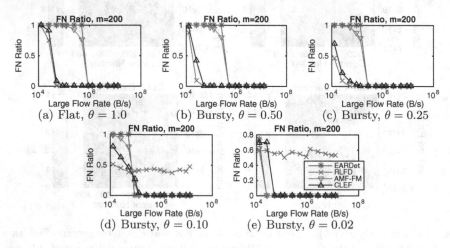

Fig. 6. FN ratio in a 200-s detection for large flows at different average rate R_{atk} (in Byte/s) and duty cycle θ. Each detection scheme uses 200 counters in total. CLEF is able to detect (FN < 1.0) low-rate flows undetectable (FN = 1.0) by AMF-FM or EARDet.

Figure 4 demonstrates the damage caused by large flows at different average rates, duty cycles, and number of detector counters during 200-s experiments; the lighter the color, the higher the damage. The damage $\geq 5 \times 10^8$ Byte is represented by the color white. Figures 5(a) to (e) compare damage in cases of different detectors with 200 counters. Figures 6(a) to (e) show the percentage of FNs produced by each detection scheme with 200 counters within 200 s. We cannot run infinitely-long experiments to show the $+\infty$ damage produced by detectors like EARDet and AMF-FM over low-rate flows, so we use the FN ratio to suggest it here. An FN of 1.0 means that the detector fails to identify any large flow in 200 s and is likely to miss large flows in the future. Thus, an infinite damage is assigned. On the contrary, if a detector has FN rate < 1.0, it is able to detect remaining large flows at some point in the future.

CLEF Ensures Low Damage Against Flat Flows. Figures 4, 5(a), and 6(a) show that RLFD and CLEF work effectively at detecting low-rate flat large flows and guaranteeing low damage. On the contrary, such flows cause much higher damage against EARDet and AMF-FM. The nearly-black figure (in Fig. 4) for CLEF shows that CLEF is effective for both high-rate and low-rate flat flows with different memory limits. Figure 5(a) shows a clear damage comparison among detector schemes. CLEF, EARDet, and AMF-FM all limit the damage to nearly zero for high-rate flat flows. However, the damage limited by CLEF is much lower than that limited by AMF-FM and EARDet for the low-rate flat flows. EARDet and AMF-FM results show a sharp top boundary that reflects the damage dropping to zero at the guaranteed-detection rates.

The damage limited by an individual RLFD is proportional to the large-flow rate when the flow rate is high. Figure 6(a) suggests that AMF-FM and EARDet are unable to catch most low-rate flat flows ($R_{atk} < 10^6$ Byte/sec), which explains the high damage by low-rate flat flows against these two schemes.

CLEF Ensures Low Damage Against Various Bursty Flows. Figures 5(b) to (e) demonstrate the damage caused by bursty flows with different duty cycle θ. The smaller the θ is, the burstier the flow. As the large flows become burstier, the EARDet and AMF-FM schemes improve at detecting flows whose average rate is low. Because the rate at the burst is R_{atk}/θ, which increases as θ decreases, thus EARDet and AMF-FM are able to detect these flows even though their average rates are low. For a single RLFD, the burstier the flows are, the harder it becomes to detect the large flows and limit the damage. As we discussed in Sect. 4.4, when the burst duration θT_b of flows is smaller than the RLFD detection cycle T_c, a single RLFD has nearly zero probability of detecting such attack flows. Thus, we need Twin-RLFD in CLEF to detect bursty flows missed by EARDet in CLEF, so that CLEF's damage is still low as the figures show. When the flow is very bursty (e.g., $\theta \leq 0.1$), the damage limitation of the CLEF scheme is dominated by EARDet.

Figures 5(b) to (e) present a clear comparison among different schemes against bursty flows. The damage limited by CLEF is lower than that limited by AMF-FM and EARDet, when θ is not too small (e.g., $\theta \geq 0.25$). Even though AMF-FM and EARDet have lower damage for very bursty flows (e.g., $\theta \leq 0.1$) than the damage limited by CLEF, the results are close because CLEF is assisted by an EARDet with $m/2$ counters. Thus, CLEF guarantees a low damage limit for a wider range of large flows than the other schemes.

CLEF Outperforms Others in Terms of FN and FP. To make our comparison more convincing, we examine schemes with classic metrics: FN and FP.

Since we know all four schemes have no FP, we simply check the FN ratios in Figs. 6(a) to (e). Generally, CLEF has a lower FN ratio than AMF-FM and EARDet do. CLEF can detect large flows at a much lower rate with zero FN ratio, and is competitive to AMF-FM and EARDet against very bursty flows (e.g., Figs. 6(b) and (e)).

CLEF is Memory-Efficient. Figure 4 shows that the damage limited by RLFD is relatively insensitive to the number of counters. This suggests that RLFD can work with limited memory and is scalable to larger links without requiring a large amount of high-speed memory. This can be explained by RLFD's recursive subdivision, by which we simply add one or more levels when the memory limit is low. Thus, we choose RLFD to complement EARDet in CLEF.

In Fig. 4, CLEF ensures a low damage (shown in black) with tens of counters, while AMF-FM suffers from a high damage (shown in light colors), even with 400 counters.

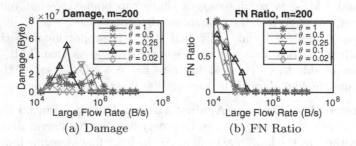

(a) Damage   (b) FN Ratio

Fig. 7. Damage and FN ratio for large flows at different average rate R_{atk} (in Byte/s) and duty cycle θ under detection of CLEF with $m = 200$ counters. CLEF is insensitive to bursty flows across duty cycles: (1) the damages are around the same scale (not keep increasing as duty cycle decrease, because of EARDet), (2) the FN ratios are stable and similar.

CLEF is Effective Against Various Types of Bursty Flows. Figures 7(a) and (b) demonstrate the changes of damage and FN ratio versus different duty cycles θ when CLEF is used to detect bursty flows. In the 200-s evaluation, as θ decreases, the maximum damage across different average flow rates increases first by ($\theta \geq 0.1$) and then decreases by ($\theta < 0.1$). The damage increases when $\theta \geq 0.1$ because Twin-RLFD (in CLEF) gradually loses its capability to detect bursty flows. The damage therefore increases due to the increase in detection delay.

However, the maximum damage does not increase all the way as θ decreases, because when θ is getting smaller, EARDet is able to catch bursty flows with a lower average rate. This explains the lower damage from large flows in the 200-s timeframe. Figure 7(b) shows that the FN ratio curve changes within a small range as θ decreases, which also indicates the stable performance of CLEF against various bursty flows. Moreover, the FN ratios are all below 1.0, which means that CLEF can eventually catch large flows, whereas EARDet and AMF-FM cannot.

CLEF Operates at High Speed. We also evaluated the performance of a Golang-based implementation under real-world traffic trace from the CAIDA [6] dataset. The implementation is able to process 11.8 M packets per second, which is sufficient for a 10 Gbps Ethernet link, which has a capacity of 14.4 M packets per second.

6   Related Work

The most closely related large-flow detection algorithms are described in Sect. 3.1 and compared in Sect. 5 and further in our technical report [33]. This section discusses other related schemes.

Frequent-Item Finding. Algorithms that find frequent items in a stream can be applied to large-flow detection. For example, Lossy Counting [24] maintains a lower bound and an upper bound of each item's count. It saves memory by periodically removing items with an upper bound below a threshold, but loses the ability to catch items close to the threshold. However, the theoretical memory lower bound of one-pass exact detection is linear to the number of large flows, which is unaffordable by in-core routers. By combining a frequent-item finding scheme with RLFD, CLEF can rapidly detect high-rate large flows and confine low-rate large flows using limited memory.

Collision-Rich Schemes. To reduce memory requirement in large-flow utilization, a common technique is hashing flows into a small number of bins. However, hash collisions may cause FPs, and FPs increase as the available memory shrinks. For example, both multistage filters [11,12] and space-code Bloom filters [18] suffer from high FPs when memory is limited.

Sampling-Based Schemes. Sampling-based schemes estimate the size of a flow based on sampled packets. However, with extremely limited memory and thus a low sampling rate, neither packet sampling (e.g., Sampled Netflow [8]) nor flow sampling (e.g., Sample and Hold [12] and Sticky Sampling [24]) can robustly identify large flows due to insufficient information. In contrast, RLFD in CLEF progressively narrows down the candidate set of large flows, thereby effectively confining the damage caused by large flows.

Top-k Detection. Top-k heavy hitter algorithms can be used to identify flows that use more than $1/k$ of bandwidth. Space Saving [25] finds the top-k frequent items by evicting the item with the lowest counter value. HashPipe [30] improves upon Space Saving so that it can be practically implemented on switching hardware. However, HashPipe still requires keeping 80 KB to detect large flows that use more than 0.3% of link capacity, whereas CLEF can enforce flow specifications as low as 10^{-6} of the link capacity using only 10 KB of memory. Tong et al. [31] propose an efficient heavy hitter detector implemented on FPGA but the enforceable flow specifications are several orders looser than CLEF.

Moreover, misbehaving flows close to the flow specification can easily bypass such heavy hitter detectors. The FPs caused by heavy hitters prevent network operators from applying strong punishment to the detected flows.

Chen et al. [7] and Xiao et al. [35] propose memory-efficient algorithms for estimating per-flow cardinality (e.g., the number of packets). These algorithms, however, cannot guarantee large-flow detection in adversarial environments due to under- or over-estimation of the flow size.

Liu et al. [22] propose a generic network monitoring framework called UniMon that allows extraction of various flow statistics. It creates flow statistics for all flows, but has high FP and FN when used to detect large flows.

7   Conclusion

In this paper we propose new efficient large-flow detection algorithms. First, we develop a randomized Recursive Large-Flow Detection (RLFD) scheme, which uses very little memory yet provides eventual detection of persistently large flows. Second, we develop CLEF, which scales to Internet core routers and is resilient against worst-case traffic. None of the prior approaches can achieve the same level of resilience with the same memory limitations. To compare attack resilience among various detectors, we define a damage metric that summarizes the impact of attack traffic on legitimate traffic. CLEF can confine damage even when faced with the worst-case background traffic because it combines a deterministic EARDet for the rapid detection of very large flows and two RLFDs to detect near-threshold large flows. We denomstrated that CLEF is able to guarantee low-damage large-flow detection against various attack flows with limited memory, outperforming other schemes even with CLEF's worst-case background traffic. Further experimental evaluation confirms the findings of our theoretical analysis and shows that CLEF has the lowest worst-case damage among all detectors and consistently low damage over a wide range of attack flows.

Acknowledgments. We thank Pratyaksh Sharma and Prateesh Goyal for early work on this project as part of their summer internship at ETH in Summer 2015. We also thank the anonymous reviewers, whose feedback helped to improve the paper.

The research leading to these results has received funding from the European Research Council under the European Union's Seventh Framework Programme (FP7/2007-2013), ERC grant agreement 617605, the Ministry of Science and Technology of Taiwan under grant number MOST 107-2636-E-002-005, and the US National Science Foundation under grant numbers CNS-1717313 and CNS-0953600. We also gratefully acknowledge support from ETH Zurich and from the Zurich Information Security and Privacy Center (ZISC).

References

1. Andersen, D.G., Balakrishnan, H., Feamster, N., Koponen, T., Moon, D., Shenker, S.: Accountable internet protocol (AIP). In: Proceedings of ACM SIGCOMM (2008). https://doi.org/10.1145/1402958.1402997
2. Anderson, T., et al.: The NEBULA future internet architecture. In: Galis, A., Gavras, A. (eds.) FIA 2013. LNCS, vol. 7858, pp. 16–26. Springer, Heidelberg (2013). https://doi.org/10.1007/978-3-642-38082-2_2
3. Antonakakis, M., et al.: Understanding the Mirai botnet. In: USENIX Security Symposium (2017)
4. Basescu, C., et al.: SIBRA: scalable internet bandwidth reservation architecture. In: Proceedings of Network and Distributed System Security Symposium (NDSS), February 2016
5. Braden, R., Clark, D., Shenker, S.: Integrated services in the internet architecture: an overview. RFC 1633 (Informational), June 1994. http://www.ietf.org/rfc/rfc1633.txt
6. CAIDA: CAIDA Anonymized Internet Traces 2016 (2016). https://data.caida.org/datasets/passive-2016/
7. Chen, M., Chen, S., Cai, Z.: Counter tree: a scalable counter architecture for per-flow traffic measurement. IEEE/ACM Trans. Netw. (TON) **25**(2), 1249–1262 (2017)
8. Claise, B.: Cisco Systems NetFlow Services Export Version 9, RFC 3954 (Informational), October 2004. http://www.ietf.org/rfc/rfc3954.txt
9. Cormode, G., Muthukrishnan, S.: An improved data stream summary: the count-min sketch and its applications. J. Algorithms **55**(1), 58–75 (2005). https://doi.org/10.1016/j.jalgor.2003.12.001
10. Demaine, E.D., López-Ortiz, A., Munro, J.I.: Frequency estimation of internet packet streams with limited space. In: Möhring, R., Raman, R. (eds.) ESA 2002. LNCS, vol. 2461, pp. 348–360. Springer, Heidelberg (2002). https://doi.org/10.1007/3-540-45749-6_33
11. Estan, C.: Internet traffic measurement: what's going on in my network? Ph.D. thesis (2003)
12. Estan, C., Varghese, G.: New directions in traffic measurement and accounting: focusing on the elephants, ignoring the mice. ACM Trans. Comput. Syst. (TOCS) **21**(3), 270–313 (2003). http://dl.acm.org/citation.cfm?id=859719
13. Fang, M., Shivakumar, N.: Computing iceberg queries efficiently. In: Proceedings of VLDB (1999). http://ilpubs.stanford.edu:8090/423/
14. Han, D., et al.: XIA: efficient support for evolvable internetworking. In: Proceedings of the 9th USENIX NSDI, San Jose, CA, April 2012
15. Intel: Intel Xeon Processor E7 v4 Family (2016). https://ark.intel.com/products/series/93797/Intel-Xeon-Processor-E7-v4-Family
16. Karp, R.M., Shenker, S., Papadimitriou, C.H.: A simple algorithm for finding frequent elements in streams and bags. ACM Trans. Database Syst. **28**(1), 51–55 (2003). https://doi.org/10.1145/762471.762473
17. Kim, T.H.J., Basescu, C., Jia, L., Lee, S.B., Hu, Y.C., Perrig, A.: Lightweight source authentication and path validation. In: ACM SIGCOMM Computer Communication Review, vol. 44, pp. 271–282. ACM (2014)
18. Kumar, A., Xu, J., Wang, J.: Space-code bloom filter for efficient per-flow traffic measurement. IEEE J. Sel. Areas Commun. **24**(12), 2327–2339 (2006)

19. Lee, S.B., Kang, M.S., Gligor, V.D.: CoDef: collaborative defense against large-scale link-flooding attacks. In: Proceedings of CoNext (2013)
20. Li, A., Liu, X., Yang, X.: Bootstrapping accountability in the internet we have. In: Proceedings of USENIX/ACM NSDI, March 2011
21. Liu, X., Li, A., Yang, X., Wetherall, D.: Passport: secure and adoptable source authentication. In: Proceedings of USENIX/ACM NSDI (2008). http://www.usenix.org/event/nsdi08/tech/full_papers/liu_xin/liu_xin_html/
22. Liu, Z., Manousis, A., Vorsanger, G., Sekar, V., Braverman, V.: One sketch to rule them all: rethinking network flow monitoring with UnivMon. In: ACM SIGCOMM (2016). https://doi.org/10.1145/2934872.2934906
23. Liu, Z., Jin, H., Hu, Y.C., Bailey, M.: MiddlePolice: toward enforcing destination-defined policies in the middle of the internet. In: Proceedings of ACM CCS, October 2016
24. Manku, G., Motwani, R.: Approximate frequency counts over data streams. In: Proceedings of VLDB (2002). http://dl.acm.org/citation.cfm?id=1287400
25. Metwally, A., Agrawal, D., El Abbadi, A.: Efficient computation of frequent and top-k elements in data streams. In: Eiter, T., Libkin, L. (eds.) ICDT 2005. LNCS, vol. 3363, pp. 398–412. Springer, Heidelberg (2004). https://doi.org/10.1007/978-3-540-30570-5_27
26. Misra, J., Gries, D.: Finding repeated elements. Sci. Comput. Program. **2**(2), 143–152 (1982)
27. Naous, J., Walfish, M., Nicolosi, A., Mazières, D., Miller, M., Seehra, A.: Verifying and enforcing network paths with ICING. In: Proceedings of ACM CoNEXT (2011). https://doi.org/10.1145/2079296.2079326
28. Pagh, R., Rodler, F.F.: Cuckoo hashing. In: auf der Heide, F.M. (ed.) ESA 2001. LNCS, vol. 2161, pp. 121–133. Springer, Heidelberg (2001). https://doi.org/10.1007/3-540-44676-1_10
29. Shenker, S., Partridge, C., Guerin, R.: Specification of guaranteed quality of service, RFC 2212 (Proposed Standard), September 1997. http://www.ietf.org/rfc/rfc2212.txt
30. Sivaraman, V., Narayana, S., Rottenstreich, O., Muthukrishnan, S., Rexford, J.: Heavy-hitter detection entirely in the data plane. In: Proceedings of the Symposium on SDN Research, pp. 164–176. ACM (2017)
31. Tong, D., Prasanna, V.: High throughput sketch based online heavy hitter detection on FPGA. ACM SIGARCH Comput. Arch. News **43**(4), 70–75 (2016)
32. Trybulec, W.A.: Pigeon hole principle. J. Formaliz. Math. **2**, 4 (1990)
33. Wu, H., Hsiao, H.C., Asoni, D.E., Scherrer, S., Perrig, A., Hu, Y.C.: CLEF: limiting the damage caused by large flows in the internet core. Technical report, arXiv:1807.05652 [cs.NI], arXiv (2018). https://arxiv.org/abs/1807.05652
34. Wu, H., Hsiao, H.C., Hu, Y.C.: Efficient large flow detection over arbitrary windows: an algorithm exact outside an ambiguity region. In: Proceedings of the 2014 Conference on Internet Measurement Conference, pp. 209–222. ACM (2014)
35. Xiao, Q., Chen, S., Chen, M., Ling, Y.: Hyper-compact virtual estimators for big network data based on register sharing. In: ACM SIGMETRICS Performance Evaluation Review, vol. 43, pp. 417–428. ACM (2015)
36. Zhang, X., Hsiao, H.C., Hasker, G., Chan, H., Perrig, A., Andersen, D.G.: SCION: scalability, control, and isolation on next-generation networks. In: IEEE Symposium on Security and Privacy, pp. 212–227 (2011)

Towards Video Compression
in the Encrypted Domain: A Case-Study
on the H264 and HEVC Macroblock
Processing Pipeline

Donald Nokam Kuate[1,2(✉)], Sebastien Canard[1], and Renaud Sirdey[2]

[1] Orange Labs, Applied Crypto Group, Caen, France
donald.nokamkuate@orange.com
[2] CEA, LIST, Gif-sur-Yvette, France

Abstract. Image/video compression is a widely used operation in our everyday life. Such an operation usually proceeds independantly on small rectangular portions, so-called macroblocks, and is mainly divided into four operations: color conversion, Discrete Cosine Transform (DCT), quantization and entropic encoding. This operation is carried out easily on non-encrypted image. In this paper, we consider the case where such an execution is done in the encrypted domain. In fact, this is today one central question related to individuals' privacy since such image/video compression is most of the time done on the premises of a service provider data center, and pictures are potentially sensitive personal data. Thus, the capacity for such entity to perform an action "blindfolded", that is not knowing the underlying input in plain, is an important topic since it permits to obtain both individual privacy and data usability.

In this context, one of the main cryptographic tool is (fully) homomorphic encryption (FHE), that permits to perform operations while keeping the data encrypted. We here consider two different instantiations of FHE, one for which the plaintext space is binary ($\mathbb{Z}_2$) and the other a modular space ($\mathbb{Z}_p$ for an integer $p > 2$), and compare them when running the well-known H264 and HEVC macroblock processing pipelines.

Our contribution is twofold. On one hand, we provide an exhaustive comparison between FHEs over $\mathbb{Z}_2$ and FHEs over $\mathbb{Z}_p$ ($p > 2$) in terms of functional capabilities, multiplicative depth and real performances using several existing FHE implementations, over libraries such as `Cingulata`, `SEAL` and `TFHE`. On the other hand, we apply this to image compression in the encrypted domain, being the first to "crypto-compress" a full encrypted photograph with practically relevant performances.

1 Introduction

Homomorphic encryption is a set of cryptographic techniques which allow to compute algebraic functions on encrypted data and obtain correct results after

This work was supported in part by projects PerSoCLoud (for the two first authors) and CRYPTOCOMP (for the third author).

J. Camenisch and P. Papadimitratos (Eds.): CANS 2018, LNCS 11124, pp. 109–129, 2018.
https://doi.org/10.1007/978-3-030-00434-7_6

decryption. This idea was born with the work of Rivest et al. [23] on *privacy homomorphisms*. In that work, they also proposed some additive homomorphic schemes which, unfortunately, were broken a few years later. The idea of a Fully Homomorphic Encryption (FHE) remained speculative for more than 30 years.

The first theoretical construction of an encryption scheme able to perform both homomorphic addition and multiplication operations in an arbitrary manner came from the work of Gentry in 2009 [17]. To obtain a FHE scheme, Gentry's initial idea has been to use a somewhat homomorphic scheme (SHE) i.e., a scheme capable to perform a limited number of homomorphic additions and multiplications, and to associate it with what he has called *bootstrapping*. Indeed, SHE schemes necessarily introduce noise at the time of encryption, this noise increases in the ciphertext with operations to the point where the latter cannot be decrypted correctly. Bootstrapping solves this issue by allowing to "refresh" the ciphertext by reducing the noise back to a constant small-enough amplitude, thus allowing further homomorphic calculations. Starting from this technique, several S/FHE schemes have emerged, and among them we can mention the most know ones as BGV [3] that can be found in the `HElib` library [18] and FV [15] found in `SEAL` [8] and in `Cingulata` [20]. We can also mention the scheme TFHE [11] found in the library of the same name [10].

The implementation of these algorithms is carried out according to two main types of techniques: the first one (called Type I in this paper) consists in working with a plaintext equal to $\mathbb{Z}_2$ and makes it possible to easily transform a binary operation in the clear domain to the encrypted one; the second technique (called Type II) uses $\mathbb{Z}_p$ (for an integer $p > 2$) as plaintext which trades off better execution times for more limited functionalities in relation to the clear domain. In this paper, our first result is to provide a detailed comparative study of these two types of FHE usage.

To get concrete, we confront both approaches through the (encrypted-domain) execution of the compression pipeline of a video/image. More precisely, we study both the H264 and HEVC macroblock processing pipelines and their underlying algorithms: (i) color space conversion RGB to and from YCrCb, (ii) Discrete Cosine Transform (DCT) and (iii) quantization. For each of them, we study and compare the different implementation strategies for Type I and Type II FHE schemes and finally compare the final result when using the best strategy of each. We think that this case study is a good choice for studying homomorphic encryption schemes since it includes a number of well-defined algorithms of moderate complexity. It also corresponds to a real-world need since it may permit to manipulate images and videos by some non-trusted entities, in an encrypted way. Such tool can be very useful to protect sensitive data, and to protect the personal data (and thus the privacy) of individuals. In fact, our study gives a precise idea of which mechanism to use if we want to make the compression of image or video in the homomorphic domain.

1.1 Related Work

Some comparison work between certain FHE cryptosystems have already been done in the past. In particular, Lepoint and Naehrig [19] propose a comparison between the FV and YASHE schemes by using them both to (homomorphically) evaluate the symmetric block cipher SIMON. Their aim was to give meaningful insights into which scheme to use according to the desired application. For this purpose, they study the parameters to be used in each case and provide a C implementation of both schemes. In [12], Costache and Smart provide a comparison between NTRU/YASHE and BGV/FV. The way they analyze both families is quite similar to the strategy used in [19], but they consider more variants (especially in relation to key and modulus switching), they do not restrict to characteristic two and they implement both schemes using the same API and the same optimizations. We here consider a very different approach by studying the way a given algorithm executed in the encrypted domain can be derived depending on the input SHE scheme (and its main properties). We do not re-implement those schemes but consider existing libraries, namely `Cingulata`, `SEAL` and `TFHE`.

Encrypted image compression is a problem that has also been addressed in the past, mainly in the medical field, for the protection of medical images to be stored on a remote server. With that respect, we can cite the work in [26] which uses secret key encryption to encrypt images and resize them in the discrete cosine domain. We can also mention the work in [25] which uses a modified version of BGV to perform some functions on the images. In [6], the authors analyse the elementary Run-Length Encoding (RLE) compression algorithm using the `Cingulata` implementation of the FV scheme. As far as we know, no previous work has attempted to implement a complete version of real-world image compression algorithms, namely H264 and HEVC, when the data are encrypted.

1.2 Our Contributions

As a summary, we investigate in this work the execution of a macroblock compression pipeline on encrypted data using two approaches: one, called Type I, with an FHE over $\mathbb{Z}_2$ (i.e. with bit-by-bit encryption) and another, called Type II, with an FHE over $\mathbb{Z}_p$ (where $p > 2$ is chosen large enough). For our case study, we take both H264 and HEVC compression algorithms and give details on their main three steps: (i) the conversion of RGB based original image to a YCrCb representation, (ii) the Discrete Cosine Transform (DCT) to transform the representation of block's coefficients into the frequency domain and (iii) the quantization to finally achieve (lossy) compression. We recall the way each step is usually performed, and then give details on the way it should be done in the encrypted domain when using either a Type I FHE or a Type II FHE. We finally compare the results we obtain in each case. As a proof that FHE is today quite close to practicality in the image/video compression domain, we apply our results to the H.264 and HEVC compression of a true 128×128 image and show that the performances are non-prohibitive.

Our contribution is then both a complete study on the way such compression algorithms can be almost practically implemented in the encrypted domain, and a full comparison on the way to manipulate FHE schemes over $\mathbb{Z}_2$ and over $\mathbb{Z}_p$ ($p > 2$) in practice. We believe that both insights, of independent interest, will be in the future useful for homomorphic encryption real deployment in privacy-preserving services.

1.3   Organization of the Paper

This paper is organized as follows. In Sect. 2, we give some preliminaries on both compression pipeline and homomorphic encryption. Section 3 compares the two approaches (Type I and Type II) for homomorphic encryption, in terms of plaintext representation, ciphertext representation, and possible gate operations. In Sect. 4, we details our approaches for the execution of conversion, DCT and quantization in the encrypted domain. Section 5 is devoted to the implementation and show our practical results. We finally conclude in Sect. 6.

2   Preliminaries

2.1   Notation

Throughout this paper, we use the following notation. $\mathbb{Z}$ is the ring of integers. For an integer $p > 0$, $\mathbb{Z}_p$ is the ring of integers modulo p. We note R to refer to the ring of polynomials $\frac{\mathbb{Z}[x]}{\varPhi}$ modulo an irreducible polynomial monic $\varPhi$. In practice, one often chooses $\varPhi$ to be the m-th cyclotomic polynomial, with m a power of 2. For an integer p, $R_p = \frac{\mathbb{Z}[x]}{(\varPhi, p)}$ is the ring of polynomials modulo $\varPhi$ with coefficients in $\mathbb{Z}_p$. $\mathbb{T}$ refers to the torus $\frac{\mathbb{R}[x]}{(\varPhi, 1)}$ which is the ring of polynomials modulo polynomial $\varPhi$, with coefficients in interval $[0, 1[$. We note a polynomial and its coefficients in lowercase. A matrix and its coefficients are represented in bold uppercase; i.e. if $\mathbf{A}$ is a matrix, $\mathbf{A}_{i,j}$ is its coefficient at position (i, j). We note $\mathbf{A}^T$ the transposed of a matrix $\mathbf{A}$.

We use $\oplus$ and $\otimes$ to represent the operations XOR and AND respectively between two clear or encrypted bits. When there is no ambiguity, we use $\cdot$ in place of $\otimes$. $\ll$ and $\gg$ represent the left and right shift respectively. We use MSB to indicate the most significant bit for both clear and encrypted bit representations (see Type I FHE below). We use $[x]$ to refer to a ciphertext which encrypts the plaintext x. For a rational number a, we note $\lfloor a \rceil$ the nearest integer to a and $\lfloor a \rfloor$ the integer part of a. In the FHE field, one usually consider the (multiplicative) depth of a circuit as the largest number of multiplication gates (or gate AND, see below) in an input-to-output path in the circuit. Addition gates are generally ignored. We use this definition throughout this work.

2.2   Compressor/Decompressor

A digital image is the discretization of a natural image obtained through analog-digital conversion techniques. A freshly captured image usually contains a lot of redundant informations. To be used later, for storage and distribution, it is necessary to suppress this useless informations by means of a *compression* algorithm. Image and video compression involves applying a well-defined sequence of basic algorithms to an input digital image. Its purpose is to reduce its size and transmission rate without reducing the quality (or in a controlled way). Over the time, several standards for image and video compression have been defined and the most well-known ones are *JPEG, MPEG2 to MPEG4* or *H261 to H265/HEVC*. But in fact, all of them share the same set of core algorithms (given in Fig. 1 for the case of the *JPEG* compression algorithm):

– the **RGB to YCrCb color space conversion algorithm** which aims at transforming a RGB representation of the color space into a YCrCb representation which is a more convenient domain for color manipulations. This conversion is given by a linear transformation on coordinates;
– the **Discrete Cosine Transform (DCT)** which is used for its capacity to compact a signal information since this latter can be concentrated into a few low-frequency components of the DCT. As the Discrete Fourier Transform, a DCT is a mathematical decomposition (a sum of sinusoids) of a finite number of regularly sampled discrete data points;
– the **quantization** is finally a process permitting to reduce the range of DCT coefficients and defines the quality of output image.

More details on each step will be given in Sect. 4, which also includes the decompression part, which one corresponds to the inverses of the three same steps, with some specificities that will be detailed further.

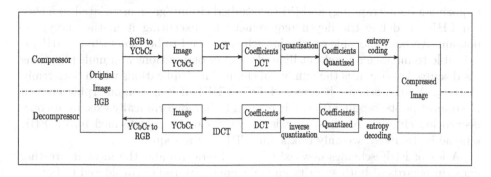

Fig. 1. Model of compressor/decompressor pipeline of type jpeg

In this paper, our objective is to work on those three algorithms in the encrypted domain. For that purpose, we have to describe each of them so as to be compatible with FHE schemes.

2.3   FHE with Binary/Digital Plaintext

An homomorphic encryption (HE) scheme consists in the specification of four algorithms KeyGen, Enc, Dec, Eval defined as follows:

- KeyGen takes as input the security parameter λ and returns a secret key sk, a public key k and an evaluation key evk;
- Enc takes as input a message m, a public key pk and returns a ciphertext ct which encrypts m;
- Dec takes as input a ciphertext ct which encrypts m under pk, a secret key sk associated to pk and returns the plaintext m;
- Eval takes as input a homomorphic description of a n entries circuit $\mathcal{C}$, n ciphertexts $ct_1, \ldots, ct_n$ encrypting respectively $m_1, \ldots, m_n$ under pk and the evaluation key evk. It returns a ciphertext $ct_{\mathcal{C}}$ which encrypts message $\mathcal{C}(m_1, \ldots, m_n)$ under pk.

In practice, a circuit is composed of a succession of basic gates and a HE scheme is capable of executing such basic gates in the encrypted domain. Any Turing machine can be described by a succession of additions (XOR gate) and multiplications (AND gate) but there are also some other basic gates that can be used in a circuit (as we will explain in the next section). In practical SHE constructions, each gate executed in the encrypted domain produces new ciphertexts with increased noise such that the latter, given on input to the Dec procedure, may give an incorrect plaintext if the noise is too important. This phenomenon is almost negligible for the XOR gate, and much more problematic for the AND one, so that most of the time, only the latter is taken into account. The purpose of the so-called *bootstrapping* operation [17] is to remove most of this noise, and then perform more operations in the encrypted domain. The notion of (multiplicative) *depth* is then usually used both for (i) the homomorphic encryption scheme to define the number of AND gates that the scheme can manage (before requiring a bootstrapping) and (ii) the studied circuit/gate, associated to a chosen FHE, to define the depth requirement for executing it in the encrypted domain. An homomorphic encryption scheme is said to be "somewhat" (SHE) if it is able to manage a fixed but limited number of additions and multiplications (as discussed above, it is the number of chained multiplications which does really matter). A SHE scheme becomes "fully" (FHE), if it is homomorphic enough to support bootstrapping (meaning enough to homomorphically execute its own decryption circuit). As most of existing SHE can be transformed into a FHE scheme by this way, we only talk about FHE in the sequel.

A lot of FHE schemes now exist in the literature and the most interesting ones (in regards of both security and efficiency) are today considered to be:

- the Brakerski-Gentry-Vaikuntanathan [3] scheme (**BGV**) which is implemented, with a bootsptrapping mechanism, in HElib [18];

- the Fan-Vercauteren [15] scheme (**FV**), implemented in SEAL [8] and in the compiler toochain `Cingulata`[1] [20]. Today, both implementations do not integrate the bootstrapping even if this is feasible for the FV scheme, as shown in [7,15] (related to the SEAL library);
- the **TFHE** [11] scheme which directly includes a bootstrapping and for which an implementation can be found in [10].

FHE schemes are also split into several so-called *generations*, defined following the underground algebraic structure in the scheme (integer, lattice, ideal-lattice, torus structure), capacities of schemes (SHE, leveled-FHE, SHE with bootstrapping, etc.) and also their effectiveness. The two first schemes above belong to the so-called *2nd generation*, and the last one to the *4th generation*.

Our aim is now to compare those different FHE instantiations and implementations and the way to use them for concrete use cases (in our case, image/video compression). A first step is done in the next section.

3   Capacities and Limitations of Main Stream FHE Class

To evaluate an algorithm in the encrypted domain, we need to transform it into a circuit that is compatible with a FHE scheme. In practice, a circuit can be described as a succession of basic gates that can be evaluated with encrypted inputs using the Eval procedure of the FHE scheme. Regarding the details of existing FHE implementations (see above), one can remark that there are different strategies on the way to encode the input plaintext. More than that, from one FHE scheme, several instantiations are possible (see the discussion below). The main point is that, when considering the circuit to be executed in the encrypted domain, the way input data are encoded is an essential information since it influences the way to describe the circuit, and the basic gates to be used. The aim of this section is exactly to describe the different possible strategies.

- **Type I FHE:** the input is encoded bitwise and the encryption then consists in one ciphertext for each bit of the plaintext.
- **Type II FHE:** the input is directly encoded using a polynomial or an integer and, in this case, the ciphertext is directly the encryption of the whole plaintext.

We now present in details these two encoding types and their respective properties. We first give some precisions on the input representation, then on the ciphertext one. We then focus on the possible basic operations that can be performed using such representation. In fact, even if the data is not encrypted, the way to describe an algorithm depends on the way the inputs are encoded. Moreover, as we want to execute such algorithms in the encrypted domain, the different options are closely related to the real feasibility to execute such gates

---

[1] `Cingulata` transforms a C++ program in the boolean circuit and execute it over bitewise encrypted data. It also enables to choose the underground FHE which encrypts input data. The current version is based on the FV FHE scheme.

and the efficiency of the resulted execution (as we will see below), in particular regarding the depth's growth.

Note that each FHE scheme can be instantiated in different manners, and implementing a FHE scheme necessitates to choose first one possible instantiation. It is easy to remark that a Type II FHE scheme can also be instantiated (and then the implementation) as a Type I FHE. For example, the FV scheme [15] is instantiated as a Type I FHE in `Cingulata` [20] and as Type II FHE in `SEAL` [8]. Similarly, the BGV scheme [3] can described in both types, and the `HElib` library [18] has chosen to instantiate it in the Type II case.

3.1   Type I: FHE over Binary Plaintext Space

In Type I FHEs, the idea is to reproduce the way a classic microprocessor is working. We here give some more details on the plaintext space and then go the case of the ciphertext. We then redefine some useful gates such that they become compatible with the ciphertext representation of a Type I FHE.

Plaintext Space $\mathcal{M}_I$. In existing works, there are three main classes of plaintext spaces for a Type I FHE

In general, the plaintext space associated to a Type I FHE can simply be seen as the set $\{0, 1\}$. Then, the encoding of an input consists in taking its binary decomposition.

Ciphertext Representation. Using the bitwise encoding, each bit of the input is then encrypted independently. Thus, the ciphertext related to the input is a set of encrypted bits and the relation between them is done as for the plaintext.

Operations. We now consider a set of gates that are at the basis of most of circuits, and especially those useful in our running example of compression. We consider the way each of them can be performed using a Type I FHE. We then consider two plaintexts a and b and their corresponding ciphertexts denoted, using the bitwise representation, $[a] = [a_n] [a_{n-1}] \ldots [a_0]$ and $[b] = [b_n] [b_{n-1}] \ldots [b_0]$.

- Addition: taking on input both ciphertexts $[a]$ and $[b]$, the addition in the encrypted domain is given by the relation

$$[a + b] = [s] = [c_{n+1}] [s_n] [s_{n-1}] \ldots [s_0]$$

where encrypted bits of $[s]$ are defined by the following relation, $[c_i]$ being the carry,

$$[s_0] = [a_0] \oplus [b_0], \quad [c_0] = [a_0] \cdot [b_0];$$
$$\text{and } [s_{i>0}] = [a_i] \oplus [b_i] \oplus [c_{i-1}], \quad [c_{i>0}] = [a_0] \cdot [b_0] \oplus [c_{i-1}] ([a_i] \oplus [b_i]).$$

- Multiplication: using on input $[a]$ and $[b]$, the multiplication can here be constructed in "a pencil and paper way", using some tricks with additions and shifts (see [24]).

- Scalar multiplication: on input a ciphertext $[a]$ and a scalar $t = t_0 + t_1 2 + \ldots t_n 2^n$, the scalar multiplication is done as

$$[t \cdot a] = (t_0 \cdot [a]) + ((t_1 \cdot [a]) \ll 1) + \cdots + ((t_n \cdot [a]) \ll (n-1)).$$

- Shift: let $r < n$ and $[x] = [x_r][x_{r-1}]\ldots[x_0]$ be a ciphertext, and let m be an integer. The shift operation ($\ll$ or $\gg$) is given by

$$[x \ll m] = [x_r][x_{r-1}]\ldots[x_0]\underbrace{[0][0]\ldots[0]}_{m} \quad \text{for } m \leq n - r$$

$$[x \gg m] = \underbrace{[0][0]\ldots[0]}_{m}[x_r][x_{r-1}]\ldots[x_{r-m}] \quad \text{for } m \leq r$$

(a signed right shift can also be performed by replication of the encrypted sign bit).
- Scalar division: for the scalar division, the idea is to obtain $[a/t]$ given a ciphertext $[a]$ and a scalar $t = t_0 + t_1 2 + \ldots t_n 2^n$. A simple approach consists in first multiplying (in the clear domain) $1/t$ by a power of two, say 2^m for a chosen m, obtaining t' and then returning $\left[(a \cdot t') \gg m\right]$ using scalar multiplication and shift gates above. When t is not equal to a power of two, this result is only an approximation of the real scalar division. To get an appropriate precision, one should take a larger value for m.
- Comparison: using bitwise representation, one possible strategy to perform comparison, that is obtain $[a > b]$ given $[a]$ and $[b]$, is to do

$$[a > b] = MSB([a - b]), \text{the most significant encrypted bit of } [a - b].$$

One can also find some more sophisticated strategies in the literature [16], essentially constructed for Multi-Party Computation but which can be adapted to the case of homomorphic encryption, but we only consider this one in the sequel, essentially for its simplicity and better efficiency.
- Conditional assignment: finally, the conditional assignment if ϵ, then a, else b, on input an encrypted bit $[\epsilon]$ and two ciphertexts $[a]$ and $[b]$, is given by:

$$[c] = [\epsilon]?[a]:[b] \Leftrightarrow [c] = [\epsilon \cdot a + (1 \oplus \epsilon) \cdot b]$$

which can be executed using the above basic methods.

Using a Type I FHE scheme, all these algorithms can then be efficiently implemented. The corresponding multiplicative depth is then given in Table 1 (left part) and they will be used as a basis of compression algorithms in the next section, with performances are given in Sect. 5. The advantage of Type I FHEs is that they have no real limitations on what can be executed in the encrypted domain (at least in principle, see below). Some of them are even very cheap, such as the scalar multiplication by a power of 2 which can be done with a simple left shift.

Also note that the intrinsic semantic security of a FHE scheme allows to execute only static control-structure programs. This is well-known for the "while" loop but this has also been noted for more complex algorithms, such as in [6]. Fortunately, general programs can in principle (automatically) be turned into static control-structure ones with only logarithmic overhead.

Table 1. Comparison of functional capabilities of Type I and Type II FHEs.

Operations	Type I		Type II	
	Possible?	Depth	Possible?	Depth
Addition	Yes	$n-1$	Yes	0
Multiplication	Yes	$n-1$	Yes	1
Scalar division	Yes	See Remark 1	Yes	1
Scalar mult.	Yes	See Remark 1	Yes	0
Shift	Yes	0	Yes	1
Comparison	Yes	$\log_2 n$	No	-
Cond. assignment	Yes	$\log_2 n$	No	-

Remark 1. With Type I FHE the number of operations (and the multiplicative depth) required to perform a multiplication or a division by a public scalar depends on the scalar value itself. In fact, when a computation mixes encrypted and cleartext inputs, some FHE operations can be simplified (e.g., adding 0 to a ciphertext gives the same ciphertext, as multiplying a ciphertext by 1, etc.).

3.2   Type II: FHEs with Polynomial Ring over $\mathbb{Z}_{p>2}$

We now consider Type II FHE schemes and again give some details on the plaintext and ciphertext spaces and then indicates how to implement basic gates in this case.

Plaintext Space $\mathcal{M}_{II}$. In Type II FHEs, the plaintext space is either an integer ring modulo $p > 2$, denoted $\mathbb{Z}_p$, or a polynomial ring modulo a cyclotomic polynomial having coefficients in $\mathbb{Z}_p$, denoted R_p. Even if there may be some other mathematical structures falling into this case, these are the two main used ones in FHE schemes. The case of integers has been used in several theoretical papers in the past but, essentially for efficiency reasons, the polynomial representation is today preferred (e.g., in the `HElib` and `SEAL` libraries). To encode the inputs of an algorithm in this case, we need to transform them (i) into integers in $\mathbb{Z}_p$, thanks for example to first a scalar multiplication by a large integer and then a rounding to the nearest integer, or (ii) into elements in R_p, using for example the method given in [9,13]. In general, this is done by decomposing a given input in some fixed basis B and by defining the plaintext as a polynomial which coefficients are those of the decomposition in that base.

Example 1. For $B = 3$ in the SEAL library, we have the following decomposition, where n is the degree of the cyclotomic polynomial for the ring R_p

$$a = 13 = 1 + 3 + 3^2 \rightarrow \text{ plaintext } a(x) = 1 + x + x^2;$$

$$b = \frac{328}{27} = 3^2 + 3 + 3^{-2} + 3^{-3} \rightarrow \text{ plaintext } b(x) = x^2 + x - x^{n-2} - x^{n-3}$$

Note that the way to represent a plaintext in $\mathcal{M}_{II}$ is in practice done in accordance with the homomorphic operations.

Ciphertext Representation. The ciphertext corresponding to an input is then obtained by the encryption of the polynomial representing the plaintext. For an input a, the ciphertext is equal to $[a(x)]$.

Operations. From two plaintexts a and b and their corresponding ciphertexts $[a]$ and $[b]$, we again consider the basic gates that have been studied for Type I and consider now the case of Type II.

– Addition: the way to perform an addition depends on used FHE and is defined in accordance with the addition of elements of $\mathbb{Z}_p$ or R_p.
– Multiplication: the way to proceed is similar to the one for addition.
– Scalar multiplication: simple multiplication of the coefficients of the ciphertext by the input scalar.
– Scalar Division: given a ciphertext $[a]$ and a scalar t, the best idea is to encode the inverse of t and use it as in a scalar multiplication. For example, the computation of $[5/8]$ is done by encoding $5/8 = 2^{-1} + 2^{-3}$ in $x^{n-1} + x^{n-3}$ and then returning $[a \cdot (x^{n-1} + x^{n-3})]$. Another (less efficient) way to proceed is to encrypt t^{-1} and then multiply it by $[a]$.
– Shift: this operation is not directly provided in Type II FHE (contrary to the Type I). It can however be obtained by scaling the ciphertext by an encoding of a power of 2. For example, to compute $[a \ll m]$, one first encodes 2^m in x^m and then returns $[a \cdot x^m]$. Similarly, for $[a \gg m]$, one encodes 2^{-m} in polynomial x^{n-m} and returns $[a \cdot x^{n-m}]$.
– Comparison: There is no known method for Type II FHE to provide a comparison in the encrypted domain. Some solutions exist for Multi-Party Computation [14] but cannot be transposed into the world of fully homomorphic encryption in which we focus. More than that, the way to provide a test that a given value is or is not equal to 0 using only additions and multiplications over $\mathbb{Z}_p$ seems infeasible!
– Conditional Assignment: similarly, the conditional assignment seems hard to obtain since it requires to perform one addition modulo 2 on the plaintext.

Again, the corresponding multiplicative depth is given in Table 1 (right part).

Because of the compact form of a polynomial-based input encoding, several operations of a usual processor cannot be performed using a Type II FHE, while this is always possible with a Type I FHE (see Table 1). The consequence is that, using a Type II FHE scheme, some circuits cannot be transformed to be executed in the encrypted domain (e.g., a circuit requiring a comparison or a conditional assignment). However, this approach presents some major advantages. Looking at Table 1, most of the basic operations only consume zero or one level of multiplicative depth, while the impact is much more important when using a Type I FHE scheme. This has also an impact on the real execution time of a circuit evaluation in the encrypted domain, as we will show in Sect. 5.

Last but not least, a Type II FHE permits to store all the information about an input into only one single polynomial. This contributes to the reduction of the expansion factor, compare to a Type I FHE.

4   Macroblock Compression in the Encrypted Domain

In this section, we present the different algorithms involved in an image compression pipeline at the macroblock level. For each of them, we give some details on how to implement them using both Type I and Type II FHE. Recall that, FHE encryption schemes being probabilistic, redundant image parts lead to different ciphertexts and that all ciphertexts are polynomialy indistinguishable with respect to a reference mathematical problem (lattice-based in the case of the FHEs used in this paper). As image and video compression is a wide domain, we focus our work on algorithms used in the mainstream video compression standards H.264 and HEVC. In the sequel, we consider colored images rather than grayscale ones.

4.1   Color Space Conversion: RGB to and from YCrCb

A digital image is made of pixels which are triplets of integers R, G and B. Each integer R, G, B is encoded using the same number of bits (say 8 to 12 bits) and represents the quantity of colors red, green and blue respectively making the pixel color. This representation system is appropriate for display devices, but for compression and image transmission, the YCrCb system is more relevant due to biological reasons (the human eye has different sensitivity to colors and brightness). In a nutshell, the YCrCb system has one component of luminance Y, and two of chrominance blue, Cb, and red, Cr. The luminance contains informations about the pixel brightness, being similar to pixel grayscale in the original image. Chrominance components, on the other hand, contain informations about the pixel color. Using this encoding method, one can reduce the amount of information in chrominance components without the human eye observing a too significant difference in the image. Letting the latter details aside, the conversion from RGB to YCrCb is a linear transformation defined as follows:

$$
\begin{bmatrix} Y \\ Cb \\ Cr \end{bmatrix} = \begin{bmatrix} ca & (1-ca-cb) & cb \\ \frac{-ca}{2(1-ca)} & \frac{(ca+cb-1)}{2(1-ca)} & \frac{(1-cb)}{2(1-ca)} \\ \frac{1-ca}{2(1-cb)} & \frac{(ca+cb-1)}{2(1-cb)} & \frac{-cb}{2(1-cb)} \end{bmatrix} \cdot \begin{bmatrix} R \\ G \\ B \end{bmatrix} , \tag{1}
$$

where the coefficients ca and cb are defined following the biology of the human eye. In ITU-R recommendation BT.601 [4], these coefficients are set to $ca = 0.299$

and $cb = 0.114$. This transformation is invertible and its inverse is also a linear transformation depending on the coefficients ca and cb.

After this first step of color space change, each component Y, Cr, Cb is divided into blocks of a few pixels, known as macroblocks, and the subsequent transformations of the compression pipeline are applied independently on each of these blocks. We now turn to implementation details for this algorithm targeting the two types of FHE considered in this paper.

RGB to and from YCrCb with Type I FHE. The first step towards porting this algorithm for an execution over encrypted data is to transform the coefficients of the matrix given in Eq. (1) into integers representing fixed-precision numbers. To do this, we simply scale each coefficient of that matrix by a power of two and round the result. Then, we compute the matrix/vector multiplication and shift the result to the left to get the correct values for coefficients YCrCb. For example, to compute the luminance Y component, we perform the following operations:

$$[Y] = (ca' [R] + (1 - ca' - cb') [G] + cb' [B]) \gg n;$$

where $ca' = \lfloor ca \times 2^n \rceil$ and $cb' = \lfloor cb \times 2^n \rceil$.

The second step corresponds to the management of the output range. In fact when RGB coefficients take their values in $[0, 255]$, Y, Cr and Cb end up with values in $[0, 255]$, $[-180, 180]$ and $[-225, 226]$ respectively. Still, in practice, it is required that the luminance and chrominance coefficients ends up in the same range. To accomplish that, there are two standard methods.

- *Method 1*: normalize the chrominance coefficients such that they range in -128 to 128 and add an offset equal to 128 to shift the result to the appropriate range (see [4]).
- *Method 2* [5]: clip the chrominance coefficients which are below 0 to 0 and above 255 to 255. E.g., if x is the output value of line 2 of Eq. (1), then

$$C_b = \mathsf{clip}(x) = \min\{255; \max\{0; x\}\}.$$

For the first method, the normalization operation can be included directly in the chrominance coefficients of (1) before we transform it into an integer. In the second method we need to transform the clip function in a circuit matching with operations allowed by Type IFHE. For that, we can use a conditional assignment as follows:

$$[z] = \mathsf{clip}([x]) \Leftrightarrow [z] = [y < 255] \cdot [y] + (1 \oplus [y < 255]) \cdot [255]$$
$$\text{where } [y] = [0 < x] \cdot [x] + (1 \oplus [0 < x]) \cdot [0].$$

Using a Type I FHE, we now compare 3 different strategies for our conversion: (i) using the basic RGB to YCrCb Eq. (1) without adjusting the range of the coefficients, (ii) using *Method 1* or (iii) using *Method 2*. For each strategy, we count the number of XOR, AND and OR (bit-level) operations that need to be performed. Our results are given in Table 2 (left side).

Table 2. Number of operations for two methods in conversion RGB to YCrCb with Type I (left) and Type II (right)

Algorithm	XOR	AND	OR
RGB to YCrCb	1556	484	1
Method 1	1556	482	3
Method 2	1992	712	11

Algorithm	ADD	SCALAR MULT.
RGB to YCrCb	6	9
Method 1	9	12
Method 2	no	no

A simple implementation of Eq. (1) requires 6 additions, 9 scalar multiplications, which corresponds to line 1 in Table 2 (left side). When we apply *Method 1*, we only add a scalar addition for each row in Eq. (1). This does not increase much the number of bit-level operations (see line 2 in Table 2 left side). Applying *Method 2* adds 12 more additions and 12 more ciphertextwise multiplications, leading to a significant increase of bit-level operations (see line 3 in Table 2) (left side).

RGB to and from YCrCb with Type II FHE. A Type II FHE allows to encode both integers and rational numbers so that both solutions are possible for the conversion of the coefficients of the matrix in Eq. (1). So as to truly compare Type I and Type II FHEs, we consider the same three strategies: basic equation, *Method 1* and *Method 2*. This first means that shift operations ($\gg n$) should be replaced, in this case, by a multiplication by a rational encoding of ($\frac{1}{2^n}$).

Yet, among the two above methods, only *Method 1* can really be implemented using a Type II FHE. In fact, to implement *Method 2*, one needs to perform a comparison, or execute at least some form of conditional assignment to realize the clip operator, and we have explained in Sect. 3 that this is not possible with a Type II FHE.

Our results in the Type II FHE case are given in Table 2 (right side). Complexity is here defined measured by the number of additions, multiplications and scaling, since this type of FHE does not implement bit-level FHE operations.

4.2   Discrete Cosine Transform (DCT)

The DCT is generally the second algorithm in a macroblock compression pipeline. It changes the representation of the block coefficients to the frequency domain. This transformation uncorrelates the coefficients and concentrates their energy in the low frequencies, i.e., after the DCT, the coefficients that contain the important informations are on the top-left side of the resulting block. For a block $\mathbf{X}$ of size $N \times N$, its DCT is given by the following equation

$$\mathbf{Y} = \mathrm{DCT}(\mathbf{X}) = \mathbf{A}\mathbf{X}\mathbf{A}^T, \text{ where } \mathbf{A} = (\mathbf{A}_{ij})_{ij} \text{ is a matrix with}$$

$$\mathbf{A}_{ij} = c_i \cos \frac{(2j+1)\,i\pi}{2N}; \quad c_i = \sqrt{\frac{1}{N}}\,(i = 0)\,; \quad c_i = \sqrt{\frac{2}{N}}\,(i > 0)\,. \tag{2}$$

The DCT is a reversible transformation. Its inverse, denoted IDCT, is similar to forward DCT and is used in the decompressor. Its equation is defined by

$$\mathbf{X} = \mathsf{IDCT}(\mathbf{Y}) = \mathbf{A}^{T}\mathbf{Y}\mathbf{A}, \text{ where } \mathbf{A} \text{ is defined as in the forward DCT.}$$

DCT for Type I FHE. The implementation of the DCT in the encrypted domain, using a Type I FHE, cannot directly use the coefficients of the matrix A in Eq. (2). In fact, this requires using floating points, requiring many multiplications (about 2×64 for a 8×8-DCT), which one is the most costly operation of nowadays homomorphic encryption schemes. Then, instead of using Eq. (2) directly, one can use an integer approximation of the DCT. There are three ways to obtain this:

- scale each matrix coefficient with some large number (typically between 2^5 and 2^{16}) and then round to the closest integer [21];
- decompose the matrix $\mathbf{A}$ as a product of two matrices $\mathbf{D} \cdot \mathbf{B}$ where $\mathbf{D}$ is a diagonal matrix with rational coefficients and $\mathbf{B}$ is a matrix with integer coefficients. The matrix $\mathbf{B}$ is then decomposed into a product of sparse integer matrices. Following the decomposition obtained for $\mathbf{B}$, the number of multiplications is lower [2];
- hand-tune the coefficients of matrix $\mathbf{A}$ such that they satisfy some conditions defined by standard HEVC [1] (orthogonality, good compaction energy, equal norm of column matrix, etc.).

In the sequel, we focus our attention on the two last methods, using the standard implementations defined in H.264 (which uses the second method on 4×4 blocks) and HEVC, which gives us several advantages. At first, these two standards are among the most deployed ones in practice. Moreover, for our purpose, they propose approximate DCT with integer coefficients (the rational part of the DCT being included in the quantization step studied below). Indeed, they can be implemented using only additions and shifts. Table 3 then gives the number of bit-level operations for both standards to compute such approx-DCT.

Table 3. Number of operations in DCT-4×4 for H.264 and HEVC with Type I FHE

Algorithms	XOR	AND	OR
Approx-DCT for H.264 [22]	1828	569	20
Approx-DCT for HEVC [1]	7738	2369	26

DCT for Type II FHE. For a Type II FHE, it may be possible to work with the basic definition of the DCT, since it permits to handle rational numbers. But, as in the non-encrypted domain, this leads to some accuracy errors between the encoder and the decoder. We then similarly work with the expressions defined in H.264 and HEVC, given above. The way to proceed is similar to Type I FHE, except that the shift operation becomes a scalar (rational) multiplication. Table 4 gives the number of basic operations for performing a DCT in this context.

Table 4. Number of operations in DCT-4 × 4 for H.264 and HEVC with Type II FHE

Algorithm	ADD	SCALAR MULT.
Approx-DCT for H.264 [22]	96	16
Approx-DCT for HEVC [1]	64	76

4.3 Quantization

Quantization is directly correlated to the DCT step defined previously. It consists in dividing the frequency coefficients derived from the DCT by a matrix $\mathbf{Q}$, and to further round them. The coefficients of the matrix $\mathbf{Q}$ are defined following a quantization parameter which regulates the compression ratio. For a DCT coefficient $\mathbf{Y}$, the equation of quantization is the following:

$$\mathbf{Z}_{i,j} = \left\lfloor \frac{\mathbf{Y}_{i,j}}{\mathbf{Q}_{i,j}} \right\rceil. \tag{3}$$

The quantization parameter defines the quality of the output image. Quantization is then a lossy transformation since it is not possible to determine the exact value of the original fractional number from the rounded integer. In the decompression step, one uses a transformation which is an approximate reversion of the forward quantization. Its equation is the following:

$$\mathbf{Y}_{i,j} = \mathbf{Z}_{i,j} \cdot \mathbf{Q}_{i,j}.$$

For further implementation details, we refer the reader to the description of quantization in the H.264 standard [22]. In this case, the DCT transformation is decomposed in the product $\mathbf{AXA}^T \otimes \mathbf{E}_f$ where the coefficients of $\mathbf{A}$ are in $\{-1, -2, 1, 2\}$ and those of $\mathbf{E}_f$ in $\{a^2, \frac{b^2}{4}, \frac{ab}{2}\}$, $a = \frac{1}{2}, b = \sqrt{\frac{2}{5}}$. The symbol $\otimes$ here represents the coefficient-wise multiplication of the matrix. Then, $\mathbf{AXA}^T$ represents the forward DCT in H.264 and $\mathbf{E}_f$ is included in the quantization step. So Eq. (3) becomes

$$\mathbf{Z}_{i,j} = \left\lfloor \mathbf{Y}_{i,j} \frac{\mathbf{E}_{i,j}}{\mathbf{Q}_{i,j}} \right\rceil, \tag{4}$$

where $\mathbf{E}_{i,j}$ refers to the coefficients of matrix $\mathbf{E}_f$. In order to simplify arithmetic implementations, the H.264 standard suggests to replace the fraction $\frac{\mathbf{E}_{i,j}}{\mathbf{Q}_{i,j}}$ by $\frac{\mathbf{M}_{i,j}}{2^{qbits}}$ such that $\frac{\mathbf{M}_{i,j}}{2^{qbits}} = \frac{\mathbf{E}_{i,j}}{\mathbf{Q}_{i,j}}$ and to implement Eq. (4) as

$$|\mathbf{Z}_{i,j}| = (|\mathbf{Y}_{i,j}| \cdot \mathbf{M}_{i,j} + f) \gg qbits, \quad sign(\mathbf{Z}_{i,j}) = sign(\mathbf{Y}_{i,j}) \tag{5}$$

where $qbits = 15 + \lfloor QP/6 \rfloor$ and $f = \frac{2^{qbits}}{3}$.

Quantization for Type I FHE. In this case, we use Eq. (5) for implementing the quantization step. To obtain the absolute value of an integer y, we first extract the (encrypted) sign bit of y and then use the conditional assignment defined above. With a Type I FHE, the sign of a ciphertext $[y]$ is simply the leftmost ciphertext bit. For a ciphertext $[y]$ represented by 16 ciphertext bits, Eq. (5) can then be computed as follows:

$$[b] = MSB([y]);$$
$$[y'] = [b] \left(2^{16} - 1 - [y]\right) + (1 \oplus [b])[y];$$
$$[z] = ([y'] \cdot \mathbf{M}_{i,j} + f) \gg qbit, \quad MSB([z]) = [b].$$

Quantization for Type II FHE. In the case of Type II FHE we cannot use Eq. (5) as recommended in the H.264 standard. Indeed, extracting the (encrypted) sign of a given ciphertext is not possible. So, we rather use Eq. (4) which evaluation does not depend on the sign of the ciphertext. In order to avoid the problem of the round function of this equation, we add the scalar $\frac{1}{2}$ to $\mathbf{Y}_{i,j} \frac{\mathbf{E}_{i,j}}{\mathbf{Q}_{i,j}}$ and after decryption of a quantized ciphertext, we decode it as an integer rather than as a rational number.

The last step of the compression pipeline is the *entropic coding*. It is composed of an RLE compression followed by an arithmetic or Huffman coding. Running RLE compression on encrypted data has already been studied in [6]. It remains the arithmetic or Huffman coding, which one is out of the scope of our paper and remains an interesting problem to study.

5   Experimental Results and Interpretation

The previous section has given our theoretical view of a macroblock processing pipeline in the encrypted world. We have shown that, depending on the FHE instantiation (Type I or Type II), the strategy on the way to implement each step (color conversion, DCT and quantization) can be quite different. We have proposed several versions and gave the advantages and drawbacks of each, before giving our theoretical conclusions. We now go one step further by going deep inside a real implementation. More precisely, in this section, we evaluate the performances, in terms of execution time, when the compression algorithms is executed using two different FHE implementations: one falling in the Type I case and the other based on a Type II FHE instance.

To obtain our real-world benchmarks, we have used both

- the `Cingulata` library, which implements the FV FHE scheme with a Type I instance and,
- the `SEAL` library, which also implements the FV FHE scheme but using a Type II instance.

In our implementations, we have set the parameters of the two FHEs to reach a 128-bit security, using [9]. More precisely, we have chosen $n = 2048$ and $\log_2 q = 56$ for the degree of the cyclotomic polynomial and the ciphertext modulus respectively. For the plaintext modulus, we have set $t = 2$ for `Cingulata` and $t = 2^8$ for SEAL. Finally, regarding the compression algorithm we have implemented in the encrypted world, we have also made some choices on the input parameters, depending on the FHE type.

– *Color space conversion*: we have first used as input the encryption of a single RGB triplet (YCrCb one for the inverse function), but the results can easily be extended to a full image. Using Cingulata, the input is encoded with the Integer8 class. During homomorphic operations, we have used instead the Integer32 class as an accumulator to store our ciphertext since it permits to avoid the precision error due to carry propagation. More precisely, we multiply the coefficients of the matrix color conversion by 2^{15} (see Sect. 4). Since the encrypted input coefficients are 8-bit ciphertexts, we should use at least a Integer24 class for this computation. For the SEAL library, as it corresponds to a Type II FHE, we do not have such problem since the inputs are encoded as coefficients of a polynomial.
– *DCT and Quantization*: in these algorithms, we have chosen a 4×4 macroblock. This size is the basic one for blocks used in H264. For our comparison, we use the same size when testing the HEVC compression algorithm. In Cingulata, we represent the encrypted input in the Integer16 class. As for color space conversion, we use an intermediary Integer32 representation to avoid precision errors.

We have run these algorithms on an Intel(R) Xeon(R) with a E5-2620 CPU with 16 core running at 2.10 GHz under a 64-bit Arch-linux OS.

Table 5 gives the benchmarks of our implementation in term of numbers of operations for each type of FHE It also gives the execution time for each pipeline compression algorithm. Let us emphasize that the execution times given for Type I/*4th generation* FHE in the Table 5 correspond to a theoretical estimate of a real execution time for TFHE. Indeed, in the TFHE scheme, all bitwise operations take exactly the same time: about 15ms. Then, using the information about the binary gates in the compression sub-algorithms taken from our implementation using Cingulata, we obtain the execution times for TFHE using the equation

$$\text{time}(\text{TFHE}) = (\#\text{XOR} + \#\text{AND} + \#\text{OR}) \times 15\,\text{ms}. \tag{6}$$

Contrary to FV, TFHE has an efficient bootstrapping procedure which is run after each gate (in the initial version of that cryptosystem). Hence, the computation results obtained with TFHE are not dependant upon the multiplicative depth of the algorithms, a fact which explains the large difference between type I FV and TFHE in Table 5.

The first thing we observe in Table 5 is the gap between the execution time for a Type I and for a Type II FHE. In fact, this gap was quite predictable since a Type I FHE is by definition some Type II FHE for a modulus plaintext set to 2 and arranged in such a way that it reproduces the functionalities of a classic processor. Yet, as shown is Table 5, the Type I/Type II gap is significantly reduced when using a 4th generation Type I FHE such as TFHE. Still, a Type I FHE gives far more possibilities regarding the operations that can be executed in

Table 5. Execution times of algorithms of pipeline image/video compression in function of Type I and Type II FHE. We use FV as a *2nd generation* FHE and TFHE as *4th generation* FHE.

		Type I						Type II				
		AND	XOR	OR	Depth	*2nd generation time(s)*	*4th generation time(s)*	ADD	MULT	SCALAR MULT.	Depth	*2nd generation time(s)*
RGB to YCrCb	*Method 1*	482	1556	3	22	164	3.062	9	0	12	0	0.0029
	Method 2	712	1992	11	37	250	4.073	n.a	n.a	n.a	n.a	n.a.
YCrCb to RGB	*Method 1*	377	1129	2	21	132	2.262	7	0	8	0	0.0021
	Method 2	346	1027	444	30	135	2.726	n.a	n.a	n.a	n.a	n.a.
DCT for H.264	Forward	516	1456	4	15	54	2.964	96	0	16	0	0.0078
	Inverse	1186	3455	8	16	63	6.974	96	0	48	0	0.0147
DCT for HEVC	Forward	2369	7738	26	24	343	15.200	64	0	76	0	0.0213
	Inverse	372	1326	4	26	88	2.553	64	0	76	0	0.0210
Quantization for H.264	Forward	2100	6892	0	29	64	13.448	16	0	32	0	0.0072
	Inverse	216	892	12	12	65	1.680	0	0	32	0	0.0066
Quantization for HEVC	Forward	1968	6688	0	29	365	12.984	16	0	48	0	0.0075
	Inverse	144	624	16	10	30	1.176	16	0	48	0	0.0100

the encrypted domain. This is due to the used structure that is more accessible than the polynomial structure of a Type II FHE. Clearly, this latter limits the operations in the encrypted world to the existing ones in the polynomial ring.

We have put together our above implementations in an attempt to execute the compression/decompression pipeline on a complete real 128×128 image. We have done so for the algorithms sets of both H264 and HEVC standards. Yet, as the SEAL library seems to be the most efficient, we limited ourselves to our results on Type II FHE. Hence, the image crosses successively the following algorithms: encryption of pixels, DCT with block size 4×4, quantization, inverse quantization, inverse DCT with block size 4×4 and finally a decryption of the resulting pixel. Figures 2, 3 and 4 gives the resulting images obtained after applying the above pipeline to the grayscale well-known picture of Lena with size 128×128. Compressing the full image takes about 244s (H.264) and 149s (HEVC) on a single core, which is clearly not prohibitive. Needless to emphasize, of course, that, since the image macroblocks are processed independently, significant speedups can be further obtained by means of parallelization. Of course, as we have run the first three steps of the compression pipeline without the RLE and the subsequent entropic coding steps, we have only achieved limited compression. Still, as discussed in our preceding paper on RLE [6], completing the full compression pipeline in the encrypted domain will require to target an a priori fixed compression ratio as variable-length, lossless compression is not achievable in the FHE setting.

Still, to the best of our knowledge, this is the first "crypto-compression" of a full image, yet of moderate resolution.

Fig. 2. Lena original   **Fig. 3.** Lena (H.264)   **Fig. 4.** Lena (HEVC)

6   Conclusion

In this work, we show that there are today two different ways to use FHE schemes: Type I which performed encrypted bitwise operations, and Type II which makes use of polynomial ring operations. We apply these two types of FHE to the main blocks of a pipeline of image/video compression. We observe, in line with our a priori intuitions, that Type II FHEs are faster than Type I, but that the latter has more flexibility in term of operations that can be executed in the encrypted domain. This work opens many other interesting problems, such as the optimization of our circuit to reduce the execution time, the definition of new operations like conditional assignment for a Type II FHE, and why not the definition of an operator which allows to switch between Type I and Type II, then obtaining the advantage of both types.

References

1. Budagavi, M., Fuldseth, A., Bjøntegaard, G., Sze, V., Sadafale, M.: Core transform design in the high efficiency video coding (HEVC) standard. J. Sel. Top. Sig. Process. **7**(6), 1029–1041 (2013)
2. Cintra, R.J., Bayer, F.M., Coutinho, V.A., Kulasekera, S., Madanayake, A.: DCT-like transform for image and video compression requires 10 additions only. CoRR abs/1402.5979 (2014)
3. Brakerski, Z., Gentry, C., Vaikuntanathan, V.: (Leveled) fully homomorphic encryption without bootstrapping. In: ITCS (2012)
4. Recommendation ITU-R BT. Studio encoding parameters of digital television for standard 4: 3 and wide-screen 16:9 aspect ratios (1995)
5. Recommendation ITU-T BT. ITU-T H.265: High efficiency video coding (2013)
6. Canard, S., Carpov, S., Kuate, D.N., Sirdey, R.: Running compression algorithms in the encrypted domain: a case-study on the homomorphic execution of RLE. In: Proceedings of Privacy, Security and Trust (2017, to appear)
7. Chen, H., Han, K.: Homomorphic lower digits removal and improved FHE bootstrapping. In: Nielsen, J.B., Rijmen, V. (eds.) EUROCRYPT 2018. LNCS, vol. 10820, pp. 315–337. Springer, Cham (2018). https://doi.org/10.1007/978-3-319-78381-9_12

8. Chen, H., Laine, K., Player, R.: Simple encrypted arithmetic library (SEAL). https://www.microsoft.com/en-us/research/project/simple-encrypted-arithmetic-library/
9. Chen, H., Laine, K., Player, R.: Simple encrypted arithmetic library - SEAL v2.1. In: Brenner, M. (ed.) FC 2017. LNCS, vol. 10323, pp. 3–18. Springer, Cham (2017). https://doi.org/10.1007/978-3-319-70278-0_1
10. Chillotti, I., Gama, N., Georgieva, M., Izabachène, M.: TFHE: fast fully homomorphic encryption library over the torus. https://github.com/tfhe/tfhe
11. Chillotti, I., Gama, N., Georgieva, M., Izabachène, M.: Improving TFHE: faster packed homomorphic operations and efficient circuit bootstrapping (2017). https://eprint.iacr.org/2017/430
12. Costache, A., Smart, N.P.: Which ring based somewhat homomorphic encryption scheme is best? In: Sako, K. (ed.) CT-RSA 2016. LNCS, vol. 9610, pp. 325–340. Springer, Cham (2016). https://doi.org/10.1007/978-3-319-29485-8_19
13. Costache, A., Smart, N.P., Vivek, S., Waller, A.: Fixed-point arithmetic in SHE schemes. In: Avanzi, R., Heys, H. (eds.) SAC 2016. LNCS, vol. 10532, pp. 401–422. Springer, Cham (2017). https://doi.org/10.1007/978-3-319-69453-5_22
14. Damgård, I., Geisler, M., Krøigaard, M.: Homomorphic encryption and secure comparison. Int. J. Appl. Crypt. 1(1), 22–31 (2008)
15. Fan, J., Vercauteren, F.: Somewhat practical fully homomorphic encryption (2012). https://eprint.iacr.org/2012/144
16. Garay, J., Schoenmakers, B., Villegas, J.: Practical and secure solutions for integer comparison. In: Okamoto, T., Wang, X. (eds.) PKC 2007. LNCS, vol. 4450, pp. 330–342. Springer, Heidelberg (2007). https://doi.org/10.1007/978-3-540-71677-8_22
17. Gentry, C.: A fully homomorphic encryption scheme. Ph.D. (2009)
18. Halevi, S., Shoup, V.: HElib an implementation of homomorphic encryption. https://github.com/shaih/HElib
19. Lepoint, T., Naehrig, M.: A comparison of the homomorphic encryption schemes FV and YASHE. In: Pointcheval, D., Vergnaud, D. (eds.) AFRICACRYPT 2014. LNCS, vol. 8469, pp. 318–335. Springer, Cham (2014). https://doi.org/10.1007/978-3-319-06734-6_20
20. CEA LIST. Cingulata: compiler toolchain and RTE for running programs over encrypted data. https://github.com/CEA-LIST/Cingulata
21. Malvar, H.S., Hallapuro, A., Karczewicz, M., Kerofsky, L.: Low-complexity transform and quantization in H.264/AVC. IEEE Trans. Circuits Syst. Video Technol. 13(7), 598–603 (2003)
22. Richardson, I.E.: H. 264 and MPEG-4 Video Compression: Video Coding for Next-Generation Multimedia. Wiley, New York (2004)
23. Rivest, R.L., Adleman, L., Dertouzos, M.L.: On data banks and privacy homomorphisms (1978)
24. Xu, C., Chen, J., Wu, W., Feng, Y.: Homomorphically encrypted arithmetic operations over the integer ring. In: Bao, F., Chen, L., Deng, R.H., Wang, G. (eds.) ISPEC 2016. LNCS, vol. 10060, pp. 167–181. Springer, Cham (2016). https://doi.org/10.1007/978-3-319-49151-6_12
25. Yang, P., Gui, X., An, J., Tian, F., Wang, J.: An encrypted image editing scheme based on homomorphic encryption. In: INFOCOM WKSHPS. IEEE (2015)
26. Zheng, P., Huang, J.: An efficient image homomorphic encryption scheme with small ciphertext expansion. In: ACMMULTIMEDIA. ACM (2013)

Malware

Malware Tolerant (Mesh-)Networks

Michael Denzel[✉] and Mark Dermot Ryan

University of Birmingham, Birmingham B15 2TT, UK
{m.denzel,m.d.ryan}@cs.bham.ac.uk

Abstract. Mesh networks, like e.g. smart-homes, are networks where every node has routing capabilities. These networks are usually flat, which means that one compromised device can potentially overtake the whole infrastructure, especially considering clone attacks.

To counter attacks, we propose a network architecture which enhances flat networks, especially mesh networks, with isolation and automatic containment of malicious devices. Our approach consists of unprivileged devices, clustered into groups, and privileged "bridge" devices which can cooperatively apply filter rules like a distributed firewall. Since there is no ultimate authority (not even bridges) to control the whole network, our approach has no single point-of-failure – so-called intrusion or malware tolerance. That means, attacks on a single device will not compromise the whole infrastructure and are tolerated. Previous research on mesh networks [3,8–10] relied on a single point-of-failure and is, thus, not intrusion or malware tolerant.

Our architecture is dynamic in the sense that bridge devices can change, misbehaving devices can be isolated by outvoting them, and cryptographic keys evolve. This effectively turns the entire network into a moving target.

We used the protocol verifier ProVerif to prove the security properties of our network architecture.

Keywords: Mesh network · Malware tolerance
Self-management · Network security

1 Introduction

Recently, smart-homes and Internet of Things (IoT) devices gain popularity through e.g. Google's Nest[1], Samsung SmartThings[2], Philips Hue[3], and Amazon Echo[4]. These smart-homes increasingly employ mesh routing, a technique where every device can forward messages. Google WiFi[5] routers already form mesh

---

[1] https://nest.com/uk/about/.
[2] http://www.samsung.com/uk/smartthings/.
[3] http://www2.meethue.com/.
[4] https://www.amazon.co.uk/Amazon-SK705DI-Echo-Black/dp/B01GAGVIE4.
[5] https://madeby.google.com/wifi/.

© Springer Nature Switzerland AG 2018
J. Camenisch and P. Papadimitratos (Eds.): CANS 2018, LNCS 11124, pp. 133–153, 2018.
https://doi.org/10.1007/978-3-030-00434-7_7

networks for performance reasons and to support non-uniformly shaped network areas (like a long stretched, narrow flat).

Mesh networks were originally used in isolated settings, e.g. by rescue teams in remote areas, and thus the main focus was on reliability and safety. Nowadays, these networks are more and more applied in consumer scenarios like smart-home networks, Wireless Ad-Hoc Networks (WANETs), Vehicular Ad-Hoc Networks (VANETs) and Wireless Sensor Networks (WSNs). However, with features and time-to-market influencing the strategy of the IoT industry, devices often lack security features. Various forms of attacks like black hole attacks, Denial of Service (DoS), routing table overflows, and impersonation [14] exist in addition to well-known attacks like buffer overflows and similar. As mesh networks are usually flat, compromised devices immediately supply an adversary with access to the entire network instead of part of it. This is in particular of concern when taking node capture attacks into account, where the adversary hijacks a device in wide area networks (e.g. a network of weather stations).

While some of the previous research already proposed self-healing techniques for mesh networks [3,8], they rely on a single point-of-failure – usually a trusted base station – which could be attacked by an adversary to still successfully compromise the architecture.

Our aim is to ensure that most of the network still operates securely when parts of it are entirely controlled by an adversary and that the attack is contained and limited from spreading further. There shall be no ultimate authority with access to everything – an approach called intrusion tolerance [19] or malware tolerance [7]. Note that our method takes place *after* the initial infection where the adversary already has control over the first system.

In our research we focus on mesh networks since they are used in smart-homes.

Contributions:

1. We design the architecture of a malware-tolerant mesh network that isolates devices into groups. Groups are able to communicate with each other via a special bridge group that can enforce security properties and filtering like a firewall. The network also applies automatic containment based on voting to identify and quarantine threats, and is in this regard self-managing.
   It is malware-tolerant, that means none of the devices, bridge groups, components, software, or accounts alone is sufficient to take over the whole network, i.e. there is no single point-of-failure.
2. To prove our network architecture we utilise state-of-the-art protocol verifier ProVerif[6]. The proofs can be found online[7].

2   Overview

Let us consider a smart-home setting in the near future with smart light bulbs, smart fridge, smart door locks, entertainment zone, tablets, phones, laptops,

---

[6] http://proverif.inria.fr.

[7] https://github.com/mdenzel/malware-tolerant_mesh_network_proofs.

etc. (see e.g. Figure 1a). The WiFi of the gateway (the router) does not reach all devices (e.g. due to the long stretched layout of the house and interference) and a flat mesh network similar to Google WiFi is used: All devices route packets. While the laptops and PCs in the network employ a firewall and an anti-virus, e.g. the light bulbs and fridge lack these defences and are easier to compromise. Thus, an attacker might get access to a light bulb and start infecting the network.

To protect the other devices from attacks (e.g. the data on the laptop), we suggest to (1) isolate different device types. We propose to setup e.g. a group for the light bulbs, one for the entertainment devices, one for the work devices, etc. This already limits the adversary to the group of the compromised device.

If an old light bulb is compromised and starts attacking the newer ones, we (2) automatically contain the attack when we detect this behaviour. All devices are allowed to apply detection and will then vote against dishonest devices. A configurable threshold of votes (we used 2) is enough to trigger a quarantine. The method of detection is hereby interchangeable, every device could employ its own detection technique or even rely on the other devices.

Lastly, there should also be (3) no single point-of-failure (malware tolerance) because this would only shift the target. E.g. if we used the PC to setup the entire network, the adversary would only have to compromise the PC to succeed. This must not be the case for our architecture.

Let us illustrate the detection in an example: Suppose the adversary compromised a light bulb in the hallway and tries to scan the ports of the PC in the living room. The traffic is e.g. routed via the dishwasher in the kitchen and two light bulbs to the PC (see red path in Fig. 1a). In addition, all the light bulbs in the hallway see the traffic because it is wireless traffic. Let us say the light bulbs have old signatures and do not detect the attack. PC and dishwasher detect the attack and vote to quarantine the compromised light bulb. These two votes satisfy our threshold and a bridge device (e.g. the TV) would isolate the compromised light bulb and trigger a renewal of the light bulb key. Note that no device would give evidence for its vote. This could be optionally possible but the result is triggered by the amount of votes not by convincing others. It relies on the assumption that most of the nodes are honest.

2.1   Assumptions

Since the Dolev-Yao attacker alone is insufficient for certain types of attacks [17], especially in mesh networks with e.g. node capture attacks, we extended the Dolev-Yao attacker with further capabilities.

We make the following assumptions for our architecture:

1. Attacker Model: We are looking at the state where the adversary compromised the first device (e.g. through a buffer overflow). The adversary has access to this one device on the network, including all its cryptographic keys, but we are initially not aware which device this is. Additionally, the adversary has Dolev-Yao capabilities through e.g. an arp spoof or similar. However, the attacker does not (yet) have any other keys and can only access devices outside of

his group through plaintext messages, fake encryption, etc. This behaviour is likely noticed by the honest devices around him and detected as suspicious activities (an IDS is not even necessary to detect this). The attacker can try to compromise further devices but a careful attacker is limited to his own group.

2. Every device is able to execute cryptography. We expect applicable CPUs to become so small in the near future that they fit into e.g. a smart light-bulb.
3. We assume the network has a high connectivity and it is not partitioned. Low connectivity enables the adversary to compromise a device that is situated at interconnections enabling him to block messages completely. As light-bulbs are normally in every room of a flat or house, this assumption is justifiable in a smart-home setting with smart light-bulbs (and further smart devices).
4. Attacks on the cryptographic algorithms itself are out of scope. I.e. we assume that e.g. AES is still secure. If it becomes insecure, the algorithm can be swapped out with the new standard.

2.2 Proposed Architecture

Our network architecture consists of two virtual types of devices: non-privileged devices and privileged "bridge" devices. Non-privileged devices are clustered into groups with every group having one symmetric group key – like a standalone WiFi network. All messages are encrypted (as it is also common nowadays in WiFi networks) and devices can only communicate with devices in their group. To enable groups to talk to each other, we promote a small amount of devices of each group (≥ 2) to bridge devices.

These bridges have two tasks:

- First, they enable communication between the device groups. A bridge device of one group and a bridge device of another group can re-encrypt and forward messages between those two groups. Filtering, similar to a firewall, works in a distributed fashion, namely at bridges.
- Second, bridges certify keys of non-privileged devices. For this, bridges are divided into two subgroups: bridge group A and B, each of which has an asymmetric key. A key of a non-privileged device is valid, if it was certified by both bridge groups A and B (i.e. by at least two different bridge devices).

Through this, we created a virtual overlay over the geographical layout of the network. An example is shown in Fig. 1 where the network is divided into three groups: light bulbs (circles), kitchen devices (triangles), and entertainment devices (squares). Non-privileged group devices are black shapes while bridge devices are white with their subgroup (A or B) written inside the shape. Connections are shown as black lines and as blue dotted circle for the router. Not every device is connected to any other one because walls and electronic currents limit connectivity. E.g. the router cannot directly reach the HiFi stereo system. Figure 1(b) displays the virtual layout of this network with the particular cryptographic keys.

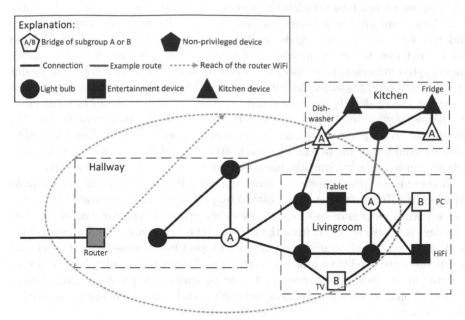

(a) Geographic network layout showing actual data links

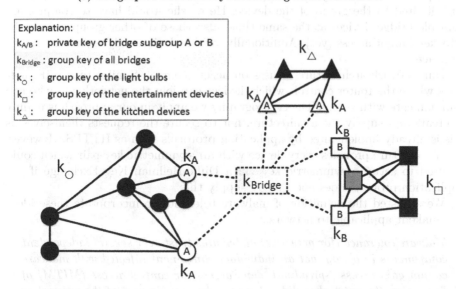

(b) Virtual network layout showing the links in each of the groups and the cryptographic keys. Additionally to the displayed keys, each device has its own asymmetric key pair (identity key).

Fig. 1. Example of the same mesh network with its geographic and virtual network layout (Color figure online)

In order to react to attacks, the proposed architecture should be dynamic. Any device can *vote to promote* another device in its group to a bridge device and can *vote to exclude* any device in *any* group from the network. We do not restrict how to detect malicious behaviour; honest devices could e.g. notice unencrypted messages, protocol errors, ongoing DoS attacks or a malicious device which is dropping packages. An Intrusion Detection System (IDS), anti-virus, or honeypot could identify malware delivered from a certain source. In these cases the honest device would vote to exclude that particular dishonest device. We would like to emphasise that not every device needs an IDS. Low capability systems could rely on others to detect attacks and forego detection or only detect simple misbehaviour like unencrypted messages or protocol errors.

If there is a certain number of votes against a device (minimum two to avoid attacks), the distrusted device is isolated by placing it into a separate new group and revoking its permission to join any other group. If the isolated device was a bridge, it is also removed from the bridges (the keys evolve) and a new bridge is elected. To forbid quarantined devices to promote themselves, at least two group votes are needed to promote a device and devices are only allowed to vote to promote in their group (note that vote to exclude is possible against every device). Thus, we create a dynamic network architecture that applies a moving target defence.

A potential adversary who compromised one device in the network is, therefore, limited to the group of the device. He or she would have to compromise multiple bridge devices at the same time, also those of other groups which the attacker cannot access (yet). Additionally, bridge devices only expose a reduced interface.

Our network architecture focuses on access control. Similar to a WiFi network where the router controls which devices can join the network and who can communicate with whom. The cryptography we apply in our approach is mainly to create and supply the architecture, not to secure the requests themselves as this is already implemented by application protocols such as HTTPS. However, our architecture provides every device with an asymmetric key pair which could be used to setup a symmetric key via a Diffie-Hellman Key Exchange if the application protocol does not already supply this.

We adjusted the definition of malware tolerance to incorporate these ideas and make it applicable to networks:

Malware tolerance (for networks) distributes trust over several independent components in a way that an individual component infected with malware cannot gain access (spreading), deny access, or control access (MITM) of devices on the network it did not control before. No part of the network is assumed invulnerable to attacks.

In the literature, security is usually defined in a binary fashion: a system can be secure or compromised. Malware tolerance, in contrast, has flexible trust assumptions: a compromised system can still work securely.

To achieve our self-managing, malware-tolerant network architecture, six operations are necessary. At the beginning, the network has to be bootstrapped:

1. SETUP

For the non-privileged groups there are three operations:

2. GET TICKET/JOIN GROUP
3. SEND
4. VOTE TO EXCLUDE/LEAVE GROUP

The bridges have two operations:

5. VOTE TO PROMOTE/BRIDGE JOIN
6. VOTE TO EXCLUDE/BRIDGE LEAVE

We will now introduce the underlying cryptography and these six operations.

Basic Cryptography: The architecture utilises four different types of keys as already mentioned in Fig. 1(b):

1. Each device has its own asymmetric key pair – the identity key (e.g. $[k_{fridge}^{pub},$ $k_{fridge}^{priv}]$).
2. Each device is part of one group and has this particular symmetric group key (e.g. the light bulb key k_o).
3. Bridge devices are additionally part of the bridge group with the symmetric bridge key k_{AB}.
4. All bridge devices of one group have exactly one of two private keys, k_A or k_B. E.g. both bridge devices of the kitchen group (Fig. 1(b)) have key k_A, but not key k_B. The combination of k_A and k_B is used to certify the identity key of each device. For this, we use the Intrusion Resilient Signature (IRS) scheme of Itkis et al. [15,16] A second similar cryptosystem, Intrusion Resilient Encryption (IRE), was proposed by Dodis et al. [11,12].

The basis of IRS (and IRE) is a static public key and an evolving private key. In IRS, messages can be verified with the public key and the time period in which the signature was created. The private key material consists of the evolving private key and an evolving base secret which is kept separate at a different device. To evolve the private key, a contribution of the base secret is necessary. There are two ways to modify the private key which Itkis et al. called *update* and *refresh*. An update changes to the next time period while a refresh only changes the private secrets and leaves public key and time period unaffected. If an attacker compromised the secret key, he can read messages of the corresponding time period but does not get further keys. The attacker would have to compromise both the base and the secret key, at the same time in order to succeed. We refer the interested reader to the original papers [11,12,15,16] and a summary by Franklin [13] for more information.

Our architecture uses two bridge IRS keys (k_A and k_B) who both run an IRS scheme with the base secret being managed by the corresponding other bridge group. That means bridge key management is securely interleaved between the two bridge groups due to the properties of IRS. Certificates need to be signed with both keys to be considered trustworthy.

IRS is limited to $N = 2^t$ time periods with t being the bit length of the time variable. That means for a 32-bit time variable, we would have $N = 2^{32}$ or roughly 4 billion time periods. Assuming the network is used 100 years this corresponds to roughly 1 time period every second. Updating the secrets will likely take longer than this, limiting even DoS attacks. At the point this might run out, a re-setup of the architecture is recommended. If a DoS manages to exhaust all these time periods regardless of the aforementioned restriction, human intervention is necessary.

In the following, $E(k, m)$ refers to an authenticated symmetric encryption of message m with key k e.g. AES-GCM, $E(k^{pub}, m)$ denotes an asymmetric encryption, $S(k^{priv}, m)$ is a digital signature, $H(k, m)$ is a secure keyed hash function, and $IRS(k^{priv}, m)$ is the Intrusion Resilient Signature scheme. $m_0|m_1$ represents a concatenation of two messages. Also, by *time* we mean time-periods of IRS.

SETUP: Initially, four devices A_1, A_2, B_1, B_2 are selected to become bridges, each generating an asymmetric identity key-pair. Either the user sets these devices up with all of the other public keys (a simple option to establish these channels would be QR codes or a USB stick), or the devices send the keys to each other with Diffie-Hellman Key Exchange and the user verifies the fingerprints of the keys.

Afterwards, A_1 and B_1 generate k_A^{priv} stored at A_1 and $base_A$ stored at B_1 of IRS (see Distributed Key Generation of Itkis et al. [16]). Similarly, A_2 and B_2 generate k_B^{priv} at B_2 and $base_B$ at A_2. A_1 and A_2 share their secrets with each other, i.e. k_A^{priv} and $base_B$, and similarly do B_1 and B_2. This establishes the initially needed keys. Key management is interleaved between groups A and B; A has the base secret of B and vice versa.

Two bridge IRS keys can support any number $n \geq 2$ of non-privileged groups. For additional security, three bridge IRS groups (A, B, and C) could be similarly setup. However, this comes at the cost of performance and convenience hence we suggest two bridge groups.

GET TICKET/JOIN: First, we have to define how devices join the network. A base of four bridge devices was already setup, thus we can rely on them.

If the user wants to connect a new device d (e.g. a smart light bulb) to group g, he or she logs in at two devices d_1, d_2 (e.g. phone and PC) both different from d. Then, the user would request a new one-time password via d_1 and d_2 to sign up the new device d to group g. Half of the password is displayed on d_1 and the other half on d_2.

The total password consists of four shares (pw_{A1}, pw_{A2}, pw_{B1}, pw_{B2}). Two of the shares identify to one bridge group: e.g. half-password $pw_A = pw_{A1}|pw_{A2}$ is needed to authenticate to group A (similar for B). Each bridge IRS group generates the shares by hashing k_A^{priv} or k_B^{priv}, the requesting device (d_1 or d_2),

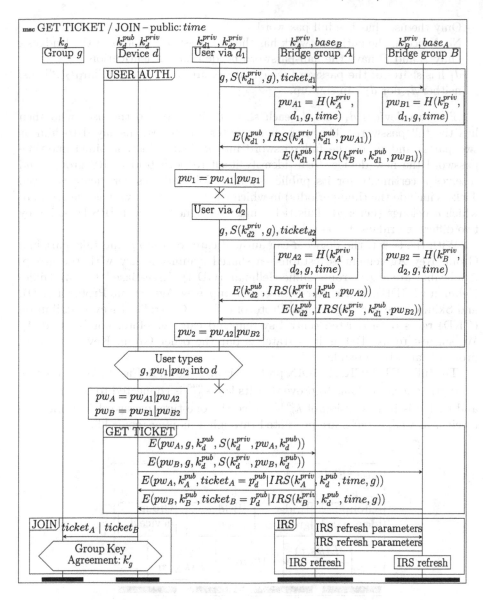

Fig. 2. GET TICKET/JOIN protocol: device d gets a ticket and joins group g. The user logs in with two devices d_1 and d_2.

g, and the time. This way, any bridge device in the particular bridge IRS group can re-calculate the shares.

To avoid attacks of d_1 or d_2, the half-passwords are sent interleaved. E.g. d_1 would receive $pw_1 = pw_{A1}|pw_{B1}$ and d_2 receives $pw_2 = pw_{A2}|pw_{B2}$. The result is that:

- Only the user has the full password.
- No device in the entire network has the full password (not even the bridges).
- Only A and B have the half-password needed for authentication.
- d_1 has shares of the password which, alone, are worthless (similar d_2). Thus, neither d_1 nor d_2 can sign up.

The two devices d_1 and d_2 each show their shares to the user who then has the full password. The user concatenates all shares (displayed to him as two parts) and types the full password into d. With this combined one-time password the new device d can identify itself to both bridge IRS groups and receives a certificate for its public key k_d^{pub}. We call this certificate a *ticket*. Tickets include the time-period(s) in which they are valid as well as the group to which d belongs (here: g). This ticket must be signed by both IRS keys, i.e. by two different bridges, to be valid.

With the ticket, the device d can authenticate to group g and take part in a Group Key Agreement to establish a shared symmetric key with the group. Applicable are e.g. Group Diffie-Hellman (GDH), Tree-Based Group Diffie-Hellman (TGDH), Burmester-Desmedt Group Key Agreement Protocol (BD), and Skinny Tree Key Agreement Protocol (STR). Centralised Key Distribution (CKD) relies on a trusted central system and can, therefore, not be used [1]. We suggest to use BD as it is stateless but the other Group Key Agreement protocols are also possible.

The full GET TICKET/JOIN protocol is also shown in Fig. 2. We sign before encrypting because d has to prove that its key k_d^{pub} is connected to pw_A or pw_B, and that d is in possession of k_d^{priv}. Since the one-time password identifies the receiver as well, attacks are prevented through a naming repair [6].

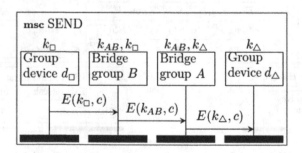

Fig. 3. SEND protocol

SEND: Each group device can communicate via the group key with devices in its group. However, there might be exceptional cases where two devices have to communicate over two groups. E.g. the user wants to check cooking recipes on a tablet (entertainment group) for the content of the fridge (kitchen group).

Sending messages to another group (Fig. 3) requires that bridges re-encrypt the packet from one group key ($k_\square$) to another group key ($k_\triangle$). The sending device $d_\square$ (e.g. the tablet) would send the packet to a bridge of group $\square$ which re-encrypts the message with the bridge key k_{AB} and sends it to a bridge of group $\triangle$. The second bridge re-encrypts the message from k_{AB} to $k_\triangle$ and sends it to the recipient (e.g. the fridge).

This re-encryption realises filtered communication between the groups. To setup a more efficient connection after the initial SEND protocol, an application protocol (e.g. HTTPS) could provide a session key. Alternatively, such a tunnel could be setup via the certified identity keys of the two devices, i.e. running an authenticated Diffie-Hellman Key Exchange via SEND.

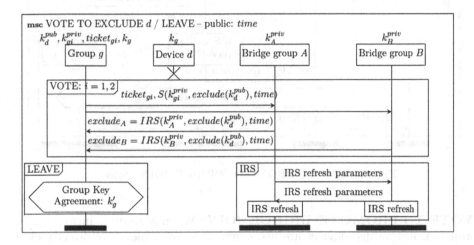

Fig. 4. VOTE TO EXCLUDE/LEAVE protocol

VOTE to EXCLUDE/LEAVE: If devices are misbehaving, bridges must be able to isolate these devices. We force misbehaving devices out of a group by re-establishing the group key – so-called leave event in Group Key Agreement protocols.

Misbehaving devices can be identified by any other device which then casts a vote to quarantine the misbehaving device(s) to all bridges. If a certain threshold of votes is received (Fig. 4 indicates this by i votes), the misbehaving device is forced to leave the group and the user is informed about the attack. Devices without group are quarantined and cannot communicate with any other device. This way, malware cannot spread further and is automatically contained. Optionally, one could allow quarantined devices to communicate with bridge devices in order to access the internet.

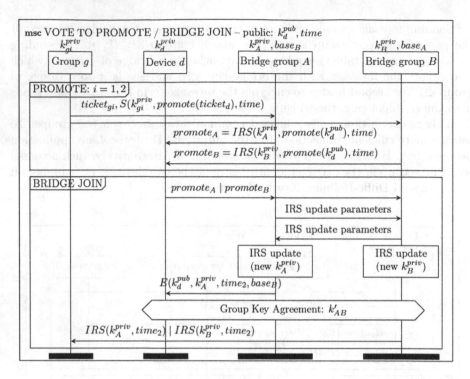

Fig. 5. VOTE TO PROMOTE/BRIDGE JOIN protocol

VOTE TO PROMOTE/BRIDGE JOIN: When a group is introduced or updated, new bridge devices are necessary. The group members directly elect these devices which are picked depending on their resources, geographic location, and/or trustworthiness. We propose that every device sends a signed message with a device for promotion but this can be replaced by any other voting algorithm that tolerates malicious nodes. This *promote* message is signed with private key of the voter and sent to both bridge IRS groups. Bridge devices can verify the signature and record the vote. Devices which do not have the capabilities (e.g. battery), can opt-out by adding this to their vote. Self-election is possible but at least two votes are necessary to elect a bridge. At the end of the election, both bridge groups issue a promotion ticket which is sent to the promoted device to verify that it agrees to being elected. Promotion tickets must expire in the next time period to avoid devices joining twice. The bridge group which the new device should join (A or B, not both), must be fixed and reproducible. We suggest to use a hash like $H(k_d^{pub}, time, k_{AB})$.

Promoted devices can join the bridge group similar to the JOIN operation. The new device d sends the promotion ticket to the bridge group and participates in a Group Key Agreement to get the bridge key k_{AB}. The difference to JOIN is that bridge devices also share the asymmetric key and base secret of IRS in order to certify other keys in the GET TICKET protocol. This key material

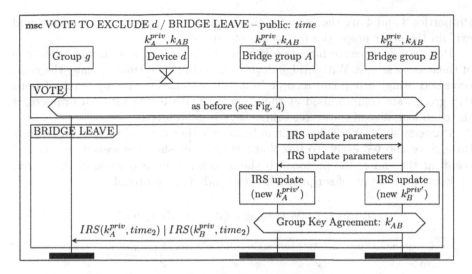

Fig. 6. VOTE TO EXCLUDE/BRIDGE LEAVE protocol

needs to be updated and shared with the new bridge device; i.e. to join bridge group A, d gets k_A^{priv} and $base_B$ (see Fig. 5). Optionally, this message could be signed with the key of the device sharing the secrets k_{A1}^{priv} and include k_d^{pub} as naming repair (see also [6]). This detects attacks of bridge device A_1.

VOTE TO EXCLUDE/BRIDGE LEAVE: Analogous to VOTE TO EXCLUDE/LEAVE, devices can also vote against a bridge device. While the vote phase works exactly as before (see Fig. 4), BRIDGE LEAVE requires that bridge secrets (for bridge group A: k_A^{priv} and $base_B$) and bridge group key k_{AB} are also updated. Additionally, a new bridge needs to be promoted. Figure 6 shows the details of BRIDGE LEAVE. Depending on the used Group Key Agreement, it might be more efficient to run a Group Key Agreement leave protocol first and use the renewed bridge group key to run IRS update.

3   Security Analysis

We evaluated our architecture using state-of-the-art protocol verifier ProVerif. The proofs are available online (see footnote 7). Each proof one by one assumes every combination of devices compromised and analyses four properties:

1. if the main purpose of the protocol is guaranteed,
2. if a second group cannot interfere with the protocol,
3. if at least one bridge IRS key is secure,
4. if the proof script ran through.

Properties 3 and 4 are the same for all proofs. We will introduce them first and explain the other properties for each protocol below.

Property 3: Since we have two IRS bridge groups, it is sufficient when one of them stays secure. With bridge devices changing from time to time, the compromised bridge group can recover from the attack. This is impossible if both IRS groups are compromised at the same time. We tested for each protocol, if the confidentiality of the secret bridge keys is guaranteed.

Property 4: ProVerif does not indicate whether a proof script ran entirely through or aborted early. To test that the proof finished, we leaked an artificial secret at the end of the protocol. If the attacker is in possession of the secret, we know that the proof script reached the end of the protocol.

Table 1. ProVerif results: GET TICKET/JOIN

No	Compromised devices	Authentication	Group 2 join	k_A/k_B secure	End reached
1	None	✓	✓	✓	✓
2	d	✓	✓	✓	✓
3	d_1	✓	✓	✓	✓
4	d_2	✓	✓	✓	✓
5	A	✓	✓	✓	✓
6	B	✓	✓	✓	✓
7	d, A	✓	✓	✓	✓
8	d, B	✓	✓	✓	✓
9	d, d_1	✓	✓	✓	✓
10	d_1, A	✓	✓	✓	✓
11	d_1, B	✓	✓	✓	✓
12	d_1, d_2		✓	✓	✓
13	A, B				✓
14	d, d_1, A	✓	✓	✓	✓
15	d, d_2, A	✓	✓	✓	✓
16	d, A, B				✓
17	d, d_1, d_2		✓	✓	✓
18	d_1, d_2, A		✓	✓	✓
19	d_1, A, B				✓
20	All				✓

GET TICKET/JOIN proves that (1) authentication via the user and the two devices is correct, and that (2) only the right group can be joined with a ticket. Table 1 shows the results of the proofs with d_1 and d_2 being the two devices for authentication. Important are cases 1 to 6 where the attacker controls up to one device. The protocol is even much stronger than this requirement and only fails if either both bridge IRS groups A and B, or d_1 and d_2 are compromised.

For VOTE TO EXCLUDE/LEAVE, we proved that (1) a minimum of two votes is needed and that (2) the exclusion will only take place in the correct

Table 2. ProVerif results: VOTE TO EXCLUDE/LEAVE

No	Compromised devices	Vote	Group 2 leave	k_A/k_B secure	End reached
1	None	✓	✓	✓	✓
2	d	✓	✓	✓	✓
3	A	✓	✓	✓	✓
4	B	✓	✓	✓	✓
5	d, A	✓	✓	✓	✓
6	d, B	✓	✓	✓	✓
7	A, B			✓	
8	All				✓

group. This is true for all cases apart from the ones where both bridge IRS groups are compromised (see Table 2).

The SEND protocol is trivial and therefore we did not formulate a proof in ProVerif. If device $d_\square$ only accepts messages signed with $k_\square$ and device $d_\triangle$ is not in possession of the key, isolation is achieved.

Table 3. ProVerif results: VOTE TO PROMOTE/BRIDGE JOIN

No	Compromised devices	Promote	Group 2 vote	k_A/k_B secure	End reached
1	None	✓	✓	✓	✓
2	d	✓	✓	✓	✓
3	A	✓	✓	✓	✓
4	B	✓	✓	✓	✓
5	d, A		✓	✓	✓
6	d, B	✓			✓
7	A, B				✓
8	All				✓

VOTE TO PROMOTE/BRIDGE JOIN proves that (1) one honest device voted for d and at least two promote messages were received. All devices are allowed to vote, that means also potentially malicious devices cast votes. However, there must be at least one honest device agreeing to proof the absence of attacks. Furthermore, we proved that (2) devices of another group cannot promote devices of the original group. This protocol only holds for the basic requirement (one compromised device) as displayed in Table 3. The reason is that a compromised A can always leak its secrets to d (case 5) and that also a compromised d correctly receives the secrets of A at the end of the protocol. It can then leak them to compromised B (case 6). However, malware tolerance is still guaranteed because the protocol holds for one compromised device (case 1 to 4).

Since Group Key Agreement and IRS cryptography scheme are already proven by the original papers, VOTE TO EXCLUDE/BRIDGE LEAVE is equivalent to VOTE TO EXCLUDE/LEAVE and, therefore, does not need additional proofs.

All in all, our architecture is secure for one compromised device. As expected, none of the protocols holds if both bridge IRS groups are compromised.

4   Discussion

Our security analysis proves that our architecture is tolerant against attacks (malware-tolerant) and can even recover from infected bridge devices. Devices are isolated in their groups and can only communicate to another group if bridge devices allow this – similar to a firewall. This also enables the architecture to proxy vulnerable or outdated devices by simply moving them into an empty group. Services to the network of the device can be made available or turned off per connection.

4.1   Attacks on Multiple Devices

In order to control the whole network, an attacker would have to compromise the two bridge IRS groups A and B in the same time-period. The adversary could either compromise a device of each of the two IRS groups or compromise enough nodes to promote him or herself in multiple groups. The former is the worst case where the architecture is tolerant against only one compromised device in total. In the latter case, a maximum of one compromised device *per group* can be tolerated and half of those can be bridge devices (if they are in the same IRS group). If the threshold for elections is greater than two, even more compromised (non-privileged) devices can be tolerated. However, we assume a powerful attacker and thus the worst case is more realistic.

4.2   Attacks on One Device

Noisy Attack: Let us assume the adversary compromised one light bulb with a buffer overflow or similar. The identity key of that light bulb and the group key of the light bulbs is compromised. The attacker can now participate (incl. read/write access) inside the light bulb group and he or she can communicate with the bridge group. Let us further assume the adversary then launches some attacks without focusing on stealth – like network scans, a spambot, cryptominer, black hole attacks dropping all network traffic, or communication to a known Command-and-Control server. For simplicity we will now only discuss the network scan, the other attacks would be similar.

A network scan can be detected by the victim and all devices that route the traffic or are in the proximity of the adversary since WiFi is not limited through cables. For example there could be two devices around the compromised light bulb, three devices routing traffic, and the victim (as seen before by the red path in Fig. 1a). Not all of these six devices might notice the attack but if we assume a threshold of two votes to exclude, only 33% of those devices need to detect and report the attack through a vote to exclude to the bridges. All the rest of the network does not know of the attack but this is not necessary.

After receiving the two votes to exclude, the compromised light bulb will be quarantined through revoking the identity key of it and renewing the light bulb group key. If the light bulb was a bridge device, the bridge keys are also renewed.

Stealthy Attack: If the adversary compromises a light bulb but stays hidden, he or she can eavesdrop, manipulate and attack the light bulb group and attack the limited interface of the bridge group.

Our architecture will not automatically defend against this, however, an adversary is restricted to the own group. A compromised bridge light bulb would give access to two groups (the light bulbs and the bridges) but cannot interfere with other groups. We estimate that the system will converge to a trusted state in the long run, because as soon as any attack becomes visible (e.g. through signature updates) the device will be automatically isolated. The infrastructure becomes a moving target for the adversary which is harder to compromise.

Physical Attacks (Clone Attacks): An adversary who physically attacks a device and clones it, only gets access to one identity key. Since we incorporated the user into the GET TICKET protocol, we defend against this kind of attack.

Apart from this, it does not matter for the architecture, if the attacker compromises nodes physically or through e.g. a buffer overflow. A compromised node gives the attacker all the secrets of that node. Thus, physical attacks are equal to the attacks discussed above.

Denial of Service: DoS attacks targeting the cryptographic routines are unavoidable but they are easily identified, resulting in the misbehaving device being quickly removed from the network (similar to noisy attacks). If the DoS focuses on the compromised device (e.g. a CryptoLocker), that device is not available any more but the attack can only spread in that one group.

Phishing: Our architecture gives the user full access. By employing two devices in the authentication process, phishing attacks are more complicated. However, the user does have full control over the architecture and phishing could leverage this.

4.3   Performance and Adoption

A major concern for all types of network is performance. Our inter-group communication requires three symmetric encryptions until the session key is setup. Hence, devices which communicate a lot with each other should be organised in the same group, such that communication between the groups is an exception. With the expensive operations JOIN and LEAVE occurring seldom – during setup, failures, and attacks – the performance is approximately similar to symmetric key encryption. Adding devices to multiple groups would improve performance, but bypasses the bridge devices and undermines the distributed firewall. Non-privileged devices only need public key cryptography during setup and for voting. However, resource-constrained devices could rely on other devices to some point. Bridges rely on public key cryptography to add or remove devices but only one bridge of each IRS group needs to answer requests. Hence, these operations can be distributed. If overhead is a concern for bridges, we could promote more bridges to distribute computations more and lower the overhead at the single bridge.

Another concern is that one bridge device of group A and B has to stay online. Considering that fridge, smartphone, router, smart-meters, and smart thermostats are already online around-the-clock we expect this to be less of an issue when smart devices are widespread.

Lastly, also old devices which do not support the protocol could be assigned to a (possibly static) group. They can communicate with the rest of the network without supporting the protocol because the SEND operation is transparent to the sender and receiver. While these old devices do not gain all the benefits, they can rely on other devices to verify and run the network.

Setting devices up works in the same fashion as with normal WiFi networks apart from our password being longer. So, if a device (e.g. a smart light-bulb) has no interface, we would setup the password as before. For light bulbs this usually includes connecting to it via a default WiFi and adding WiFi name and password of the home user. In our case, these are the group identifier instead of the WiFi name and a one-time password instead of the WiFi password. For less technically aware users, devices could be automatically allocated to groups depending on their identifier.

4.4   Improvements

We see two areas for future work. Firstly, the more expensive cryptography routines for GET TICKET, BRIDGE JOIN, and BRIDGE LEAVE could be improved. We imagine a combination of IRS and mediated RSA (mRSA) [4,5]. In mRSA the private key is split into two additive shares, which could be split between bridge group A and B removing the need for two public keys. But, a new cryptographic scheme was beyond our scope.

Secondly, we would like to improve the usability of the GET TICKET procedure. Instead of employing two different devices, we could allow GET TICKET from one device (e.g. a smartphone) and store or re-compute old one-time passwords. If a password is used twice, either the setup device (the smartphone) or the new device (e.g. the new smart light bulb) misbehaved. At the moment, this would require to store all one-time passwords.

5   Related Work and Comparison

In the literature, mesh networks are usually analysed in their applied forms, i.e. Wireless Sensor Networks, Wireless Ad-Hoc Networks, Mobile Ad-Hoc Networks, and Vehicular Ad-Hoc Networks.

While there are more mesh architectures with hierarchies or clustered devices, usually their cryptographic key or the base station is the single point-of-failure. For brevity we only included a few.

Diop et al. [10] deployed isolation to WSNs by utilising secret sharing and a network-wide symmetric key. The base station uses secret sharing to setup keys for clusters. Each head of a cluster derives the keys for the sensor nodes. Through this key infrastructure, sensor data is delivered via the cluster heads to the base station and isolation is achieved between the clusters. The authors assume a trusted base station with an IDS, unlimited resources, and table of all nodes in the network. The base station is a single point-of-failure and the architecture is, thus, not malware-tolerant.

The SASHA architecture [3] proposes a self-healing approach for sensor networks that is inspired by the immune system. The objectives of this work are automatic fault recognition, adaptive network monitoring, and a coordinated response. To detect faults, the network has a definition of itself in the form of a neural network. Base station, Thymus system, and Lymph system are single points-of-failure making the architecture vulnerable to targeted attacks.

Posh [8] is a proactive self-healing mechanism for WSNs. The sink periodically re-initialises sensor nodes with a new key and a secret seed. The nodes then also share some randomness with their neighbours to make it more difficult for the adversary to derive keys if nodes are compromised. Since the sink is in possession of all secrets, it can recompute the keys and read the data. However, the sink is a trusted entity and a single point-of-failure.

The authors [9] later improved their architecture with a moving target defence system. Data is moved either once or continuously, and then re-encrypted with one of three cryptographic schemes: symmetric encryption, symmetric encryption with key evolution, and asymmetric encryption. This way an adversary cannot easily delete data as the location of the data is unknown. Also in the extended architecture, the sink is assumed trustworthy which is not malware-tolerant.

The concept of intrusion-tolerant systems was already proposed and theoretically analysed by Verissimo et al. [19] They also created a self-healing, intrusion-tolerant system aimed at Industrial Control Systems (ICSs) [2]. A slightly different self-healing, malware-tolerant ICS was proposed in [7].

Sousa et al. [18] designed together with Verissimo an intrusion-tolerant, distributed replication system built on top of *critical utility infrastructural resilience information switches*, a firewall device which they previously developed. The approach uses proactive and reactive recovery to self-heal failed replicas. The devices are rejuvenated periodically and upon detection of malicious or faulty behaviour. To agree on firewall decisions, the replicas communicate through a synchronous, trusted channel between the replicas called wormhole. If a majority of replicas approve a network message, it is signed with a key unknown to the replicas in the wormhole subsystem. Local machines behind the firewall can verify the signature to identify trusted packages. The approach is similar to ours but, instead of deploying protection mechanisms in front of the network, we spread our firewall over the network and enforce it with cryptography. On the other side, our approach can only automatically quarantine devices. Self-healing would be optionally possible since it is orthogonal to our infrastructure but we doubt there is a general purpose solution to securely rejuvenate consumer devices of different manufacturers.

6   Conclusion

All in all, our architecture can provide isolation for flat, interconnected networks and networks where geographic and virtual layout differ. It enables them to automatically contain compromised devices while distributing trust over the entire architecture without single point-of-failure, i.e. malware tolerance.

References

1. Amir, Y., Kim, Y., Nita-Rotaru, C., Tsudik, G.: On the performance of group key agreement protocols. ACM Trans. Inf. Syst. Secur. (TISSEC) **7**(3), 457–488 (2004)
2. Bessani, A.N., Sousa, P., Correia, M., Neves, N.F., Verissimo, P.: The crutial way of critical infrastructure protection. IEEE Secur. Priv. **6**(6), 44–51 (2008)
3. Bokareva, T., Bulusu, N., Jha, S.: SASHA: toward a self-healing hybrid sensor network architecture. In: The Second IEEE Workshop on Embedded Networked Sensors, pp. 71–78. Citeseer (2005)
4. Boneh, D., Ding, X., Tsudik, G.: Identity-based mediated RSA. In: 3rd Workshop on Information Security Application [5]
5. Boneh, D., Ding, X., Tsudik, G., Wong, C.M.: A method for fast revocation of public key certificates and security capabilities. In: USENIX Security Symposium (2001)
6. Davis, D.: Defective sign & encrypt in S/MIME, PKCS#7, MOSS, PEM, PGP, and XML. In: USENIX Annual Technical Conf., General Track, pp. 65–78 (2001)
7. Denzel, M., Ryan, M., Ritter, E.: A malware-tolerant, self-healing industrial control system framework. In: De Capitani di Vimercati, S., Martinelli, F. (eds.) SEC 2017. IAICT, vol. 502, pp. 46–60. Springer, Cham (2017). https://doi.org/10.1007/978-3-319-58469-0_4
8. Di Pietro, R., Ma, D., Soriente, C., Tsudik, G.: POSH: proactive co-operative self-healing in unattended wireless sensor networks. In: IEEE Symposium on Reliable Distributed Systems, pp. 185–194. IEEE (2008)
9. Di Pietro, R., Mancini, L.V., Soriente, C., Spognardi, A., Tsudik, G.: Playing hide-and-seek with a focused mobile adversary in unattended wireless sensor networks. Ad Hoc Netw. **7**(8), 1463–1475 (2009)
10. Diop, A., Qi, Y., Wang, Q.: Efficient group key management using symmetric key and threshold cryptography for cluster based wireless sensor networks. Int. J. Comput. Netw. Inf. Secur. **6**(8), 9 (2014)

11. Dodis, Y., Franklin, M., Katz, J., Miyaji, A., Yung, M.: Intrusion-resilient public-key encryption. In: Joye, M. (ed.) CT-RSA 2003. LNCS, vol. 2612, pp. 19–32. Springer, Heidelberg (2003). https://doi.org/10.1007/3-540-36563-X_2

12. Dodis, Y., Franklin, M., Katz, J., Miyaji, A., Yung, M.: A generic construction for intrusion-resilient public-key encryption. In: Cryptographers' Track at the RSA Conference [11], pp. 81–988

13. Franklin, M.: A survey of key evolving cryptosystems. Int. J. Secur. Netw. 1(1–2), 46–53 (2006)

14. Hu, Y.C., Perrig, A.: A survey of secure wireless ad hoc routing. IEEE Secur. Priv. 2(3), 28–39 (2004)

15. Itkis, G.: Intrusion-resilient signatures: generic constructions, or defeating strong adversary with minimal assumptions. In: International Conference on Security in Communication Networks [16], pp. 102–118

16. Itkis, G., Reyzin, L.: Sibir: signer-base intrusion-resilient signatures. Adv. Cryptol.-Crypto 2002, 101–116 (2002)

17. Parno, B., Perrig, A., Gligor, V.: Distributed detection of node replication attacks in sensor networks. In: IEEE Symposium on Security and Privacy, pp. 49–63. IEEE (2005)

18. Sousa, P., Bessani, A.N., Correia, M., Neves, N.F., Verissimo, P.: Highly available intrusion-tolerant services with proactive-reactive recovery. IEEE Trans. Parallel Distrib. Syst. 21(4), 452–465 (2010)

19. Veríssimo, P.E., Neves, N.F., Correia, M.P.: Intrusion-tolerant architectures: concepts and design. In: de Lemos, R., Gacek, C., Romanovsky, A. (eds.) WADS 2002. LNCS, vol. 2677, pp. 3–36. Springer, Heidelberg (2003). https://doi.org/10.1007/3-540-45177-3_1

Inside GandCrab Ransomware

Yassine Lemmou[✉] and El Mamoun Souidi

Faculty of Sciences, LabMIASI, Mohammed V University in Rabat, BP 1014 RP,
1000 Rabat, Morocco
yassine.lemmou@gmail.com, emsouidi@gmail.com

Abstract. A special category of malware named ransomware has
become very popular for cyber-criminals to extort money. This category
limits users from accessing their machines (computers, mobile phones
and IoT devices) unless a ransom is paid. Every month, security experts
report many forms of ransomware attacks, termed as ransomware families. An example of these families is the GandCrab ransomware that
was released at the end of January 2018. In this paper, we present a full
depth malware analysis of this ransomware following some recent work
and findings on ransomware detection and prevention.

Keywords: GandCrab · Ransomware · Analysis · Infection
Detection prevention · Overinfection · Self-reproduction

1 Introduction

The `AIDS Information Trojan` or `PC Cyborg` was the first ransomware, developed by the anthropologist Joseph Popp in 1989. It was distributed via post mail:
a floppy disk labelled AIDS Information Introductory Diskette. After 90 reboots,
it delivered its payload, which encoded the names of its target files without
encrypting the contents. Ransomware reappeared in the following years, starting
from 2005: `GPCoder.AC` in 2005, `CryZip` in 2006, `GPCoder.ak` in 2008, `WinLock`
in 2010, `Pantanilla` in 2012, which was the first ransomware that infected the
Master Boot Record (MBR) and prevented the operating system from loading. In 2013, we saw `CryptoLocker` and `CryptoWall`. In 2014, `CTB-Locker` and
`TorrentLocker`. The frequency of ransomware attacks has significantly grown
since 2015 when "Researchers saw more than four million samples of ransomware
in the second quarter of 2015, including 1.2 million that were new" [7]. `TorDroid`,
`TorrentLocker` and `CTB-Locker` were among the ransomware that spread that
year. In 2016, the Internet Security Threat Report 2017 [35] mentioned that
the number of new ransomware families increased dramatically (about 100 new
families in 2016 against 30 new families in 2015). `Cerber` and `Locky` are two
of the most widespread ransomware families. The situation was not different in
2017, when ransomware kept its dominant position in the cybersecurity land-
scape. It was the most common type of malware delivered by Exploit Kits and
spams [30]. `Spora`, `BTCWare`, `WannaCry` and other families appeared in this year.

© Springer Nature Switzerland AG 2018
J. Camenisch and P. Papadimitratos (Eds.): CANS 2018, LNCS 11124, pp. 154–174, 2018.
https://doi.org/10.1007/978-3-030-00434-7_8

In 2018, ransomware continues to evolve and remains a problem for individuals and companies because of its destructive effects [39]. At the beginning of this year, new ransomware/variants were released, like `MMM`, `LazagneCrypt`, `Rapid`, `Velso`, `DexLocker`, `Saturn`, `GandCrab` (the subject of this paper), `Jigsaw` in two variants, `Globelmposter` in three variants and `Blind` in the `.[email].leon` variant.

This paper presents a full analysis (static, dynamic and reverse engineering) of the version (`V1`) of the `GandCrab` ransomware. The analysis is based on related work on ransomware detection and prevention and also on our discussions with the `GandCrab` developers, who agreed to answer our questions. This work allows us to discover the hidden side of `GandCrab`: we discuss self-reproduction, over-infection and some ransomware behaviours that can be used for detection.

The first version of `GandCrab` was first discovered by the security researcher David Montenegro at the end of January 2018 and was distributed via two exploit kits: `RIG EK` and `GrandSoft EK` [31]. Then, in early February 2018, it was delivered via the `Necurs` malicious spam and the `EITest Campaign` [31]. Until the end of February, the research community found more than seven subversions of this version, namely `v1.0`, `v1.1`, `v2.1`, `v2.1r`, `v2.2r`, `v2.3r` and `v2.3.1r`. This analysis focusses on the subversions `v1.0` and `v2.2r`, which allowed us to conclude that there are no major differences between the core modules of these versions (the packing methods were changed). This result was confirmed by the ransomware developers, who mentioned that all these subversions are only to fix bugs and distribute the ransomware by all possible ways. On 28 February 2018, Bitdefender released a ransomware decryption tool for `GandCrab` to recover files that were encrypted by the first version [11]. The `GandCrab` developers mentioned in our support chat that their servers were hacked and the database was leaked. In a personal communication with Michael Gillespie, creator of `ID Ransomware`[1], and Lawrence Abrams, owner of `Bleepingcomputer`[2], they confirmed this comment. Then, on 6 March, the `GandCrab` developers released a new version labelled `GANDCRAB V2.0` [2] with a new `.CRAB` extension and other changes. The developers stated that this version includes a secure C&C server in order to prevent a similar compromise like the first version.

This paper is organized as follows: Sect. 2 describes the static analysis. We detail the hidden side of this ransomware by a dynamic analysis and a reverse engineering in Sect. 3. We present some detection behaviours in Sect. 4 and we conclude in Sect. 5.

1.1   Related Work

Young and Yung [40, 41] presented the idea of cryptovirology (cryptography and virology) related to ransomware. While some researchers [5, 34] categorize the ransomware as a cryptovirus, the ransomware is in general not a cryptovirus. Indeed there is no self-reproduction as defined the first time by Cohen in [12] in

---

[1] https://id-ransomware.malwarehunterteam.com/.

[2] https://www.bleepingcomputer.com/.

1986. Indeed, much ransomware like `PrincessLocker`, `Striked` and `Locky` do not copy their code into other directories. For `GandCrab`, we prove that it is a virus, thus a cryptovirus like `TeslaCrypt`.

`GandCrab` confirmed the results of Gallegos-Segovia *et al.* [15] and Shinde *et al.* [38] who showed the dependence of ransomware on social engineering and demographics like age and education to compromise machines. Indeed, `GandCrab` (all its versions) is delivered via many possible ways using spams and exploit kits through social engineering. For example, the last version `v4`, released in July 2018, was distributed via fake crack sites [32].

The first ransomware analysis was published in 2010 by Alexandre Gazet [16], who described a comparative analysis of four families: `Filecode`, `Kroten`, `Dirt` and `Gpcode`. Similar works were seen in 2017; for example, Caivano *et al.* [9] discussed the common behaviours of 76 samples of 12 families, John MacRae *et al.* [29] examined the `Locky` ransomware and our previous work focused on `PrincessLocker`, `Spora` and `TeslaCrypt` [26–28]. This paper is close to these works, but offers not only an analysis of `GandCrab`, but also some detection and prevention measures are proposed, following related work. The first attempt was by Kharraz *et al.* [21] in 2015, when they suggested that monitoring abnormal file system activities can be used to design a practical defense against crypto-ransomware. The result of this study was used one year later by a dynamic analysis system called `UNVEIL`, which could be used to detect ransomware [19]. More work on ransomware detection was published in 2016/2017, for instance, `CryptoDrop` [37], a tool based on file system activities, `ShieldFS` [13], `Redemption` [20] and others. Prevention examples include `PayBreak` [23], a tool that hooks the encryption functions in a standard libraries and stores the used encryption keys, `CloudRPS` [24], a cloud analysis service for ransomware prevention, `FlashGuard` [18], `CLDsafe` [42] and others.

There are some existing analyses of `GandGrab`, for example [3,6,10] or [31], which they present `GandCrab` from another point of view different to our analysis. This paper has as goal to analyze `GandCrab`, extract its behaviours that can be used for its detection or the detection of other ransomware. In particular, this paper bridges the existing analyses on ransomware and the scientific papers on the subject. We suggest that the ransomware analyses (for `GandCrab` or other ransomware) should extract and identify the common ransomware behaviours to build a large set of common behaviours that can be used for detection and prevention.

2   Static Analysis

The seven subversions `v1.0`, `v1.1`, `v2.1`, `v2.1r`, `v2.2r`, `v2.3r` and `v2.3.1r` were detected by many antivirus engines in their first submission in `VirusTotal`. Figure 1 presents some information about them. The compilation timestamp contains the compilation date of the binary file; this field could be modified by the developers to contain a false date. This field and the first submission date field are close, which leads us to think that the field of compilation date was not modified. Figure 2 summarises our findings from the static analysis of the version v1.0 of GandCrab.

MD5	Subversion	Compilation Timestamp	First Submission	Last Analysis	Detection Ratio
a635d6a35c2fc054042b6868ef52a0c3	v1.0	26/01/2018 04:08:06	26/01/2018 07:04:11	27/01/2018 17:56:41	40/56
6866d8d8bf8565d94e0e1479978cf1e5	v1.1	28/01/2018 21:11:08	29/01/2018 00:44:12	24/02/2018 18:32:19	55/68
*	v2.0	*	*	*	*
*	v2.1	*	*	*	*
6393f064aeb0381fbfa67593f636d6b5	v2.1r	06/02/2018 11:39:42	07/02/2018 10:49:23	11/02/2018 04:50:47	46/66
a450ab3289624206b95c2ac03aad34ed	v2.2r	12/02/2018 12:22:07	12/02/2018 13:00:19	13/02/2018 09:51:06	50/67
1c20431db2283ec63a03696e03f54a57	v2.3r	20/02/2018 17:29:26	21/02/2018 16:33:27	25/02/2018 19:11:58	47/65
483625472264044dd03c0b193f5ce53a	v2.3.1r	26/02/2018 08:41:46	26/02/2018 16:17:10	27/02/2018 01:06:23	32/66

Fig. 1. GandCrab compilation timestamp and detection ratio.

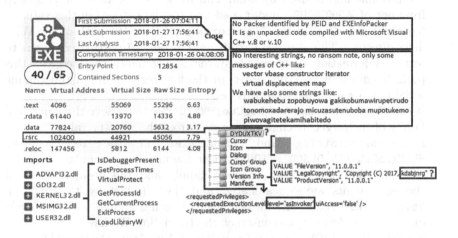

Fig. 2. GandCrab v1.0 static analysis.

These subversions contain some incomprehensible words like kdabjnrg in the subversion v1.0 or GELUMIROHIPETU in the subversion v2.2r. The security configuration item AsInvoker means that they will run with the same permission as the process that started them and can be elevated to a higher permission level by selecting Run as Administrator. We did not find any packers identified by the PEiD and EXEInfoPacker tools, no interesting strings like the ransom note strings or the names of the imports of some cryptographic functions. We suppose that they are packed by an unknown packer or obfuscated. We found the same results for the recent versions V2, V3 and V4.

3 Dynamic Analysis and Reverse Engineering

We built an isolated malware analysis sandbox using VirtualBox. This environment included a set of test data files with different file extensions within a Windows 7 Virtual Machine (VM specifications are not important) with no antivirus. All executions of the tested samples ran with local administrator privileges.

3.1   Initialisation: Mutex and Self-reproduction

After unpacking the binary files (v1.0 and v2.2r), GandCrab starts creating a mutex to prevent itself from running more than one instance of itself. To create the mutex name, GandCrab performs the following steps:

1. It calls function sub_XXXX39B0 to retrieve the following field strings that will be used in the mutex name: pc_group and ransom_id.
2. In function sub_XXXX7230:
   - GandCrab calls sub_XXXX71B0 to retrieve the Domain registry value from the registry key HKLM\SYSTEM\CurrentControlSet\services\ tcpip\Parameters using the functions RegOpenKeyExW and RegQuery ValueExW. This value key specifies the DNS domain name of the target machine and is used by GandCrab to define the value of pc_group from one of WORKGROUP, undefined and the data stored in this value.
   - GandCrab calls GetWindowsDirectoryW to retrieve the path of the Windows directory. The returned path is used by GetVolumeInformationW to retrieve information about the file system and volume associated with this path. GandCrab is only interested in the first eight digits of the volume serial number returned from this call.
   - It calls RegOpenKeyExW and RegQueryValueExW to retrieve the name and family of the target machine's processor from the registry value ProcessorNameString and Identifier in the registry key HKLM\HARDW-ARE\DESCRIPTION\System\CentralProcessor\0.
   - The processor name, the processor family and the decimal value of the eight digits are concatenated and then hashed by the function RtlCompu-te-Crc32. The hashed result is concatenated with the eight digits (not in decimal) to construct the ID victim. We have: ransom_id=CRC32(Decimal(8_FirstHex_VolumeSerialNumber)|| ProcessorName||ProcessorFamily)||8_FirstHex_VolumeSerialNumber.
3. The string Global\ is concatenated with the results of the second item to construct the name of the mutex (Fig. 3): Global\pc_group=<PcGroup> &ransom_id=<ID_Victim>.

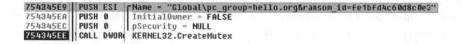

```
754345E9 ||| PUSH ESI    ┌Name = "Global\pc_group=hello.org&ransom_id=fe1bfd4c60d8c0e3"
754345EA ||| PUSH 0      │ InitialOwner = FALSE
754345EC ||| PUSH 0      │ pSecurity = NULL
754345EE ||| CALL DWOR(  │ KERNEL32.CreateMutex
```

Fig. 3. CreateMutex function in GandCrab.

Self-reproduction is defined in [28] as the ability of a program to reproduce/copy itself to other locations. Generally, ransomware does not copy itself to other directories (e.g., Cerber, Locky and BTCWare), but some ransomware, like CryptoLocker, TeslaCrypt, Alpha, Diamond and GandCrab, perform this process to hide themselves in other locations or to propagate themselves, for instance, Spora. GandCrab is a cryptovirus that uses a strange method to copy itself to the %AppData%\Microsoft\ directory. It creates a thread to create a window with a mutex name firefox browser and labels this window as firefox. This window is displayed by the function ShowWindow and loads a code that copies the binary code in the desired directory. The self-reproduction in GandCrab is performed as long as the binary is not executed in a directory in %AppData%. The copy (not hidden like the copy of TeslaCrypt v3.1) is identical to the executed binary, but named a random name of six letters generated using the function CryptGenRandom. Malware-Bytes [31] did not understand the benefits of launching a window to perform the self-reproduction. The GandCrab developers, in our communication with them, suppose that some antivirus solutions do not detect this method of loading the persistent code. Even given this answer, their method remains unclear for us and it should be tested by antivirus researchers. The full path of the created copy is used by this thread to put it in the registry key HKCU\Software\Microsoft\Windows\CurrentVersion\RunOnce. The registry value will run GandCrab once in the machine restart to encrypt any newly created file, then it will be deleted and not executed again. If an user executes (many clicks) GandCrab n times concurrently in any directory different to %AppData% directory or its subdirectories, it will create n copies in %AppData%\Microsoft\ and n registry values in RunOnce. In the following boot of the target machine, the created mutex leaves only one copy to maintain its execution, but the created copies remain in %AppData%\Microsoft\. In other ransomware that create a copy, like CryptoLocker or TeslaCrypt, the original ransomware terminates its execution and the copy continues the execution and the encryption process (in same cases the original ransomware is deleted). In GandCrab, the copy is used only in reboot and the original ransomware continues its infection normally without executing its copy.

3.2   Enumerating Running Processes and First POST to C&C

Much ransomware like Alpha or TeslaCrypt v3.1 enumerate the running processes to avoid their detection by some monitoring tools or antivirus softwares. In sub_XXXX4640, GandCrab enumerates the running processes using the functions CreateToolhelp32Snapshot, Process32FirstW and Process32NextW to kill the following processes: oracle.exe, ocssd.exe, msftesql.exe, mspub.exe, dbsnmp.exe, sqlagent.exe, sqlbrowser.exe, sqlservr.exe, excel.exe, agntsvc.exe, sqlwriter.exe, synctime.exe, agntsvc.exe, agntsvc.exe, isqlplussvc.exe, xfssvccon.exe, thebat.exe, steam.exe, agntsvc.exe, encsvc.exe, firefoxconfig.exe, ocomm.exe, mysqld.exe, powerpnt.exe, mysqld-nt.exe, mysqld-opt.exe, dbeng50.exe, inmydesktopservice.exe, fopath.exe, visio.exe, msaccess.exe, onenote.exe, ocautoupds.exe, mydsqbcoreservice.exe, outlook.exe, thebat64.exe, thunderbird.exe, wordpad.exe, esktopqos.exe, winword.exe, tbirdconfig.exe.

This list does not contain any monitoring tool or antivirus. Therefore, the cause of this enumeration is to terminate these processes (using a call to `OpenProcess` with `PROCESS_TERMINATE` in `DesiredAccess` followed by a call to `TerminateProcess`) in order to encrypt correctly the files, for example, without `Sharing violation` if the file is opened by another process.

At this point, `GandCrab` calls `sub_XXXX40A0` at `XXXX4911` to create the submitted data to C&C:

1. `GandCrab` calls again the functions `sub_XXXX39B0` and `sub_XXXX7230` to build the victim ID with the same operations described in the Subsect. 3.1. Then, using `sub_XXXX6E40` it makes the string `pc_group=<PcGroup>& ransom_id=<ID_Victim>` (Fig. 4).
2. The remaining operations in this function are used to construct the content of the text ransom note.

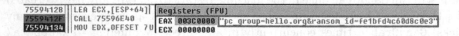

Fig. 4. `pc_group` and `ransom id`.

Next, `GandCrab` calls `sub_XXXX6370` to generate the keys that will be used for encryption. It generates a public/private key pair using API calls from `ADVAPI32.dll`. Specifically, it calls `CryptGenKey` with `A400=CALG_RSA_KEYX` in `Algid` to generate a random cryptographic RSA public/private key pair. Then, it exports these keys by two calls to `CryptExportKey`. `GandCrab` calls other functions from the function `sub_XXXX7230` to retrieve additional information about the target machine:

1. `GetUserNameW` to retrieve the name of the user who launched the ransomware and `GetComputerNameW` to retrieve the NetBIOS name of the target machine.
2. `GandCrab` calls again `sub_XXXX71B0` to retrieve the value of the field `pc_group`. This call is followed by a call to `RegOpenKeyExW` and `RegQueryValueExW` to retrieve the current language of the machine from the value `LocaleName` in the registry key `HKCU\Control Panel\International`.
3. `GandCrab` loops through the registry values in the key `HKCU\Keyboard Layout \ Preload` to check the Russian language `0x00000419=ru` in the keyboard layout. If it finds this value, `GandCrab` will exit this loop and take 1 as a value of the field `pc_keyb`. Otherwise, the field will take the value 0. This value is used by `GandCrab` to avoid infecting the users of CIS contries[3].
4. `GandCrab` retrieves the Windows product name from the registry value `HKLM\SOFTWARE\Wow6432Node\Microsoft\Windows NT\CurrentVersion\ProductName`. Then, it retrieves the information about the current system by a call to `GetNativeSystemInfo`.

---

[3] The Commonwealth of Independent States, also called the Russian Commonwealth.

5. Another process of enumeration is performed by the function sub_XXXX79C0 at XXXX75E9. This enumeration is performed to retrieve the antiviruses installed on the machine (without TerminateProcess): AVP.EXE, ekrn.exe, avgnt.exe, ashDisp.exe, Mcshield.exe, fsguiexe.exe, persfw.exe NortonAntiBot.exe, cmdagent.exe, smc.exe, cfp.exe, msmpeng.exe. This enumeration defines the field av (antivirus) to take the number of antiviruses installed on the machine. We think that this field is used for data gathering purposes.

6. GandCrab performs the same operations mentioned above to create again the victim ID. Then, for each letter from A to Z, it calls GetDriveTypeW to determine the type of disk drive. The returned value of this call is compared to 0x02=DRIVE_REMOVABLE and 0x05=CD-ROM drive in order to not call the function GetDiskFreeSpaceW for the type of drive 0x00=DRIVE_UNKNOWN, 0x01=DRIVE_NO_ROOT_DIR, 0x02=DRIVE_REMOVABLE and 0x05=DRIVE_CDROM. GandCrab does not encrypt the files on removable and media drives, but it encrypts the files on fixed drives and mounted shared directories.

   For each available target drive, GandCrab makes the following string using the two previous calls: <DriverLetter>:<TypeDrive>_<NbrBytesIn AllCluste-rs>\<NbrBytesUsed>. Contrary to GandCrab that loops from A to Z, much ransomware call firstly GetLogicalDrives to retrieve the available disk drives then, GetDriveType to determine their type.

7. GandCrab calls the function sub_XXXX6D90 to retrieve the external IP address of the victim by a GET request to ipv4bot.whatismyipaddress.com. The Host in Fig. 5 was changed by HttpAddRequestHeadersW. Despite this invalid Host header, the request returns the IP victim. The ransomware developers mentioned to us that the reason of this error was a code typing mistake.

   Despite the fact that GandCrab encrypts the files even when it does not receive an answer for this request, this mistake could give valuable information to researchers working in the field of network traffic analysis. Indeed, we can make a signature-based Snort rule (Fig. 6) to alert the network administrator for any machine being infected. In this case, they may have a chance to stop the infection by isolating the target machine (to not encrypt the shared directories) or isolating its network from the external network (GandCrab does not encrypt the files until it finds the C&C by the following POST request).

GandCrab calls CryptBinaryToStringA with the parameter 40000001 = CRYPT_STRING_NOCRLF & CRYPT_STRING_BASE64 in dwFlags, which means that the keys BLOB (exported keys) will be converted to base64 without any new line characters to the encoded keys. Then, it calls lstrcat to assemble the previous collected data: Action=call&ip=<item7>pc_user=<item1>&pc_name=<item1> &pc_group=<item2>&pc_lang=<item2>&pc_keyb=<item3>&os_major=<item4> &os_bit=<item4>&ransom_id=<item6>&hdd=<item6>&pub_key=<pubkey> &priv_key=<privkey>&version=<Subversion>. In our case, GandCrab neglects the field av for antivirus because there was no antivirus installed in the machine. Generally, it neglects any field whose value it cannot retrieve. Figure 7 presents the data sent to C&C before encryption.

```
GET / HTTP/1.1
Host: nomoreransom.coin
User-Agent: Mozilla/5.0 (Windows NT 6.1; WOW64) AppleWebKit/537.36
(KHTML, like Gecko) Chrome/55.0.2883.87 Safari/537.36
Cache-Control: no-cache
HTTP/1.1 200 OK
Cache-Control: private
Content-Type: text/html
Server:
Date: Tue, 06 Mar 2018 00:18:30 GMT
Connection: close
Content-Length: 14
<Victim Address IP>
```

Fig. 5. Wireshark capture on retrieving the external IP victim.

```
alert tcp $HOME_NET any -> $EXTERNAL_NET $HTTP_PORTS
(msg:"GandCrab V1 Ransomware"; flow:established,to_server;
content:"Host|3A| nomoreransom.coin"; nocase; http_header;
classtype:ransomware-activity; sid:2000001; rev:1;)
```

Fig. 6. Alert Snort rule for GET request.

This data is encrypted via the RC4 algorithm using the key aeriedjD#shasj (the function sub_XXXX5CC0 creates and initializes the substitution box and the function sub_XXXX5D70 generates the key stream and encrypts this data), encoded to base64 using CryptBinaryToString, then, sent to C&C.

To send this data (almost 5797 bytes), Gandcrab enters in an infinite loop of IP requests until it finds the IP address of nomoreransom.coin, nomoreransom.bit or gandcrab.bit using nslookup. Therefore, it does not encrypt files until it receives an answer from its C&C. Once it finds its C&C, it sends the transformed data by a POST request to <C&C address>/curl.php?token=1027. The token (4 numbers) is taken from the beginning of GandCrab binary file (Fig. 8).

Following the above, we can drop or reject any communication to gandcrab.bit, nomoreransom.coin or nomoreransom.bit. Like the previous Snort rule, we propose the rule in Fig. 9 to alert the network administrator for any attempt by GandCrab to communicate with its C&C.

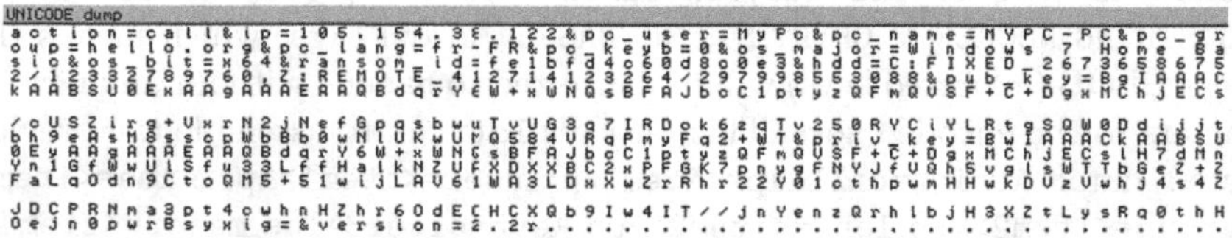

Fig. 7. The data sent before encryption and transformation.

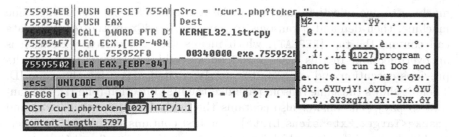

Fig. 8. The used `token` in the `POST` request.

```
alert tcp $HOME_NET any -> $EXTERNAL_NET $HTTP_PORTS
(msg:"GandCrab V1 Ransomware"; flow:established,to_server;
content:"/curl.php?token="; nocase; http_header;
pcre:/\/curl.php?token=[0-9]{4}/; classtype:ransomware-activity;
sid:2000002; rev:1;)
```

Fig. 9. Alert Snort signature for `POST` request.

3.3   C&C Response and Encryption Process

GandCrab uses the submitted data in the previous POST to create an onion ransom web page for the victim. At this point, the victim can view its ransom page before the encryption process. The response of the previous POST is used by GandCrab to redirect its flow of execution:

- If GandCrab does not receive any response from its C&C, it will return again to create the data sent to C&C, then submit it.
- For any token used in the POST request, the C&C answers by "Invalid token key". We do not know if any number other than 1027 is valid; all we tested failed. In this case, GandCrab performs the encryption process. We think that this token is used to make the reverse engineering of this version more complex and avoid the researchers to receive a response from the C&C.
- Otherwise, the C&C answers with some encrypted data (almost 5201 bytes).

The received response is decoded from Base64 using CryptStringToBinary. If it is not decoded, GandCrab will return to create the data sent to C&C and submit it again. Otherwise, it decrypts the data with the same key aeriedjD#shasj using the RC4 algorithm. Then, it verifies its content with the function sub_XXXX33E0:

- GandCrab compares the number of occurrences of { and }. If the number of occurrences of { is 0 or the number of occurrences of { and } are different, GandCrab will call ExitProcess to terminate its execution.
- Overinfection is defined in [26,28] as any infection that follows the first infection in the same machine by the same malware. Much ransomware like PrincessLocker or Striked do not assemble all their infections in the same

machine to one infection and they make n IDs in n executions in the same machine, then demand n ransoms to pay. For GandCrab, the received data can contain the tag {REPEAT}, which means that the current execution is an overinfection. In this case, GandCrab assembles this execution with its previous execution and encrypts the newly created files using the same ID. Then, it shows the same ransom page like the first infection (one ID, one ransom to pay). The answer also contains the fields {pub_key=<PubKey>} and {mask=<Target_Extensions_List>}. The first contains the public key generated in the first infection, which is used for encryption using CryptImportKey. The second contains the target extensions. The ransomware developers mentioned in our support chat that they wanted to have the ability to change extensions by their C&C. But, the team decided to use only the extensions inside the code.

- In the case of CIS countries (keyb=1 and the ip address is a CIS ip), the C&C answers only by the tag {DELETE}. This tag redirects the ransomware to delete itself and terminate its execution by ShellExecuteW and ExitProcess (Fig. 10).
- In the first infection, the received data from the C&C contains the tag {OK} and the variable {mask=<Target_Extensions_List>}.

In short, the infection process is as follows. GandCrab differentiates between the first infection and the overinfections using its ID: in the two cases, the public/private keys are generated, then submitted with the ID to C&C, which searches for this ID in its database. If it exists, the current infection is an overinfection and the C&C answers with the existed public key in its database. In this case, GandCrab neglects the generated keys and encrypts the files using the received key. In the first infection, GandCrab uses the generated public key in the current execution to encrypt files.

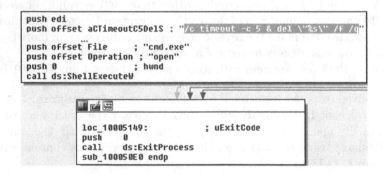

Fig. 10. Executed operations in {DELETE} tag.

GandCrab calls GetTickCount to count the encryption time, which is only used for statistical purposes, according to the GandCrab developers; the second call to the function is after completion of the encryption threads, which are created per drive, as follows. `GandCrab` loops again from A to Z and calls for each letter the function `GetDriveTypeW` to enumerate the available target drives. Then, it creates for each target drive a thread to encrypt its content. This thread calls recursively the function `sub_XXXX6B90` for each directory to perform the following operations:

1. It calls the function `sub_XXXX6590` to load the avoided directories and compare them to the current directory. `GandCrab` does not encrypt the files in: `ProgramData`, `Program Files`, `Tor Browser`, `Ransomware`, `All Users`, `Local Settings` and `Windows`. It also avoids other directories retrieved using a call to `SHGetSpecialFolderPathW`.

2. `GandCrab` calls `sub_XXXX6940` to extract the extension of each file in the current directory and compare it to `.sql`. If it is an SQL file and its size is less than `0x40000000` bytes, `GandCrab` will read the content of this file to search for the string `*******************`. Then, it calls `sub_XXXX68E0`. We supposed that `GandCrab` avoids encrypting any SQL file, but generally, it encrypts the SQL files and any file containing the previous string. We asked the ransomware developers about this operation; their response is shown in the Fig. 11, which mentions that their ransomware can detect some detection methods using decoy files. We were not able to discover which methods of decoy files they target.

   Ransomware detection using decoy files is used in some tools like [14] and mentioned in many papers, while two papers [17,25] focus particularly on describing this method. Generally, we are doubtful about ransomware detection methods based only on decoy files. Any ransomware can change the order of enumerating its target files or detect these decoy file like `GandCrab` does (if the answer in Fig. 11 is true). We suggest that the decoy files can be used along with other indicators in ransomware detection.

3. If this directory is not avoided, `GandCrab` will put the text ransom note, even if the directory is empty or does not contain target files.

4. If this directory is not avoided and contains some files, `GandCrab` will call `sub_XXXX6850` to enumerate the target files and encrypt them.

Support:	2018-02-11 11:02:25
There is a certain algorithm, including weight and certain symbols.	
You:	2018-02-11 10:36:37
i don't understand, i put the * in a sql file but the file is encrypted !!!	
Support:	2018-02-11 09:25:45
Anti-Canary.	
You:	2018-02-11 09:20:27
What about searching for 19x* in any sql file in any folder ??	

Fig. 11. `GandCrab` developers response about the 19x*.

In `sub_XXXX6850`, `GandCrab` calls the function `sub_XXXX67A0` to compare the extension of each file to its target extensions (`GandCrab` targets around 4400 extensions, as confirmed by GandCrab developers). It calls sub_XXXX66E0 to compare the file names to: desktop.ini, autorun.inf, boot.ini, thumbs.db, iconcache.db, bootsect.bak, ntuser.dat.log and its text ransom note GDCB-DECRYPT.txt. GandCrab does not encrypt these files. Then, it calls sub_XXXX35E0 to perform the following operations:

1. GandCrab calls GetFileAttributesW to retrieve the file system attributes of the target file. Then, it calls SetFileAttributesW to set the attribute FILE_ATTRIBUTE_ARCHIVE to this file to mark it for backup or removal.
2. GandCrab makes two calls to sub_XXXX8250 to generate 16 random bytes, then 32 random bytes using CryptGenRandom.
3. In sub_XXXX6480, GandCrab calls CryptImportKey to transfer the generated public key (received from C&C in overinfection or generated in the current execution in first infection) from a key BLOB into a Cryptographic Service Provider (CSP). This call is followed by a call to CryptGetKeyParam, then CryptEncrypt to encrypt the 32 bytes using the imported RSA public key. sub_XXXX6480 is called again to encrypt the 16 bytes using the same key.
4. GandCrab reads the contents of the target file using ReadFile. Then, it calls sub_XXXX3500 to encrypt the contents using the Cipher Block Chaining (CBC) mode (Fig. 12). The function sub_XXXX1020 encrypts the contents without any imported function like CryptEncrypt. The ransomware developers mentioned in our discussion that they encrypt the files using the AES256 algorithm from TrueCrypt7.1 in [4]. The developers also shared with us two pictures in imgur[4], which showed the encryption function in IDA Pro and the source code of the encryption process.
5. It appends to the end of the target file the encrypted value of the 32 bytes, the encrypted value of 16 bytes and the file size before encryption. Then, it renames the file using MoveFileW to append the extension GDCB to the name.

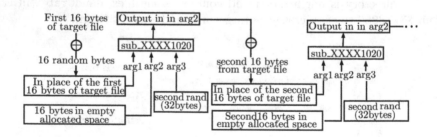

Fig. 12. GandCrab encryption process.

---

[4] https://i.imgur.com/NLaFqkv.png and https://i.imgur.com/FVtXFuu.png.

3.4 The End of the Execution and the Onion Ransom Note

The encryption threads are followed by the second call to `GetTickCount`. Then, GandCrab calls `sub_XXXX55C0` to perform the second `POST` to its C&C. The created data is encrypted using the RC4 algorithm with the same key mentioned above, encoded to `Base64`. Then, to submit this data, it enters in an infinit loop of IP requests until it finds its C&C using `nslookup` like the first `POST`. The data sent before encryption is: `action=result&e_files=<NbrEncryptedFiles>&e_size=` `<SizeEncryptedFiles>&e_time=<DurationEncryption>&pc_group= <FromDom ainRegValue>&ransom_id=<ID_Victim>`. For this data, the C&C answers by `OK` encoded to `Base64` and encrypted using RC4 (Fig. 13).

In this case, any network rule based on this `POST` request/reply (like the one in Fig. 14), has no effect on stopping the current infection of GandCrab in the target machine, but it can alert the network administrator to an infection that has been occurred, then limit the infection only to the first infection.

```
POST /curl.php?token=1016 HTTP/1.1
Host: nomoreransom.coin
Content-Type: application/x-www-form-urlencoded
User-Agent: Mozilla/5.0 (Windows NT 6.1; WOW64) AppleWebKit/537.36 (KHTML, like
Gecko) Chrome/55.0.2883.87 Safari/537.36
Content-Length: 277
Cache-Control: no-cache

data=mdU+mIEkDgfqAIOO+CE60IMj4I4KH7R1B4Gz5B/kfHeve0qnMlZCiTfpjFRL3mRkX1p/
ni9m43rGbQRqp6Hd8P6/u0uPEQzxpf
+Iwb4mdSdc76fKPbK1MHfmYYPYGBPuUXpcpvqK1c7EQicqN7C8k8Cx2eo
+izu0dVM6nFaMIVBiJ2ICLYqm5ln7zRKCVzSK3qIOAksRlfZKqaNPuw7dRfv/
dZcj6az5YcvFu2Pq8IWglyDyP4auPG3nr0PFLsroTmWD1qvsNlX5Wg==

HTTP/1.1 200 OK
...
g5oW5Q==
```

Fig. 13. The second `POST` and the C&C answer.

```
alert tcp $HOME_NET any -> $EXTERNAL_NET $HTTP_PORTS
(msg:"GandCrab V1 Ransomware"; flow:established,to_server;
content: "data="; nocase; pcre:data=[a-zA-Z0-9+/]{0,288}==;
classtype:ransomware-activity; sid:2000003; rev:1;)
```

Fig. 14. Alert Snort rule for the second `POST` request.

After this `POST`, GandCrab calls `ShellExecuteW` to delete the volume shadow copies of the machine using the command: `<Path>\wmic.exe shadow copies delete`. At the end of its execution, it opens in the default web browser the created ransom note (Fig. 15) named `gdcbghvjyqy7jclk.onion/<ID>` using the `top` or `casa` gateways. The ransom note includes information on:

– The target machine: IP address, country, PC name/group/lang and target drives. This information is submitted in the first `POST` and remain fixed during all infections/overinfections.

– The encrypted data, like the amount of encrypted files and size of encrypted data. This information is submitted in the second POST and is changed in each infection/overinfection. For example, the size of encrypted files is increased in any infection/overinfection by the size of new encrypted files.
– The requested ransom is in the DASH currency, which was not seen before in ransomware [1], the offer of one file decryption for free and a support chat (like the Spora ransomware) in a second tab. The developers mentioned that GandCrab can infect all the world except the CIS countries which we confirmed above and the requested ransom is basically fixed with some differences for some countries.

4   GandCrab Detection and Prevention

In this section, we present some behaviours that can be used for GandCrab detection and the detection of other ransomware. The behaviours could be used in combination for more efficient detection.

AS FAR AS WE KNOW:	
Country	Morocco - 41.251.181.200
OS	Windows 7 Home Basic (x64 bit)
PC User	MyPc
PC Name	MyPc
PC Group	WORKGROUP
PC Lang.	fr-FR
HDD	C
Date of encrypt	2018-02-02 16:25:35
Amount of your files	39321
Volume of your files	2147483647

Fig. 15. A part of the GandCrab ransom note.

– GandCrab creates a mutex named Global\pc_group=<PcGroup>&ransom _id=<ID_Victim> to prevent itself from running more than one instance of itself. Antiviruses can look for this name to spot the presence of GandCrab on the system.
– Much ransomware like GandCrab, TeslaCrypt, CryptoLocker and others perform the self-reproduction at the beginning of their execution. We proved in [28] that the process of copying the code to another location is also a behaviour that can be monitored to increase the efficiency of the ransomware detection, especially if it does not trigger any false alarm during a legitimate copy process. We can generalize this by monitoring any process (for example, GandCrab and TeslaCrypt) that copies itself to a sucpicious location under a different name possibly using the difference in entropy between the original name and the copy's name.

- `GandCrab` adds a registry value named as a random name in `RunOnce`. Therefore, monitoring some specified registry keys can also be an indicator for detection, especially if this value is added before encryption. An example is monitoring the process that adds any unknown, random or suspicious value in the `RunOnce`, `Run` key or startup directory.
- Much ransomware like `TeslaCrypt`, `CryptoLocker` and `Alpha` loop through the running processes in a target machine to end the execution of some detection or monitoring tools like `TaskMge` and `Process Explorer`. `GandCrab` loops twice to search the running antiviruses and some specified processes. The enumeration of the running processes in a target machine is a suspicious behaviour that can be used for `GandCrab` or other ransomware detection.
- Many calls and operations are repeated to create the victim's ID (four times). We do not know the benefits of creating the ID every time whenever `GandCrab` needs it.
- `GandCrab` creates the content of its ransom note before the encryption files. Monitoring the used ranges of memory by `GandCrab` for specified strings like `All your files`, `.GDCB`, `private key`, `Tor Browser` can be used for its detection and generalized to other ransomware that create their ransom notes before the encryption or put them in directories before encrypting the files in this directory.
- Kolodenker *et al.* [23] proposed `PayBreak` that intercepts the used keys by `CryptEncrypt` and stores them in a key vault. The keys will be used later to decrypt the encrypted files. Although we could not test `PayBreak` on `GandCrab` in our VM, we think that it is able to intercept the used keys by `CryptEncrypt` to encrypt the files. Furthermore, we can adjust the idea of `PayBreak` by hooking the calls to `CryptGenKey`, `CryptImportkey` and `CryptExportKey` to retrieve the used key in the encryption of the generated random bytes for each file. In the same way, another work [36] proposed the interception of calls to Microsoft Cryptographic API.
- Kim *et al.* [22] proposed a dynamic ransomware protection method that replaces the random number generator of the OS with a defined generator. For `GandCrab`, the generated random bytes (by `CryptGenRandom`) must be intercepted, or created for each target file and stored correctly in a database keeping the link between the file and the used random bytes in its encryption. This method cannot be generalized for all ransomware because some ransomware use a predefined functions to generate the random bytes.
- `GandCrab` calls `GetDriveTypeW` at least 52 times to retrieve the available drives. This behaviour is performed before the encryption, so we think that it can be used as a behaviour for the detection of `GandCrab`. The same goes for a call to `SHGetSpecialFolderPathW` (three calls for each target directory).
- Cabaj *et al.* [8] presented a Software-Defined Networking detection based on the network communications of `CryptoWall` and `Locky` ransomware families. For `GandCrab`, we suppose that the pattern of its network communications (the `GET` request to `ipv4bot.whatismyipaddress.com`, the `nslookup` loops and the first `POST` to its C&C) can be used for its detection. Figure 16 summarises the network communication of `GandCrab`.

- All ransomware have an avoided directories list or a target directories list to encrypt some directories and avoid encrypting the others. The most commonly avoided directory is `Windows` directory. `GandCrab` also avoids other directories like `ProgramData, Program Files` and `Local Settings`. Moore [33] proposed a ransomware detection using honeypot directories; we take this idea to propose a fake `windows` directory (or other avoided directories) in `C` drive in order to differentiate between a legitimate process like a zip process and the process of encryption by ransomware. The first encrypts the files in this fake directory and the second avoids them.

  Like the `Blind` ransomware (`Napoleon` version), `GandCrab` does not infect the removable drives. They can be also used as a decoy directories for `GandCrab`.
- The previous item can also be adapted for the target/avoided extensions and the target/avoided files names, for example, the avoided `GDCB` extension and the avoided file `boot.ini`.
- Scaife *et al.* presented `CryptoDrop` [37], a ransomware detection tool based on some behaviours like entropy (encrypted files by `GandCrab` have high entropy), file type changes (some ransomware like `GandCrab` change the extension of target files) and other indicators. We tested `CryptoDrop` (the free version that protects a limited number of directories) in our VM and it stopped `GandCrab` after encrypting 6 files in the monitored directories.
- `ShieldFS` [13] monitors the low level system activity of any running process and compares it to a set of adaptive models that was created by analysing 1.7 billion of low-level I/O filesystem requests generated by thousands of benign applications. `GandCrab` has different patterns of behaviour of other benign applications like directories listing, files read/write and for each target file three fixed `WriteFile` (256 bytes, 256 bytes then 16 bytes). We suppose that these behaviours allow this tool to detect `GandCrab`.
- `GandCrab` deletes the shadow copies at the end of its infection. Some ransomware like `Blind` (`napoleon` version) delete them before the encryption process. Monitoring this behaviour can be used in ransomware detection.
- We tested some other ransomware detection tools on `GandCrab`, and we found:
  ○

Tool	Method of detection	`GandCrab` detection
Anti Ransom V3	Decoy files	Detected after encrypting 12 files of decoy files
CybereasonRansomFree	Decoy files	Detected after encrypting 7 files of decoy files
Kaspersky Anti-Ransomware Tool	Behavioral and reputation detection (System Watcher and Kaspersky Security Network)	Detected after encrypting 24 user files

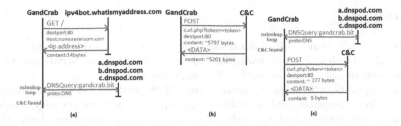

Fig. 16. GandCrab network communication.

4.1 A Quick Overview on the Other Versions

We performed a quick dynamic analysis of other versions of GandCrab (V2, V3, V4 and V4.1). GandCrab keeps the loop by nslookup searching for its C&C in V2 and V3. In V4, it does not communicate with its C&C (but the C&C connection is back in V4.1), the software demands the victims to follow some instructions in the ransom note to submit the data sent by a POST request in the other versions. Compared to the previous versions, some changes were spotted in V4, were GandCrab focuses on encrypting files without self-reproduction, the search for the external IP of the victim or the search for its C&C. Generally, V1, V2 and V3 keeps the same behaviours in their execution with a little differences in V2, which does not perform the self-reproduction or setting its copy in RunOnce registry key. We think that the behaviours discussed above can be used or adapted to detect these versions with other new behaviours, especially in the recent version V4.1 which is the running version until now (mid-June).

5 Conclusions

In this paper, we presented a malware analysis of the first version of GandCrab, mainly focusing on self-reproduction, overinfection and detection. Self-reproduction, the main characteristic of viruses, is performed by GandCrab to copy itself in the %AppData% directory. Using cryptographic functions to encrypt files, we found that it is a cryptovirus. The overinfection is managed by infecting and reinfecting the target machine with the same ID, keeping the same ransom onion page and demanding one ransom to pay. Some detection behaviours are proposed and described in this paper and can be generalized and adapted to construct a ransomware detector or identifier based on common ransomware behaviours in future work. At the end of this paper, we provide some evaluation and discussion on some tools/works on ransomware detection. Finally, we think that the story of GandCrab will not end soon, perhaps new versions with new features are coming.

References

1. Abrams, L.: GandCrab ransomware distributed by exploit kits, appends GDCB extension. https://www.bleepingcomputer.com/news/security/gandcrab-ransomware-distributed-by-exploit-kits-appends-gdcb-extension
2. Abrams, L.: GandCrab ransomware version 2 released with new .Crab extension and other changes.https://www.bleepingcomputer.com/news/security/gandcrab-ransomware-version-2-released-with-new-crab-extension-and-other-changes/
3. Abrams, L.: GandCrab version 3 released with autorun feature and desktop background. https://www.bleepingcomputer.com/news/security/gandcrab-version-3-released-with-autorun-feature-and-desktop-background/
4. AuditProject: truecrypt-verified-mirror Crypto the AES files.https://github.com/AuditProject/truecrypt-verified-mirror/tree/master/Source
5. Bajpai, P., Sood, A.K., Enbody, R.: A key-management-based taxonomy for ransomware. In: 2018 APWG Symposium on Electronic Crime Research (eCrime), pp. 1–12, May 2018
6. Biasini, N.: Gandcrab ransomware walks its way onto compromised sites. https://blog.talosintelligence.com/2018/05/gandcrab-compromised-sites.html/
7. Brewer, R.: Ransomware attacks: detection, prevention and cure. Netw. Secur. **2016**(9), 5–9 (2016)
8. Cabaj, K., Gregorczyk, M., Mazurczyk, W.: Software-defined networking-based crypto ransomware detection using HTTP traffic characteristics. CoRR abs/1611.08294 (2016)
9. Caivano, D., Canfora, G., Cocomazzi, A., Pirozzi, A., Visaggio, C.A.: Ransomware at x-rays. In: 2017 IEEE International Conference on Internet of Things (iThings) and IEEE Green Computing and Communications (GreenCom) and IEEE Cyber, Physical and Social Computing (CPSCom) and IEEE Smart Data (SmartData), Exeter, United Kingdom, 21–23 June 2017, pp. 348–353 (2017)
10. Checkpoint: The GandCrab ransomware mindset. https://research.checkpoint.com/gandcrab-ransomware-mindset/
11. Cimpanu, C.: Free decrypter available for GandCrab ransomware victims. https://bleepingcomputer.com/news/security/free-decrypter-available-for-gandcrab-ransomware-victims/
12. Cohen, F.: Computer viruses, Ph.D. thesis. University of Southern California (1986)
13. Continella, A., et al.: ShieldFS: a self-healing, ransomware-aware filesystem. In: Proceedings of the 32nd Annual Conference on Computer Security Applications, ACSAC 2016, Los Angeles, CA, USA, 5–9 December 2016, pp. 336–347 (2016)
14. Cybereason: Ransomfree. https://ransomfree.cybereason.com/
15. Gallegos-Segovia, P.L., Bravo-Torres, J.F., Larios-Rosillo, V.M., Vintimilla-Tapia, P.E., Yuquilima-Albarado, I.F., Jara-Saltos, J.D.: Social engineering as an attack vector for ransomware. In: 2017 CHILEAN Conference on Electrical, Electronics Engineering, Information and Communication Technologies, pp. 1–6, October 2017
16. Gazet, A.: Comparative analysis of various ransomware virii. J. Comput. Virol. **6**(1), 77–90 (2010)
17. Gómez-Hernández, J.A., Álvarez-González, L., García-Teodoro, P.: R-locker: thwarting ransomware action through a honeyfile-based approach. Comput. Secur. **73**, 389–398 (2018)

18. Huang, J., Xu, J., Xing, X., Liu, P., Qureshi, M.K.: FlashGuard: leveraging intrinsic flash properties to defend against encryption ransomware. In: Proceedings of the 2017 ACM SIGSAC Conference on Computer and Communications Security, CCS 2017, Dallas, TX, USA, 30 October–03 November 2017, pp. 2231–2244 (2017)

19. Kharraz, A., Arshad, S., Mulliner, C., Robertson, W.K., Kirda, E.: UNVEIL: a large-scale, automated approach to detecting ransomware. In: 25th USENIX Security Symposium, USENIX Security 16, Austin, TX, USA, 10–12 August 2016, pp. 757–772 (2016)

20. Kharraz, A., Kirda, E.: Redemption: real-time protection against ransomware at end-hosts. In: Dacier, M., Bailey, M., Polychronakis, M., Antonakakis, M. (eds.) RAID 2017. LNCS, vol. 10453, pp. 98–119. Springer, Cham (2017). https://doi.org/10.1007/978-3-319-66332-6_5

21. Kharraz, A., Robertson, W., Balzarotti, D., Bilge, L., Kirda, E.: Cutting the Gordian Knot: a look under the hood of ransomware attacks. In: Almgren, M., Gulisano, V., Maggi, F. (eds.) DIMVA 2015. LNCS, vol. 9148, pp. 3–24. Springer, Cham (2015). https://doi.org/10.1007/978-3-319-20550-2_1

22. Kim, H., Yoo, D., Kang, J.S., Yeom, Y.: Dynamic ransomware protection using deterministic random bit generator. In: 2017 IEEE Conference on Application, Information and Network Security (AINS), pp. 64–68, November 2017

23. Kolodenker, E., Koch, W., Stringhini, G., Egele, M.: PayBreak: defense against cryptographic ransomware. In: Proceedings of the 2017 ACM on Asia Conference on Computer and Communications Security, AsiaCCS 2017, Abu Dhabi, United Arab Emirates, 2–6 April 2017, pp. 599–611 (2017)

24. Lee, J.K., Moon, S.Y., Park, J.H.: CloudRPS: a cloud analysis based enhanced ransomware prevention system. J. Supercomput. 73(7), 3065–3084 (2017)

25. Lee, J., Lee, J., Hong, J.: How to make efficient decoy files for ransomware detection? In: Proceedings of the International Conference on Research in Adaptive and Convergent Systems, RACS 2017, Krakow, Poland, 20–23 September 2017, pp. 208–212 (2017)

26. Lemmou, Y., Souidi, E.M.: Princesslocker analysis. In: 2017 International Conference on Cyber Security and Protection Of Digital Services (Cyber Security), pp. 1–10, June 2017

27. Lemmou, Y., Souidi, E.M.: Infection, self-reproduction and overinfection in ransomware: the case of teslacrypt. In: 2018 International Conference on Cyber Security And Protection Of Digital Services (Cyber Security) (2018)

28. Lemmou, Y., Souidi, E.M.: An overview on Spora ransomware. In: Thampi, S.M., Martínez Pérez, G., Westphall, C.B., Hu, J., Fan, C.I., Gómez Mármol, F. (eds.) SSCC 2017. CCIS, vol. 746, pp. 259–275. Springer, Singapore (2017). https://doi.org/10.1007/978-981-10-6898-0_22

29. MacRae, J., Franqueira, V.N.L.: On locky ransomware, Al Capone and Brexit. In: Matoušek, P., Schmiedecker, M. (eds.) ICDF2C 2017. LNICST, vol. 216, pp. 33–45. Springer, Cham (2018). https://doi.org/10.1007/978-3-319-73697-6_3

30. Malwarebytes: Cybercrime tactics and techniques Q1 2017. malwarebytes.com/pdf/labs/Cybercrime-Tactics-and-Techniques-Q1-2017.pdf

31. MalwarebytesLabs: GandCrab distributed by RIG and grandsoft exploit kits. https://blog.malwarebytes.com/threat-analysis/2018/01/gandcrab-ransomware-distributed-by-rig-and-grandsoft-exploit-kit

32. MalwarebytesLabs: GandCrab V4 released with the new .KRAB extension for encrypted files. https://www.bleepingcomputer.com/news/security/gandcrab-v4-released-with-the-new-krab-extension-for-encrypted-files/

33. Moore, C.: Detecting ransomware with honeypot techniques. In: 2016 Cybersecurity and Cyberforensics Conference (CCC), pp. 77–81, August 2016
34. Nadir, I., Bakhshi, T.: Contemporary cybercrime: a taxonomy of ransomware threats mitigation techniques. In: 2018 International Conference on Computing, Mathematics and Engineering Technologies (iCoMET), pp. 1–7, March 2018
35. O'Brien, D.: Internet security threat report ransomware 2017, an ISTR special report. Symantec. https://www.symantec.com/content/dam/symantec/docs/security-center/white-papers/istr-ransomware-2017-en.pdf
36. Palisse, A., Le Bouder, H., Lanet, J.-L., Le Guernic, C., Legay, A.: Ransomware and the legacy crypto API. In: Cuppens, F., Cuppens, N., Lanet, J.-L., Legay, A. (eds.) CRiSIS 2016. LNCS, vol. 10158, pp. 11–28. Springer, Cham (2017). https://doi.org/10.1007/978-3-319-54876-0_2
37. Scaife, N., Carter, H., Traynor, P., Butler, K.R.B.: Cryptolock (and drop it): stopping ransomware attacks on user data. In: 36th IEEE International Conference on Distributed Computing Systems, ICDCS 2016, Nara, Japan, 27–30 June 2016, pp. 303–312 (2016)
38. Shinde, R., der Veeken, P.V., Schooten, S.V., van den Berg, J.: Ransomware: Studying transfer and mitigation. In: 2016 International Conference on Computing, Analytics and Security Trends (CAST) (2016)
39. Sophos: Sophoslabs 2018 malware forecast. https://sophos.com/en-us/en-us/medialibrary/PDFs/technical-papers/malware-forecast-2018.pdf
40. Young, A., Yung, M.: Cryptovirology: extortion-based security threats and countermeasures. In: Proceedings 1996 IEEE Symposium on Security and Privacy, pp. 129–140, May 1996
41. Young, A.L., Yung, M.: Cryptovirology: the birth, neglect, and explosion of ransomware. Commun. ACM **60**(7), 24–26 (2017)
42. Yun, J., Hur, J., Shin, Y., Koo, D.: CLDSafe: an efficient file backup system in cloud storage against ransomware. IEICE Trans. Inf. Syst. 100-D(9), 2228–2231 (2017)

Symmetric Key Cryptography

The Relation Between CENC and NEMO

Bart Mennink[✉]

Digital Security Group, Radboud University, Nijmegen, The Netherlands
b.mennink@cs.ru.nl

Abstract. Counter mode encryption uses a blockcipher to generate a
key stream, which is subsequently used to encrypt data. The mode is
known to achieve security up to the birthday bound. In this work we consider two approaches in literature to improve it to beyond birthday bound
security: CENC by Iwata (FSE 2006) and its generalization NEMO by
Lefranc et al. (SAC 2007). Whereas recent discoveries on CENC argued
optimal security, the state of the art of NEMO is still sub-optimal. We
draw connections among various instantiations of CENC and NEMO,
and particularly prove that the improved optimal security bound on the
CENC family carries over to a large class of variants of NEMO. We further conjecture that it also applies to the remaining variants, and discuss
bottlenecks in proving so.

Keywords: CENC · NEMO · Optimality · Linear codes

1 Introduction

The most well-known blockcipher based encryption mode is counter mode
encryption: given an n-bit keyed blockcipher E_k, a message M of (without loss
of generality) length $\ell \cdot n$ bits is encrypted by generating a random looking key
stream of ℓ blocks,

$$E_k(N) \parallel E_k(N + 1) \parallel \cdots \parallel E_k(N + \ell - 1), \qquad (1)$$

and XORing this key stream to the message M. Here, N is an initial value that
needs to meet certain criteria irrelevant for the current treatment. This mode
is known to be birthday bound secure: as E is a blockcipher, the generated key
stream does not expose collisions whereas after the generation of around $2^{n/2}$
blocks a truly random key stream would expose collisions.

Beyond birthday bound encryption modes aim to achieve security beyond this
bound. A simple way of achieving beyond birthday bound security for counter
mode is by implementing it with a PRF, the most logical choice being the sum
of permutations, where every key stream block is constituted of the sum of two
blockcipher calls. For example, the first key stream block would be

$$E_k(N \parallel 0) \oplus E_k(N \parallel 1), \qquad (2)$$

© Springer Nature Switzerland AG 2018
J. Camenisch and P. Papadimitratos (Eds.): CANS 2018, LNCS 11124, pp. 177–189, 2018.
https://doi.org/10.1007/978-3-030-00434-7_9

where the nonce is now an $(n-1)$-bit string. After a long line of research [2, 3, 10, 14], Patarin [15] and later Dai et al. [5] proved that this construction is secure up to 2^n key stream block generations. Unfortunately, the construction is expensive, requiring two blockcipher calls per data block.

In 2006, Iwata introduced CENC, an elegant and relatively cheap adjustment of counter mode that also achieves security beyond the birthday bound. At a high level, for a predetermined value $w \geq 1$, in every chunk of $w + 1$ blockcipher calls, the first one is "sacrificed:" it is not used as key stream but rather used to mask the remaining w chunks. It only allows for nonces of size m bits with $m < n$, and generates its first w key stream blocks as

$$E_k(N\|0_s) \oplus E_k(N\|1_s) \| \cdots \| E_k(N\|0_s) \oplus E_k(N\|w_s), \qquad (3)$$

after which N is incremented and w new blocks are generated. Here, i_s denotes the encoding of i as an $s = (n-m)$-bit string. Iwata proved security of CENC[w] for $w \geq 1$ up to around $2^{2n/3}$ key stream block generations, and conjectured security up to around $2^n/w$ key stream block generations. Only recently, Iwata et al. [7] confirmed this bound, pointing out that it was a direct consequence of Patarin's Mirror Theory [11–13, 15]. Bhattacharya and Nandi [4] derived a comparable bound using the Chi Squared Theory [5]. See also Sect. 3.1.

Soon after the introduction of CENC, Lefranc et al. [9] introduced a generalization called NEMO. Rather than being parametrized by w and using $w + 1$ blockcipher outputs per w keystream blocks, NEMO[G] is instantiated using a matrix G of size $w \times v$ and it generates w keystream blocks using v blockcipher outputs as

$$G \cdot \begin{pmatrix} E_k(N\|0_s) \\ E_k(N\|1_s) \\ \cdots \\ E_k(N\|(v-1)_s) \end{pmatrix}. \qquad (4)$$

Lefranc et al. proved that if G is the generator matrix of a $[v, w, d]$ code, where d is the distance of the code (see Sect. 2.4), then the resulting scheme achieves security up to approximately $(2^n/v)^{d/(d+1)}$ key stream block generations (simplified, assuming that $w \approx v^{d/(d+1)}$). See also Sect. 3.2. The term is quite complicated, but important is the exponent $d/(d+1)$, where for small d it gives suboptimal security. For larger d the bound goes to optimal security, but the mode becomes less efficient: by the Singleton bound [16], one requires $v \geq w + d - 1$ blockcipher evaluations to generate w blocks with distance d.

1.1   Equivalences

One can consider counter mode with the sum of permutations as a special case of CENC (with $w = 1$). What is more, one can consider the general CENC[w] as a special case of NEMO, namely with generator matrix

$$G_{\mathsf{CENC}[w]} = \begin{bmatrix} 1 & 1 & 0 & \cdots & 0 \\ 1 & 0 & 1 & \cdots & 0 \\ \vdots & \vdots & \vdots & \ddots & \vdots \\ 1 & 0 & 0 & \cdots & 1 \end{bmatrix}. \tag{5}$$

In light of this, the state of the art on NEMO appears to be outdated.

In this work, we further explore the connection between the generalized CENC[w] (for arbitrary w) and NEMO[G] (for arbitrary generator matrix G). First, noting that for efficiency reasons, one would prefer G to be binary and Maximum Distance Separable (MDS). Textbook results dictate that only three such codes exist, namely the trivial $[v, v, 1]$, $[v, 1, v]$, and $[v, v - 1, 2]$ codes [17, Proposition 9.2].

- Binary $[v, v, 1]$ MDS code. This code corresponds to plain counter mode of (1), giving tight $2^{n/2}$ birthday bound security.
- Binary $[v, 1, v]$ MDS code. This code corresponds to counter mode based on the sum of permutations of (2),[1] giving tight 2^n security.
- Binary $[v, v - 1, 2]$ MDS code. This code, finally, is generated among others by $G_{\mathsf{CENC}[w]}$ of (5), i.e., corresponds to CENC.

Inspired by this, one may argue that any other implementation of NEMO[G] performs sub-optimally compared with state of the art.

We further investigate the security of NEMO[G] for arbitrary matrices and derive two results. First, in Sect. 4.1 we prove that for any G generating a binary $[v, w, d]$ code with even-weight codewords only, NEMO[G] is at least as secure as CENC[$v - 1$]. Second, in Sect. 4.2 we explore the possibilities for arbitrary generator matrices G (that have odd-weight codewords) and conjecture that a similar bound can be obtained. The state of the art and the new bounds are compared in Table 1.

1.2   Understanding the Equivalences

In Sect. 5 we elaborate on possible alternatives of CENC[w], where a different generator matrix of the $[v, v - 1, 2]$ code is applied. A particularly interesting approach would be to use

$$G_{\mathsf{CENC}'[w]} = \begin{bmatrix} 1 & 1 & 0 & \cdots & 0 & 0 \\ 0 & 1 & 1 & \cdots & 0 & 0 \\ \vdots & \vdots & \vdots & \ddots & \vdots & \vdots \\ 0 & 0 & 0 & \cdots & 1 & 1 \end{bmatrix} \tag{6}$$

instead of $G_{\mathsf{CENC}[w]}$ of (5). This diagonalized version of CENC[w] gives the exact same level of security (by Lemma 1 in Sect. 4.1), but may allow for more elegant implementations and easier interpretations. In addition, it allows for drawing a

---

[1] This follows from looking at the modes at a pseudorandom function level, i.e., isolating the pseudorandom function $F_k(N) = E_k(N\|0) \oplus E_k(N\|1)$ from the mode.

Table 1. Rate (key stream blocks per blockcipher evaluations) and security (up to the number of key stream blocks) and for all variants of counter mode. $\mathsf{NEMO}[v, w, d]$ is short for $\mathsf{NEMO}[G]$ for generator matrix G of a binary $[v, w, d]$ code. For state of the art, only the most recent citations are given.

Mode	Rate	Security	Reference
Plain counter (1)	1	$2^{n/2}$	[1]
Sum of permutation (2)	$1/2$	2^n	[5, 15]
$\mathsf{CENC}[w]$ (3)	$w/(w+1)$	$2^n/w$	[4, 7]
$\mathsf{NEMO}[v, w, d]$ (4)	w/v	$(2^n/v)^{d/d+1}$	[9]
		$2^n/v$	Sect. 4.1[a]
		$2^n/v$	Sect. 4.2[b]

   [a] for even-weight code only
   [b] conjectured bound for arbitrary code

different connection between $\mathsf{CENC}[w]$ and counter mode based on the sum of permutations of (2), as the latter can be obtained from $\mathsf{CENC}'[w]$ by discarding every second key stream block.

2 Preliminaries

For $m, n \in \mathbb{N}$, we denote by $\{0, 1\}^n$ the set of all n-bit strings. We denote by $\mathsf{P}(n)$ the set of all permutations on $\{0, 1\}^n$, $\mathsf{F}(m, n)$ the set of all functions from $\{0, 1\}^m$ to $\{0, 1\}^n$, and m_n the encoding of the number m as an n-bit string. For a set $\mathcal{S}$, $s \xleftarrow{\$} \mathcal{S}$ denotes uniformly random sampling of s from $\mathcal{S}$.

2.1 Blockcipher

A blockcipher $E : \{0, 1\}^\kappa \times \{0, 1\}^n \to \{0, 1\}^n$ is a family of permutations indexed by a key $k \in \{0, 1\}^\kappa$. We denote by $\mathbf{Adv}_E^{\mathrm{prp}}(\mathcal{D})$ the advantage of a distinguisher $\mathcal{D}$ in distinguishing E from an ideal permutation $\pi \xleftarrow{\$} \mathsf{P}(n)$:

$$\mathbf{Adv}_E^{\mathrm{prp}}(\mathcal{D}) = \mathbf{Pr}\left(k \xleftarrow{\$} \{0, 1\}^\kappa \; : \; \mathcal{D}^{E_k} \to 1\right) - \mathbf{Pr}\left(\pi \xleftarrow{\$} \mathsf{P}(n) \; : \; \mathcal{D}^\pi \to 1\right). \tag{7}$$

We denote $\mathbf{Adv}_E^{\mathrm{prp}}(q, t) = \sup_{\mathcal{D}} \mathbf{Adv}_E^{\mathrm{prp}}(\mathcal{D})$, where the supremum is taken over all distinguishers that can make q queries and operate in t time.

2.2 Pseudorandom Function

A pseudorandom function $F : \{0, 1\}^\kappa \times \{0, 1\}^m \to \{0, 1\}^n$ is a family of functions in $\mathsf{F}(m, n)$ indexed by a key $k \in \{0, 1\}^\kappa$. We denote by $\mathbf{Adv}_F^{\mathrm{prf}}(\mathcal{D})$ the advantage of a distinguisher $\mathcal{D}$ in distinguishing F from an ideal function $\rho \xleftarrow{\$} \mathsf{F}(m, n)$:

$$\mathbf{Adv}_F^{\mathrm{prf}}(\mathcal{D}) = \mathbf{Pr}\left(k \xleftarrow{\$} \{0,1\}^\kappa : \mathcal{D}^{F_k} \to 1\right) - \mathbf{Pr}\left(\rho \xleftarrow{\$} \mathsf{F}(m,n) : \mathcal{D}^\rho \to 1\right).$$
(8)

We denote $\mathbf{Adv}_F^{\mathrm{prf}}(q,t) = \sup_{\mathcal{D}} \mathbf{Adv}_F^{\mathrm{prf}}(q,t)$, where the supremum is taken over all distinguishers that can make q queries and operate in t time.

2.3   Encryption

A nonce based encryption scheme $\mathcal{E} : \{0,1\}^\kappa \times \{0,1\}^n \times \{0,1\}^* \to \{0,1\}^*$ is a function that operates on a secret key k. On input of a nonce N and an arbitrarily length message M, it returns a ciphertext C of length $|M|$. We denote by $\mathbf{Adv}_{\mathcal{E}}^{\mathrm{cpa}}(\mathcal{D})$ the advantage of a distinguisher $\mathcal{D}$ in distinguishing $\mathcal{E}$ from a random function $\$$ that for every query (N, M) returns a random ciphertext C of size $|M|$:

$$\mathbf{Adv}_{\mathcal{E}}^{\mathrm{cpa}}(\mathcal{D}) = \mathbf{Pr}\left(k \xleftarrow{\$} \{0,1\}^\kappa : \mathcal{D}^{\mathcal{E}_k} \to 1\right) - \mathbf{Pr}\left(\$ \xleftarrow{\$} \mathsf{F}(n+*,*) : \mathcal{D}^\$ \to 1\right),$$

where, with abuse of notation, $\mathsf{F}(n + *, *)$ is the set of all functions that get as input an n-bit block and an arbitrarily length block, and output a string of the same size as the arbitrarily length block. Distinguisher $\mathcal{D}$ is required to be nonce-respecting, meaning that it should not repeat nonces. We denote $\mathbf{Adv}_{\mathcal{E}}^{\mathrm{cpa}}(q, \ell, t) = \sup_{\mathcal{D}} \mathbf{Adv}_{\mathcal{E}}^{\mathrm{cpa}}(\mathcal{D})$, where the supremum is taken over all distinguishers that can make q queries of length ℓ n-bit blocks and operate in t time.

2.4   Linear Codes

Let $v, w \in \mathbb{N}$ be such that $v \geq w$. A binary linear code of length v and rank w transforms vectors in $\{0,1\}^w$ into vectors in $\{0,1\}^v$ using a generator matrix $\boldsymbol{G} \in \{0,1\}^{w \times v}$.[2] The distance of the code is defined as

$$d := \min_{\substack{\boldsymbol{x} \in \{0,1\}^w \\ \boldsymbol{x} \neq 0}} \left|\boldsymbol{x}^\top \cdot \boldsymbol{G}\right|.$$
(9)

The code C is referred to as a $[v, w, d]$ code. We call a code *even-weight* if all code words have even weight (hence the name). The rows of the generator matrix form a basis of the code, and hence, for any generator matrix $\boldsymbol{G} \in \{0,1\}^{w \times v}$ and invertible $\boldsymbol{P} \in \{0,1\}^{w \times w}$, the generator matrices $\boldsymbol{G}$ and $\boldsymbol{G}' = \boldsymbol{P} \cdot \boldsymbol{G}$ correspond to the same code.

According to the well-known Singleton bound [16], the code necessarily satisfies $v - w \geq d - 1$. A Maximum Distance Separable (MDS) code is a code

---

[2] In this work we are only concerned with *binary* linear codes.

that achieves equality in the Singleton bound. An elementary result [17, Proposition 9.2] states that the only binary MDS codes are the trivial $[v, v, 1]$, $[v, 1, v]$, and $[v, v-1, 2]$ codes. The second of the two is the repetition code (encode a bit by a v-fold repetition of that bit) and the latter is its dual that can be generated by the following matrix:

$$G_{v-1}^{\star} := \begin{bmatrix} 1 & 0 & \cdots & 0 & 1 \\ 0 & 1 & \cdots & 0 & 1 \\ \vdots & \vdots & \ddots & \vdots & \vdots \\ 0 & 0 & \cdots & 1 & 1 \end{bmatrix} \in \{0,1\}^{(v-1) \times v}. \tag{10}$$

3 CENC and NEMO

Let $\kappa, m, n, v, w \in \mathbb{N}$ such that $v \geq w$ and $m + s = n$ for $s = \lceil \log_2(v) \rceil$. Let $E \in \mathsf{B}(\kappa, n)$. Both CENC and NEMO can be described by a pseudorandom function $F : \{0,1\}^\kappa \times \{0,1\}^m \to \{0,1\}^{wn}$ based on v evaluations of E_k. This pseudorandom function is then evaluated in counter mode, in such a way that F_k is never evaluated twice for the same input. The following theorem is a straightforward exercise.

Theorem 1. *Let $F : \{0,1\}^\kappa \times \{0,1\}^m \to \{0,1\}^{wn}$ be a pseudorandom function (in this work, F is either the pseudorandom function of* CENC *or of* NEMO*), and let $\mathcal{E}$ be counter mode encryption based on F. We have,*

$$\mathbf{Adv}_{\mathcal{E}}^{\mathrm{cpa}}(q, \ell, t) \leq \mathbf{Adv}_{F}^{\mathrm{prf}}(\lceil \ell/w \rceil q, t). \tag{11}$$

The proof is trivial and henceforth omitted. We proceed discussing the pseudorandom function of CENC and NEMO.

3.1 CENC Pseudorandom Function

CENC was introduced by Iwata [6], but we rephrase it in our terminology. The pseudorandom function $\mathsf{CENC}[w] : \{0,1\}^\kappa \times \{0,1\}^m \to \{0,1\}^{wn}$ has $v = w + 1$, hence it makes $w + 1$ calls to the underlying blockcipher, and is defined as

$$\mathsf{CENC}[w]_k(x) = \underbrace{\begin{bmatrix} 1 & 1 & 0 & \cdots & 0 \\ 1 & 0 & 1 & \cdots & 0 \\ \vdots & \vdots & \vdots & \ddots & \vdots \\ 1 & 0 & 0 & \cdots & 1 \end{bmatrix}}_{=:G_{\mathsf{CENC}[w]}} \cdot \begin{pmatrix} E_k(x\|0_s) \\ E_k(x\|1_s) \\ \cdots \\ E_k(x\|w_s) \end{pmatrix}, \tag{12}$$

recalling that $s = \lceil \log_2(w + 1) \rceil$ and $m + s = n$. Note that $G_{\mathsf{CENC}[w]}$ can be obtained from $G_w^\star$ of (10) by left multiplication with an invertible matrix, and hence, the two matrices generate the same code.

Iwata et al. [7] derived the following bound on $\mathsf{CENC}[w]$ using the Mirror Theory [11–13, 15]:

Theorem 2 (Iwata et al. [7]). *We have, provided $wq \leq 2^n/67$,*

$$\mathbf{Adv}^{\mathrm{prf}}_{\mathsf{CENC}[w]}(q,t) \leq \frac{w^2q}{2^n} + \mathbf{Adv}^{\mathrm{prp}}_E((w+1)q,t). \tag{13}$$

Bhattacharya and Nandi [4] derived a comparable bound using the Chi Squared Theory [5]:

Theorem 3 (Bhattacharya and Nandi [4]). *We have,*

$$\mathbf{Adv}^{\mathrm{prf}}_{\mathsf{CENC}[w]}(q,t) \leq \frac{(1+\sqrt{2})(w+1)^2q}{2^n} + \mathbf{Adv}^{\mathrm{prp}}_E((w+1)q,t). \tag{14}$$

3.2 NEMO Pseudorandom Function

NEMO was introduced by Lefranc et al. [9]. Let G be the generator matrix of a $[v,w,d]$ code. Then the pseudorandom function $\mathsf{NEMO}[G] : \{0,1\}^\kappa \times \{0,1\}^m \to \{0,1\}^{wn}$ makes v calls to the underlying blockcipher, and is defined as

$$\mathsf{NEMO}[G]_k(x) = G \cdot \begin{pmatrix} E_k(x\|0_s) \\ E_k(x\|1_s) \\ \dots \\ E_k(x\|v-1_s) \end{pmatrix}, \tag{15}$$

recalling that $s = \lceil \log_2(v) \rceil$ and $m + s = n$.

Lefranc et al. [9] derived the following bound on $\mathsf{NEMO}[G]$ for any generator matrix of binary $[v,w,d]$ code:

Theorem 4. *Let G be the generator matrix of a binary $[v,w,d]$ code. We have,*

$$\mathbf{Adv}^{\mathrm{prf}}_{\mathsf{NEMO}[G]}(q,t) \leq \frac{v^2q}{2^n} + \frac{v^{2d}q^{d+1}}{2^{dn}} + \mathbf{Adv}^{\mathrm{prp}}_E(vq,t). \tag{16}$$

4 Equivalences

It is obvious from the definitions of the pseudorandom functions of CENC in (12) and NEMO in (15) that NEMO is a direct generalization of CENC, in the sense that

$$\mathsf{NEMO}[G_{\mathsf{CENC}[w]}] = \mathsf{CENC}[w]. \tag{17}$$

However, the generic security bounds on $\mathsf{CENC}[w]$ in Theorems 2 and 3 are better than that of $\mathsf{NEMO}[G]$ in Theorem 4, regardless of the generator matrix in use. In this section, we will explore the connection further, draw equivalences and reductions among the various instantiations of $\mathsf{CENC}[w]$ and $\mathsf{NEMO}[G]$.

First, in Sect. 4.1, we focus on generator matrices G for even-weight linear codes of length v, and demonstrate that their induced $\mathsf{NEMO}[G]$'s are at least as secure as $\mathsf{CENC}[v-1]$. In Sect. 4.2, we look beyond even-weight codes, conjecture that a similar result can be obtained for arbitrary generator matrices, and discuss bottlenecks in the analysis.

4.1   Even-Weight Linear Code

We will reduce the security of NEMO[G] for a generator matrix G of an even-weight $[v, w, d]$ code to the security of CENC[$v - 1$].

Theorem 5 (Security of NEMO for even-weight binary code). *Let G be a generator matrix of a binary even-weight $[v, w, d]$ code with $v \geq w$. We have,*

$$\mathbf{Adv}^{\mathrm{prf}}_{\mathsf{NEMO}[G]}(q, t) \leq \mathbf{Adv}^{\mathrm{prf}}_{\mathsf{CENC}[v-1]}(q, t). \tag{18}$$

Proof. Let G be a generator matrix of a binary even-weight $[v, w, d]$ code. Define the matrix

$$A = \begin{bmatrix} \mathbf{0}_{(v-w-1)\times w} & G^\star_{v-w-1} \end{bmatrix} \in \{0, 1\}^{(v-w-1)\times v}, \tag{19}$$

where $G^\star_{v-w-1}$ is the matrix of (10) corresponding to the trivial $[v-w, v-w-1, 2]$ MDS code.

First Step. As a first step, we will prove that the following two matrices are row equivalent:

$$\begin{bmatrix} G \\ A \end{bmatrix} \sim G^\star_{v-1}, \tag{20}$$

where $G^\star_{v-1}$ of (10) corresponds to the trivial $[v, v - 1, 2]$ MDS code. To prove (20), row reduction on G demonstrates the existence of a matrix $B \in \{0, 1\}^{w \times (v-w)}$ such that $G \sim \begin{bmatrix} I_w & B \end{bmatrix}$. Thus:

$$\begin{bmatrix} G \\ A \end{bmatrix} \sim \begin{bmatrix} I_w & B \\ \mathbf{0}_{(v-w-1)\times w} & G^\star_{v-w-1} \end{bmatrix}. \tag{21}$$

As G is an even-weight generator matrix, every row in B has odd weight. Consider any row $[b_1 \ b_2 \ \dots \ b_{v-w}]$ in B. For each $i \in \{1, \dots, v - w - 1\}$ such that $b_i = 1$, add the i-th row of $G^\star_{v-w-1}$ (or, equivalently, the $(w + i)$-th row of the entire matrix) to this row in B. As the original row has odd weight, and each row in $G^\star_{v-w-1}$ has even weight, the resulting row in B has odd weight, and is in particular of the form $[0 \ 0 \ \dots \ 1]$. Performing this elimination algorithm for all rows in B, we subsequently have

$$\begin{bmatrix} I_w & B \\ \mathbf{0}_{(v-w-1)\times w} & G^\star_{v-w-1} \end{bmatrix} \sim G^\star_{v-1}, \tag{22}$$

completing the proof of (20).

Second Step. The second step is to note that $G^\star_{v-1}$ is row equivalent to $G_{\mathsf{CENC}[v-1]}$ of (5):

$$G^\star_{v-1} \sim G_{\mathsf{CENC}[v-1]}. \tag{23}$$

This equivalence is immediate and does not require further discussion.

Third Step. Combining (20) and (23), there exists an invertible matrix $\boldsymbol{P} \in \{0,1\}^{(v-1)\times(v-1)}$ such that

$$\boldsymbol{P} \circ \boldsymbol{G}_{\mathsf{CENC}[v-1]} = \begin{bmatrix} \boldsymbol{G} \\ \boldsymbol{A} \end{bmatrix}. \tag{24}$$

This immediately completes the proof using Lemmas 1 and 2 below, as

$$\mathbf{Adv}^{\mathrm{prf}}_{\mathsf{NEMO}[\boldsymbol{G}]}(q,t) \le \mathbf{Adv}^{\mathrm{prf}}_{\mathsf{NEMO}[\boldsymbol{P}\circ\boldsymbol{G}_{\mathsf{CENC}[v-1]}]}(q,t) \text{ by Lemma 2 and (24),} \tag{25}$$

$$= \mathbf{Adv}^{\mathrm{prf}}_{\mathsf{NEMO}[\boldsymbol{G}_{\mathsf{CENC}[v-1]}]}(q,t) \text{ by Lemma 1,} \tag{26}$$

$$= \mathbf{Adv}^{\mathrm{prf}}_{\mathsf{CENC}[v-1]}(q,t) \text{ by (17).} \tag{27}$$

□

Lemma 1. *Let* $\boldsymbol{G}, \boldsymbol{G}' \in \{0,1\}^{w\times v}$ *be two generator matrices such that* $\boldsymbol{G}' = \boldsymbol{P}\cdot\boldsymbol{G}$ *for some invertible matrix* $\boldsymbol{P} \in \{0,1\}^{w\times w}$. *We have,*

$$\mathbf{Adv}^{\mathrm{prf}}_{\mathsf{NEMO}[\boldsymbol{G}]}(q,t) = \mathbf{Adv}^{\mathrm{prf}}_{\mathsf{NEMO}[\boldsymbol{G}']}(q,t). \tag{28}$$

Proof. The proof is a trivial consequence of the fact that $\boldsymbol{G}$ and $\boldsymbol{G}'$ generate the same code. Let $\mathcal{D}$ be a distinguisher against $\mathsf{NEMO}[\boldsymbol{G}]$, we will construct a distinguisher $\mathcal{D}'$ against $\mathsf{NEMO}[\boldsymbol{G}']$ with at least the same success probability at $\mathcal{D}$. For each query x that $\mathcal{D}$ makes, $\mathcal{D}'$ queries x to its own oracle, receives a wn-bit string y. Treating it as a vector of w n-bit blocks $\boldsymbol{y}$, it computes $\boldsymbol{P}^{-1}\boldsymbol{y}$ and sends it to $\mathcal{D}$. Then, if $\mathcal{D}$ makes its final decision, $\mathcal{D}'$ forwards its choice. Distinguisher $\mathcal{D}'$ succeeds if $\mathcal{D}$ succeeds. This holds for any distinguisher $\mathcal{D}$, and hence, $\mathbf{Adv}^{\mathrm{prf}}_{\mathsf{NEMO}[\boldsymbol{G}]}(q,t) \le \mathbf{Adv}^{\mathrm{prf}}_{\mathsf{NEMO}[\boldsymbol{G}']}(q,t)$. As $\boldsymbol{P}$ is invertible, the proof in reverse direction is symmetric. □

Lemma 2. *Let* $\boldsymbol{G} \in \{0,1\}^{w\times v}$ *and* $\boldsymbol{G}' \in \{0,1\}^{w'\times v}$ *be two generator matrices such that* $\boldsymbol{G}' = \begin{bmatrix} \boldsymbol{G} \\ \boldsymbol{A} \end{bmatrix}$ *for some matrix* $\boldsymbol{A} \in \{0,1\}^{(w'-w)\times v}$. *We have,*

$$\mathbf{Adv}^{\mathrm{prf}}_{\mathsf{NEMO}[\boldsymbol{G}]}(q,t) \le \mathbf{Adv}^{\mathrm{prf}}_{\mathsf{NEMO}[\boldsymbol{G}']}(q,t). \tag{29}$$

Proof. The proof is a trivial consequence of the fact that $\boldsymbol{G}$ can be obtained from "expurgating" $\boldsymbol{G}'$ [17, Sect. 5.4.2]. Let $\mathcal{D}$ be a distinguisher against $\mathsf{NEMO}[\boldsymbol{G}]$, we will construct a distinguisher $\mathcal{D}'$ against $\mathsf{NEMO}[\boldsymbol{G}']$ with at least the same success probability at $\mathcal{D}$. For each query x that $\mathcal{D}$ makes, $\mathcal{D}'$ queries x to its own oracle, receives a $w'n$-bit string y. It forwards the first wn bits to $\mathcal{D}$. Then, if $\mathcal{D}$ makes its final decision, $\mathcal{D}'$ forwards its choice. Distinguisher $\mathcal{D}'$ succeeds if $\mathcal{D}$ succeeds. This holds for any distinguisher $\mathcal{D}$, and hence, $\mathbf{Adv}^{\mathrm{prf}}_{\mathsf{NEMO}[\boldsymbol{G}]}(q,t) \le \mathbf{Adv}^{\mathrm{prf}}_{\mathsf{NEMO}[\boldsymbol{G}']}(q,t)$. □

Remark 1. We remark that, due to its generality, the bound of Theorem 5 is non-optimal. Consider, for example, generator matrix

$$G_{\mathsf{XOP}[w]} = \begin{bmatrix} 1 & 1 & 0 & 0 & \cdots & 0 & 0 \\ 0 & 0 & 1 & 1 & \cdots & 0 & 0 \\ \vdots & \vdots & \vdots & \vdots & \ddots & \vdots & \vdots \\ 0 & 0 & 0 & 0 & \cdots & 1 & 1 \end{bmatrix} \in \{0,1\}^{w \times 2w}, \tag{30}$$

for which $\mathsf{NEMO}[G_{\mathsf{XOP}[w]}]$ corresponds to a parallel evaluation of w sums of permutations. Patarin [15] and later Dai et al. [5] demonstrated that this construction is secure up to around $wq/2^n$. The proof of Theorem 5 augments the generator matrix to

$$\begin{bmatrix} 1 & 1 & 0 & 0 & \cdots & 0 & 0 \\ 0 & 0 & 1 & 1 & \cdots & 0 & 0 \\ \vdots & \vdots & \vdots & \vdots & \ddots & \vdots & \vdots \\ 0 & 0 & 0 & 0 & \cdots & 1 & 1 \\ \hline 0 & 1 & 0 & 0 & \cdots & 0 & 1 \\ 0 & 0 & 0 & 1 & \cdots & 0 & 1 \\ \vdots & \vdots & \vdots & \vdots & \ddots & \vdots & \vdots \\ 0 & 0 & 0 & 0 & \cdots & 0 & 1 \end{bmatrix} \in \{0,1\}^{(2w-1)\times 2w}, \tag{31}$$

which generates the same code as $G_{2w-1}^{\star}$ of (10) and $G_{\mathsf{CENC}[2w-1]}$ of (12), and it gives an upper bound of around $(2w)^2 q/2^n$.

4.2 Arbitrary Linear Codes

We conjecture that the result of Theorem 5 extends to arbitrary binary linear codes.

Conjecture 1 (Security of NEMO for arbitrary binary code). Let G be a generator matrix of a binary $[v, w, d]$ code with $v \geq w$. We have,

$$\mathbf{Adv}_{\mathsf{NEMO}[G]}^{\mathrm{prf}}(q,t) \leq \mathbf{Adv}_{\mathsf{CENC}[v-1]}^{\mathrm{prf}}(q,t). \tag{32}$$

The result is intuitively appealing. As $G_{\mathsf{CENC}[v-1]}$ corresponds to a binary $[v, v-1, 2]$ MDS code, it gives the most one can get off v blocks of randomness. Stated differently, $v-1$ output blocks are generated using v blocks of randomness. Outputting another block would degrade the security of the scheme to the birthday bound. Conversely, any other $[v, w, d]$ code for $d \geq 2$ outputs less data, hence exposes less of the v blocks of randomness, and is likely to be more secure.

The proof of Theorem 5 does not stretch to Conjecture 1, and the reason is that an arbitrary generator matrix G cannot necessarily be augmented to $G_{v-1}^{\star}$ for binary $[v, v-1, 2]$ code. A simple example is given by

$$G_{\mathrm{bad}} := \begin{bmatrix} 1 & 1 & 1 \end{bmatrix}. \tag{33}$$

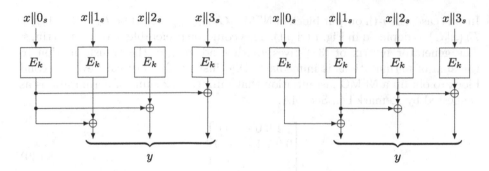

Fig. 1. CENC$[3]_k$ of (12) (left) and CENC$'[3]_k$ of (38) (right)

For this matrix, NEMO$[G_{bad}]$ implements the function

$$\text{NEMO}[G_{bad}]_k(x) = E_k(x\|0_s) \oplus E_k(x\|1_s) \oplus E_k(x\|2_s), \quad (34)$$

which is seemingly more secure than

$$\text{CENC}[2]_k(x) = E_k(x\|0_s) \oplus E_k(x\|1_s) \,\|\, E_k(x\|0_s) \oplus E_k(x\|2_s). \quad (35)$$

Yet, there appears to be no simple reduction to argue this formally. In particularly, G_{bad} cannot be augmented to $G_2^\star$ of (10).

5   Understanding Equivalences

Recall $G_{\text{CENC}[w]}$ of (12):

$$G_{\text{CENC}[w]} := \begin{bmatrix} 1 & 1 & 0 & \cdots & 0 \\ 1 & 0 & 1 & \cdots & 0 \\ \vdots & \vdots & \vdots & \ddots & \vdots \\ 1 & 0 & 0 & \cdots & 1 \end{bmatrix} \in \{0,1\}^{w\times(w+1)}. \quad (36)$$

By Lemma 1, left multiplication with an invertible matrix $P \in \{0,1\}^{w\times w}$ does not decrease the security:

$$\mathbf{Adv}^{\text{prf}}_{\text{NEMO}[P\cdot G_{\text{CENC}[w]}]}(q,t) = \mathbf{Adv}^{\text{prf}}_{\text{NEMO}[G_{\text{CENC}[w]}]}(q,t) = \mathbf{Adv}^{\text{prf}}_{\text{CENC}[w]}(q,t), \quad (37)$$

recalling that NEMO$[G_{\text{CENC}[w]}] = \text{CENC}[w]$.

Note that an implementation of CENC$[w]_k$ would have to compute $E_k(x\|0_s)$, store it, and add it to $E_k(x\|i_s)$ for $i = 1, \ldots, w$. See also Fig. 1 (left). An alternative to CENC$[w]$ would be CENC$'[w]$ based on generator matrix

$$G_{\text{CENC}'[w]} := \begin{bmatrix} 1 & 1 & 0 & \cdots & 0 & 0 \\ 0 & 1 & 1 & \cdots & 0 & 0 \\ \vdots & \vdots & \vdots & \ddots & \vdots & \vdots \\ 0 & 0 & 0 & \cdots & 1 & 1 \end{bmatrix} = \underbrace{\begin{bmatrix} 1 & 0 & \cdots & 0 & 0 \\ 1 & 1 & \cdots & 0 & 0 \\ \vdots & \vdots & \ddots & \vdots & \vdots \\ 0 & 0 & \cdots & 1 & 1 \end{bmatrix}}_{=:P} \cdot G_{\text{CENC}[w]}. \quad (38)$$

In this case, the i-th output block of $\mathsf{NEMO}[G_{\mathsf{CENC'}[w]}]$ would be $E_k(x\|(i-1)_s) \oplus E_k(x\|i_s)$ as depicted in Fig. 1 (right). This could be preferable in certain settings. The generator matrix of (38) gives another advantage: the transformation to the sum of permutations is immediate. One just needs to discard every second block to obtain a NEMO instantiation that mimics $w/2$ sums of permutations as suggested by Remark 1 in Sect. 4.1:

$$
\begin{bmatrix}
1 & 1 & 0 & 0 & \cdots & 0 & 0 \\
0 & 0 & 1 & 1 & \cdots & 0 & 0 \\
\vdots & \vdots & \vdots & \vdots & \ddots & \vdots & \vdots \\
0 & 0 & 0 & 0 & \cdots & 1 & 1
\end{bmatrix}.
\tag{39}
$$

As mentioned in Remark 1, this scheme gives around $q/2^n$ security for the generation of q output blocks.

Acknowledgments. Bart Mennink is supported by a postdoctoral fellowship from the Netherlands Organisation for Scientific Research (NWO) under Veni grant 016.Veni.173.017.

References

1. Bellare, M., Desai, A., Jokipii, E., Rogaway, P.: A concrete security treatment of symmetric encryption. In: 38th Annual Symposium on Foundations of Computer Science, FOCS 1997, Miami Beach, Florida, USA, 19–22 October 1997, pp. 394–403. IEEE Computer Society (1997). https://doi.org/10.1109/SFCS.1997.646128
2. Bellare, M., Impagliazzo, R.: A tool for obtaining tighter security analyses of pseudorandom function based constructions, with applications to PRP to PRF conversion. Cryptology ePrint Archive, Report 1999/024 (1999). http://eprint.iacr.org/1999/024
3. Bellare, M., Krovetz, T., Rogaway, P.: Luby-Rackoff backwards: increasing security by making block ciphers non-invertible. In: Nyberg, K. (ed.) EUROCRYPT 1998. LNCS, vol. 1403, pp. 266–280. Springer, Heidelberg (1998). https://doi.org/10.1007/BFb0054132
4. Bhattacharya, S., Nandi, M.: Revisiting variable output length XOR pseudorandom function. IACR Trans. Symmetric Cryptol. **2018**(1), 314–335 (2018). https://doi.org/10.13154/tosc.v2018.i1.314-335
5. Dai, W., Hoang, V.T., Tessaro, S.: Information-theoretic indistinguishability via the Chi-squared method. In: Katz and Shacham [8], pp. 497–523. https://doi.org/10.1007/978-3-319-63697-9_17
6. Iwata, T.: New blockcipher modes of operation with beyond the birthday bound security. In: Robshaw, M. (ed.) FSE 2006. LNCS, vol. 4047, pp. 310–327. Springer, Heidelberg (2006). https://doi.org/10.1007/11799313_20
7. Iwata, T., Mennink, B., Vizár, D.: CENC is optimally secure. Cryptology ePrint Archive, Report 2016/1087 (2016). http://eprint.iacr.org/2016/1087
8. Katz, J., Shacham, H. (eds.): CRYPTO 2017. LNCS, vol. 10403. Springer, Cham (2017). https://doi.org/10.1007/978-3-319-63697-9

9. Lefranc, D., Painchault, P., Rouat, V., Mayer, E.: A generic method to design modes of operation beyond the birthday bound. In: Adams, C., Miri, A., Wiener, M. (eds.) SAC 2007. LNCS, vol. 4876, pp. 328–343. Springer, Heidelberg (2007). https://doi.org/10.1007/978-3-540-77360-3_21

10. Lucks, S.: The sum of PRPs is a secure PRF. In: Preneel, B. (ed.) EUROCRYPT 2000. LNCS, vol. 1807, pp. 470–484. Springer, Heidelberg (2000). https://doi.org/10.1007/3-540-45539-6_34

11. Mennink, B., Neves, S.: Encrypted Davies-Meyer and its dual: towards optimal security using mirror theory. In: Katz and Shacham [8], pp. 556–583. https://doi.org/10.1007/978-3-319-63697-9_19

12. Nachef, V., Patarin, J., Volte, E.: Feistel Ciphers - Security Proofs and Cryptanalysis. Springer, Cham (2017). https://doi.org/10.1007/978-3-319-49530-9

13. Patarin, J.: On linear systems of equations with distinct variables and small block size. In: Won, D.H., Kim, S. (eds.) ICISC 2005. LNCS, vol. 3935, pp. 299–321. Springer, Heidelberg (2006). https://doi.org/10.1007/11734727_25

14. Patarin, J.: A proof of security in $O(2^n)$ for the Xor of two random permutations. In: Safavi-Naini, R. (ed.) ICITS 2008. LNCS, vol. 5155, pp. 232–248. Springer, Heidelberg (2008). https://doi.org/10.1007/978-3-540-85093-9_22

15. Patarin, J.: Introduction to mirror theory: analysis of systems of linear equalities and linear non equalities for cryptography. Cryptology ePrint Archive, Report 2010/287 (2010). http://eprint.iacr.org/2010/287

16. Singleton, R.C.: Maximum distance q-nary codes. IEEE Trans. Inf. Theory 10(2), 116–118 (1964). https://doi.org/10.1109/TIT.1964.1053661

17. Vermani, L.R.: Elements of Algebraic Coding Theory. CRC Press, Boca Raton (1996)

On the Efficiency of ZMAC-Type Modes

Yusuke Naito$^{(\boxtimes)}$

Mitsubishi Electric Corporation, Kanagawa, Japan
`Naito.Yusuke@ce.MitsubishiElectric.co.jp`

Abstract. In this paper, we study the efficiency of ZMAC-type message authentication codes (MACs). ZMAC was proposed by Iwata et al. (CRYPTO 2017) and is a highly efficient and highly secure MAC based on tweakable blockcipher (TBC). ZMAC achieves the so-called beyond-birthday-bound security: security up to $2^{\min\{b,(b+t)/2\}}$ TBC calls, using a TBC with the input-block space $\{0,1\}^b$ and the tweak space $\mathcal{TW} = \mathcal{I} \times \{0,1\}^t$ where $\mathcal{I}$ is a set with $|\mathcal{I}| = 5$ and is used for tweak separations. In the hash function, the b-bit and t-bit spaces are used to take message blocks (in previous MACs, only the b-bit input-block space is used). In the finalization function, a TBC is called twice, and these spaces are not used. List and Nandi (ToSC 2017, Issue 4) proposed ZMAC$^+$, a variant of ZMAC, where one TBC call is removed from the finalization function. Although both the b-bit and t-bit spaces in the hash function are used to take message blocks, those in the finalization function are not used. That rises the following question with the aim of improving the efficiency: can these spaces be used while retaining the same level of security as ZMAC? In this paper, we consider the following three ZMAC-type MACs.
- ZMACb: only the b-bit space is used.
- ZMACt: only the t-bit space is used.
- ZMACbt: both the b-bit and t-bit spaces are used.

We show that none of the above MACs achieve the same level of security as ZMAC$^{(+)}$. Hence, ZMAC$^+$ is the most efficient MAC in the ZMAC-type ones with $2^{\min\{b,(b+t)/2\}}$-security.

We next consider whether the tweak separations can be removed (i.e., $\mathcal{I}$ can be used to take a message block), with the aim of improving the efficiency of ZMAC$^+$. Iwata et al. mentioned that the tweak separations can be removed by using distinct field multiplications such as multiplications by 3 and 7, but these render the implementation much more complex (note that in ZMAC, field multiplications by 2 are used). For this problem, we show that the tweak separations can be removed without the field multiplications except for the multiplications by 2, that is, all spaces $\mathcal{TW}$ and $\{0,1\}^b$ in the hash function can be used to take message blocks without such complex implementations.

Keywords: MAC · Tweakable blockcipher · ZMAC · BBB-security

1 Introduction

Message authentication code (MAC) is a fundamental symmetric-key primitive that provides the authenticity of messages. A number of MACs are realized by

© Springer Nature Switzerland AG 2018
J. Camenisch and P. Papadimitratos (Eds.): CANS 2018, LNCS 11124, pp. 190–210, 2018.
https://doi.org/10.1007/978-3-030-00434-7_10

using blockciphers via modes of operation. Most of them are reasonably efficient, i.e., a b-bit blockcipher is called once for each b-bit message block such as [2,5,20]. The efficient MACs have the so-called birthday-bound security (security up to $O(2^{b/2})$ blockcipher calls). However, birthday-bound security becomes unreliable, when large amounts of data are processed, or when a large number of connections are needed. For this reason, designing an efficient and beyond-birthday-bound(BBB)-secure MAC is an important research topic.

Blockcipher-Based MACs with BBB-Security. The first attempt to design BBB-secure MACs was made in ISO 9797-1 [9] (without proofs of security), where six CBC-type MACs are defined. Yasuda [21] proved that Algorithm 6 achieves BBB-security (security up to $O(2^{2b/3})$ blockcipher calls), and proposed a variant of the MAC called SUM-ECBC, where the number of blockcipher keys is reduced from 6 to 4. After that, several BBB-secure MACs have been proposed, e.g., PMAC_Plus [22], 1-k-PMAC_Plus [4] (security up to $O(2^{2b/3})$ blockcipher calls), F_r [7] and LightMAC_Plus(2) [17,18] (security up to $O(2^{rb/(r+1)})$ queries for the parameter r).

Tweakable Blockcipher-Based MACs. Another approach to achieve BBB-security is to use tweakable blockcipher (TBC). The advantage of TBC-based design over blockcipher-based one is that a highly efficient and optimally secure $(O(2^b)$-secure) MAC can be designed. TBC whose concept was introduced by Liskov et al. [10] is a generalization of classical blockcipher. A TBC takes an input called tweak in addition to key and input block. Tweak is a public parameter, where a retweaking (changing a tweak) offers the same functionality as changing its secret key but should be less costly. A TBC can be either constructed in a generic way from a blockcipher through a mode of operation such as XEX [20], or as a dedicated design such as Deoxys-BC [8] and SKINNY [1], following the so-called TWEAKEY framework [8].

Naito [16] proposed PMAC_TBC1k, a combination of PMAC1 proposed by Rogaway [20] and PMAC_Plus that is a secure MAC up to $O(2^b)$ queries when using a TBC with the input-block space $\{0,1\}^b$ and the tweak space $\mathcal{TW} = \mathcal{I} \times \{0,1\}^t$ such that $\mathcal{I}$ is a set with $|\mathcal{I}| = 3$ and $b \leq t$. In PMAC_TBC1k, for each i-th message block M_i of b bits, M_i is input to the input block space and the counter value i is input to the tweak space $\{0,1\}^t$ (counter-based construction from PMAC1), and then the b-bit outputs are extended to $2b$ bits (PMAC_Plus's technique). Note that $\mathcal{I}$ is used for tweak separations. The counter-based construction avoids a collision in inputs to TBC calls at distinct positions, and PMAC_Plus's technique avoids the $O(2^{b/2})$ birthday attack. Thus, these techniques realize the optimal $O(2^b)$ security. List and Nandi [11] pointed out a flow of his security proof, and gave a valid proof. They also proposed PMAC2x which extends the output size of PMAC_TBC1k from b to $2b$ bits without harming efficiency nor security, and PMACx which is a modification of PMAC_TBC1k with b-bit outputs. Minematsu and Iwata [15] reported a flaw of the security result, and List and Nandi [11] modified their proposals so that the flaw is fixed.

Iwata et al. [6] proposed ZMAC, a highly efficient and BBB-secure MAC that is a secure MAC up to $O(2^{\min\{b,(b+t)/2\}})$ TBC calls, using a TBC with the input-block space $\{0,1\}^b$ and the tweak space $\mathcal{TW} = \mathcal{I} \times \{0,1\}^t$ with $|\mathcal{I}| = 6$. In ZMAC, both the b-bit and t-bit spaces are used to take message blocks. Hence, ZMAC is roughly $(b+t)/b$ times faster than previous TBC-based MACs with respect to the number of TBC calls. In stead of the counter-based construction in PMAC_TBC1k, ZMAC employs the XT(X) tweak extension [14] in order to securely use the t-bit space: two secret maskings defined by the powering-up scheme [20] are applied to the b-bit and t-bit spaces. Hence, in the hash function ZHASH, each message block of $b+t$ bits is input to the underlying TBC via XT(X) tweak extension, and then using the TBC outputs, a $b+t$-bit hash value is defined. In the finalization function ZFIN, a tag of ZMAC is defined by the xor of two TBCs.

List and Nandi [12] proposed ZMAC$^+$, a variant of ZMAC, where one TBC call is removed from ZFIN, while retaining the $O(2^{\min\{b,(b+t)/2\}})$-security. In addition, the size of $\mathcal{I}$ for tweak separations is reduced from 6 bits to 4 bits.[1]

Question 1. In the hash function of ZMAC$^+$, both b-bit and t-bit spaces are used to take message blocks, whereas in the finalization function, those are not used. That raises the following question, with the aim of improving the efficiency of ZMAC($^+$): can these spaces be used to take message blocks, while retaining the $O(2^{\min\{b,(b+t)/2\}})$-security? In particular, what is an optimally efficient construction in ZMAC design?

Contribution 1. For this question, the following three ZMAC-type MACs naturally come up.

1. ZMACb: only the b-bit space is used.
2. ZMACt: only the t-bit space is used.
3. ZMACbt: both the b-bit and t-bit spaces are used.

We show that none of the above MACs achieve the same level of security as ZMAC($^+$), i.e., there exist forgery attacks with $O(2^{b/2})$ TBC calls. Our results show that ZMAC$^+$ is the most efficient MAC in the ZMAC-type MACs (note that our results consider only ZMAC design, and does not rule out the possibility of other design with better efficiency).

Question 2. The above results consider ZMAC-type MACs where the b-bit and t-bit spaces are used and the remaining space $\mathcal{I}$ for the tweak separations is not. Iwata et al. [6] mentioned that the tweak separations can be removed (in other words, $\mathcal{I}$ is used to take message blocks), by using distinct field multiplications (e.g., multiplications by 3 and 7), but these render the implementation much more complex (note that ZMAC uses field multiplications by 2). Hence, the

---

[1] Usually, the tweak separations are realized by using one byte in the tweak space of each TBC call. In this case, there is no impact on the efficiency from the modification.

next question is: can the tweak separations be removed without such complex implementations?

Contribution 2. We show that the tweak separations can be removed without the distinct field multiplications, while retaining the $O(2^{\min\{b,(b+t)/2\}})$-security, that is, the complex implementations can be avoided. The resultant MAC is called ZMAC1. In ZMAC1, $\mathcal{I}$ can be used to take message blocks, and thus the efficiency of ZMAC($^+$) is improved without the complex implementations. Normally, when $\mathcal{I}$ is not empty and the tweak size is t' bits, one byte in the tweak space is used to realize $\mathcal{I}$ and the remaining tweak space of $t' - 8$ bits is used to realize $\{0,1\}^t$. In this setting, ZMAC1 is roughly $(b + t')/(b + t' - 8)$ times faster than ZMAC($^+$) with respect to the number of TBC calls. Note that our contribution 1 can be applied to the ZMAC-type MACs without the tweak separations, thereby ZMAC1 is the most efficient MAC in ZMAC design.

Further Related Work. Cogliati et al. [3] proposed Hat, a MAC based on a TBC and two universal hash functions. Hat requires three keys (one TBC key and two hash keys), whereas the ZMAC-type MACs require only a single key.

2   Preliminaries

Notation. Let λ be an empty string and $\{0,1\}^*$ the set of all bit strings. For an integer $i \geq 0$, let $\{0,1\}^i$ the set of all i-bit strings, $(\{0,1\}^i)^*$ the set of all bit strings whose lengths are multiples of i, and 0^i resp. 1^i the bit string of i-bit zeroes resp. ones. For an integer $i \geq 1$, let $[i] := \{1,2,\ldots,i\}$. For a non-empty set $\mathcal{T}$, $T \xleftarrow{\$} \mathcal{T}$ means that an element is chosen uniformly at random from $\mathcal{T}$ and is assigned to T. The concatenation of two bit strings X and Y is written as $X \| Y$ or XY when no confusion is possible. For integers $0 \leq i \leq j$ and $X \in \{0,1\}^j$, let $\mathsf{msb}_i(X)$ resp. $\mathsf{lsb}_i(X)$ be the most resp. least significant i bits of X. For integers i and j with $0 \leq i < 2^j$, let $\mathsf{str}_j(i)$ be the j-bit binary representation of i. For integers $i,j \geq 0$ and a bit string $X \in \{0,1\}^{i+j}$, we define the parsing into i-bit and j-bit strings, denoted $(L,R) \xleftarrow{i,j} X$ where $L = \mathsf{msb}_i(X)$ and $R = \mathsf{lsb}_j(X)$. For integers $i,j \geq 0$ and an ij-bit string M, we define the parsing into fixed-length j-bit strings, denoted $(M_1, M_2, \ldots, M_i) \xleftarrow{b} M$, where $M = M_1 \| M_2 \| \cdots \| M_i$. For integers $t,b \geq 0$, $X \in \{0,1\}^t$ and $Y \in \{0,1\}^b$, $X \oplus_t Y := X \oplus (Y \| 0^{t-b})$ if $b \leq t$, and $X \oplus_t Y := X \oplus \mathsf{msb}_t(Y)$ if $b > t$.

Binary Fields. The set $\{0,1\}^b$ can be considered as the finite field $GF(2^b)$ consisting of 2^b elements. To do this, we represent of $GF(2^b)$ as a polynomial over the field $GF(2)$ of degree less than b. A string $a_{b-1} \cdots a_1 a_0 \in \{0,1\}^b$ corresponds to the polynomial $a_{b-1} \mathsf{z}^{b-1} + \cdots + a_1 \mathsf{z} + a_0 \in GF(2^b)$. The addition in the field is just the addition of polynomials over $GF(2)$ (bitwise XOR $\oplus$). To define multiplication in the field, we fix an irreducible polynomial

$a(\mathbf{z}) = \mathbf{z}^b + a_{b-1}\mathbf{z}^{b-1} + \cdots + a_1\mathbf{z} + a_0$ of degree b over the field $GF(2)$. Given two elements $u(\mathbf{z}), v(\mathbf{z}) \in GF(2^b)$, their product is defined as $u(\mathbf{z})v(\mathbf{z}) \mod a(\mathbf{z})$ (polynomial multiplication over the field $GF(2)$ reduced modulo $a(\mathbf{z})$). The multiplication is simply written as $u(\mathbf{z})v(\mathbf{z})$, $u(\mathbf{z}) \cdot v(\mathbf{z})$, or $u(\mathbf{z}) \otimes v(\mathbf{z})$.

The set $\{0,1\}^b$ can be also regarded as a set of integers ranging from 0 to $2^b - 1$. A string $a_{b-1} \cdots a_1 a_0 \in \{0,1\}^b$ corresponds to the integer $a_{b-1}2^{b-1} + a_{b-2}2^{b-2} + \cdots + a_1 2 + a_0$. We often write elements of $GF(2^b)$ as integers, based on these conversions. For instance, $2 = \mathbf{z}$.

Though this paper, we assume that an irreducible polynomial has the property that the element $2 = \mathbf{z}$ generates the entire multiplication group $GF(2^b)^*$ of order $2^b - 1$. The irreducible polynomials for $b = 64$ and $b = 128$ are e.g., $a(\mathbf{z}) = \mathbf{z}^{64} + \mathbf{z}^4 + \mathbf{z}^3 + \mathbf{z} + 1$ and $a(\mathbf{z}) = \mathbf{z}^{128} + \mathbf{z}^7 + \mathbf{z}^2 + \mathbf{z} + 1$.

Tweakable Blockcipher. A tweakable blockcipher (TBC) is a set of permutations indexed by a key and a public input called tweak. Let $\mathcal{K}$ be the key spece, $\mathcal{TW}$ the tweak space, and b the input/output-block size. In this paper, a TBC is denoted by $\widetilde{E} : \mathcal{K} \times \mathcal{TW} \times \{0,1\}^b \to \{0,1\}^b$.

In this paper, the security proofs are given in the information theoretic model where the underlying keyed TBC is replaced with a tweakable random permutation (TRP). A tweakable permutation (TP) $\widetilde{P} : \mathcal{TW} \times \{0,1\}^b \to \{0,1\}^b$ is a set of b-bit permutations indexed by a tweak in $\mathcal{TW}$. Let $\widetilde{\mathsf{Perm}}(\mathcal{TW}, \{0,1\}^b)$ be the set of all TPs: $\mathcal{TW} \times \{0,1\}^b \to \{0,1\}^b$. Then a TRP is defined as $\widetilde{P} \xleftarrow{\$} \widetilde{\mathsf{Perm}}(\mathcal{TW}, \{0,1\}^b)$. Hence, tweakable pseudo-random-permutation (TPRP) security is considered. TPRP-security is defined in terms of indistinguishability between a keyed TBC and a TRP. An adversary $\mathbf{A}$ has access to either the keyed TBC or a TRP, and returns a decision bit $y \in \{0,1\}$ after the interaction. The output of $\mathbf{A}$ with access to $\mathcal{O}$ is denoted by $\mathbf{A}^{\mathcal{O}}$. The advantage function of $\mathbf{A}$ is defined as

$$\mathbf{Adv}_{\widetilde{E}}^{\mathrm{tprp}}(\mathbf{A}) := \Pr\left[K \xleftarrow{\$} \mathcal{K}; \mathbf{A}^{\widetilde{E}_K} = 1\right] - \Pr\left[\widetilde{P} \xleftarrow{\$} \widetilde{\mathsf{Perm}}(\mathcal{TW}, \{0,1\}^b); \mathbf{A}^{\widetilde{P}} = 1\right],$$

where the probabilities are taken over $K, \widetilde{P}$ and $\mathbf{A}$. Note that using a TBC $\widetilde{E}$ in a MAC, the advantage function for the TBC is introduced in addition to the security bound of the MAC using a TRP.

Security Definitions for MACs. Through this paper, an adversary $\mathbf{A}$ is a computationally unbounded algorithm. Its complexity is solely measured by the number of queries made to its oracles. Let $F[\widetilde{P}]$ be a MAC function with τ-bit outputs using a TP $\widetilde{P}$. Hereafter, the definitions of PRF-security and MAC-security are given. Note that PRF-security is a stronger security notion than MAC-security. Hence, the PRF-security of $F[\widetilde{P}]$ ensures the MAC-security, and an attack breaking the MAC-security of $F[\widetilde{P}]$ (forgery attack to $F[\widetilde{P}]$) offers an attack breaking the PRF-security.

PRF-SECURITY. The pseudo-random-function (PRF) security of $F[\widetilde{P}]$ is defined in terms of indistinguishability between the real and ideal worlds. In the real world, $\mathbf{A}$ has access to $F[\widetilde{P}]$ for $\widetilde{P} \xleftarrow{\$} \widetilde{\mathsf{Perm}}(\mathcal{TW}, \{0,1\}^b)$. In the ideal world, it has access to a random function $\mathcal{R}$, where a random function is defined as $\mathcal{R} \xleftarrow{\$} \mathsf{Func}(\{0,1\}^\tau)$ where $\mathsf{Func}(\{0,1\}^\tau)$ be the set of all functions from $\{0,1\}^*$ to $\{0,1\}^\tau$. After the interaction, $\mathbf{A}$ outputs a decision bit $y \in \{0,1\}$. The advantage function of $\mathbf{A}$ is defined as

$$\mathbf{Adv}_F^{\mathsf{prf}}(\mathbf{A}) := \Pr\left[\widetilde{P} \xleftarrow{\$} \mathsf{Perm}(\mathcal{TW}, \{0,1\}^b); \mathbf{A}^{F[\widetilde{P}]} = 1\right] -$$
$$\Pr\left[\mathcal{R} \xleftarrow{\$} \mathsf{Func}(\{0,1\}^\tau); \mathbf{A}^{\mathcal{R}} = 1\right],$$

where the probabilities are taken over $\mathbf{P}, \mathcal{R}$ and $\mathbf{A}$.

MAC-SECURITY. The MAC-security of $F[\widetilde{P}]$ is defined in terms of unforgeability under a chosen-message attack. An adversary $\mathbf{A}$ has access to $F[\widetilde{P}]$ and the verification function $\mathsf{Verif}[F[\widetilde{P}]]$. $\mathsf{Verif}[F[\widetilde{P}]]$ is defined as follows: For a query (M, T), it returns accept if $F[\widetilde{P}](M) = T$, and returns reject otherwise. We call a query to $F[\widetilde{P}]$ "a tagging query" and a query to $\mathsf{Verif}[F[\widetilde{P}]]$ "a verification query." The advantage function of $\mathbf{A}$ is defined as

$$\mathbf{Adv}_F^{\mathsf{mac}}(\mathbf{A}) := \Pr\left[\widetilde{P} \xleftarrow{\$} \mathsf{Perm}(\mathcal{TW}, \{0,1\}^b); \mathbf{A}^{F[\widetilde{P}], \mathsf{Verif}[F[\widetilde{P}]]} \text{ forges}\right],$$

where the probabilities are taken over $\widetilde{P}$ and $\mathbf{A}$. "$\mathbf{A}$ forges" means that $\mathbf{A}$ makes a verification query (M, T) such that the tagging query M has not been made and accept is returned. Note that if $\mathbf{Adv}_F^{\mathsf{prf}}(\mathbf{A}) \leq \varepsilon$ for any adversary $\mathbf{A}$ making q queries, we have $\mathbf{Adv}_F^{\mathsf{mac}}(\mathcal{B}) \leq \varepsilon + q_v/2^\tau$ for any adversary $\mathcal{B}$ making q_t tagging queries and q_v verification queries such that $q = q_t + q_v$.

ZMAC [6]. ZMAC : $\mathcal{K} \times \{0,1\}^* \to \{0,1\}^\tau$ is defined in Algorithm 1 and is illustrated in Fig. 1, where $\tau > 0$ is an integer. The tweak space of the underlying TBC $\widetilde{E}$ consists of two spaces $\mathcal{I} := \{0,1,2,3,4,5\}$ and $\{0,1\}^t$, i.e., $\mathcal{TW} = \mathcal{I} \times \{0,1\}^t$. Though this paper, $\widetilde{E}$ having $K \in \mathcal{K}$, $tw \in \{0,1\}^t$, $i \in \mathcal{I}$ and $M \in \{0,1\}^b$ is denoted by $\widetilde{E}_K^i(tw, M)$. ozp : $\{0,1\}^* \to (\{0,1\}^{b+t})^*$ is a one-zero padding: if $|M| \neq 0$ and $|M| \bmod (b+t) = 0$ then $\mathsf{ozp}(M) = M$; otherwise $\mathsf{ozp}(M) = M\|10^p$ where $p = (b+t) - (|M| \bmod (b+t)) - 1$. ZMAC consists of a hash function ZHASH : $(\{0,1\}^{b+t})^* \to \{0,1\}^b \times \{0,1\}^t$ and a finalization function ZFIN : $\{0,1\}^b \times \{0,1\}^t \to \{0,1\}^\tau$. In ZHASH, each message block of $b+t$ bits is input to $\widetilde{E}_K^1$ via the XT tweak extension [14] with secret maskings $2^j \cdot \Delta_L$ and $2^j \cdot \Delta_R$.

In [6], the following PRF-security bound is given, i.e., ZMAC is a secure PRF up to $O(2^{\min\{b,(b+t)/2\}})$ TRP calls.

Algorithm 1. ZMAC

▶ Main Procedure $\mathsf{ZMAC}[\widetilde{E}_K](M)$

1: $M^* \leftarrow \mathsf{ozp}(M); (U, V) \leftarrow \mathsf{ZHASH}[\widetilde{E}_K](M^*)$

2: **if** $|M| = 0$ or $|M| \bmod (b+t) \neq 0$ **then** $T \leftarrow \widetilde{E}_K^2(V, U) \oplus \widetilde{E}_K^4(V, U)$ ▷ ZFIN

3: **if** $|M| \neq 0$ and $|M| \bmod (b+t) = 0$ **then** $T \leftarrow \widetilde{E}_K^3(V, U) \oplus \widetilde{E}_K^5(V, U)$ ▷ ZFIN

4: **return** $\mathsf{msb}_\tau(T)$ ▷ ZFIN

▶ Subroutine $\mathsf{ZHASH}[\widetilde{E}_K](M^*)$

1: $M_1, \ldots, M_m \xleftarrow{b+t} M^*; U \leftarrow 0^b; V \leftarrow 0^t$

2: **for** $i = 1, \ldots, m$ **do**

3: $\quad (L_i, R_i) \xleftarrow{b,t} M_i; Y_i \leftarrow \mathsf{XT}[\widetilde{E}_K]((i-1, R_i), L_i); Z_i \leftarrow Y_i \oplus_t L_i$

4: $\quad V \leftarrow V \oplus Z_i; U \leftarrow 2 \cdot (U \oplus Y_i)$

5: **end for**

6: **return** (U, V)

▶ Subroutine $\mathsf{XT}[\widetilde{E}_K]((j, R), L)$

1: $\Delta_L \leftarrow \widetilde{E}_K^0(0^t, 0^b); \Delta_R \leftarrow \widetilde{E}_K^0(0^{t-1}1, 0^b); X \leftarrow 2^j \cdot \Delta_L \oplus L; W \leftarrow 2^j \cdot \Delta_R \oplus_t R$

2: $Y \leftarrow \widetilde{E}_K^1(W, X)$

3: **return** Y

Theorem 1 (PRF-Security of ZMAC [6]). *Let* **A** *be an adversary making* q *queries of* σ *TRP calls in total. Then we have*

$$\mathbf{Adv}_{\mathsf{ZMAC}}^{\mathrm{prf}}(\mathbf{A}) \leq \frac{2.5\sigma^2}{2^{b+\min\{b,t\}}} + 4\left(\frac{q}{2^b}\right)^{3/2}.$$

ZMAC$^+$ [12]. In ZMAC$^+$, one TBC call is removed from ZFIN while retaining the same level of security as ZMAC, that is, $\widetilde{E}_K^4$ and $\widetilde{E}_K^5$ are removed, and thus a TBC is called once in the finalization function.[2] The modified ZFIN is called ZFIN$^+$. By the modification, $\mathcal{I}$ is modified as $\mathcal{I} = \{0, 1, 2, 3\}$, and ZMAC$^+$ is faster than ZMAC by one TBC call.

3   On the Efficiency of **ZMAC** Type MACs

In this section, we study whether the b-bit and t-bit spaces of the TBC in ZFIN$^+$ can be used to take message blocks, i.e., the following three ZMAC-type MACs are considered.

– ZMACb: only the b-bit space is used.
– ZMACt: only the t-bit space is used.
– ZMACbt: both the b-bit and t-bit spaces are used.

---

[2] ZMAC$^+$ can produce variable-length outputs, where each b-bit output is defined by one TBC call. Using ZMAC$^+$ as a MAC, the b-bit output length is enough to ensure the $2^{\min\{b,(b+t)/2\}}$-security, where a TBC is called once. In [12], the security bound is improved to $O(q/2^b + q\sigma/2^{b+\min\{b,t\}})$.

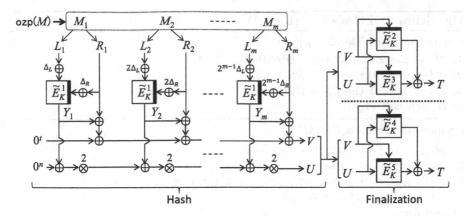

Fig. 1. ZMAC where $\Delta_L \leftarrow \widetilde{E}_K^0(0^t, 0^b)$ and $\Delta_R \leftarrow \widetilde{E}_K^0(0^{t-1}1, 0^b)$.

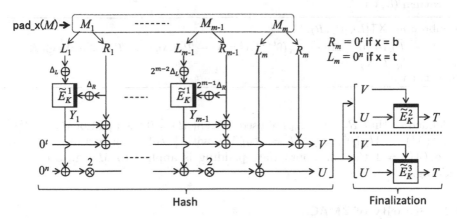

Fig. 2. ZMACx where $\Delta_L \leftarrow \widetilde{E}_K^0(0^t, 0^b)$ and $\Delta_R \leftarrow \widetilde{E}_K^0(0^{t-1}1, 0^b)$.

We show that ZMACb and ZMACt are not secure MACs after $2^{b/2}$ TBC calls. Since these MACs are the special cases of ZMACbt, these results hold for ZMACbt. Hence, ZMAC$^+$ is the most efficient MAC in the ZMAC-type ones with the $2^{\min\{b,(b+t)/2\}}$-security.

3.1   Specifications of ZMACx for x $\in$ {b, t, bt}:

ZMACx : $\mathcal{K} \times \{0,1\}^* \rightarrow \{0,1\}^\tau$ where x $\in$ {b, t, bt} is defined in Algorithm 2 and is illustrated in Fig. 2, where $t, \tau > 0$ are integers and the tweak space consists of two spaces $\{0,1\}^t$ and $\mathcal{I} = \{0,1,2,3\}$, i.e., $\mathcal{TW} = \{0,1\}^t \times \mathcal{I}$. Len is a boolean function: $\mathsf{Len}(M) = 0$ if for some integer $a \geq 0$ $|M| = (b+t)a + x$; $\mathsf{Len}(M) \neq 0$ otherwise, where $x = b$ if x = b; $x = t$ if x = t; $x = b+t$ if x = bt. $\mathsf{pad\_x} : \{0,1\}^* \rightarrow (\{0,1\}^{b+t})^+$ is a padding function: if x = b, it is defined so that L_m is used to take message blocks and R_m is not used, i.e., $R_m = 0^t$; if x = t, it is defined so that R_m is used and L_m is not used, i.e., $L_m = 0^b$; if x = bt, it

---

Algorithm 2. ZMACx $(x \in \{b, t, bt\})$

▶ Main Procedure ZMACx$[\widetilde{E}_K](M)$

1: $M^* \leftarrow \texttt{pad\_x}(M)$; $(U, V) \leftarrow$ ZHASHx$[\widetilde{E}_K](M^*)$
2: **if** $\mathsf{Len}(M) = 0$ **then** $T \leftarrow \widetilde{E}_K^2(V, U)$
3: **if** $\mathsf{Len}(M) = 1$ **then** $T \leftarrow \widetilde{E}_K^3(V, U)$
4: **return** $\mathsf{msb}_\tau(T)$

▶ Subroutine ZHASHx$[\widetilde{E}_K](M^*)$

1: $M_1, \ldots, M_m \xleftarrow{b+t} M^*$; $U \leftarrow 0^b$; $V \leftarrow 0^t$
2: **for** $i = 1, \ldots, m - 1$ **do**
3:    $(L_i, R_i) \xleftarrow{b,t} M_i$; $Y_i \leftarrow$ XT$[\widetilde{E}_K]((i-1, R_i), L_i)$; $Z_i \leftarrow Y_i \oplus_t L_i$
4:    $V \leftarrow V \oplus Z_i$; $U \leftarrow 2 \cdot (U \oplus Y_i)$
5: **end for**
6: $(L_m, R_m) \xleftarrow{b,t} M_m$; $V \leftarrow V \oplus L_m$; $U \leftarrow U \oplus R_m$
7: **return** (U, V)

▶ Subroutine XT$[\widetilde{E}_K]((j, R), L)$

1: $\Delta_L \leftarrow \widetilde{E}_K^0(0^t, 0^b)$; $\Delta_R \leftarrow \widetilde{E}_K^0(0^{t-1}1, 0^b)$; $X \leftarrow 2^j \cdot \Delta_L \oplus L$; $T \leftarrow 2^j \cdot \Delta_R \oplus_t R$
2: $Y \leftarrow \widetilde{E}_K^1(T, X)$
3: **return** Y

---

is defined so that R_m and L_m are used. If $\mathsf{Len}(M) = 0$ then $\texttt{pad\_b}(M) = M \| 0^t$; $\texttt{pad\_t}(M) = M_B \| 0^b \| M_E$ ($M = M_B \| M_E$ with $|M_E| = t$); $\texttt{pad\_bt}(M) = M$. If $\mathsf{Len}(M) = 1$ then an appropriate padding is applied to M e.g., a one-zero padding.

3.2   Security of ZMACt

The lower-bound of the MAC-security of ZMACt is given below where $\tau = b$, and the proof is given in Sect. 3.4.

Theorem 2. *Assume that $\tau = b$. There exists an adversary* **A** *making q_t tagging queries and one verification query such that* $\mathbf{Adv}_{\mathsf{ZMACt}}^{\mathsf{mac}}(\mathbf{A}) = \Omega(q_t^2/2^b)$.

The lower-bound shows that ZMACt is not a secure MAC after $2^{b/2}$ TRP calls, thereby ZMACt cannot achieve the same level of security as ZMAC$(^+)$.

3.3   Security of ZMACb

The lower-bound of the MAC-security of ZMACb is given below where $\tau = b$, and the proofs for ZMACb is given in Subsect. 3.5.

Theorem 3. *Assume that $\tau = b$. There exists an adversary* **A** *making q_t tagging queries and one verification query such that* $\mathbf{Adv}_{\mathsf{ZMACx}}^{\mathsf{mac}}(\mathbf{A}) = \Omega\left(q_t^2/2^b\right)$.

The lower-bound shows that ZMACb is not a secure MAC after $2^{b/2}$ TRP calls, thereby ZMACb cannot achieve the same level of security as ZMAC$(^+)$.

Algorithm 3. Adversarial Procedure

▶ Main Procedure of $\mathbf{A}^{\mathsf{ZMACt}[\widetilde{P}],\mathsf{Verif}[\mathsf{ZMACt}[\widetilde{P}]]}$
1: **for** $i \in [q_t/2 - 1]$ **do** $R_1^{(i)} = R_2^{(i)} = \mathsf{str}_t(i);\ L_1^{(i)} = 0^b$
2: **for** $i \in [q_t/2 - 1]$ **do** make tagging query $M^{(i)} = (R_1^{(i)}, L_1^{(i)}, R_2^{(i)})$; obtain the tag $T^{(i)}$
3: **for** $i \in [q_t/2 - 1]$ **do** make tagging query $\hat{M}^{(i)} = (R_1^{(i)}, L_1^{(i)}, 0^b, 0^t, R_2^{(i)})$; obtain the tag $\hat{T}^{(i)}$
4: **if** $\exists \alpha, \beta \in [q_t/2 - 1]$ s.t. $T^{(\alpha)} = T^{(\beta)}$ and $\hat{T}^{(\alpha)} = \hat{T}^{(\beta)}$ **then**
5:     Make a tagging query $M = (R_1^{(\alpha)}, L_1^{(\alpha)}, 1^b, 0^t, R_2^{(\alpha)})$ and obtain the response T
6:     Define $M' = (R_1^{(\beta)}, L_1^{(\beta)}, 1^b, 0^t, R_2^{(\beta)})$ and make a verification query (M', T)
7: **end if**

3.4   Proof of Theorem 2

We show a forgery attack on ZMACt using a TRP $\widetilde{P}$. The adversarial procedure of $\mathbf{A}$ is defined in Algorithm 3. In this attack, the two types of message with $\mathsf{Len}(M) = 0$ are considered. The first type is that the length of a message M is $(b+t)+b$ bits. The second type is that the length of a message $\hat{M}$ is $2(b+t)+b$ bits. In the adversarial procedure, first $q_t/2-1$ tagging queries are defined where the tweak values $R_1^{(i)}$ are distinct. Hence, the outputs of $\widetilde{P}$, $Y_1^{(1)}, \ldots, Y_1^{(q_t/2-1)}$ are independently and randomly drawn. In this case, the probability that a collision occurs in the outputs is $(0.5q_t - 1)(0.5q_t - 2)/2^{b+1} = \Omega(q_t^2/2^b)$. Here, we assume that for $\alpha, \beta \in [q_t/2 - 1]$, $Y_1^{(\alpha)} = Y_1^{(\beta)}$. For $i \in \{\alpha, \beta\}$, the hash value $(U^{(i)}, V^{(i)}) = \mathsf{ZHASHt}[\widetilde{P}](M^{(i)})$ is defined as follows.

$$U^{(i)} = 2 \cdot Y_1^{(i)}, \ V^{(i)} = (R_1^{(i)} \oplus R_2^{(i)}) \oplus_t Y_1^{(i)} = 0^t \oplus_t Y_1^{(i)}$$

Hence, the hash collision $(U^{(\alpha)}, V^{(\alpha)}) = (U^{(\beta)}, V^{(\beta)})$ occurs, and offers the tag collision $T^{(\alpha)} = T^{(\beta)}$. Then, for $i \in \{\alpha, \beta\}$, the hash value $(\hat{U}^{(i)}, \hat{V}^{(i)}) = \mathsf{ZHASHt}[\widetilde{P}](\hat{M}^{(i)})$ is defined as follows.

$$\hat{U}^{(i)} = 2^2 \cdot Y_1^{(i)} \oplus 2 \cdot Y_2 = 2 \cdot U^{(i)} \oplus 2 \cdot Y_2, \ \hat{V}^{(i)} = (Y_1 \oplus_t R_1^{(i)}) \oplus (Y_2 \oplus_t R_2^{(i)}) = V^{(i)} \oplus_t Y_2$$

where $Y_2 = \widetilde{P}^1(0^t, 0^b)$. Hence, the hash collision $(\hat{U}^{(\alpha)}, \hat{V}^{(\alpha)}) = (\hat{U}^{(\beta)}, \hat{V}^{(\beta)})$ occurs, and offers the tag collision $\hat{T}^{(\alpha)} = \hat{T}^{(\beta)}$. By the above analysis, the probability that the tag collisions occur in Step 4 is $\Omega(q_t^2/2^b)$. After the collisions occur, by the same analysis as the tag collision $\hat{T}^{(\alpha)} = \hat{T}^{(\beta)}$, the tag collision for M and M' occurs, thereby accept is returned at Step 6.

Note that there are cases where in Step 4 the tag collisions $T^{(\alpha)} = T^{(\beta)}$ and $\hat{T}^{(\alpha)} = \hat{T}^{(\beta)}$ occur without the hash collisions. In this case, the probability that there exist the tag collisions without the hash collisions is at most $O(q_t^2/2^b \times 1/2^b) = O(q_t^2/2^{2b})$: the probability of the tag collision $T^{(\alpha)} = T^{(\beta)}$ is $O(q_t^2/2^b)$ and the probability of the tag collision $\hat{T}^{(\alpha)} = \hat{T}^{(\beta)}$ is $O(1/2^b)$ (note that there are two cases for the tag collision $\hat{T}^{(\alpha)} = \hat{T}^{(\beta)}$ where α and β are fixed: (1) the tag collision occurs by the hash collision and (2) the tag collision occurs without

---

Algorithm 4. Adversarial Procedure

▶ Main Procedure of $\mathbf{A}^{\mathsf{ZMACb}[\widetilde{P}],\mathsf{Verif}[\mathsf{ZMACb}[\widetilde{P}]]}$

1: **for** $i \in [q_t/2 - 1]$ **do** $r^{(i)} \xleftarrow{\$} \{0,1\}^b$; $R_1^{(i)} = r^{(i)} \| 0^{t-b}$; $L_1^{(i)} = \mathsf{str}_b(i)$; $L_2^{(i)} = 2 \cdot r^{(i)}$

2: **for** $i \in [q_t/2 - 1]$ **do** make a tagging query $M^{(i)} = (R_1^{(i)}, L_1^{(i)}, L_2^{(i)})$; obtain the tag $T^{(i)}$

3: **for** $i \in [q_t/2 - 1]$ **do** make a tagging query $\hat{M}^{(i)} = (R_1^{(i)}, L_1^{(i)}, 0^b, 0^t, 2 \cdot L_2^{(i)})$; obtain the tag $\hat{T}^{(i)}$

4: **if** $\exists \alpha, \beta \in [q_t/2 - 1]$ s.t. $T^{(\alpha)} = T^{(\beta)}$ and $\hat{T}^{(\alpha)} = \hat{T}^{(\beta)}$ **then**

5:    Make a tagging query $M = (R_1^{(\alpha)}, L_1^{(\alpha)}, 1^b, 0^t, 2L_2^{(\alpha)})$; obtain the tag T

6:    Define $M' = (R_1^{(\beta)}, L_1^{(\beta)}, 1^b, 0^t, 2L_2^{(\beta)})$; make a verification query (M', T)

7: **end if**

---

the hash collision. The probabilities for the tag collisions are equal to or less than roughly $1/2^b$).

Since $q_t^2/2^{2b} < q_t^2/2^b$, the probability that $\mathbf{A}$ forges is $\Omega(q_t^2/2^b)$.

3.5   Proof of Theorem 3

We first show a forgery attack on ZMACb using a TRP $\widetilde{P}$ with $b \leq t$. The adversarial procedure of $\mathbf{A}$ is defined in Algorithm 4. In the forgery attack, the two types of message are considered. The first type is that the length of a message M is $(b + t) + t$ bits. The second type is that the length of a message $\hat{M}$ is $2(b + t) + t$ bits. By the adversarial procedure, the hash value $(U^{(i)}, V^{(i)}) = \mathsf{ZHASHb}[\widetilde{P}](M^{(i)})$ for $i \in [q_t/2 - 1]$ is defined as follows.

$$U^{(i)} = 2 \cdot Y_1^{(i)} \oplus L_2^{(i)} = 2 \cdot \left(Y_1^{(i)} \oplus r^{(i)}\right), \; V^{(i)} = Y_1^{(i)} \oplus_t R_1^{(i)} = \left(Y_1^{(i)} \oplus r^{(i)}\right) \| 0^{t-b}$$

Hence, for $\alpha, \beta \in [q_t/2 - 1]$ with $\alpha \neq \beta$ if $Y_1^{(\alpha)} \oplus r^{(\alpha)} = Y_1^{(\beta)} \oplus r^{(\beta)}$, then the hash collision $(U^{(\alpha)}, V^{(\alpha)}) = (U^{(\beta)}, V^{(\beta)})$ occurs, and offers the tag collision $T^{(\alpha)} = T^{(\beta)}$. Since all $r^{(i)}$ values are randomly and independently drawn, the collision probability is $\binom{q_t/2-1}{2} \cdot 1/2^b = \Omega(q_t^2/2^b)$. Here, we assume that for $\alpha, \beta \in [q_t/2 - 1]$, the hash collision occurs. Then, for $i \in \{\alpha, \beta\}$ the hash value $(\hat{U}^{(i)}, \hat{V}^{(i)}) = \mathsf{ZHASHb}[\widetilde{P}](\hat{M}^{(i)})$ is defined as follows.

$$\hat{U}^{(i)} = 2^2 \cdot Y_1^{(i)} \oplus 2 \cdot Y_2 \oplus 2 \cdot L_2^{(i)} = 2 \cdot U^{(i)} \oplus 2 \cdot Y_2$$
$$\hat{V}^{(i)} = Y_1^{(i)} \oplus_t R_1^{(i)} \oplus Y_2 = V^{(i)} \oplus Y_2$$

where $Y_2 = \widetilde{P}^1(0^t, 0^b)$. Hence, the hash collision $(\hat{U}^{(\alpha)}, \hat{V}^{(\alpha)}) = (\hat{U}^{(\beta)}, \hat{V}^{(\beta)})$ occurs, and offers the tag collision $\hat{T}^{(\alpha)} = \hat{T}^{(\beta)}$. By the above analysis, the probability that the tag collisions occur in Step 4 is $\Omega(q_t^2/2^b)$. After the tag collisions occur, by the same analysis as the tag collision $\hat{T}^{(\alpha)} = \hat{T}^{(\beta)}$, the tag collision for messages M and M' occurs, thereby at Step 6 accept is returned.

Note that there are cases where in Step 4 the tag collisions occur without the hash collisions. In the cases, the probability that there exist the tag collisions

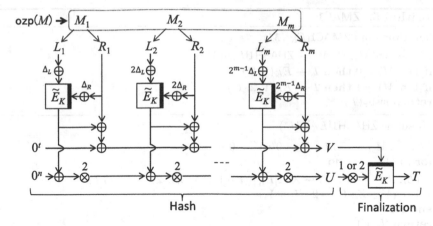

Fig. 3. ZMAC1 where $\Delta_L \leftarrow \widetilde{E}_K^0(0^t, 0^b)$ and $\Delta_R \leftarrow \widetilde{E}_K^0(0^{t-1}1, 0^b)$.

$T^{(\alpha)} = T^{(\beta)}$ and $\hat{T}^{(\alpha)} = \hat{T}^{(\beta)}$ in Step 4 without the hash collisions is at most $O(q_t^2/2^b \times 1/2^b) = O(q_t^2/2^{2b})$: the probability of the tag collision $T^{(\alpha)} = T^{(\beta)}$ is $O(q_t^2/2^b)$ and the probability of the tag collision $\hat{T}^{(\alpha)} = \hat{T}^{(\beta)}$ is $O(1/2^b)$ (note that there are two cases for the tag collision $\hat{T}^{(\alpha)} = \hat{T}^{(\beta)}$: (1) the tag collision occurs by the hash collision and (2) the tag collision occurs without the hash collision. The probabilities for the tag collisions are equal to or less than roughly $1/2^b$.).

Since $q_t^2/2^{2b} < q_t^2/2^b$, the probability that **A** forges is $\Omega(q_t^2/2^b)$.

Regarding the case where $b > t$, by the same strategy as the case where $b \leq t$, we can prove that the success probability of the forgery attack is $\Omega(q_t^2/2^b)$.

4   ZMAC Without Tweak Separations

In this section, we consider a variant of ZMAC($^+$): the tweak space for tweak separations, $\mathcal{I}$, is removed but only field multiplications by 2 are used. We call the variant ZMAC1. We show that ZMAC1 achieves the same level of PRF-security as ZMAC (security up to $O(2^{\min\{b,(b+t)/2\}})$ TRP calls).

4.1   Specification of ZMAC1

The tweak space of the underlying TBC $\widetilde{E}$ is defined as $\mathcal{TW} = \{0,1\}^t$ for an integer $t \geq 0$. ZMAC1 : $\mathcal{K} \times \{0,1\}^b \rightarrow \{0,1\}^\tau$ is defined in Algorithm 5 and illustrated in Fig. 3. Len : $\{0,1\}^* \rightarrow \{0,1\}$ is a boolean function: $\mathsf{Len}(M) = 0$ if $|M| = 0$ or $|M| \bmod (b+t) \neq 0$; $\mathsf{Len}(M) = 1$ if $|M| \neq 0$ and $|M| \bmod (b+t) = 0$. ozp is a one-zero padding function: for a message M, $\mathsf{ozp}(M) = M$ if $\mathsf{Len}(M) = 0$; $\mathsf{ozp}(M) = M\|10^p$ ($p = (|M| \bmod (b+t)) - 1$) if $\mathsf{Len}(M) = 1$. In ZMAC1, in order to avoid an additional TBC call by a padding, the multiplication by 2 is applied to U in the finalization function (Step 3).

Algorithm 5. ZMAC1

▶ Main Procedure $\mathsf{ZMAC1}[\widetilde{E}_K](M)$

1: $M^* \leftarrow \mathsf{ozp}(M)$; $(U, V) \leftarrow \mathsf{ZHASH1}[\widetilde{E}_K](M^*)$
2: **if** $\mathsf{Len}(M) = 0$ **then** $T \leftarrow \widetilde{E}_K(V, U)$
3: **if** $\mathsf{Len}(M) = 1$ **then** $T \leftarrow \widetilde{E}_K(V, 2 \cdot U)$
4: **return** $\mathsf{msb}_\tau(T)$

▶ Subroutine $\mathsf{ZHASH1}[\widetilde{E}_K](M^*)$

1: $M_1, \ldots, M_m \xleftarrow{b+t} M^*$; $U \leftarrow 0^b$; $V \leftarrow 0^t$
2: **for** $i = 1, \ldots, m$ **do**
3:    $(L_i, R_i) \xleftarrow{b,t} M_i$; $Y_i \leftarrow \mathsf{XT1}[\widetilde{E}_K]((i-1, R_i), L_i)$; $Z_i \leftarrow Y_i \oplus_t L_i$
4:    $V \leftarrow V \oplus Z_i$; $U \leftarrow 2 \cdot (U \oplus Y_i)$
5: **end for**
6: **return** (U, V)

▶ Subroutine $\mathsf{XT1}[\widetilde{E}_K]((j, R), L)$

1: $\Delta_L \leftarrow \widetilde{E}_K(0^t, 0^b)$; $\Delta_R \leftarrow \widetilde{E}_K(0^{t-1}1, 0^b)$; $X \leftarrow 2^j \cdot \Delta_L \oplus L$; $W \leftarrow 2^j \cdot \Delta_R \oplus_t R$
2: $Y \leftarrow \widetilde{E}_K(W, X)$
3: **return** Y

Algorithm 6. ZMAC1

▶ Main Procedure $\mathbb{ZMAC1}[\widetilde{P}, \widetilde{P}_\mathsf{H}](M)$

1: $M^* \leftarrow \mathsf{ozp}(M)$; $(U, V) \leftarrow \mathbb{ZHASH1}[\widetilde{P}_\mathsf{H}](M^*)$
2: **if** $\mathsf{Len}(M) = 0$ **then** $T \leftarrow \widetilde{P}(V, U)$
3: **if** $\mathsf{Len}(M) = 1$ **then** $T \leftarrow \widetilde{P}(V, 2 \cdot U)$
4: **return** $\mathsf{msb}_\tau(T)$

▶ Subroutine $\mathbb{ZHASH1}[\widetilde{P}_\mathsf{H}](M^*)$

1: $M_1, \ldots, M_m \xleftarrow{b+t} M^*$; $U \leftarrow 0^b$; $V \leftarrow 0^t$
2: **for** $i = 1, \ldots, m-1$ **do**
3:    $(L_i, R_i) \xleftarrow{b,t} M_i - 1$; $Y_i \leftarrow \widetilde{P}_\mathsf{H}((i-1, R_i), L_i)$; $Z_i \leftarrow Y_i \oplus L_i$
4:    $U \leftarrow 2 \cdot (U \oplus Y_i)$; $V \leftarrow V \oplus Z_i$
5: **end for**
6: **return** (U, V)

4.2   PRF-Security of ZMAC1

Theorem 4. *Let* **A** *be an adversary making* q *queries of* σ *TRP calls in total. Then we have*

$$\mathbf{Adv}^{\mathsf{prf}}_{\mathsf{ZMAC1}}(\mathbf{A}) \leq \frac{q}{2^b} + \frac{6.5\sigma^2}{2^{b+\min\{b,t\}}}.$$

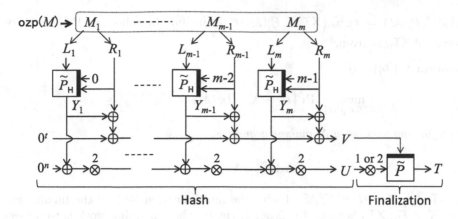

Fig. 4. ZMAC1.

4.3   Proof of Theorem 4

XT1 Tweak Extension. Firstly, the subroutine XT1 is replaced with a TRP $\widetilde{P}_\mathsf{H}$. Let $m_{\max}$ be the maximum block length of messages, i.e., $m \leq m_{\max}$. A TRP is defined as $\widetilde{P}_\mathsf{H} \xleftarrow{\$} \widetilde{\mathsf{Perm}} \left(([m_{\max}] \times \{0,1\}^t), \{0,1\}^b \right)$, where $[m_{\max}] \times \{0,1\}^t$ is the tweak space and $\{0,1\}^b$ is the input-block space. The modified ZMAC1 called $\mathbb{ZMAC}1$ is defined in Algorithm 6 and illustrated in Fig. 4. For this modification, we consider indistinguishability between the following worlds.

$$\mathsf{World}_1 = \left(\widetilde{P} \xleftarrow{\$} \mathsf{Perm}(\mathcal{TW}, \{0,1\}^b) : \mathbf{A}^{\mathbb{ZMAC}1[\widetilde{P}]} = 1 \right)$$

$$\mathsf{World}_2 = \left(\widetilde{P} \xleftarrow{\$} \mathsf{Perm}(\mathcal{TW}, \{0,1\}^b), \right.$$
$$\left. \widetilde{P}_\mathsf{H} \xleftarrow{\$} \widetilde{\mathsf{Perm}} \left(([m_{\max}] \times \{0,1\}^t), \{0,1\}^b \right) : \mathbf{A}^{\mathbb{ZMAC}1[\widetilde{P}, \widetilde{P}_\mathsf{H}]} = 1 \right).$$

The indistinguishable bound is given in the following, and the proof is given in Subsect. 4.4.

$$\Pr\left[\mathsf{World}_1\right] - \Pr\left[\mathsf{World}_2\right] \leq \frac{q}{2^b} + \frac{3.5\sigma^2}{2^{b+\min\{b,t\}}}. \tag{1}$$

PRF-Security of $\mathbb{ZMAC}1$. We next upper-bound the PRF-security of $\mathbb{ZMAC}1$. This analysis uses the security result of the tweak extension scheme XT given in [6]. XT uses a keyed hash function $H : \mathcal{K} \times \{0,1\}^* \to \mathcal{TW} \times \{0,1\}^b$ and a TP $\widetilde{P} \in \mathsf{Perm}(\mathcal{TW}, \{0,1\}^b)$, where $\mathcal{K}$ is the key space. Then, for a key K, a tweak $tw \in \{0,1\}^*$, and an input block $X \in \{0,1\}^b$, the output block of XT is defined as

$$\mathsf{XT}[K, \widetilde{P}](tw, X) = \widetilde{P}(V^*, U \oplus X) \text{ where } (V^*, U) = H_K(tw).$$

Hereafter, XT with $X = 0^b$ (the input block is fixed to 0^b) and a $(b-\tau)$-bit output truncation is considered. XT with $X = 0^b$ is denoted by XT_0, and is defined as

$\mathsf{XT}_0[K, \widetilde{P}](M) = \mathsf{msb}_\tau \left(\mathsf{XT}[K, \widetilde{P}](M, 0^b) \right)$. In [6], the following PRF-security bound of XT_0 is given.[3]

Lemma 1 ([6]). *If*

$$\max_{M \neq M' \in \{0,1\}^*} \Pr\left[K \xleftarrow{\$} \mathcal{K} : H_K(M) = H_K(M') \right] \leq \epsilon,$$

then for any adversary **A** *making q queries,*

$$\mathbf{Adv}_{\mathsf{XT}_0}^{\mathsf{prf}}(\mathbf{A}) \leq \frac{q^2 \epsilon}{2}.$$

In XT_0, putting $H = \mathrm{ZHASH1}$ with the multiplication by 2 in the finalization and $K = \widetilde{P}_\mathsf{H}$, XT_0 is equal to $\mathrm{ZMAC1}$. Hence, the remaining work is to upper-bound $\max_{M \neq M' \in \{0,1\}^*} \Pr[\mathsf{Coll}(M, M')]$. Here, $\mathsf{Coll}(M, M') = \mathsf{Coll}_0(M, M') \vee \mathsf{Coll}_1(M, M')$, and $\mathsf{Coll}_0(M, M')$ and $\mathsf{Coll}_1(M, M')$ are defined as follows.

$$\mathsf{Coll}_0(M, M') \Leftrightarrow \left(\mathsf{Len}(M) = \mathsf{Len}(M') \right) \wedge \left(U = U' \wedge V = V' \right)$$

$$\mathsf{Coll}_1(M, M') \Leftrightarrow \left(\mathsf{Len}(M) \neq \mathsf{Len}(M') = 1 \right) \wedge \left(U = 2 \cdot U' \wedge V = V' \right),$$

where $(U, V) = \mathrm{ZHASH1}[\widetilde{P}, \widetilde{P}_\mathsf{H}](\mathsf{ozp}(M))$ and $(U', V') = \mathrm{ZHASH1}[\widetilde{P}, \widetilde{P}_\mathsf{H}]$ $(\mathsf{ozp}(M'))$.

Coll_0 implies that a collision of $\mathrm{ZHASH1}$ occurs. $\mathrm{ZHASH1}$ is the same as ZHASH defined in [6] (ZHASH is introduced in the security proof of ZMAC), and the collision probability is evaluated which is at most $4/2^{b+\min\{b,t\}}$. Hence, we have

$$\max_{M \neq M' \in \{0,1\}^*} \Pr\left[\mathsf{Coll}_0(M, M') \right] \leq \frac{4}{2^{b+\min\{b,t\}}}.$$

In Subsect. 4.5. the following upper-bound is given.

$$\max_{M \neq M' \in \{0,1\}^*} \Pr\left[\mathsf{Coll}_1(M, M') \right] \leq \frac{2}{2^{b+\min\{b,t\}}}.$$

Combining these upper-bounds with Lemma 1 gives

$$\mathbf{Adv}_{\mathrm{ZMAC1}}^{\mathsf{prf}}(\mathbf{A}) \leq \frac{q^2}{2} \cdot \max_{M \neq M' \in \{0,1\}^*} \Pr[\mathsf{Coll}(M, M')]$$

$$\leq \frac{q^2}{2} \cdot \left(\max_{M \neq M' \in \{0,1\}^*} \Pr[\mathsf{Coll}_0(M, M')] + \max_{M \neq M' \in \{0,1\}^*} \Pr[\mathsf{Coll}_1(M, M')] \right)$$

$$\leq \frac{3q^2}{2^{b+\min\{b,t\}}}. \tag{2}$$

---

[3] In [6] (Lemma 1), the TPRP-security of XT is considered. Since a TRP with a constant input block, i.e., the input block is fixed to some constant, behaves like a random function, the PRF-security of XT_0 is obtained from the TPRP-security of XT.

Conclusion of the Proof. By Eqs. (1) and (2), we have

$$\mathbf{Adv}^{\mathrm{prf}}_{\mathbb{ZMAC1}}(\mathbf{A}) = \Pr[\mathsf{World}_1] - \Pr[\mathsf{World}_2] + \mathbf{Adv}^{\mathrm{prf}}_{\mathbb{ZMAC1}}(\mathbf{A}) \leq \frac{q}{2^b} + \frac{6.5\sigma^2}{2^{b+\min\{b,t\}}}.$$

4.4 Upper-Bound of $\Pr[\mathsf{World}_1] - \Pr[\mathsf{World}_2]$

First we modify World_2 as follows.

$$\mathsf{World}_2^* = \Big(\widetilde{P} \xleftarrow{\$} \mathrm{Perm}(\mathcal{TW}, \{0,1\}^b), \widetilde{P}_\Delta \xleftarrow{\$} \mathrm{Perm}(\{0,1\}^t, \{0,1\}^b),$$
$$\widetilde{P}_\mathsf{H} \xleftarrow{\$} \widetilde{\mathrm{Perm}}\left(([m_{\max}] \times \{0,1\}^t), \{0,1\}^b\right) : \mathbf{A}^{\mathbb{ZMAC1}[\widetilde{P}, \widetilde{P}_\mathsf{H}]} = 1\Big).$$

$\widetilde{P}_\Delta$ is not used in $\mathbb{ZMAC1}$ but is used in the following proof. Since the modification does not change the adversarial behavior, we have $\Pr[\mathsf{World}_2] = \Pr[\mathsf{World}_2^*]$. Hereafter, $\Pr[\mathsf{World}_2^*]$ is upper-bounded.

In this proof, for $\alpha \in [q]$, the length m at the α-th query is denoted by m_α, and a value v defined at the α-th query are denoted by $v^{(\alpha)}$, e.g., $Y_1^{(\alpha)}, V^{(\alpha)}$, etc. In this proof, we permit for $\mathbf{A}$ to obtain secret values (Δ_L, Δ_R) and all X, W, Y, U, V, T values after its interaction and before returning a decision bit. Hence, in both worlds, $\mathbf{A}$ obtains $(0^t, 0^b, \Delta_L)$, $(0^{t-1}1, 0^b, \Delta_R)$, $(W_i^{(\alpha)}, X_i^{(\alpha)}, Y_i^{(\alpha)})$, $(U_L^{(\alpha)}, V^{(\alpha)}, T^{(\alpha)})$ for $\alpha \in [q], i \in [m_\alpha]$. We note that $U_L^{(\alpha)} = U^{(\alpha)}$ if $\mathrm{Len}(M^{(\alpha)}) = 0$; $U_L^{(\alpha)} = 2 \cdot U^{(\alpha)}$ if $\mathrm{Len}(M^{(\alpha)}) = 1$; $W_i^{(\alpha)} = 2^{i-1} \cdot \Delta_R \oplus_t R_i^{(\alpha)}$; $X_i^{(\alpha)} = 2^{i-1} \cdot \Delta_L \oplus L_i^{(\alpha)}$. We also note that in World_2^*, $\Delta_L = \widetilde{P}_\Delta(0^t, 0^b)$ and $\Delta_R = \widetilde{P}_\Delta(0^{t-1}1, 0^b)$. Thus, after the interaction, $\mathbf{A}$ obtains the following set that is called "transcript."

$$\tau = \Big((0^t, 0^b, \Delta_L), (0^{t-1}1, 0^b, \Delta_R),$$
$$(W_i^{(\alpha)}, X_i^{(\alpha)}, Y_i^{(\alpha)}), (V^{(\alpha)}, U_L^{(\alpha)}, T^{(\alpha)}) \text{ for } \alpha \in [q], i \in [m_\alpha]\Big).$$

Note that this modification does not reduce the advantage of $\mathbf{A}$. Let T_1 be the transcript in World_1 obtained by sampling $\widetilde{P} \xleftarrow{\$} \widetilde{\mathrm{Perm}}(\{0,1\}^t, \{0,1\}^b)$. Let T_2 be the transcript in World_2 obtained by sampling $\widetilde{P}_\mathsf{H} \xleftarrow{\$} \widetilde{\mathrm{Perm}}([m_{\max}] \times \{0,1\}^t, \{0,1\}^b), \widetilde{P}_\Delta \xleftarrow{\$} \mathrm{Perm}(\{0,1\}^t, \{0,1\}^b)$ and $\widetilde{P} \xleftarrow{\$} \widetilde{\mathrm{Perm}}(\{0,1\}^t, \{0,1\}^b)$. We call a transcript τ *valid* if $\Pr[\mathsf{T}_2 = \tau] > 0$. Let $\mathcal{T}$ be all valid transcript. Then

$$\Pr[\mathsf{World}_1] - \Pr[\mathsf{World}_2^*] = \mathsf{SD}(\mathsf{T}_1, \mathsf{T}_2) = \frac{1}{2}\sum_{\tau \in \mathcal{T}} |\Pr[\mathsf{T}_1 = \tau] - \Pr[\mathsf{T}_2 = \tau]|.$$

The statistical distance $\mathsf{SD}(\mathsf{T}_1, \mathsf{T}_2)$ can be upper-bounded by the coefficient H technique [19]. In this technique, $\mathcal{T}$ is partitioned into two transcripts: good transcripts $\mathcal{T}_{\mathrm{good}}$ and bad transcripts $\mathcal{T}_{\mathrm{bad}}$. Then $\mathsf{SD}(\mathsf{T}_1, \mathsf{T}_2)$ is upper-bounded by the following lemma.

Lemma 2. *Let $0 \leq \varepsilon \leq 1$ be such that for all $\tau \in \mathcal{T}_{\text{good}}$, $\frac{\Pr[T_1 = \tau]}{\Pr[T_2 = \tau]} \geq 1 - \varepsilon$. Then,* $\mathsf{SD}(T_1, T_2) \leq \Pr[T_2 \in \mathcal{T}_{\text{bad}}] + \varepsilon$.

Hereafter, first good and bad transcripts are defined. Then ε and $\Pr[T_2 \in \mathcal{T}_{\text{bad}}]$ are upper-bounded. Finally, by the above lemma, the upper-bound of $\Pr[\text{World}_1] - \Pr[\text{World}_2]$ ($= \mathsf{SD}(T_1, T_2)$) is obtained.

$\mathcal{T}_{\text{good}}$ **and** $\mathcal{T}_{\text{bad}}$. $\mathcal{T}_{\text{bad}}$ is defined so that one of the following conditions is satisfied, and $\mathcal{T}_{\text{good}}$ is defined as $\mathcal{T}_{\text{good}} = \mathcal{T} \backslash \mathcal{T}_{\text{bad}}$.

$$\mathsf{Coll}_\Delta \Leftrightarrow \exists \alpha \in [q] \text{ s.t. } \left((V^{(\alpha)}, U_L^{(\alpha)}) = (0^t, 0^b) \text{ or } (0^{t-1}1, 0^b) \right)$$
$$\vee \left(\exists i \in [m_\alpha] \text{ s.t. } (W_i^{(\alpha)}, X_i^{(\alpha)}) = (0^t, 0^b) \text{ or } (0^{t-1}1, 0^b) \right)$$
$$\mathsf{Coll}_{WX,UV} \Leftrightarrow \exists \alpha, \beta \in [q], i \in [m_\alpha] \text{ s.t. } (W_i^{(\alpha)}, X_i^{(\alpha)}) = (V^{(\beta)}, U_L^{(\beta)})$$
$$\mathsf{Coll}_{WX} \Leftrightarrow \exists \alpha, \beta \in [q], i \in [m_\alpha], j \in [m_\beta] \text{ s.t. } \left(i \neq j \right)$$
$$\wedge \left((W_i^{(\alpha)}, X_i^{(\alpha)}) = (W_j^{(\beta)}, X_j^{(\beta)}) \right)$$

Upper-Bound of $\Pr[T_2 \in \mathcal{T}_{\text{bad}}]$. Note that

$$\Pr[T_2 \in \mathcal{T}_{\text{bad}}] \leq \Pr[\mathsf{Coll}_\Delta] + \Pr[\mathsf{Coll}_{WX,UV}] + \Pr[\mathsf{Coll}_{WX}].$$

Firstly, $\Pr[\mathsf{Coll}_\Delta]$ is upper-bounded.

- The first condition $\left(\exists \alpha \in [q] \text{ s.t. } (V^{(\alpha)}, U_L^{(\alpha)}) = (0^t, 0^b) \text{ or } (0^{t-1}1, 0^b) \right)$ is considered. Fix $\alpha \in [q]$. Then $U_L^{(\alpha)}$ is defined as

$$U_L^{(\alpha)} = \left(2^{m_\alpha} \cdot Y_1 \oplus 2^{m_\alpha - 1} \cdot Y_2 \oplus \cdots \oplus 2 \cdot Y_{m_\alpha} \right) \cdot \omega,$$

where $\omega = 1$ or 2. Since the number of possibilities for Y_1 is 2^b, the probability that the above equality is satisfied is $1/2^b$. Hence, the probability that the first condition is satisfied is at most $q/2^b$.

- The second condition $\left(\exists \alpha \in [q], i \in [m_\alpha] \text{ s.t. } (W_i^{(\alpha)}, X_i^{(\alpha)}) = (0^t, 0^b) \text{ or } (0^{t-1}1, 0^b) \right)$ is considered. First, fix $\alpha \in [q]$ and $i \in [m_\alpha]$. Then $(W_i^{(\alpha)}, X_i^{(\alpha)})$ are defined as

$$W_i^{(\alpha)} = 2^{i-1} \cdot \Delta_R \oplus_t R_i^{(\alpha)} \text{ and } X_i^{(\alpha)} = 2^{i-1} \cdot \Delta_L \oplus L_i^{(\alpha)}.$$

Since Δ_L and Δ_R are independently and randomly drawn, the probability that $(W_i^{(\alpha)}, X_i^{(\alpha)}) = (0^t, 0^b)$ or $(0^{t-1}1, 0^b)$ is at most $2/2^{\min\{b,t\}} \cdot 1/2^b = 2/2^{b+\min\{b,t\}}$. Hence, the probability that the second condition is satisfied is at most $2\sigma/2^{b+\min\{b,t\}}$.

The above bounds give $\Pr[\mathrm{Coll}_\Delta] \leq q/2^b + 2\sigma/2^{b+\min\{b,t\}}$.

Secondly, $\Pr[\mathrm{Coll}_{WX,UV}]$ is upper-bounded. First, fix $\alpha, \beta \in [q], i \in [m_\alpha]$. Then $(W_i^{(\alpha)}, X_i^{(\alpha)})$ are defined as

$$W_i^{(\alpha)} = 2^{i-1} \cdot \Delta_R \oplus_t R_i^{(\alpha)} \text{ and } X_i^{(\alpha)} = 2^{i-1} \cdot \Delta_L \oplus L_i^{(\alpha)}.$$

Since Δ_L and Δ_R are independently and randomly drawn, the probability that $(W_i^{(\alpha)}, X_i^{(\alpha)}) = (V^{(\beta)}, U_L^{(\beta)})$ is at most $1/2^{\min\{b,t\}} \cdot 1/2^b = 1/2^{b+\min\{b,t\}}$. Hence, we have $\Pr[\mathrm{Coll}_{WX,UV}] \leq q\sigma/2^{b+\min\{b,t\}}$.

Thirdly, $\Pr[\mathrm{Coll}_{WX}]$ is upper-bounded. Fix $\alpha, \beta \in [q], i \in [m_\alpha], j \in [m_\beta]$ with $i \neq j$. Then, similar to the above cases, since Δ_L and Δ_R are independently and randomly drawn, the probability that $(W_i^{(\alpha)}, X_i^{(\alpha)}) = (W_j^{(\beta)}, X_j^{(\beta)})$ is at most $1/2^{\min\{b,t\}} \cdot 1/2^b = 1/2^{b+\min\{b,t\}}$. Hence, we have $\Pr[\mathrm{Coll}_{WX}] \leq \binom{\sigma}{2} \cdot 1/2^{b+\min\{b,t\}} \leq 0.5\sigma^2/2^{b+\min\{b,t\}}$.

Finally, the above upper-bounds give

$$\Pr[T_2 \in \mathcal{T}_{\mathsf{bad}}] \leq \frac{q}{2^b} + \frac{3.5\sigma^2}{2^{b+\min\{b,t\}}}.$$

Upper-Bound of ε. In World_1, only the TRP $\widetilde{P}$ is used, whereas in World_2^*, TRPs $\widetilde{P}, \widetilde{P}_\Delta$ and $\widehat{P}$ are used. Hence, $\mathcal{T}_{\mathsf{good}}$ is defined so that for any distinct positions in ZHASH1, the inputs to $\widetilde{P}$ do not overlap with each other (by Coll_{WX}), inputs to $\widetilde{P}$ in ZHASH1 do not overlap with those to $\widehat{P}$ in the finalization function (by $\mathrm{Coll}_{WX,UV}$), and inputs to $\widetilde{P}$ do not overlap with those to $\widetilde{P}_\Delta$ (by Coll_Δ). By the definition of $\mathcal{T}_{\mathsf{good}}$, we can prove that $\varepsilon = 0$ (The proof is similar to the existing proofs using the coefficient H technique e.g., [13]).

Upper-Bound of $\Pr[\mathsf{world}_1] - \Pr[\mathsf{world}_2]$. The above upper-bounds give

$$\Pr[\mathrm{World}_1] - \Pr[\mathrm{World}_2] \leq \frac{q}{2^b} + \frac{3.5\sigma^2}{2^{b+\min\{b,t\}}}.$$

$\square$

4.5   Upper-Bound of $\Pr[\mathrm{Coll}_1(M, M')]$

In this proof, a value v corresponding with the message M' is denoted by v', e.g., R_1', m', etc. For two distinct messages M, M' with $m \geq m'$, we define an index set $I^{\neq}(M, M')$ that includes indexes with distinct message blocks.

$$I^{\neq}(M, M') := \{i \in [m] | M_i \neq M_i'\},$$

where $M_i' := \lambda$ for $i \in [m'+1, m]$.

Hereafter, the following cases are considered.

1. $(m = m')$: Let $\alpha \in I^{\neq}(M; M')$. Then

$$V = V' \Leftrightarrow (Y_\alpha \oplus Y'_\alpha) \oplus_t \delta_V = 0^t$$

$$U = 2 \cdot U' \Leftrightarrow \bigoplus_{i=1}^{m} 2^{m-i+1} \cdot \left(Y_i \oplus 2 \cdot Y'_i\right) = 0^b \Leftrightarrow Y_\alpha \oplus 2 \cdot Y'_\alpha = \delta_U,$$

where $\delta_V = (Y_\alpha \oplus Y'_\alpha) \oplus_t (V \oplus V')$ and $\delta_U = (Y_\alpha \oplus 2 \cdot Y'_\alpha) \oplus 2^{-(m-\alpha+1)} \cdot (U \oplus 2 \cdot U')$.

- We consider the case where $b \leq t$. Fixing δ_V and δ_U, $V = V'$ and $U = 2 \cdot U'$ offer a unique solution for Y_α and Y'_α. Since Y_α resp. Y'_α is randomly drawn from at least 2^b resp. $2^b - 1$ values, $\max_{M \neq M' \in \{0,1\}^*} \Pr[\mathsf{Coll}_1(M, M')] \leq 1/(2^b(2^b - 1)) \leq 2/2^{2b}$.

- We next consider the case where $b > t$. Note that $\Pr[V = V', U = 2 \cdot U']$

$$= \Pr \begin{bmatrix} \mathsf{msb}_t(Y_\alpha \oplus Y'_\alpha) = \delta_V \\ Y_\alpha \oplus 2 \cdot Y'_\alpha = \delta_U \end{bmatrix} \leq \sum_{\delta \in \{0,1\}^{b-t}} \Pr \begin{bmatrix} Y_\alpha \oplus Y'_\alpha = \delta_V \| \delta \\ Y_\alpha \oplus 2 \cdot Y'_\alpha = \delta_U \end{bmatrix}.$$

$Y_\alpha \oplus Y'_\alpha = \delta_V \| \delta$ and $Y_\alpha \oplus 2 \cdot Y'_\alpha = \delta_U$ offer a unique solution for Y_α and Y'_α. Since Y_α resp. Y'_α is randomly drawn from at least 2^b resp. $2^b - 1$ values, we have $\max_{M \neq M' \in \{0,1\}^*} \Pr[\mathsf{Coll}_1(M, M')] \leq 2^{b-t} \cdot 1/(2^b(2^b - 1)) \leq 2/2^{b+t}$.

2. $(m > m')$: Let $\alpha \in I^{\neq}(M, M')$. In this case,

$$V = V' \Leftrightarrow (Y_\alpha \oplus Y'_\alpha) \oplus_t \delta_V = 0^t$$

$$U = 2 \cdot U' \Leftrightarrow \left(\bigoplus_{i=m'+1}^{m} 2^{m-i+1} \cdot Y_i\right) \oplus \bigoplus_{i=1}^{m'} 2^{m'-i+1} \cdot \left(Y_i \oplus 2 \cdot Y'_i\right) = 0^b$$

$$\Leftrightarrow Y_1 \oplus 2 \cdot Y'_1 = \delta_U,$$

where $\delta_V = (Y_\alpha \oplus Y'_\alpha) \oplus_t (V \oplus V')$ and $\delta_U = (Y_1 \oplus 2 \cdot Y'_1) \oplus 2^{-m'} \cdot (U \oplus 2 \cdot U')$. Note that if $\alpha > m'$ then $Y'_\alpha = \lambda$.

- If $\alpha = 1$ then we can apply the same analysis as the first case, and thus $\Pr[U = 2 \cdot U', V = V'] \leq 2/2^{b+\min\{b,t\}}$.

- If $\alpha \neq 1$ then Y_α is randomly drawn from $\{0,1\}^b$, thereby the probability that $V = V'$ is satisfied is $1/2^{\min\{b,t\}}$; Y_1 is randomly drawn from $\{0,1\}^b$, thereby the probability that $U = 2 \cdot U'$ is satisfied is $1/2^b$. Hence, we have $\max_{M \neq M' \in \{0,1\}^*} \Pr[\mathsf{Coll}_1(M, M')] \leq 1/2^{b+\min\{b,t\}}$.

3. $(m < m')$: In this case,

$$V = V' \Leftrightarrow (Y_\alpha \oplus Y'_\alpha) \oplus_t \delta_V = 0^t$$

$$U = 2 \cdot U' \Leftrightarrow \left(\bigoplus_{i=m+1}^{m'} 2^{m'-i+1} \cdot Y_i\right) \oplus \bigoplus_{i=1}^{m} 2^{m-i+1} \cdot \left(Y_i \oplus 2 \cdot Y'_i\right) = 0^b$$

$$\Leftrightarrow Y_1 \oplus 2 \cdot Y'_1 = \delta_U,$$

where $\delta_V = (Y_\alpha \oplus Y'_\alpha) \oplus_t (V \oplus V')$ and $\delta_U = (Y_1 \oplus 2 \cdot Y'_1) \oplus 2^{-m'} \cdot (U \oplus 2 \cdot U')$. Note that if $\alpha > m$ then $Y_\alpha = \lambda$. Hence, we can apply the same analysis as the second case, and thus $\max_{M \neq M' \in \{0,1\}^*} \Pr[\mathsf{Coll}_1(M, M')] \leq 2/2^{b+\min\{b,t\}}$.

The above upper-bounds give $\max_{M \neq M' \in \{0,1\}^*} \Pr\left[\mathsf{Coll}_1(M, M')\right] \leq 2/2^{b+\min\{b,t\}}$.

References

1. Beierle, C., et al.: The SKINNY family of block ciphers and its low-latency variant MANTIS. In: Robshaw, M., Katz, J. (eds.) CRYPTO 2016. LNCS, vol. 9815, pp. 123–153. Springer, Heidelberg (2016). https://doi.org/10.1007/978-3-662-53008-5_5

2. Black, J., Rogaway, P.: A block-cipher mode of operation for parallelizable message authentication. In: Knudsen, L.R. (ed.) EUROCRYPT 2002. LNCS, vol. 2332, pp. 384–397. Springer, Heidelberg (2002). https://doi.org/10.1007/3-540-46035-7_25

3. Cogliati, B., Lee, J., Seurin, Y.: New constructions of MACs from (tweakable) block ciphers. IACR Trans. Symmetric Cryptol. **2017**(2), 27–58 (2017)

4. Datta, N., Dutta, A., Nandi, M., Paul, G., Zhang, L.: Single key variant of PMAC_Plus. IACR Trans. Symmetric Cryptol. **2017**(4), 268–305 (2017)

5. Iwata, T., Kurosawa, K.: OMAC: one-key CBC MAC. In: Johansson, T. (ed.) FSE 2003. LNCS, vol. 2887, pp. 129–153. Springer, Heidelberg (2003). https://doi.org/10.1007/978-3-540-39887-5_11

6. Iwata, T., Minematsu, K., Peyrin, T., Seurin, Y.: ZMAC: a fast tweakable block cipher mode for highly secure message authentication. In: Katz, J., Shacham, H. (eds.) CRYPTO 2017. LNCS, vol. 10403, pp. 34–65. Springer, Cham (2017). https://doi.org/10.1007/978-3-319-63697-9_2. IACR Cryptology ePrint Archive 2017, 535 (2017)

7. Iwata, T., Seurin, Y.: Reconsidering the security bound of AES-GCM-SIV. IACR Trans. Symmetric Cryptol. **2017**(4), 240–267 (2017)

8. Jean, J., Nikolić, I., Peyrin, T.: Tweaks and keys for block ciphers: the TWEAKEY framework. In: Sarkar, P., Iwata, T. (eds.) ASIACRYPT 2014. LNCS, vol. 8874, pp. 274–288. Springer, Heidelberg (2014). https://doi.org/10.1007/978-3-662-45608-8_15

9. JTC1: ISO/IEC 9797–1:1999 Information technology – Security techniques – Message Authentication Codes (MACs)–Part 1: Mechanisms using a block cipher (1999)

10. Liskov, M., Rivest, R.L., Wagner, D.: Tweakable block ciphers. In: Yung, M. (ed.) CRYPTO 2002. LNCS, vol. 2442, pp. 31–46. Springer, Heidelberg (2002). https://doi.org/10.1007/3-540-45708-9_3

11. List, E., Nandi, M.: Revisiting full-PRF-secure PMAC and using it for beyond-birthday authenticated encryption. In: Handschuh, H. (ed.) CT-RSA 2017. LNCS, vol. 10159, pp. 258–274. Springer, Cham (2017). https://doi.org/10.1007/978-3-319-52153-4_15

12. List, E., Nandi, M.: ZMAC+ - an efficient variable-output-length variant of ZMAC. IACR Trans. Symmetric Cryptol. **2017**(4), 306–325 (2017)

13. Mennink, B.: Optimally secure tweakable blockciphers. In: Leander, G. (ed.) FSE 2015. LNCS, vol. 9054, pp. 428–448. Springer, Heidelberg (2015). https://doi.org/10.1007/978-3-662-48116-5_21

14. Minematsu, K., Iwata, T.: Tweak-length extension for tweakable blockciphers. In: Groth, J. (ed.) IMACC 2015. LNCS, vol. 9496, pp. 77–93. Springer, Cham (2015). https://doi.org/10.1007/978-3-319-27239-9_5

15. Minematsu, K., Iwata, T.: Cryptanalysis of PMACx, PMAC2x, and SIVx. IACR Trans. Symmetric Cryptol. **2017**(2), 162–176 (2017)

16. Naito, Y.: Full PRF-secure message authentication code based on tweakable block cipher. In: Au, M.-H., Miyaji, A. (eds.) ProvSec 2015. LNCS, vol. 9451, pp. 167–182. Springer, Cham (2015). https://doi.org/10.1007/978-3-319-26059-4_9

17. Naito, Y.: Blockcipher-based MACs: beyond the birthday bound without message length. In: Takagi, T., Peyrin, T. (eds.) ASIACRYPT 2017, Part III. LNCS, vol. 10626, pp. 446–470. Springer, Cham (2017). https://doi.org/10.1007/978-3-319-70700-6_16

18. Naito, Y.: Improved security bound of LightMAC_Plus and its single-key variant. In: Smart, N.P. (ed.) CT-RSA 2018. LNCS, vol. 10808, pp. 300–318. Springer, Cham (2018). https://doi.org/10.1007/978-3-319-76953-0_16

19. Patarin, J.: The "Coefficients H" technique. In: Avanzi, R.M., Keliher, L., Sica, F. (eds.) SAC 2008. LNCS, vol. 5381, pp. 328–345. Springer, Heidelberg (2009). https://doi.org/10.1007/978-3-642-04159-4_21

20. Rogaway, P.: Efficient instantiations of tweakable blockciphers and refinements to modes OCB and PMAC. In: Lee, P.J. (ed.) ASIACRYPT 2004. LNCS, vol. 3329, pp. 16–31. Springer, Heidelberg (2004). https://doi.org/10.1007/978-3-540-30539-2_2

21. Yasuda, K.: The sum of CBC MACs is a secure PRF. In: Pieprzyk, J. (ed.) CT-RSA 2010. LNCS, vol. 5985, pp. 366–381. Springer, Heidelberg (2010). https://doi.org/10.1007/978-3-642-11925-5_25

22. Yasuda, K.: A new variant of PMAC: beyond the birthday bound. In: Rogaway, P. (ed.) CRYPTO 2011. LNCS, vol. 6841, pp. 596–609. Springer, Heidelberg (2011). https://doi.org/10.1007/978-3-642-22792-9_34

Signatures

Hierarchical Attribute-Based Signatures

Constantin-Cătălin Drăgan, Daniel Gardham[✉], and Mark Manulis

Surrey Centre for Cyber Security, University of Surrey, Guildford, UK
{c.dragan,d.gardham}@surrey.ac.uk, mark@manulis.eu

Abstract. Attribute-based Signatures (ABS) are a powerful tool allowing users with attributes issued by authorities to sign messages while also proving that their attributes satisfy some policy. ABS schemes provide a flexible and privacy-preserving approach to authentication since the signer's identity and attributes remain hidden within the anonymity set of users sharing policy-conform attributes. Current ABS schemes exhibit some limitations when it comes to the management and issue of attributes. In this paper we address the lack of support for hierarchical attribute management, a property that is prevalent in traditional PKIs where certification authorities are organised into hierarchies and signatures are verified along roots of trust.

Hierarchical Attribute-based Signatures (HABS) introduced in this work support delegation of attributes along paths from the top-level authority down to the users while also ensuring that signatures produced by these users do not leak their delegation paths, thus extending the original privacy guarantees of ABS schemes. Our generic HABS construction also ensures unforgeability of signatures in the presence of collusion attacks and contains an extended traceability property allowing a dedicated tracing authority to identify the signer and reveal its attribute delegation paths. We include a public verification procedure for the accountability of the tracing authority.

We anticipate that HABS will be useful for privacy-preserving authentication in applications requiring hierarchical delegation of attribute-issuing rights and where knowledge of delegation paths might leak information about signers and their attributes, e.g., in intelligent transport systems where vehicles may require certain attributes to authenticate themselves to the infrastructure but remain untrackable by the latter.

1 Introduction

Attribute-based Signatures. ABS schemes, introduced independently in [31, 32], offer a flexible, privacy preserving primitive for authenticating messages. When presented with an attribute-based signature, verifiers are convinced that the signer owns a set of attributes satisfying the signing policy, however, they do not learn the signer's identity nor the set of attributes and hence provide for signer's anonymity within a set of users holding policy-conform attributes. Users who are not in possession of such attributes are not able to produce valid ABS signatures, even if they collude and try to pool their attributes together. We note

© Springer Nature Switzerland AG 2018
J. Camenisch and P. Papadimitratos (Eds.): CANS 2018, LNCS 11124, pp. 213–234, 2018.
https://doi.org/10.1007/978-3-030-00434-7_11

that while [32] enjoys an expressive policy, [31] drops this fine-grained control in favour of a more efficient threshold-based construction and such trade-off has commonly been seen in some later ABS schemes, e.g. [21,26,31]. ABS schemes can also be generalised to policy-based signatures [4].

Existing ABS constructions typically rely on zero-knowledge proofs in the signature generation phase, with a vast majority of schemes, e.g. [4,17–19,22, 34,35], being proposed in the standard model based on bilinear maps and Groth-Sahai proofs [24]. A notable exception is the scheme in [26], which uses the RSA setting yet requires random oracles.

While anonymity makes ABS schemes interesting for fine-grained privacy-preserving authentication, the ability to trace and identify signers for account-ability is another useful property that has been considered in the context of several ABS schemes [15,18,22].

Hierarchy and Delegation. Requiring that all signers obtain their attributes from a single authority introduces scalability issues if the universe of signers or attributes becomes large. Therefore, some ABS schemes, e.g. [18,22,32,34], explicitly consider the case where multiple, possibly independent authorities can issue attributes directly to the signers. On the other hand, if the ability to issue attributes requires authorisation then some additional control mechanisms for *delegation* of attribute-issuing rights would be needed.

From a more general view, it would require an ABS scheme to support a hierarchy of attribute authorities, managed by some top-level (root) authority, and enable delegation of issuing rights (for subsets of attributes) along various delegation paths consisting of intermediate authorities. With such hierarchy, signers would be able to obtain attributes only from authorities that are authorised to issue them. For practical purposes the hierarchy should be dynamically expandable, i.e., it should be possible to add intermediate authorities (at any level) at any time. This setting resembles conceptual similarity with traditional PKIs where certification authorities form a hierarchy. The main difference is that, in the context of ABS schemes, such hierarchical delegation imposes additional challenges on the privacy of signers since leakage of the delegation path from the ABS signature may compromise the signer's anonymity by leaking information about the subsets of attributes that the signer might possess, e.g. if some authority is only responsible for a small number of attributes or otherwise has some identifying information (for example, geographic location) that could also be used to identify the signer. We note that a hybrid solution whereby the hierarchy is defined by the CAs, delegation is performed via traditional PKI certification and credentials issued to signers are standard ABS credentials would suffer from the same privacy-leaking problems. Therefore, hierarchical ABS schemes must incorporate a proof of validity of the delegation paths without disclosing any information about intermediate authorities, implying that verification must be done in relation to the public key of the top-level authority and not of the intermediate authorities.

This brings further challenges when it comes to accountability. The associated tracing mechanism needs to identify not only the signer (as in the case of existing ABS constructions) but also delegation paths through which attributes were obtained. This is because the root authority may not be aware that some particular user was issued attributes by an intermediate authority. In addition, malicious intermediate authorities in the hierarchy can try to misuse their delegation rights and create further fake authorities or users to issue rogue ABS signatures. The delegation paths disclosed by the tracing algorithm would be able to detect this behaviour, thus extending accountability to intermediate authorities.

Our Contribution: Hierarchical ABS. In this paper (see also the full version in [16]) we solve the aforementioned challenges by proposing *Hierarchical ABS (HABS)* to enable hierarchical management by a root authority and delegation of attribute-issuing rights. HABS extends the anonymity guarantees by hiding not only the signers and their attributes but also the delegation paths (i.e., intermediate authorities) that were used for these attributes. We call this new property *path anonymity*. HABS supports dynamic hierarchies, enables delegation of attribute-issuing rights to new authorities, and allows signers to obtain attributes from multiple authorities within the hierarchy with guarantees that the entire delegation path (incl. the signer) can be revealed by an independent tracing authority. Moreover, we require public verifiability for the output of this tracing procedure to address the case where the tracing authority tries to cheat. Needless to say, HABS offers extended unforgeability guarantees, expressed through the *non-frameability* requirement, ensuring that only holders of policy-conform attributes can sign, and in particular, preventing collusions between signers and authorities. We formally define HABS and propose its generic construction from public key encryption, digital signatures and non-interactive zero-knowledge proofs of knowledge. Our HABS scheme can be instantiated using bilinear maps in the standard model under the DLIN, q-SDH and Simultaneous Flexible Pairing (SFP) [1] assumptions. Our HABS scheme supports a more general scenario where intermediate authorities and users can become part of multiple independent hierarchies, each managed by a separate root authority. We also discuss the revocation of delegation and signing rights in the context of HABS, which is known to be notoriously challenging for all hierarchical signature schemes (incl. PKIs).

Applications. HABS can find applications in traditional ABS scenarios (cf. [32]) while enabling hierarchical delegation of attributes. Due to their distinctive path-anonymity and path-traceability properties we anticipate further applications in privacy-preserving authentication where there is a need to also hide the intermediate authorities that were involved in issuing the attributes.

For example, in intelligent transport systems [39] there is a challenge to authenticate messages sent by vehicles to other parties (e.g. other vehicles, infrastructure, police, etc.) while preventing that vehicles can be tracked. Existing approaches, based either on pseudonymous PKI certificates [23,27], group signatures [25,38] or identity-based signatures [29,40] have all their limitations with regard to scalability and/or limited expressivity (cf. survey in [36]). As noted in [33] an attribute-based approach would bring substantial benefits and while [33] aims at realisations with heavier attribute-based credential systems, we believe that HABS could offer a more lightweight alternative. For example, the root authority can be some regulatory authority while manufacturers, authorized dealerships, local garages or testing facilities would define the hierarchy. Assume some town has a policy that bans diesel vehicles that did not pass an emission test. By viewing a vehicle's fuel type and its emission test results as attributes issued by the manufacturer and some local testing facility, respectively, the vehicle would be able to prove its compliance with the town's policy without disclosing any other information such as its make or which local facility performed the test.

Further Related Work. As explained in [32], group signatures [14] and ring signatures [37] can be viewed as special cases of ABS satisfying policies that would contain only disjunctions over the attributes (identities). The proposed constructions of hierarchical group [41] and ring [30] signatures, seen as special cases of HABS, also lack this richer expressivity of the attribute-based setting. Mesh signatures [7], a generalization of ring signatures to monotone access structures that can be satisfied by combinations of atomic signatures would not provide unforgeability against colluding signers and would leak verification keys (attributes) for all atomic signatures used in the clauses. As discussed in [32], anonymous credentials (AC) [12,13], used for privacy-preserving attribute-based credentials [11], are a more powerful, yet also less efficient, primitive than ABS. AC schemes require costly zero-knowledge proofs during attribute acquisition since their goal is to prevent that authorities can link users to whom they issue attributes. This property is not provided by (H)ABS and may not even be needed for its applications (as in our example above where it does not make sense to hide the manufacturer of a vehicle from the local testing authority that carries out the emission test). Nonetheless, we note that the concept of delegation has also been explored for AC schemes [3] where some delegation mechanisms also require zero-knowledge proofs to provide similar guarantees as in the issue of anonymous credentials and in addition to prove that the delegator is L levels away from the (top-level) authority, a property that is not needed for HABS where intermediate authorities know their delegation paths. Anonymous credentials in this setting have also been proposed [9]. Whilst the construction is more efficient, it only supports attribute issuance along one delegation path and in particular, all attributes owned by an authority in the path are required for verification. We also note the construction of a non-delegatable AC scheme built from (homomorphic) ABS [28], where multiple root authorities issue attribute credentials directly to the signers. However, to combine attributes obtained from distinct authorities requires online collaboration of these authorities. In contrast, our scheme supports delegation and non-interactive combination of attributes obtained from multiple authorities. Additionally, anonymous proxy signatures [20] bear similarities with HABS in that the delegation path for the proxy signer is not revealed upon verification of proxy signatures but can be traced through a dedicated authority. These signatures are not attribute-based since tasks delegated to the proxy signer, when viewed as attributes, are not hidden. Functional signatures [2,8] are another primitive that allow for controlled delegation of signing rights. A signing key is created w.r.t a function f, and one can only sign a message if it is in the range of f, and in the case of delegatable schemes [2] allow signatures to be modified by another specified party. When the message m is viewed as a set of attributes satisfying some policy f, signers require separate signing keys for each possible policy in the system, which is impractical. Another related primitive are homomorphic signatures, which have been claimed to be equivalent to ABS [42]. This implication has only been shown in the single user setting and thus does not capture the strong unforgeability requirements provided by HABS. Similarly, in relation to policy-based signatures [4] (which imply ABS), we observe that, so far, the only delegation mechanism proposed for these schemes in [4] neither supports separation between users and authorities nor distinguishes between the signers. This allows authorities to forge signatures on behalf of users (cf. Remark 1) and excludes the possibility of tracing signatures.

2   Model of Hierarchical Attribute-Based Signatures

In this section we describe the entities, their roles and define the algorithms for HABS. The involved entities are attribute authorities, users (signers), and a dedicated tracing authority.

Attribute Authorities. The *root authority (RA)* with its key pair (ask_0, apk_0) is at the top of HABS hierarchy and defines its universe of attributes $\mathbb{A}$. The RA can delegate subsets from $\mathbb{A}$ to other authorities in the scheme, who are then able to delegate attributes from their subsets further, creating a dynamically expandable hierarchy of attributes (see Fig. 1). In order to be admitted to the hierarchy, each *intermediate authority (IA)* needs to generate its own key pair (ask_i, apk_i), $i > 0$ and become authorised by some already admitted authority by obtaining a subset of attributes. In addition to delegation of attributes, each authority can issue attributes from its set to the end users (signers). It is assumed that admitting authorities make sufficient checks on whether the entities they admit are eligible to receive the attributes.

Users. Upon joining, each user generates its own key pair (usk, upk) and is issued with a subset of attributes by one or more authorities from the hierarchy. Any admitted user can generate a valid HABS signature on a message m with respect to some *predicate* Ψ using the secret key usk and the set of issued attributes A as long as this set contains some subset $A' \subseteq A$ that are needed to

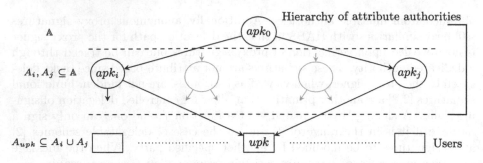

Fig. 1. Example of a HABS hierarchy where a user with public key upk receives its set of attributes $A_{upk} \subseteq A_i \cup A_j$ from two IAs i and j, who in turn receive their attribute sets A_i and A_j from the RA.

satisfy Ψ, i.e. $\Psi(A') = 1$. HABS signatures will be verified with respect to Ψ and the RA's public key apk_0. Note that, unlike authorities, users cannot delegate their attributes to other entities and can be viewed as the lowest level of the hierarchy (see Fig. 1). We make use of a label $\star$ to denote the end of the delegation path, and prevent the user from further delegating his attributes. Note we sometimes use j to differentiate users.

Warrants. For delegation of attributes to intermediate authorities and for their issue to the signers it is convenient to use warrants. That is, upon admission each HABS entity (IAs and signer) obtains a *warrant* **warr** that contains *all* attributes $a \in \mathbb{A}$ (along with their delegation paths) that the entity receives from the authority. However, upon signing we assume that a "reduced warrant" **warr** containing only a reduced attribute set A' for which $\Psi(A') = 1$ will be used by the signer. Note that by **warr**$[a]$, for $a \in$ **warr**, we denote the *delegation path* $(apk_0, \ldots, \{apk_i, \{upk, \star\}\})$, starting with RA's public key apk_0 and ending with the entity's public key, i.e. apk_i for the IA i or upk followed by a fixed label $\star$ (which is used to denote that this path cannot be extended further) for the corresponding user. We use $|$**warr**$|$ to denote the total number of attributes in **warr** and use $|$**warr**$[a]|$ to refer to the length of the delegation path for the attribute a.

Tracing Authority. A dedicated *tracing authority (TA)* with its own key pair (tsk, tpk) is responsible for tracing HABS signatures. The extended tracing procedure in HABS outputs **warr** used by the signer. This means that tracing reveals all attributes and their delegation paths from used **warr** and also the identity of the signer since its delegation paths include upk. Note that since users can use reduced warrants, the tracing procedure does not necessarily reveal all attributes held by the user but only those that were used to produce the signature. For accountability purposes we require that the output of TA is publicly verifiable, i.e. is accompanied by some proof that can be verified using a public judgment procedure.

Definition 1 (Hierarchical ABS Scheme). HABS := (Setup, KGen, AttIssue, Sign, Verify, Trace, Judge) *consists of the following seven processes:*

- Setup(1^λ) *is the initialisation process where based on some security parameter* $\lambda \in \mathbb{N}$, *the public parameters* pp *of the scheme are defined, and the root and tracing authority independently generate their own key pair, i.e. RA's* (ask_0, apk_0) *and TA's* (tsk, tpk). *In addition, RA defines the universe* $\mathbb{A}$ *of attributes, and a label* $\star$ *for users. We stress that due to dynamic hierarchy, the system can be initialised by publishing* (pp, apk_0, tpk) *with* $\mathbb{A}$ *and* $\star$ *contained in* pp.
- KGen(pp) *is a key generation algorithm executed independently by intermediate authorities and users. Each entity generates its own key pair, i.e.,* (ask_i, apk_i) *for* $i > 0$ *or* (usk, upk).
- AttIssue (ask_i, **warr**$_i$, A, $\{apk_j | upk_j\}$) *is an algorithm that is used to delegate attributes to an authority with* apk_j *or issue them to the user with* upk. *On input of an authority's secret key* ask_i, $i \in \mathbb{N}_0$, *its warrant* **warr**$_i$, *a subset of attributes* A *from* **warr**$_i$, *and the public key of the entity to which attributes are delegated or issued, it outputs a new warrant* **warr** *for that entity.*
- Sign ((usk, **warr**), m, Ψ) *is the signing algorithm. On input of the signer's* usk *and (possibly reduced)* **warr**, *a message* m *and a predicate* Ψ *it outputs a signature* σ.
- Verify (apk_0, (m, Ψ, σ)) *is a deterministic algorithm that outputs 1 if a candidate signature* σ *on a message* m *is valid with respect to the predicate* Ψ *and 0 otherwise.*
- Trace (tsk, apk_0, (m, Ψ, σ)) *is an algorithm executed by the TA on input of its private key* tsk *and outputs either a triple* (upk, **warr**, $\hat{\pi}$) *if the tracing is successful or* $\bot$ *to indicate its failure. Note that* **warr** *contains attributes and delegation paths that were used by the signer.*
- Judge (tpk, apk_0, (m, Ψ, σ), (upk, **warr**, $\hat{\pi}$)) *is a deterministic algorithm that checks a candidate triple* (upk, **warr**, $\hat{\pi}$) *from the tracing algorithm and outputs 1 if the triple is valid and 0 otherwise.*

The *correctness* property of HABS requires that any signature σ output by any signer with usk in possession of a legitimately issued warrant **warr** that contains attributes $a \in \mathbb{A}$ satisfying Ψ can be successfully verified and traced, and that a triple (upk, **warr**, $\hat{\pi}$) output by the tracing algorithm for such σ passes the public judgment procedure.

2.1 Security Properties

In this section, we define three security properties of HABS schemes: *path anonymity*, *non-frameability*, and *path traceability* and use game-based definitions assuming some PPT adversary $\mathcal{A}$ that interacts with the entities using oracles.

$$
\begin{array}{ll}
\hline
O_{\mathrm{Reg}}(\ \cdot\ )\ \text{with}\ (\ \cdot\ )=(\,i\,)\ \text{and}\ i\notin HU & O_{\mathrm{Att}}(\ \cdot\ ) \\
\hline
\end{array}
$$

$O_{\mathrm{Reg}}(\ \cdot\ )$ with $(\ \cdot\ )=(\,i\,)$ and $i\notin HU$	$O_{\mathrm{Att}}(\ \cdot\ )$
1 : $(sk_i, pk_i) \leftarrow \mathtt{KGen}(\mathrm{pp})$	$(\ \cdot\ ) = (i, \mathbf{warr}_i, a, \{apk_j | upk_j\})$
2 : $List \leftarrow List \cup \{(i, pk_i, sk_i)\}$	1 : $L := \{a | (a, pk_a, sk_a) \in List\}$
3 : $HU \leftarrow HU \cup \{i\}$	2 : if $i \in L \wedge j \in L$ then
4 : return pk_i	3 : $\quad$ warr $\leftarrow \mathtt{AttIssue}(ask_i,$
	$\qquad\qquad$ $\mathbf{warr}_i, a, \{apk_j | upk_j\})$
$O_{\mathrm{Corr}}(\ \cdot\ )$ with $(\ \cdot\ )=(\,i\,)$	4 : $\quad$ return warr
1 : if $i \in HU$ then	5 : return $\perp$
2 : $\quad HU \leftarrow HU - \{i\}$	
3 : return sk_i from $List$	$O_{\mathrm{Sig}}(\ \cdot\ )$ with $(\ \cdot\ )=(i, \mathbf{warr}, \mathrm{m}, \varPsi)$
	1 : $A \leftarrow \{a | a \in \mathbf{warr}\}$
$O_{\mathrm{Tr}}(\ \cdot\ )$ with $(\ \cdot\ )=(\mathrm{m}, \varPsi, \sigma)$	2 : if $i \in HU \wedge \varPsi(A)$ then
1 : return $\mathtt{Trace}(tsk, apk_0, (\mathrm{m}, \varPsi, \sigma))$	3 : $\quad \sigma \leftarrow \mathtt{Sign}((usk_i, \mathbf{warr}), \mathrm{m}, \varPsi)$
	4 : $\quad$ return σ
	5 : return $\perp$

Fig. 2. Oracles used in the HABS security experiments.

We note that our definitions extend earlier definitions for (multi-authority) ABS schemes, e.g. [4,18,22,32], to account for the hierarchical setting and potential corruptions within the hierarchy. In addition, our definitions of *path-anonymity* and *path-traceability* focus on hiding resp. verifiable traceability of delegation paths from the signer's warrant, a distinctive feature of HABS. Our modeling techniques for these properties are inspired by definitions behind anonymous proxy signatures [20] which do not apply directly to the attribute-based setting.

Oracles for $\mathcal{A}$. The oracles available to a PPT adversary $\mathcal{A}$ are defined in Fig. 2 and their high-level description is provided in the following. In our oracles we take into account that only authorities can delegate and issue attributes whereas only signers can generate HABS signatures.

- O_{Reg}: $\mathcal{A}$ can register new IAs and users for whom, in response, a key pair will be honestly generated and the public key given to $\mathcal{A}$. The oracle uses lists to keep track of the established entities and their keys. Upon registration all entities are initially considered to be honest.
- O_{Corr}: $\mathcal{A}$ can corrupt established entities. On input of the entity's public key $\mathcal{A}$ receives the corresponding private key, as long as this entity has been previously established. The oracle keeps track of entities who were corrupted.
- O_{Att}: $\mathcal{A}$ can ask an authority to either delegate attributes for another IA or to issue attributes to a user, as long as both involved entities are registered. Note that $\mathcal{A}$ can define which attributes the oracle should use. If both entities are registered and the issuing entity has rights to issue attributes provided by $\mathcal{A}$ then the output warrant **warr** is given to $\mathcal{A}$.

$\mathbf{Exp}_{\mathsf{HABS},\mathcal{A}}^{\mathrm{pa}\text{-}b}(\lambda)$

1 : $(\mathsf{pp}, ask_0, tsk) \leftarrow \mathtt{Setup}(1^{\lambda})$

2 : $(\mathsf{st}, (usk_0, \mathbf{warr}_0), (usk_1, \mathbf{warr}_1), m, \Psi) \leftarrow \mathcal{A}_1(\mathsf{pp}, ask_0 : O_{\mathrm{Reg}}, O_{\mathrm{Corr}}, O_{\mathrm{Tr}})$

3 : $\mathbf{if}\ |\mathbf{warr}_0| = |\mathbf{warr}_1|\ \mathbf{then}$

4 : $\sigma_0 \leftarrow \mathtt{Sign}((usk_0, \mathbf{warr}_0), \mathrm{m}, \Psi),\ \ \sigma_1 \leftarrow \mathtt{Sign}((usk_1, \mathbf{warr}_1), \mathrm{m}, \Psi)$

5 : $\mathbf{if}\ \mathtt{Verify}(apk_0, (m, \Psi, \sigma_0)) = 1\ \text{and}\ \mathtt{Verify}(apk_0, (m, \Psi, \sigma_1)) = 1\ \mathbf{then}$

6 : $b' \leftarrow \mathcal{A}_2(\mathsf{st}, \sigma_b : O_{\mathrm{Tr}})$

7 : $\mathbf{return}\ b' \wedge \mathcal{A}_2\ \text{did not query}\ O_{\mathrm{Tr}}(tsk, (m, \Psi, \sigma_b))$

8 : $\mathbf{return}\ 0$

Fig. 3. Path-anonymity experiment

- O_{Sig}: $\mathcal{A}$ can ask a signer to produce a HABS signature using the input warrant **warr**, a message m and a predicate Ψ. If the provided warrant contains a set of attributes A satisfying Ψ and the signer is not corrupted then the signature will be given to $\mathcal{A}$.
- O_{Tr}: $\mathcal{A}$ can ask the TA to perform the tracing procedure on its input, in which case its output (which can also be $\bot$) is returned to $\mathcal{A}$.

Path Anonymity. For HABS we extend the anonymity property of traditional ABS schemes to achieve privacy of the delegation path, i.e., not only to hide the signer but also all intermediate authorities that were involved in the delegation of attributes for that signer. Our game for *path anonymity* in Fig. 3 requires the adversary to decide which user's warrant and private key were used in the generation of the challenge HABS signature σ_b. We consider a powerful two-stage PPT adversary $\mathcal{A} = (\mathcal{A}_1, \mathcal{A}_2)$, who knows the private keys of the candidate signers and can moreover establish its own HABS hierarchy (with IAs and users) by learning the secret key ask_0 of the root authority. This also means that the adversary comes up with the candidate warrants **warr**$_0$ and **warr**$_1$ for the two users in the challenge phase. Since HABS signatures do not aim to hide the length of the delegation paths nor the number of attributes used to satisfy the policy we require that both warrants are of the same size and that they both satisfy the predicate Ψ output by the adversary. Since attributes are contained in warrants our definition also implies attribute-hiding.

Definition 2 (Path Anonymity). *A HABS scheme offers path anonymity if no PPT adversary $\mathcal{A}$ can distinguish between $\mathbf{Exp}_{\mathsf{HABS},\mathcal{A}}^{\mathrm{pa}\text{-}0}$ and $\mathbf{Exp}_{\mathsf{HABS},\mathcal{A}}^{\mathrm{pa}\text{-}1}$ defined in Fig. 3, i.e., the following advantage is negligible in λ:*

$$\mathsf{Adv}_{\mathsf{HABS},\mathcal{A}}^{\mathrm{pa}}(\lambda) = \left| \Pr\left[\mathbf{Exp}_{\mathsf{HABS},\mathcal{A}}^{\mathrm{pa}\text{-}0}(\lambda) = 1 \right] - \Pr\left[\mathbf{Exp}_{\mathsf{HABS},\mathcal{A}}^{\mathrm{pa}\text{-}1}(\lambda) = 1 \right] \right|.$$

$\mathbf{Exp}_{\text{HABS},\mathcal{A}}^{\text{nf}}(\lambda)$

1 : $(pp, ask_0, tsk) \leftarrow \mathtt{Setup}(1^\lambda)$

2 : $((\sigma, m, \Psi), (upk_j, \mathbf{warr}, \hat{\pi})) \leftarrow \mathcal{A}(pp, ask_0, tsk : O_{\text{Att}}, O_{\text{Sig}}, O_{\text{Corr}}, O_{\text{Reg}})$

3 : $\mathbf{if}\ \mathtt{Verify}(apk_0, (m, \Psi, \sigma))\ \wedge\ \mathtt{Judge}(tpk, apk_0, (m, \Psi, \sigma), (upk_j, \mathbf{warr}, \hat{\pi}))\ \mathbf{then}$

4 : $\mathbf{if}\ j \in HU \wedge \mathcal{A}\ \text{did not query}\ O_{\text{Sig}}((usk_j, \mathbf{warr}), m, \Psi)\ \mathbf{then,}\quad \mathbf{return}\ 1$

5 : $\mathbf{if}\ \exists a.\ a \in \mathbf{warr} \implies (apk_0, apk_1, \ldots, apk_n, upk_j, \star) = \mathbf{warr}[a]\ \wedge$

6 : $((\exists i \in [0, n-1].\ \mathcal{A}\ \text{did not query}\ O_{\text{Att}}(i,\ \cdot\ , a, apk_{i+1}) \wedge i \in HU)\ \vee$

7 : $(\mathcal{A}\ \text{did not query}\ O_{\text{Att}}(n,\ \cdot\ , a, upk_j)\ \wedge n \in HU)\ )\ \mathbf{then, return}\ 1$

8 : $\mathbf{return}\ 0$

Fig. 4. Non-frameability experiment

Non-Frameability. Another fundamental property for HABS is *non-frameabili-ty* that extends unforgeability to ensure only authorized authorities can delegate and only attribute policy-compliant users can sign. This property is formalized in Fig. 4, and requires the adversary $\mathcal{A}$ to produce valid authorizations for attributes he does not satisfy: either as a valid HABS signature σ for some honest user with upk, or as a valid tracing information that includes a warrant $\mathbf{warr}$ issued by an honest authority. In the latter, it is enough for $\mathcal{A}$ to provide a single attribute a for which the delegation path contains one honest authority i or an honest user with upk without querying O_{Att} for that authority or user. We consider a PPT adversary $\mathcal{A}$, who can admit IAs to the HABS hierarchy using the RA's private key ask_0, and act on behalf of the TA using tsk.

Definition 3 (Non-Frameability). *A HABS scheme is non-frameable, if no PPT adversary $\mathcal{A}$ can win the experiment $\mathbf{Exp}_{\text{HABS},\mathcal{A}}^{\text{nf}}$ defined in Fig. 4, i.e., the following advantage is negligible in λ:*

$$\mathsf{Adv}_{\text{HABS},\mathcal{A}}^{\text{nf}}(\lambda) = \Pr\left[\mathbf{Exp}_{\text{HABS},\mathcal{A}}^{\text{nf}}(\lambda) = 1\right].$$

Remark 1. In the non-frameability experiment we consider a strong adversary that has full control of the hierarchy through the O_{Reg} and O_{Att} oracles. We capture the notion that malicious authorities and colluding users should not be able to produce signatures on behalf of, and therefore framing, honest users. This is a stronger notion of security than considered in some existing ABS schemes [4, 32].

Path Traceability. The final property we consider for HABS is *path traceability* in Fig. 5 that offers accountability for the entire delegation path and the tracing authority, but also validity of the entities in that delegation path. The adversary $\mathcal{A}$ is required to produce a valid HABS signature σ that either cannot be traced, or can be traced to a warrant $\mathbf{warr}$ that contains at least one "rogue" entity

---

$\mathbf{Exp}^{tr}_{HABS,\mathcal{A}}(\lambda)$

1 : $(pp, ask_0, tsk) \leftarrow \mathtt{Setup}(1^\lambda)$

2 : $((\sigma, m, \Psi), (upk, \mathbf{warr}, \hat{\pi})) \leftarrow \mathcal{A}(pp, tsk : O_{\mathrm{Att}}, O_{\mathrm{Corr}}, O_{\mathrm{Reg}})$

3 : **if** $\mathtt{Verify}(apk_0, (m, \Psi, \sigma))$ **then**

4 :   **if** $\mathtt{Trace}(tsk, (m, \Psi, \sigma)) = \perp$ **then**   **return** 1

5 :   **if** $\mathtt{Judge}(tpk, apk_0, (m, \Psi, \sigma), (upk, \mathbf{warr}, \hat{\pi})) \wedge$

6 : $(\exists a.\ a \in \mathbf{warr} \implies (apk_0, apk_1, \ldots, apk_n, upk, \star) = \mathbf{warr}[a] \wedge$

7 : $(\ (\exists i \in [0, n-1].\ i \in HU \wedge (i+1, apk_{i+1}, ask_{i+1}) \notin List) \vee$

8 : $(n \in HU \wedge (\ \cdot\ , upk, usk) \notin List)\ )\ )$ **then**   **return** 1

9 : **return** 0

Fig. 5. Path-traceability experiment.

(some authority i or user with upk) within any of its delegation paths that has not been previously registered through the registration oracle, i.e., is not contained in $List$. For honest and registered authorities $\mathcal{A}$ can use the attribute-issuing oracle, which internally checks whether the public key of the entity for which the warrant needs to be issued has been registered before. This excludes a trivial attack where $\mathcal{A}$ obtains a legitimate warrant for some rogue entity from some honest authority. In its attack we also equip $\mathcal{A}$ with the TA's private key.

Definition 4 (Path Traceability) . *A* HABS *scheme offers path traceability if no PPT adversary $\mathcal{A}$ can win the experiment $\mathbf{Exp}^{tr}_{HABS,\mathcal{A}}$ defined in Fig. 5, i.e., the following advantage is negligible in λ:*

$$\mathsf{Adv}^{tr}_{HABS,\mathcal{A}}(\lambda) = \Pr\left[\mathbf{Exp}^{tr}_{HABS,\mathcal{A}}(\lambda) = 1\right].$$

3 Construction

In this section we describe and analyse our general construction for HABS that we build from several well-known building blocks.

3.1 Building Blocks

Our construction relies on standard notions of IND-CCA2 secure *public key encryption* PKE := (KGen, Enc, Dec) [10] and an unforgeable *digital signature* DS:=(KGen, Sign, Verify) [1] that withstands chosen-message attacks. We rely further on an unforgeable *tagged signature* TS := (KGen, Sign, Verify) [1] that can sign blocks of messages, also used in [18], where an additional tag t is used as input to the signing algorithm and the signature will not verify unless the verifier uses the same tag. The adversary is allowed to query its signing oracle on tags that it can use later to create a forgery. Although any unforgeable DS scheme can be used as a tagged signature if its message space admits signing pairs (t, m), the explicit separation of t allows usage of different spaces for tags and messages. Our HABS scheme further relies on a strongly unforgeable *one-time signature* OTS := (KGen, Sign, Verify) [6], for which the signing oracle can be queried only once and the adversary succeeds even if it can output a different signature on the message that it queried. Finally, our HABS construction uses *non-interactive zero-knowledge proofs* NIZK = (Setup, Prove, Verify, SimSetup, Sim) [5,24] for a language $\mathcal{L} = \{x \mid \exists w.\ R(w, x) = 1\}$, where R is some relation over a witness w and a statement x. Typically, NIZK proofs require a common reference string crs output during the setup phase. From NIZK we require the standard properties of completeness, soundness, and zero-knowledge.

3.2   Generic Construction

We use the above general building blocks to construct our HABS scheme, which is specified in Fig. 6. In the following we provide a high-level intuition behind its construction. Attribute authorities (RA and IAs) generate their key pairs (ask_i, apk_i), $i \in \mathbb{N}_0$ for the tagged signature scheme TS. The TA holds a key pair (tsk, tpk) for the public key encryption scheme PKE. The public parameters pp_of the scheme also contain trusted common reference strings crs_1 and crs_2 for the corresponding NIZK proofs.

Attributes $a \in \mathbb{A}$ are viewed as tags of the TS scheme whereas delegation paths $attL := (apk_0, \ldots, \{apk_i, \{upk_{i+1}, \star\}\})$ are treated as messages. In order to create a warrant **warr** for some authority or signer, the corresponding IA with its ask_i will produce a TS signature on each attribute a and its delegation path and include this signature into **warr**[a] as part of the list $sigL$. Thus, a separate TS signature is used for each attribute and its path such that the signer can later reduce its **warr** to attributes that are needed for a policy Ψ.

Each signer, after initialisation, holds a key pair (usk, upk) for the digital signature scheme DS. A signer with usk and a reduced **warr** that satisfies Ψ can generate a HABS signature σ for some message m. The reduced **warr** together with the signer's public key upk and a digital signature σ_s with message $otsvk$ are encrypted in a PKE ciphertext C under the TA's public key tpk with randomness μ. The signer generates a key pair $(otssk, otsvk)$ for the one-time signature scheme OTS and uses its usk to compute a digital signature σ_s on $otsvk$.

We model Ψ as a span program $\mathbf{S}$ with a labelling function ρ that maps rows from $\mathbf{S}$ to attributes in $\mathbb{A}$. The signer attests the satisfiability of Ψ w.r.t its attributes from the reduced **warr** by computing a vector of integers $\mathbf{z}$ such that $\mathbf{zS} = [1, 0, \ldots, 0]$ and for any $z_i \neq 0$ we have $\rho(i) \in$ **warr**.

Then, the signer computes a NIZK$_1$ proof π for the statement (C, $otsvk$, tpk, apk_0, Ψ) using as witness the previously computed $(upk, \mu, \mathbf{z}, \mathbf{warr}, \sigma_s)$ such that the following relation is satisfied:

$\texttt{AttIssue}(ask_i, \textbf{warr}_i, A, \{apk_j | upk_j\})$

1 : $\quad$ **warr** $:= \emptyset$

2 : $\quad$ **for** $a \in A$ **do**

3 : $\qquad \sigma_a \leftarrow \texttt{TS.Sign}(ask_i, a, (apk_1, \ldots, apk_i, \{apk_j | \{upk_j, \star\}\}))$

4 : $\qquad$ **warr**$[a] \leftarrow \textbf{warr}_i[a] \cup \{apk_j | \{upk_j, \star\}\} \cup \{\sigma_a\}$

5 : $\quad$ **return warr**

$\texttt{Sign}((usk, \textbf{warr}), \text{m}, \Psi)$

1 : $\quad (otsvk, otssk) \leftarrow \texttt{OTS.KGen}(1^\lambda)$

2 : $\quad \sigma_s \leftarrow \texttt{DS.Sign}(usk, otsvk);$ C $\leftarrow \texttt{PKE.Enc}(tpk, (upk, \textbf{warr}, \sigma_s, otsvk); \mu)$

3 : $\quad$ compute $\mathbf{z}$ $s.t.$ $\mathbf{z}\mathbf{S} = [1, 0, \ldots, 0]$

4 : $\quad \pi \leftarrow \texttt{NIZK}_1.\texttt{Prove}\big((upk, \mu, \mathbf{z}, \textbf{warr}, \sigma_s) : (\text{C}, otsvk, tpk, apk_0, \Psi)\big)$

5 : $\quad \sigma_o \leftarrow \texttt{OTS.Sign}(otssk, (\text{m}, \Psi, \text{C}, \pi))$

6 : $\quad \sigma \leftarrow (\sigma_o, \text{C}, \pi, otsvk),$ **return** σ

$\texttt{Verify}(apk_0, (\text{m}, \Psi, \sigma))$ with $\sigma = (\sigma_o, \text{C}, \pi, otsvk)$

---

return $\texttt{NIZK}_1.\texttt{Verify}((\text{C}, otsvk, tpk, apk_0, \Psi), \pi) \wedge \texttt{OTS.Verify}(otsvk, (\text{m}, \Psi, \text{C}, \pi), \sigma_o)$

$\texttt{Trace}(tsk, apk_0, (\text{m}, \Psi, \sigma))$ with $\sigma = (\sigma_o, \text{C}, \pi, otsvk)$

---

1 : $\quad$ **if** $\texttt{Verify}(apk_0, (\sigma, \text{m}, \Psi))$ **then**

2 : $\qquad (upk, \textbf{warr}, \sigma_s, otsvk') \leftarrow \texttt{PKE.Dec}(tsk, \text{C})$

3 : $\qquad \hat{\pi} \leftarrow \texttt{NIZK}_2.\texttt{Prove}(tsk \; : (otsvk, \text{C}, tpk, upk, \textbf{warr}, \sigma_s))$

4 : $\qquad$ **if** $otsvk' = otsvk$ **then return** $(upk, \textbf{warr}, (\hat{\pi}, \sigma_s))$

5 : $\quad$ **return** $\perp$

$\texttt{Judge}(tpk, apk_0, (\text{m}, \Psi, \sigma), (upk, \textbf{warr}, (\hat{\pi}, \sigma_s)))$ with $\sigma = (\sigma_o, \pi, \text{C}, otsvk)$

---

return $\texttt{Verify}(apk_0, (\text{m}, \Psi, \sigma)) \wedge \texttt{NIZK}_2.\texttt{Verify}(tpk, (otsvk, \text{C}, upk, \textbf{warr}, \sigma_s), \hat{\pi})$

Fig. 6. Algorithms of our general HABS scheme.

$\texttt{PKE.Enc}(tpk, (upk, \textbf{warr}, \sigma_s, otsvk); \mu) = \text{C} \wedge \texttt{DS.Verify}(upk, otsvk, \sigma_s)$

$\qquad \wedge \; \mathbf{z}\mathbf{S} = [1, 0, \ldots, 0] \; \wedge \; (\forall i. \; z_i \neq 0 \implies a_i = \rho(i)$

$\qquad \wedge \; ((apk_0, apk_{i_1}, \ldots, apk_{i_n}, upk, \star)(\sigma_{i_1}, \ldots, \sigma_{i_n}, \sigma_u)) = \textbf{warr}[a_i]$

$\qquad \wedge \; (\forall 1 \leq j \leq n. \; \texttt{TS.Verify}(apk_{i_{(j-1)}}, \sigma_{i_j}, a_i, (apk_0, apk_{i_1}, \ldots, apk_{i_j})))$

$\qquad \wedge \; \texttt{TS.Verify}(apk_{i_n}, \sigma_u, a_i, (apk_0, apk_{i_1}, \ldots, apk_{i_n}, upk, \star))).$

The resulting HABS signature σ contains the aforementioned C, π, and $otsvk$, along with an OTS signature σ_o, generated using $otssk$ to bind these value together with the message m and Ψ. The validity of such HABS signature σ can be verified using public parameters of the scheme and RA's public key apk_0 by checking the validity of the NIZK$_1$ proof π and the OTS signature σ_o.

The tracing algorithm, on input of a valid HABS signature $((\sigma_o, C, \pi, otsvk), m, \Psi)$ uses tsk to decrypt the warrant **warr** from the ciphertext C. The decrypted warrant contains all attributes and delegation paths, incl. signer's public key upk, and signature σ_s with message $otsvk'$. Then, it checks whether $otsvk = otsvk'$. If true, TA outputs a NIZK$_2$ proof $\hat{\pi}$ for the statement $(otsvk, C, tpk, (apk_0, \mathbf{warr}, \sigma_s))$ using tsk as its witness to prove the following relation:

$$\text{PKE.Dec}(tsk, C) = (upk, \mathbf{warr}, \sigma_s, otsvk').$$

The output of TA on a valid HABS signature can be publicly judged by checking the validity of the NIZK$_2$ proof $\hat{\pi}$.

3.3 Security Analysis

In this section we show that our general HABS construction in Fig. 6 satisfies path-anonymity, non-frameability and path-traceability from assumptions of its underlying cryptographic building blocks.

Lemma 1. HABS *defined in Fig. 6 offers path anonymity, if* NIZK$_1$ *and* NIZK$_2$ *are zero-knowledge,* PKE *is IND-CCA2, and* OTS *is strongly unforgeable.*

Proof. We follow a game-based approach and show that the advantage of the PPT adversary $\mathcal{A}$ in the path-anonymity experiment for the HABS construction from Fig. 6, is bounded by the advantages of the constructed adversaries for the underlying primitives.

Game G_0: Let this be the experiment corresponding to $\text{Exp}^{\text{pa-}b}_{\text{HABS},\mathcal{A}}(\lambda)$ in Fig. 3, where the adversary $\mathcal{A} = (\mathcal{A}_1, \mathcal{A}_2)$ is required to distinguish between the signatures $\sigma_0 = (\sigma_o^0, C_0, \pi_0, otsvk_0)$ and $\sigma_1 = (\sigma_o^1, C_1, \pi_1, otsvk_1)$.

Game G_1: This game is obtained from the game G_0 where the restriction "$\mathcal{A}_2$ did not query $O_{\text{Tr}}(m, \Psi, \sigma_b)$" is enforced by the O_{Tr} oracle available to $\mathcal{A}_2$. This is done by aborting the game, if $\mathcal{A}_2$ queries (m, Ψ, σ_b). We model this by adding the line "if $(\sigma_o, C, \pi, otsvk) = (\sigma_{o,b}, C_b, \pi_b, otsvk_b)$ then return **abort**", when the adversary calls $O_{\text{Tr}}(m, \Psi, (\sigma_o, C, \pi, otsvk))$ and $\sigma_b = (\sigma_{o,b}, C_b, \pi_b, otsvk_b)$. The games G_1 and G_0 preserve the exact same probability.

Game G_2: We define G_2 as game G_1 except on the outputs of O_{Tr}, where we replace the NIZK$_2$ proof $\hat{\pi}$ with a proof $\hat{\pi}'$, provided by the simulator NIZK$_2$.Sim. Additionally, in game G_2 for NIZK$_2$ we replace Setup by SimSetup. These changes are done to avoid the case where $\mathcal{A}$ may "extract"tsk from NIZK$_2$ proofs. Thus, for all future O_{Tr} oracle call we make use of a simulated NIZK$_2$ proof. These two games are indistinguishable due to the zero-knowledge of NIZK$_2$.

Game G_3: Let G_3 be the game obtained from G_2 where the real NIZK$_1$ proof π_b from the challenge signature $\sigma_b = (\sigma_{o,b}, C_b, \pi_b, otsvk_b)$ is replaced with the simulated proof π_b' by calling NIZK$_1$.Sim on the inputs $(C_b, otsvk_b, tpk, apk_0, \Psi)$. Similar to the previous step, by now for NIZK$_1$ we replace Setup by SimSetup.

We bound the capabilities of $\mathcal{A}$ to distinguish between games G_3 and G_2 by the advantage of the zero-knowledge adversary for NIZK_1.

Game G_4: Game G_4 is identical to game G_3, except we abort if $\mathcal{A}_2$ queries $O_{\text{Tr}}(m, \Psi, (\sigma_o, \text{C}, \pi, otsvk))$ if $(\text{C}, otsvk) = (\text{C}_b, otsvk_b)$. The adversary $\mathcal{A}$ is able to distinguish between G_3 and G_4, only if he can produce a valid OTS signature σ_o for a statement $(\text{C}_b, \pi, m, \Psi)$ and verification key $otsvk_b$, without knowledge of the signing key $otssk_b$. Essentially, breaking the strong unforgeability of OTS.

Game G_5: This game G_5 is the same as G_4, except we abort if $\mathcal{A}_2$ queries $O_{\text{Tr}}(m, \Psi, (\sigma_o, \text{C}, \pi, otsvk))$ when $\text{C} = \text{C}_b$. The output of O_{Tr} remains unchanged between these two games, as the oracle return $\perp$ if $otsvk_b$ from C is different from $otsvk$ received as input. Game G_5 preserves the same probability as G_4.

Game G_6: Let G_6 be the game obtained from G_5 where the ciphertext C_b from the challenge signature $\sigma_b = (\sigma_{o,b}, \text{C}_b, \pi_b', otsvk_b)$ is replaced with C_0. The distinguishing capabilities of the adversary $\mathcal{A}_2$ are bounded by the advantage of the IND-CCA2 adversary for the PKE scheme.

The experiment G_6 provides as challenge to $\mathcal{A}$ the exact same values independent of the random bit b that $\mathcal{A}$ is asked to guess. Additionally, due to zero-knowledge of NIZK_2 used in G_2, $\mathcal{A}$ does not have access to tsk. Therefore, the advantage of $\mathcal{A}$ in winning this experiment is 0. $\qquad\square$

Lemma 2. *The generic HABS construction from Fig. 6 is non-frameable, if NIZK_1 is sound, TS and DS are unforgeable, and OTS is strongly unforgeable.*

Proof. We model our proof by dividing the non-frameability experiment from Fig. 4 into two experiments based on the winning condition of the adversary $\mathcal{A}$. The first experiment, E_1, captures the probability of the adversary $\mathcal{A}$ to create a forgery. The second experiments E_2 follows the exact same steps as E_1 except that "$j \in HU \wedge \mathcal{A}$ did not query $O_{\text{Sig}}((usk_j, \textbf{warr}), \Psi, \text{m})$" is replaced by

"$\exists a.\ a \in \textbf{warr} \implies (apk_0, apk_1, \ldots, apk_n, upk_j, \star) = \textbf{warr}[a] \wedge$
$(\ (\exists 0 \leq i \leq n-1.\ \mathcal{A}$ did not call $O_{\text{Att}}(i, \cdot, a, apk_{i+1}) \wedge i \in HU) \vee$
$(\mathcal{A}$ did not call $O_{\text{Att}}(n, \cdot, a, upk_j)\ \wedge n \in HU))$"

The probability of winning the non-frameability experiment is bounded by the probability of $\mathcal{A}$ winning either E_1 or E_2:

$$\Pr\left[\textbf{Exp}_{\text{HABS},\mathcal{A}}^{\text{nf}}(\lambda)\right] \leq \Pr[E_1 = 1] + \Pr[E_2 = 1].$$

We start with the first experiment E_1 that we will show has a negligible probability of success. Intuitively, we want to argue over all the values $(upk', \textbf{warr}', m', \Psi'), (\sigma_o', \text{C}', \pi', otsvk')$ that correspond to the input and output of the O_{Sig} oracle. We show that they are not sufficient for the adversary $\mathcal{A}$ to create valid proofs and signatures $(\sigma_o, \text{C}, \pi, otsvk)$ for the values $(upk_j, \textbf{warr}, m, \Psi)$ different from $(upk', \textbf{warr}', m', \Psi')$. More precisely, we take each element of the tuple $(upk_j, \textbf{warr}, m, \Psi)$ and try to reason about their relation with their prime counterpart from $(upk', \textbf{warr}', m', \Psi')$.

The first step considers if"there has been any O_{Sig} request that contains upk", which sets the direction for the rest of the proof. Next, we follow the same methodology by reasoning that the values $\mathbf{warr}', m', \Psi'$ and $otsvk'$ have to coincide with $\mathbf{warr}, m, \Psi, otsvk$ for $\mathcal{A}$ to actually produce valid proofs and signatures that pass the verification conditions in E_1.

Game G_0. The game G_0 is defined exactly as E_1 except on line "$\mathcal{A}$ did not query $O_{\mathrm{Sig}}((usk_j, \mathbf{warr}), m, \Psi)$" that is replaced with a membership check $(upk_j, \mathbf{warr}, m, \Psi) \notin sL$ for the list sL. This list sL is initialized empty at the beginning of the experiment, and gets updated with the inputs of the O_{Sig} oracle. Additionally, we introduce the list spL that stores the input and output of the O_{Sig} oracle. We have that E_1 and G_0 have the same probability.

Game G_1. This game is defined exactly as G_0 with the exception the additional test $\mathrm{DS.Verify}(upk_j, otsvk, \sigma_s)$ performed over the output of the adversary $(((\sigma_o, \mathrm{C}, \pi, otsvk), m, \Psi), (upk_j, \mathbf{warr}, (\hat{\pi}, \sigma_s)))$. G_1 is indistinguishable from G_0 due to the soundness of NIZK_1: the probability of generating a valid NIZK_1 proof for a false statement (that does not pass DS verification).

Game G_2. This game uses the exact steps performed by game G_1, except it returns false if the adversary has not queried at least one signature that contains user upk_j. The adversary $\mathcal{A}$ is able to distinguish between these two games if he can produce a valid digital signature σ_s for upk_j that passes DS verification without having access to the user's secret key (as $j \in HU$). Thus, breaking unforgeability for DS.

Game G_3. We define game G_3 exactly as G_2, except we replace the test on where $\mathcal{A}$ has queried O_{Sig} for user upk_j: line $(upk_j, \star, \star, \star) \in sL$ with

$$\exists\, \mathbf{warr}'.\, m'.\, \Psi'.\, \sigma_o'.\, \mathrm{C}'.\, \pi'.\, otsvk'.\, ((upk_j, \mathbf{warr}', m', \Psi'), (\sigma_o', \mathrm{C}', \pi', otsvk')) \in spL.$$

We have $(\mathbf{warr}, m, \Psi) \neq (\mathbf{warr}', m', \Psi')$, because of $(upk_j, \mathbf{warr}, m, \Psi) \notin sL$ and $(upk_j, \mathbf{warr}', m', \Psi') \in sL$.

Game G_4. We define G_4 as the game G_3, except we extend the condition "$\exists\, \mathbf{warr}' \ldots ((upk_j, \mathbf{warr}', m', \Psi'), (\sigma_o', \mathrm{C}', \pi', otsvk')) \in spL$" to include $otsvk = otsvk'$. The capabilities of the adversary $\mathcal{A}$ to distinguish between G_4 and G_3 are bounded by the unforgeability of the DS.

Game G_5. We define game G_5 as the game G_4, where we add the restriction $(m, \Psi) = (m', \Psi')$, on the same line and in the same manner as the changes done in game G_4. The adversary $\mathcal{A}$ is able to distinguish between these two games, if he can provide a forgery for the OTS scheme by signing a message that contains (m', Ψ') without knowledge of $otssk$.

Game G_6. We define game G_6 as the game G_5, except we add $\mathrm{C} \neq \mathrm{C}'$ to the same line that was modified in game G_5. Because of the restriction $(\mathbf{warr}, m, \Psi) \neq (\mathbf{warr}', m', \Psi')$, we have $\mathbf{warr}' \neq \mathbf{warr}$ in game G_6. Given $\mathbf{warr} \neq \mathbf{warr}'$, we now show that $\mathrm{C} \neq \mathrm{C}'$. This is guaranteed by the correctness property of the encryption scheme PKE that builds C'. There should not be possible to find $\mathbf{warr}$ such that C (equal to C') decrypts to it. We take $m_0 = (upk_j, \mathbf{warr}, \sigma_s, otsvk)$ and $m_1 = (upk_j, \mathbf{warr}', \sigma_s', otsvk)$ be two different messages that both encrypt to C'. According to the correctness of PKE, C' must decrypt with overwhelming probability to one of the two message.

The probability of adversary $\mathcal{A}$ to win G_6 is bounded by the probability of creating a OTS forgery without knowledge of $otssk$, that passed the verification in the body of experiment G_6.

From the sequence of games starting $G_0, \ldots, G_6$, it follows that the probability of E_1 are bounded by unforgeability of DS, strong unforgeability of OTS, and zero-knowledge of NIZK_1.

The experiment E_2 models the case where the adversary $\mathcal{A}$ is able to provide a forged TS signature for an honest authority apk_i and some attribute a. The capabilities of the adversary $\mathcal{A}$ in this case is bounded by the unforgeability adversary for TS. □

Lemma 3. *The generic HABS construction from Fig. 6 offers path traceability, if NIZK_1 is sound and TS is unforgeable.*

Proof. See full version in [16].

Theorem 1. *The proposed HABS construction in Fig. 6 offers path anonymity, non-frameability, and path traceability under the assumptions that PKE is IND-CCA2 secure, TS and DS are unforgeable, OTS is strongly unforgeable, NIZK_1 and NIZK_2 are both sound zero-knowledge proofs.*

Proof. The proof follows from Lemmas 1, 2 and 3.

3.4   Instantiating the HABS Building Blocks

Instantiation. We instantiate HABS in the bilinear group setting. For the digital signature DS we use the constant-sized structure preserving scheme by Abe et al. [1], whereas for TS we use their unbounded-message version of their scheme. These are unforgeable under the Simultaneous Flexible Pairing (SFP) [1] assumption. We use an encryption scheme by Camenish et al. [10] that is capable of encrypting message vectors for our IND-CCA2 PKE, which relies on the DLIN assumption. Finally, for the one-time signature OTS we use the full Boneh-Boyen signature scheme [6], which is strongly unforgeable under the q-Strong Diffie-Hellman (q-SDH) assumption.

For the proofs NIZK_1 and NIZK_2, we use Groth-Sahai (GS) proof systems [24], the security of which is also based on the DLIN assumption in the symmetric setting. These are efficient, non-interactive proof systems in the CRS model that are complete, sound, and zero-knowledge. Briefly, the GS proof system works by commiting to the elements of the witness and then showing they satisfy the source equation. The equation must take the form of either a Pairing Product Equation (PPE), a Multi-Scalar Multiplication Equation (MSME) or a Quadratic Equation (QE). We refer to [24] for full details and give an overview of our constructions for NIZK_1 and NIZK_2 in the full version [16].

Efficiency. We briefly consider the efficiency of our HABS scheme. For our instantiation of OTS, the public key requires 4 group elements and the short signature only requires 3 elements from $\mathbb{G}$ and one element from $\mathbb{Z}_p$. The ciphertext C computed using PKE requires $n + 8$ elements from $\mathbb{G}$, where n is the number of elements in the public keys and tagged-signatures from the delegation paths in the warrant. However, the size of TS used to delegate and issue attributes depends linearly on the distance of the intermediate authority from the root authority in the delegation path, simply because the number of messages (authorities' public keys) increases by one with each delegation. Therefore, the proof NIZK$_1$ that includes a proof that the warrant contains a valid path also grows linearly in this parameter.

To prove satisfiability of the signing predicate Ψ, a proof containing 2β elements from $\mathbb{Z}_p$ is constructed, where β is the size of the span program $\mathbf{S}$. The proof that DS verifies is of constant size and requires 72 elements of $\mathbb{G}$.

Finally, the size of the proof in NIZK$_1$ that C was encrypted correctly is linear in the number of delegations in the warrant, this is inevitable since we need to prove the validity for each authority-signature pair on the delegation path. Similarly, this is also the case for the proof of correctness for decryption of C in NIZK$_2$.

We note that if we consider HABS in the setting where the maximum delegation path of an attribute has length 1, then the size of a HABS signature is linear in the size of the policy Ψ, which is consistent with other ABS schemes that also offer flexible signing policies, e.g., [18, 22, 32].

3.5   Other Properties

In the following we discuss some further properties that can be adopted within our general HABS construction.

Revocation. Our generic HABS construction can be extended to support revocation of attribute authorites and users by means of public revocations lists RL authenticated by the root authority. These lists would include public keys of revoked authorities and users. To enable detection of revoked entities upon verification of HABS signatures, the proof NIZK$_1$ can be extended to prove that for all attributes used to satisfy the policy none of the public keys in the corresponding delegation paths within the signer's warrant **warr** is included into these lists. Since HABS signatures hide delegation paths this approach would preserve privacy by ensuring that no verifier can identify the revoked signer. Due to its complexity, $O(r \sum_a |\mathbf{warr}[a]|)$ where r is the number of revoked public keys, this method might not scale well and hence finding more efficient revocation mechanisms can be seen as an interesting open problem.

Independent Hierarchies. Assume there are multiple HABS hierarchies, each managed by an independent root authority, and any (intermediate) authority or user should be able to receive attributes from different such hierarchies. Our general HABS construction naturally supports this scenario. In particular, warrants can include attributes (along with their signed delegation paths) that were issued to the entity by authorities belonging to other hierarchies and consequently the proof $\mathtt{NIZK_1}$ can enable generation of HABS signatures for predicates Ψ requiring possession of attributes from these hierarchies.

4 Conclusion

The notion of Hierarchical ABS (HABS) introduced in this paper extends the functionality for existing (multi-authority) ABS schemes with some useful properties that can help to expand the application domain of ABS signatures, e.g. to intelligent transport systems. The extended properties of HABS include: (1) support for dynamically expandable hierarchical formation of attribute authorities, managed by some root authority, (2) hierarchical delegation of attribute-issuing rights amongst the authorities, (3) the ability to issue attributes to signers by multiple authorities, possibly located at different levels of the hierarchy, (4) generated ABS signatures that hide signers, their attributes together with their delegation paths, (5) support for a publicly verifiable tracing procedure that enables accountability for all entities that were involved in the delegation and issue of an attribute to a signer. This brings ABS schemes closer to traditional hierarchically-organised PKIs while preserving the valuable privacy properties and security guarantees of the attribute-based setting. The proposed generic HABS construction makes use of standard cryptographic building blocks that can be instantiated in the setting of bilinear maps based on the DLIN, q-SDH and SFP assumptions. We discussed further how our HABS construction offers natural support for scenarios where the same authority or user is admitted to multiple, independently managed hierarchies and needs to bundle attributes obtained in these hierarchies to satisfy some predicate, and how it can be extended to revoke attribute authorities and signers.

Acknowledgements. DG was supported by the UK Government PhD studentship scheme. CD and MM were supported by the EPSRC project TAPESTRY (EP/N02799X). The authors also thank the reviewers of CANS 2018 and Alfredo Rial for valuable comments.

References

1. Abe, M., Fuchsbauer, G., Groth, J., Haralambiev, K., Ohkubo, M.: Structure-preserving signatures and commitments to group elements. In: Rabin, T. (ed.) CRYPTO 2010. LNCS, vol. 6223, pp. 209–236. Springer, Heidelberg (2010). https://doi.org/10.1007/978-3-642-14623-7_12

2. Backes, M., Meiser, S., Schröder, D.: Delegatable functional signatures. In: Cheng, C.-M., Chung, K.-M., Persiano, G., Yang, B.-Y. (eds.) PKC 2016. LNCS, vol. 9614, pp. 357–386. Springer, Heidelberg (2016). https://doi.org/10.1007/978-3-662-49384-7_14

3. Belenkiy, M., Camenisch, J., Chase, M., Kohlweiss, M., Lysyanskaya, A., Shacham, H.: Randomizable proofs and delegatable anonymous credentials. In: Halevi, S. (ed.) CRYPTO 2009. LNCS, vol. 5677, pp. 108–125. Springer, Heidelberg (2009). https://doi.org/10.1007/978-3-642-03356-8_7

4. Bellare, M., Fuchsbauer, G.: Policy-based signatures. In: Krawczyk, H. (ed.) PKC 2014. LNCS, vol. 8383, pp. 520–537. Springer, Heidelberg (2014). https://doi.org/10.1007/978-3-642-54631-0_30

5. Blum, M., Feldman, P., Micali, S.: Non-interactive zero-knowledge and its applications. In: STOC 1988, pp. 103–112 (1988)

6. Boneh, D., Boyen, X.: Short signatures without random oracles. In: Cachin, C., Camenisch, J.L. (eds.) EUROCRYPT 2004. LNCS, vol. 3027, pp. 56–73. Springer, Heidelberg (2004). https://doi.org/10.1007/978-3-540-24676-3_4

7. Boyen, X.: Mesh signatures. In: Naor, M. (ed.) EUROCRYPT 2007. LNCS, vol. 4515, pp. 210–227. Springer, Heidelberg (2007). https://doi.org/10.1007/978-3-540-72540-4_12

8. Boyle, E., Goldwasser, S., Ivan, I.: Functional signatures and pseudorandom functions. In: Krawczyk, H. (ed.) PKC 2014. LNCS, vol. 8383, pp. 501–519. Springer, Heidelberg (2014). https://doi.org/10.1007/978-3-642-54631-0_29

9. Camenisch, J., Drijvers, M., Dubovitskaya, M.: Practical UC-secure delegatable credentials with attributes and their application to blockchain. In: ACMCCS 2017, pp. 683–699 (2017)

10. Camenisch, J., Haralambiev, K., Kohlweiss, M., Lapon, J., Naessens, V.: Structure preserving CCA secure encryption and its application to oblivious third parties. Cryptology ePrint Archive, Report 2011/319 (2011)

11. Camenisch, J., Krontiris, I., Lehmann, A., Neven, G., Paquin, C., Rannenberg, K., Zwingelberg, H.: H2.1 abc4trust architecture for developers (2011). abc4trust.eu

12. Camenisch, J., Lysyanskaya, A.: A signature scheme with efficient protocols. In: Cimato, S., Persiano, G., Galdi, C. (eds.) SCN 2002. LNCS, vol. 2576, pp. 268–289. Springer, Heidelberg (2003). https://doi.org/10.1007/3-540-36413-7_20

13. Chaum, D.: Security without identification: transaction systems to make big brother obsolete. Commun. ACM **28**(10), 1030–1044 (1985)

14. Chaum, D., van Heyst, E.: Group signatures. In: Davies, D.W. (ed.) EUROCRYPT 1991. LNCS, vol. 547, pp. 257–265. Springer, Heidelberg (1991). https://doi.org/10.1007/3-540-46416-6_22

15. Ding, S., Zhao, Y., Liu, Y.: Efficient traceable attribute-based signature. In: IEEE TRUSTCOM 2014, pp. 582–589 (2014)

16. Dragan, C.-C., Gardham, D., Manulis, M.: Hierarchical attribute-based signatures. IACR Cryptology ePrint Archive (2018). https://eprint.iacr.org/2018/610

17. El Kaafarani, A., Ghadafi, E.: Attribute-based signatures with user-controlled linkability without random oracles. In: O'Neill, M. (ed.) IMACC 2017. LNCS, vol. 10655, pp. 161–184. Springer, Cham (2017). https://doi.org/10.1007/978-3-319-71045-7_9

18. El Kaafarani, A., Ghadafi, E., Khader, D.: Decentralized traceable attribute-based signatures. In: Benaloh, J. (ed.) CT-RSA 2014. LNCS, vol. 8366, pp. 327–348. Springer, Cham (2014). https://doi.org/10.1007/978-3-319-04852-9_17

19. Escala, A., Herranz, J., Morillo, P.: Revocable attribute-based signatures with adaptive security in the standard model. In: Nitaj, A., Pointcheval, D. (eds.) AFRICACRYPT 2011. LNCS, vol. 6737, pp. 224–241. Springer, Heidelberg (2011). https://doi.org/10.1007/978-3-642-21969-6_14

20. Fuchsbauer, G., Pointcheval, D.: Anonymous proxy signatures. In: Ostrovsky, R., De Prisco, R., Visconti, I. (eds.) SCN 2008. LNCS, vol. 5229, pp. 201–217. Springer, Heidelberg (2008). https://doi.org/10.1007/978-3-540-85855-3_14

21. Gagné, M., Narayan, S., Safavi-Naini, R.: Short pairing-efficient threshold-attribute-based signature. In: Abdalla, M., Lange, T. (eds.) Pairing 2012. LNCS, vol. 7708, pp. 295–313. Springer, Heidelberg (2013). https://doi.org/10.1007/978-3-642-36334-4_19

22. Ghadafi, E.: Stronger security notions for decentralized traceable attribute-based signatures and more efficient constructions. In: Nyberg, K. (ed.) CT-RSA 2015. LNCS, vol. 9048, pp. 391–409. Springer, Cham (2015). https://doi.org/10.1007/978-3-319-16715-2_21

23. Gisdakis, S., Lagana, M., Giannetsos, T., Papadimitratos, P.: SEROSA: service oriented security architecture for vehicular communications. In: IEEE VNC 2013, pp. 111–118 (2013)

24. Groth, J., Sahai, A.: Efficient non-interactive proof systems for bilinear groups. In: Smart, N. (ed.) EUROCRYPT 2008. LNCS, vol. 4965, pp. 415–432. Springer, Heidelberg (2008). https://doi.org/10.1007/978-3-540-78967-3_24

25. Guo, J., Baugh, J.P., Wang, S.: A group signature based secure and privacy-preserving vehicular communication framework. In: Mobile NVE 2007, pp. 103–108 (2007)

26. Herranz, J.: Attribute-based signatures from RSA. TCS **527**, 73–82 (2014)

27. Hubaux, J.-P., Čapkun, S., Luo, J.: The security and privacy of smart vehicles. IEEE Secur. Priv. **2**(3), 49–55 (2004)

28. Kaaniche, N., Laurent, M., Rocher, P.-O., Kiennert, C., Garcia-Alfaro, J.: $\mathcal{PCS}$, A privacy-preserving certification scheme. In: Garcia-Alfaro, J., Navarro-Arribas, G., Hartenstein, H., Herrera-Joancomartí, J. (eds.) ESORICS/DPM/CBT -2017. LNCS, vol. 10436, pp. 239–256. Springer, Cham (2017). https://doi.org/10.1007/978-3-319-67816-0_14

29. Kamat, P., Baliga, A., Trappe, W.: An identity-based security framework for vanets. In: ACM VANET 2006, pp. 94–95. ACM (2006)

30. Krzywiecki, Ł., Sulkowska, M., Zagórski, F.: Hierarchical ring signatures revisited – unconditionally and perfectly anonymous schnorr version. In: Chakraborty, R.S., Schwabe, P., Solworth, J. (eds.) SPACE 2015. LNCS, vol. 9354, pp. 329–346. Springer, Cham (2015). https://doi.org/10.1007/978-3-319-24126-5_19

31. Li, J., Au, M.H., Susilo, W., Xie, D., Ren, K.: Attribute-based signature and its applications. In: ACM ASIACCS 2010, pp. 60–69. ACM (2010)

32. Maji, H.K., Prabhakaran, M., Rosulek, M.: Attribute-based signatures. In: Kiayias, A. (ed.) CT-RSA 2011. LNCS, vol. 6558, pp. 376–392. Springer, Heidelberg (2011). https://doi.org/10.1007/978-3-642-19074-2_24

33. Neven, G., Baldini, G., Camenisch, J., Neisse, R.: Privacy-preserving attribute-based credentials in cooperative intelligent transport systems. In: IEEE VNC 2017, pp. 131–138 (2017)

34. Okamoto, T., Takashima, K.: Decentralized attribute-based signatures. In: Kurosawa, K., Hanaoka, G. (eds.) PKC 2013. LNCS, vol. 7778, pp. 125–142. Springer, Heidelberg (2013). https://doi.org/10.1007/978-3-642-36362-7_9

35. Okamoto, T., Takashima, K.: Efficient attribute-based signatures for non-monotone predicates in the standard model. In: Catalano, D., Fazio, N., Gennaro, R., Nicolosi, A. (eds.) PKC 2011. LNCS, vol. 6571, pp. 35–52. Springer, Heidelberg (2011). https://doi.org/10.1007/978-3-642-19379-8_3

36. Petit, J., Schaub, F., Feiri, M., Kargl, F.: Pseudonym schemes in vehicular networks: a survey. IEEE Commun. Surv. Tutor. **17**(1), 228–255 (2015)

37. Rivest, R.L., Shamir, A., Tauman, Y.: How to leak a secret. In: Boyd, C. (ed.) ASIACRYPT 2001. LNCS, vol. 2248, pp. 552–565. Springer, Heidelberg (2001). https://doi.org/10.1007/3-540-45682-1_32
38. Sampigethaya, K., Li, M., Huang, L., Poovendran, R.: AMOEBA: robust location privacy scheme for VANET. IEEE J.-SAC **25**(8), 1569–1589 (2007)
39. Schaub, F., Ma, Z., Kargl, F.: Privacy requirements in vehicular communication systems. In: CSE 2009, pp. 139–145 (2009)
40. Sun, J., Zhang, C., Zhang, Y., Fang, Y.M.: An identity-based security system for user privacy in vehicular ad hoc networks. IEEE Trans. Parallel Distrib. Syst. **21**(9), 1227–1239 (2010)
41. Trolin, M., Wikström, D.: Hierarchical Group Signatures. In: Caires, L., Italiano, G.F., Monteiro, L., Palamidessi, C., Yung, M. (eds.) ICALP 2005. LNCS, vol. 3580, pp. 446–458. Springer, Heidelberg (2005). https://doi.org/10.1007/11523468_37
42. Tsabary, R.: An equivalence between attribute-based signatures and homomorphic signatures, and new constructions for both. In: Kalai, Y., Reyzin, L. (eds.) TCC 2017. LNCS, vol. 10678, pp. 489–518. Springer, Cham (2017). https://doi.org/10.1007/978-3-319-70503-3_16

Enhanced Security of Attribute-Based Signatures

Johannes Blömer, Fabian Eidens$^{(\boxtimes)}$, and Jakob Juhnke

Department of Computer Science, Paderborn University, Paderborn, Germany
{bloemer,feidens,juhnke}@mail.uni-paderborn.de

Abstract. Despite the recent advances in attribute-based signatures (ABS), no schemes have yet been considered under a strong privacy definition. We enhance the security of ABS by presenting a strengthened simulation-based privacy definition and the first attribute-based signature functionality in the framework of universal composability (UC). Additionally, we show that the UC definition is equivalent to our strengthened experiment-based security definitions. To achieve this we rely on a general unforgeability and a simulation-based privacy definition that is stronger than standard indistinguishability-based privacy. Further, we show that two extant concrete ABS constructions satisfy this simulation-based privacy definition and are therefore UC secure. The two concrete constructions are the schemes by Sakai et al. (PKC'16) and by Maji et al. (CT-RSA'11). Additionally, we identify the common feature that allows these schemes to meet our privacy definition, giving us further insights into the security requirements of ABS.

Keywords: Attribute-based signatures · Privacy ·
Universal composability

1 Introduction

Attribute-based signature schemes and an experiment-based security definition were introduced by Maji, Prabhakaran and Rosulek [15]. The concept of attribute-based signatures considers several signers and an authority that issues secret keys to them. Secret keys encode an attribute set. Attribute-based signatures are computed on message-policy pairs under a secret key. Policies are for example Boolean formulas over the attributes. To generate a valid signature a signer has to possess a secret key where the encoded attributes satisfy the given policy. Given an attribute-based signature everyone is able to verify whether it was generated by a signer that possesses attributes satisfying the given policy.

J. Blömer, F. Eidens and J. Juhnke—This author was partially supported by the German Research Foundation (DFG) within the Collaborative Research Centre On-The-Fly Computing (SFB 901).

J. Blömer and J. Juhnke—This author was supported by the Ministry of Education and Research, grant 16SV7055, project "KogniHome".

© Springer Nature Switzerland AG 2018
J. Camenisch and P. Papadimitratos (Eds.): CANS 2018, LNCS 11124, pp. 235–255, 2018.
https://doi.org/10.1007/978-3-030-00434-7_12

The validity of a signature is therefore not bound to a single signer's identity but rather to a group of signers, namely those with satisfying attributes.

A secure ABS must be unforgeable and (perfectly) private. Unforgeability means that a valid signature on a message-policy pair can only be generated by a signer, whose attributes satisfy the policy. Further, no group of colluding signers can generate a signature on a message-policy pair if none of them has attributes satisfying the policy. Privacy captures that a signature is independent of the secret key used to generate it.

1.1   Related Work

Throughout the literature experiment-based security definitions covering unforgeability and privacy for ABS schemes have been proposed, cf. [4,10,15–17]. A general unforgeability definition is given by Okamoto and Takashima [16], where the definitions in [10,15,17] are restricted to specific policy classes.

Regarding privacy there are two definitions, perfect and computational privacy. Computational privacy is defined by an experiment with explicit capabilities of bounded adversaries, cf. [4,10,12]. For unbounded adversaries perfect privacy is defined considering distributions of signatures [14–17]. In particular one demands that the distributions are independent of the secret keys. Another notion of privacy is called simulation-based privacy and was originally presented by Bellare and Fuchsbauer [4] in the context of policy-based signatures, a more general concept than ABS. The authors [4] also show that policy-based signatures imply attribute-based signatures in the model of Maji et al. [15]. Hence their security definitions can be specialized to ABS.

Recent advances in ABS led to efficient schemes that support large classes of policies. The recent scheme by Sakai et al. [17] supports arbitrary circuits of unbounded size and depth. A further efficient scheme is presented by Okamoto and Takashima [16], supporting non-monotone span programs as policies. A generic ABS construction with monotone span programs as policies is presented by Maji et al. [15]. All these ABS schemes and security definitions look at ABS as an isolated primitive. However, in real applications ABS is combined and composed with other cryptographic primitives to achieve more comprehensive security goals. For example, ABS can be deployed as an authentication mechanism for service providers, i.e. in a challenge-response protocol. In such a protocol the user is asked to sign a policy and a nonce given by the service provider. Such authentication mechanisms are deployed in large scale applications. Canetti [7] introduced the universal composable framework (UC) to describe and prove security for such applications. UC guarantees security even if an arbitrary number of cryptographic primitives are executed concurrently and it is based on the simulation-paradigm.

Regarding the experiment-based and UC security of a cryptographic primitive there are four questions that have to be answered. First, is there a general experiment-based security definition that precisely captures the security aspect of the cryptographic primitive? Second, whether there exist schemes that are secure with respect to the experiment-based security definition. The third question is, how to define security for that primitive in the UC framework? The last question is, whether the experiment-based security definition and the UC security definition are equivalent. With respect to ABS the first question can be answered by the general unforgeability definition in [16] and the simulation-based privacy definition presented in [4]. However, the answer is not yet satisfactory for achieving UC security. To the best of our knowledge, no one has yet answered the remaining three questions in the context of ABS. However the three questions have been considered for other related primitives. With respect to the third question Ateniese et al. [3] construct a UC secure group signature scheme and Camenisch et al. [5] present a UC secure anonymous credential system. Regarding the fourth question Canetti shows in [8] that his ideal digital signature functionality is equivalent to the standard security definition (EUF-CMA) [11].

1.2 Our Contribution

In this paper we answer the four questions for attribute-based signatures. First, we give a strengthened experiment-based security definition using a simulation-based privacy definition. Second, we show that existing schemes satisfy this definition. Third, we model the first (to our knowledge) universally composable attribute-based signature functionality. Considering the fourth question, our main theorem shows the equivalence of the experiment-based and UC security of attribute-based signatures under standard requirements on the environment. The theorem is shown considering adaptive corruption of parties with erasure of ephemeral randomness and secure communication channels. We explain the requirements in detail in Sect. 3.1. Our results show that existing ABS schemes achieve UC security with only minor modifications.

In this paper we argue that the security definitions for ABS used so far do not guarantee the desired privacy and as a consequence our definition should be used. Our experiment-based security definition is based on existing unforgeability and privacy definitions. It incorporates the general ABS unforgeability definition by Okamoto and Takashima [16]. For our perfect simulation-based privacy definition we use as a basis the computational simulation privacy definition by Bellare and Fuchsbauer [4]. The authors [4] show for policy-based signatures that *computational* simulation privacy is stronger than *computational* privacy used in [2,10,14–17]. Based on our security definitions for ABS we show that *perfect* simulation privacy is stronger than *perfect* privacy.

Our UC ideal ABS functionality is based on the ideal digital signatures from Canetti [8], extended to support multiple signing parties and signature creation on message-policy pairs under secret keys with attributes. Therefore, our ideal ABS functionality is one of a few functionalities that consider multiple parties concurrently executing cryptographic tasks. Other such functionalities include the multi-commitments by Lindell [13], the group signatures by Ateniese et al. [3], and the anonymous credentials by Camenisch et al. [5].

Further, we show that our experiment-based security definition implies UC security for attribute-based signature schemes with minimal restrictions on the environment. In our proof the simulation aspect of the privacy definition is the essential ingredient. We also show the reverse direction, i.e. a UC secure ABS scheme also satisfies our experiment-based security definition. The proof of this result is inspired by the work of Abe and Ohkubo [1] on UC secure blind signature schemes. To show the applicability of our results we prove that the generic ABS constructions by Sakai et al. [17] and by Maji et al. [15] satisfy our simulation-based privacy definition and therefore achieve UC security. Since originally for both schemes weaker privacy guarantees were shown, we think that simulation-based privacy is interesting on its own.

2   Attribute-Based Signatures

In the following we formally define attribute-based signature (ABS) schemes and their experiment-based security notions.

Definition 1. *An ABS scheme Π_{ABS} consists of four algorithms:*

Setup(1^λ) *Probabilistic algorithm that takes as input security parameter 1^λ and outputs public parameters and master secret* $(\mathsf{pp}, \mathsf{msk})$, *where* pp *includes a description of the attribute universe denoted by* $\mathbb{U}(\mathsf{pp})$.

KeyGen$(\mathsf{pp}, \mathsf{msk}, \mathbb{A})$ *Probabilistic algorithm that takes as input* pp, msk, *and a set of attributes* $\mathbb{A} \subseteq \mathbb{U}(\mathsf{pp})$. *It outputs a signing key* $\mathsf{sk}_{\mathbb{A}}$.

Sign$(\mathsf{pp}, \mathsf{sk}_{\mathbb{A}}, m, \mathbb{P})$ *Probabilistic algorithm that takes as input public parameters* pp, *a message m, a policy $\mathbb{P}$ over the attributes of* $\mathbb{U}(\mathsf{pp})$, *and a signing key* $\mathsf{sk}_{\mathbb{A}}$, *such that* $\mathbb{P}(\mathbb{A}) = 1$. *It outputs a signature σ.*

Verify$(\mathsf{pp}, m, \mathbb{P}, \sigma)$ *Probabilistic algorithm that takes as input* pp, *a message m, a policy $\mathbb{P}$, and a signature σ. It outputs* $b \in \{0, 1\}$; *valid $= 1$, invalid $= 0$.*

How the universe, attributes, and policies are encoded and interpreted depends on the concrete scheme. We denote attributes $\mathbb{A}$ as subsets of $\mathbb{U}(\mathsf{pp})$ and a policy $\mathbb{P}$ is a map $\mathbb{P} : 2^{\mathbb{U}(\mathsf{pp})} \to \{0, 1\}$. Alternatively, we could also write $\mathbb{A} \in \mathbb{U}(\mathsf{pp})$ and $\mathbb{P} : \mathbb{U}(\mathsf{pp}) \to \{0, 1\}$ which is better suited for ABS schemes supporting attribute vectors of fixed length as in [17]. With $\mathbb{P} \in \mathbb{U}(\mathsf{pp})$ we denote that the policy $\mathbb{P}$ is defined over the attributes of the universe $\mathbb{U}(\mathsf{pp})$.

Definition 2 (Correctness). *An scheme Π_{ABS} is correct, if for all* $(\mathsf{pp}, \mathsf{msk}) \leftarrow \mathrm{Setup}(1^\lambda)$, *all m, all attribute sets $\mathbb{A} \subseteq \mathbb{U}(\mathsf{pp})$, all $\mathsf{sk}_{\mathbb{A}} \leftarrow$ KeyGen$(\mathsf{pp}, \mathsf{msk}, \mathbb{A})$, all policies $\mathbb{P} \in \mathbb{U}(\mathsf{pp})$ such that $\mathbb{P}(\mathbb{A}) = 1$, and all $\sigma \leftarrow$ Sign$(\mathsf{pp}, \mathsf{sk}_{\mathbb{A}}, m, \mathbb{P})$, it holds that* Verify$(\mathsf{pp}, m, \mathbb{P}, \sigma) = 0$ *with at most negligible probability $\epsilon(\lambda)$ where the probability is over the random choices of Sign and Verify.*

Correctness guarantees under honestly generated setup parameters, that signatures, computed with honestly generated secret keys, on message-policy pairs are valid with overwhelming probability.

Definition 3 (Consistency). *An ABS scheme Π_{ABS} is consistent, if for all m, $\mathbb{P}$, and σ it holds that there exists $b \in \{0,1\}$ such that $\Pr[(\mathsf{pp}, \mathsf{msk}) \leftarrow \mathrm{Setup}(1^\lambda)\colon \mathrm{Verify}(\mathsf{pp}, m, \mathbb{P}, \sigma) \neq b] \leq \epsilon(\lambda)$, where $\epsilon(\lambda)$ is negligible in λ and the probability is over randomness of Setup and Verify.*

Our definition of ABS considers a probabilistic Verify algorithm. Therefore, consistency guarantees that a signature that was once declared by Verify as valid will be declared as invalid by an independent run of Verify only with negligible probability (and vice versa).

Definition 4. *For a forger F, we define the experiment $\mathrm{Exp}_F^{\mathrm{UF}}(\lambda)$ as follows:*

1. *Run $(\mathsf{pp}, \mathsf{msk}) \leftarrow \mathrm{Setup}(1^\lambda)$, start $F(\mathsf{pp})$.*
2. *F may adaptively make queries of the following type:*
   $\mathcal{O}_{\mathsf{pp},\mathsf{msk}}^{\mathrm{KeyGen}}(\mathbb{A}_i)$: On i-th query, given attribute set $\mathbb{A}_i \subseteq \mathbb{U}(\mathsf{pp})$ it generates $\mathsf{sk}_{\mathbb{A}_i} \leftarrow \mathrm{KeyGen}(\mathsf{pp}, \mathsf{msk}, \mathbb{A}_i)$ and records $(i, \mathsf{sk}_{\mathbb{A}_i})$.
   $\mathcal{O}^{\mathrm{Reveal}}(i)$: Given i specifying an already queried secret key for $\mathbb{A}_i$, it outputs the corresponding secret key $\mathsf{sk}_{\mathbb{A}_i}$.
   $\mathcal{O}_{\mathsf{pp},\mathsf{msk}}^{\mathrm{Sign}}(i, m_j, \mathbb{P}_j)$: On j-th query, given $(i, m_j, \mathbb{P}_j)$ for an already queried $\mathbb{A}_i$ where $\mathbb{P}_j(\mathbb{A}_i) = 1$, $\mathbb{P}_j \in \mathbb{U}(\mathsf{pp})$, it returns $\sigma \leftarrow \mathrm{Sign}(\mathsf{pp}, \mathsf{sk}_{\mathbb{A}_i}, m_j, \mathbb{P}_j)$ for message m_j, policy $\mathbb{P}_j$ and secret key $\mathsf{sk}_{\mathbb{A}_i}$.
3. *Eventually F outputs a triple $(m^*, \mathbb{P}^*, \sigma^*)$*
4. *The output is 1, if all of the following conditions hold, else it is 0,*
   (a) a signature for $(m^*, \mathbb{P}^*)$ was never queried and
   (b) for all $\mathbb{A}_i$, where the corresponding secret key $\mathsf{sk}_{\mathbb{A}_i}$ was output by the reveal oracle $\mathcal{O}^{\mathrm{Reveal}}$, it holds that $\mathbb{P}^*(\mathbb{A}_i) \neq 1$, and
   (c) $\mathrm{Verify}(\mathsf{pp}, m^*, \mathbb{P}^*, \sigma^*) = 1$.

Definition 5 (Unforgeability). *An ABS scheme is unforgeable regarding an adaptive attack if for all ppt forger F, $\Pr\left[\mathrm{Exp}_F^{\mathrm{UF}}(\lambda) = 1\right]$ is negligible in λ.*

The above definition originally presented in [16] guarantees collusion resistance in the following sense. The adversary can get secret keys on attribute sets of his choice by first querying $\mathcal{O}_{\mathsf{pp},\mathsf{msk}}^{\mathrm{KeyGen}}$ and then $\mathcal{O}^{\mathrm{Reveal}}$. Even with secret keys of his choice he can not output a valid signature for $\mathbb{P}^*$ if none of the revealed secret keys (representing a group of colluding signers) would be sufficient to satisfy $\mathbb{P}^*$.

2.1 Privacy

We present two privacy definitions. The first one captures that an adversary choosing two secret keys should not be able to tell which secret key was used to generate a signature. The second definition is simulation-based and requires that even the attributes used to generate a signature are hidden. For both definitions we specialize the definitions for policy-based signatures presented in [4] to ABS.

Standard Privacy. Contrary to the privacy definition based on distributions of signatures used in [12,15–17] we define an experiment similar to [4], where the capabilities of the adversary are explicitly stated.

Definition 6. *For an ABS scheme* $\Pi_{\mathrm{ABS}} = (\mathrm{Setup}, \mathrm{KeyGen}, \mathrm{Sign}, \mathrm{Verify})$ *and dist.* D *we define the privacy experiment* $\mathrm{P}_D^{\Pi_{\mathrm{ABS}}}(\lambda, b)$ *for* $b \in \{0, 1\}$ *as follows.*

$\mathrm{P}_D^{\Pi_{\mathrm{ABS}}}(\lambda, b)$:

  $(\mathsf{pp}, \mathsf{msk}) \leftarrow \mathrm{Setup}(1^\lambda)$

  $\tilde{b} \leftarrow D^{\mathcal{O}_{\mathsf{pp,msk}}^b}(\mathsf{pp}, \mathsf{msk})$

  return $\tilde{b}$

$\mathcal{O}_{\mathsf{pp,msk}}^b(m, \mathbb{P}, \mathbb{A}_0, \mathbb{A}_1)$:

  If $\mathbb{P}(\mathbb{A}_0) = 1$, $\mathbb{P}(\mathbb{A}_1) = 1$, *and* $\mathbb{P} \in$

  $\mathbb{U}(\mathsf{pp})$, *it generates:*

    $\mathsf{sk}_{\mathbb{A}_0} \leftarrow \mathrm{KeyGen}(\mathsf{pp}, \mathsf{msk}, \mathbb{A}_0)$,

    $\mathsf{sk}_{\mathbb{A}_1} \leftarrow \mathrm{KeyGen}(\mathsf{pp}, \mathsf{msk}, \mathbb{A}_1)$,

    $\sigma \leftarrow \mathrm{Sign}\,(\mathsf{pp}, \mathsf{sk}_{\mathbb{A}_b}, m, \mathbb{P})$,

  and returns $(\sigma, \mathsf{sk}_{\mathbb{A}_1}, \mathsf{sk}_{\mathbb{A}_2})$

Definition 7 (Privacy). *For an ABS scheme* $\Pi_{\mathrm{ABS}} = (\mathrm{Setup}, \mathrm{KeyGen}, \mathrm{Sign}, \mathrm{Verify})$ *we define:*

Perfect Privacy Π_{ABS} *is* PP *if for every distinguisher* D *it holds that*

$$\mathrm{Adv}_D^{\mathrm{PP}}(\lambda) = \left| \Pr\left[\mathrm{P}_D^{\Pi_{\mathrm{ABS}}}(\lambda, 0) = 1 \right] - \Pr\left[\mathrm{P}_D^{\Pi_{\mathrm{ABS}}}(\lambda, 1) = 1 \right] \right| = 0 \ .$$

Computational Privacy Π_{ABS} *is* CP, *if for every ppt dist.* D *it holds that*

$$\mathrm{Adv}_D^{\mathrm{CP}}(\lambda) = \left| \Pr\left[\mathrm{P}_D^{\Pi_{\mathrm{ABS}}}(\lambda, 0) = 1 \right] - \Pr\left[\mathrm{P}_D^{\Pi_{\mathrm{ABS}}}(\lambda, 1) = 1 \right] \right| = \epsilon(\lambda) \ ,$$

where $\epsilon(\lambda)$ *is a negligible function in* λ.

The privacy in Definition 7 only states that the relation between the signature and the secret keys is hidden. In particular, an adversary can not determine which signer issued a signature. Another way to describe privacy, is that given a valid signature σ on a policy $\mathbb{P}$ an adversary should not be able to learn which attributes are necessary to satisfy $\mathbb{P}$ from σ, except for what it can compute from $\mathbb{P}$. Simulation privacy achieves this privacy level. To argue why simulation privacy is desirable in practice consider the following example. A similar example is presented in [4] for policy-based signatures. For the example assume a perfectly private ABS scheme according to Definition 7. Additionally, assume for every $\mathbb{P}$ there is just one satisfying attribute set $\mathbb{A}$. Hence, given a policy $\mathbb{P}$ the adversary knows the corresponding satisfying $\mathbb{A}$. Therefore, the adversary in experiment $\mathrm{P}^{\Pi_{\mathrm{ABS}}}$ has to input $\mathbb{A}_0 = \mathbb{A}_1$ for $\mathbb{P}$ to its challenge oracle $\mathcal{O}_{\mathsf{pp,msk}}^b$. Let us modify algorithm Sign such that it appends the attribute set to each signature. As a result, the returned signatures are still indistinguishable as required in Definition 7, but the used attribute set is known after a signature is shown. This is not the desired privacy guarantee in a real world application, where the attributes are secret or the satisfying set of a policy is a secret or hard to compute. To achieve the privacy level that is demanded in such applications we define simulation privacy.

Simulation Privacy. With the simulation-based definition of privacy we require that the signatures are independent of the used attributes. Therefore, simulation privacy is based on a simulation signature algorithm. The normal signature algorithm in ABS gets a secret key for an attribute set as an input, whereas the simulation signature algorithm does not. No adversary should be able to distinguish whether a signature was generated by the normal signature algorithm or by the simulation signature algorithm. Obviously, if signatures can be simulated without a given secret key for satisfying attributes (regarding the given policy), then the signatures themselves does not leak any information about the attributes used to generate it. The following simulation-based definition is originally presented in [4] for policy-based signatures.

Definition 8. *For an ABS scheme* $\Pi_{ABS} = (\text{Setup}, \text{KeyGen}, \text{Sign}, \text{Verify})$, *a 3-tuple of ppt algorithms* $(\text{SimSetup}, \text{SimKeyGen}, \text{SimSign})$ *and distinguisher D we define the simulation privacy experiment* $\text{SP}_D^{\Pi_{ABS}}(\lambda, b)$ *for $b \in \{0, 1\}$ as follows.*

$\text{SP}_D^{\Pi_{ABS}}(\lambda, 1)$:

$(\text{pp}, \text{msk}) \leftarrow \text{Setup}(1^\lambda)$

$\tilde{b} \leftarrow D^{\mathcal{O}_{\text{pp,msk}}^{\text{KeyGen}_1}, \mathcal{O}_{\text{pp,msk}}^{\text{Sign}_1}}(\text{pp}, \text{msk})$

return $\tilde{b}$

$\text{SP}_D^{\Pi_{ABS}}(\lambda, 0)$:

$(\text{pp}, \text{msk}) \leftarrow \text{SimSetup}(1^\lambda)$

$\tilde{b} \leftarrow D^{\mathcal{O}_{\text{pp,msk}}^{\text{KeyGen}_0}, \mathcal{O}_{\text{pp,msk}}^{\text{Sign}_0}}(\text{pp}, \text{msk})$

return $\tilde{b}$

$\mathcal{O}_{\text{pp,msk}}^{\text{KeyGen}_1}(\mathbb{A}_i)$: *On i-th query, given attribute set $\mathbb{A}_i \subseteq \mathbb{U}(\text{pp})$ it outputs* $\text{sk}_{\mathbb{A}_i} \leftarrow \text{KeyGen}(\text{pp}, \text{msk}, \mathbb{A}_i)$ *and records* $(i, \text{sk}_{\mathbb{A}_i})$.

$\mathcal{O}_{\text{pp,msk}}^{\text{KeyGen}_0}(\mathbb{A}_i)$: *On i-th query, given attribute set $\mathbb{A}_i \subseteq \mathbb{U}(\text{pp})$ it outputs* $\text{sk}_{\mathbb{A}_i} \leftarrow \text{SimKeyGen}(\text{pp}, \text{msk}, \mathbb{A}_i)$ *and records* $(i, \text{sk}_{\mathbb{A}_i})$.

$\mathcal{O}_{\text{pp,msk}}^{\text{Sign}_1}(i, m_j, \mathbb{P}_j)$: *On j-th query, given $(i, m_j, \mathbb{P}_j)$ for an already recorded i where $\mathbb{P}_j(\mathbb{A}_i) = 1$, and $\mathbb{P}_j \in \mathbb{U}(\text{pp})$ it returns* $\sigma \leftarrow \text{Sign}(\text{pp}, \text{sk}_{\mathbb{A}_i}, m_j, \mathbb{P}_j)$.

$\mathcal{O}_{\text{pp,msk}}^{\text{Sign}_0}(i, m_j, \mathbb{P}_j)$: *On j-th query, given $(i, m_j, \mathbb{P}_j)$ for an already recorded i where $\mathbb{P}_j(\mathbb{A}_i) = 1$, and $\mathbb{P}_j \in \mathbb{U}(\text{pp})$ it ignores $\mathbb{A}_i$ and $\text{sk}_{\mathbb{A}_i}$. It returns signature* $\sigma \leftarrow \text{SimSign}(\text{pp}, \text{msk}, m_j, \mathbb{P}_j)$.

Definition 9 (Simulation Privacy). *For an attribute-based signature scheme* $\Pi_{ABS} = (\text{Setup}, \text{KeyGen}, \text{Sign}, \text{Verify})$ *we define:*

Perfect Simulation Privacy Π_{ABS} *is PSimP, if there exists a 3-tuple of ppt algorithms* $(\text{SimSetup}, \text{SimKeyGen}, \text{SimSign})$ *such that for all dist. D*

$$\text{Adv}_D^{\text{PSimP}}(\lambda) = \left| \Pr\left[\text{SP}_D^{\Pi_{ABS}}(\lambda, 0) = 1\right] - \Pr\left[\text{SP}_D^{\Pi_{ABS}}(\lambda, 1) = 1\right] \right| = 0 .$$

Comp. Simulation Privacy Π_{ABS} *is CSimP if there exists a 3-tuple of ppt algorithms* $(\text{SimSetup}, \text{SimKeyGen}, \text{SimSign})$ *s.t. for all ppt dist. D it holds*

$$\text{Adv}_D^{\text{CSimP}}(\lambda) = \left| \Pr\left[\text{SP}_D^{\Pi_{ABS}}(\lambda, 0) = 1\right] - \Pr\left[\text{SP}_D^{\Pi_{ABS}}(\lambda, 1) = 1\right] \right| = \epsilon(\lambda) ,$$

where $\epsilon(\lambda)$ is a negligible function in λ.

Theorem 1. *An ABS scheme Π_{ABS} that is perfectly simulation private (Definition 9) is also perfectly private (Definition 7).*

Proof. Assume that Π_{ABS} is not perfectly private then there is a dist. A such that the advantage $\text{Adv}_A^{\text{PP}}(\lambda) = \Pr[\text{P}_A^{\Pi_{\text{ABS}}}(\lambda,1) = 1] - \Pr[\text{P}_A^{\Pi_{\text{ABS}}}(\lambda,0) = 1] > 0$. We construct a distinguisher D for PSimP using A as a black-box. D in $\text{SP}_D^{\Pi_{\text{ABS}}}(\lambda,b)$ works as follows.

1. Given (pp, msk) from challenger C of $\text{SP}_D^{\Pi_{\text{ABS}}}(\lambda,b)$, D runs $A(\text{pp}, \text{msk})$.
2. D flips a coin $d \leftarrow \{0,1\}$.
3. D on the k-th oracle query $(m, \mathbb{P}, \mathbb{A}_0, \mathbb{A}_1)$ where $\mathbb{A}_0, \mathbb{A}_1 \subseteq U(\text{pp})$:
   (a) It checks whether $\mathbb{P}_i(\mathbb{A}_0^*) = 1$ and $\mathbb{P}_i(\mathbb{A}_1^*) = 1$ hold, if not ignore query
   (b) Get $\text{sk}_{\mathbb{A}_0} \leftarrow \mathcal{O}_{\text{pp},\text{msk}}^{\text{KeyGen}_b}(\mathbb{A}_0)$ and $\text{sk}_{\mathbb{A}_1} \leftarrow \mathcal{O}_{\text{pp},\text{msk}}^{\text{KeyGen}_b}(\mathbb{A}_1)$
   (c) Get $\sigma_d \leftarrow \mathcal{O}_{\text{pp},\text{msk}}^{\text{Sign}_b}(2k - 1 + d, m, \mathbb{P})$
   (d) Return $(\sigma_d, \text{sk}_{\mathbb{A}_0}, \text{sk}_{\mathbb{A}_1})$
4. Eventually A outputs $\tilde{d}$.
5. D sets $\tilde{b} := 1$ if $d = \tilde{d}$, otherwise $\tilde{b} := 0$ and outputs $\tilde{b}$.

Let us analyze the advantage of D, $\text{Adv}_D^{\text{PSimP}}(\lambda) = |\Pr[\text{SP}_D^{\Pi_{\text{ABS}}}(\lambda,0) = 1] - \Pr[\text{SP}_D^{\Pi_{\text{ABS}}}(\lambda,1) = 1]|$. Let us first analyze the case where D is in the experiment $\text{SP}_D^{\Pi_{\text{ABS}}}(\lambda, b = 1)$. With $b = 1$ the challenger and the provided oracles use the normal algorithms (Setup, KeyGen, Sign). Hence, we get the following.

$$
\begin{aligned}
\Pr\left[\tilde{b} = 1\right] &= \Pr\left[\tilde{d} = 1 \mid d = 1\right] \cdot \Pr\left[d = 1\right] + \Pr\left[\tilde{d} = 0 \mid d = 0\right] \cdot \Pr\left[d = 0\right] \\
&= \frac{1}{2}\left(\Pr\left[\tilde{d} = 1 \mid d = 1\right] - \Pr\left[\tilde{d} = 1 \mid d = 0\right]\right) + \frac{1}{2} \\
&= \frac{1}{2}\left(\Pr\left[\text{P}_A^{\Pi_{\text{ABS}}}(\lambda,1) = 1\right] - \Pr\left[\text{P}_A^{\Pi_{\text{ABS}}}(\lambda,0) = 1\right]\right) + \frac{1}{2} \\
&= \frac{1}{2}\text{Adv}_A^{\text{PP}}(\lambda) + \frac{1}{2}
\end{aligned}
$$

In the other case $\text{SP}_D^{\Pi_{\text{ABS}}}(\lambda, b = 0)$, the signatures are generated independently from the bit d that D chooses. The signature oracle $\mathcal{O}_{\text{pp},\text{msk}}^{\text{Sign}_0}$ generates signatures with $\text{SimSign}(\text{pp}, \text{msk}, m, \mathbb{P})$. SimSign generates the signature in both cases ($d = 0$, $d = 1$) only with the public parameters, master secret, message and policy as input. Hence, independent of the secret key for the attribute set $\mathbb{A}_d^*$. Consequently, the view of A is independent of d. Therefore, $\Pr[\tilde{b} = 1] = \Pr[d = \tilde{d}] = \frac{1}{2}$. Consequently, it holds that $\text{Adv}_D^{\text{PSimP}}(\lambda) = \frac{1}{2}\text{Adv}_A^{\text{PP}}(\lambda)$. □

The following corollary originally shown in [4] follows from Theorem 1 and that the reduction given in the proof of Theorem 1 is efficient.

Corollary 1. *An ABS scheme Π_{ABS} that is computationally simulation private (Definition 9) is also computationally private (Definition 7).*

For policy-based signatures the authors show in [4] that without restricting the polices the reverse direction of Corollary 1 does not hold, by presenting a counterexample. Since, ABS is a special variant of policy-based signatures, the counterexample can also be applied to the reverse direction of Theorem 1. In the following we will restate the counterexample. To see that simulation-based privacy is a stronger notion than standard privacy, let us consider our example scheme above, where the Sign algorithms appends the used attribute set to the signature. Assume a policy class where computing a satisfying attribute set is computationally hard (satisfiability of CNF formulas). Obviously, the example scheme with this policy class is not perfectly simulation private, since under usual assumptions there is no probabilistic polynomial-time algorithm SimSign that given just the master secret and message, computes the satisfying attribute set and appends it to the signature.

2.2   On the Security of Existing Schemes

In Sect. 3 we present a wrapper protocol that transforms an ABS scheme to be UC compatible. Our main result Theorem 4 shows that if and only if the wrapped ABS scheme is correct, consistent, unforgeable, and simulation private then the wrapper protocol achieves UC security.

In the following we show for two existing ABS schemes [15,17] that they satisfy our perfect simulation privacy definition. Therefore, our main theorem (Theorem 4) shows that the two schemes can be used in the wrapper protocol to achieve UC security. Both schemes were originally shown to satisfy correctness, consistency, unforgeability, and the weaker notion perfect privacy. To show that an ABS schemes is perfectly simulation private we have to define three algorithms (SimSetup, SimKeyGen, SimSign) and prove that they satisfy Definition 9. To achieve this for the ABS schemes [15,17] we only apply minor modifications to the signature algorithms to define simulation signature algorithms SimSign. In particular these modifications do not imply changes to the setup and key generation algorithms.

Both ABS schemes [15,17] are generic constructions. To define a SimSign for the schemes, we exploit a commonality in the normal signature algorithms of both schemes. The normal signature algorithms fulfill two basic properties. First, the signature on a message-policy pair proves that the signer knows a valid secret key on attributes satisfying the policy. Second, it binds the policy to the signed message. In detail for [15,17], a signature on a message-policy pair $(m, \mathbb{P})$ of the normal signature algorithm Sign, proves that the signer knows a secret key for attributes satisfying the given policy $\mathbb{P}$ *OR* that he knows a special signature on $(m, \mathbb{P})$. We exploit the second property to define the SimSign algorithms for both schemes [15,17].

Generic ABS Construction by Sakai et al. [17]. The SimSign algorithm that we present is implicitly given in the unforgeability proof in [17] (Theorem 1 Game 2). For simplicity we just give a high-level description of the algorithm. The scheme [17] uses a non-interactive perfect witness indistinguishable (NIWI) proof system, a collision-resistant hash function H, a secure structure-preserving signature scheme and supports circuits C as policies. For further details especially for the NIWI proofs we refer to [17]. Basically, SimSign is the original signature algorithm Sign of the ABS scheme [17] executed with a special secret key generated on the hash value of the message-policy pair (m, C). This can only be done with the master secret.

SimSign $(\mathsf{pp}, \mathsf{msk}, m, C)$ On input public parameter pp, master secret msk, message m and policy C (policy is a circuit): Step 1 of Sign is modified such that it first computes a special secret key sk_{x^*}. Therefore, it first computes $h \leftarrow \mathrm{H}(\mathsf{hk}, \langle m, C \rangle)$, sets $h := (h_1 \| \ldots \| h_{l_\mathrm{H}})$ and $x^* := (g^1, g^{h_1}, \ldots, g^{h_{l_\mathrm{H}}}, 1, \ldots, 1) \in \mathbb{G}_1^{l+1}$. Then it computes a structure-preserving signature θ^* on x^* and sets $\mathsf{sk}_{x^*} := (x^*, \theta^*)$. Then it expands the circuit C to $\hat{C}$ as in Sign, goes on with steps $2-10$ of Sign and generates a NIWI proof π with θ^* as the witness. At the end of step 10 it outputs signature $\sigma := \pi$.

Changes to Setup and KeyGen are not necessary, since SimSign uses the master secret msk which is already output by Setup. Therefore, we use Setup as SimSetup and KeyGen as SimKeyGen.

Theorem 2. Π_{Sakai} *from [17] combined with* (SimSetup, SimKeyGen, SimSign) *as defined above is perfectly simulation private (Definition 9).*

Proof. Since SimSetup is Setup and SimKeyGen is KeyGen their distribution is unchanged. What is left to show is, that SimSign generates the same distribution as Sign. The output of SimSign and Sign is a proof π that was generated by a perfectly witness indistinguishable proof system. Sign uses the secret key of the signer as the witness, whereas SimSign generates a special secret key x^*, θ^* on-demand with the help of the master secret msk and uses this secret key as the witness. Notice, that both algorithms expand the given circuit C such that it is also satisfied by the hash value used to compute the special secret key. From the perfect witness indistinguishability of the proof system it follows that the distributions of SimSign and Sign are equivalent. □

Generic ABS Construction by Maji et al. [15]. Maji, Prabhakaran and Rosulek present in [15] a generic construction of ABS supporting monotone boolean functions as policies. The construction is based on a NIWI proof systems and so called credential bundles. A secure credential bundle $\mathrm{CB} = \{\mathsf{Setup}, \mathsf{Gen}, \mathsf{Ver}\}$, in its simplest from, can be instantiated with a secure digital signature scheme, cf. [15]. The approach of the SimSign algorithm for this construction is similar to the one that we used above for [17]. Again it is possible to generate a special element using the master secret. The scheme [15] supports a universe of attributes that contains a pseudo-attribute for every message-policy pair $(m, \mathbb{P})$. The scheme in [15] defines a normal signature algorithm Sign that on input $(m, \mathbb{P})$ and a secret key sk first extends the policy to $\mathbb{P}' := \mathbb{P} \vee$ "pseudo-attribute $(m, \mathbb{P})$". Second, it uses the signers secret key sk to generate the signature. For the simulation signature algorithm SimSign we use the master secret to issue a special secret key sk_* for the pseudo-attribute $(m, \mathbb{P})$ and use the extended $\mathbb{P}'$ to generate a signature in the same way as Sign generates it.

First we adapt the syntax and then present the SimSign algorithm in detail. The generic ABS construction in [15] describes five algorithms TSetup, ASetup, AttrGen, Sign and Verify. They define two setup algorithms to separate the setup of the NIWI proofs from the setup for key generation. We define Setup such that it combines TSetup and ASetup in one algorithm. Further, let KeyGen run AttrGen. Accordingly, we define the ABS scheme as $\Pi_{\mathrm{Maji}} = (\mathrm{Setup}, \mathrm{KeyGen}, \mathrm{Sign}, \mathrm{Verify})$. Let $\mathbb{U}$ be the universe of attributes. Let $\mathbb{U}'$ denote the space of pseudo-attributes, where $\mathbb{U} \cap \mathbb{U}' = \emptyset$. One pseudo-attribute $a_{m,\Upsilon} \in \mathbb{U}'$ is added for each pair of message m and policy Υ. A policy is defined as a monotone boolean function $\Upsilon \colon 2^{\mathbb{U}} \to \{0, 1\}$. For perfect simulation privacy we have to provide a SimSetup, SimKeyGen, and SimSign algorithm. We use Setup as SimSetup and KeyGen as SimKeyGen. The following SimSign algorithm is partially given in the proof of Theorem 1 in the original work [15].

SimSign $(\mathsf{pp}, \mathsf{tsk}, m, \Upsilon)$ On input public parameter pp, master secret tsk, message m and policy Υ: Generate a special secret key sk_* with the pseudo-attribute $a_{m,\Upsilon}$ for (m, Υ), $\mathsf{sk}_* := (\tau, \varsigma) \leftarrow \mathrm{CB.Gen}(\mathsf{tsk}, a_{m,\Upsilon})$ output $\pi \leftarrow \mathrm{Sign}(\mathsf{pp}, sk_*, m, \Upsilon)$.

Theorem 3. Π_{Maji} *from [15] combined with* $(\mathrm{SimSetup}, \mathrm{SimKeyGen}, \mathrm{SimSign})$ *as defined above is perfectly simulation private (Definition 9).*

The signatures generated by Sign and SimSign are NIWI proofs with different witnesses. Hence, as in Theorem 2 the above theorem follows from the perfect witness indistinguishability of the proof system.

3   Universal Composable Attribute-Based Signature Schemes

We first give a brief introduction to Canetti's Universal Composability framework [7] and responsive environments [6]. Based on this we present our universally composable ideal functionality for attribute-based signatures. After that we introduce a wrapper protocol that transforms ABS schemes into an UC compatible formulation. In Sect. 4 we show that the wrapper protocol is a secure UC-realization of our ideal ABS functionality if and only if the wrapped ABS scheme is correct, consistent, unforgeable and computationally simulation private.

3.1   Preliminaries: Universal Composability Framework

We briefly summarize the important parts of the Universal Composability framework [7]. For a detailed description we refer to [9]. In the UC framework a task or a scheme is described as an ideal functionality $\mathcal{F}$ and compared to a execution of a protocol π. The protocol π involves an adversary and parties that handle their tasks on their own. Each of the parties runs an instance of the protocol. The ideal functionality models a trusted party that handles all tasks in the name of all other parties. Here the parties are just dummies. In both settings, there is an environment $\mathcal{E}$ that controls the input and activations of parties. The environment is considered as the execution environment of the tasks, since in reality protocols do not exist in a vacuum. The UC security is based on a simulation paradigm. Protocol π is called UC secure, if for every adversary $\mathcal{A}$ against the protocol π, there exists a simulator $\mathcal{S}$ considered as the ideal adversary against $\mathcal{F}$, such that no environment $\mathcal{E}$ can distinguish if it talks to $\mathcal{F}$ with $\mathcal{S}$ or to π with $\mathcal{A}$. To be more precise, let the random variable $\mathcal{E}\left[\pi, \mathcal{A}\right](\lambda, z)$ denote the output of $\mathcal{E}$ when interacting with π and $\mathcal{A}$ with security parameter $\lambda \in \mathbb{N}$ on input $z \in \{0,1\}^*$. Accordingly, let $\mathcal{E}\left[\mathcal{F}, \mathcal{S}^{\mathcal{A}}\right](\lambda, z)$ be the random variable that denotes the output of $\mathcal{E}$ when interacting with $\mathcal{F}$ and $\mathcal{S}^{\mathcal{A}}$ with $\lambda \in \mathbb{N}$ on input $z \in \{0,1\}^*$, where $\mathcal{S}^{\mathcal{A}}$ denotes black-box access to adversary $\mathcal{A}$. The former random variable is defined over the randomness of all parties and $\mathcal{A}$ and the latter is defined over the randomness of $\mathcal{S}^{\mathcal{A}}$. For an ideal functionality $\mathcal{F}$ and protocol π, we say π realizes $\mathcal{F}$ (short π is UC secure) if for all adversaries $\mathcal{A}$, there is a simulator $\mathcal{S}^{\mathcal{A}}$ such that, for all environments $\mathcal{E}$ and all $z \in \{0,1\}^*$, $\mathcal{E}\left[\mathcal{F}, \mathcal{S}^{\mathcal{A}}\right](\lambda, z)$ and $\mathcal{E}\left[\pi, \mathcal{A}\right](\lambda, z)$ are computationally indistinguishable in λ. In the following we assume that $\mathcal{E}$, $\mathcal{A}$, $\mathcal{S}^{(\cdot)}$ are probabilistic polynomial-time algorithms with respect to the security parameter λ. In our notation we omit the security parameter λ and input z. We refer to an interaction of $\mathcal{E}$ with $[\mathcal{F}, \mathcal{S}^{(\cdot)}]$ as the ideal setting and with $[\pi, \mathcal{A}]$ as the real setting. For simplicity one can always assume the so called standard (dummy) adversary $\mathcal{A}$, that forwards every message received with no delay and is inactive apart from that. Canetti [7] showed that the standard adversary is the strongest adversary in UC, since $\mathcal{E}$ takes over the responsibilities of $\mathcal{A}$.

We consider adaptive corruption in the sense that at any time the adversary $\mathcal{A}$ can trigger a corruption of a party. $\mathcal{A}$ is in full control of a corrupted party. We restrict the corruption such that the party responsible for the setup of the scheme can only be corrupted after an honest setup was completed. This restriction is denoted as adaptive* and is explained in more detail in Sect. 4. Further, we consider the erasure model, where honest parties erase ephemeral randomness immediately after usage. This means that on corruption the adversary $\mathcal{A}$ only gets the result of previous computations but not the randomness used. For communication between the parties to send secret information such as secret keys, we rely on secure channels. Accordingly our results are shown in an adaptive*, erasure, secure channels model, denoted as $\mathcal{F}$ [adaptive*, erasure, secure channels].

In UC the ideal functionality and simulator often exchange some meta-data for modeling reasons. Typically protocol designers assume that the simulator answers immediately where according to the UC framework the simulator can do anything he likes after receiving a message from the ideal functionality. This introduces not anticipated state changes of parties and unexpected behavior of the ideal functionality. Therefore, the handling of the exchanged data, and responses of the simulator makes the description of the ideal functionality more complex for protocol designers. Then again the side effects of meta-data exchanges should not be ignored as Camenisch et al. highlight in [6]. To circumvent the problems the authors [6] define responsive environments where the adversary and the environment are bound to answer to so called restricting messages immediately. We model or ideal functionality for responsive environments. Therefore, we employ the generic restriction defined by Camenisch et al. [6] where every message prefixed with "Respond" is restricting.

3.2   Ideal ABS Functionality

The ideal functionality for ABS models a scheme with an unique setup party P_{Setup}. After a Setup activation through P_{Setup} was completed any party P can ask for a secret key. All activations are instantiated by the environment $\mathcal{E}$. The activation to query a secret key, given an attribute set, is called Key Generation. A signing party can generate a signature on a message and a policy by a Signature activation and any party can verify a signature through a Verify activation.

In Fig. 1 the ideal ABS functionality $\mathcal{F}_{\text{ABS}}$ with access to a simulator $\mathcal{S}$ is given. The algorithms S.Setup, S.KG, S.Sign and S.Verify output by $\mathcal{S}$ are stateless ppt algorithms. In UC each ideal functionality instance has a unique session id sid. The sid can be determined in several ways (cf. [9], Sect. 3.1.3). For simplicity, we let the first Setup activation determine the sid, which consists of the unique setup party's identifier and an unique session identifier sid'. The inputs for Setup, Key Generation, Signature and Verify activations are determined by the environment $\mathcal{E}$. Note, messages prefixed with "Respond" are answered immediately by the simulator [6] and a public delayed output is an output to a party that first has to be acknowledged by the simulator.

Setup: In the Setup activation the simulator $\mathcal{S}$ is responsible for providing ppt algorithms S.Setup, S.KG, S.Sign, and S.Verify. These have to be stateless ppt algorithms such that the outputs of $\mathcal{F}_{\text{ABS}}$ generated with these algorithms are independent of the internal state of the simulator and previous activations. Further, this modeling allows us to give a technically sound equivalence proof in Sect. 4). The algorithm S.Setup is used to generate and fix the public parameters pp and the master secret msk of the functionality instance. The algorithm S.KG and S.Sign always take as input the recorded (pp, msk). They are only given as an explicit input to highlight that we use the recorded pair.

Key Generation: This activation models an exchange between a party P_i that just queries a key on a given attribute set (KeyGenRequest) and the party P_{Setup} responsible for the actual key generation (KeyGen). The activation for P_{Setup} models that it is triggered after receiving the output (KeyGenRequest, sid, kid, pp, $\mathbb{A}$, P_i) from the activation of P_i; telling the setup party that P_i asks for a key on $\mathbb{A}$. This modeling also encompasses that P_{Setup} can decide whether to answer a key generation request. P_{Setup} proceeds only if there is an unprocessed key generation request with the key identifier kid for the party P_i. For honest P_{Setup} the ideal functionality $\mathcal{F}_{\text{ABS}}$ first checks that

Setup On input (Setup, sid) from a party P_{Setup}
1. If sid $= (P_{\text{Setup}}, \text{sid}')$ for some sid$'$ continue, else ignore.
2. If there is no record (sid$'$, P_{Setup}, pp, msk), send (Respond, (Setup, sid)) to $\mathcal{S}$. Upon (Setup, sid, S.Setup, S.KG, S.Sign, S.Verify) from $\mathcal{S}$ do:
   (a) Generate (pp, msk) $\leftarrow$ S.Setup
   (b) Record (sid$'$, P_{Setup}, pp, msk) and (S.Setup, S.KG, S.Sign, S.Verify).
3. Else, use recorded (sid$'$, P_{Setup}, pp, msk).
4. In both cases output (Public Params, sid, pp) to P_{Setup}.

Key Generation On input (KeyGenRequest, sid, kid, $\mathbb{A}$) from party P_i
1. If sid $= (P_{\text{Setup}}, \text{sid}')$ continue, else ignore. Mark the request as unprocessed.
2. Send public delayed output (KeyGenRequest, sid, kid, pp, $\mathbb{A}$, P_i) to P_{Setup}

Key Generation On input (KeyGen, sid, kid) from party P_{Setup}
1. If sid $= (P_{\text{Setup}}, \text{sid}')$ and there is an unprocessed (KeyGenRequest, sid, kid, $\mathbb{A}$) from party P_i, mark it processed and continue. Else ignore.
2. If P_{Setup} is corrupt record (KeyGen, sid, kid, $\bot$, $\bot$, $\mathbb{A}$, $\bot$) and send public delayed output (KeyGen, sid, kid, $\mathbb{A}$) to P_i.
3. Else, check $\mathbb{A} \subseteq \mathbb{U}(\text{pp})$ for recorded (sid$'$, P_{Setup}, pp, msk), if not ignore.
   (a) Generate secret key $\text{sk}_{\mathbb{A}} \leftarrow$ S.KG(pp, msk, $\mathbb{A}$) and record (KeyGen, sid, kid, $\bot$, pp, $\mathbb{A}$, $\text{sk}_{\mathbb{A}}$). Send (Respond, KeyGen, sid, kid, $\mathbb{A}$, P_i, $\text{sk}_{\mathbb{A}}$) to $\mathcal{S}$.
   (b) Upon receiving (KeyGen, sid, kid, $\mathbb{A}$, P_i, $\text{sk}_{\mathbb{A}}$, 1) send public delayed output (KeyGen, sid, kid, $\mathbb{A}$) to P_i.
4. When (KeyGen, sid, kid, $\mathbb{A}$) is delivered to P_i update the record by adding the party to (KeyGen, sid, kid, P_i, $\cdot$, $\mathbb{A}$, $\cdot$)

Signature On input (Signature, sid, kid, pp$'$, $\mathbb{A}$, m, $\mathbb{P}$) from some party P_i
1. If sid $= (P_{\text{Setup}}, \text{sid}')$, $\mathbb{A} \subseteq \mathbb{U}(\text{pp}')$ and $\mathbb{P} \in \mathbb{U}(\text{pp}')$ continue, else ignore.
2. Check for (KeyGen, sid, kid, P_i, pp$'$, $\mathbb{A}$, $\cdot$) where $\mathbb{P}(\mathbb{A}) = 1$, if not ignore.
3. If pp$' =$ pp, run S.Sign(pp, msk, m, $\mathbb{P}$) and get σ. (guarantees privacy)
4. Else send (Respond, (Signature, sid, kid, pp$'$, $\mathbb{A}$, m, $\mathbb{P}$)) to $\mathcal{S}$ and receive message (Signature, sid, kid, pp$'$, $\mathbb{A}$, m, $\mathbb{P}$, σ).
5. If a record (Signature, sid, kid, pp$'$, m, $\mathbb{P}$, σ, 0) exists, output error and halt.
6. Else, record (Signature, sid, kid, pp$'$, m, $\mathbb{P}$, σ, 1) and output (Signature, sid, kid, $\mathbb{A}$, m, $\mathbb{P}$, σ) to P_i.

Verify On input (Verify, sid, pp$'$, m, $\mathbb{P}$, σ) from some party P
1. Get $b \leftarrow$ S.Verify(pp$'$, m, $\mathbb{P}$, σ)
   I. If pp$' =$ pp for recorded pp then
      i. If (Signature, sid, kid, pp, m, $\mathbb{P}$, σ, f) recorded for any f, then set $f_{\text{out}} := f$ (guarantees correctness/consistency)
      ii. Else, if for any σ' entry (Signature, sid, kid, pp, m, $\mathbb{P}$, σ', 1) exists or P_{Setup} is corrupt or there exists at least one corrupted P_i with a record (KeyGen, sid, kid, P_i, pp, $\mathbb{A}'$, $\cdot$) where $\mathbb{P}(\mathbb{A}') = 1$, then set $f_{\text{out}} := b$ and record (Signature, sid, $\bot$, pp, m, $\mathbb{P}$, σ, f_{out})
      iii. Else, set bit $f_{\text{out}} := 0$ and record (Signature, sid, $\bot$, pp, m, $\mathbb{P}$, σ, 0). (guarantees unforgeability)
   II. If pp$' \neq$ pp for recorded pp then
      i. If (Signature, sid, kid, pp$'$, m, $\mathbb{P}$, σ, f) is recorded, set $f_{\text{out}} := f$
      ii. Else $f_{\text{out}} := b$ and record (Signature, sid, $\bot$, pp$'$, m, $\mathbb{P}$, σ, f_{out})
2. Output (Verified, sid, m, $\mathbb{P}$, σ, f_{out}) to P

Fig. 1. Attribute-based signature ideal functionality $\mathcal{F}_{\text{ABS}}$

the attribute set is valid and then it uses the algorithm S.KG provided by $\mathcal{S}$ to generate the secret key for $\mathbb{A}$. Next, $\mathcal{S}$ is informed about the key generation. This is necessary since $\mathcal{S}$ has to simulate the transmission of the secret key to the party P_i. If the final output to P_i is delivered, $\mathcal{F}_{\text{ABS}}$ is assured that the simulator transmitted the secret key and $\mathcal{F}_{\text{ABS}}$ can record a successful key generation for P_i. In the case of corrupted P_{Setup}, $\mathcal{F}_{\text{ABS}}$ records a key generation request ($\bot$ for unknown). Therefore, in the Signature activation $\mathcal{F}_{\text{ABS}}$ can ask the simulator $\mathcal{S}$ to sign the message. This is delegated to $\mathcal{S}$ since if P_{Setup} is corrupt $\mathcal{F}_{\text{ABS}}$ can not record the generated secret keys.

Signature: After a check if the inputs are valid the Signature activation checks if the activated party has a satisfying secret key for the given policy. If the activation is under registered pp, it utilizes S.Sign to output a signature without using the secret key of the party and without the activated party's identity as an input to S.Sign. Otherwise it asks $\mathcal{S}$ for a signature under unregistered public parameters. In general, each signature generated in $\mathcal{F}_{\text{ABS}}$ is recorded as valid.

Verify: In this activation we handle any public parameters. Hence, we cover the cases where pp' is invalid or belongs to another instance, even if the activated party is honest. The simplest verify case is if there is no corrupt party. Then $\mathcal{F}_{\text{ABS}}$ verifies all signatures where the corresponding message and policy was not signed in a Signature activation as invalid (Verify I.iii, $f_{\text{out}} := 0$). Verify step I.ii handles two cases. First, a presumably manipulated signature (e.g. randomized) that was not recorded in a Signature activation. Second, the existence of corrupted parties. In any case, to decide whether a signature is valid we use the algorithm S.Verify, provided by $\mathcal{S}$, and the results is recorded by $\mathcal{F}_{\text{ABS}}$.

Scope of Security: The signatures functionality by Canetti [8] supports the verification under any public key. This allows the functionality to be more modular and to be used in different applications. $\mathcal{F}_{\text{ABS}}$ is based on that idea and supports Signature and Verify activations with unregistered public parameters pp'. $\mathcal{F}_{\text{ABS}}$ only guarantees security under the registered public parameters. Therefore we have to check in Key Generation, Signature and Verify if the given public parameters pp' are equal to the registered public parameters pp. For unregistered public parameters in the Signature activation (step 4) we ask the simulator $\mathcal{S}$ or we rely on the algorithm given by $\mathcal{S}$ in the Verify activation (step 1). In this case the guarantees are determined by $\mathcal{S}$. We also allow the corruption of any party with the restriction that P_{Setup} can only be corrupted after the Setup activation was executed once.

Correctness/Consistency: For an honest signer, a Signature activation like (Signature, sid, kid, pp', $\mathbb{A}$, m, $\mathbb{P}$) always records (Signature, sid, kid, pp', m, $\mathbb{P}$, σ, $f := 1$). This leads to a verification output with $f_{\text{out}} = 1$ in a corresponding Verify activation (step I.i). Thus, correctness is guaranteed. Consistency is captured by the steps I.i and II.i. There we just output what is recorded. To verify $(m, \mathbb{P}, \sigma)$ where $\mathcal{F}_{\text{ABS}}$ already generated a different signature σ' for $(m, \mathbb{P})$ we employ step I.ii and use the bit output by S.Verify. The step I.ii also handles the case of corrupted parties. Corrupted parties generate signatures without the involvement of $\mathcal{F}_{\mathrm{ABS}}$ and may share their secret keys. In these cases, we have to use the output b of S.Verify. Hence, the guarantees are those provided by the simulator $\mathcal{S}$ and the algorithms that $\mathcal{S}$ outputs.

Non Colluding: Is handled in the Signature activation step 2. There we check if the activated party has a single secret key for attributes that satisfy the given policy.

Privacy: Privacy for honest users under registered public parameters is guaranteed by the input restriction on the algorithms returned by $\mathcal{S}$. In particular, the S.Sign generates signatures with the public parameters, the master secret, a message, and a policy as input. Therefore it generates signatures without the parties secret key or attributes as an input. Hence, for honest signing parties and under the registered pp we guarantee that the signatures output by $\mathcal{F}_{\mathrm{ABS}}$ are independent of the attribute sets encoded in the secret keys of the signing parties. Therefore, the signatures can not be linked to a party, an attribute set, and to a secret key by an adversary. Since, $\mathcal{F}_{\mathrm{ABS}}$ only guarantees privacy under the registered public parameters pp, we can ask $\mathcal{S}$ for a signature under unregistered public parameters pp' or if P_{Setup} was already corrupted during the corresponding key generation (Signature activation step 4). In a Key Generation activation with honest P_{Setup} we guarantee, that the secret key is independent of the party's identifier. Therefore, we use the S.KG algorithm where the identifier P_i is not an input. Even if P_{Setup} is corrupted after a successful key generation with party P_i, we require that a signature can be generated without the knowledge of P_i's secret key by using S.Sign with the registered (pp, msk) pair.

Unforgeability: It is guaranteed through the Verify step I.iii. Here we set the bit f_{out} to 0, if all parties are honest and we have checked that the corresponding message and policy was not signed by $\mathcal{F}_{\mathrm{ABS}}$ in a Signature activation.

3.3   Protocol

We present our ABS wrapper protocol π_{ABS} in Fig. 2. It serves as a generic transformation of an ABS scheme Π_{ABS} to the UC framework. The protocol activations Setup, Key Generation, Signature and Verify use the algorithms of Π_{ABS} as a black-box. We will show that the protocol π_{ABS} realizes the ideal functionality $\mathcal{F}_{\mathrm{ABS}}$. The Setup activation of the protocol is run by a unique party with the identifier P_{Setup}, it also runs the corresponding side of the Key Generation. The other side of Key Generation as well as the Signature and Verify protocol parts can be executed by any party. Each party runs an instance of the protocol. For example, a party P that is triggered by the environment and wants to generate a signature, executes the Signature protocol part, given in Fig. 2. Notice, secret keys are never output to $\mathcal{E}$ in the protocol π_{ABS}, since in a real world application a honest party should never reveal its secret keys.

Setup When party P_{Setup} receives first input $(\mathsf{Setup}, \mathsf{sid})$ from $\mathcal{E}$
1. If $\mathsf{sid} = (P_{\mathsf{Setup}}, \mathsf{sid}')$ for some sid' continue, else ignore.
2. P_{Setup} runs $(\mathsf{pp}, \mathsf{msk}) \leftarrow \mathsf{Setup}\,(1^{\lambda})$ and records $(\mathsf{sid}', P_{\mathsf{Setup}}, \mathsf{pp}, \mathsf{msk})$.
3. Outputs $(\mathsf{Public\,Params}, \mathsf{sid}, \mathsf{pp})$ to $\mathcal{E}$.

Key Generation
When party P_i receives $(\mathsf{KeyGenRequest}, \mathsf{sid}, \mathsf{kid}, \mathbb{A})$ from $\mathcal{E}$
1. If sid has the form $(P_{\mathsf{Setup}}, \mathsf{sid}')$ continue, else ignore.
2. P_i sends $(\mathsf{KeyGenRequest}, \mathsf{sid}, \mathsf{kid}, \mathbb{A})$ to P_{Setup}.
3. On receiving $(\mathsf{KeyGenRequest}, \mathsf{sid}, \mathsf{kid}, \mathbb{A})$, P_{Setup} records the request from P_i and outputs $(\mathsf{KeyGenRequest}, \mathsf{sid}, \mathsf{kid}, \mathsf{pp}, \mathbb{A}, P_i)$ to $\mathcal{E}$.
4. On receiving $(\mathsf{KeyGen}, \mathsf{sid}, \mathsf{kid}, \mathsf{pp}, \mathbb{A}, \mathsf{sk}_{\mathbb{A}})$ as an answer from P_{Setup}
   (a) If $(\mathsf{sk}_{\mathbb{A}}, \mathbb{A})$ is valid under received pp, P_i appends record $(\mathsf{KeyGen}, \mathsf{sid}, \mathsf{kid}, \mathsf{pp}, \mathbb{A}, \mathsf{sk}_{\mathbb{A}})$ and outputs $(\mathsf{KeyGen}, \mathsf{sid}, \mathsf{kid}, \mathbb{A})$ to $\mathcal{E}$.

When party P_{Setup} receives $(\mathsf{KeyGen}, \mathsf{sid}, \mathsf{kid})$ from $\mathcal{E}$
1. If $\mathsf{sid} = (P_{\mathsf{Setup}}, \mathsf{sid}')$ continue, else ignore.
2. Look up request record $(\mathsf{KeyGenRequest}, \mathsf{sid}, \mathsf{kid}, \mathbb{A})$ from P_i.
3. If $(\mathsf{sid}', P_{\mathsf{Setup}}, \mathsf{pp}, \mathsf{msk})$ is not recorded by P_{Setup} or $\mathbb{A} \not\subseteq \mathbb{U}(\mathsf{pp})$ ignore.
4. Else P_{Setup} computes $\mathsf{sk}_{\mathbb{A}} \leftarrow \mathsf{KeyGen}\,(\mathsf{pp}, \mathsf{msk}, \mathbb{A})$ and sends $(\mathsf{KeyGen}, \mathsf{sid}, \mathsf{kid}, \mathsf{pp}, \mathbb{A}, \mathsf{sk}_{\mathbb{A}})$ to P_i.

Signature When party P_i receives $(\mathsf{Signature}, \mathsf{sid}, \mathsf{kid}, \mathsf{pp}', \mathbb{A}, m, \mathbb{P})$ from $\mathcal{E}$
1. If $\mathsf{sid} = (P_{\mathsf{Setup}}, \mathsf{sid}')$, $\mathbb{A} \subseteq \mathbb{U}(\mathsf{pp}')$ and $\mathbb{P} \in \mathbb{U}(\mathsf{pp}')$ continue, else ignore;
2. P_i looks up last record $(\mathsf{KeyGen}, \mathsf{sid}, \mathsf{kid}, \mathsf{pp}', \mathbb{A}, \mathsf{sk}_{\mathbb{A}})$ where $\mathbb{P}\,(\mathbb{A}) = 1$.
3. If there is no record, then P_i ignores the activation.
4. Else, P_i computes $\sigma \leftarrow \mathsf{Sign}(\mathsf{pp}', \mathsf{sk}_{\mathbb{A}}, m, \mathbb{P})$ and outputs $(\mathsf{Signature}, \mathsf{sid}, \mathsf{kid}, \mathbb{A}, m, \mathbb{P}, \sigma)$ to $\mathcal{E}$

Verify When party P_i receives $(\mathsf{Verify}, \mathsf{sid}, \mathsf{pp}', m, \mathbb{P}, \sigma)$ from $\mathcal{E}$
1. P_i runs $b \leftarrow \mathsf{Verify}\,(\mathsf{pp}', m, \mathbb{P}, \sigma)$ and outputs $(\mathsf{Verified}, \mathsf{sid}, m, \mathbb{P}, \sigma, b)$

Fig. 2. Attribute-based signature protocol π_{ABS}

4 Security

The UC-realization is proven under the assumption that the setup party can only be corrupted after the setup activation was executed once. This is a restriction on the UC environment and is denoted as adaptive*. It models the guarantees of our privacy definitions (Definitions 7 and 9) and mirrors existing experiment-based secure ABS schemes that are defined with an honest setup [2,10,14–17]. The restrictions can be avoided by defining ABS in the CRS model, similar to the blind signatures by Abe and Ohkubo [1].

Theorem 4. *ABS scheme Π_{ABS} is correct, consistent, unforgeable and computationally simulation private if and only if π_{ABS} realizes $\mathcal{F}_{\mathrm{ABS}}[adaptive^*, erasure, secure\ channels]$.*

We split the theorem in two parts. Due to lack of space, we only give proof sketches. The detailed proofs are deferred to the full version of this paper.

Setup On input (Respond, (Setup, sid)) from $\mathcal{F}_{ABS}$
    1. Send (Setup, sid, SimSetup(1^λ), SimKeyGen, SimSign, Verify) to $\mathcal{F}_{ABS}$
Key Generation: If P_i is honest
    1. On seeing the public delayed output (KeyGenRequest, sid, kid, pp, $\mathbb{A}$, P_i) for
        P_{Setup} by $\mathcal{F}_{ABS}$ send (KeyGenRequest, sid, kid, $\mathbb{A}$) from P_i to P_{Setup}
Key Generation: If P_{Setup} is honest
    • On (Respond, (KeyGen, sid, kid, $\mathbb{A}$, P_i, $\mathsf{sk}_\mathbb{A}$)) from $\mathcal{F}_{ABS}$ record (KeyGen,
       sid, kid, pp, $\mathbb{A}$, P_i, $\mathsf{sk}_\mathbb{A}$) and send (KeyGen, sid, kid, $\mathbb{A}$, P_i, $\mathsf{sk}_\mathbb{A}$, 1) to $\mathcal{F}_{ABS}$.
    1. On seeing the public delayed output (KeyGen, sid, kid, $\mathbb{A}$) for P_i by $\mathcal{F}_{ABS}$
        simulate the P_{Setup} key generation part:
    2. Check for (KeyGen, sid, kid, pp, $\mathbb{A}$, P_i, $\mathsf{sk}_\mathbb{A}$) record and send (KeyGen, sid,
        kid, pp, $\mathbb{A}$, $\mathsf{sk}_\mathbb{A}$) from P_{Setup} to P_i.
Key Generation: If P_i is corrupt
    1. On receiving (KeyGenRequest, sid, kid, $\mathbb{A}$) sent to P_{Setup} from P_i (controlled
        by $\mathcal{A}$). Send (KeyGenRequest, sid, kid, $\mathbb{A}$) on behalf of P_i to $\mathcal{F}_{ABS}$.
Key Generation: If P_{Setup} is corrupt
    1. On (KeyGen, sid, kid, pp′, $\mathbb{A}$, sk) from P_{Setup} (controlled by $\mathcal{A}$). If (sk, $\mathbb{A}$) is
        valid under pp′, send (KeyGen, sid, kid) on behalf of P_{Setup} to $\mathcal{F}_{ABS}$.
    2. On seeing the public delayed output (KeyGen, sid, kid, $\mathbb{A}$) for P_i by $\mathcal{F}_{ABS}$
        record (KeyGen, sid, kid, pp′, $\mathbb{A}$, P_i, sk)
Signature On input (Respond, (Signature, sid, kid, pp′, $\mathbb{A}$, m, $\mathbb{P}$)) from $\mathcal{F}_{ABS}$
    1. Check for record (KeyGen, sid, kid, pp′, $\mathbb{A}$, P_i, $\mathsf{sk}_\mathbb{A}$), if not ignore. Else, $\sigma \leftarrow$
        Sign(pp′, $\mathsf{sk}_\mathbb{A}$, m, $\mathbb{P}$) and send (Signature, sid, kid, pp′, $\mathbb{A}$, m, $\mathbb{P}$, σ) to $\mathcal{F}_{ABS}$.
Others On (corrupt, P) from $\mathcal{A}$. Inform $\mathcal{F}_{ABS}$ with (corrupt, P), to get all input,
    output and exchanged messages for P. Send all data to $\mathcal{A}$. Further, public
    delayed output send to honest parties is delivered after the steps are processed.
    For corrupted parties it is never delivered.

Fig. 3. Simulator $\mathcal{S}_0^{\mathcal{A}}$

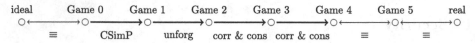

Fig. 4. Sequence of games

Experiment-Based Security implies UC Security. The UC security is shown
with respect to our ideal ABS functionality $\mathcal{F}_{ABS}$ (Fig. 1) and the ABS protocol
π_{ABS} (Fig. 2) which is a wrapper for an ABS scheme Π_{ABS}.

Theorem 5. *If Π_{ABS} is correct, consistent, unforgeable and comp. simulation
private, then $\mathcal{F}_{ABS}$ [adaptive*, erasure, secure channels] is realized by π_{ABS}.*

In the following we define one simulator $\mathcal{S}^{(\cdot)}$ that, for any given adversary $\mathcal{A}$, interacts with $\mathcal{F}_{ABS}$ such that for all environments $\mathcal{E}$, it holds that
$[\mathcal{F}_{ABS}, \mathcal{S}_0^{\mathcal{A}}]$ and $[\pi_{ABS}, \mathcal{A}]$ are indistinguishable. For an ABS scheme $\Pi_{ABS} =$
(Setup, KeyGen, Sign, Verify, SimKeyGen, SimSetup, SimSign), any adversary
$\mathcal{A}$ and $\mathcal{F}_{ABS}$ we define the simulator $\mathcal{S}_0^{\mathcal{A}}$ in Fig. 3, where $\mathcal{S}_0^{\mathcal{A}}$ has black-box

access to $\mathcal{A}$. In case of a corruption of P_{Setup}, $\mathcal{E}$ gets the master secret stored in P_{Setup}. Hence, $\mathcal{E}$ can issue arbitrary secret keys. This includes the issuing of secret keys to honest parties. If a corrupted party interacts with a honest party the interaction is handled by $\mathcal{S}_0^{\mathcal{A}}$ as described in Fig. 3.

The proof of Theorem 5 is done through a sequence of games. Starting in Game 0 with the ideal setting and ending in Game 5 with the real setting. In particular, if $\mathcal{E}$ can distinguish the ideal setting and the real setting then it has to distinguish one of the consecutive games. In the sequence of games we gradually modify $\mathcal{F}_{\text{ABS}}$ and $\mathcal{S}_0^{\mathcal{A}}$ in each step. Thereby, every game expands the modifications introduced in the games before. With each modification we show that if an environment $\mathcal{E}$ can distinguish Game i-1 and Game i, then there is an adversary that breaks one of the security guarantees of ABS. The proofs are deferred to the full version. In the following we outline the games and steps. In Fig. 4 we present the sequence of games and the related security guarantees; computational simulation privacy, unforgeability, correctness and consistency.

Game 0 Let $\mathcal{E}$ interact with $\mathcal{F}_{\text{ABS}}$ and the simulator $\mathcal{S}_0^{\mathcal{A}}$.

Game 1 The simulation algorithms (SimSetup, SimKeyGen, SimSign) are removed from $\mathcal{S}_0^{\mathcal{A}}$. Instead $\mathcal{S}_0^{\mathcal{A}}$ uses (Setup, KeyGen, Sign) as in π_{ABS}.

Game 2 The Verify step I.iii. (see Fig. 1) is modified where $f_{\text{out}} := 0$ is set. This step is changed to $f_{\text{out}} := b$, where b is the output of the verification done with Verify. This removes the absolute unforgeability guarantee of $\mathcal{F}_{\text{ABS}}$ and moves the responsibility to the ABS scheme Π_{ABS}. With absolute unforgeability we refer to the property that for honest parties under registered pp, the unchanged $\mathcal{F}_{\text{ABS}}$ guarantees unforgeability with probability 1.

Game 3 In the Verification activation of $\mathcal{F}_{\text{ABS}}$ all the verification checks are removed and replaced by a run of the Verify algorithm of the scheme Π_{ABS}.

Game 4 We remove from $\mathcal{F}_{\text{ABS}}$ the halting condition in step 5 of the Signature activation and directly record (Signature, sid, kid, pp, m, $\mathbb{P}$, σ, 1).

Game 5 Since in Game 3 we changed the Verification activation to just output what Verify outputs the Signature records were never read. Hence we can remove them without any side effects.

Let $\mathcal{F}_5$ and $\mathcal{S}_5^{\mathcal{A}}$ be the resulting ideal functionality and simulator in Game 5. At this point $\mathcal{F}_{\text{ABS}}$ was changed through the games to $\mathcal{F}_5$ such that for every activation, the output of $\mathcal{F}_5$ is now determined by the output of $\mathcal{S}_5^{\mathcal{A}}$ and the algorithms (Setup, KeyGen, Sign, Verify) used in the simulator. Furthermore, the simulator was modified such that $\mathcal{S}_5^{\mathcal{A}}$ effectively resembles π_{ABS}.

UC Security implies Experiment-Based Security. We state the second part of Theorem 4 in the following.

Theorem 6. *If π_{ABS} realizes $\mathcal{F}_{\text{ABS}}$ [adaptive*, erasure, secure channels], then Π_{ABS} is correct, consistent, unforgeable and computationally simulation private.*

In the following we give a proof outline to highlight the important steps. Detailed proofs are deferred to the full version. We use the contraposition of Theorem 6: Π_{ABS} is **not** (correct $\wedge$ consistent $\wedge$ computationally simulation private $\wedge$ unforgeable) implies that π_{ABS} does not realize $\mathcal{F}_{\text{ABS}}$. We say that π_{ABS} does not realize $\mathcal{F}_{\text{ABS}}$, this means that there is an adversary $\mathcal{A}$ such that for all simulators $\mathcal{S}$, there exists an environment $\mathcal{E}$ such that $\mathcal{E}[\mathcal{F}_{\text{ABS}}, \mathcal{S}]$ and $\mathcal{E}[\pi_{\text{ABS}}, \mathcal{A}]$ are not computationally indistinguishable. To outline the proof we successively assume that the k-th property is the first that is not satisfied, i.e. we first assume that the scheme is not correct but all other properties are satisfied. The proofs for the first two properties are similar. Assuming the ABS scheme Π_{ABS} is not correct or Π_{ABS} is not consistent we define an environment $\mathcal{E}$ that triggers an invalid verification of an genuine signature in the real setting. Since in the ideal setting this will never happen, $\mathcal{E}$ can easily distinguish the settings.

Next, assuming the ABS scheme Π_{ABS} is not computationally simulation private we define an environment that distinguishes the output of the simulation algorithms used the ideal setting and the output of the non-simulation algorithms used in the real setting. The detailed proof is technically more challenging, since we first have to prove the existence of appropriate simulation algorithms in the ideal setting. For this we need that $\mathcal{S}_0^{(\cdot)}$ (Fig. 3) outputs stateless ppt algorithms during the Setup activation.

The last step of the proof is to define a distinguishing environment $\mathcal{E}$ assuming that the scheme Π_{ABS} is not unforgeable. Given an forger F against Π_{ABS}, we define $\mathcal{E}$ such that it answers F's oracle queries (KeyGen, Reveal, Sign) by sending the corresponding ideal activation to a party. $\mathcal{E}$'s final output is the verification result of the potential forgery that F outputs. Since, ideal setting $[\mathcal{F}_{\text{ABS}}, \mathcal{S}^{(\cdot)}]$ guarantees absolute unforgeability it verifies every signature that was not signed inside $\mathcal{F}_{\text{ABS}}$ as invalid. To be successful F's potential forgery has to be generated outside $\mathcal{F}_{\text{ABS}}$. Hence, in the ideal setting it is declared as valid with probability 0. Since we assumed that Π_{ABS} is not unforgeable, the potential forgery will be valid with non-negligible probability in the real setting $[\pi_{\text{ABS}}, \Pi_{\text{ABS}}]$.

References

1. Abe, M., Ohkubo, M.: A framework for universally composable non-committing blind signatures. IJACT **2**(3), 229–249 (2012)
2. Anada, H., Arita, S., Sakurai, K.: Proof of knowledge on monotone predicates and its application to attribute-based identifications and signatures. IACR ePrint 2016, vol. 483 (2016)
3. Ateniese, G., Camenisch, J., Hohenberger, S., de Medeiros, B.: Practical group signatures without random oracles. IACR ePrint 2005 (2005). http://ia.cr/2005/385
4. Bellare, M., Fuchsbauer, G.: Policy-based signatures. In: Krawczyk, H. (ed.) PKC 2014. LNCS, vol. 8383, pp. 520–537. Springer, Heidelberg (2014). https://doi.org/10.1007/978-3-642-54631-0_30
5. Camenisch, J., Dubovitskaya, M., Haralambiev, K., Kohlweiss, M.: Composable and modular anonymous credentials: definitions and practical constructions. In: Iwata, T., Cheon, J.H. (eds.) ASIACRYPT 2015. LNCS, vol. 9453, pp. 262–288. Springer, Heidelberg (2015). https://doi.org/10.1007/978-3-662-48800-3_11

6. Camenisch, J., Enderlein, R.R., Krenn, S., Küsters, R., Rausch, D.: Universal composition with responsive environments. In: Cheon, J.H., Takagi, T. (eds.) ASIACRYPT 2016. LNCS, vol. 10032, pp. 807–840. Springer, Heidelberg (2016). https://doi.org/10.1007/978-3-662-53890-6_27
7. Canetti, R.: Universally composable security: a new paradigm for cryptographic protocols. In: FOCS, pp. 136–145. IEEE Computer Society (2001)
8. Canetti, R.: Universally composable signatures, certification and authentication. IACR ePrint 2003 (2003). http://ia.cr/2003/239
9. Canetti, R.: Universally composable security: a new paradigm for cryptographic protocols. IACR ePrint 2013 (2013). http://ia.cr/2000/067
10. Escala, A., Herranz, J., Morillo, P.: Revocable attribute-based signatures with adaptive security in the standard model. In: Nitaj, A., Pointcheval, D. (eds.) AFRICACRYPT 2011. LNCS, vol. 6737, pp. 224–241. Springer, Heidelberg (2011). https://doi.org/10.1007/978-3-642-21969-6_14
11. Goldwasser, S., Micali, S., Rivest, R.L.: A digital signature scheme secure against adaptive chosen-message attacks. SIAM J. Comput. **17**(2), 281–308 (1988)
12. Herranz, J.: Attribute-based versions of Schnorr and ElGamal. Appl. Algebra Eng. Commun. Comput. **27**(1), 17–57 (2016)
13. Lindell, Y.: Highly-efficient universally-composable commitments based on the DDH assumption. In: Paterson, K.G. (ed.) EUROCRYPT 2011. LNCS, vol. 6632, pp. 446–466. Springer, Heidelberg (2011). https://doi.org/10.1007/978-3-642-20465-4_25
14. Maji, H.K., Prabhakaran, M., Rosulek, M.: Attribute-based signatures: achieving attribute-privacy and collusion-resistance. IACR ePrint 2008 (2008). http://ia.cr/2008/328
15. Maji, H.K., Prabhakaran, M., Rosulek, M.: Attribute-based signatures. In: Kiayias, A. (ed.) CT-RSA 2011. LNCS, vol. 6558, pp. 376–392. Springer, Heidelberg (2011). https://doi.org/10.1007/978-3-642-19074-2_24
16. Okamoto, T., Takashima, K.: Efficient attribute-based signatures for non-monotone predicates in the standard model. IEEE Trans. Cloud Comput. **2**(4), 409–421 (2014)
17. Sakai, Y., Attrapadung, N., Hanaoka, G.: Attribute-based signatures for circuits from bilinear map. In: Cheng, C.-M., Chung, K.-M., Persiano, G., Yang, B.-Y. (eds.) PKC 2016. LNCS, vol. 9614, pp. 283–300. Springer, Heidelberg (2016). https://doi.org/10.1007/978-3-662-49384-7_11

Protean Signature Schemes

Stephan Krenn[1], Henrich C. Pöhls[2], Kai Samelin[3,4(✉)], and Daniel Slamanig[1]

[1] AIT Austrian Institute of Technology, Vienna, Austria
{stephan.krenn,daniel.slamanig}@ait.ac.at
[2] ISL & Chair of IT-Security, University of Passau, Passau, Germany
hp@sec.uni-passau.de
[3] TÜV Rheinland i-sec GmbH, Hallbergmoos, Germany
kaispapers@gmail.com
[4] TU Darmstadt, Darmstadt, Germany

Abstract. We introduce the notion of Protean Signature schemes. This novel type of signature scheme allows to remove and edit signer-chosen parts of signed messages by a semi-trusted third party simultaneously. In existing work, one is either allowed to remove or edit parts of signed messages, but not both at the same time. Which and how parts of the signed messages can be modified is chosen by the signer. Thus, our new primitive generalizes both redactable (Steinfeld et al., ICISC '01, Johnson et al., CT-RSA '02 & Brzuska et al., ACNS '10) and sanitizable signatures schemes (Ateniese et al., ESORICS '05 & Brzuska et al., PKC '09). We showcase a scenario where either primitive alone is not sufficient. Our provably secure construction (offering both strong notions of transparency and invisibility) makes only black-box access to sanitizable and redactable signature schemes, which can be considered standard tools nowadays. Finally, we have implemented our scheme; Our evaluation shows that the performance is reasonable.

1 Introduction

Standard unforgeable digital signature schemes do not allow for any alterations of signed messages, i.e., an adversary cannot generate validating signatures for messages not explicitly endorsed by the signer [26]. However, this is too limiting in many real-life scenarios. The standard use-case usually given as an example to clarify this situation is the handling of patient data. In particular, assume that a medical doctor signs a complete record consisting of the patient's name, insurance number and the received treatments. After the patient is released, the hospital's accountant receives the complete signed record related to the patient in question to prepare the bill for the insurance company.

This research was supported by European Union's Horizon 2020 research and innovation programme under grant agreement No 644962 PRISMACLOUD, No 653454 CREDENTIAL, No 783119 SECREDAS and No 321310 PERCY.

K. Samelin—Part of this work was done while the third author was also at IBM Research – Zurich.

© Springer Nature Switzerland AG 2018
J. Camenisch and P. Papadimitratos (Eds.): CANS 2018, LNCS 11124, pp. 256–276, 2018.
https://doi.org/10.1007/978-3-030-00434-7_13

Obviously, this is not very privacy-friendly, especially from the patient's point of view, as the accountant receives all information, even though some data is irrelevant for the task carried out. So, the obvious solution is to only give the treatments and the insurance number to the accountant, effectively anonymizing the paperwork. However, as standard signatures do not allow for such alterations, the medical doctor either needs to re-sign the document in this case or an additional trusted entity does it for the doctor. Still, both solutions are not very satisfactory, as it induces additional overhead and may also be impossible in certain scenarios, e.g., if the medical doctor is no longer employed. Thus, modifying signed messages in a controlled way has its merits.

Motivation and Contribution. We introduce the notion of "Protean Signature schemes" (PS). In such schemes, parts of a message can be removed, while the rest of this message remains authenticated, i.e., can be verified using the corresponding public key pk. However, in contrast to redactable signature schemes [31, 41] (RSS), which only allow removal of parts, our primitive also allows to alter signer-chosen blocks to arbitrary bit-strings, much like sanitizable signature schemes [2] (SSS), while also adding accountability.

In the above (minimal) example, removal is enough to anonymize the data in question. However, in some scenarios, it is also necessary to edit some parts of a signed message and not only to remove parts. For example, to achieve k-anonymity [42], one may want to coarsen (generalize) the ZIP-code by replacing the last digits of it with a special symbol, e.g., $*$. However, a problem here is that for more complex data, i.e., beyond ZIP-codes, the decision of which and how data may be anonymized depends on the actual data gathered and additional knowledge. Thus, there are scenarios where this information – and therefore the knowledge what to redact – is not available to the entity generating the signature and hence not known at the time of signature generation. Namely, coming back to the use-case with the patient data, data may be grouped based on side-effects on the type of medication given, while certain information must be completely removed, i.e., identifiers such as names. So, as new medications enter the market almost on a daily basis, even if based on existing agents, how should the signer be aware of potential side-effects or new treatments ahead of time, especially considering that the data must be grouped and anonymized w.r.t. to these values? Thus, a coexistence of the possibility to remove and edit signed data becomes a necessity to successfully protect privacy while maintaining data quality in certain scenarios.

This paper tackles this situation by introducing Protean Signature schemes (PS), where a semi-trusted third party can remove and edit signer-chosen parts of the message (blocks), also answering an open question by Bilzhause et al. [4] and de Meer et al. [18]. Thus, our new primitive can be seen as a generalization of both SSSs and RSSs.

In more detail, we introduce a formal security framework for PSs and a provably secure construction. Our construction is based on existing work on SSSs and RSSs, combining both concepts. The corresponding efficiency analysis and implementation shows that our construction is reasonably efficient, especially considering its possibilities.

Related Work. Malleable signatures received a lot of attention in the recent past, as it became clear that there are many application scenarios where signed messages need to be modified in a controlled way [1,4,19,24]. This weakens the standard unforgeability definition, where the messages protected by signatures cannot be altered at all, which is clearly not avoidable, if one wants to allow for modifications or derivations.

Essentially, existing work can be grouped into three, sometimes overlapping, directions. The first direction are homomorphic signatures [1,5,31,43], and some other closely related concepts [6,44]. Homomorphic signatures take several (signed) messages as input and can be used to compute functions on authenticated data-sets. Here, an entity not holding any secrets can derive a new (valid) signature σ' on $f(m)$, where the function f is public.

Directly related are RSSs, where anyone (i.e., no secrets are involved) can publish a subset of signed data, along with a new signature σ'. To illustrate this, let $m = $ (I, do, not, like, fish) along with a valid redactable signature σ. Anyone can then derive a signature σ' on $m' = $ (I, like, fish), i.e., redact the second and third block $m^2 = $ do and $m^3 = $ not. The original ideas of RSSs [31,41] were later formalized [7,34]. Then, RSSs have been extended to allow for additional use-cases, including adding accountability [37], discussing their relation to SSSs [18], allowing for redactable structure [39], prohibiting additional redactions [28–30,36], yet also defining dependencies between different parts of a message [40]. Moreover, there are also some real-world implementations of this primitive proving that they are practical [38,45]. All these approaches (but accountability) have later been unified into a generalized framework by Derler et al. [20]. Note, the work by Izu et al. [29] addresses the case of "sanitizable and deletable signatures". However, they actually address the case of RSSs and not SSSs. In particular, in their scheme, a third party can decide whether a redaction is visible or not, but does not allow for any other alterations. We follow the nomenclature clarified by Bilzhause et al. [4] and thus classify the work by Izu et al. [29] as an RSS.

Likewise, SSSs allow to alter signer-chosen blocks of signed messages by a semi-trusted entity named the sanitizer [2]. In particular, the sanitizer holds its own secret key and can derive new messages, along with the corresponding signatures, but cannot completely redact blocks. For example, if $m = $ (I, do, not, like, fish) (and m^5 is admissible, i.e., modifiable), then the sanitizer can, e.g., derive a new signature σ' on the message $m' = $ (I, do, not, like, meat). Even though this seems to be off the limits, it turned out that this primitive has many real-life application scenarios, see, e.g., Bilzhause et al. [4]. After the initial ideas by Ateniese et al. [2], SSSs also received a lot of attention in the recent past. Namely, the first thorough security model was given by Brzuska et al. [8] (later slightly modified by Gong et al. [27]), which was later extended for multiple signers/sanitizers [9,15], unlinkability (which means a derived signatures cannot be linked to its original) [10,12,23,35], trapdoor SSSs (where a signer can choose additional sanitizers after signature generation) [16,46], non-interactive public-accountability (an outsider can determine which party is accountable for a given valid message/signature pair) [11], limiting the sanitizer to signer-chosen values [14,21,32], invisibility (meaning that an outsider cannot derive which parts of a message are sanitizable) [3,13,22] and the case of strongly unforgeable signatures [33]. All these extensions allow for additional use-cases of this primitive [4].

Additional related work is given in some recent surveys [4,19,25]. We stress that a slightly altered SSS can be used to "mimic" an RSS by defining a special symbol to which the specific block is sanitized to mark the block as "redacted". However, as shown by de Meer et al. [18], this has a negative impact on the privacy guarantees of the resulting scheme because the special symbol remains visible. For example, $m' = $ (I, like, fish) is clearly different from $m' = $ (I, $\perp, \perp$, like, fish). We stress that our scheme supports both possibilities, i.e., visible and non-visible (transparent) redactions, adding additional freedom for the signer.

2   Preliminaries and Notation

We now give our notation and the required preliminaries. These include labeled IND-CCA2 secure encryption schemes, sanitizable signatures and redactable signatures.

The formal definitions can be found in the full version of this paper.

Notation. The main security parameter is denoted by $\kappa \in \mathbb{N}$. All algorithms implicitly take 1^κ as an additional input. We write $a \leftarrow A(x)$ if a is assigned to the output of the deterministic algorithm A with input x. If an algorithm A is probabilistic, we write $a \leftarrow_r A(x)$. An algorithm is efficient if it runs in probabilistic polynomial time (PPT) in the length of its input. For the remainder of this paper, all algorithms are PPT if not explicitly mentioned otherwise. Most algorithms may return a special error symbol $\perp \notin \{0,1\}^*$, denoting an exception. If S is a set, we write $a \leftarrow_r S$ to denote that a is chosen uniformly at random from S. In the definitions, we speak of a general message space $\mathcal{M}$ to be as generic as possible. What $\mathcal{M}$ is concretely, is defined in the instantiations. For a message $m = (m^1, m^2, \ldots, m^{\ell_m})$, m^i is called a block and $\ell_m \in \mathbb{N}$ denotes the number of blocks in m. If m is clear from the context, it is dropped from ℓ_m. A function $\nu : \mathbb{N} \to \mathbb{R}_{\geq 0}$ is negligible, if it vanishes faster than every inverse polynomial, i.e., $\forall k \in \mathbb{N}, \exists n_0 \in \mathbb{N}$ such that $\nu(n) \leq n^{-k}, \forall n > n_0$.

Labeled Public-Key Encryption Schemes. A labeled public-key encryption scheme $\Pi = \{\mathsf{PPGen}^\Pi, \mathsf{KGen}^\Pi, \mathsf{Enc}^\Pi, \mathsf{Dec}^\Pi\}$ allows to encrypt a message m using a given public key pk_Π and label $\vartheta \in \{0,1\}^*$. In a nutshell, the given ciphertext leaks no information about the contained message, except its length, if the corresponding secret key sk_Π is not known. We require IND-CCA2 security to make our construction secure.

Sanitizable Signature Schemes. Subsequently, we restate the definitions of SSSs [3,8,33]. In a nutshell, a SSS allows a semi-trusted third party, named the sanitizer, to alter signer-chosen blocks to arbitrary bit-strings. The sanitizer holds its own key-pair and can be held accountable, if it sanitizes a message.

The following framework is essentially the one given by Camenisch et al. [13], which is itself based on existing work [8]. However, some additional notation is required beforehand. The variable $\mathsf{ADM}^{\mathsf{SSS}}$ contains the set of indices of the modifiable blocks, as well as ℓ, denoting the total number of blocks in the message m. For example, let $\mathsf{ADM}^{\mathsf{SSS}} = (\{1,2,4\},4)$. Then, m must contain four blocks ($\ell = 4$) and all but the third are admissible. The variable $\mathsf{MOD}^{\mathsf{SSS}}$ is a set containing pairs $(i, m^{i'})$ for those blocks that are modified, meaning that m^i is replaced by $m^{i'}$. We use the shorthand notation $m' \leftarrow \mathsf{MOD}^{\mathsf{SSS}}(m)$ to denote the result of this replacement, while $\mathsf{MOD}^{\mathsf{SSS}} \prec (m, \mathsf{ADM}^{\mathsf{SSS}})$ means that $\mathsf{MOD}^{\mathsf{SSS}}$ is a valid modification instruction w.r.t. m and $\mathsf{ADM}^{\mathsf{SSS}}$. Likewise, we use $\mathsf{ADM}^{\mathsf{SSS}} \prec m$ to denote that $\mathsf{ADM}^{\mathsf{SSS}}$ is valid description of the admissible blocks w.r.t. m.

Definition 1 (Sanitizable Signatures). *A sanitizable signature scheme* SSS *consists of the following eight ppt algorithms* $\{\mathsf{PPGen}^{\mathsf{SSS}}, \mathsf{KGen}^{\mathsf{SSS}}_{\mathsf{sig}}, \mathsf{KGen}^{\mathsf{SSS}}_{\mathsf{san}}, \mathsf{Sign}^{\mathsf{SSS}}, \mathsf{Verify}^{\mathsf{SSS}}, \mathsf{Sanitize}^{\mathsf{SSS}}, \mathsf{Proof}^{\mathsf{SSS}}, \mathsf{Judge}^{\mathsf{SSS}}\}$ *such that:*

$\mathsf{PPGen}^{\mathsf{SSS}}$. *The algorithm* $\mathsf{PPGen}^{\mathsf{SSS}}$ *generates the public parameters:*

$$\mathsf{pp}_{\mathsf{SSS}} \leftarrow_r \mathsf{PPGen}^{\mathsf{SSS}}(1^\kappa)$$

We assume that $\mathsf{pp}_{\mathsf{SSS}}$ *is implicitly input to all other algorithms.*
$\mathsf{KGen}^{\mathsf{SSS}}_{\mathsf{sig}}$. *The algorithm* $\mathsf{KGen}^{\mathsf{SSS}}_{\mathsf{sig}}$ *generates the key pair of the signer:*

$$(\mathsf{sk}^{\mathsf{SSS}}_{\mathsf{sig}}, \mathsf{pk}^{\mathsf{SSS}}_{\mathsf{sig}}) \leftarrow_r \mathsf{KGen}^{\mathsf{SSS}}_{\mathsf{sig}}(\mathsf{pp}_{\mathsf{SSS}})$$

$\mathsf{KGen}^{\mathsf{SSS}}_{\mathsf{san}}$. *The algorithm* $\mathsf{KGen}^{\mathsf{SSS}}_{\mathsf{san}}$ *generates the key pair of the sanitizer:*

$$(\mathsf{sk}^{\mathsf{SSS}}_{\mathsf{san}}, \mathsf{pk}^{\mathsf{SSS}}_{\mathsf{san}}) \leftarrow_r \mathsf{KGen}^{\mathsf{SSS}}_{\mathsf{san}}(\mathsf{pp}_{\mathsf{SSS}})$$

$\mathsf{Sign}^{\mathsf{SSS}}$. *The algorithm* $\mathsf{Sign}^{\mathsf{SSS}}$ *generates a signature* σ^{SSS} *on input of the public key* $\mathsf{pk}^{\mathsf{SSS}}_{\mathsf{san}}$, $\mathsf{ADM}^{\mathsf{SSS}}$, *a message* m *and* $\mathsf{sk}^{\mathsf{SSS}}_{\mathsf{sig}}$:

$$\sigma^{\mathsf{SSS}} \leftarrow_r \mathsf{Sign}^{\mathsf{SSS}}(\mathsf{sk}^{\mathsf{SSS}}_{\mathsf{sig}}, \mathsf{pk}^{\mathsf{SSS}}_{\mathsf{san}}, m, \mathsf{ADM}^{\mathsf{SSS}})$$

$\mathsf{Verify}^{\mathsf{SSS}}$. *The deterministic algorithm* $\mathsf{Verify}^{\mathsf{SSS}}$ *verifies a signature* σ^{SSS}, *i.e., outputs a decision* $d \in \{0,1\}$ *w.r.t.* $\mathsf{pk}^{\mathsf{SSS}}_{\mathsf{san}}$, $\mathsf{pk}^{\mathsf{SSS}}_{\mathsf{sig}}$ *and a message* m:

$$d \leftarrow \mathsf{Verify}^{\mathsf{SSS}}(\mathsf{pk}^{\mathsf{SSS}}_{\mathsf{sig}}, \mathsf{pk}^{\mathsf{SSS}}_{\mathsf{san}}, m, \sigma^{\mathsf{SSS}})$$

Sanitize^{SSS}. *The algorithm* Sanitize^{SSS} *generates a sanitized signature* $\sigma^{\text{SSS}\prime}$ *on input* sk$_{\text{san}}^{\text{SSS}}$, ADM^{SSS}, *a message* m *and* pk$_{\text{sig}}^{\text{SSS}}$:

$$(m', \sigma^{\text{SSS}\prime}) \leftarrow_r \text{Sanitize}^{\text{SSS}}(\text{sk}_{\text{san}}^{\text{SSS}}, \text{pk}_{\text{sig}}^{\text{SSS}}, m, \sigma^{\text{SSS}}, \text{MOD}^{\text{SSS}})$$

Proof^{SSS}. *The algorithm* Proof^{SSS} *outputs a proof* π^{SSS} *on input* m, σ^{SSS}, sk$_{\text{sig}}^{\text{SSS}}$, pk$_{\text{san}}^{\text{SSS}}$ *and a set of polynomially many additional signature/message pairs* $\{(\sigma_i^{\text{SSS}}, m_i)\}$. *The proof* π^{SSS} *is used by the next algorithm to pinpoint the accountable party for a given signature:*

$$\pi^{\text{SSS}} \leftarrow_r \text{Proof}^{\text{SSS}}(\text{sk}_{\text{sig}}^{\text{SSS}}, \text{pk}_{\text{san}}^{\text{SSS}}, m, \sigma^{\text{SSS}}, \{(\sigma_i^{\text{SSS}}, m_i)\})$$

Judge^{SSS}. *The deterministic algorithm* Judge^{SSS} *outputs a decision* $d \in \{\text{Sig}^{\text{PS}}, \text{San}^{\text{PS}}, \bot\}$ *indicating whether the message/signature pair has been created by the signer, or the sanitizer:*

$$d \leftarrow \text{Judge}^{\text{SSS}}(\text{pk}_{\text{sig}}^{\text{SSS}}, \text{pk}_{\text{san}}^{\text{SSS}}, m, \sigma^{\text{SSS}}, \pi^{\text{SSS}})$$

Security Requirements. Due to space restrictions, we only sketch the security requirements here. The formal game-based definitions are given in the full version of this paper. We stress that we use the strong definitions by Beck et al. [3].

Unforgeability. An outsider must not be able to create any new valid signatures.

Immutability. The sanitizer should, even if it can create it's own key pair, only sanitize admissible blocks and neither append or remove a block.

Privacy. An outsider not holding any secret keys should not be able to derive which message was contained before a sanitization took place.

Transparency. An outsider should not be able to decide whether a signature was created by the signer or the sanitizer.

Sanitizer-Accountability. The sanitizer should not be able to create a signature which points to the signer, even though the signer did not create it.

Signer-Accountability. The signer should not be able to create a proof for a signature which points to the sanitizer, even though the sanitizer did not create that signature.

Invisibility. An outsider not holding any secret keys should not be able to decide which parts of a signed message are admissible. It depends on the context if this notion is required.

Redactable Signature Schemes. The following definitions for RSSs are taken from Derler et al. [20], but extended to support parameter generation to match the definitions of SSSs. In particular, let $m = (m^1, m^2, \ldots, m^\ell)$ be some message, while ADM$^{\text{RSS}} \in \{1, 2, \ldots, \ell\}$ denotes the admissible redactions, i.e., if $i \in \text{ADM}^{\text{RSS}}$, then m^i can be redacted by *anyone*, i.e., no additional secrets are involved.[1] The variable $\mathsf{MOD}^{\mathsf{RSS}} \subseteq \{1, 2, \ldots, \ell\}$ denotes how a message m is to be modified, i.e., each block m^i, $i \in \mathsf{MOD}^{\mathsf{RSS}}$, is removed from m to form the redacted message m'. In comparison to Derler et al. [20], however, we already define how those data-structures look like for preciseness. Moreover, as done for SSSs, we use the shorthand notation $m' \leftarrow \mathsf{MOD}^{\mathsf{RSS}}(m)$ to denote a redaction. The notation $\mathsf{MOD}^{\mathsf{RSS}} \prec (m, \mathsf{ADM}^{\mathsf{RSS}})$ means that $\mathsf{MOD}^{\mathsf{RSS}}$ is a valid modification instruction w.r.t. m and $\mathsf{ADM}^{\mathsf{RSS}}$. Likewise, we use $\mathsf{ADM}^{\mathsf{RSS}} \prec m$ to denote that $\mathsf{ADM}^{\mathsf{RSS}}$ is valid description of the admissible blocks w.r.t. m. The "redaction information" $\mathsf{RED}^{\mathsf{RSS}}$ is some auxiliary string which may be used by some RSSs to improve the efficiency of the scheme [20]. We do not define what this string is, as we use RSSs as a black-box and thus it does not matter in our case.

Definition 2 (Redactable Signatures). *A redactable signature scheme* RSS *consists of the following five algorithms, i.e.,* $\{\mathsf{PPGen}^{\mathsf{RSS}}, \mathsf{KGen}^{\mathsf{RSS}}, \mathsf{Sign}^{\mathsf{RSS}},$ $\mathsf{Verify}^{\mathsf{RSS}}, \mathsf{Redact}^{\mathsf{RSS}}\}$, *such that:*

$\mathsf{PPGen}^{\mathsf{RSS}}$. *The algorithm* $\mathsf{PPGen}^{\mathsf{RSS}}$ *generates the public parameters:*

$$\mathsf{pp}_{\mathsf{RSS}} \leftarrow_r \mathsf{PPGen}^{\mathsf{RSS}}(1^\kappa)$$

We assume that $\mathsf{pp}_{\mathsf{RSS}}$ *is implicitly input to all other algorithms.*
$\mathsf{KGen}^{\mathsf{RSS}}$. *The algorithm* $\mathsf{KGen}^{\mathsf{RSS}}$ *generates a key pair:*

$$(\mathsf{sk}^{\mathsf{RSS}}_{\mathsf{sig}}, \mathsf{pk}^{\mathsf{RSS}}_{\mathsf{sig}}) \leftarrow_r \mathsf{KGen}^{\mathsf{RSS}}(\mathsf{pp}_{\mathsf{RSS}})$$

$\mathsf{Sign}^{\mathsf{RSS}}$. *The algorithm* $\mathsf{Sign}^{\mathsf{RSS}}$ *outputs a signature* σ^{RSS} *and some redaction information* $\mathsf{RED}^{\mathsf{RSS}}$ *on input of* $\mathsf{sk}^{\mathsf{RSS}}_{\mathsf{sig}}$, $\mathsf{ADM}^{\mathsf{RSS}}$ *and a message* m:

$$(\sigma^{\mathsf{RSS}}, \mathsf{RED}^{\mathsf{RSS}}) \leftarrow_r \mathsf{Sign}^{\mathsf{RSS}}(\mathsf{sk}^{\mathsf{RSS}}_{\mathsf{sig}}, m, \mathsf{ADM}^{\mathsf{RSS}})$$

Note, it is assumed that $\mathsf{ADM}^{\mathsf{RSS}}$ *can always be derived.*
$\mathsf{Verify}^{\mathsf{RSS}}$. *The deterministic algorithm* $\mathsf{Verify}^{\mathsf{RSS}}$ *verifies a signature* σ^{RSS}, *i.e., outputs a decision* $d \in \{0, 1\}$ *w.r.t.* $\mathsf{pk}^{\mathsf{RSS}}_{\mathsf{sig}}$ *and a message* m:

$$d \leftarrow \mathsf{Verify}^{\mathsf{RSS}}(\mathsf{pk}^{\mathsf{RSS}}_{\mathsf{sig}}, m, \sigma^{\mathsf{RSS}})$$

$\mathsf{Redact}^{\mathsf{RSS}}$. *The algorithm* $\mathsf{Redact}^{\mathsf{RSS}}$ *outputs a derived signature* $\sigma^{\mathsf{RSS}\prime}$ *and a derived message* m' *on input of* $\mathsf{pk}^{\mathsf{RSS}}_{\mathsf{sig}}$, *a signature* σ^{RSS}, *some modification instruction* $\mathsf{MOD}^{\mathsf{RSS}}$ *and some redaction information* $\mathsf{RED}^{\mathsf{RSS}}$:

$$(\sigma^{\mathsf{RSS}\prime}, m', \mathsf{RED}^{\mathsf{RSS}\prime}) \leftarrow_r \mathsf{Redact}^{\mathsf{RSS}}(\mathsf{pk}^{\mathsf{RSS}}_{\mathsf{sig}}, m, \sigma^{\mathsf{RSS}}, \mathsf{MOD}^{\mathsf{RSS}}, \mathsf{RED}^{\mathsf{RSS}})$$

---

[1] Strictly speaking, there are approaches with additional secret keys, but they are not required for our construction [37].

Note, to make our construction provably secure, we require that the redaction information RED^{RSS} and its derivatives $RED^{RSS'}$, are always of constant size w.r.t. to κ. This is actually the case in the constructions by Derler et al. [20]. Note, Derler et al. require that even without RED^{RSS} a redactor can redact [20]. Thus, this auxiliary string is only meant to make redactions more efficient.

Security Requirements. Due to space restrictions, we only sketch the security requirements here. The formal game-based definitions are given in the full version of this paper.

Note, even though these definitions seem to be related to the ones for SSSs, one needs to take care that in standard definition of RSSs, only one key pair exists. Thus, neither accountability nor immutability are meaningful. Moreover, the unforgeability definition does not take signatures into account, but only messages, as everyone can redact.

Unforgeability. No one should, without holding the signing key, create valid signatures on messages not endorsed by the signer, i.e., forgeries exclude valid redactions.

Privacy. An outsider not holding any secret keys should not be able to derive which message was contained before a redaction took place.

Transparency. An outsider should not be able to decide whether a signature was the result of a redaction or not.

3   Protean Signatures

We now present our framework for PSs. To recap, a PS allows to remove and alter signer-chosen parts of a signed message by a semi-trusted third party, i.e., the sanitizer. The sanitizer can also be held accountable, if it chose to edit a signed message. For the framework, we need to settle some additional notation, which is derived from the ones used for RSSs and SSSs to ease understanding.

Protean Signature Schemes. For the framework, we use the following notation. The variable ADM^{PS} is a list containing the set of indices of the editable blocks, as well as the blocks which can be redacted. For example, let $ADM^{PS} = (\{1,2\},\{4\})$. Then, the first and second block are editable, while only the fourth block can be redacted. The variable MOD^{PS} is a list containing a set of pairs $(i, m^{i'})$ for those blocks that are modified, meaning that m^i is replaced by $m^{i'}$ and a set of indices to be redacted. In more detail, if $MOD^{PS} = (\{(1,b),(2,b)\},\{3\})$ means that the first two blocks are altered to contain a b, while the third block is redacted.

We use the shorthand notation $m' \leftarrow MOD^{PS}(m)$ to denote the result of this replacement, while $MOD^{PS} \prec (m, ADM^{PS})$ means that MOD^{PS} is a valid modification instruction w.r.t. m and ADM^{PS}. Likewise, we use $ADM^{PS} \prec m$ to denote that ADM^{PS} is valid description of the admissible blocks w.r.t. m.

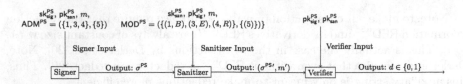

Fig. 1. Example workflow of a PS. The message m is set to (H, E, L, L, O) and is modified to (B, E, E, R).

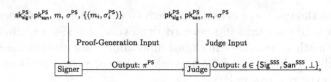

Fig. 2. Proof-generation and Judge^{PS}

An example workflow is depicted in Figs. 1 and 2. Note, that this is very similar to SSSs. To ease understanding and the description of our construction, we define that the replacements are done first and the redactions afterwards.

Definition 3 (Protean Signature). *A Protean Signature scheme PS consists of the following eight ppt algorithms* $(\text{PPGen}^{\text{PS}}, \text{KGen}_{\text{sig}}^{\text{PS}}, \text{KGen}_{\text{san}}^{\text{PS}}, \text{Sign}^{\text{PS}}, \text{Verify}^{\text{PS}}, \text{Edit}^{\text{PS}}, \text{Proof}^{\text{PS}}, \text{Judge}^{\text{PS}})$ *such that:*

PPGen^{PS}. *The algorithm* PPGen^{PS} *generates the public parameters:*

$$\text{pp}_{\text{PS}} \leftarrow_r \text{PPGen}^{\text{PS}}(1^\kappa)$$

We assume that pp_{PS} *is implicitly input to all other algorithms.*
$\text{KGen}_{\text{sig}}^{\text{PS}}$. *The algorithm* $\text{KGen}_{\text{sig}}^{\text{PS}}$ *generates the key pair of the signer:*

$$(\text{sk}_{\text{sig}}^{\text{PS}}, \text{pk}_{\text{sig}}^{\text{PS}}) \leftarrow_r \text{KGen}_{\text{sig}}^{\text{PS}}(\text{pp}_{\text{PS}})$$

$\text{KGen}_{\text{san}}^{\text{PS}}$. *The algorithm* $\text{KGen}_{\text{san}}^{\text{SSS}}$ *generates the key pair of the sanitizer:*

$$(\text{sk}_{\text{san}}^{\text{PS}}, \text{pk}_{\text{san}}^{\text{PS}}) \leftarrow_r \text{KGen}_{\text{san}}^{\text{PS}}(\text{pp}_{\text{PS}})$$

Sign^{PS}. *The algorithm* Sign^{PS} *generates a signature* σ^{PS} *on input of the public key* $\text{pk}_{\text{san}}^{\text{PS}}$, ADM^{PS}, *a message* m, *and* $\text{sk}_{\text{sig}}^{\text{PS}}$:

$$\sigma^{\text{PS}} \leftarrow_r \text{Sign}^{\text{PS}}(\text{sk}_{\text{sig}}^{\text{PS}}, \text{pk}_{\text{san}}^{\text{PS}}, m, \text{ADM}^{\text{PS}})$$

It is assumed that ADM^{PS} *can be derived from any verifying signature* σ^{PS}, *if* $\text{sk}_{\text{san}}^{\text{PS}}$ *is known.*
$\text{Verify}^{\text{PS}}$. *The deterministic algorithm* $\text{Verify}^{\text{PS}}$ *verifies a signature* σ^{PS}, *i.e., outputs a decision* $d \in \{0, 1\}$ *w.r.t.* $\text{pk}_{\text{san}}^{\text{PS}}$, $\text{pk}_{\text{sig}}^{\text{PS}}$, *and a message* m:

$$d \leftarrow \text{Verify}^{\text{PS}}(\text{pk}_{\text{sig}}^{\text{PS}}, \text{pk}_{\text{san}}^{\text{PS}}, m, \sigma^{\text{PS}})$$

Experiment $\mathsf{Unforgeability}_{\mathcal{A}}^{\mathsf{PS}}(\kappa)$

   $\mathsf{pp}_{\mathsf{PS}} \leftarrow_r \mathsf{PPGen}^{\mathsf{PS}}(1^\kappa)$

   $(\mathsf{sk}_{\mathsf{sig}}^{\mathsf{PS}}, \mathsf{pk}_{\mathsf{sig}}^{\mathsf{PS}}) \leftarrow_r \mathsf{KGen}_{\mathsf{sig}}^{\mathsf{PS}}(\mathsf{pp}_{\mathsf{PS}})$

   $(\mathsf{sk}_{\mathsf{san}}^{\mathsf{PS}}, \mathsf{pk}_{\mathsf{san}}^{\mathsf{PS}}) \leftarrow_r \mathsf{KGen}_{\mathsf{san}}^{\mathsf{PS}}(\mathsf{pp}_{\mathsf{PS}})$

   $(m^*, \sigma^{\mathsf{PS}*}) \leftarrow_r \mathcal{A}^{\mathsf{Sign}^{\mathsf{PS}}(\mathsf{sk}_{\mathsf{sig}}^{\mathsf{PS}},\cdot,\cdot,\cdot), \mathsf{Edit}^{\mathsf{PS}}(\mathsf{sk}_{\mathsf{san}}^{\mathsf{PS}},\cdot,\cdot,\cdot,\cdot), \mathsf{Proof}^{\mathsf{PS}}(\mathsf{sk}_{\mathsf{sig}}^{\mathsf{PS}},\cdot,\cdot,\cdot,\cdot)}(\mathsf{pk}_{\mathsf{sig}}^{\mathsf{PS}}, \mathsf{pk}_{\mathsf{san}}^{\mathsf{PS}})$

     for $i = 1, 2, \ldots, q$ let $(\mathsf{pk}_{\mathsf{san},i}^{\mathsf{PS}}, m_i, \mathsf{ADM}_i^{\mathsf{PS}})$ and σ_i^{PS}

     index the queries/answers to/from $\mathsf{Sign}^{\mathsf{PS}}$

     for $j = 1, 2, \ldots, q'$ let $(\mathsf{pk}_{\mathsf{sig},j}^{\mathsf{PS}}, m_j, \sigma_j^{\mathsf{PS}}, \mathsf{MOD}_j)$ and $(m_j', \sigma_j^{\mathsf{PS}'}, \mathsf{ADM}^{\mathsf{PS}'}_j)$

     index the queries/answers to/from $\mathsf{Edit}^{\mathsf{PS}}$

   return 1, if $\mathsf{Verify}^{\mathsf{PS}}(\mathsf{pk}_{\mathsf{sig}}^{\mathsf{PS}}, \mathsf{pk}_{\mathsf{san}}^{\mathsf{PS}}, m^*, \sigma^{\mathsf{PS}*}) = 1 \wedge$

     $\forall i \in \{1, 2, \ldots, q\} : (\mathsf{pk}_{\mathsf{san}}^{\mathsf{PS}}, m^*, \sigma^{\mathsf{PS}*}) \neq (\mathsf{pk}_{\mathsf{san},i}^{\mathsf{PS}}, m_i, \sigma_i^{\mathsf{PS}}) \wedge$

     $\forall j \in \{1, 2, \ldots, q'\} : (\mathsf{pk}_{\mathsf{sig}}^{\mathsf{PS}}, m^*, \sigma^{\mathsf{PS}*}) \neq (\mathsf{pk}_{\mathsf{sig},j}^{\mathsf{PS}}, m_j', \sigma_j^{\mathsf{PS}'})$

   return 0

Fig. 3. PS unforgeability

$\mathsf{Edit}^{\mathsf{PS}}$. *The algorithm* $\mathsf{Edit}^{\mathsf{PS}}$ *generates a sanitized signature* $\sigma^{\mathsf{PS}'}$ *and updated* $\mathsf{ADM}^{\mathsf{PS}'}$, *given inputs* $\mathsf{sk}_{\mathsf{san}}^{\mathsf{PS}}$, $\mathsf{ADM}^{\mathsf{PS}}$, *a message* m, *and* $\mathsf{pk}_{\mathsf{sig}}^{\mathsf{PS}}$:

$$(m', \sigma^{\mathsf{PS}'}, \mathsf{ADM}^{\mathsf{PS}'}) \leftarrow_r \mathsf{Edit}^{\mathsf{PS}}(\mathsf{sk}_{\mathsf{san}}^{\mathsf{PS}}, \mathsf{pk}_{\mathsf{sig}}^{\mathsf{PS}}, m, \mathsf{MOD}^{\mathsf{PS}})$$

$\mathsf{Proof}^{\mathsf{PS}}$. *The algorithm* $\mathsf{Proof}^{\mathsf{PS}}$ *outputs a proof* π^{PS} *on input* m, σ^{PS}, $\mathsf{sk}_{\mathsf{sig}}^{\mathsf{PS}}$, $\mathsf{pk}_{\mathsf{san}}^{\mathsf{PS}}$, *and a set of polynomially many additional signature/message pairs* $\{(\sigma_i^{\mathsf{PS}}, m^i)\}$. *The proof* π^{PS} *is used by the next algorithm to pinpoint the accountable party for a given signature:*

$$\pi^{\mathsf{PS}} \leftarrow_r \mathsf{Proof}^{\mathsf{PS}}(\mathsf{sk}_{\mathsf{sig}}^{\mathsf{PS}}, \mathsf{pk}_{\mathsf{san}}^{\mathsf{PS}}, m, \sigma^{\mathsf{PS}}, \{(\sigma_i^{\mathsf{PS}}, m^i)\})$$

$\mathsf{Judge}^{\mathsf{PS}}$. *The deterministic algorithm* $\mathsf{Judge}^{\mathsf{PS}}$ *outputs a decision* $d \in \{\mathsf{Sig}^{\mathsf{PS}}, \mathsf{San}^{\mathsf{PS}}, \perp\}$ *indicating whether the message/signature pair has been created by the signer, or the sanitizer:*

$$d \leftarrow \mathsf{Judge}^{\mathsf{PS}}(\mathsf{pk}_{\mathsf{sig}}^{\mathsf{PS}}, \mathsf{pk}_{\mathsf{san}}^{\mathsf{PS}}, m, \sigma^{\mathsf{PS}}, \pi^{\mathsf{PS}})$$

PSs Security Definitions. We now introduce the security properties for PSs. Clearly, the goals are similar to the ones for SSSs and RSSs. However, due to the extended capabilities, the semantic is quite different, while we need to take extra care for changed indices after redactions.

Unforgeability. This definition requires that an adversary $\mathcal{A}$ not having any secret keys is not able to produce any valid signature $\sigma^{\mathsf{PS}*}$ on a message m^* which it has never not seen, even if $\mathcal{A}$ has full oracle access, i.e., this captures "strong unforgeability" [33].

Definition 4 (Unforgeability). *A PS is unforgeable, if for any PPT adversary* $\mathcal{A}$ *there exists a negligible function* ν *such that* $\Pr[\mathsf{Unforgeability}_{\mathcal{A}}^{\mathsf{PS}}(\kappa) = 1] \leq \nu(\kappa)$, *where the corresponding experiment is defined in Fig. 3.*

Immutability. This definition prohibits that an adversary $\mathcal{A}$ can generate a verifying signature $\sigma^{\mathsf{PS}*}$ for a message m^* not derivable from the signatures given by an honest signer, even if it can generate the editor's key pair.

Experiment $\mathsf{Immutability}_{\mathcal{A}}^{\mathsf{PS}}(\kappa)$

   $\mathsf{pp}_{\mathsf{PS}} \leftarrow_r \mathsf{PPGen}^{\mathsf{PS}}(1^{\kappa})$

   $(\mathsf{sk}_{\mathsf{sig}}^{\mathsf{PS}}, \mathsf{pk}_{\mathsf{sig}}^{\mathsf{PS}}) \leftarrow_r \mathsf{KGen}_{\mathsf{sig}}^{\mathsf{PS}}(\mathsf{pp}_{\mathsf{PS}})$

   $(m^*, \sigma^{\mathsf{PS}*}, \mathsf{pk}_{\mathsf{san}}^{\mathsf{PS}*}) \leftarrow_r \mathcal{A}^{\mathsf{Sign}^{\mathsf{PS}}(\mathsf{sk}_{\mathsf{sig}}^{\mathsf{PS}}, \cdot, \cdot, \cdot), \mathsf{Proof}^{\mathsf{PS}}(\mathsf{sk}_{\mathsf{sig}}^{\mathsf{PS}}, \cdot, \cdot, \cdot)}(\mathsf{pk}_{\mathsf{sig}}^{\mathsf{PS}})$

     for $i = 1, 2, \ldots, q$ let $(\mathsf{pk}_{\mathsf{san},i}^{\mathsf{PS}}, m_i, \mathsf{ADM}_i^{\mathsf{PS}})$

     index the queries to $\mathsf{Sign}^{\mathsf{PS}}$

   return 1, if $\mathsf{Verify}^{\mathsf{PS}}(\mathsf{pk}_{\mathsf{sig}}^{\mathsf{PS}}, \mathsf{pk}_{\mathsf{san}}^{\mathsf{PS}*}, m^*, \sigma^{\mathsf{PS}*}) = 1 \wedge$

     $\forall i \in \{1, 2, \ldots, q\} : (\mathsf{pk}_{\mathsf{san}}^{\mathsf{PS}*} \neq \mathsf{pk}_{\mathsf{san},i}^{\mathsf{PS}} \vee$

     $m^* \notin \{\mathsf{MOD}(m_i) \mid \mathsf{MOD} \text{ with } \mathsf{MOD} \prec (m_i, \mathsf{ADM}_i^{\mathsf{PS}})\})$

   return 0

Fig. 4. PS immutability

Experiment $\mathsf{Privacy}_{\mathcal{A}}^{\mathsf{PS}}(\kappa)$

   $\mathsf{pp}_{\mathsf{PS}} \leftarrow_r \mathsf{PPGen}^{\mathsf{PS}}(1^{\kappa})$

   $(\mathsf{sk}_{\mathsf{sig}}^{\mathsf{PS}}, \mathsf{pk}_{\mathsf{sig}}^{\mathsf{PS}}) \leftarrow_r \mathsf{KGen}_{\mathsf{sig}}^{\mathsf{PS}}(\mathsf{pp}_{\mathsf{PS}})$

   $(\mathsf{sk}_{\mathsf{san}}^{\mathsf{PS}}, \mathsf{pk}_{\mathsf{san}}^{\mathsf{PS}}) \leftarrow_r \mathsf{KGen}_{\mathsf{san}}^{\mathsf{PS}}(\mathsf{pp}_{\mathsf{PS}})$

   $b \leftarrow_r \{0, 1\}$

   $a \leftarrow_r \mathcal{A}^{\mathsf{Sign}^{\mathsf{PS}}(\mathsf{sk}_{\mathsf{sig}}^{\mathsf{PS}}, \cdot, \cdot, \cdot), \mathsf{Edit}^{\mathsf{PS}}(\mathsf{sk}_{\mathsf{san}}^{\mathsf{PS}}, \cdot, \cdot, \cdot, \cdot, \cdot), \mathsf{Proof}^{\mathsf{PS}}(\mathsf{sk}_{\mathsf{sig}}^{\mathsf{PS}}, \cdot, \cdot, \cdot, \cdot), \mathsf{LoREdit}(\cdot, \cdot, \cdot, \cdot, \cdot, \mathsf{sk}_{\mathsf{sig}}^{\mathsf{PS}}, \mathsf{sk}_{\mathsf{san}}^{\mathsf{PS}}, b)}(\mathsf{pk}_{\mathsf{sig}}^{\mathsf{PS}}, \mathsf{pk}_{\mathsf{san}}^{\mathsf{PS}})$

     where oracle $\mathsf{LoREdit}$ on input of $m_0, m_1, \mathsf{MOD}_0^{\mathsf{PS}}, \mathsf{MOD}_1^{\mathsf{PS}}, \mathsf{ADM}_0^{\mathsf{PS}}, \mathsf{ADM}_1^{\mathsf{PS}}, \mathsf{sk}_{\mathsf{sig}}^{\mathsf{PS}}, \mathsf{sk}_{\mathsf{san}}^{\mathsf{PS}}, b$

     let $\sigma_i^{\mathsf{PS}} \leftarrow_r \mathsf{Sign}^{\mathsf{PS}}(\mathsf{sk}_{\mathsf{sig}}^{\mathsf{PS}}, \mathsf{pk}_{\mathsf{san}}^{\mathsf{PS}}, m_i, \mathsf{ADM}_i^{\mathsf{PS}})$ for $i \in \{0, 1\}$

     let $(m_i', \sigma_i^{\mathsf{PS}\prime}, \mathsf{ADM}_i^{\mathsf{PS}\prime}) \leftarrow_r \mathsf{Edit}^{\mathsf{PS}}(\mathsf{sk}_{\mathsf{san}}^{\mathsf{PS}}, \mathsf{pk}_{\mathsf{sig}}^{\mathsf{PS}}, m_i, \sigma_i^{\mathsf{PS}}, \mathsf{MOD}_i^{\mathsf{PS}})$ for $i \in \{0, 1\}$

     return $\perp$, if $m_0' \neq m_1' \vee \mathsf{ADM}_0^{\mathsf{PS}\prime} \neq \mathsf{ADM}_1^{\mathsf{PS}\prime}$

     return $(m_b', \sigma_b^{\mathsf{PS}\prime}, \mathsf{ADM}_b^{\mathsf{PS}\prime})$

   return 1, if $a = b$

   return 0

Fig. 5. PS privacy

Definition 5 (Immutability). *A* PS *is immutable, if for any PPT adversary $\mathcal{A}$ there exists a negligible function ν such that* $\Pr[\mathsf{Immutability}_{\mathcal{A}}^{\mathsf{PS}}(\kappa) = 1] \leq \nu(\kappa)$, *where the corresponding experiment is defined in Fig. 4.*

Privacy. This definition prohibits that an adversary $\mathcal{A}$ can learn anything about edited (redacted or sanitized) parts.

Definition 6 (Privacy). *A* PS *is private, if for any PPT adversary $\mathcal{A}$ there exists a negligible function ν such that* $\left|\Pr[\mathsf{Privacy}_{\mathcal{A}}^{\mathsf{PS}}(\kappa)] - 1/2\right| \leq \nu(\kappa)$, *where the corresponding experiment is defined in Fig. 5.*

Transparency. This definition requires that an adversary $\mathcal{A}$ does not learn whether a signature σ^{PS} was generated through $\mathsf{Sign}^{\mathsf{PS}}$ or $\mathsf{Edit}^{\mathsf{PS}}$.

Definition 7 (Transparency). *A* PS *is transparent, if for any PPT adversary $\mathcal{A}$ there exists a negligible function ν such that* $\left|\Pr[\mathsf{Transparency}_{\mathcal{A}}^{\mathsf{PS}}(\kappa)] - 1/2\right| \leq \nu(\kappa)$, *where the corresponding experiment is defined in Fig. 6.*

Signer-Accountability. Signer-accountability prohibits that an adversary can generate a bogus proof that makes $\mathsf{Judge}^{\mathsf{PS}}$ decide that the sanitizer is responsible

Experiment $\text{Transparency}_{\mathcal{A}}^{\text{PS}}(\kappa)$

$\quad \text{pp}_{\text{PS}} \leftarrow_r \text{PPGen}^{\text{PS}}(1^\kappa)$

$\quad (\text{sk}_{\text{sig}}^{\text{PS}}, \text{pk}_{\text{sig}}^{\text{PS}}) \leftarrow_r \text{KGen}_{\text{sig}}^{\text{PS}}(\text{pp}_{\text{PS}})$

$\quad (\text{sk}_{\text{san}}^{\text{PS}}, \text{pk}_{\text{san}}^{\text{PS}}) \leftarrow_r \text{KGen}_{\text{san}}^{\text{PS}}(\text{pp}_{\text{PS}})$

$\quad b \leftarrow_r \{0,1\}$

$\quad \mathcal{Q} \leftarrow \emptyset$

$\quad a \leftarrow_r \mathcal{A}^{\text{Sign}^{\text{PS}}(\text{sk}_{\text{sig}}^{\text{PS}}, \cdot, \cdot, \cdot), \text{Edit}^{\text{PS}}(\text{sk}_{\text{san}}^{\text{PS}}, \cdot, \cdot, \cdot, \cdot), \text{Proof}^{\text{PS}\prime}(\text{sk}_{\text{sig}}^{\text{PS}}, \cdot, \cdot, \cdot, \cdot), \text{Sign}/\text{Edit}(\cdot, \cdot, \cdot, \text{sk}_{\text{sig}}^{\text{PS}}, \text{sk}_{\text{san}}^{\text{PS}}, b)}(\text{pk}_{\text{sig}}^{\text{PS}}, \text{pk}_{\text{san}}^{\text{PS}})$

$\quad\quad$ where oracle $\text{Proof}^{\text{PS}\prime}$ on input of $\text{sk}_{\text{sig}}^{\text{PS}}, m, \sigma^{\text{PS}}, \{(m_i, \sigma_i^{\text{PS}}) \mid i \in \mathbb{N}\}$:

$\quad\quad\quad$ return $\bot$, if $\text{pk}_{\text{san}}^{\text{PS}\prime} = \text{pk}_{\text{san}}^{\text{PS}} \wedge ((m, \sigma^{\text{PS}}) \in \mathcal{Q} \vee \mathcal{Q} \cap \{(m_i, \sigma_i^{\text{PS}})\} \neq \emptyset)$

$\quad\quad\quad$ return $\text{Proof}^{\text{PS}}(\text{sk}_{\text{sig}}^{\text{PS}}, \text{pk}_{\text{san}}^{\text{PS}\prime}, m, \sigma^{\text{PS}}, \{(m_i, \sigma_i^{\text{PS}})\})$

$\quad\quad$ where oracle Sign/Edit on input of $m, \text{MOD}^{\text{PS}}, \text{ADM}^{\text{PS}}, \text{sk}_{\text{sig}}^{\text{PS}}, \text{sk}_{\text{san}}^{\text{PS}}, b$:

$\quad\quad\quad \sigma^{\text{PS}} \leftarrow_r \text{Sign}^{\text{PS}}(\text{sk}_{\text{sig}}^{\text{PS}}, \text{pk}_{\text{san}}^{\text{PS}}, m, \text{ADM}^{\text{PS}})$

$\quad\quad\quad (m', \sigma^{\text{PS}\prime}, \text{ADM}^{\text{PS}\prime}) \leftarrow_r \text{Edit}^{\text{PS}}(\text{sk}_{\text{san}}^{\text{PS}}, \text{pk}_{\text{sig}}^{\text{PS}}, m, \sigma^{\text{PS}}, \text{MOD}^{\text{PS}})$

$\quad\quad\quad$ if $b = 1$:

$\quad\quad\quad\quad \sigma^{\text{PS}\prime} \leftarrow_r \text{Sign}^{\text{PS}}(\text{sk}_{\text{sig}}^{\text{PS}}, \text{pk}_{\text{san}}^{\text{PS}}, m', \text{ADM}^{\text{PS}\prime})$

$\quad\quad\quad$ if $\sigma^{\text{PS}\prime} \neq \bot$, set $\mathcal{Q} \leftarrow \mathcal{Q} \cup \{(m', \sigma^{\text{PS}\prime})\}$

$\quad\quad\quad$ return $(m', \sigma^{\text{PS}\prime})$

$\quad$ return 1, if $a = b$

$\quad$ return 0

Fig. 6. PS transparency

for a given signature/message pair $(m^*, \sigma^{\text{PS}*})$, but the sanitizer has never generated this pair. This is even true, if the adversary can generate the signer's key pair.

Experiment $\text{SigAccountability}_{\mathcal{A}}^{\text{PS}}(\kappa)$

$\quad \text{pp}_{\text{PS}} \leftarrow_r \text{PPGen}^{\text{PS}}(1^\kappa)$

$\quad (\text{sk}_{\text{san}}^{\text{PS}}, \text{pk}_{\text{san}}^{\text{PS}}) \leftarrow_r \text{KGen}_{\text{san}}^{\text{PS}}(\text{pp}_{\text{PS}})$

$\quad (\text{pk}_{\text{sig}}^{\text{PS}*}, \pi^{\text{PS}*}, m^*, \sigma^{\text{PS}*}) \leftarrow_r \mathcal{A}^{\text{Edit}^{\text{PS}}(\text{sk}_{\text{san}}^{\text{PS}}, \cdot, \cdot, \cdot, \cdot)}(\text{pk}_{\text{san}}^{\text{PS}})$

$\quad\quad$ for $i = 1, 2, \ldots, q$ let $(m_i', \sigma_i^{\text{PS}\prime}, \text{ADM}^{\text{PS}}_j)$ and $(m_i, \text{MOD}_i^{\text{PS}}, \sigma_i^{\text{PS}}, \text{pk}_{\text{sig},i}^{\text{PS}})$

$\quad\quad$ index the answers/queries from/to Edit^{PS}

$\quad\quad$ return 1, if $\text{Verify}^{\text{PS}}(\text{pk}_{\text{sig}}^{\text{PS}*}, \text{pk}_{\text{san}}^{\text{PS}}, m^*, \sigma^{\text{PS}*}) = 1 \wedge$

$\quad\quad \forall i \in \{1, 2, \ldots, q\} : (\text{pk}_{\text{sig}}^{\text{PS}*}, m^*, \sigma^{\text{PS}*}) \neq (\text{pk}_{\text{sig},i}^{\text{PS}}, m_i', \sigma_i^{\text{PS}\prime}) \wedge$

$\quad\quad \text{Judge}^{\text{PS}}(\text{pk}_{\text{sig}}^{\text{PS}}, \text{pk}_{\text{san}}^{\text{PS}}, m^*, \sigma^{\text{PS}*}, \pi^{\text{PS}*}) = \text{San}^{\text{PS}}$

$\quad$ return 0

Fig. 7. PS signer-accountability

Definition 8 (Signer-Accountability). *A* PS *is signer-accountable, if for any PPT adversary* $\mathcal{A}$ *there exists a negligible function* ν *such that* $\Pr[\text{SigAccountability}_{\mathcal{A}}^{\text{PS}}(\kappa) = 1] \leq \nu(\kappa)$, *where the corresponding experiment is defined in Fig. 7.*

Sanitizer-Accountability. Sanitizer-accountability prohibits that an adversary can generate a bogus signature/message pair $(m^*, \sigma^{\text{PS}*})$ that makes $\text{Proof}^{\text{SSS}}$ output an honestly generated proof π^{PS} which points to the signer, but $(m^*, \sigma^{\text{PS}*})$

Experiment SanAccountability$_{\mathcal{A}}^{PS}(\kappa)$

$pp_{PS} \leftarrow_r PPGen^{PS}(1^\kappa)$

$(sk_{sig}^{PS}, pk_{sig}^{PS}) \leftarrow_r KGen_{sig}^{PS}(pp_{PS})$

$(m^*, \sigma^{PS*}, pk_{san}^{PS*}) \leftarrow_r \mathcal{A}^{Sign^{PS}(sk_{sig}^{PS}, \cdot, \cdot, \cdot), Proof^{PS}(sk_{sig}^{PS}, \cdot, \cdot, \cdot, \cdot)}(pk_{sig}^{PS})$

    for $i = 1, 2, \ldots, q$ let $(pk_{san,i}^{PS}, m_i, ADM_i^{PS})$ and σ_i^{PS}

    index the queries/answers to/from $Sign^{PS}$

$\pi^{PS} \leftarrow_r Proof^{PS}(sk_{sig}, pk_{san}^{PS*}, m^*, \sigma^{PS*}, \{(m_i, \sigma_i^{PS}) \mid 0 < i \leq q\})$

return 1, if $Verify^{PS}(pk_{sig}^{PS}, pk_{san}^{PS*}, m^*, \sigma^{PS*}) = 1 \wedge$

    $\forall i \in \{1, 2, \ldots, q\} : (pk_{san}^{PS*}, m^*, \sigma^{PS*}) \neq (pk_{san,i}^{PS}, m_i, \sigma_i^{PS}) \wedge$

    $Judge^{PS}(pk_{sig}^{PS}, pk_{san}^{PS*}, m^*, \sigma^{PS*}, \pi^{PS}) = Sig^{PS}$

return 0

Fig. 8. PS sanitizer-accountability

Experiment Invisibility$_{\mathcal{A}}^{PS}(\kappa)$

$pp_{PS} \leftarrow_r PPGen^{PS}(1^\kappa)$

$(sk_{sig}^{PS}, pk_{sig}^{PS}) \leftarrow_r KGen_{sig}^{PS}(pp_{PS})$

$(sk_{san}^{PS}, pk_{san}^{PS}) \leftarrow_r KGen_{san}^{PS}(pp_{PS})$

$b \leftarrow_r \{0, 1\}$

$\mathcal{Q} \leftarrow \emptyset$

$a \leftarrow_r \mathcal{A}^{Edit^{PS\prime}(sk_{san}^{PS}, \cdot, \cdot, \cdot, \cdot), Proof^{PS}(sk_{sig}^{PS}, \cdot, \cdot, \cdot, \cdot), LoRADM(sk_{sig}^{PS}, \cdot, \cdot, \cdot, \cdot, b)}(pk_{sig}^{PS}, pk_{san}^{PS})$

    where oracle LoRADM on input of $sk_{sig}, pk_{san}^{PS\prime}, m, ADM_0^{PS}, ADM_1^{PS}, b$:

    return $\bot$, if $ADM_0^{PS}.2 \neq ADM_1^{PS}.2 \vee ADM_0^{PS} \not\preceq m \wedge ADM_1^{PS} \not\preceq m$

    return $\bot$, if $pk_{san}^{PS} \neq pk_{san}^{PS\prime} \wedge ADM_0^{PS} \neq ADM_1^{PS}$

    let $\sigma^{PS} \leftarrow_r Sign^{PS}(sk_{sig}^{PS}, pk_{san}^{PS\prime}, m, ADM_b^{PS})$

    if $pk_{san}^{PS\prime} = pk_{san}^{PS}$, let $\mathcal{Q} \leftarrow \mathcal{Q} \cup \{(m, \sigma^{PS}, ((ADM_0^{PS}.1 \cap ADM_1^{PS}.1), ADM_0^{PS}.2))\}$

    return σ^{PS}

    where oracle $Edit^{PS\prime}$ on input of $pk_{sig}^{PS\prime}, sk_{san}^{PS}, m, MOD^{PS}, \sigma^{PS}$:

    return $\bot$, if $pk_{sig}^{PS\prime} = pk_{sig}^{PS} \wedge \nexists (m, \sigma^{PS}, ADM) \in \mathcal{Q} : MOD^{PS} \prec (m, ADM)$

    let $(m', \sigma^{PS\prime}, ADM^{PS\prime\prime}) \leftarrow_r Edit^{PS}(pk_{sig}^{PS\prime}, sk_{san}^{PS}, m, MOD^{PS}, \sigma^{PS})$

    if $pk_{sig}^{PS\prime} = pk_{sig}^{PS} \wedge \exists (m, \sigma^{PS}, ADM^{PS\prime}) \in \mathcal{Q} : MOD^{PS} \prec (m, ADM^{PS\prime})$,

        let $\mathcal{Q} \leftarrow \mathcal{Q} \cup \{(m', \sigma^{PS\prime}, ADM^{PS\prime\prime})\}$

    return $(m', \sigma^{PS\prime})$

return 1, if $a = b$

return 0

Fig. 9. PS invisibility

has never been generated by the signer. This is even true, if the adversary can generate the sanitizer's key pair.

Definition 9 (Sanitizer-Accountability). *A PS is sanitizer-accountable, if for any PPT adversary $\mathcal{A}$ there exists a negligible function ν such that* $\Pr[SanAccountability_{\mathcal{A}}^{PS}(\kappa) = 1] \leq \nu(\kappa)$, *where the corresponding experiment is defined in Fig. 8.*

Invisibility. Invisibility prohibits that an outsider can decide which blocks can be edited. However, as there are no RSSs which prohibit to decide which elements are redactable (as redactions are always public), we restrict ourselves to the case of which blocks can be edited by the sanitizer. This is a very strong privacy notion and might be required, or not, depending on the use-case. However, we want to point out that achieving this notion is possible with our construction, even though it comes at a high price (cf. Sect. 4). The main idea is that the adversary has to decide which blocks are admissible — the oracle either uses $\mathsf{ADM}_0^{\mathsf{PS}}.1$ or $\mathsf{ADM}_1^{\mathsf{PS}}.1$. Here, $\mathsf{ADM}_1^{\mathsf{PS}}.b$, where $b \in \{1, 2\}$ means the bth element of the list. To avoid trivial attacks, the adversary needs to be limited to further edit messages where $(\mathsf{ADM}_0^{\mathsf{PS}}.1 \cap \mathsf{ADM}_1^{\mathsf{PS}}.1)$. Note, the signing oracle can be simulated by using the same $\mathsf{ADM}^{\mathsf{PS}}$ in the LoRADM oracle.

Definition 10 (Invisibility). *A PS is invisible, if for any PPT adversary $\mathcal{A}$ there exists a negligible function ν such that $\left| \Pr[\mathsf{Invisibility}_{\mathcal{A}}^{\mathsf{PS}}(\kappa)] - 1/2 \right| \leq \nu(\kappa)$, where the corresponding experiment is defined in Fig. 9.*

We conclude with a final definition.

Definition 11 (Secure PSs). *A PS is secure, if it unforgeable, private, transparent, immutable, signer-accountable, and sanitizer-accountable.*

If invisibility is required, depends on the use-case.

In the full version we prove that PSs generalize both SSSs and RSSs.

4   Construction

In this section, we introduce our construction for PSs. The basic idea is to combine RSSs and SSSs by bridging them using unique tags. In more detail, each block $m^i \in m$ is signed using an SSS, while an additional (non-admissible) tag τ is used to identify the "overall" message m the block m^i belongs to. Moreover, each block m^i is also assigned a (non-admissible) additional tag τ_i, along with all public keys, used by the RSS to allow for redactions. Thus, there are $\ell_m\ \sigma_i^{\mathsf{SSS}}$, where each signature protects $(m^i, \tau, \tau_i, \mathsf{pk}_{\mathsf{sig}}^{\mathsf{PS}}, \mathsf{pk}_{\mathsf{san}}^{\mathsf{PS}})$. If a block m_i is sanitizable, it is marked as admissible within $\mathsf{ADM}_i^{\mathsf{SSS}}$. This allows to sanitize the block m^i. Then, each tag τ_i is put into an RSS to allow for transparent redactions, additionally bound to the non-redactable "overall" tag τ and all (non-redactable) public keys. If a block m^i is non-redactable, this is marked in $\mathsf{ADM}^{\mathsf{RSS}}$. Thus, σ^{RSS} protects $(\tau_1, \ldots, \tau_{\ell_m}, \tau, \mathsf{pk}_{\mathsf{sig}}^{\mathsf{PS}}, \mathsf{pk}_{\mathsf{san}}^{\mathsf{PS}})$. For technical reason, namely to make the auxiliary redaction information $\mathsf{RED}^{\mathsf{RSS}}$ available to the sanitizer, we also encrypt this information as c; to achieve stateless signers and sanitizers, this information is also "self-encrypted" by the redactor itself upon editing. Finally, to achieve accountability, all tags, all signatures generated so far, the resulting ciphertext and public keys are signed again using an additional SSS, while in this outer SSS everything, but the public keys and the tag τ are admissible. To maintain transparency, the overall message m is a single block in the outer SSS.

In more detail, the outer signature σ_0^{SSS} protects $(m, \sigma^{\mathsf{RSS}}, c, (\tau_i, \sigma_i^{\mathsf{SSS}})_i, \tau, \mathsf{pk}_{\mathsf{sig}}^{\mathsf{PS}}, \mathsf{pk}_{\mathsf{san}}^{\mathsf{PS}})$. Thus, changing the message or any signature requires changing σ_0^{SSS}, implying accountability. Upon sanitization of a block m^i, σ_i^{SSS} is sanitized, while the outer signature σ_0^{SSS} needs to be adjusted as well. For redaction of a block

m^i, σ^{RSS} is adjusted and the corresponding signature is no longer given out. This also means that σ_0^{SSS} must be adjusted.

Our resulting construction is depicted in Construction 1. To give a graphical overview of the construction idea, see Fig. 10 (before editing) and Fig. 11 (after editing). We stress that this idea seems to be straightforward, but there are a lot of details to make the construction provably secure. Moreover, we do not consider unlinkability [10], as it seems to be very hard to achieve with the underlying construction paradigm, especially considering that there are no SSSs yet which are unlinkable and invisible at the same time.

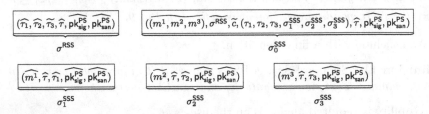

Fig. 10. Our main construction idea. Let $\mathsf{ADM}^{\mathsf{PS}} = (\{2\}, \{3\})$ and $m = (m^1, m^2, m^3)$ for preciseness, i.e., only the second block of m are sanitizable, while only the last block of m is redactable. Redactable elements for the RSS (or sanitizable for the SSS) are marked with a tilde, i.e., $\widetilde{\cdot}$. Blocks which are not redactable (or sanitizable resp.) are marked with a hat, i.e., $\widehat{\cdot}$.

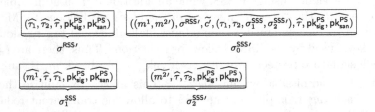

Fig. 11. State after sanitization. Here, block m^3 was redacted and m^2 was changed to $m^{2\prime}$. Block m^1 must stay the same.

Security. The proof of the following Theorem is found in the full version of this paper.

Theorem 1. *The scheme given in Construction 1 is secure (and invisible), if Π, SSS and RSS are secure (and SSS is also invisible).*

Proof (Sketch). Transparency and privacy follow from the transparency and privacy of the underlying primitives, the uniform distribution of the tags, and the IND-CCA2-security of Π. Immutability follows from the unforgeability of the RSS and the immutability of the SSSs. Accountability directly follows from the accountability of the outer SSS. Likewise, invisibility follows from the invisibility of the used SSSs.

$\mathsf{PPGen}^{\mathsf{PS}}(1^\kappa)$. Let $\mathsf{pp}_\Pi \leftarrow_r \mathsf{PPGen}^\Pi(1^\kappa)$, $\mathsf{pp}_{\mathsf{SSS}} \leftarrow_r \mathsf{PPGen}^{\mathsf{SSS}}(1^\kappa)$ and $\mathsf{pp}_{\mathsf{RSS}} \leftarrow_r$ $\mathsf{PPGen}^{\mathsf{RSS}}(1^\kappa)$. Return $\mathsf{pp}_{\mathsf{PS}} = (\mathsf{pp}_\Pi, \mathsf{pp}_{\mathsf{SSS}}, \mathsf{pp}_{\mathsf{RSS}})$.

$\mathsf{KGen}^{\mathsf{PS}}_{\mathsf{sig}}(\mathsf{pp}_{\mathsf{PS}})$. Let $(\mathsf{sk}^{\mathsf{SSS}}_{\mathsf{sig}}, \mathsf{pk}^{\mathsf{SSS}}_{\mathsf{sig}}) \leftarrow_r \mathsf{KGen}^{\mathsf{SSS}}_{\mathsf{sig}}(\mathsf{pp}_{\mathsf{SSS}})$ and $(\mathsf{sk}^{\mathsf{RSS}}_{\mathsf{sig}}, \mathsf{pk}^{\mathsf{RSS}}_{\mathsf{sig}}) \leftarrow_r$ $\mathsf{Sign}^{\mathsf{RSS}}(\mathsf{pp}_{\mathsf{RSS}})$. Return $(\mathsf{sk}^{\mathsf{PS}}_{\mathsf{sig}}, \mathsf{pk}^{\mathsf{PS}}_{\mathsf{sig}}) = ((\mathsf{sk}^{\mathsf{SSS}}_{\mathsf{sig}}, \mathsf{sk}^{\mathsf{RSS}}_{\mathsf{sig}}), (\mathsf{pk}^{\mathsf{SSS}}_{\mathsf{sig}}, \mathsf{pk}^{\mathsf{RSS}}_{\mathsf{sig}}))$.

$\mathsf{KGen}^{\mathsf{PS}}_{\mathsf{san}}(\mathsf{pp}_{\mathsf{PS}})$. Let $(\mathsf{sk}^{\mathsf{SSS}}_{\mathsf{san}}, \mathsf{pk}^{\mathsf{SSS}}_{\mathsf{san}}) \leftarrow_r \mathsf{KGen}^{\mathsf{SSS}}_{\mathsf{san}}(\mathsf{pp}_{\mathsf{SSS}})$ and $(\mathsf{sk}_\Pi, \mathsf{pk}_\Pi) \leftarrow_r \mathsf{KGen}^\Pi(\mathsf{pp}_\Pi)$. Return $(\mathsf{sk}^{\mathsf{PS}}_{\mathsf{san}}, \mathsf{pk}^{\mathsf{PS}}_{\mathsf{san}}) = ((\mathsf{sk}^{\mathsf{SSS}}_{\mathsf{san}}, \mathsf{sk}_\Pi), (\mathsf{pk}^{\mathsf{SSS}}_{\mathsf{san}}, \mathsf{pk}_\Pi))$.

$\mathsf{Sign}^{\mathsf{PS}}(\mathsf{sk}^{\mathsf{PS}}_{\mathsf{sig}}, \mathsf{pk}^{\mathsf{PS}}_{\mathsf{san}}, m, \mathsf{ADM}^{\mathsf{PS}})$. If $\mathsf{ADM}^{\mathsf{PS}} \prec m$, where $m = (m^1, m^2, \ldots, m^\ell)$, continue. Otherwise, return $\bot$. Parse $\mathsf{ADM}^{\mathsf{PS}} = (\mathsf{ADM}^{\mathsf{PS}}_1, \mathsf{ADM}^{\mathsf{PS}}_2)$. Draw $\tau \leftarrow_r \{0,1\}^\kappa$. Do $(\forall i \in \{1, 2, \ldots, \ell_m\})$: $\sigma^{\mathsf{SSS}}_i \leftarrow_r \mathsf{Sign}^{\mathsf{SSS}}(\mathsf{sk}^{\mathsf{SSS}}_{\mathsf{sig}}, \mathsf{pk}^{\mathsf{SSS}}_{\mathsf{san}}, (m^i, \tau, \tau_i, \mathsf{pk}^{\mathsf{PS}}_{\mathsf{sig}}, \mathsf{pk}^{\mathsf{PS}}_{\mathsf{san}}), \mathsf{ADM}^{\mathsf{SSS}}_i)$, where each $\tau_i \leftarrow_r \{0,1\}^\kappa$ and, if $i \in \mathsf{ADM}^{\mathsf{PS}}_1$, let $\mathsf{ADM}^{\mathsf{SSS}}_i = (\{1\}, 5)$ and $\mathsf{ADM}^{\mathsf{SSS}}_i = (\emptyset, 5)$ otherwise. Next, let $(\sigma^{\mathsf{RSS}}, \mathsf{RED}^{\mathsf{RSS}}) \leftarrow_r \mathsf{Sign}^{\mathsf{RSS}}(\mathsf{sk}^{\mathsf{RSS}}_{\mathsf{sig}}, m', \mathsf{ADM}^{\mathsf{RSS}})$, where $\mathsf{ADM}^{\mathsf{RSS}} = \mathsf{ADM}^{\mathsf{PS}}_2$ and the message $m' = (\tau_1, \tau_2, \ldots, \tau_\ell, \tau, \mathsf{pk}^{\mathsf{PS}}_{\mathsf{sig}}, \mathsf{pk}^{\mathsf{PS}}_{\mathsf{san}})$. Next, let $c \leftarrow_r \mathsf{Enc}^\Pi(\mathsf{pk}_\Pi, \mathsf{RED}^{\mathsf{RSS}}, (\tau, \mathsf{pk}^{\mathsf{PS}}_{\mathsf{sig}}, \mathsf{pk}^{\mathsf{PS}}_{\mathsf{san}}))$. Finally, generate the signature $\sigma^{\mathsf{SSS}}_0 \leftarrow_r \mathsf{Sign}^{\mathsf{SSS}}(\mathsf{sk}^{\mathsf{SSS}}_{\mathsf{sig}}, \mathsf{pk}^{\mathsf{SSS}}_{\mathsf{san}}, (m, \sigma^{\mathsf{RSS}}, c, (\tau_i, \sigma^{\mathsf{SSS}}_i)_{1 \le i \le \ell_m}, \tau, \mathsf{pk}^{\mathsf{PS}}_{\mathsf{sig}}, \mathsf{pk}^{\mathsf{PS}}_{\mathsf{san}}), \mathsf{ADM}^{\mathsf{SSS}}_0)$, where $\mathsf{ADM}^{\mathsf{SSS}}_0 = (\{1, 2, 3, 4\}, 7)$. Return $((\sigma^{\mathsf{SSS}}_i)_{0 \le i \le \ell_m}, \sigma^{\mathsf{RSS}}, c, \tau, (\tau_i)_{1 \le i \le \ell_m})$.

$\mathsf{Verify}^{\mathsf{PS}}(\mathsf{pk}^{\mathsf{PS}}_{\mathsf{sig}}, \mathsf{pk}^{\mathsf{PS}}_{\mathsf{san}}, m, \sigma^{\mathsf{PS}})$. If $\mathsf{Verify}^{\mathsf{SSS}}(\mathsf{pk}^{\mathsf{SSS}}_{\mathsf{sig}}, \mathsf{pk}^{\mathsf{SSS}}_{\mathsf{san}}, (m, \sigma^{\mathsf{RSS}}, c, \tau, (\tau_i, \sigma^{\mathsf{SSS}}_i)_{1 \le i \le \ell_m}, \mathsf{pk}^{\mathsf{PS}}_{\mathsf{sig}}, \mathsf{pk}^{\mathsf{PS}}_{\mathsf{san}}), \sigma^{\mathsf{SSS}}_0) = 0$, return 0. If $0 = \mathsf{Verify}^{\mathsf{RSS}}(\mathsf{pk}^{\mathsf{RSS}}_{\mathsf{sig}}, (\tau_1, \tau_2, \ldots, \tau_\ell, \tau, \mathsf{pk}^{\mathsf{PS}}_{\mathsf{sig}}, \mathsf{pk}^{\mathsf{PS}}_{\mathsf{san}}), \sigma^{\mathsf{RSS}})$, return 0. If for any $i \in \{1, 2, \ldots, \ell_m\} : 0 = \mathsf{Verify}^{\mathsf{SSS}}(\mathsf{pk}^{\mathsf{SSS}}_{\mathsf{sig}}, \mathsf{pk}^{\mathsf{SSS}}_{\mathsf{san}}, (m^i, \tau, \tau_i, \mathsf{pk}^{\mathsf{PS}}_{\mathsf{sig}}, \mathsf{pk}^{\mathsf{PS}}_{\mathsf{san}}), \sigma^{\mathsf{SSS}}_i)$, return 0. Return 1.

$\mathsf{Edit}^{\mathsf{PS}}(\mathsf{sk}^{\mathsf{PS}}_{\mathsf{san}}, \mathsf{pk}^{\mathsf{PS}}_{\mathsf{sig}}, m, \mathsf{MOD}^{\mathsf{PS}})$. If $0 = \mathsf{Verify}^{\mathsf{PS}}(\mathsf{pk}^{\mathsf{PS}}_{\mathsf{sig}}, \mathsf{pk}^{\mathsf{PS}}_{\mathsf{san}}, m, \sigma^{\mathsf{PS}})$, return $\bot$. Parse $\mathsf{MOD}^{\mathsf{PS}} = (\mathsf{MOD}^{\mathsf{PS}}_1, \mathsf{MOD}^{\mathsf{PS}}_2)$. Further do $(\forall(i, m^{i'}) \in \mathsf{MOD}^{\mathsf{PS}}_1)$: $(m^{i'}, \sigma^{\mathsf{SSS}'}_i) \leftarrow_r \mathsf{Sanitize}^{\mathsf{SSS}}(\mathsf{sk}^{\mathsf{SSS}}_{\mathsf{san}}, \mathsf{pk}^{\mathsf{SSS}}_{\mathsf{sig}}, (m^i, \tau, \tau_i, \mathsf{pk}^{\mathsf{PS}}_{\mathsf{sig}}, \mathsf{pk}^{\mathsf{PS}}_{\mathsf{san}}), \sigma^{\mathsf{SSS}}_i, \{(0, m^{i'})\})$. If any $\sigma^{\mathsf{SSS}'}_i = \bot$, return $\bot$. Let $\vartheta = (\tau, \mathsf{pk}^{\mathsf{PS}}_{\mathsf{sig}}, \mathsf{pk}^{\mathsf{PS}}_{\mathsf{san}})$ and $\mathsf{RED}^{\mathsf{RSS}} \leftarrow \mathsf{Dec}^\Pi(\mathsf{sk}_\Pi, c, \vartheta)$. If $\mathsf{RED}^{\mathsf{RSS}} = \bot$, return $\bot$. Generate $(\sigma^{\mathsf{RSS}'}, m', \mathsf{RED}^{\mathsf{RSS}'}) \leftarrow_r \mathsf{Redact}^{\mathsf{RSS}}(\mathsf{pk}^{\mathsf{RSS}}_{\mathsf{sig}}, m'', \sigma^{\mathsf{RSS}}, \mathsf{MOD}^{\mathsf{RSS}}_2, \mathsf{RED}^{\mathsf{RSS}})$, where $m'' = (\tau_1, \tau_2, \ldots, \tau_\ell, \tau, \mathsf{pk}^{\mathsf{PS}}_{\mathsf{sig}}, \mathsf{pk}^{\mathsf{PS}}_{\mathsf{san}})$. If $\sigma^{\mathsf{RSS}'} = \bot$, return $\bot$. Let $c' \leftarrow_r \mathsf{Enc}^\Pi(\mathsf{pk}_\Pi, \mathsf{RED}^{\mathsf{RSS}'}, \vartheta)$ and $(m'_0, \sigma^{\mathsf{SSS}}_0) \leftarrow_r \mathsf{Sanitize}^{\mathsf{SSS}}(\mathsf{sk}^{\mathsf{SSS}}_{\mathsf{san}}, \mathsf{pk}^{\mathsf{SSS}}_{\mathsf{sig}}, (m, \sigma^{\mathsf{RSS}}, c, (\tau_i \sigma^{\mathsf{SSS}}_i)_{1 \le i \le \ell_m}, \tau, \mathsf{pk}^{\mathsf{PS}}_{\mathsf{sig}}, \mathsf{pk}^{\mathsf{PS}}_{\mathsf{san}}), \sigma^{\mathsf{SSS}}_0, \{(1, m'), (2, \sigma^{\mathsf{RSS}'}), (3, c'), (4, (\tau_i, \sigma^{\mathsf{SSS}'}_i)_{i \in \{1,2,\ldots,\ell\} \backslash \mathsf{MOD}^{\mathsf{PS}}_2})\})$. If $\sigma^{\mathsf{SSS}'}_0 = \bot$, return $\bot$. Update $\mathsf{ADM}^{\mathsf{PS}}$ to $\mathsf{ADM}^{\mathsf{PS}'}$ by removing all indices in $\mathsf{MOD}^{\mathsf{PS}}_2$ and adjusting the remaining indices by reducing each i in $\mathsf{ADM}^{\mathsf{PS}}$ by $\#\{j \in \mathsf{MOD}^{\mathsf{PS}}_2 : j < i\}$. Return $(\mathsf{MOD}^{\mathsf{PS}}(m), ((\sigma^{\mathsf{SSS}}_i)_{i \in \{1,2,\ldots,\ell\} \backslash \mathsf{MOD}^{\mathsf{PS}}_2}, \sigma^{\mathsf{RSS}'}, c', \tau, (\tau_i)_{i \in \{1,2,\ldots,\ell\} \backslash \mathsf{MOD}^{\mathsf{PS}}_2}), \mathsf{ADM}^{\mathsf{PS}'})$.

$\mathsf{Proof}^{\mathsf{PS}}(\mathsf{sk}^{\mathsf{PS}}_{\mathsf{sig}}, \mathsf{pk}^{\mathsf{PS}}_{\mathsf{san}}, m, \sigma^{\mathsf{PS}}, \{(\sigma^{\mathsf{PS}}_i, m^i)\})$. If for any $(\sigma^{\mathsf{PS}}_i, m_i)$, $0 = \mathsf{Verify}^{\mathsf{PS}}(\mathsf{pk}^{\mathsf{PS}}_{\mathsf{sig}}, \mathsf{pk}^{\mathsf{PS}}_{\mathsf{san}}, m_i, \sigma^{\mathsf{PS}}_i)$, return $\bot$. If $0 = \mathsf{Verify}^{\mathsf{PS}}(\mathsf{pk}^{\mathsf{PS}}_{\mathsf{sig}}, \mathsf{pk}^{\mathsf{PS}}_{\mathsf{san}}, m, \sigma^{\mathsf{PS}})$, return $\bot$. Return $\mathsf{Proof}^{\mathsf{SSS}}(\mathsf{sk}^{\mathsf{SSS}}_{\mathsf{sig}}, \mathsf{pk}^{\mathsf{SSS}}_{\mathsf{san}}, m', \sigma^{\mathsf{SSS}}, \{(\sigma^{\mathsf{SSS}}_i, m'_i)\})$, where $m' = (m, \sigma^{\mathsf{RSS}}, c, (\tau_i)_{1 \le i \le \ell_m}, \tau, \mathsf{pk}^{\mathsf{PS}}_{\mathsf{sig}}, \mathsf{pk}^{\mathsf{PS}}_{\mathsf{san}})$ and each $m'_i = (m_i, \sigma^{\mathsf{RSS}}_i, c_i, (\tau_{i,j})_{1 \le j \le \ell_{m_i}}, \tau_i, \mathsf{pk}^{\mathsf{PS}}_{\mathsf{sig}}, \mathsf{pk}^{\mathsf{PS}}_{\mathsf{san}})$.

$\mathsf{Judge}^{\mathsf{PS}}(\mathsf{pk}^{\mathsf{PS}}_{\mathsf{sig}}, \mathsf{pk}^{\mathsf{PS}}_{\mathsf{san}}, m, \sigma^{\mathsf{PS}}, \pi^{\mathsf{PS}})$. If $0 = \mathsf{Verify}^{\mathsf{PS}}(\mathsf{pk}^{\mathsf{PS}}_{\mathsf{sig}}, \mathsf{pk}^{\mathsf{PS}}_{\mathsf{san}}, m, \sigma^{\mathsf{PS}})$, return $\bot$. Return $\mathsf{Judge}^{\mathsf{SSS}}(\mathsf{pk}^{\mathsf{SSS}}_{\mathsf{sig}}, \mathsf{pk}^{\mathsf{SSS}}_{\mathsf{san}}, m', \sigma^{\mathsf{SSS}}, \pi^{\mathsf{PS}})$, where $m' = (m, \sigma^{\mathsf{RSS}}, c, (\tau_i)_{1 \le i \le \ell_m}, \tau, \mathsf{pk}^{\mathsf{PS}}_{\mathsf{sig}}, \mathsf{pk}^{\mathsf{PS}}_{\mathsf{san}})$.

Construction 1: Our PS scheme

Notes on the Construction. We stress that one does not strictly require to use an SSS for a block which is not admissible at signing, but could use a standard signature scheme instead. However, this was not done for two reasons.

First, this would further blow up the description. Second, we achieve a stronger form of privacy, i.e., invisibility, if the underlying SSS supports this notion.

Moreover, one may notice that the inner SSSs do not need to be accountable, as the outer SSS is used for this purpose. However, as there are (for obvious reasons) no notions of non-accountable SSSs, there is no way around this, while defining such a notion is not the goal of this paper. Moreover, this can be turned into a useful additional feature, i.e., one can actually generate a proof which blocks have been altered, based on the ideas by Brzuska et al. [11]. How this can be achieved (along with additional extensions) is discussed in the full version of this paper.

Implementation. To demonstrate that our scheme is realizable, it was implemented in Java. We chose to implement the version giving the most privacy guarantees, i.e., with invisibility. This was done to show the absolute lower bound of our construction. We discuss this in more depth at the end of the this section. We use the implementation by Beck et al. [3] as the underlying SSS, also using their chameleon-hash with 2,048 Bit RSA moduli and the RSS presented in the full version of this paper with 2,048 Bit RSA-FDH signatures, based on the ideas by Brzuska et al. [7]. The security parameter κ is fixed to 512. Furthermore, we stress that the implemented RSS does not have any redaction information $(\mathsf{RED}^{\mathsf{RSS}} = \emptyset)$, and thus c is always $\bot$. The measurements were performed on a Lenovo W530 with an Intel i7-3470QM@2.70 Ghz, and 16 GiB of RAM. No performance optimization such as CRT were implemented and only a single thread does the computations. We evaluated our implementation with 32 blocks, wheres 25% were marked as admissible and an additional 25% as redactable. For editing, 50% of the admissible blocks were sanitized and redacted. We omit proof generation and the judge, as they are simple database look-ups, and parameter generation as it is a one-time setup. The overall results are depicted in Table 1 and are based on 500 runs, while verification was measured after sanitization. A more detailed evaluation is given in the full version of this paper.

Table 1. Performance measurements in ms

	$\mathsf{KGen}^{\mathsf{PS}}_{\mathsf{sig}}$	$\mathsf{KGen}^{\mathsf{PS}}_{\mathsf{san}}$	$\mathsf{Sign}^{\mathsf{PS}}$	$\mathsf{Edit}^{\mathsf{PS}}$	$\mathsf{Verify}^{\mathsf{PS}}$
Min.	275	76	24'619	7'825	4'701
25th PCTL	784	260	27'672	8'230	4'847
Median	1'172	353	28'655	8'650	4'993
75th PCTL	1'795	494	29'788	9'475	5'287
90th PCTL	2'698	650	31'009	11'361	5'918
95th PCTL	3'464	787	31'842	13'653	6'453
Max.	8'332	1'356	43'164	44'273	47'713
Average	1'450	394	28'655	10'937	5'333
SD	1'004	188	1'938	2'974	2'095

As demonstrated, signing is the most expensive operation. Moreover, as already explained, we chose to implement the most expensive version, i.e., the one with invisibility. As this involves rather expensive primitives, i.e., the SSS presented by Beck et al. [3], it is "obvious" that the runtime is not very satisfactory. However, we chose to do this to present a lower bound. In other words, if one is willing to drop invisibility and deploys a weaker SSS (e.g., Brzuska et al [8]; Runtimes are given by de Meer et al. [17]), our resulting construction becomes much more efficient.

5 Conclusion

We have introduced the notion of Protean Signature schemes (PS). This new primitive allows to modify and redact signer-chosen parts of a signed message without additional involvement of the signer. We proposed a formal security model and a provably secure black-box construction from sanitizable (SSS) and redactable signature schemes (RSS). Our new primitive generalizes both SSSs and RSSs, while our performance estimates show that our corresponding construction can be considered efficient. However, it remains an open question whether we can construct "designated redactor" RSSs which hide which parts of a message are redactable to achieve a stronger invisibility notion, hiding which blocks are redactable. Likewise, it remains an open question if we can add unlinkability.

References

1. Ahn, J.H., Boneh, D., Camenisch, J., Hohenberger, S., Shelat, A., Waters, B.: Computing on authenticated data. J. Cryptol. **28**(2), 351–395 (2015). https://doi.org/10.1007/s00145-014-9182-0
2. Ateniese, G., Chou, D.H., de Medeiros, B., Tsudik, G.: Sanitizable signatures. In: di Vimercati, S.C., Syverson, P., Gollmann, D. (eds.) ESORICS 2005. LNCS, vol. 3679, pp. 159–177. Springer, Heidelberg (2005). https://doi.org/10.1007/11555827_10
3. Beck, M.T., et al.: Practical strongly invisible and strongly accountable sanitizable signatures. In: Pieprzyk, J., Suriadi, S. (eds.) ACISP 2017. LNCS, vol. 10342, pp. 437–452. Springer, Cham (2017). https://doi.org/10.1007/978-3-319-60055-0_23
4. Bilzhause, A., Pöhls, H.C., Samelin, K.: Position paper: the past, present, and future of sanitizable and redactable signatures. In: Ares, pp. 87:1–87:9 (2017)
5. Boneh, D., Freeman, D.M.: Homomorphic signatures for polynomial functions. In: Paterson, K.G. (ed.) EUROCRYPT 2011. LNCS, vol. 6632, pp. 149–168. Springer, Heidelberg (2011). https://doi.org/10.1007/978-3-642-20465-4_10
6. Boyle, E., Goldwasser, S., Ivan, I.: Functional signatures and pseudorandom functions. In: Krawczyk, H. (ed.) PKC 2014. LNCS, vol. 8383, pp. 501–519. Springer, Heidelberg (2014). https://doi.org/10.1007/978-3-642-54631-0_29
7. Brzuska, C., et al.: Redactable signatures for tree-structured data: definitions and constructions. In: Zhou, J., Yung, M. (eds.) ACNS 2010. LNCS, vol. 6123, pp. 87–104. Springer, Heidelberg (2010). https://doi.org/10.1007/978-3-642-13708-2_6

8. Brzuska, C., et al.: Security of sanitizable signatures revisited. In: Jarecki, S., Tsudik, G. (eds.) PKC 2009. LNCS, vol. 5443, pp. 317–336. Springer, Heidelberg (2009). https://doi.org/10.1007/978-3-642-00468-1_18

9. Brzuska, C., Fischlin, M., Lehmann, A., Schröder, D.: Santizable signatures: how to partially delegate control for authenticated data. In: BIOSIG (2009)

10. Brzuska, C., Fischlin, M., Lehmann, A., Schröder, D.: Unlinkability of sanitizable signatures. In: Nguyen, P.Q., Pointcheval, D. (eds.) PKC 2010. LNCS, vol. 6056, pp. 444–461. Springer, Heidelberg (2010). https://doi.org/10.1007/978-3-642-13013-7_26

11. Brzuska, C., Pöhls, H.C., Samelin, K.: Non-interactive public accountability for sanitizable signatures. In: De Capitani di Vimercati, S., Mitchell, C. (eds.) EuroPKI 2012. LNCS, vol. 7868, pp. 178–193. Springer, Heidelberg (2013). https://doi.org/10.1007/978-3-642-40012-4_12

12. Brzuska, C., Pöhls, H.C., Samelin, K.: Efficient and perfectly unlinkable sanitizable signatures without group signatures. In: Katsikas, S., Agudo, I. (eds.) EuroPKI 2013. LNCS, vol. 8341, pp. 12–30. Springer, Heidelberg (2014). https://doi.org/10.1007/978-3-642-53997-8_2

13. Camenisch, J., Derler, D., Krenn, S., Pöhls, H.C., Samelin, K., Slamanig, D.: Chameleon-hashes with ephemeral trapdoors. In: Fehr, S. (ed.) PKC 2017. LNCS, vol. 10175, pp. 152–182. Springer, Heidelberg (2017). https://doi.org/10.1007/978-3-662-54388-7_6

14. Canard, S., Jambert, A.: On extended sanitizable signature schemes. In: Pieprzyk, J. (ed.) CT-RSA 2010. LNCS, vol. 5985, pp. 179–194. Springer, Heidelberg (2010). https://doi.org/10.1007/978-3-642-11925-5_13

15. Canard, S., Jambert, A., Lescuyer, R.: Sanitizable signatures with several signers and sanitizers. In: Mitrokotsa, A., Vaudenay, S. (eds.) AFRICACRYPT 2012. LNCS, vol. 7374, pp. 35–52. Springer, Heidelberg (2012). https://doi.org/10.1007/978-3-642-31410-0_3

16. Canard, S., Laguillaumie, F., Milhau, M.: Trapdoor sanitizable signatures and their application to content protection. In: Bellovin, S.M., Gennaro, R., Keromytis, A., Yung, M. (eds.) ACNS 2008. LNCS, vol. 5037, pp. 258–276. Springer, Heidelberg (2008). https://doi.org/10.1007/978-3-540-68914-0_16

17. de Meer, H., Pöhls, H.C., Posegga, J., Samelin, K.: Scope of security properties of sanitizable signatures revisited. In: Ares, pp. 188–197 (2013)

18. de Meer, H., Pöhls, H.C., Posegga, J., Samelin, K.: On the relation between redactable and sanitizable signature schemes. In: Jürjens, J., Piessens, F., Bielova, N. (eds.) ESSoS 2014. LNCS, vol. 8364, pp. 113–130. Springer, Cham (2014). https://doi.org/10.1007/978-3-319-04897-0_8

19. Demirel, D., Derler, D., Hanser, C., Pöhls, H.C., Slamanig, D., Traverso, G.: PRISMACLOUD D4.4: overview of functional and malleable signature schemes. Technical report, H2020 Prismacloud (2015). www.prismacloud.eu

20. Derler, D., Pöhls, H.C., Samelin, K., Slamanig, D.: A general framework for redactable signatures and new constructions. In: Kwon, S., Yun, A. (eds.) ICISC 2015. LNCS, vol. 9558, pp. 3–19. Springer, Cham (2016). https://doi.org/10.1007/978-3-319-30840-1_1

21. Derler, D., Slamanig, D.: Rethinking privacy for extended sanitizable signatures and a black-box construction of strongly private schemes. In: Au, M.-H., Miyaji, A. (eds.) ProvSec 2015. LNCS, vol. 9451, pp. 455–474. Springer, Cham (2015). https://doi.org/10.1007/978-3-319-26059-4_25

22. Fischlin, M., Harasser, P.: Invisible sanitizable signatures and public-key encryption are equivalent. In: Preneel, B., Vercauteren, F. (eds.) ACNS 2018. LNCS, vol. 10892, pp. 202–220. Springer, Cham (2018). https://doi.org/10.1007/978-3-319-93387-0_11

23. Fleischhacker, N., Krupp, J., Malavolta, G., Schneider, J., Schröder, D., Simkin, M.: Efficient unlinkable sanitizable signatures from signatures with re-randomizable keys. In: Cheng, C.-M., Chung, K.-M., Persiano, G., Yang, B.-Y. (eds.) PKC 2016. LNCS, vol. 9614, pp. 301–330. Springer, Heidelberg (2016). https://doi.org/10.1007/978-3-662-49384-7_12

24. Ghosh, E., Goodrich, M.T., Ohrimenko, O., Tamassia, R.: Verifiable zero-knowledge order queries and updates for fully dynamic lists and trees. In: Zikas, V., De Prisco, R. (eds.) SCN 2016. LNCS, vol. 9841, pp. 216–236. Springer, Cham (2016). https://doi.org/10.1007/978-3-319-44618-9_12

25. Ghosh, E., Ohrimenko, O., Tamassia, R.: Zero-knowledge authenticated order queries and order statistics on a list. In: Malkin, T., Kolesnikov, V., Lewko, A.B., Polychronakis, M. (eds.) ACNS 2015. LNCS, vol. 9092, pp. 149–171. Springer, Cham (2015). https://doi.org/10.1007/978-3-319-28166-7_8

26. Goldwasser, S., Micali, S., Rivest, R.L.: A digital signature scheme secure against adaptive chosen-message attacks. SIAM J. Comput. **17**(2), 281–308 (1988)

27. Gong, J., Qian, H., Zhou, Y.: Fully-secure and practical sanitizable signatures. In: Lai, X., Yung, M., Lin, D. (eds.) Inscrypt 2010. LNCS, vol. 6584, pp. 300–317. Springer, Heidelberg (2011). https://doi.org/10.1007/978-3-642-21518-6_21

28. Haber, S., et al.: Efficient signature schemes supporting redaction, pseudonymization, and data deidentification. In: AsiaCCS, pp. 353–362 (2008)

29. Izu, T., Kunihiro, N., Ohta, K., Sano, M., Takenaka, M.: Sanitizable and deletable signature. In: Chung, K.-I., Sohn, K., Yung, M. (eds.) WISA 2008. LNCS, vol. 5379, pp. 130–144. Springer, Heidelberg (2009). https://doi.org/10.1007/978-3-642-00306-6_10

30. Izu, T., Kunihiro, N., Ohta, K., Sano, M., Takenaka, M.: Yet another sanitizable signature from bilinear maps. In: Ares, pp. 941–946 (2009)

31. Johnson, R., Molnar, D., Song, D., Wagner, D.: Homomorphic signature schemes. In: Preneel, B. (ed.) CT-RSA 2002. LNCS, vol. 2271, pp. 244–262. Springer, Heidelberg (2002). https://doi.org/10.1007/3-540-45760-7_17

32. Klonowski, M., Lauks, A.: Extended sanitizable signatures. In: Rhee, M.S., Lee, B. (eds.) ICISC 2006. LNCS, vol. 4296, pp. 343–355. Springer, Heidelberg (2006). https://doi.org/10.1007/11927587_28

33. Krenn, S., Samelin, K., Sommer, D.: Stronger security for sanitizable signatures. In: Garcia-Alfaro, J., Navarro-Arribas, G., Aldini, A., Martinelli, F., Suri, N. (eds.) DPM/QASA -2015. LNCS, vol. 9481, pp. 100–117. Springer, Cham (2016). https://doi.org/10.1007/978-3-319-29883-2_7

34. Kundu, A., Bertino, E.: Privacy-preserving authentication of trees and graphs. Int. J. Inf. Secur. **12**(6), 467–494 (2013). https://doi.org/10.1007/s10207-013-0198-5

35. Lai, R.W.F., Zhang, T., Chow, S.S.M., Schröder, D.: Efficient sanitizable signatures without random oracles. In: Askoxylakis, I., Ioannidis, S., Katsikas, S., Meadows, C. (eds.) ESORICS 2016. LNCS, vol. 9878, pp. 363–380. Springer, Cham (2016). https://doi.org/10.1007/978-3-319-45744-4_18

36. Miyazaki, K.: Digitally signed document sanitizing scheme with disclosure condition control. IEICE Trans. **88−A**(1), 239–246 (2005)

37. Pöhls, H.C., Samelin, K.: Accountable redactable signatures. In: Ares, pp. 60–69 (2015)

38. Pöhls, H.C., Samelin, K., Posegga, J.: Sanitizable signatures in XML signature—performance, mixing properties, and revisiting the property of transparency. In: Lopez, J., Tsudik, G. (eds.) ACNS 2011. LNCS, vol. 6715, pp. 166–182. Springer, Heidelberg (2011). https://doi.org/10.1007/978-3-642-21554-4_10

39. Samelin, K., Pöhls, H.C., Bilzhause, A., Posegga, J., de Meer, H.: Redactable signatures for independent removal of structure and content. In: Ryan, M.D., Smyth, B., Wang, G. (eds.) ISPEC 2012. LNCS, vol. 7232, pp. 17–33. Springer, Heidelberg (2012). https://doi.org/10.1007/978-3-642-29101-2_2

40. Slamanig, D., Rass, S.: Generalizations and extensions of redactable signatures with applications to electronic healthcare. In: De Decker, B., Schaumüller-Bichl, I. (eds.) CMS 2010. LNCS, vol. 6109, pp. 201–213. Springer, Heidelberg (2010). https://doi.org/10.1007/978-3-642-13241-4_19

41. Steinfeld, R., Bull, L., Zheng, Y.: Content extraction signatures. In: Kim, K. (ed.) ICISC 2001. LNCS, vol. 2288, pp. 285–304. Springer, Heidelberg (2002). https://doi.org/10.1007/3-540-45861-1_22

42. Sweeney, L.: k-anonymity: a model for protecting privacy. Int. J. Uncertain. Fuzziness Knowl.-Based Syst. **10**(5), 557–570 (2002)

43. Traverso, G., Demirel, D., Buchmann, J.A.: Homomorphic Signature Schemes - A Survey. Springer Briefs in Computer Science. Springer, Heidelberg (2016). https://doi.org/10.1007/978-3-319-32115-8

44. Tsabary, R.: An equivalence between attribute-based signatures and homomorphic signatures, and new constructions for both. In: Kalai, Y., Reyzin, L. (eds.) TCC 2017. LNCS, vol. 10678, pp. 489–518. Springer, Cham (2017). https://doi.org/10.1007/978-3-319-70503-3_16

45. Wu, Z.Y., Hsueh, C.-W., Tsai, C.-Y., Lai, F., Lee, H.-C., Chung, Y.-F.: Redactable signatures for signed CDA documents. J. Med. Syst. **36**(3), 1795–1808 (2012). https://doi.org/10.1007/s10916-010-9639-0

46. Yum, D.H., Seo, J.W., Lee, P.J.: Trapdoor sanitizable signatures made easy. In: Zhou, J., Yung, M. (eds.) ACNS 2010. LNCS, vol. 6123, pp. 53–68. Springer, Heidelberg (2010). https://doi.org/10.1007/978-3-642-13708-2_4

Code-Based Signature Schemes
from Identification Protocols
in the Rank Metric

Emanuele Bellini[✉], Florian Caullery, Alexandros Hasikos, Marcos Manzano,
and Victor Mateu

Darkmatter LLC, Abu Dhabi, UAE
eemanuele.bellini@gmail.com

Abstract. We present two code-based identification protocols and signature schemes in the rank metric, providing detailed pseudocode and
selecting practical parameters. The proposals are derived from their analogue in the Hamming metric. We discuss their security in the post-
quantum scenario. With respect to other signature schemes based on
codes, our constructions maintain a similar efficiency, possess large but
still practical signatures, and the smallest key and public key sizes.

Keywords: Code-based cryptography · Signature scheme
Identification protocol · Fiat-Shamir transform · Rank metric

1   Introduction

Quantum computers have evolved considerably in the last decade. Recently
Google announced Bristlecone, a new 72 qubits quantum processor [24]. Such
advances pose a real threat to traditional public-key cryptography based on
number theory [41]. As a consequence, there has been a burst of interest in
Post-Quantum Cryptography (PQC), which has raised as the preferred solution
to face quantum computer-aided attacks. The National Institute of Standards
and Technology (NIST) is running a PQC standardization process in order to
define the next standards for public-key encryption, digital signatures and key-
exchange schemes [11,35]. At the time of writing such process is already at
Round 1 stage [36]. Due to the early stage of post-quantum algorithm research,
it is of paramount importance to provide the full range of quantum secure cryptographic primitives (signatures, key exchange, etc.) for all the main mathematical
problems cryptography relies on. This way, it will be easier to switch from one
scheme to the other in the case one of the problems turns out to be insecure in
the quantum model.

Code-based cryptography is a strong candidate in the so-called PQC NIST
competition [40], given that it is the oldest PQC family and, hence, the most
thoroughly studied among all the contenders. This work focuses on code-based
cryptography digital signature schemes. Designing such schemes efficiently has

© Springer Nature Switzerland AG 2018
J. Camenisch and P. Papadimitratos (Eds.): CANS 2018, LNCS 11124, pp. 277–298, 2018.
https://doi.org/10.1007/978-3-030-00434-7_14

been a grueling challenge and different approaches have been followed, with very little success. One of them uses the Fiat-Shamir transform to turn a zero-knowledge identification scheme into a signature scheme, as initially proposed by Stern [43], and later improved by Veron [48] and Cayrel, Veron and El Yousfi Alaoui (CVE) [9]. These three schemes are based on the Hamming metric, as most of the classical code-based cryptographic solutions. However, it is also possible to use the rank metric to build secure schemes. This metric was introduced by Gabidulin in [19], and is recently gaining attention as a valid alternative in code-based cryptography, since it yields much smaller key sizes, which is usually the main drawback of these type of schemes.

In this manuscript we consider the work of Veron and CVE, and propose an analogue construction for the rank metric (Stern was already converted to rank metric in [22]). In addition, we show how an attacker could forge signatures for the original Stern and Veron schemes if the proper number of rounds is not wisely selected. Our constructions are resistant to the aforementioned attack. We provide the detailed pseudo-code for the two schemes, and present four set of parameters for 80 bit of classical security and for 128, 192, 256 of post-quantum security. Finally, we compare our proposals with the state-of-the-art code-based signature schemes.

The paper is organized as follows: Sect. 2 provides an overview of previous works. In Sect. 3 we provide some notation, basic facts from code-based cryptography, a discussion on the difficulty of solving the Rank Syndrome Decoding problem, and some remarks on the post-quantum security of the Fiat-Shamir transform. Section 4 presents our two identification schemes based on rank metric, Sect. 5 describes our analogue signature schemes for the rank metric, Sect. 6 details the attack against the original Stern and Veron digital signature schemes, Sect. 7 considers the parameters for our schemes, Sect. 8 argues about the complexity of our schemes, Sect. 9 shows a comparison between our proposals and other well-known signature schemes, and Sect. 10 presents the conclusions and future work.

2   Related Works

The first practical signature scheme whose security is based on the difficulty of Syndrome Decoding problem is called CFS (Courtois-Finiasz-Sendrier), and has been presented in [12]. This is a trapdoor based signature scheme derived from the Niederreiter cryptosystem [34]. In this scheme the parity-check matrix of a structured linear code with fast decoding is used as private key, while the public key is obtained from the private key by multiplying it on the right and on the left by two random invertible matrices. In this way the public key becomes indistinguishable from the parity-check matrix of a random linear code, which is not efficiently decodable. The first proposal of [12] used Goppa codes as the underlying hidden code. Many other signature schemes have been proposed based on the same idea, and using a different underlying code with the intent of reducing either the keys or the signature size, and to provide better security. For example,

Low Density Generator Matrix codes are used in [4], but a recent efficient attack has been published [38], which breaks the scheme when the attacker has at his disposal enough signatures obtained from the same secret key. Another example is in [31], where convolutional codes are exploited. Nevertheless, this scheme has been efficiently attacked in [27]. A third example, proposed in [21], involves Low Rank Parity Check codes, which are defined using a different metric than the Hamming metric, called the *rank metric*. This scheme, under the name of RankSign, is one of the candidates of the NIST competition for selecting new quantum-resistant signature schemes. At the time of writing this manuscript, the authors of RankSign withdrew their proposal from the competition due to an attack by Debris-Alazard and Tillich [14]. There are two other NIST competition proposals for code-based signatures. While the first one, called RaCoSS [39], has a somehow original construction, the second one, called pqsignRM [28], is a CFS-like scheme using punctured Reed-Muller codes instead of Goppa codes. Some attacks, available in the comments section of the NIST competition website, are currently being evaluated for both schemes. Even though CFS has short signature size and reasonably fast software implementation for 80 bit of classical security, the parameters of the Goppa code do not scale well when increasing the security level. Furthermore, an unpublished attack by Bleichenbacher (described in [18]), forced the original parameters to be increased even more. Because of this attack, another proposal called Parallel-CFS [17] has been published.

All CFS-like signature schemes require to decode a random vector, which is usually the output of a hash function. When a code has the property of being able to decode any random vector, then it is said to have *complete decoding*. If the code does not have this property then it has *non-zero decoding failure probability*. Each of the previously presented schemes has a non-zero decoding failure probability, and the lower this probability is, the higher the parameters become. Furthermore, there exist only a few families of codes which are well suited to achieve efficient complete decoding (with a very small decoding failure probability), and in particular, as far as it concerns rank metric codes, there is no analogue of the Goppa codes, and the only viable option in this metric seems to be the one used in [21].

To overcome this problem two other approaches have been followed, which avoid the use of trapdoors. The first, usually referred to as KKS (Kabatianskii-Krouk-Smeets), has been presented in [25], and evolved in the BMS (Barreto-Misoczki-Simplicio) scheme [5]. These two schemes can be instantiated on top of general linear codes. KKS and BMS have a good balance between public key and signature size, but they can only be considered one-time signature schemes.

A last approach is to convert an identification protocol to a signature scheme. For the Hamming metric, this approach has been explored by Stern [43], Veron [48], and Cayrel-Veron-El Yousfi Alaoui (CVE) [9]. The first two signature schemes are obtained from a 3-pass identification protocol via the Fiat-Shamir transform [16], while the third one is obtained from a generalization of the Fiat Shamir transform recently analyzed in [13]. A version of Stern scheme in the rank metric has also been proposed in [22].

In general, there exist variations of code-based encryption schemes (i.e. [6] and [33]) that use quasi-cyclic and quasi-dyadic constructions codes in order to produce a smaller public key. However, all these constructions have been subject to structural attacks such as [44] and [15]. Thus, to remain on the safe side, we will propose two schemes which are based on random linear codes.

The purpose of this work is to provide the analogue constructions of Veron, and CVE schemes in the rank metric, and to compare these constructions against their Hamming metric version and against the most important existing signature schemes based on codes at the moment of writing.

3   Preliminaries

In this section we provide notations and definitions that are used throughout the paper.

3.1   Notation

We use the notation $[a, b, c]$ to indicate a list (or sequence) of elements not necessarily belonging to the same set.

We denote with $x \leftarrow_{\$} A$ the uniform random choice of x among the elements of a set A.

We indicate with $\mathbb{F}_q$ the field of q elements, and with $\mathbb{F}_{q^m}$ a m-degree extension of $\mathbb{F}_q$.

A vector $v \in (\mathbb{F}_{q^m})^n$ will be either represented as a vector of n elements $(v_1, \ldots, v_n), v_j \in \mathbb{F}_{q^m}, j = 1, \ldots, n$, or as a $m \times n$ q-ary matrix, called *associated matrix*, whose entries are denoted $v_{i,j} \in \mathbb{F}_q$ with $i = 1, \ldots, m$ and $j = 1, \ldots, n$, where $(v_{1,j}, \ldots, v_{m,j})$ is the expansion of v_j with respect to some base $\{b_1, \ldots, b_m\}$ of $\mathbb{F}_{q^m}$ seen as a vector space over $\mathbb{F}_q$.

We denote with S_n the set of all permutations of n elements. For any $\sigma \in S_n$ and sequence $s = [s_1, \ldots, s_n]$ of n elements, we write $\sigma(s)$ to be the sequence $[s_{\sigma(1)}, \ldots, s_{\sigma(n)}]$. A similar notation is applied to vectors and matrices. In this last case, given matrix M of m rows and n columns whose entries are $m_{i,j}, i \in \{1, \ldots, m\}, j \in \{1, \ldots, n\}$, we write $\sigma(M)$ to denote the matrix with entries $m_{i,\sigma(j)}$, i.e. where the columns are affected by the permutation.

We will denote with H a cryptographically secure hash function, and with h its output bit length.

Given a sequence $v = (v_1, \ldots, v_n)$ we define $v^{(i)} := (v_1^i, \ldots, v_n^i)$.

We will denote by λ the security level of the scheme.

3.2   Coding Theory and Rank Metric Preliminaries

A linear $(n, k)_q$-code C is vector subspace of $(\mathbb{F}_q)^n$ of dimension k, where k and n are positive integers such that $k < n$, q is a prime power, and $\mathbb{F}_q$ is the finite field with q elements. Elements of the vector space are called vectors or words, while elements of the code are called codewords.

It is possible to define a distance function d : $(\mathbb{F}_q)^n \mapsto \mathbb{R}^{\geq}$. This function is called a *metric* if for all $a, b, c \in (\mathbb{F}_q)^n$ it holds that (1) $\mathrm{d}(a, b) \geq 0$, where $\mathrm{d}(a, b) = 0$ if and only if $a = b$, (2) $\mathrm{d}(a, b) = \mathrm{d}(b, a)$, and (3) $\mathrm{d}(a, b) + \mathrm{d}(b, c) \geq \mathrm{d}(a, c)$. Given a metric it is possible to define the *distance* between two vectors a, b as $\mathrm{d}(a, b)$, the *weight* of a vector a as $\mathrm{d}(a, 0)$ and the *minimum distance* of a code as $\min_{c,c' \in C, c \neq c'} \{\mathrm{d}(c, c')\}$. Based on the minimum distance d of a linear code, we can define its correction capability as $t = \lfloor \frac{d-1}{2} \rfloor$.

Definition 1 (Generator and Parity-check matrix). *Let C be a linear $(n, k)_q$-code over $\mathbb{F}_q$. A matrix $G \in \mathbb{F}_q^{k \times n}$ is called a generator matrix of C if its rows form a basis of C, i.e. $C = \{x \cdot G : x \in (\mathbb{F}_q)^k\}$. A matrix $H \in \mathbb{F}_q^{(n-k) \times n}$ is called a parity-check matrix of C if $C = \{x \in (\mathbb{F}_q)^n : H \cdot x^T = 0\}$.*

Classical error-correcting codes are defined in the *Hamming metric*. The *Hamming weight* and *Hamming distance* can be defined as follows.

Definition 2 (Hamming weight and distance). *Let $a, b \in (\mathbb{F}_{q^m})^n$. The Hamming weight of a is the number of its non-zero elements as a vector over $\mathbb{F}_{q^m}$, i.e. $\mathrm{w_H}(a) = |\{i : a_i \neq 0, a_i \in \mathbb{F}_{q^m}, i = 1, \ldots, n\}|$. The Hamming distance of a and b is the Hamming weight of their difference, i.e. $\mathrm{d_H}(a, b) = \mathrm{w_H}(a - b) = |\{i : a_i - b_i \neq 0, a_i, b_i \in \mathbb{F}_{q^m}, i = 1, \ldots, n\}|$.*

In this paper we also consider codes in the *rank metric*.
The *rank weight* and *rank distance* can be defined as follows.

Definition 3 (Rank weight and distance). *Let $a, b \in (\mathbb{F}_{q^m})^n$. Then we define the rank weight of a as the rank of its q-ary matrix representation, i.e.*

$$
\mathrm{w_r}(a) = \mathrm{Rank} \left(\begin{pmatrix} a_{1,1} & \cdots & a_{1,m} \\ \vdots & \ddots & \vdots \\ a_{m,1} & \cdots & a_{m,m} \end{pmatrix} \right),
$$

with $a_{i,j} \in \mathbb{F}_q, i = 1, \ldots, m, j = 1, \ldots, n$. The rank distance between a, b is then given by the rank of the q-ary matrix representation of the matrix difference of a and b (in matrix form), i.e.

$$
\mathrm{d_r}(a, b) = \mathrm{w_r}(a - b) = \mathrm{Rank} \left(\begin{pmatrix} a_{1,1} - b_{1,1} & \cdots & a_{1,m} - b_{1,m} \\ \vdots & \ddots & \vdots \\ a_{m,1} - b_{m,1} & \cdots & a_{m,m} - b_{m,m} \end{pmatrix} \right),
$$

with $a_{i,j}, b_{i,j} \in \mathbb{F}_q, i = 1, \ldots, m, j = 1, \ldots, n$.

We denote by $\begin{bmatrix} n \\ s \end{bmatrix} = \prod_{i=0}^{s-1} \frac{q^n - q^i}{q^s - q^i}$ the number of s-dimensional vector subspaces of $(\mathbb{F}_q)^n$ over $\mathbb{F}_q$.

A *ball* $B_R^r(a)$ in the rank metric of radius r centered in a vector $a \in (\mathbb{F}_{q^m})^n$ is the set of all vectors in rank distance at most r from a. It can be shown [49] that $|B_R^r(a)| = \sum_{i=1}^{r} \begin{bmatrix} m \\ i \end{bmatrix} \prod_{j=0}^{i-1} (q^n - q^j)$, which does not depend on a.

The following bound plays an important role in the choice of the parameters of our schemes.

Theorem 1 (q-ary Gilbert-Varshamov Bound in rank metric [19]). *Let $A_{q^m}^R(n,d)$ be the maximum cardinality of a linear block code over $\mathbb{F}_{q^m}$ of length n, size M, and minimum distance d in the rank metric. Then $A_{q^m}^R(n,d) \geq \frac{q^{mn}}{|B_R^{d-1}(0)|}$.*

Both in the Hamming and in the rank metric, random codes over $\mathbb{F}_q$ asymptotically achieve the Gilbert-Varshamov bound. Furthermore, they have close to optimal correction capability [29]. This result is important for the scheme that we propose as it allows to choose random generator (or parity-check) matrices as long as the code parameters respect the bound.

The two identification and corresponding signature schemes that we analyze base their security on the difficulty of solving two problems, namely the Bounded Distance Decoding (BDD) problem and the Rank Syndrome Decoding (RSD) problem. Both are defined next:

Problem 1 (Bounded distance q^m-ary rank decoding (BDD(C, t, y))).
Instance:

- A q^m-ary code C with generator matrix $G \in \mathbb{F}_{q^m}^{k \times n}$
- An integer r
- $y \in (\mathbb{F}_{q^m})^n$

Problem: find if exists $x \in (\mathbb{F}_{q^m})^k$ and $e \in (\mathbb{F}_{q^m})^n$ of rank weight r, such that $y = x \cdot G + e$.

The dual of this problem is

Problem 2 (Rank q^m-ary syndrome decoding (RSD(C, t, s))).
Instance:

- A q^m-ary code C with parity-check matrix $H \in \mathbb{F}_{q^m}^{(n-k) \times n}$
- An integer r
- $s \in (\mathbb{F}_{q^m})^{n-k}$

Problem: find if exists $x \in (\mathbb{F}_{q^m})^n$ of rank weight r, such that $s = H \cdot x^T$.

It is not known if BDD problem is NP-complete. However, in [23] or [20], there are arguments that show that the RSD problem is hard.

3.3   Complexity of Solving RSD Problem

Many efforts have been put to solve the RSD problem, or, equivalently, the BDD problem. The first two main combinatorial attempts can be found in [10] (the attack has an exponential term of $q^{(m-r)(r-1)}$) and [37] (exponential term of $q^{(k+1)(r-1)}$). Both complexity of these attacks do not have the length n of the code in their exponent. An algebraic attack in [47] only offers limited results for recovering errors of rank r greater than 2 or 3.

The most performing attack which can recover an error of rank weight r is in [3], which improves a combinatorial algorithm in [20]. In [3] the complexity of the attack is

$$\mathcal{O}\left((n-k)^3 m^3 q^{r\left\lfloor\frac{(k+1)m}{n}\right\rfloor - m}\right),\tag{1}$$

while the combinatorial attack in [20] requires

$$\min\left\{\mathcal{O}\left((n-k)^3 m^3 q^{r\left\lfloor\frac{km}{n}\right\rfloor}\right),\mathcal{O}\left((n-k)^3 m^3 q^{(r-1)\left\lfloor\frac{(k+1)m}{n}\right\rfloor}\right)\right\}\tag{2}$$

operations in $\mathbb{F}_q$.

In [20] an algebraic attack is also presented, which aims at solving the RSD problem by reducing it to the problem of solving a polynomial system. This attack can be implemented following two approaches.

The first approach uses linearization techniques, and if $n \geq (r+1)(k+1)-1$ then the complexity of solving the rank decoding problem is polynomial with $((r+1)(k+1)-1)^3$ operations in $\mathbb{F}_{q^m}$. In general, if $k \geq \left\lceil\frac{(r+1)(k+1)-(n+1)}{r}\right\rceil$ the error can be recovered with complexity $\mathcal{O}\left(r^3 k^3 q^{r\left\lceil\frac{(r+1)(k+1)-(n+1)}{r}\right\rceil}\right)$. The second approach uses Gröbner basis and its complexity seems harder to be evaluated compared to experimental results. This approach improves the linearization approach as long as $n > r(k+1)$, and it yields a complexity of $\mathcal{O}\left(n^{\binom{(k+1)r+d_{reg}}{d_{reg}}}\right)$, where d_{reg} is the degree of regularity of the polynomial system (see [20] for more details). This last complexity is very high, but the authors noted a discrepancy by the theoretical complexity and the actual experiment complexity. The authors of [20] also propose an hybrid approach and conclude that *in practice the algebraic attacks do not work necessarily for all type of parameters but these attacks were more efficient than the first generic combinatorial attack on the parameters we attacked.*

A final remark is that in [30], where a McEliece-like post-quantum cryptosystem based on the rank metric and Gabidulin code [19] is presented, the parameters of the scheme are chosen considering that RSD has a complexity of

$$m^3 q^{(r-1)\left\lfloor k\frac{\min\{m,n\}}{n}\right\rfloor},\tag{3}$$

which is less conservative than the one in [20]. Unfortunately no attack is presented in [30] having such complexity, but instead the results of [20] are referred.

As far as it concerns post-quantum security, the author of [30], in line with [7], presents some arguments showing that the post-quantum complexity of RSD is computed by square-rooting the exponential term in the classical complexity formula, i.e. giving $m^3 q^{(r-1)\left\lfloor k\frac{\min\{m,n\}}{2n}\right\rfloor}$.

Since our proposed schemes rely on the difficulty of solving RSD problem, we take into consideration the above mentioned complexities to choose the proper parameters of the schemes (Sect. 7).

In what follows, we will denote by $\mathrm{WF}_{\mathcal{P}^{\mathcal{A}}}(m,n,k,r)$ the work factor of algorithm $\mathcal{A}$ for solving problem $\mathcal{P}$ with input m,n,k,r, or simply $\mathrm{WF}_{\mathcal{P}}(m,n,k,r)$

when referring to the work factor of solving problem $\mathcal{P}$ with the best known applicable algorithm.

We conclude this section by recalling that, up to the authors knowledge, the worst-case complexity of decoding[1] a random binary code in the Hamming metric is $2^{0.0473n}$ [32]. We will use this estimate to compare the presented schemes with their analogues in the Hamming metric.

3.4 Post-quantum Security of the Fiat-Shamir Transform

It is well known that the Fiat-Shamir transform is secure in the random oracle model (ROM), see e.g. [26]. However, when the adversary has a quantum access to the oracle, i.e. in the quantum random oracle model (QROM), the situation is somehow more complex, and recently many results have been published (e.g. [8,26,45,46]). Since most of the schemes we compare to do not take into account this scenario, we also omit it, and leave it to future research.

An alternative quantum secure transform by Unruh [45] could be used instead of the Fiat-Shamir one, yielding though a considerably less efficient signature, since multiple executions of the underlying identification scheme are required.

In [46], it is proven that if a sigma-protocol has honest-verifier zero-knowledge and statistical soundness with a dual-mode hard instance generator, then the resulting Fiat-Shamir signature scheme is unforgeable in the quantum scenario. It is easy to see that our proposal has a dual-mode hard instant generator and honest-verifier (computational) zero-knowledge. Though, by applying for example the attack of Sect. 6 with a computationally unbounded adversary, statistical soundness cannot be achieved. Thus we cannot apply the theorem of [46] to our proposal. Still, to the best of our knowledge, no quantum attack has been published to our specific construction.

4 Identification Schemes Description

In this section we provide the description of the two rank metric variants of the identification schemes presented in [9,48], which we will refer to, respectively, as Veron and CVE, Identification and Signature Protocols. While the first scheme can be converted from Hamming metric to rank metric in a straightforward way (we work on the field $(\mathbb{F}_{q^m})^n$ instead of on a binary field, and we need to replace the Hamming weight with the rank weight when choosing the private key), it is not obvious how to convert the third scheme in order to obtain a much more efficient scheme, because of the use of a special function that it is used inside the scheme (see below). This function has the property of preserving the rank of a vector in $(\mathbb{F}_{q^m})^n$, as it first apply a linear transformation and then a permutation to its coordinates (see Definition 4).

---

[1] Here decoding is referring to the half distance decoding scenario (with $n \approx 2k$), which is the one of interest in the cryptographic setting.

Veron: $\mathsf{KGen}(1^\lambda)$	CVE: $\mathsf{KGen}(1^\lambda)$
1 : Define m, n, k, r	1 : Define m, n, k, r
as in Sect. 7	as in Sect. 7
2 : $x \leftarrow\!\!\$\ (\mathbb{F}_{q^m})^k$	2 : $s \leftarrow\!\!\$\ (\mathbb{F}_{q^m})^n$
3 : $e \leftarrow\!\!\$\ (\mathbb{F}_{q^m})^n$	s.t. $\mathrm{w_r}(s) = r$
s.t. $\mathrm{w_r}(s) = r$	3 : $\mathsf{sk} \leftarrow s$
4 : $\mathsf{sk} \leftarrow (x, e)$	4 : $H \leftarrow\!\!\$\ (\mathbb{F}_{q^m})^{(n-k)\times n}$
5 : $G \leftarrow\!\!\$\ (\mathbb{F}_{q^m})^{k\times n}$	5 : $y_i \leftarrow H \cdot (s^{(i)})^T,$
6 : $y \leftarrow x \cdot G + e$	$i = 1, \ldots, m$
7 : $\mathsf{pk} \leftarrow (y, G, r)$	6 : $\mathsf{pk} \leftarrow (y_i, H, r)$
8 : $\textbf{return sk}, \mathsf{pk}$	7 : $\textbf{return sk}, \mathsf{pk}$

Fig. 1. Veron and CVE key generation algorithm in the rank metric

The security of the CVE scheme is based on the Rank Syndrome Decoding problem, while the one of the Veron scheme is based on the Bounded Distance Rank Decoding problem.

Recall that we will denote by λ the security level of the scheme. The two key generation algorithms are listed in Fig. 1. The Veron, and CVE identification protocols are listed, respectively, in Figs. 2, and 3.

As far as it concern the CVE protocol, we need the following function.

Definition 4. *Given a q-ary $(m \times m)$-matrix $\Gamma = \Gamma_{i,j}, i = 1, \ldots, m, j = 1, \ldots, n$ a permutation $\Sigma \in S_n$, and a vector $v \in (\mathbb{F}_{q^m})^n$, we define the following function*

$$\Pi_{\Gamma, \Sigma} : (\mathbb{F}_{q^m})^n \mapsto (\mathbb{F}_{q^m})^n$$
$$(v_1, \ldots, v_n) \mapsto (\pi_1, \ldots, \pi_n)$$

where, for $j = 1, \ldots, n$, $\pi_j := (\Gamma_{1,1}v_{1,\Sigma(j)} + \cdots + \Gamma_{1,m}v_{m,\Sigma(j)}, \ldots, \Gamma_{m,1}v_{1,\Sigma(j)} + \cdots + \Gamma_{m,m}v_{m,\Sigma(j)})$

The formula to compute the function $\Pi_{\Gamma, \Sigma}(v)$ comes from applying the permutation Σ to the multiplication of Γ and v seen as q-ary matrices, as follows:

$$\Pi_{\Gamma,\Sigma}(v) := \Sigma \left(\begin{pmatrix} \Gamma_{1,1} & \cdots & \Gamma_{1,m} \\ \vdots & \ddots & \vdots \\ \Gamma_{m,1} & \cdots & \Gamma_{m,m} \end{pmatrix} \cdot \begin{pmatrix} v_{1,1} & \cdots & v_{1,n} \\ \vdots & \ddots & \vdots \\ v_{m,1} & \cdots & v_{m,n} \end{pmatrix} \right)$$

$$= \begin{pmatrix} \Gamma_{1,1}v_{1,\Sigma(1)} + \cdots + \Gamma_{1,m}v_{m,\Sigma(1)} & \cdots & \Gamma_{1,1}v_{1,\Sigma(n)} + \cdots + \Gamma_{1,m}v_{m,\Sigma(n)} \\ \vdots & \ddots & \vdots \\ \Gamma_{m,1}v_{1,\Sigma(1)} + \cdots + \Gamma_{m,m}v_{m,\Sigma(1)} & \cdots & \Gamma_{m,1}v_{1,\Sigma(n)} + \cdots + \Gamma_{m,m}v_{m,\Sigma(n)} \end{pmatrix}$$

$$= (\pi_1, \ldots, \pi_n) \in (\mathbb{F}_{q^m})^n .$$

Notice that the correctness of the protocol is given by the following properties:
$H \cdot \Pi_{\Sigma,\Gamma}^{-1}(\beta) - \sum_{i=1}^m \alpha_i y_i = H \cdot u^T$, and $\beta - \sum_{i+1}^m \alpha_i \mathsf{rsp}_{1,i} = \Pi_{\Gamma, \Sigma}(u)$.

Prover	Verifier
sk, pk $= (x, e), (y, G, r) \leftarrow$ KGen	pk

$u \leftarrow_\$ (\mathbb{F}_q m)^k, \sigma \leftarrow_\$ S_n$
$c_1 \leftarrow H(\sigma)$
$c_2 \leftarrow H(\sigma((u + x) \cdot G))$

$c_3 \leftarrow H(\sigma(u \cdot G + y))$ $\qquad \xrightarrow{\ c_1, c_2, c_3\ }$

$\qquad\qquad\qquad\qquad\quad \xleftarrow{\quad b \quad} \quad b \leftarrow_\$ \{0, 1, 2\}$

if $b = 0$

$\quad$ rsp$_1 \leftarrow \sigma$, rsp$_2 \leftarrow u + x$ $\quad \xrightarrow{\text{rsp}_1, \text{rsp}_2}$ **if** $c_1 = H(\text{rsp}_1) \wedge$

$\qquad\qquad\qquad\qquad\qquad\qquad\qquad\quad c_2 = H(\text{rsp}_1(\text{rsp}_2 \cdot G))$
$\qquad\qquad\qquad\qquad\qquad\qquad\qquad\quad$ **return true**

if $b = 1$

$\quad$ rsp$_1 \leftarrow \sigma((u + x) \cdot G)$, rsp$_2 \leftarrow \sigma(e)$ $\xrightarrow{\text{rsp}_1, \text{rsp}_2}$ **if** $c_2 = H(\text{rsp}_1) \wedge$

$\qquad\qquad\qquad\qquad\qquad\qquad\qquad\quad c_3 = H(\text{rsp}_1 + \text{rsp}_2) \wedge$
$\qquad\qquad\qquad\qquad\qquad\qquad\qquad\quad w_r(\text{rsp}_2) = r$
$\qquad\qquad\qquad\qquad\qquad\qquad\qquad\quad$ **return true**

if $b = 2$

$\quad$ rsp$_1 \leftarrow \sigma$, rsp$_2 \leftarrow u$ $\qquad \xrightarrow{\text{rsp}_1, \text{rsp}_2}$ **if** $c_1 = H(\text{rsp}_1) \wedge$

$\qquad\qquad\qquad\qquad\qquad\qquad\qquad\quad c_3 = H(\text{rsp}_1(\text{rsp}_2 \cdot G + y))$
$\qquad\qquad\qquad\qquad\qquad\qquad\qquad\quad$ **return true**

Fig. 2. Veron identification protocol in the rank metric

5 Signature Schemes Description

In this section we provide the description of the two rank metric variants of the signature schemes derived from Veron, and CVE identification protocols, which we will refer to, respectively, as Veron, and CVE signature schemes. Up to the authors knowledge, with the exception of [2] (and [13] for CVE), a detailed pseudo-code for such signature schemes has never been provided. The security of the CVE scheme is based on the RSD problem, while the one of Veron is based on the BDR Decoding problem.

We first present the Veron signature and verification algorithm in the rank metric, which can be observed in Fig. 4. Key generation is the same as in Sect. 4. Let $f(x, y)$ be the function that maps the bits x, y to the set $\{0, 1, 2\}$ following the rule $00 \mapsto 0, 01 \mapsto 1, 10 \mapsto 2$ and 11 maps to either $0, 1, 2$ in a cyclic fashion. In the following algorithms, if 2δ is greater than h, then it is possible to compute the challenge as ch $\leftarrow H(\text{cmt} \| \text{msg} \| 1) \| \dots \| H(\text{cmt} \| \text{msg} \| l) \in (\mathbb{F}_2)^{l \cdot h}$, where $l \leftarrow \lfloor 2\delta/h \rfloor + 1$.

Prover	Verifier
$\mathsf{sk} = s \leftarrow \mathsf{KGen}$	
$\mathsf{pk} = (y_i, H, r) \leftarrow \mathsf{KGen}$	pk
$i = 1, \ldots, m$	

$u \leftarrow_\$ (\mathbb{F}_{q^m})^n$

$\Gamma \leftarrow_\$ (\mathbb{F}_q)^{m \times m}$ invertible

$\Sigma \leftarrow_\$ S_n$

$c_1 \leftarrow H(\Sigma, \Gamma, H \cdot u^T)$

$c_2 \leftarrow H(\Pi_{\Gamma,\Sigma}(u), \Pi_{\Gamma,\Sigma}(s))$ $\xrightarrow{\quad c_1, c_2 \quad}$

$\xleftarrow{\quad \alpha \quad}$ $\alpha = (\alpha_1, \ldots, \alpha_n) \leftarrow_\$ (\mathbb{F}_{q^m})^n$

$\beta = \Pi_{\Gamma,\Sigma}\left(u + \sum_{i=1}^{m} \alpha_i s^{(i)}\right)$ $\xrightarrow{\quad \beta \quad}$

$\xleftarrow{\quad b \quad}$ $b \leftarrow_\$ \{0, 1\}$

if $b = 0$

$\quad \mathsf{rsp}_1 \leftarrow \Sigma, \mathsf{rsp}_2 \leftarrow \Gamma$ $\xrightarrow{\quad \mathsf{rsp}_1, \mathsf{rsp}_2 \quad}$ **if** $c_1 = H\left(\Sigma, \Gamma, H \cdot \Pi_{\Sigma,\Gamma}^{-1}(\beta) - \sum_{i=1}^{m} \alpha_i y_i\right)$

$\quad\quad\quad\quad\quad\quad\quad\quad\quad\quad\quad\quad$ **return** true

if $b = 1$

$\quad \mathsf{rsp}_{1,i} \leftarrow \Pi_{\Gamma,\Sigma}(s^{(i)})$ $\xrightarrow{\quad \mathsf{rsp}_{1,i} \quad}$ **if** $c_2 = H\left(\beta - \sum_{i+1}^{m} \alpha_i \mathsf{rsp}_{1,i}, \mathsf{rsp}_{1,1}\right) \wedge$
$\quad\quad\quad i=1,\ldots,m$

$\quad\quad\quad\quad\quad\quad\quad\quad\quad\quad\quad\quad$ $\mathsf{w}_r(\mathsf{rsp}_{1,1}) = r$

$\quad\quad\quad\quad\quad\quad\quad\quad\quad\quad\quad\quad$ **return** true

Fig. 3. CVE identification protocol in the rank metric

We now present CVE signature and verification algorithm in the rank metric, which is shown in Fig. 5. The security of the scheme is based on the RSD problem. Key generation is the same as in Sect. 4.

The scheme we present is an instantiation of the one presented in [13], using the Hamming metric. The combinations of Step 8 and 9 are the instantiation of the first oracle of the scheme, while the second oracle is instantiated in Step 13. Notice that $\alpha_i \in (\mathbb{F}_2)^m, \mathsf{cmt}_{1,i} \in (\mathbb{F}_{2^m})^n, \mathsf{ch}_1, \mathsf{ch}_2 \in (\mathbb{F}_2)^h$.

6   Forging Signatures with Stern and Veron Signature Protocols

In this section we show how to obtain a forged signature of the Stern scheme if the number of rounds is too low (for Veron scheme the attack works in the same way). In this case the attacker gains the ability to force the signature in a way that the verifier never checks if the private key is tied to the public key.

The aim of the attacker is to create a fake signature which is successfully verified. The attacker must perform the following steps:

Veron: Sign(sk, pk, msg, δ)

$sk = (x, e) \leftarrow$ KGen
$pk = (y, G, r) \leftarrow$ KGen
msg, message
δ, number of rounds as defined in Sect. 7.1

```
1 :   for i = 1..δ do
2 :       u_i ←$ (F_{q^m})^k
3 :       σ_i ←$ S_n
4 :       c_{i,1} ← H(σ_i)
5 :       c_{i,2} ← H(σ_i((u_i + x) · G))
6 :       c_{i,3} ← H(σ_i(u_i · G + y))
7 :   cmt ← c_{1,1}‖c_{1,2}‖c_{1,3}‖ · · · ‖c_{δ,1}‖c_{δ,2}‖c_{δ,3}
8 :   ch ← H(cmt‖msg) ∈ (F_2)^h
9 :   for i = 1..δ do
10 :      b_i ← f(ch_{2i}, ch_{2i+1})
11 :      if b_i = 0
12 :          rsp_i ← [σ_i, u_i + x]
13 :      if b_i = 1
14 :          rsp_i ← [σ_i((u_i + x) · G), σ(e))]
15 :      if b_i = 2
16 :          rsp_i ← [σ_i, u_i]
17 :   sgn ← [cmt, rsp]
18 :   return sgn
```

Veron: Verify(pk, msg, δ, sgn)

$pk = (y, G, r) \leftarrow$ KGen
msg, message
δ, number of rounds as defined in Sect. 7.1
sgn = [cmt, rsp], signature

```
1 :   ch ← H(cmt‖msg) ∈ (F_2)^h
2 :   for i = 1..δ do
3 :       c_{i,1} ← cmt_{[3(i−1)h+1,...,(3(i−1)+1)h]}
4 :       c_{i,2} ← cmt_{[(3(i−1)+1)h+1,...,(3(i−1)+2)h]}
5 :       c_{i,3} ← cmt_{[(3(i−1)+2)h+1,...,3ih]}
6 :       b_i ← f(ch_{2i}, ch_{2i+1})
7 :       if b_i = 0
8 :           if c_{i,1} ≠ H(rsp_{i,1})∨
                   c_{i,2} ≠ H(rsp_{i,1}(rsp_{i,2} · G))
9 :               return false
10 :      if b_i = 1
11 :          if c_{i,2} ≠ H(rsp_{i,1}) ∨ w_r(rsp_{i,2}) ≠ r∨
                   c_{i,3} ≠ H(rsp_{i,1} + rsp_{i,2})
12 :              return false
13 :      if b_i = 2
14 :          if c_{i,1} ≠ H(rsp_{i,1})∨
                   c_{i,3} ≠ H(rsp_{i,1}(rsp_{i,2} · G + y))
15 :              return false
16 :   return true
```

Fig. 4. Veron signature and verification algorithms in the rank metric

- for each $i = 1, \ldots, \delta - 1$
  - choose randomly $u_i \in (\mathbb{F}_{q^m})^n$, $\sigma_i \in S_n$, and $s \in (\mathbb{F}_{q^m})^n$ s.t. $\mathrm{w_r}(s) = r$
  - compute $c_{i,1} \leftarrow \mathsf{H}(\sigma_i \| H \cdot u_i^T)$, $c_{i,2} \leftarrow \mathsf{H}(\sigma_i(u_i))$, and $c_{i,3} \leftarrow \mathsf{H}(\sigma_i(u_i + s))$
- compute $\mathrm{cmt}' \leftarrow c_{1,1} \| c_{1,2} \| c_{1,3} \| \ldots \| c_{\delta-1,1} \| c_{\delta-1,2} \| c_{\delta-1,3}$
- choose u_δ, σ_δ and s in such a way that the first δ bit pairs of $\mathsf{H}(\mathrm{cmt}' \| c_{\delta,1} \| c_{\delta,2} \| c_{\delta,3} \| \mathrm{msg})$ are either 00 or 10
- set $\mathrm{cmt} = \mathrm{cmt}' \| c_{\delta,1} \| c_{\delta,2} \| c_{\delta,3}$
- construct rsp as in the signing procedure.

Notice that in this way, b_i is never 1. Also notice that the probability of finding the hash output of the required form, by picking u_δ, σ_δ and s randomly, is $(\frac{1}{2})^{\delta+1}$. It can be easily seen that such constructed signature will be successfully verified. This is because the $b_i = 1$ branch, which is where the bond between the public and the secret key is checked, is never reached.

To avoid such an attack, a possible countermeasure seems to be increasing the number of rounds, and consequently the signature size, in order to make the special hash output search infeasible.

CVE: Sign(sk, pk, msg, δ)	CVE: Verify(pk, msg, δ, sgn)
sk $= s \leftarrow$ KGen	pk $= (y_i, H, r) \leftarrow$ KGen
pk $= (y_i, H, r) \leftarrow$ KGen	msg, message
msg, message	δ, number of rounds as defined in Sect. 7.1
δ, number of rounds as defined in Sect. 7.1	sgn $= [\text{cmt}_0, \text{ch}_1, \text{cmt}_1, \text{ch}_2, \text{rsp}]$, signature

// Step 1
1 :   **for** $i = 1..\delta$ **do**
2 : $u_i \leftarrow\!\!\$ \, (\mathbb{F}_{q^m})^n$
3 : $\Gamma_i \leftarrow\!\!\$ \, (\mathbb{F}_q)^{m \times m}$ invertible
4 : $\Sigma_i \leftarrow\!\!\$ \, S_n$
5 : $c_{i,0} \leftarrow \mathsf{H}(\Sigma_i, \Gamma_i, H \cdot u_i^T)$
6 : $c_{i,1} \leftarrow \mathsf{H}(\Pi_{\Gamma_i, \Sigma_i}(u_i), \Pi_{\Gamma_i, \Sigma_i}(s))$
7 : $\text{cmt}_0 \leftarrow c_{1,0} \| c_{1,1} \| \ldots \| c_{\delta,0} \| c_{\delta,1}$
// Step 2
8 : $\text{ch}_1 \leftarrow \mathsf{H}(\text{cmt}_0 \| \text{msg})$
9 :   Truncate rightmost bits in ch_1
      so that it has $m\delta$ bits
// Step 3
10 : **for** $i = 1..\delta$ **do**
11 : $\alpha_i \leftarrow (\text{ch}_{1,m(i-1)+1}, \ldots, \text{ch}_{1,mi})$
12 : $\text{cmt}_{1,i} \leftarrow \Pi_{\Gamma_i, \Sigma_i}\left(u_i + \sum_{i=1}^{m} \alpha_{i,j} s^{(j)}\right)$
// Step 4
13 : $\text{ch}_2 \leftarrow \mathsf{H}(\text{cmt}_1 \| 1) \| \ldots \| \mathsf{H}(\text{cmt}_1 \| l)$
// Step 5
14 : **for** $i = 1..\delta$ **do**
15 :   **if** $\text{ch}_{2,i} = 0$
16 : $\text{rsp}_i \leftarrow [\Sigma_i, \Gamma_i]$
17 :   **if** $\text{ch}_{2,i} = 1$
18 : $\text{rsp}_i \leftarrow (\Pi_{\Gamma_i, \Sigma_i}(s^{(1)}), \ldots, \Pi_{\Gamma_i, \Sigma_i}(s^{(m)}))$
19 : $\text{sgn} \leftarrow [\text{cmt}_0, \text{ch}_1, \text{cmt}_1, \text{ch}_2, \text{rsp}]$
20 : **return** sgn

1 :   **for** $i = 1..\delta$ **do**
2 : $\alpha_i \leftarrow (\text{ch}_{1,m(i-1)+1}, \ldots, \text{ch}_{1,mi})$
3 :   **if** $\text{ch}_{2,i} = 0$
4 : $c_{i,1} \leftarrow \text{cmt}_{0[2h(i-1)+1,\ldots,2h(i-1)+h]}$
5 : $t \leftarrow H \cdot \Pi^{-1}_{\text{rsp}_{i,1}, \text{rsp}_{i,2}}(\text{cmt}_{1,i}) - \sum_{j=1}^{m} \alpha_{i,j} y_j$
6 :   **if** $c_{i,1} \neq \mathsf{H}(\text{rsp}_{i,1}, \text{rsp}_{i,2}, t)$
7 :   **return** false
8 :   **if** $\text{ch}_{2,i} = 1$
9 : $c_{i,2} \leftarrow \text{cmt}_{0[2h(i-1)+h)+1,\ldots,2hi]}$
10 :   **if** $c_{i,2} \neq \mathsf{H}\left(\text{cmt}_{1,i} - \sum_{j=1}^{m} \alpha_{i,j} \text{rsp}_j, \text{rsp}_1\right) \vee$
                   $w_r(\text{rsp}_1) \neq r$
11 :   **return** false
12 : **return** true

Fig. 5. CVE signature and verification algorithms in the rank metric

7   Parameters Choice

In this section we first provide a set of requirements that the scheme parameters must meet in order to provide enough security against known attacks. Once the requirement are set we choose a set of parameters for 80 bit security in the classical scenario, and 128, 192, and 256 bit security in the post-quantum scenario.

7.1   Requirements

Code Size. All the schemes presented in this work rely their security on the difficulty of decoding a random linear q-ary code in the rank metric. In order to choose the proper parameters for our codes we need to choose m, n, k, r satisfying the following conditions:

- it should not be possible to apply the polynomial-time algebraic attacks of [20], i.e. $n < (r+1)(k+1) - 1$ and $n \leq r(k+1)$;
- if the algebraic attack of [20] is applicabale in the more generic scenario of $k < \left\lceil \frac{(r+1)(k+1) - (n+1)}{r} \right\rceil$, then we should have $\log_2 \left(r^3 k^3 q^{r \left\lceil \frac{(r+1)(k+1) - (n+1)}{r} \right\rceil} \right) \geq \lambda$.
- the complexity of the best known generic combinatorial attack [3], should be such that $\log_2 \left((n-k)^3 m^3 q^{r \frac{(k+1)m}{n} - m} \right) \geq \lambda$. We also consider a set of parameters with regards of the less conservative complexity $m^3 q^{(r-1) \lfloor k \frac{\min\{m,n\}}{n} \rfloor}$, where given by the attack referred in [30].

For the case of parameters which are secure even in the post-quantum setting we will simply square-root the exponential term of the complexity formula of each attack.

To summarize, we have the following two requirements respectively for the classical and the post-quantum scenario:

Requirement 1 (Classical scenario). *If conditions* $k < \left\lceil \frac{(r+1)(k+1) - (n+1)}{r} \right\rceil$, $n < (r+1)(k+1) - 1$, *and* $n \leq r(k+1)$ *are met, in the classical scenario we require*

$$\min \left\{ r^3 k^3 q^{r \left\lceil \frac{(r+1)(k+1) - (n+1)}{r} \right\rceil}, (n-k)^3 m^3 q^{r \frac{(k+1)m}{n} - m}, m^3 q^{(r-1) \lfloor k \frac{\min\{m,n\}}{n} \rfloor} \right\} \geq 2^\lambda.$$

while, in the post-quantum scenario we require

$$\min \left\{ r^3 k^3 q^{r \left\lceil \frac{(r+1)(k+1) - (n+1)}{2r} \right\rceil}, (n-k)^3 m^3 q^{r \frac{(k+1)m}{2n} - m}, m^3 q^{(r-1) \lfloor k \frac{\min\{m,n\}}{2n} \rfloor} \right\} \geq 2^\lambda.$$

Choice of r. As suggested in [43], it is better to choose r slightly below the theoretical t provided by the Gilbert-Varshamov bound[2], in order to avoid possible small rank attacks similar to small weight codewords attack such as [42].

Number of Rounds. We also need to choose the number of rounds δ in order to decrease the impersonation probability to our needs. As far as it concern the identification protocols, for Stern and Veron the impersonation probability of one single round is $2/3$, while for CVE is $1/2$. In [2] the authors state that they choose the number of rounds according to the norm ISO/IEC-9798-5 [1], which defines the weak and strong authentication probabilities to be 2^{-16} and 2^{-32}. To achieve these probabilities, they need respectively 28 and 55 rounds for Stern and Veron schemes, while 16 and 32 rounds for CVE. In general, to reach a security level l with an impersonation probability of q, i.e. to compute the number of round δ, we need to set $\delta = \log_q(1/2^l)$. This results in $\delta = 137, 218, 329, 438$ for Stern and Veron, and $\delta = 80, 128, 192, 256$ for CVE, respectively, for 80 bit

---

[2] Recall that the bounds provides d and than $t = \lfloor (d-1)/2 \rfloor$.

security level in the classical scenario and 128, 256, 512 bit security level in the post-quantum scenario. The number of rounds provided is enough to avoid the attack described in Sect. 6.

7.2 Proposed Parameters

We now propose 4 sets of parameters, respectively for the 80 bit security level in the classical scenario, Table 1, and for 128, 192, and 256 bit security level in the post-quantum scenario, Table 2. For all the proposed parameters it holds the condition $k < \left\lceil \frac{(r+1)(k+1)-(n+1)}{r} \right\rceil$, so the algebraic attack of [20] must be taken into consideration while evaluating the security.

Table 1. Classical scenario. $A = r^3 k^3 q^{r \left\lceil \frac{(r+1)(k+1)-(n+1)}{r} \right\rceil}$, $B = (n-k)^3 m^3$ $q^{r \frac{(k+1)m}{n} - m}$, $C = m^3 q^{(r-1) \left\lfloor k \frac{\min\{m,n\}}{n} \right\rfloor}$.

Parameters							Security level		
q	m	n	k	r	δ	h	$\log_2 A$	$\log_2 B$	$\log_2 C$
2	48	35	16	5	137 (Stern, Veron), 80 (CVE)	160	89	98	80

Table 2. Post-quantum scenario. $A = (n-k)^3 m^3 q^{r \frac{(k+1)m}{2n} - m}$, $B = m^3 q^{(r-1) \left\lfloor k \frac{\min\{m,n\}}{2n} \right\rfloor}$, $C = r^3 k^3 q^{r \left\lceil \frac{(r+1)(k+1)-(n+1)}{2r} \right\rceil}$.

Parameters							Security level		
q	m	n	k	r	δ	h	$\log_2 A$	$\log_2 B$	$\log_2 C$
2	80	64	30	9	218 (Stern, Veron), 128 (CVE)	256	128.60	138.97	150.23
2	96	72	32	12	329 (Stern, Veron), 192 (CVE)	384	203.72	195.75	205.75
2	128	80	32	16	438 (Stern, Veron), 256 (CVE)	512	332.15	261.00	267.00

8   Signature and Verification Cost

The cost of Stern, Veron, and CVE key generation algorithm is dominated by the multiplication by either the generator (Veron) or the parity-check (Stern, CVE) matrix. In the case of Stern and Veron only one multiplication is needed, while for CVE m of such multiplications are needed to generate the public key. On the other hand, the cost of Stern, Veron, and CVE signature and verification algorithms are dominated by the number of rounds and the cost of the underlying hash function.

In particular, in the case of Stern and Veron schemes, $3\delta + \lfloor 2\delta/h \rfloor + 1$ hashes have to be computed for the signature, while, $2\delta + \lfloor 2\delta/h \rfloor + 1$ hashes must be computed for verification.

As far as it concern the CVE scheme, $2\delta + 2\lceil m\delta/h \rceil$ hashes have to be computed for the signature, while, only δ hashes must be computed for verification.

9   Key and Signature Size Comparison

Veron Scheme. In the rank metric version of the Veron signature scheme we have the following keys and signature size:

- $|\mathsf{sk}| = |x| + |e| = m(k + n)$,
- $|\mathsf{pk}| = |y| + |G| + |r| = mn + mkk + \log_2(r)$,
- the average size of the signature is $|\mathsf{sgn}| = |\mathsf{cmt}| + |\mathsf{rsp}| = 3h\delta + \frac{2}{3}\delta n(2m + \log_2(n))$, where $|\mathsf{rsp}| = \frac{2}{3}\delta(mn + n\log_2(n)) + \frac{1}{3}\delta nm$, since 2/3 of the times the i-th component of rsp is made by a permutation in S_n and a vector in $(\mathbb{F}_{2^m})^n$, while the other 1/3 of the times is made by two vectors in $(\mathbb{F}_{2^m})^n$.

CVE Scheme. In the rank metric version of the CVE signature scheme we have the following keys and signature size:

- $|\mathsf{sk}| = |s| = mn$,
- $|\mathsf{pk}| = \sum_{i=1}^{m} |y_i| + |H| + |r| = m^2(n - k) + m(n - k)(n - k) + \log_2(r)$,
- the average size of the signature is $|\mathsf{sgn}| = |\mathsf{cmt}_0| + |\mathsf{ch}_1| + |\mathsf{cmt}_1| + |\mathsf{ch}_2| + |\mathsf{rsp}| = \delta 2h + 2\lceil\frac{m\delta}{h}\rceil h + \delta mn + \frac{1}{2}\delta(m^2 + n\log_2(n) + m^2 n)$,
  where $|\mathsf{rsp}| = \frac{1}{2}\delta(m^2 + n\log_2(n)) + \frac{1}{2}\delta(m^2 n)$, since 1/2 of the times the i-th component of rsp is made by a $m \times m$-binary matrix and permutation in S_n, while the other 1/2 of the times is made by m vectors in $(\mathbb{F}_{2^m})^n$.

Comparison. In Table 3 we report some key and signature bit sizes for other signature schemes based on codes. In particular we report the results provided in [17] for Parallel-CFS, the results for the only three NIST competitors for signatures based on codes, RankSign [21], RaCoSS [39], and pqsignRM [28], and the results from [2] of the Hamming variants of our proposals. Recall that for all three NIST competititors some attacks have been found, so either the parameters should be made larger or some modification of the scheme will be proposed in the future.

In Appendix A we recall how the key and signature sizes are derived from the parameters of the other schemes.

An interesting consideration regarding the CVE scheme is that, unlike in the Hamming metric, when using the rank metric the scheme is not the best performing, neither has the smallest signature and public key compared to Stern and Veron schemes.

Overall, compared to Parallel-CFS and to the three NIST submissions, the two schemes presented in this manuscript provide the smallest private key size and the second smallest public key size (only RankSign offers a smaller public key[3]), but the largest signature size. Thus, the use of these type of signatures is suggested in an environment where having small keys is more important than small signatures, as it would be the case in some IoT scenarios.

---

[3] Recall that RankSign scheme has been proven to be broken with the above mentioned parameters.

Table 3. Comparison of keys and signature bit sizes with the most popular code-based signature schemes. The superscript c indicates classical scenario security.

λ	Scheme	Metric	Scheme parameters	|sgn|	|sk|	|pk|
			(m, t, δ, i)			
81^c	Parallel-CFS	Hamm.	$(20, 8, 2, 3)$	294	20 971 680	167 746 560
80^c	Parallel-CFS	Hamm.	$(17, 10, 2, 2)$	196	2 228 394	22 253 340
			(n, k, ω, γ)			
177	RaCoSS	Hamm.	$(2400, 2060, 48, 0.07)$	4800	5 760 000	816 000
177	RaCoSS (Compr.)	Hamm.	$(2400, 2060, 48, 0.07)$	2436	1 382 400	816 000
			$(q, m, n, k, d, t, t', r)$			
128	RankSign I	Rank	$(2^{32}, 21, 20, 10, 2, 2, 1, 8)$	11 008	540 288	80 640
128	RankSign II	Rank	$(2^{24}, 24, 24, 12, 2, 2, 2, 10)$	12 000	652 032	96 768
192	RankSign III	Rank	$(2^{32}, 27, 24, 12, 2, 3, 1, 10)$	17 280	1 034 208	155 520
256	RankSign IV	Rank	$(2^{32}, 30, 28, 14, 2, 3, 2, 12)$	23 424	1 527 360	228 480
			(r, m, p, w)			
128	pqsignRM-4-12	Hamm.	$(4, 12, 16, 1295)$	4 224	27 749 002	2 621 788
196	pqsignRM-6-12	Hamm.	$(6, 12, 8, 311)$	4 224	19 326 902	3 980 860
256	pqsignRM-6-13	Hamm.	$(6, 13, 16, 1441)$	8 320	16 777 216	84 020 992
			(q, n, k, w, δ, h)			
80^c	Stern	Hamm.	$(2, 768, 384, 76, 141, 160)$	904 022	768	147 846
80^c	Veron	Hamm.	$(2, 768, 384, 76, 141, 160)$	904 022	1 152	148 230
80^c	CVE	Hamm.	$(2^8, 144, 72, 55, 80, 160)$	531 539	1 152	42 053
			$(q, m, n, k, r, \delta, h)$			
80^c	Veron	Rank	$(2, 48, 35, 16, 5, 137, 160)$	389 037	2 448	13 971
128	Veron	Rank	$(2, 80, 64, 30, 9, 219, 256)$	1 719 296	7 520	77 124
192	Veron	Rank	$(2, 96, 72, 32, 12, 329, 384)$	3 508 508	9 984	105 220
256	Veron	Rank	$(2, 128, 80, 32, 16, 438, 512)$	6 800 609	14 336	141 316
80^c	CVE	Rank	$(2, 48, 35, 16, 5, 80, 160)$	3 492 621	1 680	61 107
128	CVE	Rank	$(2, 80, 64, 30, 9, 128, 256)$	27 389 952	5 120	310 084
192	CVE	Rank	$(2, 96, 72, 32, 12, 192, 384)$	66 139 799	6 912	522 244
256	CVE	Rank	$(2, 128, 80, 32, 16, 256, 512)$	172 883 169	10 240	1 081 348

10 Conclusions

We have presented two cryptographic signature schemes based on codes in the rank metric derived from their analogue in the Hamming metric. For all of the schemes we proposed four sets of parameters which hold 80 bit security in the classical scenario, and 128, 192, and 256 bit security in the post-quantum scenario. The two schemes with these parameters offer a similar cost complexity as other post-quantum signature schemes. A disadvantage of the schemes is the large signature size, while on the other hand they present very small secret and public keys, namely the smallest among all known signature schemes based on codes.

We have also described a practical attack to one instantiation of the original Stern and Veron scheme presented in [2]. Our proposal is immune to such attack.

Among the two schemes proposed, the first is the most efficient and presents the smallest key sizes. Since it is derived from an identification protocol through the Fiat-Shamir transform, a proof of security in the quantum random oracle model of the transform for this specific case should be provided. We leave this topic to future research.

A   Key and Signature Size Derivation for Other Code-Based Signature Schemes

As far as it concerns Parallel-CFS, we recall that the scheme is defined by the parameters m, t, δ, i, which yield a code of length $n = 2^m$ and dimension $k = 2^m - mt$. The parameter t is the correction capability of the underlying Goppa code and also the degree of its defining polynomial g over $\mathbb{F}_{2^m}$. The parameter i is the number of parallel hashes, which also determines the linear increase of the signature time and size with respect to the original scheme. The parameter δ can be thought of as the increase that needs to be added to t in order for $t + \delta$ to provide complete decoding. The public key is a hidden $mt \times n$ parity-check matrix $H \in \{0,1\}^{mt \times n}$ in systematic form of the Goppa code, which can then be represented using $(n - k)k = mt(2^m - mt)$ bits. The private key has size $mt + mn$, since it is formed by g and the so called support $(\alpha_1, \ldots, \alpha_n) \in (\mathbb{F}_{2^m})^n$ of the code. There are shortening techniques that can be used to represent the signature, depending on whether a larger signature or a slower scheme is desired. To obtain fast signature verification, a possible trade-off gives a size of $i \log_2 \binom{n}{t+\delta-1}$ bits. To obtain short signatures with a longer verification, a possible trade-off gives a size of $i \log_2 \binom{n/m}{t+\delta-3}$ bits. We report the two extremes presented in [17] for a security of at least 80 bits. For higher security levels or for the post-quantum scenario the key sizes become prohibitive.

The code parameters of RaCoSS are the length of the code n, its dimension k, its minimum distance ω, and a real constant γ. The private and the public key of RaCoSS scheme are, respectively, a $n \times n$ and a $(n-k) \times n$ binary matrix. The signature is composed by the elements z and c of size n bits each. The authors also use a compression technique to reduce the size of the secret key to $n\omega \lceil \log_2 n \rceil$ and the signature to $n + \lfloor \gamma\omega \rfloor \lceil \log_2 n \rceil$.

The parameters of the RankSign scheme are the cardinality q of the base field, the length n, the dimension k, and the weight d of the LRPC code, the extension degree m, the number t of random columns added to the LRPC code to obtain the augmented LRPC code, the rank weight t' of the error, and the rank weight r of the signature of a message. The public key is given by a parity-check matrix in systematic form of size $(n - k) \times (n + t)$, with entries in $\mathbb{F}_{q^m}$, which can be represented with $(n-k)(t+k)m\lceil \log_2 q \rceil$ bits. The secret key is composed by 3 matrices of size $(n - k) \times (n - k)$, $(n + t) \times (n + t)$, and $(n - k) \times (n + t)$, for a total size of $((n - k)^2 + (n + t)^2 + (n - k)(n + t))m \log_2 q$. The signature has size $r(m + n + t)\lceil \log_2 q \rceil$.

The parameters of pqsignRM are the integers r, m defining the Reed-Mueller code of length $n = 2^m$ and dimension $k = \sum_{i=0}^{r} \binom{m}{i}$, a positive integer p as the puncturing parameter, and the error weight parameter w. The public key is a binary $(n - k) \times n$ parity-check matrix in systematic form, thus requiring $(n - k)k$ bits for its representation. The secret key is made by 3 binary matrices of size, respectively, $(n - k) \times (n - k)$, $n \times n$, and $p \times (n - p)$, plus a vector of size $n - k$. The signature is given by a vector e of n bits and integer $i < 2^{128}$.

References

1. ISO/IEC 9798-5:2009 Information technology - Security techniques - Entity authentication - Part 5: Mechanisms using zero-knowledge techniques, December 2009. https://www.iso.org/standard/50456.html
2. El Yousfi Alaoui, S.M., Cayrel, P.-L., El Bansarkhani, R., Hoffmann, G.: Code-based identification and signature schemes in software. In: Cuzzocrea, A., Kittl, C., Simos, D.E., Weippl, E., Xu, L. (eds.) CD-ARES 2013. LNCS, vol. 8128, pp. 122–136. Springer, Heidelberg (2013). https://doi.org/10.1007/978-3-642-40588-4_9
3. Aragon, N., Gaborit, P., Hauteville, A., Tillich, J.P.: Improvement of generic attacks on the rank syndrome decoding problem (2017)
4. Baldi, M., Bianchi, M., Chiaraluce, F., Rosenthal, J., Schipani, D.: Using LDGM codes and sparse syndromes to achieve digital signatures. In: Gaborit, P. (ed.) PQCrypto 2013. LNCS, vol. 7932, pp. 1–15. Springer, Heidelberg (2013). https://doi.org/10.1007/978-3-642-38616-9_1
5. Barreto, P.S., Misoczki, R., Simplicio Jr., M.A.: One-time signature scheme from syndrome decoding over generic error-correcting codes. J. Syst. Softw. **84**(2), 198–204 (2011)
6. Berger, T.P., Cayrel, P.-L., Gaborit, P., Otmani, A.: Reducing key length of the McEliece cryptosystem. In: Preneel, B. (ed.) AFRICACRYPT 2009. LNCS, vol. 5580, pp. 77–97. Springer, Heidelberg (2009). https://doi.org/10.1007/978-3-642-02384-2_6
7. Bernstein, D.J.: Grover vs. McEliece. In: Sendrier, N. (ed.) PQCrypto 2010. LNCS, vol. 6061, pp. 73–80. Springer, Heidelberg (2010). https://doi.org/10.1007/978-3-642-12929-2_6
8. Boneh, D., et al.: Random oracles in a quantum world. In: Lee, D.H., Wang, X. (eds.) ASIACRYPT 2011. LNCS, vol. 7073, pp. 41–69. Springer, Heidelberg (2011). https://doi.org/10.1007/978-3-642-25385-0_3
9. Cayrel, P.-L., Véron, P., El Yousfi Alaoui, S.M.: A zero-knowledge identification scheme based on the q-ary Syndrome decoding problem. In: Biryukov, A., Gong, G., Stinson, D.R. (eds.) SAC 2010. LNCS, vol. 6544, pp. 171–186. Springer, Heidelberg (2011). https://doi.org/10.1007/978-3-642-19574-7_12
10. Chabaud, F., Stern, J.: The cryptographic security of the syndrome decoding problem for rank distance codes. In: Kim, K., Matsumoto, T. (eds.) ASIACRYPT 1996. LNCS, vol. 1163, pp. 368–381. Springer, Heidelberg (1996). https://doi.org/10.1007/BFb0034862
11. Chen, L., et al.: Report on Post-quantum Cryptography (2016). https://doi.org/10.6028/NIST.IR.8105

12. Courtois, N.T., Finiasz, M., Sendrier, N.: How to achieve a McEliece-based digital signature scheme. In: Boyd, C. (ed.) ASIACRYPT 2001. LNCS, vol. 2248, pp. 157–174. Springer, Heidelberg (2001). https://doi.org/10.1007/3-540-45682-1_10

13. Dagdelen, Ö., Galindo, D., Véron, P., Alaoui, S.M.E.Y., Cayrel, P.L.: Extended security arguments for signature schemes. Des. Codes Cryptogr. **78**(2), 441–461 (2016)

14. Debris-Alazard, T., Tillich, J.P.: An attack on a NIST proposal: RankSign, a code-based signature in rank metric. arXiv preprint arXiv:1804.02556 (2018)

15. Faugère, J.-C., Otmani, A., Perret, L., Tillich, J.-P.: Algebraic cryptanalysis of McEliece variants with compact keys. In: Gilbert, H. (ed.) EUROCRYPT 2010. LNCS, vol. 6110, pp. 279–298. Springer, Heidelberg (2010). https://doi.org/10. 1007/978-3-642-13190-5_14

16. Fiat, A., Shamir, A.: How to prove yourself: practical solutions to identification and signature problems. In: Odlyzko, A.M. (ed.) CRYPTO 1986. LNCS, vol. 263, pp. 186–194. Springer, Heidelberg (1987). https://doi.org/10.1007/3-540-47721-7_12

17. Finiasz, M.: Parallel-CFS. In: Biryukov, A., Gong, G., Stinson, D.R. (eds.) SAC 2010. LNCS, vol. 6544, pp. 159–170. Springer, Heidelberg (2011). https://doi.org/ 10.1007/978-3-642-19574-7_11

18. Finiasz, M., Sendrier, N.: Security bounds for the design of code-based cryptosystems. In: Matsui, M. (ed.) ASIACRYPT 2009. LNCS, vol. 5912, pp. 88–105. Springer, Heidelberg (2009). https://doi.org/10.1007/978-3-642-10366-7_6

19. Gabidulin, E.M.: Theory of codes with maximum rank distance. Probl. Peredachi Informatsii **21**(1), 3–16 (1985)

20. Gaborit, P., Ruatta, O., Schrek, J.: On the complexity of the rank syndrome decoding problem. IEEE Trans. Inf. Theory **62**(2), 1006–1019 (2016)

21. Gaborit, P., Ruatta, O., Schrek, J., Zémor, G.: RankSign: an efficient signature algorithm based on the rank metric. In: Mosca, M. (ed.) PQCrypto 2014. LNCS, vol. 8772, pp. 88–107. Springer, Cham (2014). https://doi.org/10.1007/978-3-319-11659-4_6

22. Gaborit, P., Schrek, J., Zémor, G.: Full cryptanalysis of the Chen identification protocol. In: Yang, B.-Y. (ed.) PQCrypto 2011. LNCS, vol. 7071, pp. 35–50. Springer, Heidelberg (2011). https://doi.org/10.1007/978-3-642-25405-5_3

23. Gaborit, P., Zémor, G.: On the hardness of the decoding and the minimum distance problems for rank codes. IEEE Trans. Inf. Theory **62**(12), 7245–7252 (2016)

24. Google: A preview of Bristlecone, Google's new quantum processor (2018). https:// research.googleblog.com/2018/03/a-preview-of-bristlecone-googles-new.html

25. Kabatianskii, G., Krouk, E., Smeets, B.: A digital signature scheme based on random error-correcting codes. In: Darnell, M. (ed.) Cryptography and Coding 1997. LNCS, vol. 1355, pp. 161–167. Springer, Heidelberg (1997). https://doi.org/10. 1007/BFb0024461

26. Kiltz, E., Lyubashevsky, V., Schaffner, C.: A concrete treatment of Fiat-Shamir signatures in the quantum random-oracle model. In: Nielsen, J.B., Rijmen, V. (eds.) EUROCRYPT 2018. LNCS, vol. 10822, pp. 552–586. Springer, Cham (2018). https://doi.org/10.1007/978-3-319-78372-7_18

27. Landais, G., Tillich, J.-P.: An efficient attack of a McEliece cryptosystem variant based on convolutional codes. In: Gaborit, P. (ed.) PQCrypto 2013. LNCS, vol. 7932, pp. 102–117. Springer, Heidelberg (2013). https://doi.org/10.1007/978-3-642-38616-9_7

28. Lee, W., Kim, Y.S., Lee, Y.W., No, J.S.: Post quantum signature scheme based on modified Reed-Muller code, Post-Quantum Cryptography, Round

1 Submissions, November 2017. https://csrc.nist.gov/Projects/Post-Quantum-Cryptography/Round-1-Submissions

29. Loidreau, P.: Properties of codes in rank metric. arXiv preprint cs/0610057 (2006)

30. Loidreau, P.: A new rank metric codes based encryption scheme. In: Lange, T., Takagi, T. (eds.) PQCrypto 2017. LNCS, vol. 10346, pp. 3–17. Springer, Cham (2017). https://doi.org/10.1007/978-3-319-59879-6_1

31. Löndahl, C., Johansson, T.: A new version of McEliece PKC based on convolutional codes. In: Chim, T.W., Yuen, T.H. (eds.) ICICS 2012. LNCS, vol. 7618, pp. 461–470. Springer, Heidelberg (2012). https://doi.org/10.1007/978-3-642-34129-8_45

32. May, A., Ozerov, I.: On computing nearest neighbors with applications to decoding of binary linear codes. In: Oswald, E., Fischlin, M. (eds.) EUROCRYPT 2015. LNCS, vol. 9056, pp. 203–228. Springer, Heidelberg (2015). https://doi.org/10.1007/978-3-662-46800-5_9

33. Misoczki, R., Barreto, P.S.L.M.: Compact McEliece keys from Goppa codes. In: Jacobson, M.J., Rijmen, V., Safavi-Naini, R. (eds.) SAC 2009. LNCS, vol. 5867, pp. 376–392. Springer, Heidelberg (2009). https://doi.org/10.1007/978-3-642-05445-7_24

34. Niederreiter, H.: Knapsack-type cryptosystems and algebraic coding theory. Prob. Control Inf. Theory 15(2), 159–166 (1986)

35. NIST: Call for proposals (2018). https://csrc.nist.gov/Projects/Post-Quantum-Cryptography/Post-Quantum-Cryptography-Standardization/Call-for-Proposals

36. NIST: Round 1 submissions (2018). https://csrc.nist.gov/Projects/Post-Quantum-Cryptography/Round-1-Submissions

37. Ourivski, A.V., Johansson, T.: New technique for decoding codes in the rank metric and its cryptography applications. Prob. Inf. Trans. 38(3), 237–246 (2002)

38. Phesso, A., Tillich, J.-P.: An efficient attack on a code-based signature scheme. In: Takagi, T. (ed.) PQCrypto 2016. LNCS, vol. 9606, pp. 86–103. Springer, Cham (2016). https://doi.org/10.1007/978-3-319-29360-8_7

39. Roy, P.S., Xu, R., Fukushima, K., Kiyomoto, S., Morozov, K., Takagi, T.: Supporting documentation of RaCoSS, post-Quantum Cryptography, Round 1 Submissions (2017). https://csrc.nist.gov/Projects/Post-Quantum-Cryptography/Round-1-Submissions

40. Sendrier, N.: Code-based cryptography: state of the art and perspectives. IEEE Secur. Priv. 15(4), 44–50 (2017)

41. Shor, P.W.: Polynomial-time algorithms for prime factorization and discrete logarithms on a quantum computer. SIAM J. Comput. 26(5), 1484–1509 (1997)

42. Stern, J.: A method for finding codewords of small weight. In: Cohen, G., Wolfmann, J. (eds.) Coding Theory 1988. LNCS, vol. 388, pp. 106–113. Springer, Heidelberg (1989). https://doi.org/10.1007/BFb0019850

43. Stern, J.: A new identification scheme based on syndrome decoding. In: Stinson, D.R. (ed.) CRYPTO 1993. LNCS, vol. 773, pp. 13–21. Springer, Heidelberg (1994). https://doi.org/10.1007/3-540-48329-2_2

44. Umana, V.G., Leander, G.: Practical key recovery attacks on two McEliece variants. In: International Conference on Symbolic Computation and Cryptography-SCC, vol. 2010, p. 62 (2010)

45. Unruh, D.: Non-interactive zero-knowledge proofs in the quantum random oracle model. In: Oswald, E., Fischlin, M. (eds.) EUROCRYPT 2015. LNCS, vol. 9057, pp. 755–784. Springer, Heidelberg (2015). https://doi.org/10.1007/978-3-662-46803-6_25

46. Unruh, D.: Post-quantum security of Fiat-Shamir. In: Takagi, T., Peyrin, T. (eds.) ASIACRYPT 2017. LNCS, vol. 10624, pp. 65–95. Springer, Cham (2017). https://doi.org/10.1007/978-3-319-70694-8_3
47. Levy-dit Vehel, F., Perret, L.: Algebraic decoding of rank metric codes. In: Proceedings of YACC (2006)
48. Véron, P.: Improved identification schemes based on error-correcting codes. Appl. Algebra Eng. Commun. Comput. 8(1), 57–69 (1997)
49. Wachter-Zeh, A.: Decoding of block and convolutional codes in rank metric. Ph.D. thesis, Universität Ulm (2013)

SETLA: Signature and Encryption
from Lattices

François Gérard$^{(\boxtimes)}$ and Keno Merckx

Université libre de Bruxelles, Brussels, Belgium
{fragerar,kmerckx}@ulb.ac.be

Abstract. In data security, the main objectives one tries to achieve are *confidentiality, data integrity* and *authentication*. In a public-key setting, *confidentiality* is reached through asymmetric encryption and both *data integrity* and *authentication* through signature. Meeting all the security objectives for data exchange requires to use a concatenation of those primitives in an encrypt-then-sign or sign-then-encrypt fashion. Signcryption aims at providing all the security requirements in one single primitive at a lower cost than using encryption and signature together. Most existing signcryption schemes are using ElGamal-based or pairing-based techniques and thus rely on the decisional Diffie-Hellman assumption. With the current growth of a quantum threat, we seek for post-quantum counterparts to a vast majority of public-key primitives. In this work, we propose a lattice-based signcryption scheme in the random oracle model inspired from a construction of Malone-Lee. It comes in two flavors, one integrating the usual lattice-based key exchange into the signature and the other merging the scheme with a RLWE encryption. Our instantiation is based on a ring version of the scheme of Bai and Galbraith as was done in ring-TESLA and TESLA♯. It targets 128 bits of classical security and offers a save in bandwidth over a naive concatenation of state-of-the-art key exchanges and signatures from the literature. Another lightweight instantiation derived from GLP is feasible but raises long-term security concerns since the base scheme is somewhat outdated.

1 Introduction

Enabling secure communication between two parties over a public channel is the most natural task one can ask from cryptography. Nevertheless, it is not necessarily obvious what is meant by secure. Since the channel is public, the first difficulty to overcome is to prevent unauthorized people from accessing the transiting data, that is to say, ensuring *confidentiality* of data. Confidentiality is enabled by using an encryption scheme. This scheme transforms a plaintext m in an encrypted message c called ciphertext. Using a secret key, the authorized receiver will be able to reverse this transformation but no polynomial time adversary should be able to retrieve any meaningful information on m given only c. Having data secretly transmitted is clearly a milestone in securing communication but cannot be seen as the final answer. While answering all the real-life

© Springer Nature Switzerland AG 2018
J. Camenisch and P. Papadimitratos (Eds.): CANS 2018, LNCS 11124, pp. 299–320, 2018.
https://doi.org/10.1007/978-3-030-00434-7_15

security threats of a communication system seems unfortunately not possible relying solely on mathematics, two common issues in practice are impersonation and data corruption. Hence, *data integrity* (data were not modified) and *authentication* (sender is actually the one they claim to be) should be guaranteed. In a public-key setting, these properties are both ensured by digital signatures which allow a signer to create a signature $\sigma(m)$ on a message m, verifiable by anyone knowing their public key.

Those cryptographic primitives have been developed somewhat independently and can be used separately, depending on the context. If the adversary is passive, i.e. they can only read the channel but not write on it, encryption can be enough. If the secrecy of the message is not important, signing can be enough. Yet, in a situation in which an active adversary is present during a sensitive communication, *confidentiality*, *data integrity* and *authentication* must all be guaranteed at the same time. It is clearly possible to use encryption and signature together but it implies accepting the overhead of using two building blocks and forces a careful security analysis since concatenating two cryptographic primitives in a naive way can be dangerous.

In private-key cryptography, a lot of effort has been put toward the development of *authenticated encryption* schemes. The idea is to merge a symmetric encryption scheme with a message authentication code in a single block providing all the security properties listed above. This work gave rise to a dedicated workshop (DIAC) and a (currently ongoing) competition to establish a portfolio called CAESAR.

On the public-key side, the equivalent primitive is called *signcryption*. The goal of a signcryption scheme is to provide the security properties of both encryption and signature at a lower cost than concatenating them. The (academic) story started at CRYPTO in 1997 with the original paper of Zheng [34]. In this work, the author used a clever combination of ElGamal encryption and signature to create an efficient scheme leading a line of research aiming at formalizing, studying security and enhancing signcryption [15].

Unfortunately, the techniques used were based on the Diffie-Hellman (or RSA) assumption and their security would be compromised in case of the emergence of a large quantum computing power. Now, even though it is not clear when or even if a large enough quantum computer will be built, the importance of ensuring the security of communication in today's world is so critical that no risks can be taken and cryptography should be able to answer at the right moment. Designing and analyzing new cryptosystems takes time and trust can only be developed in the long run when the research community has put a huge amount of effort over the years to break it. Furthermore, the quantum threat could also be already present now if an adversary is currently recording long-term confidential encrypted data in order to decrypt it in the future. For those reasons, the post-quantum community is trying to push, as soon as possible, for development, both on theoretical and practical side, of quantum-resistant cryptography.

Our Contribution. In this paper, we introduce a construction of a signcryption scheme in the Fiat-Shamir with aborts framework of Lyubashevsky based on the signature of Bai and Galbraith [7]. It is inspired from a Schnorr-like variant of the original work of Zheng [34] proposed by Malone-Lee [28]. We provide two versions of the scheme, both relying on the concept of sharing a key while signing and forwarding a symmetric encryption of the message under this key. The first one uses a usual lattice-based key exchange while the second one encrypts the key in a KEM (key encapsulation mechanism) fashion. Those two flavors of the scheme provide a tradeoff between efficiency and storage. The key exchange version is slower but uses less memory/bandwidth. We also provide a concrete instantiation with parameters chosen according to the methodology of [7] enabling correctness of the scheme and compares the gains of using this specific scheme instead of a naive concatenation of signature and key exchange.

Previous Work. Signcryption has not been extensively studied in the post-quantum world yet. Some works on lattice-based schemes exist [22, 24, 32, 32, 33], however, they are all based on trapdoors and thus provide less practical instantiations. Our work is, to our knowledge, the first one studying signcryption using the Fiat-Shamir with aborts technique on lattices. We call the scheme SETLA (Signature and EncrypTion from LAttices) as a tribute to the TESLA family of signatures and to facilitate references to it in the text.

Organization of the Paper. Section 2 formalizes signcryption and recalls basic tools needed in the construction. Section 3 presents the two versions of SETLA and points out their differences. Sections 4 and 5 argue the security, correctness and efficiency of the schemes and Sect. 6 concludes.

2   Preliminaries

2.1   Notations

Let us first explain which notations will be used through the paper. For the sake of simplicity and readability, they are similar to what is commonly used in the recent literature on the topic. We write polynomials with bold lower cases, e.g. $\mathbf{a} \in \mathbb{Z}[X]$. When a value v is sampled from a distribution χ, we use the notation $v \xleftarrow{r} \chi$. This notation is extended in a natural way to polynomials (of a given degree), $\mathbf{v} \xleftarrow{r} \chi$ means that the coefficients of $\mathbf{v}$ are all sampled independently from χ. The uniform distribution over a set S is written $\mathcal{U}(S)$. We use $v \xleftarrow{r} S$ as a shorthand for $v \xleftarrow{r} \mathcal{U}(S)$. For an odd q, we use the representative in $\left[\frac{-(q-1)}{2}, \frac{q-1}{2}\right]$ to identify cosets of $\mathbb{Z}_q$. We use the notation $\lfloor x \rceil_d = (x - [x]_{2^d})/2^d$ with $[x]_{2^d}$ the integer in $(-2^{d-1}, 2^{d-1}]$ congruent to x modulo 2^d to denote the d-bit modular rounding of x and also extend it to vectors.

2.2   Signcryption

A signcryption scheme is a cryptographic primitive aiming to act at the same time as encryption and signature on some data. The usual situation is that of a sender (a.k.a Alice) willing to send a message m to a receiver (a.k.a Bob) while ensuring at the same time confidentiality, integrity and authentication. It is the public-key analog of authenticated encryption.

Definition 1. Formally, a signcryption scheme with message space $\mathcal{M}$ and sign-cryptext space $\mathcal{C}$ is a tuple $\Gamma_{\mathcal{M},\mathcal{C}} = (\texttt{ParamGen}, \texttt{KeyGenSender}, \texttt{KeyGenReceiver}, \texttt{Signcrypt}, \texttt{Unsigncrypt})$ composed of the five following algorithms:

- $\texttt{ParamGen}(\lambda)$: a randomized algorithm taking as input the security parameter λ and outputting the parameters $\texttt{params}$ of the system. We consider $\texttt{params}$ as an implicit input of all the algorithms.
- $\texttt{KeyGenSender}()$: a randomized algorithm generating a key pair (sk_a, pk_a) for the sender (Alice). We will call sk_a the secret signing key and pk_a the public verification key.
- $\texttt{KeyGenReceiver}()$: a randomized algorithm generating a key pair (sk_b, pk_b) for the receiver (Bob). We will call sk_b the secret decryption key and pk_b the public encryption key.
- $\texttt{Signcrypt}(sk_a, pk_b, m)$: a randomized algorithm taking as input Alice's secret signing key sk_a, Bob's public encryption key pk_b, a message $m \in \mathcal{M}$ and outputting a signcryptext $C \in \mathcal{C}$.
- $\texttt{Unsigncrypt}(pk_a, sk_b, C)$: a deterministic algorithm taking as input Alice's public verification key pk_a, Bob's secret decryption key sk_b, a signcryptext $C \in \mathcal{C}$ and outputting a either a message $m \in \mathcal{M}$ if the signcryptext is valid or a failure symbol $\perp$.

It should be noted that, for efficiency and simplicity reasons, the two key generation algorithms can be merged in a single $\texttt{KeyGen}$ algorithm outputting a key pair (sk, pk) in which sk act simultaneously as decryption and signing key and pk as verification and encryption key.

Non-repudiation. There is no settled answer to the question of non-repudiation for a signcryption scheme. Indeed, since we want confidentiality of the message, it is not clear if a public verification mechanism is required. But if Alice can later repudiate the message in front of a judge, can we really call it a signature? The consensus is to set up a mechanism allowing Bob to generate a signature from the signcryptext at the price of revealing the message. Hence, if at some point Alice tries to be dishonest, he can create a publicly verifiable signature and present it to the judge. Hence, we extend the signcryption scheme with two optional algorithms:

- $\texttt{SignExtract}(pk_a, sk_b, C)$: a deterministic algorithm taking the same inputs as $\texttt{Unsigncrypt}$ and outputting a publicly verifiable signature $\sigma(m)$.
- $\texttt{PublicVerif}(pk_a, \sigma(m))$: a deterministic algorithm taking as input the parameters of the system, the public key of Alice and a signature on m and outputting 1 if $\sigma(m)$ is a valid signature on m, 0 otherwise.

In practice, the $\texttt{SignExtract}$ algorithm can be merged with $\texttt{Unsigncrypt}$ to output at the same time m together with its signature $\sigma(m)$.

2.3   Ring Learning with Errors and Decisional Compact Knapsack

The ring learning with errors (RLWE) [27] problem is a variant of the learning with errors problem offering higher efficiency, both in memory and computing power at the price of a globally less understood security. It is parametrized by a positive integer q, an irreducible polynomial $p(X)$ of degree n defining the polynomial ring $\mathcal{R} = \mathbb{Z}[X]/\langle p(X) \rangle$ together with its "mod q version" $\mathcal{R}_q = \mathcal{R}/q\mathcal{R}$ and a narrow error distribution χ of zero mean over $\mathbb{Z}$. To enable efficient computation, we take the usual well-known ring $\mathcal{R}_q = \mathbb{Z}_q[X]/\langle X^n + 1 \rangle$ with $q \equiv 1$ mod $2n$. Through the paper, elements in $\mathcal{R}_q$ will be seen alternatively as polynomials or vectors in $\mathbb{Z}_q$ together with negacyclic convolution as multiplication. It should be clear from context which view we use. To denote the set of elements with coefficients in the range $[-B, B]$ we write $\mathcal{R}_{q,[B]}$. We define the following problems, all believed to be hard, even for an adversary in possession of a large-scale quantum computer:

Definition 2. (*Search-RLWE*) for a secret $\mathcal{R}_q$ and a (polynomially bounded) number of samples $\mathbf{a}_i \cdot \mathbf{s} + \mathbf{e}_i \in \mathcal{R}_q$ with $\mathbf{a}_i \xleftarrow{} \mathcal{R}_q$ and $\mathbf{e}_i \in \mathcal{R}$ with coefficients sampled from χ, find $\mathbf{s}$.

Definition 3. (*Decisional-RLWE*) for a secret $\mathbf{s} \in \mathcal{R}_q$ and a (polynomially bounded) number of samples $\mathbf{t}_i = \mathbf{a}_i \cdot \mathbf{s} + \mathbf{e}_i \in \mathcal{R}_q$ with $\mathbf{a}_i$ and $\mathbf{e}_i$ sampled as above, distinguish, with non-negligible probability, the distribution of the $\mathbf{t}_i$ from $\mathcal{U}(\mathcal{R}_q)$.

Definition 4. (*Decisional Compact Knapsack*) In [19], the authors use a small parameters version of decisional RLWE called the decisional Compact Knapsack problem (DCK). In that version, the secret and error distributions are $\mathcal{U}(\{-1, 0, 1\})$ which means that the adversary receives tuples of the form $(\mathbf{a}, \mathbf{a} \cdot \mathbf{s} + \mathbf{e})$ with $\mathbf{a} \xleftarrow{r} \mathcal{R}_q$ and $(\mathbf{s}, \mathbf{e}) \xleftarrow{r} (\mathcal{R}_{q,[1]} \times \mathcal{R}_{q,[1]})$, and must distinguish them from samples from $\mathcal{U}(\mathcal{R}_q \times \mathcal{R}_q)$. One can also naturally define the corresponding search problem.

2.4   RLWE Encryption

It is possible to construct an ElGamal-like CPA-secure encryption from RLWE. This ideal lattices version has been studied in the literature under the name RLWE encryption [14,23,27,31] and can be found in Fig. 1. This scheme is really similar to ElGamal encryption, the difference lies in the fact that Bob will recover a noisy version of the ring element representing the message. This is why an encoding and a decoding algorithms are used. Basically the encoding function maps the message as a bitstring to a polynomial by encoding one bit per coefficient. The bit b in position i is encoded as $\frac{q-1}{2} \cdot b$. A threshold decoder is applied to recover the message. If the coefficient at position i is closer to $\lfloor \frac{q}{2} \rfloor$ than 0, we set the bit at the same position to 1, else, we set it to 0. Hence, as long as no coefficients are modified by more than $\frac{q}{4}$, the decoding algorithm will recover the correct message. Since χ is a narrow distribution of zero mean, this should happen with overwhelming probability.

Public parameter: $\mathbf{a}$
Decryption key: $\mathbf{s} \xleftarrow{r} \chi$
Encryption key: $\mathbf{pk} = \mathbf{a} \cdot \mathbf{s} + \mathbf{e}$ with $\mathbf{e} \xleftarrow{r} \chi$

RLWE Encrypt($\mathbf{pk}, m$):

1: $\mathbf{y_1}, \mathbf{y_2}, \mathbf{y_3} \xleftarrow{r} \chi$
2: $\mathbf{c_1} \leftarrow \mathbf{a} \cdot \mathbf{y_1} + \mathbf{y_2}$
3: $\mathbf{c_2} \leftarrow \mathbf{pk} \cdot \mathbf{y_1} + \mathbf{y_3} + \text{Encode}(m)$
4: return $\mathbf{c_1}, \mathbf{c_2}$

RLWE Decrypt($\mathbf{c_1}, \mathbf{c_2}, \mathbf{s}$):

1: $\mathbf{m} = \mathbf{c_2} - \mathbf{c_1} \cdot \mathbf{s} \approx \text{Encode}(m)$
2: $m = \text{Decode}(\mathbf{m})$
3: return m

Encode(m):

1: for i in $1...n$
2: $\quad \mathbf{m}[i] = m[i] \cdot \lfloor \frac{q-1}{2} \rfloor$
3: return $\mathbf{m}$

Decode($\mathbf{m}$):

1: for i in $1...n$
2: $\quad$ if $\mathbf{m}[i]$ in $\left[-\lceil \frac{q}{4} \rceil, \lceil \frac{q}{4} \rceil - 1 \right]$
3: $\quad\quad m[i] = 1$
4: $\quad$ else
5: $\quad\quad m[i] = 0$
6: return m

Fig. 1. RLWE encryption

2.5 Reconciliation Mechanism

A common issue in learning with errors key exchanges [5,11,12,20,29] is that both parties end up with two values that are close to each other but not exactly the same. It is due to the fact that, as in the encryption scheme, it is often made of ElGamal-like cryptography but with noisy elements. For example in the RLWE version, Alice eventually computes $\mathbf{ass'} + \mathbf{e's}$ while Bob has $\mathbf{ass'} + \mathbf{es'}$ (this can really be seen has them agreeing on a noisy version of g^{ab} in Diffie-Hellman). Obviously, the key exchange cannot be considered successful if each party has a different value. The solution is to use a reconciliation mechanism deriving a common value from noisy data (a.k.a fuzzy extractor [16]). For example let us assume we work in $\mathbb{Z}_q$ with elements represented as values in $[-(q-1)/2, \ldots, (q-1)/2]$. Alice possesses a and Bob $b = a + e$ for a small e. They could map their values to, say, $\{0,1\}$ by partitioning $\mathbb{Z}_q$ in $S_0 = [-\lceil q/4 \rceil, \lceil q/4 \rceil - 1]$ and $S_1 = [\lceil q/4 \rceil, (q-1)/2] \cup [-(q-1)/2, -\lceil q/4 \rceil - 1]$ and outputting in which subset lies their value. This works well if a and b are close to 0 or $q/2$ but can fail if they are close to $q/4$ or $-q/4$. To overcome that possibility, Alice can send a reconciliation value $v \in \{0,1\}$ indicating if a is in $[0, \lceil q/4 \rceil] \cup [-(q-1)/2, \lfloor -q/4 \rfloor]$ or $[\lceil q/4 \rceil + 1, (q-1)/2] \cup [\lceil -q/4 \rceil - 1, -1]$. The value v thus conveys no information about the partition in which a lies but helps Bob to reconcile on the correct value using his knowledge of b. This approach has been used by Peikert in [29], by applying the above technique separately on each coefficients of an element of $\mathcal{R}_q$ (with a slight modification dealing with the fact that an odd q cannot be split in two equal parts).

Clearly, any reconciliation technique has an error tolerance threshold over which agreement cannot be reached. To increase the threshold, a possibility is to use *multiple* values to agree on a common bit. The motivation is that polynomials used in RWLE-based are often of size 512 or 1024 to ensure the security of the underlying lattice problem while symmetric secrets of bit size 256 appear to be enough, even in a post-quantum world. Hence we should use mappings from $\mathbb{Z}_q^n$ to $\{0,1\}^{256}$ with $n \in \{512, 1024\}$. Of course mappings for higher n or larger symmetric keys can be used but in practice, those parameters are good enough. For the key exchange version of our construction, we borrow the notations from NewHope [5]. In their paper, they show how to agree on a n bit key from either a polynomial of degree $2n$ or $4n$. The description of their whole reconciliation mechanism is quite tedious and takes a lot of space. Hence we redirect the interested reader to their paper for a full explanation and analysis. By borrowing their notations, we mean that we will use two algorithms $\text{HelpRec}(\mathbf{x})$ and $\text{Rec}(\mathbf{x}', \mathbf{hr})$ (as defined below) but that the scheme is unaffected by how those functions work under the hood, they could implement any reconciliation mechanism.

- $\text{HelpRec}(\mathbf{x})$ taking as input a ring element and outputting a reconciliation vector $\mathbf{hr}$
- $\text{Rec}(\mathbf{x}', \mathbf{hr})$ taking as input a ring element and a reconciliation vector and outputting a symmetric key K.

If $\mathbf{x}$ and $\mathbf{x}'$ are close to each other (the distance between their coefficients is small), the output of $\text{Rec}(\mathbf{x}, \mathbf{hr})$ and $\text{Rec}(\mathbf{x}', \mathbf{hr})$ are the same.

2.6 Fiat-Shamir Lattice-Based Signatures

In [25], Lyubashevsky presented the Fiat-Shamir with aborts technique to construct digital signatures in the random oracle model. It spawned a long line of research enabling practical instantiations of lattice-based signatures such as BLISS, Dilithium or qTESLA. The construction is following the same pattern as Schnorr signatures. It starts by defining an identification scheme with a Σ protocol and then use the generic Fiat-Shamir transformation to create a signature scheme. As Schnorr identification protocol acts as a zero-knowledge proof for a discrete logarithm, Lyubashevsky's protocol acts as a zero-knowledge proof for a LWE/SIS instance. In Fig. 2 we informally recall such a signature instantiated with RLWE. The public parameter $\mathbf{a}$ is uniform in the ring, E and Y denote two small distributions (with Y significantly larger then E but still small in comparison to the modulus q). The crucial difference between this signature

---

Public parameter: $\mathbf{a}$
Secret key: $\mathbf{s}, \mathbf{e} \xleftarrow{r} E$
Public key: $\mathbf{t} \leftarrow \mathbf{a} \cdot \mathbf{s} + \mathbf{e}$

$\underline{\text{Sign}(\mathbf{s}, m):}$
1: **do**
2:   $\mathbf{y}_1, \mathbf{y}_2 \xleftarrow{r} Y$
3:   $\mathbf{c} \leftarrow H(\mathbf{a} \cdot \mathbf{y}_1 + \mathbf{y}_2, m)$
4:   $\mathbf{z}_1 \leftarrow \mathbf{s} \cdot \mathbf{c} + \mathbf{y}_1, \mathbf{z}_2 \leftarrow \mathbf{e} \cdot \mathbf{c} + \mathbf{y}_2$
5: **while** $\text{Rejected}(\mathbf{z}_1, \mathbf{z}_2)$
6: **return** $\mathbf{z}_1, \mathbf{z}_2, \mathbf{c}$

$\underline{\text{Verify}(\mathbf{z}_1, \mathbf{z}_2, \mathbf{c}, \mathbf{t}, m):}$
1: $\mathbf{v} \leftarrow \mathbf{a} \cdot \mathbf{z}_1 + \mathbf{z}_2 - \mathbf{t} \cdot \mathbf{c}$
2: **return** 1 if $\mathbf{c} = H(\mathbf{v}, m)$ and both $\mathbf{z}_i$
   are small else 0

Fig. 2. Generic RLWE variant of the signature scheme of [26]. H is modeled as a random oracle.

and Schnorr's scheme is the rejection sampling step performed after generating the z_i. It is required in order to avoid leakage of the secret over the release of signatures. Indeed, since the y_i are not sampled uniformly over the whole ring, they do not act as a one-time pad perfectly hiding the value $s \cdot c$. The rejection sampling procedure will reject some signatures such that the output distribution of the z_i is statistically independent of the secret and hence do not reveal anything about it.

3 Lattice-Based Signcryption Schemes

Hereunder, we describe both versions of our scheme. The discussion in Sect. 5 will only be made for the first version for the sake of brevity but the analysis is basically the same. In the following, when we talk about lattice signatures, we mean lattice-based signatures obtained from the Fiat-Shamir transformation.

3.1 SETLA-KEX Signcryption

First we describe how to integrate encryption into a lattice signature, following the steps of the ElGamal modification of Zheng. From a high-level point of view, the idea of the original signcryption scheme is to sign a message with an ElGamal signature and to realize a non-interactive Diffie-Hellman ephemeral key exchange (KEX) at the same time reusing the "commit" value of the signature. The gain in efficiency comes from the fact that the same operation is used in both primitives. Subsequently, the message is symmetrically encrypted with the key derived from the exchange and forwarded to the receiver. While the first scheme of Zheng was not directly translatable in a lattice version, one of its derivative due to Malone-Lee [28] caught our attention. Indeed, even though its primary advantage over Zheng in pre-quantum cryptography was to enable non-interactive non-repudiation, namely that Bob alone can create a valid signature from a signcryptext, the second difference is that it is based on Schnorr signature. The lattice-based signatures schemes coming from identification schemes through Fiat-Shamir transform being Schnorr-like [3,7,17,26], this is where post-quantum can meet signcryption. We use a ring version of the signature proposed by Bai and Galbraith as a base to construct the scheme but it can be generalized to most signatures derived from the original work of Lyubashevsky as long as the parameters offer at the same time security and correctness for the key reconciliation. We actually also have a construction based on GLP working out of the box with the original parameters which is omitted in this conference version of the paper for the sake of compactness.

Key Generation. (Algorithm 1) The key generation is simple and straightforward for a scheme using ideal lattices cryptography. It uses some public parameters a_1, a_2 shared among all users and output two RLWE samples $pk = (t_1, t_2)$ together with a secret polynomial s. The error and secret distributions are the same and output a polynomial with uniform coefficients in $\{-1, 0, 1\}$. The choice

---

Algorithm 1. SETLA Key generation

Input: Public parameter $\mathbf{a_1}, \mathbf{a_2}$
Output: Key pair $\mathbf{pk} = (\mathbf{t_1}, \mathbf{t_2}), \mathbf{sk} = (\mathbf{s}, \mathbf{e_1}, \mathbf{e_2})$
1: $\mathbf{s}, \mathbf{e_1}, \mathbf{e_2} \leftarrow \mathcal{R}_{q,[1]}$
2: $\mathbf{t_1} \leftarrow \mathbf{a_1} \cdot \mathbf{s} + \mathbf{e_1}, \mathbf{t_2} \leftarrow \mathbf{a_2} \cdot \mathbf{s} + \mathbf{e_2}$
3: **return** $\mathbf{pk} = (\mathbf{t_1}, \mathbf{t_2}), \mathbf{sk} = (\mathbf{s}, \mathbf{e_1}, \mathbf{e_2})$

---

of such a distribution is suboptimal in terms of security since it has low variance and its special structure may enable specialized attacks but has been made for reasons that will come clear later. Note that in the context of signcryption, both Alice and Bob will run the key generation procedure to retrieve their keys since two key pairs are used in the full signcrypt/unsigncrypt procedure. In the following, we use subscripts (e.g. $\mathbf{pk}_a = (\mathbf{t}_{a,1}, \mathbf{t}_{a,2})$) to differentiate them.

Algorithm 2. SETLA-KEX Signcrypt

Input: Public parameters $\mathbf{a_1}, \mathbf{a_2}$, Bob's public key $\mathbf{pk}_b$, Alice's keys $(\mathbf{s}_a, \mathbf{e}_{a,1}, \mathbf{e}_{a,2}, \mathbf{pk}_a)$, a message m, random oracle $H : * \rightarrow \{\mathbf{v} \mid \mathbf{v} \in \mathcal{R}_{q,[1]}, \|\mathbf{v}\|_1 = \omega\}$, symmetric encryption algorithm E
Output: a signcryptext of m: $C = (\mathbf{z}, \mathbf{c}, \mathcal{E}, \mathbf{r})$
2: $\quad \mathbf{y}, \mathbf{y'} \overset{r}{\leftarrow} \mathcal{R}_{q,[B]}$
3: $\quad \mathbf{v} \leftarrow \mathbf{t}_{b,1} \cdot \mathbf{y} + \mathbf{y'} = \mathbf{a_1} \cdot \mathbf{s}_b \cdot \mathbf{y} + \mathbf{e}_{b,1} \cdot \mathbf{y} + \mathbf{y'}$
4: $\quad \mathbf{r} \leftarrow \mathsf{HelpRec}(\mathbf{v})$
5: $\quad K \leftarrow \mathsf{Rec}(\mathbf{v}, \mathbf{r})$
6: $\quad \mathbf{c} \leftarrow H(\lfloor \mathbf{a_1} \cdot \mathbf{y} \rceil_d, \lfloor \mathbf{a_2} \cdot \mathbf{y} \rceil_d, m, K, \mathbf{pk}_a, \mathbf{pk}_b)$
7: $\quad \mathbf{z} \leftarrow \mathbf{s}_a \cdot \mathbf{c} + \mathbf{y}$
8: $\quad \mathbf{w_1} \leftarrow \mathbf{a_1} \cdot \mathbf{y} - \mathbf{e}_{a,1} \cdot \mathbf{c}, \mathbf{w_2} \leftarrow \mathbf{a_2} \cdot \mathbf{y} - \mathbf{e}_{a,2} \cdot \mathbf{c}$
9: **while not**($\mathbf{z}$ in $\mathcal{R}_{q,[B-\omega]}$ **and** $\lfloor \mathbf{a_1} \cdot \mathbf{y} \rceil_d = \lfloor \mathbf{w_1} \rceil_d$ **and** $\lfloor \mathbf{a_2} \cdot \mathbf{y} \rceil_d = \lfloor \mathbf{w_2} \rceil_d$)
10: $\mathcal{E} \leftarrow E_K(m)$
11: **return** $\mathbf{z}, \mathbf{c}, \mathcal{E}, \mathbf{r}$

SETLA-KEX Signcrypt. (Algorithm 2) The signcrypt procedure contains three interleaved parts: signature, key exchange and encryption. The signature follows the structure of [1,8] as a Fiat-Shamir signature from a Σ protocol. First, a commitment consisting of two rounded polynomials $\lfloor \mathbf{a_1} \cdot \mathbf{y} \rceil_d, \lfloor \mathbf{a_2} \cdot \mathbf{y} \rceil_d$ depending on a masking value $\mathbf{y}$ is computed. Then, an unpredictable challenge $\mathbf{c}$ is retrieved by simulating a verifier with a random oracle H taking inputs depending on the commitment. Finally, the response consists of a polynomial of the form $\mathbf{z} = \mathbf{s} \cdot \mathbf{c} + \mathbf{y}$. Note that for reasons related specifically to signcryption schemes, the random oracle should take as input a symmetric key K and both public identities. If the key was not included in the input, the adversary playing a signcryption specific CCA2 game would easily be able to distinguish between two messages m_0, m_1 by computing both $H(., m_i, ., .)$ and verify the equality with $\mathbf{c}$. Having the public identities in the hash is a common practice in signcryption schemes to prove security in advanced models [15].

The key exchange part is performed by deriving a secret value K from a noisy version of $\mathbf{a}_1 \cdot \mathbf{s}_b \cdot \mathbf{y}$. Alice cannot find the exact value since it means she would know Bob's secret key but she can find an approximate value from Bob's public key by computing $\mathbf{t}_{b,1} \cdot \mathbf{y} = \mathbf{a}_1 \cdot \mathbf{s}_b \cdot \mathbf{y} + \mathbf{e}'_{b,1} \cdot \mathbf{y} \approx \mathbf{a}_1 \cdot \mathbf{s}_b \cdot \mathbf{y}$. This is exactly the technique employed in lattice-based key exchanges such as NewHope. The efficiency gain comes from the fact that Bob will later be able to retrieve an approximation version of $\mathbf{a}_1 \cdot \mathbf{y}$ *without* sending him any other ring element than the polynomials computed in the signature $(\mathbf{z}, \mathbf{c})$. As in [5,12], Alice gets a symmetric key by applying a reconciliation procedure on the noisy shared value. The last part is straightforward, now that a key is available, a symmetric cipher E is used to encrypt the data.

Finally, Alice outputs the signature $(\mathbf{z}, \mathbf{c})$, the symmetric ciphertext $\mathcal{E}$ and a small reconciliation vector $\mathbf{r}$. It means that the message was at the same time encrypted and authenticated in an asymmetric manner with only the overhead of sending a symmetric ciphertext (obviously we need to send something at least as long as the message for encryption) and a small reconciliation vector on the top of the signature.

Algorithm 3. SETLA-KEX Unsigncrypt

Input: Public parameters $\mathbf{a}_1, \mathbf{a}_2$, Bob's keys $(\mathbf{s}_b, \mathbf{pk}_b)$, Alice's public key $\mathbf{pk}_a$, a signcryptext $C = (\mathbf{z}, \mathbf{c}, \mathcal{E}, \mathbf{r})$, random oracle $H : * \to \{\mathbf{v} \mid \mathbf{v} \in \mathcal{R}_{q,[1]}, \|\mathbf{v}\|_1 = \omega\}$, symmetric encryption algorithm E
Output: A message m or failure symbol $\perp$

1: $\mathbf{w}_1 \leftarrow \mathbf{a}_1 \cdot \mathbf{z} - \mathbf{t}_{a,1} \cdot \mathbf{c}$, $\mathbf{w}_2 \leftarrow \mathbf{a}_2 \cdot \mathbf{z} - \mathbf{t}_{a,2} \cdot \mathbf{c}$
2: $K \leftarrow \mathrm{Rec}(\mathbf{w}_1 \cdot \mathbf{s}_b, \mathbf{r})$
3: $m \leftarrow E_K^{-1}(\mathcal{E})$
4: **return** m if $\mathbf{c} = H(\lfloor \mathbf{w}_1 \rceil_d, \lfloor \mathbf{w}_2 \rceil_d, m, K, \mathbf{pk}_a, \mathbf{pk}_b)$ and $\mathbf{z} \in \mathcal{R}_{q,[B-\omega]}$ **else** $\perp$

SETLA-KEX Unsigncrypt. (Algorithm 3) The goal of this algorithm is to allow Bob to find the secret key to decrypt the symmetric cipher and at the same, to provide authentication of the message through a signature.

First, Bob will recover the commitment part of the signature by rounding the values $\mathbf{w}_1 \leftarrow \mathbf{a}_1 \cdot \mathbf{z} - \mathbf{t}_{a,1} \cdot \mathbf{c}$ and $\mathbf{w}_2 \leftarrow \mathbf{a}_2 \cdot \mathbf{z} - \mathbf{t}_{a,2} \cdot \mathbf{c}$. Without rounding, $\mathbf{c}$ would have been different since Alice queried the random oracle with $\lfloor \mathbf{a}_1 \cdot \mathbf{y} \rceil_d$ and $\lfloor \mathbf{a}_2 \cdot \mathbf{y} \rceil_d$. The difference with the original signature scheme is that Bob must now find the key K and the message in order to verify the hash value. To recover it, he shall use the reconciliation vector $\mathbf{r}$ with an approximate version of $\mathbf{a}_1 \cdot \mathbf{s}_b \cdot \mathbf{y}$. Such a value can be found by computing the product $\mathbf{w}_1 \cdot \mathbf{s}_b = \mathbf{a}_1 \cdot \mathbf{s}_b \cdot \mathbf{y} + \mathbf{e}_{a,1} \cdot \mathbf{s}_b \cdot \mathbf{c} \approx \mathbf{a}_1 \cdot \mathbf{s}_b \cdot \mathbf{y}$. Once the message is decrypted, Bob verifies the signature by checking the size of $\mathbf{z}$ and the hash value. He outputs the message if everything is correct and a failure symbol otherwise.

SETLA-KEX SignExtract. This scheme also inherits the capability to perform a signature extraction from the signcryption of Malone-Lee. It is a simple transformation of the unsigncrypt procedure and can be found in Appendix B.

3.2 SETLA-KEM Signcryption

Now, we describe the second version of the scheme based on key encapsulation instead of direct key exchange. The approach is similar to the one used in NewHope-Simple [4] or Kyber [10]. The high-level perspective is now to perform a noisy ElGamal encryption of a chosen key during signature instead of noisy Diffie-Hellman. While in NewHope-Simple the goal of the new approach is to make the protocol simpler by getting rid of the reconciliation mechanism but not really to enhance the scheme, here, using an encryption based method leads to better performances in terms of speed and can enable parallelism, at the cost of a significantly bigger signcryptext.

Algorithm 4. SETLA-KEM Signcrypt

Input: Public parameters a_1, a_2, Bob's public key pk_b, Alice's key $(s_a, e_{a,1}, e_{a,2}, pk_a)$, a message m, random oracle $H : * \to \{v \mid v \in \mathcal{R}_{q,[1]}, \|v\|_1 = \omega\}$, symmetric encryption algorithm E

Output: a signcryptext of m: $C = (z, c, x, \mathcal{E})$

1: $K \xleftarrow{r} \{0,1\}^{256}$
2: **do**
3:    $y \xleftarrow{r} \mathcal{R}_{q,[B]}$
4:    $c \leftarrow H(\lfloor a_1 \cdot y \rceil_d, \lfloor a_2 \cdot y \rceil_d, m, K, pk_a, pk_b)$
5:    $z \leftarrow s_a \cdot c + y$
6:    $w_1 \leftarrow a_1 \cdot y - e_{a,1} \cdot c, \ w_2 \leftarrow a_2 \cdot y - e_{a,2} \cdot c$
7: **while not**(z in $\mathcal{R}_{q,[B-\omega]}$ and $\lfloor a_1 \cdot y \rceil_d = \lfloor w_1 \rceil_d$ and $\lfloor a_2 \cdot y \rceil_d = \lfloor w_2 \rceil_d$)
8: $y' \xleftarrow{r} \mathcal{R}_{q,[B]}$
9: $x \leftarrow t_{b,1} \cdot y + y' + \text{Encode}(K)$
10: $\mathcal{E} \leftarrow E_K(m)$
11: **return** $z, c, x, \mathcal{E}$

SETLA-KEM Signcrypt. (Algorithm 4) In the same way as before, one can find three phases: signature, key encapsulation and symmetric encryption. The signature is now more isolated and almost exactly the same as in [8], the small difference is that the random oracle (as in the KEX version) takes as input the message, the symmetric decryption key and the public identities.

The key encapsulation part is a RLWE encryption of a randomly sampled key K. Such an encryption consists of two ciphertexts $c_1 = a \cdot y_1 + y_2$ and $c_2 = pk_b \cdot y_1 + y_3$. Basically, c_2 is the message masked with a ring element depending on the public-key looking random under the decisional-RLWE assumption and c_1 is a value allowing the owner of s_b to remove the mask without conveying any (computable) information on y_1 under the search-RLWE assumption. Here we gain efficiency by having the value $\lfloor a_1 \cdot y \rceil_d$ acting at the same time as the commitment of the signature and the c_1 part of the encryption scheme.

Globally, the KEM version is adding a lot of overhead on the size of the signcryptext which is problematic since this is where we are looking for efficiency. Nevertheless, we see two advantages of using encryption instead of key exchange. First, the scheme is faster because it has less computation in the rejection sampling loop (which can run several times depending on the parameters) and we can now parallelize the symmetric encryption algorithm. Indeed, in the KEX version, the key depends on $\mathbf{y}$ and was not known until the end of the rejection sampling procedure, hence, everything had to be sequential and a multiplication with $\mathbf{t}_{b,1}$ had to be done at each iteration. Now, the symmetric encryption can start at the same time as the rejection sampling. It is fair to say that in general symmetric operations are lightweight in comparison to polynomial multiplication. Nevertheless, if a really large message has to be encrypted, say such that $E_K(m)$ takes as long as the **do. . . while** loop, the saving becomes non-negligible. Obviously, this argument only makes sense if the rejection sampling procedure itself is not affected by the size of the message. One solution would be to pre-hash the message before the loop and only inject this hash in the random oracle. Actually this issue is not specific to signcryption, all the signature schemes using rejection sampling would be badly affected by a really long message if the hash function cannot restart from its previous sate. Hence, in this case, hashing the message once before would save some computation. This small modification could be done in the KEX version as well as in existing Fiat-Shamir lattice-based signatures.

Second, depending on the parameters, if the correctness during reconciliation is a real issue, having the key encoded as a polynomial with coefficients in $\{0, \frac{q-1}{2}\}$ is optimal for the since they are at "maximum distance" in $\mathbb{Z}_q$. Also, because the symmetric key needed being often smaller than the encoding polynomial, having control over the value eases the process of embedding an error-correcting code in the extra space. Even though in the current state of affairs and with the parameters proposed in the next section the KEM version would not outperform neither the KEX version nor the naive concatenation of efficient schemes, we think the construction may be of interest in some contexts.

Algorithm 5. SETLA-KEM Unsigncrypt

Input: Public parameter $\mathbf{a}_1, \mathbf{a}_2$, Bob's key $(\mathbf{s}_b, \mathbf{s}_b', \mathbf{pk}_b)$, Alice's public key $\mathbf{pk}_a$, a signcryptext $C = (\mathbf{z}, \mathbf{c}, \mathbf{x}, \mathcal{E}, \mathbf{r})$, random oracle $H : * \to \{\mathbf{v} \mid \mathbf{v} \in \mathcal{R}_{q,[1]}, \|\mathbf{v}\|_1 = \omega\}$, symmetric encryption algorithm E
Output: A message m or failure symbol $\perp$

1: $\mathbf{w}_1 \leftarrow \mathbf{a}_1 \cdot \mathbf{z} - \mathbf{t}_{a,1} \cdot \mathbf{c}$
2: $\mathbf{w}_2 \leftarrow \mathbf{a}_2 \cdot \mathbf{z} - \mathbf{t}_{a,2} \cdot \mathbf{c}$
3: $K \leftarrow \text{Decode}(\mathbf{x} - \mathbf{w}_1 \cdot \mathbf{s}_b)$
4: $m \leftarrow E^{-1}(\mathcal{E})$
5: **return** m if $\mathbf{c} = H(\mathbf{v}, m, K, \mathbf{pk}_a, \mathbf{pk}_b)$ and $\mathbf{z} \in \mathcal{R}_{q,[k-\omega]}$ **else** $\perp$

SETLA-KEM Unsigncrypt. (Algorithm 5) The unsigncrypt algorithm follows in the obvious manner. Bob retrieves the $\mathbf{c}_1$ part of the RLWE encryption from the signature and run the decryption algorithm to find the key. Then, he decrypts the symmetric ciphertext and verifies the signature.

4   Security Arguments

The security aspects of interest for signcryption are unforgeability and privacy. The construction combining both a signature scheme using the Fiat-Shamir heuristic and a public key encryption scheme, we argue the security by using the forking lemma [30] and a standard hybrid argument. This does not provide a formal argument of security in a signcryption specific security model since it does not consider the primitive as an encryption *and* a signature but rather successively as an encryption *or* a signature. We do not claim that this is a sufficient analysis, nevertheless, having both unforgeability and privacy of the two underlying schemes is a good pointer toward the fact the design is sound. Providing a formal argument in advanced signcryption models is a tedious task (see [6]) and we do not attempt to do so here.

4.1   Unforgeability

The underlying signature of the signcryption scheme is the ring variant of the Bai-Galbraith signature which is itself a derivative of the original proposal of Lyubashevsky [26]. The full security argument can be found in [7] but the idea is to use the forking lemma to get two different signatures for the same commitment that would allow us to solve a special SIS instance. We use the adversary to get two forgeries $\mathbf{z}, \mathbf{c}$ and $\mathbf{z}', \mathbf{c}'$ for different random oracles but the same random tape (hence the same $\mathbf{y}$). We have (providing the argument for only one RLWE sample instead of two as in the signature for the sake of simplicity) $\lfloor \mathbf{a} \cdot \mathbf{z} - \mathbf{t}_a \cdot \mathbf{c} \rceil_d = \lfloor \mathbf{a} \cdot \mathbf{z}' - \mathbf{t}_a \cdot \mathbf{c}' \rceil_d = \lfloor \mathbf{a} \cdot \mathbf{y} \rceil_d$. This means that for some small $\mathbf{e}$, $\mathbf{a} \cdot \mathbf{z} - \mathbf{t}_a \cdot \mathbf{c} = \mathbf{a} \cdot \mathbf{z}' - \mathbf{t}_a \cdot \mathbf{c}' + \mathbf{e}$ and thus, with $\mathbf{t}_a = \mathbf{a} \cdot \mathbf{s}_a + \mathbf{e}_a$, $\mathbf{a} \cdot (\mathbf{z} - \mathbf{z}' - \mathbf{s}_a \cdot \mathbf{c} + \mathbf{s}_a \cdot \mathbf{c}') + (\mathbf{e}_a \cdot (\mathbf{c}' - \mathbf{c}) + \mathbf{e}) = 0$. As pointed in [7] Sect. 4.2, (if $\mathbf{z} - \mathbf{z}' - \mathbf{s}_a \cdot \mathbf{c} + \mathbf{s}_a \cdot \mathbf{c}'$ and $\mathbf{e}_a \cdot (\mathbf{c}' - \mathbf{c}) + \mathbf{e}$ are non-zero) we have found a solution to the SIS instance. This argument still holds for the signcryption scheme.

4.2   Confidentiality

We argue the confidentiality of the scheme with a sequence of games showing semantic security under the **DCK** assumption in the random oracle model. We model the adversary as a tuple of two algorithms $\mathcal{A} = (\mathcal{A}_1, \mathcal{A}_2)$, the first choosing messages for the game according to the public keys and the second trying to guess which one was signcrypted. The encryption scheme E is seen as an ideal primitive. The sequence of games for the KEX version can be found in Fig. 4. Games for the KEM version are really similar and can be found in Appendix A (Fig. 3).

Game 0: Game 0 is the usual CPA game against SETLA, the adversary chooses two messages m_0, m_1 and tries to guess which one was signcrypted.

Game 1: By virtue of the rejection sampling performed during signcryption, the output distribution of $\mathbf{z}$ should be exactly the same as a uniform over $\mathcal{R}_{q, [k-\omega]}$.

Game 0:
1: $(m_0, m_1) \leftarrow \mathcal{A}_1(\mathbf{pk}_a, \mathbf{pk}_b)$
2: $b \xleftarrow{r} \{0, 1\}$
3: $\mathbf{y}, \mathbf{y'} \xleftarrow{r} \mathcal{R}_{q, [B]}$
4: $\mathbf{v} \leftarrow \mathbf{t}_{b,1} \cdot \mathbf{y} + \mathbf{y'}$
5: $\mathbf{r} \leftarrow \mathsf{HelpRec}(\mathbf{v})$
6: $K \leftarrow \mathsf{Rec}(\mathbf{v}, \mathbf{r})$
7: $\mathbf{h}_1 \leftarrow \lfloor \mathbf{a}_1 \cdot \mathbf{y} \rfloor_d, \mathbf{h}_2 \leftarrow \lfloor \mathbf{a}_2 \cdot \mathbf{y} \rfloor_d$
8: $\mathbf{c} \leftarrow H(\mathbf{h}_1, \mathbf{h}_2, m, K, \mathbf{pk}_a, \mathbf{pk}_b)$
9: $\mathbf{z} \leftarrow \mathbf{s}_a \cdot \mathbf{c} + \mathbf{y}$
10: $\mathbf{w}_1 \leftarrow \mathbf{a}_1 \cdot \mathbf{y} - \mathbf{e}_{a,1} \cdot \mathbf{c}, \mathbf{w}_2 \leftarrow \mathbf{a}_2 \cdot \mathbf{y} - \mathbf{e}_{a,2} \cdot \mathbf{c}$
11: **if** $\mathbf{h}_1 \neq \lfloor \mathbf{w}_1 \rfloor_d$ **or** $\mathbf{h}_1 \neq \lfloor \mathbf{w}_2 \rfloor_d$, **goto** 3
12: **if** $\mathbf{z}$ not in $\mathcal{R}_{q, [B-\omega]}$, **goto** 3
13: $\mathcal{E} \leftarrow E_K(m)$
14: $\hat{b} \leftarrow \mathcal{A}_2(\mathbf{z}, \mathbf{c}, \mathcal{E}, \mathbf{r})$
15: **return** $\hat{b}$

Game 1:
1: $(m_0, m_1) \leftarrow \mathcal{A}_1(\mathbf{pk}_a, \mathbf{pk}_b)$
2: $b \xleftarrow{r} \{0, 1\}$
3: $\mathbf{y}, \mathbf{y'} \xleftarrow{r} \mathcal{R}_{q, [B]}$
4: $\mathbf{v} \leftarrow \mathbf{t}_{b,1} \cdot \mathbf{y} + \mathbf{y'}$
5: $\mathbf{r} \leftarrow \mathsf{HelpRec}(\mathbf{v})$
6: $K \leftarrow \mathsf{Rec}(\mathbf{v}, \mathbf{r})$
7: $\mathbf{h}_1 \leftarrow \lfloor \mathbf{a}_1 \cdot \mathbf{y} \rfloor_d, \mathbf{h}_2 \leftarrow \lfloor \mathbf{a}_2 \cdot \mathbf{y} \rfloor_d$
8: $\mathbf{c} \leftarrow H(\mathbf{h}_1, \mathbf{h}_2, m, K, \mathbf{pk}_a, \mathbf{pk}_b)$
9: $\mathbf{z} \xleftarrow{r} \mathcal{R}_{q, [B-\omega]}$
10: $\mathbf{w}_1 \leftarrow \mathbf{a}_1 \cdot \mathbf{y} - \mathbf{e}_{a,1} \cdot \mathbf{c}, \mathbf{w}_2 \leftarrow \mathbf{a}_2 \cdot \mathbf{y} - \mathbf{e}_{a,2} \cdot \mathbf{c}$
11: **if** $\mathbf{h}_1 \neq \lfloor \mathbf{w}_1 \rfloor_d$ **or** $\mathbf{h}_1 \neq \lfloor \mathbf{w}_2 \rfloor_d$, **goto** 3
12: with probability P, **goto** 3
13: $\mathcal{E} \leftarrow E_K(m)$
14: $\hat{b} \leftarrow \mathcal{A}_2(\mathbf{z}, \mathbf{c}, \mathcal{E}, \mathbf{r})$
15: **return** $\hat{b}$

Game 2:
1: $(m_0, m_1) \leftarrow \mathcal{A}_1(\mathbf{pk}_a, \mathbf{pk}_b)$
2: $b \xleftarrow{r} \{0, 1\}$
3: $\mathbf{y}, \mathbf{y'} \xleftarrow{r} \mathcal{R}_{q, [B]}$
4: $\mathbf{a'} \xleftarrow{r} \mathcal{R}_q$
5: $\mathbf{v} \leftarrow \mathbf{a'} \cdot \mathbf{y} + \mathbf{y'}$
6: $\mathbf{r} \leftarrow \mathsf{HelpRec}(\mathbf{v})$
7: $K \leftarrow \mathsf{Rec}(\mathbf{v}, \mathbf{r})$
8: $\mathbf{h}_1 \leftarrow \lfloor \mathbf{a}_1 \cdot \mathbf{y} \rfloor_d, \mathbf{h}_2 \leftarrow \lfloor \mathbf{a}_2 \cdot \mathbf{y} \rfloor_d$
9: $\mathbf{c} \leftarrow H(\mathbf{h}_1, \mathbf{h}_2, m, K, \mathbf{pk}_a, \mathbf{pk}_b)$
10: $\mathbf{z} \xleftarrow{r} \mathcal{R}_{q, [B-\omega]}$
11: $\mathbf{w}_1 \leftarrow \mathbf{a}_1 \cdot \mathbf{y} - \mathbf{e}_{a,1} \cdot \mathbf{c}, \mathbf{w}_2 \leftarrow \mathbf{a}_2 \cdot \mathbf{y} - \mathbf{e}_{a,2} \cdot \mathbf{c}$
12: **if** $\mathbf{h}_1 \neq \lfloor \mathbf{w}_1 \rfloor_d$ **or** $\mathbf{h}_1 \neq \lfloor \mathbf{w}_2 \rfloor_d$, **goto** 3
13: with probability P, **goto** 3
14: $\mathcal{E} \leftarrow E_K(m)$
15: $\hat{b} \leftarrow \mathcal{A}_2(\mathbf{z}, \mathbf{c}, \mathcal{E}, \mathbf{r})$
16: **return** $\hat{b}$

Game 3:
1: $(m_0, m_1) \leftarrow \mathcal{A}_1(\mathbf{pk}_a, \mathbf{pk}_b)$
2: $b \xleftarrow{r} \{0, 1\}$
3: $\mathbf{y}, \mathbf{y'} \xleftarrow{r} \mathcal{R}_{q, [B]}$
4: $\mathbf{v} \xleftarrow{r} \mathcal{R}_q$
5: $\mathbf{r} \leftarrow \mathsf{HelpRec}(\mathbf{v})$
6: $K \leftarrow \mathsf{Rec}(\mathbf{v}, \mathbf{r})$
7: $\mathbf{h}_1 \leftarrow \lfloor \mathbf{a}_1 \cdot \mathbf{y} \rfloor_d, \mathbf{h}_2 \leftarrow \lfloor \mathbf{a}_2 \cdot \mathbf{y} \rfloor_d$
8: $\mathbf{c} \leftarrow H(\mathbf{h}_1, \mathbf{h}_2, m, K, \mathbf{pk}_a, \mathbf{pk}_b)$
9: $\mathbf{z} \xleftarrow{r} \mathcal{R}_{q, [B-\omega]}$
10: $\mathbf{w}_1 \leftarrow \mathbf{a}_1 \cdot \mathbf{y} - \mathbf{e}_{a,1} \cdot \mathbf{c}, \mathbf{w}_2 \leftarrow \mathbf{a}_2 \cdot \mathbf{y} - \mathbf{e}_{a,2} \cdot \mathbf{c}$
11: **if** $\mathbf{h}_1 \neq \lfloor \mathbf{w}_1 \rfloor_d$ **or** $\mathbf{h}_1 \neq \lfloor \mathbf{w}_2 \rfloor_d$, **goto** 3
12: with probability P, **goto** 3
13: $\mathcal{E} \leftarrow E_K(m)$
14: $\hat{b} \leftarrow \mathcal{A}_2(\mathbf{z}, \mathbf{c}, \mathcal{E}, \mathbf{r})$
15: **return** $\hat{b}$

Fig. 3. Sequence of games for the KEX version

Hence, we can replace $\mathbf{z}$ by random elements over this range without modifying the view of the adversary.

Game 2: Using the **RLWE** assumption, we can replace the public key of Bob by a random element in $\mathcal{R}_q$ without being detected by the polynomial time adversary.

Game 3: In game 3, we use the same argument again to replace $\mathbf{v}$ by a uniformly random value (and hence K is uniform as well by design of Rec).

In conclusion, using the fact that both $H(.)$ and $E(.)$ are modeled as ideal primitives and that H takes one random unknown to the adversary value (K) uncorrelated to the message, they do not reveal anything about their inputs.

Hence, the values given to $\mathcal{A}_2$ looks all random and independent from the messages. Thus, the adversary cannot guess which one was signcrypted.

4.3 ROM vs QROM

It is known that the forking lemma cannot be used if the adversary has quantum access to the random oracle. This issue has been recently discussed a lot in the literature on lattice-based signatures and some schemes took it into consideration [3] while others ignored it to focus on performances [18]. Since our goal is to improve practicability, we decided to stick to the classical ROM. Having a classical reduction is essential to claim provable security but the implications of the QROM issue in practice are not clear enough to require QROM security for all the schemes. We redirect the interested reader to [9,21] for more details.

5 Analysis and Parameters

5.1 Parameter Selection

To select the parameters, we followed the methodology described in [7]. It allows the scheme to reduce to worst-case problems on ideal lattices. Be careful that it does not mean that the parameters are chosen such that the problem we reduce to is hard (since the proofs are non-tight) but merely that the reduction works. This is a common practice and as pointed in [21], it is reasonable to assume that it does not create any security issue. Our parameters can be found in Table 1. The dimension n has been set to 1024 because it seems to be the minimal lattice dimension such that RLWE is hard with such a small error distribution. The value m represents the number of rows of the LWE instance written in matrix form. Here it means that we work with two polynomials (which are explicit in the construction) since $m = 2n$. The entropy of the output of the random oracle is given by $\kappa = \log_2\left(2^\omega \binom{n}{\omega}\right)$, that is to say the logarithm of the cardinality of the set $\{\mathbf{v} \mid \mathbf{v} \in \mathcal{R}_{q,[1]}, \|\mathbf{v}\|_1 = \omega\}$. The modulus $q = 2^{25} - 2^{12} + 1$ is a prime such that $q \equiv 1 \mod 2n$. The parameters d and B are chosen such that the rejection probability of the signature is not too high in order to keep the runtime reasonable and $q^{m-n} \geq \frac{2^{(d+1)m+\kappa}}{(2B)^n}$.

To assess the security of the scheme, we used the *LWE-Estimator* tool of Albrecht et al. [2]. We ran the estimator with the following command:

```
n = 1024; q = 33550337;
stddev = sqrt(2/3); alpha = alphaf(sigmaf(stddev), q)
_ = estimate_lwe(n, alpha, q,
        secret_distribution=(-1,1),reduction_cost_model=BKZ.sieve)
```

It estimates a bit security of 131 against the most efficient attack. The estimation of the hardness of directly forging the signature without recovering the private key has been made in the same way as in [13]. It gave overwhelming results, which is not a surprise since the parameters are a harder version of the most secure parameters set of [19].

Table 1. Parameters targeting 128 bits of classical security.

n	m	ω	d	B	q	κ
1024	2048	16	15	2^{15}	$33550337 \approx 2^{25}$	131

5.2 Failure Probability

The main bottleneck of the signcryption scheme is the correctness regarding decryption. Indeed, as in a lot of RLWE-based protocols, the two parties end up with two ring elements close to each other but not exactly the same. In our case, the difference between the value of Alice and the value of Bob is $\Delta_{ab} = \mathbf{e}_{b,1} \cdot \mathbf{y} - \mathbf{e}_{a,1} \cdot \mathbf{c} \cdot \mathbf{s}_b + \mathbf{y}'$. While in those schemes the parameters are chosen in order to get correctness with overwhelming probability, we face here a strong constraint which is that the parameters should also be compatible with the signature scheme. In their case, the $\mathbf{y}$ is coming from the error distribution and hence is very small. In our case, it is the masking polynomial for the signature $\mathbf{s} \cdot \mathbf{c} + \mathbf{y}$ which should be significantly larger. Obviously, one strategy to reduce the norm of Δ_{ab} is to reduce B. This would give better results for correctness but unfortunately decrease the speed of the scheme since the rejection sampling loop would have to run longer to find a small enough $\mathbf{z}$. This is the reason why we decided to use such a small distribution for the secret and the errors. Of course, it is possible to work with slightly larger distributions in a more specific context in which correctness matters less.

We now provide an analysis of the failure probability for the KEX-version. Using the reconciliation method of [5], the KEX-Unsigncrypt algorithm recovers the correct key if $\|\Delta_{ab}\|_\infty < \lfloor \frac{3q}{8} \rfloor$ (actually the requirement is that the ℓ_1 norm of packs of 4 coefficients should be smaller than $\lfloor \frac{3q}{4} \rfloor - 2$). In the following, we write $(\mathbf{p})_i$, to denote the i-th coefficient of a polynomial $\mathbf{p}$.

We shall bound the magnitude of one coefficient $(\Delta'_{ab})_i = (\mathbf{e}'_{b,1} \cdot \mathbf{y})_i$. Since the polynomial product is computed modulo $\langle X^n + 1 \rangle$ and all distributions are symmetric, one such coefficient is the result of a sum of n products between a coefficient of a polynomial in $\mathcal{R}_{q,[1]}$ and a polynomial in $\mathcal{R}_{q,[B]}$.

Let $S \sim \mathcal{U}(\{-1,0,1\})$ and $Y \sim \mathcal{U}([-B,B])$ be random variables, we denote their product SY. Each coefficient of Δ'_{ab} is the sum of n samples from SY, hence $(\Delta'_{ab})_i \sim \sum_{i=1}^n (SY)_i$. Fortunately, computing the exact distribution SY is easy:

$$\mathbb{P}[SY = 0] = \frac{2B+3}{6B+3}$$

$$\mathbb{P}[SY = z \mid z \in [-B,B]\backslash\{0\}] = \frac{2}{6B+3}$$

Since the value of B is reasonable, to find the distribution of Δ'_{ab}, one could hope to compute $\log(n)$ time the convolution of the distribution with itself. Unfortunately, this approach failed to give accurate results because of numerical stability issues. Instead, as in [5], we use the Chernoff-Cramer inequality to bound the sum of the random variables.

Chernoff-Cramer Inequality. Let χ be a distribution over $\mathbb{R}$ and let $X_1, \ldots, X_n$ be i.i.d. symmetric random variables of law χ. Then, for any t such that $M_\chi(t) = \mathbb{E}[e^{tX}] < \infty$ it holds that

$$\mathbb{P}\left[\left|\sum_{i=1}^{n} x_i\right| > \alpha\right] < 2e^{-\alpha t + n \log(M_\chi(t))}.$$

Using the above inequality with

$$M_{SY}(t) = \frac{2B+3}{6B+3} + \frac{2}{6B+3} \cdot \left(\frac{e^{t(B+1)}-1}{e^t-1} + \frac{e^{-t(B+1)}-1}{e^{-t}-1} - 2\right)$$

and setting $\alpha = \lfloor \frac{q}{4} \rfloor - B - n\omega$, $t \approx 2.5 \cdot 10^{-5}$, $n = 1024$ and $k = 2^{15}$ (our parameters from the previous section), we find that $\mathbb{P}\left[(\Delta'_{ab})_i > \lfloor \frac{3q}{16} \rfloor\right] \approx 2^{-115}$. By virtue of the union bound on the 1024 coefficients, we get that the failure probability is $\approx 2^{-105}$.

5.3 Performances

Even if the construction of the signcryption scheme is conceptually interesting on its own, its usage only makes sense if we gain something over the trivial solution of concatenating an encryption/key exchange and a signature scheme. In Table 2, we compare the performances regarding bandwidth between SETLA and a selection of schemes of the same kind. Since lattice-based schemes are already doing great in terms of speed, especially when they can take advantage of SIMD (Single Instruction Multiple Data) instructions, reducing bandwidth will a major factor for adoption in the future. We decided to compare SETLA to the pairs given in the table for the following reasons:

- Dilithium + Kyber: They were very recently designed and are part of the same family of algorithms.
- qTESLA + NewHope: They are the two up-to-date RLWE based schemes and are both candidates for future standardization.
- TESLA♯ + Kyber: This seems to be the most efficient pair regarding compactness out of the reasonably secure Fiat-Shamir/key exchange schemes in the literature.

For the record, we also indicates the performances of the GLP version of signcryption that is using the original parameters of the signature [19]. It obviously gives goods results since we get the key exchange for free without modifying the parameters but the security has been reduced so much over the years that it does not seem reasonable to use it without further modifications. The signcryptext size for SETLA was computed without the symmetric cipher (since it depends on the size of the message itself and should be added to the naive construction as well[1]) and with Peikert's reconciliation which is less efficient but

---

[1] The considered naive constructions are actually KEM + signature and not directly encryption + signature.

more compact than the one of NewHope but still gives good correctness results in practice. The last column compares the gain in compactness of signcryptext when using SETLA instead of the mentioned scheme. We see that at the price of a larger public key, SETLA outperforms the naive concatenation of popular schemes by a significant margin. This is not a surprise since we only have to output a signature and the key exchange is done implicitly. The large public key comes partially from the lack of flexibility of RLWE which limits fast implementations to power of two cyclotomics and m as a multiple of n. We also evaluated the speed of a research oriented implementation made to verify that the design of the scheme is sound. The SETLA-KEX signcrypt procedure took 1 735 234 cycles while the unsigncrypt procedure took 391 944 cycles. Those tests were made on an Intel Core i7-4600M processor using a reasonable but unoptimized implementation and can be greatly improved using AVX2 parallel instructions for the polynomial operations, even if the scheme is already quite fast.

Table 2. Comparison between similar schemes using the naive construction. Values are given in bytes.

Scheme	|sk|	|pk|	|Signcryptext|	Gain
Dilithium [18] + Kyber [10]	2863(=463 + 2400)	2560(=1472 + 1088)	3852(=2700 + 1152)	48%
qTESLA + NewHope [5]	3648(=1856 + 1792)	4800(=2976 + 1824)	4896(=2720 + 2176)	60%
TESLA♯ [8] + Kyber	4512(=2112 + 2400)	4416(=3328 + 1088)	2768(=1616 + 2176)	29%
SETLA-KEX	608	6400	1972	-
GLP-Signcrypt	202	1475	1247	-

6   Conclusion

In this work we presented a lattice-based signcryption scheme called SETLA. We chose a scheme of Malone-Lee as a starting point and proposed two construction both using the Bai-Galbraith signature at their cores. The first construction directly embeds a RLWE key exchange in the signature exactly as in the classical signcryption scheme while the second one uses RLWE encrypt as a key encapsulation mechanism. The KEX version seems to globally outperform the KEM version since even if it is heavier in terms of computation, this is not the main issue with lattices. We proposed a set of parameters targeting 128 bits of classical security following the reduction of Bai and Galbraith. We provided an analysis of correctness and a comparison with most recent schemes (using the naive construction) in the literature regarding signcryptext size. We also made a research oriented implementation to verify the soundness of the scheme while providing reasonable benchmarks. We conclude that it is possible to instantiate SETLA with parameters providing security, correctness and efficiency while still outperforming the naive construction of encrypt-then-sign with state-of-the-art schemes.

A   Security Games for the KEM Version

Game 0:

1: $(m_0, m_1) \leftarrow \mathcal{A}_1(\mathbf{pk}_a, \mathbf{pk}_b)$
2: $b \xleftarrow{r} \{0,1\}$
3: $K \xleftarrow{r} \{0,1\}^{256}$
4: $\mathbf{y} \xleftarrow{r} \mathcal{R}_{q,[B]}$
5: $\mathbf{h}_1 \leftarrow \lfloor \mathbf{a}_1 \cdot \mathbf{y} \rceil_d, \mathbf{h}_2 \leftarrow \lfloor \mathbf{a}_2 \cdot \mathbf{y} \rceil_d$
6: $\mathbf{c} \leftarrow H(\mathbf{h}_1, \mathbf{h}_2, m, K, \mathbf{pk}_a, \mathbf{pk}_b)$
7: $\mathbf{z} \leftarrow \mathbf{s}_a \cdot \mathbf{c} + \mathbf{y}$
8: $\mathbf{w}_1 \leftarrow \mathbf{a}_1 \cdot \mathbf{y} - \mathbf{e}_{a,1} \cdot \mathbf{c}, \mathbf{w}_2 \leftarrow \mathbf{a}_2 \cdot \mathbf{y} - \mathbf{e}_{a,2} \cdot \mathbf{c}$
9: **if** $\mathbf{h}_1 \neq \lfloor \mathbf{w}_1 \rceil_d$ **or** $\mathbf{h}_1 \neq \lfloor \mathbf{w}_2 \rceil_d$, **goto** 3
10: **if** $\mathbf{z}$ **not in** $\mathcal{R}_{q,[B-\omega]}$, **goto** 3
11: $\mathbf{y}' \xleftarrow{r} \mathcal{R}_{q,[B]}$
12: $\mathbf{x} \leftarrow \mathbf{t}_{b,1} \cdot \mathbf{y} + \mathbf{y}' + \mathtt{Encode}(K)$
13: $\mathcal{E} \leftarrow E_K(m)$
14: $\hat{b} \leftarrow \mathcal{A}_2(\mathbf{z}, \mathbf{c}, \mathbf{x}, \mathcal{E})$
15: **return** $\hat{b}$

Game 1:

1: $(m_0, m_1) \leftarrow \mathcal{A}_1(\mathbf{pk}_a, \mathbf{pk}_b)$
2: $b \xleftarrow{r} \{0,1\}$
3: $K \xleftarrow{r} \{0,1\}^{256}$
4: $\mathbf{y} \xleftarrow{r} \mathcal{R}_{q,[B]}$
5: $\mathbf{h}_1 \leftarrow \lfloor \mathbf{a}_1 \cdot \mathbf{y} \rceil_d, \mathbf{h}_2 \leftarrow \lfloor \mathbf{a}_2 \cdot \mathbf{y} \rceil_d$
6: $\mathbf{c} \leftarrow H(\mathbf{h}_1, \mathbf{h}_2, m, K, \mathbf{pk}_a, \mathbf{pk}_b)$
7: $\mathbf{z} \xleftarrow{r} \mathcal{R}_{q,[B-\omega]}$
8: $\mathbf{w}_1 \leftarrow \mathbf{a}_1 \cdot \mathbf{y} - \mathbf{e}_{a,1} \cdot \mathbf{c}, \mathbf{w}_2 \leftarrow \mathbf{a}_2 \cdot \mathbf{y} - \mathbf{e}_{a,2} \cdot \mathbf{c}$
9: **if** $\mathbf{h}_1 \neq \lfloor \mathbf{w}_1 \rceil_d$ **or** $\mathbf{h}_1 \neq \lfloor \mathbf{w}_2 \rceil_d$, **goto** 3
10: **with probability** P, **goto** 3
11: $\mathbf{y}' \xleftarrow{r} \mathcal{R}_{q,[B]}$
12: $\mathbf{x} \leftarrow \mathbf{t}_{b,1} \cdot \mathbf{y} + \mathbf{y}' + \mathtt{Encode}(K)$
13: $\mathcal{E} \leftarrow E_K(m)$
14: $\hat{b} \leftarrow \mathcal{A}_2(\mathbf{z}, \mathbf{c}, \mathbf{x}, \mathcal{E})$
15: **return** $\hat{b}$

Game 2:

1: $(m_0, m_1) \leftarrow \mathcal{A}_1(\mathbf{pk}_a, \mathbf{pk}_b)$
2: $b \xleftarrow{r} \{0,1\}$
3: $K \xleftarrow{r} \{0,1\}^{256}$
4: $\mathbf{y} \xleftarrow{r} \mathcal{R}_{q,[B]}$
5: $\mathbf{h}_1 \leftarrow \lfloor \mathbf{a}_1 \cdot \mathbf{y} \rceil_d, \mathbf{h}_2 \leftarrow \lfloor \mathbf{a}_2 \cdot \mathbf{y} \rceil_d$
6: $\mathbf{c} \leftarrow H(\mathbf{h}_1, \mathbf{h}_2, m, K, \mathbf{pk}_a, \mathbf{pk}_b)$
7: $\mathbf{z} \xleftarrow{r} \mathcal{R}_{q,[B-\omega]}$
8: $\mathbf{w}_1 \leftarrow \mathbf{a}_1 \cdot \mathbf{y} - \mathbf{e}_{a,1} \cdot \mathbf{c}, \mathbf{w}_2 \leftarrow \mathbf{a}_2 \cdot \mathbf{y} - \mathbf{e}_{a,2} \cdot \mathbf{c}$
9: **if** $\mathbf{h}_1 \neq \lfloor \mathbf{w}_1 \rceil_d$ **or** $\mathbf{h}_1 \neq \lfloor \mathbf{w}_2 \rceil_d$, **goto** 3
10: **with probability** P, **goto** 3
11: $\mathbf{y}' \xleftarrow{r} \mathcal{R}_{q,[B]}$
12: $\mathbf{a}' \xleftarrow{r} \mathcal{R}_q$
13: $\mathbf{x} \leftarrow \mathbf{a}' \cdot \mathbf{y} + \mathbf{y}' + \mathtt{Encode}(K)$
14: $\mathcal{E} \leftarrow E_K(m)$
15: $\hat{b} \leftarrow \mathcal{A}_2(\mathbf{z}, \mathbf{c}, \mathbf{x}, \mathcal{E})$
16: **return** $\hat{b}$

Game 3:

1: $(m_0, m_1) \leftarrow \mathcal{A}_1(\mathbf{pk}_a, \mathbf{pk}_b)$
2: $b \xleftarrow{r} \{0,1\}$
3: $K \xleftarrow{r} \{0,1\}^{256}$
4: $\mathbf{y} \xleftarrow{r} \mathcal{R}_{q,[B]}$
5: $\mathbf{h}_1 \leftarrow \lfloor \mathbf{a}_1 \cdot \mathbf{y} \rceil_d, \mathbf{h}_2 \leftarrow \lfloor \mathbf{a}_2 \cdot \mathbf{y} \rceil_d$
6: $\mathbf{c} \leftarrow H(\mathbf{h}_1, \mathbf{h}_2, m, K, \mathbf{pk}_a, \mathbf{pk}_b)$
7: $\mathbf{z} \xleftarrow{r} \mathcal{R}_{q,[B-\omega]}$
8: $\mathbf{w}_1 \leftarrow \mathbf{a}_1 \cdot \mathbf{y} - \mathbf{e}_{a,1} \cdot \mathbf{c}, \mathbf{w}_2 \leftarrow \mathbf{a}_2 \cdot \mathbf{y} - \mathbf{e}_{a,2} \cdot \mathbf{c}$
9: **if** $\mathbf{h}_1 \neq \lfloor \mathbf{w}_1 \rceil_d$ **or** $\mathbf{h}_1 \neq \lfloor \mathbf{w}_2 \rceil_d$, **goto** 3
10: **with probability** P, **goto** 3
11: $\mathbf{x} \xleftarrow{r} \mathcal{R}_q$
12: $\mathcal{E} \leftarrow E_K(m)$
13: $\hat{b} \leftarrow \mathcal{A}_2(\mathbf{z}, \mathbf{c}, \mathbf{x}, \mathcal{E})$
14: **return** $\hat{b}$

Fig. 4. Sequence of games for the KEM version

Game 0 $\rightarrow$ **Game 1**: Rejection sampling
Game 1 $\rightarrow$ **Game 2**: Decisional Compact Knapsack/RLWE
Game 2 $\rightarrow$ **Game 3**: Decisional Compact Knapsack/RLWE

B   Publicly Verifiable Signature from Signcryptext

An interesting feature of Malone-Lee's signcryption scheme is that the receiver Bob can himself create a fully valid publicly verifiable signature under Alice's secret key on the message he unsigncrypted. Even if we chose to start from this scheme for its similarity with Schnorr signature (and thus, lattice-based signature), this really helpful feature carries to our construction. Below are the algorithms for the KEX version but the same technique can trivially be applied to the KEM version.

Algorithm 6. SETLA-KEX SignExtract

Input: Public parameters $\mathbf{a_1}, \mathbf{a_2}$, Bob's keys $(\mathbf{s}_b, \mathbf{pk}_b)$, Alice's public key $\mathbf{pk}_a$, a signcryptext $C = (\mathbf{z}, \mathbf{c}, \mathcal{E}, \mathbf{r})$, random oracle $H : * \rightarrow \{\mathbf{v} \mid \mathbf{v} \in \mathcal{R}_{q,[1]}, \|\mathbf{v}\|_1 = \omega\}$, symmetric encryption algorithm E
Output: A message m together with its signature $\sigma(m)$ or a failure symbol

1: $\mathbf{w}_1 \leftarrow \mathbf{a}_1 \cdot \mathbf{z} - \mathbf{t}_{a,1} \cdot \mathbf{c}$, $\mathbf{w}_2 \leftarrow \mathbf{a}_2 \cdot \mathbf{z} - \mathbf{t}_{a,2} \cdot \mathbf{c}$
2: $K \leftarrow \mathsf{Rec}(\mathbf{w}_1 \cdot \mathbf{s}_b, \mathbf{r})$
3: $m \leftarrow E_K^{-1}(\mathcal{E})$
4: $b \leftarrow \mathbf{c} = H(\lfloor \mathbf{w}_1 \rceil_d, \lfloor \mathbf{w}_2 \rceil_d, m, K, \mathbf{pk}_a, \mathbf{pk}_b)$ **and** $\mathbf{z} \in \mathcal{R}_{q,[B-\omega]}$
5: **return** $m, \sigma(m) = (K, \mathbf{z}_1, \mathbf{z}_2, \mathbf{c})$ **if** $b = 1$ **else** $\perp$

SETLA-KEX SignExtract. (Algorithm 6) To extract a publicly verifiable signature $\sigma(m)$ from a signcryptext, Bob will use the fact that the output of KEX-Signcrypt is essentially equivalent to a TESLA♯ signature on m with a nonce depending on $K, \mathbf{pk}_a$ and $\mathbf{pk}_b$ queried to the random oracle. Since a verifier should obviously know the message to validate the signature, the confidentiality of the key K is not required anymore. Thus, KEX-SignExctract will output m and K together with the signature and anyone will be able to perform the verification.

Algorithm 7. PublicVerif

Input: Public parameters $\mathbf{a_1}, \mathbf{a_2}$, Alice's public key $\mathbf{pk}_a$, Bob's public key $\mathbf{pk}_b$, a message m, a signature $\sigma(m) = (K, \mathbf{z}, \mathbf{c})$, hash function $H : * \rightarrow \{\mathbf{v} \mid \mathbf{v} \in \mathcal{R}_{q,[1]}, \|\mathbf{v}\|_1 = \omega\}$
Output: 1 if the signature is valid, 0 otherwise

1: $\mathbf{w}_1 \leftarrow \mathbf{a}_1 \cdot \mathbf{z} - \mathbf{t}_{a,1} \cdot \mathbf{c}$, $\mathbf{w}_2$
2: **return** 1 **if** $\mathbf{c} = H(\lfloor \mathbf{w}_1 \rceil_d, \lfloor \mathbf{w}_2 \rceil_d, m, K, \mathbf{pk}_a, \mathbf{pk}_b)$ **and** $\mathbf{z} \in \mathcal{R}_{q,[B-\omega]}$ **else** 0

PublicVerif. (Algorithm 7) The public verification is the same as in usual lattice-based signatures, except that the hash function also takes as input $K, \mathbf{pk}_a$ and $\mathbf{pk}_b$.

References

1. Akleylek, S., Bindel, N., Buchmann, J., Krmer, J., Marson, G.A.: An efficient lattice-based signature scheme with provably secure instantiation. Cryptology ePrint Archive, Report 2016/030 (2016). https://eprint.iacr.org/2016/030
2. Albrecht, M.R., Player, R., Scott, S.: On the concrete hardness of learning with errors. Cryptology ePrint Archive, Report 2015/046 (2015). https://bitbucket.org/malb/lwe-estimator
3. Alkim, E., et al.: Revisiting TESLA in the quantum random oracle model. Cryptology ePrint Archive, Report 2015/755 (2015). http://eprint.iacr.org/2015/755
4. Alkim, E., Ducas, L., Pöppelmann, T., Schwabe, P.: Newhope without reconciliation. Cryptology ePrint Archive, Report 2016/1157 (2016). http://eprint.iacr.org/2016/1157
5. Alkim, E., Ducas, L., Pöppelmann, T., Schwabe, P.: Post-quantum key exchange—a new hope. In: 25th USENIX Security Symposium (USENIX Security 2016), Austin, TX, pp. 327–343. USENIX Association (2016)
6. Baek, J., Steinfeld, R., Zheng, Y.: Formal proofs for the security of signcryption. J. Cryptol. **20**(2), 203–235 (2007)
7. Bai, S., Galbraith, S.D.: An improved compression technique for signatures based on learning with errors. In: Benaloh, J. (ed.) CT-RSA 2014. LNCS, vol. 8366, pp. 28–47. Springer, Cham (2014). https://doi.org/10.1007/978-3-319-04852-9_2
8. Barreto, P.S.L.M., Longa, P., Naehrig, M., Ricardini, J.E., Zanon, G.: Sharper ring-LWE signatures. Cryptology ePrint Archive, Report 2016/1026 (2016). https://eprint.iacr.org/2016/1026
9. Boneh, D., Dagdelen, Ö., Fischlin, M., Lehmann, A., Schaffner, C., Zhandry, M.: Random oracles in a quantum world. Cryptology ePrint Archive, Report 2010/428 (2010). https://eprint.iacr.org/2010/428
10. Bos, J., et al.: Crystals - kyber: a CCA-secure module-lattice-based KEM. Cryptology ePrint Archive, Report 2017/634 (2017). http://eprint.iacr.org/2017/634
11. Bos, J.W., et al.: Frodo: take off the ring! Practical, quantum-secure key exchange from LWE (2016)
12. Bos, J.W., Costello, C., Naehrig, M., Stebila, D.: Post-quantum key exchange for the TLS protocol from the ring learning with errors problem. In: 2015 IEEE Symposium on Security and Privacy, pp. 553–570, May 2015
13. Dagdelen, Ö., et al.: High-speed signatures from standard lattices. In: Aranha, D.F., Menezes, A. (eds.) LATINCRYPT 2014. LNCS, vol. 8895, pp. 84–103. Springer, Cham (2015). https://doi.org/10.1007/978-3-319-16295-9_5
14. de Clercq, R., Roy, S.S., Vercauteren, F., Verbauwhede, I.: Efficient software implementation of ring-LWE encryption. In: Proceedings of the 2015 Design, Automation & Test in Europe Conference & Exhibition, DATE 2015, San Jose, CA, USA, pp. 339–344, EDA Consortium (2015)
15. Dent, A.W., Zheng, Y.: Practical Signcryption. Springer, Heidelberg (2010). https://doi.org/10.1007/978-3-540-89411-7
16. Dodis, Y., Reyzin, L., Smith, A.: Fuzzy extractors: how to generate strong keys from biometrics and other noisy data. In: Cachin, C., Camenisch, J.L. (eds.) EUROCRYPT 2004. LNCS, vol. 3027, pp. 523–540. Springer, Heidelberg (2004). https://doi.org/10.1007/978-3-540-24676-3_31
17. Ducas, L., Durmus, A., Lepoint, T., Lyubashevsky, V.: Lattice signatures and bimodal gaussians. In: Canetti, R., Garay, J.A. (eds.) CRYPTO 2013. LNCS, vol. 8042, pp. 40–56. Springer, Heidelberg (2013). https://doi.org/10.1007/978-3-642-40041-4_3

18. Ducas, L., Lepoint, T., Lyubashevsky, V., Schwabe, P., Seiler, G., Stehle, D.: Crystals - dilithium: digital signatures from module lattices. Cryptology ePrint Archive, Report 2017/633 (2017). https://eprint.iacr.org/2017/633
19. Güneysu, T., Lyubashevsky, V., Pöppelmann, T.: Practical lattice-based cryptography: a signature scheme for embedded systems. In: Prouff, E., Schaumont, P. (eds.) CHES 2012. LNCS, vol. 7428, pp. 530–547. Springer, Heidelberg (2012). https://doi.org/10.1007/978-3-642-33027-8_31
20. Lin, X., Ding, J., Xie, X.: A simple provably secure key exchange scheme based on the learning with errors problem. Cryptology ePrint Archive, Report 2012/688 (2012). https://eprint.iacr.org/2012/688
21. Kiltz, E., Lyubashevsky, V., Schaffner, C.: A concrete treatment of fiat-shamir signatures in the quantum random-oracle model. In: Nielsen, J.B., Rijmen, V. (eds.) EUROCRYPT 2018. LNCS, vol. 10822, pp. 552–586. Springer, Cham (2018). https://doi.org/10.1007/978-3-319-78372-7_18
22. Li, F., Bin Muhaya, F.T., Khan, M.K., Takagi, T., Takagi, T.: Lattice-based signcryption. Concur. Comput. Pract. Exp. **25**(14), 2112–2122 (2013)
23. Liu, Z., Seo, H., Sinha Roy, S., Großschädl, J., Kim, H., Verbauwhede, I.: Efficient ring-LWE encryption on 8-bit avr processors. In: Güneysu, T., Handschuh, H. (eds.) CHES 2015. LNCS, vol. 9293, pp. 663–682. Springer, Heidelberg (2015). https://doi.org/10.1007/978-3-662-48324-4_33
24. Lu, X., Wen, Q., Jin, Z., Wang, L., Yang, C.: A lattice-based signcryption scheme without random oracles. Front. Comput. Sci. **8**(4), 667–675 (2014)
25. Lyubashevsky, V.: Fiat-shamir with aborts: applications to lattice and factoring-based signatures. In: Matsui, M. (ed.) ASIACRYPT 2009. LNCS, vol. 5912, pp. 598–616. Springer, Heidelberg (2009). https://doi.org/10.1007/978-3-642-10366-7_35
26. Lyubashevsky, V.: Lattice signatures without trapdoors. In: Pointcheval, D., Johansson, T. (eds.) EUROCRYPT 2012. LNCS, vol. 7237, pp. 738–755. Springer, Heidelberg (2012). https://doi.org/10.1007/978-3-642-29011-4_43
27. Lyubashevsky, V., Peikert, C., Regev, O.: On ideal lattices and learning with errors over rings. J. ACM **60**(6), 43:1–43:35 (2013)
28. Malone-Lee, J.: Signcryption with non-interactive non-repudiation. Des. Codes Crypt. **37**(1), 81–109 (2005)
29. Peikert, C.: Lattice cryptography for the internet. In: Mosca, M. (ed.) PQCrypto 2014. LNCS, vol. 8772, pp. 197–219. Springer, Cham (2014). https://doi.org/10.1007/978-3-319-11659-4_12
30. Pointcheval, D., Stern, J.: Security arguments for digital signatures and blind signatures. J. Crypt. **13**(3), 361–396 (2000)
31. Pöppelmann, T., Oder, T., Güneysu, T.: High-performance ideal lattice-based cryptography on 8-bit ATxmega microcontrollers. In: Lauter, K., Rodríguez-Henríquez, F. (eds.) LATINCRYPT 2015. LNCS, vol. 9230, pp. 346–365. Springer, Cham (2015). https://doi.org/10.1007/978-3-319-22174-8_19
32. Sato, S., Shikata, J.: Lattice-based signcryption without random oracles. In: Lange, T., Steinwandt, R. (eds.) PQCrypto 2018. LNCS, vol. 10786, pp. 331–351. Springer, Cham (2018). https://doi.org/10.1007/978-3-319-79063-3_16
33. Yan, J., Wang, L., Wang, L., Yang, Y., Yao, W.: Efficient lattice-based signcryption in standard model. Math. Prob. Eng. **2013**, 1–18 (2013)
34. Zheng, Y.: Digital signcryption or how to achieve cost(signature & encryption) & cost(signature) + cost(encryption). In: Kaliski, B.S. (ed.) Advances in Cryptology – CRYPTO 1997. Lecture Notes in Computer Science, vol. 1294, pp. 165–179. Springer, Heidelberg (1997). https://doi.org/10.1007/BFb0052234

Cryptanalysis

Assessing and Countering Reaction Attacks Against Post-Quantum Public-Key Cryptosystems Based on QC-LDPC Codes

Paolo Santini, Marco Baldi[✉], and Franco Chiaraluce

Università Politecnica delle Marche, Ancona, Italy
p.santini@pm.univpm.it,{m.baldi,f.chiaraluce}@univpm.it

Abstract. Code-based public-key cryptosystems based on QC-LDPC and QC-MDPC codes are promising post-quantum candidates to replace quantum-vulnerable classical alternatives. However, a new type of attacks based on Bob's reactions have recently been introduced and appear to significantly reduce the length of the life of any keypair used in these systems. In this paper we estimate the complexity of all known reaction attacks against QC-LDPC and QC-MDPC code-based variants of the McEliece cryptosystem. We also show how the structure of the secret key and, in particular, the secret code rate affect the complexity of these attacks. It follows from our results that QC-LDPC code-based systems can indeed withstand reaction attacks, on condition that some specific decoding algorithms are used and the secret code has a sufficiently high rate.

Keywords: Code-based cryptography · McEliece cryptosystem
Niederreiter cryptosystem · Post-quantum cryptography
Quasi-cyclic low-density parity-check codes

1 Introduction

Research in the area of post-quantum cryptography, that is, the design of cryptographic primitives able to withstand attacks based on quantum computers has known a dramatic acceleration in recent years, also due to the ongoing NIST standardization initiative of post-quantum cryptosystems [19]. In this scenario, one of the most promising candidates is represented by code-based cryptosystems, that were initiated by McEliece in 1978 [17]. Security of the McEliece cryptosystem relies on the hardness of decoding a random linear code: a common instance of this problem is known as syndrome decoding problem (SDP) and no polynomial-time algorithm exists for its solution [8,16]. In particular, the best SDP solvers are known as information set decoding (ISD) algorithms

P. Santini—The work of Paolo Santini was partially supported by Namirial S.p.A.

J. Camenisch and P. Papadimitratos (Eds.): CANS 2018, LNCS 11124, pp. 323–343, 2018.
https://doi.org/10.1007/978-3-030-00434-7_16

[7, 20, 22], and are characterized by an exponential complexity, even considering attackers provided with quantum computers [9].

Despite these security properties, a large-scale adoption of the McEliece cryptosystem has not occurred in the past, mostly due to the large size of its public keys: in the original proposal, the public key is the generator matrix of a Goppa code with length 1024 and dimension 524, requiring more than 67 kB of memory for being stored. Replacing Goppa codes with other families of more structured codes may lead to a reduction in the public key size, but at the same time might endanger the system security because of such an additional structure. An overview of these variants can be found in [3].

Among these variants, a prominent role is played by those exploiting quasi-cyclic low-density parity-check (QC-LDPC) [2, 6] and quasi-cyclic moderatedensity parity-check (QC-MDPC) codes [18] as private codes, because of their very compact public keys. Some of these variants are also at the basis of post-quantum primitives that are currently under review for possible standardization by NIST [1, 5]. QC-LDPC and QC-MDPC codes are decoded through iterative algorithms that are characterized by a non-zero decryption failure rate (DFR), differently from classical bounded distance decoders used for Goppa codes. The values of DFR achieved by these decoders are usually very small (in the order of 10^{-6} or less), but are bounded away from zero.

In the event of a decoding failure, Bob must acknowledge Alice in order to let her encrypt the plaintext again. It has recently been shown that the occurrence of these events might be exploited by an opponent to recover information about the secret key [11, 12, 14]. Attacks of this type are known as *reaction attacks*, and exploit the information leakage associated to the dependence of the DFR on the error vector used during encryption and the structure of the private key. These attacks have been shown to be successful against some cryptosystems based on QC-LDPC and QC-MDPC codes, but their complexity has not been assessed yet, to the best of our knowledge.

In this paper, we consider all known reaction attacks against QC-LDPC and QC-MDPC code-based systems, and provide closed form expressions for their complexity. Based on this analysis, we devise some instances of QC-LDPC code-based systems that are able to withstand these attacks. The paper is organized as follows. In Sect. 2 we give a description of the QC-LDPC and QC-MDPC code-based McEliece cryptosystems. In Sect. 3 we describe known reaction attacks. In particular, we generalize existing procedures, applying them to codes having whichever parameters and take the code structure into account, with the aim to provide complexity estimations for the attacks. In Sect. 4 we make a comparison between all the analyzed attacks, and consider the impact of the decoder on the feasibility of some attacks. We show that QC-LDPC code-based McEliece cryptosystems have an intrinsic resistance to reaction attacks. This is due to the presence of a secret transformation matrix that implies Bob to decode an error pattern that is different from the one used during encryption. When the system parameters are properly chosen, recovering the secret key can hence become computationally unfeasible for an opponent.

2   System Description

Public-key cryptosystems and key encapsulation mechanisms based on QC-LDPC codes [2,5] are built upon a secret QC-LDPC code with length $n = n_0 p$ and dimension $k = (n_0 - 1)p$, with n_0 being a small integer and p being a prime. The latter choice is recommended to avoid reductions in the security level due to the applicability of folding attacks of the type in [21]. The code is described through a parity-check matrix in the form:

$$H = [H_0 | H_1 | \cdots | H_{n_0 - 1}], \tag{1}$$

where each block H_i is a $p \times p$ circulant matrix, with weight equal to d_v.

2.1   Key Generation

The private key is formed by H and by a transformation matrix Q, which is an $n \times n$ matrix in quasi-cyclic (QC) form (i.e., it is formed by $n_0 \times n_0$ circulant blocks of size p). The row and column weights of Q are constant and equal to $m \ll n$. The matrix Q is generated according to the following rules:

- the weights of the circulant blocks forming Q can be written in an $n_0 \times n_0$ circulant matrix $w(Q)$ whose first row is $\bar{m} = [m_0, m_1, \cdots, m_{n_0-1}]$, such that $\sum_{i=0}^{n_0-1} m_i = m$; the weight of the (i,j)-th block in Q corresponds to the (i,j)-th element of $w(Q)$;
- the permanent of $w(Q)$ must be odd for the non-singularity of Q; if it is also $< p$, then Q is surely non-singular.

In order to obtain the public key from the private key, we first compute the matrix $\tilde{H}$ as:

$$\tilde{H} = HQ = \left[\tilde{H}_0 \middle| \tilde{H}_1 \middle| \cdots \middle| \tilde{H}_{n_0-1} \right], \tag{2}$$

from which the public key is obtained as:

$$G' = \left[I_{(n_0-1)p} \middle| \begin{array}{c} \left(\tilde{H}_{n_0-1}^{-1} \tilde{H}_0 \right)^T \\ \left(\tilde{H}_{n_0-1}^{-1} \tilde{H}_1 \right)^T \\ \vdots \\ \left(\tilde{H}_{n_0-1}^{-1} \tilde{H}_{n_0-2} \right)^T \end{array} \right], \tag{3}$$

where $I_{(n_0-1)p}$ is the identity matrix of size $(n_0 - 1)p$. The matrix G' is the generator matrix of the public code and can be in systematic form since we suppose that a suitable conversion is adopted to achieve indistinguishability under adaptive chosen ciphertext attack (CCA2) [15].

2.2 Encryption

Let u be a k-bit information message to be encrypted, and let e be an n-bit intentional error vector with weight t. The ciphertext x is then obtained as:

$$x = uG' + e. \tag{4}$$

When a CCA2 conversion is used, the error vector is obtained as a deterministic transformation of a string resulting from certain public operations, including one-way functions (like hash functions), that involve the plaintext and some randomness generated during encryption. Since the same relationships are used by Bob to check the integrity of the received message, in the case with CCA2 conversion performing an arbitrary modification of the error vector in (4) is not possible. Analogously, choosing an error vector and computing a consistent plaintext is not possible, because it would require inverting a hash function. As we will see next, this affects reaction attacks, since it implies that the error vector cannot be freely chosen by an opponent. Basically, this turns out into the following simple criterion: in the case with CCA2 conversion, the error vector used for each encryption has to be considered as a randomly extracted n-tuple of weight t.

2.3 Decryption

Decryption starts with the computation of the syndrome as:

$$s = xQ^T H^T = eQ^T H^T = e'H^T, \tag{5}$$

which corresponds to the syndrome of an *expanded error vector* $e' = eQ^T$, computed through H^T. Then, a syndrome decoding algorithm is applied to s, in order to recover e. A common choice to decode s is the bit flipping (BF) decoder, firstly introduced in [13], or one of its variants. In the special setting used in QC-LDPC code-based systems, decoding can also be performed through a special algorithm named *Q-decoder* [5], which is a modified version of the classical BF decoder and exploits the fact that e' is obtained as the sum of rows from Q^T. The choice of the decoder might strongly influence the probability of success of reaction attacks, as it will be discussed afterwards.

QC-MDPC code-based systems introduced in [18] can be seen as a particular case of the QC-LDPC code-based scheme, corresponding to $Q = I_{n_0 p}$. Encryption and decryption work in the same way, and syndrome decoding is performed through BF. We point out that the classical BF decoder can be considered as a particular case of the Q-decoder, corresponding to $Q = I_{n_0 p}$.

2.4 Q-decoder

The novelty of the Q-decoder, with respect to the classical BF decoder, is in the fact that it exploits the knowledge of the matrix Q to improve the decoding performance. A detailed description of the Q-decoder can be found in [5]. In the Q-decoder, decisions about error positions are taken on the basis of some *correlation* values that are computed as:

$$R = s * H * Q = \Sigma * Q, \tag{6}$$

where $*$ denotes the integer inner product and $\Sigma = s * H$. In a classical BF decoder, the metric used for the reliability of the bits is only based on Σ, which is a vector collecting the number of unsatisfied parity-check equations per position. In QC-LDPC code-based systems, the syndrome s corresponds to the syndrome of the expanded error vector $e' = eQ^T$: this fact means that the error positions in e' are not uniformly distributed, because they depend on Q. The Q-decoder takes into account this fact through the integer multiplication by Q [5, Sect. 2.3], and the vector R is used to estimate the error positions in e (instead of e').

In the case of QC-MDPC codes, a classical BF decoder is used, and it can be seen as a special instance of the Q-decoder, corresponding to $Q = I_{n_{op}}$. As explained in [5, Sect. 2.5], from the performance standpoint the Q-decoder approximates a BF decoder working on $\tilde{H} = HQ$. However, by exploiting H and Q separately, the Q-decoder achieves lower complexity than BF decoding working on $\tilde{H}$. The aforementioned performance equivalence is motivated by the following relation:

$$
\begin{aligned}
R &= s * H * Q \\
&= eQ^T H^T * H * Q \\
&= e\tilde{H}^T * H * Q \\
&\approx e\tilde{H}^T * \tilde{H}, \tag{7}
\end{aligned}
$$

where the approximation $HQ \approx H * Q$ comes from the sparsity of both H and Q. Thus, Eq. (7) shows how the decision metric considered in the Q-decoder approximates that used in a BF decoder working on $\tilde{H}$.

3   Reaction Attacks

In order to describe recent reaction attacks proposed in [11,12,14], let us introduce the following notation.

Given two ones at positions j_1 and j_2 in the same row of a circulant block, the distance between them is defined as $\delta(j_1, j_2) = \min\{\pm(j_1 - j_2) \bmod p\}$. Given a vector v, we define its distance spectrum $\Delta(v)$ as the set of all distances between any couple of ones. The multiplicity $\mu_d^{(v)}$ of a distance d is equal to the number of distinct couples of ones producing that distance; if a distance does not appear in the distance spectrum of v, we say that it has zero multiplicity (i.e., $\mu_d^{(v)} = 0$), with respect to that distance. Since the distance spectrum is invariant to cyclic shifts, all the rows of a circulant matrix share the same distance spectrum; thus, we can define the distance spectrum of a circulant matrix as the distance spectrum of any of its rows (the first one for the sake of convenience).

The main intuition behind reaction attacks is the fact that the DFR depends on the correlation between the distances in the error vector used during encryption and those in H and Q. In fact, common distances produce cancellations of ones in the syndrome, and this affects the decoding procedure [10], by slightly reducing the DFR. In general terms, a reaction attack is based on the following stages:

i. The opponent sends T queries to a decryption oracle. For the i-th query, the opponent records the error vector used for encryption $(e^{(i)})$ and the corresponding oracle's answer $(\Im^{(i)})$. The latter is 1 in the case of a decoding failure, 0 otherwise.
ii. The analysis of the collected couples $\{e^{(i)}, \Im^{(i)}\}$ provides the opponent with some information about the distance spectrum of the secret key.
iii. The opponent exploits this information to reconstruct the secret key (or an equivalent representation of it).

We point out that these attacks can affect code-based systems achieving security against both chosen plaintext attack (CPA) and CCA2. However, in this paper we only focus on systems with CCA2 security, which represent the most interesting case. Therefore, we assume that each decryption query uses an error vector randomly picked among all the n-tuples with weight t (see Sect. 2).

3.1 Matrix Reconstruction from the Distance Spectrum

In [11, Sect. 3.4] the problem of recovering the support of a vector from its distance spectrum has been defined as Distance Spectrum Reconstruction (DSR) problem, and can be formulated as follows:

Distance Spectrum Reconstruction (DSR)
Given $\Delta(v)$, with v being a p-bit vector with weight w, find a set of integers $\Theta^* = \{v_0^*, v_1^*, \cdots, v_{w-1}^* \mid v_i^* < p\}$ such that Θ^* is the support of a p-bit vector v^* and $\Delta(v^*) = \Delta(v)$.
This problem is characterized by the following properties:

– each vector obtained as the cyclic shift of v is a valid solution to the problem; the search for a solution can then be made easier by setting $v_0^* = 0$ and $v_1^* = \min\{\pm d \mod p \mid d \in \Delta(v)\}$;
– the elements of Θ^* must satisfy the following property:

$$\forall v_i^* > 0 \ \exists d \in \Delta(v) \ \text{s.t.} \ (v_i^* = d) \vee (v_i^* = p - d), \tag{8}$$

since it must be $\delta(0, v_i^*) = \min\{v_i^*, p - v_i^*\} \in \Delta(v)$.
– for every solution Θ^*, there always exists another solution Θ' such that:

$$\forall v_i^* \in \Theta^* \ \exists! \ v_i' \in \Theta' \ \text{s.t.} \ v_i' = (p - v_i^*) \mod p; \tag{9}$$

– the DSR problem can be represented through a graph $\mathcal{G}$, containing nodes with values $0, 1, \cdots, p - 1$: there is an edge between any two nodes i and j if and only if $\delta(i, j) \in \Delta(v)$. In the graph $\mathcal{G}$, a solution Θ^* (and Θ') is represented by a size-w clique.

Reaction attacks against QC-MDPC code-based systems are based on the DSR problem. Instead, in the case of QC-LDPC code-based systems, an attacker aiming at recovering the secret QC-LDPC code has to solve the following problem:

Distance Spectrum Distinguishing and Reconstruction (DSDR)
Given $\bigcup_{i=0}^{z-1} \Delta\left(v^{(i)}\right)$, where each $v^{(i)}$ is a p-bit vector with weight $w^{(i)}$, find z sets $\Theta^{*(i)} = \left\{v_0^{*(i)}, v_1^{*(i)}, \cdots, v_{w^{(i)}-1}^{*(i)} \mid v_j^{*(i)} < p\right\}$ such that each $\Theta^{*(i)}$ is the support of a p-bit vector $v^{*(i)}$ and $\bigcup_{i=0}^{z-1} \Delta\left(v^{*(i)}\right) = \bigcup_{i=0}^{z-1} \Delta\left(v^{(i)}\right)$.

Also in this case, the problem can be represented with a graph, where solutions of the DSDR problem are defined by cliques of proper size and are coupled as described by (9). On average, solving these problems is easy: the associated graphs are sparse (the number of edges is relatively small), so the probability of having spurious cliques (i.e., cliques that are not associated to the actual distance spectrum), is in general extremely low. In addition, the complexity of finding the solutions is significantly smaller than that of the previous steps of the attack, so it can be neglected [11,14]. From now on, we conservatively assume that these problems always have the smallest number of solutions, that is equal to 2 for the DSR case and to $2z$ for the DSDR case.

3.2 GJS Attack

The first reaction attack exploiting decoding failures has been proposed in [14], and is tailored to QC-MDPC code-based systems. Therefore, we describe it considering $Q = I_{n_0 p}$, $\tilde{H} = H$, and we refer to it as the GJS attack. In this attack, the distance spectrum recovery is performed through Algorithm 1. The vectors a and b estimated through Algorithm 1 are then used by the opponent to guess the multiplicity of each distance in the spectrum of H_{n_0-1}. Indeed, the ratios $p_d = \frac{a_d}{b_d}$ follow different and distinguishable distributions, with mean values depending on the multiplicity of d. This way, the analysis of the values p_d allows the opponent to recover $\Delta(H_{n_0-1})$.

Solving the DSR problem associated to $\Delta(H_{n_0-1})$ allows the opponent to obtain a matrix $H_{n_0-1}^* = \Pi H_{n_0-1}$, with Π being an unknown circulant permutation matrix. Decoding of intercepted ciphertexts can be done just with $H_{n_0-1}^*$. In fact, according to (3), the public key can be written as $G' = [I|P]$, with:

$$P = \begin{bmatrix} P_0 \\ P_1 \\ \vdots \\ P_{n_0-2} \end{bmatrix} = \begin{bmatrix} \left(H_{n_0-1}^{-1} H_0\right)^T \\ \left(H_{n_0-1}^{-1} H_1\right)^T \\ \vdots \\ \left(H_{n_0-1}^{-1} H_{n_0-2}\right)^T \end{bmatrix}. \tag{10}$$

The opponent can then compute the products:

$$H_{n_0-1}^* P_i^T = \Pi H_i = H_i^*, \tag{11}$$

Algorithm 1. GJS distance spectrum recovery

$a \leftarrow$ zero initialized vector of length $\left\lfloor \frac{p}{2} \right\rfloor$
$b \leftarrow$ zero initialized vector of length $\left\lfloor \frac{p}{2} \right\rfloor$
for $\{i = 0, 1, \cdots, T-1\}$ **do**
    $x^{(i)} \leftarrow$ ciphertext encrypted with the error vector $e^{(i)}$
    Divide $e^{(i)}$ as $\left[e_0^{(i)}, \cdots, e_{n_0-1}^{(i)} \right]$, where each $e_j^{(i)}$ has length p
    $\Delta(e_{n_0-1}^{(i)}) \leftarrow$ distance spectrum of $e_{n_0-1}^{(i)}$
    for $\left\{ d \in \Delta \left(e_{n_0-1}^{(i)} \right) \right\}$ **do**
       $b_d \leftarrow b_d + 1$
       $a_d \leftarrow a_d + \Im^{(i)}$
    end for
end for

---

in order to obtain a matrix $H^* = \left[H_0^*, H_1^*, \cdots, H_{n_0-1}^* \right] = \Pi H$. This matrix can be used to efficiently decode the intercepted ciphertexts, since:

$$xH^{*T} = eH^T \Pi^T = s^T \Pi^T = s^{*T}. \tag{12}$$

Applying a decoding algorithm on s^{*T}, with the parity-check matrix H^*, will return e as output. The corresponding plaintext can then be easily recovered by considering the first k positions of $x + e$.

As mentioned in Sect. 3.1, the complexity of solving the DSR problem can be neglected, which means that the complexity of the GJS attack can be approximated with the one of Algorithm 1. First of all, we denote as $C_{\texttt{dist}}$ the number of operations that the opponent must perform, for each decryption query, in order to compute the distance spectrum of $e^{(i)}$ and update the estimates a and b. The p-bit block $e_{n_0-1}^{(i)}$ can have weight between 0 and t; let us suppose that its weight is t_p, which occurs with probability

$$p_{t_p} = \frac{\binom{p}{t_p}\binom{n-p}{t-t_p}}{\binom{n}{t}}. \tag{13}$$

We can assume that in e_{n_0-1} there are no distances with multiplicity ≥ 2 (this is reasonable when e is sparse). The average number of distances in e_{n_0-1} can thus be estimated as $\sum_{t_p=0}^{t} p_{t_p} \binom{t_p}{2}$, which also gives the number of operations needed to obtain the spectrum of e_{n_0-1}. Each of these distances is associated to two additional operations: the update of b, which is performed for each decryption query, and the update of a, which is performed only in the case of a decryption failure. Thus, if we denote as ϵ the DFR of the system and as $C_{\texttt{enc}}$ and $C_{\texttt{dec}}$ the complexities of one encryption and one decryption, respectively, the average complexity of each decryption query can be estimated as:

$$C_q = C_{\texttt{enc}} + C_{\texttt{dec}} + (2 + \epsilon) \sum_{t_p=0}^{t} p_{t_p} \binom{t_p}{2}. \tag{14}$$

Thus, the complexity of the attack, in terms of work factor, can be estimated as:

$$WF_{\text{GJS}} \approx T\,C_q = T\left[C_{\text{enc}} + C_{\text{dec}} + (2+\epsilon)\sum_{t_p=0}^{t} p_{t_p}\binom{t_p}{2}\right]. \tag{15}$$

3.3   FHS$^+$ Attack

More recently, a reaction attack specifically tailored to QC-LDPC code-based systems has been proposed in [11], and takes into account the effect of the matrix Q. We refer to this attack as the FHS$^+$ attack. The collection phase in the FHS$^+$ attack is performed through Algorithm 2. We point out that we consider a slightly different (and improved) version of the attack in [11].

Algorithm 2. FHS$^+$ distance spectrum recovery

$a \leftarrow$ zero initialized vector of length $\left\lfloor\frac{p}{2}\right\rfloor$
$b \leftarrow$ zero initialized vector of length $\left\lfloor\frac{p}{2}\right\rfloor$
$u \leftarrow$ zero initialized vector of length $\left\lfloor\frac{p}{2}\right\rfloor$
$v \leftarrow$ zero initialized vector of length $\left\lfloor\frac{p}{2}\right\rfloor$
for $\{i = 0, 1, \cdots, T-1\}$ **do**
    $x^{(i)} \leftarrow$ ciphertext encrypted with the error vector $e^{(i)}$
    for $\{j = 0, 1, \cdots, n_0-1\}$ **do**
        Divide $e^{(i)}$ as $\left[e_0^{(i)}, \cdots, e_{n_0-1}^{(i)}\right]$, where each $e_j^{(i)}$ has length p
        $\Delta\left(e_j^{(i)}\right) \leftarrow$ distance spectrum of $e_j^{(i)}$
    end for
    $\Delta\left(e^{(i)}\right) = \bigcup_{j=0}^{n_0-1}\Delta\left(e_j^{(i)}\right)$
    for $\left\{d \in \Delta\left(e^{(i)}\right)\right\}$ **do**
        $b_d \leftarrow b_d + 1$
        $a_d \leftarrow a_d + \Im^{(i)}$
    end for
    for $\left\{d \in \Delta\left(e_{n_0-1}^{(i)}\right)\right\}$ **do**
        $v_d \leftarrow v_d + 1$
        $u_d \leftarrow u_d + \Im^{(i)}$
    end for
end for

As in the GJS attack, the estimates $\frac{a_d}{b_d}$ are then used by the opponent to guess the distances appearing in the blocks of H. In particular, every block $e_j^{(i)}$ gets multiplied by all the blocks H_j, so the analysis based on $\frac{a_d}{b_d}$ reveals $\Delta(H) = \bigcup_{j=0}^{n_0-1}\Delta(H_j)$. In the same way, the estimates $\frac{u_d}{v_d}$ are used to guess the distances appearing in the blocks belonging to the last block row of Q^T. Indeed, the block $e_{n_0-1}^{(i)}$ gets multiplied by all the blocks Q_{j,n_0-1}^T. Since a circulant matrix and its transpose share the same distance spectrum, the opponent is indeed guessing distances in the first block column of Q. In other words, the analysis based on $\frac{u_d}{v_d}$ reveals $\Delta(Q) = \bigcup_{j=0}^{n_0-1} \Delta(Q_{j,n_0-1})$.

The opponent must then solve two instances of the DSDR problem in order to obtain candidates for H_j and Q_{j,n_0-1}, for $j = 0, 1, \cdots, n_0 - 1$. As described in Sect. 3.1, we can conservatively suppose that the solution of the DSDR problem for $\Delta(H)$ is represented by two sets $\Gamma_h^* = \left\{ \Theta_h^{*(0)}, \cdots, \Theta_h^{*(n_0-1)} \right\}$ and $\Gamma_h' = \left\{ \Theta_h'^{(0)}, \cdots, \Theta_h'^{(n_0-1)} \right\}$, with each couple $\left\{ \Theta_h^{*(j)}, \Theta_h'^{(j)} \right\}$ satisfying (9). Each solution $\Theta^{*(j)}$ (as well as the corresponding $\Theta'^{(j)}$) represents a candidate for one of the blocks in H, up to a cyclic shift. In addition, we must also consider that the opponent has no information about the correspondence between cliques in the graph and blocks in H: in other words, even if the opponent correctly guesses all the circulant blocks of H, he does not know their order and hence must consider all their possible permutations. Considering the well-known isomorphism between $p \times p$ binary circulant matrices and polynomials in $GF_2[x]/(x^p + 1)$, the matrix H can be expressed in polynomial form as:

$$H(x) = \left[x^{\alpha_0^{(h)}} h_{\pi^{(h)}(0)}(x), x^{\alpha_1^{(h)}} h_{\pi^{(h)}(1)}(x), \cdots, x^{\alpha_{n_0-1}^{(h)}} h_{\pi^{(h)}(n_0-1)}(x) \right], \quad (16)$$

with $\alpha_j^{(h)} \in [0, p-1]$, $\pi^{(h)}$ being a permutation of $\{0, 1, \cdots, n_0 - 1\}$ (so that $\pi^{(h)}(j)$ denotes the position of the element j in $\pi^{(h)}$), and each $h_j(x)$ is the polynomial associated to the support $\Theta_h^{*(j)}$ or $\Theta_h'^{(j)}$. In the same way, solving the DSDR problem for $\Delta(Q)$ gives the same number of candidates for the last column of Q, which are denoted as $q_{j,n_0-1}(x)$ in polynomial notation. This means that for the last column of $Q(x)$ we have an expression similar to (16), with n_0 coefficients $\alpha_j^{(q)} \in [0, p-1]$ and a permutation $\pi^{(q)}$. The opponent must then combine these candidates, in order to obtain candidates for the last block of the matrix $\tilde{H} = HQ$, which is denoted as $\tilde{h}_{n_0-1}(x)$ in polynomial form. Indeed, once $\tilde{h}_{n_0-1}(x)$ is known, the opponent can proceed as in the GJS attack for recovering $\tilde{H}$. Taking into account that $\tilde{H} = HQ$, the polynomial $\tilde{h}_{n_0-1}(x)$ can be expressed as:

$$\tilde{h}_{n_0-1}(x) = \sum_{j=0}^{n_0-1} x^{\alpha_j^{(h)}} h_{\pi^{(h)}(j)}(x) x^{\alpha_j^{(q)}} q_{\pi^{(q)}(j),n_0-1}(x). \quad (17)$$

Because of the commutative property of the addition, the opponent can look only for permutations of the polynomials $q_{j,n_0-1}(x)$. Then, (17) can be replaced by:

$$\tilde{h}_{n_0-1}(x) = \sum_{j=0}^{n_0-1} x^{\alpha_j^{(h)}} h_j(x) x^{\alpha_j^{(q)}} q_{\pi^{(q)}(j),n_0-1}(x), \quad (18)$$

which can be rearranged as:

$$\tilde{h}_{n_0-1}(x) = \sum_{j=0}^{n_0-1} x^{\alpha_j} h_j(x) q_{\pi^{(q)}(j),n_0-1}(x), \quad (19)$$

with $\alpha_j = \alpha_j^{(h)} + \alpha_j^{(q)}$ mod p. Since whichever row-permuted version of $\tilde{H}$ can be used to decode intercepted ciphertexts, we can write:

$$\tilde{h}'_{n_0-1}(x) = x^{-\alpha_0} \tilde{h}_{n_0-1}(x)$$

$$= x^{-\alpha_0} \sum_{j=0}^{n_0-1} x^{\alpha_j} h_j(x) q_{\pi^{(q)}(j),n_0-1}(x)$$

$$= \sum_{j=0}^{n_0-1} x^{\beta_j} h_j(x) q_{\pi^{(q)}(j),n_0-1}(x), \tag{20}$$

with $\beta_0 = 0$ and $\beta_j \in \{0, 1, \cdots, p-1\}$.

We must now consider the fact that, in the case of blocks Q_{j,n_0-1} having weight ≤ 2 (we suppose that the weights of the blocks H_j are all > 2), the number of candidates for $\tilde{h}'_{n_0-1}(x)$ is reduced. Indeed, let us suppose that there are $n^{(2)}$ and $n^{(1)}$ blocks $Q_{j,n_0-1}(x)$ with weights 2 and 1, respectively. Let us also suppose that there is no null block in Q. These assumptions are often verified for the parameter choices we consider. For blocks with weight 1 there is no distance to guess, which means that the associated polynomial is just $x^0 = 1$. In the case of a block with weight 2, the two possible candidates are in the form $x^0 + x^d$ and $x^0 + x^{p-d}$. However, since $x^0 + x^d = x^d\left(x^0 + x^{p-d}\right)$, the opponent can consider only one of the two solutions defined by (9).

Hence, the number of possible choices for the polynomials $h_j(x)$ and $q_{j,0}(x)$ in (20) is equal to $2^{2n_0-n^{(2)}-n^{(1)}}$. In addition, the presence of blocks with weight 1 reduces the number of independent configurations of $\pi^{(q)}$: if we look at (18), it is clear that any two permutations $\pi_1^{(q)}$ and $\pi_2^{(q)}$ that differ only in the positions of the polynomials with weight 1 lead to two identical sets of candidates. Based on these considerations, we can compute the number of different candidates in (20) as:

$$N_c = \frac{n_0!}{n^{(1)}!} 2^{2n_0-n^{(1)}-n^{(2)}} p^{n_0-1}. \tag{21}$$

The complexity for computing each of these candidates is low: indeed, the computations in (20) involve sparse polynomials, and so they require a small number of operations. For this reason, we neglect the complexity of this step in the computation of the attack work factor. After computing each candidate, the opponent has to compute the remaining polynomials forming $\tilde{H}(x)$ through multiplications by the polynomials appearing in the non-systematic part of the public key (see (3)). In fact, it is enough to multiply any candidate for $\tilde{h}_{n_0-1}(x)$ by the polynomials included in the non-systematic part of G' (see (3)). When the right candidate for $\tilde{h}_{n_0-1}(x)$ is tested, the polynomials resulting from such a multiplication will be sparse, with weight $\leq md_v$. The check on the weight can be initiated right after performing the first multiplication: if the weight of the first polynomial obtained is $> md_v$, then the candidate is discarded, otherwise the other polynomials are computed and tested. Thus, we can conservatively assume that for each candidate the opponent performs only one multiplication.

Considering fast polynomial multiplication algorithms, complexity can be estimated in $C_c = p \log_2(p)$. Neglecting the final check on the weights of the vectors obtained, the complexity of computing and checking each one of the candidates of $\tilde{h}_{n_0-1}(x)$ can be expressed as:

$$WF_{\text{FHS+}} \geq N_c C_c = 2^{2n_0 - n^{(1)} - n^{(2)}} \frac{n_0!}{n^{(1)}!} p^{n_0} \log_2(p). \tag{22}$$

The execution of Algorithm 2 has a complexity which can be estimated in a similar way as done for the GJS attack (see Eq. (15)). However, unless the DFR of the system is significantly low (such that T is in the order of the work factor expressed by (22)), collecting the required number of cyphertexts for the attack is negligible from the complexity standpoint [11], so (22) provides a (tight) lower bound on the complexity of the attack.

3.4   FHZ Attack

The FHZ attack has been proposed in [12], and is another attack procedure specifically tailored to QC-LDPC code-based systems. The attack starts from the assumption that the number of decryption queries to the oracle is properly bounded, such that the opponent cannot recover the spectrum of H (this is the design criterion followed by the authors of LEDApkc [4]). However, it may happen that such a bounded amount of ciphertexts is enough for recovering the spectrum of Q: in such a case, the opponent might succeed in reconstructing a shifted version of H, with the help of ISD. The distance spectrum recovery procedure for this attack is described in Algorithm 3.

Algorithm 3. FHZ distance spectrum recovery

---

for $\{j = 0, 1, \cdots, n_0 - 1\}$ **do**

  $a^{(j)} \leftarrow$ zero initialized vector of length $\lfloor \frac{p}{2} \rfloor$

  $b^{(j)} \leftarrow$ zero initialized vector of length $\lfloor \frac{p}{2} \rfloor$

end for

for $\{i = 0, 1, \cdots, M\}$ **do**

  $x^{(i)} \leftarrow$ ciphertext encrypted with the error vector $e^{(i)}$

  Divide $e^{(i)}$ as $\left[e_0^{(i)}, \cdots, e_{n_0-1}^{(i)} \right]$, where each $e_j^{(i)}$ has length p

  for $\{j = 0, 1, \cdots, n_0 - 1\}$ **do**

    $\Delta\left(e_j^{(i)} \right) \leftarrow$ distance spectrum of $e_j^{(i)}$

    for $\left\{ d \in \Delta\left(e_j^{(i)} \right) \right\}$ **do**

      $b_d^{(j)} \leftarrow b_d + 1$

      $a_d^{(j)} \leftarrow a_d + \Im^{(i)}$

    end for

  end for

end for

The estimates $\frac{a_d^{(i)}}{b_d^{(i)}}$ are then used to guess distances in $\bigcup_{j=0}^{n_0-1} \Delta(Q_{j,i})$; solving the related DSDR problems gives the opponent proper candidates for the blocks of Q. These candidates can then be used to build sets of candidates for Q^T, which will be in the form:

$$Q^T(x) = \begin{bmatrix} x^{\alpha_0}\tilde{q}_0(x) & x^{\alpha_{n_0}}\tilde{q}_{n_0}(x) & \cdots & x^{\alpha_{n_0(n_0-1)}}\tilde{q}_{n_0(n_0-1)}(x) \\ x^{\alpha_1}\tilde{q}_1(x) & x^{\alpha_{n_0+1}}\tilde{q}_{n_0+1}(x) & \cdots & x^{\alpha_{n_0(n_0-1)+1}}\tilde{q}_{n_0(n_0-1)+1}(x) \\ \vdots & \vdots & \ddots & \vdots \\ x^{\alpha_{n_0-1}}\tilde{q}_{n_0-1}(x) & x^{\alpha_{2n_0-1}}\tilde{q}_{2n_0-1}(x) & \cdots & x^{\alpha_{n_0^2-1}}\tilde{q}_{n_0^2-1}(x) \end{bmatrix},$$

(23)

where each polynomial $\tilde{q}_j(x)$ is obtained through the solution of the DSDR problem (in order to ease the notation, the polynomial entries of $Q^T(x)$ in (23) have been put in sequential order, such that we can use only one subscript to denote each of them). Let us denote as $\bar{m} = [m_0, m_1, \cdots, m_{n_0-1}]$ the sequence of weights defining the first row of $w(Q)$, as explained in Sect. 2. The solutions of the DSDR problem for the first row of Q^T will then give two polynomials for each weight. The number of candidates for $Q^T(x)$ depends on the distribution of the weights in $\bar{m}$: let us consider, for the sake of simplicity, the case of $m_0 = m_1$, while all the other weights in $\bar{m}$ are distinct. In this situation, the graph associated to the DSDR problem will contain (at least) two couples of cliques with size $m_0 = m_1$ (see Sect. 3.1). For the sake of simplicity, let us look at the first row of $Q^T(x)$: in such a case, the solution is represented by the sets $\Gamma^{(1)} = \{\Theta^{*(1)}, \Theta'^{(1)}\}$ and $\Gamma^{(2)} = \{\Theta^{*(2)}, \Theta'^{(2)}\}$, where each couple of cliques $\Theta^{*(i)}$ and $\Theta'^{(i)}$ is described by (9). In order to construct a candidate for $Q^T(x)$, as in (23), the opponent must guess whether $\Gamma^{(1)}$ is associated to $\tilde{q}_0(x)$ (and $\Gamma^{(2)}$ is associated to $\tilde{q}_{n_0}(x)$) or to $\tilde{q}_1(x)$; then, he must pick one clique from each $\Gamma^{(i)}$. The number of candidates for the first row of $Q^T(x)$ is hence $2^{n_0}2! = 2^{n_0}2$. Since there are n_0 rows, the number of possible choices for the polynomials in (23) is then equal to $(2!)^{n_0}2^{n_0^2} = 2^{n_0}2^{n_0^2}$. If we have $m_0 = m_1 = m_2$, then this number is equal to $(3!)^{n_0}2^{n_0^2}$. In order to generalize this reasoning, we can suppose that $\bar{m}$ contains z distinct integers $\hat{m}_0, \hat{m}_1, \cdots, \hat{m}_{z-1}$, with multiplicities $j_0, j_1, \cdots, j_{z-1}$, that is:

$$j_i = \#_l\{m_l = \hat{m}_i\}.$$

(24)

Thus, also taking into account the fact that for polynomials with weight ≤ 2 we have only one candidate (instead of 2), the number of different choices for the entries of $Q^T(x)$ in (23) can be computed as:

$$N_Q = 2^{n_0^2 - n_0 n^{(2)} - n_0 n^{(1)}} \left[\prod_{\substack{i=0 \\ \hat{m}_i \geq 2}}^{z} j_i! \right]^{n_0},$$

(25)

with $n^{(2)}$ and $n^{(1)}$ being the number of entries of $\bar{m}$ that are equal to 2 and 1, respectively. Considering (23), the i-th row of Q^T can be expressed as $\bar{q}_i(x)S_i(x)$, with:

$$\bar{q}_i(x) = \left[\tilde{q}_i(x), \tilde{q}_{n_0+i}(x), \cdots, \tilde{q}_{n_0(n_0-1)+i}(x) \right],$$

(26)

and $S_i(x)$ being a diagonal matrix:

$$S_i(x) = \begin{bmatrix} x^{\alpha_i} & & & & \\ & x^{\alpha_{n_0+1+i}} & & & \\ & & x^{\alpha_{2n_0+3+i}} & & \\ & & & \ddots & \\ & & & & x^{\alpha_{n_0(n_0-1)+i}} \end{bmatrix}. \tag{27}$$

Let $G'(x)$ denote the public key; then, the matrix $G''(x) = G'(x)Q^T(x)$ is a generator matrix of the secret code. In particular, we have:

$$G''(x) = G'(x)Q^T(x) =$$

$$= \begin{bmatrix} 1 & & & & g_0(x) \\ & 1 & & & g_1(x) \\ & & \ddots & & \vdots \\ & & & 1 & g_{n_0-2}(x) \end{bmatrix} \cdot \begin{bmatrix} \bar{q}_0(x)S_0(x) \\ \bar{q}_1(x)S_1(x) \\ \vdots \\ \bar{q}_{n_0-1}(x)S_{n_0-1}(x) \end{bmatrix}$$

$$= \begin{bmatrix} \bar{q}_0(x)S_0(x) + g_0(x)\bar{q}_{n_0-1}(x)S_{n_0-1}(x) \\ \bar{q}_1(x)S_1(x) + g_1(x)\bar{q}_{n_0-1}(x)S_{n_0-1}(x) \\ \vdots \\ \bar{q}_{n_0-2}(x)S_{n_0-2}(x) + g_{n_0-2}(x)\bar{q}_{n_0-1}(x)S_{n_0-1}(x) \end{bmatrix}, \tag{28}$$

where $g_i(x)$ denotes the polynomial representation of the circulant obtained as $\left(\tilde{H}_{n_0-1}\tilde{H}_i\right)^T$. The multiplication of every row of $G''(x)$ by whichever polynomial returns a matrix which generates the same code as $G''(x)$. In particular, we can multiply the first row of $G''(x)$ by $x^{-\alpha_0}$, the second row by $x^{-\alpha_1}$, and so on. The resulting matrix can then be expressed as:

$$G(x) = \begin{bmatrix} x^{-\alpha_0} & & & \\ & x^{-\alpha_1} & & \\ & & \ddots & \\ & & & x^{-\alpha_{n_0-2}} \end{bmatrix} G''(x)$$

$$= \begin{bmatrix} x^{-\alpha_0}\left[\bar{q}_0(x)S_0(x) + g_0(x)\bar{q}_{n_0-1}(x)S_{n_0-1}(x)\right] \\ x^{-\alpha_1}\left[\bar{q}_1(x)S_1(x) + g_1(x)\bar{q}_{n_0-1}(x)S_{n_0-1}(x)\right] \\ \vdots \\ x^{-\alpha_{n_0-2}}\left[\bar{q}_{n_0-2}(x)S_{n_0-2}(x) + g_{n_0-2}(x)\bar{q}_{n_0-1}(x)S_{n_0-1}(x)\right] \end{bmatrix}. \tag{29}$$

Taking into account (27), we can define:

$$S_i^*(x) = x^{-\alpha_i}S_i(x)$$

$$= \begin{bmatrix} 1 & & & & \\ & x^{\alpha_{n_0+1+i}-\alpha_i} & & & \\ & & x^{\alpha_{2n_0+3+i}-\alpha_i} & & \\ & & & \ddots & \\ & & & & x^{\alpha_{n_0(n_0-1)+i}-\alpha_i} \end{bmatrix}, \tag{30}$$

which holds for $i \leq n_0 - 2$. We can now express $G(x)$ as:

$$G(x) = \begin{bmatrix} \bar{q}_0(x)S_0^*(x) + g_0(x)\bar{q}_{n_0-1}(x)x^{-\alpha_0}S_{n_0-1}(x) \\ \bar{q}_1(x)S_1^*(x) + g_1(x)\bar{q}_{n_0-1}(x)x^{-\alpha_1}S_{n_0-1}(x) \\ \vdots \\ \bar{q}_{n_0-2}(x)S_{n_0-2}^*(x) + g_{n_0-2}(x)\bar{q}_{n_0-1}(x)x^{-\alpha_{n_0-1}}S_{n_0-1}(x) \end{bmatrix}. \tag{31}$$

As anticipated, $G(x)$ is a generator matrix for the secret code, which means that it admits $H(x)$ as a corresponding sparse parity-check matrix. Then, any row of the binary matrix corresponding to $[h_0(x), h_1(x), \cdots, h_{n_0-1}(x)]$ is a low-weight codeword in the dual of the code generated by $G(x)$. Thus, an opponent can apply an ISD algorithm to search for vectors with weight $n_0 d_v$, denoted as $\bar{v}(x)$ in polynomial notation, such that $G(x)\bar{v}^T(x) = 0$. Finding one of these vectors results in determining a row of the secret parity-check matrix.

For every non-singular matrix $A(x)$, we can define $G^*(x) = G(x)A(x)$ and $\bar{w}(x) = \bar{v}(x)A^{-T}(x)$, such that:

$$\begin{aligned} G^*(x)\bar{w}^T(x) &= G(x)A(x)\bar{w}^T(x) \\ &= G(x)A(x)A^{-1}(x)\bar{v}^T(x) \\ &= G(x)\bar{v}^T(x) = 0. \end{aligned} \tag{32}$$

The opponent can apply ISD on $G^*(x)$, searching for solutions $\bar{w}(x)$, and then obtain the corresponding vectors $\bar{v}(x)$ as $\bar{v}(x) = \bar{w}(x)A^T(x)$. In particular, he can choose $A(x) = S_0^{*-1}(x)$, that is:

$$A(x) = \begin{bmatrix} 1 & & & & \\ & x^{\alpha_0 - \alpha_{n_0}+1} & & & \\ & & x^{\alpha_0 - \alpha_{2n_0}+3} & & \\ & & & \ddots & \\ & & & & x^{\alpha_0 - \alpha_{n_0(n_0-1)}} \end{bmatrix}. \tag{33}$$

Let us denote as $\bar{g}_i^*(x)$ the i-th row of $G^*(x)$, and as $\bar{g}_i(x)$ the i-th row of $G(x)$; we have:

$$\bar{g}_i^*(x) = \bar{g}_i(x)A(x), \tag{34}$$

which can be expressed as:

$$\bar{g}_i^*(x) = \left[\bar{q}_i(x)S_i^*(x) + g_i(x)\bar{q}_{n_0-1}(x)x^{-\alpha_i}S_{n_0-1}(x)\right]S_0^{*-1}(x). \tag{35}$$

For the first row of $G^*(x)$ (i.e., $i = 0$), we have:

$$\begin{aligned} \bar{g}_0^*(x) &= \left[\bar{q}_0(x)S_0^*(x) + g_0(x)\bar{q}_{n_0-1}(x)x^{-\alpha_0}S_{n_0-1}(x)\right]S_0^{*-1}(x) \\ &= \bar{q}_0(x) + g_0(x)\bar{q}_{n_0-1}(x)x^{-\alpha_0}S_{n_0-1}(x)S_0^{*-1}(x) \\ &= \bar{q}_0(x) + g_0(x)\bar{q}_{n_0-1}(x)D(x), \end{aligned} \tag{36}$$

with $D(x) = x^{-\alpha_0}S_{n_0-1}(x)S_0^{*-1}(x)$ being a diagonal matrix with monomial entries only. Once the polynomials $\bar{q}_0(x)$ and $\bar{q}_{n_0-1}$ have been picked, $\bar{g}_0^*(x)$

depends only on the values of the matrix $D(x)$. This results in p^{n_0} possible different candidates for $\bar{g}_0^*(x)$.

We can now look at the other rows of G; in general, the i-th row (with $i \geq 1$) is in the form:

$$
\begin{aligned}
\bar{g}_i^*(x) &= \left[\bar{q}_i(x)S_i^*(x) + g_i(x)\bar{q}_{n_0-1}(x)x^{-\alpha_i}S_{n_0-1}(x)\right]S_0^{*-1}(x) \\
&= \bar{q}_i(x)S_i^*(x)S_0^{*-1}(x) + g_i(x)\bar{q}_{n_0-1}(x)x^{-\alpha_i}S_{n_0-1}(x)S_0^{*-1}(x) \\
&= \bar{q}_i(x)S_i^*(x)S_0^{*-1}(x) + g_i(x)\bar{q}_{n_0-1}(x)x^{\alpha_0-\alpha_i}D(x). \qquad (37)
\end{aligned}
$$

From (37) we see that the row $\bar{g}_i^*(x)$ is defined by n_0 independent parameters: indeed, $S_i^*(x)S_0^{*-1}(x)$ always has the first element equal to 1, with all the other $n_0 - 1$ ones taking values in $[0, p-1]$, while the only other additional degree of freedom comes from the choice of $(\alpha_0 - \alpha_i) \in [0, p-1]$.

Based on the above considerations, we can finally obtain the total number of candidates for $G^*(x)$: starting from a choice of polynomials $\tilde{q}_0(x), \cdots, \tilde{q}_{n_0^2-1}(x)$, the opponent has p^{n_0} independent possible choices for each row of $G^*(x)$. Since the matrix has $n_0 - 1$ rows, the total number of candidates for $G^*(x)$ is then equal to:

$$
N_G = (p^{n_0})^{n_0-1} = p^{n_0^2-n_0}. \qquad (38)
$$

For each candidate of $G^*(x)$, the opponent performs ISD, searching for vectors $\bar{w}(x)$. Since $A(x)$ is a permutation, the weight of $\bar{w}(x)$ is equal to that of $\bar{v}(x)$. Thus, the complexity of this last step is equal to that of ISD running on a code with length $n = n_0 p$, dimension p (the opponent attacks the dual of the code generated by $G^*(x)$), searching for a codeword with weight $n_0 d_v$, and can be denoted as $C_{\text{ISD}}(n_0 p, p, n_0 d_v)$.

As for the FHS$^+$ attack, unless the DFR of the system is significantly low, we can neglect the complexity of Algorithm 3, and estimate the complexity of the FHZ attack as:

$$
WF_{\text{FHZ}} = N_Q N_G C_{\text{ISD}}(n_0 p, p, n_0 d_v), \qquad (39)
$$

where N_Q and N_G are given by (25) and (38), respectively.

4   Efficiency of Reaction Attacks

In the previous sections we have described reaction attacks against QC-MDPC and QC-LDPC code-based McEliece cryptosystems. In particular, we have computed the number of candidates an opponent has to consider for general choices of the system parameters, and devised tight complexity estimations. Based on the analysis developed in the previous sections, in this section we study and compare the efficiency of all the aforementioned attack procedures. First of all, we must consider the fact that the GJS attack can be applied to a QC-LDPC code-based cryptosystem as well, on condition that Q-decoding is used for decryption. In fact, as explained in Sect. 2.4, the Q-decoder approximates a BF decoder working in $\tilde{H}$, therefore an attacker could focus on $\tilde{H}$ as the target of a reaction attack.

Based on this consideration, we can expect the GJS attack to be successful when Q-decoding is used: in such a case, the recovered distance spectrum is that of $\tilde{H}_{n_0-1}$ (see Eq. (2)). In order to verify this intuition, we have simulated the attack on a code with parameters $n_0 = 2$, $p = 4801$, $d_v = 9$, $m = 5$. The corresponding estimates $\frac{a_d}{b_d}$, obtained through Algorithm 1, are shown in Fig. 1. As we can see from the figure, the distances tend to group into distinct bands, depending on the associated multiplicity in the spectrum. In this case, the opponent can reconstruct the matrix $\tilde{H}_{n_0-1}$ by solving the related DSR problem, searching for cliques of size $\leq md_v$.

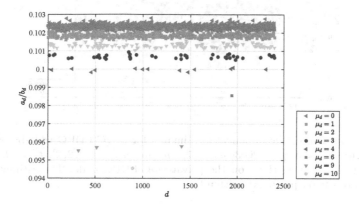

Fig. 1. Distribution of the opponent's estimates for a QC-LDPC code-based system instance with $n_0 = 2$, $p = 4801$, $d_v = 9$, $[m_0, m_1] = [2,3]$, $t = 95$, decoded through the Q-decoder. The estimates a_d/b_d correspond to the output of Algorithm 1.

Instead, the same attack cannot be applied against a QC-LDPC code-based system instance if BF decoding working on the private code is exploited. In order to justify this fact, let us consider the generic expression of a block of $\tilde{H}$, say the first one:

$$\tilde{h}_0(x) = \sum_{j=0}^{n_0-1} q_{j,0}(x)h_j(x) = \sum_{j=0}^{n_0-1} a_j(x), \qquad (40)$$

with $a_j = q_{j,0}(x)h_j(x)$. Each $a_j(x)$ can be seen as a sum of replicas of $h_j(x)$ (resp. $q_{j,0}(x)$) placed at positions depending on $q_{j,0}(x)$ (resp. $h_j(x)$). Since all these polynomials are sparse, the expected number of cancellations occurring in such a sum is small. This means that, with high probability, distances in $q_{j,0}(x)$ or $h_j(x)$ are present also in $a_j(x)$. Since the BF decoder performance depends on distances in both H and Q, the opponent can correctly identify these distances by analyzing Bob's reactions. However, the spectrum of $\tilde{h}_0(x)$ also contains a new set of *inter-block* distances, i.e., distances formed by one entry of $a_i(x)$ and one entry of $a_j(x)$, with $i \neq j$. These distances cannot be revealed by the opponent, because they do not affect the decoding performance when a BF decoder working on the private code is used. To confirm this statement, an example of the opponent estimates, obtained though Algorithm 1 for a QC-LDPC code-based system instance exploiting BF decoding over the private QC-LDPC code, is shown in Fig. 2. From the figure we notice that, differently from the previous case, the two sets of distances are indistinguishable.

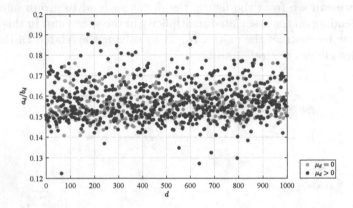

Fig. 2. Distribution of the opponent's estimates for a QC-LDPC code-based system instance with $n_0 = 3$, $p = 2003$, $d_v = 7$, $[m_0, m_1, m_2] = [3, 2, 2]$, $t = 12$, decoded through BF decoding working on the private QC-LDPC code. The estimates a_d/b_d correspond to the output of Algorithm 1.

We can now sum up all the results regarding reaction attacks against the considered systems, and this is done in Table 1, where the applicability of each attack against each of the considered systems is summarized, together with the relevant complexity.

Table 1. Applicability of reaction attacks, for different McEliece variants

Attack	Complexity	QC-MDPC	QC-LDPC (Q-decoder)	QC-LDPC (BF decoder)
GJS	Eq. (15)	✓	✓	✗
FHS⁺	Eq. (22)	✗	✓	✓
FHZ	Eq. (39)	✗	✓	✓

The QC-MDPC code-based system and the QC-LDPC code-based system with Q-decoding are both exposed to the GJS attack. For these systems, such an attack can be avoided only by achieving sufficiently low DFR values, which is a solution that obviously prevents all reaction attacks. Another solution consists in properly bounding the lifetime of a key-pair, which means that the same key-pair is used only for a limited amount of encryptions/decryptions, before being discarded. Basically, this is equivalent to assume that the opponent can only exploit a bounded number of decryption queries. The most conservative choice

Table 2. Sets of parameters of QC-LDPC code-based system instances using BF decoding on the private code and achieving a security level of 2^{80} or more against FHS$^+$, FHZ and ISD based attacks.

n_0	d_v	p	$\bar{m}$	t
5	9	8539	$[3, 3, 2, 2, 1]$	38
5	9	7549	$[3, 2, 2, 1, 1]$	37
6	9	5557	$[3, 2, 1, 1, 1, 1]$	34
6	11	5417	$[2, 1, 1, 1, 1, 1]$	34

Table 3. Sets of parameters of QC-LDPC code-based system instances using BF decoding on the private code and achieving a security level of 2^{128} or more against FHS$^+$, FHZ and ISD based attacks.

n_0	d_v	p	$\bar{m}$	t
8	9	13367	$[2, 2, 2, 2, 2, 1, 1, 1]$	45
8	11	14323	$[2, 2, 2, 2, 2, 1, 1, 1]$	44
9	9	10657	$[2, 2, 1, 1, 1, 1, 1, 1, 1]$	42
9	11	11597	$[2, 2, 1, 1, 1, 1, 1, 1, 1]$	42

consists in using ephemeral keys, i.e., refreshing the key-pair after decrypting each ciphertext [1,5]. This choice allows avoiding reaction attacks of any type, but necessarily decreases the system efficiency. Relaxing this condition would obviously be welcome, but estimating a safe amount of observed ciphertexts might be a hard task. A less drastic but still quite conservative choice might be bounding the lifetime of a key-pair as DFR^{-1} (this means that, on average, the opponent has only one decryption query for each key-pair). Actually, recent proposals achieve DFR values in the order of 10^{-9} or less [5], resulting into very long lifetimes for a key-pair.

When we consider classical BF decoding in the QC-LDPC code-based system, the scenario is different. In such a case, for a non-negligible DFR, we have to consider the complexities of both FHS$^+$ and FHZ attacks. Since for both attacks we have a precise estimation of the complexity, we can choose proper parameters to achieve attack work factors that are above the target security level. In Tables 2 and 3 we provide some parameter choices able to guarantee that both reaction and ISD attacks have a complexity of at least 2^{80} and 2^{128} operations, respectively. We point out that, when n_0 increases, satisfying the conditions that ensure non-singularity of Q according to Sect. 2.1 is no longer possible. However, these conditions are sufficient but not necessary. This means that, in some cases, the generation of Q should be repeated, until a non-singular matrix is obtained. We point out that the use of the BF decoder obviously leads to an increase in the code length (with respect to the Q-decoder), and this is the price to pay for withstanding state-of-the-art reaction attacks.

5   Conclusion

In this paper we have analyzed recent reaction attacks against McEliece cryptosystems based on iteratively decoded codes. We have generalized the attack procedures for all possible system variants and parameter choices, and provided estimates for their complexity.

For QC-MDPC code-based systems, preventing reaction attacks requires achieving negligible DFR, and the same occurs for QC-LDPC code-based systems exploiting Q-decoding. However, in the case of QC-LDPC code-based systems, such attacks can be made infeasible by using the BF decoder and choosing proper parameters. This choice comes with the inevitable drawback of increasing the public key size, since the BF decoder is characterized by a worse performance than the Q-decoder.

In our analysis we have neglected the fact that, in all the attacks against QC-LDPC code-based systems using BF decoding, the opponent must solve instances of the DSDR problem. This problem can be made more difficult by appropriately choosing the distances in the spectrum of Q. In other words, we can choose the blocks of Q such that the union of the spectra $\bigcup_{j=0}^{n_0-1} (Q_{j,n_0-1})$ forms a clique having size larger than the maximum value appearing in $\bar{m}$. In this case, the number of solutions to the DSDR problem should be significantly increased. This, however, is left for future works.

Acknowledgment. The authors wish to thank Tomáš Fabšič for fruitful discussion about the FHZ attack.

References

1. Aragon, N., et al.: BIKE: Bit Flipping Key Encapsulation. NIST Post-Quantum Cryptography Project: First Round Candidate Algorithms, December 2017. http://bikesuite.org/
2. Baldi, M., Bodrato, M., Chiaraluce, F.: A new analysis of the McEliece cryptosystem based on QC-LDPC codes. In: Ostrovsky, R., De Prisco, R., Visconti, I. (eds.) SCN 2008. LNCS, vol. 5229, pp. 246–262. Springer, Heidelberg (2008). https://doi.org/10.1007/978-3-540-85855-3_17
3. Baldi, M., Santini, P., Cancellieri, G.: Post-quantum cryptography based on codes: state of the art and open challenges. In: 2017 AEIT International Annual Conference, pp. 1–6, September 2017
4. Baldi, M., Barenghi, A., Chiaraluce, F., Pelosi, G., Santini, P.: LEDApkc: Low dEnsity coDe-bAsed public key cryptosystem. NIST Post-Quantum Cryptography Project: First Round Candidate Algorithms, December 2017. https://www.ledacrypt.org/
5. Baldi, M., Barenghi, A., Chiaraluce, F., Pelosi, G., Santini, P.: LEDAkem: a post-quantum key encapsulation mechanism based on QC-LDPC codes. In: Lange, T., Steinwandt, R. (eds.) PQCrypto 2018. LNCS, vol. 10786, pp. 3–24. Springer, Cham (2018). https://doi.org/10.1007/978-3-319-79063-3_1
6. Baldi, M., Bianchi, M., Chiaraluce, F.: Security and complexity of the McEliece cryptosystem based on QC-LDPC codes. IET Inf. Secur. **7**(3), 212–220 (2012)

7. Becker, A., Joux, A., May, A., Meurer, A.: Decoding random binary linear codes in $2^{n/20}$: how $1 + 1 = 0$ improves information set decoding. In: Pointcheval, D., Johansson, T. (eds.) EUROCRYPT 2012. LNCS, vol. 7237, pp. 520–536. Springer, Heidelberg (2012). https://doi.org/10.1007/978-3-642-29011-4_31

8. Berlekamp, E., McEliece, R., van Tilborg, H.: On the inherent intractability of certain coding problems. IEEE Trans. Inf. Theory **24**(3), 384–386 (1978)

9. Bernstein, D.J.: Grover vs. McEliece. In: Sendrier, N. (ed.) PQCrypto 2010. LNCS, vol. 6061, pp. 73–80. Springer, Heidelberg (2010). https://doi.org/10.1007/978-3-642-12929-2_6

10. Eaton, E., Lequesne, M., Parent, A., Sendrier, N.: QC-MDPC: a timing attack and a CCA2 KEM. In: Lange, T., Steinwandt, R. (eds.) PQCrypto 2018. LNCS, vol. 10786, pp. 47–76. Springer, Cham (2018). https://doi.org/10.1007/978-3-319-79063-3_3

11. Fabšič, T., Hromada, V., Stankovski, P., Zajac, P., Guo, Q., Johansson, T.: A reaction attack on the QC-LDPC McEliece cryptosystem. In: Lange, T., Takagi, T. (eds.) PQCrypto 2017. LNCS, vol. 10346, pp. 51–68. Springer, Cham (2017). https://doi.org/10.1007/978-3-319-59879-6_4

12. Fabsic, T., Hromada, V., Zajac, P.: A reaction attack on LEDApkc. Cryptology ePrint Archive, Report 2018/140 (2018). https://eprint.iacr.org/2018/140

13. Gallager, R.G.: Low-Density Parity-Check Codes. MIT Press, Cambridge (1963)

14. Guo, Q., Johansson, T., Stankovski, P.: A key recovery attack on MDPC with CCA security using decoding errors. In: Cheon, J.H., Takagi, T. (eds.) ASIACRYPT 2016. LNCS, vol. 10031, pp. 789–815. Springer, Heidelberg (2016). https://doi.org/10.1007/978-3-662-53887-6_29

15. Kobara, K., Imai, H.: Semantically secure McEliece public-key cryptosystems - conversions for McEliece PKC. In: Kim, K. (ed.) PKC 2001. LNCS, vol. 1992, pp. 19–35. Springer, Heidelberg (2001). https://doi.org/10.1007/3-540-44586-2_2. citeseer.ist.psu.edu/kobara01semantically.html

16. May, A., Meurer, A., Thomae, E.: Decoding random linear codes in $\tilde{\mathcal{O}}(2^{0.054n})$. In: Lee, D.H., Wang, X. (eds.) ASIACRYPT 2011. LNCS, vol. 7073, pp. 107–124. Springer, Heidelberg (2011). https://doi.org/10.1007/978-3-642-25385-0_6

17. McEliece, R.J.: A public-key cryptosystem based on algebraic coding theory. DSN Progress Report, pp. 114–116 (1978)

18. Misoczki, R., Tillich, J.P., Sendrier, N., Barreto, P.S.L.M.: MDPC-McEliece: new McEliece variants from moderate density parity-check codes. In: 2013 IEEE International Symposium on Information Theory, pp. 2069–2073, July 2013

19. National Institute of Standards and Technology: Post-quantum crypto project, December 2016. http://csrc.nist.gov/groups/ST/post-quantum-crypto/

20. Prange, E.: The use of information sets in decoding cyclic codes. IRE Trans. Inf. Theory **8**(5), 5–9 (1962)

21. Shooshtari, M.K., Ahmadian-Attari, M., Johansson, T., Aref, M.R.: Cryptanalysis of McEliece cryptosystem variants based on quasi-cyclic low-density parity check codes. IET Inf. Secur. **10**(4), 194–202 (2016)

22. Stern, J.: A method for finding codewords of small weight. In: Cohen, G., Wolfmann, J. (eds.) Coding Theory 1988. LNCS, vol. 388, pp. 106–113. Springer, Heidelberg (1989). https://doi.org/10.1007/BFb0019850

Breaking the Hardness Assumption and IND-CPA Security of HQC Submitted to NIST PQC Project

Zhen Liu[1,2], Yanbin Pan[1,2(✉)], and Tianyuan Xie[1,2]

[1] Key Laboratory of Mathematics Mechanization, NCMIS,
Academy of Mathematics and Systems Science, Chinese Academy of Sciences,
Beijing 100190, China
panyanbin@amss.ac.cn
[2] School of Mathematical Sciences, University of Chinese Academy of Sciences,
Beijing 100049, China
{liuzhen16,xietianyuan15}@mails.ucas.ac.cn

Abstract. HQC (Hamming Quasi-Cyclic) cryptosystem, proposed by Aguilar Melchor *et al.*, is a code-based key encapsulation mechanism (KEM) running for standardization to NIST's competition in the category "post-quantum public key encryption scheme". The underlying hard mathematical problem of HQC is presented as the s-DQCSD (Decision Quasi-Cyclic Syndrome Decoding) problem, which refers to the question of distinguishing whether a given instance came from the s-QCSD distribution or the uniform distribution. Under the assumption that 2-DQCSD and 3-DQCSD are hard, HQC, viewed as a PKE scheme, is proven to be IND-CPA secure, and can be transformed into an IND-CCA2 secure KEM. However, in this paper, we are going to show that s-DQCSD problem is actually not intractable. More precisely, we can efficiently distinguish the s-QCSD distribution instances from the uniform distribution instances with at least a constant advantage. Furthermore, with a similar technique, we show that HQC can not attain IND-CPA security with all the proposed parameter sets.

Keywords: HQC · Coding theory · Post-quantum cryptography s-DQCSD problem · IND-CPA

1 Introduction

The classical public key schemes based on the number theoretical hard problem are severely threatened since the proposal of the remarkable quantum algorithm—Shor's algorithm [10,11]. If practical quantum computers were ever

This work was supported in part by the NNSF of China (No. 61572490, and No. 11471314), the National Center for Mathematics and Interdisciplinary Sciences, CAS.

J. Camenisch and P. Papadimitratos (Eds.): CANS 2018, LNCS 11124, pp. 344–356, 2018.
https://doi.org/10.1007/978-3-030-00434-7_17

built, many of our modern cryptosystems would be vulnerable to quantum attack. Therefore, more and more attentions have been drawn to the post quantum cryptography.

NIST initiated a process to solicit, evaluate, and standardize one or more quantum-resistant public-key cryptographic algorithms since 2016 [3]. It called for proposals of post quantum cryptosystems including public key encryption, digital signature and key encapsulation. In December of 2017, Round 1 submissions were published by NIST for public comment.

About thirty percent of the Round 1 submissions are code-based cryptosystems, which are believed to be quantum-attack resistant. It is well known that the first code-based cryptosystem was proposed by McEliece in 1978 [7], which disguises the binary Goppa codes that is easy to decode as a general linear code that seems hard to decode. Although McEliece cryptosystem is thought to be secure by now, its key size is very large. Therefore, many variants based on alternative codes have been proposed to pursue better efficiency and security, but have turned out to be flawed later.

HQC (Hamming Quasi-Cyclic) cryptosystem, proposed by Aguilar Melchor *et al.* [1], is a code-based key encapsulation mechanism (KEM) running for standardization to NIST's competition in the category "post-quantum public key encryption scheme". Its security relates to the hardness of syndrome decoding problem on some structured code [2,8]. More precisely, HQC employs a framework similar to Regev's scheme [9], and two types of codes: a random quasi-cyclic code to ensure the security and an efficiently decodable code to ensure the correctness of decryption.

To present a formal security proof, the underlying mathematical problem of HQC is summarized as the s-DQCSD (Decision Quasi-Cyclic Syndrome Decoding) problem, which refers to the question of distinguishing whether a given instance came from the s-QCSD distribution (See Definition 10 for more details) or the uniform distribution. Under the assumption that 2-DQCSD and 3-DQCSD are hard, HQC, viewed as a PKE scheme, is proven to be IND-CPA secure, and can be transformed into an IND-CCA2 secure KEM [4].

However, we are going to show that s-DQCSD problem is actually not intractable under the HQC setting. More precisely, we can efficiently distinguish the instances from s-QCSD distribution and the uniform distribution with advantage $1/2 - 1/2^s$. Taking 2-DQCSD problem as an example to explain our idea, we find that for the instance (h, y) from 2-QCSD distribution, the weight (mod 2) of h and the weight (mod 2) of y are not independent. They have some fixed relation, or in another word, the weight (mod 2) of h decides the weight (mod 2) of y. In contrast, for the instance (h, y) from the uniform distribution, the weight (mod 2) of h and the weight (mod 2) of y must be independent. By this observation, we can solve the 2-DQCSD problem by checking if the relation holds or not.

Furthermore, with a similar technique, we observe that the Hamming weight (mod 2) of the ciphertext depends on the weight (mod 2) of the message. By choosing two messages carefully, we can easily distinguish which message the given ciphertext comes from in the corresponding IND-CPA game, which implies that HQC can not attain IND-CPA security.

We have to point out that although the hardness assumption and the IND-CPA security do not hold for HQC, we can not recover the private key or recover the message without the private key by now. Furthermore, we also present some possible ways to make HQC resistant to our attack.

Roadmap. The remainder of the paper is organized as follows. First we present some notations and preliminaries on coding theory and cryptography in Sect. 2. Then we describe the HQC cryptosystem in Sect. 3, show that the hardness assumption does not hold for HQC in Sect. 4 and break the IND-CPA security of HQC in Sect. 5. Finally a short conclusion is given in Sect. 6.

2   Preliminaries

We denote by $\mathbb{Z}$ the ring of integers, by $\mathbb{F}_2$ the binary finite field, by $\mathbb{F}_2^n$ a vector space of dimension n over $\mathbb{F}_2$ for some positive $n \in \mathbb{Z}$, and by $\omega(v)$ the Hamming weight of a vector v, $i.e.$ the number of its non-zero coordinates.

Every element $v = (v_0, \cdots, v_{n-1}) \in \mathbb{F}_2^n$ can be interchangeably considered as row vector in $\mathbb{F}_2^n$ or polynomial in $\mathcal{R} = \mathbb{F}_2[x]/(x^n - 1)$ by the bijection from $(v_0, \cdots, v_{n-1})$ to $\sum_{i=0}^{n-1} v_i x^i$. Vectors/polynomials (resp. matrices) will be represented by lower-case (resp. upper-case) letters.

2.1   Coding Theory

For completeness, we will recall some basic definitions and properties about coding theory. Please see [1] for more details.

A linear code $\mathcal{C}$ of length n and dimension k is a linear subspace with dimension k of the vector space $\mathbb{F}_q^n$, where $\mathbb{F}_q$ is a finite field with q elements. In this paper, we will focus on $q = 2$. Elements of $\mathcal{C}$ are referred to as codewords, and the minimum distance of $\mathcal{C}$ is the minimum weight of any nonzero codeword. The code $\mathcal{C}$ is called an $[n, k, d]$ code.

We say that $G \in \mathbb{F}_2^{k \times n}$ is a generator matrix for the $[n, k, d]$ code $\mathcal{C}$ if

$$\mathcal{C} = \left\{ mG : for\ m \in \mathbb{F}_2^k \right\},$$

and $H \in \mathbb{F}_2^{(n-k) \times n}$ is a parity-check matrix for $\mathcal{C}$ if H is a generator matrix of the dual code $\mathcal{C}^\perp = \{v \in \mathbb{F}_2^n : \forall c \in \mathcal{C}, <c, v> = 0\}$.

We can construct new linear code from known linear codes, such as:

Definition 1 (Tensor Product Code). *Let $\mathcal{C}_1$ (resp. $\mathcal{C}_2$) be an $[n_1, k_1, d_1]$ (resp. $[n_2, k_2, d_2]$) linear code over $\mathbb{F}_2$ generated by $G_1 = (g_{ij}) \in \mathbb{F}_2^{k_1 \times n_1}$ (resp.*

$G_2 = (g'_{ij}) \in \mathbb{F}_2^{k_2 \times n_2})$. The tensor Product Code of C_1 and C_2, denoted by $C_1 \otimes C_2$, is generated by

$$
G_1 \otimes G_2 = \begin{bmatrix} g_{11}G_2 & g_{12}G_2 & \cdots & g_{1n_1}G_2 \\ g_{21}G_2 & g_{22}G_2 & \cdots & g_{2n_1}G_2 \\ \vdots & \vdots & \ddots & \vdots \\ g_{k_11}G_2 & g_{k_12}G_2 & \cdots & g_{k_1n_1}G_2 \end{bmatrix},
$$

where $C_1 \otimes C_2$ is an $[n_1 n_2, k_1 k_2, d_1 d_2]$ linear code.

2.2 Cyclic Code

A linear code C is called cyclic if every cyclic shift of a codeword in C is also a codeword; namely, if $(v_0, \cdots, v_{n-1}) \in C$, then $(v_{n-1}, v_0, \cdots, v_{n-2}) \in C$.

A cyclic code C over $\mathbb{F}_2$ can also be viewed as an ideal which is principal in $\mathcal{R} = \mathbb{F}_2[x]/(x^n - 1)$, since for any vector $v = (v_0, \cdots, v_{n-1}) \in \mathbb{F}_2^n$, we can map it to the polynomial $\sum_{i=0}^{n-1} v_i x^i \in \mathcal{R}$ and the multiplication by x in $\mathcal{R}$ corresponds to a cyclic shift of a codeword. Hence a cyclic code C can be written as $C = \langle g(x) \rangle$, where $g(x)$ is called the generator polynomial of C.

BCH code is an important class of cyclic codes. The binary BCH code C over $\mathbb{F}_2$ has the following parameters: the length $n = 2^m - 1$, where m is any positive integer greater than two; the minimum distance d which is capable of decoding arbitrary patterns of up to $\delta = \lfloor \frac{d-1}{2} \rfloor$ errors of C; the number of parity-check digits is $n - k \le m\delta$ and k is the number of information bits. We can construct BCH code as below. Let α be a primitive element of $\mathbb{F}_{2^m}$. For any positive integer i, let $m_i(x)$ be the minimal polynomial of α^i over $\mathbb{F}_2$. The generator polynomial of the BCH code is defined as the least common multiple

$$
g(x) = lcm(m_1(x), \cdots, m_{2\delta}(x)).
$$

We denote this code by $[n, k, \delta]$.

From cyclic code, we can construct shorten cyclic code.

Definition 2 (Shorten Cyclic Code [6]**).** *Given an $[n, k, \delta]$ cyclic code C, consider the set of code vectors for which the l leading high-order information digits are identical to zero. There are 2^{k-l} such code vectors and they form a linear subcode of C, if the l zero information digits are deleted of these code vectors, we obtain a set of 2^{k-l} vectors of length $n-l$. These 2^{k-l} shorten vectors form an $[n - l, k - l]$ linear code, this code is called a shortened cyclic code.*

We can also generalize the cyclic code to a quasi-cyclic code.

Definition 3 (Quasi-Cyclic Codes). *View a vector $c = (c_1, c_2, \cdots, c_s)$ of $\mathbb{F}_2^{sn}$ as successive blocks(n-tuple). An $[sn, k, d]$ linear code C is Quasi-Cyclic (QC) of index s, if for any $c = (c_1, c_2, \cdots, c_s) \in C$, the vector obtained after applying a simultaneous circular shift to every block $c_1, c_2, \cdots, c_s$ is also a codeword. More formally, by considering each block c_i as a polynomial in $\mathcal{R}$, the code C is Quasi-Cyclic of index s if for any $c = (c_1, c_2, \cdots, c_s) \in C$ it holds that $(x \cdot c_1, \cdots, x \cdot c_s) \in C$.*

Definition 4 (Systematic Quasi-Cyclic Codes). *A systematic Quasi-Cyclic* $[sn, n]$ *code of index* s *and rate* $\frac{1}{s}$ *is a quasi-cyclic code with an* $(s-1)n \times sn$ *parity-check matrix of the form:*

$$
H = \begin{bmatrix} I_n & 0 & \cdots & 0 & A_1 \\ 0 & I_n & \cdots & 0 & A_2 \\ \vdots & \vdots & \ddots & \vdots & \vdots \\ 0 & 0 & \cdots & I_n & A_{s-1} \end{bmatrix},
$$

where $A_1, \cdots, A_{s-1}$ *are circulant* $n \times n$ *matrix. The case* $s = 2$ *corresponds to double circulant codes with generator matrix of the form* $(I_n|A)$ *for* A *a circulant matrix.*

2.3 Some Facts for $\mathcal{R} = \mathbb{F}_2[x]/(x^n - 1)$

Recall that we can map any vector $v = (v_0, \cdots, v_{n-1}) \in \mathbb{F}_2^n$ to the polynomial $\sum_{i=0}^{n-1} v_i x^i \in \mathcal{R}$. We have

Lemma 1. *For any two vectors* $u, v \in \mathbb{F}_2^n$, *the polynomial corresponding to* $rot(u)v^T$ *is exactly* $u \cdot v \in \mathcal{R}$ *when taking* u, v *as the polynomials in* $\mathcal{R}$, *where* $rot(u)$ *is the circulant matrix induced by* $u = (u_0, \cdots, u_{n-1})$:

$$
rot(u) = \begin{pmatrix} u_0 & u_{n-1} & \cdots & u_1 \\ u_1 & u_0 & \cdots & u_2 \\ \vdots & \vdots & \ddots & \vdots \\ u_{n-1} & u_{n-2} & \cdots & u_0 \end{pmatrix}.
$$

The following lemma is the key observation of our attack.

Lemma 2. *For any two representatives* $u, v \in \mathbb{F}_2[x]$ *for the same equivalence class in* $\mathcal{R}$, *the evaluations of* u, v *at 1 are identical in* $\mathbb{F}_2$. *More precisely, if* $u = v \in \mathcal{R}$, *then* $u(1) = v(1) \in \mathbb{F}_2$.

Proof. Since $u = v \in \mathcal{R}$, there exists some $d \in \mathbb{F}_2[x]$ such that $u = v + d \cdot (x^n - 1)$ in $\mathbb{F}_2[x]$, which implies that $u(1) = v(1) + d(1) \cdot 0 = v(1) \in \mathbb{F}_2$ immediately.

2.4 The s-QCSD Problem

HQC employs quasi-cyclic codes, and the hard problems that the cryptosystem relies on are presented as follows.

Definition 5 (s-QCSD distribution). *For positive integers* n, w *and* s, *the* s-*QCSD(n, w) distribution chooses uniformly at a random a parity matrix sample* $H \xleftarrow{\$} \mathbb{F}_2^{(sn-n) \times sn}$ *of a systematic QC code* $\mathcal{C}$ *of index* s *and rate* $\frac{1}{s}$ *together with a vector sample* $x = (x_1, \cdots, x_s) \xleftarrow{\$} \mathbb{F}_2^{sn}$ *such that* $\omega(x_i) = w$, $i = 1, \cdots, s$, *and outputs* (H, xH^T).

Definition 6 (Search s-QCSD Problem). *For positive integers n,w and s, a random parity check matrix H of a systematic QC code C of index s and sample $y \xleftarrow{\$} \mathbb{F}_2^{sn-n}$, the search s-Quasi-Cyclic SD problem s-QCSD(n,w) asks to find sample $x = (x_1, \cdots, x_s) \xleftarrow{\$} \mathbb{F}_2^{sn}$ such that $\omega(x_i) = w$, $i = 1, \cdots, s$, and $y = xH^T$.*

Definition 7 (Decision s-QCSD Problem(s-$DQCSD$)). *For positive integers n, w and s, a random parity check matrix H of a systematic QC code C and sample $y \xleftarrow{\$} \mathbb{F}_2^{sn-n}$, the Decision s-Quasi-Cyclic SD problem s-DQCSD(n,w) asks to decide with non-negligible advantage whether (H,y) came from the s-QCSD(n,w) distribution or the uniform distribution over $\mathbb{F}_2^{(sn-n) \times n} \times \mathbb{F}_2^{sn-n}$.*

We now formalize the indistinguishability game $\mathcal{D}_{\mathcal{A},\mathcal{H}}(n,w,s,\lambda)$ relative to the s-DQCSD problem in Fig. 1. Denote by $\mathcal{A}$ any possible probabilistic polynomial-time adversary, by $\mathcal{H}$ the set of all random parity check matrices of a systematic QC code $C[sn,n]$, and by λ the security parameter.

$\mathcal{D}_{\mathcal{A},\mathcal{H}}(n,w,s,\lambda)$

---

1 : $H \xleftarrow{\$} \mathcal{H}$

2 : $b \xleftarrow{\$} \{0,1\}$

3 : **if** $b = 0$

4 :   **then** $x \xleftarrow{\$} \{(x_1, \cdots, x_s) \in \mathbb{F}_2^{sn} | x_i \in \mathbb{F}_2^n, \omega(x_i) = w\}, y = xH^T$

5 : **else** $y \xleftarrow{\$} \mathbb{F}_2^n$

6 : $b' \leftarrow \mathcal{A}(H, y, w, \lambda)$

7 : **return** 1 if $b' = b$ and 0 otherwise.

Fig. 1. Game of distinguishing s-QCSD instance from uniform instance

Definition 8 (Hardness of s-DQCSD problem). *The s-DQCSD problem is hard, if for every polynomial-time adversary $\mathcal{A}$ in $\mathcal{D}_{\mathcal{A},\mathcal{H}}(n,w,s,\lambda)$, the advantage that $\mathcal{A}$ wins the indistinguishability game above is negligible in security parameter λ, that is*

$$Pr[\mathcal{D}_{\mathcal{A},\mathcal{H}}(n,w,s,\lambda) = 1] - \frac{1}{2} \leq \mathsf{negl}(\lambda).$$

2.5   The IND-CPA Security

Given the public-key encryption scheme $\Pi = (\mathsf{KGen}, \mathsf{Enc}, \mathsf{Dec})$ and an adversary $\mathcal{A}$, the IND-CPA security is related to the indistinguishability game $PubK_{\mathcal{A},\Pi}^{cpa}(\lambda)$ in Fig. 2.

$$
\begin{array}{l}
\hline
PubK^{cpa}_{\mathcal{A},\Pi}(\lambda) \\
\hline
1: \quad (\mathsf{pk},\mathsf{sk}) \leftarrow \mathsf{KGen}(1^{\lambda}) \\
2: \quad (m_0, m_1) \leftarrow \mathcal{A}(1^{\lambda}, \mathsf{pk}) \\
3: \quad b \xleftarrow{\$} \{0,1\} \\
4: \quad c \leftarrow \mathsf{Enc}(\mathsf{pk}, m_b) \\
5: \quad b' \leftarrow \mathcal{A}(1^{\lambda}, \mathsf{pk}, c) \\
6: \quad \textbf{return } 1 \text{ if } b' = b \text{ and } 0 \text{ otherwise.} \\
\hline
\end{array}
$$

Fig. 2. Chosen plaintext attack

Definition 9 (IND-CPA [5]**).** *A public key encryption scheme* $\Pi =$ (KGen, Enc, Dec) *has indistinguishable encryptions under a chosen-plaintext attack, or is* IND-CPA *secure, if for all probabilistic polynomial-time adversaries* $\mathcal{A}$ *there is a negligible function* $\mathsf{negl}(\lambda)$ *such that*

$$
Pr[PubK^{cpa}_{\mathcal{A},\Pi}(\lambda) = 1] \leq \frac{1}{2} + \mathsf{negl}(\lambda).
$$

3 The HQC Public Key Encryption Scheme

3.1 The Description of HQC Encryption Scheme

The following polynomial-time algorithms constitute the HQC PKE scheme. Note that the all the operations are in the ring $\mathcal{R} = \mathbb{F}_2[x]/(x^n - 1)$.

- **KGen**(1^{λ}): Generate the global parameter param $= (n, k, \delta, w, w_r, w_e)$. Sample

$$
h \xleftarrow{\$} \mathcal{R}, x, y \xleftarrow{\$} \{v \in \mathcal{R} | \omega(v) = w\}.
$$

Generate the generator matrix $G \in \mathbb{F}_2^{k \times n}$ for some efficiently decodable code $\mathcal{C}$. Set private key sk and public key pk as

$$
\mathsf{sk} = (x, y) \text{ and } \mathsf{pk} = (h, s = x + h \cdot y).
$$

return $(G, \mathsf{pk}, \mathsf{sk})$.
- **Encrypt** (pk, m): To encrypt message $m \in \mathbb{F}_2^k$, first sample

$$
r_1, r_2 \xleftarrow{\$} \{v \in \mathcal{R} | \omega(v) = w_r\}, e \xleftarrow{\$} \{v \in \mathcal{R} | \omega(v) = w_e\},
$$

then compute
$$
u = r_1 + h \cdot r_2 \text{ and } v = mG + s \cdot r_2 + e.
$$

return the ciphertext $c = (u, v)$.
- **Decrypt**(sk, c): return $\mathcal{C}.\textbf{Decode}(v - u \cdot y)$.

3.2   The Efficiently Decodable Code $\mathcal{C}$ in HQC

Aguilar Melchor et al. [1] suggested employing a tensor product code $\mathcal{C} = \text{BCH-S}(n_1, k, \delta) \otimes \mathbf{1}_{n_2}$ as the efficiently decodable code in HQC, where BCH-S is a shortened BCH code and $\mathbf{1}_{n_2} = \{a(1, 1, \cdots, 1) : a \in \mathbb{F}_2\}$ is the repetition code.

Roughly speaking, we first construct a primitive BCH code with generator polynomial $g(x)$ and then shorten it into the shortened BCH-S code as in Definition 2. For example, [1] suggested the BCH code and shortened BCH-S code with the following parameters (Table 1).

Table 1. Parameter sets for the primitive BCH code and the shortened BCH code

Code	n_1	k	δ
Primitive BCH-1	1023	513	57
Primitive BCH-2	1023	483	60
BCH-S1	766	256	57
BCH-S2	796	256	60

Note that the codewords in BCH-S1 (resp. BCH-S2) can be obtained by dropping 257 (resp. 227) zero information bits in the codewords in BCH-1 (resp. BCH-2) code.

When getting the shortened code BCH-S(n_1, k, δ), we construct the tensor product code by just repeating every component of any codeword in BCH-S code n_2 times.

For example, to encode a message $m \in \mathbb{F}_2^k$ into a codeword $\tilde{m} \in \mathbb{F}_2^{n_1 n_2}$, we first encode it into $\bar{m} \in \mathbb{F}_2^{n_1}$ with shortened code BCH-S(n_1, k, δ), and then each coordinate $\bar{m}_i$ of $\bar{m}$ is encoded into $(\bar{m}_i, \bar{m}_i, \cdots, \bar{m}_i) \in \mathbb{F}_2^{n_2}$ with repetition code $\mathbf{1}_{n_2}$. At last $m \in \mathbb{F}_2^k$ is encoded as

$$\tilde{m} = (\bar{m}_1, \bar{m}_1, \cdots, \bar{m}_1, \bar{m}_2, \bar{m}_2, \cdots, \bar{m}_2, \cdots, \bar{m}_{n_1}, \bar{m}_{n_1}, \cdots, \bar{m}_{n_1}).$$

Note that the shorten BCH code has a generator matrix in $\mathbb{F}_2^{k \times n_1}$ of the form

$$G_1 = \begin{pmatrix} v_0 & 1 & 0 & \cdots & 0 \\ v_1 & 0 & 1 & \cdots & 0 \\ \vdots & \vdots & \vdots & \ddots & \vdots \\ v_{k-1} & 0 & 0 & \cdots & 1 \end{pmatrix},$$

with $v_i = \left(v_{i0}, \cdots, v_{i(n_1-k-1)}\right) \in \mathbb{F}_2^{n_1-k}$, where $x^{n_1-k+i} \equiv \sum_{j=0}^{n_1-k-1} v_{ij} x^j$ mod $g(x)$, for $0 \leq i \leq k-1$. Let $G_2 = (1, \cdots, 1) \in \mathbb{F}_2^{n_2}$, then we have $\tilde{m} = mG_1 \otimes G_2$. We can summarize the encoding procedure as in Algorithm 1:

Algorithm 1. The Tensor Product Encoding Scheme

Input: message: $\mathbf{m} \in \mathbb{F}_2^k$; k: the message length; n_1: the shorten BCH code length; n_2: the repetition code length; g: the generator polynomial of BCH code.
Output: the codeword $\mathbf{c}' \in \mathbb{F}_2^{n_1 n_2}$
  view $\mathbf{m}$ as a polynomial m in $\mathbb{F}_2[x]$. compute r that satisfies $x^{n_1-k}m = qg + r$, where q is a polynomial in $\mathbb{F}_2[x]$ and $\deg(r) < \deg(g)$.
  compute $c = x^{n_1-k}m + r$, where c is viewed as a shorten code vector $\mathbf{c} \in \mathbb{F}_2^{n_1}$
  for $i = 1$; $i <= n_1$; i++ **do**
    $c_i' = (c_i, \cdots, c_i)$, $c_i' \in \mathbb{F}_2^{n_2}$
  end for
  return $\mathbf{c}' = (c_1', \cdots, c_{n_2}') \in \mathbb{F}_2^{n_1 n_2}$

3.3 Parameter Sets for HQC

Aguilar Melchor *et al.* [1] proposed several sets of parameters for HQC, targeting different levels of security. We list them as below (Table 2).

Table 2. Parameter sets for the shortened BCH code and the Hamming weight used in the HQC public key encryption.

Instance	n_1	n_2	n	k	δ	w	$w_r = w_e$
Basic-I	766	29	22229	256	57	67	77
Basic-II	766	31	23747	256	57	67	77
Basic-III	796	31	24677	256	60	67	77
Advanced-I	796	51	40597	256	60	101	117
Advanced-II	766	57	43669	256	57	101	117
Advanced-III	766	61	46747	256	57	101	117
Paranoiac-I	766	77	59011	256	57	133	153
Paranoiac-II	766	83	63587	256	57	133	153
Paranoiac-III	796	85	67699	256	60	133	153
Paranoiac-IV	796	83	70853	256	60	133	153

4 Breaking the Hardness Assumption for the HQC PKE

4.1 The s-DQCSD Problem is Easy

To present a formal security proof, the underlying mathematical problem of HQC is summarized as the s-DQCSD problem, which refers to the question of distinguishing whether a given instance came from the s-QCSD distribution or the uniform distribution. Under the assumption that 2-DQCSD and 3-DQCSD are hard, HQC, viewed as a PKE scheme, is proven to be IND-CPA secure, and can be transformed into an IND-CCA2 secure KEM [4].

However, we will show that s-DQCSD problem is actually not intractable under the HQC setting.

Taking 2-DQCSD problem as an example, we have

Proposition 1. *There exists a polynomial-time adversary $\mathcal{A}$ that solves 2-DQCSD problem over $\mathbb{F}_2$ with advantage $\frac{1}{4}$.*

Proof. We now describe a adversary $\mathcal{A}$ who distinguishes the 2-QCSD instance from uniform instance in game $\mathcal{D}_{\mathcal{A},\mathcal{H}}(n, w, 2, \lambda)$ in Fig. 1 as follows.

- A challenger samples $H \xleftarrow{\$} \mathcal{H}$, where $\mathcal{H}$ denotes the set of all random parity check matrices of systematic QC code $\mathcal{C}[2n, n]$.
- The challenger chooses $b \xleftarrow{\$} \{0, 1\}$. If $b = 0$, the challenger uniformly samples $x = (x_1, x_2) \in \mathbb{F}_2^{2n}$ such that $w(x_1) = w(x_2) = w$, and sets $y = xH^T$. If $b = 1$, the challenger samples $y \xleftarrow{\$} \mathbb{F}_2^n$.
- The challenger gives the sample (H, y, w, λ) to $\mathcal{A}$.
- Note that by the definition of the parity check matrix of systematic QC code $\mathcal{C}[2n, n]$, $H = [I_n, rot(h)]$ where $h \in \mathcal{R}$. Therefore $\mathcal{A}$ can first recover the polynomial h from H. Considering y as a polynomial in $\mathcal{R}$ also, $\mathcal{A}$ then evaluates the polynomials h and y at 1. If $y(1) = w + w \cdot h(1) \mod 2$, $\mathcal{A}$ outputs $b' = 0$, otherwise outputs $b' = 1$.
- If $b' = b$, the challenger outputs 1, otherwise outputs 0.

We now compute the advantage of $\mathcal{A}$ winning the game $\mathcal{D}_{\mathcal{A},\mathcal{H}}(n, w, 2, \lambda)$.

If $b = 0$, that is, (H, y, w, λ) is a 2-QCSD instance satisfying $y = xH^T$, taking x_1 and x_2 as the polynomials in $\mathcal{R}$, by Lemma 1 we know that in $\mathcal{R}$

$$y = x_1 + x_2 \cdot h.$$

Hence, by Lemma 2 it must hold that

$$y(1) = x_1(1) + x_2(1) \cdot h(1) \mod 2 = w + w \cdot h(1) \mod 2.$$

If $b = 1$, that is, (H, y, w, λ) is uniform instance, the relation

$$y(1) = w + w \cdot h(1) \mod 2.$$

holds just with probability $1/2$.

Then we know that

$$\Pr[\mathcal{D}_{\mathcal{A},\mathcal{H}}(n, w, 2, \lambda) = 1] = \Pr[b = 0] + \Pr[b = 1 \wedge y(1) \neq w + w \cdot h(1) \mod 2]$$
$$= \frac{1}{2} + \Pr[y(1) \neq w + w \cdot h(1) \mod 2 \mid b = 1] \cdot \Pr[b = 1]$$
$$= \frac{1}{2} + \frac{1}{2} \cdot \frac{1}{2}$$
$$= \frac{3}{4}.$$

Then the advantage of $\mathcal{A}$ winning the game $\mathcal{D}_{\mathcal{A},\mathcal{H}}(n, w, 2, \lambda)$ is $1/4$.

Similarly, for $s > 2$, the adversary $\mathcal{A}$ can distinguish the s-QCSD instance from the uniform instance by checking if the $s - 1$ relations $y_i(1) = w + w \cdot h_i(1)$ mod 2 ($i = 1, 2, \cdots, s - 1$) hold at the same time. If they all hold, $\mathcal{A}$ outputs 0 and if there exists a relation that does not hold, $\mathcal{A}$ outputs 1. A similar analysis shows that the probability that $\mathcal{A}$ wins the game $\mathcal{D}_{\mathcal{A}, \mathcal{H}}(n, w, s, \lambda)$ is $1 - 1/2^s$. Finally we have

Theorem 1. *For any positive integer $s \geq 2$, there exists a polynomial-time adversary $\mathcal{A}$ that solves s-DQCSD problem over $\mathbb{F}_2$ with advantage $\frac{1}{2} - \frac{1}{2^s}$.*

Since $1/2 - 1/2^s$ is definitely non-negligible, the assumption that s-DQCSD problem is hard does not hold.

4.2   A Variant of s-DQCSD Problem

Note that our attack against the hardness assumption of HQC depends on the fact that x_i has a fixed weight w. By choosing x_i with variable weight, we propose a variant of s-DQCSD problem that seems hard.

Definition 10 (s-QCSD distribution with variable weight). *For positive integers n, w and s, the s-QCSD(n, w) distribution with variable weight chooses uniformly at a random a parity matrix sample $H \xleftarrow{\$} \mathbb{F}_2^{(sn-n) \times sn}$ of a systematic QC code $\mathcal{C}$ of index s and rate $\frac{1}{s}$ together with a vector sample $x = (x_1, \cdots, x_s) \xleftarrow{\$} \mathbb{F}_2^{sn}$ where for each $i = 1, \cdots, s$, x_i is chosen independently such that $\omega(x_i) = w$ with probability $1/2$ and $\omega(x_i) = w - 1$ with probability $1/2$, and outputs (H, xH^T).*

Definition 11 (Decision s-QCSD Problem with variable weight). *For positive integers n, w and s, a random parity check matrix H of a systematic QC code $\mathcal{C}$ and sample $y \xleftarrow{\$} \mathbb{F}_2^{sn-n}$, the Decision s-QCSD Problem with variable weight asks to decide with non-negligible advantage whether (H, y) came from s-QCSD(n, w) distribution with variable weight or the uniform distribution over $\mathbb{F}_2^{(sn-n) \times n} \times \mathbb{F}_2^{sn-n}$.*

5   Breaking the IND-CPA Security of the HQC PKE

Recall that the second part of the ciphertext is $v = mG + s \cdot r_2 + e$. Note that the evaluation of v at 1 leaks some information about message. We have that

Theorem 2. *With all the proposed parameter sets, HQC is not IND-CPA secure.*

Proof. We show there is a polynomial-time adversary $\mathcal{A}$ that always wins the indistinguishability game in Fig. 2 as below:

- KGen(1^λ) is run to obtain (pk, sk).
- $\mathcal{A}$ obtains pk and outputs a pair of equal-length messages (m_0, m_1), where $m_0 \in \mathbb{F}_2^{k_1}$ is the zero vector $(0, 0, \cdots, 0)$, and $m_1 \in \mathbb{F}_2^{k_1}$ is the vector whose nonzero component is just the first component, that is, $(1, 0, \cdots, 0)$.
- A bit b is chosen uniformly at random from $\{0, 1\}$, and then the challenge ciphertext $c_b = (u_b, v_b) \leftarrow$ Enc(pk, m_b) is computed and given to $\mathcal{A}$.
- With pk $= (h, s = x + h \cdot y)$ and $c_b = (u_b, v_b)$, $\mathcal{A}$ evaluates v_b at 1, and checks if $v_b(1) = h(1) \mod 2$ or not. $\mathcal{A}$ outputs $b' = 0$ if $v_b(1) = h(1) \mod 2$, and outputs $b' = 1$ otherwise.
- The challenger outputs 1 if $b' = b$, otherwise outputs 0.

We next show that $\mathcal{A}$ always wins the game. Recall that

$$v = mG + s \cdot r_2 + e.$$

If m_0 is encrypted, then the corresponding codeword $m_0 G$ is 0. Hence,

$$v_0(1) = s(1) \cdot r_2(1) + e(1) \mod 2,$$

which is in fact

$$v_0(1) = (w + w \cdot h(1)) \cdot w_r + w_e \mod 2.$$

By the choice of the parameters, w, w_r and w_e are all odd. Thus

$$v_0(1) = h(1) \mod 2. \tag{1}$$

If m_1 is encrypted, the codeword is $m_1 G$. Taking $m_1 G$ as a polynomial, we also have

$$v_1(1) = m_1 G(1) + s(1) \cdot r_2(1) + e(1) \mod 2.$$

Note that $m_1 G(1)$ is just the weight of codeword $m_1 G$. By the fact the length n_2 of the repetition code is odd and the weight of g that generates the BCH code is odd (see the source codes of HQC implementation in [1], where the weight is either 267 or 261), the weight of $m_1 G$ is also odd, which implies that $m_1 G(1) = 1 \mod 2$. Together with the fact that $s(1) \cdot r_2(1) + e(1) = h(1) \mod 2$, we finally get

$$v_1(1) = 1 + h(1) \mod 2. \tag{2}$$

Combining Eqs. (1) and (2), it can be easily concluded that $\mathcal{A}$ always wins the game.

Remark 1. *The adversary can choose any two equal-length messages (m_0, m_1) such that $m_0 G(1) \neq m_1 G(1) \mod 2$ to complete the attack.*

Remark 2. *To resist such an attack, we can also choose x_1, x_2, e with variable weights instead of fixed ones as in Subsect. 4.2.*

6   Conclusion

In this paper, we show that the hardness assumption for HQC that s-DQCSD problem is hard does not hold. Furthermore, HQC can not attain IND-CPA security with all the proposed parameter sets. Some possible ways to resist our attack are also proposed.

Acknowledgments. We very thank the anonymous referees for their valuable suggestions on how to improve the presentation of this paper.

References

1. Aguilar, C., et al.: HQC Submission (2017). https://csrc.nist.gov/Projects/Post-Quantum-Cryptography/Round-1-Submissions
2. Aguilar, C., Blazy, O., Deneuville, J.C., Gaborit, P., Zémor, G.: Efficient encryption from random quasi-cyclic codes. arXiv preprint arXiv:1612.05572 (2016)
3. Chen, L., Jordan, S., et al.: Report on post-quantum cryptography (2016). http://nvlpubs.nist.gov/nistpubs/ir/2016/NIST.IR.8105.pdf
4. Dennis Hofheinz, K.H., Kiltz, E.: A modular analysis of the Fujisaki-Okamoto transformation. Cryptology ePrint Archive Report 2017/604 (2017)
5. Katz, J., Lindell, Y.: Introduction to Modern Cryptography. Chapman & Hall/CRC, Boca Raton (2007)
6. Lin, S., Costello, D.J.: Error control coding. Princ. Mob. Commun. **44**(2), 607–610 (1983)
7. Mceliece, R.J.: A public-key cryptosystem based on algebraic coding theory. Coding Thv **4244**, 114–116 (1978)
8. Misoczki, R., Tillich, J.P., Sendrier, N., Barreto, P.S.L.M.: MDPC-McEliece: new McEliece variants from moderate density parity-check codes. In: IEEE International Symposium on Information Theory Proceedings, pp. 2069–2073 (2013)
9. Regev, O.: On lattices, learning with errors, random linear codes, and cryptography. In: 37th STOC, pp. 84–93 (2005)
10. Shor, P.W.: Algorithms for quantum computation: discrete logarithms and factoring. In: 1994 Proceedings of 35th Annual Symposium on Foundations of Computer Science, pp. 124–134. IEEE (1994)
11. Shor, P.W.: Polynomial-time algorithms for prime factorization and discrete logarithms on a quantum computer. SIAM Rev. **41**(2), 303–332 (1999)

Solving LWR via BDD Strategy: Modulus Switching Approach

Huy Quoc Le[1]([envelope]), Pradeep Kumar Mishra[1], Dung Hoang Duong[2],
and Masaya Yasuda[3,4]

[1] Graduate School of Mathematics, Kyushu University, 744 Motooka, Nishi-ku,
Fukuoka-shi, Fukuoka-ken 819-0395, Japan
{q-le,p-mishra}@math.kyushu-u.ac.jp
[2] School of Computing and Information Technology, University of Wollongong,
Northfields Avenue, Wollongong, NSW 2522, Australia
hduong@uow.edu.au
[3] Institute of Mathematics for Industry, Kyushu University, 744 Motooka, Nishi-ku,
Fukuoka-shi, Fukuoka-ken 819-0395, Japan
yasuda@imi.kyushu-u.ac.jp
[4] JST, CREST, 4-1-8 Honcho, Kawaguchi, Saitama 332-0012, Japan

Abstract. The typical approach in attacking an $\mathrm{LWR}_{m,n,q,p}(\chi_s)$ instance parameterized by four integers m, n, q, p ($q \geq p$) and a probability distribution χ_s is just by simply regarding it as a Learning with Errors (LWE) modulo q instance and then trying to adapt known LWE attacks to this LWE instance. In this paper, we show that for an $\mathrm{LWR}_{m,n,q,p}(\chi_s)$ instance whose parameters satisfy a certain sufficient condition, one can use the BDD strategy to recover the secret with higher advantages if one transforms the LWR instance to an LWE modulo q' instance with q' chosen appropriately instead of an LWE modulo q instance. The optimal modulus q' used in our BDD attack is quite close to p as well as typically smaller than q. Especially, our experiments confirm that our BDD attack is much better in solving search-LWR in terms of root Hermite factor, success probability and even running time either in case the ratio $\log(q)/\log(p)$ is big or/and the dimension n is sufficiently large.

Keywords: Learning with Errors (LWE)
Learning with rounding (LWR)
Bounded distance decoding (BDD) strategy · Modulus switching
Lattice basis reduction · Babai's Nearest Plane (BNP) algorithm

1 Introduction

The LWR problem introduced by Banerjee, Peikert and Rosen in [6] is a derandomization variant of the well-known LWE problem in which a (q, p)-modulo rounding function (denoted by $\lfloor \cdot \rceil_{q,p}$) is used to hide the secret instead of using an error e drawn from some distribution. Specifically, for $x \in \mathbb{Z}_q$ we have $\lfloor x \rceil_{q,p} = \lfloor (p/q) \cdot x \rceil \in \mathbb{Z}_p$, where $\lfloor x \rceil$ rounds the real number x to the nearest integer. Let

© Springer Nature Switzerland AG 2018
J. Camenisch and P. Papadimitratos (Eds.): CANS 2018, LNCS 11124, pp. 357–376, 2018.
https://doi.org/10.1007/978-3-030-00434-7_18

$n \geq 1$, $q \geq p \geq 2$, and given a secret vector $\mathbf{s} \in \mathbb{Z}_q^n$, an LWR sample is the pair $(\mathbf{a}, c) \in \mathbb{Z}_q^n \times \mathbb{Z}_p$, in which the vector $\mathbf{a} \leftarrow \mathbb{Z}_q^n$ uniformly at random and $c := \lfloor \langle \mathbf{a}, \mathbf{s} \rangle \rceil_{q,p} \in \mathbb{Z}_p$.

Several LWR-based cryptosystems have recently been submitted to NIST for Post-Quantum Cryptography Standardization, for instance Round2 [4] and Lizard [12]. In their proposals, for efficiency goal, the secret is sampled from (even sparse) small sets. For example, in [12], the authors consider the binary secrets $\{0,1\}^*$ or trinary secrets $\{-1,0,1\}^*$ or even the secret $\mathbf{s}$ is sampled from some uniform distribution over $\{-1,0,1\}^*$ in which $\mathbf{s}$ contains h nonzeros for some fixed integer $h > 0$.

A typical approach in attacking LWR is to transform an LWR instance to an LWE modulo q. More specifically, the following method, called q-*reduction*, is used to lift an LWR instance $(\mathbf{a}, c = \lfloor \langle \mathbf{a}, \mathbf{s} \rangle \rceil_{q,p}) \in \mathbb{Z}_q^n \times \mathbb{Z}_p$ to an LWE instance modulo q of the form $(\mathbf{a}, c' = \langle \mathbf{a}, \mathbf{s} \rangle + e) \in \mathbb{Z}_q^n \times \mathbb{Z}_q$, where $c' = \left\lfloor \frac{q}{p} c \right\rceil$ and $e \in \left(-\frac{q}{2p}, \frac{q}{2p} \right]$. Most of techniques for solving LWR are adapted from attacks against an LWE modulo q instance [4,12,13] such as SIS strategy, BDD strategy, uSVP strategy, algebraic strategy [3] and so on (cf. [2] for more details). In this work, we just focus on the BDD strategy which aims to reduce a search-LWE instance to the closest vector problem (CVP), then use a practical lattice basis reduction algorithm (such as Lenstra-Lenstra-Lovász (LLL) algorithm [19] or the blockwise Korkine-Zolotarev (BKZ) algorithm [23]) along with the Babai's Nearest Plane (BNP) algorithm [5] to solve this CVP instance.

Some questions can be raised here that if it is possible to transform an $\text{LWR}_{m,n,q,p}(\chi_s)$ instance to an LWE instance modulo q' (called q'-*approach*) other than an LWE modulo q (called q-*approach*), with $q' < q$ or even $q' > q$, that if the q'-approach is better for specific attacks (such as the BDD strategy we are going to focus on) than the q-approach and that if so, how to choose the optimal q'. Note that, in the case of $q' < q$, the transformation is the so-called *modulus switching* technique. The technique allows to transform an LWE modulo q instance to an LWE modulo q' instance with q' is typically chosen as

$$q' \approx \frac{\sigma_s}{\sigma} \cdot \sqrt{\frac{n}{12}} \cdot q, \tag{1}$$

where n is the length of the secret and σ_s, σ are standard deviations of the secret and the error of the original LWE mod q instance, respectively (cf. [2, Lemma 2] for more details). The modulus switching technique was used for the first time aiming to speed up the homomorphic encryption operations [10]. Then the technique was also used to evaluate the classical hardness of LWE problem [9]. Recently, the technique was modified to combine with BKW algorithm on LWE [1]. Until now, however, the effect of the technique on other attacks against LWE and LWR has not been studied carefully.

Our Contribution. We evaluate the impact of modulus switching on the BDD strategy in solving search LWR problem. We achieved the following:

1. We reduce an $\text{LWR}_{m,n,q,p}(\chi_s)$ instance to an LWE modulo q instance and obtain an induced error e. Some previous works stated that the error *heuristically* follows a uniform distribution over $(-q/2p, q/2p]$ (see, e.g., [12, Sec. 4.2.1]) then its variance is roughly $\frac{q^2}{12p^2}$. We will confirm that the error actually follows a discrete uniform distribution and hence we compute its variance that is more precisely equal to $\frac{q^2+2pq}{12p^2}$, which is much larger than $\frac{q^2}{12p^2}$ if $q \gg p$. This helps us to estimate q' (mentioned below) more exactly than previous works.

2. We also determine the successful range in which LWR instances can be solved by the BDD strategy using practical lattice reduction algorithms (e.g., LLL or BKZ) accompanied with the BNP algorithm [5].

3. We theoretically and experimentally convince that one can transform an $\text{LWR}_{m,n,q,p}(\chi_s)$ instance to an LWE modulo $q' \approx \sqrt{\frac{(m-n)(n\sigma_s^2+1)p^2q^2}{n(q^2+2q)}}$ which can be solved more "efficiently" by the BDD strategy under a sufficient condition. By "efficiently", we mean that we will have either higher success probability and smaller root Hermite factor or/and smaller running time in solving this LWE instance depending on how much the size of α is. Our approach is especially suitable for LWR instances with short secret, i.e., σ_s small.

Our main technical tool is a heuristic evaluation on the success probability of the BDD strategy. To the best of our knowledge, this work is the first attempt to evaluate carefully the modulus switching's effect to the BDD strategy on LWR problem. We expect that our work will provide with a different perspective in exploiting modulus switching technique not only to solve LWR (even LWE) (by the BDD strategy or even other strategies) but also in other application scenarios.

Notation. If $A = \{a_1, \cdots, a_m\}$ with $a_i \in \mathbb{R}$ then $k \cdot A = \{k \cdot a_1, \cdots, k \cdot a_m\}$ for any $k \in \mathbb{R}$. The logarithm of base 2 (resp., the natural logarithm) of a positive real number x will be written as $\log(x)$ (resp., $\ln(x)$). We use $\mathcal{U}(A)$ to indicate the uniform distribution over the set A. The rounding operation $\lfloor a \rceil$ outputs the integer closest to a and in the case of a tie, it outputs the integer next to a. For any positive integer q, we denote by $\mathbb{Z}_q = \{0, 1, \cdots, q-1\}$ the set of integers modulo q. We write $x \leftarrow \chi$ to say that the random variable x follows the probability distribution χ or x is sampled from the distribution χ. For a real number k, the notation $y \leftarrow k \cdot \chi$ means that $y = k \cdot x$ for some x that follows the probability distribution χ.

2   Preliminaries

2.1   Lattices

The lattice $\mathcal{L} = \mathcal{L}(\mathbf{A})$ generated by the column matrix $\mathbf{A} = [\mathbf{a}_1, \cdots, \mathbf{a}_m] \in \mathbb{Z}^{n \times m}$ of m linearly independent vectors is defined to be the set of all linear integral combinations of $\mathbf{a}_i$'s, i.e., $\mathcal{L}(\mathbf{A}) = \{\mathbf{A}.\mathbf{x} : \mathbf{x} \in \mathbb{Z}^m\} = \{\sum_{i=1}^m x_i\mathbf{a}_i : x_i \in \mathbb{Z}\}$. We call the matrix $\mathbf{A}$ *a basis* of $\mathcal{L}$ and call each $\mathbf{a}_i$ *a basis vector*. The rank of the lattice is the number of basis vector (i.e., m). The dimension of the lattice is the number of entries in each basis vector (i.e., n). If $m = n$, the lattice is called to be *full-rank*. Note that, every lattice has infinitely many bases up to a unimodular matrix of determinant ± 1. Hence, if $\mathbf{A}$ and $\mathbf{B}$ are two different bases of the lattice $\mathcal{L}$, then $\det(\mathbf{A}^T\mathbf{A}) = \det(\mathbf{B}^T\mathbf{B})$. We call $\det(\mathcal{L}(\mathbf{A})) := \sqrt{\det(\mathbf{A}^T\mathbf{A})}$ the *determinant* (or *volume*) of the lattice $\mathcal{L}(\mathbf{A})$.

The *Gram-Schmidt* matrix $\mathbf{A}^* = \{\mathbf{a}_1^*, \cdots, \mathbf{a}_m^*\}$ for a basis $\mathbf{A} = \{\mathbf{a}_1, \cdots, \mathbf{a}_m\}$ is defined by setting $\mathbf{a}_1^* = \mathbf{a}_1$ and $\mathbf{a}_i^* = \mathbf{a}_i - \sum_{j=1}^{i-1} \frac{\langle \mathbf{a}_i, \mathbf{a}_j^* \rangle}{\|\mathbf{a}_j^*\|^2}, i = 2, \cdots, m$. Note that $\det(\mathcal{L}(\mathbf{A})) = \prod_{i=1}^{m} \|\mathbf{a}_i^*\|$. The *fundamental parallelepiped* associated with a basis $\mathbf{A} = \{\mathbf{a}_1, \cdots, \mathbf{a}_m\}$ is $\mathcal{P}_{1/2}(\mathbf{A}) = \{\sum_{i=1}^{m} x_i\mathbf{a}_i : x_i \in [-\frac{1}{2}, \frac{1}{2})\}$. We define the fundamental parallelepiped $\mathcal{P}_{1/2}(\mathbf{A}^*)$ for the Gram-Schmidt matrix $\mathbf{A}^*$ in the same way.

For integers q, m, n $(m \geq n)$, given a random matrix $\mathbf{A} \in \mathbb{Z}_q^{m \times n}$, we consider the so-called *q-ary lattice* $\Lambda_q(\mathbf{A}) = \{\mathbf{u} \in \mathbb{Z}^m : \mathbf{u} = \mathbf{A}\mathbf{s} \bmod q \text{ for some } \mathbf{s} \in \mathbb{Z}^n\}$. It is well known that $\det(\Lambda_q(\mathbf{A})) = q^{m-n}$ with high probability.

2.2   Lattice Basis Reduction Algorithms and Root Hermite Factor

A basis of a lattice can be reduced using the so-called *lattice basis reduction* (LBR) algorithms to obtain a new basis consisting of short and nearly orthogonal lattice vectors. Such two algorithms typically used in practice are LLL [19] and BKZ [23]. The former is a polynomial-time algorithm and the latter is a block version of the former with exponential complexity.

Let $\mathcal{L}$ be a lattice of rank m and $\mathbf{A}$ be a reduced lattice basis obtained using some LBR algorithm, say $\mathcal{A}$, the *root Hermite factor* (rHF) $\delta_{\mathcal{A}}$ of $\mathcal{A}$ with respect to $\mathbf{A}$ is the constant given by

$$\delta_{\mathcal{A}} = \left(\frac{\|\mathbf{u}_1\|}{\det(\mathcal{L})^{1/m}} \right)^{\frac{1}{m}}, \tag{2}$$

where $\mathbf{u}_1$ is the shortest non-zero vector of $\mathbf{A}$. Gama and Nguyen in [15] attempted to estimate the rHF of LLL and BKZ for random matrices. Namely, they estimated that the rHF of LLL is $\delta_{\text{LLL}} \approx 1.0219$ on average in high dimension ≥ 100 while that of BKZ with blocksize $\beta = 20^1$ is $\delta_{\text{BKZ}} \approx 1.0128$.

Unfortunately, however, these experimental results of [15] for random matrices may be not perfectly fit for q-ary lattices. That is the reason why Kudo et al. in [17] conducted intensively an experiment on q-ary lattices to estimate the quantity $\min_{i=1}^{m} \|\mathbf{b}_i^*\|$ from which they defined an alternative measure as follows:

$$c_{\mathcal{A}} := \left(\frac{\min_{i=1}^{m} \|\mathbf{b}_i^*\|}{\det(\Lambda_q(\mathbf{A}))^{1/m}} \right)^{\frac{1}{m}}, \tag{3}$$

---

[1] BKZ of blocksize 20 is usually used in practice because of its time/quality trade-off property.

where $\mathbf{b}_i^*$'s are Gram-Schmidt vectors of a basis of the q-ary lattice $\Lambda_q(\mathbf{A})$, say $\mathbf{B} = \{\mathbf{b}_1, \cdots, \mathbf{b}_m\}$, that is already reduced by some LBR algorithm $\mathcal{A}$. Note that $c_\mathcal{A} \leq 1$ since $\min_{i=1}^m \|\mathbf{b}_i^*\| \leq (\prod_{i=1}^m \|\mathbf{b}_i^*\|)^{1/m} = \det(\Lambda_q(\mathbf{A}))^{1/m}$. Especially, Kudo et al. [17] estimated that $c_{\text{LLL}} = 0.9775$ whereas using BKZ with blocksize $\beta = 20$, they got $c_{\text{BKZ}} = 0.9868$ (cf. [17, Table 1]).

If we still denote the rHF for q-ary lattices by $\delta_\mathcal{A}$ then it seems that $\delta_\mathcal{A} \approx 1/c_\mathcal{A}$. For instance, with $c_{\text{LLL}} = 0.9775$ and $c_{\text{BKZ}} = 0.9868$, we have $1/c_{\text{LLL}} = 1.0230$ and $1/c_{\text{BKZ}} = 1.0139$, respectively, that are quite close to the rHF for random matrices mentioned above.

We will use (3) to reach an important heuristic that is useful for our work (see Subsect. 2.4).

2.3   Probability

Variance of Random Variables. We denote the variance of a random variable X by σ_X. For $a, b \in \mathbb{Z}$, the variance of a random variable X following the discrete uniform distribution $\mathcal{U}(\{a, a+1, \cdots, b-1, b\})$ is $\sigma_X^2 = ((b-a+1)^2 - 1)/12$. If X follows the continuous uniform distribution $\mathcal{U}(a, b)$ then $\sigma_X^2 = (b-a)^2/12$. Assuming that $Z = X + Y$ where X, Y are independent random variables then $\sigma_Z^2 = \sigma_X^2 + \sigma_Y^2$. Finally, for every random variable X and for every constant $k \in \mathbb{R}$, let $Y = kX$, then we have $\sigma_Y^2 = k^2\sigma_X^2$.

Gaussian Distribution. For any real numbers $\mu, x \in \mathbb{R}$ and any real number $\sigma > 0$, the one dimensional continuous Gaussian distribution $\mathcal{D}_{\mu,\sigma}$ of mean μ and variance σ^2 is defined by its probability density function (pdf) $\mathcal{D}_{\mu,\sigma}(x) = \frac{1}{\sqrt{2\pi\sigma^2}} \cdot e^{-\frac{(x-\mu)^2}{2\sigma^2}}, \forall x \in \mathbb{R}$.

Convolution of Two Distributions. Let X and Y be continuously distributed independent random variables with pdfs f_X and f_Y. Then the pdf of the random variable $Z = X + Y$ is the convolution of f_X and f_Y given by

$$f_Z(z) = (f_X * f_Y)(z) = \int_{-\infty}^{+\infty} f_X(t)f_Y(z-t)dt = \int_{-\infty}^{+\infty} f_X(z-t)f_Y(t)dt. \quad (4)$$

2.4   Search-LWE and BDD Strategy

LWE problem proposed in [22] has been playing important role in lattice-based cryptography. The hardness of most of the lattice-based cryptosystems is based on the LWE problem which has two versions: one is decision version and another is search version. Here, we recall the search version of the LWE problem.

Definition 1 (Search-LWE Problem). *Given positive integers n, q, a fixed secret vector $\mathbf{s}$ whose each component is sampled from some distribution χ_s and another probability distribution χ_e on $\mathbb{Z}$, the search-$\text{LWE}_{m,n,q,\chi_s,\chi_e}$ problem is to find the secret $\mathbf{s}$ from m LWE samples of the form $(\mathbf{a}, c = \langle \mathbf{a}, \mathbf{s} \rangle + e \mod q) \in \mathbb{Z}_q^n \times \mathbb{Z}_q$, where $\mathbf{a} \in \mathbb{Z}_q^n$ is drawn uniformly at random, and the error term $e \leftarrow \chi_e$.*

If we have such m samples $(\mathbf{a}_i, c_i = \langle \mathbf{a}, \mathbf{s} \rangle + e_i)$ for $i = 1, \cdots, m$, we can collect them as $(\mathbf{A}, \mathbf{c} = \mathbf{A}.\mathbf{s} + \mathbf{e})$ in which $\mathbf{A}$ is an $(m \times n)$- matrix whose i-th row is $\mathbf{a}_i$, $\mathbf{c} = (c_1, c_2, \cdots, c_m)^T$, and $\mathbf{e} = (e_1, e_2, \cdots, e_m)^T$.

BDD Strategy. The BDD strategy for solving search-LWE proposed by Lindner and Peikert [20] is based on the close relation between search-LWE problem and BDD problem. Given a lattice and a target vector unusually close to the lattice, BDD problem asks to find the lattice vector closest to the target.

Let $(\mathbf{A}, \mathbf{c} = \mathbf{A}\mathbf{s} + \mathbf{e} \mod q) \in \mathbb{Z}_q^{m \times n} \times \mathbb{Z}_q^m$ be a search-LWE$_{m,n,q,\chi_s,\chi_e}$ instance. Also let $\Lambda_q(\mathbf{A}) = \{ \mathbf{u} \in \mathbb{Z}^m : \mathbf{u} = \mathbf{A}\mathbf{s} \mod q \text{ for some } \mathbf{s} \in \mathbb{Z}^n \}$ be the q-ary lattice spanned by columns of $\mathbf{A}$ and we call it *the associated q-ary lattice* of the search-LWE problem $(\mathbf{A}, \mathbf{c})$. To solve search-LWE problem via the BDD strategy, we reduce it to a CVP. In fact, if the error $\mathbf{e}$ is sufficiently short then $\mathbf{c}$ is closest to some lattice point $\mathbf{u} = \mathbf{A}\mathbf{s} \mod q \in \Lambda_q(\mathbf{A})$ since we have $\mathbf{e} = \mathbf{c} - \mathbf{A}\mathbf{s}$. Thus, finding the secret $\mathbf{s}$ is equivalent to finding $\mathbf{u}$, i.e., solving a CVP problem over q-ary lattice $\Lambda_q(\mathbf{A})$.

The most basic tools used in solving search-LWE via BDD strategy are some basis reduction algorithm, say $\mathcal{A}$ (e.g., LLL or BKZ), and the BNP algorithm. The BNP algorithm takes as input the vector $\mathbf{c}$ and a basis $\mathbf{B} = \{ \mathbf{b}_1, \cdots, \mathbf{b}_m \}$ of $\Lambda_q(\mathbf{A})$ that is already reduced by $\mathcal{A}$. Finally, the BNP algorithm outputs the lattice point $\mathbf{u} \in \Lambda_q(\mathbf{A})$ such that $\mathbf{e} = \mathbf{c} - \mathbf{u} \in \mathcal{P}_{1/2}(\mathbf{B}^*)$.

From now on, by "BDD strategy" or "BDD attack", we mean the BDD strategy associated with the BNP algorithm.

Success Probability of the BDD Strategy. The success probability of the BDD strategy in solving search-LWE is measured by the probability of the event that the error $\mathbf{e}$ lies in $\mathcal{P}_{1/2}(\mathbf{B}^*)$. Depending on which distribution the error $\mathbf{e}$ follows, we have some formulas to compute the probability in literature: (i) if $\mathbf{e}$ is uniform then we can estimate the probability by

$$\Pr\left[\mathbf{e} \in \mathcal{P}_{1/2}(\mathbf{B}^*) \right] = \prod_{i=1}^{m} \left(\frac{\|\mathbf{b}_i^*\|}{2\sigma_e \sqrt{3}} \right), \tag{5}$$

(ii) in the case of a Gaussian error $\mathbf{e}$, we can use the formula taken from [20]

$$\Pr\left[\mathbf{e} \in \mathcal{P}_{1/2}(\mathbf{B}^*) \right] = \prod_{i=1}^{m} \mathrm{erf}\left(\frac{\|\mathbf{b}^*_i\|}{2\sigma_e \sqrt{2}} \right), \tag{6}$$

where σ_e^2 is the variance of the error $\mathbf{e}$ according to its distribution and $\mathrm{erf}(\cdot)$ is the Gaussian error function $\mathrm{erf}(z) = \frac{2}{\sqrt{\pi}} \int_0^z \exp(-t^2) dt$, $z \in [0, +\infty]$. However, (5) and (6) are really not helpful for our work[2]. Therefore, we have to look for another way to estimate the success probability for the BDD strategy regardless

---

[2] We cannot use either (5) or (6) if the error $\mathbf{e}$ has a complex behavior. Such a kind of error is the q'-error that we will see in Sect. 5.

of the error's distribution. Fortunately, we can use a heuristic analysis appeared in [17] as follows:

We have $\Pr\left[\mathbf{e} \in \mathcal{P}_{1/2}(\mathbf{B}^*)\right] = \Pr\left[|\langle \mathbf{e}, \mathbf{b}_i^* \rangle| < \|\mathbf{b}_i^*\|^2/2, \forall i = 1, ..., m\right]$. Using the heuristics $|\langle \mathbf{e}, \mathbf{b}_i^* \rangle| \approx \|\mathbf{e}\| \cdot \|\mathbf{b}_i^*\|/\sqrt{m}$ and $\|\mathbf{e}\| \approx \sigma_e \cdot \sqrt{m}$, we have $2\sigma_e \leq \|\mathbf{b}_i^*\|$ for all $i = 1, ..., m$, which is equivalent to

$$2\sigma_e \leq \min_{i=1,...,m} \|\mathbf{b}_i^*\|. \tag{7}$$

Combining (7) with (3) yields the following heuristic that will be very useful for our work:

Heuristic 1. *Let $c_{\mathcal{A}}$ is defined as in (3). Heuristically, the success probability for the BDD strategy in solving search-LWE problem $(\mathbf{A}, \mathbf{c} = \mathbf{As} + \mathbf{e} \mod q) \in \mathbb{Z}_q^{m \times n} \times \mathbb{Z}_q^m$ can be measured by the probability $\Pr\left[2\sigma_e \leq c_{\mathcal{A}}^m \cdot \det(\Lambda_q(\mathbf{A}))^{1/m}\right]$, namely, $\Pr\left[2\sigma_e \leq c_{\mathcal{A}}^m \cdot q^{(m-n)/m}\right]$ which is equivalent to*

$$\Pr\left[\frac{q^{m-n}}{\sigma_e^m} \geq \frac{2^m}{c_{\mathcal{A}}^{m^2}}\right], \tag{8}$$

where $\mathcal{A}$ is the LBR algorithm used within the BDD strategy.

BDD Strategy and Root Hermite Factor. It is conventional that the quality of the reduced basis (which is characterized by the rHF obtained using by some LBR algorithm) has the most significant effect on the success probability of the BNP algorithm (see, e.g., [2, Sect. 5.4], [7, 16]), hence the BDD strategy. Namely, smaller rHF means that the corresponding basis is reduced better, hence the BNP algorithm may return the closest vector more precisely, so the efficacy of the BDD strategy may be higher.

Assume the BDD strategy uses the LBR algorithm named $\mathcal{A}$. And suppose that we want to compare the efficacy of the BDD strategy in solving a search-LWE problem $(\mathbf{A}_1, \mathbf{c}_1)$ with that in solving a search-LWE problem $(\mathbf{A}_2, \mathbf{c}_2)$. Then instead of success probability, we can compare the rHFs of $\mathcal{A}$ with respect to the reduced bases of the associated q-ary lattices $\Lambda_q(\mathbf{A}_1)$ and $\Lambda_q(\mathbf{A}_2)$.

2.5   Search LWR and a Reduction from LWR to LWE

Let p, q be two moduli such that $2 \leq p \leq q$. Recall that, the (q, p)-modulo rounding operation, denoted by $\lfloor . \rceil_{q,p}$, is defined as follows: for $x \in \mathbb{Z}_q$ $\lfloor x \rceil_{q,p} = \lfloor (p/q) \cdot x \rceil \in \mathbb{Z}_p$. We can extend the operation for vectors, matrices by taking it component-wise, such as for $\mathbf{x} = (x_1, \cdots, x_n) \in \mathbb{Z}_q^n$, we have $\lfloor \mathbf{x} \rceil_{q,p} = (\lfloor x_1 \rceil_{q,p}, \cdots, \lfloor x_n \rceil_{q,p})$.

Definition 2 (LWR Sample). *For a secret vector $\mathbf{s} \leftarrow \chi_s$ where χ_s is some distribution of variance σ_s^2, an $LWR_{m,n,q,p}(\chi_s)$ sample is obtained by choosing a vector $\mathbf{a} \leftarrow \mathbb{Z}_q^n$ uniformly at random and outputting $(\mathbf{a}, c = \lfloor \langle \mathbf{a}, \mathbf{s} \rangle \rceil_{q,p}) \in \mathbb{Z}_q^n \times \mathbb{Z}_p$.*

Assuming that we have such m LWR samples then we can write them as $(\mathbf{A}, \mathbf{c} = \lfloor \mathbf{As} \rceil_{q,p}) \in \mathbb{Z}_q^{m \times n} \times \mathbb{Z}_p^m$, where $\mathbf{A}$ is a matrix whose rows are $\mathbf{a}_i$ and $\mathbf{c}$ is a column vector whose elements are c_i.

Definition 3 (Search-LWR). *Given m LWR samples $(\mathbf{A}, \mathbf{c} = \lfloor \mathbf{As} \rceil_{q,p}) \in \mathbb{Z}_q^{m \times n} \times \mathbb{Z}_p^m$, the search-LWR$_{m,n,p,q}(\chi_s)$ problem is to find the secret $\mathbf{s}$.*

Reducing LWR$_{m,n,q,p}(\chi_s)$ to LWE Modulo q. The following reduction, called *q-reduction*, is used to transform an LWR instance consisting of samples of the form $(\mathbf{a}, c = \lfloor \langle \mathbf{a}, \mathbf{s} \rangle \rceil_{q,p}) \in \mathbb{Z}_q^n \times \mathbb{Z}_p$ to an LWE modulo q instance of the form $(\mathbf{a}, c_1) \in \mathbb{Z}_q^n \times \mathbb{Z}_q$ in which

$$
\begin{aligned}
c_1 &= \left\lfloor \frac{q}{p} \cdot c \right\rceil \bmod q \\
&= \left\lfloor \frac{q}{p} \cdot \left(\frac{p}{q} \cdot (\langle \mathbf{a}, \mathbf{s} \rangle + qu) + e_1 \right) \right\rceil \bmod q, \text{with } e_1 \in \left(-\frac{1}{2}, \frac{1}{2} \right], u \in \mathbb{Z}, \quad (9) \\
&= (\langle \mathbf{a}, \mathbf{s} \rangle + e) \bmod q = \langle \mathbf{a}, \mathbf{s} \rangle \bmod q + e, \text{ where } e := \lfloor (q/p) \cdot e_1 \rceil .
\end{aligned}
$$

For short, we call the error e *q-error*.

Note that, in the reduction above, we used the following assumption:

Assumption 1. *We assume that in our work, the error induced by reduction from an LWR instance to a corresponding LWE instance is not changed by a modulo operation. Formally, for an LWE sample $(\mathbf{a}, (\langle \mathbf{a}, \mathbf{s} \rangle + e) \bmod q) \in \mathbb{Z}_q^n \times \mathbb{Z}_q$, we assume that*

$$(\langle \mathbf{a}, \mathbf{s} \rangle + e) \bmod q = \langle \mathbf{a}, \mathbf{s} \rangle \bmod q + e.$$

This assumption was also used in many previous works relating to LWE such as [8,10,11,17,18]. We still use this assumption in Sect. 5.

3   Distribution of the q-Error

The q-reduction above has been typically considered in recent works relating to the LWR problem (see, e.g., [4,12,14]). In these works, it is heuristically assumed that e is continuously uniform over $(-q/2p, q/2p]$. If so, the variance is just $\sigma^2 \approx q^2/(12p^2)$. In this section, we show that e is actually distributed according to a discrete uniform distribution over the set $\{-\lfloor \lfloor q/2 \rfloor /p \rfloor, \cdots, \lfloor \lfloor q/2 \rfloor /p \rfloor\}$, hence its variance is actually $\sigma^2 \approx (q^2 + 2pq)/(12p^2)$ which is significantly greater than $q^2/(12p^2)$ in the case $q \gg p$.

To begin with, we state a simple lemma on rounding operation via discrete uniform distribution.

Lemma 1. *Given a nonzero real number b. Set $b_0 := -\lfloor b \rceil$, $b_1 := -\lfloor b \rceil + 1$, $\cdots, b_{t-1} := \lfloor b \rceil - 1$ and $b_t := \lfloor b \rceil$ and define the set $B := \{b_0, \cdots, b_t\}$. Let x be a real number taken uniformly at random from $[-b, b]$. Then*

$$\Pr[\lfloor x \rceil = b_i | b_i \in B] = \Pr[\lfloor x \rceil = b_j | b_j \in B], \text{ for all } i, j \in \{1, ..., t-1\}.$$

In particular,

$$\Pr[\lfloor x \rceil = b_0] = \Pr[\lfloor x \rceil = b_t] \leq \Pr[\lfloor x \rceil = b_i | b_i \in B], \forall i \in \{1, ..., t-1\}.$$

Proof. The idea for the proof is easy. Firstly, note that, for $1 \leq i \leq t-1$, we have

$$\Pr[\lfloor x \rceil = b_i] = \Pr[x \in [b_i - 1/2, b_i + 1/2)],$$

which implies the first statement in the lemma. Secondly, since $b_0 = -\lfloor b \rceil$ and $b_t = \lfloor b \rceil$, so $b_0 - 1/2 \leq -b < b_0 + 1/2$ and $b_t - 1/2 \leq b < b_t + 1/2$,

$$\Pr[\lfloor x \rceil = b_0] = \Pr[x \in [-b, b_0 + 1/2)] \leq \Pr[x \in [b_0 - 1/2, b_0 + 1/2)],$$

and

$$\Pr[\lfloor x \rceil = b_t] = \Pr[x \in [b_t - 1/2, b]] \leq \Pr[x \in [b_t - 1/2, b_t + 1/2)].$$

$\square$

Now we give the theorem describing the behavior of q-error e.

Theorem 1. *Set $b := \frac{\lfloor q/2 \rfloor}{p}$ and $A := \{-\lfloor b \rceil + 1, \cdots, \lfloor b \rceil - 1\}$. Also let e be the q-error defined as in (9). Then we have:*

$$\Pr[e = a | a \in A] = \frac{1}{2b}, \text{ and } \Pr[e = -\lfloor b \rceil] = \Pr[e = \lfloor b \rceil] = \frac{b - \lfloor b \rceil + \frac{1}{2}}{2b} \leq \frac{1}{2b}.$$

However, less precisely, we can say that e is uniform over

$$B := \{-\lfloor b \rceil, -\lfloor b \rceil + 1, \cdots, \lfloor b \rceil - 1, \lfloor b \rceil\}.$$

Then the variance of q-error e is

$$\sigma^2 \approx \frac{\left(2\left\lfloor \frac{\lfloor q/2 \rfloor}{p} \right\rfloor + 1\right)^2 - 1}{12} \approx \frac{q^2 + 2qp}{12p^2}. \tag{10}$$

Proof. First, we show that the error e_1 appears in (9) is distributed uniformly over $\frac{1}{q} \cdot \{-\lfloor q/2 \rfloor, \cdots, \lfloor q/2 \rfloor\}$. Note that, we fix the secret **s** which is sampled from some probability distribution χ_s beforehand. It is true that if we take $\mathbf{a} \in \mathbb{Z}_q^n$ uniformly at random then $(\langle \mathbf{a}, \mathbf{s} \rangle \bmod q)$ is also uniform over $\mathbb{Z}_q$. Hence, $\frac{p}{q} \cdot (\langle \mathbf{a}, \mathbf{s} \rangle \bmod q)$ is also uniform over $\frac{p}{q} \cdot \mathbb{Z}_q = \{0, p/q, \cdots, p \cdot (q-1)/q\}$. Suppose that $\langle \mathbf{a}, \mathbf{s} \rangle \bmod q = k$, for some $k \leftarrow \mathcal{U}(\{0, \cdots, q-1\})$. There always exist integers w and v such that $kp = qw + v$, $-\lfloor q/2 \rfloor \leq v \leq \lfloor q/2 \rfloor$, and $0 \leq w \leq p$. Certainly, v is uniform over the set $\{-\lfloor q/2 \rfloor, \cdots, \lfloor q/2 \rfloor\}$. Thus, $(p/q) \cdot (\langle \mathbf{a}, \mathbf{s} \rangle \bmod q) = kp/q = w + v/q$, where $-\lfloor q/2 \rfloor/q \leq v/q \leq \lfloor q/2 \rfloor/q$. Consequently, $\lfloor (p/q) \cdot (\langle \mathbf{a}, \mathbf{s} \rangle \bmod q) \rceil = w \in \{0, \cdots, p\}$, and hence

$$e_1 := \frac{p}{q}(\langle \mathbf{a}, \mathbf{s} \rangle \bmod q) - \left\lfloor \frac{p}{q}(\langle \mathbf{a}, \mathbf{s} \rangle \bmod q) \right\rceil = \frac{v}{q}$$

is uniform over $(1/q) \cdot \{-\lfloor q/2 \rfloor, \cdots, \lfloor q/2 \rfloor\}$. As a result, $(q/p) \cdot e_1 = v/p$ is uniform over $\{-\lfloor q/2 \rfloor/p, \cdots, \lfloor q/2 \rfloor/p\}$.

Recall that, the q-error $e = \lfloor (q/p) \cdot e_1 \rceil$. Applying Lemma 1 to $b := \lfloor q/2 \rfloor/p$, $B := \{-\lfloor b \rfloor, -\lfloor b \rfloor + 1, \cdots, \lfloor b \rfloor - 1, \lfloor b \rfloor\}$ and $x := (q/p) \cdot e_1$ and $e := \lfloor x \rceil$, the theorem follows. The variance of e is computed using the discrete uniform distribution over $B \subset \mathbb{Z}$. $\qquad\square$

4   Estimating the Successful Range for BDD Strategy in Solving LWR

Our purpose in this section is to find a condition of q so as to the $\text{LWR}_{m,n,q,p}(\chi_s)$ instance can be solved by the BDD strategy. The condition depends only on dimension n, the used LBR algorithm $\mathcal{A}$ (through its constant $c_{\mathcal{A}}$ defined as in (3)) as well as the bit ratio between q and p. According to the q-reduction, we say that a search-$\text{LWR}_{m,n,q,p}(\chi_s)$ instance is solvable by the BDD strategy if the corresponding LWE modulo q can be solved by the strategy.

Let $(\mathbf{a}, c = \lfloor \langle \mathbf{a}, \mathbf{s} \rangle \rceil_{q,p}) \in \mathbb{Z}_q^n \times \mathbb{Z}_p$ be an $\text{LWR}_{m,n,q,p}(\chi_s)$ instance and its corresponding LWE instance defined as in (9), the q-error e has variance σ defined as in (10). By Heuristic 1, we need $2\sigma \le c_{\mathcal{A}}^m \cdot q^{(m-n)/m}$ happens with probability 1. Note that $\sigma = \sqrt{\frac{q^2 + 2qp}{12p^2}} \le \frac{q}{2p}$ as $pq \le q^2$, yielding that $2\sigma \le \frac{q}{p}$. To estimate the successful range, we should consider the following slightly stronger condition

$$\frac{q}{p} \le c_{\mathcal{A}}^m \cdot q^{(m-n)/m},$$

from which we obtain $\frac{q^n}{p^m} \le c_{\mathcal{A}}^{m^2}$. Given $0 < \alpha < 1$ such that $p = q^\alpha$, from the previous equation we get

$$(m\alpha - n)\log(q) \ge -m^2 \log(c_{\mathcal{A}}). \qquad (11)$$

It is easy to see that (11) just makes sense as long as $m > \frac{n}{\alpha}$. So with this condition, we can rewrite (11) as $\log(q) \ge \frac{-m^2 \log(c_{\mathcal{A}})}{m\alpha - n}$. Hence we have that

$$\log(q) \ge \frac{-4n \log(c_{\mathcal{A}})}{\alpha^2},$$

since $\min_m \left\{ \frac{-m^2 \log(c_{\mathcal{A}})}{m\alpha - n} \right\} = \frac{-4n \log(c_{\mathcal{A}})}{\alpha^2}$ obtained at $m = \frac{2n}{\alpha}$. For given α, let $q_{\min}$ be the integer such that

$$\log(q_{\min}) = \lceil -4n \log(c_{\mathcal{A}})/\alpha^2 \rceil, \qquad (12)$$

then $\log(q_{\min})$ is a function in n whose graph is a straight line (called *the boundary line*). The line divides the plane into two half-planes: the upper half-plane indicates the successful range in which LWR instances are solvable by the BDD strategy, while the lower half-plane indicates the failure range in which LWR instances are unsolvable by the BDD strategy, (see Fig. 1).

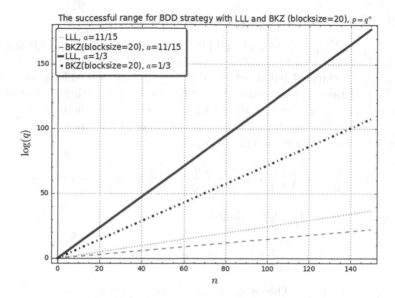

Fig. 1. We plot the graphs of the lines $\log(q_{\min}) = \lceil -4n \log(c_\mathcal{A})/\alpha^2 \rceil$ corresponding to $\alpha = 11/15$ and $\alpha = 1/3$. For LLL, we use $c_{\mathrm{LLL}} = 0.9775$ and for BKZ of block size 20 we use $c_{\mathrm{BKZ}} = 0.9868$.

Remark 1. It is easy to see from (12) that either n grows or/and α decreases makes the value $\log(q_{\min})$ increase. This seems to mean that large n and/or smaller α should be chosen for LWR-based cryptosystems. However, as we will see later in our experiments, larger n and/or smaller α provide our modulus switching approach with more advantages (see Sects. 5, 6).

Optimal Number of LWR Samples for BDD Strategy. The optimal number of LWR samples m should be chosen such that the right hand side of $2\sigma \leq c_\mathcal{A}^m q^{\frac{m-n}{m}}$ is maximum. So the optimal value of m should be:

$$m = \left\lfloor \sqrt{\frac{n \log(q)}{-\log(c_\mathcal{A})}} \right\rceil. \tag{13}$$

Remind that, the optimal number of samples typically used in attacking LWE problems (e.g., see [20,21]) is $m = \left\lfloor \sqrt{\frac{n \log(q)}{\log(\delta_\mathcal{A})}} \right\rceil$, which along with (13) again convince us that $\delta_\mathcal{A} \approx 1/c_\mathcal{A}$ (see Subsect. 2.2).

5 Modulus Switching for BDD Strategy on LWR

We will analyze the so-called q'-reduction which reduces an $\mathrm{LWR}_{m,n,q,p}(\chi_s)$ instance to an LWE modulo q' instance. Then we estimate the optimal q' and an associated condition such that the BDD strategy on LWE modulo q' instance is more efficient than the BDD strategy on LWE modulo q instance.

5.1   Reducing LWR$_{m,n,q,p}(\chi_s)$ to LWE Modulo q'

Let $(\mathbf{a}, c = \lfloor \langle \mathbf{a}, \mathbf{s} \rangle \rceil_{q,p}) \in \mathbb{Z}_q^n \times \mathbb{Z}_p$ be an LWR sample. We reduce this LWR sample to the LWE sample modulo q' of the form $(\mathbf{a}', c' = \langle \mathbf{a}', \mathbf{s} \rangle + e') \in \mathbb{Z}_{q'}^n \times \mathbb{Z}_{q'}$ with $c' = \lfloor (q'/q) \cdot c \rceil$ clarified below where $\mathbf{a}' = \lfloor (q'/q) \cdot \mathbf{a} \rceil$. We call the error e' q'-error. We now take a closer look into the process of generating e'. Recall that, $c = \lfloor \langle \mathbf{a}, \mathbf{s} \rangle \rceil_{q,p} = (p/q) \cdot \langle \mathbf{a}, \mathbf{s} \rangle + p \cdot u + e_1$ for some $u \in \mathbb{Z}$, where $e_1 \leftarrow \frac{1}{q} \cdot \mathcal{U}(T)$ with $T = \{-\lfloor q/2 \rfloor, ..., \lfloor q/2 \rfloor\}$ (see (9) and the proof of Theorem 1).

Now with q'-reduction we will obtain

$$c_2 := \frac{q'}{p} \cdot c = \left\langle \left\lfloor \frac{q'}{q} \mathbf{a} \right\rceil, \mathbf{s} \right\rangle + \left\langle \frac{q'}{q} \mathbf{a} - \left\lfloor \frac{q'}{q} \mathbf{a} \right\rceil, \mathbf{s} \right\rangle + q' \cdot u + e_2,$$

where $e_2 := \frac{q'}{p} \cdot e_1 \leftarrow \frac{q'}{pq} \cdot \mathcal{U}(T)$. Hence

$$c' := \lfloor c_2 \rceil \bmod q' = \left\langle \left\lfloor \frac{q'}{q} \mathbf{a} \right\rceil, \mathbf{s} \right\rangle \bmod q' + \left\langle \frac{q'}{q} \mathbf{a} - \left\lfloor \frac{q'}{q} \mathbf{a} \right\rceil, \mathbf{s} \right\rangle + e_2 + e_3,$$

where $e_3 \in (-\frac{1}{2}, \frac{1}{2}]$. The q'-error is $e' := e_2 + e_3 + e_4$, with $e_4 := \left\langle \frac{q'}{q} \mathbf{a} - \left\lfloor \frac{q'}{q} \mathbf{a} \right\rceil, \mathbf{s} \right\rangle = \sum_1^n \left(\frac{q'}{q} a_i - \left\lfloor \frac{q'}{q} a_i \right\rceil \right) \cdot s_i$.

Distribution of q'-Error. The behavior of q'-error is mainly affected by that of e_2 (following a uniform distribution (cf. Sect. 3)) and e_4 (following a Gaussian distribution via Central Limit Theorem (cf. [2, Lemma 2])). Then, using the Eq. (4) on the convolution of two distributions, the probability density function of e' can be approximated by

$$f(y) = \frac{p\sqrt{6}}{q'\sqrt{\pi n \sigma_s^2}} \int_{-\frac{q'}{2p}}^{\frac{q'}{2p}} \exp\left(-\frac{6(x-y)^2}{n\sigma_s^2} \right) dx = \frac{p}{q'\sqrt{\pi}} \int_{\frac{\sqrt{6}\left(-\frac{q'}{2p}-y\right)}{\sqrt{n}\sigma_s}}^{\frac{\sqrt{6}\left(\frac{q'}{2p}-y\right)}{\sqrt{n}\sigma_s}} \exp(-\zeta^2) d\zeta$$

$$= \frac{p}{2q'} \cdot \left[\mathrm{erf}\left(\frac{\sqrt{6}\left(\frac{q'}{2p}-y\right)}{\sqrt{n}\sigma_s} \right) + \mathrm{erf}\left(\frac{\sqrt{6}\left(\frac{q'}{2p}+y\right)}{\sqrt{n}\sigma_s} \right) \right]. \tag{14}$$

Its derivative is

$$f'(y) = \frac{\sqrt{6}p}{2\sqrt{\pi}nq'\sigma_s} \cdot \left[-\exp\left(\frac{-6\left(\frac{q'}{2p}-y\right)^2}{n\sigma_s^2} \right) + \exp\left(\frac{-6\left(\frac{q'}{2p}+y\right)^2}{n\sigma_s^2} \right) \right].$$

The function $f(y)$ is symmetric through origin and it has convex bell-shaped curve reaching its highest value $h(q') = (p/q') \cdot \mathrm{erf}\left((\sqrt{6}q')/(2p\sqrt{n}\sigma_s)\right)$ at $y = 0$. Note that the functions $f'(y)$ and $h(q')$ tend to 0 as q' increases. Thus, if $q' \gg p$, the error e' will tend to follow a uniform distribution. By contrast, when $q' \approx p$, the error e' will tend to be distributed via a Gaussian distribution.

The behavior of q'-error e' is complex, therefore we cannot use (5) or (6) to estimate the success probability of the BDD strategy in solving the LWE modulo q'. Also, on the other hand, we cannot compare the success probability of the BDD strategy on LWE modulo q' with that on LWE modulo q using the formulas (5) or (6). This is why we need to use Heuristic 1.

Variance of q'-Error. We consider the variances of e_2, e_3 and e_4. The variance of e_2 will be $\sigma_2^2 := \left(q'^2/(q^2 p^2)\right) \cdot \left(\left((2\lfloor q/2 \rfloor + 1)^2 - 1\right)/12\right)$, the variance of e_3 is $\sigma_3^2 = \frac{1}{12}$. The variance σ_4^2 of e_4 can be approximated as sum of n summands in which each summand is uniform on $(-\frac{1}{2}\sigma_s, \frac{1}{2}\sigma_s]$ where σ_s is the variance of the secret $\mathbf{s}$. Hence $\sigma_4^2 = \frac{n}{12}\sigma_s^2$. We assume that e_2, e_3 and e_4 are three independent random variables, then the variance of e' is estimated by

$$\sigma'^2 := \sigma_2^2 + \sigma_3^2 + \sigma_4^2 \approx \frac{1}{12}\left(n\sigma_s^2 + \frac{q'^2}{q^2 p^2}\left(q^2 + 2q\right) + 1\right) = \frac{1}{12}\left(Mq'^2 + N\right), \quad (15)$$

where $M := (q^2 + 2q)/(p^2 q^2)$ and $N := n\sigma_s^2 + 1$.

5.2 Optimizing q' for BDD Strategy

Assume that we have m LWR samples each of which is a pair $(\mathbf{a}, c = \lfloor \langle \mathbf{a}, \mathbf{s} \rangle \rceil_{q,p}) \in \mathbb{Z}_q^n \times \mathbb{Z}_p$. We reduce the LWR instance to:

- The LWE modulo q instance consists of m LWE samples of the form $(\mathbf{a}, c_1) \in \mathbb{Z}_q^n \times \mathbb{Z}_q$ where $c_1 = \langle \mathbf{a}, \mathbf{s} \rangle \bmod q + e$ where q-error e has variance of $\sigma^2 \approx \frac{q^2 + 2qp}{12p^2}$. We call this approach q-approach.
- The LWE modulo q' instance consists of m LWE samples of the form $(\mathbf{a}', c') \in \mathbb{Z}_{q'}^n \times \mathbb{Z}_{q'}$ where $c' = \langle \mathbf{a}', \mathbf{s} \rangle \bmod q' + e'$ and $\mathbf{a}' = \lfloor (q'/q) \cdot \mathbf{a} \rceil$, and the q'-error e' has variance of $\sigma'^2 \approx \frac{1}{12}\left(Mq'^2 + N\right)$, with $M = (q^2 + 2q)/(p^2 q^2)$ and $N = n\sigma_s^2 + 1$. We call this approach q'-approach.

For short, we say that the success probability of the BDD strategy in solving the LWE modulo q instance (resp., the LWE modulo q instance) as *the success probability of the q-approach* (resp., the success probability of the q'-approach). Notice that, in this section, the number of samples m is arbitrary as long as $m > n$. However, m will be optimally chosen via (13) in our experiments.

Our goal is to choose q' such that the success probability of the q'-approach is highest and certainly higher than that of the q-approach. The key idea is to use Heuristic 1. According to the heuristic, the success probability of the q-approach is

$$\Pr\left[\frac{q^{m-n}}{\sigma^m} \geq \frac{2^m}{c_{\mathcal{A}}^{m^2}}\right]. \quad (16)$$

Similarly, that of the q'-approach is

$$\Pr\left[\frac{q'^{m-n}}{\sigma'^m} \geq \frac{2^m}{c_{\mathcal{A}}^{m^2}}\right]. \quad (17)$$

Set $P' := \frac{q'^{m-n}}{\sigma'^m}$ and $P := \frac{q^{m-n}}{\sigma^m}$. The Eqs. (16) and (17) say that if $P' \geq P$ then the success probability of the q'-approach will be higher than that of the q-approach. Hence in order to achieve our goal, we can choose q' such that $P' \geq P$ and

$$P' \text{ is maximum.} \tag{18}$$

The condition $P' \geq P$ is equivalent to

$$\frac{q'^{m-n}}{\sqrt{(Mq'^2 + N)^m}} \geq \frac{q^{m-n}}{\sqrt{(\frac{q^2+2qp}{p^2})^m}}. \tag{19}$$

The Eq. (19) can be rewritten as

$$q'^{2(m-n)} \cdot (q^2 + 2qp)^m \geq q^{2(m-n)} \cdot p^{2m} \cdot (Mq'^2 + N)^m. \tag{20}$$

Now, it is the time to state the main theorem of this section.

Theorem 2. (i) *The optimal choice for q' satisfying* (18) *is*

$$q' \approx \sqrt{\frac{(m-n)(n\sigma_s^2 + 1)p^2q^2}{n(q^2 + 2q)}}. \tag{21}$$

(ii) *The sufficient condition under which the q'-approach has success probability higher than that of the q-approach is that*

$$(n\sigma_s^2 + 1)p^2 \leq q^2 + 2q. \tag{22}$$

Proof. Set $M := (q^2 + 2q)/(p^2q^2)$ and $N := n\sigma_s^2 + 1$ as in (15).

For (i), we have $P' = \frac{q'^{m-n}}{\sigma'^m} = \frac{q'^{m-n}\sqrt{12^m}}{\sqrt{(Mq'^2+N)^m}}$. Define $t := q'^2$, then $P'^2 = \frac{t^{m-n}12^m}{(Mt+N)^m}$. It is easy to see that $t_0 := \frac{(m-n)N}{nM}$ maximizes P'^2. So we should choose $q' \approx \sqrt{t_0} = \sqrt{\frac{(m-n)N}{nM}}$.

For (ii), by plugging $q'^2 = t_0$ into (20) and after some calculations, we get

$$[(m-n)N]^{m-n} \cdot (q^2 + 2qp)^m \cdot n^n \geq q^{2(m-n)} \cdot p^{2m} \cdot (mN)^m \cdot M^{m-n}. \tag{23}$$

Now taking the natural logarithm on (23) we have

$$(m-n)\ln(m-n) + (m-n)\ln(N) + m\ln(q^2 + 2qp) + n\ln(n)$$
$$\geq 2(m-n)\ln(q) + 2m\ln(p) + m\ln(m) + m\ln(N) + (m-n)\ln(M).$$

Using the facts that $m\ln(q^2+2qp) \geq m\ln(q^2+2q)$, and that $(m-n)\ln(m-n) + n\ln(n) \geq m\ln(m)$[3] along with some simple calculations, we imply the sufficient condition for (20) to hold is that $\ln(N) + [\ln(p^2) - \ln(q^2 + 2q)] \leq 0$ which is equivalent to

$$(n\sigma_s^2 + 1)p^2 \leq q^2 + 2q.$$

$\square$

---

[3] It is easy to check that the function $x\ln(x)$ is concave over $(0, +\infty)$.

Remark 2. The Eq. (21) looks like the same as the Eq. (1). The main difference between them is that the Eq. (21) gets involved with the number of samples m. This suggests that in order to apply the modulus switching technique for the BDD strategy on LWE, one should find the new q' rather than using the one in (1).

Remark 3. Recall that, if (22) holds then so does the (20), hence (19) also holds. Thus the gap

$$\mathtt{GAP} := (q^2 + 2q) - (n\sigma_s^2 + 1)p^2 \tag{24}$$

can be used to estimate the gap between two approaches. Obviously, the bigger the gap $\mathtt{GAP}$ is, the better the q'-approach is in comparison with the q-approach. The Eq. (24) yields that: (i) the q'-approach is more suitable for short secret LWR instances which have σ_s small; (ii) in the case that p close to q, i.e., $\alpha \approx 1$, the q'-approach is not more efficient than the q-approach and (iii) by contrast, in the case p is much smaller than q, i.e., $\alpha \ll 1$, the q'-approach is much more efficient than the q-approach.

Remark 4. By Remark 1, given α, if n increases then $\log(q_{\min})$ also increases. This is likely to make the gap $\mathtt{GAP}$ increase. We can see this trend from the columns entitled "GAP" in the Tables 2, 3, 4 and 5.

6   Implementation and Experimental Results

We implemented the BDD strategy on LWR problem to evaluate the efficacy of the q'-approach in comparison with the q-approach. In our experiments, we used SageMath version 8.1 [24] to implement the BDD strategy. The LBR algorithm used in our experiments is LLL [19]. We used the the function".LLL()" to call the floating point implementation of LLL in the *fplll* library which is included in SageMath with the default reduction parameter 0.99. By using such an LLL algorithm, we have the corresponding constant mentioned in (3) is $c_{\mathrm{LLL}} = 0.9775$ (see Sect. 2.2).

Table 1. How to proceed with our experiments?

1. First, choose α, then choose n and compute $\log(q_{\min})$ by (12)
2. Next, choose $\log(q)$ to be around $\log(q_{\min})$, from which we have q and p. After that we compute q' by (21) and compute m by (13)
3. For each tuple $(\alpha, n, q_{\min}, q, p, q')$, sample 10 LWR instances or 5 LWR instances up to α and n. (For $\alpha = 11/15$, we sample 10 LWR instances. For the rest of α's, we sample 5 LWR instances.)
4. For each LWR instance, transform it to LWE modulo q and LWE modulo q'
5. Finally, run BDD attack on these two LWE instances

We introduce some parameters and notations presented in our experimental results: α is the bit ratio of p and q, i.e., $\alpha = \log(p)/\log(q)$; n is the dimension of secret; $\log(q_{\min})$ is the smallest bit size of q computed by (12) given α, n; $\log(q')$, $\log(q)$, $\log(p)$ are the bit size of modulo q' computed by (21), of moduli q and p, respectively; m is the optimal number of LWR samples for BDD attack computed by (13) (we use the same number of samples m in both the q-approach and q'- approach); the columns entitled "GAP", "succ(q)", "succ(q')", "rHF(q)" and "rHF(q')" represent the size of the gap GAP in (24), the success probability of the q-approach and of the q'-approach, the rHF of the q-approach and of the q'-approach, respectively. Note that, rHF(q) and rHF(q') are computed using the formula (3).

Table 2. Compare q'-approach with the q-approach ($\alpha = 11/15$)

$(n, \log(q_{\min}))$	$\log(q)$	$\log(p)$	$\log(q')$	m	GAP	succ(q)	succ(q')	rHF(q)	rHF(q')
(60, 15)	15	11	14	166	9.5776e8	0%	60%	1.0202	1.0200
	17	12	15	176	1.6716e10	100%	100%	1.0203	1.0197
(80, 20)	17	12	15	204	1.6567e10	0%	0%	1.0209	1.0200
	18	13	16	209	6.6267e10	20%	80%	1.0205	1.0200
	20	15	19	221	1.0603e12	80%	100%	1.0209	1.0200
	22	16	20	232	1.7435e13	100%	100%	1.0205	1.0200
(100, 25)	20	15	19	247	1.0507e12	20%	60%	1.0210	1.0203
	25	18	22	276	1.1228e15	100%	100%	1.0212	1.0195

Table 3. Compare the q'-approach with the q-approach ($\alpha = 2/3$)

$(n, \log(q_{\min}))$	$\log(q)$	$\log(p)$	$\log(q')$	m	GAP	succ(q)	succ(q')	rHF(q)	rHF(q')
(60, 18)	16	11	14	171	4.1791e9	80%	80%	1.0203	1.0199
	17	11	14	176	1.7064e10	20%	60%	1.0201	1.0188
	18	12	15	181	6.8256e10	100%	100%	1.0202	1.0191
(80, 24)	21	14	18	226	4.3882e12	20%	100%	1.0203	1.0187
	23	15	19	237	7.0330e13	40%	100%	1.0215	1.0180
	24	16	20	242	2.8132e14	100%	100%	1.0208	1.0183
(100, 30)	24	16	20	270	2.8128e14	0%	80%	1.0211	1.0184
	26	17	21	281	4.5028e15	0%	100%	1.0211	1.0179
	28	19	23	292	7.2045e16	100%	100%	1.0213	1.0182

The experimental results are summarized in the Tables 2, 3, 4 and 5 each of which corresponds to one value α. The small secret s is drawn uniformly at random over $\{-1, 0, 1\}^n$. The first $\alpha = 11/15$ is inspired from choosing parameters

Table 4. Compare the q'-approach with the q-approach ($\alpha = 1/2$)

$(n, \log(q_{\min}))$	$\log(q)$	$\log(p)$	$\log(q')$	m	GAP	$\mathrm{succ}(q)$	$\mathrm{succ}(q')$	$\mathrm{rHF}(q)$	$\mathrm{rHF}(q')$
$(60, 32)$	**26**	13	**17**	218	4.5036e15	**0%**	**100%**	1.0210	1.0142
	30	15	**19**	234	1.1529e18	**20%**	**100%**	1.0201	1.0140
$(80, 43)$	**27**	17	**21**	256	1.8014e16	**0%**	**80%**	1.0208	1.0146
	35	18	**22**	292	1.1806e21	**0%**	**100%**	1.0209	1.0140
$(100, 53)$	**31**	16	**20**	307	4.5036e15	**0%**	**60%**	1.0214	1.0143
	37	19	**23**	336	1.8889e22	**0%**	**100%**	1.0213	1.0138

Table 5. Compare the q'-approach with the q-approach ($\alpha = 1/3$)

$(n, \log(q_{\min}))$	$\log(q)$	$\log(p)$	$\log(q')$	m	GAP	$\mathrm{succ}(q)$	$\mathrm{succ}(q')$	$\mathrm{rHF}(q)$	$\mathrm{rHF}(q')$
$(40, 48)$	**38**	13	**17**	215	7.5558e22	**0%**	**100%**	1.0212	1.0096
$(60, 71)$	**49**	16	**20**	299	3.1691e29	**0%**	**100%**	1.0215	1.0091
$(80, 95)$	**61**	20	**24**	386	5.3169e36	**0%**	**100%**	1.0214	1.0088
$(100, 119)$	**59**	20	**24**	424	3.3231e35	**0%**	**100%**	1.0213	1.0091

in the work of [4], the last one $\alpha = 1/3$ comes from [13] whilst two middle ones $\alpha = 2/3$ and $\alpha = 1/2$ are additionally suggested by us. We refer to Table 1 for generating parameters, sampling LWR instances, as well as running BDD attack on the corresponding LWE instances.

We highlight some noticeable things from our experimental results:

- In all cases, the rHF of the q-approach is always bigger than that of the q'-approach. Interestingly, the rHF of the q'-approach becomes smaller once α declines while the rHF of the q-approach does not seem to change, namely, $\mathrm{rHF}(q') \approx 1.0201$ for all considered α's. Recall that, smaller root Hermite factor means that the LWE modulo q' instance is more easily solved by BDD strategy than the LWE modulo q instance (see Sect. 2.4).
- When α is close to 1, such as $\alpha = 11/15$, the q'-approach does not outweigh the q-approach much (see Table 2). In contrast, when α is closer to 0 than 1, e.g., $\alpha = 1/3$, q' approach is much efficient than the q-approach in terms of success probability, rHF and even running time (although we do not add the runtime data in the tables due to lacking of space) since q' is quite close to p (see Table 5). For example, with $\alpha = 1/3, n = 100$, we log$(q') = 59$ that is much less than $\log(q) = 119$.
- The bit size $\log(q')$ is quite close to $\log(p)$. Namely, in all considered cases, we have $\log(q') - \log(p)$ equals to 3 or 4. It seems that the difference $\log(q') - \log(p)$ increases (but slowly) once either n increases or/and α decreases.
- With fixed α, the successful range for BDD strategy seems to be widen when n grows. For instance, consider $\alpha = 11/15$: in case $n = 60$ we have $\log(q_{\min}) = 15$, if choose $\log(q) = 15$ then $\mathrm{succ}(q) = 0\%$; by contrast, with $n = 80$, we have

$\log(q_{\min}) = 20$, hence if $\log(q) = 20$ then $\mathrm{succ}(q)=80\%$. Similarly, for $n = 100$, $\log(q_{\min}) = 25$ then $\mathrm{succ}(q)=100\%$ with if $\log(q) = 25$.

- With fixed α, it seems that when n grows the difference $\mathrm{succ}(q')-\mathrm{succ}(q)$ between two approaches also increases. Take $\alpha = 2/3$ for example, we can compare the difference $\mathrm{succ}(q')-\mathrm{succ}(q)$ for $n = 60$ with the difference $\mathrm{succ}(q')-\mathrm{succ}(q)$ for $n = 100$ (see Table 3). This suggests that for large n, q'-approach actually outweighs q-approach.
- Also, fixed α and n, the difference $\mathrm{succ}(q')-\mathrm{succ}(q)$ seems to depend on choosing q around $q_{\min}$. If q is much less than $q_{\min}$ then both $\mathrm{succ}(q)$ and $\mathrm{succ}(q')$ are 0%. For example, for $\alpha = 11/15, n = 80$, we have $\log(q_{\min}) = 20$, if we choose $\log(q) = 17$ then $\log(q') = 15$ and $\mathrm{succ}(q)=\mathrm{succ}(q')=0\%$. However, for the case q is sufficiently bigger than $q_{\min}$, the success probability of two approaches is 1. Certainly, in that case, depending on which one is smaller (typically, q' is smaller than q), we choose the corresponding approach to reduce the running time of BDD attack.
- Remarkably, when α is close to 0 (e.g., $\alpha = 1/3$), the q'-approach significantly widens the successful range. For instance, with $\alpha = 1/3$, $n = 80$ and $\log(q_{\min}) = 95$, if we choose $\log(q) = 61$, then $\log(q') = 24$ and $\mathrm{succ}(q)=0\%$ but $\mathrm{succ}(q')=100\%$ (see Table 5).

The experimental phenomena listed above can be theoretically explained by our theoretical results. Our experimental results, in turn, also strongly support our reasonings. From our experiments, we can conclude that for LWR-based cryptosystems, one should choose two moduli q and p that are not so far from each other.

7 Conclusion

In this paper, we concentrated on applying the idea of the modulus switching technique for solving LWR instances. To do that, we scrutinized the behavior of LWR errors in order to evaluate their variances more precisely. Furthermore, the successful range in which a search LWR instance can be solved by the BDD strategy associated with Babai's Nearest Plane algorithm was also determined. Based on the successful range, we take LWR instances that are consistent with our experiments. Experimental results support our theoretical result that applying modulus switching technique for the BDD strategy on (small secret) search-$\mathrm{LWR}_{m,n,q,p}(\chi_s)$ will be very efficient, especially if the bit ratio $\log(p)/\log(q)$ is close to 0 and/or n is sufficiently large. While our experiments were just proceeded with toy examples in which n is quite small, we believe that our modulus switching approach still performs very well for large n's used in practice.

Although our work does not give any warning to current LWR-based cryptosystems, it suggests that the modulus switching technique should be carefully considered in security analyses of prospective LWR-based (maybe even LWE-based) cryptosystems due to its remarkable effects. Considering effects of the modulus switching on other attacking strategies against LWR problem (even LWE) and analyzing its runtime effectiveness are our future works.

Acknowledgments. This work was supported by JST CREST Grant Number JPMJCR14D6, Japan. This work was also supported by JSPS KAKENHI Grant Number 16H02830. We would like to thank the anonymous reviewers for their careful reading as well as very helpful comments and suggestions.

References

1. Albrecht, M.R., Faugère, J.-C., Fitzpatrick, R., Perret, L.: Lazy modulus switching for the BKW algorithm on LWE. In: Krawczyk, H. (ed.) PKC 2014. LNCS, vol. 8383, pp. 429–445. Springer, Heidelberg (2014). https://doi.org/10.1007/978-3-642-54631-0_25

2. Albrecht, M.R., Player, R., Scott, S.: On the concrete hardness of learning with errors. Cryptology ePrint Archive, Report 2015/046 (2015). https://eprint.iacr.org/2015/046

3. Arora, S., Ge, R.: New algorithms for learning in presence of errors. In: Aceto, L., Henzinger, M., Sgall, J. (eds.) ICALP 2011. LNCS, vol. 6755, pp. 403–415. Springer, Heidelberg (2011). https://doi.org/10.1007/978-3-642-22006-7_34

4. Baan, H., et al.: Round2: KEM and PKE based on GLWR. Submission to NIST proposal, Round 1 (2017). https://csrc.nist.gov/Projects/Post-Quantum-Cryptography/Round-1-Submissions

5. Babai, L.: On lovász' lattice reduction and the nearest lattice point problem. Combinatorica **6**(1), 1–13 (1986). https://doi.org/10.1007/BF02579403

6. Banerjee, A., Peikert, C., Rosen, A.: Pseudorandom functions and lattices. In: Pointcheval, D., Johansson, T. (eds.) EUROCRYPT 2012. LNCS, vol. 7237, pp. 719–737. Springer, Heidelberg (2012). https://doi.org/10.1007/978-3-642-29011-4_42

7. Bischof, C., Buchmann, J., Dagdelen, Ö., Fitzpatrick, R., Göpfert, F., Mariano, A.: Nearest planes in practice. In: Ors, B., Preneel, B. (eds.) Cryptography and Information Security in the Balkans, pp. 203–215. Springer International Publishing, Cham (2015)

8. Brakerski, Z., Gentry, C., Vaikuntanathan, V.: (Leveled) fully homomorphic encryption without bootstrapping. In: Proceedings of the 3rd Innovations in Theoretical Computer Science Conference, ITCS 2012, pp. 309–325. ACM, New York (2012). https://doi.org/10.1145/2090236.2090262

9. Brakerski, Z., Langlois, A., Peikert, C., Regev, O., Stehlé, D.: Classical hardness of learning with errors. In: Proceedings of the Forty-Fifth Annual ACM Symposium on Theory of Computing, STOC 2013, pp. 575–584. ACM, New York (2013). https://doi.org/10.1145/2488608.2488680

10. Brakerski, Z., Vaikuntanathan, V.: Efficient fully homomorphic encryption from (standard) LWE. In: Proceedings of the 2011 IEEE 52nd Annual Symposium on Foundations of Computer Science, FOCS 2011, pp. 97–106. IEEE Computer Society, Washington (2011). https://doi.org/10.1109/FOCS.2011.12

11. Brakerski, Z., Vaikuntanathan, V.: Fully homomorphic encryption from ring-LWE and security for key dependent messages. In: Rogaway, P. (ed.) CRYPTO 2011. LNCS, vol. 6841, pp. 505–524. Springer, Heidelberg (2011). https://doi.org/10.1007/978-3-642-22792-9_29

12. Cheon, J.H., Kim, D., Lee, J., Song, Y.: Lizard public key encryption. Submission to NIST proposal, Round 1 (2017). https://csrc.nist.gov/Projects/Post-Quantum-Cryptography/Round-1-Submissions

13. Duc, A., Tramér, F., Vaudenay, S.: Better algorithms for LWE and LWR. Cryptology ePrint Archive, Report 2015/056 (2015). https://eprint.iacr.org/2015/056
14. Fang, F., Li, B., Lu, X., Liu, Y., Jia, D., Xue, H.: (Deterministic) hierarchical identity-based encryption from learning with rounding over small modulus. In: Proceedings of the 11th ACM on Asia Conference on Computer and Communications Security, ASIA CCS 2016, pp. 907–912. ACM, New York (2016). https://doi.org/10.1145/2897845.2897922
15. Gama, N., Nguyen, P.Q.: Predicting lattice reduction. In: Smart, N. (ed.) EUROCRYPT 2008. LNCS, vol. 4965, pp. 31–51. Springer, Heidelberg (2008). https://doi.org/10.1007/978-3-540-78967-3_3
16. Göpfert, F., van Vredendaal, C., Wunderer, T.: A hybrid lattice basis reduction and quantum search attack on LWE. In: Lange, T., Takagi, T. (eds.) PQCrypto 2017. LNCS, vol. 10346, pp. 184–202. Springer, Cham (2017). https://doi.org/10.1007/978-3-319-59879-6_11
17. Kudo, M., Yamaguchi, J., Guo, Y., Yasuda, M.: Practical analysis of key recovery attack against search-LWE problem. In: Ogawa, K., Yoshioka, K. (eds.) IWSEC 2016. LNCS, vol. 9836, pp. 164–181. Springer, Cham (2016). https://doi.org/10.1007/978-3-319-44524-3_10
18. Laine, K., Lauter, K.: Key recovery for LWE in polynomial time. Cryptology ePrint Archive, Report 2015/176 (2015). https://eprint.iacr.org/2015/176
19. Lenstra, A.K., Lenstra, H.W., Lovasz, L.: Factoring polynomials with rational coefficients. Math. Ann. **261**, 515–534 (1982)
20. Lindner, R., Peikert, C.: Better key sizes (and attacks) for LWE-based encryption. In: Kiayias, A. (ed.) CT-RSA 2011. LNCS, vol. 6558, pp. 319–339. Springer, Heidelberg (2011). https://doi.org/10.1007/978-3-642-19074-2_21
21. Micciancio, D., Regev, O.: Lattice-based cryptography. In: Bernstein, D.J., Buchmann, J., Dahmen, E. (eds.) Post-Quantum Cryptography, pp. 147–191. Springer, Heidelberg (2009). https://doi.org/10.1007/978-3-540-88702-7_5
22. Regev, O.: On lattices, learning with errors, random linear codes, and cryptography. J. ACM **56**(6), 34:1–34:40 (2009). https://doi.org/10.1145/1568318.1568324
23. Schnorr, C.P., Euchner, M.: Lattice basis reduction: improved practical algorithms and solving subset sum problems. Math. Program. **66**(1), 181–199 (1994). https://doi.org/10.1007/BF01581144
24. Stein, W., et al.: Sage Mathematics Software (Version 8.1). The Sage Development Team (2018). http://www.sagemath.org

Acceleration of Index Calculus for Solving ECDLP over Prime Fields and Its Limitation

Momonari Kudo[1], Yuki Yokota[2], Yasushi Takahashi[2], and Masaya Yasuda[3(✉)]

[1] Kobe City College of Technology,
8-3, Gakuen-Higashimachi, Nishi-ku, Kobe 651-2194, Japan
[2] Graduate School of Mathematics, Kyushu University,
744 Motooka, Nishi-ku, Fukuoka 819-0395, Japan
[3] Institute of Mathematics for Industry, Kyushu University,
744 Motooka, Nishi-ku, Fukuoka 819-0395, Japan
yasuda@imi.kyushu-u.ac.jp

Abstract. In 2018, Amadori et al. proposed a new variant of index calculus to solve the elliptic curve discrete logarithm problem (ECDLP), using Semaev's summation polynomials. The variant drastically decreases the number of required Gröbner basis computations, and it outperforms other index calculus algorithms for the ECDLP over prime fields. In this paper, we provide several improvements to accelerate to solve systems of multivariate equations arising in the variant. A main improvement is to apply the hybrid method, which mixes exhaustive search and Gröbner bases techniques to solve multivariate systems over finite fields. We also make use of symmetries of summation polynomials. We show experimental results of our improvements, and give their complexity analysis to discuss a limitation of our acceleration in both theory and practice.

Keywords: ECDLP · Index calculus · Summation polynomials
Gröbner basis algorithms

1 Introduction

After Rivest, Shamir, and Adleman [27] in 1977 proposed the RSA cryptosystem, Koblitz [21] and Miller [24] independently proposed elliptic curve cryptography (ECC) in 1985. These cryptosystems have been most widely used in modern information society. While the security of RSA is based on the computational hardness of the integer factorization problem (IFP), that of ECC relies on the ECDLP defined as follows; Given an elliptic curve E over a finite field $\mathbb{F}_q$ with q elements, a point $P \in E(\mathbb{F}_q)$ of prime order n, and a point $Q \in \langle P \rangle$, the ECDLP is to find the unique integer $0 \leq d \leq n - 1$ satisfying $Q = dP$. Subexponential time algorithms have been known to solve the IFP. For the ECDLP, Pollard's rho method [26] is the best known algorithm except special cases such as

© Springer Nature Switzerland AG 2018
J. Camenisch and P. Papadimitratos (Eds.): CANS 2018, LNCS 11124, pp. 377–393, 2018.
https://doi.org/10.1007/978-3-030-00434-7_19

supersingular [23] and anomalous curves [28,29,34] (see also textbooks [4,8,18]). The rho method has fully exponential time. This ensures that smaller ECC key sizes can provide the same security level as RSA, and hence ECC can be embedded into devices with limited storage or/and power supply. While the current world record for solving the IFP is 768-bit [20], the records of the order n for solving the ECDLP are 112-bit over prime fields (secp112r1) [5], 117.35-bit over binary fields (target117) [2], and 113-bit over Koblitz curves [35], which were all solved by the parallelized rho method (see also [36] for a comparison of the hardness of the IFP and the ECDLP). Recently, Kusaka et al. [22] announced a new record for solving the ECDLP in a Barreto-Naehrig curve over a prime field of 114-bit (it took about 6 months using 2000 CPU cores).

Index calculus is a useful method to solve the DLP over a cyclic group $G = \langle P \rangle$ of order n (we represent G *additively* to conform to the ECDLP); Fix a *factor base* $\mathcal{F} \subseteq G$. Given a target element $Q \in G$, we randomly generate $u, v \in \mathbb{Z}$, and try to decompose $R = uP + vQ$ as a *relation*

$$uP + vQ = \sum_{P_i \in \mathcal{F}} e_i P_i.$$

In case of success, we store (u, v) and (e_i) as a row of a relation matrix. After we collect at least $\#\mathcal{F}$ relations, we apply linear algebra modulo n for the relation matrix to obtain $\lambda P + \mu Q = 0$ in G. If μ is invertible modulo n, the discrete logarithm of Q with base P is given as $d \equiv -\lambda/\mu \bmod n$. In 2004, Semaev [30] introduced *summation polynomials* S_ℓ associated with an elliptic curve, and showed a way to collect a relation for the ECDLP by solving a system of S_ℓ-equations. In the literature, a number of index calculus algorithms have been proposed for the ECDLP over binary fields (e.g., see the survey paper [14]). As typical works, Gaudry [17] and Diem [9] fully developed the approach of Semaev [30] based on a Weil descent. In 2012, Faugère et al. [13] showed that systems arising in algorithms based on a Weil descent have special structures, and the structures make it easier to solve the systems by Gröbner basis algorithms. Since the work of [13], the asymptotic complexity of index calculus algorithms for the ECDLP over binary fields have been analyzed and discussed (see [14, Sect. 10.2]). On the other hand, for the ECDLP over prime fields, the algorithm by Semaev [31] is applicable, in which a combination of multiple S_3-equations is used to lower the degree of a system of equations at the expense of more variables. In 2016, Petit et al. [25] provided a new approach of index calculus, called the *algebraic approach*. In particular, they showed that the algebraic approach works efficiently when $p-1$ has a smooth large factor. In 2018, Amadori et al. [1] proposed a new variant of index calculus for solving arbitrary ECDLP instance. Their variant drastically decreases the required number of Gröbner basis computations, and it outperforms both [25,31].

In this paper, we provide several improvements to accelerate to solve systems of multivariate equations arising in Amadori et al.'s variant [1]. (cf., Some improvements for Petit et al.'s algebraic approach were proposed in [37].) For cryptanalysis of multivariate schemes, Bettale et al. [3] proposed a hybrid method, which mixes exhaustive search and Gröbner bases techniques to efficiently solve systems of multivariate equations over finite fields. As our main improvement, we adopt the hybrid method to Amadori et al.'s variant. We also make use of symmetries of summation polynomials for further efficiency. We show experimental results of our improvements over the computer algebra software MAGMA, together with our implementation results of Petit et al.'s algebraic approach [25] and Amadori et al.'s original systems [1] for a comparison. Furthermore, we estimate the complexity of Gröbner basis algorithms for solving our systems, and discuss a limitation of our acceleration in both theory and practice.

2   Index Calculus for ECDLP over Prime Fields

In this section, we review the algebraic approach by Petit et al. [25] and the new variant of index calculus by Amadori et al. [1] for solving the ECDLP over prime fields $\mathbb{F}_p$ using Semaev's summation polynomials [30]. We begin to present the summation polynomials and their properties.

2.1   Summation Polynomials

Let $E : y^2 = x^3 + ax + b$ be an elliptic curve over a field K of characteristic $p \geq 5$. The summation polynomials S_ℓ associated with E are defined as follows [30, Theorem 1]; $S_2(X_1, X_2) = X_1 - X_2$ and

$$
\begin{aligned}
S_3(X_1, X_2, X_3) =& (X_1 - X_2)^2 X_3^2 - 2\left\{(X_1 + X_2)(X_1 X_2 + a) + 2b\right\} X_3 \\
& + \left\{(X_1 X_2 - a)^2 - 4b(X_1 + X_2)\right\}.
\end{aligned}
\tag{1}
$$

For $\ell \geq 4$, the ℓ-th summation polynomial $S_\ell(X_1, \ldots, X_\ell)$ is defined by

$$
\mathrm{Res}_X\left(S_{\ell-j}(X_1, \ldots, X_{\ell-j-1}, X), S_{j+2}(X_{\ell-j}, X_{\ell-j+1}, \ldots, X_\ell, X)\right)
$$

for any $1 \leq j \leq \ell - 3$, where 'Res_X' denotes the resultant with respect to a variable X. The polynomial S_ℓ is symmetric and of degree $2^{\ell-2}$ in each variable X_i for any $\ell \geq 3$. Moreover, the polynomial is absolutely irreducible.

For $x_1, \ldots, x_\ell \in \overline{K}$, we have $S_\ell(x_1, \ldots, x_\ell) = 0$ if and only if there exist $y_1, \ldots, y_\ell \in \overline{K}$ such that $P_i = (x_i, y_i) \in E(\overline{K})$ for $1 \leq i \leq \ell$ and $P_1 + \cdots + P_\ell = \infty$ in the Mordell-Weil group $E(\overline{K})$, where $\overline{K}$ is the algebraic closure of K and ∞ is the point at infinity (it is the zero element in the group).

2.2   Algebraic Approach by Petit et al. [25]

Here we review the algebraic approach proposed by Petit, Kosters and Messeng [25] for the ECDLP over prime fields. It requires the following conditions to solve multivariate systems efficiently with Gröbner basis algorithms:

Requirement. Let $(E/\mathbb{F}_p, P, Q, n)$ be an ECDLP instance. Given a parameter k of the size of factor base, a main idea of the algebraic approach is to use an algebraic or a rational map L over $\mathbb{F}_p$ satisfying the following two conditions:

- We have $\#\{x \in \mathbb{F}_p \mid L(x) = 0\} \approx \#\{x \in \overline{\mathbb{F}}_p \mid L(x) = 0\} \approx p^{1/k}$.
- The map L can be represented as a composition of maps L_j of low degrees.

Remark 1. In [25, Sect. 3.3], a specific way to take a suitable map L is shown when $p - 1$ has a large smooth factor as

$$p - 1 = hN, \quad N = \prod_{i=1}^{r} p_i \approx p^{1/k}, \tag{2}$$

where h is a cofactor, primes p_i are not necessarily distinct and all smaller than a given bound $B > 0$ (e.g., we take $B = 2$ or 3). Take $L(x) = 1 - x^N$ for $x \in \overline{\mathbb{F}}_p$. Set $L_j(x) = x^{p_j}$ for $1 \leq j \leq r - 1$ and $L_r(x) = 1 - x^{p_r}$. Then we have $L(x) = (L_r \circ L_{r-1} \circ \cdots \circ L_1)(x)$ for any $x \in \overline{\mathbb{F}}_p$. In other words, the map L is a composition of algebraic maps L_j of degree $p_j \leq B$.

For arbitrary p, an attack is shown in [25, Sect. 3.4]. However, the attack requires the knowledge of an auxiliary elliptic curve E' isogeneous to E over $\mathbb{F}_p$, which has a large smooth factor like Eq. (2). A way to find such an auxiliary curve has been discussed in [25, Sect. 3.5]. However, the way seems very costly, and hence the algebraic approach might be inefficient if $p - 1$ has not a large smooth factor.

Factor Base. For the map L, let $V = \{x \in \mathbb{F}_p \mid L(x) = 0\}$. We set

$$\mathcal{F} = \{(x, y) \in E(\mathbb{F}_p) \mid x \in V\} \tag{3}$$

as a factor base. Given a point $R = uP + vQ = (x_R, y_R) \in E(\mathbb{F}_p)$ with randomly chosen integers u and v, we consider

$$S_{k+1}(X_1, \ldots, X_k, x_R) = 0 \tag{4}$$

with variables X_i $(1 \leq i \leq k)$. If a solution $(x_1, \ldots, x_k) \in \mathbb{F}_p^k$ is found with $x_i \in V$ for $1 \leq i \leq k$, then we obtain a relation

$$P_1 + \cdots + P_k = R = uP + vQ \tag{5}$$

for some $P_i \in \mathcal{F}$, from the property of the summation polynomial S_{k+1}.

System to Be Solved. Since the map L is composed of maps L_j of low degrees for $1 \leq j \leq r$, the algebraic approach requires to solve a system

$$\begin{cases} S_{k+1}(X_{1,1}, \ldots, X_{k,1}, x_R) = 0 & \\ L_j(X_{i,j}) = X_{i,j+1} & (1 \leq i \leq k, 1 \leq j \leq r - 1) \\ L_r(X_{i,r}) = 0 & (1 \leq i \leq k) \end{cases} \tag{6}$$

with variables $X_{i,j}$, where every variable X_i in (4) is decomposed as equations

$$X_i = X_{i,1}, L_1(X_{i,1}) = X_{i,2}, \ldots, L_{r-1}(X_{i,r-1}) = X_{i,r} \text{ and } L_r(X_{i,r}) = 0.$$

Advantages and Limitations. As in the basic framework of index calculus, the algebraic approach requires to solve the system (6) at least $\#\mathcal{F} \approx p^{1/k}$ times for different points $R \in E(\mathbb{F}_p)$. Large k can reduce the total number of solving the system, but only $k = 2$ and 3 cases work in practice due to the degree of S_{k+1} (in fact, $k = 2$ was used in experiments of [25, Sect. 4], and see also Table 1 below for our experimental results). Main advantages of the algebraic approach are as follows; (i) Most solutions of the system (6) are defined over $\mathbb{F}_p$. (ii) All the polynomial equations in (6) have low degrees, which implies that we can solve the system (6) efficiently by Gröbner basis algorithms. On the other hand, applicable ECDLP instances are very limited since the algebraic approach works only when $p - 1$ has a large smooth factor as described in Remark 1.

2.3   New Variant by Amadori et al. [1]

Here we present the new variant of index calculus proposed by Amadori, Pintore and Sala [1] for solving the ECDLP over prime fields. Different from the basic framework of index calculus, this variant requires to find a *single solution* of a system, that is, only a relation like (5) is required. Furthermore, different from the algebraic approach, this variant is applicable to arbitrary ECDLP instances.

Factor Base. Given an ECDLP instance $(E/\mathbb{F}_p, P, Q, n)$, set

$$\mathcal{F} = \{\pm R \in E(\mathbb{F}_p) \mid R = uP + vQ \text{ for randomly chosen } 0 \leq u, v \leq n - 1\}$$

as a factor base. This is slightly different from the factor base in [1, Section 3], and we here take the factor base $\mathcal{F}$ so that the negative $-R$ of every $R \in \mathcal{F}$ is also included in $\mathcal{F}$. Like Pollard's rho method [26] or Shank's baby-step giant-step (BSGS) method [32], this variant requires to randomly generate two integers $0 \leq u, v \leq n - 1$, and compute $R = uP + vQ \in E(\mathbb{F}_p)$ to build the factor base $\mathcal{F}$ (cf., the algebraic approach does not require such computation for a factor base). The final size of $\mathcal{F}$ depends on a parameter m, which shall be described later in more detail (we take $\#\mathcal{F} \approx p^{1/m}$ *roughly*).

Systems to Be Solved. The following two systems are shown in [1, Sect. 3.1]:

– *Original system*: Let V denote the set of x-coordinates of points $R \in \mathcal{F}$. The original system to be solved with m variables $X_1, \ldots, X_m$ is as follows:

$$\begin{cases} S_m(X_1, \ldots, X_m) = 0 \\ \quad f(X_1) = 0 \\ \qquad \vdots \\ \quad f(X_m) = 0 \end{cases} \tag{7}$$

where let $f(X)$ denote the polynomial generating the vanishing ideal of $V \subseteq \mathbb{F}_p$ for a variable X, that is,

$$f(X) = \prod_{v \in V} (X - v) \in \mathbb{F}_p[X].$$

Once a solution of (7) is found, we can obtain a relation $P_1 + \cdots + P_m = \infty$ for some $P_i \in \mathcal{F}$, from the property of the summation polynomial S_m. From the construction of the factor base $\mathcal{F}$, every point P_i equals to $u_i P + v_i Q$ for some known integers $u_i, v_i \in \mathbb{Z}$. This induces the linear congruence $\lambda P + \mu Q = \infty$ with $\lambda, \mu \in \mathbb{Z}$, which is a main key point of [1].

- *Improved system*: The degree of $f(X)$ in the system (7) is equal to $\#V \approx \frac{\#\mathcal{F}}{2}$ by the construction of the factor base $\mathcal{F}$. In order to lower the degrees in the system (7), the authors of [1] partition the factor base $\mathcal{F}$ into m partitions $\mathcal{F}_1, \ldots, \mathcal{F}_m$ with almost same size, that is, $\mathcal{F} = \bigsqcup_{i=1}^{m} \mathcal{F}_i$ and $\#\mathcal{F}_i \approx \#\mathcal{F}_j$ for $i \neq j$ (the idea of partitioning the factor base is based on [15]). For each $1 \leq i \leq m$, let V_i denote the set of x-coordinates of points in the partition $\mathcal{F}_i$. Now consider a system

$$
\begin{cases}
S_m(X_1, \ldots, X_m) = 0 \\
\quad f_1(X_1) = 0 \\
\qquad \vdots \\
\quad f_m(X_m) = 0
\end{cases}
\tag{8}
$$

where $f_i(X)$ is the polynomial generating the vanishing ideal of V_i for every $1 \leq i \leq m$. Then the degree of every $f_i(X)$ equals to $\#V_i$, which is roughly equal to $\frac{\#V}{m}$ since $V = \bigsqcup_{i=1}^{m} V_i$ and $\#V_i \approx \#V_j$ for $i \neq j$.

Size of Factor Base. Let s denote the size of the factor base $\mathcal{F}$. The expected number of combinations $P_1 + \cdots + P_m \in E(\mathbb{F}_p)$ with all $P_i \in \mathcal{F}$ is approximately equal to $\frac{s^m}{m!}$. Since the order of the group $E(\mathbb{F}_p)$ is approximately equal to p (precisely, $\#E(\mathbb{F}_p) = p + 1 - t$ with $|t| \leq 2\sqrt{p}$ by the Hasse theorem, e.g., see [33, Theorem 1.1 in Chap. V]), we roughly estimate that the original system (7) has a solution when

$$
\frac{s^m}{m!} \geq p \iff s \geq (m! \times p)^{1/m}.
\tag{9}
$$

On the other hand, the expected number of combinations $P_1 + \cdots + P_m \in E(\mathbb{F}_p)$ with $P_i \in \mathcal{F}_i$ for every $1 \leq i \leq m$ is approximately equal to

$$
\#\mathcal{F}_1 \times \cdots \times \#\mathcal{F}_m \approx \left(\frac{s}{m} \right)^m
$$

since the partitions $\mathcal{F}_1, \ldots, \mathcal{F}_m$ are disjoint. Therefore we roughly estimate that the improved system (8) has a solution when

$$
\left(\frac{s}{m} \right)^m \geq p \iff s \geq m p^{1/m}.
\tag{10}
$$

3   Acceleration for Amadori et al.'s Variant

In this section, we accelerate Amadori et al.'s variant of index calculus, and report experimental results on our acceleration for solving several ECDLP instances over prime fields $\mathbb{F}_p$. Specifically, we adopt some methods to accelerate to solve the *original system* (7) while Amadori et al. in [1, Table 2] reported some experimental results of solving the improved system (8). Furthermore, we focus on $m = 3$, which is more efficient than $m = 4$ and 5 for p larger than 20-bit from experimental results [1, Table 2]. From our experiments (see Table 1 below), the running time of solving the original system (7) is considerably slower than the improved system (8) with Gröbner basis algorithms. However, the original system is more suitable to use symmetries for acceleration, and it is easier to analyze the complexity. From these reasons, we focus on the original system (7).

3.1 Three Improvements for Solving Systems

In this subsection, we present three improvements to accelerate to solve system (7) with $m = 3$.

(A) Adoption of the Hybrid Approach. Bettale, Faugère and Perret [3] proposed an improved approach, called the *hybrid approach*, to solve multivariate systems over finite fields. Their idea is to mix exhaustive search and Gröbner basis algorithms for efficiency, but there is a trade-off between them. Here we apply the hybrid approach to solve the system (7) with $m = 3$; For a randomly chosen element z from the set V, consider

$$\begin{cases} S_3(X_1, X_2, z) = 0 \\ \quad\quad f(X_1) = 0 \\ \quad\quad f(X_2) = 0 \end{cases} \tag{11}$$

where $f(X)$ is the same polynomial in system (7) (note that since $z \in V$ means $f(z) = 0$, the equation $f(X_3) = 0$ is unnecessary in the hybrid approach). This approach requires $\#V$ times of exhaustive search for different elements z in order to obtain a solution of (11) (note that $\#V \approx \frac{\#\mathcal{F}}{2} \approx p^{1/3}$). On the other hand, the system (11) has only two variables, and this enables to efficiently solve the system for every $z \in V$ (note that the system has no solution for most $z \in V$).

(B) Using Symmetries in the Hybrid Approach. As is described in [14, Sect. 9.1], we can potentially lower the degree of every summation polynomial by using its symmetry. Here we make use of the symmetry of $S_3(X_1, X_2, z)$ in system (11). Set $T_1 = X_1 + X_2$ and $T_2 = X_1 X_2$ as elementary symmetric polynomials. Then the polynomial $S_3(X_1, X_2, z)$ is rewritten as

$$S_3'(T_1, T_2, z) = (T_1^2 - 4T_2)z^2 - 2\left(T_1 T_2 + aT_1 + 2b\right)z + (T_2 - a)^2 - 4bT_1,$$

which has total degree 2 (cf., the original polynomial $S_3(X_1, X_2, z)$ has total degree 4, see Eq. (1)). On the other hand, since neither $f(X_1)$ nor $f(X_2)$ has any symmetry, system (11) cannot be rewritten with two variables T_1 and T_2.

In order to reconstruct the system with T_1 and T_2, we consider

$$f(X_1) + f(X_2) = \prod_{v \in V}(X_1 - v) + \prod_{v \in V}(X_2 - v)$$

$$= X_1^t + X_2^t - \sum_{v \in V} v(X_1^{t-1} + X_2^{t-1}) + \cdots =: g_+(T_1, T_2),$$

$$f(X_1) \times f(X_2) = \prod_{v \in V}(X_1 - v)(X_2 - v)$$

$$= \prod_{v \in V}(T_2 - vT_1 + v^2) =: g_\times(T_1, T_2),$$

where we set $\#V = t$. Note that every $X_1^j + X_2^j$ for $1 \leq j \leq t$ can be converted into certain polynomial with two variables T_1 and T_2. Then we consider

$$\begin{cases} S_3'(T_1, T_2, z) = 0 \\ g_+(T_1, T_2) = 0 \\ g_\times(T_1, T_2) = 0 \end{cases} \tag{12}$$

as a system alternative to (11) with variables T_1 and T_2.

Let $(t_1, t_2) \in \mathbb{F}_p^2$ be a solution of the system (12). For any pair $(\alpha, \beta) \in \overline{\mathbb{F}}_p^2$ with $t_1 = \alpha + \beta$ and $t_2 = \alpha\beta$, we have $f(\alpha) + f(\beta) = g_+(t_1, t_2) = 0$ and $f(\alpha) \times f(\beta) = g_\times(t_1, t_2) = 0$. From this, we have $f(\alpha) = f(\beta) = 0$, and hence $\alpha, \beta \in V \subseteq \mathbb{F}_p$. Since $S_3(\alpha, \beta, z) = S_3'(t_1, t_2, z) = 0$, we obtain a desired relation

$$P_1 + P_2 + P_3 = \infty \tag{13}$$

with $P_1, P_2, P_3 \in \mathcal{F}$. Since both $g_+(T_1, T_2)$ and $g_\times(T_1, T_2)$ have the same total degrees as $f(X)$, the degrees in the new system (12) are smaller than the old system (11). Therefore we expect that we could solve the system (12) with Gröbner basis algorithms more efficiently than the old system. Furthermore, two polynomials $g_+(T_1, T_2)$ and $g_\times(T_1, T_2)$ depend only on the set V, and hence we can compute them in a pre-computation of the hybrid approach.

(C) **Solving via GCD Computation.** It is very fast to solve a univariate system via GCD computation. To solve the system (11) for every $z \in V$ efficiently, we compute

$$h_{w,z}(X_1) := \gcd(S_3(X_1, w, z), f(X_1)) \in \mathbb{F}_p[X_1]$$

for randomly chosen elements w from V. If the degree of $h_{w,z}(X_1)$ is greater than 0, then it follows from the form of $f(X_1)$ that $(X - v)$ divides $h_{w,z}(X_1)$ for some $v \in V$. Since $S_3(v, w, z) = 0$, we have a desired relation (13).

Remark 2. With resultant and GCD computations, we can solve the system (11) as follows; We first compute $r_z(X_1) := \mathrm{Res}_{X_2}(S_3(X_1, X_2, z), f(X_2)) \in \mathbb{F}_p[X_1]$, and then compute $\gcd(r_z(X_1), f(X_1))$ to find a relation. Since the degree of $r_z(X_1)$ is large due to $\deg f(X_2) = \#V \approx p^{1/3}$, the resultant computation is costly for large p. Hence we do not use the resultant in our acceleration.

Remark 3. In our improvement (C), the number of required elements $w, z \in V$ in exhaustive search is $(\#V)^2 \approx p^{2/3}$. This complexity is much worse than that of both Pollard's rho method and Shank's BSGS method, whose complexity is roughly equal to $p^{1/2}$. On the other hand, both improvements (A) and (B) *potentially* have a better complexity than the rho method and the BSGS method. However, the complexity depends on Gröbner basis algorithms for solving systems (11) and (12), which shall be analyzed in more detail in Subsect. 3.3 below (see also Table 1 below for our experimental results).

Table 1. The running time (seconds) of solving several ECDLP instances over prime fields $\mathbb{F}_p$, where $p - 1$ is divisible by $N = 2^r \approx p^{1/2}$ for some $r \in \mathbb{N}$ for the requirement of Petit et al.'s algebraic approach [25] with parameter $k = 2$ and bound $B = 2$ (all methods except the BSGS method use the third summation polynomial S_3)

Bitsize of p	Petit et al.'s approach [25]	Amadori et al.'s variant [1]		Our improvements for [1]			BSGS method
		System (7)	System (8)	(A)	(B)	(C)	
16	794.480	10.850	0.274	0.085	0.052	0.008	0.004
18	8694.720	88.704	1.938	0.344	0.210	0.012	0.008
20	137803.170	718.937	12.522	1.618	0.736	0.040	0.019
22	—	—	118.635	6.389	2.688	0.110	0.045
24	—	—	—	24.072	12.599	0.297	0.099
26	—	—	—	100.965	63.920	1.145	0.277
28	—	—	—	566.302	202.647	3.641	0.531
30	—	—	—	—	1344.293	13.934	1.177

3.2 Experimental Results

In Table 1, we report experimental results of solving several ECDLP instances over prime fields $\mathbb{F}_p$ with our improvements, together with our implementation results of Petit et al.'s algebraic approach [25], Amadori et al.'s variant [1], and the BSGS method [32] for a comparison. All methods except the BSGS method use the third summation polynomial S_3. Due to extensive running time, we did not perform experiments for both the algebraic approach and Amadori et al.'s variant for most primes p larger 22-bit. We used primes p for which $p - 1$ is divisible by $N = 2^r \approx p^{1/2}$ for some $r \in \mathbb{N}$ to satisfy the requirement of the algebraic approach with parameter $k = 2$ and bound $B = 2$. For each p, we randomly chose an elliptic curve E over $\mathbb{F}_p$ of prime order $n = \#E(\mathbb{F}_p)$. All our experiments were performed on a CPU with Intel Core i7-4770K at 3.50 GHz (the Operating System was Linux version 4.4.0-47-generic). We used MAGMA V2.22-7 in its 64-bit version. In particular, we implemented a Gröbner basis algorithm to solve a multivariate system with some MAGMA functions such as GroebnerBasis (we did not use the Variety function). On the other hand, we used the GCD function for our improvement (C).

Setting. We adopted the graded reverse lexicographic (grevlex) order in solving a multivariate system by our Gröbner basis algorithm. We also set the order of variables so that a system becomes almost homogeneous for efficiency; For the algebraic approach, we set

$$X_{2,r} \succ X_{1,r} \succ X_{2,r-1} \succ X_{1,r-1} \succ \cdots \succ X_{2,1} \succ X_{1,1}$$

for the system (6) with $k = 2$. For Amadori et al.'s variant, we set $X_1 \succ X_2 \succ X_3$ for both the original system (7) and the improved system (8) with $m = 3$. For our improvements, we set $X_1 \succ X_2$ and $T_1 \succ T_2$ for systems (11) and (12), respectively. For Amadori et al.'s variant, we set the size $s = \#\mathcal{F}$ of the factor base as $s = 3p^{1/3}$ to satisfy both conditions (9) and (10) with $m = 3$. In this setting, each of both systems (7) and (8) has a solution with high probability, and we have to solve only a single system for solving every ECDLP instance.

Comparison with Known Implementation Results. In [25, Sect. 4], Petit et al.'s reported the running time of solving the system (6) with Gröbner basis algorithms in MAGMA V2.18-5 on a CPU with 16-cores Intel Xeon Processor 5550 at 2.67 GHz. According to their report, it took 9.09, 59.87 and 454.79 s on average to solve the system (6) with $k = 2$ for $16, 18$ and 20-bits p, respectively. In contrast, Table 1 shows the total running time of solving an ECDLP instance, in which we solved the system (6) $p^{1/2}$ times for different $R \in E(\mathbb{F}_p)$. From our experimental data, we estimate that it took about 3.10, 16.98 and 134.57 s on average to solve the system (6) *once* for $16, 18$ and 20-bits p, respectively. Our data are about 3 times faster than [25] for Petit et al.'s algebraic approach, due to the difference of MAGMA versions.

In [1, Table 2], Amadori et al. reported the running time of solving the system (8) with almost the same setting as ours, on a CPU with an Intel Xeon Processor 5460 at 3.16 GHz (the MAGMA version is not given in [1]). According to their report, it took 3.303, 28.230 and 267.659 s on average to solve system (8) with $m = 3$ for $18, 20$ and 22-bits p. In contrast, from Table 1, it took 1.938, 12.522 and 118.635 s to solve the same system with our Gröbner basis algorithm for the same bits p. Our data are about twice faster than [1].

Comparison for Methods. As is shown in [1, Table 2], we see from our experiments that Amadori et al.'s variant [1] is much faster than Petit et al.'s algebraic approach [25] even under condition where the algebraic approach can work efficiently. We also see from Table 1 that our improvements considerably accelerated Amadori et al.'s variant. In particular, our improvement (C) is the fastest among our three improvements, and it is hundreds times faster than Amadori et al.'s variant for primes p around 20-bit. However, our improvement (C) was slower than the BSGS method (note that our implementation for the BSGS method is not optimal at all). Since the complexity of (C) is at least $p^{2/3}$ as described in Remark 3, our improvement (C) can never be faster than the BSGS method for large primes p. On the other hand, as is also described in Remark 3, our improvements (A) and (B) have a possibility that they are *asymptotically* faster than (C) and the BSGS method. In the following subsection, we shall analyze the complexity of (A) and (B).

Remark 4. Recently, the authors in [16] proposed a brute-force algorithm to find a relation in the framework of Amadori et al.'s index calculus for the ECDLP over $\mathbb{F}_p$ (see [16, Algorithm 4.1] for the algorithm), without using Gröbner basis algorithms and summation polynomials. According to their experimental data [16, Table 4], their algorithm took 66.25, 1126 and 6848 s for primes p of 27, 32, and 34 bits, respectively. In contrast, our improvement (C) took only 3.641 and 13.934 s for primes p of 28 and 30 bits, respectively, from Table 1. Since the complexity of their method is $O(p)$ from [16, Theorem 5.14], their brute-force method could never be faster than our improvement (C) for large p.

3.3   Complexity Analysis of (A) and (B)

The complexity of Gröbner basis algorithms (such as F_4 [11] and F_5 [12]) is not completely understood, especially when the input polynomials are *non-homogeneous* (the algorithm F_4 is the default algorithm for computing Gröbner bases in MAGMA, and F_5 might be more efficient). Recently, Caminata and Gorla proved the following result [6, Proposition 3.16]:

Proposition 1. *Let K be a field, and $R = K[X_1, \ldots, X_n]$ the polynomial ring of n variables. Let $f_1, \ldots, f_\ell$ be a system of non-homogeneous polynomials in R, defining an ideal I. Let $s =$ solv. $\deg(I)$ denote the solving degree, that is, the highest degree of the polynomials involved in the computation of a Gröbner basis of I (we fix the grevlex order for Gröbner bases). Let d_i be the degree of f_i for $1 \leq i \leq \ell$, and*

$$m = \sum_{i=1}^{\ell} \binom{n + s - d_i}{s - d_i}.$$

Then the number of operations in K required to compute a Gröbner basis of I is

$$O\left(\binom{n + s}{s} m^{\omega - 1}\right) \text{ if } m \leq \binom{n + s}{s}, \text{ and } O\left(m \binom{n + s}{s}^{\omega - 1}\right) \text{ otherwise,}$$

where $2 \leq \omega \leq 3$ is the exponent of matrix multiplication.

For our improvement (A), let

$$I_z = \langle S_3(X_1, X_2, z), f(X_1), f(X_2)\rangle \tag{14}$$

denote the ideal in the ring $\mathbb{F}_p[X_1, X_2]$ generated from the polynomials in the system (11) for an element $z \in V \subseteq \mathbb{F}_p$. Since the solving degree is not less than the maximum degree of input polynomials, we have

$$\text{solv. } \deg(I_z) \geq \deg(f) \approx p^{1/3}$$

(in the next section, we will prove solv. $\deg(I_z) = O(p^{1/3})$, see Lemma 3 below). By Proposition 1, the number of operations in $\mathbb{F}_p$ required to compute a Gröbner basis of I_z is at least $p^{1/3}$. Since our improvement (A) requires to solve the system (11) $p^{1/3}$ times for different elements $z \in V$, our improvement (A) has complexity at least $p^{1/3} \times p^{1/3} = p^{2/3}$. This complexity is worse than the complexities of both our improvement (C) and the BSGS method, and hence our improvement (A) can never be faster than both our improvement (C) and the BSGS method for large primes p.

From a similar discussion as above, our improvement (B) can never be faster than both our improvement (C) and the BSGS method. In fact, our improvement (B) is just a transformation of (A) using the symmetry of S_3-polynomial, and we see from Table 1 that (B) is about twice faster than (A) for all primes p.

4   Theoretical Investigation on the Ideal I_z

In this section, we give a theoretical analysis on the ideal I_z given by (14), in order to analyze the complexity of our improvement (A).

4.1   Definitions of Regularities

Here we present some definitions of regularities. Let $R = K[X_1, \ldots, X_n]$ be the polynomial ring of n variables over a field K. Let R_d denote the set of homogeneous elements of R of degree $d \geq 0$, and then $R = \bigoplus_{d \geq 0} R_d$. In both algebraic geometry and commutative algebra, the regularity of a finitely generated graded R-module is defined as follows:

Definition 1 (Castelnuovo-Mumford regularity). *Let M be a finitely generated graded R-module, and let*

$$0 \longrightarrow F_\ell \xrightarrow{\varphi_\ell} \cdots \xrightarrow{\varphi_2} F_1 \xrightarrow{\varphi_1} F_0 \xrightarrow{\varphi_0} M \longrightarrow 0, \quad (15)$$

be its minimal free resolution, where for $0 \leq i \leq \ell$ each F_i is a free R-module given by

$$F_i = \bigoplus_{j=1}^{\beta_i} R(-e_{i,j})$$

for some integers β_i and $e_{i,j}$ (here we let $R(e)$ denote the e-twist of R for an integer e). The Castelnuovo-Mumford regularity of M is defined as

$$\mathrm{reg}(M) := \max\{e_{i,j} - i : 0 \leq i \leq \ell\}.$$

Remark 5. If a graded R-module $M = \bigoplus M_i$ is of finite length, the regularity $\mathrm{reg}(M)$ is equal to the maximal integer i with $M_i \neq 0$, see [10, Corollay 4.4].

For a non-homogeneous polynomial $f \in R$, we denote by $f^h \in R[Y] = K[X_1, \ldots, X_n, Y]$ its homogenization with respect to an extra variable Y. For an ideal $I \subset R$, we also denote by I^h the homogeneous ideal in $R[Y]$ generated by $\{f^h : f \in I\}$. The ideal I^h only depends on the ideal I, and especially it is independent of the choice of generators. On the other hand, for a set $\{f_1, \ldots, f_k\}$ of generators of I, we denote by $\widetilde{I}$ the homogeneous ideal $\langle f_1^h, \ldots, f_k^h \rangle \subset R[Y]$. Note that we have $\widetilde{I} \subset I^h$, but the equality does not hold in general.

In the following, we state the definition of the degree of regularity given by M. Bardet in his PhD thesis at 2004:

Definition 2 (Degree of regularity d_{reg}).

- *Homogeneous Case. Let $I = \bigoplus I_d$ be the homogeneous ideal generated by homogeneous polynomials $f_1, \ldots, f_k$ in R. Assume that I is zero-dimensional. The degree of regularity of I, denoted by $d_{\text{reg}}(I)$, is defined as the minimal integer d with $R_d = I_d$. In particular, for any zero-dimensional homogeneous ideal I, we have*

$$d_{\text{reg}}(I) = \text{reg}(R/I) + 1.$$

- *Non-Homogeneous Case. Let $I \subset R$ be the ideal generated by non-homogeneous polynomials $f_1, \ldots, f_k$ in R. In this case, the degree of regularity of the (not necessarily homogeneous) ideal I is defined as follows: Let $f_i^{(h)}$ denote the homogeneous part of highest total degree in f_i for each $1 \le i \le k$. We define*

$$d_{\text{reg}}(I) = \text{reg}(\langle f_1^{(h)}, \ldots, f_k^{(h)} \rangle).$$

The homogeneous ideal $\langle f_1^{(h)}, \ldots, f_k^{(h)} \rangle$ depends on the choice of generators $f_1, \ldots, f_k$, but it is denoted by $I^{(h)}$ when the set of generators of I is clear from the context.

4.2 Analysis for the Ideal I_z

Here we shall analyze the degree of regularity $d_{\text{reg}}(I_z)$ and the solving degree solv. $\deg(I_z)$ of the non-homogeneous ideal $I_z \subset \mathbb{F}_p[X_1, X_2]$, given by (14). For simplicity, we write $f_1 := f(X_1)$ and $f_2 := f(X_2)$. Recall that $\widetilde{I}_z$ is defined as the homogeneous ideal generated by the homogenizations f_1^h, f_2^h and S_3^h in $\mathbb{F}_p[X_1, X_2, Y]$, where Y is an extra variable. Since the homogeneous ideal $\widetilde{I}_z \subset \mathbb{F}_p[X_1, X_2, Y]$ is generated by three homogeneous polynomials of at most degree $t = \#V \approx p^{1/3}$ (recall that V is the set of x-coordinates of the factor base $\mathcal{F}$), we have

$$\text{reg}(\widetilde{I}_z) \le (2t)^{2^{3-2}} = 4t^2 = O(p^{2/3})$$

from the bound of the regularity shown in [7]. Thus we obtain the following from [6, Corollary 3.14] (in this section, we fix the grevlex order for Gröbner bases):

Lemma 1. *We have*

$$\text{solv. } \deg(I_z) = \text{solv. } \deg(\widetilde{I}_z) = \text{max. GB. } \deg(\widetilde{I}_z) \le \text{reg}(\widetilde{I}_z) \le 4t^2 = O(p^{2/3}),$$

where max. GB. $\deg(I)$ denotes the maximum degree of a polynomial appearing in a reduced Gröbner basis of an ideal I.

Remark 6. The sequence (f_1^h, f_2^h, S_3^h) (or its permutation) is not necessarily $\mathbb{F}_p[X_1, X_2, Y]$-regular in general, which we have confirmed in our experiments. Thus we can not use the upper bound for the solving degree of a regular sequence, whereas we will obtain the same bound in Lemma 3 below.

The Degree of Regularity of I_z. We set

$$g_1 := f_1^{(h)} = X_1^t, \quad g_2 := f_2^{(h)} = X_2^t \quad \text{and} \quad g_3 := S_3^{(h)} = X_1^2 X_2^2.$$

as the homogeneous parts of highest total degrees in f_1, f_2, S_3, respectively. Let $I_z^{(h)}$ denote the homogeneous ideal in $R := \mathbb{F}_p[X_1, X_2]$ generated by three polynomials g_1, g_2 and g_3. Since $d_{\text{reg}}(I_z) = \text{reg}(I_z^{(h)})$, we have the following:

Lemma 2. *There is an exact sequence of graded R-modules*

$$0 \longrightarrow R(-t-2)^{\oplus 2} \xrightarrow{\varphi_2} R(-t)^{\oplus 2} \oplus R(-4) \xrightarrow{\varphi_1} R \xrightarrow{\varphi_0} R/I_z^{(h)} \longrightarrow 0, \quad (16)$$

where φ_0 is the canonical homomorphism and two homomorphisms φ_1, φ_2 are, respectively, represented by two matrices

$$A_1 = \begin{bmatrix} g_1 \\ g_2 \\ g_3 \end{bmatrix}, A_2 = \begin{bmatrix} 0 & X_1^2 & -X_2^{t-2} \\ X_2^2 & 0 & -X_1^{t-2} \end{bmatrix}. \quad (17)$$

Hence we have $\text{reg}(R/I_z^{(h)}) = t$ by definition, and thus

$$d_{\text{reg}}(I_z) = \text{reg}(I_z^{(h)}) = \text{reg}(R/I_z^{(h)}) + 1 = t + 1.$$

Proof. We clearly see that $\text{Ker}(\varphi_0) = \text{Im}(\varphi_1)$ and φ_2 (resp., φ_0) is injective (resp., surjective). We shall show $\text{Ker}(\varphi_1) = \text{Im}(\varphi_2)$. Put $\mathbf{u}_1 = [0, X_1^2, -X_2^{t-2}]$ and $\mathbf{u}_2 = [X_2^2, 0, -X_1^{t-2}]$, which generates $\text{Im}(\varphi_2)$ over R. Let $[h_1, h_2, h_3]$ be an arbitrary element in the submodule $\text{Ker}(\varphi_1)$. Then

$$\varphi_1([h_1, h_2, h_3]) = f_1 h_1 + f_2 h_2 + f_3 h_3 = X_1^t h_1 + X_2^t h_2 + X_1^2 X_2^2 h_3 = 0,$$

and thus $X_1^2(X_2^2 h_3 + X_1^{t-2} h_1) = -X_2^t h_2$. There exists $h_2' \in R$ with $h_2 = X_1^2 h_2'$. Similarly, we have $h_1 = X_2^2 h_1'$ for some h_1', and

$$X_1^t X_2^2 h_1' + X_2^t X_1^2 h_2' + X_1^2 X_2^2 h_3 = 0.$$

Thus $h_3 = -X_1^{t-2} h_1' - X_2^{t-2} h_2'$. Hence we have

$$[h_1, h_2, h_3] = [0, X_1^2 h_2', -X_2^{t-2} h_2'] + [X_2^2 h_1', 0, -X_1^{t-2} h_1'] = h_2' \mathbf{u}_1 + h_1' \mathbf{u}_2.$$

Conversely, we have $\varphi_1([0, X_1^2, -X_2^{t-2}]) = (X_2^t) X_1^2 + (X_1^2 X_2^2)(-X_2^{t-2}) = 0$, and

$$\varphi_1([X_2^2, 0, -X_1^{t-2}]) = (X_1^t) X_2^2 + (X_1^2 X_2^2)(-X_1^{t-2}) = 0.$$

Thus It follows that $\text{Ker}(\varphi_1) = \langle \mathbf{u}_1, \mathbf{u}_2 \rangle_R$, that is, $\text{Ker}(\varphi_1) = \text{Im}(\varphi_2)$. $\square$

Shape Bound for solv.deg(I_z). We prove $t \leq \max. \text{GB.deg}(\tilde{I}_z) \leq 2t + 2$ to apply a upper bound of $\max. \text{GB.deg}(\tilde{I}_z)$, provided in the proof of [19, Theorem 5.3]. When we apply the bound, we have to check the following two conditions:

(i) $\tilde{I}_z$ is in quasi stable position, that is, for any leading term $m \in \mathrm{LT}(I_z)$ and for all integers i, j, s with $1 \leq j < i \leq 3$, such that $X_i^s | m$, there exists $t > 0$ such that $X_j^t(m/X_i^s) \in \mathrm{LT}(I_z)$.

(ii) $\dim(\tilde{I}_z) \leq 1$, that is, the dimension of the affine variety $V(f_1^h, f_2^h, S_3^h) \subset \mathbb{A}^3(\overline{K})$ is one.

The condition (i) is clear since $X_1^t = \mathrm{LT}(f_1^h) \in \mathrm{LT}(I_z)$. For the condition (ii), the dimension of the projective zero-locus $V_{\mathrm{p}}(f_1^h, f_2^h, S_3^h)$ is 0 as a projective variety in $\mathbb{P}^2(\overline{K})$ where $K = \mathbb{F}_p$. Indeed, the projective curve $V_{\mathrm{p}}(f_1^h) \subset \mathbb{P}^2(\overline{K})$ has dimension 1. Since f_2^h is not a zero-divisor in $\mathbb{F}_p[X_1, X_2, Y]/\langle f_1^h \rangle$, we have $\dim V_{\mathrm{p}}(f_1^h, f_2^h) = \dim V_{\mathrm{p}}(f_1^h) - 1 = 0$. Thus we have

$$\dim V_{\mathrm{p}}(f_1^h, f_2^h, S_3^h) \leq \dim V_{\mathrm{p}}(f_1^h, f_2^h) = 0.$$

Now the affine zero-locus $V(f_1^h, f_2^h, S_3^h)$ is the affine cone of $V_{\mathrm{p}}(f_1^h, f_2^h, S_3^h)$, and thus we have $\dim V(f_1^h, f_2^h, S_3^h) = \dim V_{\mathrm{p}}(f_1^h, f_2^h, S_3^h) + 1 = 1$. Hence it follows from the proof of [19, Theorem 5.3] that

$$\mathrm{max.\, GB.\, deg}(\tilde{I}_z) \leq \deg(f_1^h) + \deg(f_2^h) + \deg(S_3^h) - 3 + 1 = 2t + 2.$$

Thus we obtain the following:

Lemma 3. *We have*

$$\mathrm{solv.\, deg}(I_z) = \mathrm{solv.\, deg}(\tilde{I}_z) = \mathrm{max.\, GB.\, deg}(\tilde{I}_z) \leq 2t + 2 = O(p^{1/3}).$$

Thus $\mathrm{solv.\, deg}(I_z) = O(p^{1/3})$.

Remark 7. Reduced Gröbner bases for $\tilde{I}_z$ in our experiments have the maximal degrees $2t + 1$ with $\mathrm{reg}(\tilde{I}_z) = 2t + 1$. This satisfies both of the bounds given in Lemmas 1 and 3, and implies that there is still a room to improve the bounds.

5   Conclusion

Based on the hybrid approach [3] for multivariate systems and the symmetry of the S_3-summation polynomial, we *drastically* accelerated to solve the system arising in Amadori et al.'s variant of index calculus [1] for solving the ECDLP over prime fields. With our acceleration, we had solved the ECDLP over prime fields $\mathbb{F}_p$ for primes p up to 30-bit over MAGMA. However, the complexity of our acceleration with Gröbner basis algorithms is worse than that of both the BSGS and the rho methods. Specifically, while both the BSGS and the rho methods have asymptotic complexity $p^{1/2}$, our improvements of [1] with Gröbner basis algorithms have at least $p^{2/3}$. Therefore our accelerated index calculus can never be faster than the BSGS nor the rho methods for large primes p. This is due to the expensive complexity of *current* Gröbner basis algorithms for solving multivariate systems (on the other hand, it might emerge new efficient specific algorithms for solving multivariate systems arising in index calculus). As a conclusion, compared to both the BSGS and the rho methods, index calculus with current Gröbner basis algorithms is quite infeasible for solving the ECDLP of cryptographic sizes such as 160-bit primes p.

Acknowledgments. This work was supported by JST CREST Grant Number JPMJCR14D6, Japan.

References

1. Amadori, A., Pintore, F., Sala, M.: On the discrete logarithm problem for prime-field elliptic curves. Finite Fields Appl. **51**, 168–182 (2018)
2. Bernstein, D.J., et al.: Faster elliptic-curve discrete logarithms on FPGAs. IACR Cryptology ePrint Archive 2016/382 (2016)
3. Bettale, L., Faugère, J.C., Perret, L.: Hybrid approach for solving multivariate systems over finite fields. J. Math. Cryptol. **3**(3), 177–197 (2009)
4. Blake, I.F., Seroussi, G., Smart, N.: Elliptic Curves in Cryptography, vol. 265. Cambridge University Press, Cambridge (1999)
5. Bos, J.W., Kaihara, M.E., Kleinjung, T., Lenstra, A.K., Montgomery, P.L.: Solving a 112-bit prime elliptic curve discrete logarithm problem on game consoles using sloppy reduction. Int. J. Appl. Cryptogr. **2**(3), 212–228 (2012)
6. Caminata, A., Gorla, E.: Solving multivariate polynomial systems and an invariant from commutative algebra. arXiv preprint arXiv:1706.06319 (2017)
7. Caviglia, G., Sbarra, E.: Characteristic-free bounds for the castelnuovo-mumford regularity. Compos. Math. **141**(6), 1365–1373 (2005)
8. Cohen, H., et al.: Handbook of Elliptic and Hyperelliptic Curve Cryptography. CRC Press, Boca Raton (2005)
9. Diem, C.: On the discrete logarithm problem in elliptic curves. Compos. Math. **147**(01), 75–104 (2011)
10. Eisenbud, D.: The Geometry of Syzygies: A Second Course in Algebraic Geometry and Commutative Algebra. Graduate Texts in Mathematics, vol. 229. Springer, New York (2005). https://doi.org/10.1007/b137572
11. Faugère, J.C.: A new efficient algorithm for computing Gröbner bases (F4). J. Pure Appl. Algebra **139**(1–3), 61–88 (1999)
12. Faugère, J.C.: A new efficient algorithm for computing Gröbner bases without reduction to zero (F5). In: International Symposium on Symbolic and Algebraic Computation-ISSAC 2002, pp. 75–83. ACM (2002)
13. Faugère, J.-C., Perret, L., Petit, C., Renault, G.: Improving the complexity of index calculus algorithms in elliptic curves over binary fields. In: Pointcheval, D., Johansson, T. (eds.) EUROCRYPT 2012. LNCS, vol. 7237, pp. 27–44. Springer, Heidelberg (2012). https://doi.org/10.1007/978-3-642-29011-4_4
14. Galbraith, S.D., Gaudry, P.: Recent progress on the elliptic curve discrete logarithm problem. Des. Codes Cryptogr. **78**(1), 51–72 (2016)
15. Galbraith, S.D., Gebregiyorgis, S.W.: Summation polynomial algorithms for elliptic curves in characteristic two. In: Meier, W., Mukhopadhyay, D. (eds.) INDOCRYPT 2014. LNCS, vol. 8885, pp. 409–427. Springer, Cham (2014). https://doi.org/10.1007/978-3-319-13039-2_24
16. Gary, M., Daniela, M.: A few more index calculus algorithms for the elliptic curve discrete logarithm problem. Cryptology ePrint Archive: Report 2017/1262 (2017). https://eprint.iacr.org/2017/1262
17. Gaudry, P.: Index calculus for abelian varieties of small dimension and the elliptic curve discrete logarithm problem. J. Symb. Comput. **44**(12), 1690–1702 (2009)
18. Hankerson, D., Menezes, A.J., Vanstone, S.: Guide to Elliptic Curve Cryptography. Springer, New York (2006). https://doi.org/10.1007/b97644

19. Hashemi, A., Seiler, W.M.: Dimension-dependent upper bounds for grobner bases. arXiv preprint arXiv:1705.02776 (2017). https://arxiv.org/abs/1705.02776

20. Kleinjung, T., et al.: Factorization of a 768-bit RSA modulus. In: Rabin, T. (ed.) CRYPTO 2010. LNCS, vol. 6223, pp. 333–350. Springer, Heidelberg (2010). https://doi.org/10.1007/978-3-642-14623-7_18

21. Koblitz, N.: Elliptic curve cryptosystems. Math. Comput. **48**(177), 203–209 (1987)

22. Kusaka, T., et al.: Solving 114-bit ECDLP for a barreto-naehrig curve. In: Kim, H., Kim, D.-C. (eds.) ICISC 2017. LNCS, vol. 10779, pp. 231–244. Springer, Cham (2018). https://doi.org/10.1007/978-3-319-78556-1_13

23. Menezes, A.J., Okamoto, T., Vanstone, S.A.: Reducing elliptic curve logarithms to logarithms in a finite field. IEEE Trans. Inf. Theory **39**(5), 1639–1646 (1993)

24. Miller, V.S.: Use of elliptic curves in cryptography. In: Williams, H.C. (ed.) CRYPTO 1985. LNCS, vol. 218, pp. 417–426. Springer, Heidelberg (1986). https://doi.org/10.1007/3-540-39799-X_31

25. Petit, C., Kosters, M., Messeng, A.: Algebraic approaches for the elliptic curve discrete logarithm problem over prime fields. In: Cheng, C.-M., Chung, K.-M., Persiano, G., Yang, B.-Y. (eds.) PKC 2016. LNCS, vol. 9615, pp. 3–18. Springer, Heidelberg (2016). https://doi.org/10.1007/978-3-662-49387-8_1

26. Pollard, J.M.: Monte Carlo methods for index computation (mod p). Math. Comput. **32**(143), 918–924 (1978)

27. Rivest, R.L., Shamir, A., Adleman, L.: A method for obtaining digital signatures and public-key cryptosystems. Commun. ACM **21**(2), 120–126 (1978)

28. Satoh, T., Araki, K.: Fermat quotients and the polynomial time discrete log algorithm for anomalous elliptic curves. Comment. Math. Univ. Sancti Pauli **47**(1), 81–92 (1998)

29. Semaev, I.A.: Evaluation of discrete logarithms in a group of p-torsion points of an elliptic curve in characteristic p. Math. Comput. **67**(221), 353–356 (1998)

30. Semaev, I.A.: Summation polynomials and the discrete logarithm problem on elliptic curves. IACR Cryptology ePrint Archive 2004/031 (2004)

31. Semaev, I.A.: New algorithm for the discrete logarithm problem on elliptic curves. IACR Cryptology eprint Archive 2015/310 (2015)

32. Shanks, D.: Class number, a theory of factorization, and genera. In: Proceedings of Symposium of Pure Mathematics, vol. 20, pp. 41–440 (1971)

33. Silverman, J.H.: The Arithmetic of Elliptic Curves. Graduate Texts in Mathematics, vol. 106, 2nd edn. Springer, New York (2009). https://doi.org/10.1007/978-0-387-09494-6

34. Smart, N.P.: The discrete logarithm problem on elliptic curves of trace one. J. Cryptol. **12**(3), 193–196 (1999)

35. Wenger, E., Wolfger, P.: Solving the discrete logarithm of a 113-bit Koblitz curve with an FPGA cluster. In: Joux, A., Youssef, A. (eds.) SAC 2014. LNCS, vol. 8781, pp. 363–379. Springer, Cham (2014). https://doi.org/10.1007/978-3-319-13051-4_22

36. Yasuda, M., Shimoyama, T., Kogure, J., Izu, T.: Computational hardness of IFP and ECDLP. Appl. Algebra Eng. Commun. Comput. **27**(6), 493–521 (2016)

37. Yokota, Y., Kudo, M., Yasuda, M.: Practical limit of index calculus algorithms for ECDLP over prime fields. In: International Workshop on Coding and Cryptography-WCC 2017 (2017). http://wcc2017.suai.ru/proceedings.html

Several MILP-Aided Attacks Against SNOW 2.0

Yuki Funabiki[1](✉), Yosuke Todo[2], Takanori Isobe[3], and Masakatu Morii[1]

[1] Kobe University, 1-1 Rokkodai-cho, Nada-ku, Kobe, Hyogo 657-8501, Japan
funabiki@stu.kobe-u.ac.jp,mmorii@kobe-u.ac.jp
[2] NTT Secure Platform Laboratories,
3-9-11 Midori-cho, Musashino, Tokyo 180-8585, Japan
todo.yosuke@lab.ntt.co.jp
[3] University of Hyogo,
7-1-28 Minatojima-minamimachi, Chuo-ku, Kobe, Hyogo 650-0047, Japan
takanori.isobe@ai.u-hyogo.ac.jp

Abstract. SNOW 2.0 is a software-oriented stream cipher and internationally standardized by ISO/IEC 18033-4. In this paper, we present three attacks on SNOW 2.0 by MILP-aided automatic search algorithms. First, we present an efficient algorithm to find linear masks with the high correlation. It enables us to improve time and data complexities of the known fast correlation attacks. Then we propose a 17-round integral distinguisher out of 32 rounds by evaluating the propagation of the division property. Moreover, we propose a cube attack on the 14-round SNOW 2.0. The time complexity is $2^{61.59}$ where 2^{39} chosen IVs are required. As far as we know, these are the first investigations about integral and cube attacks of SNOW 2.0, respectively.

Keywords: Stream cipher · SNOW 2.0 · Fast correlation attack
Division property · Integral distinguisher · Cube attack · MILP

1 Introduction

1.1 Background

Since a Mixed Integer Linear Programming (MILP) was first introduced into cryptanalyses by Mouha et al. [17], the MILP-aided search has been successfully applied to search several cryptographic characteristics such as differential [22,23], linear [22], impossible differential [5,19], zero-correlation linear [5], and integral characteristics (using the division property) [30].

SNOW 2.0 [9] was proposed by Ekdahl and Johansson in 2002 as a strengthened version of SNOW 1.0 [8], which was a NESSIE candidate and broken by the guess-and-determine attack [11] and distinguishing attack [4]. Currently, SNOW 2.0 is considered one of the most important stream ciphers and it is internationally standardized by ISO/IEC 18033-4 [12].

© Springer Nature Switzerland AG 2018
J. Camenisch and P. Papadimitratos (Eds.): CANS 2018, LNCS 11124, pp. 394–413, 2018.
https://doi.org/10.1007/978-3-030-00434-7_20

1.2   Our Contributions

In this paper, we improve a fast correlation attack on SNOW 2.0 by the MILP-aided search [10] which enables us to search linear masks more efficiently. Moreover, we propose an integral attack and a cube attack on the reduced-round SNOW 2.0 by using the MILP-aided tool and division property [24,26,30].

Fast Correlation Attack. Our purpose is to find linear masks with the higher correlation by using the MILP-aided tool. To efficiently perform the MILP-aided search on SNOW 2.0, we need to model six operations: XOR, Three-forked branch, SubBytes, MixColumns, 2-input addition modulo 2^{32} and 3-input addition modulo 2^{32}. Most of them have the established modeling method. However, the method for linear approximations of the 3-input addition has not been established yet as discussed in [10]. To overcome this problem, we leverage a linear relaxation model and then utilize existing linear approximation methods by Nyberg and Wallén [18] to efficiently search linear masks. By this approach, we are able to get linear masks whose correlation is sufficiently higher than known results [13,18]. Using the linear masks and several techniques for fast correlation attacks, e.g. k-tree algorithm [31], we develop an improved fast correlation attack on SNOW 2.0. Table 1 shows previous results and our result on SNOW 2.0. The required time and data complexities of our attack are less than the half of the previous attack [31], while it still requires more than time complexity of 2^{128}.

Table 1. Comparison of related works on SNOW 2.0

Attack type	Data	Time	Reference
Distinguishing attack	2^{174}	2^{174}	[18]
Key recovery attack	$2^{198.77}$	$2^{212.38}$	[13]
Key recovery attack	$2^{163.59}$	$2^{164.15}$	[31]
Key recovery attack	$\mathbf{2^{162.34}}$	$\mathbf{2^{162.91}}$	**This paper**

Integral Attack. We consider an integral distinguisher of the reduced-round SNOW 2.0 by the MILP-aided search. We construct a MILP model based on the division property and its propagation rules [24,26]. The point for constructing an integral distinguisher is how to arrange the positions of active bits in the field of initialization vector (IV). As a result, we are able to construct an integral distinguisher on the 17-round SNOW 2.0 out of 32 rounds with 2^3 chosen IVs. As far as we know, this is the first investigation about the integral distinguisher of SNOW 2.0. While a 13-round integral distinguisher of SNOW 3G, which is a variant of SNOW 2.0 and standard cipher for 3GPP, was found [2]. Our result reveals that the security margin of SNOW 2.0 against integral distinguisher is smaller than that of SNOW 3G.

Cube Attack. We also consider a cube attack on the reduced-round SNOW 2.0. For the cube attack, we construct the same MILP model in the integral attack by the bit-based division property [25]. Moreover, we update this model by the latest study about the algebraic degree [28]. Like considering integral distinguisher, the point is how to arrange the positions of active bits in the IV's field. As a result, we can mount a key recovery attack on the 14-round SNOW 2.0 with $2^{61.59}$ time complexity and 2^{39} chosen IVs. As far as we know, this is the first result of the cube attack on the reduced-round SNOW 2.0.

Paper Organization: This paper is organized as follows: We present some preliminaries about our works in Sect. 2. In Sect. 3, we propose an improved MILP-aided search algorithm for linear masks with the high correlation. Moreover, we present the best key recovery attack on SNOW 2.0 by using the found linear masks. In Sect. 4, we propose how to get new 17-round integral distinguishers by evaluating the propagation of the division property. Then, we also present 14-round cube attacks by exploiting the algebraic degree in Sect. 5. Section 6 concludes this paper.

2 Preliminaries

2.1 Specification of SNOW 2.0

The stream cipher SNOW 2.0 uses a 128-bit secret key and a 128-bit initialization vector (IV). It consists of a Linear Feedback Shift Register (LFSR) with 16 words of 32-bit length and a Finite State Machine (FSM) with 2 words as shown in Fig. 1. Here, $\oplus$ denotes the XOR and $\boxplus$ denotes the addition modulo 2^{32}. The feedback polynomial of the LFSR is represented as

$$s_{t+16} = \alpha^{-1} \cdot s_{t+11} \oplus s_{t+2} \oplus \alpha \cdot s_t,$$

where α is a root of the polynomial $x^4 + \beta^{23} x^3 + \beta^{245} x^2 + \beta^{48} x + \beta^{239} \in GF(2^8)[x]$ and β is a root of the polynomial $x^8 + x^7 + x^5 + x^3 + 1 \in GF(2)[x]$. The FSM is updated as $R1_{t+1} = s_{t+5} \boxplus R2_t$ and $R2_{t+1} = S(R1_t)$ where S is a 32-bit to 32-bit function defined as a combination of SubBytes and MixColumns which are the well-known components in AES [6].

SNOW 2.0 is initialized with the key $K = (k_3, k_2, k_1, k_0)$ and the $IV = (IV_3, IV_2, IV_1, IV_0)$. Let $\mathbf{1}$ be the all-one word, first load the LFSR as follows.

$$s_{15} = k_3 \oplus IV_0, \quad s_{14} = k_2, \qquad s_{13} = k_1, \qquad s_{12} = k_0 \oplus IV_1,$$
$$s_{11} = k_3 \oplus \mathbf{1}, \quad s_{10} = k_2 \oplus \mathbf{1} \oplus IV_2, \quad s_9 = k_1 \oplus \mathbf{1} \oplus IV_3, \quad s_8 = k_0 \oplus \mathbf{1},$$
$$s_7 = k_3, \qquad s_6 = k_2, \qquad s_5 = k_1, \qquad s_4 = k_0,$$
$$s_3 = k_3 \oplus \mathbf{1}, \qquad s_2 = k_2 \oplus \mathbf{1}, \qquad s_1 = k_1 \oplus \mathbf{1}, \qquad s_0 = k_0 \oplus \mathbf{1}.$$

The FSM is initialized with $R1_0 = R2_0 = 0$. Then run the cipher 32 times with the feedback of the LFSR is XORed with the FSM output and no keystream is generated. After this, the cipher is switched into the keystream generation mode, but the first keystream word is discarded. The keystream word generated at clock t is $z_t = (s_{t+15} \boxplus R1_t) \oplus R2_t \oplus s_t$.

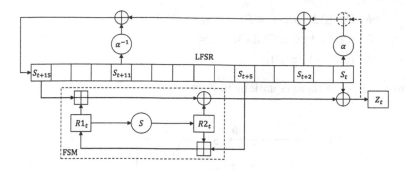

Fig. 1. Keystream generation of SNOW 2.0

2.2 Mixed Integer Linear Programming

A Mixed Integer Linear Programming (MILP) is an optimization or feasibility program where variables are restricted to integers. A MILP model $\mathcal{M}$ consists of variables $\mathcal{M}.var$, constraints $\mathcal{M}.con$, and an objective function $\mathcal{M}.obj$. A MILP solver can solve such an optimization program, and it returns *infeasible* if there is no feasible solution. Moreover, if there is no objective function, the MILP solver only evaluates whether the model is feasible or not. We used Gurobi optimization [1] as the solver in our experiments.

2.3 Linear Approximation for Fast Correlation Attack

Linear Mask and Correlation. In the linear cryptanalysis [15], we first extract some bits from plaintext P, ciphertext C and secret key K, and generate the linear approximation as $\Gamma_P \cdot P \oplus \Gamma_C \cdot C = \Gamma_K \cdot K$, where $x \cdot y$ is defined as the inner product of x and y on $GF(2)$. Also, $\Gamma_P, \Gamma_C, \Gamma_K$ is called a linear mask and is an operation for extracting a specific bit, respectively. The probability Pr that equation holds can be expressed as $\Pr = \frac{1}{2} + \epsilon$, where ϵ denotes the bias. Attackers substitute the value obtained by the known plaintexts attack into that equation and derive the bias from the result. Therefore, the greatest interest in the linear cryptanalysis is directed to search for a linear approximation that maximizes the absolute value of the bias. The total bias is produced by *piling up lemma* [15] is generally calculated by $\Pr = \frac{1}{2} + 2^{m-1} \prod_{i=1}^{m} \epsilon_i$, where ϵ_i represents the i-th bias. By considering correlation κ_i corresponding to $\kappa_i = 2\epsilon_i$, the calculation process is simplified as $2\Pr = 1 + \prod_{i=1}^{m} \kappa_i$.

Known Linear Approximations of SNOW 2.0. Several linear approximations on SNOW 2.0 have already been proposed [18,29]. The related states and linear masks are shown in Fig. 2. The linear approximation equations were obtained as follows.

$$\Phi \cdot R1_t \boxplus \Gamma \cdot s_{t+15} = \Gamma(z_t \oplus s_t \oplus R2_t),$$
$$\Gamma \cdot R2_t \boxplus \Lambda \cdot s_{t+5} \boxplus \Lambda \cdot s_{t+16} = \Lambda \cdot (z_{t+1} \oplus s_{t+1} \oplus S(R1_t)),$$
$$\Phi \cdot R1_t = \Lambda \cdot S(R1_t).$$

We aim to improve these equations in Sect. 3.

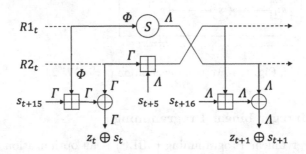

Fig. 2. Known linear approximation of SNOW 2.0

2.4   Division Property

The division property, which was proposed in [24,26], is a general method to find integral distinguisher. We first prepare the division property of the chosen plaintexts and then calculate the division property of the corresponding ciphertexts by evaluating the propagation for every round function.

Some propagation rules for the division property are proven in [24,26]. Attackers determine indices $I = \{i_1, i_2, \ldots, i_{|I|}\}$ and prepare $2^{|I|}$ chosen plaintexts where variables indexed by I are taking all possible combinations of values. If the division property of the corresponding ciphertexts does not have a unit vector e_i whose only i-th element is 1, the i-th bit of r-round ciphertexts is balanced. For the division property on stream ciphers, we regard the initialization vectors (IVs) as plaintexts and the keystream as ciphertexts.

2.5   Cube Attack

The cube attack is a key recovery attack proposed by Dinur and Shamir [7]. Considering a stream cipher with n-bit secret information $x = (x_1, x_2, \ldots, x_n)$ and m-bit public initialization vector $v = (v_1, v_2, \ldots, v_m)$, one bit of the keystream can be regarded as a polynomial of x and v referred as $f(x, v)$. For a set of indices $I = \{i_1, i_2, \ldots, i_{|I|}\} \subset \{1, 2, \ldots, n\}$, which is referred as cube indices, t_I denotes the monomial as $t_I = v_{i_1} \cdots v_{i_{|I|}}$. The algebraic normal form (ANF) of $f(x, v)$ can be uniquely decomposed as $f(x, v) = t_I \cdot p(x, v) + q(x, v)$.

Let C_I, which is referred as a cube (defined by I), be a set of $2^{|I|}$ values where variables in $\{v_{i_1}, v_{i_2}, \ldots, v_{i_{|I|}}\}$ are taking all possible combinations of values, and all remaining variables are fixed to some arbitrary values. Then the sum of f overall values of the cube C_I is

$$\bigoplus_{C_I} f(\boldsymbol{x}, \boldsymbol{v}) = \bigoplus_{C_I} t_I \cdot p(\boldsymbol{x}, \boldsymbol{v}) + \bigoplus_{C_I} q(\boldsymbol{x}, \boldsymbol{v}) = p(\boldsymbol{x}, \boldsymbol{v}).$$

The first term is reduced to $p(\boldsymbol{x}, \boldsymbol{v})$ because t_I becomes 1 for only one case in C_I. The second term is always canceled out because $q(\boldsymbol{x}, \boldsymbol{v})$ misses at least one variable from $\{v_{i_1}, v_{i_2}, \ldots, v_{i_{|I|}}\}$. Then, $p(\boldsymbol{x}, \boldsymbol{v})$ is called the superpoly of the cube C_I. Since public variables $\boldsymbol{v}$ are known and selectable by attackers, the ANF of $p_v(\boldsymbol{x}) = p(\boldsymbol{v}, \boldsymbol{x})$ can be evaluated. The goal of attackers is to recover $p_v(\boldsymbol{x})$ whose $\boldsymbol{v}$ is fixed. Once the superpoly $p_v(\boldsymbol{x})$ is recovered, attackers query the cube to an encryption oracle and compute the sum of $f(\boldsymbol{x}, \boldsymbol{v})$ over the cube. Then, attackers can get one polynomial about secret variables.

3   New MILP Modeling Method for Linear Masks and Application to Fast Correlation Attack

For improving the fast correlation attack, we aim to find more efficient linear masks with the high correlation by the MILP-aided search. In this section, we first describe our target linear approximation. Then, we propose new modeling methods and search for linear masks. Finally, we show how to applicate our linear masks to the fast correlation attack.

In the linear masking method [4] for SNOW 2.0, we prepare the set of linear masks is shown in Fig. 3.

We obtain the linear approximation equations as

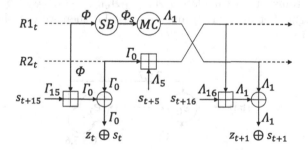

Fig. 3. Our linear approximation of SNOW 2.0

$$\Phi \cdot R1_t \boxplus \Gamma_{15} \cdot s_{t+15} = \Gamma_0 \cdot (z_t \oplus s_t \oplus R2_t), \tag{1}$$
$$\Gamma_0 \cdot R2_t \boxplus \Lambda_5 \cdot s_{t+5} \boxplus \Lambda_{16} \cdot s_{t+16} = \Lambda_1 \cdot (z_{t+1} \oplus s_{t+1} \oplus MC(SB(R1_t))), \tag{2}$$
$$\Phi \cdot R1_t = \Phi_S \cdot SB(R1_t) = \Lambda_1 \cdot MC(SB(R1_t)). \tag{3}$$

These equations involve six operations: XOR, Three-forked branch, SubBytes, MixColumns, 2-input addition modulo 2^{32} and 3-input addition modulo 2^{32}. The MILP modeling methods of the first four operations have already established in [22,23]. Hence, we describe new modeling methods for the last two operations.

3.1   Improved Modeling Method for 2-Input Addition Modulo 2^{32}

Nyberg and Wallén proposed an efficient algorithm for computing the correlation of linear approximations of the addition modulo 2^n with k inputs in [18,27]. Based on this algorithm, Fu et al. proposed the MILP modeling method for 2-input addition modulo 2^{32} in [10]. At first, we describe these previous methods. Then, we show the improved modeling method.

Theorem 1 (see [18,27]). *For the linear approximation of the 2-input addition modulo 2^n, we consider the input masks $\Lambda_\alpha, \Lambda_\beta$ and output mask Γ. These masks are defined as $\Lambda_\alpha, \Lambda_\beta, \Gamma \in \mathbb{F}_2^n$ and $\Lambda_\alpha = (\Lambda_\alpha[n-1], \ldots, \Lambda_\alpha[0]), \Lambda_\beta = (\Lambda_\beta[n-1], \ldots, \Lambda_\beta[0]), \Gamma = (\Gamma[n-1], \ldots, \Gamma[0])$. We define the vector $u = (u[n-1], \ldots, u[0])$ where $u[i] = 4\Gamma[i] + 2\Lambda_\alpha[i] + \Lambda_\beta[i], 0 \le u[i] < 8, 0 \le i < n$. The correlation κ_2 can be computed with the following linear representation,*

$$\kappa_2 = L A_{u[n-1]} A_{u[n-2]} \cdots A_{u[0]} C,$$

where $A_r, r = 0, \ldots, 7$, is 2×2 matrices,

$$A_0 = \frac{1}{2}\begin{pmatrix} 2 & 0 \\ 0 & 1 \end{pmatrix}, A_1 = A_2 = -A_4 = \frac{1}{2}\begin{pmatrix} 0 & 0 \\ 1 & 0 \end{pmatrix},$$

$$A_7 = \frac{1}{2}\begin{pmatrix} 0 & 2 \\ 1 & 0 \end{pmatrix}, -A_3 = A_5 = A_6 = \frac{1}{2}\begin{pmatrix} 0 & 0 \\ 0 & 1 \end{pmatrix}.$$

L is a row vector $L = (1,0)$, and C is a column vector $C = (1,1)^T$.

In order to provide a fast implementation for Theorem 1, Nyberg and Wallén utilized the automaton to calculate $L A_{u[n-1]} A_{u[n-2]} \cdots A_{u[0]} C$ by multiplying from left to right. Let $e_0 = (1,0)$ and $e_1 = (0,1)$, then we can show the state transitions in Fig. 4.

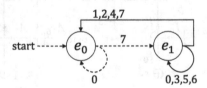

Fig. 4. State transitions on automaton

Fu et al.'s Modeling Method [10]. Based on the Fig. 4, they showed Proposition 1 to calculate the correlation κ_2 for the 2-input addition modulo 2^{32}.

Proposition 1. *For the linear approximation of the 2-input addition modulo 2^n with input masks $\Lambda_\alpha, \Lambda_\beta$ and output mask Γ, the state transitions of the automaton are shown in Fig. 4, where $u[i] = 4\Gamma[i] + 2\Lambda_\alpha[i] + \Lambda_\beta[i], 0 \le u[i] <$*

$8, 0 \leq i < n$ and $\epsilon_j \in \{e_0, e_1\}, 0 \leq j < n$. If the correlation for the linear approximation is non-zero, the absolute value of the correlation can be computed as follows,

$$|\kappa_2| = 2^{-\#\{0<i<n|\epsilon_i=e_1\}}.$$

They use the **inequality generator()** function in the **sage. geometry. polyhedron** class of SAGE [20] and the greedy algorithm in [22] to get 8 linear inequalities satisfying all 10 possible transitions. Note that there is an additional constraint $\epsilon_n = e_0$. Hence, for the linear approximation of the 2-input addition modulo 2^n, the constraints contain $8 \times n + 1$ linear inequalities and the absolute value of correlation is $2^{-\sum_{i=1}^{n-1} s[i]}$, where the bit variable $s[i]$ is defined as $s[i] = 0$ if $\epsilon_i = e_0$, and $s[i] = 1$ if $\epsilon_i = e_1$.

Our Modeling Method. We focus on the dedicated method by the following truth table from Fig. 4. In the Table 2, we find a characteristic of 10 possible transitions which are marked T with each hamming weight. This constraint is represented as

$$s[i+1] + \Gamma[i] + \Lambda_\alpha[i] + \Lambda_\beta[i] + s[i] = 2d, \quad d = 0 \text{ or } 1 \text{ or } 2.$$

This equation restricts the possible transitions to X_H, where $X = T$ or F. Therefore, we have to make the equations which prohibit the F_Hs.

$$\begin{cases} s[i+1] + \Gamma[i] - \Lambda_\beta[i] \geq 0, \\ s[i+1] - \Lambda_\alpha[i] + \Lambda_\beta[i] \geq 0, \\ s[i+1] - \Gamma[i] + \Lambda_\alpha[i] \geq 0. \end{cases}$$

These equations make partial cells where $s[i] = 0$ and $1 \leq u[i] \leq 6$ are banned. In this way, our constraints contain $4 \times n + 1$ linear inequalities.

Table 2. Truth table for 2-input addition modulo 2^{32}

$u[i]$	$s[i] = 0$								$s[i] = 1$							
	0	1	2	3	4	5	6	7	0	1	2	3	4	5	6	7
$s[i+1] = 0$	T_H	F	F	F_H	F	F_H	F_H	F	F	T_H	T_H	F	T_H	F	F	T_H
$s[i+1] = 1$	F	F_H	F_H	F	F_H	F	F	T_H	T_H	F	F	T_H	F	T_H	T_H	F

3.2   New Modeling Method for 3-Input Addition Modulo 2^{32}

The modeling method for the 3-input addition modulo 2^{32} has been the open problem. In this paper, we attempt to solve this problem. Before we describe our method, we show how to compute the correlation of the 3-input addition modulo 2^{32}. Nyberg et al. described the computing the correlation of linear approximations of the 3-input addition modulo 2^n in [18,27].

Theorem 2 (see [18,27]). *For the linear approximation of the 3-input addition modulo 2^n, we consider the input masks $\Lambda_\alpha, \Lambda_\beta, \Lambda_\gamma$ and output mask Γ. These masks are defined as $\Lambda_\alpha, \Lambda_\beta, \Lambda_\gamma, \Gamma \in \mathbb{F}_2^n$ and $\Lambda_\alpha = (\Lambda_\alpha[n-1], \ldots, \Lambda_\alpha[0]), \Lambda_\beta = (\Lambda_\beta[n-1], \ldots, \Lambda_\beta[0]), \Lambda_\gamma = (\Lambda_\gamma[n-1], \ldots, \Lambda_\gamma[0]), \Gamma = (\Gamma[n-1], \ldots, \Gamma[0])$. We define the vector $u = (u[n-1], \ldots, u[0])$ where $u[i] = 8\Gamma[i] + 4\Lambda_\alpha[i] + 2\Lambda_\beta[i] + \Lambda_\gamma[i], 0 \le u[i] < 16, 0 \le i < n$. The correlation κ_3 can be computed with the following linear representation,*

$$\kappa_3 = LA_{u[n-1]}A_{u[n-2]} \cdots A_{u[0]}C,$$

where $A_r, r = 0, \ldots, 15$, is 3×3 matrices,

$$A_0 = \frac{1}{8}\begin{pmatrix} 4 & 1 & 0 \\ 4 & 6 & 4 \\ 0 & 1 & 4 \end{pmatrix}, A_1 = A_2 = A_3 = -A_8 = \frac{1}{8}\begin{pmatrix} 2 & 1 & 0 \\ -2 & 0 & 2 \\ 0 & -1 & -2 \end{pmatrix},$$

$$A_3 = A_5 = A_6 = -A_9 = -A_{10} = -A_{12} = \frac{1}{8}\begin{pmatrix} 0 & 1 & 0 \\ 0 & -2 & 0 \\ 0 & 1 & 0 \end{pmatrix},$$

$$A_7 = -A_{11} = -A_{13} = -A_{14} = \frac{1}{8}\begin{pmatrix} -2 & 1 & 0 \\ 2 & 0 & -2 \\ 0 & -1 & 2 \end{pmatrix}, A_{15} = \frac{1}{8}\begin{pmatrix} 4 & -1 & 0 \\ 4 & -6 & 4 \\ 0 & -1 & 4 \end{pmatrix}.$$

L is a row vector $L = (1,1,1)$, and C is a column vector $C = (1,0,0)^T$.

According to Theorem 2, we can calculate the correlation of the 3-input addition modulo 2^{32}. If we can convert this calculation to the MILP model, the open problem will be solved. However, such model demands huge constraints and the solution cannot be obtained within the practical time. Therefore, we aim to construct the rough MILP model (which is called a linear relaxation model) and check the solution outside the model by this calculation.

At first, we calculate the partial correlations for each nibble-wise unit. Since there are 5 types of matrices, that is A_0, A_1, A_3, A_7 and A_{15}, we can get the list of partial correlations with 5^4 computations. Then, we link the index $u[i]$ to the matrix number $j = \{0,1,3,7,15\}$ and the 4-bit sequence of u corresponds to the partial correlation of this list. By this procedure, we can get rough MILP model which is restricted for each nibble instead of bit. Since this MILP model can be solved within a practical time, only we have to do is to evaluate the whole correlation outside of the model.

Moreover, we set some constraints to our model for more efficient search. If the most significant bits of input and output masks produce $u[n-1] = 0$, the same sequence continues until $u[i] = 15$ appears. This characteristic is restricted by following equations.

$$\begin{cases} s[i] + s[i-1] - \Gamma[i] \ge 0 \\ s[i] + s[i-1] - \Lambda_\alpha[i] \ge 0 \\ s[i] + s[i-1] - \Lambda_\beta[i] \ge 0 \\ s[i] + s[i-1] - \Lambda_\gamma[i] \ge 0 \end{cases}, \begin{cases} s[i] - s[i-1] + \Gamma[i] \ge 0 \\ s[i] - s[i-1] + \Lambda_\alpha[i] \ge 0 \\ s[i] - s[i-1] + \Lambda_\beta[i] \ge 0 \\ s[i] - s[i-1] + \Lambda_\gamma[i] \ge 0 \end{cases}, s[i] \le s[i-1].$$

First 4 constraints restrict to the propagation of $u[i] = 0 \rightarrow u[i-1] = 0$. And next 4 constraints restrict to the propagation of $u[i] = 0 \rightarrow u[i-1] = 15$. Last constraint means that above constraints are invalidated once $u[i] = 15$ appears. Furthermore, the following patterns in multiplications of matrices derive zero-correlation.

$$A_1 A_3 = A_1 A_0 A_3 = A_1 A_1 A_1 = A_1 A_1 A_7 = A_3 A_7 A_3 = 0.$$

Hence, we prohibit these patterns in our MILP model.

3.3 Our MILP Model for Linear Masks on SNOW 2.0

Our search algorithm is shown in Algorithm 1 We first prepare 7 linear masks

---

Algorithm 1. MILP model for linear masks on SNOW 2.0

1: **procedure** searchMasks
2:    Prepare empty MILP Model $\mathcal{M}$
3:    $\mathcal{M}.var \leftarrow \Gamma_0, \Gamma_{15}, \Lambda_1, \Lambda_5, \Lambda_{16}, \Phi, \Phi_s$ as 32-bit vectors
4:    $\mathcal{M}.var \leftarrow \kappa_2$ as integer
5:    $\mathcal{M}.var \leftarrow \kappa_3, \kappa_s$ as continuous value
6:    $(\mathcal{M}, \kappa_s) = \text{subBytes}(\mathcal{M}, \Phi, \Phi_s)$
7:    $\mathcal{M} = \text{mixColumns}(\mathcal{M}, \Phi_s, \Lambda_1)$
8:    $(\mathcal{M}, \kappa_2) = \text{modAdd2}(\mathcal{M}, \Gamma_{15}, \Phi, \Gamma_0)$
9:    $(\mathcal{M}, \kappa_3) = \text{modAdd3}(\mathcal{M}, \Gamma_0, \Lambda_5, \Lambda_{16}, \Lambda_1)$
10:    $(\mathcal{M}.con \leftarrow \Gamma_0 = \Lambda_1) \leftarrow$ *Added later*
11:    $\mathcal{M}.obj \leftarrow$ Minimize $\kappa_2 + \kappa_3 + \kappa_s$
12:    **repeat**
13:        solve MILP
14:        **if** $\mathcal{M}$ is feasible **then**
15:            recalculate correlations $\kappa'_{2,3,s} \leftarrow \kappa_{2,3,s}$, respectively
16:            **if** $\kappa'_{2,3,s} > 0$ **then**
17:                list $\leftarrow$ linearHull$(\Gamma_0, \Gamma_{15}, \Lambda_1, \Lambda_5, \Lambda_{16})$
18:            **end if**
19:            banMasks$(\Gamma_0, \Gamma_{15}, \Lambda_1, \Lambda_5, \Lambda_{16}, \Phi, \Phi_s)$
20:        **end if**
21:    **until** $\mathcal{M}$ is feasible
22:    **return** list
23: **end procedure**

---

and 3 correlations which are produced by the Eq.(1–3), where each correlation variable κ is defined as the exponent part of the correlation like $2^{-\kappa}$. In particular, κ_3 and κ_s are defined as continuous values in order to calculate more accurate correlations. These linear masks and correlations are restricted by subBytes, mixColumns, modAdd2 and modAdd3 which are defined by Sub-Bytes, MixColumns, 2-input addition modulo 2^{32} and 3-input addition modulo 2^{32}, respectively. Then, we set the objective function that minimizes the total correlation $\kappa_2 + \kappa_3 + \kappa_s$ and optimize the MILP model. If the model is feasible, we recalculate the correlations by Nyberg et al.'s method. If the real correlations have no problem, we also check the *linear hull effect* [15] by `linearHull`. Because 5 linear masks are used in our linear approximation and the remaining 2 linear masks are arbitrary values. Then, regardless of whether the total correlation is obtained, we restrict the current solution by `banMasks` and go on to the next solution. By continuing this algorithm until the model is infeasible, we can get the list of linear masks and the total correlations.

3.4   Search Result

Unfortunately, our search which targets all cases did not work in practical time. Therefore, we added one constraint which $\Gamma_0 = \Lambda_1$ to the MILP model. This constraint reduced the load on the 3-input addition modulo 2^{32} and we could obtain the list of total correlations.

   We compare the results of linear approximations in the Table 3. Our result is the best high correlation. However, we have to note that the known linear approximation was searched to be suitable for the distinguishing attack. Anyway, we could obtain new optimal linear masks for the fast correlation attack.

Table 3. Comparison of linear masks and its correlations

Mask value	Correlation	Reference
0x0303600c	$2^{-23.48}$	[29]
0x00018001	$2^{-14.496}$	[18]
0x01800001	$2^{-14.411}$	**This paper**

3.5   Application to Fast Correlation Attack

The fast correlation attack [16] is known as an effective analysis method for the LFSR type stream cipher. Moreover, the fast correlation attack can be replaced with a linear code using a Discrete Memory Channel (DMC). A linear code C can be calculated from the generator matrix G.

   Now, we describe the procedure of this attack and how to applicate our linear masks. First, a linear approximation is obtained from the relation between the internal state of the LFSR and the keystream. The internal state is derived from the initial state by the generator matrix G. A (N, n) linear code C_1 can be generated from the generator matrix G, and the parity check equations for the attack can be derived from this C_1. However, these parity check equations cannot be used for the attack. In general, the initial state size n is larger than the key size k. Therefore, Zhang et al. proposed using the k-tree algorithm for solving the partial sum problem k-tree algorithm [31]. It enables us to reduce the involved initial state to m less than k. At this time, the number of parity check equations becomes M_k and the correlation decreases. By the method, the parity check equations are derived from the (M_k, m) linear code C_2 obtained by compressing the generator matrix G. The number of compressed parity check equations M_k is derived from the discrete memory channel capacity C_{DMC} and the correlation κ_k as follows [31].

$$M_k = \frac{m}{C_{DMC}} = \frac{2m \ln(2)}{\kappa_k}.$$

The time and data complexities in this compressed process can be estimated by $O(M_k^{1/(1+\log_2(k))} \times k \times 2^{(n-m)/(1+\log_2(k))})$. Finally, after guessing the initial state of the m bit, calculate and evaluate the parity check equations by using the Fast Walsh Hadamard Transform (FWHT) [3, 14]. This time complexity is required as $O(M_k + (m+2)2^m)$. Since our correlation of the linear approximation is $\kappa = 2^{-14.411}$, the correlation κ_k of the whole parity check equations after the compression is $2^{-2 \times 14.411k} = 2^{-28.822k}$. The required number of parity check equations M_k after the compression is $2m \ln(2) \times 2^{28.822k}$.

We searched for parameters that minimize the time and data complexities. As a result, we got the best result when $k = 4, m = 154$. The number of parity check equations after the compression is $M_k = 2^{123.03}$. The data/time complexity is both $2^{162.34}$ in the compressing process. Moreover, the time complexity by FWHT is $2^{161.29}$. Then, the total time complexity is $2^{162.91}$. By these computations, 154 bits among the 512 bits of the initial state of the LFSR are determined and the time complexity of the rest bits can be ignored compared with the complexity. After the recovery of the whole initial LFSR state, we also recover the initial FSM state by the exhaustive search. Since the initialization of SNOW 2.0 is a reversible process, we can recover the secret key from the initial state. Finally, our attack performance is regarded as $2^{162.91}$. We compare the performance of the known attacks in Table 4. It can be said that the result of our work is superior in terms of time/data complexity compared with the known attacks.

Table 4. Performance comparison of fast correlation attacks

Data	Time	Reference
$2^{198.77}$	$2^{212.38}$	[13]
$2^{163.59}$	$2^{164.15}$	[31]
$2^{162.34}$	$2^{162.91}$	This paper

4   17-Round Integral Distinguisher of SNOW 2.0

Let us consider $f(x, v)$ as a stream cipher, where x and v denote the secret and pubic variables, respectively. The polynomial f is designed by using iterative structure. For the indices I where the variables in $\{v_{i_1}, v_{i_2}, \ldots, v_{i_{|I|}}\}$ are taking all possible combinations of values, the propagation of the division property enables us to evaluate whether or not the sum of $f(\boldsymbol{x}, \boldsymbol{v})$ over all values of the indices I is balanced. In this way, we aim to find zero-sum integral distinguishers.

4.1   Our MILP Model for Integral Distinguisher of SNOW 2.0

We first describe how to construct a MILP model for SNOW 2.0. At ASI-ACRYPT 2016, Xiang et al. showed that the propagation of the division property is efficiently evaluated by the MILP-aided search. Please refer to [30] for more detailed descriptions.

Framework. We can evaluate which secret variables are involved to the distinguisher. If the distinguisher involves any secret variable, it does not work. Therefore, we have to check whether no secret variable is involved in the distinguisher. Algorithm 2 shows the algorithm supported by MILP. The input $\mathcal{M}$ is a MILP model, where the target stream cipher is represented by the context of the division property. Now, how to construct $\mathcal{M}$ for SNOW 2.0 is described. First, we construct the MILP model $\mathcal{M}$ by `Snow2Core` and pick MILP variables $\boldsymbol{x}$ and $\boldsymbol{v}$ from $\mathcal{M}$, where $\boldsymbol{x}$ and $\boldsymbol{v}$ correspond to MILP variables for secret and public variables, respectively. Then, the input division property is defined with $\boldsymbol{v}$ indexed by I. Since at least one element in secret variables is 1, the sum of $\boldsymbol{x}$ is constrained to 1. Next, we solve this MILP model by using the solver. If $\mathcal{M}$ is infeasible, there is no involved secret variable and $\bigoplus_I f(\boldsymbol{x}, \boldsymbol{v})$ is always constant.

Algorithm 2. Evaluate integral distinguisher by MILP

1: **procedure** evaluateDistinguisher(MILP model $\mathcal{M}$, Indices I)
2:     **for** $j = 1$ to n **do**
3:         Declare a MILP model $\mathcal{M} \leftarrow$ Snow2Core(R)
4:         Let $\boldsymbol{x}$ be n MILP variables of $\mathcal{M}$ corresponding to secret variables
5:         Let $\boldsymbol{v}$ be m MILP variables of $\mathcal{M}$ corresponding to public variables
6:         $\mathcal{M}.con \leftarrow v_i = 1$ for all $i \in I$ and $v_i = 0$ for all $i \in (\{1, 2, \ldots, m\} - I)$
7:         $\mathcal{M}.con \leftarrow \sum_{i=1}^{n} x_i = 1$ and $x_j = 1$
8:         solve MILP model $\mathcal{M}$
9:         **if** $\mathcal{M}$ is feasible **then**
10:            **return** $false$
11:         **end if**
12:     **end for**
13:     **return** $true$
14: **end procedure**

Search Model. Snow2Core in Algorithm 3 generates a MILP model $\mathcal{M}$ as the input of Algorithm 2, and the model $\mathcal{M}$ can evaluate all division trails for SNOW 2.0 whose initialization rounds are reduced to R. The function of loadKIV divides K into 4×4 components by copy rule, and set to register according to the initialization of SNOW 2.0. The function of modAdd has been established in [21]. The function of funcSB consist of sbox rule as follows [24]. The functions of funcMC, funcAlpha and funcInvAlpha have consistent characteristic. The sum of input equal to the sum of output in terms of the division property, because these functions consist of only linear constraints. The functions of shift, fbk and ksg are defined as a circular shift, feedback and keystream generation and consist of copy and xor rules, respectively.

Algorithm 3. MILP model of division property for SNOW 2.0

1: **procedure** Snow2Core(round R)
2:    Prepare empty MILP Model $\mathcal{M}$
3:    $\mathcal{M}.var \leftarrow S_i^0$ for $i \in \{1, 2, \ldots, 512\}$ and $R1_i^0, R2_i^0$ for $i \in \{1, 2, \ldots, 32\}$.
4:    $\mathcal{M}.var \leftarrow K_i, IV_i$ for $i \in \{1, 2, \ldots, 128\}$.
5:    $(\mathcal{M}, \boldsymbol{S^0}, \boldsymbol{R1^0}, \boldsymbol{R2^0}) = \text{loadKIV}(\mathcal{M}, \boldsymbol{K}, \boldsymbol{IV})$
6:    **for** $r = 1$ to R **do**
7:        $(\mathcal{M}, \boldsymbol{R1^r}) = \text{modAdd}(\mathcal{M}, \boldsymbol{R2}^{r-1}, S_{161,\ldots,192}^{r-1})$
8:        $(\mathcal{M}, \boldsymbol{T}) = \text{funcSB}(\mathcal{M}, \boldsymbol{R1}^{r-1})$
9:        $(\mathcal{M}, \boldsymbol{R2^r}) = \text{funcMC}(\mathcal{M}, \boldsymbol{T})$
10:       $(\mathcal{M}, \boldsymbol{U}) = \text{modAdd}(\mathcal{M}, \boldsymbol{R1}^{r-1}, S_{481,\ldots,512}^{r-1})$
11:       $(\mathcal{M}, \boldsymbol{V}) = \text{funcAlpha}(\mathcal{M}, S_{1,\ldots,32}^{r-1})$
12:       $(\mathcal{M}, \boldsymbol{W}) = \text{funcInvAlpha}(\mathcal{M}, S_{353,\ldots,384}^{r-1})$
13:       $(\mathcal{M}, S_{1,\ldots,480}^r, \boldsymbol{R1^r}, \boldsymbol{R2^r}) = \text{shift}(\mathcal{M}, S_{33,\ldots,512}^{r-1}, \boldsymbol{R1}^{r-1}, \boldsymbol{R2}^{r-1})$
14:   **end for**
15:   **for** $r = 1$ to $R - 2$ **do**
16:       $(\mathcal{M}, S_{481,\ldots,512}^r) = \text{fbk}(\mathcal{M}, \boldsymbol{U}, \boldsymbol{V}, \boldsymbol{W}, \boldsymbol{R2}^{r-1}, S_{65,\ldots,96}^{r-1})$
17:   **end for**
18:   **for** $r = R - 1$ to R **do**
19:       $(\mathcal{M}, S_{481,\ldots,512}^r) = \text{fbk}(\mathcal{M}, \boldsymbol{V}, \boldsymbol{W}, S_{65,\ldots,96}^{r-1})$
20:       $(\mathcal{M}, \boldsymbol{Z^r}) = \text{ksg}(\mathcal{M}, \boldsymbol{U}, \boldsymbol{R2}^{r-1}, S_{1,\ldots,32}^{r-1})$
21:   **end for**
22:   **for** $i = 1$ to 512 **do**
23:       $\mathcal{M}.con \leftarrow S_i^R = 0$.
24:   **end for**
25:   **for** $i = 1$ to 32 **do**
26:       $\mathcal{M}.con \leftarrow R1_i^R = R2_i^R = Z_i^{R-1} = 0$.
27:   **end for**
28:   $\mathcal{M}.con \leftarrow \sum_{i=1}^{32} Z_i^R = 1$.
29:   **return** $\mathcal{M}$
30: **end procedure**

4.2   Search Result

By the addition modulo 2^{32}, the computation of MSB is more complicated than LSB. Therefore, we focus on the cases that the LSB of the output is balanced. At first, we prepare all IVs are active and check the output after R-round initializations. Then, we find that the LSB of 17-round is balanced and one of 18-round is unbalanced. Moreover, we choose the MSB of each byte in IVs as an active bit. For 1-bit and 2-bit active, we check the $\binom{16}{1}$ and $\binom{16}{2}$ solutions. Unfortunately, we did not find the integral distinguisher. For 3-bit active, we check the $\binom{16}{3}$ solutions and find the integral distinguisher. Furthermore, we change the position of active bits within the same byte which has the original active bit and check the distinguisher. In any case, we can confirm the effectiveness of the 17-round integral distinguisher.

Now, we show the detail of our results. At first, we prepare the IVs which takes all possible values are defined by following rules.

$$\sum_{i=24}^{31} IV_0[i] = 1, \quad \sum_{i=0}^{31} IV_2[i] = 1, \quad \sum_{i=0}^{31} IV_3[i] = 1, \quad \text{the others are 0.}$$

It means that one bit of the most significant byte of IV_0 is active, and each one bit of the IV_2 and IV_3 is active. The others are fixed with constants. There are 2^3 chosen IVs that meet these conditions. After 17-round initializations and one key generation, we get the output keystreams. We find that the LSB of the sum of keystreams is balanced. This is the first investigation about the integral distinguisher of SNOW 2.0. Moreover, we confirm this integral distinguisher. Here, we verify that our new integral distinguisher does work or not. At first, we prepare 8 chosen IVs. In this time, we choose each MSB of IV_3, IV_2 and IV_0 as an active bit. Then, we fix the secret key to `0x 3549073d f264d471 f468616e d6442ac2`. After 17-round initializations and one key generation, we get the output keystreams. Since the sum of the LSB is 0, we can say that this example works as the 17-round integral distinguisher. We checked such a test 100 times. In any case, the sum of LSB is balanced.

5   Cube Attack on 14-Round SNOW 2.0

5.1   MILP Modeling Method for Search Cube Index

In CRYPTO 2017, Todo et al. proposed a method for determining a set J, which is key indices $J \subseteq \{1, \ldots, m\}$ s.t. for arbitrary $v \in \mathbb{F}_2^m$, $p(x, v)$ can only be related to x_j's $(j \in J)$ by using the bit-based division property [25]. Moreover, Wang et al. introduced some techniques about exploiting various algebraic properties of the superpoly [28]. For an $IV \in \mathbb{F}_2^m$ s.t. $p_{IV}(x) \neq 0$, the ANF of $p_{IV}(x)$ can be represented as

$$p_{IV}(x) = \sum_{u \in \mathbb{F}_2^n} a_u x^u,$$

where a_u is determined by the values of the non-cube IVs. If the degree of the superpoly is upper bounded by d, then for all u's with the hamming weight satisfying $hw(u) > d$, attackers constantly have $a_u = 0$. In this case, attackers no longer have to build the whole truth table to recover the superpoly. Instead, attackers only need to determine the coefficients a_u for $hw(u) \leq d$. Therefore, attackers select $\sum_{i=0}^{d} \binom{|J|}{i}$ different x's and construct a linear system with $(\sum_{i=0}^{d} \binom{|J|}{i})$ variables and the coefficients as well as the whole ANF of $p_{IV}(x)$ can be recovered by solving such a linear system.

According to Wang et al.s' study, the knowledge of the algebraic degree of superpolys can largely benefit the efficiency of the cube attack. They showed how to estimate the algebraic degree of superpolys by the division property.

Proposition 2. *Let $f(x, v)$ be a polynomial, where x and v denote the secret and public variables, respectively. For a set of indices $I = \{i_1, i_2, \ldots, i_{|I|}\} \subset \{1, 2, \ldots, m\}$, let C_I be a set of $2^{|I|}$ values where the variables in $\{v_{i_1}, v_{i_2}, \ldots, v_{i_{|I|}}\}$ are taking all possible combinations of values. Let k_I be an m-dimensional bit vector such that $v^{k_I} = t_I = v_{i_1} v_{i_2} \cdots v_{i_{|I|}}$. Let k_Λ be an n-dimensional bit vector. Assuming there is no division trail such that $(k_\Lambda \| k_I) \xrightarrow{f} 1$, the monomial x^{k_Λ} is not involved in the superpoly of the cube C_I.*

According to Proposition 2, the existence of the division trail $(k_\Lambda, k_I) \xrightarrow{f} 1$ is in accordance with the existence of the monomial x^{k_Λ} in the superpoly of the cube C_I. They showed that the algebraic degree of the superpoly is bounded by d. Using the MILP, d can be naturally modeled as the maximum of the objective function $\sum_{j=1}^{n} x_j$.

In this paper, we construct an appropriate MILP model for SNOW 2.0 based on their theory. We use the Algorithm 4 where the `Snow2Core` is defined by Algorithm 2. First, we pick MILP variables x and v from $\mathcal{M}$, where x and v correspond to MILP variables for secret and public variables, respectively. Then, the input division property is defined with v indexed by I. We set the objective function as a maximization of $\sum_{i=1}^{n} x_i$. Then, we solve this MILP model by using the solver and get the upper bound of algebraic degree on the superpoly.

Algorithm 4. Evaluate upper bound of algebraic degree on the superpoly

---

1: **procedure** evaluateDegree(Cube indices I)
2:     Declare a MILP model $\mathcal{M} \leftarrow$ Snow2Core(R)
3:     Let x be n MILP variables of $\mathcal{M}$ corresponding to secret variables
4:     Let v be m MILP variables of $\mathcal{M}$ corresponding to public variables
5:     $\mathcal{M}.con \leftarrow v_i = 1$ for all $i \in I$ and $v_i = 0$ for all $i \in (\{1, 2, \ldots, m\} - I)$
6:     Set the objective function $\mathcal{M}.obj \leftarrow \max \{\sum_{i=1}^{n} x_i\}$
7:     solve MILP model $\mathcal{M}$
8:     **return** The solution of $\mathcal{M}$
9: **end procedure**

5.2   14-Round Key Recovery Attack on SNOW 2.0

Considering IV's Space. In the phase of setting cube indices I, we can choose all bits as an active bit candidate. However, the number of its candidates is 2^{128} and we have to consider the strategy about active bits pattern.

For the byte-wise division property, there are three characteristics: *all* ($\mathcal{A} = $ 0xff), *balance* ($\mathcal{B} = $ 0xfe, ..., 0x01) and *constant* ($\mathcal{C} = $ 0x00). Therefore, we can consider the active byte as three types, which are represented as 0xff, 0xfe and 0x00, respectively. This idea reduces the number of candidates for active bytes pattern to 3^{16}. Moreover, for the addition modulo 2^{32}, we can use the same strategy in Sect. 4 which the active bit pattern is filled with 1 from MSB to LSB in order. Hence, we finally consider the active word pattern with 9^4 as follows.

$$\{ \texttt{0xffffffff}, \texttt{0xfffffffe}, \texttt{0xffffff00}, \texttt{0xfffffe00}, \texttt{0xffff0000},$$

$$\texttt{0xfffe0000}, \texttt{0xff000000}, \texttt{0xfe000000}, \texttt{0x00000000} \}^4 .$$

Search Result. We searched the upper bound of the algebraic degree on the superpoly each round 14 to 17 in order of above active words pattern. These results are shown in Table 5. Unfortunately, the cube over 14-rounds involve all key variables. Therefore, we attack 14-round initializations of SNOW 2.0.

Table 5. Cube indices on reduced-round SNOW 2.0

Round	Example of cube indices	Involved key	d
14	0x fffffffe ff000000 00000000 00000000	K_3	13
15	0x fe000000 ffffff00 fe000000 00000000	$K_3 K_2 K_1 K_0$	65
16	0x fe000000 00000000 ffffffff ff000000	$K_3 K_2 K_1 K_0$	126
17	0x 00000000 00000000 00000000 fe000000	$K_3 K_2 K_1 K_0$	128

14-Round Key Recovery Attack. When attacker already gets the cube index I and index of involved secret variable J, attacker's strategy to recover secret variables consists of three phases: *offline phase*, *online phase* and *brute-force search phase*.

1. **Offline Phase (Superpoly Recovery).** For all $\binom{|J|}{\leq d}$ $\boldsymbol{x}$'s satisfying $hw(\boldsymbol{x}) \leq d$ and $\bigoplus_{j \in J} e_j \succeq \boldsymbol{x}$, compute the values of the superpolys as $p_{IV}(\boldsymbol{x})$ by summing over the cube $C_I(\boldsymbol{IV})$ and generate a linear system of the $\binom{|J|}{\leq d}$ coefficients $a_{\boldsymbol{u}}$ ($hw(\boldsymbol{u}) \leq d$). Solve the linear system, determine the coefficient $a_{\boldsymbol{u}}$ of the $\binom{|J|}{\leq d}$ terms and store them in a lookup table T. The ANF of the $p_{IV}(\boldsymbol{x})$ can be determined with the lookup table.
2. **Online Phase (Partial Key Recovery).** Query the encryption oracle and sum over the cube $C_I(\boldsymbol{IV})$ and acquire the exact value of $p_{IV}(\boldsymbol{x})$. For each of the $2^{|J|}$ possible values of $\{x_{j_1}, \ldots, x_{j_{|J|}}\}$, compute the values of the superpoly and identify the correct key candidates.

3. **Brute-Force Search Phase.** Attackers guess the remaining secret variables to recover the entire value in secret variables.

The complexity of Phase 1 becomes $2^{|I|} \times \binom{|J|}{\leq d}$. Phase 2 now requires $2^{|I|}$ encryptions and $2^{|J|} \times \binom{|J|}{\leq d}$ table lookups, so the complexity can be regarded as $2^{|I|} + 2^{|J|} \times \binom{|J|}{\leq d}$. The complexity of Phase 3 remains 2^{n-1}. Therefore, the number of encryptions an available attack requires is

$$\max \left\{ 2^{|I|} \times \binom{|J|}{\leq d}, 2^{|I|} + 2^{|J|} \times \binom{|J|}{\leq d} \right\} < 2^n.$$

According to Table 5, 14-round SNOW 2.0 involved 32-bit key variables and its algebraic degree of the superpoly is 13. Therefore, we succeeded to cube attack on 14-round SNOW 2.0 with $2^{61.59}$ time complexity and 2^{39} chosen IVs.

6 Conclusion

In this paper, we proposed a new MILP modeling method of the 3-input addition modulo 2^{32} which was difficult with the conventional modeling methods. Our new MILP model performs an automatic search for more efficient linear masks in order to improve the fast correlation attack on SNOW 2.0. As a result of our search, new linear masks were obtained and it makes our new attack more superior in terms of both time and data complexities compared with the known best attack. Moreover, we found new 17-round integral distinguishers of SNOW 2.0. There is no paper discusses the integral distinguisher of SNOW 2.0 until now. Therefore, our investigation will be the first step about this theme. Furthermore, we propose a cube attack on the 14-round SNOW 2.0 with $2^{61.59}$ time complexity and 2^{39} chosen IVs. This attack also will be the first investigation about cube attacks on the reduced-round SNOW 2.0.

Acknowledgment. This work was supported by JSPS KAKENHI Grant Numbers JP17K00184, JP17K12698.

References

1. http://www.gurobi.com/
2. Biryukov, A., Priemuth-Schmid, D., Zhang, B.: Multiset collision attacks on reduced-round SNOW 3G and SNOW 3G$^{(+)}$. In: Zhou, J., Yung, M. (eds.) ACNS 2010. LNCS, vol. 6123, pp. 139–153. Springer, Heidelberg (2010). https://doi.org/10.1007/978-3-642-13708-2_9
3. Chose, P., Joux, A., Mitton, M.: Fast correlation attacks: an algorithmic point of view. In: Knudsen, L.R. (ed.) EUROCRYPT 2002. LNCS, vol. 2332, pp. 209–221. Springer, Heidelberg (2002). https://doi.org/10.1007/3-540-46035-7_14
4. Coppersmith, D., Halevi, S., Jutla, C.: Cryptanalysis of stream ciphers with linear masking. In: Yung, M. (ed.) CRYPTO 2002. LNCS, vol. 2442, pp. 515–532. Springer, Heidelberg (2002). https://doi.org/10.1007/3-540-45708-9_33

5. Cui, T., Jia, K., Fu, K., Chen, S., Wang, M.: New automatic search tool for impossible differentials and zero-correlation linear approximations. IACR Cryptology ePrint Archive 2016, p. 689 (2016)
6. Daemen, J., Rijmen, V.: The Design of Rijndael: AES - The Advanced Encryption Standard. Information Security and Cryptography. Springer, Heidelberg (2002). https://doi.org/10.1007/978-3-662-04722-4
7. Dinur, I., Shamir, A.: Cube attacks on tweakable black box polynomials. In: Joux, A. (ed.) EUROCRYPT 2009. LNCS, vol. 5479, pp. 278–299. Springer, Heidelberg (2009). https://doi.org/10.1007/978-3-642-01001-9_16
8. Ekdahl, P., Johansson, T.: SNOW-a new stream cipher. In: Proceedings of First Open NESSIE Workshop, pp. 167–168 (2000)
9. Ekdahl, P., Johansson, T.: A new version of the stream cipher SNOW. In: Nyberg, K., Heys, H. (eds.) SAC 2002. LNCS, vol. 2595, pp. 47–61. Springer, Heidelberg (2003). https://doi.org/10.1007/3-540-36492-7_5
10. Fu, K., Wang, M., Guo, Y., Sun, S., Hu, L.: MILP-based automatic search algorithms for differential and linear trails for speck. In: Peyrin, T. (ed.) FSE 2016. LNCS, vol. 9783, pp. 268–288. Springer, Heidelberg (2016). https://doi.org/10.1007/978-3-662-52993-5_14
11. Hawkes, P., Rose, G.G.: Guess-and-determine attacks on SNOW. In: Nyberg, K., Heys, H. (eds.) SAC 2002. LNCS, vol. 2595, pp. 37–46. Springer, Heidelberg (2003). https://doi.org/10.1007/3-540-36492-7_4
12. ISO/IEC: JTC1: ISO/IEC 18033–4: Information technology - security techniques - encryption algorithms - part 4: Stream ciphers (2011)
13. Lee, J.-K., Lee, D.H., Park, S.: Cryptanalysis of sosemanuk and SNOW 2.0 using linear masks. In: Pieprzyk, J. (ed.) ASIACRYPT 2008. LNCS, vol. 5350, pp. 524–538. Springer, Heidelberg (2008). https://doi.org/10.1007/978-3-540-89255-7_32
14. Lu, Y., Vaudenay, S.: Faster correlation attack on bluetooth keystream generator E0. In: Franklin, M. (ed.) CRYPTO 2004. LNCS, vol. 3152, pp. 407–425. Springer, Heidelberg (2004). https://doi.org/10.1007/978-3-540-28628-8_25
15. Matsui, M.: Linear cryptanalysis method for DES cipher. In: Helleseth, T. (ed.) EUROCRYPT 1993. LNCS, vol. 765, pp. 386–397. Springer, Heidelberg (1994). https://doi.org/10.1007/3-540-48285-7_33
16. Meier, W., Staffelbach, O.: Fast correlation attacks on certain stream ciphers. J. Cryptol. 1(3), 159–176 (1989)
17. Mouha, N., Wang, Q., Gu, D., Preneel, B.: Differential and linear cryptanalysis using mixed-integer linear programming. In: Wu, C.-K., Yung, M., Lin, D. (eds.) Inscrypt 2011. LNCS, vol. 7537, pp. 57–76. Springer, Heidelberg (2012). https://doi.org/10.1007/978-3-642-34704-7_5
18. Nyberg, K., Wallén, J.: Improved linear distinguishers for SNOW 2.0. In: Robshaw, M. (ed.) FSE 2006. LNCS, vol. 4047, pp. 144–162. Springer, Heidelberg (2006). https://doi.org/10.1007/11799313_10
19. Sasaki, Y., Todo, Y.: New impossible differential search tool from design and cryptanalysis aspects. In: Coron, J.-S., Nielsen, J.B. (eds.) EUROCRYPT 2017. LNCS, vol. 10212, pp. 185–215. Springer, Cham (2017). https://doi.org/10.1007/978-3-319-56617-7_7
20. Stein, W., et al.: Sage: Open Source Mathematical Software (2008)
21. Sun, L., Wang, W., Wang, M.: Automatic search of bit-based division property for ARX ciphers and word-based division property. In: Takagi, T., Peyrin, T. (eds.) ASIACRYPT 2017. LNCS, vol. 10624, pp. 128–157. Springer, Cham (2017). https://doi.org/10.1007/978-3-319-70694-8_5

22. Sun, S., et al.: Towards finding the best characteristics of some bit-oriented block ciphers and automatic enumeration of (related-key) differential and linear characteristics with predefined properties. Technical report, Cryptology ePrint Archive, Report 2014/747 (2014)

23. Sun, S., Hu, L., Wang, P., Qiao, K., Ma, X., Song, L.: Automatic security evaluation and (related-key) differential characteristic search: application to SIMON, PRESENT, LBlock, DES(L) and other bit-oriented block ciphers. In: Sarkar, P., Iwata, T. (eds.) ASIACRYPT 2014. LNCS, vol. 8873, pp. 158–178. Springer, Heidelberg (2014). https://doi.org/10.1007/978-3-662-45611-8_9

24. Todo, Y.: Structural evaluation by generalized integral property. In: Oswald, E., Fischlin, M. (eds.) EUROCRYPT 2015. LNCS, vol. 9056, pp. 287–314. Springer, Heidelberg (2015). https://doi.org/10.1007/978-3-662-46800-5_12

25. Todo, Y., Isobe, T., Hao, Y., Meier, W.: Cube attacks on non-blackbox polynomials based on division property. In: Katz, J., Shacham, H. (eds.) CRYPTO 2017. LNCS, vol. 10403, pp. 250–279. Springer, Cham (2017). https://doi.org/10.1007/978-3-319-63697-9_9

26. Todo, Y., Morii, M.: Bit-based division property and application to SIMON family. In: Peyrin, T. (ed.) FSE 2016. LNCS, vol. 9783, pp. 357–377. Springer, Heidelberg (2016). https://doi.org/10.1007/978-3-662-52993-5_18

27. Wallén, J.: Linear approximations of addition modulo 2^n. In: Johansson, T. (ed.) FSE 2003. LNCS, vol. 2887, pp. 261–273. Springer, Heidelberg (2003). https://doi.org/10.1007/978-3-540-39887-5_20

28. Wang, Q., Hao, Y., Todo, Y., Li, C., Isobe, T., Meier, W.: Improved division property based cube attacks exploiting algebraic properties of superpoly. IACR Cryptology ePrint Archive 2017, p. 1063 (2017)

29. Watanabe, D., Biryukov, A., De Cannière, C.: A distinguishing attack of SNOW 2.0 with linear masking method. In: Matsui, M., Zuccherato, R.J. (eds.) SAC 2003. LNCS, vol. 3006, pp. 222–233. Springer, Heidelberg (2004). https://doi.org/10.1007/978-3-540-24654-1_16

30. Xiang, Z., Zhang, W., Bao, Z., Lin, D.: Applying MILP method to searching integral distinguishers based on division property for 6 lightweight block ciphers. In: Cheon, J.H., Takagi, T. (eds.) ASIACRYPT 2016. LNCS, vol. 10031, pp. 648–678. Springer, Heidelberg (2016). https://doi.org/10.1007/978-3-662-53887-6_24

31. Zhang, B., Xu, C., Meier, W.: Fast correlation attacks over extension fields, large-unit linear approximation and cryptanalysis of SNOW 2.0. In: Gennaro, R., Robshaw, M. (eds.) CRYPTO 2015. LNCS, vol. 9215, pp. 643–662. Springer, Heidelberg (2015). https://doi.org/10.1007/978-3-662-47989-6_31

Cryptographic Primitives

Identity-Based Encryption Resilient to Auxiliary Leakage under the Decisional Linear Assumption

Masahito Ishizaka$^{(\boxtimes)}$ and Kanta Matsuura

Institute of Industrial Science, The University of Tokyo, Tokyo, Japan
{ishimasa,kanta}@iis.u-tokyo.ac.jp

Abstract. Leakage-resilience guarantees that even if some information about the secret key is partially leaked, the security is maintained. Several security models considering leakage-resilience have been proposed. Among them, auxiliary leakage model proposed by Dodis et al. in STOC'09 is especially important, since it can deal with a leakage caused by a function which information-theoretically reveals the secret key, e.g., one-way permutation.

Contribution of this work is two-fold. Firstly, we propose an identity-based encryption (IBE) scheme and prove that it is fully secure and resilient to the auxiliary leakage under the decisional linear assumption in the standard model. Secondly, although the IBE scheme proposed by Yuen et al. in Eurocrypt'12 has been considered to be the only IBE scheme resilient to auxiliary leakage, we prove that the security proof for the IBE scheme is defective. We insist that our IBE scheme is the only IBE scheme resilient to auxiliary leakage.

Keywords: Identity-based encryption · Leakage-resilience
Auxiliary leakage

1 Introduction

Background. Identity-based encryption (IBE) is one type of public-key encryption (PKE), and has an advantage such that we can use an identifier $ID \in \{0,1\}^*$ (e.g., a mail address, telephone number) as the public key. The idea of IBE was presented by Shamir [32] in Crypto'84. The first concrete IBE scheme which utilizes a bilinear map was proposed by Boneh et al. [7]. Although the IBE scheme by Boneh et al. was proven to be secure in the random oracle model, large number of IBE schemes have been proven to be secure in the standard model, e.g., [4,5,15,33,34]. Large number of lattice-based IBE schemes have been proposed, e.g., [1,22].

Every one of the IBE schemes mentioned above is not considering leakage-resilience. Leakage-resilience is a property which guarantees that even if secret information such as the secret key is partially leaked, the security is maintained.

© Springer Nature Switzerland AG 2018
J. Camenisch and P. Papadimitratos (Eds.): CANS 2018, LNCS 11124, pp. 417–439, 2018.
https://doi.org/10.1007/978-3-030-00434-7_21

Any scheme whose security has been proven only in a security model without leakage-resilience is not guaranteed to be secure when some information about the secret information is leaked. Considering the situation where some side-channel attacks, e.g., [23], are real threats, leakage-resilient cryptographic schemes are practically more desirable than non-leakage-resilient ones.

In security models considering the leakage-resilience, a side-channel attack caused by an adversary is modelled as a polynomial time computable function f : $\{0,1\}^{|Secret|} \to \{0,1\}^{*1}$. Any adversary is allowed to choose a leakage function f arbitrarily and query the function to a leakage oracle, then learns a leakage information $f(Secret)$. Let us consider a case where the identity map is chosen as the leakage function. In that case, any adversary acquires full bits of the secret key and breaks the security model. Hence, we have to impose a restriction on the leakage function f whom the adversary is allowed to choose. Several security models which impose different type of restrictions on the leakage function f have been proposed.

In bounded leakage (BL) model [3], the output bit-length of the leakage function f is restricted. More concretely, only function f satisfying $f : \{0,1\}^{|Secret|} \to \{0,1\}^{l(k)}$ such that $l(k) < k$ is allowed for the adversary to choose[2]. To remove the restriction on the output bit-length of the leakage function in the BL model, noisy leakage (NL) model [30] was proposed. In the NL model, only function $f : \{0,1\}^{|Secret|} \to \{0,1\}^*$ such that when we observe $f(Secret)$, the minimum entropy of the secret key sk drops by at most $l(k) < k$ is allowed to choose. Note that functions which reveal the secret key sk information-theoretically are not allowed to choose in either one of the BL model and NL model. Hence, for instance, one-way permutation is not allowed to choose in either one of the models. To remove such a restriction, auxiliary (input) leakage (AL) model [20] was proposed. In the AL model, the function f is a hard-to-invert function. More concretely, only function f such that no PPT algorithm which is given $f(Secret)$ can identify sk with probability larger than $\mu(k)$ is allowed to choose, where $\mu(\cdot)$ is a negligible function such that $\mu(k) > 2^{-k}$. Note that the bigger $\mu(k)$ is, the bigger the function class of f is. The AL model is considered to be a generalization of the BL model and NL model, so the AL model has a larger function class. Moreover, the AL model is useful in the composition. There may be the case where people want to use the pair of public key and secret key of an auxiliary leakage-resilient encryption system for other cryptographic systems such as digital signature or identification. Their composition remains secure as long as these other systems have been proven to be secure in the standard, i.e., non-leakage-resilient, security model [16,36].

In the above models, the secret key cannot be updated, so the secret key leaks its partial information repeatedly throughout the lifetime of the cryptographic system. In continual leakage (CL) model [10,17], meanwhile, the situation where the secret key can be updated periodically is considered. Although for any time

---

[1] *Secret* denotes the secret information. $|Secret|$ denotes the bit-length of *Secret*.

[2] k denotes the minimum entropy of the secret key sk. If the secret-key is generated uniformly at random, k is equivalent to the bit-length of the secret-key $|sk|$.

period t and the secret key sk_t in the time period, the restriction imposed on the leakage function for sk_t is the same as the model without the continual leakage-resilience such as the normal BL model, the total number of times of secret-key update is unbounded. So, generally, the amount of leakage in the CL model is unbounded, hence it is much larger than the model without the continual leakage-resilience.

Related Works. Large number of schemes secure in the BL model have been proposed. For instance, digital signature schemes [2,12,18,19], identification schemes [2,18,19], and authenticated key agreement (AKA) schemes [2,18,19] have been proposed. PKE schemes have been proposed by Akavia et al. [3], Dodis et al. [18,19], Brakerski et al. [8], and others. IBE schemes have been proposed by Chow et al. [14], Lewko et al. [27], Kurosawa et al. [24], and others. ABE schemes have been proposed by Lewko et al. [27], Zhang et al. [37], and others. As schemes secure in the continual bounded leakage (CBL) model combining the BL model and the CL model, digital signature schemes [10,17,25,26], identification scheme [17], AKA scheme [17], PKE schemes [10,25,26], IBE schemes [10,24,27], and ABE scheme [27] have been proposed. Moreover, Bellare et al. [11] proposed a security model which introduces the forward security into the CBL model, and proposed a digital signature scheme and a PKE scheme secure in the security model.

Several schemes secure in the AL model have been proposed. Symmetric-key encryption scheme [20] and digital signature scheme [21] have been proposed. PKE scheme has been proposed by Dodis et al. [16]. An IBE scheme has been proposed by Yuen et al. [36]. Yuen et al. [36] proposed not only the IBE scheme secure in the AL model, but also an IBE scheme secure in continual auxiliary leakage (CAL) model which combines the AL model and CL model. ABE schemes (secure in the AL model) have been proposed by Zhang et al. [38] and Wang et al. [35].

Our Results. Firstly, we present an IBE construction and prove that it is fully secure, i.e., adaptively secure, and resilient to auxiliary leakage under the decisional linear (DLIN) assumption [6] in the standard model. Secondly, we show that the proof of security of the IBE scheme by Yuen et al. [36] proposed in Eurocrypt'12 is wrong. Yuen et al. insist that the IBE scheme is correctly proven to be fully secure and resilient to auxiliary leakage under the decisional subgroup (DSG) assumptions [29] in the standard model. As far as we know, among the previous works, the IBE scheme has been the only one which is proven to be resilient to auxiliary leakage. Therefore, our IBE construction is the only one proven to be fully secure and resilient to auxiliary leakage under standard assumptions. Below, we explain each result in more detail.

Result 1: Presenting an IBE Construction Fully Secure and Resilient to Auxiliary Leakage under the DLIN Assumption. Our security model for IBE scheme is a model adding a leakage oracle leaking information from a secret-key for the target ID to the standard full security model without leakage-resilience such as one in [33]. The leakage oracle is added between the two phases "Phase 1" and

"Challenge". The leakage oracle takes as inputs an ID ID^* as the target ID and a function f, then generates a secret-key sk^* for ID^* and returns $f(sk^*)$. The leakage function f is a function included in a function class $\mathcal{F}_{pk,mk,\mathcal{L},ID^*}(\xi(\lambda))$ parameterized by variables such as the system public-key pk and master-key mk generated in the security game, the target ID ID^*, and a negligible function $\xi(\lambda)$. And, the definition of $\mathcal{F}_{pk,mk,\mathcal{L},ID^*}(\xi(\lambda))$ is as follows. It consists of every function f s.t. for every PPT $\mathcal{B}$, it holds that $\Pr[\mathcal{B}(pk,mk,\mathcal{L},ID^*,OUT, f,f(sk^*)) \rightarrow sk^*|(sk^*,OUT) \leftarrow \textbf{KeyGen}'_{IN}(pk,mk,ID^*)] < \xi(\lambda)$, where the algorithm $\textbf{KeyGen}'_{IN}(pk,mk,ID^*)$ is a key-generation algorithm such that the secret-key sk^* is generated in the same manner as the "normal" key-generation algorithm $\textbf{KeyGen}$ and the variable OUT includes some information about the secret-key sk^*.

Our IBE scheme is a modified variant of one presented by Kurosawa and Phong [24] which has been proven to fully secure and resilient to bounded leakage under the DLIN assumption. We introduce an assumption "assumption X parameterized by (an integer) l" which is implied by the DLIN assumption. We prove that our IBE construction is secure in our security model (mentioned earlier) with auxiliary leakage parameter $\xi(\lambda) = 2^{-m^\epsilon}$ under the assumption X parameterized by m, where the integer m is set to $m := (4\lambda)^{1/\epsilon}$ by using a constant $0 < \epsilon < 1$. Actually, m is related to the number of elements included in a secret-key for each ID. Specifically, secret-key space is $\mathbb{Z}_p^{2m}$, where p is a prime. Both the IBE constructions presented in our work and the work [24] are proven to be secure under the DLIN assumption, reduction cost to the assumption achieved by each work is different. Ours is determined by the parameter m only. On the other hand, one in [24] is determined by the bit-length of an ID and the total number of oracle queries made by an adversary in security game. The difference can be interesting.

Result 2: Showing that Security Proof for the IBE Construction Proposed by Yuen et al. [36] is Wrong. Although Yuen et al. describes a proof sketch in [36], they have not disclosed the full version of the proof. Based on the proof sketch, we show that their proof is wrong. Specifically, we introduce several concrete examples of polynomial-time adversary as counterexamples, each one of which becomes an evidence that their proof is wrong[3]. The proof by Yuen et al. is done by a hybrid argument using a sequence of games. They insist that a lemma guarantees that two successive games are indistinguishable since it can be reduced to an indistinguishability-type assumption, i.e., a DSG assumption [29]. However, each one of our counterexamples distinguishes the two games with a non-negligible advantage. Thus, the lemma at least does not hold.

Yuen et al. also presents an IBE scheme resilient to continual auxiliary leakage. We can show that properly modified variants of the counterexamples for the scheme resilient to auxiliary leakage work effectively against it as well[3].

---

[3] Note that each one of our counterexamples indicates that their current proof is wrong, but not that their scheme cannot be proven to be secure in their security model. Thus, it is possible that their scheme is proven to be secure if the proof is done in another manner.

Although the ABE schemes by Zhang et al. [38] and Wang et al. [35] have been considered to be the only ABE schemes proven to be resilient to auxiliary leakage, we show that their security proofs are defective. For details, see Subsect. 5.5.

Organization of the Paper. This paper is organized as follows. In Sect. 2, basic notations, bilinear groups of prime order, the decisional linear (DLIN) assumption, and Goldreich-Levin theorem for large fields [16] are described. In Subsects. 3.1 and 3.2, the syntax of IBE scheme and the definition of security of IBE scheme are given, respectively. In Subsect. 4.1, the concrete construction of our IBE scheme is given. We prove its security and consider its leakage-resilience in Subsects. 4.2 and 4.3, respectively. In Sect. 5, the results by Yuen et al. [36] are described. Specifically, the security of an IBE scheme defined by them and the IBE construction proposed by them are described in Subsects. 5.1 and 5.2, respectively. And, the definitions of semi-functional secret-key and ciphertexts by Yuen et al. and the sketch of the security proof by them are given in Subsects. 5.3 and 5.4, respectively. In Subsect. 5.5, we show some counterexamples against the security proof by Yuen et al.

2   Preliminaries

Notations. PPT is an abbreviation of probabilistic polynomial time. For $\lambda \in \mathbb{N}$, 1^λ denotes a security parameter. For a set A, $a \xleftarrow{U} A$ indicates a procedure which we extract an element a from A uniformly at random. Given a matrix $\mathbf{A}$ of size $m \times n$ whose (i,j)-th element is denoted by $a_{i,j}$, $g^{\mathbf{A}}$ denotes a matrix of size $m \times n$ whose (i,j)-th element is $g^{a_{i,j}}$. $\mathbf{I}_m$ denotes the identity matrix of size m.

2.1   Bilinear Groups of Prime Order

$\mathcal{G}_{bg}$ denotes a generator of bilinear groups of prime order. $\mathcal{G}_{bg}$ takes 1^λ as input, and outputs $(p, \mathbb{G}, \mathbb{G}_T, \hat{e})$, where p is a prime of λ-bit, $\mathbb{G}$ and $\mathbb{G}_T$ are cyclic groups of order p, and $\hat{e} : \mathbb{G} \times \mathbb{G} \to \mathbb{G}_T$ is a map computable in polynomial time which satisfies the following conditions. For every $g, h \in \mathbb{G}$ and $a, b \in \mathbb{Z}_p$, it holds that $\hat{e}(g^a, h^b) = \hat{e}(g, h)^{ab}$. If g is a generator of $\mathbb{G}$, $\hat{e}(g, g)$ becomes a generator of $\mathbb{G}_T$.

2.2   Decisional Linear (DLIN) Assumption [6]

$\mathcal{G}$ denotes a generator of a group with prime order. $\mathcal{G}$ takes 1^λ, where $\lambda \in \mathbb{N}$, as input, then outputs $(p, \mathbb{G})$, where p is a prime number of bit-size λ and $\mathbb{G}$ is a cyclic group of order p. The decisional linear assumption [6] says that for any PPT $\mathcal{A}$ and any $\lambda \in \mathbb{N}$, $\mathsf{Adv}_{\mathcal{A}}^{\mathrm{DLIN}}(\lambda) := |\Pr[\mathcal{A}(p, \mathbb{G}, g_1, g_2, g_3, g_1^{r_1}, g_2^{r_2}, g_3^{s_b}) \to b |$ $(p, \mathbb{G}) \leftarrow \mathcal{G}(1^\lambda), g_1, g_2, g_3 \xleftarrow{U} \mathbb{G}, r_1, r_2, s_0 \xleftarrow{U} \mathbb{Z}_p, s_1 := r_1 + r_2, b \xleftarrow{U} \{0,1\}] - 1/2|$ is negligible.

2.3   Goldreich-Levin Theorem for Large Fields [16]

The following Goldreich-Levin theorem for large fields was proven by Dodis et al. [16].

Theorem 1. *Let p denote a prime number. Let H denote an arbitrary subset of $GF(p)$. $f : H^{m \times 1} \to \{0,1\}^*$ is an arbitrary function. If there is a distinguisher $\mathcal{D}$ running in time t such that*

$$\delta := \left| \Pr\left[\mathcal{D}(f(\mathbf{s}), \mathbf{r}, \mathbf{rs}) = 1 \middle| \mathbf{s} \xleftarrow{U} H^{m \times 1}, \mathbf{r} \xleftarrow{U} \mathbb{Z}_p^{1 \times m} \right] - \right.$$
$$\left. \Pr\left[\mathcal{D}(f(\mathbf{s}), \mathbf{r}, u) = 1 \middle| \mathbf{s} \xleftarrow{U} H^{m \times 1}, \mathbf{r} \xleftarrow{U} \mathbb{Z}_p^{1 \times m}, u \xleftarrow{U} \mathbb{Z}_p \right] \right|,$$

then there is an inverter $\mathcal{B}$ running in time $t' = t \cdot \mathrm{poly}(m, |H|, 1/\delta)$ such that

$$\Pr\left[\mathcal{B}(f(\mathbf{s})) = \mathbf{s} \middle| \mathbf{s} \xleftarrow{U} H^{m \times 1} \right] \geq \delta^3/512 \cdot m \cdot p^2.$$

3   Identity-Based Encryption

3.1   Syntax

Identity-based encryption (IBE) consists of the following 4 polynomial-time algorithms:

- **Setup**$(1^\lambda) \to (\mathrm{pk}, \mathrm{mk})$: Setup algorithm takes a security parameter 1^λ as an input, and outputs a system public key pk and a master key mk. pk determines the ID space $\mathcal{I}$ and plaintext space $\mathcal{M}$ uniquely.
- **KeyGen**$(\mathrm{pk}, \mathrm{mk}, ID) \to \mathrm{sk}$: User's secret key generation algorithm takes pk, mk, and $ID \in \mathcal{I}$ as inputs, and outputs an secret key sk for ID.
- **Enc**$(\mathrm{pk}, M, ID) \to C$: Encryption algorithm takes pk, a plaintext $M \in \mathcal{M}$, and $ID \in \mathcal{I}$ as inputs, and outputs a ciphertext C.
- **Dec**$(\mathrm{pk}, C, \mathrm{sk}) \to M/\bot$: Decryption algorithm takes pk, a ciphertext C, and a secret key sk as inputs, and outputs a plaintext M or $\bot$, where $\bot$ indicates a failure of decryption.

Every IBE scheme must be correct. An IBE scheme $\Pi = \{\textbf{Setup}, \textbf{KeyGen}, \textbf{Enc}, \textbf{Dec}\}$ is correct, if it holds that $\forall \lambda \in \mathbb{N}$, $\forall (\mathrm{pk}, \mathrm{mk}) \leftarrow \textbf{Setup}(1^\lambda)$, $\forall ID \in \mathcal{I}$, $\forall \mathrm{sk} \leftarrow \textbf{KeyGen}(\mathrm{pk}, \mathrm{mk}, ID)$, $\forall M \in \mathcal{M}$, $\forall C \leftarrow \textbf{Enc}(\mathrm{pk}, M, ID)$, $\Pr[M \leftarrow \textbf{Dec}(\mathrm{pk}, C, \mathrm{sk})] = 1$.

3.2   Definition of Security

We define ciphertext indistinguishability in the auxiliary leakage (AL) model for an IBE scheme $\Pi_{IBE} = \{\textbf{Setup}, \textbf{KeyGen}, \textbf{Enc}, \textbf{Dec}\}$. Before its concrete definition, we define a probabilistic polynomial-time algorithm $\textbf{KeyGen}'_{IN}$ as follows.

- **KeyGen$'_{IN}$**(pk, mk, ID) → (sk, OUT): This algorithm takes the system public key pk, the master key mk, $ID \in I$, and an input-information $IN \in \{0,1\}^*$ as inputs, and outputs a user's secret key sk for ID, and an output-information $OUT \in \{0,1\}^*$ which actually is an information about the secret-key sk.

The algorithm is used in the definition of the ciphertext indistinguishability of an IBE scheme. The secret-key generated by the algorithm must be generated in the same manner as the secret-key generated by the normal secret-key generation algorithm **KeyGen**.

Let us define the ciphertext indistinguishability for IBE. Firstly, we define a security game $\xi(\lambda)$-AL-IND-ID-CPA for an IBE scheme $\Pi_{IBE} = \{$**Setup**, **KeyGen**, **Enc**, **Dec**$\}$ and its algorithm **KeyGen$'_{IN}$**, which is played between an adversary $\mathcal{A}$ and challenger C. Here, AL-IND-ID-CPA indicates ciphertext indistinguishability against adaptively chosen ID and plaintexts attacks in the auxiliary leakage model. The parameter $\xi(\cdot)$ whom we call auxiliary leakage parameter, is a negligible function s.t. $\xi(\lambda) > 2^{-k}$, where k denotes the minimum entropy of the user's secret key. Concrete definition of the game is as follows.

Setup: C runs (pk, mk) ← **Setup**(1^λ). C sends pk to $\mathcal{A}$. C initializes the list $\mathcal{L}$ by an empty set $\emptyset$.

Phase 1: $\mathcal{A}$ is allowed to use the key-revelation oracle **Reveal** adaptively.
   Reveal(ID): $\mathcal{A}$ issues an ID as a query. C runs sk ← **KeyGen**(pk, mk, ID), then returns sk to $\mathcal{A}$. Then, C sets $\mathcal{L} := \mathcal{L} \cup \{(ID, sk)\}$.

Leak($ID^*, f \in \mathcal{F}_{pk,mk,\mathcal{L},ID^*}(\xi(\lambda))$): $\mathcal{A}$ sends an ID ID^* which was not queried to **Reveal** in **Phase 1** and a function $f \in \mathcal{F}_{pk,mk,\mathcal{L},ID^*}(\xi(\lambda))$. Definition of the function class $\mathcal{F}_{pk,mk,\mathcal{L},ID^*}(\xi(\lambda))$ is given below the game. C computes a secret user-key for the ID ID^* by running sk* ← **KeyGen**(pk, mk, ID^*). Then, C computes $f(sk^*; r)$, where r is a randomness of the function.

Challenge(M_0, M_1): $\mathcal{A}$ sends two distinct plaintexts $M_0, M_1 \in \mathcal{M}$. C sets $b \xleftarrow{U} \{0,1\}$, runs C^* ← **Enc**(pk, M_b, ID^*), and sends C^* to $\mathcal{A}$.

Phase 2: $\mathcal{A}$ uses the oracle **Reveal** adaptively in the same manner as **Phase 1** except that he cannot query ID^* to the oracle.

Guess($b' \in \{0,1\}$): $\mathcal{A}$ sends a guess $b' \in \{0,1\}$ for b.

Advantage of $\mathcal{A}$ is defined as $\mathrm{Adv}_{\Pi_{IBE},\mathbf{KeyGen}'_{IN},\mathcal{A}}^{\xi(\lambda)-AL-IND-ID-CPA}(\lambda) := |\Pr[b = b'] - 1/2|$. The function class $\mathcal{F}_{pk,mk,\mathcal{L},ID^*}(\xi(\lambda))$ consists of every probabilistic or deterministic polynomial-time function $f : \{0,1\}^{|sk|} \to \{0,1\}^*$ such that for every PPT $\mathcal{B}$, it holds that $\Pr[\mathcal{B}(pk, mk, \mathcal{L}, ID^*, OUT, f, f(sk^*)) \to sk^*|(sk^*, OUT) \leftarrow \mathbf{KeyGen}'_{IN}(pk, mk, ID^*)] < \xi(\lambda)$.

Definition 1. *A scheme* $\Pi_{IBE} = \{$**Setup**, **KeyGen**, **Enc**, **Dec**$\}$ *is* $(\xi(\lambda))$-*AL-IND-ID-CPA w.r.t.* **KeyGen$'_{IN}$**, *if for every PPT* $\mathcal{A}$, $\mathrm{Adv}_{\Pi_{IBE},\mathbf{KeyGen}'_{IN},\mathcal{A}}^{\xi(\lambda)-AL-IND-ID-CPA}$ (λ) *is negligible.*

Comparison with the Security Model in [36]. Our security model is different from one in [36]. For the definition of the latter model, see [36] or Subsect. 5.1 of this paper.

Actually, our security model is weaker than one in [36]. For instance, the following three properties make our security model weaker. Firstly, our security model lacks leakage-resilience for the master-key. Secondly, ours does not allow the adversary to use adaptively in the phase 1 an oracle which reveals secret-keys for IDs other than the target ID ID^* and an oracle which leaks some information from secret-key(s) for ID^*. Thirdly, ours does not allow the adversary to use the leakage oracle multiple times.

On the other hand, our security model is superior to one in [36] in some respects. One of them is related to the definition of the leakage function class.

In [36], the authors define the leakage function class in a way that any PPT cannot find any secret-key for the target ID ID^* with a probability larger than a concrete negligible function. It is hard for us to present a concrete example of function which satisfy the definition. It is uncertain that even a function which outputs 1 bit of a secret-key for ID^* really satisfies the definition. Actually, in [36], any specific example which satisfies the definition is not given.

We define the leakage function class in a way that any PPT which is given a leakage-information from a single secret-key sk^* for ID^* cannot identify sk^* with a probability larger than a concrete negligible function. A benefit whom we obtain by using such a definition is that it is possible for us to present a concrete example which satisfies the definition. Note that in the definition, the inverter $\mathcal{B}$ is given a variable OUT which includes some information about the target secret-key sk^*. It is obvious that if $OUT = sk^*$, no function satisfies the definition. So, we should make the information about sk^* which is revealed by OUT as small as possible. In Subsect. 4.3, we consider what kind of leakage functions satisfy the definition. We show that not only a function which reveals 1 bit of sk^*, but also various concrete functions, can satisfy the definition.

4 Our IBE Scheme

In Subsect. 4.1, concrete construction of our IBE scheme Π_{IBE} is given. In Subsect. 4.2, its security, i.e., ciphertext indistinguishability, is proven. In Subsect. 4.3, we consider the leakage allowed for our IBE scheme.

4.1 Concrete Construction

The scheme $\Pi_{IBE} = \{\textbf{Setup}, \textbf{KeyGen}, \textbf{Enc}, \textbf{Dec}\}$ is defined as follows.

Setup$(1^\lambda, n)$: Run $(p, \mathbb{G}, \mathbb{G}_T, \hat{e}) \leftarrow \mathcal{G}_{bg}(1^\lambda)$, where $\mathcal{G}_{bg}$ is the generator of bilinear groups which was defined in Subsect. 2.1. Let g denote a randomly chosen generator of the group $\mathbb{G}$. Each one of ID space and plaintext space is set as $\mathcal{I} := \{0,1\}^n$ and $\mathcal{M} := \mathbb{G}_T$, respectively. For $\epsilon \in \mathbb{R}$ such that $0 < \epsilon < 1$, set $m := (4\lambda)^{1/\epsilon}$. $\mathbf{A}_0$ and $\mathbf{E}$ are set as $\mathbf{A}_0 \xleftarrow{U} \mathbb{Z}_p^{2 \times m}$ and $\mathbf{E} \xleftarrow{U} \mathbb{Z}_p^{m \times 1}$, respectively. For $i \in [0, n]$, set $r_i \xleftarrow{U} \mathbb{Z}_p$. Set $\mathbf{A}_0' \in \mathbb{Z}_p^{2 \times m}$, $\mathbf{A}_i \in \mathbb{Z}_p^{2 \times m}$, where $i \in [1, n]$, and $\mathbf{D} \in \mathbb{Z}_p^{2 \times 1}$ as $\mathbf{A}_0' := r_0 \mathbf{A}_0$, $\mathbf{A}_i := r_i \mathbf{A}_0$, and $\mathbf{D} := \mathbf{A}_0 \mathbf{E}$, respectively.

Return (pk, mk), where $pk := (p, \mathbb{G}, \mathbb{G}_T, \hat{e}, g, g^{\mathbf{A}_0}, g^{\mathbf{A}_0'}, g^{\mathbf{A}_1}, \cdots, g^{\mathbf{A}_n}, g^{\mathbf{D}})$ and $mk := (r_0, r_1, \cdots, r_n, \mathbf{E})$.

Hereafter, for an $ID \in \mathcal{I}$, $ID[i] \in \{0,1\}$ denotes the i-th bit of ID. An $ID \in \mathcal{I}$ is associated to a matrix $\mathbf{F}(ID) \in \mathbb{Z}_p^{2 \times 2m}$ which is defined as $\mathbf{F}(ID) = [\mathbf{A}_0 | \mathbf{A}_0' + \Sigma_{i=1}^n ID[i]\mathbf{A}_i] = \mathbf{A}_0 [\mathbf{I}_m | (r_0 + \Sigma_{i=1}^n ID[i]r_i)\mathbf{I}_m]$.

KeyGen$(\text{pk}, \text{mk}, ID)$: For $i \in [m+1, 2m]$, set $v_i \xleftarrow{U} \mathbb{Z}_p$. For $i \in [1, m]$, set $v_i := E_i - (r_0 + \sum_{k=1}^n ID[k]r_k)v_{m+i}$, where E_i is the $(i, 1)$-th element of the vector $\mathbf{E} \in \mathbb{Z}_p^{m \times 1}$. Set sk $:= g^{\mathbf{v}}$, where the $(i, 1)$-th element of $\mathbf{v} \in \mathbb{Z}_p^{2m \times 1}$ is set as v_i[4]. **Return** sk.

Enc(pk, M, ID) : Set $\mathbf{z} \xleftarrow{U} \mathbb{Z}_p^{1 \times 2}$. Calculate $C_1 := g^{\mathbf{zF}(ID)} \in \mathbb{G}^{1 \times 2m}$ and $C_2 := \hat{e}(g,g)^{\mathbf{zD}} \cdot M \in \mathbb{G}_T$. **Return** $C := (C_1, C_2)$.

Dec$(\text{pk}, C, \text{sk})$: C is parsed as (C_1, C_2). By using $\mathbf{c} \in \mathbb{Z}_p^{1 \times 2m}$, C_1 is written as $g^{\mathbf{c}} \in \mathbb{G}^{1 \times 2m}$. By using $\mathbf{v} \in \mathbb{Z}_p^{1 \times 2m}$, sk is written as $g^{\mathbf{v}} \in \mathbb{G}^{2m \times 1}$. Calculate $K := \hat{e}(g,g)^{\mathbf{cv}} \in \mathbb{G}_T$. **Return** C_2/K.

The IBE scheme is correct. We consider a ciphertext for an ID ID and a plaintext M generated properly, i.e., $C = (C_1, C_2) = (g^{\mathbf{zF}(ID)}, \hat{e}(g,g)^{\mathbf{zD}} \cdot M)$, and a secret user-key for the same ID ID generated properly, i.e., sk $= g^{\mathbf{v}}$. When C is decrypted by using sk, the calculated value of K becomes $K = \hat{e}(g,g)^{\mathbf{zF}(ID)\mathbf{v}} = \hat{e}(g,g)^{\mathbf{zD}}$ since $\mathbf{F}(ID)\mathbf{v} = \mathbf{D}$. Hence, M is correctly obtained.

The algorithm **KeyGen**$'$ is defined as follows, where l is a polynomial function.

KeyGen$'_l(\text{pk}, \text{mk}, ID)$: For $i \in [m+1, 2m]$, set $v_i \xleftarrow{U} \mathbb{Z}_p$. For $i \in [1, m]$, set $v_i := E_i - (r_0 + \sum_{k=1}^n ID[k]r_k)v_{m+i}$, where E_i is the $(i, 1)$-th element of the vector $\mathbf{E} \in \mathbb{Z}_p^{m \times 1}$. For every $i \in [1, m]$, do the following:

- Set $H_i := \{v_i\}$ and $H_{m+i} := \{v_{m+i}\}$. For every $j \in [2, l]$, do the following:
  - Set $v_{m+i,j} \xleftarrow{U} \mathbb{Z}_p \setminus H_{m+i}$ and $v_{i,j} := E_i - (r_0 + \sum_{k=1}^n ID[k]r_k)v_{m+i,j}$. Set $H_i := H_i \cup \{v_{i,j}\}$ and $H_{m+i} := H_{m+i} \cup \{v_{m+i,j}\}$.

Set $H^* := H_1 \cup \cdots \cup H_{2m}$. Set sk $:= g^{\mathbf{v}}$, where the $(i, 1)$-th element of $\mathbf{v} \in \mathbb{Z}_p^{2m \times 1}$ is set as v_i. **Return** (sk, H^*).

Obviously, for any $ID \in \mathcal{I}$, the secret user-key outputted by **KeyGen**$'_l$ is generated in the same manner as the secret user-key outputted by **KeyGen**.

4.2 Security of Our IBE Scheme

In this subsection, security, i.e., ciphertext indistinguishability in the AL model, of the IBE scheme Π_{IBE} is proven. We give the following theorem.

Theorem 2. *IBE scheme Π_{IBE} is (2^{-m^ϵ})-AL-IND-ID-CPA-secure with respect to **KeyGen**$'_l$ under the assumption X parameterized by m.*

---

[4] It obviously holds that $[\mathbf{I}_m | (r_0 + \Sigma_{i=1}^n ID[i]r_i)\mathbf{I}_m] \mathbf{v} = \mathbf{E}$. Note that by pre-multiplying this equation by $\mathbf{A}_0$, we obtain $\mathbf{F}(ID)\mathbf{v} = \mathbf{D}$.

The assumption X parameterized by an integer l is an assumption which says that for every PPT $\mathcal{A}$ and $\lambda \in \mathbb{N}$,

$$\left| \Pr \left[\mathcal{A}(p, \mathbb{G}, g, g^{\mathbf{A}_b}) \to b \mid (p, \mathbb{G}) \leftarrow \mathcal{G}(1^\lambda), g \xleftarrow{\text{U}} \mathbb{G}, \mathbf{x}, \mathbf{y}, \mathbf{z} \xleftarrow{\text{U}} \mathbb{Z}_p^{1 \times l}, s, t, \xleftarrow{\text{U}} \mathbb{Z}_p, \right. \right.$$

$$\left. \left. \mathbf{A}_0 := \begin{bmatrix} \mathbf{x} \\ \mathbf{y} \\ \mathbf{z} \end{bmatrix} \in \mathbb{Z}_p^{3 \times l}, \mathbf{A}_1 := \begin{bmatrix} \mathbf{x} \\ \mathbf{y} \\ s\mathbf{x} + t\mathbf{y} \end{bmatrix} \in \mathbb{Z}_p^{3 \times l}, b \xleftarrow{\text{U}} \{0, 1\} \right] - 1/2 \right|$$

is negligible. Validity of the assumption is guaranteed by the following theorem whose proof is given in the full version of this paper.

Theorem 3. *For any $l \in \mathbb{N}$, the assumption X parameterized by l is implied by the DLIN assumption.*

Proof of Theorem 2. Game_i, where $i \in \{0, 1, 2\}$, is defined as follows.

Game_0: This is a normal (2^{-m^ϵ})-AL-IND-ID-CPA game for the IBE scheme Π_{IBE} and $\mathbf{KeyGen}'_l$ which is played between a PPT adversary $\mathcal{A}$ and challenger $\mathcal{C}$.

Game_1: This game is the same as Game_0 except that the challenge ciphertext $C^* = (C_1^*, C_2^*)$ is generated as follows: $C_1^* := g^{[\mathbf{y}^* | r^* \mathbf{y}^*]} \in \mathbb{G}^{1 \times 2m}$ and $C_2^* := \hat{e}(g, g)^{[\mathbf{y}^* | r^* \mathbf{y}^*] \mathbf{v}^*} \cdot M_b \in \mathbb{G}_T$, where $\mathbf{y}^* \xleftarrow{\text{U}} \mathbb{Z}_p^{1 \times m}$, $r^* := r_0 + \Sigma_{i=1}^n ID^*[i] r_i$, and $\mathbf{v}^* \in \mathbb{Z}_p^{2m \times 1}$ is the exponent of the secret-key $\mathsf{sk}^* = g^{\mathbf{v}^*}$ for ID^*.

Game_2: This game is the same as Game_1 except that C_2^* of the challenge ciphertext C^* is set to $C_2^* := \hat{e}(g, g)^u \cdot M_b$, where $u \xleftarrow{\text{U}} \mathbb{Z}_p$.

For $i \in \{0, 1, 2\}$, W_i denotes the event where $\mathcal{A}$ outputs b' such that $b' = b$ in Game_i. The advantage of an adversary $\mathcal{A}$ playing the game of (2^{-m^ϵ})-AL-IND-ID-CPA for the IBE scheme Π_{IBE} and $\mathbf{KeyGen}'_l$ satisfies $\mathbf{Adv}_{\Pi_{IBE}, \mathbf{KeyGen}'_l, \mathcal{A}}^{(2^{-m^\epsilon})-AL-IND-ID-CPA}(\lambda) = |\Pr[W_0] - 1/2| \leq |\Pr[W_0] - \Pr[W_1]| + |\Pr[W_1] - \Pr[W_2]| + |\Pr[W_2] - 1/2|$.

By the above inequality and the following three lemmas, Theorem 2 is proven. $\square$

Lemma 1. $|\Pr[W_0] - \Pr[W_1]|$ *is negligible under the assumption X parameterized by m.*

Lemma 2. $|\Pr[W_1] - \Pr[W_2]|$ *is negligible.*

Lemma 3. $|\Pr[W_2] - 1/2|$ *is negligible.*

We prove the first two lemmas. Since Lemma 3 is true obviously, its proof is not needed.

Proof of Lemma 1. We prove the lemma by contradiction. Specifically, we prove that if there exists a PPT $\mathcal{A}$ which makes $|\Pr[W_0] - \Pr[W_1]|$ non-negligible, then a PPT simulator $\mathcal{S}$ which breaks the assumption X parameterized by m can be constructed.

The simulator $\mathcal{S}$ is given a matrix $g^{\bar{\mathbf{A}}} \in \mathbb{G}^{3 \times m}$ as an instance of the problem X, then simulates Game_0 (resp. Game_1) against $\mathcal{A}$ if $\bar{\mathbf{A}}$ is the matrix $\mathbf{A}_1$ (resp. $\mathbf{A}_0$) whose third row vector is a linear combination of the first two row vectors (resp. a randomly generated one). The concrete behaviour by $\mathcal{S}$ is as follows.

Setup: $(p, \mathbb{G}, \mathbb{G}_T, \hat{e}) \leftarrow \mathcal{G}_{bg}(1^\lambda)$ is run. g denotes a generator of $\mathbb{G}$. $\mathcal{S}$ is given $(g, g^{\bar{\mathbf{A}}})$ as an instance of the problem in the assumption X, where $\bar{\mathbf{A}} \in \mathbb{Z}_p^{3 \times m}$. $\mathcal{S}$ sets the first (resp. second) row vector of $g^{\mathbf{A}_0}$ as the first (resp. second) row vector of $g^{\bar{\mathbf{A}}}$.
$\mathcal{S}$ sets $r_i \overset{U}{\leftarrow} \mathbb{Z}_p$ where $i \in [1, n]$, and $\mathbf{E} \overset{U}{\leftarrow} \mathbb{Z}_p^{m \times 1}$. $\mathcal{S}$ computes $g^{\mathbf{A}_0'}, g^{\mathbf{A}_i}$, where $i \in [1, n]$, and $g^{\mathbf{D}}$ by using $g^{\mathbf{A}_0}, r_i$, where $i \in [1, n]$, and $\mathbf{E}$, where $\mathbf{A}_0' = r_0 \mathbf{A}_0$, $\mathbf{A}_i = r_i \mathbf{A}_0$, and $\mathbf{D} = \mathbf{A}_0 \mathbf{E}$.
$\mathbf{F}(ID)$ is defined as $\mathbf{F}(ID) = [\mathbf{A}_0 | \mathbf{A}_0' + \Sigma_{i=1}^n ID[i]\mathbf{A}_i] = \mathbf{A}_0[\mathbf{I}_m | (r_0 + \Sigma_{i=1}^n ID[i]r_i)\mathbf{I}_m]$. $\mathcal{S}$ sets $\mathrm{pk} := (q, \mathbb{G}, \mathbb{G}_T, \hat{e}, g, g^{\mathbf{A}_0}, g^{\mathbf{A}_0'}, g^{\mathbf{A}_1}, \cdots, g^{\mathbf{A}_n}, g^{\mathbf{D}})$ and $\mathrm{mk} := (r_0, r_1, \cdots, r_n, \mathbf{E})$.
$\mathcal{S}$ sends pk to $\mathcal{A}$. $\mathcal{S}$ initializes the list $\mathcal{L}$ as an empty set $\emptyset$.

Phase 1: When $\mathcal{A}$ issues a query to the oracle **Reveal**, $\mathcal{S}$ behaves as follows:
Reveal($ID \neq ID^*$): $\mathcal{S}$ randomly chooses $\mathbf{v} \in \mathbb{Z}_p^{2m \times 1}$ satisfying
$$[\mathbf{I}_m | (r_0 + \Sigma_{i=1}^n ID[i]r_i)\mathbf{I}_m] \mathbf{v} = \mathbf{E},$$ and sets sk $:= g^{\mathbf{v}}$. $\mathcal{S}$ sets $\mathcal{L} := \mathcal{L} \cup \{(ID, \mathrm{sk})\}$.
Leak(ID^*, f): $\mathcal{S}$ randomly chooses $\mathbf{v}^* \in \mathbb{Z}_p^{2m \times 1}$ satisfying $[\mathbf{I}_m | (r_0 + \Sigma_{i=1}^n ID^*[i]r_i)\mathbf{I}_m]\mathbf{v}^* = \mathbf{E}$, then sets sk $:= g^{\mathbf{v}^*}$. $\mathcal{S}$ computes $f(\mathrm{sk}^*)$, then gives it to $\mathcal{A}$.

Challenge(M_0, M_1): $\mathcal{S}$ receives two plaintexts (M_0, M_1). $b \in \{0, 1\}$ is set as $b \overset{U}{\leftarrow} \{0, 1\}$. $r^* \in \mathbb{Z}_p$ is set as $r^* := r_0 + \Sigma_{i=1}^n ID^*[i]r_i$. $g^{\mathbf{y}} \in \mathbb{G}^{1 \times m}$ is set as the third row vector of $g^{\bar{\mathbf{A}}} \in \mathbb{G}^{3 \times m}$. $\mathbf{v}^* \in \mathbb{Z}_p^{2m \times 1}$ is the exponent of sk$^* = g^{\mathbf{v}^*} \in \mathbb{G}^{2m \times 1}$ which was generated in **Leak**. $\mathcal{S}$ sets the challenge ciphertext C^* to $C^* := (C_1^*, C_2^*) := (g^{[\mathbf{y} | r^*\mathbf{y}]}, \hat{e}(g, g)^{[\mathbf{y} | r^*\mathbf{y}]\mathbf{v}^*} \cdot M_b)$, then sends it to $\mathcal{A}$.
Phase 2: If $\mathcal{A}$ issues a query to the oracle **Reveal**, $\mathcal{S}$ behaves in the same manner as **Phase 1**.
Guess(b'): $\mathcal{S}$ receives $b' \in \{0, 1\}$ sent by $\mathcal{A}$. $\mathcal{S}$ outputs $\beta' := 1$ if $b' = b$. $\mathcal{S}$ outputs $\beta' := 0$ if $b' \neq b$.

We now verify that $\mathcal{S}$ simulates Game_0 (resp. Game_1) against $\mathcal{A}$ perfectly when the matrix $\bar{\mathbf{A}} \in \mathbb{Z}_p^{3 \times m}$ is the matrix $\mathbf{A}_1$ (resp. $\mathbf{A}_0$).

Firstly, we consider the case that $\bar{\mathbf{A}}$ is $\mathbf{A}_1$. In this case, the third row of $\bar{\mathbf{A}}$, i.e., $\mathbf{y} \in \mathbb{Z}_p^{1 \times m}$, is a linear combination of the first row and the second row of $\bar{\mathbf{A}}$, so there is $\mathbf{z}^* \in \mathbb{Z}_p^{1 \times 2}$ such that $\mathbf{y} = \mathbf{z}^* \mathbf{A}_0$. Hence, we obtain $[\mathbf{y} | r^*\mathbf{y}] = [\mathbf{z}^* \mathbf{A}_0 | \mathbf{z}^*(r^* \mathbf{A}_0)] = \mathbf{z}^* \mathbf{F}(ID^*)$, and $[\mathbf{y} | r^*\mathbf{y}]\mathbf{v}^* = \mathbf{z}^*\mathbf{F}(ID^*)\mathbf{v}^* = \mathbf{z}^* \mathbf{D}$. Therefore, the challenge ciphertext is written as $C^* = (C_1^*, C_2^*) = (g^{\mathbf{z}^* \mathbf{F}(ID^*)}, \hat{e}(g, g)^{\mathbf{z}^* \mathbf{D}} \cdot M_b)$. The challenge ciphertext C^* is the proper challenge ciphertext in Game_0. Hence, if $\bar{\mathbf{A}}$ is $\mathbf{A}_1$, then $\mathcal{S}$ simulates Game_0 to $\mathcal{A}$ perfectly.

Next, we consider another case that $\bar{\mathbf{A}}$ is $\mathbf{A}_0$. In this case, the third row of $\bar{\mathbf{A}}$, i.e., $\mathbf{y} \in \mathbb{Z}_p^{1 \times m}$, distributes equivalently to a vector chosen uniformly at random, so the challenge ciphertext C^* generated by S is the proper challenge ciphertext in Game_1 exactly. Hence, S simulates Game_1 against $\mathcal{A}$ perfectly.

Therefore, we obtain $\mathbf{Adv}_S^{\mathrm{DLIN}} = |\Pr[W_1] - \Pr[W_0]|$.   □

Proof of Lemma 2. At first, we define three events $U^{(\mathrm{pk,mk})}$, $V_{(\mathrm{pk,mk})}^{\mathcal{L}}$ and $V_{(\mathrm{pk,mk}),\mathcal{L}}^{ID^*,f}$ for the game Game_1 or Game_2. Here, $(\mathrm{pk,mk})$ is a pair of a system public-key pk and master-key mk generated in the phase **Setup**, $\mathcal{L}$ is a list generated in the phase **Phase 1** under the queries issued by the adversary $\mathcal{A}$ given $(\mathrm{pk,mk})$ in **Setup**, and (ID^*, f) is the pair of a target ID and a leakage function chosen by $\mathcal{A}$ in the phase **Leak** when $(\mathrm{pk,mk})$ and $\mathcal{L}$ were generated.

The probability for each event $U^{(\mathrm{pk,mk})}$, $V_{(\mathrm{pk,mk})}^{\mathcal{L}}$ and $V_{(\mathrm{pk,mk}),\mathcal{L}}^{ID^*,f}$ to happen is denoted by $\Pr[U^{(\mathrm{pk,mk})}]$, $\Pr[V_{(\mathrm{pk,mk})}^{\mathcal{L}}]$ and $\Pr[V_{(\mathrm{pk,mk}),\mathcal{L}}^{ID^*,f}]$. We define a set $\mathbb{Q}_{(\mathrm{pk,mk})}^{\mathcal{L}}$ as $\{\mathcal{L} \text{ s.t. } \Pr[V_{(\mathrm{pk,mk})}^{\mathcal{L}}] > 0\}$. Likewise, we define a set $\mathbb{Q}_{(\mathrm{pk,mk}),\mathcal{L}}^{ID^*,f}$ as $\{(ID^*, f) \text{ s.t. } \Pr[V_{(\mathrm{pk,mk}),\mathcal{L}}^{ID^*,f}] > 0\}$.

We define games $\mathsf{Game}_1^{(\mathrm{pk,mk}),\mathcal{L},(ID^*,f)}$ and $\mathsf{Game}_2^{(\mathrm{pk,mk}),\mathcal{L},(ID^*,f)}$, and events $W_1^{(\mathrm{pk,mk}),\mathcal{L},(ID^*,f)}$ and $W_2^{(\mathrm{pk,mk}),\mathcal{L},(ID^*,f)}$. $\mathsf{Game}_1^{(\mathrm{pk,mk}),\mathcal{L},(ID^*,f)}$ is the following game where a PPT adversary $\mathcal{A}$ and a challenger C communicate each other:

Setup: C runs $\mathrm{sk}^* \leftarrow \mathbf{KeyGen}(\mathrm{pk}, \mathrm{mk}, ID^*)$, then C computes $f(\mathrm{sk}^*)$. C sends $(\mathrm{pk}, \mathcal{L}, ID^*, f, f(\mathrm{sk}^*))$ to $\mathcal{A}$.

Challenge(M_0, M_1): C receives two distinct plaintexts $M_0, M_1 \in \mathcal{M}$ from $\mathcal{A}$. C sets $C_1^* := g^{[\mathbf{y}|r^*\mathbf{y}]}$ and $C_2^* := \hat{e}(g,g)^{[\mathbf{y}|r^*\mathbf{y}]\mathbf{v}^*} \cdot M_b$, where $b \xleftarrow{\mathrm{U}} \{0,1\}$, $\mathbf{y} \xleftarrow{\mathrm{U}} \mathbb{Z}_p^{1 \times m}$, $r^* := r_0 + \sum_{i=1}^n r_i \cdot ID^*[i]$, and $\mathbf{v}^* \in \mathbb{Z}_p^{1 \times 2m}$ is the exponent of the secret-key $\mathrm{sk}^* := g^{\mathbf{v}^*}$. C sends $C^* := (C_1^*, C_2^*)$ to $\mathcal{A}$.

Phase 2: $\mathcal{A}$ is allowed to use the oracle **Reveal** adaptively.

  Reveal$(ID \neq ID^*)$: C runs $\mathrm{sk} \leftarrow \mathbf{KeyGen}(\mathrm{pk}, \mathrm{mk}, ID)$, then sends it to $\mathcal{A}$.

Guess$(b' \in \{0,1\})$: $\mathcal{A}$ sends a guess $b' \in \{0,1\}$ for b.

$\mathsf{Game}_2^{(\mathrm{pk,mk}),\mathcal{L},(ID^*,f)}$ is the same as $\mathsf{Game}_1^{(\mathrm{pk,mk}),\mathcal{L},(ID^*,f)}$ except that the second element C_2^* of the challenge ciphertext C^* is set to $C_2^* := \hat{e}(g,g)^u$, where $u \xleftarrow{\mathrm{U}} \mathbb{Z}_p$.

Let $W_{1,(\mathrm{pk,mk}),\mathcal{L},(ID^*,f)}$ (resp. $W_{2,(\mathrm{pk,mk}),\mathcal{L},(ID^*,f)}$) denote the event where $\mathcal{A}$ outputs b' such that $b' = b$ in $\mathsf{Game}_1^{(\mathrm{pk,mk}),\mathcal{L},(ID^*,f)}$ (resp. $\mathsf{Game}_2^{(\mathrm{pk,mk}),\mathcal{L},(ID^*,f)}$).

By the definitions of W_1, $U^{(\mathrm{pk,mk})}$, $V_{(\mathrm{pk,mk})}^{\mathcal{L}}$, $V_{(\mathrm{pk,mk}),\mathcal{L}}^{ID^*,f}$ and $W_{2,(\mathrm{pk,mk}),\mathcal{L},(ID^*,f)}$, we obtain

$$\Pr[W_1] = \sum_{(\mathrm{pk,mk}) \leftarrow \mathbf{Setup}(1^\lambda)} \sum_{\mathcal{L} \in \mathbb{Q}_{(\mathrm{pk,mk})}^{\mathcal{L}}} \sum_{(ID^*,f) \in \mathbb{Q}_{(\mathrm{pk,mk}),\mathcal{L}}^{(ID^*,f)}} \Pr\left[W_{1,(\mathrm{pk,mk}),\mathcal{L},(ID^*,f)}\right]$$
$$\cdot \Pr\left[V_{(\mathrm{pk,mk}),\mathcal{L}}^{ID^*,f}\right] \cdot \Pr\left[V_{(\mathrm{pk,mk})}^{\mathcal{L}}\right] \cdot \Pr\left[U^{(\mathrm{pk,mk})}\right] \tag{1}$$

Likewise, we obtain an equation for $\Pr[W_2]$. Hence, we obtain

$$|\Pr[W_1] - \Pr[W_2]| = \left| \sum_{(\mathrm{pk,mk}) \leftarrow \mathbf{Setup}(1^\lambda)} \sum_{\mathcal{L} \in \mathbb{Q}^{\mathcal{L}}_{(\mathrm{pk,mk})}} \sum_{(ID^*,f) \in \mathbb{Q}^{(ID^*,f)}_{(\mathrm{pk,mk}),\mathcal{L}}} \right.$$

$$\left(\Pr\left[W_{1,(\mathrm{pk,mk}),\mathcal{L},(ID^*,f)}\right] - \Pr\left[W_{2,(\mathrm{pk,mk}),\mathcal{L},(ID^*,f)}\right] \right)$$

$$\left. \cdot \Pr\left[V^{ID^*,f}_{(\mathrm{pk,mk}),\mathcal{L}}\right] \cdot \Pr\left[V^{\mathcal{L}}_{(\mathrm{pk,mk})}\right] \cdot \Pr\left[U^{(\mathrm{pk,mk})}\right] \right|$$

$$\leq \sum_{(\mathrm{pk,mk}) \leftarrow \mathbf{Setup}(1^\lambda)} \sum_{\mathcal{L} \in \mathbb{Q}^{\mathcal{L}}_{(\mathrm{pk,mk})}} \sum_{(ID^*,f) \in \mathbb{Q}^{(ID^*,f)}_{(\mathrm{pk,mk}),\mathcal{L}}}$$

$$\left| \Pr\left[W_{1,(\mathrm{pk,mk}),\mathcal{L},(ID^*,f)}\right] - \Pr\left[W_{2,(\mathrm{pk,mk}),\mathcal{L},(ID^*,f)}\right] \right|$$

$$\cdot \Pr\left[V^{ID^*,f}_{(\mathrm{pk,mk}),\mathcal{L}}\right] \cdot \Pr\left[V^{\mathcal{L}}_{(\mathrm{pk,mk})}\right] \cdot \Pr\left[U^{(\mathrm{pk,mk})}\right].$$

By Lemma 4, there exists a negligible function $negl(\lambda)$ s.t.

$$|\Pr[W_1] - \Pr[W_2]| \leq negl(\lambda) \cdot \left\{ \sum_{(\mathrm{pk,mk}) \leftarrow \mathbf{Setup}(1^\lambda)} \sum_{\mathcal{L} \in \mathbb{Q}^{\mathcal{L}}_{(\mathrm{pk,mk})}} \sum_{(ID^*,f) \in \mathbb{Q}^{(ID^*,f)}_{(\mathrm{pk,mk}),\mathcal{L}}} \right.$$

$$\left. \Pr\left[V^{ID^*,f}_{(\mathrm{pk,mk}),\mathcal{L}}\right] \cdot \Pr\left[V^{\mathcal{L}}_{(\mathrm{pk,mk})}\right] \cdot \Pr\left[U^{(\mathrm{pk,mk})}\right] \right\}. \tag{2}$$

We give three facts. It holds that $\sum_{(\mathrm{pk,mk}) \leftarrow \mathbf{Setup}(1^\lambda)} \Pr\left[U^{(\mathrm{pk,mk})}\right] = 1$. It also holds that for any $(\mathrm{pk,mk}) \leftarrow \mathbf{Setup}(1^\lambda)$, $\sum_{\mathcal{L} \in \mathbb{Q}^{\mathcal{L}}_{(\mathrm{pk,mk})}} \Pr\left[V^{\mathcal{L}}_{(\mathrm{pk,mk})}\right] = 1$. It also holds that for any $(\mathrm{pk,mk}) \leftarrow \mathbf{Setup}(1^\lambda)$ and any $\mathcal{L} \in \mathbb{Q}^{\mathcal{L}}_{(\mathrm{pk,mk})}$, $\sum_{(ID^*,f) \in \mathbb{Q}^{ID^*,f}_{(\mathrm{pk,mk}),\mathcal{L}}} \Pr\left[V^{ID^*,f}_{(\mathrm{pk,mk}),\mathcal{L}}\right] = 1$.

By the above three facts and (2), it is true that for any PPT $\mathcal{A}$, there exists a negligible function $negl(\lambda)$ such that $|\Pr[W_1] - \Pr[W_2]| \leq negl(\lambda)$. □

Lemma 4. *For any PPT $\mathcal{A}$, any $\lambda \in \mathbb{N}$, any $(\mathrm{pk,mk}) \leftarrow \mathbf{Setup}(1^\lambda)$, any $\mathcal{L} \in \mathbb{Q}^{\mathcal{L}}_{(\mathrm{pk,mk})}$ and any $(ID^*,f) \in \mathbb{Q}^{ID^*,f}_{(\mathrm{pk,mk}),\mathcal{L}}$, there exists $negl(\lambda)$ such that $|\Pr[W_{1,(\mathrm{pk,mk}),\mathcal{L},(ID^*,f)}] - \Pr[W_{2,(\mathrm{pk,mk}),\mathcal{L},(ID^*,f)}]| \leq negl(\lambda)$.*

Proof of Lemma 4. To prove the lemma, we use Lemma 5.

We consider a PPT simulator S. S behaves as the distinguisher $\mathcal{D}$ in Lemma 5. S behaves concurrently as the challenger in $\mathbf{Game}_1^{(\mathrm{pk,mk})}$ or $\mathbf{Game}_2^{(\mathrm{pk,mk})}$, so S has to simulate each game against $\mathcal{A}$. The concrete behaviour of S is as follows:

Setup: S is the distinguisher $\mathcal{D}$ in Lemma 5, so S is given $(\mathrm{pk,mk}, \mathcal{L}, ID^*, f, f(\mathrm{sk}^*), [\mathbf{y}|r^*\mathbf{y}], s)$, where $s \in \mathbb{Z}_p$ is $[\mathbf{y}|r^*\mathbf{y}]\mathbf{v}^*$ or u. S sends $(\mathrm{pk}, \mathcal{L}, ID^*, f, f(\mathrm{sk}^*))$ to $\mathcal{A}$.

Challenge(M_0, M_1): S receives two plaintexts $M_0, M_1 \in M$ sent from $\mathcal{A}$. S sets $b \xleftarrow{U} \{0,1\}$, then sets $C_1^* := g^{[\mathbf{y}|r^*\mathbf{y}]} \in \mathbb{G}^{1 \times 2m}$ and $C_2^* := \hat{e}(g, g)^s \cdot M_b$. After that, S sends $C^* := (C_1^*, C_2^*)$ to $\mathcal{A}$.

Phase 2: When $\mathcal{A}$ issues a query to **Reveal**, S acts as follows:

Reveal$(ID \neq ID^*)$: S runs sk $\leftarrow$ **KeyGen**(pk, mk, ID), then sends sk to $\mathcal{A}$.

Guess$(b' \in \{0,1\})$: S receives $b' \in \{0,1\}$ from $\mathcal{A}$. If $b' = b$, then S outputs $\beta' := 1$. Otherwise, then S outputs $\beta' := 0$.

For any PPT $\mathcal{A}$, any $\lambda \in \mathbb{N}$, any (pk, mk) $\leftarrow$ **Setup**(1^λ), any $\mathcal{L} \in \mathbb{Q}_{(\mathrm{pk,mk})}^{\mathcal{L}}$ and any $(ID^*, f) \in \mathbb{Q}_{(\mathrm{pk,mk}),\mathcal{L}}^{ID^*,f}$, we obtain $\Pr[W_{1,(\mathrm{pk,mk}),\mathcal{L},(ID^*,f)}] = \Pr[S(\mathrm{pk}, \mathrm{mk}, \mathcal{L}, ID^*, f, f(\mathrm{sk}^*), [\mathbf{y}|r^*\mathbf{y}], [\mathbf{y}|r^*\mathbf{y}]\mathbf{v}^*) \rightarrow 1 | (\mathrm{sk}^*, H^*) \leftarrow$ **KeyGen**$'_l(\mathrm{pk}, \mathrm{mk}, ID^*), \mathbf{y} \xleftarrow{U} \mathbb{Z}_p^{1 \times m}]$ and $\Pr[W_{2,(\mathrm{pk,mk}),\mathcal{L},(ID^*,f)}] = \Pr[S(\mathrm{pk}, \mathrm{mk}, \mathcal{L}, ID^*, f, f(\mathrm{sk}^*), [\mathbf{y}|r^*\mathbf{y}], u) \rightarrow 1 |$

$(\mathrm{sk}^*, H^*) \leftarrow$ **KeyGen**$'_l(\mathrm{pk}, \mathrm{mk}, ID^*), \mathbf{y} \xleftarrow{U} \mathbb{Z}_p^{1 \times m}, u \xleftarrow{U} \mathbb{Z}_p]$.

Hence, we obtain

$$\delta := \left| \Pr\left[W_{1,(\mathrm{pk,mk}),\mathcal{L},(ID^*,f)}\right] - \Pr\left[W_{2,(\mathrm{pk,mk}),\mathcal{L},(ID^*,f)}\right] \right|$$
$$= |\Pr\left[S\left(\mathrm{pk}, \mathrm{mk}, \mathcal{L}, ID^*, f, f(\mathrm{sk}^*), [\mathbf{y}|r^*\mathbf{y}], [\mathbf{y}|r^*\mathbf{y}]\,\mathbf{v}^*\right) \rightarrow 1\right.$$
$$\left.\left|(\mathrm{sk}^*, H^*) \leftarrow \text{\textbf{KeyGen}}'_l(\mathrm{pk}, \mathrm{mk}, ID^*), \mathbf{y} \xleftarrow{U} \mathbb{Z}_p^{1 \times m}\right]\right.$$
$$- \Pr\left[S\left(\mathrm{pk}, \mathrm{mk}, \mathcal{L}, ID^*, f, f(\mathrm{sk}^*), [\mathbf{y}|r^*\mathbf{y}], u\right) \rightarrow 1\right.$$
$$\left.\left|(\mathrm{sk}^*, H^*) \leftarrow \text{\textbf{KeyGen}}'_l(\mathrm{pk}, \mathrm{mk}, ID^*), \mathbf{y} \xleftarrow{U} \mathbb{Z}_p^{1 \times m}, u \xleftarrow{U} \mathbb{Z}_p\right]\right|. \qquad (3)$$

Lemma 5 guarantees that there exists a PPT inverter $\mathcal{B}$ such that

$$\Pr\left[\mathcal{B}\left(\mathrm{pk}, \mathrm{mk}, \mathcal{L}, ID^*, f, f(\mathrm{sk}^*), H^*\right) \rightarrow \mathrm{sk}^*\right.$$
$$\left.\left|(\mathrm{sk}^*, H^*) \leftarrow \text{\textbf{KeyGen}}'_l(\mathrm{pk}, \mathrm{mk}, ID^*)\right] \geq \frac{\delta^3}{1024 \cdot m^2 \cdot p^3 \cdot l}. \qquad (4)$$

We assume that there exists a polynomial function $poly(\lambda)$ such that $\delta \geq 1/poly(\lambda)$. Since p is $p < 2^\lambda$, m is $m = (4\lambda)^{1/\epsilon}$, and l can be written as a polynomial function $poly^*(\lambda)$, we obtain

$$\frac{\delta^3}{1024 \cdot m^2 \cdot p^3 \cdot l} > \frac{1}{1024 \cdot (4\lambda)^{2/\epsilon} \cdot 2^{3\lambda} \cdot poly(\lambda)^3 \cdot poly^*(\lambda)}$$
$$> 2^{-3\lambda} \cdot 2^{-\lambda} = 2^{-4\lambda} = 2^{-m^\epsilon}. \qquad (5)$$

(4) and (5) lead us to a contradiction against the fact that $f \in \mathcal{F}_{(\mathrm{pk,mk}),\mathcal{L},(ID^*,f)}(2^{-m^\epsilon})$. Hence, there are no polynomial functions $poly(\lambda)$ such that $\delta \geq 1/poly(\lambda)$. Therefore, by (3), for any PPT $\mathcal{A}$, any $\lambda \in \mathbb{N}$, any (pk, mk) $\leftarrow$ **Setup**(1^λ), any $\mathcal{L} \in \mathbb{Q}_{(\mathrm{pk,mk})}^{\mathcal{L}}$ and any $(ID^*, f) \in \mathbb{Q}_{(\mathrm{pk,mk}),\mathcal{L}}^{ID^*,f}$, $\left|\Pr\left[W_{1,(\mathrm{pk,mk}),\mathcal{L},(ID^*,f)}\right] - \Pr\left[W_{2,(\mathrm{pk,mk}),\mathcal{L},(ID^*,f)}\right]\right|$ is negligible. $\square$

Lemma 5 is given below. Proof of this lemma is shown in the full version of this paper. The proof is similar to the proof of Goldreich-Levin theorem for large fields [16].

Lemma 5. *The notations of* pk, mk, $\mathcal{L}$, ID^* *and* f *are the same as the ones in the proof of Lemma 2.* pk *and* mk *are parsed as* pk $= (p, \mathbb{G}, \mathbb{G}_T, \hat{e}, g, g^{\mathbf{A}_0}, g^{\mathbf{A}_0'}, g^{\mathbf{A}_1}, \cdots, g^{\mathbf{A}_n}, g^{\mathbf{D}})$ *and* mk $= (r_0, r_1, \cdots, r_n, \mathbf{E})$, *respectively.* r^* *is set as* $r^* := r_0 + \sum_{i=1}^{n} r_i \cdot ID^*[i]$.
We assume that there exists a distinguisher $\mathcal{D}$ *running in time* t *such that*

$$\delta := \left| \Pr\left[\mathcal{D}(\mathrm{pk}, \mathrm{mk}, \mathcal{L}, ID^*, f, f(\mathrm{sk}^*), [\mathbf{y}|r^*\mathbf{y}], [\mathbf{y}|r^*\mathbf{y}]\,\mathbf{v}^*) \to 1 \right.\right.$$
$$\left| (\mathrm{sk}^*, H^*) \leftarrow \mathbf{KeyGen}'_l(\mathrm{pk}, \mathrm{mk}, ID^*), \mathbf{y} \xleftarrow{\mathsf{U}} \mathbb{Z}_p^{1 \times m} \right]$$
$$- \Pr\left[\mathcal{D}(\mathrm{pk}, \mathrm{mk}, \mathcal{L}, ID^*, f, f(\mathrm{sk}^*), [\mathbf{y}|r^*\mathbf{y}], u \qquad) \to 1 \right.$$
$$\left.\left| (\mathrm{sk}^*, H^*) \leftarrow \mathbf{KeyGen}'_l(\mathrm{pk}, \mathrm{mk}, ID^*), \mathbf{y} \xleftarrow{\mathsf{U}} \mathbb{Z}_p^{1 \times m}, u \xleftarrow{\mathsf{U}} \mathbb{Z}_p \right]\right|,$$

where $\mathrm{sk}^* = g^{\mathbf{v}^*}$ *and* $\mathbf{v}^* \in \mathbb{Z}_p^{2m \times 1}$. *If such a distinguisher exists, we can construct an inverter* $\mathcal{B}$ *running in time* $t' = t \cdot \mathrm{poly}(m, l, \frac{1}{\delta})$ *such that*

$$\Pr\left[\mathcal{B}(\mathrm{pk}, \mathrm{mk}, \mathcal{L}, ID^*, f, f(\mathrm{sk}^*), H^*) \to \mathrm{sk}^* \right.$$
$$\left| (\mathrm{sk}^*, H^*) \leftarrow \mathbf{KeyGen}'_l(\mathrm{pk}, \mathrm{mk}, ID^*) \right] \geq \frac{\delta^3}{1024 \cdot m^2 \cdot p^3 \cdot l}.$$

4.3   Leakage Allowed for Our IBE Scheme

In this subsection, we consider the leakage allowed for our IBE scheme Π_{IBE}. We write the secret user-key sk^* as $\mathrm{sk}^* = g^{\mathbf{v}^*} \in \mathbb{G}^{2m \times 1}$, where $\mathbf{v}^* \in \mathbb{Z}_p^{2m \times 1}$. For $i \in [1, 2m]$, the $(i, 1)$-th element of $\mathbf{v}^*$ is denoted by v_i^*.

At first, we consider the case that the leakage function leaks no information about sk^*. As is obvious from the concrete construction of our IBE scheme, for any $i \in [1, m]$, v_i^* and v_{m+i}^* are dependent each other. Hence, any PPT $\mathcal{B}$ in the definition of leakage-function class which is given some information about v_i^* can get some information about v_{m+i}^*, and vice versa. On the contrary, if neither information about v_i^* nor v_{m+i}^* is leaked, any PPT $\mathcal{B}$ cannot identify either v_i^* or v_{m+i}^* with probability greater than $1/l$, information-theoretically. Therefore, the following statement is true, information-theoretically: for any $\lambda \in \mathbb{N}$, any $(\mathrm{pk}, \mathrm{mk}) \leftarrow \mathbf{Setup}(1^\lambda)$, any $\mathcal{L} \in \mathbb{Q}_{(\mathrm{pk}, \mathrm{mk})}^{\mathcal{L}}$, any ID^* which is not in the list $\mathcal{L}$, any function f which leaks no information about sk^*, and any PPT $\mathcal{B}$, it holds that $\Pr[\mathcal{B}(\mathrm{pk}, \mathrm{mk}, \mathcal{L}, ID^*, f, f(\mathrm{sk}^*), H^*) \to \mathrm{sk}^* | (\mathrm{sk}^*, H^*) \leftarrow \mathbf{KeyGen}'_l(\mathrm{pk}, \mathrm{mk}, ID^*)] \leq 1/l^m$. Since $m > 4\lambda$, if we set l such that $l > 2$, then $l^{-m} < 2^{-4\lambda} = 2^{-m^\epsilon}$. Hence, for any $\lambda \in \mathbb{N}$, any $(\mathrm{pk}, \mathrm{mk}) \leftarrow \mathbf{Setup}(1^\lambda)$, any $\mathcal{L} \in \mathbb{Q}_{(\mathrm{pk}, \mathrm{mk})}^{\mathcal{L}}$ and any ID^* which is not in the list $\mathcal{L}$, any leakage function f which leaks no information about sk^* is allowed to query.

Next, we consider the case that the leakage function leaks some information about sk^*. Obviously, the leakage function which fully leaks sk^* is not an allowed one, because any PPT $\mathcal{B}$ given the leakage information can identify sk^* with probability 1. Hereafter, we let c be a constant positive real number, and we consider a leakage function which satisfies the following condition: among m "pairs" of $(v_1^*, v_{m+1}^*), \cdots, (v_{m-1}^*, v_{2m}^*)$, there are at least $4\lambda/c$ pairs of (v_i^*, v_{m+i}^*), where $i \in [1, m]$, such that the leakage function does not leak any information about either v_i^* or v_{m+i}^*.

The following statement is true, information-theoretically: for any $\lambda \in \mathbb{N}$, any $(\text{pk}, \text{mk}) \leftarrow \textbf{Setup}(1^\lambda)$, any $\mathcal{L} \in \mathbb{Q}_{(\text{pk},\text{mk})}^{\mathcal{L}}$, any ID^* which is not in the list $\mathcal{L}$, any leakage function f which satisfies the above condition, and any PPT $\mathcal{B}$, it holds that $\Pr[\mathcal{B}(\text{pk}, \text{mk}, \mathcal{L}, ID^*, f, f(\text{sk}^*), H^*) \to \text{sk}^*|(\text{sk}^*, H^*) \to \textbf{KeyGen}_l'(\text{pk}, \text{mk}, ID^*)] \leq 1/l^{4\lambda/c}$. If we set l such that $l > 2^c$, then $l^{-4\lambda/c} < 2^{-4\lambda} = 2^{-m^\epsilon}$. Hence, For any $\lambda \in \mathbb{N}$, any $(\text{pk}, \text{mk}) \leftarrow \textbf{Setup}(1^\lambda)$, any $\mathcal{L} \in \mathbb{Q}_{(\text{pk},\text{mk})}^{\mathcal{L}}$, any ID^* which is not in the list $\mathcal{L}$, any leakage function f which satisfies the above condition is allowed to query.

How Large is the Amount of Leakage Allowed for Our IBE Scheme? In the above, we considered a leakage function such that there are at least $4\lambda/c$ pairs of (v_j^*, v_{m+j}^*), where $j \in [1, m]$, any one of which does not leak any information about either v_j^* or v_{m+j}^*. We did not impose any restriction on the leakage function regarding the remaining $m - 4\lambda/c$ pairs. We can allow the function to fully leak every one of the $m - 4\lambda/c$ pairs. The bigger the parameter $m = (4\lambda)^{1/\epsilon}$ whose ϵ is $0 < \epsilon < 1$ is, the bigger the number $m - 4\lambda/c$ of pairs which can be fully leaked is. Therefore, the amount of allowed leakage linearly increases with the size of the secret user-key.

5   The Results by Yuen et al. [36]

In this section, the results by Yuen et al. [36] is described. In Subsects. 5.1 and 5.2, their definition of the ciphertext indistinguishability for an IBE scheme and their concrete construction of IBE scheme are described, respectively. They adopts the dual system encryption methodology, so defining the semi-functional secret-key and ciphertext is required. The definitions are given in Subsect. 5.3. The proof sketch for the security of their IBE construction is given in Subsect. 5.4. Our counterexamples against their security proof are described in Subsect. 5.5.

5.1   Definition of Security for IBE Scheme in [36]

Yuen et al. define $g^u(k_u)$-AL-IND-ID-CPA game for an IBE scheme $\Pi_{IBE} = \{\textbf{Setup}, \textbf{KeyGen}, \textbf{Enc}, \textbf{Dec}\}$ as follows, where k_u denotes the minimum entropy of the secret user-key, and $g^u(k_u)$ denotes a negligible function such that $g^u(k_u) > 2^{-k_u}$.

Setup : C runs $(\text{pk}, \text{mk}) \leftarrow \textbf{Setup}(1^\lambda)$. C sends pk to $\mathcal{A}$.

Phase 1: $\mathcal{A}$ is allowed to use extraction oracle $\mathcal{KEO}$, leakage oracle $\mathcal{LO}$, and update oracle $\mathcal{UO}$ adaptively.

   $\mathcal{KEO}(ID, i)$: i should be $i \in \mathbb{N}^+$, and $ID \in \mathcal{I}$ should be such that list $\mathcal{L}_{ID}$ for the ID has been generated. C finds out the tuple in the form of (sk_{ID}, ID, j) in $\mathcal{L}_{ID}$ whose third element is the biggest among all tuples in the list. Let $j^\dagger \in \mathbb{N}^+$ denote the biggest integer. If $i \leq j^\dagger$, then C retrieves the tuple $(\text{sk}_{ID}', ID, i) \in \mathcal{L}_{ID}$, and sends sk_{ID}' to $\mathcal{A}$.

$\mathcal{LO}(f_i, ID)$: f_i should be $f_i \in \mathcal{F}_i(g^u(k_u))$, and $ID \in \mathcal{I}$ should be such that list $\mathcal{L}_{ID}$ for the ID has been generated. The index i of f_i indicates that this query is the i-th query to the leakage oracle. The definition of the function class $\mathcal{F}_i(g^u(k_u))$ is described after the definition of the game. C computes $f_i(\text{pk}, \text{mk}, \mathcal{L}_{ID}, ID)$, then sends it to $\mathcal{A}$.

$\mathcal{UO}(ID)$: ID should be $ID \in \mathcal{I}$. If the list $\mathcal{L}_{ID}$ for ID has not been generated, C generates the list $\mathcal{L}_{ID}$ initialized by $\emptyset$, and sets $j^\dagger := 0$. Otherwise, C finds out the tuple in the form of (sk_{ID}, ID, j) in $\mathcal{L}_{ID}$ whose third element is the biggest integer among all tuples in the list, and sets $j^\dagger$ to the biggest integer.

C runs $\text{sk}'_{ID} \leftarrow \textbf{KeyGen}(\text{pk}, \text{mk}, ID)$, and sets $\mathcal{L}_{ID} := \mathcal{L}_{ID} \cup \{(\text{sk}'_{ID}, ID, j^\dagger + 1)\}$.

Challenge(M_0, M_1, ID^*): $\mathcal{A}$ sends two plaintexts M_0, M_1 and an ID ID^*. C sets $b \xleftarrow{U} \{0,1\}$ and calculates $C^* \leftarrow \textbf{Enc}(\text{pk}, M_b, ID^*)$. C sends C^* to $\mathcal{A}$.

Phase 2: $\mathcal{A}$ is allowed to use the oracle $\mathcal{KEO}$ in the same manner as **Phase 1**.

Guess(b'): $\mathcal{A}$ sends a bit $b' \in \{0,1\}$ to C as a guess for b.

Every ID queried to $\mathcal{KEO}$ in **Phase 1** or **Phase 2** should not be ID^*. Advantage of $\mathcal{A}$ is defined as $\textbf{Adv}_{\Pi_{IBE}, \mathcal{A}}^{(g^u(k_u))-AL-IND-ID-CPA}(\lambda) := |\Pr[b' = b] - 1/2|$.

Definition 2. *We say that an IBE scheme $\Pi_{IBE} = \{\textbf{Setup}, \textbf{KeyGen}, \textbf{Enc}, \textbf{Dec}\}$ is $(g^u(k_u))$-AL-IND-ID-CPA secure, if for every PPT adversary $\mathcal{A}$ in the game of $(g^u(k_u))$-AL-IND-ID-CPA for Π_{IBE}, $\mathcal{A}$'s advantage $\textbf{Adv}_{\Pi, \mathcal{A}}^{(g^u(k_u))-AL-IND-ID-CPA}(\lambda)$ is negligibly small.*

The definition of the function class $\mathcal{F}_i(g^u(k_u))$, where $i \in [1, q_l]$, is as follows. $\mathcal{F}_i(g^u(k_u))$ is a set consists of every function f_i which is computable in polynomial time and satisfies the following condition: for every PPT $\mathcal{B}$, it holds that $\Pr[\mathcal{B}(\text{pk}, ID^*, S, \{f_j(\text{pk}, \text{mk}, \mathcal{L}_{ID_j,j}, ID_j)\}_{j \in [1,i]}) \rightarrow \text{sk}_{ID^*}$ such that $\text{sk}_{ID^*} \in S^*] \leq g^u(k_u)$. Here, S is the set of all secret keys which has been extracted until the i-th leakage oracle query (f_i, ID_i) is issued, S^* is the set of all secret keys for ID^*, and f_j and ID_j, where $j \in [1, i-1]$, are the function and ID in the j-th leakage oracle query (f_j, ID_j) respectively. Every element of the tuple $(\text{pk}, \text{mk}, S, S^*, \{f_j(\text{pk}, \text{mk}, \mathcal{L}_{ID_j,j}, ID_j)\}_{j \in [1,i]})$ is randomly generated.

5.2 Concrete IBE Construction in [36]

Each algorithm of the concrete IBE construction $\Pi_{IBE}^{YCZY12} = \{\textbf{Setup}, \textbf{KeyGen}, \textbf{Enc}, \textbf{Dec}\}$ proposed by Yuen et al. is described below:

Setup(1^λ): Run $(N = p_1 p_2 p_3, \mathbb{G}, \mathbb{G}_T, \hat{e}) \leftarrow \mathcal{G}_{comp}(1^\lambda)$, where $\mathcal{G}_{comp}$ is a generator of bilinear groups of composite order. Set $g_1, u, h \xleftarrow{U} \mathbb{G}_{p_1}, X_3 \xleftarrow{U} \mathbb{G}_{p_3}$, and $m := (3\lambda)^{1/\epsilon}$, where $0 < \epsilon < 1$. For every $i \in [1, m]$, set $\alpha_i, t_i \xleftarrow{U} \mathbb{Z}_N$, $v_i \xleftarrow{U} \mathbb{G}_{p_1}, T_{1,i}, T_{2,i}, T_{3,i} \xleftarrow{U} \mathbb{G}_{p_3}, K_{1,i} := g_1^{\alpha_i} \cdot h^{t_i} \cdot T_{1,i}, K_{2,i} := u^{t_i} \cdot T_{2,i}$, and $K_{3,i} := v_i^{t_i} \cdot T_{3,i}$. **Return** (pk, mk), where $\text{pk} := (N, \mathbb{G}, \mathbb{G}_T, \hat{e}, g_1, u, h, X_3, \{v_i, y_i := \hat{e}(g_1, v_i)^{\alpha_i}\}_{i \in [1,m]})$ and $\text{mk} := (\{K_{1,i}, K_{2,i}, K_{3,i}\}_{i \in [1,m]})$. ID space (resp. plaintext space) is $\mathcal{I} = \mathbb{Z}_N$ (resp. $\mathcal{M} = \mathbb{G}_T$).

KeyGen(pk, mk, ID): For every $i \in [1, m]$, set $r_i \xleftarrow{U} \mathbb{Z}_N$ and $R_{1,i}, R_{2,i} \xleftarrow{U} \mathbb{G}_{p_3}$. **Return** sk$_{ID} := (\{D_i, E_i\}_{i \in [1,m]})$, where $D_i := K_{1,i} \cdot K_{2,i}^{ID} \cdot (u^{ID} \cdot h)^{r_i} \cdot R_{1,i}$, and $E_i := K_{3,i} \cdot v_i^{r_i} \cdot R_{2,i}$.

Enc(pk, M, ID): For every $i \in [1, m]$, set $s_i \xleftarrow{U} \mathbb{Z}_N$. **Return** $C := (A, \{B_i, C_i\}_{i \in [1,m]})$, where $A := M \cdot \prod_{i \in [1,m]} y_i^{s_i}$, $B := v_i^{s_i}$, and $C_i := (u^{ID} \cdot h)^{s_i}$.

Dec(pk, C, ID): **Return** $A \cdot \prod_{i \in [1,m]} \hat{e}(C_i, E_i) / \prod_{i \in [1,m]} \hat{e}(B_i, D_i)$.

5.3   Semi-functional Secret-Key and Ciphertext in [36]

Under the dual system encryption framework, Yuen et al. define semi-functional (SF) master-key, secret user-key, and ciphertext, each one of which is perturbed by an element in $\mathbb{G}_{p_2}$. Below, each one of $\bar{g}_2$ and $\hat{g}_2$ denotes a generator of $\mathbb{G}_{p_2}$.

Given a normal sk $= (\{D_i, E_i\}_{i \in [1,m]})$, a SF secret user-key sk$'$ is computed as follows: sk$' := (\{C_i', E_i'\}_{i \in [1,m]}) := (\{C_i \cdot \bar{g}_2^{\kappa_i}, E_i \cdot \bar{g}_2^{z_i}\})$, where $\kappa_1, z_1, \cdots, \kappa_m, z_m \xleftarrow{U} \mathbb{Z}_N$.

Given a normal $C = (A, \{B_i, C_i\}_{i \in [1,m]})$, a SF ciphertext C' is computed as follows: $C' := (A', \{B_i', C_i'\}) := (A, \{B_i \cdot \hat{g}_2^{\delta_i}, C_i \cdot \hat{g}_2^{x_i}\})$, where $\delta_1, x_1, \cdots, \delta_m, x_m \xleftarrow{U} \mathbb{Z}_N$.

Decrypting a SF ciphertext for ID by using a SF secret user-key for the same ID almost always fails, because the decryption results in a blinded message by a factor $\hat{e}(\bar{g}_2, \hat{g}_2)^{\sum_{i=1}^m \{z_i x_i - \kappa_i \delta_i\}}$. We say that a SF secret user-key sk$' = (\{D_i', E_i'\}_{i \in [1,m]})$ for ID is nominally semi-functional (NSF) for a SF ciphertext $C' = (A', \{B_i', C_i'\})$ for the same ID, or a SF ciphertext C' for ID is NSF for a SF secret user key sk$'$ for the same ID, if it holds that $\sum_{i=1}^m \{z_i x_i - \kappa_i \delta_i\} \equiv 0 \pmod{p_2}$. If a SF secret user-key (resp. ciphertext) is not NSF, we say that the key (resp. ciphertext) is truly semi-functional (TSF).

5.4   Proof of Security in [36]

Yuen et al. claim that security of their IBE scheme is guaranteed by the following.

Theorem 4 [36]. *IBE scheme Π_{IBE}^{YCZY12} is (2^{-m^e})-AL-ID-CPA secure if DSG assumptions 1, 2, 3, given in [36], hold.*

The definition of the games whom Yuen et al. use to prove Theorem 4 is as follows: Game$_{real}$ is the normal (2^{-m^e})-AL-IND-ID-CPA game for Π_{IBE}^{YCZY12} in which an adversary $\mathcal{A}$ plays with a challenger C. Let q_e, q_l and q_u denote the number of times which $\mathcal{A}$ uses $\mathcal{KEO}$, $\mathcal{LO}$ and $\mathcal{UO}$, respectively. q denotes $q = q_e + q_l + q_u$.

Game$_{restricted}$ is the same as Game$_{real}$ except that every ID queried to the extraction oracle satisfies $ID \neq ID^* \mod p_2$.

Game$_0$ is the same as Game$_{restricted}$ except that a generator $\hat{g}_2$ of $\mathbb{G}_{p_2}$ is randomly generated in **Setup**, and the challenge ciphertext is semi-functional one.

Game$_i$, where $i \in [1, q]$, is the same as Game$_0$ except that a generator $\bar{g}_2$ of $\mathbb{G}_{p_2}$ is randomly generated in **Setup**, and for every $j \in [1, i]$, the reply against the j-th oracle query is computed by using secret-keys in the semi-functional form.

Game$_{final}$ is the same as Game$_q$ except that the challenge ciphertext is generated as a (semi-functional) ciphertext for a uniformly chosen plaintext $M' \xleftarrow{U} \mathcal{M}$.

Adv$_X$, where $X \in \{real, restricted, 0, 1, \cdots, q, final\}$, denotes the advantage of $\mathcal{A}$ in Game$_X$. For the advantage of $\mathcal{A}$ in the game of (2^{-m^ϵ})-AL-IND-ID-CPA for the IBE scheme Π_{IBE}^{YCZY12}, it holds that

$$\mathbf{Adv}_{\Pi_{IBE}^{YCZY12},\mathcal{A}}^{(2^{-m^\epsilon})-AL-IND-ID-CPA}(\lambda) = \mathbf{Adv}_{real} \leq |\Pr[\mathbf{Adv}_{real}] - \Pr[\mathbf{Adv}_{restricted}]| +$$
$$|\Pr[\mathbf{Adv}_{restricted}] - \Pr[\mathbf{Adv}_0]| + \sum_{i=1}^{q} |\Pr[\mathbf{Adv}_{i-1}] - \Pr[\mathbf{Adv}_i]| + |\Pr[\mathbf{Adv}_q] - \Pr[\mathbf{Adv}_{final}]| + \Pr[\mathbf{Adv}_{final}].$$

One of the lemmas required to prove Theorem 4 is the following lemma.

Lemma 6. *If DSG assumption 2* [36] *holds, then for any* $i \in [1, q]$, $|\Pr[\mathbf{Adv}_{i-1}] - \Pr[\mathbf{Adv}_i]|$ *is negligible.*

5.5 Counterexamples against the Security Proof in [36]

Although we have not been able to find a cryptanalysis of their scheme, we have found some counterexamples of adversaries each one of which indicates that their proof of Theorem 4, specifically Lemma 6, is wrong. Below, we describe one of such counterexamples. The counterexample $\mathcal{A}_1$ behaves in Game$_{real}$ as follows.

1. In **Setup**, $\mathcal{A}_1$ receives pk. pk is parsed as $(N, \mathbb{G}, \mathbb{G}_T, \hat{e}, g_1, u, h, X_3, \{v_i, y_i\}_{i \in [1,m]})$.
2. In **Phase 1**, $\mathcal{A}_1$ queries ID^* to $\mathcal{UO}$, where $ID^* \xleftarrow{U} \mathbb{Z}_N$. After that, $\mathcal{A}_1$ queries ID^* and a function f_1 in Fig. 1 to $\mathcal{LO}$, then receives $(D_1, E_1) \in \mathbb{G}^2$. After that, $\mathcal{A}_1$ queries ID^* and a function f_2 in Fig. 1 to $\mathcal{LO}$, then receives $(D_1', E_1') \in \mathbb{G}^2$.
3. In **Challenge**, $\mathcal{A}_1$ queries two plaintexts $M_0, M_1 \xleftarrow{U} \mathbb{G}_T$ and ID^*, and receives a challenge ciphertext $C^* = (A^*, \{B_i^*, C_i^*\}_{i \in [1,m]})$.
4. In **Guess**, $\mathcal{A}_1$ calculates $K_1 := \hat{e}(C_1^*, E_1)$, $K_2 := \hat{e}(B_1^*, D_1)$, $K_1' := \hat{e}(C_1^*, E_1')$, and $K_2' := \hat{e}(B_1^*, D_1')$. $\mathcal{A}_1$ outputs 1 if $K_2/K_1 = K_2'/K_1'$, and outputs 0 otherwise.

Yuen et al. [36] insist that $|\Pr[W_1] - [W_2]|$ is proven to be negligible because it can be reduced to the DSG assumption 2 [36]. If so, any PPT adversary must not be able to distinguish Game$_1$ from Game$_2$ with a non-negligible advantage. However, $\mathcal{A}_1$ is able to do that. Specifically, in Game$_1$ or Game$_2$, $\mathcal{A}_1$ and C behave as follows.

Setup: C runs $(pk, mk) \leftarrow$ **Setup**(1^λ). pk and mk are parsed as pk $= (N = p_1 p_2 p_3, \mathbb{G}, \mathbb{G}_T, \hat{e}, g_1, u, h, X_3, \{v_i, y_i := \hat{e}(g_1, v_i)^{\alpha_i}\}_{i \in [1,m]})$ and mk $= (\{K_{1,i}, K_{2,i}, K_{3,i}\})$, where $K_{1,i} := g_1^{\alpha_i} \cdot h^{t_i} \cdot T_{1,i}$, $K_{2,i} := u^{t_i} \cdot T_{2,i}$, and $K_{3,i} := v_i^{t_i} \cdot T_{3,i}$, respectively. C sends pk to $\mathcal{A}_1$. Generators of $\mathbb{G}_{p_2}$-part of semi-functional secret key and challenge ciphertext are randomly chosen, and they are denoted by $\bar{g}_2$ and $\hat{g}_2$ respectively.

Phase 1: If $\mathcal{A}_1$ issues the following three queries sequentially, C acts as follows.

$\mathcal{UO}(ID^*)$: For every $i \in [1, m]$, after C sets $r_i, \kappa_i, z_i \xleftarrow{\mathrm{U}} \mathbb{Z}_N$ and $R_{1,i}, R_{2,i} \xleftarrow{\mathrm{U}} \mathbb{G}_{p_3}$, C sets D_i and E_i as $D_i := K_{1,i} \cdot K_{2,i}^{ID^*} \cdot (u^{ID^*} \cdot h)^{r_i} \cdot R_{1,i} \cdot \bar{g}_2^{\kappa_i} = g_1^{\alpha_i} \cdot (u^{ID^*} \cdot h)^{r_i + t_i} \cdot T_{1,i} \cdot T_{2,i}^{ID^*} \cdot R_{1,i} \cdot \bar{g}_2^{\kappa_i}$ and $E_i := K_{3,i} \cdot v_i^{r_i} \cdot R_{2,i} = v_i^{r_i + t_i} \cdot T_{3,i} \cdot R_{2,i} \cdot \bar{g}_2^{z_i}$, respectively. After that if the game is Game_2, C sets $\mathrm{sk}_{ID^*} := (\{D_i, E_i\}_{i \in [1,m]})$, and if the game is Game_1, C sets $\mathrm{sk}_{ID^*} := (\{D_i / \bar{g}_2^{\kappa_i}, E_i / \bar{g}_2^{z_i}\}_{i \in [1,m]})$. After that, C sets $\mathcal{L}_{ID^*} := \{(\mathrm{sk}_{ID^*}, ID^*, 1)\}$.

$\mathcal{LO}(f_1, ID^*)$: C calculates $f_1(\mathrm{pk}, \mathrm{mk}, \mathcal{L}_{ID^*}, ID^*)$, and returns it to $\mathcal{A}_1$. After that, in Game_2, the tuple $(\mathrm{sk}_{ID^*}, ID^*, 1) \in \mathcal{L}_{ID^*}$ is retrieved, and the secret-key $\mathrm{sk}_{ID^*} = (\{D_i, E_i\}_{i \in [1,m]})$ is changed to $\mathrm{sk}'_{ID^*} := (\{D_i / \bar{g}_2^{\kappa_i}, E_i / \bar{g}_2^{z_i}\}_{i \in [1,m]})$.

$\mathcal{LO}(f_2, ID^*)$: C calculates $f_2(\mathrm{pk}, \mathrm{mk}, \mathcal{L}_{ID^*}, ID^*)$, and returns it to $\mathcal{A}_1$.

Challenge(M_0, M_1, ID^*): C sets $b \xleftarrow{\mathrm{U}} \{0, 1\}$. For every $i \in [1, m]$, after setting $s_i, \delta_i, x_i \xleftarrow{\mathrm{U}} \mathbb{Z}_N$, C sets $A^* := M_b \cdot \prod_{i \in [1,m]} y_i^{s_i}$, $B_i^* := v_i^{s_i} \cdot \hat{g}_2^{\delta_i}$ and $C_i^* := (u^{ID^*} \cdot h)^{s_i} \cdot \hat{g}_2^{x_i}$. After that, C sends $C^* = (A^*, \{B_i^*, C_i^*\}_{i \in [1,m]})$ to $\mathcal{A}_1$.

Guess(b'): C receives b' from $\mathcal{A}_1$, where b' is set as 1 iff $K_2/K_1 = K_2'/K_1'$.

In Game_1, $K_2/K_1 = K_2'/K_1' = \hat{e}(v_1, g_1)^{s_1 \alpha_1}$ with probability 1. Thus, $\mathcal{A}_1$ outputs $b' = 1$ with probability 1. In Game_2, $K_2/K_1 = K_2'/K_1' = \hat{e}(v_1, g_1)^{s_1 \alpha_1}$ with probability $1/p_2$, and $K_2/K_1 = \hat{e}(v_1, g_1)^{s_1 \alpha_1} \cdot \hat{e}(\bar{g}_2, \hat{g}_2)^{\delta_1 \kappa_1 - x_1 z_1} \neq K_2'/K_1' = \hat{e}(v_1, g_1)^{s_1 \alpha_1}$ with probability $1 - 1/p_2$. Thus, $\mathcal{A}_1$ outputs $b' = 1$ (resp. $b' = 0$) with probability $1/p_2$ (resp. $1 - 1/p_2$). Hence, $\mathcal{A}_1$ distinguishes Game_1 from Game_2 with a non-negligible advantage $|\Pr[b' = 1 \mid \mathsf{Game}_1] - \Pr[b' = 1 \mid \mathsf{Game}_2]| = |1 - 1/p_2| = 1 - 1/p_2$.

In the above, we explained how one of our counterexamples, i.e., $\mathcal{A}_1$, effectively works. We have found some other counterexamples. One of them issues an ID ID^* twice to $\mathcal{UO}$, then issues f_1 and f_3 in Fig. 1 to $\mathcal{LO}$. The other one issues an ID ID^* to $\mathcal{UO}$, then issues f_1 and f_4 in Fig. 1 to $\mathcal{LO}$. They effectively work as $\mathcal{A}_1$ does.

$f_1(\mathrm{pk}, \mathrm{mk}, \mathcal{L}_{ID^*}, ID^*)$: $\mathcal{L}_{ID^*}$ is parsed as $\{(\mathrm{sk}_{ID^*}, ID^*, 1)\}$, sk_{ID^*} is parsed as $(\{D_i, E_i\}_{i \in [1,m]})$, **Return** (D_1, E_1)
$f_2(\mathrm{pk}, \mathrm{mk}, \mathcal{L}_{ID^*}, ID^*)$:   pk is parsed as $\mathrm{pk} := (N, \mathbb{G}, \mathbb{G}_T, \hat{e}, g_1, u, h, X_3, \{v_i, y_i\}_{i \in [1,m]})$, $\mathcal{L}_{ID^*}$ is parsed as $\{(\mathrm{sk}_{ID^*}, ID^*, 1)\}$ sk_{ID^*} is parsed as $(\{D_i, E_i\}_{i \in [1,m]})$, $r_1' \xleftarrow{\mathrm{U}} \mathbb{Z}_N$, $D_1' := D_1 \cdot (u^{ID} \cdot h)^{r_1'}$, $E_1' := E_1 \cdot v^{r_1'}$ **Return** (D_1', E_1')
$f_3(\mathrm{pk}, \mathrm{mk}, \mathcal{L}_{ID^*}, ID^*)$: $\mathcal{L}_{ID^*}$ is parsed as $\{(\mathrm{sk}_{ID^*}, ID^*, 1), (\mathrm{sk}'_{ID^*}, ID^*, 2)\}$, sk'_{ID^*} is parsed as $(\{D_i', E_i'\}_{i \in [1,m]})$ **Return** (D_1', E_1')
$f_4(\mathrm{pk}, \mathrm{mk}, \mathcal{L}_{ID^*}, ID^*)$: $\mathrm{sk}'_{ID^*} \leftarrow \mathsf{KeyGen}(\mathrm{pk}, \mathrm{mk}, ID^*)$, sk'_{ID^*} is parsed as $(\{D_i', E_i'\}_{i \in [1,m]})$, **Return** (D_1', E_1')

Fig. 1. Functions f_1, f_2, f_3 and f_4.

Deficiency of Security Proofs by Zhang et al. [38] *and Wang et al.* [35]. We have found some defective parts in the full security proof of the ABE schemes by Zhang et al. [38] and Wang et al. [35].

Zhang et al. do not use the GL theorem properly in the proof of Lemma 5.4, so the proof of the lemma is not correct. And, we have found some concrete PPT adversaries, or counterexamples, which indicate that the proof of Lemma 5.3 is wrong. The counterexamples behave similarly to ones against the proof of Yuen et al.

Wang et al. [35] do not use the GL theorem anywhere in their security proof, so their scheme lacks the guarantee for the leakage-resilience.

References

1. Agrawal, S., Boneh, D., Boyen, X.: Efficient lattice (H)IBE in the standard model. In: Gilbert, H. (ed.) EUROCRYPT 2010. LNCS, vol. 6110, pp. 553–572. Springer, Heidelberg (2010). https://doi.org/10.1007/978-3-642-13190-5_28
2. Alwen, J., Dodis, Y., Wichs, D.: Leakage-resilient public-key cryptography in the bounded-retrieval model. In: Halevi, S. (ed.) CRYPTO 2009. LNCS, vol. 5677, pp. 36–54. Springer, Heidelberg (2009). https://doi.org/10.1007/978-3-642-03356-8_3
3. Akavia, A., Goldwasser, S., Vaikuntanathan, V.: Simultaneous hardcore bits and cryptography against memory attacks. In: Reingold, O. (ed.) TCC 2009. LNCS, vol. 5444, pp. 474–495. Springer, Heidelberg (2009). https://doi.org/10.1007/978-3-642-00457-5_28
4. Boneh, D., Boyen, X.: Efficient selective-ID secure identity-based encryption without random oracles. In: Cachin, C., Camenisch, J.L. (eds.) EUROCRYPT 2004. LNCS, vol. 3027, pp. 223–238. Springer, Heidelberg (2004). https://doi.org/10.1007/978-3-540-24676-3_14
5. Boneh, D., Boyen, X.: Secure identity based encryption without random oracles. In: Franklin, M. (ed.) CRYPTO 2004. LNCS, vol. 3152, pp. 443–459. Springer, Heidelberg (2004). https://doi.org/10.1007/978-3-540-28628-8_27
6. Boneh, D., Boyen, X., Shacham, H.: Short group signatures. In: Franklin, M. (ed.) CRYPTO 2004. LNCS, vol. 3152, pp. 41–55. Springer, Heidelberg (2004). https://doi.org/10.1007/978-3-540-28628-8_3
7. Boneh, D., Franklin, M.: Identity-based encryption from the Weil pairing. In: Kilian, J. (ed.) CRYPTO 2001. LNCS, vol. 2139, pp. 213–229. Springer, Heidelberg (2001). https://doi.org/10.1007/3-540-44647-8_13
8. Brakerski, Z., Goldwasser, S.: Circular and leakage resilient public-key encryption under subgroup indistinguishability. In: Rabin, T. (ed.) CRYPTO 2010. LNCS, vol. 6223, pp. 1–20. Springer, Heidelberg (2010). https://doi.org/10.1007/978-3-642-14623-7_1
9. Boneh, D., et al.: Fully key-homomorphic encryption, arithmetic circuit ABE and compact garbled circuits. In: Nguyen, P.Q., Oswald, E. (eds.) EUROCRYPT 2014. LNCS, vol. 8441, pp. 533–556. Springer, Heidelberg (2014). https://doi.org/10.1007/978-3-642-55220-5_30
10. Brakerski, Z., Kalai, Y.T., Katz, J., Vaikuntanathan, V.: Overcoming the hole in the bucket: public-key cryptography resilient to continual memory leakage. In: FOCS 2010, pp. 501–510 (2010)
11. Bellare, M., O'Neill, A., Stepanovs, I.: Forward-security under continual leakage. Cryptology ePrint Archive: Report 2017/476 (2017)

12. Boyle, E., Segev, G., Wichs, D.: Fully leakage-resilient signatures. In: Paterson, K.G. (ed.) EUROCRYPT 2011. LNCS, vol. 6632, pp. 89–108. Springer, Heidelberg (2011). https://doi.org/10.1007/978-3-642-20465-4_7

13. Cocks, C.: An identity based encryption scheme based on quadratic residues. In: Honary, B. (ed.) Cryptography and Coding 2001. LNCS, vol. 2260, pp. 360–363. Springer, Heidelberg (2001). https://doi.org/10.1007/3-540-45325-3_32

14. Chow, S.S.M., Dodis, Y., Rouselakis, Y., Waters, B.: Practical leakage-resilient identity-based encryption from simple assumptions. In: ACMCCS 2010, pp. 152–161 (2010)

15. Canetti, R., Halevi, S., Katz, J.: A forward-secure public-key encryption scheme. In: Biham, E. (ed.) EUROCRYPT 2003. LNCS, vol. 2656, pp. 255–271. Springer, Heidelberg (2003). https://doi.org/10.1007/3-540-39200-9_16

16. Dodis, Y., Goldwasser, S., Tauman Kalai, Y., Peikert, C., Vaikuntanathan, V.: Public-key encryption schemes with auxiliary inputs. In: Micciancio, D. (ed.) TCC 2010. LNCS, vol. 5978, pp. 361–381. Springer, Heidelberg (2010). https://doi.org/10.1007/978-3-642-11799-2_22

17. Dodis, Y., Haralambiev, K., López-Alt, A., Wichs, D.: Cryptography against continuous memory attacks. In: FOCS 2010, pp. 511–520 (2010)

18. Dodis, Y., Haralambiev, K., López-Alt, A., Wichs, D.: Efficient public-key cryptography in the presence of key leakage. In: Abe, M. (ed.) ASIACRYPT 2010. LNCS, vol. 6477, pp. 613–631. Springer, Heidelberg (2010). https://doi.org/10.1007/978-3-642-17373-8_35

19. Dodis, Y., Haralambiev, K., López-Alt, A., Wichs, D.: Efficient public-key cryptography in the presence of key leakage. Cryptology ePrint Archive: Report 2010/154 (2010)

20. Dodis, Y., Kalai, Y.T., Lovett, S.: On cryptography with auxiliary input. In: STOC 2009, pp. 621–630 (2009)

21. Faust, S., Hazay, C., Nielsen, J.B., Nordholt, P.S., Zottarel, A.: Signature schemes secure against hard-to-invert leakage. In: Wang, X., Sako, K. (eds.) ASIACRYPT 2012. LNCS, vol. 7658, pp. 98–115. Springer, Heidelberg (2012). https://doi.org/10.1007/978-3-642-34961-4_8

22. Gentry, C., Peikert, C., Vaikuntanathan, V.: Trapdoors for hard lattices and new cryptographic constructions. In: STOC 2008, pp. 197–206 (2008)

23. Halderman, J.A., et al.: Lest we remember: cold boot attacks on encryption keys. In: USENIX Security Symposium, pp. 45–60 (2008)

24. Kurosawa, K., Trieu Phong, L.: Leakage resilient IBE and IPE under the DLIN assumption. In: Jacobson, M., Locasto, M., Mohassel, P., Safavi-Naini, R. (eds.) ACNS 2013. LNCS, vol. 7954, pp. 487–501. Springer, Heidelberg (2013). https://doi.org/10.1007/978-3-642-38980-1_31

25. Lewko, A., Lewko, M., Waters, B.: How to leak on key updates. Cryptology ePrint Archive: Report 2010/562 (2010)

26. Lewko, A., Lewko, M., Waters, B.: How to leak on key updates. In: STOC 2011, pp. 725–734 (2011)

27. Lewko, A., Rouselakis, Y., Waters, B.: Achieving leakage resilience through dual system encryption. In: Ishai, Y. (ed.) TCC 2011. LNCS, vol. 6597, pp. 70–88. Springer, Heidelberg (2011). https://doi.org/10.1007/978-3-642-19571-6_6

28. Lewko, A., Okamoto, T., Sahai, A., Takashima, K., Waters, B.: Fully secure functional encryption: attribute-based encryption and (hierarchical) inner product encryption. In: Gilbert, H. (ed.) EUROCRYPT 2010. LNCS, vol. 6110, pp. 62–91. Springer, Heidelberg (2010). https://doi.org/10.1007/978-3-642-13190-5_4

29. Lewko, A., Waters, B.: New techniques for dual system encryption and fully secure HIBE with short ciphertexts. In: Micciancio, D. (ed.) TCC 2010. LNCS, vol. 5978, pp. 455–479. Springer, Heidelberg (2010). https://doi.org/10.1007/978-3-642-11799-2_27

30. Naor, M., Segev, G.: Public-key cryptosystems resilient to key leakage. In: Halevi, S. (ed.) CRYPTO 2009. LNCS, vol. 5677, pp. 18–35. Springer, Heidelberg (2009). https://doi.org/10.1007/978-3-642-03356-8_2

31. Okamoto, T., Takashima, K.: Fully secure functional encryption with general relations from the decisional linear assumption. In: Rabin, T. (ed.) CRYPTO 2010. LNCS, vol. 6223, pp. 191–208. Springer, Heidelberg (2010). https://doi.org/10.1007/978-3-642-14623-7_11

32. Shamir, A.: Identity-based cryptosystems and signature schemes. In: Blakley, G.R., Chaum, D. (eds.) CRYPTO 1984. LNCS, vol. 196, pp. 47–53. Springer, Heidelberg (1985). https://doi.org/10.1007/3-540-39568-7_5

33. Waters, B.: Efficient identity-based encryption without random oracles. In: Cramer, R. (ed.) EUROCRYPT 2005. LNCS, vol. 3494, pp. 114–127. Springer, Heidelberg (2005). https://doi.org/10.1007/11426639_7

34. Waters, B.: Dual system encryption: realizing fully secure IBE and HIBE under simple assumptions. In: Halevi, S. (ed.) CRYPTO 2009. LNCS, vol. 5677, pp. 619–636. Springer, Heidelberg (2009). https://doi.org/10.1007/978-3-642-03356-8_36

35. Wang, Z., Yiu, S.M.: Attribute-based encryption resilient to auxiliary input. In: Au, M.-H., Miyaji, A. (eds.) ProvSec 2015. LNCS, vol. 9451, pp. 371–390. Springer, Cham (2015). https://doi.org/10.1007/978-3-319-26059-4_21

36. Yuen, T.H., Chow, S.S.M., Zhang, Y., Yiu, S.M.: Identity-based encryption resilient to continual auxiliary leakage. In: Pointcheval, D., Johansson, T. (eds.) EUROCRYPT 2012. LNCS, vol. 7237, pp. 117–134. Springer, Heidelberg (2012). https://doi.org/10.1007/978-3-642-29011-4_9

37. Zhang, M.: New model and construction of ABE: achieving key resilient-leakage and attribute direct-revocation. In: Susilo, W., Mu, Y. (eds.) ACISP 2014. LNCS, vol. 8544, pp. 192–208. Springer, Cham (2014). https://doi.org/10.1007/978-3-319-08344-5_13

38. Zhang, M., Wang, C., Takagi, T., Mu, Y.: Functional encryption resilient to hard-to-invert leakage. Comput. J. (2013). https://doi.org/10.1093/comjnl/bxt105

Adaptive-Secure VRFs with Shorter Keys from Static Assumptions

Răzvan Roşie[1,2](✉)

[1] ENS, CNRS, PSL Research University, 75005 Paris, France
razvan.rosie@ens.fr
[2] Inria, Paris, France

Abstract. Verifiable random functions are pseudorandom functions producing publicly verifiable proofs for their outputs, allowing for efficient checks of the correctness of their computation. In this work, we introduce a new computational hypothesis, the n-Eigen-Value assumption, which can be seen as a particularization of the $\mathcal{U}_{l,k}$-MDDH assumption for the case $l = k + 1$, and prove its equivalence with the n-Rank problem. Based on the newly introduced computational hypothesis, we build the core of a verifiable random function having an exponentially large input space and reaching adaptive security under a static assumption. The final construction achieves shorter public and secret keys compared to the existing schemes reaching the same properties.

Keywords: VRF · Matrix-DDH · Eigenvalue assumption

1 Introduction

The notion of a pseudorandom function (PRF), introduced in the seminal work of Goldreich, Goldwasser and Micali [7], is a foundational building block in theoretical cryptography. A PRF is a *keyed* functionality guaranteeing the randomness of its output under various assumptions. PRFs found applications in the construction of both symmetric and public-key primitives. Since the inception of their investigation, various number-theoretical constructions targeted efficiency [12,16] or enhancing the security guarantees [2].

A stronger, related and theoretically relevant concept, the notion of verifiable random function (VRF), has been put forward by Micali, Rabin and Vadhan [15] in 1999. A verifiable random function behaves similarly to its simpler pseudorandom counterpart, but in addition to its output value y, it also creates a publicly verifiable proof π allowing for efficient verification of the correctness of the computation. Among their proposed applications, Micali and Rivest mention simple, non-interactive lottery systems [13], while Micali and Reyzin found applications in reducing the number of rounds to 3 in zero-knowledge proofs [14]. More recently, VRFs found more *practical applications* in preventing zone enumeration attacks against the DNS Security Extensions (DNSSEC). The work

© Springer Nature Switzerland AG 2018
J. Camenisch and P. Papadimitratos (Eds.): CANS 2018, LNCS 11124, pp. 440–459, 2018.
https://doi.org/10.1007/978-3-030-00434-7_22

of Goldberg et al. [8] puts forward a new solution (NSEC5) where the prevention step follows from the *privacy* property of the NSEC5 construction, which is achieved through the means of a verifiable random function.

The first VRF construction was introduced in [15] and was based on the RSA $s(k)$-hardness assumption, obtaining a scheme with unrestricted input lengths. Since then, various works targeted constructions that accomplish: (1) adaptive security [11], (2) security under standard assumptions [5], or (3) exponentially large input spaces [11]. However, the realization of VRFs that simultaneously achieve these three requirements, but without having to rely on a q-type assumption has been proven a difficult task until the recent work of Hofheinz and Jager [9]. The impeding constraint in achieving adaptive security resides in the lack of techniques for removing the q-type assumptions from the security proofs. As described by [3], q-type assumptions get stronger with the increase of the parameter q. Recently, an interesting, lattice-based approach has been recently proposed in [17]: although the computational hypothesis used is still not static, we point out the reduced sizes of proofs and secret keys obtained in the constructions introduced in [17]. This work targets VRFs under static assumptions using the framework introduced in [9].

The VRF by Hofheinz and Jager. The core of the construction by Hofheinz and Jager is inspired by the scheme introduced by Lysyanskaya in [12], where the output corresponding to $x \in \{0,1\}^k$ is defined as $y \leftarrow g^{\prod_{i=1}^{k} a_{i,x_i}}$. The novel technique presented in [9] consists in replacing the set of (uniform) unidimensional exponents $a_{i,0/1}$ with matrix exponents. The crux point is to benefit from the algebraic properties enabled by the chain of matrix multiplications (linear maps in this case) in order to remove the need for q-type assumptions. The full realization of the VRF in [9] involves an extra *generic* step of post-processing the vectorial output of the matrix construction via a final multiplication with a randomness extractor. The size of matrices and the issued proofs (proportional to the binary length of the input) constitutes the main downside of the construction introduced by Hofheinz and Jager. Therefore, an interesting open problem resides in obtaining constructions with *shorter parameters* or *proofs*.

Our Contributions. A first contribution is the introduction of a novel computational assumption (the n-Eigen-Value assumption), that we show equivalent to the n-Rank assumption (Sect. 3). Informally, it states that given an encoding of a uniform $n \times n$ matrix having (at least) one eigenvalue in $\mathbb{Z}_p$, a computationally bounded adversary cannot distinguish between an encoding of its eigenvalue ($[\lambda] := g^\lambda$) and an encoding of a uniformly sampled element. Finally, we provide a VRF based on the framework introduced in [9] and prove its adaptive security under the aforementioned assumption. In essence, we adopt the same methodology of obtaining the output through matrix multiplications. Comparing it with the previous work, we are able to reduce the size of the keys, by eliminating n elements from each pair of $n \times n$ matrix needed. For efficient implementation over bilinear maps, where the dimension of the matrices is 3×3, the result translates in reducing the size of the *secret* and *verification* keys by a factor of one sixth.

Our Technique. We give a brief overview of the proof technique we use and explain the difficulty encountered while attempting to reduce the dimensions of the matrix-based keys even with a constant factor. For brevity, consider a simplified version of our construction having the output generated as: $g^{\mathbf{v}^{\top}} \leftarrow g^{\mathbf{u}^{\top} \prod_{i=1}^{k}(\mathbf{M}_i - \mathbf{P}_{i,x_i})}$. The crucial property we want to achieve is a linear mapping between $\mathbf{v}^{(j-1)} \leftarrow \mathbf{u}^{\top} \cdot \prod_{i=1}^{j-1}(\mathbf{M}_i - \mathbf{P}_{i,x_i})$ and $\mathbf{v}^{(j)} \leftarrow \mathbf{u}^{\top} \cdot \prod_{i=1}^{j}(\mathbf{M}_i - \mathbf{P}_{i,x_i})$ through the means of $\mathbf{M}_j - \mathbf{P}_{j,x_j}$. If $\mathbf{v}^{(j-1)}$ belongs to a pre-established subspace $\mathcal{S}_{j-1}$, we intend to map it to $\mathcal{S}_j$ by multiplication with $\mathbf{M}_j - \mathbf{P}_{j,x_j}$; otherwise ($\mathbf{v}^{(j-1)} \notin \mathcal{S}_{j-1}$), the matrix multiplication should guarantee that $\mathbf{v}^{(j)} \notin \mathcal{S}_j$. To ensure this, we consider an **orthogonal component n** sucht that $\mathbf{n} \perp \mathcal{S}_{j-1}$ and attempt to "hide" it in $\mathbf{P}_{j,0}$ or $\mathbf{P}_{j,1}$ (in fact in their difference depending on the challenge $X^{(0)}$). Thus if $\mathbf{v}^{(j-1)} \in \mathcal{S}_{j-1}$, then the inner-product $\mathbf{n}^{\top} \cdot \mathbf{v}^{(j-1)} = 0$ (and $\neq 0$ for $\mathbf{v}^{(j-1)} \notin \mathcal{S}_{j-1}$).

The second idea that we will apply is to consider a representation of $\mathbf{n}$ where its last entry is set to 1; put differently $\mathbf{n}^{\top} = (\alpha_1, \ldots, \alpha_{n-1}, 1)$. Setting the last component to 1 enables us to *save a row* per index in the matrix construction we give. In some sense, the main difficulty in going beyond one row elimination consists in the number of constant components we can obtain in $\mathbf{n}$. The basic construction – a programmable vector hash function or PVHF – is presented in Sect. 4, while an adaptive PVHF is presented in Sect. 5. Finally, we simply get the VRF on top of a PVHF through the generic transform introduced in [9] (stated in Theorem 3, Appendix A).

2 Preliminaries

We denote by $s \xleftarrow{\$} S$ the fact that s is picked uniformly at random from a finite set S. Variables in bold capital letters stand for matrices (e.g. $\mathbf{M}$) while bold lowercase letters represent vectors (e.g. $\mathbf{u}$). A subscript i on a vector $\mathbf{u}$ (e.g. $\mathbf{u}_i$) stands for the i-th component of the vector. An analogue convention is used for matrices. By $[a] := g^a$ we denote the "encoding of an element" w.r.t. a group generator $g \in \mathbb{G}$, while through $[\mathbf{M}]$ and $[\mathbf{u}]$, we denote the encodings of a matrix, respectively vector. $\overline{\mathbf{W}}$ denotes the matrix formed by the top $n - 1$ rows of a matrix $\mathbf{W}$ of size $n \times n$. When working with a family of vectors $\mathbf{v}$, we use the upper script to distinguish between them: $\mathbf{v}^{(0)}, \mathbf{v}^{(1)}, \ldots$. We abuse notation and extend it to bilinear maps by writing $e([\mathbf{A}], [\mathbf{B}]) = e(g, g)^{\mathbf{A} \cdot \mathbf{B}} = [\mathbf{A} \cdot \mathbf{B}]$ to denote the matrix obtained by multiplying the exponents and obtaining the pairing of entries. By $C(\mathbf{A})$, we denote the columnspace of a matrix $\mathbf{A}$, and by $C(\mathbf{A}^{\top})$, we denote its rowspace. We denote the security parameter by $\lambda \in \mathbb{N}^*$ and we assume it is given to all algorithms in the unary representation 1^{λ}. We regard an algorithm as being randomized (unless stated) and being modeled by a Turing machine. PPT stands for "probabilistic polynomial-time." Given a randomized algorithm $\mathcal{A}$ we denote the action of running $\mathcal{A}$ on input(s) $(1^{\lambda}, x_1, \ldots)$ with uniform random coins r and assigning the output(s) to $(y_1, \ldots)$ by $(y_1, \ldots) \xleftarrow{\$} \mathcal{A}(1^{\lambda}, x_1, \ldots; r)$. We denote the set of all negligible functions by NEGL. With $\bar{x} \prec x$, we denote a bitstring prefix.

2.1   Definitions

We recall the standard definition of a VRF and the novel notion of verifiable vector hash function from [9].

Definition 1 (Verifiable Random Function). *A verifiable random function consists of a tuple of three PPT algorithms* VRF $:=$ (VRF.Gen, VRF.Eval, VRF.Vfy), *defined as:*

- VRF.Gen *takes as input the security parameter* 1^λ *(in unary), and outputs a secret key sk together with a verification key vk;*
- VRF.Eval *takes as inputs a secret key sk and a string* $X \in \{0,1\}^k$ *and outputs a function value* $Y \in \mathcal{Y}$ *(where* $\mathcal{Y}$ *is a finite set) and a proof* π;
- VRF.Vfy *takes as inputs a verification key vk, a string* $X \in \{0,1\}^k$, *a value* $Y \in \mathcal{Y}$, *and a proof* π, *and outputs a bit.*

Moreover, we require the following three properties to hold:

- Correctness: $\Pr\left[\text{VRF.Vfy}(vk, Y, X, \pi) = 1 \;\middle|\; \begin{matrix} (sk, vk) \xleftarrow{\$} \text{VRF.Gen}(1^\lambda) \\ (Y, \pi) \xleftarrow{\$} \text{VRF.Eval}(sk, X) \end{matrix} \right] = 1$
- Unique Provability: *for any* (vk, sk) *(even maliciously generated) and any* $X \in \{0,1\}^k$, *there does not exist any* (Y_0, π_0, Y_1, π_1) *such that* $Y_0 \neq Y_1$ *and* VRF.Vfy$(vk, X, Y_0, \pi_0) = $ VRF.Vfy$(vk, X, Y_1, \pi_1) = 1$.
- Pseudorandomness: *for any PPT adversary* $\mathcal{A} = (\mathcal{A}_0, \mathcal{A}_1)$, *its advantage:*

$$\mathbf{Adv}^{\text{vrf}}_{\text{VRF}}(\mathcal{A}, \lambda) := 2 \cdot \Pr\left[\text{ExpVRF}^{\mathcal{A}}_{\text{VRF}}(\lambda) = 1 \right] - 1 \in \text{NEGL}$$

is negligible, where ExpVRF$^{\mathcal{A}}_{\text{VRF}}$ *is defined in Fig. 1, and where the adversary never repeats a query twice (in particular, it cannot query the challenge* X^* *to the oracle* $\mathcal{O}$). *We define the security experiments for both* selective *and* adaptive *security — selective security being similar except the challenge* X^* *is chosen by the adversary before seeing a verification key.*

Vector hash functions (VHFs) are extensions of programmable hash functions [10], with outputs represented vectorially. Programmable hash functions are number theoretic hashes that work in two indistinguishable modes: using standard keys, the hash behaves "normally", but under trapdoor keys, the output follows a particular algebraic specification.

Definition 2 (Verifiable Vector Hash Function). *A verifiable vector hash function consists in a tuple of three algorithms* VHF = (VHF.Gen, VHF.Eval, VHF.Vfy) *defined as:*

- VHF.Gen *takes as input a certified bilinear group* Π *for a security parameter* 1^λ, *and outputs an evaluation key and a verification key* (ek, vk);
- VHF.Eval *takes as input an evaluation key ek and an input* X *and outputs a vector of group encodings* $[\mathbf{v}] \in \mathbb{G}^n$ *together with a proof of correctness* $\pi \in \{0,1\}^*$;

$$
\begin{array}{l|l}
\hline
\mathsf{ExpVRF}_{\mathsf{VRF}}^{\mathcal{A}}(1^\lambda): & \mathcal{O}(X): \\
\boxed{(X^*, st) \xleftarrow{\$} \mathcal{A}_0(1^\lambda)} & \overline{(Y, \pi)} \leftarrow \mathsf{VRF.Eval}(sk, X) \\
& \text{Return } (Y, \pi) \\
(sk, vk) \xleftarrow{\$} \mathsf{VRF.Gen}(1^\lambda) & \\
b \xleftarrow{\$} \{0,1\} & \mathsf{Chal}(X^*, b): \\
\boxed{\boxed{(X^*, st) \xleftarrow{\$} \mathcal{A}_0^{\mathcal{O}(\cdot)}(vk)}} & \text{If } b = 0 \text{ then} \\
Y^* \leftarrow \mathsf{Chal}(X^*, b) & (Y^*, \pi) \leftarrow \mathsf{VRF.Eval}(sk, X^*) \\
b' \xleftarrow{\$} \mathcal{A}_1^{\mathcal{O}(\cdot)}(st, Y^*) & \text{Else} \\
\text{Return } b = b' & Y^* \xleftarrow{\$} \mathcal{Y} \\
& \text{Return } Y^* \\
\hline
\end{array}
$$

$$
\begin{array}{l|l}
\hline
\boxed{\mathsf{Sel}}\,\mathsf{TrapInd}_{\mathsf{VHF}}^{\mathcal{A}}(\lambda): & \mathcal{O}_0(X): \\
b \xleftarrow{\$} \{0,1\} & ([\mathbf{v}], \pi) \xleftarrow{\$} \mathsf{VHF.Eval}(ek_0, X) \\
\Pi \xleftarrow{\$} \mathsf{GrpGen}(1^\lambda) & \text{Return } ([\mathbf{v}], \pi) \\
\boxed{(X^{(0)}, st) \xleftarrow{\$} \mathcal{A}_0(1^\lambda)} & \\
& \mathcal{O}_1(X): \\
(vk_0, ek_0) \xleftarrow{\$} \mathsf{VHF.Gen}(\Pi) & \overline{(\boldsymbol{\beta}, \pi)} \leftarrow \mathsf{VHF.TrapEval}(ek_1, X) \\
\mathbf{B} \xleftarrow{\$} \mathsf{GL}_n(\mathbb{Z}_p) & [\mathbf{v}] := [\mathbf{B}] \cdot \boldsymbol{\beta} \\
(vk_1, ek_1) \xleftarrow{\$} \mathsf{VHF.TrapGen}(\Pi, [\mathbf{B}], \boxed{X^{(0)}}) & \text{Return } ([\mathbf{v}], \pi) \\
& \\
& \mathcal{O}_{\mathsf{check}}(X): \\
b' \xleftarrow{\$} \mathcal{A}^{\mathcal{O}_b(\cdot),\, \boxed{\boxed{\mathcal{O}_{\mathsf{check}}(\cdot)}}}(st, vk_b) & \overline{(\boldsymbol{\beta}, \pi)} \leftarrow \mathsf{VHF.TrapEval}(ek_1, X) \\
\text{Return } b = b' & (\beta_1, \ldots, \beta_n) := \boldsymbol{\beta} \\
& \text{If } \beta_n \neq 0 \text{ then Return } 1 \\
& \text{Else Return } 0 \\
\hline
\end{array}
$$

Fig. 1. The experiment (game) defining the pseudorandomness of a VRF (top). The experiment and oracles defining indistinguishability for selective/adaptive programmable VHFs (down). A $\boxed{\text{boxed value}}$ is included in the $\boxed{\text{selective}}$ game, $\boxed{\boxed{\text{double-boxed}}}$ in the adaptive game.

- VHF.Vfy *takes as input a verification key* vk, *an input* X, *a vector* $[\mathbf{v}]$, *and a proof* π, *and outputs a bit* b,

and such that they satisfy the following two properties, termed correctness *and* unique provability:

- *For* **correctness**, *we require that:*

$$
\Pr\left[\mathsf{VHF.Vfy}(vk, [\mathbf{v}], X, \pi) = 1; \left| \begin{array}{l} \Pi \xleftarrow{\$} \mathsf{GrpGen}(1^\lambda) \wedge \\ (vk, ek) \leftarrow \mathsf{VHF.Gen}(\Pi) \wedge \\ ([\mathbf{v}], \pi) \leftarrow \mathsf{VHF.Eval}(ek, X) \end{array} \right. \right] = 1 \quad (1)
$$

- **Unique provability** *requires that, for any verification key* vk *and any input* X, *there does not exist any tuple* $([\mathbf{v}]_1, \pi_{\mathbf{v}}, [\mathbf{w}], \pi_{\mathbf{w}})$ *with* $[\mathbf{v}] \neq [\mathbf{w}]$ *such that:*

$$
\mathsf{VHF.Vfy}(vk, X, [\mathbf{v}], \pi_{\mathbf{v}}) = \mathsf{VHF.Vfy}(vk, X, [\mathbf{w}], \pi_{\mathbf{w}}) = 1 . \quad (2)
$$

We require that a VHF reaches selective/adaptive programmability with respect to trapdoor procedures (to be used in security proofs) as introduced in [9]. We also denote them as PVHFs (programmable VHFs). The adaptive programmability is similar and is defined in Definition 4.

Definition 3 (Selective Programmability). *A verifiable vector hash function* VHF = (VHF.Gen, VHF.Eval, VHF.Vfy) *is selectively programmable if there exist two PPT algorithms* (VHF.TrapGen, VHF.TrapEval):

- VHF.TrapGen *takes as input* $\Pi \xleftarrow{\$} \mathsf{GrpGen}(1^\lambda)$, *a matrix* $[\mathbf{B}] \in \mathbb{G}^{n \times n}$, *and* $X^{(0)} \in \{0,1\}^k$ *and outputs a verification key* vk *and a trapdoor evaluation key* td;
- VHF.TrapEval *takes as input a trapdoor evaluation key and a string* $X \in \{0,1\}^k$, *and outputs a vector* $\boldsymbol{\beta} \in \mathbb{Z}_p^n$ *and a proof* $\pi \in \{0,1\}^*$,

such that the following three properties hold:

- Correctness:

$$\Pr\left[\begin{array}{c} \text{VHF.Vfy}(vk, [\mathbf{v}], \\ X, \pi) = 1 \end{array} \middle| \begin{array}{l} \Pi \xleftarrow{\$} \mathsf{GrpGen}(1^\lambda) \wedge \\ (vk, td) \xleftarrow{\$} \text{VHF.TrapGen}(\Pi, [\mathbf{B}], X^{(0)}) \\ \wedge (\boldsymbol{\beta}, \pi) \xleftarrow{\$} \text{VHF.TrapEval}(td, X) \wedge \\ [\mathbf{v}] := [\mathbf{B}] \cdot \boldsymbol{\beta} \end{array} \right] = 1$$

- Well-Distributed Outputs: *for* $q = q(\lambda)$ *a polynomial, there exists a polynomial* poly *such that for any* $X^{(0)}, X^{(1)}, \ldots, X^{(q)} \in (\{0,1\}^k)^{q+1}$ *with* $X^{(i)} \neq X^{(0)}$ *for all* $i \in \{1, \ldots, q\}$, *we have:*

$$\Pr\left[\begin{array}{l} \beta_n^{(0)} \neq 0 \wedge \\ \beta_n^{(i)} = 0; \\ \forall i = 1, \ldots, q \end{array} \middle| \begin{array}{l} \Pi \xleftarrow{\$} \mathsf{GrpGen}(1^\lambda) \wedge \mathbf{B} \xleftarrow{\$} \mathrm{GL}_n(\mathbb{Z}_p) \wedge \\ (vk, td) \xleftarrow{\$} \text{VHF.TrapGen}(\Pi, [\mathbf{B}], X^{(0)}) \\ \wedge (\boldsymbol{\beta}^{(i)}, \pi) \xleftarrow{\$} \text{VHF.TrapEval}(td, X^{(i)}) \end{array} \right] \geq \frac{1}{poly(k)} \quad (3)$$

where $\beta_n^{(i)}$ *denotes the* n-*th component of* $\boldsymbol{\beta}^{(i)}$.

- Indistinguishability: *for any PPT adversary* $\mathcal{A} = (\mathcal{A}_0, \mathcal{A}_1)$, *its advantage:*

$$\mathbf{Adv}_{\text{VHF}}^{\text{sel-ind-vhf}}(\mathcal{A}, \lambda) := 2 \cdot \Pr\left[\text{SelTrapInd}_{\text{VHF}}^{\mathcal{A}}(\lambda) = 1 \right] - 1$$

is negligible, where experiment SelTrapInd$_{\text{VHF}}$ *is defined in Fig. 1. Intuitively, we require that verification keys generated using* VHF.Gen *are indistinguishable from those generated using* VHF.TrapGen.

Definition 4 (Adaptive Programmability). *A verifiable vector hash function* VHF = (VHF.Gen, VHF.Eval, VHF.Vfy) *is adaptively programmable, if algorithms* (VHF.TrapGen, VHF.TrapEval), *defined as above except that* VHF.TrapGen *takes as input only* Π *and* $[\mathbf{B}]$ *(and no longer an input* $X^{(0)}$*), exist, and satisfy the above correctness, well-distribution, and such that the advantage of any PPT adversary* $\mathcal{A}$, *defined as:*

$$\mathbf{Adv}_{\text{VHF}}^{\text{ind-vhf}}(\mathcal{A}, \lambda) := 2 \cdot \Pr\left[\text{TrapInd}_{\text{VHF}}^{\mathcal{A}}(\lambda) = 1 \right] - 1 \,,$$

is negligible, where experiment SelTrapInd$_{\text{VHF}}$ *is defined in Fig. 1.*

3   The Eigenvalue Assumption

In this section, we propose a new assumption, termed the n-Eigen-Value assumption, which we prove to be equivalent to the n-Rank assumption, whose definition is also recalled below. The purpose of this assumption is to offer more flexibility than the n-Rank assumption; we then use the n-Eigen-Value to prove the security of our construction (which then holds under the standard n-Rank assumption). Before giving the formal definition of our assumption, let us recall the definition of the n-Rank assumption in a group $\mathbb{G}$:

Definition 5 (*n-Rank Assumption*). *Let $\mathbf{M}_i$ denote a $n \times n$ matrix ($n \geq 2$) of rank i sampled uniformly at random from $\left\{ \mathbf{W} \mid \mathbf{W} \in \mathbb{Z}_p^{n \times n} \wedge \mathrm{RANK}(\mathbf{W}) = i \right\}$. Let $\mathcal{A}$ be any PPT adversary. Then the advantage of $\mathcal{A}$ against the n-Rank problem in a group $\mathbb{G}$, defined as:*

$$\mathbf{Adv}_{\mathbb{G}}^{n\text{-rank}}(\mathcal{A}, \lambda) := \Pr\left[\mathcal{A}\big([\mathbf{M}_n], 1^\lambda \big) = 1 \right] - \Pr\left[\mathcal{A}\big([\mathbf{M}_{n-1}], 1^\lambda \big) = 1 \right] ,$$

is negligible.

Remark 1 (Computational vs Decisional n-Rank). Note that Definition 5 implicitly makes the n-Rank assumption "computational": distinguishing between the two ranks implicitly gives the rank of the matrix.

The natural n-Eigen-Value counterpart of the n-Rank assumption, roughly saying that $\big([\mathbf{M}], [\lambda] \big) \approx_c \big([\mathbf{M}], [\$] \big)$ — the encoding of an eigenvalue for a randomly sampled matrix $\mathbf{M}$ is indistinguishable from the encoding of a random element, needs a more careful definitional setting. This happens because not every $\mathbf{M}$ defined over $\mathbb{Z}_p^{n \times n}$ has its eigenvalues belonging to $\mathbb{Z}_p$. Concretely, the (monic) characteristic polynomial of $\mathbf{M}$ is irreducible with probability:

$$\mu = \frac{1}{n} + \mathbf{O}\big(p^{-n/2} \cdot \sqrt{n}\big) . \tag{4}$$

For large p, μ approaches $1/n$. Thus, the probability that a random matrix $\mathbf{M}$ has eigenvalues in $\mathbb{Z}_p$ tends to $1 - 1/n$. Still, practical applications would benefit for small values of n, and the aforementioned probability in Eq. (4) is significant, so we employ a different strategy.

Based on the previous observation, we now define the n-Eigen-Value assumption as follows: let $\mathbf{A}, \mathbf{B}$ be two matrices of ranks $n - 1$ respectively n, and $\mathbf{L}$ be randomly sampled from $\mathbb{Z}_p^{n \times n}$ (which has rank n with overwhelming probability). We set $\mathbf{M}_{n-1} \leftarrow \mathbf{L} \cdot \mathbf{A} + \lambda \cdot \mathbf{I}_n$ and $\mathbf{M}_n \leftarrow \mathbf{B}$. We now claim that the two distributions — $\big([\mathbf{M}_{n-1}], [\lambda] \big)$ and $\big([\mathbf{M}_n], [\$] \big)$ — are indeed computationally indistinguishable.

Definition 6 (*n-Eigen-Value*). *Let $\mathbf{A} \xleftarrow{\$} \left\{ \mathbf{W} \mid \mathbf{W} \in \mathbb{Z}_p^{n \times n} \wedge rank(\mathbf{W}) = n - 1 \right\}$, $\mathbf{B} \xleftarrow{\$} \mathbb{Z}_p^{n \times n}$ and $\mathbf{L} \xleftarrow{\$} \mathrm{GL}_n(\mathbb{Z}_p)$. The advantage of any PPT adversary $\mathcal{A}$ against the n-Eigen-Value problem in a group $\mathbb{G}$, defined as:*

$$\mathbf{Adv}_{\mathbb{G}}^{n\text{-ev}}(\mathcal{A}, \lambda) := \Pr\left[\mathcal{A}\big([\mathbf{M}], [\lambda], 1^\lambda \big) = 1 \right] - \Pr\left[\mathcal{A}\big([\mathbf{N}], [r], 1^\lambda \big) = 1 \right] ,$$

is negligible, where $\mathbf{M} \leftarrow \mathbf{L} \cdot \mathbf{A} + \lambda \cdot \mathbf{I}_n$, $\mathbf{N} \leftarrow \mathbf{B}$ and $r \xleftarrow{\$} \mathbb{Z}_p$.

Theorem 1. *The n-Rank assumption holds in $\mathbb{G}$ if and only if the n-Eigen-Value assumption holds in $\mathbb{G}$.*

Proof. We prove this statement by proving both implications separately.

n-Rank $\Rightarrow$ n-Eigen-Value Let $\mathcal{A}$ be an adversary against the n-Eigen-Value problem in $\mathbb{G}$. We then build an adversary $\mathcal{B}$ against the n-Rank problem in $\mathbb{G}$ as follows: $\mathcal{B}$ is given a matrix of group elements $[\mathbf{M}]$ with $\mathbf{M}$ being of rank $n-1$ or n. It then picks uniformly at random an invertible matrix $\mathbf{L} \xleftarrow{\$} \mathrm{GL}_n(\mathbb{Z}_p)$, a scalar $\lambda \xleftarrow{\$} \mathbb{Z}_p$ and computes $[\mathbf{B}] = [\mathbf{M} \cdot \mathbf{L} + \lambda \cdot \mathbf{I}_n]$. Finally, it sends $([\mathbf{B}], [\lambda])$ to $\mathcal{A}$. When $\mathcal{A}$ returns some bit b, $\mathcal{B}$ simply outputs b.

Then, assuming $\mathbf{M}$ is a rank n matrix, $\det(\mathbf{B} - \lambda \cdot \mathbf{I}_n) = \det(\mathbf{M} \cdot \mathbf{L}) \neq 0$, since $\mathbf{M}$ and $\mathbf{L}$ are rank n matrices, and then λ is not an eigenvalue of $\mathbf{B}$, and $\mathcal{B}$ simulates precisely the setting $([\mathbf{B}], [r])$ (with overwhelming probability). Now, if $\mathbf{M}$ is a rank $n-1$ matrix, so is $\mathbf{M} \cdot \mathbf{L}$, and then $\det(\mathbf{B} - \lambda \cdot \mathbf{I}_n) = 0$, which implies that λ is an eigen value of $\mathbf{B}$. Then, $\mathcal{B}$ simulates exactly the setting $([\mathbf{B}], [\lambda])$.

n-Eigen-Value $\Rightarrow$ n-Rank Let now $\mathcal{A}$ denote an adversary against the n-Rank problem in $\mathbb{G}$. Then we build an adversary $\mathcal{B}$ against the n-Eigen-Value problem in $\mathbb{G}$ as follows: $\mathcal{B}$ is given a tuple $([\mathbf{M}], [\lambda])$ with λ being either random or an eigenvalue of $\mathbf{M}$ (for the second case, $\mathbf{M} = \mathbf{L} \cdot \mathbf{A} + \lambda \cdot \mathbf{I}_n$). Then, $\mathcal{B}$ simply computes $[\mathbf{M} - \lambda \cdot \mathbf{I}_n]$ and sends it to $\mathcal{A}$. When $\mathcal{A}$ halts with some bit b, $\mathcal{B}$ outputs b.

Indeed, if λ is not an eigenvalue and $\mathbf{M}$ is uniformly sampled, $\mathbf{M} - \lambda \cdot \mathbf{I}_n$ is just a uniform matrix in $\mathbb{Z}_p^{n \times n}$, which is then of rank n with overwhelming probability, and $\mathcal{B}$ simulates correctly the case where the input matrix for the n-Rank adversary has rank n. However, if λ is indeed an eigenvalue, then $\det(\mathbf{M} - \lambda \cdot \mathbf{I}_n) = 0$, which implies that $\mathbf{M} - \lambda \cdot \mathbf{I}_n$ has rank at most $n-1$ (rank $n-1$ with overwhelming probability). In this case, $\mathcal{B}$ simulates the case where the input matrix to the n-Rank solver has rank $n-1$.

This concludes the proof of Theorem 1.   □

4 A New Programmable Vector Hash Function

Verifiable random functions can be built generically on top of programmable verifiable vector hash functions. We recall their transform allowing to obtain PVHF-based VRFs in Appendix A. In what follows, we contribute by introducing a new PVHF construction with smaller public and secret keys compared to the construction proposed in [9], and relying on a new technique.

4.1   A New PVHF Construction

For $e : \mathbb{G} \times \mathbb{G} \to \mathbb{G}_T$ a symmetric pairing with $|\mathbb{G}| = p$ (p prime), let $\mathcal{D}_0$ and $\mathcal{D}_1$ be the following "pattern" matrix distributions:

$$
\mathcal{D}_0 = \begin{pmatrix} d_{1,1} & d_{1,2} & \cdots & d_{1,n} \\ 0 & 0 & \cdots & 0 \\ 0 & 0 & \cdots & 0 \\ \vdots & \vdots & \cdots & \vdots \\ 0 & 0 & \cdots & 0 \end{pmatrix} \quad \mathcal{D}_1 = \begin{pmatrix} 0 & 0 & \cdots & 0 \\ d_{2,1} & d_{2,2} & \cdots & d_{2,n} \\ \cdots & \cdots & \cdots & \cdots \\ d_{n-1,1} & d_{n-1,2} & \cdots & d_{n-1,n} \\ 0 & 0 & \cdots & 1 \end{pmatrix}, \text{ where } \begin{cases} d_{i,j} \xleftarrow{\$} \mathbb{Z}_p, \\ i \in [n-1], \\ j \in [n]. \end{cases}
$$

VHF.Gen(1^λ):

$\mathbf{u} \xleftarrow{\$} \mathbb{Z}_p^n$

$(\mathbf{M}_i, \mathbf{P}_{i,0}, \mathbf{P}_{i,1}) \xleftarrow{\$} \mathbb{Z}_p^{n \times n} \times \mathcal{D}_0 \times \mathcal{D}_1, \forall i \in [k-1]$

$(\mathbf{M}_{k,0}, \mathbf{M}_{k,1}) \xleftarrow{\$} \mathbb{Z}_p^{n \times n} \times \mathbb{Z}_p^{n \times n}$

$vk \leftarrow \Big([\mathbf{u}], \{[\mathbf{M}_i, \mathbf{P}_{i,b}, \mathbf{M}_{k,b}]\}_{i \in [k-1], b \in \{0,1\}} \Big)$

$sk \leftarrow \Big(\mathbf{u}, \{\mathbf{M}_i, \mathbf{P}_{i,b}, \mathbf{M}_{k,b}\}_{i \in [k-1], b \in \{0,1\}} \Big)$

Return (vk, sk)

VHF.Eval(x, sk):

$[\mathbf{v}] := [\mathbf{u}^\mathsf{T} \cdot \mathbf{M}_x]$

$\pi := \{[\mathbf{u}^\mathsf{T} \cdot \mathbf{M}_{\bar{x}}] : \forall \bar{x} \prec x\}$

Return $([\mathbf{v}], \pi)$

VRF.Vfy($x, vk, [y], \pi$):

check $e([\mathbf{u}^\mathsf{T} \cdot \mathbf{M}_{\bar{x}}^{(i)}], [\mathbf{1}]) \overset{?}{=}$
$e([\mathbf{M}_{i,x_i}], [\mathbf{u}^\mathsf{T} \cdot \mathbf{M}_{\bar{x}}^{(i-1)}])$

Fig. 2. The underlying VHF construction, used to construct a selective PVHF for inputs of length k. We use the following notation $\mathbf{M}_x := \prod_{i=1}^{k-1} (\mathbf{M}_i - \mathbf{P}_{i,x_i}) \cdot \mathbf{M}_{k,x_k}$. We **emphasize** the representation size of $\mathbf{P}_{i,0}, \mathbf{P}_{i,1}$ is $n^2\text{-}n$, which translates in 6 elements for efficient construction using 3×3 matrices, thus obtaining a more efficient construction in terms of both public and secret keys when comparing to the one in [9].

Overview of the Construction. We define a VHF construction in Fig. 2, show its correctness and unique provability, then introduce the trapdoor algorithms in Sect. 4.2 and prove programmability.

- The VHF.Gen algorithm of the proposed scheme generates a set of uniform matrices $(\mathbf{M}_j, \mathbf{P}_{j,0}, \mathbf{P}_{j,1})$, $\forall j \in [k\text{-}1]$, sampled according to the appropriate distributions. The set of "plain" matrices form the secret key sk, while the vk is set to be their encodings.
- The VHF.Eval procedure under sk, corresponding to $x \in \{0,1\}^k$ outputs:

$$\left[\mathbf{u}^{\top} \cdot \left(\prod_{i=1}^{k-1} (\mathbf{M}_i - \mathbf{P}_{i,x_i})\right) \cdot \mathbf{M}_{k,x_k}\right].$$

In some sense, our evaluation procedure is similar to the one described in [12], but we use a matrix multiplication construction rather than a unidimensional product.

- The VHF.Vfy procedure checks if all the pairings of (1) the vectors constituting the proof π, with (2) the matrices forming the public key, are correct.

Fine tunning the VHF *to achieve well-distributed outputs.* We also justify the need for uniform matrices corresponding to position k. Well-distributed outputs, as formulated in Definition 3 (Fig. 1), enforces the last subspace ($\mathcal{W}$) we work to be the one spanned by the first $n-1$ canonical vectors. The reason for this constraint, resides in the proof for pseudorandomness: the outcome of the trapdoor evaluation is multiplied by a (n-LIN-distributed - cf. [6], page 9) matrix $\mathbf{B}$. To cope with this subtlety, we "fine-tune" the PVHF, by doing the following change: we replace the matrices in the last position $(\mathbf{M}_k, \mathbf{P}_{k,0}, \mathbf{P}_{k,1})$ with two "proper", random matrices $(\mathbf{M}_{k,0}, \mathbf{M}_{k,1})$.

4.1.1   Correctness and Unique Provability

Correctness (1) follows immediately from the construction. Unique provability (2) follows from the deterministic evaluation. We prove it formally below:

Lemma 1. *The* VHF *construction presented in Fig. 2 achieves unique provability, according to Definition 2.*

Proof. Suppose there exists a public key vk, a strings X of length k, and a tuple $([\mathbf{v}], \pi, [\mathbf{w}], \phi)$ with $[\mathbf{v}] \neq [\mathbf{w}]$ and $[\mathbf{v}], [\mathbf{w}] \in \mathbb{G}^n$ such that: VHF.Vfy$(vk, X, [\mathbf{v}], \pi) =$ VHF.Vfy$(vk, X, [\mathbf{w}], \phi) = 1$.

To prove uniqueness (2), we refer to the properties of the construction. Suppose there exists a vector index $j \in [n]$ such that $[\mathbf{v}_j] \neq [\mathbf{w}_j]$. We expand $[\mathbf{v}_j] \neq [\mathbf{w}_j]$ and obtain:

$$\left(\mathbf{u}^{\top} \cdot \prod_{i=1}^{k-1}(\mathbf{M}_i - \mathbf{P}_{i,x_i}) \cdot \mathbf{M}_{k,x_k}\right)_j \neq \left(\mathbf{u}^{\top} \cdot \prod_{i=1}^{k-1}(\mathbf{M}_i - \mathbf{P}_{i,x_i}) \cdot \mathbf{M}_{k,x_k}\right)_j \quad (5)$$

The extended equation shows the output values are uniquely determined by the secret key and the input string x, in a fully deterministic procedure. Hence, from Eq. (5), it follows the unique provability property.   □

4.2   Proving Selective Programmability

As usual, provable security is achieved via a reduction to a computationally hard problem; we rely on the n-Eigen-Value assumption (detailed in Sect. 3).

Overview. To prove selective programmability (Definition 3) w.r.t. a challenge $X^{(0)}$ for the VHF in Fig. 2, we *gradually* replace the relevant rows in $\mathbf{P}_{j,0}, \mathbf{P}_{j,1}$

with vectors lying in the rowspace defined by the challenge n-Eigen-Value tuple $([\mathbf{A}], [e])$ (i.e. the eigenspace of $[\mathbf{A} - e \cdot \mathbf{I}_n]$). Among these vectors, we attempt to "hide" the orthogonality components for the rowspace defined by the matrices corresponding to position j-1 (Fig. 3). We also replace $\mathbf{M}_j$ such that $(\mathbf{M}_j - \mathbf{P}_{j,X_j^{(0)}})$ linearly maps vectors between rowspaces defined by $(\mathbf{M}_{j-1} - \mathbf{P}_{j-1,1-X_{j-1}^{(0)}})$ and $(\mathbf{M}_j - \mathbf{P}_{j,1-X_j^{(0)}})$. Then, given the k pairs of matrices $\{(\mathbf{M}_1 - \mathbf{P}_{1,0}, \mathbf{M}_1 - \mathbf{P}_{1,1}), \ldots, (\mathbf{M}_{k-1} - \mathbf{P}_{k-1,0}, \mathbf{M}_{k-1} - \mathbf{P}_{k-1,1}), (\mathbf{M}_{k,0}, \mathbf{M}_{k,1})\}$, the value $\mathbf{u}^\mathsf{T} \cdot \mathbf{M}_{X^{(0)}}$ completely determines $\mathbf{u}$ (since $\mathbf{M}_{X^{(0)}}$ has full rank w.h.p.), whereas for any $x \neq X^{(0)}$, $\mathbf{M}_x$ is a matrix of rank $n - 1$ (because for some j, $\mathbf{M}_j - \mathbf{P}_{j,1-X_j^{(0)}}$ has rank $n - 1$ and it's a term in the product represented by $\mathbf{M}_x$), so $\mathbf{u}^\mathsf{T} \cdot \mathbf{M}_x$ *loses* information about $\mathbf{u}$.

   The trapdoor mode algorithms VHF.TrapGen and VHF.TrapEval are described below:

1. VHF.TrapGen sets all the matrices $(\mathbf{M}_j, \mathbf{P}_{j,0}, \mathbf{P}_{j,1})$ such that:
   - it first generates, uniformly at random, a subspace of dimension $n - 1$, denoted $\mathcal{S}_0$ and a uniform $\mathbf{u} \xleftarrow{\$} \mathbb{Z}_p^n$, which with overwhelming probability will not belong to $\mathcal{S}_0$.
   - it incrementally constructs the challenge-related matrices such that $\mathbf{M}_j - \mathbf{P}_{j,1-X^{(0)}}$ defines a rowspace of rank $n-1$, denoted $\mathcal{S}_j$. Also, $\mathbf{M}_j - \mathbf{P}_{j,X^{(0)}}$ defines a **linear map** between the subspaces $\mathcal{S}_{j-1}$ and $\mathcal{S}_j$; formally $(\mathbf{M}_j - \mathbf{P}_{j,X^{(0)}}) : \mathcal{S}_{j-1} \rightarrow \mathcal{S}_j$.

   Achieving the linear map property is more subtle, and requires a careful programming of the matrices $\mathbf{M}_j, \mathbf{P}_{j,0}, \mathbf{P}_{j,1}$. The VHF.TrapGen begins by sampling $\mathbf{L}_j \xleftarrow{\$} \mathbb{Z}_p^{n \times n}$. It also samples $\mathbf{S}_j \xleftarrow{\$} \mathbb{Z}_p^{(n-1) \times n}$ such that its rowspace defines $\mathcal{S}_j$. A **normal vector** $(\alpha_1, \ldots, \alpha_{n-1}, 1)$, orthogonal on $\mathcal{S}_{j-1}$ is also computed. Finally the matrices can be set as in Fig. 3:

   The **intuition** behind this setting is given by the orthogonal component. The value of the inner product between $\mathbf{v}^{(j-1)}$ and the orthogonal component on $\mathcal{S}_{j-1}$ will enable/disable the membership of $\mathbf{v}^{(j)}$ to $\mathcal{S}_j$: a zero inner product means that $\mathbf{v}^{(j-1)} \in \mathcal{S}_{j-1}$, otherwise $\mathbf{v}^{(j-1)} \notin \mathcal{S}_j$. Finally $\mathbf{M}_{k,1-X^{(0)}}$ is sampled from $\mathcal{S}_k$, while $\mathbf{M}_{k,X^{(0)}}$ is set to map $\mathcal{S}_{k-1} \xrightarrow{C^{-1}} \mathcal{W} \xrightarrow{C'} \mathcal{S}_k$, where $\mathcal{W}$ is the subspace spanned by the first n-1 vectors from the canonical basis.

2. VHF.TrapEval behaves exactly as the VHF.Eval with the noticeable difference, that for a trapdoor algorithm, the resulting vector is multiplied with the matrix $\mathbf{B}$, as specified in Fig. 1.

We now prove *well-distributed* outputs and *indistinguishability*.

4.2.1   Well-Distributed Outputs

Lemma 2. *The* PVHF *construction presented in Fig. 2 has well-distributed outputs according to Definition 3.*

Proof. The triple $(\mathbf{M}_j, \mathbf{P}_{j,0}, \mathbf{P}_{j,1})_{j \in [k-1]}$ — as defined in Fig. 3 — can be used to construct matrices with the properties enumerated below:

$$\mathbf{P}_{j,1} = \begin{pmatrix} 0 & 0 & \cdots & 0 \\ s_{2,1}^{(j)} & s_{2,2}^{(j)} & \cdots & s_{2,n}^{(j)} - \alpha_2 \\ \cdots & \cdots & \cdots & \cdots \\ s_{n-1,1}^{(j)} & s_{n-1,2}^{(j)} & \cdots & s_{n-1,n}^{(j)} - \alpha_{n-1} \\ 0 & 0 & \cdots & -1 \end{pmatrix} \quad \mathbf{P}_{j,0} = \begin{pmatrix} s_{1,1}^{(j)} & s_{1,2}^{(j)} & \cdots & s_{1,n}^{(j)} + \alpha_1 \\ 0 & 0 & \cdots & 0 \\ \cdots & \cdots & \cdots & \cdots \\ 0 & 0 & \cdots & 0 \end{pmatrix}$$

$$\mathbf{M}_j = \mathbf{L}_j \cdot \begin{pmatrix} \mathbf{S}_j \\ \mathbf{s}_j^\top \cdot \mathbf{S}_j \end{pmatrix} + \mathbf{P}_{j,1-X_j^{(0)}}, \forall j \in [k-1]$$

$$\mathbf{M}_{k,1-X_k^{(0)}} = \mathbf{L}_k \cdot \begin{pmatrix} \mathbf{S}_k \\ \mathbf{s}_k^\top \cdot \mathbf{S}_k \end{pmatrix} \qquad \mathbf{M}_{k,1-X_k^{(0)}} = \begin{pmatrix} \mathbf{L}_k' \cdot \mathbf{S}_{k-1} \\ \mathbf{r}' \end{pmatrix}^{-1} \cdot \begin{pmatrix} \mathbf{L}_k'' \cdot \mathbf{S}_k \\ \mathbf{r}'' \end{pmatrix}$$

Fig. 3. Matrices $\mathbf{M}_j, \mathbf{P}_{j,0}, \mathbf{P}_{j,1}$ for $j \in [k\text{-}1]$ generated for the trapdoor mode. The matrices $\mathbf{M}_{k,0}, \mathbf{M}_{k,1}$ are generated as in [9].

1. *Property 1.* $\mathbf{M}_j - \mathbf{P}_{j,X_j^{(0)}} = \mathbf{L}_j' \cdot \begin{pmatrix} \mathbf{S}_j \\ \mathbf{s}^\top \cdot \mathbf{S}_j \end{pmatrix} + (-1)^{X_j^{(0)}} \cdot \mathbf{N}$, where $\mathbf{N}$ is the **zero matrix** except the last column being set to $(\alpha_1, \alpha_2, \ldots, \alpha_{n-1}, 1)$.

2. *Property 2.* $\mathbf{M}_j - \mathbf{P}_{j,1-X_j^{(0)}} = \mathbf{L}_j \cdot \begin{pmatrix} \mathbf{S}_j \\ \mathbf{s}^\top \cdot \mathbf{S}_j \end{pmatrix}$.

An *invariant* is used to easily encapsulate the well-distributed outputs property:

$\exists$ matrices $\mathbf{S}_1, \ldots, \mathbf{S}_k \in \mathbb{Z}_p^{(n-1) \times n}$ of rank $n - 1$ such that for each $x \in \{0,1\}^j$ not a prefix of $X^{(0)}$, $\mathbf{M}_x$ lies in $\mathcal{S}_j$, where $C(\mathbf{S}_j^\top) = \mathcal{S}_j$.

We show the invariant is preserved under the setting of matrices shown in Fig. 3 by proving a set of simple lemmata. Essentially, the first one ensures that $(\mathbf{M}_j - \mathbf{P}_{j,1-X_j^{(0)}}) : \mathbb{Z}_p^n \to \mathcal{S}_j$. The second and third lemmata state that $\mathbf{M}_j - \mathbf{P}_{j,X_j^{(0)}}$ will map vectors from $\mathcal{S}_{j-1} \to \mathcal{S}_j$ for $j \in [k\text{-}1]$. The proofs are straightforward and we defer them for space reasons.

- **Lemma 3.** Let $\mathbf{S} \xleftarrow{\$} \mathbb{Z}_p^{(n-1) \times n}$, $\mathbf{s} \xleftarrow{\$} \mathbb{Z}_p^n$. Let $\mathbf{b} \in \mathbb{Z}_p^n$. Then $\exists \mathbf{a} \in \mathbb{Z}_p^n$ s.t: $\mathbf{b}^\top \cdot \Big(\mathbf{M}_j - \mathbf{P}_{j,1-X_j^{(0)}} \Big) = \mathbf{a}^\top \cdot \begin{pmatrix} \mathbf{S}_j \\ \mathbf{s}_j^\top \cdot \mathbf{S}_j \end{pmatrix}$.

- **Lemma 4.** Let $\mathbf{S} \xleftarrow{\$} \mathbb{Z}_p^{(n-1) \times n}$ and $\mathbf{s} \xleftarrow{\$} \mathbb{Z}_p^n$. Let $\mathbf{v} \in \mathbb{Z}_p^n$ and $\mathbf{b}^\top = \mathbf{v}^\top \cdot \begin{pmatrix} \mathbf{S}_{j-1} \\ \mathbf{s}_{j-1}^\top \cdot \mathbf{S}_{j-1} \end{pmatrix}$. Then $\exists \mathbf{a} \in \mathbb{Z}_p^n$ such that $\mathbf{b}^\top \cdot \Big(\mathbf{M}_j - \mathbf{P}_{j,1-X_j^{(0)}} \Big) = \mathbf{a}^\top \cdot \begin{pmatrix} \mathbf{S}_j \\ \mathbf{s}_j^\top \cdot \mathbf{S}_j \end{pmatrix}$.

- **Lemma 5.** Let $\mathbf{S} \xleftarrow{\$} \mathbb{Z}_p^{(n-1) \times n}$ and $\mathbf{s} \xleftarrow{\$} \mathbb{Z}_p^n$. $\forall \mathbf{v} \in \mathbb{Z}_p^n$ let $\mathbf{b}^\top \neq \mathbf{v}^\top \cdot \begin{pmatrix} \mathbf{S}_{j-1} \\ \mathbf{s}_{j-1}^\top \cdot \mathbf{S}_{j-1} \end{pmatrix}$. Then $\forall \mathbf{a} \in \mathbb{Z}_p^n$ we have $\mathbf{b}^\top \cdot \Big(\mathbf{M}_j - \mathbf{P}_{j,X_j^{(0)}} \Big) \neq \mathbf{a}^\top \cdot \begin{pmatrix} \mathbf{S}_j \\ \mathbf{s}_j^\top \cdot \mathbf{S}_j \end{pmatrix}$.

Finally, care is needed due to the special $\mathbf{M}_{k,0}$ and $\mathbf{M}_{k,1}$ are sampled. Their trapdoor form is given in Fig. 3. Moreover, according to Definiton 3, one needs to ensure that $\mathcal{S}_k = \mathcal{W}$, which implies a special form for $\mathbf{S}_k$ used to instantiate $(\mathbf{M}_{k,0}, \mathbf{M}_{k,1})$. Finally, the invariant immediately follows from the lemmata, and therefore we obtain *well-distributed outputs* for the construction in Fig. 2.   □

4.2.2 Indistinguishability Proof

The procedures VHF.Gen and VHF.TrapGen used in the indistinguishability security experiment (Definition 3) are given in Fig. 4.

VHF.Gen(Π):

$\mathbf{u} \xleftarrow{\$} \mathbb{Z}_p^n$

$(\mathbf{A}_i, \mathbf{B}_{i,0}, \mathbf{B}_{i,1}) \xleftarrow{\$} \mathbb{Z}_p^{n \times n} \times \mathcal{D}_0 \times \mathcal{D}_1$,
$\qquad i \in [k-1], b \in \{0,1\}$

$(\mathbf{D}_{k,0}, \mathbf{D}_{k,1}) \xleftarrow{\$} \mathbb{Z}_p^{n \times n} \times \mathbb{Z}_p^{n \times n}$

$vk := \Big([\mathbf{u}], \{[\mathbf{A}_i],$

$\qquad\qquad [\mathbf{B}_{i,b}], [\mathbf{D}_{k,b}]\}_{i \in [k-1], b \in \{0,1\}} \Big)$

$sk := \Big(\mathbf{u}, \{\mathbf{A}_i,$

$\qquad\qquad \mathbf{B}_{i,b}, \mathbf{D}_{k,b}\}_{i \in [k-1], b \in \{0,1\}} \Big)$

Return (vk, sk)

Eval$_0$(x):

$\mathbf{v}^\top := \mathbf{u}^\top \cdot \prod_{i=1}^{k-1}(\mathbf{A}_i - \mathbf{B}_{i,x_i}) \cdot \mathbf{D}_{k,x_k}$

Return $[\mathbf{v}]$

VHF.TrapGen($\Pi, [\mathbf{B}], X^{(0)}$):

$\mathbf{u} \xleftarrow{\$} \mathbb{Z}_p^n$

$(\mathbf{M}_i, \mathbf{P}_{i,0}, \mathbf{P}_{i,1})$ are sampled as in
$\qquad\qquad$ Figure 6

$(\mathbf{M}_{k,0}, \mathbf{M}_{k,1})$ are sampled as in
$\qquad\qquad$ Figure 6

$vk := \Big([\mathbf{u}], \{[\mathbf{M}_i],$

$\qquad\qquad [\mathbf{P}_{i,b}], [\mathbf{M}_{k,b}]\}_{i \in [k-1], b \in \{0,1\}} \Big)$

$td := \Big(\mathbf{u}, \{\mathbf{M}_i,$

$\qquad\qquad \mathbf{P}_{i,b}, \mathbf{M}_{k,b}\}_{i \in [k-1], b \in \{0,1\}}, \Big)$

Return (vk, td)

Eval$_1$(x):

$\mathbf{v}^\top := \mathbf{u}^\top \cdot \prod_{i=1}^{k-1}(\mathbf{M}_i - \mathbf{P}_{i,x_i}) \cdot \mathbf{M}_{k,x_k}$

Return $[\mathbf{B} \cdot \mathbf{v}]$

Fig. 4. The VHF.Gen and VHF.TrapGen procedures and the oracles used by the indistinguishability security experiment defined in Fig. 1. We provide explicit forms for the two evaluation oracles.

Theorem 2. *The PVHF construction presented in Fig. 2 is indistinguishable according to Defintion 3.*

Proof. Intuitively, we build the proof on transitions based on indistinguishability between **hybrid games** (Fig. 5, left side). **Game$_0$** will correspond to the setting where the matrices used by the VHF.TrapGen are sampled via the VHF.Gen procedure. A transition between the hybrids $j-1$ and j consists in replacing the first j pairs of matrices in the public key with ones sampled according to VHF.TrapGen. To facilitate the transition from **Game$_j$** to **Game$_{j+1}$** we introduce an **intermediate hybrid** security experiment, defined in Fig. 5 (right side). Lemmata 6, 7 are used to prove the transitions between **Game$_j$** → **Game$_{j,A}$** and **Game$_{j,A}$** → **Game$_{j+1}$**.

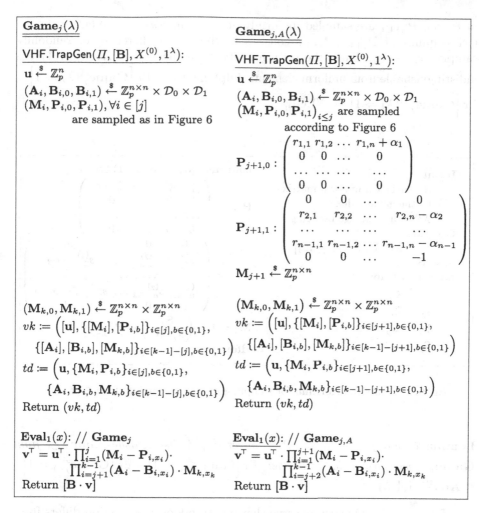

Fig. 5. We describe the VHF.TrapGen and VHF.TrapEval procedures used during the indistinguishability experiment defined in Fig. 1 for $\mathbf{Game}_{j \in [k-1]}$ (left) and $\mathbf{Game}_{j,A}$ (right). VHF.Gen and VHF.Eval are identical to ones described in Fig. 4.

Lemma 6. *Let $j \in [k-2]$. The advantage of any PPT distinguisher $\mathcal{A}$ in distinguishing between $\mathbf{Game}_j$ and $\mathbf{Game}_{j,A}$ is negligible.*

Proof (Lemma 6). We prove an adversary cannot detect the transition between $\mathbf{Game}_j$ and $\mathbf{Game}_{j+1}$, via the intermediate sub-hybrid game we have introduced. The transition between $\mathbf{Game}_j$ and $\mathbf{Game}_{j,A}$ relies on a statistical argument. In $\mathbf{Game}_j$, the tuple $\left(\mathbf{M}_{j+1}, \mathbf{P}_{j+1,0}, \mathbf{P}_{j+1,1}\right)$ corresponding to the position $j+1$ are sampled uniformly from $\mathbb{Z}_p^{n \times n} \times \mathcal{D}_0 \times \mathcal{D}_1$. In $\mathbf{Game}_{j,A}$, we sample the matrices in position $j+1$ using the trapdoor distribution. The indistinguishability follows from the fact that in $\mathbf{Game}_{j,A}$ (Fig. 5), all the entries in $\mathbf{P}_{j+1,0}, \mathbf{P}_{j+1,1}$ are sampled uniformly at random; *observe* the entries in the last columns of $\mathbf{P}_{j+1,0}, \mathbf{P}_{j+1,1}$ consists in the sum (difference) of randomly sampled $r_{i,n} + \alpha_i$. Thus, the orthogonality components $(\alpha_1, \ldots, \alpha_{n-1}, 1)$ are indistinguishable from uniform elements, implying that $\big| \Pr \big[\mathbf{Game}_j^{\mathcal{A}}(\lambda) \Rightarrow 1 \big] - \Pr \big[\mathbf{Game}_{j,A}^{\mathcal{A}}(\lambda) \Rightarrow 1 \big] \big| \in \mathrm{NEGL}.$ □

Input:

    $\mathbf{S}$ - (n-1) x n uniform matrix

    i - the game index

    $X^{(0)}$ - a challenge bitstring

Output:

    $(\mathbf{M}_j, \mathbf{P}_{j,0}, \mathbf{P}_{j,1})_{j \in [i-1]}$

$\mathbf{S}_i \leftarrow \mathbf{S}$

for j=i **to** 1 **do:**

    $\delta_j \xleftarrow{\$} \mathbb{Z}_p$

    $s_j \xleftarrow{\$} \mathbb{Z}_p^{n-1}$

    $\mathbf{L}_j \xleftarrow{\$} \mathbb{Z}_p^{n \times n}$

    $\mathbf{S}_{j-1} \xleftarrow{\$} \mathbb{Z}_p^{(n-1) \times n}$

compute $(\alpha_1, \ldots \alpha_{n-1}, 1) \perp \mathbf{S}_{j-1}$

$$\mathbf{P}_{j,0} = \begin{pmatrix} s_{1,1}^{(j)} & s_{1,2}^{(j)} & \cdots & s_{1,n}^{(j)} + \alpha_1 \\ 0 & 0 & \cdots & 0 \\ \cdots & \cdots & \cdots & \cdots \\ 0 & 0 & \cdots & 0 \end{pmatrix}$$

$$\mathbf{P}_{j,1} = \begin{pmatrix} 0 & 0 & \cdots & 0 \\ s_{2,1}^{(j)} & s_{2,2}^{(j)} & \cdots & s_{2,n}^{(j)} - \alpha_2 \\ \cdots & \cdots & \cdots & \cdots \\ s_{n-1,1}^{(j)} & s_{n-1,2}^{(j)} & \cdots & s_{n-1,n}^{(j)} - \alpha_{n-1} \\ 0 & 0 & \cdots & -1 \end{pmatrix}$$

$\mathbf{M}_j = \mathbf{L}_j \cdot \begin{pmatrix} \mathbf{S}_j \\ s_j^{\mathsf{T}} \cdot \mathbf{S}_j \end{pmatrix} + \mathbf{P}_{j,1-X_j^{(0)}}$

endfor

Fig. 6. A recursive algorithm for sampling trapdoor matrices for $i \in [k-1]$.

Lemma 7. *For* $j \in [k\text{-}2]$, *any* PPT *adversary* $\mathcal{A}$ *distinguishes* $\mathbf{Game}_{j,A}$ *from* $\mathbf{Game}_{j+1}$ *with negligible advantage:* $\big| \Pr \big[\mathbf{Game}_{j,A}^{\mathcal{A}} \Rightarrow 1 \big] - \Pr \big[\mathbf{Game}_{j+1}^{\mathcal{A}} = 1 \big] \big| \leq \mathbf{Adv}_{\mathbb{G}}^{n\text{-ev}}(\mathcal{A}, \lambda).$

Proof (Lemma 7). One can observe that our trapdoor construction differs from the one introduced in [9] from the point of view that instead of using two matrices, we use a matrix and two vectors (when $n = 3$), in a sense aiming to compress as much information as possible in the two row vectors.

Reduction to the n-Eigen-Value *assumption.* We take the contrapositive. Let $\mathcal{A}$ be a PPT adversary having a non-negligible advantage in distinguishing between $\mathbf{Game}_{j,A}$ and $\mathbf{Game}_{j+1}$. We build an adversary $\mathcal{A}'$ that wins the n-Eigen-Value game with the same probability. The n-Eigen-Value game commences by sampling a bit b. $\mathcal{A}'$ is given as input a pair $([\mathbf{A}], [e_b])$; e_0 stands for an eigenvalue for $\mathbf{A}$ and e_1 for a uniform element. We provide the internal working of $\mathcal{A}'$ (Fig. 7) in what follows:

– Input: given a tuple $([\mathbf{A}], [e_b])$, we set the $\mathbf{M}_i, \mathbf{P}_{i,0}, \mathbf{P}_{i,1}, i \in [j]$ as in the $Game_{j,A}$. We embed the challenge in $\mathbf{M}_{j+1}, \mathbf{P}_{j+1,0}, \mathbf{P}_{j+1,1}$ as depicted in Fig. 3.

– $\mathcal{A}'$ is able to construct the evaluation oracle, given that it knows the values of the matrices used, except the ones corresponding to index $j+1$ (which are encoded). This means that $\mathcal{A}'$ can interact with the evaluation oracle.

Algorithm $\mathcal{A}'\big(([\mathbf{A}], [e_b]), j, \lambda\big)$:

1. $\left[\begin{pmatrix} \mathbf{S}_{j+1} \\ \mathbf{s}_{j+1}^{\mathsf{T}} \cdot \mathbf{S}_{j+1} \end{pmatrix}\right] \leftarrow [\mathbf{A} - e_b \cdot \mathbf{I}_n]$ (last row matches $\mathbf{s}_{j+1}^{\mathsf{T}} \cdot \mathbf{S}_{j+1}$)

2. set (td, vk) as in $Game_{j,A}$; set $([\mathbf{M}_{j+1}], [\mathbf{P}_{j+1,0}], [\mathbf{P}_{j+1,1}])$ as in Figure 3

3. $\mathcal{A}'$ builds $\mathbf{Eval}(\cdot)$ as follows:

   3.1. $\mathcal{A}'$ knows all the matrices, except the one on position $j+1$

   3.2. $\mathcal{A}'$ computes $\mathbf{Eval}(x) = \left[\mathbf{u}^{\mathsf{T}} \cdot \prod_{i=1}^{k-1} \left(\mathbf{M}_i - \mathbf{P}_{i,x_i}\right) \cdot \mathbf{M}_{k,x_k}\right] = [\mathbf{v}]$ as follows:

      3.2.1. compute "in plain" $\mathbf{v}^{(j)^{\mathsf{T}}} = \mathbf{u}^{\mathsf{T}} \cdot \prod_{i=1}^{j} \left(\mathbf{M}_i - \mathbf{P}_{i,x_i}\right)$

      3.2.2. compute $[\mathbf{v}^{(j+1)^{\mathsf{T}}}] = [\mathbf{v}^{(j)^{\mathsf{T}}} \cdot \left(\mathbf{M}_{j+1} - \mathbf{P}_{j+1,x_{j+1}}\right)]$

      3.2.3. compute $[\mathbf{v}^{\mathsf{T}}] = [\mathbf{v}^{(k)^{\mathsf{T}}}] = [\mathbf{v}^{(j+1)^{\mathsf{T}}}] \cdot \prod_{i=j+2}^{k-1} \left(\mathbf{M}_i - \mathbf{P}_{i,x_i}\right) \cdot \mathbf{M}_{k,x_k}$

4. $b \leftarrow \mathcal{A}^{\mathbf{Eval}(\cdot)}$; return b

---

Fig. 7. The reduction algorithm used in the proof of Lemma 7.

Correctness of the simulation:

– if e_b is an eigenvalue for $\mathbf{A}$, then the matrices $\mathbf{M}_{j+1}, \mathbf{P}_{j+1,0}, \mathbf{P}_{j+1,1}$ are distributed as in $\mathbf{Game}_{j+1}$.

– if e_b is not an eigenvalue for $\mathbf{A}$, but a uniformly sampled element from $\mathbb{Z}_p$, the matrices are distributed exactly as in $\mathbf{Game}_{j,A}$, the argument relying on the fact that $(\mathbf{A} - e_b \cdot \mathbf{I}_n)$ is a full rank matrix:

– $\mathbf{P}_{j+1,0} = \begin{pmatrix} s_{1,1}^{(j+1)} & s_{1,2}^{(j+1)} & \cdots & s_{1,n}^{(j+1)} + \alpha_1 \\ 0 & 0 & \cdots & 0 \\ \cdots & \cdots & \cdots & \cdots \\ 0 & 0 & \cdots & 0 \end{pmatrix}$ is indistinguishable from its

   equivalent from $\mathbf{Game}_{j,A}$, due to the fact that $\left(s_{1,1}^{(j+1)}, s_{1,2}^{(j+1)}, \ldots, s_{1,n}^{(j+1)}\right)$ are uniform elements.

– $\mathbf{P}_{j+1,1} = \begin{pmatrix} 0 & 0 & \cdots & 0 \\ s_{2,1}^{(j+1)} & s_{2,2}^{(j+1)} & \cdots & s_{2,n}^{(j+1)} - \alpha_2 \\ \cdots & \cdots & \cdots & \cdots \\ s_{n-1,1}^{(j+1)} & s_{n-1,2}^{(j+1)} & \cdots & s_{n-1,n}^{(j+1)} - \alpha_{n-1} \\ 0 & 0 & \cdots & -1 \end{pmatrix}$ is indistinguishable from

   its equivalent from $\mathbf{Game}_{j,A}$, due to the fact that $\{s_{i,j}\}$ are uniform elements.

   – $\mathbf{M}_{j+1} = \mathbf{L}_{j+1} \cdot \left(\mathbf{A} - e_b \cdot \mathbf{I}_n\right) + \mathbf{P}_{j,1-X_j^{(0)}}$. We argue for pseudorandomness based on the fact that $\mathbf{L}_{j+1}$ is a uniformly sampled matrix which randomizes the left side, and the result of the multiplication with the full rank matrix $\mathbf{A} - e_b \cdot \mathbf{I}_n$ is also uniform. Thus $\mathbf{M}_{j+1}$ is a uniform matrix if e_b is not an eigenvalue for $\mathbf{A}$.

– Finally, if the adversary $\mathcal{A}$ can distinguish the way $\mathbf{M}_j, \mathbf{P}_{j+1,0}, \mathbf{P}_{j+1,1}$ are sampled based on $\mathbf{A}$ and e_b, then it can break the n-Eigen-Value assumption.   □

Hence, the advantage of an adversary distinguishing between $\mathbf{Game}_0$ and $\mathbf{Game}_{k-1}$ is bounded by: $\left| \Pr\left[\mathbf{Game}_0^{\mathcal{A}}(\lambda) \Rightarrow 1\right] - \Pr\left[\mathbf{Game}_{k-1}^{\mathcal{A}}(\lambda) \Rightarrow 1\right] \right| \leq (k-1) \cdot \mathbf{Adv}_{\mathbb{G}}^{n\text{-ev}}(\mathcal{A}, \lambda)$.

Final Games. In $\mathbf{Game}_k$ we change the setup for $(\mathbf{M}_{k,0}, \mathbf{M}_{k,1})$. We rely on the same technique as in [9]: given a challenge tuple $([\mathbf{A}], [e_b])$, we set $[\mathbf{M}_{k,x_k^*}] = [\mathbf{A} - e_b \cdot \mathbf{I}_n]$ and $[\mathbf{M}_{k,1-x_k^*}] = \mathbf{C}_k^{-1} \cdot [\mathbf{C}_k']$, where the forms of $\mathbf{C}_k$ and $\mathbf{C}_k'$ are depicted in Fig. 9. Pictorially, one can visualize $\mathbf{C}_k^{-1}$ mapping $\mathcal{S}_{k-1} \to \mathcal{W}$ and $\mathbf{C}_k'$ mapping $\mathcal{W} \to \mathcal{S}_k$. The simulator knows $\mathbf{C}_k^{-1}$ and can construct $[\mathbf{C}_k']$ based on the challenge $([\mathbf{A}], [e_b])$ (by sampling uniformly $n-1$ encodings of vectors in the subspace $\mathcal{S}_k$ defined by $\mathbf{A} - e_b \cdot \mathbf{I}_n$). e_b not an eigenvalue implies a uniformly sampled $\mathbf{C}'$, and thus we are in the setting corresponding to $\mathbf{Game}_{k-1}$. On the other hand, if e_b is an eigenvalue, then we are in the setting corresponding to $\mathbf{Game}_k$.

The final transition, from $\mathbf{Game}_k \to \mathbf{Game}_{k+1}$, consists in embedding $\mathbf{B}$ (Definition 3) in $\mathbf{M}_{k,0}$ and $\mathbf{M}_{k,1}$. This is done by setting $\mathcal{S}_k$ as $\mathcal{W}$ and multiplying the resulting $\mathbf{M}_{k,0}, \mathbf{M}_{k,1}$ with a uniformly sampled $\mathbf{B}$, which guarantees indistinguishability from random. $\mathbf{B}$ is to be used in Theorem 3 to embed the n-Lin assumption and prove the pseudorandomness of the final (generic) VRF construction. Thus: $\left| \Pr\left[\mathbf{Game}_0^{\mathcal{A}}(\lambda) \Rightarrow 1\right] - \Pr\left[\mathbf{Game}_{k+1}^{\mathcal{A}} = 1\right] \right| \leq k \cdot \mathbf{Adv}_{\mathbb{G}}^{n\text{-ev}}(\mathcal{A}, \lambda) + \mathbf{O}\left(k \cdot n/p\right)^1$. Finally, this completes the proof of Theorem 2, and shows the VHF is selectively programmable. Adaptive programmability is similar and shown in Sect. 5.   □

5   An Adaptive Programmable Vector Hash Function

The adaptive PVHF is obtained on top of the selective one defined in Fig. 2, with the additional change that we make use of an admissible hash function AHF. AHFs, introduced in [1], and used in [4], are useful tools for doing the "jump" from selective to adaptive security. In terms of the PVHF construction introduced in Sect. 4.1, the main change consists in hashing the inputs via an AHF. The resulting strings are used to feed the VHF.Eval, VHF.TrapEval algorithms defined for the PVHF. A partial change consists in the form of the matrices corresponding to positions for which $K_{\mathsf{AHF}} = \star$.

The process of sampling the trapdoor keys (td, vk) depends on the key K_{AHF}, and is done as follows:

1. If $K_{\mathsf{AHF},j} \in \{0,1\}$, then the matrices $(\mathbf{M}_j, \mathbf{P}_{j,0}, \mathbf{P}_{j,1})$ are set as in the selective case (Fig. 3).

---

[1] n/p is the probability that a matrix sampled uniformly at random in $\mathbb{Z}_p^{n \times n}$ is singular.

VHF.TrapGen($[\mathbf{B}], 1^\lambda$):

$\mathbf{u} \xleftarrow{\$} \mathbb{Z}_p^n$

$K_{\mathsf{AHF}} \xleftarrow{\$} \mathsf{KeyGen}_{\mathsf{AHF}}(1^\lambda)$

set $(\mathbf{M}_i, \mathbf{P}_{i,0}, \mathbf{P}_{i,1})$ as in Figure 9

set $(\mathbf{M}_{k,0}, \mathbf{M}_{k,1})$ as in Figure 9

$vk := \left([\mathbf{u}], \{[\mathbf{M}_i], [\mathbf{P}_{i,b}], [\mathbf{M}_{k,b}]\}_{i \in [k-1], b \in \{0,1\}}\right)$

$td := \left(\mathbf{u}, \{\mathbf{M}_i, \mathbf{P}_{i,b}, \mathbf{M}_{k,b}\}_{i \in [k-1], b \in \{0,1\}}, K_{\mathsf{AHF}}\right)$

VHF.TrapEval(x, td):

$x \leftarrow AHF_K(x)$

$\beta^\top = \mathbf{u}^\top \cdot \mathbf{M}_x$

$\pi = \left(\{[\mathbf{u}^\top \cdot \mathbf{M}_{\bar{x}}] : \forall \bar{x} \prec x\}\right)$

return $([\mathbf{B} \cdot \beta], \pi)$

VHF.Vfy($x, vk, [y], \pi$):

check $e([\mathbf{M}_{\bar{x}}^{(i)} \cdot \mathbf{u}], [1]) \overset{?}{=}$

$\qquad e([\mathbf{M}_{i,x_i}], [\mathbf{M}_{\bar{x}}^{(i-1)} \cdot \mathbf{u}])$

Fig. 8. The adaptive PVHF obtained via AHFs.

2. If $K_{\mathsf{AHF},j} = \star$, a more careful instantiation is required. If this is the case, we want that both $\mathbf{M}_j - \mathbf{P}_{j,0}$ and $\mathbf{M}_j - \mathbf{P}_{j,1}$ to map vectors between $\mathcal{S}_{j-1}$ and $\mathcal{S}_j$. For this to happen, an adaptive VHF.TrapGen will sample the matrices as in Fig. 9.

$$\mathbf{C}_j = \begin{pmatrix} s_{1,1}^{(j-1)} & s_{1,2}^{(j-1)} & \cdots & s_{1,n}^{(j-1)} \\ s_{2,1}^{(j-1)} & s_{2,2}^{(j-1)} & \cdots & s_{2,n}^{(j-1)} \\ \cdots & \cdots & \cdots & \cdots \\ r_{n,1}^{(j-1)} & r_{n,2}^{(j-1)} & \cdots & r_{n,n}^{(j-1)} \end{pmatrix} \qquad \mathbf{C}_j' = \begin{pmatrix} s_{1,1}^{(j)} & s_{1,2}^{(j)} & \cdots & s_{1,n}^{(j)} \\ s_{2,1}^{(j)} & s_{2,2}^{(j)} & \cdots & s_{2,n}^{(j)} \\ \cdots & \cdots & \cdots & \cdots \\ r_{n,1}^{(j)} & r_{n,2}^{(j)} & \cdots & r_{n,n}^{(j)} \end{pmatrix}$$

$$\mathbf{D}_j = \begin{pmatrix} \mathbf{L}_j & 0 \\ 0 & 1 \end{pmatrix} \cdot \begin{pmatrix} s_{1,1}^{(j-1)} & s_{1,2}^{(j-1)} & \cdots & s_{1,n}^{(j-1)} \\ s_{2,1}^{(j-1)} & s_{2,2}^{(j-1)} & \cdots & s_{2,n}^{(j-1)} \\ \cdots & \cdots & \cdots & \cdots \\ 0 & 0 & \cdots & \delta \end{pmatrix} \qquad \mathbf{D}_j' = \begin{pmatrix} \mathbf{L}_j' & 0 \\ 0 & 1 \end{pmatrix} \cdot \begin{pmatrix} s_{1,1}^{(j)} & s_{1,2}^{(j)} & \cdots & s_{1,n}^{(j)} \\ s_{2,1}^{(j)} & s_{2,2}^{(j)} & \cdots & s_{2,n}^{(j)} \\ \cdots & \cdots & \cdots & \cdots \\ 0 & 0 & \cdots & \delta \end{pmatrix}$$

$$\mathbf{P}_{j,0} \xleftarrow{\$} \mathcal{D}_0$$
$$\mathbf{M}_j = \mathbf{C}_j^{-1} \cdot \mathbf{C}_j' + \mathbf{P}_{j,0}$$
$$\mathbf{P}_{j,0} - \mathbf{P}_{j,1} = \mathbf{D}_j^{-1} \cdot \mathbf{D}_j'$$

Fig. 9. Matrices $\mathbf{M}_j, \mathbf{P}_{j,0}, \mathbf{P}_{j,1}$ corresponding to $K_{\mathsf{AHF},j} = \star$. For the case where $K_{\mathsf{AHF},j} \neq \star$, the matrices are sampled as in Fig. 3. Here, $\mathbf{L}_j$ and $\mathbf{L}_j'$ are uniform $(n-1) \times (n-1)$ matrices and $\delta \xleftarrow{\$} \mathbb{Z}_p$, the first $n-1$ rows in $\mathbf{C}_j$ are sampled from $\mathcal{S}_{j-1}$; $r_{x,y}$ denotes a random element in $\mathbb{Z}_p$.

Lemma 8 *The construction in Fig. 8 yields an adaptive secure PVHF.*

Proof (Lemma 8). Correctness and *unique provability* are proven as in the selective case. To motivate the *well-distributed outputs*, observe that if $K_{\mathsf{AHF},j} = \star$, then $\mathbf{D}_j^{-1} \cdot \mathbf{D}_j$ matches the pattern $\begin{pmatrix} \mathbf{R} \\ 0\,0\ldots 1 \end{pmatrix}$ where $\mathbf{R}$ stands for a uniformly sampled $(n-1) \times n$ matrix. When $K_{\mathsf{AHF},j} = \star$, then multiplying with $\mathbf{M}_j - \mathbf{P}_{j,x_j}$ will be either $\mathbf{C}_j^{-1} \cdot \mathbf{C}_j'$ or $\mathbf{C}_j^{-1} \cdot \mathbf{C}_j' + \mathbf{D}_j^{-1} \cdot \mathbf{D}_j'$. Both $\mathbf{C}_j^{-1} \cdot \mathbf{C}_j'$ and $\mathbf{D}_j^{-1} \cdot \mathbf{D}_j'$ map $\mathcal{S}_{j-1}$ to $\mathcal{S}_j$, and so does their sum.

To motivate *indistinguishability* for $K_{\mathsf{AHF},j} = \star$, observe that both $\mathbf{C}_j$ and $\mathbf{C}_j'$ are full rank matrices, and the elements in $\mathbf{C}_j'$ are uniformly sampled ($\mathcal{S}_j$ being a uniform subspace), thus $\mathbf{C}_j'$ acting as a randomness extractor. This randomizes $\mathbf{M}_j$. We also have to show that no computational adversary can distinguish $\mathbf{P}_{j,0}$ and $\mathbf{P}_{j,1}$ (thus $\mathbf{D}_j^{-1} \cdot \mathbf{D}_j'$) from a uniform matrix sampled from the same distributions. Both $\mathbf{D}_j$ and $\mathbf{D}_j'$ are pre-multiplied with two upper-corner uniform matrices acting as randomness extractors for $\overline{\mathbf{D}}_j$ and $\overline{\mathbf{D}'}_j$. The top rows of $\mathbf{D}_j$ and $\mathbf{D}_j'$ are therefore uniform. For completeness, we mention that if $K_{\mathsf{AHF},k} = \star$, we instantiate both $\mathbf{M}_{k,0}$ and $\mathbf{M}_{k,1}$ of the form $\mathbf{C}_{k,0/1}^{-1} \cdot \mathbf{C}_{k,0/1}'$.

Finally, we point out that $\mathcal{O}_{\mathsf{check}}$ oracle needed in the adaptive indistinguishability experiment defined in Fig. 1 can be implemented using K_{AHF}. □

The adaptive PVHF represents the platform used to build an adaptive secure VRF under a static assumptions via the generic transform given in Appendix A (Theorem 3). The final advantage of an adversary $\mathcal{A}$ winning the pseudorandomness game being: $\mathbf{Adv}_{\mathsf{VRF}}^{\mathsf{vrf}}(\mathcal{A}, \lambda) \leq \mathbf{Adv}_{\mathsf{PVHF}}^{\mathsf{Indist.}}(\mathcal{A}, \lambda) + \mathbf{Adv}^{\mathsf{n-LIN}}(\mathcal{A}, \lambda) = \ell_{\mathsf{AHF}} \cdot \mathbf{Adv}_{\mathbb{G}}^{n\text{-ev}}(\mathcal{A}, \lambda) + \mathbf{O}(\ell_{\mathsf{AHF}} \cdot n/p) + \mathbf{Adv}^{\mathsf{n-LIN}}(\mathcal{A}, \lambda)$.

A   Generic Constructions of **VRF** on Top of **PVHFs**

Theorem 3 (Hofheinz and Jager [9]). *Given an adaptive (selective) secure PVHF, the construction depicted in Fig. 10 yields an adaptive (selective) secure VRF under the* n − LIN *assumption.*

VRF.Gen(1^λ):

$\mathbf{v} \xleftarrow{\$} \mathbb{Z}_p^n$

$\Pi \xleftarrow{\$} \mathsf{GrpGen}(1^\lambda)$

$(vk_{\mathsf{PVHF}}, sk_{\mathsf{PVHF}}) \xleftarrow{\$} \mathsf{VHF.Gen}(\Pi, 1^\lambda)$

$vk := \left([\mathbf{v}], vk_{\mathsf{PVHF}}\right)$

$sk := \left(\mathbf{v}, sk_{\mathsf{PVHF}}\right)$

VRF.Eval(x, sk):

$([\mathbf{z}], \pi_{\mathsf{PVHF}}) \xleftarrow{\$} \mathsf{VHF.Eval}(sk, x)$

$[y] := [\mathbf{v}^\top \mathbf{z}] = [\sum_{i=1}^{k+1} \mathbf{v}_i \cdot \mathbf{z}_i]$

$\pi := \left([\mathbf{v}_1 \cdot \mathbf{z}_1], \ldots, [\mathbf{v}_{k+1} \cdot \mathbf{z}_{k+1}], \pi_{\mathsf{PVHF}}\right)$

return $([y], \pi)$

VRF.Vfy($x, vk, [y], \pi$):

check $e([\mathbf{v}_i], [\mathbf{z}_i]) \overset{?}{=} e([\mathbf{z}_i \cdot \mathbf{v}_i], [1])$

check $[y] \overset{?}{=} [\sum_{i=1}^{k+1} \mathbf{v}_i \cdot \mathbf{z}_i]$

check $\mathsf{VHF.Vfy}(vk_{\mathsf{PVHF}}, \pi_{\mathsf{PVHF}}, x, [\mathbf{z}])$

Fig. 10. The generic construction used to obtain verifiable random functions based on programmable verifiable vector hash function, as presented in [9].

References

1. Boneh, D., Boyen, X.: Secure identity based encryption without random oracles. In: Franklin, M. (ed.) CRYPTO 2004. LNCS, vol. 3152, pp. 443–459. Springer, Heidelberg (2004). https://doi.org/10.1007/978-3-540-28628-8_27

2. Boneh, D., Montgomery, H.W., Raghunathan, A.: Algebraic pseudorandom functions with improved efficiency from the augmented cascade. In: Al-Shaer, E., Keromytis, A.D., Shmatikov, V. (eds.) ACM CCS 2010, pp. 131–140. ACM Press, October 2010

3. Cheon, J.H.: Security analysis of the strong Diffie-Hellman problem. In: Vaudenay, S. (ed.) EUROCRYPT 2006. LNCS, vol. 4004, pp. 1–11. Springer, Heidelberg (2006). https://doi.org/10.1007/11761679_1

4. Cash, D., Hofheinz, D., Kiltz, E., Peikert, C.: Bonsai trees, or how to delegate a lattice basis. In: Gilbert, H. (ed.) EUROCRYPT 2010. LNCS, vol. 6110, pp. 523–552. Springer, Heidelberg (2010). https://doi.org/10.1007/978-3-642-13190-5_27

5. Dodis, Y., Yampolskiy, A.: A verifiable random function with short proofs and keys. In: Vaudenay, S. (ed.) PKC 2005. LNCS, vol. 3386, pp. 416–431. Springer, Heidelberg (2005). https://doi.org/10.1007/978-3-540-30580-4_28

6. Escala, A., Herold, G., Kiltz, E., Ràfols, C., Villar, J.: An algebraic framework for Diffie-Hellman assumptions. In: Canetti, R., Garay, J.A. (eds.) CRYPTO 2013. LNCS, vol. 8043, pp. 129–147. Springer, Heidelberg (2013). https://doi.org/10.1007/978-3-642-40084-1_8

7. Goldreich, O., Goldwasser, S., Micali, S.: How to construct random functions. J. ACM **33**(4), 792–807 (1986)

8. Goldberg, S., Naor, M., Papadopoulos, D., Reyzin, L., Vasant, S., Ziv, A.: NSEC5: provably preventing DNSSEC zone enumeration. In: NDSS 2015. The Internet Society, February 2015

9. Hofheinz, D., Jager, T.: Verifiable random functions from standard assumptions. In: Kushilevitz, E., Malkin, T. (eds.) TCC 2016. LNCS, vol. 9562, pp. 336–362. Springer, Heidelberg (2016). https://doi.org/10.1007/978-3-662-49096-9_14

10. Hofheinz, D., Kiltz, E.: Programmable hash functions and their applications. In: Wagner, D. (ed.) CRYPTO 2008. LNCS, vol. 5157, pp. 21–38. Springer, Heidelberg (2008). https://doi.org/10.1007/978-3-540-85174-5_2

11. Hohenberger, S., Waters, B.: Constructing verifiable random functions with large input spaces. In: Gilbert, H. (ed.) EUROCRYPT 2010. LNCS, vol. 6110, pp. 656–672. Springer, Heidelberg (2010). https://doi.org/10.1007/978-3-642-13190-5_33

12. Lysyanskaya, A.: Unique signatures and verifiable random functions from the DH-DDH separation. In: Yung, M. (ed.) CRYPTO 2002. LNCS, vol. 2442, pp. 597–612. Springer, Heidelberg (2002). https://doi.org/10.1007/3-540-45708-9_38

13. Micali, S., Rivest, R.L.: Micropayments revisited. In: Preneel, B. (ed.) CT-RSA 2002. LNCS, vol. 2271, pp. 149–163. Springer, Heidelberg (2002). https://doi.org/10.1007/3-540-45760-7_11

14. Micali, S., Reyzin, L.: Physically observable cryptography. In: Naor, M. (ed.) TCC 2004. LNCS, vol. 2951, pp. 278–296. Springer, Heidelberg (2004). https://doi.org/10.1007/978-3-540-24638-1_16

15. Micali, S., Rabin, M.O., Vadhan, S.P.: Verifiable random functions. In: 40th FOCS, pp. 120–130. IEEE Computer Society Press, October 1999

16. Naor, M., Reingold, O.: Number-theoretic constructions of efficient pseudo-random functions. J. ACM **51**(2), 231–262 (2004)

17. Yamada, S.: Asymptotically compact adaptively secure lattice IBEs and verifiable random functions via generalized partitioning techniques. In: Katz, J., Shacham, H. (eds.) CRYPTO 2017. LNCS, vol. 10403, pp. 161–193. Springer, Cham (2017). https://doi.org/10.1007/978-3-319-63697-9_6

Cryptographic Protocols

Secret Sharing Schemes
for (k, n)-Consecutive Access Structures

Javier Herranz[1,2]([⊠]) and Germán Sáez[1,2]

[1] Dept. Matemàtiques, Universitat Politècnica de Catalunya,
c. Jordi Girona 1-3, 08034 Barcelona, Spain
{javier.herranz,german.saez}@upc.edu
[2] CYBERCAT-Center for Cybersecurity Research of Catalonia, Barcelona, Spain

Abstract. We consider access structures over a set $\mathcal{P}$ of n participants, defined by a parameter k with $1 \leq k \leq n$ in the following way: a subset is authorized if it contains participants $i, i + 1, \ldots, i + k - 1$, for some $i \in \{1, \ldots, n-k+1\}$. We call such access structures, which may naturally appear in real applications involving distributed cryptography, (k, n)-consecutive.

We prove that these access structures are only ideal when $k = 1$, $n - 1, n$. Actually, we obtain the same result that has been obtained for other families of access structures: being ideal is equivalent to being a vector space access structure and is equivalent to having an optimal information rate strictly bigger than $\frac{2}{3}$. For the non-ideal cases, we give either the exact value of the optimal information rate, for $k = n - 2$ and $k = n - 3$, or some bounds on it.

Keywords: Secret sharing schemes · Ideal access structures
Information rate

1 Introduction

Secret sharing schemes are a cryptographic primitive of vital importance in the design of other cryptographic protocols, including attribute-based cryptosystems, distributed signature schemes or encryption schemes with distributed decryption. A secret sharing scheme is related to a set of participants $\mathcal{P} = \{1, 2, \ldots, n\}$ and a monotone increasing family of authorized subsets of participants, $\Gamma \subset 2^{\mathcal{P}}$. The idea is to distribute a secret value s into shares $s_1, \ldots, s_n$, one for each participant in $\mathcal{P}$. Later, the secret can be recovered only if participants of an authorized subset $A \in \Gamma$ put their shares together. If the secret sharing scheme is perfect, no information at all on the secret can be obtained from the shares of a non-authorized subset of participants.

Different notions have been defined to measure the quality of a secret sharing scheme, all of them involving (the relation between) the size of the secret and the size of the shares received by the participants. If the size of the share of each participant is equal to the size of the secret, then the scheme is called *ideal*.

© Springer Nature Switzerland AG 2018
J. Camenisch and P. Papadimitratos (Eds.): CANS 2018, LNCS 11124, pp. 463–480, 2018.
https://doi.org/10.1007/978-3-030-00434-7_23

In general, however, some of the shares may be larger in size than the secret. Given a particular access structure, it is thus important to obtain bounds on (the relation between) these sizes, for the perfect secret sharing schemes that realize this access structure.

The first secret sharing schemes were introduced in [2,20] for the case of (t, n)-threshold access structures, defined as $\Gamma = \{A \subset \mathcal{P} : |A| \geq t\}$ for some threshold t such that $1 \leq t \leq n$. After that, many researchers have studied the existence and quality of secret sharing schemes for many kinds of access structures. Some examples are weighted threshold access structures [1], graph-based access structures [4–6,21], access structures for five participants [8,13], hierarchical access structures [10,22], multipartite access structures [9,11,19].

In this work we follow this line of research, by considering a family of access structures that (up to our knowledge) has not been deeply studied before: (k, n)-consecutive access structures. The idea is to imagine the n participants placed in a line and to consider a subset of participants authorized only if it contains, at least, k consecutive participants. We stress that other similar access structures that appear in the literature (as k-paths in [7] or those of the secret sharing schemes across time in [14]) are not exactly (k, n)-consecutive access structures.

Our first contact with (k, n)-consecutive access structures was the reading of the paper [18]. Therein, authors propose a method to use cellular automata to design ideal secret sharing schemes. They state that the access structures realized by these ideal secret sharing schemes are (k, n)-consecutive. As we will see in this paper, this statement may not be true in general. Actually, it is easy to see that there are other subsets of participants, which do not contain k consecutive participants, that are authorized for their secret sharing schemes.

1.1   Applications of (k, n)-Consecutive Access Structures

We believe (k, n)-consecutive access structures can naturally appear in real-life situations. Here we sketch some of them, where secret sharing schemes realizing (k, n)-structures can be combined with (distributed) cryptosystems for signature or decryption.

Automatized Control. Participants can be sensors that detect the speed of cars/trains in a (rail)road. When a sensor detects a speed excess, it can broadcast an alert message, signed with its share of the secret key. If the same alert message is signed by k consecutive sensors, it means the speed excess requires some reaction by the authorities.

Similarly, in a health-oriented application, maybe each participant is the measure of the vital signs of a patient, taken by a sensor in a different period of time; if the vital signs are out of the safety area in some period i, participant i uses its share of the secret key to sign an alert message. If k consecutive participants sign the alert message, the final valid signature is produced, as a proof that the vital signs of the patient are out of the safety area during k consecutive periods of time; in such a case, the medical team can act accordingly.

Rewarding Continuous Participation. The first example in the previous item can be seen as a punishment for misbehaviours. But (k, n)-consecutive access structures can be applied also as a reward for people who show a continuous interest or (economic) implication. For instance, a researcher who attends the same conference during k consecutive years can obtain some digital prize. Similarly, a pay-per-view TV channel can send one share of a secret to each consumer who buys an episode of a series, and finally broadcast a bonus episode encrypted with the corresponding secret key, so that only people who have bought k consecutive episodes will be able to watch the bonus one.

Secure Channels Against Inconstant Eavesdroppers. Finally, and following some of the ideas proposed in [14] in the scenario of RFID security, we can consider a situation where a sender wants to send information to a receiver through a channel. Both users know that there is some adversary that sees the communication, but they also know that this adversary is inconstant: he/she is not able to eavesdrop for more than T seconds, each time that he/she gets access to the channel.

One solution is that the sender splits the information to be transmitted in packages that are sent periodically through the channel, so that any interval of T seconds contains at most $k - 1$ communications. The real information m to be sent is encrypted using a symmetric encryption scheme with secret key s, and s is distributed in shares using a secret sharing scheme for (k, n) consecutive access structures, for some big enough n which ensures that the receiver will have access to k communications, even if he is disconnected at some time. The i-th communication contains the share s_i, along with the encrypted information $c = \mathsf{Enc}_s(m)$. The inconstant eavesdropper will not have enough information to recover s, whereas the honest receiver, after obtaining k consecutive communications, can recover the secret s and decrypt c to obtain the information.

1.2   Our Contributions and Organization of the Paper

In this work we give some bounds on the optimal information rate (a quality measure that will be defined in Sect. 2) of (k, n)-consecutive access structures. In particular, we will see that a (k, n)-consecutive access structure is ideal if and only if $k = 1$ or $k = n - 1$ or $k = n$. This clearly shows that the ideal secret sharing schemes designed in [18] cannot realize (k, n)-consecutive access structures, in general.

In general, there is a quite big gap between the upper and the lower bounds that we obtain for the information rate of (k, n)-consecutive access structures. For instance, for the case $n = 2k$, we obtain that the information rate of a $(k, 2k)$-consecutive access structure is between $\frac{4}{k+4}$ and $\frac{k}{2k-1}$. Therefore, there is a lot of work to do in the future, to obtain (if possible) tighter bounds and better secret sharing schemes for these consecutive access structures. We stress that this may be a difficult problem; for instance, it has taken more than twenty years to obtain the exact value of the information rate of all the access structures defined on a set of five participants [8, 13].

In Sect. 2 we give the necessary definitions related to secret sharing schemes and the quality measure of the optimal information rate; we also recall some notions and techniques that will be used later in the paper. In Sect. 3 we define the family of (k, n)-consecutive access structures and prove some initial results, where we relate the information rate of a (k_1, n_1)-consecutive access structure with that of a (k_2, n_2)-consecutive access structure, for different configurations of (k_1, n_1) and (k_2, n_2). The case $k = 3$ is analyzed independently, in Sect. 4. After that, we prove in Sect. 5 different bounds on the information rate of $(k, 2k)$-consecutive access structures, which can be combined with the results in Sect. 3 to derive bounds on the information rate of (k, n)-consecutive access structures, for any configuration of k and n. In particular, we give a theorem to characterize some equivalent conditions for ideal (k, n)-access structures. Finally, as an example to illustrate that some of our general bounds are not optimal, we provide a better lower bound for the information rate of the $(4, 8)$-consecutive access structure.

2   Secret Sharing Schemes: Definition and Some Known Results

2.1   Definitions

Definition 1 (Access Structure). *Given a set of players* $\mathcal{P} = \{1, 2, \ldots, n\}$, *an access structure* $\Gamma \subset 2^{\mathcal{P}}$ *is a non-empty family of subsets of* $\mathcal{P}$ *which is monotone: if* $A_1 \in \Gamma$ *and* $A_1 \subset A_2$, *then* $A_2 \in \Gamma$.
The set of minimal subsets in Γ *is called the basis of* Γ *and is denoted as* Γ_0.

Definition 2 (Secret Sharing). *A secret sharing scheme* $\Sigma = (\mathcal{P}, S, S_1, \ldots, S_n, R, \mu, \mathsf{Dist}, \{\mathsf{Rec}_A\}_{A \subset \mathcal{P}})$ *in the set of players* $\mathcal{P}$ *consists of* $n + 1$ *finite sets* $S, S_1, \ldots, S_n$, *a probability distribution* μ *on a finite set* R *and then two functions:*

- *a distribution function* $\mathsf{Dist} : S \times R \to S_1 \times \ldots \times S_n$ *which, given a secret* $s \in S$ *and randomness* $r \in R$ *chosen accordingly to the distribution* μ, *produces a tuple of shares* $(s_1, \ldots, s_n) \leftarrow \mathsf{Dist}(s, r)$;
- *a reconstruction function* Rec_A *for each subset* $A = \{i_1, \ldots, i_t\} \subset \mathcal{P}$, $\mathsf{Rec}_A : S_{i_1} \times \ldots \times S_{i_t} \to S$.

Definition 3 (Perfect Secret Sharing). *The secret sharing* Σ *perfectly realizes the access structure* $\Gamma \subset 2^{\mathcal{P}}$ *if the following two properties hold (we denote as* $\mathsf{Dist}(s, r)_A$ *the projection of* $\mathsf{Dist}(s, r)$ *to the coordinates corresponding to players in* A):

(a) *for any* $A \in \Gamma$, *any secret* $s \in S$ *and any* $r \in R$ *following* μ, *we have*

$$\Pr\left[\mathsf{Rec}_A\left(\mathsf{Dist}(s, r)_A\right) = s\right] = 1$$

(b) for any $A \notin \Gamma$, any two secrets $s, s' \in S$, any $r, r' \in R$ following μ and any possible subset of shares $(s_i)_{i \in A}$, we have

$$\Pr\left[Dist(s, r)_A = (s_i)_{i \in A}\right] = \Pr\left[Dist(s', r')_A = (s_i)_{i \in A}\right]$$

Definition 4 (Linear Secret Sharing Scheme). *A secret sharing scheme Σ is linear if there exist a finite field $\mathbb{F}$ and a positive integer ℓ such that $S = \mathbb{F}^\ell$, the sets $R, S_1, \ldots, S_n$ are $\mathbb{F}$-vector spaces, μ is the uniform distribution on R and Dist is a linear function.*

To measure the efficiency of a secret sharing scheme, one possibility is to compare the size of the set S of possible secrets with the size of the set S_i of possible shares for player i, either locally or globally. Among the different possible measures considered in the literature (average, total, minimum information rate or maximum information ratio), we will consider in this work the information rate.

Definition 5 (Individual Information Rate of Σ). *The individual information rate $\rho_i(\Sigma)$ of a participant $i \in \mathcal{P}$ in a secret sharing scheme Σ is defined as*

$$\rho_i(\Sigma) = \frac{\log |S|}{\log |S_i|}$$

Definition 6 ((Minimum) Information Rate of Σ). *The (minimum) information rate $\rho(\Sigma)$ of a secret sharing scheme Σ is defined as*

$$\rho(\Sigma) = \min_{1 \leq i \leq n} \rho_i(\Sigma)$$

It is well-known that, in any perfect secret sharing scheme Σ, it holds $\rho(\Sigma) \leq \rho_i(\Sigma) \leq 1$, for any participant $i \in \mathcal{P}$. When $\rho(\Sigma) = 1$, we say that Σ is ideal and that the access structure realized by Σ is ideal, as well. A linear secret sharing scheme which is ideal is called *vector space secret sharing scheme*.

For an access structure $\Gamma \subset 2^{\mathcal{P}}$, we define its information rate (or optimal information rate) $\rho(\Gamma)$ as the supremum of the information rates of secret sharing schemes that perfectly realize Γ.

Definition 7 ((Optimal) Information Rate of Γ).

$$\rho(\Gamma) = \sup_{\Sigma \text{ perfectly realizes } \Gamma} \rho(\Sigma)$$

2.2 Two Techniques to Obtain Bounds on $\rho(\Gamma)$

The concept of independent sequence of subsets, introduced in [19], is a generalization of the concept of independent sequence of participants [3]. This concept has been used to derive upper bounds on the information rate of many access structures.

Definition 8 (Independent Sequence of Subsets). *Given a set of partici-
pants* $\mathcal{P} = \{1, \ldots, n\}$ *and an access structure* $\Gamma \subset 2^{\mathcal{P}}$*, we say that* $\emptyset = B_0 \subset
B_1 \subset B_2 \subset \ldots \subset B_m \subset \mathcal{P}$ *is independent if and only if* $B_m \notin \Gamma$ *and for every*
$i = 1, 2, \ldots, m$ *there exists* $X_i \subset \mathcal{P}$ *such that* $B_i \cup X_i \in \Gamma$ *and* $B_{i-1} \cup X_i \notin \Gamma$*.*

We say that a subset of participants $A \subset \mathcal{P}$ *makes the sequence* $B_1, B_2, \ldots, B_m$
independent if and only if $A \supset X_1 \cup X_2 \cup \ldots \cup X_m$*.*

Theorem 1 ([19]). *If* A *makes the sequence* $B_1, B_2, \ldots, B_m$ *independent then:*

(i) if $A \in \Gamma$ *then* $\rho(\Gamma) \leq \frac{|A|}{m+1}$*,*
(ii) if $A \notin \Gamma$ *then* $\rho(\Gamma) \leq \frac{|A|}{m}$*.*

Regarding lower bounds for the information rate $\rho(\Gamma)$ of an access structure,
a common technique to obtain them is that of λ-decompositions, introduced by
Stinson in [21].

Definition 9 (λ-Decomposition). *A* λ*-decomposition of* Γ *is a family of sub-
structures* $\Gamma_1, \Gamma_2, \ldots, \Gamma_v \subset \Gamma$ *such that any minimal* $A \in \Gamma_0$ *belongs to at least*
λ *of these sub-structures.*

Theorem 2 ([21]). *Given a* λ*-decomposition* $\{\Gamma_h\}_{1 \leq h \leq v}$ *of* Γ*, let* P_h *denote the
set of participants that appear in the sub-structure* Γ_h*, for each* $h = 1, 2, \ldots, v$*.
If there exists a secret sharing scheme* Σ_h *perfectly realizing* Γ_h *with individual
information rates* $\rho_j(\Sigma_h)$*, for each* $h = 1, 2, \ldots, v$ *and* $j \in P_h$*, then there exists
a secret sharing scheme* Σ *that perfectly realizes* Γ*, with*

$$\rho(\Sigma) = \frac{\lambda}{\max_{j \in \mathcal{P}} \sum_{h \text{ s.t. } j \in P_h} \frac{1}{\rho_j(\Sigma_h)}}$$

Furthermore, in this constructive result by Stinson, it holds that, if the secret
sharing scheme Σ_h for Γ_h is linear, for each $h = 1, 2, \ldots, v$, then the resulting
global secret sharing scheme Σ for Γ is also linear.

2.3   Dual Access Structures

Definition 10 (Dual Access Structure). *Given an access structure* $\Gamma \subset 2^{\mathcal{P}}$*,
the dual* Γ^* *of* Γ *is defined as*

$$\Gamma^* = \{A \subset \mathcal{P} \mid \mathcal{P} - A \notin \Gamma\}.$$

The dual of a monotone increasing access structure Γ is clearly a monotone
increasing access structure, and the relation $(\Gamma^*)^* = \Gamma$ holds. The minimal
subsets in Γ^* are the complements of the maximal non-authorized subsets of Γ.
Jackson and Martin proved in [12] the following result.

Theorem 3 ([12]). *If there exists a linear secret sharing scheme* Σ *that perfectly
realizes* Γ *with information rate* $\rho(\Sigma)$*, then there exists a linear secret sharing
scheme* Σ^* *that perfectly realizes* Γ^* *with* $\rho(\Sigma^*) = \rho(\Sigma)$*.*

2.4 Graph Access Structures

An access structure Γ where all the minimal subsets have exactly 2 players is called a graph access structure, because it can be represented by a graph: there are n vertices, one for each player $i \in \{1, \ldots, n\} = \mathcal{P}$, and two vertices i, j are connected with an edge if and only if $A = \{i, j\} \in \Gamma$.

This kind of access structures have been deeply studied in the literature. Here we recall two known results that will be used in this paper.

Theorem 4 ([5]). *A graph access structure Γ, where the corresponding graph is connected, is ideal if and only if the corresponding graph is a complete multipartite graph.*

Theorem 5 ([21]). *Let d be the maximum degree of the vertices of the graph representing a graph access structure Γ. Then $\rho(\Gamma) \geq \frac{2}{d+1}$.*

3 (k, n)-Consecutive Access Structures

Given positive integers $1 \leq k \leq n$, let us consider the family of access structures $\Gamma^{(k,n)}$ defined on $\mathcal{P} = \{1, 2, \ldots, n\}$ by their basis

$$\Gamma_0^{(k,n)} = \{\{1, 2, \ldots, k-1, k\}, \{2, 3, \ldots, k, k+1\}, \ldots, \{n-k+1, n-k+2, \ldots, n-1, n\}\}.$$

We will denote from now on the information rate of such access structures as $\rho_{(k,n)} = \rho\left(\Gamma^{(k,n)}\right)$.

For $k = 1$, we have that any single player is authorized, $i \in \Gamma^{(1,n)}$, for any $n \geq 1$ and any $i \in \mathcal{P} = \{1, \ldots, n\}$. This is clearly an ideal and linear access structure (a $(1,n)$-threshold access structure), so we have $\rho_{(1,n)} = 1$, for all $n \geq 1$.

For $n = k$, we have that $\Gamma_0^{(n,n)} = \{\{1, 2, \ldots, n\}\} = \{\mathcal{P}\}$, so the only authorized subset is the whole set of players. Again, we have an ideal and linear access structure (a (n,n)-threshold access structure), so we have $\rho_{(n,n)} = 1$, for all $n \geq 1$.

For $n = k + 1$, we have that $\Gamma_0^{(k,k+1)} = \{\{1, 2, \ldots, k\}, \{2, 3, \ldots, k+1\}\}$ contains only two minimals. Any access structure with two minimals is ideal and can be realized by a vector space secret sharing scheme, so we have $\rho_{(k,k+1)} = 1$, for all $k \geq 1$.

As we will see, these are the only cases where $\Gamma^{(k,n)}$ is an ideal access structure. For instance, for $k = 2$ and $n \geq 4$, we have that $\Gamma^{(k,n)}$ is a graph access structure, where the graph is a path of length $n - 1$. It is known [4,21] that the information rate of any path with $n \geq 4$ is exactly $2/3$, so we have $\rho_{(2,n)} = \frac{2}{3}$, for all $n \geq 4$.

We will see in the rest of the paper that, for any $2 \leq k \leq n$ satisfying $k + 2 \leq n$, we have $\rho_{(k,n)} \leq \frac{2}{3} < 1$, and so $\Gamma^{(k,n)}$ cannot be an ideal access structure in all these cases.

3.1 First Results

The first property states that the optimal information rate $\rho_{(k,n)}$ is decreasing in n:

Lemma 1. *If $k \leq n_1 < n_2$, then $\rho_{(k,n_1)} \geq \rho_{(k,n_2)}$.*

Proof. For any secret sharing scheme Σ realizing $\Gamma^{(k,n_2)}$, let us consider the secret sharing scheme Σ' for $\Gamma^{(k,n_1)}$ that simply erases the shares of participants $n_1+1, \ldots, n_2$ from algorithm Dist of Σ. Clearly, the scheme Σ' realizes the access structure $\Gamma^{(k,n_1)}$ defined for participants $1, 2, \ldots, n_1$. We have $\rho(\Sigma') \geq \rho(\Sigma)$, for any secret sharing scheme realizing $\Gamma^{(k,n_2)}$. Taking supremum values in this inequality, we have

$$\rho_{(k,n_1)} \geq \sup_{\Sigma \text{ realizes } \Gamma^{(k,n_2)}} \rho(\Sigma') \geq \sup_{\Sigma \text{ realizes } \Gamma^{(k,n_2)}} \rho(\Sigma) = \rho_{(k,n_2)} \ .$$

□

Lemma 2. *If $k < n < 2k$, then $\rho_{(k,n)} = \rho_{(n-k,2(n-k))}$.*

Proof. The $2k - n > 0$ participants $n - k + 1, n - k + 2, \ldots, k$ belong to all the minimal authorized subsets in $\Gamma^{(k,n)}$.

For any secret sharing scheme Σ realizing $\Gamma^{(k,n)}$, let us remove the common participants $n - k + 1, n - k + 2, \ldots, k$ and make their shares public. The resulting secret sharing scheme Σ' realizes $\Gamma^{(k-(2k-n),n-(2k-n))} = \Gamma^{(n-k,2(n-k))}$ with the information rate $\rho(\Sigma') \geq \rho(\Sigma)$. As in the proof of Lemma 1, taking supremum values in this inequality, for any secret sharing scheme realizing $\Gamma^{(k,n)}$, we conclude $\rho_{(n-k,2(n-k))} \geq \rho_{(k,n)}$.

To prove the other inequality, given any secret sharing scheme Σ realizing $\Gamma^{(n-k,2(n-k))}$, let S be the finite set of possible secrets of Σ. If $m = |S|$, we can identify S (if necessary, via a bijection) with the ring of integers modulus m, that is, $S = \mathbb{Z}_m$. We are going to add $2k - n$ new participants to each of the minimal subset in $\Gamma^{(n-k,2(n-k))}$. The resulting access structure is clearly $\Gamma^{(k,n)}$, and we realize it with a secret sharing scheme Σ' defined as follows: let $s \in \mathbb{Z}_m$ be a secret to be distributed; take random numbers $R_1, R_2, \ldots, R_{2k-n} \in \mathbb{Z}_m$; each of these numbers will be the share of one of the new participants. For the other (not new) $2(n - k)$ participants, distribute the secret $s - R_1 - R_2 - \cdots - R_{2k-n} \bmod m$ using algorithm Dist of Σ. It is easy to see that this new secret sharing scheme realizes $\Gamma^{(k,n)}$ with the information rate $\rho(\Sigma') = \rho(\Sigma)$. Taking supremum values for any secret sharing scheme realizing $\Gamma^{(n-k,2(n-k))}$, we have $\rho_{(k,n)} \geq \rho_{(n-k,2(n-k))}$.

□

Lemma 3. *If $k \geq 2$, then $\rho_{(k,n)} \leq \rho_{(k-1,n-\lfloor \frac{n}{k} \rfloor)}$.*

Proof. For any secret sharing scheme Σ realizing $\Gamma^{(k,n)}$ defined on $\mathcal{P} = \{1, 2, \ldots, n\}$, with information rate $\rho(\Sigma)$, let us consider a secret sharing scheme Σ' defined on the set of participants $\mathcal{P}' = \{1, 2, \ldots, n\} - \{k, 2k, 3k, \ldots, \ell k\}$ with $\ell = \lfloor \frac{n}{k} \rfloor$ and $|\mathcal{P}'| = n - \ell$. The scheme Σ' works as follows: run algorithm Dist of secret sharing scheme Σ to obtain shares of the secret to be distributed, then publish the shares of participants $k, 2k, 3k, \ldots, \ell k$. Clearly, Σ' realizes a $(k-1, n-\ell)$-consecutive access structure, with information rate $\rho(\Sigma') \geq \rho(\Sigma)$. Taking supremum values for any scheme realizing $\Gamma^{(k,n)}$, we conclude $\rho_{(k-1,n-\ell)} \geq \rho_{(k,n)}$. □

Lemma 4. If $n > 2k$, then $\rho_{(k,n)} \geq \frac{\rho_{(k,2k)}}{2}$.

Proof. First of all decompose $\Gamma^{(k,n)}$ into ℓ sub-access structures, all of them of the form $\Gamma^{(k,2k)}$ (for different sets of participants) and a last access structure of the form $\Gamma^{(k,n')}$ for $n' \leq 2k$. It is easy to see that $\ell = \lfloor \frac{n-k+1}{k+1} \rfloor$ and:

$$\Gamma_1 = \{\{1, \ldots, k\}, \{2, \ldots, k+1\}, \ldots, \{k+1, \ldots, 2k\}\}$$
$$\Gamma_2 = \{\{k+2, \ldots, 2k+1\}, \{k+3, \ldots, 2k+2\}, \ldots, \{2k+2, \ldots, 3k+1\}\}$$
$$\Gamma_3 = \{\{2k+3, \ldots, 3k+2\}, \{2k+4, \ldots, 3k+3\}, \ldots, \{3k+3, \ldots, 4k+2\}\}$$
$$\ldots$$
$$\Gamma_\ell = \{\{(k+1)\ell - k, \ldots, (k+1)\ell - 1\}, \{(k+1)\ell - k + 1, \ldots, (k+1)\ell\}, \ldots, \{(k+1)\ell, \ldots, (k+1)\ell + k - 1\}\}$$
$$\Gamma_{\ell+1} = \{\{(k+1)\ell+1, \ldots, (k+1)\ell+k\}, \{(k+1)\ell+2, \ldots, (k+1)\ell+k+1\}, \ldots, \{n - k + 1, \ldots, n\}\}$$

Let us consider the $(k, 2k)$-consecutive access structure $\Gamma'_{\ell+1}$ obtained from $\Gamma_{\ell+1}$ by adding $r = k - (n - k - (k+1)\ell)$ additional players $n+1, \ldots, n+r$ and the corresponding minimal subsets:

$$\Gamma'_{\ell+1} = \Gamma_{\ell+1} \cup \{\{n-k+2, \ldots, n+1\}, \ldots, \{n-k+s+1, \ldots, n+s\}\}.$$

If $n - k - (k+1)\ell = k$, then $s = 0$ and $\Gamma'_{\ell+1} = \Gamma_{\ell+1}$.

Now for any secret sharing scheme Σ realizing $\Gamma^{(k,2k)}$ with information rate $\rho(\Sigma)$, we define a secret sharing scheme Σ' that first uses Σ to share the same secret for each of $\Gamma_1, \ldots, \Gamma_\ell, \Gamma'_{\ell+1}$, and finally erases the shares corresponding to participants $n+1, \ldots, n+s$.

Clearly, Σ' realizes $\Gamma^{(k,n)}$. Each participant appears in at most two of the access structures $\Gamma_1, \ldots, \Gamma_\ell, \Gamma'_{\ell+1}$, so we have $\rho(\Sigma') \geq \frac{\rho(\Sigma)}{2}$. Taking supremum values in this inequality, for any secret sharing scheme Σ realizing $\Gamma^{(k,2k)}$, we obtain the desired result $\rho_{(k,n)} \geq \frac{\rho_{(k,2k)}}{2}$. □

4 The Case $k = 3$

As a warming up, we consider the case $k = 3$ independently. We know that $\rho_{(3,3)} = \rho_{(3,4)} = 1$, and applying Lemma 2, we conclude that $\rho_{(3,5)} = \rho_{(2,4)} = \frac{2}{3}$. Now we will prove that the exact value for $\rho_{(3,6)}$ is $\frac{3}{5}$, and we will give some bounds on $\rho_{(3,n)}$ for $n > 6$.

Theorem 6. $\rho_{(3,6)} = \frac{3}{5}$.

Proof. We have the basis $\left(\Gamma^{(3,6)}\right)_0 = \{\{1, 2, 3\}, \{2, 3, 4\}, \{3, 4, 5\}, \{4, 5, 6\}\}$.

To prove the upper bound $\rho_{(3,6)} \leq \frac{3}{5}$, we construct the following independent sequence of subsets:

$B_1 = \{1\}$, $B_2 = \{1,5\}$, $B_3 = \{1,2,5\}$, $B_4 = \{1,2,5,6\}$, which satisfies $\emptyset = B_0 \subset B_1 \subset B_2 \subset B_3 \subset B_4 \notin \Gamma^{(3,6)}$.

The subsets $X_1 = \{2,3\}$, $X_2 = \{3,4\}$, $X_3 = \{3\}$, $X_4 = \{4\}$ are such that $X_i \cup B_i \in \Gamma^{(3,6)}$ and $X_i \cup B_{i-1} \notin \Gamma^{(3,6)}$, for all $i = 1,\ldots,4$. Therefore, the subset $A = X_1 \cup \ldots \cup X_4 = \{2,3,4\} \in \Gamma^{(3,6)}$ makes the sequence $B_1 \subset \ldots \subset B_4$ independent. We can apply Theorem 1 with $m = 4$ and $A \in \Gamma^{(3,6)}$ with $|A| = 3$, to conclude that $\rho_{(3,6)} \le \frac{|A|}{m+1} = \frac{3}{5}$.

To prove the lower bound $\rho_{(3,6)} \ge \frac{3}{5}$, we consider the following λ-decomposition of $\Gamma^{(3,6)}$ into access structures with three minimals (we describe the basis of these access structures, below):

$\Gamma_1 = \{\{1,2,3\}, \{2,3,4\}, \{3,4,5\}\}$,
$\Gamma_2 = \{\{1,2,3\}, \{2,3,4\}, \{4,5,6\}\}$,
$\Gamma_3 = \{\{1,2,3\}, \{3,4,5\}, \{4,5,6\}\}$,
$\Gamma_4 = \{\{2,3,4\}, \{3,4,5\}, \{4,5,6\}\}$.

We have that each minimal subset of $\Gamma^{(3,6)}$ appears in $\lambda = 3$ of the access structures $\Gamma_1,\ldots,\Gamma_4$. From now on, let S be a finite field.

A secret sharing scheme Σ_1 for Γ_1, to share a secret $s \in S$, gives a random single share $s_3 \in S$ to player 3, and then distributes $\tilde{s} = s - s_3$ among the other players, by choosing s_1, s_4 randomly and independently, and defining $s_2^{(1)} = \tilde{s} - s_1$, $s_5 = s_2^{(2)} = \tilde{s} - s_4$. In this way, we have $\rho_1(\Sigma_1) = \rho_3(\Sigma_1) = \rho_4(\Sigma_1) = \rho_5(\Sigma_1) = 1$, and $\rho_2(\Sigma_1) = \frac{1}{2}$.

A secret sharing scheme Σ_2 for Γ_2, to share a secret $s \in S$, chooses random values s_2, s_3, s_5, s_6 and defines $s_1 = s_4^{(1)} = s - s_2 - s_3$ and $s_4^{(2)} = s - s_5 - s_6$. In this way, we have $\rho_1(\Sigma_2) = \rho_2(\Sigma_2) = \rho_3(\Sigma_2) = \rho_5(\Sigma_2) = \rho_6(\Sigma_2) = 1$, and $\rho_4(\Sigma_2) = \frac{1}{2}$.

A secret sharing scheme Σ_3 for Γ_3, to share a secret $s \in S$, chooses random values s_1, s_2, s_4, s_5 and defines $s_3^{(1)} = s - s_1 - s_2$ and $s_3^{(2)} = s_6 = s - s_4 - s_5$. In this way, we have $\rho_1(\Sigma_3) = \rho_2(\Sigma_3) = \rho_4(\Sigma_3) = \rho_5(\Sigma_3) = \rho_6(\Sigma_3) = 1$, and $\rho_3(\Sigma_3) = \frac{1}{2}$.

Finally, a secret sharing scheme Σ_4 for Γ_4, to share a secret $s \in S$, gives a random single share $s_4 \in S$ to player 4, and then distributes $\tilde{s} = s - s_4$ among the other players, by choosing s_3, s_6 randomly and independently, and defining $s_2 = s_5^{(1)} = \tilde{s} - s_3$, $s_5^{(2)} = \tilde{s} - s_6$. In this way, we have $\rho_2(\Sigma_4) = \rho_3(\Sigma_4) = \rho_4(\Sigma_4) = \rho_6(\Sigma_3) = 1$, and $\rho_5(\Sigma_4) = \frac{1}{2}$.

The maximum value for $\sum_{h \text{ s.t. } j \in P_h} \frac{1}{\rho_j(\Sigma_h)}$ is achieved by players $j = 2,3,4,5$, and is equal to 5. Therefore, applying Theorem 2, we obtain the lower bound $\rho_{(3,6)} \ge \frac{3}{5}$. $\square$

Proposition 1. *For any $n > 6$, it holds $\rho_{(3,n)} \ge \frac{1}{2}$.*

Proof. We consider the following λ-decomposition, with $\lambda = 1$, in $\lfloor \frac{n-1}{2} \rfloor$ ideal sub-access structures (each of them with at most 2 minimals, as described by the following basis):

$\Gamma_1 = \{\{1,2,3\},\{2,3,4\}\},$
$\Gamma_2 = \{\{3,4,5\},\{4,5,6\}\},$
...
$\Gamma_{\lfloor \frac{n-1}{2} \rfloor} = \{\{n-3,n-2,n-1\},\{n-2,n-1,n\}\}$ (if n is even) or $\Gamma_{\lfloor \frac{n-1}{2} \rfloor} = \{\{n-2,n-1,n\}\}$ (if n is odd).

Each player appears in at most two of these ideal access structures, with $\rho_j(\Sigma_h) = 1$ for all $h = 1,2,\ldots,\lfloor \frac{n-1}{2} \rfloor$ and all $j \in P_h$, so Theorem 2 leads to the lower bound $\rho_{(3,n)} \geq \frac{1}{2}$. $\qquad\square$

As a direct consequence of Theorem 6, Proposition 1 and Lemma 1, we have the following result.

Corollary 1. *For any $n > 6$, it holds $\frac{1}{2} \leq \rho_{(3,n)} \leq \frac{3}{5}$.*

5   The General Case: Bounds on $\rho_{(k,n)}$

According to the results stated in Lemmas 2 and 4, bounds on the values $\rho_{(k,n)}$ can be obtained from bounds on the values $\rho_{(k,2k)}$. In this section, we are going to prove some bounds on $\rho_{(k,2k)}$, first. Then we will give the derived bounds on the values $\rho_{(k,n)}$, in general.

5.1   Upper Bounds on $\rho_{(k,2k)}$

Theorem 7. *For any $k \geq 2$, it holds $\rho_{(k,2k)} \leq \frac{k}{2k-1}$.*

Proof. We construct the following independent sequence of $m = 2k - 2$ subsets:
$B_1 = \{1\}$, $B_2 = \{1,k+2\}$, $B_3 = \{1,2,k+2\}$, $B_4 = \{1,2,k+2,k+3\}$, ..., $B_{2k-3} = \{1,2,\ldots,k-1,k+2,k+3,\ldots,2k-1\}$, $B_{2k-2} = \{1,2,\ldots,k-1,k+2,k+3,\ldots,2k\}$, which satisfies $\emptyset = B_0 \subset B_1 \subset B_2 \subset \ldots \subset B_m \notin \Gamma^{(k,2k)}$. In other words, we have, $B_{2i-1} = \{1,2,\ldots,i,k+2,k+3,\ldots,k+i\}$ and $B_{2i} = B_{2i-1} \cup \{k+i+1\}$, for $i = 1,\ldots,k-1$.

Let us now consider the subsets $X_1 = \{2,3,\ldots,k\}$, $X_2 = \{3,4,\ldots,k,k+1\}$, $X_3 = \{3,4,\ldots,k\}$, $X_4 = \{4,5,\ldots,k,k+1\}$, ..., $X_{2k-3} = \{k\}$, $X_{2k-2} = \{k+1\}$, or in other words $X_{2i-1} = \{i+1,i+2,\ldots,k\}$ and $X_{2i} = \{i+2,i+3,\ldots,k,k+1\}$, for $i = 1,\ldots,k-1$. They satisfy $X_i \cup B_i \in \Gamma^{(k,2k)}$ and $X_i \cup B_{i-1} \notin \Gamma^{(k,2k)}$, for all $i = 1,\ldots,k-1$.

Therefore, the subset $A = X_1 \cup \ldots \cup X_{2k-2} = \{2,3,\ldots,k,k+1\} \in \Gamma^{(k,2k)}$ makes the sequence $B_1 \subset \ldots \subset B_{2k-2}$ independent. We can apply Theorem 1 with $m = 2k-2$ and $A \in \Gamma^{(k,2k)}$ with $|A| = k$, to conclude that $\rho_{(k,2k)} \leq \frac{|A|}{m+1} = \frac{k}{2k-1}$. $\qquad\square$

5.2   Lower Bounds on $\rho_{(k,2k)}$

We first prove that the dual of $\Gamma^{(k,2k)}$ is a graph access structure, where the graph is bipartite.

Proposition 2. $\left(\Gamma^{(k,2k)}\right)_0^* = \{\{i,j\} \ s.t. \ 1 \le i \le k, k+1 \le j \le k+i\}.$

Proof. Let $A \in \left(\Gamma^{(k,2k)}\right)_0^*$. Then $\mathcal{P} - A$ is a maximal non-authorized sub-set, meaning that $(\mathcal{P} - A) \cup \{i\} \in \Gamma^{(k,2k)}$ for any $i \in A$. Suppose that $A = \{i_1, i_2, \ldots, i_\ell\}$ with $i_1 < i_2 < \cdots < i_\ell$. First we will prove that $\ell = 2$. Suppose $\ell = 1$, then $i_1 - 1 < k$ and $2k - (i_1 + 1) + 1 < k$ because $\mathcal{P} - A = \mathcal{P} - \{i_1\}$ is non-authorized for $\Gamma^{(k,2k)}$. From this we deduce $i_1 < k+1$ and $i_1 > k$, a contradiction. Now we will prove that $\ell \ge 3$ also gives a contradiction. Since $(\mathcal{P} - A) \cup \{i_1\}$ and $(\mathcal{P} - A) \cup \{i_\ell\}$ are authorized, then $i_2 - 1 \ge k$ and $2k - (i_{\ell-1} + 1) + 1 \ge k$ that is, $i_2 \ge k+1$ and $i_{\ell-1} \le k$ a contradiction because $i_2 \le i_{\ell-1}$ for $\ell \ge 3$. So we have proved that $A = \{i,j\}$ must have cardinality 2. As far as $\mathcal{P} - A$ is non authorized we have $i - 1 < k$, $j - (i+1) + 1 < k$ and $2k - (j+1) + 1 < k$, that is, $i \le k$, $j \le i+k$ and $j \ge k+1$, the condition stated in the proposition.

Conversely: let $A = \{i,j\}$ with $1 \le i \le k, k+1 \le j \le k+i$; we will prove that $\mathcal{P} - A$ is a maximal non-authorized subset of $\Gamma^{(k,2k)}$. First this subset is non-authorized because $i - 1 < k$, $j - 1 - (i+1) + 1 = j - i - 1 < k$ and $2k - (j+1) + 1 = 2k - j < k$. Secondly $\mathcal{P} - A$ is maximal because $(\mathcal{P} - A) \cup \{i\}$ has the first $j - 1 \ge k$ participants and $(\mathcal{P} - A) \cup \{j\}$ has the last $2k - (j+1) + 1 = 2k - j \ge k$ participants, so both $(\mathcal{P} - A) \cup \{i\}$ and $(\mathcal{P} - A) \cup \{j\}$ are authorized. $\square$

Let us define $\rho_{(k,n)^*} = \rho\left(\left(\Gamma^{(k,n)}\right)^*\right)$. The bipartite graph representing $\left(\Gamma^{(k,2k)}\right)^*$ has maximum degree k, because player k is connected to players $k+1, \ldots, 2k$. Applying Theorem 5, we have that $\rho_{(k,2k)^*} \ge \frac{2}{k+1}$. In the rest of the section we prove a better lower bound for $\rho_{(k,2k)^*}$ and $\rho_{(k,2k)}$.

Lemma 5. *There is a λ-decomposition of $\left(\Gamma^{(k,2k)}\right)_0^*$ in ideal (and linear) access structures, for $\lambda = k$. Every participant appears in at most ℓ_k access structures, where $\ell_k = \frac{k(k+4)}{4}$ if k is even, and $\ell_k = \frac{k^2 + 4k - 1}{4}$ if k is odd.*

Proof. The proof is by induction on k. For $k = 1$, we have $\left(\Gamma^{(1,2)}\right)^* = \{\{1,2\}\}$, and the 1-decomposition consists of $\left(\Gamma^{(1,2)}\right)^*$ itself, leading to $\ell_1 = 1$.

For $k = 2$, we have $\left(\Gamma^{(2,4)}\right)_0^* = \{\{1,3\}, \{2,3\}, \{2,4\}\}$ which can be decomposed into $\Gamma_1 = \{\{1,3\}, \{2,3\}\}$, $\Gamma_2 = \{\{1,3\}, \{2,4\}\}$ and $\Gamma_3 = \{\{2,3\}, \{2,4\}\}$, a 2-decomposition in ideal linear access structures, where participants 2 and 3 appear $\ell_2 = 3$ times, satisfying the statement of the lemma.

Now suppose the statement of the lemma is true for any $k' < k$ and let us prove that it is also true for k. Let us consider the following access structures (defined by the basis below):

$$\Gamma_{0,1} = \{\{i, k+i\}_{1 \le i \le k}\},$$

$\Gamma_{1,s} = \{\{i, k + 1\}_{1 \leq i \leq s}\}$, for $s = 2, \dots, k$,
$\Gamma_{2,s} = \{\{k, i\}_{2k - s + 1 \leq i \leq 2k}\}$, for $s = 2, \dots, k$,
$\Gamma_{3,s} = \{\{i, j\}_{k - s \leq i \leq k,\ k + 1 \leq j \leq 2k - s}\}$, for $s = 1, \dots, k - 2$.

All these access structures correspond to complete bipartite graphs, and so (by Theorem 4) they can be realized by ideal linear secret sharing schemes. Participant k appears in $2k - 1$ of the access structures, and the same happens with participant $k + 1$. We stress that $2k - 1 \leq \frac{k^2 + 4k - 1}{4} < \frac{k(k + 4)}{4}$ for all $k \geq 3$.

Participant 1 appears in k access structures, and the same happens with participant $2k$. Each of the remaining participants appears in exactly $k + 1$ of the access structures.

All the edges of the bipartite graph of $\left(\Gamma^{(k,2k)}\right)_0^*$ that involve participants $1, k, k + 1, 2k$ appear exactly k times. For the remaining edges $\{i, j\}$, with $2 \leq i \leq k - 1$, $k + 2 \leq j \leq 2k - 1$ and $j \leq i + k$, we have two cases: if $j = i + k$, then edge $\{i, i + k\}$ appears in $\Gamma_{0,1}$ and in $\Gamma_{3,k-i}$; if $j > i + k$, then edge $\{i, j\}$ appears in $\Gamma_{3,k-i}$ and in $\Gamma_{3,k-i+1}$. Summing up, the remaining edges appear in at least two of the access structures.

If we remove from the graph $\left(\Gamma^{(k,2k)}\right)_0^*$ the vertices of players $1, k, k + 1, 2k$ and the edges involving them, we obtain the bipartite graph corresponding to $\left(\Gamma^{(k-2,2(k-2))}\right)_0^*$. By the induction hypothesis (applied to $k' = k - 2$), there is a $(k - 2)$-decomposition for $\left(\Gamma^{(k-2,2(k-2))}\right)_0^*$ where each of the players $2, 3, \dots, k - 1, k + 2, k + 3, \dots, 2k - 1$ appears in at most ℓ_{k-2} of the (ideal and linear) access structures.

Summing up, we finish with a k-decomposition for the initial $\left(\Gamma^{(k,2k)}\right)_0^*$, where players $1, k, k + 1, 2k$ appear in $2k - 1$ access structures, and the rest of players appear in at most $k + 1 + \ell_{k-2}$ access structures.

If k is even, we have $\ell_{k-2} = \frac{(k-2)(k+2)}{4}$ and so each player appears in at most $\ell_k = k + 1 + \frac{(k-2)(k+2)}{4} = \frac{k^2 + 4k}{4}$ access structures.

If k is odd, we have $\ell_{k-2} = \frac{(k-2)^2 + 4(k-2) - 1}{4} = \frac{k^2 - 5}{4}$ and so each player appears in at most $\ell_k = k + 1 + \frac{k^2 - 5}{4} = \frac{k^2 + 4k - 1}{4}$ access structures. $\qquad\square$

Theorem 8. *For any $k \geq 2$, it holds:*

- *if k is even, then $\rho_{(k,2k)} \geq \frac{4}{k+4}$,*
- *if k is odd, then $\rho_{(k,2k)} \geq \frac{4k}{k^2 + 4k - 1}$.*

Proof. Applying Theorem 2 to the k-decomposition of $\left(\Gamma^{(k,2k)}\right)_0^*$ described in (the proof of) Lemma 5, we conclude that:

- if k is even, then $\rho_{(k,2k)^*} \geq \frac{4}{k+4}$,
- if k is odd, then $\rho_{(k,2k)^*} \geq \frac{4k}{k^2 + 4k - 1}$.

Since all the secret sharing schemes involved in (the proof of) Theorem 2 and Lemma 5 are linear, we have (by Theorem 3) that there exist linear secret sharing schemes with the same information rates for the dual of $\left(\Gamma^{(k,2k)}\right)^*$, which is $\Gamma^{(k,2k)}$. $\qquad\square$

5.3 Bounds on $\rho_{(k,n)}$ and Characterization of Ideal (k, n)-Consecutive Access Structures

Combining the results in Theorems 7 and 8 and Lemmas 1 and 4, we obtain the following bounds on $\rho_{(k,n)}$.

Theorem 9. *Let* $1 \leq k \leq n$ *be positive integers. It holds:*

- *if* $n \leq 2k$*, then:*
  - *if* $n - k$ *is even, then* $\frac{4}{n-k+4} \leq \rho_{(k,n)} \leq \frac{n-k}{2(n-k)-1}$*,*
  - *if* $n - k$ *is odd, then* $\frac{4(n-k)}{(n-k)^2+4(n-k)-1} \leq \rho_{(k,n)} \leq \frac{n-k}{2(n-k)-1}$*,*
- *if* $n > 2k$*, then:*
  - *if* k *is even, then* $\frac{2}{k+4} \leq \rho_{(k,n)} \leq \frac{k}{2k-1}$*,*
  - *if* k *is odd, then* $\frac{2k}{k^2+4k-1} \leq \rho_{(k,n)} \leq \frac{k}{2k-1}$*.*

We can also give a theorem to characterize the ideal (k, n)-consecutive structures. The pattern of the theorem is the same as in the characterization of ideal access structures for some other families, including graph access structures [4,5,21] or bipartite access structures [19], among others [15–17]. That is, ideal and vector space access structures are equivalent, and there does not exist a (k, n)-consecutive access structure Γ with $\frac{2}{3} < \rho(\Gamma) < 1$.

Theorem 10. *Let* Γ *be a* (k, n)*-consecutive access structure on a set* $\mathcal{P}$ *of* n *participants, with* $1 \leq k \leq n$*. Then, the following conditions are equivalent:*

(i) Γ *is an ideal access structure.*
(ii) $\rho(\Gamma) > \frac{2}{3}$*.*
(iii) Γ *is a vector space access structure.*
(iv) $k = 1$*,* $k = n - 1$ *or* $k = n$*.*

Proof. We know that (iv) implies (iii), which implies (i); and trivially (i) implies (ii). From Theorem 9 we obtain that no (iv) implies $\rho(\Gamma) \leq \frac{2}{3}$, and so (ii) implies (iv). So the equivalence of the four statements is proved. $\square$

5.4 A Tighter Lower Bound on $\rho_{(4,8)}$

From the results in Sect. 5, we know that $\frac{4}{k+4} \leq \rho_{(k,2k)} \leq \frac{k}{2k-1}$. Therefore, there is a big gap between the lower and the upper bounds on $\rho_{(k,2k)}$. It is an interesting open problem to find better bounds that narrow this gap.

In particular, the lower bounds of Theorem 8 are not always tight, as we show now with a better bound for $\rho_{(4,8)}$. For $k = 4$, the lower bound obtained by applying Theorem 8 is $\rho_{(4,8)} \geq \frac{4}{k+4} = \frac{1}{2}$.

Proposition 3. $\rho_{(4,8)} \geq \frac{6}{11}$.

Proof. We have $\Gamma_0^{(4,8)} = \{\{1,2,3,4\}, \{2,3,4,5\}, \{3,4,5,6\}, \{4,5,6,7\}, \{5,6,7,8\}\}$.

We consider the following λ-decomposition of $\Gamma^{(4,8)}$ into nine access structures (we describe the basis of these access structures, below):

$$\Gamma_1 = \{\{1,2,3,4\}, \{2,3,4,5\}, \{3,4,5,6\}, \{4,5,6,7\}\},$$
$$\Gamma_2 = \{\{1,2,3,4\}, \{2,3,4,5\}, \{3,4,5,6\}, \{5,6,7,8\}\},$$
$$\Gamma_3 = \{\{1,2,3,4\}, \{2,3,4,5\}, \{4,5,6,7\}, \{5,6,7,8\}\},$$
$$\Gamma_4 = \{\{1,2,3,4\}, \{3,4,5,6\}, \{4,5,6,7\}, \{5,6,7,8\}\},$$
$$\Gamma_5 = \{\{2,3,4,5\}, \{3,4,5,6\}, \{4,5,6,7\}, \{5,6,7,8\}\},$$
$$\Gamma_6 = \{\{1,2,3,4\}, \{2,3,4,5\}, \{3,4,5,6\}\},$$
$$\Gamma_7 = \{\{3,4,5,6\}, \{4,5,6,7\}, \{5,6,7,8\}\},$$
$$\Gamma_8 = \{\{1,2,3,4\}, \{2,3,4,5\}\},$$
$$\Gamma_9 = \{\{4,5,6,7\}, \{5,6,7,8\}\}.$$

We have that each minimal subset of $\Gamma^{(3,6)}$ appears in $\lambda = 6$ of the access structures $\Gamma_1, \ldots, \Gamma_9$.

A secret sharing scheme Σ_1 for Γ_1, to share a secret $s \in S$, gives a random single share $s_4 \in S$ to player 4, and then distributes $\tilde{s} = s - s_4$ among the other players, by choosing $s_2^{(1)}, s_3^{(1)}, s_3^{(2)}, s_6^{(2)}$ randomly and independently, and defining $s_1 = \tilde{s} - s_2^{(1)} - s_3^{(1)}$, $s_2^{(2)} = s_6^{(1)} = \tilde{s} - s_5 - s_3^{(2)}$ and $s_7 = \tilde{s} - s_5 - s_6^{(2)}$. In this way, we have $\rho_1(\Sigma_1) = \rho_4(\Sigma_1) = \rho_5(\Sigma_1) = \rho_7(\Sigma_1) = 1$, and $\rho_2(\Sigma_1) = \rho_3(\Sigma_1) = \rho_6(\Sigma_1) = \frac{1}{2}$.

A secret sharing scheme Σ_2 for Γ_2, to share a secret $s \in S$, chooses random values $s_1, s_3, s_4, s_5^{(1)}, s_6^{(2)}, s_7, s_8$ randomly and independently, and defines $s_2^{(1)} = s - s_1 - s_3 - s_4$, $s_2^{(2)} = s_6^{(1)} = s - s_3 - s_4 - s_5^{(1)}$ and $s_5^{(2)} = s - s_6^{(2)} - s_7 - s_8$. In this way, we have $\rho_1(\Sigma_2) = \rho_3(\Sigma_2) = \rho_4(\Sigma_2) = \rho_7(\Sigma_2) = \rho_8(\Sigma_2) = 1$, and $\rho_2(\Sigma_2) = \rho_5(\Sigma_2) = \rho_6(\Sigma_2) = \frac{1}{2}$.

A secret sharing scheme Σ_3 for Γ_3, to share a secret $s \in S$, chooses random values $s_2, s_3, s_4^{(1)}, s_5^{(2)}, s_6, s_7$ randomly and independently, and defines $s_1 = s_4^{(1)} = s - s_2 - s_3 - s_4^{(1)}$ and $s_4^{(2)} = s_8 = s - s_5^{(2)} - s_6 - s_7$. In this way, we have $\rho_1(\Sigma_3) = \rho_2(\Sigma_3) = \rho_3(\Sigma_3) = \rho_6(\Sigma_3) = \rho_7(\Sigma_3) = \rho_8(\Sigma_3) = 1$, and $\rho_4(\Sigma_3) = \rho_5(\Sigma_3) = \frac{1}{2}$.

A secret sharing scheme Σ_4 for Γ_4, to share a secret $s \in S$, chooses random values $s_1, s_2, s_3^{(1)}, s_4^{(2)}, s_5, s_6, s_8$ randomly and independently, and defines $s_4^{(1)} = s - s_1 - s_2 - s_3^{(1)}$, $s_3^{(2)} = s_7^{(1)} = s - s_5 - s_6 - s_4^{(2)}$ and $s_7^{(2)} = s - s_5 - s_6 - s_8$. In this way, we have $\rho_1(\Sigma_4) = \rho_2(\Sigma_4) = \rho_5(\Sigma_4) = \rho_6(\Sigma_4) = \rho_8(\Sigma_4) = 1$, and $\rho_3(\Sigma_4) = \rho_4(\Sigma_4) = \rho_7(\Sigma_4) = \frac{1}{2}$.

A secret sharing scheme Σ_5 for Γ_5, to share a secret $s \in S$, gives a random single share $s_5 \in S$ to player 5, and then distributes $\tilde{s} = s - s_5$ among the other players, by choosing $s_2, s_4, s_6^{(1)}, s_6^{(2)}, s_7^{(1)}$ randomly and independently, and defining $s_3^{(1)} = \tilde{s} - s_2 - s_4$, $s_3^{(2)} = s_7^{(1)} = \tilde{s} - s_4 - s_6^{(1)}$ and $s_8 = \tilde{s} - s_6^{(2)} - s_7^{(2)}$. In this way, we have $\rho_2(\Sigma_5) = \rho_4(\Sigma_5) = \rho_5(\Sigma_5) = \rho_8(\Sigma_5) = 1$, and $\rho_3(\Sigma_5) = \rho_6(\Sigma_5) = \rho_7(\Sigma_5) = \frac{1}{2}$.

A secret sharing scheme Σ_6 for Γ_6, to share a secret $s \in S$, gives a random share $s_3 \in S$ to player 3 and a random share $s_4 \in S$ to player 4, and then distributes $\tilde{s} = s - s_3 - s_4$ among the other players, by choosing s_1, s_5 randomly and independently, and defining $s_2^{(1)} = \tilde{s} - s_1$ and $s_2^{(2)} = s_6 = \tilde{s} - s_5$. We have $\rho_1(\Sigma_6) = \rho_3(\Sigma_6) = \rho_4(\Sigma_6) = \rho_5(\Sigma_6) = \rho_6(\Sigma_6) = 1$, and $\rho_2(\Sigma_6) = \frac{1}{2}$.

A secret sharing scheme Σ_7 for Γ_7, to share a secret $s \in S$, gives a random share $s_5 \in S$ to player 5 and a random share $s_6 \in S$ to player 6, and then

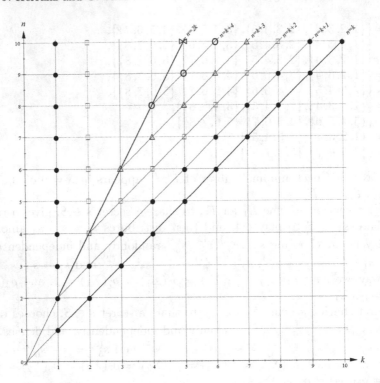

Fig. 1. Some values of $\rho_{(k,n)}$. $\bullet$ is for $\rho_{(k,n)} = 1$ (ideal access structures), $\square$ is for $\rho_{(k,n)} = \frac{2}{3}$, $\triangle$ is for $\rho_{(k,n)} = \frac{3}{5}$. Finally, $\bigcirc$ is for $\rho_{(k,n)} = \rho_{(4,8)}$ and $\bowtie$ is for $\rho_{(k,n)} = \rho_{(5,10)}$ (unknown exact values). The exact values of $\rho_{(k,n)}$ with $k \geq 3$ and $n > 2k$ are also unknown.

distributes $\tilde{s} = s - s_5 - s_6$ among the other players, by choosing s_4, s_8 randomly and independently, and defining $s_3 = s_7^{(1)} = \tilde{s} - s_4$ and $s_7^{(2)} = \tilde{s} - s_8$. We have $\rho_3(\Sigma_7) = \rho_4(\Sigma_7) = \rho_5(\Sigma_7) = \rho_6(\Sigma_7) = \rho_8(\Sigma_7) = 1$, and $\rho_7(\Sigma_7) = \frac{1}{2}$.

Finally, access structures Γ_8 and Γ_9 are both ideal, since each of them has two minimal subsets. Therefore, we have $\rho_1(\Sigma_8) = \ldots = \rho_5(\Sigma_8) = 1$ and $\rho_4(\Sigma_9) = \ldots = \rho_8(\Sigma_9) = 1$.

The maximum value for $\sum_{h \text{ s.t. } j \in P_h} \frac{1}{\rho_j(\Sigma_h)}$ is achieved by players $j = 2, 3, 4, 5, 6, 7$, and is equal to 11. Therefore, applying Theorem 2, we obtain the lower bound $\rho_{(4,8)} \geq \frac{6}{11}$. $\qquad\square$

6   Conclusions

We have studied in this work the family of (k, n)-consecutive access structures, which may appear in natural applications of distributed cryptographic protocols. We have proved that (k, n)-consecutive access structures are ideal if and only if $k = 1, n-1, n$. For the other cases, we have proved some lower and upper bounds on the information rate of these access structures. In particular, our results show that some statement made in previous work [18] is wrong.

Figure 1 illustrates some of (the connections between) the values of $\rho_{(k,n)}$ that we have proved, for $1 \leq k \leq n \leq 10$. In particular, the exact value of the optimal information rate $\rho_{(k,n)}$ is now known for all the cases $k = n, n - 1, n - 2, n - 3$.

We stress that there is in general a big gap between the upper and the lower bounds on $\rho_{(k,n)}$ that we have obtained in this paper. Narrowing this gap remains as an interesting open problem for future work.

Acknowledgments. This work is partially supported by Spanish Ministry of Economy and Competitiveness, under Project MTM2016-77213-R.

References

1. Beimel, A., Tassa, T., Weinreb, E.: Characterizing ideal weighted threshold secret sharing. SIAM J. Discret. Math. **22**(1), 360–397 (2008)
2. Blakley, G.R.: Safeguarding cryptographic keys. In: AFIPS Conference Proceedings, vol. 48, pp. 313–317 (1979)
3. Blundo, C., De Santis, A., De Simone, R., Vaccaro, U.: Tight bounds on the information rate of secret sharing schemes. Des. Codes Cryptogr. **11**(2), 107–122 (1997)
4. Blundo, C., De Santis, A., Stinson, D.R., Vaccaro, U.: Graph decompositions and secret sharing schemes. J. Cryptol. **8**(1), 39–64 (1995)
5. Brickell, E.F., Davenport, D.M.: On the classification of ideal secret sharing schemes. J. Cryptol. **4**, 123–134 (1991)
6. Csirmaz, L., Tardos, G.: Optimal information rate of secret sharing schemes on trees. IEEE Trans. Inf. Theory **59**(4), 2527–2530 (2013)
7. Di Crescenzo, G., Galdi, C.: Hypergraph decomposition and secret sharing. Discret. Appl. Math. **157**(5), 928–946 (2009)
8. Farràs, O., Kaced, T., Martín, S., Padró, C.: Improving the linear programming technique in the search for lower bounds in secret sharing. In: Nielsen, J.B., Rijmen, V. (eds.) EUROCRYPT 2018. LNCS, vol. 10820, pp. 597–621. Springer, Cham (2018). https://doi.org/10.1007/978-3-319-78381-9_22
9. Farràs, O., Martí-Farré, J., Padró, C.: Ideal multipartite secret sharing schemes. J. Cryptol. **25**(3), 434–463 (2012)
10. Farràs, O., Padró, C.: Ideal hierarchical secret sharing schemes. IEEE Trans. Inf. Theory **58**(5), 3273–3286 (2012)
11. Herranz, J., Sáez, G.: New results on multipartite access structures. IET Proc. Inf. Secur. **153**(4), 153–162 (2006)
12. Jackson, W.A., Martin, K.M.: Geometric secret sharing schemes and their duals. Des. Codes Cryptogr. **4**(1), 83–95 (1994)
13. Jackson, W.A., Martin, K.M.: Perfect secret sharing schemes on five participants. Des. Codes Cryptogr. **9**(3), 267–286 (1996)
14. Juels, A., Pappu, R., Parno, B.: Unidirectional key distribution across time and space with applications to RFID security. In: Proceedings of the USENIX Security Symposium 2008, pp. 75–90 (2008)
15. Martí-Farré, J., Padró, C.: Secret sharing schemes on sparse homogeneous access structures with rank three. Electron. J. Comb. **11**(1), 72 (2004)
16. Martí-Farré, J., Padró, C.: Secret sharing schemes with three or four minimal qualified subsets. Des. Codes Cryptogr. **34**(1), 17–34 (2005)

17. Martí-Farré, J., Padró, C.: Secret sharing schemes on access structures with intersection number equal to one. Discret. Appl. Math. **154**(3), 552–563 (2006)
18. Martín, A., Pereira, J., Rodríguez, G.: A secret sharing scheme based on cellular automata. Appl. Math. Comput. **170**(2), 1356–1364 (2005)
19. Padró, C., Sáez, G.: Secret sharing schemes with bipartite access structure. IEEE Trans. Inf. Theory **46**(7), 2596–2604 (2000)
20. Shamir, A.: How to share a secret. Commun. ACM **22**, 612–613 (1979)
21. Stinson, D.R.: Decomposition constructions for secret sharing schemes. IEEE Trans. Inf. Theory **40**(1), 118–125 (1994)
22. Tassa, T.: Hierarchical threshold secret sharing. J. Cryptol. **20**(2), 237–264 (2007)

Extending a Framework for Biometric Visual Cryptography

Koray Karabina[✉] and Angela Robinson

Florida Atlantic University, Boca Raton, USA
kkarabina@fau.edu, arobin65@my.fau.edu

Abstract. Recently, a general framework to help assess the security of extended biometric visual cryptographic schemes (e-BVC) was proposed, formalizing the notion of perfect resistance against false authentication. In this paper, we extend this framework with respect to indistinguishability and index privacy notions. Based on our definitions, we present theoretical analysis of e-BVC schemes and propose new attack strategies. We show that the general framework can be applied to derive new and quantifiable upper bounds on the security of e-BVC schemes. We also discuss the practical impact of our attacks in detail and present several case analyses for a recent implementation of a face recognition protocol.

1 Introduction

In a (t, n)-threshold secret sharing scheme [3, 11], a secret is divided into n shares, and the secret can be recovered if and only if t or more shares are available. More interestingly, any collection of at most $(t - 1)$ shares does not reveal any information about the secret. Visual cryptographic (VC) schemes [2, 7] use secret sharing algorithms as a building block, and they allow secure distribution of images over several databases in such a way that the recovery of a secret image can be performed at almost no cost. In [1, 7], it was described how to extend VC (e-VC) so that the secret shares are now meaningful images. Applications of e-VC to biometrics (e-BVC) have appeared in several research papers [5, 6, 8–10]. On the other hand, there is a lack in the formal security analysis of e-BVC schemes.

One example of an e-BVC scheme is [10]. In this work, the authors present a face recognition protocol with $t = n = 2$. A secret face image α is split into two shares so that the two shares are not sheets of random pixels, as in [7]. Instead, the two shares appear as face images. The motivation for this objective in [10] is to avoid drawing attention from an interceptor. The authors propose that a passive eavesdropper who, upon seeing shares containing random sets of pixels, would expect the presence of a secret image [10]. The authors make several security claims based on experimental results. For example, the authors claim that a single sheet image reveals nothing about the secret original image.

© Springer Nature Switzerland AG 2018
J. Camenisch and P. Papadimitratos (Eds.): CANS 2018, LNCS 11124, pp. 481–494, 2018.
https://doi.org/10.1007/978-3-030-00434-7_24

In a recent paper [4], a general framework was proposed to help assess the security of e-BVC, and a formal notion of *perfect resistance against false authentication* was presented. In particular, a new attack was proposed in [4] increasing the success probability of a false authentication attack against one of the protocols in [10] from 0.005 to 0.45. In this paper, we extend the framework in [4] with respect to *indistinguishability* and *index privacy* notions. The *index privacy* notion was not considered in [10], but we show that index recovery is a practical threat model that should be considered in a biometric authentication scheme. Our contributions can be summarized as follows:

1. In Sect. 2, we formalize the security notion of *sheet indistinguishability* and define *perfect indistinguishability* for BVC schemes. We present two attacks for challenging sheet indistinguishability, namely a *guessing attack* and a *new distinguishing attack*. As a result, we are able to provide a necessary condition for a BVC scheme to achieve *perfect indistinguishability*; see Corollary 1. Our case analysis in Sect. 2.3 shows that the face recognition protocol in [10] does not achieve perfect indistinguishability.

2. In order to demonstrate the practical impact of our indistinguishability notion, we introduce the *index recovery notion* and define *perfect index privacy* for BVC schemes in Sect. 3. We present a new index recovery attack and obtain a necessary condition for satisfying perfect index privacy; see Corollary 2. In particular, we show that [10] does not achieve *perfect index privacy*; see Sect. 3.2. We find that the success probability of an adversary can be at least twice better than that of random guess when attacking the given IMM database and Dataset G in [10]. See Sect. 3.2 for more details.

Notation. In the rest of this paper, we inherit the same notation from [4], and denote a BVC scheme by the tuple $(\Omega, S, M, \mathcal{D}_n, \mathcal{R}_t, \mathcal{M}, \mathcal{A}_m)$, where Ω is the space of biometric images, and S a space of images (not necessarily biometric). Note that Ω is a subset of S. M is a well-ordered set with "$\geq$" the comparison operator. We have the following oracles for a formal description BVC.

1. **Decomposition:**
$$\mathcal{D}_n : \Omega \to \underbrace{S \times S \times \cdots \times S}_{n \text{ copies}},$$

   which decomposes one biometric image into n images, also known as *sheets*.

2. **Reconstruction:**
$$\mathcal{R}_t : \underbrace{S \times S \times \cdots \times S}_{t \text{ copies}} \to \Omega,$$

   which takes t sheets as input, and constructs a biometric image.

3. **Matching:**
$$\mathcal{M} : \Omega \times \Omega \to M,$$

   which takes a pair of biometric images as input, and outputs a matching score $m_0 \in M$.

4. Authentication:

$$\mathcal{A}_m : \Omega \times \underbrace{S \times S \times \cdots \times S}_{t \text{ copies}} \to \{0,1\},$$

where $m \in M$ is the matching threshold of the authentication protocol. $\mathcal{A}_m$ takes a tuple $(\alpha, s_1, s_2, \ldots s_t)$, $\alpha \in \Omega$, $s_i \in S$ as input. If $\beta = \mathcal{R}_t(s_1, s_2, \ldots, s_t)$ and $m_0 = \mathcal{M}(\alpha, \beta)$, then the output of $\mathcal{A}_m$ is 1 if $m_0 \geq m$, indicating a successful authentication. Otherwise, $\mathcal{A}_m$ outputs 0.

2 Indistinguishability Notion

In this section, we define the *sheet indistinguishability* notion for BVC schemes. Our motivation is to measure the advantage of an adversary who is trying to distinguish between pairs of genuine and imposter biometric images, defined below, by exploiting the sheets of the images. Note that adversaries should not have any non-trivial advantage over random guessing in an ideal BVC scheme because a sheet of a biometric image is not supposed to reveal any information about the image itself.

First, we recall some common definitions in biometrics. A *genuine pair* is a pair of biometric images or some cryptographic transformation of images derived from the same person or entity. An *imposter pair* is a pair of biometric images which do not correspond to the same person. Given some matching oracle $\mathcal{M}$ and authentication oracle $\mathcal{A}_m$, we define a *Genuine Accept* as the event that the matching oracle $\mathcal{M}$ computes a matching score $m_0 \geq m$, given a genuine pair of biometric images. That is, $\mathcal{A}_m(\alpha, \beta) = 1$ for a genuine pair (α, β). A *False Reject* is the event that $\mathcal{A}_m(\alpha, \beta) = 0$ for a genuine pair (α, β). A *Genuine Reject* is the event that $\mathcal{M}$ computes $m_0 < m$, given an imposter pair. That is, $\mathcal{A}_m(\alpha, \beta) = 0$ for an imposter pair (α, β). A *False Accept* is the event that $\mathcal{A}_m(\alpha, \beta) = 1$ for an imposter pair (α, β). *False Reject Rate* $\mathrm{FRR}(m)$ with respect to a matching threshold m is computed by counting the number of false rejects found from a list of genuine pairs, and dividing this number by the size of the list. Similarly, *False Accept Rate* $\mathrm{FAR}(m)$ with respect to a matching threshold m is computed by counting the number of false accepts found from a list of imposter pairs, and diving this number by the size of the list.

2.1 Indistinguishability Game

Let $(\Omega, S, M, \mathcal{D}_n, \mathcal{R}_t, \mathcal{M}, \mathcal{A}_m)$ represent a BVC scheme. For simplicity, we assume $t = n = 2$. We define the sheet indistinguishability of BVC with the following game $\mathsf{G}_{\mathsf{IND}}$. Our definition is inspired from the indistinguishability definition in [12]. In $\mathsf{G}_{\mathsf{IND}}$, $\mathcal{A}$ is a computationally bounded adversary and $\mathcal{C}$ represents a challenger.

Indistinguishability Game $\mathsf{G}_{\mathsf{IND}}$

1. The challenger $\mathcal{C}$ generates a private biometric data $\alpha \in \Omega$ uniformly at random.
2. $\mathcal{C}$ selects uniformly at random a bit $b \in \{0,1\}$. If $b = 0$, then $\mathcal{C}$ generates another private biometric data $\beta \in \Omega$ uniformly at random such that (α, β) is an imposter pair. If $b = 1$, then $\mathcal{C}$ generates some private biometric data $\beta \in \Omega$ uniformly at random such that (α, β) is a genuine pair. The challenger sends the pair $(s_1(\alpha), s_1(\beta))$ to the adversary, where $\mathcal{D}_2(\alpha) = (s_1(\alpha), s_2(\alpha))$ as before.
3. $\mathcal{A}$ guesses $b' \in \{0,1\}$. $\mathcal{A}$ wins $\mathsf{G}_{\mathsf{IND}}$ if $b' = b$.

We define the success probability of $\mathcal{A}$ in $\mathsf{G}_{\mathsf{IND}}$ as $\Pr[b' = b]$, and the advantage of $\mathcal{A}$ attacking an e-BVC scheme in $\mathsf{G}_{\mathsf{IND}}$ as

$$\mathsf{Adv}_{\mathcal{A}}^{\mathsf{IND}} = \left| \Pr[b' = b] - \frac{1}{2} \right|.$$

We say that an e-BVC scheme preserves sheet indistinguishability if $\mathsf{Adv}_{\mathcal{A}}^{\mathsf{IND}}$ is negligible for all possible $\mathcal{A}$. In particular, we say an e-BVC achieves *perfect indistinguishability* if $\mathsf{Adv}_{\mathcal{A}}^{\mathsf{IND}} = 0$ for all possible $\mathcal{A}$.

2.2   Indistinguishability Attacks

In this section, we analyze the security of a general e-BVC scheme with respect to the indistinguishability notion defined in Sect. 2.1.

Guessing Attack. Suppose the adversary $\mathcal{A}$ plays the indistinguishability game $\mathsf{G}_{\mathsf{IND}}$. Then $\mathcal{A}$ receives some tuple $(s_1(\alpha), s_1(\beta))$ from the challenger $\mathcal{C}$ and tries to produce a bit b' so that $b' = b$. In the guessing attack, $\mathcal{A}$ guesses b by choosing a bit b' uniformly at random from $\{0,1\}$. Clearly, we have the following theorem.

Theorem 1. *The success probability of $\mathcal{A}$ in the guessing attack is $\Pr[b' = b] = \frac{1}{2}$ and the advantage of $\mathcal{A}$ is $\mathsf{Adv}_{\mathcal{A}}^{\mathsf{IND}} = 0$.*

In order to gain a non-trivial adversarial advantage (rather than $\mathsf{Adv}_{\mathcal{A}}^{\mathsf{IND}} = 0$ as in the case of a guessing attack), we present a new distinguishing attack (NDA), where the adversary does not simply guess a bit b'. We assume that $\mathcal{A}$ is provided with explicit definitions of algorithms and parameters in the e-BVC scheme under attack. In particular, $\mathcal{A}$ is assumed to have access to the matching oracle $\mathcal{M}$ and knows the matching threshold m. This is a valid assumption because many protocols, such as [10], employ commercial software that can be purchased by anyone.

Before we describe the NDA, we define new genuine accept and genuine reject notions. Our definitions are analogous to the standard definitions of genuine accept and genuine reject notions except that they are specifically defined for the sheets rather than the original biometric images.

Definition 1. *Let* $(\Omega, S, M, \mathcal{D}_n, \mathcal{R}_t, \mathcal{M}, \mathcal{A}_m)$ *represent an e-BVC scheme.* $\text{GAR}'(m)$ *(or simply* GAR'*) is defined to be a function of the matching threshold* m *and denotes the rate at which* $\mathcal{M}(s_1(\alpha), s_1(\beta)) \geq m$ *given that* (α, β) *is a genuine pair. Similarly,* $\text{GRR}'(m)$ *(or, simply* GRR'*) is a function of* m *and denotes the rate at which* $\mathcal{M}(s_1(\alpha), s_1(\beta)) < m$ *given that* (α, β) *is an imposter pair.*

GAR' and GRR' definitions play a key role in analyzing the success probability of adversaries in our framework. More concretely, in an ideal e-BVC scheme one would intuitively expect that $\text{GAR}' \approx 0$ and $\text{GRR}' \approx 1$ because a sheet of a biometric image is not supposed to reveal any information about the image itself. In fact, our analysis throughout this paper confirms this intuition and provides a quantitative security analysis of e-BVC schemes; see Corollarys 1 and 2.

A New Distinguishing Attack (NDA). Suppose $\mathcal{A}$ plays $\mathsf{G}_{\mathsf{IND}}$ and receives $(s_1(\alpha), s_1(\beta))$ from $\mathcal{C}$. Then $\mathcal{A}$ queries the matching oracle $\mathcal{M}$ with this pair. If the matching score $m_0 = \mathcal{M}(s_1(\alpha), s_1(\beta)) \geq m$, then the adversary outputs $b' = 1$. Otherwise, if $m_0 < m$, the adversary outputs $b' = 0$.

Theorem 2. *The success probability of* $\mathcal{A}$ *in NDA is*

$$\Pr[b' = b] = \frac{1}{2}(\text{GAR}' + \text{GRR}') \tag{1}$$

and the advantage of $\mathcal{A}$ *is*

$$\mathsf{Adv}_{\mathcal{A}}^{\mathsf{IND}} = \frac{1}{2}|\text{GAR}' + \text{GRR}' - 1|, \tag{2}$$

Proof. The success probability of $\mathcal{A}$ in NDA can be computed as

$$\Pr[b' = b] = \Pr[b = 0]\Pr[b' = 0|b = 0] + \tag{3}$$
$$\Pr[b = 1]\Pr[b' = 1|b = 1]$$

$$= \frac{1}{2}\left(\Pr[b' = 0|b = 0] + \Pr[b' = 1|b = 1]\right). \tag{4}$$

Recall that when $b = 0$, the challenger selects an imposter pair (α, β). In NDA, $\mathcal{A}$ computes the matching score $\mathcal{M}(s_1(\alpha), s_1(\beta))$ and if this value is less than m, $\mathcal{A}$ outputs $b' = 0$. Similarly, when $b = 1$, $\mathcal{C}$ selects a genuine pair (α, β). $\mathcal{A}$ computes the matching score $\mathcal{M}(s_1(\alpha), s_1(\beta))$ and if this value is greater than or equal to m, $\mathcal{A}$ outputs $b' = 1$. Therefore, we can rewrite (4) as follows:

$$\Pr[b' = b] = \frac{1}{2}\Pr[\mathcal{M}(s_1(\alpha), s_1(\beta)) < m | (\alpha, \beta) \text{ Imposter}] \tag{5}$$

$$+ \frac{1}{2}\Pr[\mathcal{M}(s_1(\alpha), s_1(\beta)) \geq m | (\alpha, \beta) \text{ Genuine}] \tag{6}$$

$$= \frac{1}{2}(\text{GRR}' + \text{GAR}') \tag{7}$$

It follows that

$$\mathsf{Adv}_{\mathcal{A}}^{\mathsf{IND}} = \left|\Pr[b' = b] - \frac{1}{2}\right| = \frac{1}{2}|(\text{GRR}' + \text{GAR}') - 1|. \tag{8}$$

Our analysis yields a necessary condition for the perfect indistinguishability of an e-BVC scheme as stated in the following corollary.

Corollary 1. *An e-BVC scheme cannot achieve perfect indistinguishability if* $\mathrm{GAR}' + \mathrm{GRR}' \neq 1$.

Proof. It is clear from (2) that $\mathrm{GAR}' + \mathrm{GRR}' = 1$ is necessary for the perfect indistinguishability of a BVC scheme.

Remark 1. Satisfying the equality $\mathrm{GAR}' + \mathrm{GRR}' = 1$ may not guarantee the perfect indistinguishability of an e-BVC scheme because NDA is just one way of attacking the system and there may exist other attack methods.

Remark 2. We have described the game $\mathsf{G}_{\mathsf{IND}}$ in which $\mathcal{A}$ receives the pair $(s_1(\alpha), s_1(\beta))$ from $\mathcal{C}$. Similarly, $\mathsf{G}_{\mathsf{IND}}$ can be defined such that $\mathcal{A}$ receives the pair $(s_2(\alpha), s_2(\beta))$ from $\mathcal{C}$. The advantage of $\mathcal{A}$ may be different in these two cases; see Sect. 2.3 for example.

2.3   A Case Analysis for RO-e-BVC

As mentioned before in Sect. 1, a visual face recognition protocol (RO-e-BVC) was proposed and implemented in [10]. Several experiments were conducted in [10] to analyze the security and privacy-preserving properties of RO-e-BVC. In particular, Experiment 7 in [10] considers the possibility of recovering a secret biometric image given only the first (second) copies of sheet images $s_1(\alpha)$ $(s_2(\alpha))$ as α runs through all enrolled images in a given database. It is noted in [10] that experimental results confirm the difficulty of exposing the identity of the secret face image by using the sheets alone. However, we are not aware of a concrete analysis or a proof of this claim. In this section, we apply our framework and security model to present a formal security analysis of the RO-e-BVC scheme with respect to the indistinguishability notion and show that RO-e-BVC does not achieve perfect indistinguishability.

In Experiment 7 in [10], 6 different subexperiments are performed. In particular, the face recognition protocol in [10] is implemented for 2 different databases (IMM and XM2VTS) and each database is considered with respect to 3 different datasets (A, F, and G) with a various number of host images. In Table IX in [10], equal error rates are reported in three different categories:

- Matching reconstructed images i.e., $\mathcal{R}_2((s_1(\alpha), s_2(\alpha))$ vs. $\mathcal{R}_2((s_1(\beta), s_2(\beta))$;
- Matching the first sheets of the decomposed images i.e., $s_1(\alpha)$ vs. $s_1(\beta)$; and
- Matching the second sheets of the decomposed images i.e., $s_2(\alpha)$ vs. $s_2(\beta)$.
  Note that, an equal error rate e in the second (and third) category yields $\mathrm{GAR}' = \mathrm{GRR}' = 1 - e$ in Theorem 2, which determines the advantage of an attacker as
  $$\mathsf{Adv}_{\mathcal{A}}^{\mathsf{IND}} = \frac{1}{2}|1 - 2e|.$$

Based on the equal error rates reported in Table IX in [10], we summarize in Table 1 the advantage of $\mathcal{A}$ in G_{IND} attacking RO-e-BVC under the new distinguishability attack (NDA).

As seen in Table 1, various databases and datasets yield various results. The adversarial advantage is non-zero in all of the cases and so RO-e-BVC does not achieve perfect indistinguishability.

Table 1. The advantage of $\mathcal{A}$ in G_{IND} (in percentages): attacking RO-e-BVC under the new distinguishability attack.

Database	IMM	XM2	IMM	XM2	IMM	XM2
Dataset	A	A	F	F	G	G
$(s_1$ vs. $s_1)$ $Adv_{\mathcal{A}}^{IND}$	5.3	14.0	14.3	18.3	16.2	12.2
$(s_2$ vs. $s_2)$ $Adv_{\mathcal{A}}^{IND}$	5.8	16.2	10.0	11.7	10.5	10.7

3 Practical Impact of the New Distinguishing Attack: Index Recovery Notion

In this section, we further explore the practical impact of the advantage of an adversary in the indistinguishability game G_{IND}. In particular, we argue that the adversarial advantage can be exploited in a more practical attack scenario. We formally define the *Index Recovery Game* G_{REC} and the notion of *index privacy*. We show that an adversary with non-zero advantage in G_{IND} can be turned into an adversary with non-zero advantage in G_{REC}; see Corollary 3. We present a case analysis for the face recognition scheme RO-e-BVC [10] and show that RO-e-BVC does not achieve *perfect index privacy*.

3.1 A Practical Attack Scenario

Consider a user, Alice, who is enrolled in two service providers, say S_1 and S_2, with her biometric images α and β, respectively. We may assume that both S_1 and S_2 employ the same biometric visual cryptographic system BVC for authentication purposes. This is a valid assumption because, for example, RO-e-BVC [10] (with the same host image datasets) can be deployed by two different service providers in practice. We further assume that the underlying BVC is represented in the framework with $(\mathcal{D}_2, \mathcal{R}_2, \mathcal{M}, \mathcal{A}_m)$. In particular, S_1 will decompose Alice's biometric information α into two sheets $s_1(\alpha)$ and $s_2(\alpha)$ and store them separately in two independent databases. Similarly, S_2 will decompose Alice's biometric information β into two sheets $s_1(\beta)$ and $s_2(\beta)$ and store them separately in two independent databases. Note that α and β may not be identical even though they form a genuine pair.

Now, suppose that an adversary $\mathcal{A}$ obtains one sheet image of Alice's biometric information, $s_1(\alpha)$, from a database of S_1 and that $\mathcal{A}$ knows Alice is a member of S_2. $\mathcal{A}$ is assumed to have access to the first sheets $s_{1,j}$ of the decomposed biometric images in S_2's database but not the second sheets $s_{2,j}$. [1] The adversary's objective is to recover the index j such that $s_{1,j} = s_1(\beta)$. Recovering index j potentially exposes sensitive information related to Alice which has been stored in the service provider. In the case of a gym or fitness center, birthdate, contact information, frequency of visits, and more may be attached to the user's index.

We formalize the index recovery attack through the index recovery game $\mathsf{G_{REC}}$. Let $(\Omega, S, M, \mathcal{D}_n, \mathcal{R}_t, \mathcal{M}, \mathcal{A}_m)$ represent a BVC scheme. For simplicity, we assume $t = n = 2$. In $\mathsf{G_{REC}}$, $\mathcal{A}$ is a computationally bounded adversary and $\mathcal{C}$ represents a challenger.

Index Recovery Game $\mathsf{G_{REC}}$

1. The challenger $\mathcal{C}$ generates a private biometric data $\alpha \in \Omega$ uniformly at random.
2. UsingFAthe decomposition oracle $\mathcal{D}_2$, $\mathcal{C}$ generates N pairs of biometric sheets $\mathcal{D}_2(\beta_j) = (s_{1,j}, s_{2,j})$ such that (α, β_j) is a genuine pair for exactly k indices chosen uniformly at random with $1 \leq k < N$. $\mathcal{C}$ also generates $\mathcal{D}_2(\alpha) = (s_1(\alpha), s_2(\alpha))$.
3. $\mathcal{C}$ sends $s_1(\alpha)$ and $\{s_{1,j}\}_{j=1}^N$ to the adversary $\mathcal{A}$.
4. $\mathcal{A}$ outputs an integer j and wins if (α, β_j) is a genuine pair.

We define the success probability of $\mathcal{A}$ in $\mathsf{G_{REC}}$ as $\Pr[j : (\alpha, \beta_j) \text{ Genuine}]$, and the advantage of $\mathcal{A}$ attacking an e-BVC scheme in $\mathsf{G_{REC}}$ as

$$\mathsf{Adv}_{\mathcal{A}}^{\mathsf{REC}} = |\Pr[j : (\alpha, \beta_j) \text{ Genuine}] - p|, \qquad (9)$$

where $0 < p = k/N < 1$. We say that an e-BVC scheme preserves *index privacy* if $\mathsf{Adv}_{\mathcal{A}}^{\mathsf{REC}}$ is negligible for all possible $\mathcal{A}$. In particular, we say an e-BVC achieves *perfect index privacy* if $\mathsf{Adv}_{\mathcal{A}}^{\mathsf{REC}} = 0$ for all possible $\mathcal{A}$.

Note that, in an index recovery attack, $\mathcal{A}$ can always choose j at random and hope that $s_{1,j} = s_1(\beta)$. This concept is formalized in the following guessing attack.

Guessing Attack. Suppose the adversary $\mathcal{A}$ plays the index recovery game $\mathsf{G_{REC}}$. Then $\mathcal{A}$ receives $s_1(\alpha)$ and $\{s_{1,j}\}_{j=1}^N$ such that, for exactly k of $s_{1,j} = s_1(\beta_j)$, (α, β_j) is a genuine pair. In the guessing attack, $\mathcal{A}$ chooses $j \in [1, N]$ uniformly at random and outputs j. Clearly, we have the following theorem.

Theorem 3. *The success probability of $\mathcal{A}$ in the guessing attack is*

$$\Pr[j : (\alpha, \beta_j) \text{ Genuine}] = k/N,$$

and the advantage of $\mathcal{A}$ is $\mathsf{Adv}_{\mathcal{A}}^{\mathsf{REC}} = 0$.

---

[1] This is a valid attack scenario because in an ideal BVC, the first sheet of a decomposed biometric image is not supposed to reveal any information about the original image.

In an ideal scheme, we would expect that $\mathcal{A}$'s success probability is no better than the success probability of a random guess and that $\mathcal{A}$ has zero advantage $\mathsf{Adv}_{\mathcal{A}}^{\mathsf{REC}} = 0$. Next, we propose a new index recovery attack and compute adversarial advantage. As a result, we obtain a necessary condition for perfect index privacy.

A New Index Recovery Attack (IND-REC). $\mathcal{A}$ receives $s_1(\alpha)$ and $\{s_{1,j}\}_{j=1}^{N}$ such that, for exactly k of $s_{1,j}$, $s_{1,j} = s_1(\beta_j)$ and (α, β_j) is a genuine pair. In the attack, $\mathcal{A}$ computes a matching score $m_j = \mathcal{M}(s_1(\alpha), s_{1,j})$ for all j, and outputs an index j for which $m_j \geq m$. If $m_j < m$ for all j, then $\mathcal{A}$ chooses $j \in [1, N]$ uniformly at random and outputs j.

Theorem 4. *Let* $p = k/N$ *with* $k \in [1, N)$. *If* $\mathrm{GAR}' = 0$, *then the success probability of* $\mathcal{A}$ *in IND-REC is* $\Pr[j : (\alpha, \beta_j) \text{ Genuine}] = p$ *and the advantage of* $\mathcal{A}$ *is* $\mathsf{Adv}_{\mathcal{A}}^{\mathsf{REC}} = 0$. *If* $\mathrm{GAR}' > 0$, *then the success probability of* $\mathcal{A}$ *in IND-REC is*

$$\Pr[j : (\alpha, \beta_j) \text{ Genuine}] = \frac{p\mathrm{GAR}'}{p\mathrm{GAR}' + (1 - p)(1 - \mathrm{GRR}')}, \tag{10}$$

and the advantage of $\mathcal{A}$ *is*

$$\mathsf{Adv}_{\mathcal{A}}^{\mathsf{REC}} = \left| \frac{(p - p^2)(\mathrm{GAR}' + \mathrm{GRR}' - 1)}{p\mathrm{GAR}' + (1 - p)(1 - \mathrm{GRR}')} \right|, \tag{11}$$

Proof. If $\mathrm{GAR}' = 0$ then $m_j = \mathcal{M}(s_1(\alpha), s_{1,j}) < m$ for all j and $\mathcal{A}$ will output $j \in [1, N]$ uniformly at random. Therefore, $\Pr[j : (\alpha, \beta_j) \text{ Genuine}] = p$ and $\mathsf{Adv}_{\mathcal{A}}^{\mathsf{REC}} = 0$. Now, assume that $\mathrm{GAR}' > 0$. The success probability of $\mathcal{A}$ in IND-REC can be computed

$$\Pr[j : (\alpha, \beta_j) \text{ Genuine}] \tag{12}$$

$$= \Pr[(\alpha, \beta_j) \text{ Genuine} | \mathcal{M}(s_1(\alpha), s_{1,j}) \geq m] \tag{13}$$

$$= \Pr[\mathcal{M}(s_1(\alpha), s_{1,j}) \geq m | (\alpha, \beta_j) \text{ Genuine}] \cdot \tag{14}$$

$$\frac{\Pr[(\alpha, \beta_j) \text{ Genuine}]}{\Pr[\mathcal{M}(s_1(\alpha), s_{1,j}) \geq m]} \tag{15}$$

$$= \mathrm{GAR}' \frac{p}{p\mathrm{GAR}' + (1 - p)(1 - \mathrm{GRR}')}, \tag{16}$$

where the last equation follows because

$$\Pr[\mathcal{M}(s_1(\alpha), s_{1,j}) \geq m]$$
$$= \Pr[(\alpha, \beta_j) \text{ Genuine}] \cdot$$
$$\Pr[\mathcal{M}(s_1(\alpha), s_{1,j}) \geq m | (\alpha, \beta_j) \text{ Genuine}]$$
$$+ \Pr[(\alpha, \beta_j) \text{ Imposter}] \cdot$$
$$\Pr[\mathcal{M}(s_1(\alpha), s_{1,j}) \geq m | (\alpha, \beta_j) \text{ Imposter}]$$
$$= \Pr[(\alpha, \beta_j) \text{ Genuine}] \cdot$$

$$\Pr[\mathcal{M}(s_1(\alpha), s_{1,j}) \geq m | (\alpha, \beta_j) \text{ Genuine}]$$
$$+ \Pr[(\alpha, \beta_j) \text{ Imposter}] \cdot$$
$$(1 - \Pr[\mathcal{M}(s_1(\alpha), s_{1,j}) < m | (\alpha, \beta) \text{ Imposter}])$$
$$= p\text{GAR}' + (1 - p)(1 - \text{GRR}')$$

Finally, we write

$$\mathsf{Adv}_{\mathcal{A}}^{\mathsf{REC}} = \left| \frac{p\text{GAR}'}{p\text{GAR}' + (1 - p)(1 - \text{GRR}')} - p \right|$$
$$= \left| \frac{(p - p^2)(\text{GAR}' + \text{GRR}' - 1)}{p\text{GAR}' + (1 - p)(1 - \text{GRR}')} \right|,$$

as required.

In Theorem 5, we derive upper and lower bounds on the success probability $\Pr[j : (\alpha, \beta_j) \text{ Genuine}]$ of an adversary in $\mathsf{G_{REC}}$.

Theorem 5. *Let p, GAR$'$, and GRR$'$ be as defined in Definition 1. If GAR$' > 0$, then the success probability $\Pr[j : (\alpha, \beta_j) \text{ Genuine}]$ of an adversary in IND-REC satisfies the following:*

1. $\Pr[j : (\alpha, \beta_j) \text{ Genuine}] = p$ *if* GAR$' +$ GRR$' = 1$.
2. $p < \Pr[j : (\alpha, \beta_j) \text{ Genuine}] < p\frac{\text{GAR}'}{1 - \text{GRR}'}$ *if* GAR$' +$ GRR$' > 1$.
3. $p\frac{\text{GAR}'}{1 - \text{GRR}'} < \Pr[j : (\alpha, \beta_j) \text{ Genuine}] < p$ *if* GAR$' +$ GRR$' < 1$.

Proof. It follows from (10) that if GAR$' +$ GRR$' = 1$, then $\Pr[j : (\alpha, \beta_j) \text{ Genuine}] = p$. If GAR$' +$ GRR$' > 1$, then, using $0 \leq (1 - \text{GRR}') < \text{GAR}'$ we can write

$$(1 - \text{GRR}') < p\text{GAR}' + (1 - p)(1 - \text{GRR}') < \text{GAR}',$$

and it follows from (10) that

$$p < \Pr[j : (\alpha, \beta_j) \text{ Genuine}] < p\frac{\text{GAR}'}{1 - \text{GRR}'}.$$

Similarly, if GAR$' +$ GRR$' < 1$, then we can show that

$$p\frac{\text{GAR}'}{1 - \text{GRR}'} < \Pr[j : (\alpha, \beta_j) \text{ Genuine}] < p.$$

Our analysis yields a necessary condition for the perfect index privacy of an e-BVC scheme as stated in the following corollary.

Corollary 2. *An e-BVC scheme cannot achieve perfect index privacy if GAR$' +$ GRR$' \neq 1$ and GAR$' > 0$. Moreover, if GAR$' +$ GRR$' \neq 1$ and GAR$' > 0$, then the advantage $\mathsf{Adv}_{\mathcal{A}}^{\mathsf{REC}}$ of an adversary in IND-REC satisfies*

$$0 < \mathsf{Adv}_{\mathcal{A}}^{\mathsf{REC}} < p \left| \frac{\text{GAR}' + \text{GRR}' - 1}{1 - \text{GRR}'} \right|. \tag{17}$$

Proof. It follows from (9), Theorems 4 and 5 that $\mathsf{Adv}_{\mathcal{A}}^{\mathsf{REC}} = 0$ if and only if $\mathsf{GAR}' + \mathsf{GRR}' = 1$ or $\mathsf{GAR}' = 0$. Therefore, perfect index privacy cannot be achieved if $\mathsf{GAR}' + \mathsf{GRR}' \neq 1$ and $\mathsf{GAR}' > 0$. The inequality (17) follows from (9) and Theorem 5.

Remark 3. Satisfying the equality $\mathsf{GAR}' + \mathsf{GRR}' = 1$ may not guarantee the perfect index privacy of an e-BVC scheme because IND-REC is just one way of attacking the system and there may exist other attack methods.

The next corollary shows that an adversary with non-zero advantage in $\mathsf{G_{IND}}$ can be turned into an adversary with non-zero advantage in $\mathsf{G_{REC}}$, and vice versa.

Corollary 3. *There exists an adversary with non-zero advantage in $\mathsf{G_{IND}}$ if and only if there exists an adversary with non-zero advantage in $\mathsf{G_{REC}}$.*

Proof. The proof follows from (2) and (11), and from the fact that $0 < p < 1$.

Remark 4. We have described the game $\mathsf{G_{REC}}$ in which $\mathcal{A}$ receives $s_1(\alpha)$ and $\{s_{1,j}\}_{j=1}^{N}$ from $\mathcal{C}$. Similarly, $\mathsf{G_{REC}}$ can be defined such that $\mathcal{A}$ receives $s_2(\alpha)$ and $\{s_{2,j}\}_{j=1}^{N}$ from $\mathcal{C}$. The advantage of $\mathcal{A}$ may be different in these two cases; see Sect. 3.2 for example.

3.2   A Case Analysis for RO-e-BVC

As an extension of our analysis in Sect. 2.3, we now analyze the advantage of $\mathcal{A}$ in $\mathsf{G_{REC}}$ attacking RO-e-BVC [10] under the new index recovery attack (IND-REC). We apply the framework and security model to present a formal security analysis of the of the RO-e-BVC scheme with respect to the index recovery notion, and show that RO-e-BVC does not achieve perfect index privacy.

Recall that in Table IX in [10], equal error rates are reported in three different categories and in the last two of these three categories, an equal error rate e yields $\mathsf{GAR}' = \mathsf{GRR}' = 1 - e$ in Theorem 4, which determines the advantage of an attacker as

$$\mathsf{Adv}_{\mathcal{A}}^{\mathsf{REC}} = \left| \frac{p(1-p)(1-2e)}{p(1-e) + (1-p)e} \right|.$$

Based on the equal error rates reported in Table IX in [10], we summarize in Table 2 the advantage of $\mathcal{A}$ in $\mathsf{G_{REC}}$ attacking RO-e-BVC under the new index recovery attack (IND-REC) for a various number of N values. We also present the success probability $\mathsf{Pr_{REC}} = \Pr[j : (\alpha, \beta_j) \text{ Genuine}]$ of an adversary in IND-REC in comparison with $\mathsf{Pr_{Guess}} = \Pr[j : (\alpha, \beta_j) \text{ Genuine}]$ in the guessing attack.

In Table 2, various databases and datasets yield various values for the adversarial advantage. $\mathsf{Adv}_{\mathcal{A}}^{\mathsf{REC}}$ is non-zero in all of the cases and so RO-e-BVC does not achieve perfect index privacy. It is also interesting to compare the values in Table 2 with our theoretical estimates for $\mathsf{Adv}_{\mathcal{A}}^{\mathsf{REC}}$ in Corollary 2. Recall that

Table 2. The advantage of $\mathcal{A}$ in G_{REC}: attacking RO-e-BVC under the new index recovery attack with $N = 100$ and $N = 1000$.

		Database IMM	XM2	IMM	XM2	IMM	XM2
		Dataset A	A	F	F	G	G
	N	100	100	100	100	100	100
(s_1 vs. $s_{1,j}$)	Pr_{Guess}	.01	.01	.01	.01	.01	.01
(s_1 vs. $s_{1,j}$)	Pr_{REC}	.01234	.01764	.01787	.02130	.01940	.01635
(s_1 vs. $s_{1,j}$)	$Adv_{\mathcal{A}}^{REC}$	.00234	.00764	.00787	.01130	.00940	.00635
	N	1000	1000	1000	1000	1000	1000
(s_1 vs. $s_{1,j}$)	Pr_{Guess}	.001	.001	.001	.001	.001	.001
(s_1 vs. $s_{1,j}$)	Pr_{REC}	.001237	.00178	.00180	.00215	.00195	.00164
(s_1 vs. $s_{1,j}$)	$Adv_{\mathcal{A}}^{REC}$	.000237	.00078	.00080	.00115	.00095	.00064
		Database IMM	XM2	IMM	XM2	IMM	XM2
		Dataset A	A	F	F	G	G
	N	100	100	100	100	100	100
(s_2 vs. $s_{2,j}$)	Pr_{Guess}	.01	.01	.01	.01	.01	.01
(s_2 vs. $s_{2,j}$)	Pr_{REC}	.01259	.01940	.01493	.01601	.01524	.01536
(s_2 vs. $s_{2,j}$)	$Adv_{\mathcal{A}}^{REC}$	.00259	.00940	.00493	.00601	.00524	.00536
	N	1000	1000	1000	1000	1000	1000
(s_2 vs. $s_{2,j}$)	Pr_{Guess}	.001	.001	.001	.001	.001	.001
(s_2 vs. $s_{2,j}$)	Pr_{REC}	.00126	.00196	.00150	.00161	.00153	.00154
(s_2 vs. $s_{2,j}$)	$Adv_{\mathcal{A}}^{REC}$	.00026	.00096	.00050	.00061	.00053	.00054

in Corollary 2, we show that if $GAR' + GRR' \neq 1$ and $GAR' > 0$, then the advantage of an adversary in IND-REC satisfies

$$0 < Adv_{\mathcal{A}}^{REC} < p \left| \frac{GAR' + GRR' - 1}{1 - GRR'} \right|.$$

For example, we derive from Table IX in [10] that $GAR' = GRR' = 0.553$ if RO-e-BVC is implemented with the IMM database and Dataset A, and if the first sheets are compared in the attack. Accordingly, we find out that

$$0 < Adv_{\mathcal{A}}^{REC} < p \left| \frac{GAR' + GRR' - 1}{1 - GRR'} \right| = 0.237p.$$

In particular, if $p = 0.01$ and $p = 0.001$, then $0 < Adv_{\mathcal{A}}^{REC} < 0.00237$ and $0 < Adv_{\mathcal{A}}^{REC} < 0.000237$, respectively. We observe in Table 2 that the actual adversarial advantage values (0.00234 and 0.000237) are in fact very close to the theoretical upper bounds. We find that the greatest adversarial advantages are obtained when RO-e-BVC is implemented with the IMM database and Dataset G (success probability and advantage are bounded by $1.958p$ and $0.958p$, respectively) and when RO-e-BVC is implemented with the XM2 database and Dataset

F (success probability and advantage bounded by $2.154p$ and $1.154p$, respectively). Therefore, the success probability of an adversary can be at least twice better than that of a random guess when attacking certain implementations of RO-e-BVC.

Remark 5. In Sects. 2 and 3 we discussed security of e-BVC schemes with respect to indistinguishability and index privacy notions. It is worth noting that the NDA and IND-REC attacks we described are conservative in the sense that they consider rather weak adversaries. We anticipate that there exist stronger attacks. For example, in NDA, the adversary $\mathcal{A}$ exploits his access to the matching oracle. $\mathcal{A}$'s advantage is likely to increase if the decomposition $\mathcal{D}_n$ or reconstruction $\mathcal{R}_t$ oracles are also accessed during the attack. Similarly, in IND-REC, the adversarial advantage is likely to increase if $\mathcal{A}$ outputs an index j such that $m_j = \mathcal{M}(s_1(\alpha), s_{1,j})$ is maximum among all $\{m_j\}_{j=1}^N$ (rather than outputting an index j with $m_j \geq m$).

4   Conclusion

We extended a previously inititiated framework for biometric visual cryptographic schemes and formalized several security notions and definitions including sheet indistinguishability, perfect indistinguishability, index recovery, and perfect index privacy. We also proposed new and generic strategies for attacking e-BVC schemes such as new distinguishing attack and new index recovery. Our quantitative analysis verifies the practical impact of the framework and offers concrete bounds on the security of e-BVC. As an application of our analysis we were able to disprove some of the security claims in [10].

Acknowledgements. This work is partially supported by US National Science Foundation (NSF) under the grant number NSF-CNS-1718109. The statements made herein are solely the responsibility of the authors.

References

1. Ateniese, G., Blundo, C., De Santis, A., Stinson, D.: Extended capabilities for visual cryptography. Theor. Comput. Sci. **250**, 143–161 (2001)
2. Ateniese, G., Blundo, C., De Santis, A., Stinson, D.R.: Visual cryptography for general access structures. Inf. Comput. **129**(2), 86–106 (1996)
3. Blakley, G.: Safeguarding cryptographic keys. In: Proceedings of the National Computer Conference, vol. 48, pp. 313–317 (1979)
4. Karabina, K., Robinson, A.: Revisiting the false acceptance rate attack on biometric visual cryptographic schemes. In: Nascimento, A.C.A., Barreto, P. (eds.) ICITS 2016. LNCS, vol. 10015, pp. 114–125. Springer, Cham (2016). https://doi.org/10. 1007/978-3-319-49175-2_6
5. Nakajima, M., Yamaguchi, Y.: Extended visual cryptography for natural images. J. WSCG **10**, 303–310 (2002)

6. Naor, M., Pinkas, B.: Visual authentication and identification. In: Kaliski, B.S. (ed.) CRYPTO 1997. LNCS, vol. 1294, pp. 322–336. Springer, Heidelberg (1997). https://doi.org/10.1007/BFb0052245
7. Naor, M., Shamir, A.: Visual cryptography. In: De Santis, A. (ed.) EUROCRYPT 1994. LNCS, vol. 950, pp. 1–12. Springer, Heidelberg (1995). https://doi.org/10.1007/BFb0053419
8. Rao, Y., Sukonkina, Y., Bhagwati, C., Singh, U.: Fingerprint based authentication application using visual cryptography methods (Improved ID card). In: TENCON 2008–2008 IEEE Region 10 Conference, pp. 1–5. IEEE (2008)
9. Revenkar, P., Anjum, A., Gandhare, W.: Secure iris authentication using visual cryptography. arXiv preprint arXiv:1004.1748 (2010)
10. Ross, A., Othman, A.: Visual cryptography for biometric privacy. IEEE Trans. Inf. Forensics Secur. **6**, 70–81 (2011)
11. Shamir, A.: How to share a secret. Commun. ACM **22**, 612–613 (1979)
12. Simoens, K., Tuyls, P., Preneel, B.: Privacy weaknesses in biometric sketches. In: Proceedings of the 2009 30th IEEE Symposium on Security and Privacy, SP 2009, pp. 188–203. IEEE Computer Society, Washington, DC (2009)

Constructions of Secure Multi-Channel Broadcast Encryption Schemes in Public Key Framework

Kamalesh Acharya[✉] and Ratna Dutta

Department of Mathematics, Indian Institute of Technology Kharagpur,
Kharagpur 721302, India
kamaleshiitkgp@gmail.com, ratna@maths.iitkgp.ernet.in

Abstract. Multi-Channel Broadcast Encryption (MCBE) introduced by Phan et al. provides a suitable way to broadcast messages efficiently to groups of recipients while usual broadcast encryption (BE) sends a message to a particular group of users, consequently increases communication bandwidth and computation cost to send different messages to different group of users by employing BE repeatedly. We have proposed two *public key multi-channel broadcast encryption* schemes while all the existing schemes are in private key setting. Our first construction achieves semi-static security against chosen plaintext attack (CPA) under Decisional Bilinear Diffie-Hellman Exponent Sum (DBDHE-sum) assumption and second scheme achieves selective security against CPA under modified squared Decisional Diffie-Hellman Exponent (m-sq-DDHE) assumption. Both of our proposed constructions have constant header size. Our second construction achieves *outsider-anonymity* which hides user identity from outsiders apart from data hiding.

Keywords: Multi-channel broadcast encryption
Complete subtree method · Chosen plaintext attack

1 Introduction

Broadcast encryption (BE) is a useful cryptographic primitive that enables the broadcaster to send an encrypted message to a group of users in such a way that users outside the group cannot decrypt. It has numerous applications in real life ranging from TV broadcast to digital right management. There have been a number of proposals for BE [1–4,6,12]. However, huge computation and communication are required if the broadcaster wants to send different ciphertexts to different groups of users by repeated use of a broadcast encryption scheme. This problem was first addressed by Phan et al. [12] who introduced a multi-channel broadcast encryption (MCBE) scheme in private key setting. In an MCBE scheme, a single header is generated for a set of different groups of users allowing all the recipients in a particular group to recover same session key. The session key for different groups are different and a single header

© Springer Nature Switzerland AG 2018
J. Camenisch and P. Papadimitratos (Eds.): CANS 2018, LNCS 11124, pp. 495–515, 2018.
https://doi.org/10.1007/978-3-030-00434-7_25

is framed that contains all the information in encrypted form that are required recover the session keys corresponding to respective groups by the corresponding users in that group. Those session key for each group is used to encrypt a message using a symmetric key encryption scheme. Broadcast encryption can be broadly classified into two: public key BE and private key BE. In private key BE, the broadcaster plays the role of the private key generation centre (PKGC) and consequently, knows sensitive information such as master secret key whose disclosure may compromise the security. The same setup cannot be used by different broadcasters in private key setting. The encrypter either stores the secret keys or computes them during the encryption. On the other hand, public key BE considers the PKGC and the broadcaster as different entities and performs encryption with the help of public parameters. It reduces workload of broadcaster by employing a PKGC, which is required in many broadcast mechanism. Following are certain situations where MCBE is applicable. Suppose a TV channel wants to broadcast different regional movies to different groups of users in different states. He can use MCBE that broadcast a single header to all the users instead of different headers to different group of users, thereby, reducing communication cost.

In the modern era of digital technology, hiding user privacy is of crucial importance apart from data hiding. For example, suppose a customer wants to subscribe a sensitive TV channel concealing his identity. *Anonymous* BE provides this feature. Most of the BE schemes do not exhibit this property. BE with *outsider-anonymity* is another variant introduced by Fazio et al. [7] in which user identities will be kept secret from the users outside the group for which the ciphertext has been generated. For instance, consider a project manager divides his project into parts. He sends each part of task to various groups of scientists in different location of the country. Each part will be solved by different groups of scientists who needs to share their documents among them selves in a group without revealing their identities to other groups. This can be managed efficiently using *outsider-anonymous* MCBE scheme (Fig. 1).

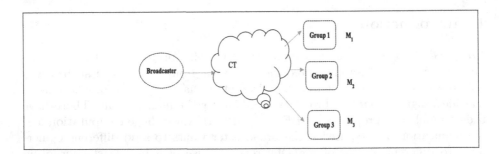

Fig. 1. Multi-channel broadcast encryption.

Phan et al. [12] used the broadcast encryption scheme of Boneh et al. [6] to develop first MCBE scheme in private key setting. They have cleverly multiplied the headers generated using the BE of [6] to provide a single header that enables to retrieve session key corresponding to a particular group by individual users in that group. The scheme has constant secret key size while public parameter size linear to the maximum number of users that can be accommodated in the system. The scheme achieves selective indistinguishability against chosen plaintext attack (IND-CPA) security under the decisional bilinear Diffie-Hellman exponent (DBDHE) assumption. In selective security model the adversary gives a challenge set to the challenger at the beginning of game. The challenger generates public key, secret key, challenge ciphertext by using the challenge set. Later, Zhao et al. [13] improved this work and provided an MCBE scheme with short public parameter by reducing the number of exponentiations in the public parameters of the MCBE of [12] (Tables 1 and 2).

Table 1. Comparative summaries of storage, communication bandwidth and security of MCBE schemes.

Scheme	$|PP|$	$|SK|$	$|Hdr|$	Public	SM	Assumption
[12]	$(3N-1)\,|G|$	$1|G|$	$2|G|$	No	Sel	N-DBDHE
[13]	$(2N+m-1)\,|G|$	$1|G|$	$2|G|$	No	Sel	N-DBDHE
Our MCBE	$(2N+m+3)\,|G|$	$1|G|$	$2|G|$	Yes	Semi-static	DBDHE-sum
Our OMCBE	$(N+2)\,|G|$	$\zeta|G|$	$1|G|+\tau m$	Yes	Sel	m-sq-DDHE

$|PP|$ = public parameter size, $sf|SK|$ = secret key size, $|Hdr|$ = header size, N = total number of users, $|G|$ = bit size of an element of G, n = number of users in each group ($= 2^{\zeta}$ for some integer ζ), $N = nm$, m = number of groups, SM = security model. τ = size of check bits.

Table 2. Comparison of computation cost for MCBE schemes.

Scheme	PP	SK	Enc		Dec	
	#exp	#exp	#exp	#pair	#exp	#pair
[12]	$3N-1$ in G	1 in G	m in G m in G_1	m	0	$1+m$
[13]	$2N+m-1$ in G	1 in G	m in G m in G_1	m	0	$1+m$
Our MCBE	$3N+m$ in G	1 in G	$N+1$ in G	1	$N-1$ in G	1
Our OMCBE	N in G	ζ in G	l^2+l+1 in G	l	0	at most ζ

PP = public parameter, SK = secret key, Enc = encryption, Dec = decryption, N = total number of users, # exp = number of exponentiations, # pair = number of pairings, m = number of groups, $n = 2^{\zeta}$, $N = nm$, l = cover size.

Our Contribution: Considering the limited development in the area, MCBE is further studied in this paper. We have put-forward two MCBE schemes in public key setting with our second construction featuring the additional property of outsider-anonymity. The closest related works to ours are that of Phan et al.

[12] and Zhao et al. [13], both of which are in private key setting. In contrast, our constructions use public key setup and allow a third party called as broadcaster to broadcast messages which is desirable in many real life applications. More precisely, we summarize our contribution below:

- We use the broadcast encryption scheme of Kim et al. [10] to achieve the first MCBE scheme with constant header size in pubic key setting which provides semi-static security without using random oracle. We have used [10] in each group of users in such a way that it has single header and provides revocation of users. This scheme has single header, public parameter size linear to the maximum number of users that can be accommodated in the system and secret key size is constant. Our scheme achieves semi-static IND-CPA security under DBDHE-sum assumption. In semi-static security adversary submits an initialization set to challenger, but in challenge phase it takes a subset of initial set as a challenge set. Thus more challenging to achieve in MCBE framework.

- Our second construction, outsider-anonymous MCBE (OMCBE) uses the complete subtree method of Naor et al. [11] to partition the subscribed users. We employs *anonymous identity-based encryption* scheme of Izabachne et al. [8] on each partition to develop first OMCBE scheme in public key setting. Each subscribed user recovers the corresponding message by decrypting the header using its own secret key. No existing MCBE design exhibits the feature. This scheme has public parameter size linear to the maximum number of users that can be accommodated in the system and secret key size is linear to the height of complete subtree in which it belongs. We achieve *outsider anonymity* by providing some check bits along with single header. Our scheme achieves selective IND-CPA security under m-sq-DBDHE assumption.

Our constructions support any user to remain active or inactive any-time without updating its public parameter and secret key and non-interactive in the sense that they do not need to interact with users after releasing the public and secret key, similar to [12,13].

2   Preliminaries

Notation: We use the notation $x \in_R S$ to denote x is a random element of S, $[m]$ to denote integers from 1 to m and $[a, b]$ to represent integers from a to b. Let $\epsilon : \mathbb{N} \to \mathbb{R}$ be a function where $\mathbb{N}$ and $\mathbb{R}$ are the sets of natural and real numbers respectively. The function ϵ is said to be a *negligible function* if for every positive integer c, $\exists$ an integer N_c such that $\epsilon(\lambda) \leq \frac{1}{\lambda^c}$ for every $\lambda > N_c$. Assume that $|S|$ denotes number of users in set S.

2.1   Multi-Channel Broadcast Encryption

In AsiaCCS 2013, Phan et al. [12] proposed *multichannel broadcast encryption* (MCBE) which is a new variant of broadcast encryption. In a MCBE, a private key generation centre (PKGC) generates public parameter and secret key. A broadcaster generates ciphertexts $\{CT_i\}_{i=1}^m$ of respective messages $\{M_i\}_{i=1}^m$ for respective groups of disjoint users $\{G_i\}_{i=1}^m$. A subscribed user $u \in G_i$ recovers corresponding message M_i using its own secret key. We start with a description of a formal model for MCBE scheme and the associated algorithms.

Syntax of MCBE: A multi-channel broadcast encryption scheme MCBE = (MCBE.Setup, MCBE.KeyGen, MCBE.Encrypt, MCBE.Decrypt) consists of 4 algorithms and works as follows.

$(PP, MK) \leftarrow MCBE.Setup(N, \lambda)$: On input the total number of users N supported in the system with security parameter λ, the PKGC generates the public parameter PP and a master key MK. It makes PP public and keeps MK secret to itself. For convenience, we take $N = mn$ where the set of N users are divided into m disjoint subsets $G_1, \ldots, G_m$ and each G_i has n users.

$(sk_u) \leftarrow MCBE.KeyGen(PP, MK, u)$: Taking as input PP, MK and a subscribed user u, the PKGC generates a secret key sk_u of user u and sends sk_u to u through a secure communication channel between the PKGC and u.

$(Hdr, \{K_i\}_{i=1}^m) \leftarrow MCBE.Encrypt(S_1, S_2, \ldots, S_m, PP)$: On input PP and group of subscribed users $S_1, S_2, \ldots, S_m$, with each $S_i \subseteq G_i$, the broadcaster produces a header Hdr and session key K_i for each group S_i. The broadcaster makes the header Hdr public and keeps the set of session keys $\{K_i\}_{i=1}^m$ secret. The session key K_i can be used to generate a ciphertext for message M_i using a symmetric key encryption algorithm. Note that some S_i may be the null set (ϕ). If $S_i = \phi$ then the broadcaster sets $K_i = \perp$.

$(K_i) \leftarrow MCBE.Decrypt(PP, sk_u, Hdr, \{S_i\}_{i=1}^m)$: A subscribed user $u \in S_i$ recovers its session key K_i corresponds to S_i using sk_u, PP, Hdr and subscribed user sets $S_1, S_2, \ldots, S_m$.

Correctness: The scheme MCBE is said to be correct if the session key K_i can be retrieved from the header Hdr by any subscribed user $u \subseteq S_i$. Suppose $(PP, MK) \leftarrow MCBE.Setup(N, \lambda)$, $(Hdr, \{K_i\}_{i=1}^m) \leftarrow MCBE.Encrypt(S_1, \ldots, S_m, PP)$ and K_i is session key of S_i. Then for every subscribed user $u \in S_i$,

$$MCBE.Decrypt\Big(PP, MCBE.KeyGen(PP, MK, u), Hdr, S_i\Big) = K_i.$$

Syntax of OMCBE: An outsider-anonymous multi-channel broadcast encryption OMCBE = (OMCBE.Setup, OMCBE.KeyGen, OMCBE.Encrypt, OMCBE.Decrypt) unlike MCBE, does not require the explicit knowledge of the set of subscribers or the set of revoked users as input during decryption.

$(PP, MK) \leftarrow OMCBE.Setup(N, \lambda)$: This is exactly the same as MCBE.Setup.

$(sk_i) \leftarrow OMCBE.KeyGen(PP, MK, i)$: This is identical to MCBE.KeyGen.

$(Hdr, \{K_i\}_{i=1}^m) \leftarrow OMCBE.Encrypt(S_1, S_2, \ldots, S_m, PP)$: On input group of subscribed users $S_1, S_2, \ldots, S_m$, with each $S_i \subseteq G_i$, public parameter PP, the broadcaster produces a header Hdr and session key $K_i = \{K_{i,j}\}_{j=1}^{L_i}$ for each group S_i, where L_i is a upper bound of the number of disjoint partitions of S_i

i.e., $S_i = \bigcup_{j=1}^{L_i} S_{i,j}$ with $S_{i,j_1} \cap S_{i,j_2} = \phi$ for $j_1 \neq j_2, 1 \leq j_1, j_2 \leq L_i$ and $K_{i,j}$ is the session key corresponding to $S_{i,j}$. If some $S_{i,j} = \phi$, set $K_{i,j}$ as random. It makes the header Hdr public and keeps the session key $\{K_i\}_{i=1}^m$ secret. The session key K_i can be used to generate a ciphertext for message M_i using a symmetric key encryption algorithm. Note that some S_i may be the null set. If $S_i = \phi$ then the broadcaster sets $K_i = \bot$.

$(K_{i,j}) \leftarrow$ OMCBE.Decrypt(PP, sk_u, Hdr): A subscribed user $u \in S_{i,j}$ ($\subseteq S_i$) recovers its session key $K_{i,j}$ corresponds to $S_{i,j}$ using sk_u, PP, Hdr. Here user u does not need set of subscribed users during decryption and it does not know the partition $S_{i,j}$ in which it belongs.

Correctness: The scheme OMCBE is said to be correct if the session key $K_{i,j}$ can be retrieved from the header Hdr by any subscribed user u. Suppose (PP, MK) $\leftarrow$ OMCBE.Setup(N, λ), (Hdr, $\{K_i\}_{i=1}^m$) $\leftarrow$ OMCBE.Encrypt($S_1, S_2, \ldots, S_m$, PP) and $K_i = \{K_{i,j}\}_{j=1}^{L_i}$ where L_i is the upper bound of the number of disjoint partitions of S_i. Then for every subscribed user $u \in S_{i,j}(\subseteq S_i)$,

$$\text{OMCBE.Decrypt}\Big(\text{PP}, \text{OMCBE.KeyGen}(\text{PP}, \text{MK}, u), \text{Hdr}\Big) = K_{i,j}.$$

2.2 Security Framework

Key Indistinguishability of MCBE Under CPA: Security of the MCBE is analyzed under the following key indistinguishability game played between a challenger $\mathcal{C}$ and an adversary $\mathcal{A}$. Let us assume that both the adversary and challenger knows m group of users $\{G_i\}_{i=1}^m$ each having n elements. The total number of users that can be accommodated in the system is $N = nm$.

Initialization: The adversary $\mathcal{A}$ selects a set of recipient sets $S_1, \ldots, S_m$ with $S_i \subseteq G_i$, an index $\gamma \leq m$ and provides it to $\mathcal{C}$. Note that some S_i may be ϕ.

Setup: The challenger $\mathcal{C}$ generates (PP, MK) $\leftarrow$ MCBE.Setup(N, λ). It keeps the master key MK secret to itself and sends the public parameter PP to $\mathcal{A}$.

Phase 1: The adversary $\mathcal{A}$ sends key generation queries for user $i \notin S_\gamma$ to $\mathcal{C}$ and receives the secret key $sk_i \leftarrow$ MCBE.KeyGen(PP, MK, i).

Challenge: The adversary $\mathcal{A}$ chooses $S'_\gamma \subset S_\gamma$ and sends to the challenger. The challenger $\mathcal{C}$ generates (Hdr, $\{K_i\}_{i=1}^m$) $\leftarrow$ MCBE.Encrypt($S_1, S_2, \ldots, S'_\gamma, \ldots, S_m$, PP) and choose a bit $b \in_R \{0,1\}$. If $b = 0$, $\mathcal{C}$ sends (Hdr, $\{K_i\}_{i=1}^m$) to $\mathcal{A}$ where K_i is session key for S_i. Otherwise, $\mathcal{C}$ replaces $K_\gamma, 1 \leq \gamma \leq m$ for the group S_γ by a random session key and provides (Hdr, $\{K_i\}_{i=1}^m$) to $\mathcal{A}$.

Phase 2: This is similar to Phase 1 key generation queries.

Guess: The adversary $\mathcal{A}$ outputs a guess $b' \in \{0,1\}$ of b and wins if $b' = b$.

Adversary's advantage in the above security game is defined as $Adv_{\mathcal{A}}^{\text{MCBE-INDK}} = |2Pr(b' = b) - 1| = |Pr[b' = 1|b = 1] - Pr[b' = 1|b = 0]|$. The probability is taken over random bits used by $\mathcal{C}$ and $\mathcal{A}$.

Definition 1. *The* MCBE *scheme is* (t, q, ϵ)*-semantic secure if* $Adv_{\mathcal{A}}^{\text{MCBE-INDK}} \leq \epsilon$ *for every probabilistic polynomial time (PPT) adversary* $\mathcal{A}$ *with running time at most* t *and making at most* q *key generation queries.*

Key Indistinguishability of OMCBE Under CPA: Security of OMCBE scheme is measured under key indistinguishability game described below.

Initialization: The adversary $\mathcal{A}$ selects 2 group of target recipient sets $\mathbb{S}_0 = \{S_{0,1}, \ldots, S_{0,m}\}$, $\mathbb{S}_1 = \{S_{1,1}, \ldots, S_{1,m}\}$ with $S_{0,i}, S_{1,i} \subseteq G_i$, $|S_{0,i}| = |S_{1,i}|$, $i \in [m]$ an index $\gamma \leq m$ and provides it to $\mathcal{C}$.

Phase 1: The adversary $\mathcal{A}$ sends key generation queries for user $u \notin (S_{0,\gamma} \bigcup S_{1,\gamma})$ and receives back secret key sk_u.

Challenge: The challenger $\mathcal{C}$ generates $(\text{Hdr}, \{K_i\}_{i=1}^m) \leftarrow$ OMCBE.Encrypt $(\mathbb{S}_0, \text{PP})$. If $b = 0$, $\mathcal{C}$ sends $(\text{Hdr}, \{K_i\}_{i=1}^m)$ to $\mathcal{A}$ where $K_i = \{K_{i,j}\}_{j=1}^{L_i}$ is session key for S_i, L_i is the theoretical upper bound of disjoint partitions of S_i i.e., $S_i = \bigcup_{j=1}^{L_i} S_{i,j}$ with $S_{i,j_1} \bigcap S_{i,j_2} = \phi$ for $j_1 \neq j_2, 1 \leq j_1, j_2 \leq L_i$ and $K_{i,j}$ is the session key corresponding to $S_{i,j}$. Otherwise, $\mathcal{C}$ generates $(\text{Hdr}, \{K_i\}_{i=1}^m) \leftarrow$ OMCBE.Encrypt$(\mathbb{S}_1, \text{PP})$ and provides $(\text{Hdr}, \{K_i\}_{i=1}^m)$ to $\mathcal{A}$.

Phase 2: This is similar to Phase 1 key generation queries. The adversary $\mathcal{A}$ sends key generation queries for user $u \notin (S_{0,\gamma} \bigcup S_{1,\gamma})$ and receives back secret key sk_u as in Phase 1.

Guess: The adversary $\mathcal{A}$ output a guess $b' \in \{0, 1\}$ of b and wins if $b' = b$.

Adversary's advantage in the above security game is defined as $Adv_{\mathcal{A}}^{\text{OMCBE-INDK}} = |2Pr(b' = b) - 1| = |Pr[b' = 1|b = 1] - Pr[b' = 1|b = 0]|$. The probability is taken over random bits used by $\mathcal{C}$ and $\mathcal{A}$.

Definition 2. *The* OMCBE *scheme is* (t, q, ϵ)*-semantic secure if* $Adv_{\mathcal{A}}^{\text{OMCBE-INDK}} \leq \epsilon$ *for every PPT adversary* $\mathcal{A}$ *with running time at most* t *and making at most* q *key generation queries.*

2.3 Complexity Assumptions

Definition 3 (Bilinear Map). *Let* $\mathbb{G}$ *and* $\mathbb{G}_1$ *be two multiplicative groups of prime order* p. *Let* g *be a generator of* $\mathbb{G}$. *A bilinear map* $e : \mathbb{G} \times \mathbb{G} \longrightarrow \mathbb{G}_1$ *is a function having the following properties:*

1. $e(u^a, v^b) = e(u, v)^{ab}$, $\forall u, v \in \mathbb{G}$ *and* $\forall a, b \in \mathbb{Z}_p$.
2. The map is non-degenerate, i.e., $e(g, g)$ *is a generator of* $\mathbb{G}_1$.

The tuple $\mathbb{S} = (p, \mathbb{G}, \mathbb{G}_1, e)$ *is called a prime order bilinear group system.*

- modified-Squared-Decisional Diffie-Hellman Exponent (m-sq-DDHE) Assumption:

  Input: $\langle Z = (\mathbb{S}, A = u^a, \{U_i, B_i, C_i\}_{i=0}^N), K \rangle$, where $u \in \mathbb{G}, U_i = u^{1/a^i}$, $B_i = u^{b/a^i}$, $C_i = u^{c/a^i}$ for $i \in [0, N]$, K is either $e(u, u)^{abc}$ or a random element X of the target group $\mathbb{G}_1$.

  Output: 0 if $K = e(u, u)^{abc}$; 1 if $K = X$ is random.

Definition 4. *The (t, ϵ) m-sq-DDHE assumption holds if for every PPT adversary $\mathcal{A}$ with running time at most t, the advantage of solving the above problem is at most ϵ, i.e., $Adv_{\mathcal{A}}^{m\text{-}sq\text{-}DDHE} = |Pr[\mathcal{A}(Z, K = e(u, u)^{abc}) = 1] - Pr[\mathcal{A}(Z, K = X) = 1]| \leq \epsilon(\lambda)$, where $\epsilon(\lambda)$ is a negligible function in security parameter λ.*

- Decisional Bilinear-Diffie-Hellman Exponent sum (DBDHE-sum) Assumption [10]:

  Input: $\langle Z = (\mathbb{S}, g^{\alpha^i}, i \in ([0, N - 2], [4N, 7N - 1], [8N, 9N - 1], [12N, 15N], [16N, 19N + 1]), K \rangle$, where g is generator of $\mathbb{G}$, $\alpha, N \in_R \mathbb{Z}_p, K$ is either $e(g, g)^{\alpha^{16N-1}}$ or a random element X of the target group $\mathbb{G}_1$.

  Output: 0 if $K = e(g, g)^{\alpha^{16N-1}}$; 1 if $K = X$ is random.

Definition 5. *The DBDHE-sum assumption holds with (T, ϵ) if for every PPT adversary $\mathcal{A}$ with running time at most T, the advantage of solving the above problem is at most ϵ, i.e., $Adv_{\mathcal{A}}^{DBDHE\text{-}sum} = |Pr[\mathcal{A}(Z, K = e(g, g)^{\alpha^{16N-1}}) = 0] - Pr[\mathcal{A}(Z, K = X) = 0]| \leq \epsilon(\lambda)$, where $\epsilon(\lambda)$ is a negligible function in security parameter λ.*

The security of DBDHE-sum, m-sq-DDHE assumption follows from the intractability of General Decisional Diffie-Hellman Exponent problem [5].

2.4   Complete Subtree Method [11]

Complete subtree (CS) method partitions subscribed users into disjoint subsets. Let U be the set of all users and R be the set of revoked users. It generates a cover which is a partition of the set of subscribed users $U \setminus R$ into a collection of disjoint subsets. In binary CS method, a complete binary tree $T(x)$ is considered with users in U located at leaf level. For a set of revoked users R, let $\mathsf{ST}(R)$ denotes the Steiner tree, i.e., the minimal subtree of $T(x)$ connecting all the members of the set of revoked users R with the root. Let $\mathsf{CS}_{x,1}, \mathsf{CS}_{x,2}, \ldots, \mathsf{CS}_{x,m}$ be the complete subtrees of tree $T(x)$ that hang of $\mathsf{ST}(R)$. These subtrees of $T(x)$ are *headed* by the vertices that hang of the vertices of outdegree 1 in $\mathsf{ST}(R)$. The leaf nodes of these subtrees form the required cover of the subscribed users. In Fig. 2, $v(x, i, j)$ denotes the j-th node at the i-th level of tree $T(x)$. The generated cover for the set of revoked users $R = \{v(x, 4, 3), v(x, 4, 4)\}$ is $S_{x,1}, S_{x,2}$ where $S_{x,1} = \{v(x, 4, 1), v(x, 4, 2)\}, S_{x,2} = \{v(x, 4, 5), v(x, 4, 6), v(x, 4, 7), v(x, 4, 8)\}$. The subcover $S_{x,1}$ is headed by $v(x, 3, 1)$ and the subcover $S_{x,2}$ is headed by $v(x, 2, 2)$. Note that $v(x, 3, 1), v(x, 2, 2)$ hang of $v(x, 2, 1), v(x, 1, 1)$ respectively of outdegree 1 in $\mathsf{ST}(R)$.

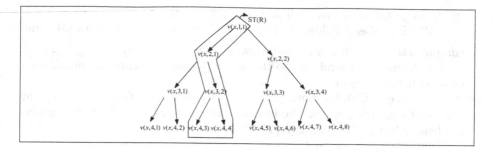

Fig. 2. Steiner tree ST(R) for the set of revoked users $R = \{v(x,4,3), v(x,4,4)\}$.

Lemma 1. *For a subscribed user u in a complete binary tree $T(x)$ with the subscribed user at leaf level, we have $|\text{Head} \cap \text{path}(u)| = 1$, where Head is the set of head node identities in a cover of the subscribed users with respect to a set of revoked users R and $\text{path}(u)$ denotes identities of nodes along the path lies between user u at leaf to the root of $T(x)$.*

Proof. Let $|\text{Head} \cap \text{path}(u)| \neq 1$ and $|\text{Head} \cap \text{path}(u)| = y > 1$. Then y many head nodes with identities in Head matches with that of $\text{path}(u)$. Therefore, user u will belong to y groups as each complete subtree with head node on $\text{path}(u)$ contains the user u. This leads to a contradict as head nodes partition subscribed users into disjoint subcovers. If $|\text{Head} \cap \text{path}(u)| = 0$, then the subscribed user u will not belong to any subcover as path nodes and head of the subcovers and are different. As the subscribed user u should lie in a subcover whose head node is in Head, a contradiction arises. Hence, $|\text{Head} \cap \text{path}(u)| = 1$.

The cover size of binary CS is at most $r \log(\frac{N}{r})$, where N is the total number of users placed at the leaf level of a complete binary tree $T(x)$ and r is the size of the set of revoked users R (Proof is given in [11]).

3 Our MCBE

Our MCBE $=$ (MCBE.Setup, MCBE.KeyGen, MCBE.GroupGen, MCBE.Verify, MCBE. Encrypt, MCBE.Decrypt) works as follows:

(PP, MK) $\leftarrow$ MCBE.Setup(N, λ): Let $N = nm$ be the total number of users supported by the system with m group of users $\{G_x\}_{x=1}^{m}$ and each group $G_x, x \in [m]$ contains n users. Using the security parameter λ, the PKGC generates the public parameter PP and a master key MK for a maximum number N of broadcast recipients by executing the following steps:

1. It first selects a bilinear group system $\mathbb{S} = (p, \mathbb{G}, \mathbb{G}_1, e)$, where $\mathbb{G}, \mathbb{G}_1$ are groups of prime order p and $e : \mathbb{G} \times \mathbb{G} \rightarrow \mathbb{G}_1$ is a bilinear mapping.
2. It picks $g_1, g_2 \in_R \mathbb{G}$ and $\alpha, \beta, \gamma, \{x_j\}_{j \in [m]} \in_R \mathbb{Z}_p$, computes $\hat{g}_1 = g_1^{\beta}, \hat{g}_2 = g_2^{\beta}$ and sets PP, MK as
$$\text{PP} = (\mathbb{S}, \{g_1^{\alpha^i}, \hat{g}_1^{\alpha^i}\}_{i \in [0,N]}, \{\hat{g}_2^{\alpha^k}\}_{k \in [0,N-2]}, \{g_1^{\gamma x_j}\}_{j \in [m]}, g_1^{\gamma}, g_1^{\alpha\gamma}),$$
$$\text{MK} = (\alpha, g_2, \gamma, \{x_i\}_{i=1}^{m}).$$

3. It keeps MK secret to itself and makes PP public.

$(sk_i) \leftarrow$ MCBE.KeyGen(PP, MK, i): The PKGC extracts α, γ, g_2 from MK, and computes the secret key $sk_i = (sk_{i,1}, sk_{i,2})$, where $sk_{i,1} = g_2^{\frac{\gamma}{\alpha+i}}$, $sk_{i,2} = x_j, i \in G_j$ for the user i. It sends sk_i to the user i through a secure communication channel between them.

(Hdr, $\{K_i\}_{i=1}^m) \leftarrow$ MCBE.Encrypt($S_1, \ldots, S_m$, PP): Let $S_x \subseteq G_x$, $x \in [m]$ be the groups of subscribed users. The broadcaster performs the following to generate header Hdr and session key $\{K_i\}_{i=1}^m$:

1. Generates polynomial $P(x)$ as

$$P(x) = \prod_{i \in S}(x+i) \prod_{i \in [N] \setminus S}(x - N + i) = \sum_{i=0}^{N} P_i x^i, \text{ where } S = \bigcup_{x=1}^{m} S_x$$

2. Selects $s \in_R \mathbb{Z}_p$ and computes

$$C_1 = \prod_{i=0}^{N} (\hat{g}_1^{\alpha^i P_i})^s = \hat{g}_1^{\left\{\sum_{i=0}^{N} \alpha^i P_i s\right\}} = \hat{g}_1^{P(\alpha)s}, C_2 = g_1^{s\gamma}$$

3. Sets Hdr $= (C_1, C_2) = \left(\hat{g}_1^{P(\alpha)s}, g_1^{s\gamma}\right)$.

4. Computes $K = e(g_1, \hat{g}_2)^{\alpha^{N-1} s\gamma}$ and sets session key $\{K_i\}_{i=1}^m$ as follows
$K = e(g_1^{\alpha\gamma}, \hat{g}_2^{\alpha^{N-2}})^s = e(g_1, \hat{g}_2)^{\alpha^{N-1} s\gamma}$, $K_i = Kg_1^{s\gamma r_i}$.

Finally, it broadcasts the Hdr and keeps $\{K_i\}_{i=1}^m$ secret to itself.

$(K_i) \leftarrow$ MCBE.Decrypt(PP, sk_i, Hdr, $\{S_i\}_{i=1}^m$): Using the secret key sk_i, the public parameter PP, the header Hdr $= (C_1, C_2)$ and the set of subscribed users $S = \bigcup_{i=1}^{m} S_i$, a subscribed user $i \in G_j$ computes $\prod_{i=0}^{N-2} \hat{g}_2^{\bar{P}_i \alpha^i} = \hat{g}_2^{P_i(\alpha)}$ where $P_i(x) = x^{N-1} - \frac{P(x)}{x+i} = \sum_{i=0}^{N-2} \bar{P}_i x^i$ and $P(x) = \prod_{i \in S}(x+i) \prod_{i \in [1,N] \setminus S}(x - N + i)$ is as in MCBE.Encrypt phase. It recovers K_i as

$$K = \{e(C_1, sk_{i,1})e(C_2, \hat{g}_2^{P_i(\alpha)})\}, K_j = Kg_1^{s\gamma \cdot sk_{i,2}} = Kg_1^{s\gamma x_j}.$$

Correctness: The correctness of MCBE.Decrypt follows as

$$K = e(C_1, sk_{i,1})e(C_2, \hat{g}_2^{P_i(\alpha)})$$
$$= e(\hat{g}_1^{P(\alpha)s}, g_2^{\frac{\gamma}{\alpha+i}})e(g_1^{s\gamma}, \hat{g}_2^{P_i(\alpha)})$$
$$= e(g_1, \hat{g}_2)^{s\gamma \frac{P(\alpha)}{\alpha+i}} e(g_1, \hat{g}_2)^{s\gamma P_i(\alpha)}$$
$$= e(g_1, \hat{g}_2)^{s\gamma(\frac{P(\alpha)}{\alpha+i} + P_i(\alpha))}$$
$$= e(g_1, \hat{g}_2)^{s\gamma(\alpha^{N-1})}$$
$$= e(g_1, \hat{g}_2)^{\alpha^{N-1} s\gamma},$$
$$K_j = Kg_1^{s\gamma x_j} = e(g_1, \hat{g}_2)^{\alpha^{N-1} s\gamma} g_1^{s\gamma x_j}.$$

Theorem 1. *(Key indistinguishability under CPA) Our proposed* MCBE *scheme described in Sect. 3 achieves semi-static IND-CPA (indistinguishable under chosen plaintext attack) security as per the key indistinguishability security game of Sect. 2.2 under the hardness of* DBDHE-*sum problem.*

Before explaining the security proof of this theorem, we will explain the following Lemma whose proof has been given by Gentry et al. in [9].

Lemma 2. *Let $f(x), g(x) \in F_p[x]$ be polynomials of degrees d_1 and d_2 respectively, whose resultant is nonzero. Let $d_3 = d_1 + d_2 - 1$ and $i \in \{d_1, \ldots, d_3\}$. There exists a polynomial $t(x) \in F_p[x]$ of degree d_3 such that $t(x)f(x)|_i = 0$ and $t(x)f(x)|_j = 1$ for $j \in \{d_1, \ldots, d_3\}\backslash i$ and $t(x)g(x)|_j = 0$ for $j \in \{d_2, \ldots, d_3\}$. Here $q(x)|_i$ denotes the coefficient of x^i in function $q(x)$.*

Proof (Theorem 1). Let us assume that both the adversary and challenger knows m group of users $\{G_x\}_{x=1}^m$ each having n elements. Also assume that users in G_x are placed in leave level of a tree $T(x)$ of height ζ. The total number of users that can be accommodated in the system is $N = nm$. Assume that there is a PPT adversary $\mathcal{A}$ that breaks the semi-static IND-CPA security of our proposed MCBE scheme with a non-negligible advantage. We construct a distinguisher $\mathcal{C}$ that attempts to solve the DBDHE-sum problem using $\mathcal{A}$ as a subroutine. Both $\mathcal{A}$ and $\mathcal{C}$ are given N, the total number of users and t, the total number of key generation queries. Let $\mathcal{C}$ be given a DBDHE-sum instance $\langle Z = (\mathbb{S}, g^{\alpha^i}, i \in ([0, N-2], [4N, 7N-1], [8N, 9N-1], [12N, 15N], [16N, 19N+1]), X \rangle$. The distinguisher $\mathcal{C}$ attempts to output 0 if $X = e(g, g)^{\alpha^{16N-1}}$ and 1 otherwise, using $\mathcal{A}$ as a subroutine. Now $\mathcal{C}$ plays the role of a challenger in the security game described in Sect. 2.2 and interacts with $\mathcal{A}$ as follows:

Initialization: The adversary $\mathcal{A}$ selects a target recipient set S_γ of k users.
Setup: Using DBDHE-sum instance $\langle Z, X \rangle$, the challenger $\mathcal{C}$ does the followings
1. Sets a polynomial $f_1(x)$ of degree $2N + k$ whose roots are not equal to $-i$ for $i \in S_\gamma$ and not equal to $(N - i)$ for $i \in [N]\backslash S_\gamma$.
2. Selects $a_0, a_1, a_2 \in_R \mathbb{Z}_p$ and sets $f(x) = \prod_{i \in [N]\backslash S_\gamma} (x + i)f_1(x)$. Obviously degree of $f(x)$ is $3N$.
3. Sets $g_1 = g^{a_1 \alpha^{16N}}, g_2 = g^{a_2 \alpha^{4N}}$, implicitly sets $\beta = a_0 \alpha^{-4N}, \gamma = f(\alpha)$.
4. Computes

$$g_1^{\alpha^j} = (g^{a_1 \alpha^{16N}})^{\alpha^j} = g^{a_1 \alpha^{16N+j}}, \qquad j \in [0, N],$$
$$\hat{g}_1^{\alpha^j} = (g^{a_0 a_1 \alpha^{12N}})^{\alpha^j} = g^{a_0 a_1 \alpha^{12N+j}}, \qquad j \in [0, N],$$
$$\hat{g}_2^{\alpha^k} = g^{a_0 a_1 \alpha^k}, \qquad k \in [0, N-2].$$

5. Selects $x_i \in_R \mathbb{Z}_p, i \in [m]$ and sets public parameter PP, master key MK as
$$PP = (\mathbb{S}, \{g_1^{\alpha^j}, \hat{g}_1^{\alpha^j}\}_{j \in [0,N]}, \{\hat{g}_2^{\alpha^k}\}_{k \in [0,N-2]}, \{g_1^{\gamma x_i}\}_{i=1}^m, g_1^\gamma, g_1^{\alpha\gamma}),$$
$$MK = (\alpha, g_2, \gamma, \{x_i\}_{i=1}^m).$$
Note that α, γ are not known to $\mathcal{C}$ explicitly.
Key Query Phase: The challenger generates secret key for user $i \notin S_\gamma$ as
1. Computes $\frac{f(x)}{x+i} = \sum_{i=0}^{3N-1} b_i x^i$ where b_i is co-efficient of x^i.

2. Also computes $sk_{i,1} = \prod_{i=0}^{3N-1} g^{a_2 b_i \alpha^{(i+4N)}} = g^{\left\{a_2 \alpha^{4N} \sum_{i=0}^{3N-1} b_i \alpha^i\right\}} = g_2^{\frac{f(\alpha)}{\alpha+i}}.$

3. Sets $sk_i = (sk_{i,1}, sk_{i,2})$ where $sk_{i,2} = x_i$ for group G_i.

Note that the distribution of $sk_{i,1} = g_2^{\frac{f(\alpha)}{\alpha+i}} = g_2^{\frac{\gamma}{\alpha+i}}$ is identical to original.

Challenge: The challenger $\mathcal{C}$ does the following

1. Selects $S'_\gamma \subseteq S_\gamma$ and computes $P(x) = \prod_{i \in S'_\gamma} (x+i) \prod_{i \in [N] \setminus S'_\gamma} (x - N + i)$.

2. Using Lemma 1, $\mathcal{C}$ finds a polynomial $t(x)$ of degree $4N - 1$ such that

$$
\begin{aligned}
t(x)f(x)|_i &= 0 \qquad \text{for } i \in [3N+1, 4N-1] \\
t(x)f(x)|_{3N} &= 1 \\
t(x)P(x)|_i &= 0 \qquad \text{for } i \in [N, 4N-1].
\end{aligned}
$$

Here notation $q(x)|_i$ denotes the coefficient of x^i in function $q(x)$.

3. Sets $g_3 = g_1^{\alpha^{-4N}} = g^{a_1 \alpha^{12N}}$, then $\hat{g}_3 = g^{a_0 a_1 \alpha^{8N}}$.

4. Let $P(x)t(x) = \sum_{i=0}^{5N-1} B_i x^i$ and $f(x)t(x) = \sum_{i=0}^{7N-1} C_i x^i$, where B_i, C_i are co-efficient of x^i.
   Obviously $C_i = 0$ for $i \in [3N+1, 4N-1]$, $C_{3N} = 1$ and $B_i = 0$ for $i \in [N, 4N-1]$.

5. Computes

$$
\prod_{i=0}^{5N-1} g^{a_0 a_1 B_i \alpha^{i+8N}} = g^{\left\{a_0 a_1 \sum_{i=0}^{5N-1} B_i \alpha^{i+8N}\right\}} = g^{\left\{a_0 a_1 \alpha^{8N} P(\alpha)t(\alpha)\right\}} = \hat{g}_3^{P(\alpha)t(\alpha)},
$$

$$
\prod_{i=0}^{7N-1} g^{a_1 C_i \alpha^{i+12N}} = g^{\left\{a_1 \sum_{i=0}^{7N-1} C_i \alpha^{i+12N}\right\}} = g^{\left\{a_1 \alpha^{12N} f(\alpha)t(\alpha)\right\}} = g_3^{f(\alpha)t(\alpha)}.
$$

6. Sets header $\mathsf{Hdr} = (\hat{g}_3^{P(\alpha)t(\alpha)}, g_3^{f(\alpha)t(\alpha)})$. Assuming $t = t(\alpha)\alpha^{-4N}$

$$
\begin{aligned}
\hat{g}_3^{P(\alpha)t(\alpha)} &= g^{a_0 a_1 \alpha^{12N} \alpha^{-4N} t(\alpha) P(\alpha)} = g^{a_0 a_1 \alpha^{12N} t P(\alpha)} = \hat{g}_1^{tP(\alpha)}, \\
g_3^{f(\alpha)t(\alpha)} &= g^{a_1 \alpha^{16N} \alpha^{-4N} t(\alpha) f(\alpha)} = \hat{g}^{a_1 \alpha^{16N} t\gamma} = g_1^{\gamma t}.
\end{aligned}
$$

Therefore simulation is perfect.

7. Let

$$
\begin{aligned}
I &= [0, N-2] \cup [4N, 7N-1], J_1 = [14N-1, 15N] \cup [16N, 17N-1], \\
J &= [N, 2N+1] \cup [3N+1, 4N], L_1 = [8N+2, 9N-1], \\
L &= [2N+2, 3N-1].
\end{aligned}
$$

8. Observe that $[0, 7N-1] \setminus \{3N\} = I \cup J \cup L \cup \{N-1\}$.

9. It computes

$$e(g^{\alpha^{14N-2}}, g^{C_{N-1}}) = e(g,g)^{\alpha^{13N-1}\alpha^{N-1}C_{N-1}}$$

$$\prod_{i\in I} e(g^{\alpha^{13N-1}}, g^{C_i\alpha^i}) = e(g,g)^{\alpha^{13N-1}\sum_{i\in I} C_i\alpha^i}$$

$$\prod_{i\in J_1} e(g, g^{C_{i-(13N-1)}\alpha^i}) = e(g,g)^{\alpha^{13N-1}\sum_{i\in J} C_i\alpha^i}$$

$$\prod_{i\in L_1} e(g^{\alpha^{7N-1}}, g^{C_{i-6N}\alpha^i}) = e(g,g)^{\alpha^{13N-1}\sum_{i\in L} C_i\alpha^i}$$

Multiplying above values we get $e(g,g)^{\left(f(\alpha)t(\alpha)\alpha^{13N-1}-\alpha^{16N-1}\right)}$.

10. Sets K and session key $\{K_i\}_{i=1}^m$ as

$$K = X^{a_0 a_1 a_2} e(g,g)^{a_0 a_1 a_2 (f(\alpha)t(\alpha)\alpha^{13N-1}-\alpha^{16N-1})},$$

$$K_i = K g_1^{t\gamma x_i}.$$

If $X = e(g,g)^{\alpha^{16N-1}}$ then

$$K = X^{a_0 a_1 a_2} e(g,g)^{a_0 a_1 a_2 (f(\alpha)t(\alpha)\alpha^{13N-1}-\alpha^{16N-1})}$$

$$= e(g,g)^{a_0 a_1 a_2 \alpha^{13N-1} f(\alpha)t(\alpha)}$$

$$= e(g^{a_1 \alpha^{16N}}, g^{a_0 a_2})^{\alpha^{N-1}\alpha^{-4N} f(\alpha)t(\alpha)}$$

$$= e(g_1, \hat{g}_2)^{\alpha^{N-1}t\gamma},$$

$$K_i = K g_1^{t\gamma x_i} = e(g_1, \hat{g}_2)^{\alpha^{N-1}t\gamma} g_1^{t\gamma x_i},$$

Therefore simulation is perfect.

11. The challenger $\mathcal{C}$ selects $b \in_R \{0,1\}$. If $b = 0$, it sends $(\mathsf{Hdr}, \{K_i\}_{i=1}^m)$ to $\mathcal{A}$, otherwise selects randomly the session key component K_γ for S_γ and sends $(\mathsf{Hdr}, \{K_i\}_{i=1}^m)$ to $\mathcal{A}$.

Phase 2: This is similar to Phase 1 key generation queries.

Guess: Finally $\mathcal{A}$ output guess b' of b and wins if $b' = b$.

We define $X = e(g,g)^{\alpha^{16N-1}}$ as real event and X a random element of $\mathbb{G}_1$ as rand event. Therefore

$$Adv_{\mathcal{C}}^{DBDHE-sum} = |Pr[b' = b|\mathsf{real}] - Pr[b' = b|\mathsf{rand}]| = |Pr[b' = b|\mathsf{real}] - \frac{1}{2}|$$

$$= \left|(\frac{1}{2}Pr[b' = 1|b = 1 \wedge \mathsf{real}] + \frac{1}{2}Pr[b' = 0|b = 0 \wedge \mathsf{real}]) - \frac{1}{2}\right|$$

$$= \left|\frac{1}{2}Pr[b' = 1|b = 1 \wedge \mathsf{real}] - \frac{1}{2}Pr[b' = 1|b = 0 \wedge \mathsf{real}]\right|.$$

$$[\,\text{as } Pr[b' = 0|b = 0 \wedge \mathsf{real}] + Pr[b' = 1|b = 0 \wedge \mathsf{real}] = 1\,]$$

In real case, the distribution of all the variables agrees with the semantic security game, thereby $Adv_{\mathcal{A}}^{MCBE-INDK} = |Pr[b' = 1|b = 1 \wedge \mathsf{real}] - Pr[b' = 1|b = 0 \wedge \mathsf{real}]|.$

This implies $Adv_{\mathcal{C}}^{DBDHE-sum} = \frac{1}{2}Adv_{\mathcal{A}}^{MCBE-INDK}$. Therefore, if $\mathcal{A}$ has a non-negligible advantage in correctly guessing b', then $\mathcal{C}$ predicts $X = e(g,g)^{\alpha^{16N-1}}$ or a random element of $\mathbb{G}_1$ i.e. solves the DBDHE-sum problem given to $\mathcal{C}$ with non-negligible advantage. Hence the theorem follows.

4   Our OMCBE

Our outsider-anonymous MCBE scheme OMCBE = (OMCBE.Setup, OMCBE. KeyGen, OMCBE.Encrypt, OMCBE.Decrypt) is described as follows.

$(\mathsf{PP}, \mathsf{MK}) \leftarrow$ OMCBE.Setup(N, λ): Let $N = nm$ be the total number of users supported by the system with m group of users $\{G_x\}_{x=1}^m$ and each group $G_x, x \in [m]$ contains $n = 2^\varsigma$ users which are placed at the leaf nodes of a complete binary tree $T(x), x \in [m]$ of height ς. Using security parameter λ and the total number of users N, the private key generation centre (PKGC) does the following to generate the public parameter PP, master key MK:

1. Chooses a bilinear group system $\mathbb{S} = (p, \mathbb{G}, \mathbb{G}_1, e)$ where $\mathbb{G}, \mathbb{G}_1$ are groups of prime order p, g is a generator of $\mathbb{G}$ and $e : \mathbb{G} \times \mathbb{G} \to \mathbb{G}_1$ is a bilinear mapping.
2. Picks a cryptographic hash function $H : \{0,1\}^* \to \mathbb{Z}_p^*$ and assigns an identity id(x, i, j) to the j-th node at the i-th level of tree $T(x), x \in [m], i \in [\varsigma], j \in [2^{i-1}]$. Let $\mathsf{ID} = \{\mathrm{id}(x,i,j)|v(x,i,j) \in T(x), x \in [m]\}$ be the collection of the identities of all the nodes in trees $T(1), \ldots, T(m)$.
3. Selects $\alpha \in_R \mathbb{Z}_p^*$, $h \in_R \mathbb{G}$ and sets $\mathsf{MK} = \alpha$, $\mathsf{PP} = (\mathbb{S}, h, g, g_1, \ldots, g_N, H, \mathsf{ID})$, where $g_i = g^{\alpha^i}$ for $1 \leq i \leq N$.
4. Keeps MK secret to itself and makes PP public.

$(sk_u) \leftarrow$ OMCBE.KeyGen$(\mathsf{PP}, \mathsf{MK}, u)$: Let user u lies in $T(x)$ and path(u) denotes the identities of the nodes along the path from user u at leaf to the root of $T(x)$. The PKGC computes $sk_{\mathrm{id}(x,i,j)} = h^{\frac{1}{\alpha + H(\mathrm{id}(x,i,j))}}$ and sets secret key sk_u as $sk_u = \{sk_{\mathrm{id}(x,i,j)} \mid \mathrm{id}(x,i,j) \in \mathsf{path}(u), u \in T(x)\}$.
The PKGC sends sk_u to user u through a secure communication channel between them.

$(\mathsf{Hdr}, \{K_i\}_{i=1}^m) \leftarrow$ OMCBE.Encrypt$(S_1, \ldots, S_m, \mathsf{PP})$: Let $S_x \subseteq G_x$, $x \in [m]$ be the groups of subscribed users. The broadcaster performs the following to generate header Hdr and session key $\{K_x\}_{x=1}^m$:

1. Generates cover $\{S_{x,1}, S_{x,2}, \ldots, S_{x,l_x}\}$ using binary CS method for each subscribed user set $S_x \subseteq G_x$ using $R_x = G_x \backslash S_x$ as the set of revoked users for each $x \in [m]$. Let the total cover size $\sum_{x=1}^m l_x$ be denoted by l. Suppose that the set of identities of the head nodes of the subcovers be $\mathsf{Head} = \{\mathrm{id}(x, i_k, j_k)|x \in [m], k \in [l_x] \text{ and } v(x, i_k, j_k) \text{ is head node of } S_{x,k}\}$. Note that a head node $v(x, i_k, j_k)$ of complete subtree $\mathsf{CS}_{x,k}$ in $T(x)$ hangs of a vertex with out degree 1 in Steiner tree $\mathsf{ST}(R_x)$ and leaf node of the complete subtree $\mathsf{CS}_{x,k}$ in $T(x)$ yields subcover $S_{x,k}$

2. Selects $r \in_R \mathbb{Z}_p^*$ and computes $C = g^\eta$ by extracting g^{α^i} values from PP. Here $\eta = r \prod_{\rho \in \text{Head}} (\alpha + H(\rho))$.

3. Sets $K_x = \{K_{x,\varrho} | \varrho \in [l_x]\}$ for $x \in [m]$ where $K_{x,\varrho} = e(g^{\eta/\xi_{x,\varrho}}, h) = e(g, h)^{\frac{\eta}{\xi_{x,\varrho}}}, \xi_{x,\varrho} = (\alpha + H(\text{id}(x, i_\varrho, j_\varrho))), \eta = r \prod_{\rho \in \text{Head}} (\alpha + H(\rho))$.

4. Let the theoretical upper bound for set G_x be L_x. It sets $K_x = \{K_{x,j} | j \in [L_x]\}$ for $x \in [m]$. Here $L_x - l_x$ components $\{K_{x,j}\}_{j=l_x+1}^{L_x}$ are random session keys.

5. Keeps $\{K_j\}_{j=1}^m$ secure to itself and makes $\text{Hdr} = (C, \{k_i\}_{i=1}^m)$ public, where $k_i = \{k_{i,j}\}_{j=1}^{L_i}$ and $k_{i,j}$ is last τ bits of $K_{i,j}$.

Note that some S_x may be ϕ. If $S_x = \phi$ then the broadcaster sets $K_x = \perp$.

$(K_{x,\varrho}) \leftarrow \text{OMCBE.Decrypt}(\text{PP}, sk_u, \text{Hdr})$: Following Lemma 1, $|\text{Head} \cap \text{path}(u)| = 1$ which implies that each subscribed user u must be in exactly one of the subset cover with a head node identity in $\text{path}(u)$. Starting from leaf level a subscribed user u lies in $\text{path}(u)$, computes $K' = e(C, sk_{\text{id}(x,i_{\varrho'}, j_{\varrho'})})$, using PP, until it recovers K' whose last τ bits matches with some $K_{x,\varrho}$. Return K' as session key $K_{x,\varrho}$.

Note that $K_{x,\varrho} = e(C, sk_{\text{id}(x,i_\varrho, j_\varrho)}) = e(g^\eta, h^{\frac{1}{\xi_{x,\varrho}}}) = e(g, h)^{\eta/\xi_{x,\varrho}}$.

Remark 1. Consider the following scheme in which public key is generated for all nodes in the complete subtree as $g^{x_i}, x_i \in_R \mathbb{Z}_p$ and each user receives the private keys corresponding to the nodes from the root to its leaf as x_i values. We can simply generate random group element g^r (set as a Header) and set session keys using the Diffie-Hellman value of g^r and the public-key corresponding to the head nodes of the subcovers of the set of receivers (i.e. $g^{x_i \cdot r}$ where g^{x_i} are the public-keys corresponding to the head nodes of the subcovers of the set of receivers and x_i is the corresponding secret-key associated with the head nodes of the subcovers of the set of receivers). We can obtain a scheme with public parameters of size $2N - m$, with user private keys of size ζ and header which consists of only 1 group element. This is another scheme which do not use pairings and is therefore more efficient than the OMCBE scheme but it can not provides outsider anonymity due to following.

Suppose, if $b = 0$, $\mathcal{C}$ sends $(\text{Hdr}, \{K_i\}_{i=1}^m) \leftarrow \text{OMCBE.Encrypt}(\mathbb{S}_0, \text{PP})$ to $\mathcal{A}$ where $K_i = \{K_{i,j}\}_{j=1}^{L_i}$ is session key for S_i, L_i is the theoretical upperbound of number of disjoint partitions of S_i i.e., $S_i = \bigcup_{j=1}^{L_i} S_{i,j}$ with $S_{i,j_1} \cap S_{i,j_2} = \phi$ for $j_1 \neq j_2, 1 \leq j_1, j_2 \leq L_i$ and $K_{i,j}$ is the session key corresponding to $S_{i,j}$. Otherwise, $\mathcal{C}$ generates $(\text{Hdr}, \{K_i\}_{i=1}^m) \leftarrow \text{OMCBE.Encrypt}(\mathbb{S}_1, \text{PP})$ and provides $(\text{Hdr}, \{K_i\}_{i=1}^m)$ to $\mathcal{A}$. Now adversary will compute $e(g^r, g^{x_i})$, if it matches with $e(g, K_i)$ then the node corresponding to g^{x_i} will be a head of a complete subtree whose leaves are subset of subscribed users. Thus outsider-anonymity will not be preserved.

Remark 2. If we use usual CS method on each group then header size for m group will be $O(\sum_{i=1}^{m} L_i)$, where L_i is the theoretical upper bound for the number of cover for i-th group. In contrast, our OMCBE needs single header.

Theorem 2. *Our proposed OMCBE scheme achieves selective semantic security as per the key indistinguishability of Sect. 2.2 under the m-sq-DDHE assumption.*

Proof: Let us assume that both the adversary and challenger knows m group of users $\{G_x\}_{x=1}^{m}$ each having n elements. Also assume that users in G_x are placed in leave level of a tree $T(x)$ of height ζ. The total number of users that can be accommodated in the system is $N = nm$. Assume that there is a PPT adversary $\mathcal{A}$ that breaks the selective semantic security of our proposed OMCBE scheme with a non-negligible advantage. We construct a distinguisher $\mathcal{C}$ that attempts to solve the m-sq-DDHE problem using $\mathcal{A}$ as a subroutine. The distinguisher $\mathcal{C}$ takes as input an m-sq-DDHE instance $\langle Z = (\mathbb{S}, A = u^a, \{U_i, B_i, C_i\}_{i=0}^{N}), X \rangle$, where $\mathbb{S} = (p, \mathbb{G}, \mathbb{G}_1, e)$ is bilinear group system, $e : \mathbb{G} \times \mathbb{G} \longrightarrow \mathbb{G}_1$ is bilinear mapping, $\mathbb{G}, \mathbb{G}_1$ are group of prime order p, $a, b, c \in_R \mathbb{Z}_p$, u is the generator of a group $\mathbb{G}$, $U_i = u^{1/a^i}$, $B_i = u^{b/a^i}$, $C_i = u^{c/a^i}$ for $i \in [0, N]$, X is either $e(u, u)^{abc}$ or a random element of the target group $\mathbb{G}_1$. The distinguisher $\mathcal{C}$ attempts to output 0 if $X = e(u, u)^{abc}$ and 1 otherwise. Now $\mathcal{C}$ plays the role of a challenger in the security game and interacts with $\mathcal{A}$ as follows:

Initialization: The adversary $\mathcal{A}$ selects 2 group of target recipient sets $\mathbb{S}_0 = \{S_{0,1}, \ldots, S_{0,m}\}$, $\mathbb{S}_1 = \{S_{1,1}, \ldots, S_{1,m}\}$ with $S_{0,i}, S_{1,i} \subseteq G_i$, $|S_{0,i}| = |S_{1,i}|$, $i \in [m]$, an index $\gamma \leq m$ and provides it to $\mathcal{C}$.

Setup: The challenger $\mathcal{C}$ generates PP, MK using Z as follows:

1. Sets $g = A = u^a$.

2. Selects $t, x_\gamma \in_R \mathbb{Z}_p^*$, and sets $\Gamma_i(x) = x(\frac{t}{x} - x_\gamma)^i = \sum_{j=0}^{i} \Gamma_{i,j}/x^{j-1}$ for $i \in [N]$. Here $\Gamma_{i,j} = (-1)^i \binom{i}{j} t^{i-j} x_\gamma^j$ are functions of t, x_γ.

   Sets $g_i = A^{\Gamma_{i,0}} \prod_{j=1}^{i} U_{j-1}^{\Gamma_{i,j}} = u^{\sum_{j=0}^{i} \Gamma_{i,j}/a^{j-1}} = u^{a(\frac{t}{a} - x_\gamma)^i} = g^{(\frac{t}{a} - x_\gamma)^i}, i \in [N]$.

3. Selects q random values $x_1, \ldots, x_q$ from $\mathbb{Z}_p^*$ and sets a polynomial of degree q,

$$P(x) = \prod_{i \in [q]} (tx + x_i) = \sum_{i=0}^{q} P_i x^i.$$

   Here P_i are function of $t, \{x_i\}_{i=1}^{q}$ that can be computed by challenger $\mathcal{C}$. Note that $P_0 = x_1 \ldots x_q$.

4. Computes $h = \prod_{i=0}^{q} C_i^{P_i} = C_0^{\sum_{i=0}^{q} P_i/a^i} = u^{cP(\frac{1}{a})}$.

5. Let $H : \{0,1\}^* \rightarrow \mathbb{Z}_p^*$ be a cryptographic hash function and $\mathsf{ID} = \{\mathsf{id}(x,i,j)|v(x,i,j) \in T(x), x \in [m], i \in [\zeta], j \in [2^i]\}$ be the identities of the nodes in $T(x), x \in [m]$.

6. Sets public parameter PP and master key MK as

$$\mathsf{PP} = (\mathbb{S}, h, g, g_1, g_2, \dots, g_N, H, \mathsf{ID}), \mathsf{MK} = \frac{t}{a} - x_\gamma = \alpha \text{ (say)}.$$

Note that $\mathsf{MK} = \alpha = \frac{t}{a} - x_\gamma$ in not known to $\mathcal{C}$ explicitly.

7. The challenger $\mathcal{C}$ sends PP to $\mathcal{A}$.

Observe that, the generated PP, MK have the same distribution as those generated by invoking $\mathsf{MCBE.Setup}(N, \lambda)$ in the real protocol. As $P(x)$ is a random polynomial, h is random element from $\mathbb{G}$.

Phase 1: The adversary $\mathcal{A}$ issues a series of key generation queries for user $u \notin S_\gamma$ to $\mathcal{C}$ who in turn generates the secret keys as described below:

1. Assume that user u lies in $T(\beta)$ and $\mathsf{id}(\beta, i_k, j_k)$ be an identity in $\mathsf{path}(u)$. To generate $sk_{\mathsf{id}(\beta, i_k, j_k)}$, the adversary $\mathcal{A}$ proceeds as follows:

   (a) Sets $Q_k(x) = P(x)/(\frac{t}{x} + x_{k'}) = \prod_{i=1}^{q}(\frac{t}{x} + x_i)/(\frac{t}{x} + x_{k'}) = \sum_{i=0}^{q-1} Q_{k,i}/x^i$.
   and $H(\mathsf{id}(\beta, i_k, j_k)) = x_\gamma + x_{k'}, x_{k'} \in \{x_1, \dots, x_q\}$.

   (b) Computes $sk_{\mathsf{id}(\beta, i_k, j_k)} = \prod_{i=0}^{q-1} C_i^{Q_{k,i}} = u^{c\sum_{j=0}^{q-1} Q_{k,i}/a^i} = u^{cQ_k(a)}$.

2. Sends $sk_u = \{sk_{\mathsf{id}(x, i_k, j_k)} \,|\, \mathsf{id}(x, i_k, j_k) \in \mathsf{path}(u), u \in T(x)\}$ to $\mathcal{A}$.

The secret key components in sk_u simulated by $\mathcal{C}$ is identical to that of real scheme as

$$u^{cQ_k(a)} = u^{cP(1/a)/(\frac{t}{a} + x_{k'})} = h^{\frac{1}{\frac{t}{a} + x_{k'}}} = h^{\frac{1}{\frac{t}{a} - x_\gamma + x_\gamma + x_{k'}}} = h^{\frac{1}{\alpha + H(\mathsf{id}(\beta, i_k, j_k))}}.$$

For δ secret key query it need $\delta\zeta$ hash values, therefore $\delta\zeta \leq q \Rightarrow \delta \leq q/\zeta$.

Challenge: The challenger $\mathcal{C}$ does the followings using m-sq-DDHE instance $\langle Z, X \rangle$ as follows:

1. Generates the cover using binary CS method with the target recipient set $\mathbb{S}_0 = \{S_{0,1}, \dots, S_{0,m}\}$.

   (a) Let l_y be the cover size for $S_{0,y}, y \in [m]$ and total cover size be $l = \sum_{i=1}^{m} l_y$ and the set of identities of the head nodes of the subset covers be $\mathsf{Head} = \{\mathsf{id}(y, i_z, j_z)|y \in [m], z \in [l_y]\}$.

   (b) Let $\mathsf{Head}' = \mathsf{Head} \setminus \mathsf{id}(\gamma, i_1, j_1)$, where γ is the preselected index provided by $\mathcal{A}$ to $\mathcal{C}$ in the initialization phase and $\mathsf{id}(\gamma, i_1, j_1)$ be identity of head node of $S_{\gamma, 1}$. If any identity ρ has not assigned a hash value before then the challenger $\mathcal{C}$ defines hash value as $H(\rho) = \begin{cases} x_\gamma + x_{z'} & \text{if } \rho \in \mathsf{Head}' \\ x_\gamma & \text{if } \rho = \mathsf{id}(\gamma, i_1, j_1) \end{cases}$. Here $x_{z'} \in_R \mathbb{Z}_p^* \setminus \{x_1, \dots, x_q\}$.

(c) Computes $C = (\prod_{i=0}^{l-1} B_i^{F_i})^s, s \in_R \mathbb{Z}_p$. Here B_i is extractable from Z and F_i are function of $t, x_\gamma, \{H(\rho)\}_{\rho \in \text{Head}}$, determined by the following polynomial

$$F(x) = \prod_{\rho \in \text{Head}'} \left(\frac{t}{x} + H(\rho) - x_\gamma\right) = \sum_{i=0}^{l-1} \frac{F_i}{x^i}. \text{ Note that distribution of}$$

C is identical to that of real protocol as

$$C = \left(\prod_{i=0}^{l-1} B_i^{F_i}\right)^s = \prod_{i=0}^{l-1} u^{\frac{sb F_i}{a^i}} = u^{sb \prod_{\rho \in \text{Head}'} \left(\frac{t}{a} + H(\rho) - x_\gamma\right)}$$

$$= u^{t \frac{sb}{t} \prod_{\rho \in \text{Head}'} (H(\rho) + \alpha)} = g^{r_1 \prod_{\rho \in \text{Head}'} (H(\rho) + \alpha)}$$

See that $u^t = u^{\frac{t}{a} a} = u^{a(x_\gamma + \frac{t}{a} - x_\gamma)} = g^{H(\text{id}(\gamma, i_1, j_1)) + \alpha}$. Assume that $sb/t = r_1$, a random number.

(d) Computes the session key $K_{\gamma,1}$ corresponding to identity $\text{id}(\gamma, i_1, j_1)$ by executing the following steps:

  i. Sets $\Delta_{\gamma,1}(x) = \prod_{\rho \in \text{Head}'} x\left(\frac{t}{x} + H(\rho) - x_\gamma\right) = \sum_{j=0}^{l-1} \Delta_{\gamma,1,j}/x^{j-1}$. Here $\Delta_{\gamma,1,j}$ are function of $t, x_\gamma, \{H(\rho)\}_{\rho \in \text{Head}}$ and computable by challenger $\mathcal{C}$.

  ii. Computes $Y_{\gamma,1} = \prod_{j=1}^{l-1} B_{j-1}^{\Delta_{\gamma,1,j}} = u^{b \sum_{j=1}^{l-1} \Delta_{\gamma,1,j}/a^{j-1}}$ and $e(Y_{\gamma,1}, h)$.

  iii. Computes
$$\prod_{i=1}^{q} e(B_0, C_{i-1}^{P_i}) = e(u^b, \prod_{i=1}^{q} C_{i-1}^{P_i}) = e(u^b, \prod_{i=1}^{q} C_i^{aP_i}) = e(u^{ab}, \prod_{i=1}^{q} C_i^{P_i}).$$
[See that $C_{i-1} = u^{\frac{c}{a^{i-1}}} = C_i^a$.]

  iv. Sets $K_{\gamma,1} = \{X^{P_0 \Delta_{\gamma,1,0}} e(Y_{\gamma,1}, h) e(u^{ab}, \prod_{i=1}^{q} C_i^{P_i})^{\Delta_{\gamma,1,0}}\}^{\frac{s}{t}}$.

If $X = e(u, u)^{abc}$ then the following calculation shows that $K_{\gamma,1}$ is a valid session key, as this simulated session key is identical to the original one.

$$K_{\gamma,1} = \{X^{P_0 \Delta_{\gamma,1,0}} e(u^{ab}, \prod_{i=1}^{q} C_i^{P_i})^{\Delta_{\gamma,1,0}} e(Y_{\gamma,1}, h)\}^{\frac{s}{t}}$$

$$= \{e(u^{ab\Delta_{\gamma,1,0}}, u^{cP_0}) e(u^{ab}, \prod_{i=1}^{q} C_i^{P_i})^{\Delta_{\gamma,1,0}} e(Y_{\gamma,1}, h)\}^{\frac{s}{t}}$$

$$= \{e(u^{ab\Delta_{\gamma,1,0}}, u^{cP_0} \prod_{i=1}^{q} C_i^{P_i}) e(Y_{\gamma,1}, h)\}^{\frac{s}{t}}$$

$$= \{e(u^{ab\Delta_{\gamma,1,0}}, \prod_{i=0}^{q} C_i^{P_i}) e(Y_{\gamma,1}, h)\}^{\frac{s}{t}} = \{e(u^{ab\Delta_{\gamma,1,0}}, h) e(Y_{\gamma,1}, h)\}^{\frac{s}{t}}$$

$$= \{e(Y_{\gamma,1} u^{ab\Delta_{\gamma,1,0}}, h)\}^{\frac{s}{t}} = \{e(u^{\; b\sum\limits_{j=0}^{l-1} \Delta_{\gamma,1,j}/a^{j-1}}, h)\}^{\frac{s}{t}}$$

$$= e(u^{b\Delta_{\gamma,1}(a)}, h)^{\frac{s}{t}} = e(u^{\Delta_{\gamma,1}(a)}, h)^{\frac{sb}{t}} = e(g, h)^{\frac{r_1 \Delta_{\gamma,1}(a)}{a}} = e(g, h)^{\frac{\eta}{\xi_{\gamma,1}}}$$

where $\eta = r_1 \prod\limits_{\rho \in \mathsf{Head}} (\alpha + H(\rho))$, $\xi_{\gamma,1} = \alpha + H(\mathsf{id}(\gamma, i_1, j_1))$, $sb/t = r_1, g = u^a$ and

$$\frac{r_1 \Delta_{\gamma,1}(a)}{a} = \frac{r_1 \prod\limits_{\rho \in \mathsf{Head}} (\alpha + H(\rho))}{\alpha + H(\mathsf{id}(\gamma, i_1, j_1))} = \frac{\eta}{\xi_{\gamma,1}}.$$

(e) Computes the session key $K_{\delta,\nu}, (\delta, \nu) \neq (\gamma, 1)$ corresponding to the identity $\mathsf{id}(\delta, i_\nu, j_\nu)$ as follows:

   i. Let us define $\mathsf{Head}'' = \mathsf{Head} \setminus \mathsf{id}(\delta, i_\nu, j_\nu)$. It sets

$$\Delta_{\delta,\nu}(x) = \prod_{\rho \in \mathsf{Head}''} x\left(\frac{t}{x} + H(\rho) - x_\gamma\right)$$

$$= \left(\frac{t}{x} + H(\mathsf{id}(\gamma, i_1, j_1)) - x_\gamma\right) \prod_{\substack{\rho \in \mathsf{Head}'' \\ \rho \neq \mathsf{id}(\gamma, i_1, j_1)}} x\left(\frac{t}{x} + H(\rho) - x_\gamma\right)$$

$$= \frac{t}{x} \prod_{\substack{\rho \in \mathsf{Head}'' \\ \rho \neq \mathsf{id}(\gamma, i_1, j_1)}} x\left(\frac{t}{x} + H(\rho) - x_\gamma\right) \; [\text{as } H(\mathsf{id}(\gamma, i_1, j_1)) = x_\gamma]$$

$$= \sum_{j=0}^{l-2} \frac{\Delta_{\delta,\nu,j}}{x^j}$$

   ii. Computes $Y_{\delta,\nu} = \prod\limits_{j=0}^{l-2} B_j^{\Delta_{\delta,\nu,j}} = u^{\; b\sum\limits_{j=0}^{l-2} \Delta_{\delta,\nu,j}/a^j} = u^{b\Delta_{\delta,\nu}(a)}.$

   iii. Sets $K_{\delta,\nu} = \{e(Y_{\delta,\nu}, h)\}^{\frac{s}{t}}.$

Note that $K_{\delta,\nu}$ has distribution similar to that in the real protocol as

$$K_{\delta,\nu} = \{e(Y_{\delta,\nu}, h)\}^{\frac{s}{t}} = \{e(u^{b\Delta_{\delta,\nu}(a)}, h)\}^{\frac{s}{t}} = \{e(g^{b\frac{\Delta_{\delta,\nu}(a)}{a}}, h)\}^{\frac{s}{t}}$$

$$= e(g^{\frac{\Delta_{\delta,\nu}(a)}{a}}, h)^{\frac{sb}{t}} = e(g, h)^{\frac{r_1\Delta_{\delta,\nu}(a)}{a}} = e(g, h)^{\frac{\eta}{\xi_{\delta,\nu}}},$$

Here $\eta = r_1 \prod_{\rho \in \mathsf{Head}} (\alpha + H(\rho))$, $\xi_{\delta,\nu} = \alpha + H(\mathsf{id}(\delta, i_\nu, j_\nu))$, $sb/t = r_1, g = u^a$ and

$$\frac{r_1\Delta_{\delta,\nu}(a)}{a} = \frac{r_1 \prod_{\rho \in \mathsf{Head}} (\alpha + H(\rho))}{\alpha + H(\mathsf{id}(\delta, i_\nu, j_\nu))} = \frac{\eta}{\xi_{\delta,\nu}}.$$

2. Similarly the challenger $\mathcal{C}$ repeats the above steps to generate C and session key for $\mathbb{S}_1$. Here in time of session key generation, it takes X as random.

3. The challenger $\mathcal{C}$ selects $b \in_R \{0, 1\}$. If $b = 0$ it sends $\mathsf{Hdr} = (C, \{k_i\}_{i=1}^m), \{K_i\}_{i=1}^m$ generated for $\mathbb{S}_0$ to $\mathcal{A}$. Here $K_i = \{K_{i,j}\}_{j=1}^{L_i}, k_i = \{k_{i,j}\}_{j=1}^{L_i}, k_{i,j}$ is last τ bits of $K_{i,j}$. If $b = 1$ it sets $K_{\gamma,1}$ of K_γ as random and sends $\mathsf{Hdr}, \{K_i\}_{i=1}^m$ (generated for $\mathbb{S}_1$ in step 2) to $\mathcal{A}$.

Phase 2: This is similar to Phase 1 key generation queries. The adversary $\mathcal{A}$ sends key generation queries for user $u \notin (S_{0,\gamma} \bigcup S_{1,\gamma})$ and receives back secret key sk_u simulated in the same manner by $\mathcal{C}$ as in Phase 1.

Guess: The adversary $\mathcal{A}$ outputs a guess $b' \in \{0, 1\}$ of b. If $b' = b$, $\mathcal{C}$ outputs 0, indicating that $X = e(u, u)^{abc}$, else outputs 1, indicating that X is random.

We define $X = e(u, u)^{abc}$ as real event and X a random element of $\mathbb{G}_1$ as rand event. Therefore

$$Adv_{\mathcal{C}}^{m-sq-DDHE} = |Pr[b' = b|\mathsf{real}] - Pr[b' = b|\mathsf{rand}]| = |Pr[b' = b|\mathsf{real}] - \frac{1}{2}|$$

$$= \left|\left(\frac{1}{2}Pr[b' = 1|b = 1 \wedge \mathsf{real}] + \frac{1}{2}Pr[b' = 0|b = 0 \wedge \mathsf{real}]\right) - \frac{1}{2}\right|$$

$$= \left|\frac{1}{2}Pr[b' = 1|b = 1 \wedge \mathsf{real}] - \frac{1}{2}Pr[b' = 1|b = 0 \wedge \mathsf{real}]\right|.$$

$$[\text{as } Pr[b' = 0|b = 0 \wedge \mathsf{real}] + Pr[b' = 1|b = 0 \wedge \mathsf{real}] = 1]$$

In real case, the distribution of all the variables agrees with the semantic security game, thereby $Adv_{\mathcal{A}}^{OMCBE-INDK} = |Pr[b' = 1|b = 1 \wedge \mathsf{real}] - Pr[b' = 1|b = 0 \wedge \mathsf{real}]|$. This implies $Adv_{\mathcal{C}}^{m-sq-DDHE} = \frac{1}{2}Adv_{\mathcal{A}}^{OMCBE-INDK}$. Therefore, if $\mathcal{A}$ has non-negligible advantage in correctly guessing b', then $\mathcal{C}$ solves m-sq-DDHE instance given to $\mathcal{C}$ with non-negligible advantage. Hence the theorem follows.

References

1. Acharya, K., Dutta, R.: Secure and efficient construction of broadcast encryption with dealership. In: Chen, L., Han, J. (eds.) ProvSec 2016. LNCS, vol. 10005, pp. 277–295. Springer, Cham (2016). https://doi.org/10.1007/978-3-319-47422-9_16

2. Acharya, K., Dutta, R.: Adaptively secure broadcast encryption with dealership. In: Hong, S., Park, J.H. (eds.) ICISC 2016. LNCS, vol. 10157, pp. 161–177. Springer, Cham (2017). https://doi.org/10.1007/978-3-319-53177-9_8

3. Acharya, K., Dutta, R.: Provable secure constructions for broadcast encryption with personalized messages. In: Okamoto, T., Yu, Y., Au, M.H., Li, Y. (eds.) ProvSec 2017. LNCS, vol. 10592, pp. 329–348. Springer, Cham (2017). https://doi.org/10.1007/978-3-319-68637-0_20

4. Acharya, K., Dutta, R.: Recipient revocable broadcast encryption schemes without random oracles. In: Kim, H., Kim, D.-C. (eds.) ICISC 2017. LNCS, vol. 10779, pp. 191–213. Springer, Cham (2018). https://doi.org/10.1007/978-3-319-78556-1_11

5. Boneh, D., Boyen, X., Goh, E.-J.: Hierarchical identity based encryption with constant size ciphertext. In: Cramer, R. (ed.) EUROCRYPT 2005. LNCS, vol. 3494, pp. 440–456. Springer, Heidelberg (2005). https://doi.org/10.1007/11426639_26

6. Boneh, D., Gentry, C., Waters, B.: Collusion resistant broadcast encryption with short ciphertexts and private keys. In: Shoup, V. (ed.) CRYPTO 2005. LNCS, vol. 3621, pp. 258–275. Springer, Heidelberg (2005). https://doi.org/10.1007/11535218_16

7. Fazio, N., Perera, I.M.: Outsider-anonymous broadcast encryption with sublinear ciphertexts. In: Fischlin, M., Buchmann, J., Manulis, M. (eds.) PKC 2012. LNCS, vol. 7293, pp. 225–242. Springer, Heidelberg (2012). https://doi.org/10.1007/978-3-642-30057-8_14

8. Izabachène, M., Pointcheval, D.: New anonymity notions for identity-based encryption. In: Cortier, V., Kirchner, C., Okada, M., Sakurada, H. (eds.) Formal to Practical Security: Papers Issued from the 2005-2008 French-Japanese Collaboration. LNCS, vol. 5458, pp. 138–157. Springer, Heidelberg (2009). https://doi.org/10.1007/978-3-642-02002-5_8

9. Gentry, C., Waters, B.: Adaptive security in broadcast encryption systems (with short ciphertexts). In: Joux, A. (ed.) EUROCRYPT 2009. LNCS, vol. 5479, pp. 171–188. Springer, Heidelberg (2009). https://doi.org/10.1007/978-3-642-01001-9_10

10. Kim, J., Susilo, W., Au, M.H., Seberry, J.: Efficient semi-static secure broadcast encryption scheme. In: Cao, Z., Zhang, F. (eds.) Pairing 2013. LNCS, vol. 8365, pp. 62–76. Springer, Cham (2014). https://doi.org/10.1007/978-3-319-04873-4_4

11. Naor, D., Naor, M., Lotspiech, J.: Revocation and tracing schemes for stateless receivers. In: Kilian, J. (ed.) CRYPTO 2001. LNCS, vol. 2139, pp. 41–62. Springer, Heidelberg (2001). https://doi.org/10.1007/3-540-44647-8_3

12. Phan, D.H., Pointcheval, D., Trinh, V.C.: Multi-channel broadcast encryption. In: ASIACCS 2013. ACM (2013)

13. Zhao, X.W., Li, H.: Improvement on a multi-channel broadcast encryption scheme. Appl. Mech. Mater. **427–429**, 2163–2169 (2013)

Author Index

Printed in the United States
By Bookmasters